TEXAS ALMANAC
2008 ★ 2009

The Source For All Things Texan Since 1857

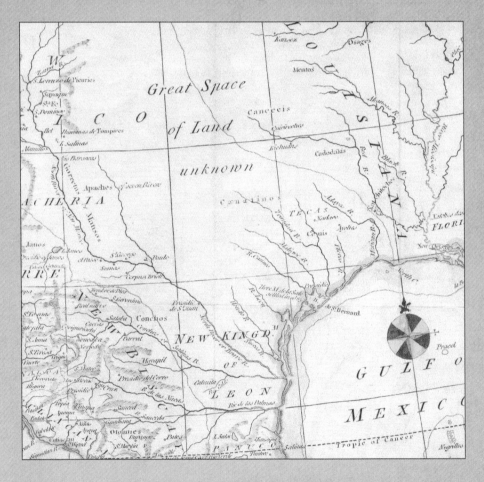

Published by
The Dallas Morning News

TEXAS ALMANAC
2008-2009

Elizabeth Cruce Alvarez
Editor

Robert Plocheck
Associate Editor

Cover design and inside page designs by
Lorin Bruckner of **Alamo Studios**, Irving, Texas.
www.alamoinc.com.

On the Cover

✶ **Clovis points and blades** found at the Gault archeological site in Bell County. Clockwise from top center: Clovis point, small serated blade, engraved stone, dart point preform, blade core, large serrated blade, blade, Clovis point, graver tip on blade, (center) clear quartz crystal Clovis point. Erich Schlegel photo.

✶ **Holly Fine Engraved Bottle**, ca. A.D. 900–1300, excavated in 1970 from a Caddo Indian grave at the Caddoan Mounds State Historic Site in Cherokee County by a crew from the University of Texas at Austin. Courtesy of the Texas Archeological Research Laboratory at the University of Texas at Austin. www.utexas.edu/research/tarl/

✶ **Vintage exploration map** from The Texas Collection, Baylor University.

On the Back Cover

✶ **Stagecoach at the Stagecoach Inn at Salado**. Randy Eli Grothe photo.

✶ **Vintage baseball card** depicting Dugey, a player for the Texas League Waco team, issued by Old Mill Cigarettes in 1910.

✶ **Pecos County map;** see page 361.

ISBN (hardcover) 978-0-914511-40-3
ISBN (softcover) 978-0-914511-41-0

Library of Congress Control Number: 2007902945

www.texasalmanac.com

Distributed by Texas A&M University Press Consortium
4354 TAMUS, College Station, Texas 77843-4354

To order by telephone, call 1-800-826-8911
To order online, log onto http://www.tamu.edu/upress/BOOKS/2007/texasalmanac.htm

The *Texas Almanac* Teacher's Guide is now available online at www.texasalmanac.com. The guide consists of lessons, activities, maps and puzzles that make use of the factually dense *Texas Almanac*. The Teacher's Guide was developed by a team of veteran social-studies teachers and curriculum writers.

Printed in the United States of America

THE SOURCE FOR ALL THINGS TEXAN SINCE 1857

Preface

This 64th edition of the *Texas Almanac* has been revised and expanded and includes more maps and photographs than previous editions. This is the second edition that has been printed in color, and beginning with the "Flags and Symbols" section and "A Brief Sketch of Texas History," we have added more photographs and maps and have continued this throughout every section of the Almanac.

There are several new articles in this edition that highlight unique features of Texas. First, there is a summary and list of archeological sites in Texas. Every area of the state has fascinating sites where artifacts and rock art can be explored. Next, we have a story about stagecoach travel in Texas. For many years this mode of transportation, though rough and rugged, was the primary way to transport people, goods and mail across the state.

Another article focuses on the great work of the Civilian Conservation Corps in Texas during the Great Depression. This army of men in the CCC built many of Texas' beautiful state, national and local parks, and the rock and wood buildings still standing in these parks are a testament to the hard work of these men.

We also offer a story about the development of minor league baseball in Texas, which began in 1888 and continues in many cities today. This story, found in the Recreation & Sports section, marks the introduction of more sports into the *Texas Almanac.* Following that article there are several pages of tables listing major league baseball statistics, Texas Olympic medalists, Sports Hall of Fame inductees, and high school champions in football and boys and girls basketball. Current University Scholastic League winners also can be found in the Education section.

In addition, we have updated all the state and county maps in the Almanac. Our county maps include relief and are the best companion when traveling throughout the state.

We also would like readers to know that the *Texas Almanac* Web site has been expanded and contains feature articles, a history timeline, tables and maps from previous editions that could not be included in this edition because of space constraints. Visit the Web site at www.texasalmanac.com and explore the many interesting features on the site. Nearly every section in the printed Almanac has a companion page on the Web site.

The Web site also includes the *Texas Almanac's* Searchable Town Database,® which contains more than 17,000 towns, existing and non-existing. The database can be used to search out a single town or look up all towns in a particular county. This is a wonderful research tool, which also lists other names associated with a town and if that town had ever been in another county (before the final list of 254 counties was established).

We hope readers enjoy this edition of the *Texas Almanac* and use it at work and take it along when traveling across this great state.

Elizabeth Cruce Alvarez
Editor, 2007

Table of Contents

Index of Maps

Index of Tables

Contents

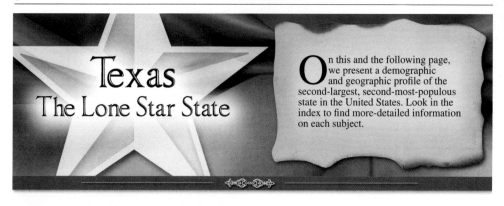

Texas
The Lone Star State

On this and the following page, we present a demographic and geographic profile of the second-largest, second-most-populous state in the United States. Look in the index to find more-detailed information on each subject.

★ The Government

Capital: Austin
Government: Bicameral Legislature
28th State to enter the Union: Dec. 29, 1845
Present Constitution adopted: 1876

State motto: Friendship (1930)
State symbols:
    Flower: Bluebonnet (1901)
    Bird: Mockingbird (1927)
    Tree: Pecan (1919)
    Song: "Texas, Our Texas" (1929)

Origin of name: Texas, or Tejas, was the Spanish pronunciation of a Caddo Indian word meaning "friends" or "allies."

Nickname: Texas is called the Lone Star State because of the design of the state flag: a broad vertical blue stripe at left centered by a single white star, and at right, horizontal bars of white (top) and red.

★ The People

Population (Jan. 2006 State Data
Center estimate) 23,507,700
Population (July 2004 U.S. Bureau
of the Census estimate) 22,490,022
Population, 2000 U.S. Census count ... 20,851,820
Population, 1990 U.S. Census count 16,986,510
Population increase, 1990–2000 .... 22.8%
Population increase, 2000–2006 .... 12.7%

Ethnicity, 2005 (for explanation of categories, see page 224):

	Number	Percent
Anglo	11,243,000	49.18%
Hispanic	8,030,000	35.12%
Black	2,673,000	11.69%
Other	926,000	4.01%

Population density (2005) .... 87.3 per sq. mi.

Voting-age population (2005) 17,033,000

(U.S. Census Bureau, The 2007 Statistical Abstract)

On an Average Day in Texas in 2004:

There were **1,042** resident live **births**.
There were **416** resident **deaths**.
There were **626** more births than deaths.
There were **488** marriages.
There were **222** divorces.

(2004 Texas Vital Statistics, Texas Dept. of Health)

★ Ten Largest Cities

Houston (Harris Co.)	2,085,737
San Antonio (Bexar Co.)	1,274,607
Dallas (Dallas Co.)	1,224,397
Austin (Travis Co.)	705,611
Fort Worth (Tarrant Co.)	638,102
El Paso (El Paso Co.)	602,112
Arlington (Tarrant Co.)	365,723
Corpus Christi (Nueces Co.)	283,384
Plano (Collin Co.)	255,593
Garland (Dallas Co.)	218,303

(January 2006 State Data Center estimate)

Number of counties 254
Number of incorporated cities 1,208
Number of cities of 100,000 pop. or more 28
Number of cities of 50,000 pop. or more 57
Number of cities of 10,000 pop. or more 205

★ Business

Gross State Product (2006) .... $1.068 trillion
Per Capita Personal Income (2005) $32,460
Civilian Labor Force (January 2005) 11,616,514

(GSP: Texas Comptroller of Public Accounts and U.S. Bureau of Economic Analysis; per capita income: U.S. Bureau of Economic Analysis; civilian labor force: Texas Workforce Commission.)

★ The Natural Environment

Area (total) .... 268,581 sq. miles
(171,891,840 acres)

Land area..................................... 261,797 sq. miles
(167,550,080 acres)

Water area .... 6,784 sq. miles
(4,341,760 acres)

Geographic center: About 15 miles northeast of
Brady in northern McCulloch County.

Highest point: Guadalupe Peak (8,749 ft.) in Culberson County in far West Texas.

Lowest point: Gulf of Mexico (sea level).

Normal average annual precipitation range:
From 60.57 inches at Jasper County in far East Texas,
to 9.43 inches at El Paso, in far West Texas.

Record highest temperature:
Seymour, August 12, 1936 .... 120°F
Monahans, June 28, 1994...................... 120°F

Record lowest temperature:
Tulia, Feb. 12, 1899................................ −23°F
Seminole, Feb. 8, 1933 .... −23°F

★ Principal Products

Manufactures: Chemicals and allied products, petroleum and coal products, food and kindred products, transportation equipment.

Farm products: Cattle, cotton, vegetables, fruits, nursery and greenhouse, dairy products.

Minerals: Petroleum, natural gas, natural gas liquids.

Finance (as of 12/31/2006):
Number of banks 608
Total deposits $181,846,927,000
Number of savings and loan associations...... 20
Total assets $64,692,927,000
Number of savings banks............................. 22
Total assets $9,393,482,000

(Banks: Federal Reserve Bank of Dallas; savings and loans and savings banks: Texas Savings and Loan Dept.)

Agriculture:
Total farm marketings, 2004 .... $16.498 billion
Number of farms, 2006.......................... 230,000
Land in farms (acres, 2006) .... 129.7 million
Cropland (acres, 2006).................... 22,617,000
Pastureland (acres, 2000) 15,914,000
Rangeland (acres, 2000)................. 95,745,000

(U.S. Census Bureau, The 2007 Statistical Abstract)

The Guadalupe Range in northwest Culberson County is the highest of the Trans-Pecos mountains. At 8,749 feet, Guadalupe Peak is the highest point in Texas. To the right of Guadalupe Peak is squared-off El Capitan, which stands 8,085 feet high. Robert Plocheck photo.

Texas' Rank Among the United States

Texas' rank among the United States in selected categories are given below. Others categories are covered in other sections in the *Texas Almanac,* such as, Agriculture, Business and Transportation, Science and Health.

Source (unless otherwise noted): The 2007 Statistical Abstract, U.S. Census Bureau; www. census.gov/compendia/statab

★ Ten Most Populous States, 2005

Rank		Population 2005	%Change 2000–2005
1.	California	36,132,000	4.8
2.	**Texas**	**22,860,000**	**6.1**
3.	New York	19,255,000	1.1
4.	Florida	17,790,000	6.5
5.	Illinois	12,763,000	1.9
6.	Pennsylvania	12,430,000	0.7
7.	Ohio	11,464,000	0.7
8.	Michigan	10,121,000	1.4
9.	Georgia	9,073,000	6.1
10.	New Jersey	8,718,000	2.7

(United States, ... 290,810,000 .... 5.3)

★ Ten Fastest Growing States, 2005

Rank	State	Population Change 2000–2005
1.	Nevada	20.8%
2.	Arizona	15.8%
3.	Florida	11.3%
4.	Georgia	10.8%
5.	Utah	10.6%
6.	Idaho	10.4%
7.	**Texas**	**9.6%**
8.	Colorado	8.4%
9.	North Carolina	7.9%
10.	Delaware	7.6%

★ States with Highest Immigration, 2005

Rank	State	Immigrants
1.	California	232,023
2.	New York	136,828
3.	Florida	122,918
4.	**Texas**	**95,958**
5.	New Jersey	56,180
6.	Illinois	52,419
7.	Massachusetts	34,236
8.	Georgia	31,535
9.	Pennsylvania	28,908
10.	Virginia	27,100

(United States .... 1,122,373)

★ States with Most Live Births, 2004

Rank	State	Births
1.	California	544,843
2.	**Texas**	**381,293**
3.	New York	249,947
4.	Florida	218,053
5.	Illinois	180,778
6.	Ohio	148,954

(United States .... 4,112,052)

★ States with Highest Birth Rates, 2004

Rank	State	Births per 1,000 Pop.
1.	Utah	21.2
2.	Montana	17.1
3.	New York	16.3
4.	Arizona	16.2
5.	**Texas**	**15.8**
6.	New Jersey	15.7

(United States .... 14.0)

★ States with Most Farms, 2006

Rank	State	No. of Farms
1.	**Texas**	**230,000**
2.	Missouri	105,000
3.	Iowa	88,600
4.	Kentucky	84,000
5.	Oklahoma	83,000
6.	Tennessee	82,000

(United States .... 2,089,790)

★ States with Most Land in Farms, 2006

Rank	State	Farm Acreage
1.	**Texas**	**129,700,000**
2.	Montana	60,100,000
3.	Kansas	47,200,000
4.	Nebraska	45,700,000
5.	New Mexico	44,500,000
6.	South Dakota	43,700,000

(United States .... 932,430,000)

State Flags and Symbols

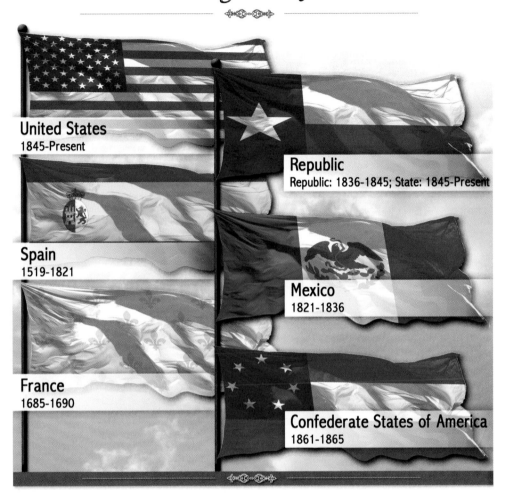

United States
1845-Present

Republic
Republic: 1836-1845; State: 1845-Present

Spain
1519-1821

Mexico
1821-1836

France
1685-1690

Confederate States of America
1861-1865

Texas often is called the **Lone Star State** because of its state flag with a single star. The state flag was also the **flag of the Republic of Texas**. The following information about historic Texas flags, the current flag and other Texas symbols may be supplemented by information available from the **Texas State Library** in Austin. (On the Web: **www.texasalmanac.com/flags.htm and www.tsl.state.tx.us/ref/abouttx/index.html#flags**)

Six Flags of Texas

Six different flags have flown over Texas during eight changes of sovereignty. The accepted sequence of these flags follows:

Spanish — 1519–1821
French — 1685–1690
Mexican — 1821–1836
Republic of Texas — 1836–1845
Confederate States of America — 1861–1865
United States — 1845 to the present.

Evolution of the Lone Star Flag

The Convention at Washington-on-the-Brazos in March 1836 allegedly adopted a flag for the Republic that was designed by Lorenzo de Zavala. The design of de Zavala's flag is unknown, but the convention journals state that a "Rainbow and star of five points above the western horizon; and a star of six points sinking below" was added to de Zavala's flag.

There was a suggestion the letters "T E X A S" be placed around the star in the flag, but there is no evidence that the Convention ever approved a final flag design. Probably because of the hasty dispersion of the Convention and loss of part of the Convention notes, nothing further was done with the Convention's proposals for a national flag. A **so-called "Zavala flag"** is sometimes flown in Texas today that consists of a blue field with a white five-pointed star in the center and letters "T E X A S" between the star points, but there is no historical evidence to support this flag's design.

The **first official flag of the Republic**, known as the **National Standard of Texas** or **David G. Burnet's**

flag, was adopted by the Texas Congress and approved by President Sam Houston on Dec. 10, 1836. The design "shall be an azure ground with a large golden star central."

The Lone Star Flag

On Jan. 25, 1839, President Mirabeau B. Lamar approved the adoption by Congress of a new national flag. This flag consisted of "a blue perpendicular stripe of the width of one third of the whole length of the flag, with a white star of five points in the centre thereof, and two horizontal stripes of equal breadth, the upper stripe white, the lower red, of the length of two thirds of the length of the whole flag." This is the **Lone Star Flag**, which later became the state flag.

Although Senator William H. Wharton proposed the adoption of the Lone Star Flag in 1838, no one knows who actually designed the flag. The legislature in 1879 inadvertently repealed the law establishing the state flag, but the legislature adopted a new law in 1933 that legally re-established the flag's design.

The red, white and blue of the state flag stand, respectively, for bravery, purity and loyalty. The proper finial for use with the state flag is either a star or a spearhead. Texas is one of only two states that has a flag that formerly served as the flag of an independent nation. The other is Hawaii.

Rules for Display of the State Flag

The Texas Flag Code was first adopted in 1933 and completely revised in 1993. Laws governing display of the state flag are found in sections 3100.051 through 3100.072 of the Texas Government Code. (On the Web: **www.tsl.state.tx.us/ref/abouttx/flagcode.html**). A summary of those rules follows:

The Texas flag should be displayed on state and national holidays and on special occasions of historical significance, and it should be displayed at every school on regular school days. **When flown out-of-doors**, the Texas flag should not be flown earlier than sunrise nor later than sunset unless properly illuminated. It should not be left out in inclement weather unless a weatherproof flag is used. It should be flown with the white stripe uppermost except in case of distress.

No flag other than the **United States flag** should be placed above or, if on the same level, to the state flag's right (observer's left). The state flag should be underneath the national flag when the two are flown from the same halyard. **When flown from adjacent flagpoles**, the national flag and the state flag should be of approximately the same size and on flagpoles of equal height; the national flag should be on the flag's own right (observer's left).

If the state flag is displayed with the flag of another U.S. state, a nation other than the U.S., or an international organization, the state flag should be, from an observer's perspective, to the left of the other flag on a separate flagpole or flagstaff, and the state flag should not be above the other flag on the same flagpole or flagstaff or on a taller flagpole or flagstaff. If the state flag and the U.S. flag are displayed from crossed flagstaffs, the state flag should be, from an observer's perspective, to the right of the U.S. flag and the state flag's flagstaff should be behind the U.S. flag's flagstaff.

When the flag is displayed horizontally, the white stripe should be above the red stripe and, from an observer's perspective, to the right of the blue stripe. **When the flag is displayed vertically**, the blue stripe should be uppermost and the white stripe should be to the state flag's right (observer's left).

If the state and national flags are both **carried in a procession**, the national flag should be on the marching right and state flag should be on the national flag's left (observer's right).

On Memorial Day, the state flag should be displayed at half-staff until noon and at that time raised to the peak of the flagpole. **On Peace Officers Memorial Day** (May 15), the state flag should be displayed at half-staff all day, unless that day is also Armed Forces Day.

The state flag should not touch anything beneath it or be dipped to any person or things except the U.S. flag. Advertising should not be fastened to a flagpole, flagstaff or halyard on which the state flag is displayed. If a state flag is no longer used or useful as an emblem for display, it should be destroyed, preferably by burning. A **flag retirement ceremony** is set out in the Texas Government Code at the Texas State Library Web site mentioned above.

Pledge to the Texas Flag

A pledge to the Texas flag was adopted in 1933 by the 43rd Legislature. It contained a phrase, "Flag of 1836," which inadvertently referred to the David G. Burnet flag instead of the Lone Star Flag adopted in 1839. In 2007, the 80th Legislature changed the pledge to its current form:

Honor the Texas flag;
I pledge allegiance to thee,
Texas, one state under
God, one and indivisible.

A person reciting the pledge to the state flag should face the flag, place the right hand over the heart and remove any easily removable hat.

The pledge to the Texas flag may be recited at all public and private meetings at which the pledge of allegiance to the national flag is recited and at state historical events and celebrations. The pledge to the Texas flag should be recited after the pledge of allegiance to the United States flag if both are recited.

State Song

The state song of Texas is **"Texas, Our Texas."** The music was written by the late William J. Marsh (who died Feb. 1, 1971, in Fort Worth at age 90), and the words by Marsh and Gladys Yoakum Wright, also of Fort Worth. It was the winner of a state song contest sponsored by the

41st legislature and was adopted in 1929. The wording has been changed once: Shortly after Alaska became a state in Jan. 1959, the word "Largest" in the third line was changed by Mr. Marsh to "Boldest."

The text follows:

 Texas, Our Texas

Texas, our Texas! All hail the mighty State!
Texas, our Texas! So wonderful, so great!
Boldest and grandest, Withstanding ev'ry test;
O Empire wide and glorious, You stand
      supremely blest.

Chorus
God bless you Texas!
And keep you brave and strong,
That you may grow in power and worth,
Thro'out the ages long.

Refrain
Texas, O Texas! Your freeborn single star,
Sends out its radiance to nations near and far.
Emblem of freedom! It sets our hearts aglow,
With thoughts of San Jacinto and glorious
      Alamo.

Texas, dear Texas! From tyrant grip now free,
Shines forth in splendor your star of destiny!
Mother of heroes! We come your children
      true,
Proclaiming our allegiance, our faith, our love
      for you.

Front of Seal

Back of Seal

State Motto
The state motto is "**Friendship**." The word Texas, or Tejas, was the Spanish pronunciation of a Caddo Indian word meaning "friends" or "allies." (41st Legislature in 1930.)

State Citizenship Designation
The people of Texas usually call themselves Texans. However, **Texian** was generally used in the early period of the state's history.

State Seal
The design of the **obverse (front)** of the State Seal consists of "a star of five points encircled by olive and live oak branches, and the words, 'The State of Texas'." (State Constitution, Art. IV, Sec. 19.) This design is a slight modification of the Great Seal of the Republic of Texas, adopted by the Congress of the Republic, Dec. 10, 1836, and readopted with modifications in 1839.

An official design for the **reverse (back)** of the seal was adopted by the 57th Legislature in 1961, but there were discrepancies between the written description and the artistic rendering that was adopted at the same time. To resolve the problems, the 72nd Legislature in 1991 adopted an official design.

The 73rd Legislature in 1993 finally adopted the reverse by law. The current description is in the Texas Government Code, section 3101.001:

"(b) The reverse side of the state seal contains a shield displaying a depiction of:

(1) the Alamo; (2) the cannon of the Battle of Gonzales; and (3) Vince's Bridge. (c)

The shield on the reverse side of the state seal is encircled by:

(1) live oak and olive branches; and (2) the unfurled flags of: (A) the Kingdom of France; (B) the Kingdom of Spain; (C) the United Mexican States: (D) the Republic of Texas; (E) the Confederate States of America; and (F) the United States of America. (d) Above the shield is emblazoned the motto, "REMEMBER THE ALAMO," and beneath the shield are the words, "TEXAS ONE AND INDIVISIBLE." (e) A white five-pointed star hangs over the shield, centered between the flags."

Texas State Symbols

State Bird — The **mockingbird** (*Mimus polyglottos*) is the state bird of Texas, adopted by the 40th Legislature of 1927 at the request of the Texas Federation of Women's Clubs.

State Flower — The state flower of Texas is the **bluebonnet**, also called **buffalo clover**, **wolf flower** and *el conejo* (the rabbit). The bluebonnet was adopted as the state flower, at the request of the Society of Colonial Dames in Texas, by the 27th Legislature in 1901. The original resolution made *Lupinus subcarnosus* the state flower, but a resolution by the 62nd Legislature in 1971 provided legal status as the state flower of Texas for "*Lupinus Texensis* and any other variety of bluebonnet."

State Tree — The **pecan tree** (*Carya illinoinensis*) is the state tree of Texas. The sentiment that led to its official adoption probably grew out of the request of Gov. James Stephen Hogg that a pecan tree be planted at his grave. The 36th Legislature in 1919 adopted the pecan tree.

Other Symbols

(In 2001, the Texas Legislature placed restrictions on the adoption of future symbols by requiring that a joint resolution to designate a symbol must specify the item's historical or cultural significance to the state.)

State Air Force — The **Commemorative Air Force** (formerly known as the Confederate Air Force), based in Midland at Midland International Airport, was proclaimed the state air force of Texas by the 71st Legislature in 1989.

State Bluebonnet City — The city of **Ennis** in Ellis County was named state bluebonnet city by the 75th Legislature in 1997.

State Bluebonnet Festival — The **Chappell Hill Bluebonnet Festival**, held in April, was named state bluebonnet festival by the 75th Legislature in 1997.

State Bluebonnet Trail — The city of Ennis was named state bluebonnet trail by the 75th Legislature in 1997.

State Bread — *Pan de campo*, translated "camp bread" and often called cowboy bread, was named the state bread by the 79th Legislature in 2005. It is a simple baking-powder bread that was a staple of early Texans and often baked in a Dutch oven.

State Cooking Implement — The **cast iron Dutch oven** was named the cooking implement of Texas by the 79th Legislature in 2005.

State Dinosaur — The **Brachiosaur Sauropod, Pleurocoelus** was designated the state dinosaur by the 75th Legislature in 1997.

State Dish — **Chili** was proclaimed the Texas state dish by the 65th Legislature in 1977.

State Dog Breed — The **Blue Lacy** was designated the state dog breed by the 79th Legislature in 2005. The Blue Lacy is a herding and hunting breed descended from greyhound, scent-hound, and coyote stock and developed by the Lacy brothers, who left Kentucky and settled near Marble Falls in 1858.

State Epic Poem — "**The Legend of Old Stone Ranch**," written by John Worth Cloud, was named the epic poem of Texas by the 61st Legislature in 1969. The work is a 400-page history of the Albany–Fort Griffin area written in verse form.

STATE BIRD

Mocking Bird
Mimus Polyglottos

STATE FLOWER

Bluebonnet
Lupinus Texensis

STATE TREE

Pecan Tree
Carya Illinoinensis

STATE DISH

Chili

STATE DOG BREED

Blue Lacy

STATE FIBER AND FABRIC

Cotton

STATE FRUIT

STATE INSECT

STATE SMALL MAMMAL

STATE NATIVE PEPPER

Monarch Butterfly
Danaus Plexippus

Texas Red Grapefruit

Armadillo
Dasypus Novemcinctus

Chiltepin

State Fiber and Fabric — **Cotton** was designated the state fiber and fabric by the 75th Legislature in 1997.

State Fish — The **Guadalupe bass**, a member of the genus *Micropterus* within the sunfish family, was named the state fish of Texas by the 71st Legislature in 1989. It is one of a group of fish collectively known as black bass.

State Flower Song — "**Bluebonnets**," written by Julia D. Booth and Lora C. Crockett, was named the state flower song by the 43rd Legislature in 1933.

State Folk Dance — The **square dance** was designated the state folk dance by the 72nd Legislature in 1991.

State Fruit — The **Texas red grapefruit** was designated the state fruit by the 73rd Legislature in 1993.

State Gem — **Texas blue topaz**, the state gem of Texas, is found in the Llano uplift area in Central Texas, especially west to northwest of Mason. It was designated by the 61st Legislature in 1969.

State Gemstone Cut — The **Lone Star Cut** was named the state gemstone cut by the 65th Legislature in 1977.

State Grass — **Sideoats grama** (*Bouteloua curtipendula*), a native grass found on many different soils, was designated the state grass of Texas by the 62nd Legislature in 1971.

State Health Nut — The **pecan** was designated the state nut by the 77th Legislature in 2001.

State Insect — The **Monarch butterfly** (*Danaus plexippus*) was designated the state insect by the 74th Legislature in 1995.

State Mammals — The **armadillo** (*Dasypus novemcinctus*) was designated the state **small mammal**; the **longhorn** was designated the state **large mammal**; and the **Mexican free-tailed bat** (*Tadarida brasiliensis*) was designated the state flying mammal by the 74th Legislature in 1995.

State Musical Instrument — The **guitar** was named the state musical instrument by the 75th Legislature in 1997.

State Native Pepper — The **chiltepin** was named the native pepper of Texas by the 75th Legislature in 1997.

State Native Shrub — The **Texas purple sage** (*leucophyllum frutescens*) was designated the state native shrub by the 79th Legislature in 2005.

State Pepper — The **jalapeño pepper** was designated the state pepper by the 74th Legislature in 1995.

State Plant — The **prickly pear cactus** was named the state plant by the 74th Legislature in 1995.

State Plays — The four official state plays of Texas are *The Lone Star, Texas, Beyond the Sundown*, and *Fandangle*. They were designated by the 66th Legislature in 1979.

STATE PEPPER

STATE PLANT

STATE REPTILE

STATE TARTAN

Jalapeño Pepper

Prickly Pear Cactus

Texas Horned Lizard
Phrynosoma Cornutum

Texas Bluebonnet Tartan

State Precious Metal — Silver was named the official precious metal by the 80th Legislature in 2007.

State Railroad — The **Texas State Railroad** was designated the state railroad by the 78th Legislature in 2003. The Texas State Railroad is a steam powered tourist excursion train operated by the Texas Parks & Wildlife Department. Its 25 miles of track meander through the East Texas piney woods and across the Neches River between the towns of Rusk and Palestine.

State Reptile — The **Texas horned lizard** (*Phrynosoma cornutum*) was named the state reptile by the 73rd Legislature in 1993.

State Seashell — The **lightning whelk** (*Busycon perversum pulleyi*) was named the state seashell by the 70th Legislature in 1987. One of the few shells that open on the left side, the lightning whelk is named for its colored stripes. It is found only on the Gulf Coast.

State Ship — The battleship **USS Texas** was designated the state ship by the 74th Legislature in 1995. The USS Texas was launched on May 18, 1912, from Newport News, VA, and commissioned on March 12, 1914. In 1919, it became the first U.S. battleship to launch an aircraft, and in 1939 it received the first commercial radar in the U.S. Navy. In 1940, the Texas was designated flagship of the U.S. Atlantic Fleet and was the last of the battleships to participate in both World Wars I and II. It was decommissioned on April 21, 1948, and is a National Historic Landmark and a National Mechanical Engineering Landmark.

State Shoe — The cowboy boot was named the state shoe by the 80th Legislature in 2007.

State Shrub — The **crape myrtle** (*Lagerstroemia indica*) was designated the official state shrub by the 75th Legislature in 1997.

State Snack — **Tortilla chips and salsa** was designated the official state snack by the 78th Legislature in 2003 at the request of second-grade students in Mission.

State Sport — **Rodeo** was named the state sport of Texas by the 75th Legislature in 1997.

State Stone — **Petrified palmwood**, found in Texas principally in eastern counties near the Texas Gulf Coast, was designated the state stone by the 61st Legislature in 1969.

State Tall Ship — The **Elissa** was named the state tall ship by the 79th Legislature in 2005. The 1877 ship makes its home at the Texas Seaport Museum at the port of Galveston.

State Tartan — The **Texas Bluebonnet Tartan** was named the official state tartan by the 71st Texas Legislature in 1989.

State Tie — The bolo tie was designated the state tie by the 80th Legislature in 2007.

State Vegetable — The **Texas sweet onion** was designated the state vegetable by the 75th Legislature in 1997.

State Vehicle — The **chuck wagon** was named the state vehicle by the 79th Legislature in 2005. Texas rancher Charles Goodnight is created with inventing the chuck wagon to carry cowboys food and supplies on trail drives.

State 10K — The **Texas Roundup 10K** was named the state 10K by the 79th Legislature in 2005 to encourage Texans to exercise and incorporate physical activity into their daily lives.

The chuck wagon is the official state vehicle.

History

Pictographs on outcroppings near Paint Rock. Matthew Minard photo.

Texas Archeology

Stagecoaching in Texas

Civilian Conservation Corps

A Brief Sketch of Texas History

ROCK ART AND ANCIENT ARTIFACTS CAN BE SEEN AND EXPLORED THROUGHOUT THE STATE

By Elizabeth Cruce Alvarez

Texas is rich in archeology. You don't have to be a scholar or student of archeology to get your fill of pictographs, arrowheads, rock shelters and burial mounds. From rugged outdoor excavations and museum exhibits to Web sites filled with photographs, some of the most important archeological finds in the United States can be seen and explored in Texas.

Although many archeological digs conducted by Texas universities are off limits to the public, such as parts of the Gault Clovis site in the Hill Country where Clovis points have been found, there are plenty of sites open to visitors. Many state parks and historic sites are famous for their Paleo-Indian and Native American sites and artifacts, such as the Caddoan Mounds State Historic Site in Cherokee County, where Early Caddo Mound Builder people lived around A.D. 800; Palo Duro Canyon State Park in Randall County, where there is evidence of 12,000 years of Indian occupation; Seminole Canyon State Park & Historic Site in Val Verde County, home of the famous Fate Bell Shelter, which contains some of North America's oldest pictographs; and Hueco Tanks State Historic Site in El Paso County, which has more pictograph mask images than any other rock art site in North America.

Archeological finds have also been discovered at Texas' national parks and monuments. Big Bend National Park contains two prehistoric sites, the Hot Springs pictograph site and the Chimneys, in addition to later Indian, Spanish and Mexican ruins and ar-

Three pieces of pottery from the excavation of a Caddo Indian village near Gilmer were discovered in a burial mound. Russell Bronson photo.

tifacts. Nearby Sul Ross State University is home to the Center for Big Bend Studies and the Museum of the Big Bend. The center conducts historical and archeological research in the Big Bend area and holds an archeological field school each summer. The museum exhibits artifacts from thousands of years of Indian occupation in the Big Bend.

Alibates Flint Quarries National Monument in Potter County was a major stone quarry for the Indians of the Southern Plains beginning about 10,000 B.C; and at Amistad National Recreation Area near Del Rio in Val Verde County, prehistoric Indian rock art located on the shores of the lake can be visited by commercial boat tours.

Visitors can also explore Lubbock Lake Landmark in Lubbock County. The site, operated by the Museum of Texas Tech University, contains a detailed record covering the past 12,000 years and is considered one of the most important Paleo-Indian sites in North America.

In addition, city and county museums across the state exhibit fascinating finds, and many of the historic forts and missions of Texas contain archeological artifacts from Plains Indian cultures, Spanish explorers and early Texans.

Then there are privately owned sites, such as Paint Rock in Concho County, which contains more than 1,500 rock art markings dating from prehistoric times through the last quarter of the 19th century. Though located on private land, the owners maintain a Web site and daily tours are given by appointment. (See list of Sites to Visit.)

The Rock Art Foundation in San Antonio maintains a Web site (www.rockart.org) filled with pictographs from the Lower Pecos region of Southwest Texas, and it conducts tours of rock art and historic sites, many of which are on private land.

Another web site devoted to teaching about archeology in Texas is the Texas Beyond History site, www.texasbeyondhistory.net, which features in-depth descriptions of excavations across Texas, along with a huge gallery of pottery, arrowheads, dig sites and interpretive drawings.

Launched in 2001, Texas Beyond History is a virtual museum and a public education service of the Texas Archeological Research Laboratory at the University of Texas at Austin, in partnership with 14 other organizations. Through this site, the research lab can share its archeological and historical research on Texas' cultural heritage.

For those who want to get involved in digs and preservation, Texas Archeological Society (www.txarch.org) offers memberships and a wide variety of hands-on activities. Since 1929, the society has studied and helped to preserve the state's historic and prehistoric treasures.

The 1,500-member society conducts field schools and brings its Texas Archeological Academy to various towns throughout the year, teaching participants how to identify, test and record archeological sites. The group participates with the Texas Historical Commission in holding events for Texas Archeology Month, which is

Dr. Michael Collins of the UT Austin Archeological Research Laboratory stands near a flint outcropping at the Gault site, an important Paleo-Indian excavation in Bell County. The abundance of flint veins account for the large amount of toolmaking discovered there, including Clovis artifacts. Eric Schlegel photo.

observed in October.

The Texas Historical Commission's Archeology Division also records and evaluates archeological sites and works on several specific projects, including the Fort St. Louis Archeological Project and the Red River War Battle Sites Project. It also conducts marine archeology programs, including the La Salle Shipwreck Project. The THC assigns archeologists to each of six regions in the state, who can be contacted if landowners believe they have an archeological site on their land.

The THC web site (www.thc.state.tx.us/archeology/aadefault.html) has a wealth of material about archeology in Texas, including its semiannual publication, *Current Archeology in Texas.*

There are archeological societies across Texas that welcome both amateur and professional members. The Texas Archeological Society lists these organization that offer memberships:

Panhandle Archeological Society
PO Box 814, Amarillo, TX 79105; 806-364-6894

Collin County Archeological Society
c/o Heard Natural Science Museum
One Nature Place, McKinney, TX 75069

Dallas Archeological Society
1900 Preston Rd., #267 PMB 123, Plano, TX 75093; info@dallasarcheology.org
www.dallasarcheology.org/

Parker County Archeological Society
Contact: Laurie Moseley at moseley@airmail.net.

Tarrant County Archeological Society
Box 24679, Fort Worth, TX 76124; 817-496-5475

East Texas Archeological Society
PO Box 632398, Nacogdoches, TX 75961; 936-875-2864

Deep East Texas Archeological Society
960 College, Jasper, TX 75951

Valley of the Caddo Archeological Society
Contact: D. Richard Proctor, President, 1-903-785-0229

Brazosport Archaeological Society
c/o Brazosport Museum of Natural Science, 400 College Dr., Clute, TX 77531
www.geocities.com/fortbendarch/

Fort Bend Archeological Society
c/o Ft. Bend Museum, 500 Houston St., Richmond, TX 77469; 1-281-342-6478

Houston Archeological Society
PO Box 6751, Houston, TX 77265-6751
www.houstonarcheology.org/

Coastal Bend Archaeological Society
4650 Hakel Dr., Corpus Christi, TX 78415-2824; 1-361-241-1090

Rio Grande Delta Archeological Society
c/o Rio RV Park Office, 8801 Boca Chica, Brownsville,TX 78521; 956-831-4653
riograndeltarch@aol.com;

Central Texas Archeological Society
4229 Mitchell Rd., Waco, TX 76710; 254-772-0027

Llano Uplift Archeological Society
Box 302, Kingsland, TX 78639
www.texasluas.org/

Travis County Archeological Society
Box 9250, Austin, TX 78766-9250

http://travis.txarch.org

Concho Valley Archeological Society
4222 North Rd. 3, Miles, TX 76861
www.geocities.com/cvas.geo/

Iraan Archeological Society
101 S. Rio, Fort Stockton, TX 79735;
915-336-5580

Midland Archeological Society
PO Box 4224, Midland, TX 79704
www.midarcsoc.org/

Big Bend Archaeological Society
PO Box 1, Big Bend National Park, TX 79834; 432-837-8179
www.bigbendarch.org

El Paso Archaeological Society
PO Box 4345; El Paso, TX 79914-4345
www.epas.com/

Southern Texas Archaeological Association
PO Box 791032, San Antonio, TX 78279-1031; www.staa.org/

Hill Country Archeological Association
PO Box 290393, Kerrville, TX 78029
Contact: sanerjr@ktc.com or sodbustr@ktc.com

Archeological Sites & Museums to Visit

Source: Texas Historical Commission and web sites of the various facilities listed below.

ALBANY, Shackelford County

Fort Griffin State Park & Historic Site. The fort was constructed in 1867 and deactivated in 1881. Partially restored ruins include mess hall, barracks, store, administration building, hospital and powder magazine. A restored bakery and replicas of enlisted men's huts are on a bluff overlooking the Clear Fork of the Brazos River. A portion of the official Texas longhorn herd resides in the park. Tours and living-history programs are available. Located 15 miles north of Albany on US Highway 283. www.tpwd.state.tx.us/spdest/findadest/parks/fort_griffin/

ALPINE and vicinity, Brewster County

Big Bend National Park. Located south of Alpine and Marathon, the 800,000-acre park contains evidence of Indian-Spanish-Mexican cultural adaptations to the Big Bend's arid environment and more than 450 historic structures and ruins related to ranching, mining, early settlement and the military. Of special interest are the Castolon Historic Compound, which includes many structures dating from the period of Pancho Villa's border raids, and the Glenn Spring area, which lies on a branch of the Comanche Trail. Two prehistoric sites, the Hot Springs pictograph site and the Chimneys, also are accessible to the public. Park headquarters is located at Panther Junction at U.S 385 and FM 170. www.nps.gov/bibe/

Center for Big Bend Studies. Located on the campus of Sul Ross State University, the center conducts historical and archeological research in the Big Bend area and holds an archeological field school each summer. Visitors welcome. www.sulross.edu/~cbbs

Museum of the Big Bend. Located on the Sul Ross State University campus, this museum's exhibits and collections include artifacts from thousands of years of Indian occupation in the Big Bend. Especially noteworthy are items such as fiber sandals that have survived in the dry caves of the region. www.sulross.edu/~museum

ALTO, Cherokee County

Caddoan Mounds State Historic Site. The park contains the remnants of two temple mounds, a burial mound and a large portion of the village area built by the Early Caddo Mound Builder people starting about A.D. 800. Visitors can take a self-guided tour around the site and view dioramas, artifact exhibits and an interpretive audiovisual program in the visitor's center. Located at 1649 State Hwy 21W. www.tpwd.state.tx.us/spdest/findadest/parks/caddoan_mounds/

AMARILLO, Potter County

Alibates Flint Quarries National Monument. Alibates was a major stone quarry for the Indians of the Southern Plains beginning about 10,000 B.C. Archeologists have recovered the distinctive Alibates flint across a wide area of Texas and the Southern Plains, indicating a widespread trade network. Access by ranger-led tours only; reservations should be made several days ahead. Located north of Amarillo, south of Fritch, off Hwy 136. www.nps.gov/alfl

AUSTIN, Travis County

Texas Memorial Museum. Located on the University of Texas campus and part of the Texas Natural Science Center, the museum exhibits collections that include materials from the prehistoric to the present. The Hall of Geology and Paleontology features 5,200 square feet of fossils of dinosaurs and other prehistoric creatures, as well as meteorites, rocks and minerals. Visitors can bring in their own fossil finds and learn about them from working paleontologists in the on-site paleo lab. The hands-on Discovery Drawers includes specimens from the Texas Natural Science Center's collections. www.tmm.utexas.edu

BORGER, Hutchinson County

Hutchinson County Historical Museum. The museum has permanent exhibits relating to Southern Plains tribes, the adventures of Billy Dixon — a civilian scout for the Army during the Red River War — and the Adobe Walls trading posts, site of the 1864 and 1874 battles of Adobe Walls. Located at 618 N. Main. www.hutchinsoncountymuseum.org/

BRACKETTVILLE, Kinney County

Fort Clark. The fort was established in 1852, abandoned by Federal troops in 1861, occupied by Confederate troops during the Civil War, and reoccupied by Federal troops in 1866. Fort Clark is perhaps best known as the home of the Seminole-Negro Indian

Scouts, who came to Fort Duncan in 1872 and then to Fort Clark. The fort was closed in 1944 and was later developed into a private recreation community. The Historic District of the fort remains much as it was in the late 1800s. A museum is maintained in the Old Fort Clark Guardhouse located on U.S. 90. The historic Seminole-Negro Indian Scout Cemetery is on FM Road 3348, west of the fort. www.fortclark.com/

BRYAN, Brazos County

Brazos Valley Museum of Natural History. The museum offers science programs, exhibits, special events and affiliated programs — such as those of Earthwatch, the Archaeological Institute of America and the Texas Cooperative Wildlife Collections. Located at 3232 Briarcrest Dr. http://bvmuseum.myriad.net

CANYON, Randall County

Palo Duro Canyon State Park. In addition to 12,000 years of Indian occupation, Palo Duro Canyon is believed to have been visited by Coronado in the 1540s. The canyon was the site of one of the last major Indian battles in Texas in 1874. Located on State Hwy 217 about 12 miles east of Canyon. www.palodurocanyon.com

Panhandle-Plains Historical Museum. The museum has extensive exhibits relating to the history of the Panhandle. The Hall of the Southern Plains Indians includes authentic materials of the Comanche, Southern Cheyenne, Arapaho, Kiowa, Kiowa Apache and Apache tribes. Artifacts document 14,000 years of habitation in the Texas Panhandle from Clovis and Folsom big-game hunters to later foragers and Southern Plains villagers living in semi-permanent houses, hunting bison, farming corn, beans and squash, and mining and trading Alibates flint. Collections also include Spanish items from the age of exploration through the colonial period, and the Ranching Hall tells the history of ranching from the Spaniards' introduction of cattle until today. Located at 2401 Fourth Ave. on the West Texas A&M University campus. www.wtamu.edu/museum

CLARENDON, Donley County

Saints' Roost Museum. Present-day Donley County was the site of several skirmishes between U.S. Army and Native American forces in the 1870s. On permanent display is a Red River War exhibit featuring a selection of Native American artifacts. The museum is housed in the former Adair Hospital, built in 1910 by Cornelia Adair for use by the JA Ranch cowboys. Other exhibits highlight the lives of cattleman Col. Charles Goodnight and Western artist Harold D. Bugbee. Located at 610 E. Harrington St. www.saintsroost.org/

CLAUDE, Armstrong County

Armstrong County Museum. The first official battle of the Red River War was waged in what is now Armstrong County on August 30, 1874. Armstrong County was also the location of the Battle of Palo Duro Canyon, the turning point of the war. An exhibit featuring Colonel Mackenzie's victory at the Battle of Palo Duro Canyon is on permanent display at the museum. Located at 120 N. Trice. www.searchtexas.com/gem-theatre/

COMSTOCK, Val Verde County

Seminole Canyon State Park & Historic Site. In the canyon is Fate Bell Shelter, which contains some of North America's oldest pictographs. Painted as long as 4,000 years ago, these fine examples of rock art can be seen on guided tours into the canyon. Headquarters exhibits interpret the human presence here from the first known evidence to present-day ranching. Park located on U.S. 90, 20 miles east of Langtry. www.tpwd.state.tx.us/spdest/findadest/parks/seminole_canyon/

CORPUS CHRISTI, Nueces County

Corpus Christi Museum of Science and History. Features a permanent display, in a dockside setting, of artifacts from 1554 Spanish shipwrecks. Permanent exhibits also include Karankawa Indian artifacts and a diorama of this group in historic times. Fees include access to museum and to full-scale replicas of Columbus' ships. Located at 1900 N. Chaparral St. www.ccmuseum.com/museum/index.cfm

CROSBYTON, Crosby County

Crosby County Pioneer Memorial Museum. In addition to the Wayne J. Parker Collection of Native American artifacts, the museum showcases a diorama of Blanco Canyon, a half-dugout reproduction and the story of peoples who made the Llano Estacado their home for more than 700 years. Relating to the Red River War are artifacts from Colonel Mackenzie's Supply Camp, located near Crosbyton, and materials relating to the Battle of Blanco Canyon, the climax of Mackenzie's 1871 campaign against the Comanches. Located at 101 W. Main. www.crosbycountymuseum.com/

DALLAS, Dallas County

Dallas Museum of Art. The museum's collections include superb works from ancient cultures, including those of native North America, Mesoamerica and South America. Located at 1717 N. Harwood. http://dallas-museumofart.org/

Dallas Museum of Natural History. In addition to featuring environmental exhibits and dioramas of native plants and animals that are essential to an understanding of prehistoric environments, the museum may feature special archeological or Native American exhibits; inquire for current exhibits. Located at Second and Grand avenues in Fair Park. www.natureandscience.org/

International Museum of Cultures. For both children and adults, the museum features exhibits such as Jungle Potters — which shows the designs and pottery-making techniques of the Lowland Quichua people of Amazonian Ecuador — that demonstrate the relationship of artifacts to cultures and culture's adaptations to their local environments. www.internationalmuseumofcultures.org/

DEL RIO and vicinity, Val Verde County

Amistad National Recreation Area. Prehistoric Indian rock art located on the shores of the lake — including Panther Cave, one of the state's most important rock art sites — can be visited by commercial boat tours. San Felipe Springs (commemorated by a marker on the grounds of the City Water Commission Building in Del Rio) was an oasis that drew both Indians and early Spanish explorers; it was a campground on the legendary Comanche War Trail. Amistad's museum collection consists almost exclusively of prehistoric artifacts excavated prior to the impoundment of waters behind Amistad Dam in 1969. Located on U.S. 290 at northern edge of Del Rio. www.nps.gov/amis

Devils River State Natural Area. Archeological evidence suggests that cultural influences from the west and east met at Devils River. Tours of remote rock art sites on a preapproved basis only. Tour fees apply. Located north of Del Rio. www.tpwd.state.tx.us/spdest/findadest/parks/devils_river/

Whitehead Memorial Museum. The museum's focus is on the historic period from the Spanish Colonial period to the present, but displays also include American Indian materials. Located at 1308 S. Main St. www.whitehead-museum.com

EL PASO and vicinity, El Paso County

El Paso Centennial Museum. The museum focuses on the natural history and the indigenous, colonial, pre-urban and folk cultures of the border regions of southwestern United States and Mexico. It promotes and shares knowledge and understanding of the natural and cultural diversity of the region and its peoples. Located at University Avenue and Wiggins Road on the University of Texas at El Paso campus. http://museum.utep.edu/

El Paso Museum of Archeology. This indoor-outdoor museum, which covers 17 acres, features exhibits and dioramas depicting human adaptation to the arid environment of the region. Replicas of a pueblo ruin, a kiva and a pithouse are on display. The museum also houses the laboratory of the El Paso Archeological Society and features special programs in observance of Archeology Awareness Month each October. Located north of El Paso at 4301 Transmountain Rd. www.epas.com/museum.htm.

Franklin Mountains State Park. Native American groups used the plant and animal resources of the Franklin Mountains for thousands of years. Evidence of their occupation remains in pictographs on boulders and in rock shelters and deep mortar pits (used to grind seeds) in rock outcrops near scattered water sources. During the past four centuries, the mountains have witnessed an endless procession of expansion, settlement, raiding and conquest. Check for availability of guided-tour hikes to learn about the cultural history of the area and the local flora and fauna (first and third weekends; reservations required). Located 3.8 miles east of Interstate-10. www.tpwd.state.tx.us/spdest/findadest/parks/franklin/

Hueco Tanks State Historical Site. A unique natural and cultural site, Hueco Tanks is one of the most impressive outdoor art galleries in the world and has more pictograph mask images than

Hueco Tanks State Historical Site contains natural basins that caught rainwater. Pictographs are also plentiful. David Kennedy photo.

any other rock art site in North America. Altogether, more than 3,000 paintings depict a multitude of human, animal and geometric figures. For centuries, Hueco Tanks has been a well-known landmark in this arid region of western Texas because of the supply of rainwater that is trapped in the natural basins, or huecos, among the rocks. Park located off U.S. 62/180, 24 miles east of El Paso, then 8 miles north on FM 2775. Guided rock art tours available Wednesday–Sunday; call in advance for reservations (915-857-1135). Note: access is limited. www.tpwd.state.tx.us/spdest/findadest/parks/hueco_tanks/

Ysleta del Sur Pueblo (including the Tigua Indian Reservation and Ysleta Mission). The Tigua Indians have inhabited this locale since about 1681 and are one of only three tribal Indian groups in Texas. Ysleta, the oldest community in present-day Texas, is now part of the city of El Paso. The Ysleta del Sur Pueblo Cultural Center is owned and operated by the Tigua Indians. Located at 119 S. Old Pueblo Rd. www.lone-star.net/mall/txtrails/ysleta.htm

FORT DAVIS, Jeff Davis County

Fort Davis National Historic Site. The story of a frontier fort's military and civilian residents, as well as the Native American inhabitants of the Trans-Pecos region, is told at Fort Davis National Historic Site. Established in 1854, the fort was abandoned during the Civil War, re-established in 1867, and operated until 1891. More than 50 historic structures — both ruins and restorations of adobe, stone and wood — date from the second era (1867–1891). Fort Davis is a showplace among frontier forts of the Southwest. www.nps.gov/foda

FORT McKAVETT, Menard County

Fort McKavett State Historic Site. The fort, established in 1852, was abandoned in 1859, reoccupied in 1868 following the Civil War, and finally abandoned in 1883. Restored buildings include the 1870 hospital (housing the interpretive center), officers' quarters, schoolhouse, barracks, post headquarters and bakery. Park offers guided group tours and, in March, an Annual Living History Event. Located west of Menard of of U.S. 190 and FM 864. www.tpwd.state.tx.us/spdest/findadest/parks/fort_mckavett/

FORT STOCKTON, Pecos County

Historic Fort Stockton. Established in 1859, the fort was abandoned in 1861, occupied by Confederate troops until 1862, and re-established by four companies of the 9th U.S. Cavalry in July 1867. Most of the soldiers garrisoned at the fort from 1867 until 1886 were African-American troops (Buffalo Soldiers), and they played a major role in the settlement and development of the American West. In 1988–1989, excavations were undertaken at the fort site to locate the foundations of two enlisted men's barracks and kitchens. The barracks and kitchens were reconstructed in 1990, and a museum/ visitor's center is maintained in the barracks. www.tourtexas.com/ fortstockton/ftstockfort.html

FORT WORTH, Tarrant County

Fort Worth Museum of Science and History. Offers social studies classroom kits using artifacts from the museum's teaching collection. Topics include Texas Archeology, Indians and the Buffalo, and Lone Star Dinosaurs, which currently is available to view online at http://lonestardinosaurs.org/exhibit/index.html and will reopen in fall 2009 when the museum opens a new facility. Located at 1501 Montgomery St. www.fwmuseum.org

GOLIAD, Goliad County

Goliad State Park & Mission Espiritu Santo State Historic Site. The park contains a refurnished replica of the mission, reconstructed by the Civilian Conservation Corps in the 1930s. The mission, established here in 1749, became the first large cattle ranch in Texas and has interpretive displays relating to the historic Indians of the area and the Spanish Colonial period. General Ignacio Zaragoza's birthplace and the ruins of Mission Nuestra Senora del Rosario, established in 1754, also are included in the park. Located 1/4 mile south of Goliad on US 183. www.tpwd.state.tx.us/spdest/findadest/ parks/goliad_and_mission_espiritu_santo/ htm

Presidio de la Bahia. The 1749 presidio was restored in the 1960s and is now a National Historic Landmark. In addition to the imposing structure, interpretive exhibits cover both Spanish Colonial and Texas revolutionary periods, and archeologically recovered materials are on display. Check for special events. Located 2 miles south of Goliad off US 183. www.presidiolabahia.org/index.html

HARLINGEN, Cameron County

Rio Grande Valley Museum. As well as materials relating to the historic bicultural heritage of the region, the museum's displays include artifacts from the nomadic Indians of South Texas. Located in Industrial Air Park, Boxwood Street.

HOUSTON, Harris County

Houston Museum of Natural Science. The 10 galleries of the John P. McGovern Hall of the Americas are fun, entertaining, educational and appealing to all who are interested in archeology. The Origins and Diversity Gallery introduces the major themes and explains the sciences of anthropology and archeology. In the Plains Gallery, objects displayed in a reconstructed tipi tell the story of the nomadic peoples of the Plains. The Southwest Gallery examines Pueblo cultures through artifacts and a full-scale re-creation of an excavated kiva. Located at One Hermann Circle Dr. www.hmns.org.

Museum of Fine Arts, Houston. The museum's American, Oceanic and African exhibit displays Precolumbian and tribal arts, including Southwestern Indian materials and Casas Grandes items. Located at 1001 Bissonnet at Main. www.mfah.org

San Jacinto Museum of History. While the museum is strong in material relating to the period of the Republic of Texas, exhibits interpret Texas history from the early American civilizations through the end of the 19th century. Located in San Jacinto Battleground State Historical Park off SH 225. www.sanjacinto-museum.org

KINGSLAND, Burnet County

Nightengale Archaeological Center. The center offers tours of the prehistoric Kingsland site, which is located on 10 acres on Lake LBJ. More than 171,000 flint tools, spear points, arrowheads and other artifacts have been recovered. Interpretive exhibits outdoors include a prehistoric hut reconstruction based on evidence found at the site. Located 9.3 miles northwest of Marble Falls and 2.5 miles southeast of Kingsland on FM 1431, then 1/2 mile west on CR 126. www.lcra.org/parks/natural_resource/nightengale.html

JACKSBORO, Jack County

Fort Richardson State Park & Historic Site. The fort, established in November 1867, was abandoned in May 1878. Restorations of original structures include post hospital, officers' quarters (housing the interpretive center), powder magazine, commissary, guardhouse and bakery. Guided historical tours are offered on weekends and by appointment. Special events held throughout the year include military reenactments and living-history presentations. Located 1/2 mile south of Jacksboro on US 281. www.tpwd.state. tx.us/spdest/findadest/parks/fort_richardson/

LAKE JACKSON, Brazoria County

Brazosport Museum of Natural Science. The museum includes both prehistoric and historic archeology among its displays and permanent collections and is home of the Brazosport Archaeological Society. Located at 400 College Dr. bcfas.org/museum

LUBBOCK, Lubbock County

Lubbock Lake Landmark. The Lubbock Lake site contains a detailed cultural, geological, faunal and floral record covering the past 12,000 years and is one of the most important Paleo-Indian sites in North America. The Interpretive Center is both an educational facility and museum. Outdoor activities include a 1-mile archeology trail and a 4-mile nature trail. Operated by the Museum of Texas Tech University and located at 2401 Landmark Dr., on northwest edge of city. interoz.com/lubbock/landmark.htm

Museum of Texas Tech University. Prehistoric cultures of both Mexico and the United States are included in the museum's permanent collections. Located at 4th Street and Indiana Avenue www.depts.ttu.edu/museumttu/

MENARD vicinity, Menard County

Fort McKavett State Historic Site. Abandoned during the Civil War, the fort was reopened after the war and completely rebuilt by members of the 9th U.S. Cavalry (Buffalo Soldiers). The fort provided supplies, scouts and troops in support of Ranald S. Mackenzie's actions against the Comanches and their allies. Composed of 15 restored buildings, a selection of artifacts from archeological excavations and a display on the history of the post can be seen in the visitor center. Located 23 miles west of Menard, U.S. 190 and FM 864. www.tpwd.state.tx.us/spdest/findadest/parks/fort_mckavett/

MIAMI, Roberts County

Roberts County Museum. The museum has a Native American room, and its art collections include works by Native American artists; noteworthy are the 1920s Kiowa silk-screen prints. Special collections relate to the area's well-known Miami Clovis site (Clovis is the oldest known prehistoric culture in Texas). Located on US 60 E in Miami. www.robertscountymuseum.org/.

MIDLAND, Midland County

Midland County Historical Museum. Museum exhibits depict the prehistory and history of the region and include a display related to the Midland site, one of the state's early, important Paleo-Indian sites. Located at 301 W. Missouri. 432-688-8947.

Museum of the Southwest. Collections focus on art and archeology of the American Southwest. Exhibits include ethnographic materials relating to Southwestern cultures. Located at 1705 W. Missouri. www.museumsw.org

Permian Basin Petroleum Museum. The west wing of the museum offers an extensive exhibit of prehistoric stone tools accompanied by an artist's views of Native American scenes and topics. Located at 1500 I-20 W. www.petroleummuseum.org

NEWCASTLE, Young County

Fort Belknap. Established in 1851, this fort was one of the largest posts in North Texas before the Civil War, and it protected early settlers and the Butterfield Overland Mail Route. The fort was abandoned in 1867. Six original buildings and one replica still stand; the site is now a county park with museum, archives and picnic facilities. Located 3 miles south off Texas 251. www.forttours.com/pages/ tocftbelknap.asp

ORANGE, Orange County

Stark Museum of Art. The museum features a collection of material crafted by American Indian tribes of the Great Plains, Southwest and Northwest Coast. Plains Indian clothing, body ornaments and beadwork are displayed, and Puebloan materials include pottery, Zuni and Hopi kachina dolls, and Navajo rugs and blankets. Located at 712 Green Ave. www.starkmuseum.org

OZONA, Crockett County

Crockett County Museum. Opened in 1939, this county museum has an Indian Room offering very good interpretive exhibits and Indian artifacts from the following periods: paleo; early, middle and late archaic; prehistoric and late pre-historic and historic period. Located at 404 11th St. www.museumsusa.com/museums/ info/1167679

PAINT ROCK, Concho County

Paint Rock. This privately owned site is one of the best-known rock art sites in Texas. The earliest paintings date from prehistoric times, while succeeding pictographs continued until the last quarter of the 19th century when Comanche Indians still hunted in the area. Daily tours by appointment to see 1,500 markings. Office about 1/2 mile north of Paint Rock on US 83. www.paintrockpictographs.com/

PAMPA, Gray County

White Deer Land Museum. Along with local and ranching heritage, permanent exhibits include displays of prehistoric stone tools and Native American art. Located in the 80-year-old restored Land Office Building at 112 S. Cuyler. www.museuminpampa.org

PANHANDLE, Carson County
Carson County Square House Museum. Native American artifacts are included in three of the museum's exhibits: Southwestern and Plains materials in the Hazlewood Building, North American prehistory and history in Freedom Hall, and Texas Panhandle prehistory in the Square House. Museum complex located at Hwy 207 and 5th streets. www.museumsusa.org/museums/info/1167449

PERRYTON, Ochiltree County
Museum of the Plains. An exhibit on Panhandle archeology includes artifacts relating to the Buried City and Wolf Creek sites, and a "What Is It?" exhibit explains stone tools for children. Regional interpretive panels include historic photographs and accompanying text. This is a fine interpretive exhibit, with a strong preservation message, in an area of major archeological significance. Located at 1200 N Main. www.museumoftheplains.com

PINE SPRINGS, Culberson County
Guadalupe Mountains National Park. People have long been lured to these mountains because of the presence of water in seeps and springs, including the Mescalero Apaches, the Butterfield Overland Mail, Buffalo Soldiers, and ranchers. Visitor Center is located on US 62/180 near Pine Springs. www.nps.gov/gumo

PLAINVIEW, Hale County
Llano Estacado Museum. Exhibits related to human cultural adaptation to the semiarid Llano Estacado (Staked Plains) from prehistoric through historic times. Permanent displays include materials relating to the Plains Indians, the role of the Buffalo Soldiers (African American regiments) during the Red River War campaign. Located at 1900 W. 8th (on Wayland Baptist University campus). www.wbu.edu/c/c05b/

PRESIDIO vicinity, Presidio County
Big Bend Ranch State Park. This rugged and remote park offers periodic educational seminars and workshops on aspects of the cultural and natural resources of Big Bend Ranch. Several times a year, park staff move the Texas Longhorn cattle between pastures, offering the public an opportunity to experience living history by helping roundup and move the livestock. Visitors must contact either Fort Leaton State Historical Park (4 miles east of Presidio on FM 170) or Barton Warnock Environmental Education Center (1 mile east of Lajitas on FM 170) to obtain permits, pay user fees. www.tpwd.state.tx.us/spdest/findadest/parks/big_bend_ranch/
Fort Leaton State Historic Site. Originally constructed by Ben Leaton in 1848 as a fortified adobe trading post known as Fort Leaton. The park offers guided tours, plus exhibits on the history from 15th century, natural history and archeological history of the area. Located 4 miles southeast of Presidio on the scenic River Road to the Big Bend (FM 170). www.tpwd.state.tx.us/spdest/findadest/parks/fort_leaton/

QUITAQUE, Briscoe County
Caprock Canyons State Park & Trailway. The Lake Theo site, a Paleo-Indian occupation, is located in the park and has been excavated. In 1997, a small herd of free-ranging Southern Plains bison were captured and transported to the facilities at Caprock Canyons. Now, some two dozen Southern Plains buffalo again roam their native range to inspire all who appreciate the wild heritage of Texas and the role these animals played in the vanished ways of the Plains Indians. www.tpwd.state.tx.us/spdest/findadest/parks/caprock_canyons/

SAN ANGELO, Tom Green County
Fort Concho National Historic Landmark. From 1867–1889 Fort Concho protected frontier settlements and transportation. Now owned and operated by the City of San Angelo, Fort Concho National Historic Landmark encompasses most of the former army post and includes 23 original and restored fort structures. Restored exhibit buildings include a headquarters building, soldier's barracks, officer's quarters, chapel/schoolhouse, and post hospital. Located at 630 S. Oakes. www.fortconcho.com

SAN ANTONIO, Bexar County
Casa Navarro State Historic Site. The original house complex of this historic architectural and archeological site was the residence of Texas hero Jose Antonio Navarro (1795–1871). Consisting of three limestone, caliche block and adobe structures, it was built about 1848. The park is dedicated to the interpretation of the Mexican history and heritage of Texas as viewed through the life of Navarro, a prominent San Antonio merchant, rancher, statesman, and signer of the Texas Declaration of Independence. Located at 228 S. Laredo St. www.tpwd.state.tx.us/spdest/findadest/parks/casa_navarro/
Institute of Texan Cultures. The institute's permanent exhibits

The Fate Bell Shelter in Seminole Canyon State Historic Site is a deeply stratified rock shelter containing many prehistoric Indian pictographs. Larry Bleiberg photo.

are designed to appeal to all ages, and it also is a source of books, audiovisuals, traveling exhibits available for rent and other materials relating to the peoples of Texas, past and present. Located at 801 S. Bowie St. www.texancultures.utsa.edu/public/index.htm
San Antonio Missions National Park. The chain of missions established along the San Antonio River in the 18th century, including San Jose, Concepcion, Espada and San Juan, represents the greatest concentration of Spanish missions in North America. The Espada Aqueduct associated with the missions is one of the oldest arched Spanish aqueducts in the United States. Visitor Center at 6701 San Jose Drive, adjacent to San Jose. www.nps.gov/saan
Witte Museum. The premier museum in San Antonio, the Witte offers an excellent interpretive exhibit of the archeology, lifeways and rock art of the prehistoric Indian hunter-gatherer societies of the Lower Pecos region. Located at 3801 Broadway. www.wittemuseum.org

SAN MARCOS, Hays County
Aquarena Center. The center's Archeological Tour allows students to step into the past as they explore the Archeology Museum of artifacts, hands-on live demonstrations, underwater and surface archeological sites, the Spanish Mission, historic houses, a gristmill and an 1890s general store. The tour also includes a 30-minute Glass-Bottom Boat ride that cruises the underwater site that first brought international attention to San Marcos. Located at Spring Lake in San Marcos. www.aquarena.txstate.edu

SHEFFIELD, Pecos County
Fort Lancaster State Historic Site. The fort was established Aug. 20, 1855, to guard the San Antonio-El Paso Road and protect the movement of supplies and immigrants. Fort Lancaster was abandoned on March 19, 1861, after Texas seceded from the Union, and only ruins remain. The park offers exhibits on history, natural history and archeology. Located 8 miles east of Sheffield, off I-10 on US Highway 290. www.tpwd.state.tx.us/spdest/findadest/parks/fort_lancaster/

WACO, McLennan County
Mayborn Museum Complex. Exhibits include collections relating to the Indians of Central Texas from prehistory through the period of Anglo American settlement. Located at 1300 S. University Parks. www.baylor.edu/mayborn/index.php?id=15383 ☆

Stagecoaching In Texas

Icons of the Old West Crisscrossed the State with People, Goods and the U.S. Mail

By Mike Cox

Early-day Texas travelers had only four choices when they needed to get from one town to another — walk, ride a horse, bounce along in a buggy or take a stagecoach.

Multi-passenger horse-drawn stagecoaches — Texas' first regularly scheduled non-maritime, for-hire public transportation — came into use soon after the Mexican province won its independence from Mexico in 1836. By 1837, only a year after the Battle of San Jacinto, a stage line connected Houston and Harrisburg, a distance of five miles.

A year later, the Telegraph and Texas Register carried a display advertisement noting availability of a "Regular Line of Stages From Houston to Washington." The stage departed an inn called the Houston House at 6 a.m. on Thursdays, and, weather permitting, rolled into Washington-on-the-Brazos 30 hours later. A stage left Washington-on-the-Brazos for Houston at 6 a.m. every Wednesday. As proprietor J.F. Brown noted in his ad, "The subscriber having the contract for carrying the mail, will run regular with a carriage to accommodate passengers."

That not-so-well-crafted sentence from 1838 summarizes the business model for stagecoaching that stood for more than 70 years in some parts of Texas. A stagecoach operator's bread-and-butter came in the form of a government mail contract. Passengers and light freight sometimes paid for themselves, sometimes not, but an annual payment from the government enhanced that profit or loss.

The first Congress of the Republic of Texas set up a postal system and established postal routes, but as with most government enterprises in the near-decade of Texas national sovereignty, a lack of money left Texans with mail service that fell far short of its model in the neighboring United States.

By 1839, with the founding of Austin as the republic's capital, a stage line carried mail, passengers and freight along a hardly improved 150-plus-mile route from Houston to the new city on the frontier.

Rolling Stock

Though "stagecoach" served as the generic description for horse-drawn conveyances carrying passengers, three types of coaches traveled the rough roads of Texas. The first, the one that comes to mind for most when they think of stagecoaches, was the Concord coach.

The distinctive teacup-on-four-wheels design of the stagecoach emerged as an icon of the Old West, but the coaches came from a manufacturer in New England. The history of the Concord coach traces to 1813, when 21-year-old Lewis Downing moved from Massachusetts to Concord, N.H., and began operating a carriage shop. Thirteen years later, Downing hired journeyman coach builder J. Stephen Abbot, who soon became his partner. In 1827, they built the first vehicle that came to be called the Concord coach.

The firm of Abbott & Downing went on to produce more than 3,000 stagecoaches, the "Cadillacs" of the industry. Pulled by either four or six horses, the coaches came in 6-, 9- or 12-passenger sizes. (Up to six passengers, including the driver and a messenger in charge of the mail sacks, also could sit on top of the coach.) Handcrafted from oak and ash, with elm wheels and a curved body of basswood, the coaches had red upholstered seats (though some had leather seats) and a leather "boot" on the back for luggage. Standing 8-½ feet high and weighing 1-¼ tons, the Concord usually came in red with yellow trim. Fancy paintings and gold scroll often decorated the coach's doors.

"It is roomy and grand, with rhythm in its roll and the play of its wheels," one happy traveler wrote of the Concord stage. "It is poetry in motion."

That "rhythm" came from the coach's innovative thoroughbraces, long, 4-inch-wide leather strips that in a latter era would be called shock absorbers. In addition to lessening the bumps associated with traveling unpaved roads, the thoroughbraces caused the stagecoach to swing from side to side. If the coach got stuck in the mud, savvy drivers knew that motion made it easier for the horses to extract it. Mark Twain, in *Roughing It*, likened a stagecoach to a "cradle on wheels."

At the height of their popularity and production, Concord coaches ranged in price from $500 to twice that. Other carriage makers, mostly smaller operations, also built coaches similar in appearance to the Concord-made vehicles. Still, the Concords saw the most use on the basis of their deserved reputation for quality.

The second commonly used vehicle was a four-horse wagon covered with a canvas tarp that could be rolled up in warm weather or tied down in cold or rainy conditions. Built on a Concord frame, these vehicles were called celerity wagons. Also known as mud wagons, they had a lower center of gravity and being lighter, could travel faster. Often pulled by mules, they usually served the shorter, less-trafficked, more rugged routes, particularly in West Texas.

In later years, two-horse hacks, also with roll-down canvas tops, plied routes connecting smaller communities with towns having rail service.

Ben Buckwalter of Anna sits atop the original 1880s Butterfield Overland stagecoach that he restored. Buckwalter takes his stagecoach to fairs and living history festivals in Texas where he gives fairgoers rides and a taste of traveling in the Old West.

Stagecoach Inns and Stations

Every stagecoach route in Texas stretched along a series of stopping points where drivers could hitch on a fresh team in 10 minutes and be on their way again. Three times a day, passengers could get a hurried meal. Long-haul stages tended to run 24-hours-a-day, but some stage stops featured overnight accommodations. The distance between stops varied depending on the terrain and the availability of water, but 15 to 30 miles apart was the norm.

In the early days of stagecoaching in Texas, especially in the more populated areas, those stops came at rural inns offering travelers bed and board. These inns ranged from log cabins with a dogtrot to handsome two-story Greek Revival–style houses. In cities, hotels often served as departure points. As Texas grew to the west and south, the stops in more remote areas tended to be less fancy. In the vastness of West Texas, a stage stop usually amounted to little more than a stone or adobe structure and a corral for the stock.

Stagecoach stop fare ranged from terrible — wormy biscuits and grease-laden meat of unknown source — to something weary travelers looked forward to. Meal prices ran from 40 cents to a dollar in the late 1850s.

A man named Sargent ran a hotel that served as the stage stop in Brackettville, the town that had grown up outside the Army garrison at Fort Clark in Kinney County. Vinton E. James, passing through on the stage in 1876, spent the night at the Sargent Hotel. He later wrote: "Next morning, after a hearty breakfast of hot cakes and coffee we told our host, Mr. Sargent, goodbye."

At most stage stations, pork or wild game, beans, bread and coffee awaited tired, dusty travelers. But at the better places, usually those in the more settled areas of East Texas, a hungry stage passenger might find a variety of wild game, oysters or fish. Biscuits or cornbread could be slathered in butter and washed down with sweet milk, as it was called.

"The fare, though rough, is better than could be expected so far from civilized districts," *New York Herald* correspondent Waterman L. Ormsby said of stagecoach stop food in Texas. "It consists of bread, tea, and fried steaks of bacon, venison, antelope, or mule flesh — the latter tough. ..." He added, "the stomach does not long remain delicate after a few days of life on the plains."

Connecting Texas Ports

Stagecoaches carried passengers inland from Texas' two busiest ports, Galveston and Indianola. "The U.S. Mail stage leaves the Planter's House on the arrival of the steamers from New Orleans and Galveston by which travelers will have a speedy and direct passage to Victoria, Cuero, Gonzales, Seguin, New Braunfels, and Austin," a Dec. 29, 1848, advertisement in the Galveston News said of the stage service available at its rival port down the coast. "Messrs. Harrison and McCullough, the well known proprietors of the line, have placed upon it an excellent coach, and will make their trips so as to enable passengers landing at Indian Point [Indianola] to proceed to the interior with as little delay as possible."

Overland Routes

The 1848 discovery of gold along the American River in California turned Sacramento and San Francisco into boom towns and stimulated the development of stagecoach transportation in Texas, half-way across the continent.

Frontiersman Henry Skillman garnered a mail contract to provide service from San Antonio to El Paso to Santa Fe in 1851, the first of his stages rolling out of San Antonio on Nov. 3, 1851. Skillman lost his contract in 1854, but after a short interval partnered with George H.

Giddings to resume the Texas-to-New Mexico service. In the summer of 1857, the operators suddenly faced a business challenge from James Birch, who landed a $150,000-a-year contract to provide through service to San Diego.

Birch owned 400 mules and horses and employed 65 men to run 50 Concord stages or celerity wagons (which saw more usage in Texas) on a 1,476-mile route that took an average of 27 days to cover. A passenger wanting to get all the way to El Paso from the Alamo City had to pony over $100. Passage to California from Texas cost twice that. Mules provided most of the motive power, giving Birch's enterprise its nickname, "The Jackass Mail." When Birch died in the fall of 1857, Giddings and R.E. Doyle bought his contract.

The Jackass Mail not being sufficient to handle all the non-maritime mail going in and out of the Golden State, U.S. Postmaster General Aaron Brown executed an ambitious mail contract with New Yorker John Butterfield in March 1857. Butterfield's contract netted him $600,000 yearly to provide twice-a-week mail service in each direction. The agreement also allowed him to collect fares for carrying passengers.

Butterfield oversaw the surveying of a route that extended 2,795 miles from St. Louis to San Francisco. The oxbow-shaped route, selected by the postmaster general because it would be usable year-round (though Brown, being a Southerner, may also have had something to do with it) crossed the Red River into Texas at Benjamin Franklin Colbert's ferry at Preston in Grayson County and continued for 740 miles toward El Paso, cutting across the upper Pecos River to Pine Springs at the foot of the Guadalupe Mountains, then via Hueco Tanks to El Paso. After mid-1859, Butterfield moved the trans-Pecos segment of the route more to the south, his stages fording the snake-like river at the legendary Horsehead Crossing. The Texas leg of the trip took eight days on average.

With significant financial support from William G. Fargo and Henry Wells (owners of Wells, Fargo & Co. and American Express), Butterfield's Overland Mail Co.

built a stage stop every 15 to 20 miles, digging cisterns and putting up corrals. The significance of the operation — the nation's first commercial transcontinental transportation system — can be judged by the level of investment: The company purchased 250 stagecoaches or celerity wagons in addition to freight and water wagons, some 1,200 horses and 600 mules, and kept nearly 800 drivers, conductors, station keeps, blacksmiths and wranglers on its payroll.

The first Butterfield stage left the St. Louis area on Sept. 16, 1858, with the initial east-bound stage having pulled out of San Francisco the day before. Butterfield's contract stipulated that the trip take less than 25 days.

"Remember boys," Butterfield famously said, "nothing on God's earth must stop the United States mail!"

Twenty-three-year-old Waterman L. Ormsby, a correspondent for the New York Herald, rode with Butterfield and his son aboard the west-bound stage when it left Missouri. In what became a classic of Western Americana, the young journalist chronicled the inaugural trip for posterity.

When the stagecoach finally reached California, Ormsby wrote: "Had I not just come over the route, I would be perfectly willing to go back, but I now know what Hell is like. I've just had 24 days of it."

Stage Lines Span the State

"As a general thing," the 1859 Texas Almanac informed its readers, "the service is as good as can be found elsewhere." Travel by stagecoach normally cost a dime a mile, though rates could be doubled when rain-swollen streams and muddy roads made operations more difficult.

The Austin-based firm of Risher & Sawyer operated two important routes in the 1850s, a line than connected Austin and San Antonio three times weekly and a Houston–Austin route. The Texas State Gazette offered its "best wishes for … success" in 1852 when Col. George W. Grant had formed a company that would run a stage "every alternate day" from Austin to Houston, making the trip in only two days. One way from the Capital City

Guards brandish their weapons as a Wells Fargo Express Co. treasure wagon transports $150,000 of gold bullion from the Great Homestake Mine in Deadwood, S.D., in 1890. John C. H. Grabill Collection.

to Houston cost $15.

From Austin to the Alamo City, one old-timer later recalled, "the trip was made in 18 hours with breakfast at the Blanco Creek, supper in New Braunfels and arrival at San Antonio sometime during the night, weather and floods permitting." In wet weather, the 75-mile trip took the worst part of a week.

Shortly before the beginning of the Civil War, Texas had 31 stage lines in operation. B. Risher and a new partner, C.K. Hall, ran 16 of those lines. They had some 300 men working for them and owned more than 1,000 horses and mules.

The Overland Mail Co. ranked as the largest stagecoach firm doing business in Texas, but Butterfield's connection to the company ended in 1860, when Fargo and the other stakeholders relieved him of his day-to-day managerial authority over a difference in operational philosophy. The Overland line continued its Texas runs until March 2, 1861, less than six weeks before the outbreak of the Civil War, when Congress moved the main mail route farther to the north.

With blue-coated U.S. cavalry troopers having been withdrawn from the state following secession, and with most able-bodied Texans off fighting Yankees, the virtually unprotected Texas frontier contracted eastward by a hundred miles or more. Indian attacks increased while stagecoach travel decreased. Except for a line connecting San Antonio and Eagle Pass, San Antonio represented the western-most extent of stage service in Confederate Texas.

Stage traffic increased, however, between the state's southern-most railhead at Alleyton in Colorado County and the Rio Grande Valley, where Southern-grown cotton was shipped to foreign markets on blockade runners via ports at the mouth of the river on the Mexican side. The route from Alleyton to Brownsville came to be called the Cotton Road.

Following the war, Texas stagecoach operations and routes expanded. Communities without service eagerly sought a connection.

"Here we are, 35 miles from a stage line, and have to send the mail that distance every week to the Post Office," the Tyler Journal lamented in November 1865. Only a few weeks later, another Tyler newspaper, *The Reporter,* informed its readers that "Sawyer, Risher & Hall have established a stage line from Marshal via Tyler, to Crockett. This is a much needed improvement and places Tyler again within reach of the balance of the world by stage."

By the early 1870s, Risher and Hall ran seven routes operating out of Austin, Brenham, Columbus, La Grange, San Antonio, Victoria and Waco. E.M. Sawyer and his brother Frederick, had four lines, including the one through Tyler. Calling them "indefatigable and enterprising," the editor of the *1867 Texas Almanac* said the state "is probably more indebted [to Sawyer, Risher and Hall] for mails … than to all others together. There is nominally a mail agent for Texas and Louisiana, but so far as Texas is concerned, he is only nominally an agent."

Ben Ficklin operated a stage line connecting Fort Smith, Ark., and San Antonio with service to El Paso beginning in 1868. After Ficklin's death in 1871, his partner F.C. Taylor took over the operation. One of their more important stations, a stop on the Concho River, be-

came, along with Fort Concho, the nucleus for the city of San Angelo.

Indian Attacks

Stagecoach travel in the less-settled areas, particularly far West Texas, remained risky even after the Civil War. The caution John Butterfield had offered his customers before the war still held sway: "You will be traveling through Indian country and the safety of your person cannot be vouchsafed by anyone but God."

During the 2 years, 5 months and 17 days that the Overland Mail Co. served Texas, it lost more than 50 employees to Indians and many of its stage stops were sacked by Indians bent on stealing mules and horses. They escaped with hundreds of head.

Before the Butterfield line supplanted the San Antonio–San Diego "Jackass Mail," Apaches killed all occupants of a west-bound stage in Quitman Canyon, southwest of present-day Sierra Blanca in what is now Hudspeth County.

"The Indians had ambuscaded the road by building blinds on each side of the road," former Texas Ranger Capt. George W. Baylor recollected in 1899. "They riddled the stage with bullets and arrows."

When searchers found the battered stage, Baylor continued, "There was a great deal of blood on the dashboard and the bottom of the stage … showing the first volley at close range must have killed or wounded most of the party [aboard the stage]."

Only one body was ever found, and it had been burned beyond recognition.

The last known Indian attack on a stagecoach occurred in January 1881, also in Quitman Canyon. Rangers trailed the warriors responsible for the raid and killed most of them in the final clash between the state officers and hostile Indians.

Robberies

Stagecoach robberies happened so often it came to be considered something of a right of passage to hand over one's money and valuables to a masked man with a gun on some lonely roadside.

"At one time," wrote journalist Alexander Sweet in his humor sheet Texas Siftings, "the traveling public became so accustomed to going through the usual ceremonies that they complained to the stage companies if they came through unmolested. Being robbed came to be regarded as a vested right."

Fifty-eight years after the fact, Austin resident Sam Moore still liked to talk about the time he faced highwaymen in 1879.

Just back from a trail drive, Moore had boarded the west-bound stage in Austin. The Capital City had rail service to points north and east, but stagecoaches remained the only form of public transportation to West Texas.

"When we reached the Peg Leg Crossing, on the San Saba River, a fellow wearing a mask rode out and unhitched the horses and ordered everyone from the coach," Moore recalled in an interview in the long-defunct Austin Dispatch in 1937.

Riding with him that day were four traveling salesman — then called "drummers" — and a young woman. Drummers usually conducted their business in cash and road agents considered them "rich pickings."

The outlaws searched the salesmen and relieved them of cash and coin. After examining the lady's purse and jewelry, the lead robber handed it back, courteously saying he didn't rob women.

Then the gunman turned his attention to Moore.

"He … punched me in the ribs with his gun, and said, 'Keep your stuff, there ain't no cowboy got a damn thing.' "

Noticing the masked man's eyes looked somewhat familiar, Moore figured the robber knew him. The young cowboy may or may not have known the robber, but he later maintained the man was Rube Burrow, "a rather notorious character with whom Uncle Sam was acquainted."

Stagecoaches were routinely held up and some travelers came to expect this inconvenience. This 1911 photo was staged to illustrate a fictitious story about stagecoach robberies.

Eventually arrested for murder in Tucson, Ariz., "Burrow" was extradited to Texas and booked into the Travis county jail, a castle-like stone structure built in 1875 across from the Capitol.

"After a time," Moore continued his tale, "a woman, representing herself to be 'Burrow's' wife, appeared at the jail to visit her husband, with food and clean clothing."

The visits continued with regularity for several months.

"Then one afternoon, when time came to let her out the 'wife' pushed a Colt into the jailers' ribs and demanded the keys. Wearing a Mother Hubbard, 'Rube Burrow' clattered down the steps and made his escape. The woman dressed in her husband's garb, remained in jail."

"Burrow," whoever he really was, never again appeared in Texas.

That was Moore's story, anyway. An Alabama-born character by the name of Rube Burrow with a Robin Hood like reputation did spend some time in Texas during the 1870s and 1880s, but his first crime is not believed to have occurred until 1886, well after the robbery Moore remembered.

The Texas Rangers eventually rounded up the Peg Leg stage robbers, but the only thing that truly put an end to stage coach robbing was the expansion of rail service in Texas. And then bandits took to robbing trains.

Hard Travel

Even without Indians or outlaws, stagecoach travel was hard going.

"To make excellent jam," the San Antonio Herald wrote with its editorial-tongue-in-cheek, "squeeze six or eight women, now-a-days, into a common stagecoach." A Nebraska newspaper published a list of stagecoach travel tips that worked just as well in Texas. "The best seat … is the one next to the driver," the newspaper advised. Three important "don'ts" included not slumping over on a fellow passenger when sleeping, not asking how far it is to the next station "until you get there," and not discussing politics or religion. Finally, "Expect annoyance, discomfort, and some hardships. If you are disappointed, thank heaven."

On the Austin–Houston route, wet weather always made the trip more difficult. "On the river and creek bottoms," one old-timer later recalled, "passengers were requested by the driver, politely or otherwise, to step out and down, and walk in the mud, packing rails to help the stage out of the mud. Then, the trip was made in five or six days. Yet, we got along very nicely."

A Baptist preacher making the 150-mile, 35-hour trip from San Antonio to Corpus Christi encountered an unexpected form of annoyance in 1879 — a "hilariously drunk" driver. The driver's boss, the San Antonio station agent, recognizing the extent of his driver's level of intoxication, decided to accompany him at least as far as the first stop to give him time to sober up.

"When [stage employees] loosed the heads of the four wild mules and jumped quickly out of the way," Dr. J.M. Carroll later recalled, "the stage left the side entrance of the Menger Hotel like it was shot out of a cannon. Away we went as fast as those mules could possibly go. No effort was made to do more than keep them in the road."

Yelling and cracking his whip, the stage driver continued to operate his coach as if there were no tomorrow, which was what the terrified passengers had come to believe.

"Our driver was still unsobered when we reached the first stand," Carroll continued, "so the agent decided to go with us to the next. … The new quartette of mules was not quite so wild, so we made it to the next stand more decently. We wanted the agent to continue with us, but he said the driver was now all right, so … the agent went back."

The Rev. A.H. Sutherland never forgot his stagecoach trip from San Antonio to El Paso in the late summer of 1881. The coach left from the Menger Hotel on Alamo Plaza.

"The stage line passed through Forts Concho, Stockton and Davis and covered a distance of 720 miles," the Methodist preacher recalled in an 1917 article in the El Paso Herald."

The trip took one week. Though 14 different drivers handled various legs of the route, Sutherland got no such relief as a passenger. When the stage pulled up in front of the Central Hotel, the preacher was "nearly dead of fatigue."

Stages to Trains

When Sutherland made that stagecoach trip halfway across Texas, two railroads had crews laying track toward El Paso.

By 1888, Texas had more than 8,000 miles of railroad with more track going down all the time. Two transcontinental routes spanned the state.

For a time, two West Texas towns, Albany and Cisco, had the distinction of being possibly the only communities in the nation where a railroad and a stagecoach line competed with each other. When the Houston & Texas Central reached Albany from Cisco, the man who operated the stagecoach between the two points vowed that the railroad would not put him out of business. Indeed, the railroad lost money on that part of its route. The result was irregular and slow service.

"Albany is a local option town," *The Dallas Morning News* reported on June 10, 1888, "and when an old toper goes up on a round-trip ticket and fails to take a supply along with him, he is cured of the alcohol habit for the want of fuel to feed the fires by the time he gets back to Cisco. It is different with the runner of the stage line. He makes, or causes to be made, a trip every day. He keeps his horses fat, and for his own part he wears diamonds and is rapidly evoluting into a bloated bondholder."

Stagecoaches Hang On

Though the stagecoach era in Texas essentially ended by the mid-1880s with the widespread availability of faster and more comfortable travel by rail, stagecoaches endured as a means of transportation in some parts of the state well beyond the declared death of the frontier.

A stage line from Alice to Brownsville remained the only form of public land transportation to the Rio Grande Valley well into the 20th century. Pulled by a four-horse team, the stage left Alice at 6 a.m. every day. With a change of horses every 10 miles, the trip to the southern tip of the state took 36 hours.

That line, the last long-haul stage route in Texas, operated until 1904, when the St. Louis, Brownsville and Mexico Railroad completed its tracks into Brownsville.

A couple of years before the railroad killed the Alice-to-Brownsville line, a family on their way from Corpus Christi to a South Texas ranch in a mule-drawn wagon saw the stagecoach as it passed them.

"We watched until they were out of sight," one member of that family later wrote, "and could see the stagecoach for a long way — it finally became only a tiny black speck on the horizon."

From 1904 to 1906, Walter Dunlap drove a stage from Ozona to San Angelo, following a route stretching 83 miles. With a two-horse team pulling a four-wheeled, canvas-topped wagon, Dunlap normally made the trip in 9-½ to 10 hours. Once, he later recalled, he raced his stage between the two towns in slightly more than 8 hours, thanks to a pair of horses he remembered fondly nearly 60 years later, "Crazy Jim" and "Goodeye."

Dunlap changed horses every 18 or 20 miles and had to stop and open 32 different ranch gates. Tiring of that and wanting to do something that earned better money, Dunlap went to work as a cowboy and later became a rancher.

Demise of the General Sam Houston

The General Sam Houston, a Concord stage named after the first President of the Texas Republic, made its first run between Austin and Brenham in 1841. Pulled by six horses or mules in good weather and eight in muddy weather, the stage later made regular Austin–to–San An-

The depot building at the Age of Steam Railroad Museum in Fair Park in Dallas was used at the Houston & Texas Central Railroad yard office in Dallas around 1900. Although the railroad killed stagecoach lines in most places by the mid-1880s, two West Texas towns, Albany and Cisco, had the distinction of being possibly the only communities in the nation where a railroad and a stagecoach line competed with each other. When the Houston & Texas Central reached Albany from Cisco, the man who operated the stagecoach between the two towns vowed the railroad would not put him out of business.

tonio runs.

But in 1873, road worn and made obsolete by Austin's connection to the state's growing network of iron rails, the General Sam Houston was parked in an alley outside Patterson's Livery Stable. And there it stayed, slowly falling apart. Finally, after more than three decades of non-use, Austin city officials ordered its removal.

Noting that a movement to save the coach for posterity had "failed to bear fruit," the Austin Statesman lamented its demise, reporting on July 17, 1909, "the 'Sam Houston' was torn to pieces yesterday and the timber cast in a waste heap."

Jehus, Reinsmen, Whips, Whipsters

Newspaper advertisements placed by stage lines promised the usual things like comfortable rides and regular service. The quality of a company's drivers also figured in their promotional efforts. One firm serving Austin and San Antonio assured potential customers that it had "pleasant and convenient coaches and fresh teams and skilled and accommodating drivers." In an ad published by the Texas State Gazette in Austin, stage operators Brown & Tarbox declared they had "after a great length of time and expense, been able to procure careful and skillful drivers; and they recommend them as punctual and honest men. ..."

This circa 1904 painting by Frederic Remington shows the perils of stagecoach travel on rough terrain.

Drivers may not always have been accommodating or honest, but they definitely had to be skilled to survive in an enterprise that involved dealing with teams of unruly animals and sometimes equally unruly passengers, not to mention protecting them and their cargo from Indians and outlaws.

One of the most famous drivers who ever cracked a whip in Texas was one-time Texas Ranger William A. "Bigfoot" Wallace, who drove a stage for a time on the San Antonio to El Paso route.

"Uncle" Jim Davis, who died in Fort Worth at 72 in the fall of 1910, was recognized as "perhaps the last of the old-time frontier stage drivers" in North Texas. From Fort Worth to Fort Concho at San Angelo, via Granbury and Brownwood, he had driven a stagecoach until railroads drove the line he worked for out of business.

Once, with 14 passengers on board, the "Lone Highwayman" held up his stage.

Davis' life symbolized the story of stagecoaches in Texas. After Fort Worth gained rail connections with most of the rest of Texas, Davis used his talent at handling teams to haul freight. In 1889, he began operating a horse-drawn cab in Cowtown and continued with that until he got too old.

Davis' life came to an end on Nov. 22, 1910, but stage coaches in Texas rolled more slowly toward the sunset of obsolescence.

Indeed, as The Dallas Morning News observed that same year, "Though modern transportation agencies have stolen away the glories of the stagecoach with its galloping spans, it can still be found in commission to those who seek it. ... In the South and West it is known and respected. Its latest commercial competitor is the rural free delivery, and as this expands and railroads find a way of profitably negotiating mountain passes and tapping regions whose resources are vastly greater than their population, the stage coach must yield what place it still has, but the process will be so slow that the lovers of the inconveniently picturesque may count for years to come on the chance of meeting the vehicle."

Throughout the early part of the 20th century, stagecoaches continued to operate in areas of the state not served by railroads. As late as May 1918, a stage line ran between Llano and Mason, Fredericksburg and Mason, and Brady and Mason. Motorbuses and automobiles operating on improved roads finally sent stagecoaches and their teams and drivers to the barn for the last time.

Last Stage Coach

The last known use of a horse-drawn vehicle for regularly scheduled public transportation came in Lake Jackson during the gasoline shortage associated with World War II.

People who lived in Lake Jackson, almost all of them connected to the newly opened Dow Chemical

The Stagecoach Mystique

The 1939 classic film *Stagecoach,* directed by John Ford and starring Claire Trevor and John Wayne, used a stagecoach as a literal stage for human drama and conflict. Set in New Mexico but filmed in Monument Valley on the Utah-Arizona border, the movie captured a colorful era in transportation history. File photo.

plant at nearby Freeport, needed a convenient way to get from their homes to downtown businesses and to get their children to the day school operating in the Community Center.

"We were building a new town and needed to interest people to live in Lake Jackson," A.C. Ray later told longtime Dow employee Bill Colegrove, author of the 1983 book *Episodes: Texas Dow 1940–76.*

Noting that Dow still used horses and mules to pull graders, someone among the business leaders suggested that the nascent town should provide its residents transportation with a modern day stagecoach.

Committee members secured a used lumber dolly and added two automobile axles with balloon tires. To accommodate a team of horses, a wooden wagon tongue went on the front of the vehicle. A row of wooden seats anchored each side of the coach, with an aisle down the middle. Passengers boarded by walking up a two-step platform on the rear of the coach. Finally, a rounded canvas top provided protection from the blistering coastal sun. The conveyance, which could carry a couple dozen people, looked more like a long covered wagon than an Old West stagecoach, but they called it their stagecoach.

Following the acquisition of two black draft horses, the Lake Jackson stagecoach began serving the community. "Pop" Crumrine, a farmer who knew how to handle a horse-drawn wagon, operated the one-vehicle, privately funded "transit system." Starting at 8:30 a.m. and continuing every 45 minutes until 4:15 p.m., the coach left downtown for the residential area and then returned to the local drug store.

Youngsters took particular delight in riding the stagecoach, though they preferred to hop on it from a running start rather than step up on it like the adults did.

Quite popular with all concerned, the stagecoach saved passengers precious motor fuel and reduced mileage on already well-worn tires with free trips from their houses to the businesses downtown. In turn, the merchants and service providers saw a much-appreciated upswing in their receipts.

But eventually a problem developed. Traditional iron horseshoes did not last long on concrete pavement. And soft horseshoes could not be had because of war-time demands for rubber. Also, with Lake Jackson having no blacksmith, Ray and fellow businessman J.T. Dunbar shoed the stagecoach horses every Sunday whether they wanted to or not.

Finally, the two men had enough of their extracurricular civic duty and the Lake Jackson stagecoach rolled into history.

Old West Icon

Long after stagecoaches had any paying passengers to haul, they continued to capture the imagination of people through outdoor spectaculars and tent shows. Col. W.F. "Buffalo Bill" Cody used a large "genuine" Concord stage coach in his Wild West shows, even shipping it to Europe when his 500-person company traveled overseas. Stagecoaches also carried many a plot line in pulp fiction magazines, Western novels and the movie screen, the most notable film being the 1939 classic *Stagecoach.* Directed by John Ford and starring Claire

Trevor and John Wayne, the movie used a stagecoach as a literal stage for human drama and conflict. Set in New Mexico but filmed in Monument Valley on the Utah-Arizona border, the movie captured a colorful era in transportation history.

In the early 1970s, the mystique of the word "stagecoach" struck the developers of a residential community and resort in Montgomery County. The acreage under development having been located on a 19th-century stagecoach route, Stagecoach is the name the owners picked for their property. In 1980 the community incorporated as a general rule city and by 2006 had a population of 537.

Impact on Texas

Given the role stagecoaches performed in the settlement of Texas — for a time they provided the state's only form of commercial transportation and communication — having a town named "Stagecoach" is a faint commemoration of the industry's impact. Particularly across West Texas, stagecoaches fostered, along with the U.S. Army, the first settlement and development.

"The Butterfield Overland and San Antonio–San Diego mail lines spurred development of the Texas portion of [the] frontier," wrote historian Glen Ely in his 2005 Texas Christian University master's thesis, "Riding the Western Frontier: Antebellum Encounters on the Butterfield Overland Mail, 1858–1861," "establishing much of the regional infrastructure that later became modern West Texas."

Indeed, the San Antonio–El Paso stage line and the long arc of the Butterfield trail can be viewed as the 19th-century equivalents of Interstate-10 and Interstate-20.

Ely continued: "The community histories of Sherman, Gainesville, Denton, Decatur, Bridgeport, Jacksboro, Belknap, Fort Stockton, Fort Davis, San Elizario, Socorro, Ysleta, and Franklin–El Paso all testify to the significant impact the Butterfield Overland Mail had upon their growth and development."

Midland historian Jack Scannell wrote in the West Texas Historical Association's 1971 Yearbook that: "Where the stagecoach led, the rails followed, and with the rails came settlers, new businesses, and prosperity. To the present day, the highways, railroads, and even the airlines follow the routes laid out by the pounding hooves and spinning wells of the stagecoach."

Referring to the stage lines that connected San Antonio with El Paso, and points west, in his landmark study "Sharps Rifles and Spanish Mules: The San Antonio–El Paso Mail, 1851–1881," historian Wayne R. Austerman used a quotation from Gen. William T. Sherman that applies to stagecoaching across all of Texas and the West. The mail companies and their stagecoaches, the Army officer said, amounted to "the skirmish line of civilization." ☆

Mike Cox, an Austin-based writer and historian, has written 13 books about Texas. His syndicated column, "Texas Tales," can be read at www.texasescapes.com/MikeCoxTexasTales/MikeCoxTexasTales.htm

Sources

Austerman, Wayne R. *Sharps Rifles and Spanish Mules: The San Antonio–El Paso Mail, 1851–1881.* College Station: Texas A&M Press, 1985.

Carter, Kathryn Turner. *Stagecoach Inns of Texas.* Austin: Eakin Press, 1994.

The Dallas Morning News Archives, 1885–1977.

Davy, Dava McGahee. "The Pinery Station: Guadalupe Mountains National Park Texas." Carlsbad, NM: Carlsbad Caverns Natural History Association, 1979.

Ely, Glen. "Riding the Western Frontier: Antebellum Encounters on the Butterfield Overland Mail, 1858–1861." Master's thesis, Texas Christian University, 2005.

The Handbook of Texas Online, www.tsha.utexas.edu/handbook/online.

McSwain, Ross. "Crazy Jim, Goodeye Helped Establish New Time On Stage Run From San Angelo to Ozona," San Angelo Standard-Times, Aug. 23, 1964.

Moody, Ralph. *Stagecoach West.* New York: Thomas Y. Crowell, 1967.

Nolen, Oran W. "By Stage From Corpus Christi to San Antonio." The Cattleman, January 1946.

Ormsby, Waterman L. *The Butterfield Overland Mail.* San Marino, CA: The Huntington Library, 1942, 1991.

Scannell, Jack C. "A Survey of the Stagecoach Mail in the Trans-Pecos 1850–1861," West Texas Historical Association Yearbook, 1971.

Smith, Marian. "The Stagecoach in Travis County." Manuscript, Austin History Center, Austin, Texas.

Texas Almanac, 1859, 1861, 1863, 1867, 1869, 1871, 1873.

Thonhoff, Robert H. *San Antonio Stage Lines, 1847–1881.* El Paso: Texas Western Press, 1971.

Wells Fargo Bank, "The Overland Stage," ND.

Wikipedia.org "Stagecoach" www.en.wikipedia.org/wiki/Stagecoach

For Further Reading

Barton, Barbara. *Stagecoach Lines and Freighters of West Texas.* Knickerbocker, TX: 2007.

Greene, A.C. *900 Miles on the Butterfield Trail.* Denton: University of North Texas Press, 1994.

The Civilian Conservation Corps In Texas

THE HARD WORK OF A "NEW DEAL" ARMY IS PRESERVED IN RUSTIC BUILDINGS, BRIDGES AND TRAILS IN 56 TEXAS PARKS

By Mary G. Ramos

Where did those rustic rock buildings in many Texas State Parks come from — the ones that look so natural, they might simply have grown out of the ground? They might be visitor centers, group shelters or cabins. Chances are that those structures were built by young men in the Civilian Conservation Corps during the 1930s and early 1940s.

The CCC developed 56 state, national and local parks in Texas between 1933 and 1942. Thirty-one of these are still in the Texas Parks & Wildlife Department. Other parks serve the public in cities and counties around the state. (See table, page 44-45.)

Born of a national economic emergency, the CCC was organized in the wink of an eye, lived a short but productive nine years, then was allowed to die. Here is its story, including its impact on Texas and Texans.

Why the CCC Was Formed: The Great Depression

Texas has lived through a number of economic disasters, but none was so thoroughly devastating as the Great Depression. There were many contributing factors

The rough-hewn rock used to build this CCC structure fits in nicely with the rugged West Texas landscape of Davis Mountains State Park. Texas Parks & Wildlife Department photo.

This unusual boathouse was built by the CCC at Bonham State Park during the 1930s. The 261-acre park, located in Fannin County, includes a 65-acre lake, rolling prairies and woodlands. Texas Parks & Wildlife Department photo.

to the Depression, but the precipitating event was the stock market crash in late October 1929 and the subsequent run on banks as people scrambled to get their money out of failing institutions. The bottom fell out of the economies of not only the United States, but also European countries and most other developed countries of the world.

President Herbert Hoover was slow to acknowledge the scope of the Depression. He rejected recommendations of direct aid to Americans, believing the problem was simply a cyclical swing that could be remedied by "voluntary cooperation" between business and govern-

ment, with business taking the lead. Since no businesses were willing to take the risks necessary for such a scheme to have a chance to work, Hoover's plan failed.

By the 1932 presidential election, unemployment was rampant, soup lines were long, agricultural prices were hitting bottom, and Americans were desperate for drastic remedies that only the government could put into action.

New York Governor Franklin Delano Roosevelt handily won the presidency in 1932. Sworn into office on March 4, 1933, Roosevelt quickly pushed a package of legislation, termed the "New Deal," through Congress

Buildings around the swimming and wading pools at Abilene State Park were constructed by the CCC in the early 1930s. Texas Parks & Wildlife Department photo.

A shelter constructed by the CCC overlooks Palo Duro Canyon. From 1933–1937, the CCC sent six companies of young men and military veterans to Palo Duro Canyon to develop road access to the canyon floor, as well as the visitor center, cabins, shelters and the park's headquarters. Palo Duro Canyon State Park opened on July 4, 1934, and comprises 16,402 acres in Armstrong and Randall counties, southeast of Amarillo. Texas Parks & Wildlife Department photo.

setting up myriad new federal agencies to funnel direct payments to suffering Americans. Most were designed to provide work on specially created government projects. Each agency targeted a particular segment of the economy — agriculture, industry, local jobs, the arts — with the Federal Deposit Insurance Corporation insuring banks against losses.

The CCC was created to employ young single men from ages 18 to 25 on outdoor conservation projects. Originally called Emergency Conservation Work, the agency was dubbed the Civilian Conservation Corps by the press and that name became official in 1937.

The minimum age was dropped to 17 later, and the maximum fluctuated, going as high as 28. Two-thirds of CCC enrollees were 20 or younger. They had to be physically fit and come from families that were on relief and to whom they were willing to send most of their pay. Each man earned $30 per month, of which $25 went directly to his family (the average CCC enrollee came from a family of eight). The large public projects were

The Group Rec Hall is among many structures constructed at Lake Brownwood State Park by the CCC in the early 1930s from timber and native rock found in the park. Texas Parks & Wildlife Department photo.

Civilian Conservation Corps workers at Fort Parker State Park construct a dam across the Navasota River in 1939, creating Fort Parker Lake. The park was created in 1935, and all of its recreational facilities were constructed by the CCC. Texas Parks & Wildlife Department photo.

mainly in rural areas so that the CCC's low wages would not compete unfairly with private businesses.

President Roosevelt signed the enabling legislation on March 31, 1933, naming Robert Fechner, a former machinists' union leader, director of the agency.

On April 17, 1933, an incredibly fast two-and-a-half weeks after Roosevelt signed the legislation, the first enrollees arrived at the first CCC camp, appropriately named Camp Roosevelt, in the George Washington National Forest near Luray, Virginia. By July 1, more than 270,000 enrollees were living in 1,330 camps across the country.

During its nine-year existence, the CCC distributed more than $2.4 billion in federal funds to employ more than 2.5 million jobless young men (up to 519,000 were enrolled at any one time) who worked in about 3,000 camps.

In the agency's first five years, enrollees planted more than 1.3 billion tree seedlings, most in forests that had been clear cut and abandoned. They erected fire towers, built truck roads and firebreaks, reclaimed thousands of acres of land from soil erosion, and constructed facilities for visitors to national forests. They also developed national, state and local parks.

The Civilian Conservation Corps was probably the most popular and successful of the New Deal agencies. It employed thousands of idle young men and trained them in useful jobs. Their work provided money for their families, as well as income for businesses near CCC camps, where CCC administrators purchased camp supplies. The enrollees taught farmers how to prevent soil erosion, and they left a legacy of forest and park improvements all over the nation that Americans continue to enjoy today.

CCC enrollees stand at attention at an evening retreat in 1936 at their camp near Mesquite. In the background are their barracks and infirmary, which once supervised a one-week quarantine during a meningitis scare. The Mesquite camp was open from 1935–1941 and housed 250 men, who worked on such soil conservation projects as planting trees, terracing and fencing on 40,000 acres of farmland in Dallas, Kaufman and Rockwall counties. Photo courtesy of the Mesquite Public Library.

A Civilian Conservation Corps company near their camp in rural Texas. Texas Parks & Wildlife Department photo.

Organization of the CCC

In order to enroll, check qualifications of, train, clothe, feed, house and transport a large number of young men in a short time, Roosevelt called on the only government agency that had the capacity and experience to do it: the U.S. Army. Their clothing was left-over World War I uniforms. Initial housing on project sites was Army tents, replaced as soon as practicable by enrollee-built barracks, mess halls and support buildings. These were, in turn, replaced by portable, reusable buildings after 1935.

A regular Army officer was appointed commander of each camp, with reserve officers assisting. After December 1933, reserve officers replaced regular officers as commanders, with specially trained enrollees assisting.

The Army divided the United States into nine "corps areas." Texas shared the Eighth Corps Area with Oklahoma, New Mexico, Arizona, Colorado and most of Wyoming, with headquarters at Fort Sam Houston in San Antonio.

Local relief agencies handled recruitment, following federal guidelines and overseen by the U.S. Department of Labor. The forest and soil-conservation projects were supervised by the U.S. Department of Agriculture; park development was coordinated by the National Park Service of the Interior Department. Classes were planned by the U.S. Office of Education. The CCC Advisory Council, composed of a representative from each of these agencies and the Army, helped the director set policy and guided the work of the CCC. State relief agencies were responsible for suggesting projects

and providing direct supervision of the work. Each CCC camp also hired "local experienced men" to help train enrollees in such vital skills as how to handle tools.

Such a complex administrative organization, with responsibility shared among many agencies at several levels of government, would appear to be, as one writer called it, a "bureaucratic monstrosity." But historian Mark Welborn explains that each agency had specific duties, and a workable communication network was in place. For the most part, the plan worked reasonably well for the limited time that it was needed.

Camps were set up in every state plus Alaska, Hawaii (both U.S. territories at the time), Puerto Rico and the Virgin Islands. When a camp completed work on one project, it might be moved to another location, so enrollees often worked in several different locations during their time in the CCC.

Soil conservation and forest management projects were on both public and private lands.

CCC workers stand in front of the picnic pavilion they constructed at Bachman Lake in Dallas between 1935–1937. CCC Company 2896 completed projects at both Bachman Lake and White Rock Lake. File photo.

A CCC enrollee planes a board while working at a camp in rural Texas. Texas Parks & Wildlife Department photo.

The original goal was to enroll 250,000 youths at a time for six-month periods, allowing them to re-enroll for an additional six months. Later, the re-enrollment period was lengthened to one year, and the boys could sign up for more than one extension.

Segregation at the Camps

The CCC was of very limited assistance to black families during the Depression, because of local bigotry and national CCC leaders' political concerns. CCC rules forbade discrimination based on race, color or creed, but local relief boards often refused to enroll blacks, particularly in the South. The political realities of the time included white enrollees' hostility to blacks being in the same camps. When they were enrolled, blacks were almost always placed in segregated camps, not only in the South, but all over the country.

In Texas camps, there was nominal integration for a couple of years, but those camps maintained segregated barracks, mess halls, latrines and recreation halls. During these years, the total number of blacks accepted by Texas CCC recruiters was only 300. After a number of ugly racial incidents, separate black camps were instituted throughout the entire CCC in 1935.

Also, when the camps in white enrollees home states were filled, they were sent to other states whose camps were not yet at capacity. Blacks were not. They were enrolled only as vacancies occurred in black camps within their home states.

By 1935, the percentage of black enrollment in Texas was finally equal to their percentage of the population. But because a larger percentage of blacks than whites were poor, they were not able to participate in proportion to their need.

The main reason administrators and camp commanders gave for not enforcing integration of camps as required by law was that the only purpose of the CCC was to provide work for the enrollees rather than to fight for civil rights.

In April 1933, President Roosevelt authorized the CCC to enroll 14,000 American Indians. They mainly served at separate camps located on 50 million acres of tribal lands in 23 states, helping mitigate the effects of a severe drought.

The following month, the president ordered the enrollment of up to 25,000 World War I veterans. They also served at separate camps.

The Texas Relief Agencies

Governor Miriam "Ma" Ferguson persuaded the Texas Legislature to create the Texas Rehabilitation and Relief Commission in spring 1933 to coordinate the state's efforts with Roosevelt's relief plans.

Lawrence Westbrook was director of Texas' CCC selection process, but much of the work until 1937 was done by assistant director Neal Guy. The forest projects were coordinated by E.O. Siecke of the State Forest Service, and State Parks Board director Wendall Mayes handled parks projects.

At its peak of operations, 96 Texas CCC camps employed about 19,200 men at a time. Although the CCC's parks work is best known to the public, most of the Texas CCC camps did soil-conservation and erosion-control work.

Life in the CCC

On acceptance, enrollees were sent to "conditioning camps" at army posts for about two weeks, where they learned to function as a group and began intense physical exercise. From there they went to individual camps, which housed about 200 men each.

The day usually started with reveille at 6 or 6:30 a.m. Morning exercises were followed by a hearty breakfast, plain but ample. After straightening the barracks and policing the camp, they went to the work site by 8 a.m. for an eight-hour day of hard physical labor. Lunch was brought to the site about 1 p.m. The workday ended about 4 p.m., with supper back at camp by 5 or 5:30 p.m., followed by leisure activities — sports, games or reading. Lights out was at 10:30 p.m.

Most of the camps had libraries, as well as sports programs, which might include baseball, softball, boxing and football, and other recreation for filling after-work hours. For example, several enrollees at the Hereford camp formed an orchestra, aided by a few townspeople. The Palo Duro camp held a semi-monthly dance. A number of camps produced their own newsletters.

Education of the CCC Enrollees

Discovering that many of the enrollees were functionally illiterate, the CCC enlisted the help of the U.S. Office of Education to provide classes in basic school subjects — English, spelling, arithmetic and writing — and vocational courses. A camp education special-ist taught some classes; others might be taken at nearby high schools. Additional courses might include radio, shorthand or geometry, as at the Brenham camp. Enrollees at Longhorn Cavern could choose from dramatics, debate, social sciences, typing, singing, mechanical drawing and penmanship. Classes at Palo Duro Canyon included not only basic academics, but also such extras as one enrollee giving "a very interesting and enlightening talk on the curing of fresh pork ..."

Nationally, by June 1937, 35,000 men had learned to read and write, more than 1,000 received the equivalent of a high-school education, and 39 had received college degrees.

The CCC Creates Parks

Texas had a State Parks Board that by 1933 had acquired several historical sites and received a few gifts of land for parks, but it had no funds to develop and maintain a park system. As did other states, Texas seized the opportunity to create a large number of state parks using CCC labor and federal relief funds. The first four CCC park camps in Texas were at the Davis Mountains, Caddo Lake, Blanco and Mineral Wells.

Texas Canyons State Park was one of those planned in 1933 and was to be built in West Texas on a strip of land along the Rio Grande encompassing several canyons. Later that year, the Chisos Mountains were added to the acreage, and the name was changed to Big Bend State Park. A CCC camp began developing the park in 1935. The transfer to federal ownership was made in 1942; it opened as Big Bend National Park in 1944.

Between 1933 and 1942, CCC enrollees built

Quaint log cabins built by the Civilian Conservation Corps in the 1930s are popular with visitors to Caddo Lake State Park. The park's original improvements were made by CCC Company 889 in 1933 and completed by Company 857 between 1934–1937. They also built a pavilion and picnic sites. Texas Parks & Wildlife Department photo.

lodges, cabins, picnic pavilions, refectories, concession buildings, support buildings, footbridges and restrooms, usually from native rock and timber. They also constructed swimming pools, strung telephone lines, planted thousands of trees, developed hiking and equestrian trails, installed guardrails, built dams to impound lakes, and constructed culverts to provide drainage.

Some Texas parks presented particular challenges: At Davis Mountains State Park, enrollees molded adobe bricks to build Indian Lodge. At Longhorn Cavern, the campers dug more than 2 million cubic yards of silt and bat guano out of the cave. The rock that they also removed was used to construct bridges and entrance gates to the park and the cavern. CCC enrollees at the Balmorhea camp built a huge, one-and-three-quarter-acre swimming pool. Still in use, the pool is 25 feet deep and is filled by San Solomon Springs' 72-degree-to-76-degree water.

The men were also on hand to help with emergencies. In 1935, enrolleees in the Big Spring camp saw a fire on Scenic Mountain. When enrollee James Cook of Plainview ran to the location, he saw, "a group of women standing by a flaming automobile trying to put the fire out with screams …" The boys phoned for a wrecker.

National Forests in Texas

When the Great Depression began, Texas had no national forests. In 1933, the Texas Legislature authorized the sale of lands in East Texas to the federal government for the development of national forests, and the land transfer was formalized in 1936. The CCC developed Texas' national forests: Davy Crockett, Angelina, Sam Houston and Sabine, which today cover 637,646 acres in parts of 12 Texas counties.

In them, the CCC reforested bare areas; erected lookout towers, water towers and observation platforms; fought forest fires; waged war against tree insects and diseases; and developed campgrounds.

Soil Conservation Work

The Great Depression coincided with the Dust Bowl across the Great Plains, adding agricultural woes to the general economic ones. Settlers had moved onto the plains in the late 19th century and plowed up most of the native grasses to raise crops. When the crops failed because of severe drought beginning in the early 1930s, there was no vegetation to hold the dirt when windstorms hit the area. Loose dirt picked up in the Great Plains was carried sometimes for thousands of miles. The "dusters" turned daylight into dark, making it hard to see more than a few feet and making it even harder to breathe.

Indian Lodge in Davis Mountains State Park is often considered the "crown jewel" of the CCC structures in Texas and the only example of Southwestern Pueblo-style architecture in Texas, according to TPWD historians. In 2006, an extensive restoration of the lodge was completed that included both interior and exterior improvements. Texas Parks & Wildlife Department photo.

Original ceilings of pine beams and rustic wood furniture built by the CCC were restored in Indian Lodge during a 5-year project. The lodge in the 2,709-acre Davis Mountains State Park has 39 rooms and hosted more than 55,000 visitors in 2006, including nearly 16,000 overnight guests and 38,000 who dined at the Black Bear Restaurant. Texas Parks & Wildlife Department photo.

Amarillo residents, for example, counted more than 190 "black blizzards" between January 1933 and February 1936. The storms that boiled across the denuded plains for almost a decade gave the afflicted area the name "Dust Bowl."

While the arid plains were blowing away, farmers farther east had a different soil problem. In Central Texas, land that once produced 200 to 300 pounds of lint cotton per acre annually yielded only 100 to 150 pounds in 1935. Farmers assumed that the soil had simply worn out. But much of their trouble stemmed from the common practice of planting crops in long, straight rows, creating ideal conditions for soil erosion. The March 1935 issue of *Farm and Ranch* magazine stated that between 1930 and 1935, loss of topsoil was as great as 65 tons per acre where corn had been grown in rows run-

A two-acre, sping-fed swimming pool is the focal point of Balmorhea State Park, which was developed by CCC Company 1856 between 1936–1941. The 45.9-acre park is located about four miles southwest of Balmorhea in the foothills of the Davis Mountains in Reeves County. The pool, an oasis for aquatic life and popular with scuba clubs, is fed by more than 22 million gallons of water that flows each day from San Solomon Springs. Other CCC structures in the park include a limestone concession building, two wooden bathhouses, an adobe superintendent residence and San Solomon Courts, an early example of the modern-day motel. All of the CCC buildings are constructed in a Spanish Colonial style with stucco exteriors and tile roofs. Texas Parks & Wildlife Department photo.

ning up and down slopes. The land was not wearing out, it was washing away.

CCC enrollees, guided by the Soil Conservation Service of the Department of Agriculture, taught 5,000 Texas farmers how to terrace their fields and use contour plowing to prevent soil loss by holding rain in place until it soaked into the dirt rather than letting it run off, carrying valuable topsoil with it.

The work of the Memphis SCS camp, opened in July 1935, was typical. Working in parts of four surrounding Texas counties, the campers surveyed contour lines and laid terraces, seeded range land, and built stock tanks and dams.

They constructed 130 miles of terraces, 1,500 check dams, and 16 stock tanks; furrowed 1,500 acres of pasture; and planted 20 miles of trees and shrubs.

The limestone-block group pavilion at Big Spring State Park in Howard County was constructed by the CCC soon after the state acquired the park property in 1934. Using limestone quarried on the site, the CCC also built the park's headquarters, residence, pump house and restroom. The largest CCC project at the 382-acre park is a three-mile scenic drive. Texas Parks & Wildlife Department photo.

The CCC at the Texas Centennial

The National Park Service and the Texas State Parks Board sponsored an extensive CCC exhibit at Fair Park in Dallas during the Texas Central Centennial Exposition, June 6 to November 29, 1936, celebrating the Texas Centennial. Around a 28,000-square-foot area, CCC enrollees erected a wall of native stone and timber. Within it, they built a weekend cabin, like the ones built in Texas State Parks, and a fieldstone and pine-log building to display exhibits by the federal agencies involved in the CCC program.

The exhibit building's rustic front door swung on large wrought-iron hinges made at the White Rock Lake CCC camp. Examples of furniture used in park cabins, handmade from Texas cedar by enrollees at Palo Duro Canyon, were part of the exhibit. Twenty-four CCC members guided visitors through the exhibit.

In the courtyard, enrollees planted a miniature forest composed of 85 varieties of native trees and shrubs from all over the state, from the mesquite and catclaw of Southwest Texas to the magnolias, pines and dogwoods of East Texas.

The Final Days of the CCC

As the Depression eased and businesses began hiring, the CCC had increasing problems attracting and keeping enrollees. Some signed up but deserted if they didn't like the work or if they found a job in the private sector. With the threat of war in Europe looming, other potential CCC members signed up for military service instead. Some CCC camps began substituting military-

The Lake Highlands High School band plays during the rededication of the shelter on Flag Pole Hill at White Rock Lake during the National Association of Civilian Conservation Corps Alumni Reunion on Sept. 28, 2006. The shelter was built by the CCC in 1936 and was refurbished before the reunion. Photo by Rex C. Curry.

Former CCC workers and their wives attend the National Association of Civilian Conservation Corps Alumni Reunion on Sept. 28, 2006, at Flag Pole Hill at White Rock Lake. From left are: Cecil Nicholas, J. Woodrow Sayre, Selma Sayre, Rita Sanchez and Tony Sanchez. Photo by Rex C. Curry.

A six-foot-tall statue at Sunset Bay at White Rock Lake in Dallas honors Civilian Conservation Corps workers. It was presented in 2004 to members of Company 2896, who built buildings and structures around White Rock Lake and Bachman Lake. Photo by Louis DeLuca.

related training for education: demolition, road and bridge construction, radio operation, first aid and cooking.

The number of camps and enrollees continued shrinking until Congress finally ended the CCC on June 30, 1942.

A total of 156,000 Texans were enrolled in the CCC during its nine years of existence, according to historian Mark Welborn. (Other writers say 50,000, the difference perhaps resulting from one writer counting an enrollee each time he re-enrolled, and another counting each individual only once.) Many of the enrollees entered the CCC undernourished and dejected. Almost to a man, they gained strength, confidence and weight, gaining an average 11¼ pounds. For the most part, CCC alumni look back on their experiences fondly. As E. Maury Wallace of Austin, who worked on Longhorn Cavern, said

in 1988: "[We] were just hard up for work. I was glad to get a job. We ate good every day and you could have all you wanted." In 2005, an alumnus of the Garner State Park camp remembered his pride in being able to pay his mother's way through beauty school with the allotment he sent home.

Former CCC enrollees have organized the National Association of Civilian Conservation Corps Alumni (NACCCA), which holds an annual meeting (the 2006 meeting was in Dallas). Some local alumni chapters exist, as well.

The immediate purpose of the CCC was to provide a living for destitute young men and their families, but the relief funds benefited all of Texas. Texans continue to enjoy the results of the hard work of this extraordinary group of young men. ☆

Mary G. Ramos, a Dallas free-lance writer, is editor emerita of the Texas Almanac.

Sources

Brophy, William J. "Black Texans and the New Deal," The Depression in the Southwest. Donald W. Whisenhunt, ed. National University Publications, Port Washington, N.Y., 1980.

Cox, Jim. "Fond Memories from a Time of National Hardship." Texas Parks and Wildlife Magazine, September 1978. Reprinted online at http://www.tpwd.state.tx.us/spdest/findadest/historic_sites/ccc/; accessed Nov. 3, 2005.

Dallas Morning News, various. "Park Service Installing Fair Exhibit," April 19, 1936; "Trees From All Parts of Texas Viewed at Fair," June 7, 1936; "Trying Out C.C.C. Furniture," June 21, 1936.

Hendrickson, Kenneth E., Jr. "Replenishing the Soil and the Soul of Texas: The CCC in the Lone Star State as an Example of State-Federal Work Relief During the Great Depression." Faculty Papers, Series 2, Vol. 1, Midwestern State University, Wichita Falls, Texas, 1974–1975.

"Index of States/Camps Listing: Texas." National Association of Civilian Conservation Corps Alumni (NACCCA) Website: http://www.cccalumni.org/states/texas1.html; accessed Jan. 19, 2007.

Lacy, Leslie Alexander. The Soil Soldiers: The Civilian Conservation Corps in the Great Depression. Chilton Book Company, Radnor, Pa., 1976.

Merrill, Perry H. Roosevelt's Forest Army: A History of the Civilian Conservation Corps, 1993–1942. Perry H. Merrill, Montpelier, Vt., 1981.

Mortimer, John L. "Farmers to Control Soil Erosion." Farm and Ranch, Farm and Ranch Publishing Co., Dallas, March 15, 1935.

Nall, Garry L. "The Struggle to Save the Land: The Soil Conservation Effort in the Dust Bowl," The Depression in the Southwest. Donald W. Whisenhunt, ed. National University Publications, Port Washington, N.Y., 1980.

Otis, Alison T., et al. The Forest Service and The Civilian Conservation Corps: 1933–42. Forest Service, FS-395, U.S. Department of Agriculture, August 1986.

Paige, John C. The Civilian Conservation Corps and the National Park Service, 1933–1942: An Administrative History. The National Park Service, Department of the Interior, 1985. Online edition: http://www.cr.nps.gov/history/online_books/ccc/ccct.htm); accessed Jan. 8, 2007.

Plainsman, The, Vol. 1, No. 2, Lubbock, Aug. 16, 1935.

Rodgers, L.W. "Civilian Conservation Corps Educational Program," Texas Centennial Magazine. Texas Centennial Publishing Co., San Antonio, March 1936.

Salmond, John A. The Civilian Conservation Corps, 1933–1942: A New Deal Case Study. Duke University Press, Durham, N.C., 1967.

Steely, James Wright. The Civilian Conservation Corps in Texas State Parks. Texas Parks and Wildlife Department, Austin, 1986.

Steely, James Wright. Parks for Texas: Enduring Landscapes of the New Deal. University of Texas Press, Austin, 1999.

Sypolt, Larry N. Civilian Conservation Corps: A Selectively Annotated Bibliography. Praeger, Westport, Conn., 2005.

Texas Almanac, various. "Texas State Parks," Texas Almanac 1936; "Texas State Parks — Public Recreation," Texas Almanac 1941–42; "National Forests and Grasslands in Texas," Texas Almanac 2006–2007. The Dallas Morning News, Dallas, Texas.

Welborn, Mark Alan. "Texas and the CCC: A Case Study in the Successful Administration of a Confederate State and Federal Program." Master's Thesis, University of North Texas, 1989.

PARKS IN TEXAS DEVELOPED
BY THE CIVILIAN CONSERVATION CORPS, 1933–1942

This table lists current parks in Texas — national, state, and local — developed by the Civilian Conservation Corps, and the nearest town to the park. CCC-built facilities remaining in these parks include refectory buildings, cabins, lodges, bridges, dams, roads, hiking trails, picnic tables and benches, observation towers or swimming pools. Not all parks contain all these elements.

PARK (Original name listed first, with current name in parentheses)	NEAREST TOWN
National Park	
Big Bend National Park	Marathon
State Parks	
Balmorhea State Park	Balmorhea
Bastrop State Park	Bastrop
Big Spring State Park	Big Spring
Blanco State Park	Blanco
Bonham State Park	Bonham
Brownwood State Park *(Lake Brownwood SP)*	Brownwood
Buescher State Park	Smithville
Caddo Lake State Park	Karnack
Cleburne State Park	Cleburne
Daingerfield State Park	Daingerfield
Davis Mountains State Park	Fort Davis
Fort Griffin State Park *(Fort Griffin State Park & Historic Site)*	Albany
Fort Parker State Park	Mexia
Garner State Park	Concan
Goliad State Park &	
Mission Espíritu Santo State Historic Site	Goliad
Goose Island State Park	Rockport
Huntsville State Park	Huntsville
Inks Lake State Park	Burnet
Lake Abilene State Park *(Abilene SP)*	Buffalo Gap
Lake Corpus Christi State Park	Mathis
Lake Mineral Wells State Park	Mineral Wells
Lockhart State Park	Lockhart
Longhorn Cavern State Park	Burnet
Meridian State Park	Meridian
Mission Tejas State Park*	Weches
Mother Neff State Park	Moody
Palmetto State Park	Gonzales
Palo Duro Canyon State Park	Canyon
Possum Kingdom State Park	Caddo
Tyler State Park	Tyler

Mission Tejas State Park, a 363.5-acre park in Houston County, 22 miles northeast of Crockett was built in 1934 by Company 888 of the Civilian Conservation Corps as a commemorative representation of Mission San Francisco de los Tejas, the first Spanish mission in the province of Texas, which was established in 1690. Activities in this park include camping, picnicking, hiking and fishing. Texas Parks & Wildlife Department photo.

PARKS IN TEXAS DEVELOPED
BY THE CIVILIAN CONSERVATION CORPS, 1933–1942

Developed as State Parks and Now on Private Land	
Palisades State Park	Canyon
Lampasas State Park	Lampasas
Stephenville State Park	Stephenville

Existing Municipal and County Parks	
Lake Austin Metropolitan Park *(Emma Long Municipal Park)*	Austin
Zilker Metropolitan Park	Austin
Tyrrell Metropolitan Park *(Tyrrell Park)*	Beaumont
Bachman–White Rock Lake Metropolitan Park (White Rock Lake Park and Bachman Lake Park)	Dallas
Grayson State Park *(Loy Park)*	Denison
Ascarate County Park	El Paso
Lake Worth Metropolitan Park *(Fort Worth Nature Center and Casino Beach)*	Fort Worth
Old Fort Parker	Groesbeck
Mackenzie State Park *(Mackenzie Park)*	Lubbock
Franklin Fields Park *(Olmos Basin Park)*	San Antonio

*Mission Tejas State Park was developed by the CCC as a forest park. It was transferred from the Texas Forest Service to Texas Parks and Wildlife Department in 1957.

Woodlake:
A New Deal Experiment in East Texas

By Mary G. Ramos

The heavily forested Piney Woods of East Texas seems an odd place for an experiment in communal farming. But the community of Woodlake, established in Trinity County by the federal government in the mid-1930s, was just such an experiment.

The Great Depression economically devastated the nation beginning with the stock market crash in October 1929. After President Franklin D. Roosevelt was sworn into office in March 1933, he launched the New Deal, a massive, multi-agency effort to bring relief to the unemployed and to reform the country's economic institutions. The new Federal Emergency Relief Administration created 28 communities for families on relief — three of them in Texas. Another 71 communities, 8 in Texas, were established by two other New Deal agencies (*see table on next page*).

Woodlake, located about halfway between Huntsville and Lufkin, was the first FERA town in Texas. Dallas architect David Williams, whose experience included creating prefabricated housing for oilfield workers near Tampico, Mexico, between 1916 and 1921, was chosen to design the East Texas community. He was enthusiastic about helping people who were, in his view, trapped in city slums. Williams believed that encouraging city families to live on farms would not only allow them to grow their food but also put them in a healthier environ.

Williams planned a modern, low-cost, but attractive and comfortable living environment with as many city conveniences as possible. The community had a core of 100 houses, each on a three-acre plot, providing enough space for each family to have its own vegetable garden.

The houses were surrounded by two 600-acre communal farm fields. Centrally located were a church, a school, a trading post, other community buildings, including a cold-storage facility, plus a 255-acre park with two lakes, a stone pavilion and a bath house. Unlike a majority of Texas farmhouses at the time, Woodlake's had running water, electricity and sanitary facilities.

Each family helped raise and market the crops and the products from a communal dairy. Pooling their purchases, their labor and their marketing efforts, Williams believed, would lead to economies of scale and would benefit all. Construction began in January 1934. Through the use of standardized industrial construction techniques and the prefabrication of components, the 100 houses and other facilities were finished and ready for occupation by June 1, 1934.

The Previous Woodlake

FERA's Woodlake should perhaps be called "Woodlake II." An earlier, smaller Woodlake had been built at the site several years before as a private philanthropic project by Helen Kerr Thompson, wife of a wealthy lumber-industry executive.

Trinity County was a center of Texas' lumbering industry for half a century. Exploitation of the area's forests took root about 1875. When the International and Great Northern Railroad laid tracks through the county in 1881, the lumbering industry expanded enormously. In those days, reforestation of cutover lands was not legally required, and most timber company owners did not believe they needed to replenish natural resources. The lumber companies cut down all the trees on their land as quickly as they could, then moved on to another tract, leaving essentially worthless land covered with nothing but stumps and brambles in their wakes.

In 1881, the Thompson and Tucker Lumber Co. began acquiring land in Trinity County, eventually amassing 12,000 acres. By spring 1882, their mill was processing 13,000 feet of lumber a day. Output increased until, by 1909, 100,000 feet of pine lumber were emerging from the company's mills daily. Two years later, all the trees were gone, and the company abandoned its land.

J. Lewis Thompson, the company's president and one of the founder's sons, moved to Houston to go into banking, but he retained ownership of the family home and the 12,000 acres of cutover land in Trinity County. When World War I began, Thompson entered the Army, deeding that land to his wife, Helen Kerr Thompson.

Mrs. Thompson, who had grown up on a farm near Sherman, was the daughter of a well-known horticulturist, John S. Kerr. The sagging economy of Trinity County worried her, and she developed a plan to turn the cutover land into a farming operation, benefiting both the land and the area's displaced lumber-industry workers. She incorporated her father's ideas of crop diversification, rebuilding the depleted soil and using organic fertilizers. Financing the project with family money, she gave tenant farmers an opportunity to buy their farms under favorable terms. By the late 1920s, 29 families were working the land, growing corn, cotton, tomatoes and chickens.

But agricultural prices fell disastrously at the onset of the Great Depression, reducing the families to bare subsistence level. In 1932, Mrs. Thompson began looking for outside financial help. She contacted Texas' relief administrator, Col. Lawrence Westbrook, suggesting that her communal farm be expanded into a relief project. Westbrook believed that a permanent solution for unemployed families was better than direct relief grants and that rural resettlement had great potential as a solution. Mrs. Thompson sold about 3,200 acres of the former Thompson and Tucker land to the Texas Rural Communities Project, on which the second Woodlake was built.

The New Deal Woodlake

The organization of the second Woodlake was similar to that of the first: A farm manager directed the work; the residents shared the labor and divided the income. While FERA initially provided guidance and financing, the community was to eventually become a self-supporting corporation owned by the farmers. Although families leased their homes for the first three years, they then

NEW DEAL COMMUNITIES IN TEXAS

In addition to the Federal Emergency Relief Administration, two other New Deal agencies created communities in the relief effort: the Division of Subsistence Homesteads and the Resettlement Administration. Of a total of 99 such colonies developed across the nation by these three agencies, those in Texas are listed below by creating agency. Information includes the name, location, type of community and number of living units. The number next to the agency name is the national total of communities developed by that agency.

NAME	LOCATION	TYPE OF COMMUNITY	NO. OF LIVING UNITS
Federal Emergency Relief Administration (28)			
Woodlake Community	Trinity County	Farm village	101
Ropesville Farms	Hockley County	Farm community	76
Wichita Valley Farms	Wichita County	Farm community	91
Division of Subsistence Homesteads (34)			
Beauxart Gardens	Beaumont	Industrial	50
Dalworthington Gardens	Arlington	Industrial	79
Houston Gardens	Houston	Industrial	100
Three Rivers Gardens	Three Rivers	Industrial	50
Wichita Gardens	Wichita Falls	Industrial	62
Resettlement Administration (37)			
McLennan Farms	McLennan County	Farm community	20
Sabine Farms	Harrison County	Farm community	80
Sam Houston Farms	Harris County	Farm community	86

Source: National New Deal Preservation Association Website: http://newdeallegacy.org/history_newdeal.htm accessed Nov. 12, 2006.

could get a low-cost, 25-year loan to buy their homes.

The experiment got off to a fairly good start. Although they didn't move in until early summer 1934, the residents had grown and preserved a large amount of food in the central food-processing plant by that fall. They planted tomatoes, cotton, corn, sugar cane and other crops. The dairy supplied the residents' needs and enough more to sell. Woodlake's chickens laid enough eggs to enable the community to sell eggs under contract to corporations year round.

But the community soon began faltering, mainly because of the people recruited to live there. Mrs. Thompson's Woodlake proved that a successful communal farm was possible with motivated families who understood the importance of cooperation. They were local families with shared traditions and a familiarity with the area and with each other.

Although the participants in FERA's Woodlake were carefully selected and briefed as to the nature of the experiment, many never understood the level of cooperation that would be required among the 100 families. FERA's participants were not from the area's farming families, but mostly from Houston's relief rolls. Many of them weren't interested in farming as a life's work. Others who had once been farmers wanted to work their own fields and market their own crops rather than help work communal fields. Those who worked the fields in the blazing sun were jealous of those who worked in the cool dairy. Some colonists sneaked to Houston to go job hunting as the economic crisis eased, then defaulted on their obligations at Woodlake if they found a job.

There was also political fallout: Commercial farmers complained that the Woodlake families were government-subsidized competition. Local politicians resented all the attention and money going to tenant farmers.

The results of the Woodlake experiment persuaded FERA not to include a communal component in their other family resettlement projects. The agency's Ropesville Farms, built west of Lubbock near the already existing town of Ropesville, encompassed 76 farms of 146 to 300 acres each, with each family responsible for its own fields and livestock. The first 33 families arrived in 1936; all the farms were occupied by the end of 1939. When the project ended in 1943, the community was transferred to individual ownership.

By the time the first Ropesville families arrived, the entire FERA program was already faltering. On June 30, 1936, most FERA communities were transferred to the Resettlement Administration. Woodlake dropped its communal experiment and became a settlement of small individual plots occupied by farm families. In 1937, Woodlake was transferred again, this time to the Farm Security Administration. Other small changes were made until, in 1943, at the end of the Depression era, the federal government auctioned off all government communities. Some of the Woodlake homes were purchased by individuals and moved away from the site, while others continued to be occupied by farm families.

A tiny community and post office on U.S. 287 bear the Woodlake name today. The last unofficial estimate of the town's population was just under 100 residents. ☆

Sources

Booker, James Terry. "The Woodlake Cooperative Community: A New Deal Experiment in Rural Living for the Unemployed." Masters Thesis, Texas A&M University, December 1976.

Handbook of Texas Online. "Thompson, Helen Kerr." http://www.tsha.utexas.edu/handbook/online/articles/TT/fthdh.html; accessed Nov. 15, 2006.

Handbook of Texas Online. "Trinity County." http://www.tsha.utexas.edu/handbook/online/articles/TT/hct9.html; accessed Nov. 15, 2006.

Handbook of Texas Online. "Woodlake, Texas (Trinity County)." http://www.tsha.utexas.edu/handbook/online/articles/WW/hlw47.html; accessed Nov 30, 2006.

Richardson, T.C. "Woodlake: An Interesting Experiment." Farm and Ranch, Oct. 1, 1935, p. 2.

Texas Historic Sites Atlas. "Ropesville Resettlement Project." Texas Historical Commission, http://atlas.thc.state.tx.us/; accessed Dec. 13, 2006.

Wade, Michael G. "Back to the Land: The Woodlake Community, 1933–1943." East Texas Historical Journal, Vol. XXI, No. 2, Stephen F. Austin State University, Nacogdoches, Texas, 1983.

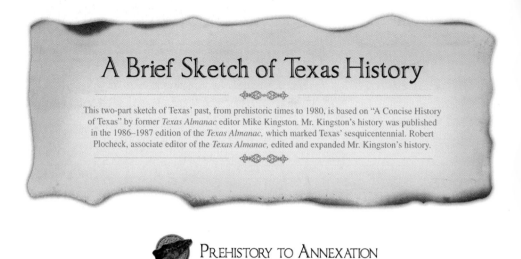

A Brief Sketch of Texas History

This two-part sketch of Texas' past, from prehistoric times to 1980, is based on "A Concise History of Texas" by former *Texas Almanac* editor Mike Kingston. Mr. Kingston's history was published in the 1986–1987 edition of the *Texas Almanac*, which marked Texas' sesquicentennial. Robert Plocheck, associate editor of the *Texas Almanac*, edited and expanded Mr. Kingston's history.

PREHISTORY TO ANNEXATION

Prehistoric Texas

Early Texans are believed to have been descendants of Asian groups that migrated across the Bering Strait during the Ice Ages of the past 50,000 years.

At intermittent periods, enough water accumulated in massive glaciers worldwide to lower the sea level several hundred feet. During these periods, the Bering Strait became a 1,300-mile-wide land bridge between North America and Asia.

These early adventurers worked their way southward for thousands of years, eventually getting as far as Tierra del Fuego in South America about 10,000 years ago.

Biologically, they were completely modern homo sapiens. No evidence has been found to indicate that any evolutionary change occurred in the New World.

Four basic stages reflecting cultural advancement of early inhabitants are used by archeologists in classifying evidence. These stages are the Paleo-Indian (20,000 to 7,000 years ago), Archaic (7,000 years ago to about the time of Christ), Woodland (time of Christ to 800–1,000 years ago), and Neo-American or Late Prehistoric (800–1,000 years ago until European contact).

Not all early people advanced through all these stages in Texas. Much cultural change occurred in adaptation to changes in climate. The Caddo tribes of East Texas, for example, reached the Neo-American stage before the Spanish and French explorers made contact in the 1500s and 1600s.

Others, such as the Karankawas of the Gulf Coast,

An ancient Indian pictograph named Speaking Rock is engraved in the rocks at Hueco Tanks State Park near El Paso. This 860-acre park also features natural rock basins that provided water for Indians and Anglo travelers. File photo.

advanced no further than the Archaic stage of civilization at the same time. Still others advanced and then regressed in the face of a changing climate.

The earliest confirmed evidence indicates that humans were in Texas between 10,000 and 13,000 years ago.

Paleo-Indians were successful big-game hunters. Artifacts from this period are found across the state but not in great number, indicating that they were a small, nomadic population.

As Texas' climate changed at the end of the Ice Age about 7,000 years ago, inhabitants adapted. Apparently the state experienced an extended period of warming and drying, and the population during the **Archaic** period increased.

These Texans began to harvest fruits and nuts, and to exploit rivers for food, as indicated by the fresh-water mussel shells in ancient garbage heaps.

The **Woodland** stage is distinguished by the development of settled societies, with crops and local wild plants providing much of their diet. The bow and arrow came into use, and the first pottery is associated with this period.

Pre-Caddoan tribes in East Texas had formed villages and were building distinctive mounds for burials and for ritual.

The **Neo-American** period is best exemplified by the highly civilized Caddoes, who had a complex culture with well-defined social stratification. They were fully agricultural and participated in trade over a wide area of North America. *(See page 18 for an overview of archeological sites in Texas.)*

The Spanish Explorations

Spain's exploration of North America was one of the first acts of a vigorous nation that was emerging from centuries of campaigns to oust the Islamic Moors from the Iberian Peninsula.

In early **1492**, the Spanish forces retook the province of Granada, completing the reconquista or reconquest.

Francisco Vasquez de Coronado explored the Texas High Plains looking for gold and silver. This drawing entitled Coronado's March — Colorado (circa 1897) by Frederic Remington is courtesy of the Library of Congress.

Later in the year, the Catholic royals of the united country, Ferdinand and Isabella, took a major stride toward shaping world history by commissioning Christopher Columbus for the voyage that was to bring Europeans to America.

As early as **1519, Capt. Alonso Alvarez de Pineda**, in the service of the governor of Jamaica, mapped the coast of Texas.

The **first recorded exploration of today's Texas** was made in the 1530s by **Alvar Núñez Cabeza de Vaca**, along with two other Spaniards and a Moorish slave named Estevanico. They were members of an expedition commanded by Panfilo de Narváez that left Cuba in 1528 to explore what is now the southeastern United States. Ill-fated from the beginning, many members of the expedition lost their lives, and others, including Cabeza de Vaca, were shipwrecked on the Texas coast. Eventually the band wandered into Mexico in 1536.

In **1540**, Francisco Vázquez de Coronado was commissioned to lead an exploration of the American Southwest. The quest took him to the land of the Pueblo Indians in what is now New Mexico. Native Americans, who had learned it was best to keep Europeans away from their homes, would suggest vast riches could be found in other areas. So Coronado pursued a fruitless search for gold and silver across the **High Plains of Texas**, Oklahoma and Kansas.

While Coronado was investigating Texas from the west, Luis de Moscoso Alvarado approached from the east. He assumed leadership of Hernando de Soto's expedition when the commander died on the banks of the Mississippi River. In **1542**, Moscoso's group ventured as far west as **Central Texas** before returning to the Mississippi.

Forty years passed after the Coronado and Moscoso expeditions before Fray Agustín Rodríguez, a Franciscan missionary, and Francisco Sánchez Chamuscado, a soldier, led an expedition into Texas and New Mexico.

Following the Río Conchos in Mexico to its confluence with the Rio Grande near present-day **Presidio** and then turning northwestward up the great river's valley, the explorers passed through the El Paso area in **1581**.

Juan de Oñate was granted the right to develop this area populated by Pueblo Indians in 1598. He blazed a trail across the desert from Santa Barbara, Chihuahua, to intersect the Rio Grande at the Pass of the North. For the next 200 years, this was the supply route from the interior of Mexico that served the northern colonies.

Texas was attractive to the Spanish in the 1600s. Small expeditions found trade possibilities, and missionaries ventured into the territory. Frays Juan de Salas and Diego López responded to a request by the Jumano Indians for religious instruction in **1629**, and for a brief time priests lived with the Indians near present-day **San Angelo**.

The first permanent settlement in Texas was established in **1681–1682** after New Mexico's Indians rebelled and drove Spanish settlers southward. The colonists retreated to the **El Paso** area, where the missions of Corpus Christi de la Isleta and Nuestra Señora del Socorro — each named for a community in New Mexico — were established. Ysleta pueblo originally was located on the south side of the Rio Grande, but as the river changed its course, the pueblo ended up on the north bank. Now part of El Paso, the community is considered the oldest European settlement in Texas.

This engraving by Jan Van Vianen, created in 1698, shows La Salle, several priests and others on shore as supplies are unloaded from a ship. While exploring near the Trinity River, LaSalle was murdered by some of his men. Image courtesy of the Library of Congress.

French Exploration

In 1682, **René Robert Cavelier, Sieur de La Salle**, explored the Mississippi River to its mouth at the Gulf of Mexico. La Salle claimed the vast territory drained by the river for France.

Two years later, La Salle returned to the New World with four ships and enough colonists to establish his country's claim. Guided by erroneous maps, this second expedition overshot the mouth of the Mississippi by 400 miles and ended up on the Texas coast. Though short of supplies because of the loss of two of the ships, the French colonists established Fort Saint Louis on Garcitas Creek several miles inland from Lavaca Bay.

In 1687, La Salle and a group of soldiers began an overland trip to find French outposts on the Mississippi River. Somewhere west of the Trinity River, the explorer was murdered by some of his men. His grave has never been found. (A more detailed account of La Salle's expedition can be found in the *Texas Almanac 1998–1999* and on the *Texas Almanac* Web site.)

In 1689, Spanish authorities sent **Capt. Alonso de León**, the governor of Coahuila (which at various times included Texas in its jurisdiction), into Texas to confront the French. He headed eastward from present-day **Eagle Pass** and eventually found the tattered remnants of Fort Saint Louis.

Indians had destroyed the settlement and killed many colonists. León continued tracking survivors of the ill-fated colony into East Texas.

Spanish Rule

Father **Damián Massanet** accompanied León on this journey. The priest was fascinated with tales about the "Tejas" Indians of the region.

Tejas meant *friendly*, but at the time the term was considered a tribal name. Actually these Indians were members of the Caddo Confederacy that controlled parts of four present states: Texas, Louisiana, Arkansas and Oklahoma.

The Caddo religion acknowledged one supreme god, and when a Tejas chief asked Father Massanet to stay and instruct his people in his faith, the Spaniards promised to return and establish a mission.

The pledge was redeemed in **1690** when the mission San Francisco de los Tejas was founded near present-day Weches in Houston County.

Twin disasters struck this missionary effort. Spanish government officials quickly lost interest when the French threat at colonization diminished. And as was the case with many New World Indians who had no resistance to European diseases, the Tejas soon were felled by an epidemic. The Indians blamed the new religion and resisted conversion. The mission languished, and it was difficult to supply it from other Spanish outposts in northern Mexico. In 1693, the Spanish officials closed the mission effort in **East Texas.**

Although Spain had not made a determined effort to settle Texas, great changes were coming to the territory. Spain introduced horses into the Southwest. By the late 1600s, Comanches were using the horses to expand their range southward across the plains, displacing the Apaches. In the **1720s**, the **Apaches** moved onto the lower Texas Plains, usurping the traditional hunting grounds of the Jumanos and others. The nomadic Coahuiltecan bands were particularly hard hit.

In 1709, Fray Antonio de San Buenaventura y Olivares had made an initial request to establish a mission at

The Ybarbo Ranch House on the grounds of Stephen F. Austin State University in Nacogdoches was built around 1774 by Antonio Gil Ybarbo, a Spanish lieutenant governor and commander of the militia in Nacogdoches in the late eighteenth century. Image courtesy of the Library of Congress.

San Pedro Springs (today's San Antonio) to minister to the Coahuiltecans. Spanish officials denied the request. However, new fears over the French movement into East Texas changed that.

Another Franciscan, **Father Francisco Hidalgo**, who had earlier served at the missions in East Texas, returned to them when he and **Father Antonio Margil de Jesús** accompanied **Capt. Diego Ramón** on an expedition to the area in 1716. In that year, the mission of San Francisco de los Neches was established near the site of the old San Francisco de los Tejas mission. Nuestra Señora de Guadalupe was located at the present-day site of Nacogdoches, and Nuestra Señora de los Dolores was placed near present-day San Augustine.

The East Texas missions did little better on the second try, and supplying the frontier missions remained difficult. It became apparent that a way station between northern Mexico and East Texas was needed.

In 1718, Spanish officials consented to Fray Olivares' request to found a mission at San Pedro Springs. That mission, called **San Antonio de Valero**, was later to be known as the **Alamo**. Because the Indians of the region often did not get along with each other, other missions were established to serve each group.

These missions flourished and each became an early ranching center. But the large herds of cattle and horses attracted trouble. The San Antonio missions began to face the wrath of the Apaches. The mission system, which attempted to convert the Indians to Christianity and to "civilize" them, was partially successful in subduing minor tribes but not larger tribes like the Apaches.

The Spanish realized that more stable colonization efforts must be made. Indians from Mexico, such as the Tlascalans who fought with Cortés against the Aztecs, were brought into Texas to serve as examples of "good" Indians for the wayward natives.

In **1731**, Spanish colonists from the **Canary Islands** were brought to Texas and founded the **Villa of San Fernando de Béxar**, the first civil jurisdiction in the province and today's **San Antonio**.

In the late 1730s, Spanish officials became concerned over the vulnerability of the large area between the Sierra Madre Oriental and the Gulf Coast in northern Mexico. The area was unsettled, a haven for runaway Indian slaves and marauders, and it was a wide-open pathway for the English or French to travel from the Gulf to the rich silver mines in Durango.

For seven years, the search for the right colonizer went on before **José de Escandón** was selected in 1746. A professional military man and successful administrator, Escandón earned a high reputation by subduing Indians in central Mexico. On receiving the assignment, he launched a broad land survey of the area running from the mountains to the Gulf and from the Río Pánuco in Tamaulipas, Mexico, to the Nueces River in Texas.

In 1747, he began placing colonists in settlements throughout the area. **Tomás Sánchez** received a land grant on the Rio Grande in 1755 from which **Laredo** developed. And other small Texas communities along the river sprang up as a result of Escandón's well-executed plan. Many old Hispanic families in Texas hold title to their land based on grants in this period.

In the following decades, a few other Spanish colonists settled around the old missions and frontier forts. **Antonio Gil Ybarbo** led one group that settled **Nacogdoches** in the **1760s and 1770s**.

The Demise of Spain

Spain's final 60 years of control of the province of Texas were marked with a few successes and a multitude of failures, all of which could be attributed to a breakdown in the administrative system.

Charles III, the fourth of the Bourbon line of kings, took the Spanish throne in 1759. He launched a series of reforms in the New World. The king's choice of administrators was excellent. In 1765, José de Gálvez was dispatched to New Spain (an area that then included all of modern Mexico and much of today's American West) with instructions to improve both the economy and the defense of the area.

Gálvez initially toured parts of the vast region, gaining first-hand insight into the practical problems of the colony. There were many that could be traced to Spain's basic concepts of colonial government. Texas, in particular, suffered from the mercantilist economic system that attempted to funnel all colonial trade through ports in Mexico.

But administrative reforms by Gálvez and his nephew, Bernardo Gálvez, namesake of Galveston, were to be followed by ill-advised policies by successors.

Problems with the Comanches, Apaches and "Norteños," as the Spanish called some tribes, continued to plague the province, too.

About the same time, Spain undertook the administration of the Louisiana Territory. One of the terms of the cession by France was that the region would enjoy certain trading privileges denied to other Spanish dependencies. So although Texas and Louisiana were neighbors, trade between the two provinces was banned.

The Spanish crown further complicated matters by placing the administration of Louisiana under authorities in Cuba, while Texas remained under the authorities in Mexico City.

The death of Charles III in 1788 and the beginning of the French Revolution a year later weakened Spain's hold on the New World dominions. Charles IV was not as good a sovereign as his predecessor, and his choice of ministers was poor. The quality of frontier administrators declined, and relations with Indians soured further.

Charles IV's major blunder, however, was to side with French royalty during the revolution, earning Spain the enmity of Napoleon Bonaparte. Spain also allied with England in an effort to thwart Napoleon, and in this losing cause, the Spanish were forced to cede Louisiana back to France.

In 1803, Napoleon broke a promise to retain the territory and sold it to the United States. Spain's problems in the New World thereby took on an altogether different dimension. Now, Anglo-Americans cast longing eyes on the vast undeveloped territory of Texas.

With certain exceptions for royalists who left the American colonies during the revolution, Spain had maintained a strict prohibition against Anglo or other non-Spanish settlers in their New World territories. But they were unprepared to police the eastern border of Texas after removing the presidios in the 1760s. What had been a provincial line became virtually overnight an international boundary, and an ill-defined one at that.

American Immigrants

Around **1800, Anglo-Americans** began to probe the Spanish frontier. Some settled in East Texas and others crossed the Red River and were tolerated by authorities.

Others, however, were thought to have nefarious designs. Philip Nolan was the first of the American filibusters to test Spanish resolve. Several times he entered Texas to capture wild horses to sell in the United States.

But in 1801, the Spanish perceived an attempted insurrection by Nolan and his followers. He was killed in a battle near present-day Waco, and his company was taken captive to work in the mines in northern Mexico.

Spanish officials were beginning to realize that the economic potential of Texas must be developed if the Anglo-Americans were to be neutralized. But Spain's

His-oo-san-chees, the Little Spaniard, was a brave of the highest order in his Comanche tribe. The Comanches, Apaches and "Norteños," as the Spanish called some tribes, often clashed with the Spanish soldiers. Image courtesy of the Smithsonian Institution.

centuries-long role in the history of Texas was almost over.

Resistance to Spanish rule had developed in the New World colonies. Liberal ideas from the American and French revolutions had grown popular, despite the crown's attempts to prevent their dissemination.

In Spain, three sovereigns — Charles IV, Napoleon's brother Joseph Bonaparte, and Ferdinand VII — claimed the throne, often issuing different edicts simultaneously. Since the time of Philip II, Spain had been a tightly centralized monarchy with the crown making most decisions. Now, chaos reigned in the colonies.

As Spain's grip on the New World slipped between 1790 and 1820, Texas was almost forgotten, an internal province of little importance. Colonization was ignored; the Spanish government had larger problems in Europe and in Mexico.

Spain's mercantile economic policy penalized colonists in the area, charging them high prices for trade goods and paying low prices for products sent to markets in the interior of New Spain. As a result, settlers from central Mexico had no incentives to come to Texas. Indeed, men of ambition in the province often prospered by turning to illegal trade with Louisiana or to smuggling. On the positive side, however, Indians in the province had been mollified through annual gifts and by developing a dependence on Spain for trade goods.

Ranching flourished. In **1795**, a census found **69 families** living on 45 ranches in the **San Antonio** area. A census in **1803** indicated that there were **100,000 head of cattle** in Texas. But aside from a few additional families in Nacogdoches and La Bahía (near present-day Goliad), the province was thinly populated.

The largest group of early immigrants from the

United States was not Anglo, but Indian.

As early as **1818, Cherokees** of the southeastern United States came to Texas, settling north of Nacogdoches on lands between the Trinity and Sabine rivers. The Cherokees had been among the first U.S. Indians to accept the federal government's offers of resettlement. As American pioneers entered the newly acquired lands of Georgia, Alabama and other areas of the Southeast, the Indians were systematically removed, through legal means or otherwise.

Some of the displaced groups settled on land provided in Arkansas Territory, but others, such as the Cherokees, came to Texas. These Cherokees were among the "Five Civilized Tribes" that had adopted agriculture and many Anglo customs in an unsuccessful attempt to get along with their new neighbors. Alabama and Coushatta tribes had exercised squatters' rights in present-day Sabine County in the early 1800s, and soon after the Cherokees arrived, groups of Shawnee, Delaware and Kickapoo Indians came from the United States.

A **second wave of Anglo** immigrants began to arrive in Texas, larger than the first and of a different character. These Anglos were not so interested in agricultural opportunities as in other schemes to quickly recoup their fortunes.

Spain recognized the danger represented by the unregulated colonization by Americans. The Spanish Cortes' colonization law of 1813 attempted to build a buffer between the eastern frontier and northern Mexico. Special permission was required for Americans to settle within 52 miles of the international boundary, although this prohibition often was ignored.

As initially envisioned, Americans would be allowed to settle the interior of Texas. Colonists from Europe and Mexico would be placed along the eastern frontier to limit contact between the Americans and the United States. Spanish officials felt that the Americans already in Texas illegally would be stable if given a stake in the province through land ownership.

Moses Austin, a former Spanish subject in the vast Louisiana Territory, applied for the first empresario grant from the Spanish government. With the intercession of Baron de Bastrop, a friend of Austin's from Missouri Territory, the request was approved in January **1821**.

Austin agreed to settle **300 families** on land bounded by the Brazos and Colorado rivers on the east and west, by El Camino Real (the old military road running from San Antonio to Nacogdoches) on the north, and by the Gulf Coast.

But Austin died in June 1821, leaving the work to his son, **Stephen F. Austin**. Problems began as soon as the first authorized colonists arrived in Texas the following December when it was learned that Mexico had gained independence from Spain.

Mexico, 1821–1836

Mexico's war for independence, 1810–1821, was savage and bloody in the interior provinces, and Texas suffered as well.

In early 1812, Mexican revolutionary José Bernardo Gutiérrez de Lara traveled to Natchitoches, La., where, with the help of U.S. agents, an expedition was organized. **Augustus W. Magee**, a West Point graduate, commanded the troop, which entered Texas in August 1812. This "Republican Army of the North" easily took Nacogdoches, where it gathered recruits.

After withstanding a siege at La Bahía, the army took San Antonio and proclaimed the First Republic of Texas in April 1813. A few months later, the republican forces were bloodily subdued at the Battle of Medina River.

Royalist Gen. Joaquín de Arredondo executed a staggering number of more than 300 republicans, including some Americans, at San Antonio, and a young lieutenant, **Antonio López de Santa Anna**, was recognized for valor under fire.

When the war finally ended in Mexico in 1821, little more had been achieved than separation from Spain.

Sensing that liberal reforms in Spain would reduce the authority of royalists in the New World, Mexican conservatives had led the revolt against the mother country. They also achieved early victories in the debate over the form of government the newly independent Mexico should adopt.

An independent Mexico was torn between advocates of centralist and federalist forms of government.

The former royalists won the opening debates, settling Emperor Agustín de Iturbide on the new Mexican throne. But he was overthrown and the Constitution of 1824, a federalist document, was adopted.

The Mexican election of 1828 was a turning point in the history of the country when the legally elected administration of Manuel Gómez Pedraza was overthrown by supporters of Vicente Guerrero, who in turn was ousted by his own vice president Anastasio Bustamante. Mexico's most chaotic political period followed. Between 1833 and 1855, the Mexican presidency changed hands 36 times.

Texas, 1821–1833

Mexico's **land policy,** like Spain's, differed from the U.S. approach. Whereas the United States sold land directly to settlers or to speculators who dealt with the pioneers, the Mexicans retained tight control of the property transfer until predetermined agreements for development were fulfilled.

But a 4,428-acre *sitio* — a square league — and a 177-acre *labor* could be obtained for only surveying costs and administrative fees as low as $50. The empresario was rewarded with grants of large tracts of land, but only when he fulfilled his quota of families to be brought to the colonies.

Considering the prices the U.S. government charged, Texas' land was indeed a bargain and a major attraction to those Americans looking for a new start.

More than 25 empresarios were commissioned to settle colonists. Empresarios included **Green DeWitt** and **Martín de León**, who in 1824 founded the city of Guadalupe Victoria (present-day Victoria).

By 1830, Texas boasted an estimated population of 15,000, with Anglo-Americans outnumbering Hispanics by a margin of four to one.

Stephen F. Austin was easily the most successful empresario. After his initial success, Austin was authorized in 1825 to bring 900 more families to Texas, and in 1831, he and his partner, **Samuel Williams**, received another concession to bring 800 Mexican and European families. Through Austin's efforts, 1,540 land titles were issued to settlers.

In the early years of colonization, the settlers busied

themselves clearing land, planting crops, building homes and fending off Indian attacks. Many were successful in establishing a subsistence economy.

One weakness of the Mexican colonial policy was that it did not provide the factors for a market economy. Although towns were established, credit, banks and good roads were not provided by the government.

Ports were established at Galveston and Matagorda bays after Mexican independence, but the colonists felt they needed more, particularly one at the mouth of the Brazos. And foreign ships were barred from coastwise trade, which posed a particular hardship because Mexico had few merchant ships.

To settle in Texas, pioneers had to become Mexican citizens and to embrace Roman Catholicism. Most of the Americans were Protestants, if they adhered to any religion, and they were fiercely defensive of the right to **religious freedom** enjoyed in the United States.

Although no more than one-fourth of the Americans ever swore allegiance to the Catholic Church, the requirement was a long-standing irritation.

Slavery, too, was a point of contention. Mexico prohibited the introduction of slavery after December 1827. Nevertheless, several efforts were made to evade the government policy. Austin got the state Legislature to recognize labor contracts under which slaves were technically free but bound themselves to their masters for life. Often entire families were covered by a single contract. While many early Anglo colonists were not slaveholders, they were Southerners, and the ownership of slaves was a cultural institution that they supported. The problem was never settled during Texas' colonial period despite the tensions it generated.

Most of the early Anglo-American colonists in Texas intended to fulfill their pledge to become good Mexican citizens. But the political turmoil following the 1828 presidential election raised doubts in the Americans' minds about the ability of Mexico to make representative government function properly.

On a tour of Texas in 1827 and 1828, Gen. Manuel Mier y Terán noted that the Texans "carried their constitutions in their pockets." And he feared the Americans' desire for more rights and liberties than the government was prepared to offer would lead to rebellion. Unrest increased in Texas when Gen. Mier y Terán began reinforcing existing garrisons and establishing new ones.

But a major factor in the discontent of Americans came with the **decree of April 6, 1830**, when the Mexican government in essence banned further American immigration into Texas and tried to control slavery. (For an account of how Texans opposed this decree at Fort Anahuac, see Texas History Features on the *Texas Almanac* Web site.)

Austin protested that the prohibition against American immigration would not stop the flow of Anglos into Texas; it would stop only stable, prosperous Americans from coming.

Austin's predictions were fulfilled. Illegal immigrants continued to come. By 1836, the estimated number of people in Texas had reached 35,000.

Prelude to Revolution

In the midst of all the turmoil, Texas was prospering. By 1834, some 7,000 bales of cotton with a value

of $315,000 were shipped to New Orleans. In the middle of the decade, Texas exports, including cotton and beaver, otter and deer skins, amounted to $500,000.

Trade ratios were out of balance, however, because $630,000 in manufactured goods were imported. And, there was little currency in Texas. Ninety percent of the business transactions were conducted with barter or credit.

In 1833 and 1834, the **Coahuila y Texas** legislature was diligently trying to respond to the complaints of the Texas colonists. The English language was recognized for official purposes. Religious toleration was approved. The court system was revised, providing Texas with an appellate court and trial by jury.

In Mexico City, however, a different scenario was developing. **Santa Anna** assumed supreme authority in April 1834 and began dismantling the federalist government. Among the most offensive changes dictated by Santa Anna was the reduction of the state militias to one man per each 500 population. The intent was to eliminate possible armed opposition to the emerging centralist government.

But liberals in the state of Zacatecas in central Mexico rebelled. Santa Anna's response was particularly brutal, as he tried to make an example of the rebels. Troops were allowed to sack the state capital after the victory over the insurgents.

Trouble also was brewing closer to the Texans.

In March 1833, the Coahuila y Texas legislature moved the state capital from Saltillo to Monclova. The Monclova legislature in 1834 gave the governor authority to sell 400 *sitios* — or 1.77 million acres of land — to finance the government and to provide for protection. A year later the lawmakers criticized Santa Anna's reputation on federalism. Seeing a chance to regain lost pres-

GENERAL D. ANTONIO LOPEZ DE SANTA-ANNA.
PRESIDENT OF THE REPUBLIC OF MEXICO.
By **A. Hoffy,** from an original likeness taken from life at **Vera-Cruz.**

General Antonio López de Santa Anna, President of the Republic of Mexico, circa 1847. Courtesy of the Library of Congress.

tige, Saltillo declared for Santa Anna and set up an opposition government. In the spring of 1835, Santa Anna sent his brother-in-law, Martín Perfecto de Cos, to break up the state government at Monclova.

Texans were appalled by the breakdown in state government, coming on the heels of so many assurances that the political situation was to improve.

Texas politics were polarizing. A "war party" advocated breaking away from Mexico altogether, while a "peace party" urged calm and riding out the political storm. Most of the settlers, however, aligned with neither group.

In January 1835, Santa Anna sent a detachment of soldiers to Anahuac to reinforce the customs office, but duties were being charged irregularly at various ports on the coast. William B. Travis, in an act not supported by all colonists, led a contingent of armed colonists against the Mexican soldiers, who withdrew without a fight.

Although some members of the peace party wrote Mexican Gen. **Martín Perfecto de Cos**, stationed at Matamoros, apologizing for the action, he was not compromising. Cos demanded that the group be arrested and turned over to him. The Texans refused.

The committees of correspondence, organized at the Convention of 1832 (which had asked that Texas be separated from Coahuila), began organizing another meeting. Because the term "convention" aroused visions of revolution in the eyes of Mexican officials, the gathering at Washington-on-the-Brazos in October 1835 was called a "consultation." But with the breakdown of the state government and with Santa Anna's repeal of the Constitution of 1824, the American settlers felt well within their rights to provide a new framework with which to govern Texas.

Fresh from brutally putting down the rebellion in Zacatecas, Santa Anna turned his attention to Texas. Gen. Cos was determined to regarrison the state, and the settlers were equally determined to keep soldiers out.

Col. **Domingo de Ugartechea**, headquartered at San Antonio, became concerned about armed rebellion when he heard of the incident at Anahuac. He recalled a six-pound cannon that had been given DeWitt colonists to fight Indians.

Ugartechea ordered Cpl. Casimira de León with five men to Gonzales to retrieve the weapon. No problems were expected, but officials at Gonzales refused to surrender the weapon. When the Mexicans reinforced Cpl. León's men, a call was sent out for volunteers to help the Gonzales officials. Dozens responded.

Oct. 2, 1835, the Texans challenged the Mexicans with a **"come-and-take-it"** flag over the cannon. After a brief skirmish, the Mexicans withdrew, but the first rounds in the Texas Revolution had been fired.

Winning Independence

As 1836 opened, Texans felt in control of their destiny and secure in their land and their liberties. The Mexican army had been driven from their soil.

But tragedy loomed. Easy victories over government forces at Anahuac, Nacogdoches, Goliad, Gonzales and San Antonio in the fall of 1835 had given them a false sense of security. That independent mood was their undoing, for no government worthy of the name coordinated the defense of Texas. Consequently, as the Mexican counterattack developed, no one was in charge.

Sam Houston was titular commander-in-chief of the Texas forces, but he had little authority.

Some even thought the Mexicans would not try to re-enter Texas. Few Texans counted on the energy and determination of Santa Anna, the dictator of Mexico.

The status of the strongholds along the San Antonio River was of concern to Houston. In mid-January, Houston sent **James Bowie** to San Antonio to determine if the Alamo was defensible. If not, Bowie had orders to destroy it and withdraw the men and artillery to Gonzales and Copano.

On Feb. 8, David Crockett of Tennessee, bringing 12 men with him, arrived to aid the revolutionaries.

On Feb. 12, 1836, Santa Anna's main force crossed the Rio Grande headed for San Antonio. The Mexican battle plan had been debated. But Mexico's national pride was bruised by the series of defeats the nation's army had suffered in 1835, capped by Gen. Cos's ouster from San Antonio in December.

On Feb. 11, the Consultation's "governor of the government" **Henry Smith**, sent **William B. Travis** to San Antonio. Immediately a split in command at the **Alamo** garrison arose. Most were American volunteers who looked to the Houston-appointed Bowie as their leader. Travis had only a handful of Texas army regulars. Bowie and Travis agreed to share the command of 150 men.

Arriving at the Alamo on Feb. 23, Santa Anna left no doubt regarding his attitude toward the defenders. He hoisted a blood-red flag, the traditional Mexican symbol of no quarter, no surrender, no mercy. Travis and Bowie defiantly answered the display with a cannon shot.

Immediately the Mexicans began surrounding the Alamo and bombarding it. Throughout the first night and nights to come, Santa Anna kept up a continual din to destroy the defenders' morale.

On Feb. 24, Bowie became ill and relinquished his share of command to Travis. Although the Mexican bombardment of the Alamo continued, none of the defenders was killed. In fact, they conducted several successful forays outside the fortress to burn buildings that were providing cover for the Mexican gunners and to gather firewood.

Messengers also successfully moved through the Mexican lines at will, and 32 reinforcements from Gonzales made it into the Alamo without a loss on March 1.

Historians disagree over which flag flew over the defenders of the Alamo.

Mexican sources have said that Santa Anna was outraged when he saw flying over the fortress a Mexican tricolor, identical to the ones carried by his troops except with the numbers "1 8 2 4" emblazoned upon it. Some Texas historians have accepted this version because the defenders of the Alamo could not have known that Texas' independence had been declared on March 2. To the knowledge of the Alamo's defenders, the last official position taken by Texas was in support of the Constitution of 1824, which the flag symbolized. But the only flag found after the battle, according to historian Walter Lord, was one flown by the **New Orleans Greys**.

By March 5, Santa Anna had 4,000 men in camp, a force he felt sufficient to subdue the Alamo.

Historians disagree on the date, but the story goes that on March 3 or 5, Travis called his command together and explained the bleak outlook. He then asked those willing to die for freedom to stay and fight; those not

Battle of the Alamo (circa 1912) by Percy Moran. Santa Anna's victory at the Alamo came at a great cost; almost one-third of his forces were killed or wounded, and the battle shook Texans out of their lethargy. Image courtesy of the Library of Congress.

for clemency for the captives. The Mexican leader issued orders for their execution. On March 27, a Palm Sunday, most of the prisoners were divided into groups and marched out of Goliad, thinking they were being transferred to other facilities. When the executions began, many escaped. But about 350 were killed.

On March 17, Houston reached the Colorado near the present city of La Grange and began receiving reinforcements. Within a week, the small force of several hundred had become almost respectable, with 1,200-1,400 men in camp.

By the time Houston reached the Colorado, the convention at Washington-on-the-Brazos was completing work. **David Burnet**, a New Jersey native, was named interim president of the new Texas government, and **Lorenzo de Zavala**, a Yucatán native, was named vice president.

willing could try to get through enemy lines to safety. Even the sick Jim Bowie vowed to stay. Only Louis (Moses) Rose, a veteran of Napoleon's retreat from Moscow slipped out of the Alamo that night.

At dawn March 6, Santa Anna's forces attacked. When the fighting stopped between 8:30 and 9 a.m., all the defenders were dead. Only a few women, children and black slaves survived the assault. **Davy Crockett**'s fate is still debated. Mexican officer Enrique de la Peña held that Crockett was captured with a few other defenders and was executed by Santa Anna.

Santa Anna's victory came at the cost of almost one-third his forces killed or wounded. Their deaths in such number set back Santa Anna's timetable. The fall of the Alamo also brutally shook Texans out of their lethargy.

Sam Houston, finally given command of the entire Texas army, left the convention at **Washington-on-the-Brazos** on the day of the fall of the Alamo.

On March 11, he arrived at Gonzales to begin organizing the troops. Two days later, **Susanna Dickinson**, the wife of one of the victims of the Alamo, and two slaves arrived at Houston's position at Gonzales with the news of the fall of the San Antonio fortress.

Houston then ordered **James Fannin** to abandon the old presidio **La Bahía** at Goliad and to retreat to Victoria. Fannin had arrived at the fort in late January with more than 400 men. As a former West Pointer, he had a background in military planning, but Fannin had refused Travis' pleas for help, and after receiving Houston's orders, Fannin waited for scouting parties to return.

Finally, on March 19, he left, but too late. Forward elements of Gen. José de Urrea's troops caught Fannin's command on an open prairie. After a brief skirmish Fannin surrendered.

Santa Anna was furious when Gen. Urrea appealed

On March 27, Houston moved his men to San Felipe on the Brazos. The Texas army was impatient for a fight, and there was talk in the ranks that, if action did not develop soon, a new commander should be elected.

As the army marched farther back toward the San Jacinto River, two Mexican couriers were captured and gave Houston the information he had hoped for. Santa Anna in his haste had led the small Mexican force in front of Houston. Now the Texans had an opportunity to win the war.

Throughout the revolt, Houston's intelligence system had operated efficiently. Scouts, commanded by **Erastus "Deaf" Smith**, kept the Texans informed of Mexican troop movements. **Hendrick Arnold**, a free black, was a valuable spy, posing as a runaway slave to enter Mexican camps to gain information.

Early on April 21, Gen. Cos reinforced Santa Anna's troops with more than 500 men. The new arrivals, who had marched all night, disrupted the camp's routine for a time, but soon all the soldiers and officers settled down for a midday rest.

About 3 p.m., Houston ordered his men to parade and the battle was launched at 4:30 p.m.

A company of Mexican-Texans, commanded by Juan Seguín, had served as the rear guard for Houston's army through much of the retreat across Texas and had fought many skirmishes with the Mexican army in the process.

Perhaps fearing the Mexican-Texans would be mistaken for Santa Anna's soldiers, Houston had assigned

army would withdraw to south of the **Rio Grande**, that prisoners would be released and that Santa Anna would be shipped to Veracruz as soon as possible.

In the secret treaty, Santa Anna agreed to recognize Texas' independence, to give diplomatic recognition, to negotiate a commercial treaty and to set the Rio Grande as the new Republic's boundary.

Republic of Texas, 1836–1845

Sam Houston was easily the most dominant figure throughout the nearly 10-year history of the Republic of Texas. While he was roundly criticized for the retreat across Texas during the revolution, the victory at San Jacinto endeared him to most of the new nation's inhabitants.

Houston handily defeated Henry Smith and Stephen F. Austin in the election called in September 1836 by the interim government, and he was inaugurated as president on Oct. 22.

In the same September election, voters overwhelmingly approved a proposal to request annexation to the United States.

The first cabinet appointed by the new president represented an attempt to heal old political wounds. Austin was named secretary of state and Smith was secretary of the treasury. But Texas suffered a major tragedy in late December 1836 when Austin, the acknowledged **"Father of Texas,"** died of pneumonia.

A host of problems faced the new government. Santa Anna was still in custody, and public opinion favored his execution. Texas' leadership wisely kept Santa Anna alive, first to keep from giving the Mexicans an emotional rallying point for launching another invasion. Second, the Texas leaders hoped that the dictator would keep his promise to work for recognition of Texas.

Santa Anna was released in November 1836 and made his way to Washington, D.C. Houston hoped the dictator could persuade U.S. President **Andrew Jackson** to recognize Texas. Jackson refused to see Santa Anna, who returned to Mexico, where he had fallen from power.

Another major challenge was the Texas army. The new commander, Felix Huston, favored an invasion of Mexico, and the troops, made up now mostly of American volunteers who came to Texas after the battle of San Jacinto, were rebellious and ready to fight.

President Houston tried to replace Felix Huston with **Albert Sidney Johnston**, but Huston seriously wounded Johnston in a duel. In May 1837, Huston was asked to the capital in Columbia to discuss the invasion. While

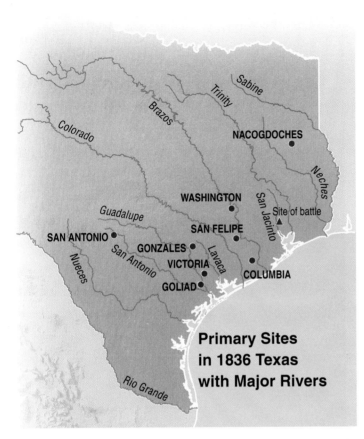

Primary Sites in 1836 Texas with Major Rivers

the company to guard duty as the battle approached. But after the men protested, they fought in the battle of San Jacinto.

Historians disagree widely on the number of troops on each side. Houston probably had about 900 while Santa Anna had between 1,100 and 1,300.

But the Texans had the decided psychological advantage. Two thirds of the fledgling Republic's army were "old Texans" who had family and land to defend. They had an investment of years of toil in building their homes. And they were eager to avenge the massacre of men at the Alamo and Goliad.

In less than 20 minutes they set the Mexican army to rout. More than 600 Mexicans were killed and hundreds more wounded or captured. Only nine of the Texans died in the fight.

It was not until the following day that Santa Anna was captured. One Texan noticed that a grubby soldier his patrol found in the high grass had a silk shirt under his filthy jacket. Although denying he was an officer, he was taken back to camp, where he was acknowledged with cries of "El Presidente" by other prisoners.

Santa Anna introduced himself when taken to the wounded Houston.

President Burnet took charge of Santa Anna, and on May 14 the dictator signed **two treaties at Velasco**, a public document and a secret one. The public agreement declared that hostilities would cease, that the Mexican

Huston was away from the troops, Houston sent **Thomas J. Rusk**, the secretary of war, to furlough the army without pay — but with generous land grants. Only 600 men were retained in the army.

The Republic's other problems were less tractable. The economy needed attention, Indians still were a threat, Mexico remained warlike, foreign relations had to be developed, and relations with the United States had to be solidified.

The greatest disappointment in Houston's first term was the failure to have the Republic annexed to the United States. Henry Morfit, President Jackson's agent, toured the new Republic in the summer of 1836. Although impressed, Morfit reported that Texas' best chance at continued independence lay in the "stupidity of the rulers of Mexico and the financial embarrassment of the Mexican government." He recommended that annexation be delayed.

Houston's foreign policy achieved initial success when **J. Pinckney Henderson** negotiated a trade treaty with Great Britain. Although the agreement was short of outright diplomatic recognition, it was progress. In the next few years, France, Belgium, The Netherlands and some German states recognized the new Republic.

Under the constitution, Houston's first term lasted only two years, and he could not succeed himself. His successor, **Mirabeau B. Lamar**, had grand visions and was a spendthrift. Houston's first term cost Texas only about $500,000, while President Lamar and the Congress spent $5 million in the next three years.

Early in 1839, Lamar gained recognition as the **"Father of Education"** in Texas when the Congress granted each of the existing 23 counties three leagues of land to be used for education. Fifty leagues of land were set aside for a university.

Despite the lip service paid to education, the government did not have the money for several years to set up a school system. Most education during the Republic was provided by private schools and churches.

Lamar's Indian policies differed greatly from those under Houston. Houston had lived with Cherokees as a youth, was adopted as a member of a tribe and advocated Indian rights long before coming to Texas. Lamar reflected more the frontier attitude toward American Indians. His first experience in public life was as secretary to Gov. George Troup of Georgia, who successfully opposed the federal government's policy of assimilation of

A copy of the Texas Declaration of Independence sits on a table in Independence Hall, a restored version of the building where the declaration was signed on March 2, 1836, at Washington-on-the-Brazos. Photo courtesy of Texas Department of Parks & Wildlife.

Indians at the time. Indians were simply removed from Georgia.

Texans first tried to negotiate the Cherokees' removal from the region, but in July 1839, the Indians were forcibly ejected from Texas at the **Battle of the Neches River** in Van Zandt County. Houston's close friend, the aging Cherokee chief **Philip Bowles**, was killed in the battle while Houston was visiting former President Jackson in Tennessee. The Cherokees moved on to Arkansas and Indian Territory.

Houston was returned to the presidency of the Republic in 1841. His second administration was even more frugal than his first; soon income almost matched expenditures.

Houston re-entered negotiations with the Indians in Central Texas in an attempt to quell the raids on settlements. A number of trading posts were opened along the frontier to pacify the Indians.

War fever reached a high pitch in Texas in 1842, and Houston grew increasingly unpopular because he would not launch an offensive war against Mexico.

In March 1842, Gen. **Rafael Vásquez** staged guerrilla raids on San Antonio, Victoria and Goliad, but quickly left the Republic.

A force of 3,500 Texas volunteers gathered at San Antonio demanding that Mexico be punished. Houston urged calm, but the clamor increased when Mexican **Gen. Adrian Woll** captured San Antonio in September. He raised the Mexican flag and declared the reconquest of Texas.

Ranger Capt. **Jack Hays** was camped nearby. Within days 600 volunteers had joined him, eager to drive the Mexican invaders from Texas soil. Gen. Woll withdrew after the **Battle of Salado.**

Alexander Somervell was ordered by Houston to follow with 700 troops and harass the Mexican army. He reached Laredo in December and found no Mexican troops. Somervell crossed the Rio Grande to find military targets. A few days later, the commander returned home, but 300 soldiers decided to continue the raid under the command of William S. Fisher. On Christmas day, this group attacked the village of **Mier**, only to be defeated by a Mexican force that outnumbered them 10-to-1.

After attempting mass escape, the survivors of the Mier expedition were marched to Mexico City where Santa Anna, again in political power, ordered their execution. When officers refused to carry out the order, it was amended to require execution of one of every 10 Texans. The prisoners drew beans to determine who would be shot; bearers of **black beans** were executed. Texans again were outraged by the treatment of prisoners, but the war fever soon subsided.

As Houston completed his second term, the United States was becoming more interested in annexation. Texas had seriously flirted with Great Britain and France, and the Americans did not want a rival republic with close foreign ties on the North American continent. Houston orchestrated the early stages of the final steps toward annexation. It was left to his successor, **Anson Jones**, to complete the process.

The Republic of Texas' main claim to fame is simply endurance. Its settlers, unlike other Americans who had military help, had cleared a large region of Indians by themselves, had established farms and communities and had persevered through extreme economic hardship.

Adroit political leadership had gained the Republic recognition from many foreign countries. Although dreams of empire may have dimmed, Texans had established an identity on a major portion of the North American continent. The frontier had been pushed to a line running from Corpus Christi through San Antonio and Austin to the Red River.

The U.S. presidential campaign of 1844 was to make Texas a part of the Union. ☆

SAM HOUSTON

Born in 1793, Sam Houston was easily the most dominant figure through the nearly 10-year history of the Republic of Texas. He served as its president from Oct. 22, 1836, to Dec. 10, 1838, and again from Dec. 13, 1841, to Dec. 9, 1844. After Texas became a state, Houston served as governor from Dec. 21, 1859, until March 16, 1861, when he resigned because of Texas' secession from the Union. Houston died in 1863.

ANNEXATION TO 1980

Annexation

Annexation to the United States was far from automatic for Texas once independence from Mexico was gained in 1836. Sam Houston noted that Texas "was more coy than forward" as negotiations reached a climax in 1845.

William H. Wharton was Texas' first representative in Washington. His instructions were to gain diplomatic recognition of the new Republic's independence.

After some squabbles, the U.S. Congress appropriated funds for a minister to Texas, and President Andrew Jackson recognized the new country in one of his last acts in office in March 1837.

Texas President **Mirabeau B. Lamar** (1838–41) opposed annexation. He held visions of empire in which Texas would rival the United States for supremacy on the North American continent.

During his administration, Great Britain began a close relationship with Texas and made strenuous efforts to get Mexico to recognize the Republic. This relationship between Great Britain and Texas raised fears in the United States that Britain might attempt to make Texas part of its empire.

Southerners feared for the future of slavery in Texas, which had renounced the importation of slaves as a concession to get a trade treaty with Great Britain, and American newspapers noted that trade with Texas had suffered after the Republic received recognition from European countries.

In Houston's second term in the Texas presidency, he instructed **Isaac Van Zandt**, his minister in Washington, to renew the annexation negotiations. Although U.S. President **John Tyler** and his cabinet were eager to annex Texas, they were worried about ratification in the U.S. Senate. The annexation question was put off.

In January 1844, Houston again gave Van Zandt instructions to propose annexation talks. This time the

This lithograph, circa 1844, is a satire on the Whig party's anti-annexation platform. The question of annexing Texas was a large issue separating presidential candidates in 1844 because of the serious implications for the future of slavery. Voters were polarized between Democrat James K. Polk, who supported slavery, and Whig candidate Henry Clay, who opposed it. Texas, personified as a young woman, stands between Clay (right, with arms folded) and Polk. Polk doffs his hat saying, "Welcome, sister, your valor has won you liberty and independence, and you have fairly won the right to be identified with 'the land of the brave, and the home of the free.'" She replies, "Shall the slanders that have been urged against your sister, sever those whose blood flows from the same fountain?" George M. Dallas, standing left of Polk, says, "Slandered as she is, let him that is without sin, cast the first stone at her!" Clay piously says, "Stand back, Madam Texas! for we are more holy than thou! Do you think we will have anything to do with gamblers, horse-racers, and licentious profligates?" A Quaker taps Clay on the shoulder and reminds him, "Softly, softly, friend Harry. Thou hast mentioned the very reason that we cannot vote for thee!" Image courtesy of the Library of Congress.

WAR WITH MEXICO

Clockwise from left: Engraving of Gen. Zach-ary Taylor, circa 1848, by Alexander Hay Ritchie. Taylor arrived in Corpus Christi in July 1845 and soon moved his troops into disputed land near the mouth of the Rio Grande, which touched off the war with Mexico. Print of the battle of Re-saca de la Palma, published June 29, 1846. Litho-graph of the Battle of Palo Alto, circa 1846, by Sarony & Major. Images courtesy of the Library of Congress.

United States agreed to Houston's standing stipulation that, for serious negotiations to take place, the United States must provide military protection to Texas. U.S. naval forces were ordered to the Gulf of Mexico and U.S. troops were positioned on the southwest border close to Texas.

On April 11, 1844, Texas and the United States signed a treaty for annexation. Texas would enter the Union as a territory, not a state, under terms of the treaty. The United States would assume Texas' debt up to $10 million and would negotiate Texas' southwestern bound-ary with Mexico.

On June 8, 1844, the U.S. Senate rejected the treaty with a vote of 35-16, with much of the opposition com-ing from the slavery abolition wing of the Whig Party.

But **westward expansion** became a major issue in the U.S. presidential election that year. James K. Polk, the Democratic nominee, was a supporter of expansion, and the party's platform called for adding Oregon and Texas to the Union.

After Polk won the election in November, President Tyler declared that the people had spoken on the issue of annexation, and he resubmitted the matter to Congress.

Several bills were introduced in the U.S. House of Representatives containing various proposals.

In **February 1845**, the U.S. Congress approved a resolution that would bring Texas into the Union as a state. Texas would cede its public property, such as forts and custom houses, to the United States, but it could keep its public lands and must retain its public debt. The region could be divided into four new states in addition to the original Texas. And the United States would nego-tiate the Rio Grande boundary claim.

British officials asked the Texas government to de-lay consideration of the U.S. offer for 90 days to attempt to get Mexico to recognize the Republic. The delay did no good: Texans' minds were made up.

President Anson Jones, who succeeded Houston in 1844, called a convention to write a **state constitution** in Austin on July 4, 1845.

Mexico finally recognized Texas' independence, but the recognition was rejected. **Texas voters overwhelm-ingly accepted** the U.S. proposal and approved the new constitution in a referendum.

On **Dec. 29, 1845**, the U.S. Congress accepted the state constitution, and Texas became the 28th state in the

Union. The first meeting of the Texas Legislature took place on Feb. 16, 1846.

1845–1860

The entry of Texas into the Union touched off the **War with Mexico**, a war that some historians now think was planned by President James K. Polk to obtain the vast American Southwest.

Gen. **Zachary Taylor** was sent to Corpus Christi, just above the Nueces River, in July 1845. In February 1846, right after Texas formally entered the Union, the general was ordered to move troops into the disputed area south of the Nueces to the mouth of the Rio Grande. Mexican officials protested the move, claiming the status of the territory was under negotiation.

After Gen. Taylor refused to leave, Mexican President **Mariano Paredes** declared the opening of a defensive war against the United States on April 24, 1846.

After initial encounters at **Palo Alto and Resaca de la Palma**, both a few miles north of today's **Brownsville**, the war was fought south of the Rio Grande.

President Polk devised a plan to raise 50,000 volunteers from every section of the United States to fight the war. About 5,000 Texans saw action in Mexico.

Steamboats provided an important supply link for U.S. forces along the Rio Grande. Historical figures such as **Richard King**, founder of the legendary King Ranch, and **Mifflin Kenedy**, another rancher and businessman, first came to the **Lower Rio Grande Valley** as steamboat operators during the war.

Much farther up the Rio Grande, the war was hardly noticed. U.S. forces moved south from Santa Fe, which had been secured in December 1846. After a minor skirmish with Mexican forces north of El Paso, the U.S. military established American jurisdiction in this part of Texas.

Gen. **Winfield Scott** brought the war to a close in March 1847 with the capture of Mexico City.

When the **Treaty of Guadalupe Hidalgo** was signed on Feb. 2, 1848, the United States had acquired the American Southwest for development. And in Texas, the Rio Grande became an international boundary.

Europeans, of whom the vast majority were **German**, rather than Anglos, were the first whites to push the Texas frontier into west Central Texas after annexation. **John O. Meusebach** became leader of the German immigration movement in Texas, and he led a wagon train of some 120 settlers to the site of **Fredericksburg** in May 1846.

Germans also migrated to the major cities, such as San Antonio and Galveston, and by 1850 there were more people of German birth or parentage in Texas than there were Mexican-Texans.

The estimated population of 150,000 at annexation grew to 212,592, including 58,161 slaves, in the first U.S. census count in Texas in 1850.

As the state's population grew, the regions developed distinct population characteristics. The southeast

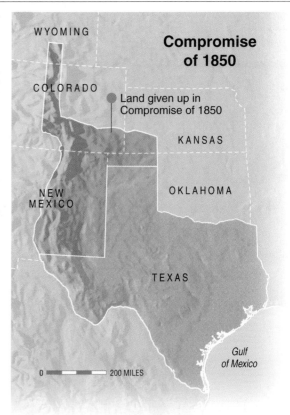

Compromise of 1850

Land given up in Compromise of 1850

WYOMING

COLORADO

KANSAS

NEW MEXICO

OKLAHOMA

TEXAS

Gulf of Mexico

0   200 MILES

and eastern sections attracted immigrants from the Lower South, the principal slaveholding states. Major plantations developed in these areas.

North Texas got more Upper Southerners and Midwesterners. These immigrants were mostly small farmers and few owned slaves.

Mexican-Texans had difficulty with Anglo immigrants. The **"cart war"** broke out in 1857. Mexican teamsters controlled the transportation of goods from the Gulf coast to San Antonio and could charge lower rates than their competition.

A campaign of terror was launched by Anglo haulers, especially around Goliad, in an attempt to drive the Mexican-Texans out of business. Intervention by the U.S. and Mexican governments finally brought the situation under control, but it stands as an example of the attitudes held by Anglo-Texans toward Mexican-Texans.

Cotton was by far the state's largest money crop, but corn, sweet potatoes, wheat and sugar also were produced. **Saw milling** and grain milling became the major industries, employing 40 percent of the manufacturing workers.

Land disputes and the public-debt issue were settled with the **Compromise of 1850**. Texas gave up claims to territory extending to Santa Fe and beyond in exchange for $10 million from the federal government. That sum was used to pay off the debt of the Republic.

Personalities, especially Sam Houston, dominated elections during early statehood, but, for most Texans, politics were unimportant. Voter turnouts were low in the 1850s until the movement toward secession gained strength.

Secession

Texas' population almost tripled in the decade between 1850 and 1860, when 604,215 people were counted, including 182,921 slaves.

Many of these new settlers came from the Lower South, a region familiar with slavery. Although three-quarters of the Texas population and two-thirds of the farmers did not own slaves, slaveowners controlled 60 to 70 percent of the wealth of the state and dominated the politics.

In 1850, 41 percent of the state's officeholders were from the slaveholding class; a decade later, more than 50 percent of the officeholders had slaves.

In addition to the political power of the slaveholders, they also provided role models for new immigrants to the state. After these newcomers got their first land, they saw slave ownership as another step up the economic ladder, whether they owned slaves or not. Slave ownership was an economic goal.

This attitude prevailed even in areas of Texas where slaveholding was not widespread or even practical.

These factors were the wind that fanned the flames of the secessionist movement throughout the late 1850s.

The appearance of the **Know-Nothing Party**, which based its platform on a pro-American, anti-immigrant foundation, began to move Texas toward party politics. Because of the large number of foreign-born settlers, the party attracted many Anglo voters.

In 1854, the Know-Nothings elected candidates to city offices in San Antonio, and a year later, the mayor of Galveston was elected with the party's backing. Also in 1855, the Know-Nothings elected 20 representatives and five senators to the Legislature.

The successes spurred the **Democrats** to serious party organization for the first time. In 1857, **Hardin Runnels** was nominated for governor at the Democratic convention held in Waco.

Sam Houston sought the governorship as an independent, but he also got Know-Nothing backing. Democrats were organized, however, and Houston was dealt the only election defeat in his political career.

Runnels was a strong states'-rights Democrat who irritated many Texans during his administration by advocating reopening the slave trade. His popularity on the frontier also dropped when Indian raids became more severe.

Most Texans still were ambivalent about secession. The Union was seen as a protector of physical and economic stability. No threats to person or property were perceived in remaining attached to the United States.

In 1859, Houston again challenged Runnels, basing his campaign on Unionism. Combined with Houston's personal popularity, his position on the secession issue apparently satisfied most voters, for they gave him a solid victory over the more radical Runnels. In addition, Unionists **A.J. Hamilton** and **John H. Reagan** won the state's two congressional seats. Texans gave the states'-rights Democrats a sound whipping at the polls.

Within a few months, however, events were to change radically the political atmosphere of the state. On the frontier, the army could not control Indian raids, and with the later refusal of a Republican-controlled Congress to provide essential aid in fighting Indians, the

This wood engraving entitiled "Destruction of the Westfield" depicts the Union vessel Westfield being destroyed Jan. 1, 1863, after running aground in Galveston Bay. As Union troops attempted to blow up the ship rather than let it fall into Confederate hands, it exploded prematurely, killing the entire crew. Image courtesy of the Library of Congress.

federal government fell into disrepute.

Secessionists played on the growing distrust. Then in the summer of 1860, a series of fires in the cities around the state aroused fears that an abolitionist plot was afoot and that a slave uprising might be at hand — a traditional concern in a slaveholding society.

Vigilantes lynched blacks and Northerners across Texas, and a siege mentality developed.

When **Abraham Lincoln** was elected president (he was not on the ballot in Texas), secessionists went to work in earnest.

Pleas were made to Gov. Houston to call the Legislature into session to consider secession. Houston refused, hoping the passions would cool. They did not. Finally, **Oran M. Roberts** and other secessionist leaders issued a call to the counties to hold elections and send delegates to a convention in Austin. Ninety-two of 122 counties responded, and on Jan. 28, 1861, the meeting convened.

Only eight delegates voted against secession, while 166 supported it. An election was called for Feb. 23, 1861, and the ensuing campaign was marked by intolerance and violence. Opponents of secession were often intimidated — except the governor, who courageously stumped the state opposing withdrawal from the Union. Houston also argued that if Texas did secede it should revert to its status as an independent republic and not join the Confederacy.

Only one-fourth of the state's population had been in Texas during the days of independence, and the argument carried no weight. On election day, 76 percent of 61,000 voters favored secession.

President Lincoln, who took office within a couple of weeks, reportedly sent the Texas governor a letter offering 50,000 federal troops to keep Texas in the Union. But after a meeting with other Unionists, Houston declined the offer. "I love Texas too well to bring strife and bloodshed upon her," the governor declared.

On March 16, Houston refused to take an oath of loyalty to the Confederacy and was replaced in office by **Lt. Gov. Edward Clark.**

See the Texas Almanac Web site for results of the Referendum on Ordinance of Secession of 1861.

Civil War

Texas did not suffer the devastation of its Southern colleagues in the Civil War. On but a few occasions did Union troops occupy territory in Texas, except in the El Paso area.

The state's cotton was important to the Confederate war effort because it could be transported from Gulf

Union prisoners (non-commissioned officers of the 19th Iowa Infantry) who had been imprisoned at Camp Ford, northeast of Tyler, are exchanged at New Orleans sometime near the end of the Civil War. Established in 1862 as a training camp, Camp Ford became a prison camp for Union POWs in 1863. About 6,000 prisoners were confined at Camp Ford from 1863 until the end of the war in 1865. It was the largest Confederate prison camp west of the Mississippi River. Photo courtesy of the Library of Congress.

ports when other Southern shipping lanes were blockaded.

Some goods became difficult to buy, but unlike other states of the Confederacy, Texas still received consumer goods because of the trade that was carried on through Mexico during the war.

Although accurate figures are not available, historians estimate that between 70,000 and 90,000 Texans fought for the South, and between 2,000 and 3,000, including some former slaves, saw service in the Union army.

Texans became disenchanted with the Confederate government early in the war. State taxes were levied for the first time since the Compromise of 1850, and by war's end, the Confederacy had collected more than $37 million from the state.

But most of the complaints about the government centered on Brig. Gen. **Paul O. Hebert**, the Confederate commander of the Department of Texas.

In April 1862, Gen. Hebert declared martial law without notifying state officials. Opposition to the South's new conscription law, which exempted persons owning more than 15 slaves among other categories of exemptions, prompted the action.

In November 1862, the commander prohibited the export of cotton except under government control, and this proved a disastrous policy.

The final blow came when Gen. Hebert failed to defend **Galveston** and it fell into Union hands in the fall of 1862.

Maj. Gen. **John B. Magruder**, who replaced Hebert, was much more popular. The new commander's first actions were to combat the Union offensive against Texas ports. Sabine Pass had been closed in September 1862 by the Union blockade, and Galveston was in Northern hands.

On Jan. 1, 1863, Magruder retook Galveston with the help of two steamboats lined with cotton bales. Sharpshooters aboard proved devastating in battles against the Union fleet. Three weeks later, Magruder used two other cotton-clad steamboats to break the Union blockade of Sabine Pass, and two of the state's major ports were re-opened.

Late in 1863, the Union launched a major offensive against the Texas coast that was partly successful. On Sept. 8, however, Lt. **Dick Dowling** and 42 men fought off a 1,500-man Union invasion force at **Sabine Pass**. In a brief battle, Dowling's command sank two Union gunboats and put the other invasion ships to flight.

Federal forces were more successful at the mouth of the Rio Grande. On Nov. 1, 1863, 7,000 Union troops landed at **Brazos Santiago**, and five days later, Union forces entered Brownsville.

Texas Unionists led by **E.J. Davis** were active in the Valley, moving as far upriver as Rio Grande City. Confederate Col. **John S. "Rip" Ford**, commanding state troops, finally pushed the Union soldiers out of Brownsville in July 1864, reopening the important port for the Confederacy.

Most Texans never saw a Union soldier during the war. The only ones they might have seen were in the **prisoner-of-war camps**. The largest, **Camp Ford**, near Tyler, housed 5,000 prisoners. Others operated in Kerr County and at Hempstead.

As the war dragged on, the mood of Texans changed. Those on the homefront began to feel they were sacrificing loved ones and suffering hardship so cotton speculators could profit.

Public order broke down as refugees flocked to Texas. And slaves from other states were sent to Texas for safekeeping. When the war ended, there were an estimated 400,000 slaves in Texas, more than double the number counted in the 1860 census.

Morale was low in Texas in early 1865. Soldiers at Galveston and Houston began to mutiny. At Austin, Confederate soldiers raided the state treasury in March and found only $5,000 in specie. Units began breaking up, and the army was beginning to dissolve before Gen.

Robert E. Lee surrendered at **Appomattox** in April 1865. He surrendered the Army of Northern Virginia, and while this assured Union victory, the surrender of other Confederate units was to follow until the last unit gave up in Oklahoma at the end of June.

The last land battle of the Civil War was fought at **Palmito Ranch** near Brownsville on May 13, 1865. After the Confederate's victory, they learned the governors of the Western Rebel states had authorized the disbanding of armies, and, a few days later, they accepted a truce with the Union forces.

Reconstruction

On June 19, 1865, **Gen. Gordon Granger**, under the command of Gen. Philip M. Sheridan, arrived in Galveston with 1,800 federal troops to begin the Union occupation of Texas. Gen. Granger proclaimed the emancipation of the slaves.

A.J. Hamilton, a Unionist and former congressman from Texas, was named provisional governor by President Andrew Johnson.

Texas was in turmoil. Thousands of the state's men had died in the conflict. Indian raids had caused as much damage as the skirmishes with the Union army, causing the frontier to recede up to 100 miles eastward in some areas.

Even worse, confusion reigned. No one knew what to expect from the conquering forces.

Gen. Granger dispatched troops to the population centers of the state to restore civil authority. But only a handful of the 50,000 federal troops that came to Texas was stationed in the interior. Most were sent to the Rio Grande as a show of force against the French forces in Mexico, and clandestine aid was supplied to Mexican President Benito Juarez in his fight against the French and Mexican royalists.

The **frontier forts**, most of which were built during the early 1850s by the federal government to protect

A man representing the Freedman's Bureau stands between armed groups of white and black Americans. Wood carving by Alfred R. Waud first published in Harper's Weekly on July 25, 1868. Image courtesy of the Library of Congress.

Richard Coke easily defeated E.J. Davis in the 1873 governor's race. Davis' administration is said to have been the most unpopular in Texas history. Photo courtesy of the Library of Congress.

western settlements, had been abandoned by the U.S. Army after secession. These were not remanned, and a prohibition against a militia denied settlers a means of self-defense against Indian raids. *(For an overview of the frontier forts, see Texas Almanac 2004–2005.)*

Thousands of freed black slaves migrated to the cities, where they felt the federal soldiers would provide protection. Still others traveled the countryside, seeking family members and loved ones from whom they had been separated during the war.

The **Freedman's Bureau**, authorized by Congress in March 1865, began operation in September 1865 under Gen. E.M. Gregory. It had the responsibility to provide education, relief aid, labor supervision and judicial protection for the newly freed slaves.

The bureau was most successful in opening schools for blacks. Education was a priority because 95 percent of the freed slaves were illiterate.

The agency also was partially successful in getting blacks back to work on plantations under reasonable labor contracts.

Some plantation owners harbored hopes that they would be paid for their property loss when the slaves were freed. In some cases, the slaves were not released from plantations for up to a year.

To add to the confusion, some former slaves had the false notion that the federal government was going to parcel out the plantation lands to them. These blacks simply bided their time, waiting for the division of land.

Under pressure from President Johnson, Gov. Hamilton called for an election of delegates to a constitutional convention in January 1866. Hamilton told the gathering what was expected: Former slaves were to be given

civil rights; the secession ordinance had to be repealed; Civil War debt had to be repudiated; and slavery was to be abolished with ratification of the Thirteenth Amendment.

Many delegates to the convention were former secessionists, and there was little support for compromise.

J.W. Throckmorton, a Unionist and one of eight men who had opposed secession in the convention of 1861, was elected chairman of the convention. But a coalition of conservative Unionists and Democrats controlled the meeting. As a consequence, Texas took limited steps toward appeasing the victorious North.

Slavery was abolished, and blacks were given some civil rights. But they still could not vote and were barred from testifying in trials against whites.

No action was taken on the Thirteenth Amendment because, the argument went, the amendment already had been ratified.

Otherwise, the constitution that was written followed closely the constitution of 1845. President Johnson in August 1866 accepted the new constitution and declared insurrection over in Texas, the last of the states of the Confederacy so accepted under **Presidential Reconstruction**.

Throckmorton was elected governor in June, along with other state and local officials. However, Texans had not learned a lesson from the war.

When the Legislature met, a series of laws limiting the rights of blacks were passed. In labor disputes, for example, the employers were to be the final arbitrators. The codes also bound an entire family's labor, not just the head of the household, to an employer.

Funding for black education would be limited to what could be provided by black taxpayers. Since few blacks owned land or had jobs, that provision effectively denied education to black children. However, the thrust of the laws and the attitude of the legislators was clear: Blacks simply were not to be considered full citizens.

Many of the laws later were overturned by the Freedman's Bureau or military authorities when, in March 1867, Congress began a **Reconstruction plan** of its own. The Southern states were declared to have no legal government and the former Confederacy was divided into districts to be administered by the military until satisfactory Reconstruction was effected. Texas and Louisiana made up the Fifth Military District under the command of Gen. Philip H. Sheridan.

Gov. Throckmorton clashed often with Gen. Sheridan. The governor thought the state had gone far enough in establishing rights for the newly freed slaves and other matters. Finally in August 1867, Throckmorton and other state officials were removed from office by Sheridan because they were considered an "impediment to the reconstruction." **E.M. Pease**, the former two-term governor and a Unionist, was named provisional governor by the military authorities.

A **new constitutional convention** was called by Gen. Winfield S. Hancock, who replaced Sheridan in November 1867. For the first time, blacks were allowed to participate in the elections that selected delegates. A total of 59,633 whites and 49,497 blacks registered. The elected delegates met on June 1, 1868. Deliberations got bogged down on partisan political matters, however, and the convention spent $200,000, an astronomical sum for the time.

THE TEXAS & PACIFIC RY.
1876

Print of Texas and Pacific Railway's old wood-burning locomotive No. 20. This engine made the historic run to Fort Worth in 1876 to mark the beginning of rail service to that frontier town. Photo courtesy of the Texas and Pacific Railway Company.

This constitution of 1869, as it came to be known, granted full rights of citizenship to blacks, created a system of education, delegated broad powers to the governor and generally reflected the views of the state's Unionists.

Gov. Pease, disgusted with the convention and with military authorities, resigned in September 1869. Texas had no chief executive until January 1870, when the newly elected **E.J. Davis** took office.

Meeting in February 1870, the Legislature created a **state militia** under the governor's control; created a **state police force**, also controlled by the governor; postponed the 1870 general election to 1872; enabled the governor to appoint more than 8,500 local officeholders; and granted subsidized **bonds for railroad construction** at a rate of $10,000 a mile.

For the first time, a system of public education was created. The law required compulsory attendance at school for four months a year, set aside one-quarter of the state's annual revenue for education and levied a poll tax to support education. Schools also were to be integrated, which enraged many white Texans.

The Davis administration was the most unpopular in Texas' history. In fairness, historians have noted that Davis did not feel that whites could be trusted to assure the rights of the newly freed blacks.

Violence was rampant in Texas. One study found that between the close of the Civil War and mid-1868, 1,035 people were murdered in Texas, including 486 blacks, mostly victims of white violence.

Gov. Davis argued that he needed broad police powers to restore order. Despite their unpopularity, the state police and militia — blacks made up 40 percent of the police and a majority of the militia — brought the lawlessness under control in many areas.

Democrats, aided by moderate Republicans, regained control of the Legislature in the 1872 elections, and, in 1873, the lawmakers set about stripping the governor of many of his powers.

The political turmoil ended with the gubernatorial election of 1873, when **Richard Coke** easily defeated Davis. Davis tried to get federal authorities to keep him in office, but President Grant refused to intervene.

In January of 1874, Democrats were in control of state government again. The end of Reconstruction concluded the turbulent Civil War era, although the attitudes that developed during the period lasted well into the 20th century.

Capital and Labor

A **constitutional convention** was called in 1875 to rewrite the 1869 constitution, a hated vestige of Radical Republican rule.

Every avenue to cutting spending at any level of government was explored. Salaries of public officials were slashed. The number of offices was reduced. Judgeships, along with most other offices, were made elective rather than appointive.

The state road program was curtailed, and the immigration bureau was eliminated.

Perhaps the worst change was the destruction of the statewide school system. The new charter created a "community system" without a power of taxation, and schools were segregated by race.

Despite the basic reactionary character, the new constitution also was visionary. Following the lead of several other states, the Democrats declared railroads to be common carriers and subject to regulation.

To meet the dual challenge of lawlessness and Indian insurrection, Gov. Coke in 1874 re-established the **Texas Rangers**.

While cowboys and cattle drives are romantic subjects for movies on the Texas of this period, the fact is that the simple cotton farmer was the backbone of the state's economy.

But neither the farmer nor the cattleman prospered throughout the last quarter of the 19th century. At the root of their problems was federal monetary policy and the lingering effects of the Civil War.

Although the issuance of paper money had brought about a business boom in the Union during the

Fourteen-year-old spinner Matty Lott works in a Brazos Valley Cotton Mill in West, in violation of the law, in November 1913. In 1903, the Texas Legislature prohibited abuse of child labor and set minimum ages at which children could work in certain industries. Photo courtesy of the Library of Congress.

war, inflation also increased. Silver was demonetized in 1873. Congress passed the Specie Resumption Act in 1875 that returned the nation to the gold standard in 1879.

Almost immediately a contraction in currency began. Between 1873 and 1891, the amount of national bank notes in circulation declined from $339 million to $168 million.

The reduction in the money supply was devastating in the defeated South. Land values plummeted. In 1870, Texas land was valued at an average of $2.62 an acre, compared with the national average of $18.26 an acre.

With the money supply declining and the national economy growing, farm prices dropped. In 1870, a bushel of wheat brought $1. In the 1890s, wheat was 60 cents a bushel. Except for a brief spurt in the early 1880s, cattle prices followed those of crops.

Between 1880 and 1890, the number of farms in Texas doubled, but the number of tenants tripled. By 1900, almost half the state's farmers were tenants.

The much-criticized crop-lien system was developed following the war to meet credit needs of the small farmers. Merchants would extend credit to farmers through the year in exchange for liens on their crops. But the result of the crop-lien system, particularly when small farmers did not have enough acreage to operate efficiently, was a state of continual debt and despair.

The work ethic held that a man would benefit from his toil. When this apparently failed, farmers looked to the monetary system and the railroads as the causes. Their discontent hence became the source of the agrarian revolt that developed in the 1880s and 1890s.

The entry of the Texas & Pacific and the Missouri-

Kansas-Texas **railroads** from the northeast changed trade patterns in the state.

Since the days of the Republic, trade generally had flowed to Gulf ports, primarily Galveston. Jefferson in Northeast Texas served as a gateway to the Mississippi River, but it never carried the volume of trade that was common at Galveston.

The earliest railroad systems in the state also were centered around Houston and Galveston, again directing trade southward. With the T&P and Katy lines, North Texas had direct access to markets in St. Louis and the East.

Problems developed with the railroads, however. In 1882, Jay Gould and Collis P. Huntington, owner of the Southern Pacific, entered into a secret agreement that amounted to creation of a monopoly of rail service in Texas. They agreed to stop competitive track extensions; to divide under a pooling arrangement freight moving from New Orleans and El Paso; to purchase all competing railroads in Texas; and to share the track between Sierra Blanca and El Paso.

The Legislature made weak attempts to regulate railroads, as provided by the state constitution. Gould thwarted an attempt to create a commission to regulate the railroads in 1881 with a visit to the state during the Legislature's debate.

The railroad tycoon subdued the lawmakers' interest with thinly disguised threats that capital would abandon Texas if the state interfered with railroad business.

As the 19th century closed, Texas remained an agricultural state. But the industrial base was growing. Between 1870 and 1900, the per capita value of manufactured goods in the United States rose from $109 to $171. In Texas, these per capita values increased from

$14 to $39, but manufacturing values in Texas industry still were only one-half of annual agricultural values.

In 1886, a new breed of Texas politician appeared. **James Stephen Hogg** was not a Confederate veteran, and he was not tied to party policies of the past.

As a reform-minded attorney general, Hogg had actively enforced the state's few railroad regulatory laws. With farmers' support, Hogg was elected governor in 1890, and at the same time, a debate on the constitutionality of a **railroad commission** was settled when voters amended the constitution to provide for one.

The reform mood of the state was evident. Voters returned only 22 of the 106 members of the Texas House in 1890.

Despite his reputation as a reformer, Hogg accepted the growing use of **Jim Crow laws** to limit blacks' access to public services. In 1891, the Legislature responded to public demands and required railroads to provide separate accommodations for blacks and whites.

The stage was being set for one of the major political campaigns in Texas history, however. Farmers did not think that Hogg had gone far enough in his reform program, and they were distressed that Hogg had not appointed a farmer to the railroad commission. Many began to look elsewhere for the solutions to their problems. The **People's Party** in Texas was formed in August 1891.

The 1892 general election was one of the most spirited in the state's history. Gov. Hogg's supporters shut conservative Democrats out of the convention in Houston, so the conservatives bolted and nominated railroad attorney George Clark for governor.

The People's Party, or **Populists**, for the first time had a presidential candidate, James Weaver, and a gubernatorial candidate, T.L. Nugent.

Texas Republicans also broke ranks. The party's strength centered in the black vote. After the death of former Gov. E.J. Davis in 1883, **Norris Wright Cuney**, a black, was party leader. Cuney was considered one of the most astute politicians of the period, and he controlled federal patronage.

White Republicans revolted against the black leadership, and these "Lily-whites" nominated **Andrew Jackson Houston**, son of Sam Houston, for governor.

Black Republicans recognized that alone their strength was limited, and throughout the latter part of the 19th century, they practiced fusion politics, backing candidates of third parties when they deemed it appropriate. Cuney led the Republicans into a coalition with the conservative Democrats in 1892, backing George Clark.

The election also marked the first time major Democratic candidates courted the black vote. Gov. Hogg's supporters organized black voter clubs, and the governor got about half of the black vote.

Black farmers were in a quandary. Their financial problems were the same as those small farmers who backed the Populists.

White Populists varied in their sympathy with the racial concerns of blacks. On the local level, some whites showed sympathy with black concerns about education, voting and law enforcement. Black farmers also were reluctant to abandon the Republican Party because it was their only political base in Texas.

Hogg was re-elected in 1892 with a 43 percent plu-

rality in a field of five candidates.

Populists continued to run well in state races until 1898. Historians have placed the beginning of the party's demise in the 1896 presidential election in which national Populists fused with the Democrats and supported **William Jennings Bryan**.

Although the Populist philosophy lived on, the party declined in importance after 1898. Farmers remained active in politics, but most returned to the Democratic Party, which usurped many of the Populists' issues.

Oil

Seldom can a people's history be profoundly changed by a single event on a single day. But Texas' entrance into the industrial age can be linked directly to the discovery of oil at **Spindletop**, three miles from **Beaumont**, on Jan. 10, 1901.

From that day, Texas' progress from a rural, agricultural state to a modern industrial giant was steady.

1900–1920

One of the greatest natural disasters ever to strike the state occurred on Sept. 8, 1900, when a **hurricane devastated Galveston**, killing 6,000 people. (For a more detailed account, see "After the Great Storm" in the 1998-1999 *Texas Almanac*). In rebuilding from that disaster, Galveston's civic leaders fashioned the **commission form of municipal government**.

Amarillo later refined the system into the council-manager organization that is widely used today.

The great Galveston storm also reinforced arguments by Houston's leadership that an inland port should be built for protection against such tragedies and disruptions of trade. The **Houston Ship Channel** was soon a reality.

The reform spirit in government was not dead after the departure of Jim Hogg. In 1901, the Legislature prohibited the issuing of railroad passes to public officials. More than 270,000 passes were issued to officials that year, and farmers claimed that the free rides increased their freight rates and influenced public policy as well.

In 1903, state Sen. **A.W. Terrell** got a major **election-reform law** approved, a measure that was further modified two years later. A was established to replace a hodgepodge of practices for nominating candidates that had led to charges of irregularities after each election.

Also in the reform spirit, the Legislature in 1903 prohibited abuse of **child labor** and set minimum ages at which children could work in certain industries. The action preceded federal child-labor laws by 13 years.

However, the state, for the first time, imposed the **poll tax** as a requirement for voting. Historians differ on whether the levy was designed to keep blacks or poor whites — or both — from voting. Certainly the poll tax cut election turnouts. Black voter participation dropped from about 100,000 in the 1890s to an estimated 5,000 in 1906.

The Democratic State Executive Committee also recommended that county committees limit participation in primaries to whites only, and most accepted the suggestion.

The election of **Thomas M. Campbell** as governor in 1906 marked the start of a progressive period in Texas politics. Interest revived in controlling corporate influence.

Under Campbell, the state's **antitrust laws** were strengthened and a **pure food and drug bill** was passed. Life insurance companies were required to invest in Texas 75 percent of their reserves on policies in the state. Less than one percent of the reserves had been invested prior to the law.

Some companies left Texas. But the law was beneficial in the capital-starved economy. In 1904, voters amended the constitution to allow the state to charter **banks** for the first time, and this eased some of the farmers' credit problems. In 1909, the Legislature approved a bank-deposit insurance plan that predated the federal program.

With corporate influence under acceptable control, attention turned to the issue of prohibition of alcohol. Progressives and prohibitionists joined forces against the conservative establishment to exert a major influence in state government for the next two decades.

Prohibitionists had long been active in Texas. They had the **local-option clause** written into the Constitution of 1876, which allowed counties or their subdivisions to be voted dry. But in 1887, a prohibition amendment to the state constitution had been defeated by a two-to-one margin, and public attention had turned to other problems.

In the early 20th century, the prohibition movement gathered strength. Most of Texas already was dry because of local option. When voters rejected a prohibition amendment by a slim margin in 1911, the state had 167 dry counties and 82 wet or partially wet counties. The heavily populated counties, however, were wet. Prohibition continued to be a major issue.

Problems along the U.S.-Mexico border escalated in 1911 as the decade-long **Mexican Revolution** broke out. Soon the revolutionaries controlled some northern Mexican states, including Chihuahua. Juarez and El Paso were major contact points. El Paso residents could stand on rooftops to observe the fighting between revolutionaries and government troops. Some Americans were killed.

After pleas to the federal government got no action, Gov. Oscar Colquitt sent state militia and Texas Rangers into the Valley in 1913 to protect Texans after Matamoros fell to the rebels. Unfortunately, the Rangers killed many innocent Mexican-Texans during the operation. In addition to problems caused by the fighting and raids, thousands of Mexican refugees flooded Texas border towns to escape the violence of the revolution.

In 1914, **James E. Ferguson** entered Texas politics and for the next three decades, "Farmer Jim" was one of the most dominating and colorful figures on the political stage. Ferguson, a banker from Temple, skirted the prohibition issue by pledging to veto any legislation pertaining to alcoholic beverages.

His strength was among farmers, however. Sixty-two percent of Texas' farmers were tenants, and Ferguson pledged to back legislation to limit tenant rents. Ferguson also was a dynamic orator. He easily won the primary and beat out three opponents in the general elec-

Drafted men report for service on Jan. 1, 1917, at Camp Travis in San Antonio. Almost 200,000 young Texans volunteered for military service during World War I, and 450 Texas women served in the nurses' corps. Five thousand lost their lives overseas, either fighting or in the influenza pandemic that swept the globe. Photo courtesy of the U.S. Department of Defense.

tion.

Ferguson's first administration was successful. The Legislature passed the law limiting tenants' rents, although it was poorly enforced, and aid to rural schools was improved.

In 1915, the border problems heated up. A Mexican national was arrested in the Lower Rio Grande Valley carrying a document outlining plans for Mexican-Americans, Indians, Japanese and blacks in Texas and the Southwest to eliminate all Anglo males over age 16 and create a new republic. The document, whose author was never determined, started a bloodbath in the Valley. Mexican soldiers participated in raids across the Rio Grande, and Gov. Ferguson sent in the Texas Rangers.

Historians differ on the number of people who were killed, but a safe assessment would be hundreds. Gov. Ferguson and Mexican President Venustiano Carranza met at Nuevo Laredo in November 1915 in an attempt to improve relations. The raids continued.

Pancho Villa raided Columbus, N.M., in early 1916; two small Texas villages in the Big Bend, Glenn Springs and Boquillas, also were attacked. In July, President **Woodrow Wilson** determined that the hostilities were critical and activated the National Guard.

Soon 100,000 U.S. troops were stationed along the border. **Fort Bliss** in El Paso housed 60,000 men, and **Fort Duncan** near Eagle Pass was home to 16,000 more.

With the exception of Gen. John J. Pershing's pursuit of Villa into Northern Mexico, few U.S. troops crossed into Mexico. But the service along the border gave soldiers basic training that was put to use when the United States entered World War I in 1917.

Ferguson was easily re-elected in 1916, and he worked well with the Legislature the following year. But after the Legislature adjourned, the governor got into a dispute with the board of regents of the **University of Texas**. The disagreement culminated in the governor's vetoing all appropriations for the school.

As the controversy swirled, the Travis County grand jury indicted Ferguson for misappropriation of funds and for embezzlement. In July 1917, Speaker of the Texas House F.O. Fuller called a special session of the Legislature to consider **impeachment** of the governor.

The Texas House voted 21 articles of impeachment, and the Senate in August 1917 convicted Ferguson on 10 of the charges. The Senate's judgment not only removed Ferguson from office, but also barred him from seeking office again. Ferguson resigned the day before the Senate rendered the decision in an attempt to avoid the prohibition against seeking further office.

Texas participated actively in **World War I**. Almost 200,000 young Texans, including 31,000 blacks, volunteered for military service, and 450 Texas women served in the nurses' corps. Five thousand lost their lives overseas, either fighting or in the **influenza pandemic** that swept the globe.

Texas also was a major training ground during the conflict, with 250,000 soldiers getting basic training in the state.

On the negative side, the war frenzy opened a period of intolerance and nativism in the state. German-Texans were suspect because of their ancestry. A law was passed to prohibit speaking against the war effort. Persons who failed to participate in patriotic activities often were punished. Gov. William P. Hobby even vetoed the appropriation for the German department at the University of Texas.

Ferguson's removal from office was a devastating blow to the anti-prohibitionists. Word that the former governor had received a $156,000 loan from members of the brewers' association while in office provided ammunition for the progressives.

In February 1918, a special session of the Legislature prohibited saloons within a 10-mile radius of military posts and ratified the national prohibition amendment, which had been introduced in Congress by Texas Sen. **Morris Sheppard**.

Women also were given the **right to vote in state primaries** at the same session.

Although national prohibition was to become effective in early 1920, the Legislature presented a prohibition amendment to voters in May 1919, and it was approved, bringing prohibition to Texas earlier than to the rest of the nation. At the same time, a woman suffrage amendment, which would have granted women the right to vote in all elections, was defeated.

Although World War I ended in November 1918, it brought many changes to Texas. Rising prices during the war had increased the militancy of labor unions.

Blacks also became more militant after the war. Discrimination against black soldiers led in 1917 to a riot in Houston in which several people were killed.

With the election of Mexican President Alvaro Obregón in 1920, the fighting along the border subsided.

In 1919, state Rep. J.T. Canales of Brownsville initiated an investigation of the **Texas Rangers'** role in the border problems. As a result of the study, the Rangers' manpower was reduced from 1,000 members to 76, and stringent limitations were placed on the agency's activities. Standards for members of the force also were upgraded.

By 1920, although still a rural state, the face of Texas was changing. Nearly one-third of the population was in the cities.

Pat M. Neff won the gubernatorial election of 1920, beating Sen. Joseph W. Bailey in the primary. As a former prosecuting attorney in McLennan County, Neff made law and order the major thrust of his administration. During his tenure the state took full responsibility for developing a **highway system**, a **gasoline tax** was imposed, and a state **park board** was established.

In 1921, a group of West Texans threatened to form a new state because Neff vetoed the creation of a new college in their area. Two years later, **Texas Technological College** (now Texas Tech University) was authorized in Lubbock and opened its doors in 1925.

Although still predominantly a rural state, Texas cities were growing. In 1900, only 17 percent of the population lived in urban areas; by 1920, that figure had almost doubled to 32 percent. A discontent developed with the growth of the cities. Rural Texans had long seen cities as hotbeds of vice and immorality. Simple rural values were cherished, and it seemed that those values were threatened in a changing world. After World War I, this transition accelerated.

KKK and Minorities

In addition, "foreigners" in the state became suspect; nativism reasserted itself. German-Texans were

The Depression Years

Clockwise from upper left: A dust storm blows through Amarillo in April 1936. A migrant farmer and a child tote water in a pail near Harlingen in February 1942. A cotton seed bag sits in front of a general store in a small Texas town in June 1937. A Texas family looks for cotton to pick in Haskell County in September 1931. Photos courtesy of the U.S. Department of Agriculture.

ing Texas the reputation as the most powerful Klan bastion in the Union. Hiram Wesley Evans of Dallas also was elected imperial wizard of the national Klan in that year.

The Klan became more directly involved in politics and planned to elect the next governor in 1924. Judge Felix Robertson of Dallas got the organization's backing in the Democratic primary. Former governor Jim Ferguson filed to run for the office, but the Texas Supreme Court ruled that he could not because of his impeachment conviction. So Ferguson placed his wife, Miriam A. Ferguson, on the ballot. Several other prominent Democrats also entered the race.

The Fergusons made no secret that Jim would have a big influence on his wife's administration. One campaign slogan was, "Two governors for the price of one." Mrs. Ferguson easily won the runoff against Robertson when many Texans decided that "Fergusonism" was preferable to the Klan in the governor's office.

Minorities began organizing in Texas to seek their civil rights. The National Association for the Advancement of Colored People (**NAACP**) opened a Texas chapter in 1912, and by 1919, there were chapters in 31 Texas communities. Similarly, Mexican-Texans formed Orden Hijos de America in 1921, and in 1929, the **League of United Latin American Citizens** (LULAC) was organized in Corpus Christi.

The Klan dominated the Legislature in 1923, passing a law barring blacks from participation in the Democratic primary. Although blacks had in fact been barred from voting in primaries for years, this law gave **Dr. Lawrence A. Nixon**, a black dentist from El Paso, the opportunity to go to court to fight the all-white primary. IIn 1927, the U.S. Supreme Court overturned the statute, but that was only the beginning of several court battles, which were not resolved until 1944.

Disgruntled Democrats and Klansmen tried to beat Mrs. Ferguson in the general election in 1924, but she was too strong. Voters also sent 91 new members to the Texas House, purging it of many of the Klan-backed representatives. After that election, the Klan's power ebbed rapidly in Texas.

Mrs. Ferguson named Emma Grigsby Meharg as

associated with the enemy in the war, and Mexican-Texans were mostly Roman Catholics and likened to the troublemakers along the border. Texas was a fertile ground for the new **Ku Klux Klan** that entered the state in late 1920. The Klan's philosophy was a mixture of patriotism, law-and-order, nativism, white supremacy and Victorian morals. Its influence spread quickly across the state, and reports of Klan violence and murder were rampant.

Prohibition had brought a widespread disrespect for law. Peace officers and other officials often ignored speakeasies and gambling. The Klan seemed to many Texans to be an appropriate instrument for restoring law and order and for maintaining morality in towns and cities. By 1922, many of the state's large communities were under direct Klan influence, and a Klan-backed candidate, Earle Mayfield, was elected to the U.S. Senate, giv-

In 1935, Texas Sen. Tom Connally authored the Hot Oil Act, which involved the federal government in regulation. Photo courtesy of the Library of Congress.

Texas' first woman secretary of state in 1925. The governors Ferguson administration was stormy. Jim was accused of cronyism in awarding highway contracts and in other matters. And "Ma" returned to her husband's practice of liberal clemency for prisoners. In two years, Mrs. Ferguson extended clemency to 3,595 inmates.

Although Jim Ferguson was at his bombastic best in the 1926 Democratic primary, young Attorney General **Dan Moody** had little trouble winning the nomination and the general election.

At age 33, Moody was the youngest person ever to become governor of Texas. Like many governors during this period, he was more progressive than the Legislature, and much of his program did not pass. Moody was successful in some government reorganization. He also cleaned up the highway department, which had been criticized under the Fergusons, and abandoned the liberal clemency policy for prisoners. And Moody worked at changing Texas' image as an anti-business state. "The day of the political trust-buster is gone," he told one Eastern journalist.

Progressives and prohibitionists still had a major influence on the Democratic Party, and 1928 was a watershed year for them. Moody easily won renomination and re-election. But the state party was drifting away from the direction of national Democrats. When **Al Smith**, a wet and a Roman Catholic, won the presidential nomination at the national Democratic convention in Houston, Texans were hard-pressed to remain faithful to the "party of the fathers." Moody, who had been considered a potential national figure, ruined his political career trying to straddle the fence, angering both wets and drys, Catholics and Protestants. Former governor O.B. Colquitt led an exodus of so-called "**Hoovercrats**" from

the state Democratic convention in 1928, and for the first time in its history, Texas gave its electoral votes to a Republican, Herbert Hoover, in the general election.

Through the 1920s, oil continued to increase in importance in Texas' economy. New discoveries were made at Mexia in 1920, Luling in 1922, Big Lake in Reagan Conty in 1923, in the Wortham Field in 1924 and in Borger in 1926. But oil still did not dominate the state's economic life.

As late as **1929**, meat packing, cottonseed processing and various milling operations exceeded the added value of petroleum refining. And as the 1920s ended, lumbering and food processing shared major economic roles with the petroleum industry. During the decade, Texas grew between 35 and 42 percent of U.S. cotton and 20-30 percent of the world crop. Irrigation and mechanization opened the South Plains to cotton growing. Eight years later, more than 1.1 million bales were grown in the region, mostly around Lubbock.

But Texas, with the rest of the nation, was on the threshhold of a major economic disaster that would have irreversible consequences. The **Great Depression** was at hand.

Depression Years

Historians have noted that the state's economic collapse was not as severe as that which struck the industrialized states. Texas' economy had sputtered through the decade of the 1920s, primarily because of the fluctuation of the price of cotton and other agricultural products. But agricultural prices were improving toward the end of the decade.

The Fergusons attempted a political comeback in the gubernatorial election of 1930. But Texans elected **Ross S. Sterling**, the founder of Humble Oil Co. Early in the Depression, Texans remained optimistic that the economic problems were temporary, another of the cyclical downturns the nation experienced periodically. Indeed, some Texans even felt that the hardships would be beneficial, ridding the economy of speculators and poor businessmen. Those attitudes gave way to increasing concern as the poor business conditions dragged on.

A piece of good luck turned into a near economic disaster for the state in late 1930. **C.M. "Dad" Joiner** struck oil near Kilgore, and soon the **East Texas oil boom** was in full swing. Millions of barrrels of new oil flooded the market, making producers and small landowners wealthy. Soon the glut of new oil drove market prices down from $1.10 a barrel in 1930 to 10 cents in 1931. Many wells had to be shut in around the state because they could not produce oil profitably at the low prices.

The Texas Railroad Commission attempted in the spring of 1931 to control production through proration, which assigned production quotas to each well (called the allowable). The first proration order limited each well to about 1,000 barrels a day of production. **Proration** had two goals: to protect reserves through conservation and to maintain prices by limiting production. But, on July 28, a federal court ruled that proration was an illegal attempt to fix prices.

In August 1931, Gov. Sterling placed four counties of the East Texas field under martial law and briefly shut down oil production there altogether. A federal court later ruled the governor's actions illegal. Gov. Sterling was roundly criticized for sending troops. Opponents said the action was taken to aid the major oil companies to the disadvantage of independent producers.

In 1932, Gov. Sterling appointed **Ernest O. Thompson** to a vacancy on the railroad commission. Thompson, who had led a coalition in favor of output regulation, is credited with fashioning a compromise between independents and major oil companies. In April 1933, the railroad commission prorated production on the basis, in part, of bottom-hole pressure in each well, and the courts upheld this approach. But enforcement remained a problem.

Finally in 1935, Texas' Sen. **Tom Connally** authored the Hot Oil Act, which involved the federal government in regulation by prohibiting oil produced in violation of state law from being sold in interstate commerce. Thereafter, Texas' producers accepted the concept of proration. Since Texas was the nation's largest oil producer, the railroad commission could set the national price of oil through proration for several decades thereafter.

Despite these problems, the oil boom helped East Texas weather the Depression better than other parts of the state. Farmers were hit particularly hard in 1931. Bumper crops had produced the familiar reduction in prices. Cotton dropped from 18 cents per pound in 1928 to six cents in 1931. That year Louisiana Gov. **Huey Long** proposed a ban on growing cotton in 1932 to eliminate the surplus. The Louisiana legislature enacted the ban, but Texas was the key state to the plan since it led the nation in cotton production. Gov. Sterling was cool to the idea, but responded to public support of it by calling a special session of the Legislature. The lawmakers passed a **cotton acreage limitation** bill in 1931, but the law was declared unconstitutional the following year.

One feature of the Depression had become the number of transients drifting from city to city looking for work. Local governments and private agencies tried to provide relief for the unemployed, but the effort was soon overwhelmed by the number of persons needing help. In Houston, blacks and Mexican-Texans were warned not to apply for relief because there was not enough money to take care of whites, and many Mexicans returned to Mexico voluntarily and otherwise.

To relieve the local governments, Gov. Sterling proposed a bond program to repay counties for highways they had built and to start a public-works program. Texans' long-held faith in self-reliance and rugged individualism was put to a severe test.

By **1932**, many were looking to the federal government to provide relief from the effects of the Depression.

U.S. Speaker of the House **John Nance Garner** of Texas was a presidential candidate when the Democrats held their national convention. To avoid a deadlocked convention, Garner maneuvered the Texans to change strategy. On the fourth ballot, the Texas delegation voted for the eventual nominee, New York Gov. **Franklin D. Roosevelt**. Garner got the second place on the ticket that swept into office in the general election.

In Texas, **Miriam Ferguson** was successful in unseating Gov. Sterling in the Democratic primary, winning by about 4,000 votes. Her second administration was less turbulent than the first. State government costs were reduced, and voters approved $20 million in so-called "bread bonds" to help provide relief. In 1933, **horse racing** came to the state, authorized through a rider on an appropriations bill legalizing pari-mutuel betting. The law was repealed in 1937. Prohibition also was repealed in 1933, although much of Texas remained dry under the **local-option** laws and the prohibition against open saloons.

State government faced a series of financial problems during Mrs. Ferguson's second term. The annual deficit climbed to $14 million, and the state had to default on the interest payments on some bonds. Voters aggravated the situation by approving a $3,000 **home-**

A farmstead in Dallas County is covered by drifting sand in this April 1938 photo. Photo courtesy of the U.S. Department of Agriculture.

U.S. Marine Corps Technical Sergeant Jack Pittman Jr. of Amarillo sits in the cockpit of a USMC F4U "CORSAIR" aircraft at Russell Island, Australia, on July 4, 1943. Pittman was an ace pilot during World War II. Photo courtesy of the U.S. Department of Defense Visual Information Center.

stead exemption. Many property owners were losing their homes because they could not pay taxes. And while the exemption saved their homesteads, it worsened the state's financial problems.

Many Texas banks failed during the Depression, as did banks nationally. One of Roosevelt's first actions was to declare a national bank holiday in 1933. Gov. Ferguson closed state banks at the same time, although she had to "assume" authority that was not in the law.

The New Deal

In Washington, Texans played an important role in shaping Roosevelt's **New Deal**. As vice president, Garner presided over the Senate and maneuvered legislation through the upper house. **Texans** also chaired major committees in the House: **Sam Rayburn**, Interstate and Foreign Commerce; **Hatton W. Sumners**, Judiciary; **Fritz G. Lanham**, Public Buildings and Grounds; **J.J. Mansfield**, Rivers and Harbors; and **James P. Buchanan**, Appropriations. With this influence, the Texas delegation supported the president's early social programs. In addition, **Jesse Jones** of Houston served as director of the Reconstruction Finance Corporation, the Federal Loan Administration and as Secretary of Commerce. Jones was one of the most influential men in Washington and second only to Roosevelt in wielding financial power to effect recovery.

Poor conservation practices had left many of the state's farmlands open to erosion. During the **Dust Bowl** days of the early and mid-1930s, for example, the weather bureau in Amarillo reported 192 dust storms within a three-year period. Cooperation between state and federal agencies helped improve farmers' conservation efforts and reduced the erosion problem by the end of the decade.

Mrs. Ferguson did not seek re-election in 1934, and Attorney General **James V. Allred** was elected. Under his administration, several social-welfare programs were initiated, including old-age pensions, teachers' retire-

ment and worker's compensation. Allred was re-elected in 1936.

Some of the New Deal's luster dimmed when the nation was struck by another recession in 1937.

Although Texas' economic condition improved toward the end of the decade, a full recovery was not realized until the beginning of World War II — when the state went through another industrial revolution.

Tragedy struck the small East Texas town of **New London** in Rusk County on March 18, 1937. At 3:05 p.m., natural gas, which had seeped undetected into an enclosed area beneath a school building from a faulty pipe connection, exploded when a shop teacher turned on a sander. Approximately 298 of the 540 students and teachers in the school died, and all but 130 of the survivors were injured. The disaster prompted the Legislature to pass a law requiring that a malodorant be added to gas so leaks could be detected by smell.

In 1938, voters elected one of the most colorful figures in the state's political history to the governor's office. **W. Lee "Pappy" O'Daniel**, a flour salesman and leader of a radio hillbilly band, came from nowhere to defeat a field of much better known candidates in the Democratic primary and to easily win the general election. When re-elected two years later, O'Daniel became the first candidate to poll more than one million votes in a Texas election.

But O'Daniel's skills of state did not equal his campaigning ability, and throughout his administration, the governor and the Legislature were in conflict. In early **1941**, long-time U.S. Senator Morris Sheppard died, and O'Daniel wanted the office. He appointed Andrew Jackson Houston, Sam Houston's aged son, to fill the vacancy. Houston died after only 24 days in office. O'Daniel won the special election for the post in a close race with a young congressman, **Lyndon B. Johnson**.

Lt. Gov. **Coke R. Stevenson** succeeded O'Daniel as governor and brought a broad knowledge of government to the office. Stevenson was elected to two full terms.

Thanks to frugal management and greatly increasing revenues during the war years, he left the state treasury with a surplus in 1947. Voters also solved the continuing deficit problem by approving a pay-as-you-go amendment to the constitution in 1942. It requires the state comptroller to certify that tax revenues will be available to support appropriations. Otherwise the money cannot be spent.

World War II

As in every war after Texas entered the Union, young Texans flocked to military service when the United States entered World War II. More than 750,000 served, including 12,000 women in the auxiliary services. In December 1942, U.S. Secretary of the Navy Frank Knox said Texas contributed the largest percentage of its male population to the armed forces of any state. Thirty Texans won Congressional Medals of Honor in the fighting. **Audie Murphy**, a young farm boy from Farmersville, became one of the most decorated soldiers of the war. Dallas-born **Sam Dealey** was the most-decorated Navy man.

Important contributions also were made at home. Texas was the site of 15 training posts, at which more than one and a quarter million men were trained, and of several prisoner-of-war camps.

World War II irrevocably changed the face of Texas. During the decade of the 1940s, the state's population switched from predominantly rural to 60 percent urban. The number of **manufacturing** workers almost doubled. And as had been the dream of Texas leaders for more than a century, the state began to attract new industries.

Conservatives vs. Liberals

The state's politics became increasingly controlled by conservative Democrats after Gov. Allred left office. In 1946, **Beauford H. Jester**, a member of the railroad commission, gained the governorship. Under Jester in 1947, the Legislature passed the state's right-to-work law, prohibiting mandatory union membership, and reorganized public education with passage of the **Gilmer-Aikin Act**.

During the Jester administration several major constitutional amendments were adopted. Also, one of Texas' greatest tragedies occurred on April 16, 1947, when the French ship SS Grandcamp, carrying a load of ammonium nitrate, exploded at **Texas City**. More than 500 died and 4,000 sustained injuries. Property damage exceeded $200 million.

In **1948**, Sen. W. Lee O'Daniel did not seek re-election. Congressman Lyndon Johnson and former Gov. Coke Stevenson vied for the Democratic nomination. In the runoff, Johnson won by a mere **87 votes** in the closest — and most hotly disputed — statewide election in Texas' history. Johnson quickly rose to a leadership position in the U.S. Senate, and, with House Speaker Sam Rayburn, gave Texas substantial influence in national political affairs.

Although re-elected in 1948, Jester died in July 1949, the only Texas governor to die in office, and Lt. Gov. **Allan Shivers** succeeded him. During Shivers' administration, state spending more than doubled, reaching $805.7 million in 1956, as the governor increased appropriations for public-health institutions, school salaries, retirement benefits, highways and old-age pensions.

Shivers broke with tradition, successfully winning three full terms as governor after completing Jester's unexpired term. Shivers also led a revolt by Texas Democrats against the national party in **1952**. The governor, who gained both the Democratic and Republican nominations for the office under the law that allowed cross-filing that year, supported Republican Dwight Eisenhower for the presidency. Many Texas Democrats broke with the national party over the so-called "**Tidelands issue**." Texas claimed land 12 miles out into the Gulf as state lands. The issue was important because revenue from oil and natural gas production from the area supported public education in the state.

Major oil companies also backed Texas' position because state royalties on minerals produced from the land were much lower than federal royalties. President Harry S. Truman vetoed legislation that would have given Texas title to the land. Democratic presidential nominee Adlai Stevenson was no more sympathetic to the issue, and Texas gave its electoral votes to Republican Dwight Eisenhower in an election that attracted a two million-vote turnout for the first time in Texas. President Eisenhower signed a measure into law guaranteeing Texas' tidelands.

Scandal struck state government in 1954 when irregularities were discovered in the handling of funds in the veterans' land program in the General Land Office. Land Commissioner Bascom Giles was convicted of several charges and sent to prison. Several insurance companies also went bankrupt in the mid-1950s, prompting a reorganization of the State Board of Insurance in 1957.

In 1954, the U.S. Supreme Court ruled unconstitutional the segregation of schools, and for the next quarter-century, **school integration** became a major political issue. By the late 1960s, most institutions were integrated, but the state's major cities continued to wage court battles against forced busing of students to attain racial balance. Blacks and Mexican-Texans also made gains in voting rights during the 1950s.

Shivers had easily defeated **Ralph W. Yarborough** in the Democratic primary in 1952, but the divisions between the party's loyalists and those who bolted ranks to join Republicans in presidential races were growing. Shivers barely led the first 1954 primary over Yarborough and won the nomination with 53 percent of the vote in the runoff. Yarborough ran an equally close race against **Price Daniel**, a U.S. Senator who sought the governorship in 1956. Upon election as governor, Daniel left the Senate, and Yarborough won a special election to fill the vacancy in 1957. Yarborough won re-election in 1964 before losing to **Lloyd Bentsen** in 1970 in the Democratic primary. Although a liberal, Yarborough proved to be unusually durable in Texas' conservative political climate.

The state budget topped $1 billion for the first time in 1958. The Legislature met for 205 days in regular and special sessions in 1961–62 and levied, over Gov. Daniel's opposition, the state's first broad-based **sales tax in 1962**.

Technological Growth

Through the 1950s and 1960s, Texas' industrial base had expanded and diversified. Petroleum production and refining remained the cornerstones, but other industries grew. Attracted by cheap electricity, the aluminum industry came to Texas. Starting from the base developed during World War II, defense industries and associated high-tech firms, specializing in electronics and computers, centered on the Dallas–Fort Worth area and Houston. One of the most important scientific breakthroughs of the century came in 1958 in Dallas. **Jack Kilby**, an engineer at **Texas Instruments**, developed and patented the integrated circuit that became the central part of computers.

Sen. Lyndon Johnson unsuccessfully sought the Democratic presidential nomination in 1960, and **John F. Kennedy** subsequently selected the Texan as his running mate. Johnson is credited with keeping several Southern states, including Texas, in the Democratic column in the close election. Kennedy was a Roman Catholic and a liberal, a combination normally rejected by the Southern states. When Johnson left the Senate to assume his new office in 1961, **John Tower** won a special election that attracted more than 70 candidates. Tower became the first Republican since Reconstruction to serve as a Texas senator.

President John F. Kennedy (left) was assassinated in downtown Dallas on Nov. 22, 1963, while riding in a motorcade. Texas Gov. John B. Connally (in front of Kennedy) was seriously wounded in the attack. File photo.

During the early 1960s, Harris County was chosen as the site for the National Aeronautics and Space Administration's manned spacecraft center. The acquisition of **NASA** further diversified Texas' industrial base.

In 1962, **John B. Connally**, a former aide to LBJ and Secretary of the Navy under Kennedy, returned to Texas to seek the governorship. Gov. Daniel sought an unprecedented fourth term and was defeated in the Democratic primary. Connally won a close Democratic run-off over liberal **Don Yarborough** and was elected easily. As governor, Connally concentrated on improving **public education, state services** and **water development**. He was re-elected in 1964 and 1966.

The Assassination

One of the major tragedies in the nation's history occurred in Dallas on **Nov. 22, 1963**, when President Kennedy was assassinated while riding in a motorcade. Gov. Connally also was seriously wounded. Lyndon Johnson was administered the oath of the presidency by Federal Judge Sarah T. Hughes of Dallas aboard Air Force One at Love Field. Lee Harvey Oswald was arrested for the murder of the president on the afternoon of the assassination, but Oswald was killed by Dallas nightclub operator Jack Ruby two days later.

An extensive investigation into the assassination of President Kennedy was conducted by the Warren Commission. The panel concluded that Oswald was the killer and that he acted alone. Ruby, who was convicted of killing Oswald, died of cancer in the Dallas County jail in 1967 while the case was being appealed.

The assassination damaged the Republican Party in Texas, however. Building strength in Texas' conservative political atmosphere in 1962, eight Republicans, the most in decades, had been elected to the Texas House. And two Republicans — Ed Foreman of Odessa and Bruce Alger of Dallas — served in Congress. All were defeated in the 1964 general election.

In the emotional aftermath of the tragedy, Johnson, who won the presidency outright in a **landslide election in 1964**, persuaded the Congress to pass a series of civil-rights and social-welfare programs that changed the face of the nation. Texas was particularly affected by the civil-rights legislation and a series of lawsuits challenging election practices. During the 1960s, the state constitutional limitation of urban representation in the Legislature was overturned. The poll tax was declared unconstitutional, and the practice of electing officials from at-large districts fell to the so-called "one-man, one-vote" ruling. As a result, more Republican, minority and liberal officials were elected, particularly from urban areas. In 1966, **Curtis Graves** and **Barbara Jordan** of Houston and **Joe Lockridge** of Dallas became the first blacks to serve in the Texas Legislature since 1898.

Lyndon Johnson did not seek re-election in 1968. The nation had become involved in an unpopular war in Vietnam, and Johnson bowed out of the race in the interest of national unity.

Sharpstown Scandal

Democrats stayed firmly in control of state government. **Preston Smith** was elected governor, and **Ben Barnes** gained the lieutenant governorship. Both were re-elected in 1970. Although state spending continued to increase, particularly on education, the Legislature otherwise was quiet. A minimum-wage law was approved, and public kindergartens were authorized in 1969.

At a special session, the **Sharpstown scandal**, one of the state's major scandals developed. Gov. Smith allowed the lawmakers to consider special banking legislation supported by Houston banker Frank Sharp. Several public officials were implicated in receiving favors from the banker for seeing that the legislation passed. Texas House Speaker Gus Mutscher and Rep. Tommy Shannon were convicted of conspiracy to accept bribes in a trial held in Abilene.

Voters in **1972** demanded a new leadership in the state capital. Smith and Barnes were defeated in the Democratic primary, and **Dolph Briscoe** was elected governor. In the fall, Texans gave presidential candidate Richard Nixon the state's electoral votes. Nixon carried 246 counties over Democrat George McGovern and received more than 65 percent of the popular vote.

The Legislature in 1973 was dominated by a reform atmosphere in the wake of the Sharpstown scandal. Price Daniel Jr., son of the former governor, was selected speaker of the House, and several laws concerning ethics and disclosure of campaign donations and spending were passed. Open meetings and open records statutes also were approved.

By 1970, Texas had become an even more urban state. The census found almost 11.2 million people in the state, ranking it sixth nationally. Three Texas cities, Houston, Dallas and San Antonio, were among the 10 largest in the nation.

Through the first half of the 1970s, several major changes were made in state policy. **Liquor-by-the-drink** became legal and the age of majority was lowered from 20 to 18, giving young people the right to vote. Also, the state's first Public Utilities Commission was created, hearing its initial case in September 1976.

Prosperity

Texas entered a period of unparalleled prosperity in 1973 when the Organization of Petroleum Exporting Countries (OPEC) boycotted the U.S. market. Severe energy shortages resulted, and the price of oil and natural gas skyrocketed. The federal government had allowed foreign oil to be imported through the 1960s, severely reducing the incentives to find and produce domestic oil. Consequently, domestic producers could not compensate for the loss in foreign oil as a result of the boycott. The Texas Railroad Commission had long complained about the importation of foreign oil, and in 1972, the panel had removed proration controls from wells in the state, allowing 100 percent production. For the rest of the decade, domestic producers mounted a major exploration effort, drilling thousands of wells. Nevertheless, **Texas' oil and gas production peaked in 1970** and has been declining since. Newly discovered oil and gas have not replaced the declining reserves. While Texans suffered from the inflation that followed, the state prospered. Tax revenues at all levels of government increased, and state revenues, basically derived from oil and gas taxes, spiraled, as did the state budget.

With the new revenue from inflation and petroleum taxes, state spending rose from $2.95 billion in 1970 to $8.6 billion in 1979, and education led the advance, moving from 42 percent of the budget to 51.5 percent. But there was no increase in state tax rates.

It was no surprise that **education** was one of the major beneficiaries of increased state spending. After World

Barbara Jordan, U.S. Representative from Houston, gave the keynote address at the Democratic National Convention in New York City on July 12, 1976. In 1966, Jordan became the first African-American woman to serve in the Texas Senate and the first African-American elected to that body since 1883. In 1972, she became the first African-American woman from the South to be elected to the U.S. Congress, where she served as a member of the House of Representatives until 1979. Jordan died in 1996. Photo courtesy of the Library of Congress.

War II, more emphasis was placed on education across the state. **Community colleges** sprang up in many cities, and a total of 109 colleges were established between the end of the war and 1980. Quantity did not assure quality, however, and Texas' public and higher education seldom were ranked among national leaders.

In 1972, voters approved an amendment authorizing the Legislature to sit as a **constitutional convention** to rewrite the 1876 charter. The lawmakers met for several months and spent $5 million, but they failed to propose anything to be considered by voters. The public was outraged, and in 1975, the Legislature presented the work of the convention to voters in the form of eight constitutional amendments. All were defeated in a special election in November 1975.

Texas voters participated in their **first presidential primary in 1976**. Jimmy Carter of Georgia won the Democratic primary, and eventually the presidency. Ronald Reagan carried the state's Republicans, but lost the party's nomination to President Gerald Ford.

The state proved politically volatile in **1978**. First, Attorney General **John Hill** defeated Gov. Dolph Briscoe in the Democratic primary. A political newcomer, Dallas businessman **William P. Clements**, upset Hill in the general election, giving Texas its first Republican governor since Reconstruction. Also for the first time since Reconstruction, state officials were elected to **four-year terms.** ☆

Environment

Davis Mountains State Park in Jeff Davis County. Ron Billings photo; Texas Forest Service.

Physical Regions

Geology

Soils

Aquifers, Rivers, Lakes

Plant Life

Forests & Grasslands

Wildlife

Environment

Texas has a natural environment of remarkable variety that extends from sea level at the Gulf of Mexico to over 8,000 feet in the Guadalupe Mountains of far West Texas and from the semitropical Lower Rio Grande Valley to the High Plains of the Panhandle. This section discusses the physical features, geology, soils, water, vegetation and wildlife that are found in the Lone Star State.

The Physical State of Texas

Area of Texas

Texas occupies about 7 percent of the total water and land area of the United States. Second in size among the states, **Texas has a land and water area of 268,580 square miles** as compared with Alaska's 663,267 square miles, according to the United States Bureau of the Census. California, the third largest state, has 163,696 square miles. Texas is as large as all of New England, New York, Pennsylvania, Ohio and North Carolina combined.

The **state's total area** consists of 261,797 square miles of land and 6,783 square miles of water.

Length and Breadth

The **longest straight-line distance** in a general north-south direction is 801 miles from the northwest corner of the Panhandle to the extreme southern tip of Texas on the Rio Grande below Brownsville. The greatest east-west distance is 773 miles from the extreme eastward bend in the Sabine River in Newton County to the extreme western bulge of the Rio Grande just above El Paso.

The **geographic center** of Texas is southwest of Mercury in northern McCulloch County at approximately 99° 20' West longitude and 31° 08' North latitude.

Texas' Boundary Lines

The boundary of Texas by segments, including only larger river bends and only the great arc of the coastline, is as follows:

BOUNDARY	MILES
Rio Grande	889.0
Coastline	367.0
Sabine River, Lake and Pass	180.0
*Sabine River to Red River	106.5
† Red River	480.0
*East Panhandle line	133.6
*North Panhandle line	167.0
*West Panhandle line	310.2
*Along 32nd parallel	209.0
TOTAL	**2,842.3**

Following the smaller meanderings of the rivers and the tidewater coastline, the following are the boundary measurements:

BOUNDARY	MILES
Rio Grande	1,254
Coastline (tidewater)	624
Sabine River, Lake and Pass	292
† Red River	726
*The five unchanged line segments above table	926
TOTAL (including segments marked *)	**3,822**

Latitude and Longitude

The extremes of latitude and longitude are as follows: From **25° 50' North latitude** at the extreme southern turn of the Rio Grande on the south line of Cameron County to **36° 30' North latitude** along the north line of the Panhandle, and from **93° 31' West longitude** at the extreme eastern point on the Sabine River on the east line of Newton County to **106° 38' West longitude** on the extreme westward point on the Rio Grande above El Paso.

Texas' Highs and Lows

The highest point in the state is **Guadalupe Peak** at **8,749 feet** above sea level. Its twin, **El Capitan**, stands at **8,085** feet and also is located in Culberson County near the New Mexico state line. Both are in Guadalupe Mountains National Park, which includes the scenic McKittrick Canyon. These elevations and the others in this article have been determined by the U.S. Geological Survey, unless otherwise noted.

Named Peaks in Texas Above 8,000 Feet

The named peaks above 8,000 feet and the counties in which they are located are listed below. These elevations may differ from those in earlier editions of the Almanac because of the more accurate measuring methods currently being used by the USGS.

NAME	COUNTY	ELEVATION
Guadalupe Peak	Culberson	8,749
Bush Mountain,	Culberson	8,001
Shumard Peak	Culberson	8,615
Bartlett Peak	Culberson	8,508
Mount Livermore (Baldy Peak)	Jeff Davis	8,378
Hunter Peak (Pine Top Mtn.)	Culberson	8,368
El Capitan	Culberson	8,085

Fort Davis in Jeff Davis County is the **highest town** of any size in Texas at 5,050 feet above sea level, and the county has the **highest average elevation.** The **highest state highway point** also is in Jeff Davis County at **McDonald Observatory** on **Mount Locke** where the road reaches 6,781 feet above sea level, as determined by the Texas Department of Transportation.

The **highest railway point** is Paisano Pass, which is 5,074 above sea level, 14 miles east of Marfa in Presidio County.

Sea level is the **lowest elevation** determined in Texas, and it can be found in all the coastal counties. No point in the state has been found by the geological survey to be below sea level. ☆

Physical Regions

This section was reviewed by Dr. David R. Butler, professor of geography at Texas State University–San Marcos.

The principal physical regions of Texas are usually listed as follows (see also **Vegetational Areas** and **Soils**):

The Gulf Coastal Plains

Texas' Gulf Coastal Plains are the western extension of the coastal plain extending from the Atlantic to beyond the Rio Grande. Its characteristic rolling to hilly surface covered with a heavy growth of pine and hardwoods extends into East Texas. In the increasingly arid west, however, its forests become secondary in nature, consisting largely of post oaks and, farther west, prairies and brushlands.

The interior limit of the Gulf Coastal Plains in Texas is the line of the **Balcones Fault and Escarpment**. This geologic fault or shearing of underground strata extends eastward from a point on the Rio Grande near Del Rio. It extends to the northwestern part of Bexar County where it turns northeastward and extends through Comal, Hays and Travis counties, intersecting the Colorado River immediately above Austin. The fault line is a single, definite geologic feature, accompanied by a line of southward- and eastward-facing hills.

The resemblance of the hills to balconies when viewed from the plain below accounts for the Spanish name for this area: *balcones.*

North of Waco, features of the fault zone are sufficiently inconspicuous that the interior boundary of the Coastal Plain follows the traditional geologic contact between upper and lower Cretaceous rocks. This contact is along the western edge of the **Eastern Cross Timbers**.

This fault line is usually accepted as the boundary between lowland and upland Texas. Below the fault line, the surface is characteristically coastal plains. Above the Balcones Fault, the surface is characteristically interior rolling plains.

Pine Belt or "Piney Woods"

The Pine Belt, called the **"Piney Woods,"** extends 75 to 125 miles into Texas from the east. From north to south, it extends from the Red River to within about 25 miles of the Gulf Coast. Interspersed among the pines are some hardwood timbers, usually in valleys of rivers and creeks. This area is the source of practically all of Texas' commercial timber production *(see Texas Forest Resources, page 109).* It was settled early in Texas' history and is an older farming area of the state.

This area's soils and climate are adaptable to production of a variety of fruit and vegetable crops. Cattle raising is widespread, accompanied by the development of pastures planted to improved grasses. Lumber production is the principal industry. There is a large iron-and-steel industry near Daingerfield in Morris County based on nearby iron deposits. Iron deposits are also worked in Rusk and one or two other counties.

A great oil field discovered in Gregg, Rusk and Smith counties in 1931 has done more than anything else to contribute to the economic growth of the area. This area has a variety of clays, lignite and other minerals as potentials for development.

Post Oak Belt

The main Post Oak Belt of Texas is wedged between the Pine Belt on the east, Blacklands on the west, and the

Cypress trees grow along a creek off Texas 16 in Bandera County. This scenic southwestern county is on the Edwards Plateau. Robert Plocheck photo.

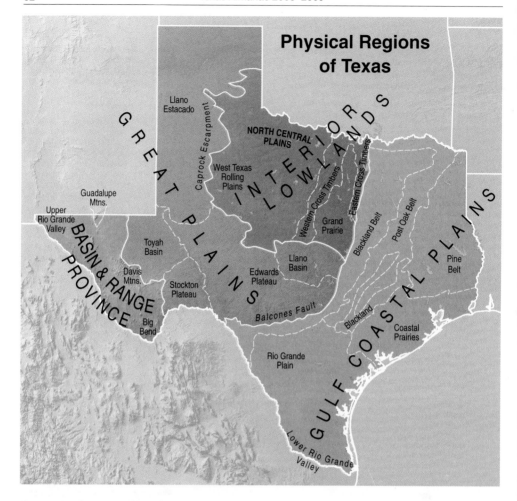

Physical Regions of Texas

Coastal Prairies on the south, covering a considerable area in East Central Texas. The principal industry is diversified farming and livestock raising. Throughout, it is spotty in character, with some insular areas of blackland soil and some that closely resemble those of the Pine Belt. There is a small isolated area of loblolly pines in Bastrop County known as the **"Lost Pines,"** the westernmost southern pines in the United States. The Post Oak Belt has lignite, commercial clays and some other minerals.

Blackland Belt

The Blackland Belt stretches from the Rio Grande to the Red River, lying just below the line of the **Balcones Fault,** and varying in width from 15 to 70 miles. It is narrowest below the segment of the Balcones Fault from the Rio Grande to Bexar County and gradually widens as it runs northeast to the Red River. Its rolling prairie, easily turned by the plow, developed rapidly as a farming area until the 1930s and was the principal cotton-producing area of Texas. Now, however, other Texas areas that are irrigated and mechanized lead in farming.

Because of the early growth, the Blackland Belt is still the most thickly populated area in the state and contains within it and along its border more of the state's large and middle-sized cities than any other area. Primarily because of this concentration of population, this belt has the most diversified manufacturing industry of the state.

Coastal Prairies

The Texas Coastal Prairies extend westward along the coast from the Sabine River, reaching inland 30 to 60 miles. Between the Sabine and Galveston Bay, the line of demarcation between the prairies and the Pine Belt forests to the north is very distinct. The Coastal Prairie extends along the Gulf from the Sabine to the Lower Rio Grande Valley.

The eastern half is covered with a heavy growth of grass; the western half, which is more arid, is covered with short grass and, in some places, with small timber and brush. The soil is heavy clay. Grass supports the densest cattle population in Texas, and cattle ranching is the principal agricultural industry. Rice is a major crop, grown under irrigation from wells and rivers. Cotton, grain sorghum and truck crops are also grown.

Coastal Prairie areas have seen the greatest industrial development in Texas history since World War II. Chief concentration has been from Orange and Beaumont to Houston, and much of the development has been in petrochemicals and the aerospace industry.

Corpus Christi, in the Coastal Bend, and Brownsville, in the Lower Rio Grande Valley, have seaports and agricultural and industrial sections. Cotton, grain, vegetables and citrus fruits are the principal crops. Cattle production is significant, with the famed King Ranch and other large ranches located here.

Lower Rio Grande Valley

The deep alluvial soils and distinctive economy cause the Lower Rio Grande Valley to be classified as a subregion of the Gulf Coastal Plain. The Lower Valley, as it is called locally, is Texas' greatest citrus-winter vegetable area because of the normal absence of freezing weather and the rich delta soils of the Rio Grande. Despite occasional damaging freezes, as in 1951 and 1961, the Lower Valley ranks high among the nation's fruit-and-truck regions. Much of the acreage is irrigated, although dry-land farming also is practiced.

Rio Grande Plain

This may be roughly defined as lying south of San Antonio between the Rio Grande and the Gulf Coast. The Rio Grande Plain shows characteristics of both the Texas Gulf Coastal Plain and the North Mexico Plains because there is similarity of topography, climate and plant life all the way from the Balcones Escarpment in Texas to the Sierra Madre Oriental in Mexico, which runs past Monterrey about 160 miles south of Laredo.

The Rio Grande Plain is partly prairie, but much of it is covered with a dense growth of **prickly pear, cactus, mesquite, dwarf oak, catclaw, guajillo, huisache, blackbrush, cenizo** and other wild shrubs. This country is devoted primarily to raising cattle, sheep and goats. The Texas Angora goat and mohair industry centers in this area and on the **Edwards Plateau,** which borders it on the north. San Antonio and Laredo are its chief commercial centers, with San Antonio dominating trade.

There is some farming, and the **Winter Garden,** centering in Dimmit and Zavala counties north of Laredo, is irrigated from wells and streams to produce vegetables in late winter and early spring. Primarily, however, the central and western part of the Rio Grande Plain is devoted to livestock raising. The rainfall is less than 25 inches annually and the hot summers bring heavy evaporation, so that cultivation without irrigation is limited. Over a large area in the central and western parts of the Rio Grande Plain, the growth of **small oaks, mesquite, prickly pear (Opuntia) cactus** and a variety of wild shrubs is very dense and it is often called the **Brush Country.** It is also referred to as the **chaparral** and the **monte.** (*Monte* is a Spanish word, one meaning of which is dense brush.)

Interior Lowlands

North Central Plains

The North Central Plains of Texas are a southwestern extension into Texas of the interior, or central, lowlands that extend northward to the Canadian border, paralleling the Great Plains to the West. The North Central Plains of Texas extend from the Blackland Belt on the east to the Caprock Escarpment on the west. From north to south they extend from the Red River to the Colorado.'

West Texas Rolling Plains

The West Texas Rolling Plains, approximately the western two-thirds of the North Central Plains in Texas, rise from east to west in altitude from about 750 feet to 2,000 feet at the base of the **Caprock Escarpment**. Annual rainfall ranges from about 30 inches on the east to 20 on the west. In general, as one progresses westward in Texas the precipitation not only declines but also becomes more variable from year to year. Temperature varies rather widely between summer's heat and winter's cold.

This area still has a large cattle-raising industry with many of the state's largest ranches. However, there is much level, cultivable land.

Grand Prairie

Near the eastern edge of the North Central Plains is the **Grand Prairie,** extending south from the Red River in an irregular band through Cooke, Montague, Wise, Denton, Tarrant, Parker, Hood, Johnson, Bosque, Coryell and some adjacent counties. It is a limestone-based area, usually treeless except along the numerous streams, and adapted primarily to livestock raising and staple-crop growing. Sometimes called the **Fort Worth Prairie,** it has an agricultural economy and largely rural population, with no large cities except Fort Worth on its eastern boundary.

Eastern and Western Cross Timbers

Hanging over the top of the Grand Prairie and dropping down on each side are the Eastern and Western Cross Timbers. The two southward-extending bands are connected by a narrow strip along the Red River. The **Eastern Cross Timbers** extend southward from the Red River through eastern Denton County and along the boundary between Dallas and Tarrant counties. It then stretches through Johnson County to the Brazos River and into Hill County.

The much larger **Western Cross Timbers** extend from the Red River south through Clay, Montague, Jack, Wise, Parker, Palo Pinto, Hood, Erath, Eastland, Comanche, Brown and Mills counties to the Colorado River, where they meet the Edwards Plateau. Their soils are adapted to fruit and vegetable crops, which reach considerable commercial production in some areas in Parker, Erath, Eastland and Comanche counties.

Great Plains

High Plains

The Great Plains, which lie to the east of the base of the Rocky Mountains, extend into Northwest Texas. This area, commonly known as the **High Plains,** is a vast, flat, high plain covered with thick layers of alluvial material. It is also known as the **Staked Plains** or the Spanish equivalent, *Llano Estacado.*

Historians differ as to the origin of this name. Some say it came from the fact that the explorer Coronado's expedition used stakes to mark its route across the trackless sea of grass so that it would be guided on its return trip. Others think that the *estacado* refers to the palisaded appearance of the Caprock in many places, especially the west-facing escarpment in New Mexico.

The **Caprock Escarpment** is the dividing line between the High Plains and the Lower Rolling Plains of West Texas. Like the Balcones Escarpment, the Caprock Escarpment is a striking physical feature, rising abruptly 200, 500 and in some places almost 1,000 feet above the plains. Unlike the **Balcones Escarpment**, the Caprock was caused by surface erosion. Where rivers issue from the eastern face of the Caprock, there frequently are notable canyons, such as **Palo Duro Canyon** on the **Prairie Dog Town Fork (main channel) of the Red River** and the breaks along the Canadian River as it crosses the Panhandle north of Amarillo.

Along the eastern edge of the Panhandle, there is a gradual descent of the land's surface from high to low plains; but at the Red River, the Caprock Escarpment becomes a striking surface feature. It continues as an east-facing wall south through Briscoe, Floyd, Motley, Dickens, Crosby, Garza and Borden counties, gradually decreasing in elevation. South of Borden County, the escarpment is less obvious, and the boundary between the High Plains and the Edwards Plateau occurs where the alluvial cover of the High Plains disappears.

Stretching over the largest level plain of its kind in the United States, the High Plains rise gradually from about 2,700 feet on the east to more than 4,000 in spots along the New Mexico border.

Chiefly because of climate and the resultant agriculture, subdivisions are called the North Plains and South Plains. The **North Plains,** from Hale County north, has primarily wheat and grain sorghum farming, but with significant ranching and petroleum developments. Amarillo is the largest city, with Plainview on the south and Borger on the north as important commercial centers.

The **South Plains,** also a leading grain sorghum region, **leads Texas in cotton production.** Lubbock is the principal city, and Lubbock County is one of the state's largest cotton producers. Irrigation from underground reservoirs, centered around Lubbock and Plainview, waters much of the crop acreage.

Edwards Plateau

Geographers usually consider that the Great Plains at the foot of the Rocky Mountains actually continue southward from the High Plains of Northwest Texas to the Rio Grande and the Balcones Escarpment. This southern and lower extension of the Great Plains in Texas is known as the **Edwards Plateau.**

It lies between the Rio Grande and the Colorado River. Its southeastern border is the **Balcones Escarpment** from the Rio Grande at Del Rio eastward to San Antonio and thence to Austin on the Colorado River. Its upper boundary is the Pecos River, though the **Stockton Plateau** is geologically and topographically classed with the Edwards Plateau.

The Edwards Plateau varies from about 750 feet high at its southern and eastern borders to about 2,700 feet in places. Almost the entire surface is a thin, limestone-based soil covered with a medium to thick growth of **cedar, small oak** and **mesquite** with a varying growth of **prickly pear.** Grass for cattle, weeds for sheep and tree foliage for the browsing goats support three industries — **cattle, goat and sheep raising** — upon which the area's economy depends. It is the **nation's leading Angora goat and mohair producing region** and one of the nation's leading sheep and wool areas. A few crops are grown.

The Hill Country

The Hill Country is a popular name for an area of hills and spring-fed streams along the edge of the **Balcones Escarpment** in the southeast portion of the Edwards Plateau south of the Llano Basin. Notable large springs include **Barton Springs** at Austin, **San Marcos Springs** at San Marcos, **Comal Springs** at New Braunfels, several springs at San Antonio, and a number of others. The Hill Country is characterized by rugged hills with relatively steep slopes and thin soils overlying limestone bedrock. High gradient streams combine with these steep hillslopes and occasionally heavy precipitation to produce an area with a significant flash-flood hazard.

Toyah Basin

To the northwest of the Edwards and Stockton plateaus is the Toyah Basin, a broad, flat remnant of an old sea floor that occupied the region as recently as Quaternary time. Located in the **Pecos River Valley,** this region, in relatively recent time, has become important for many agricultural products as a result of irrigation. Additional economic activity is afforded by local oil fields.

The Llano Basin

The Llano Basin lies at the junction of the Colorado and Llano rivers in Burnet and Llano counties. Earlier, this was known as the **"Central Mineral Region,"** because of the evidence there of a large number of minerals.

On the Colorado River in this area, a succession of dams impounds two large and five small reservoirs. Uppermost is **Lake Buchanan,** one of the large reservoirs, between Burnet and Llano counties. Below it in the western part of Travis County is **Lake Travis.** Between these two large reservoirs are three smaller ones, **Inks, L.B. Johnson** (formerly Granite Shoals) and **Marble Falls** reservoirs, used primarily for maintaining heads to produce electric power from the overflow from Lake Buchanan. **Lake Austin** is just above the city of Austin. Still another small lake, **Town Lake,** is formed by a low-water dam in Austin.

The recreational area around these lakes is called the **Highland Lakes Country.** This is an interesting area with Precambrian and Paleozoic rocks found on the surface. Granitic domes, exemplified by **Enchanted Rock** north of Fredericksburg, form the core of this area of ancient rocks.

Basin and Range Province

The Basin and Range province, with its center in Nevada, surrounds the Colorado Plateau on the west and south and enters far West Texas from southern New Mexico. It consists of broad interior drainage basins interspersed with scattered fault-block mountain ranges. Although this is the only part of Texas regarded as mountainous, these should not be confused with the Rocky Mountains. Of all the independent ranges in West Texas, only the Davis Mountains resemble the Rockies, and there is much debate about this.

Texas west of the Edwards Plateau, bounded on the north by New Mexico and on the south by the Rio Grande, is distinctive in its physical and economic conditions. Traversed from north to south by fault-block mountains, it contains all of Texas' true mountains and also is very interesting geologically.

Highest of the Trans-Pecos Mountains is the **Guadalupe Range,** which enters the state from New Mexico. It comes to an abrupt end about 20 miles south of the boundary line, where **Guadalupe Peak,** (8,749 feet, highest in Texas) and **El Capitan** (8,085 feet) are situated. El Capitan, because of perspective, appears to the observer on the plain below to be higher than Guadalupe.

Lying just west of the Guadalupe range and extending to the **Hueco Mountains** a short distance east of El Paso is the **Diablo Plateau** or basin. It has no drainage outlet to the sea. The runoff from the scant rain that falls on its surface drains into a series of salt lakes that lie just west of the Guadalupe Mountains. These lakes are dry during periods of low rainfall, exposing bottoms of solid salt, and for years they were a source of **commercial salt.**

Davis Mountains

The Davis Mountains are principally in Jeff Davis County. The highest peak, **Mount Livermore** (8,378 feet), is **one of the highest in Texas;** there are several others more than 7,000 feet high. These mountains intercept the moisture-bearing winds and receive more precipitation than elsewhere in the Trans-Pecos, so they have more vegetation than the other Trans-Pecos mountains. Noteworthy are the **San Solomon Springs** at the northern base of these mountains.

Big Bend

South of the Davis Mountains lies the Big Bend country, so called because it is encompassed on three sides by a great southward swing of the Rio Grande. It is a mountainous country of scant rainfall and sparse population. Its principal mountains, the **Chisos,** rise to 7,825 feet in **Mount Emory.**

Along the Rio Grande are the **Santa Elena, Mariscal** and **Boquillas canyons** with rim elevations of 3,500 to 3,775 feet. They are among the noteworthy canyons of the North American continent. Because of its remarkable topography and plant and animal life, the southern part of this region along the Rio Grande is home to **Big Bend National Park,** with headquarters in a deep valley in the Chisos Mountains. It is a favorite recreation area.

Upper Rio Grande Valley

The Upper Rio Grande (El Paso) Valley is a narrow strip of irrigated land running down the river from El Paso for a distance of 75 miles or more. In this area are the historic towns and missions of **Ysleta, Socorro** and **San Elizario, oldest in Texas.** Cotton is the chief product of the valley, much of it the long-staple variety. This limited area has a dense urban and rural population, in marked contrast to the territory surrounding it. ☆

Geology of Texas

Source: Bureau of Economic Geology, The University of Texas at Austin; www.beg.utexas.edu/

History in the Rocks

Mountains, seas, coastal plains, rocky plateaus, high plains, forests — all this physiographic variety in Texas is controlled by the varied rocks and structures that underlie and crop out across the state. The fascinating geologic history of Texas is recorded in the rocks — both those exposed at the surface and those penetrated by holes drilled in search of oil and natural gas.

The rocks reveal a dynamic, ever-changing earth — ancient mountains, seas, volcanoes, earthquake belts, rivers, hurricanes and winds. Today, the volcanoes and great earthquake belts are no longer active, but rivers and streams, wind and rain, and the slow, inexorable alterations of rocks at or near the surface continue to change the face of Texas.

The geologic history of Texas, as documented by the rocks, began more than a billion years ago. Its legacy is the mineral wealth and varied land forms of modern Texas.

Geologic Time Travel

The story preserved in rocks requires an understanding of the origin of strata and how they have been deformed. **Stratigraphy** is the study of the composition, sequence and origin of rocks: what rocks are made of, how they were formed and the order in which the layers were formed.

Structural geology reveals the architecture of rocks: the locations of the mountains, volcanoes, sedimentary basins and earthquake belts.

The map on the following page shows where rocks of various geologic ages are visible on the surface of Texas today. History concerns events through time, but geologic time is such a grandiose concept, most find it difficult to comprehend. So geologists have named the various chapters of earth history.

Areas along the Balcones Escarpment make for good rock climbing. Ali Romero nears the top of a rock face at Milton Reimers Ranch Park near Dripping Springs. Erich Schlegel photo.

Precambrian Eon

Precambrian rocks, more than 600 million years old, are exposed at the surface in the **Llano Uplift** of Central Texas and in scattered outcrops in **West Texas**, around and north of Van Horn and near El Paso.

These rocks, some more than a billion years old, include complexly deformed rocks that were originally formed by cooling from a liquid state as well as rocks that were altered from pre-existing rocks.

Precambrian rocks, often called the "basement complex," are thought to form the foundation of continental masses. They underlie all of Texas. The outcrop in Central Texas is only the exposed part of the **Texas Craton**, which is primarily buried by younger rocks. (A craton is a stable, almost immovable portion of the earth's crust that forms the nuclear mass of a continent.)

Paleozoic Era

During the early part of the Paleozoic Era (approximately 600 million to 350 million years ago), broad, relatively shallow seas repeatedly inundated the Texas Craton and much of North and West Texas. The evidence for these events is found exposed around the Llano Uplift and in far West Texas near Van Horn and El Paso, and also in the subsurface throughout most of West and North Texas. The evidence includes early Paleozoic rocks — sandstones, shales and limestones, similar to sediments that form in seas today — and the fossils of animals, similar to modern crustaceans — the brachiopods, clams, snails and related organisms that live in modern marine environments.

By **late Paleozoic** (approximately 350 million to 240 million years ago), the Texas Craton was bordered on the east and south by a long, deep marine basin called

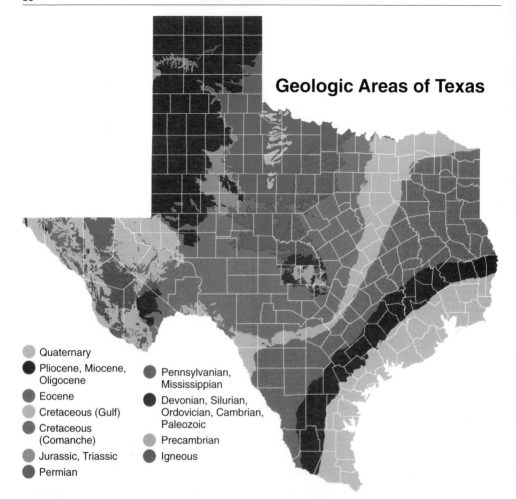

Geologic Areas of Texas

- Quaternary
- Pliocene, Miocene, Oligocene
- Eocene
- Cretaceous (Gulf)
- Cretaceous (Comanche)
- Jurassic, Triassic
- Permian
- Pennsylvanian, Mississippian
- Devonian, Silurian, Ordovician, Cambrian, Paleozoic
- Precambrian
- Igneous

the **Ouachita Trough**. Sediments slowly accumulated in this trough until late in the Paleozoic Era. Plate-tectonic theory postulates that the collision of the North American Plate (upon which the Texas Craton is located) with the European and African–South American plates uplifted the thick sediments that had accumulated in the trough to form the Ouachita Mountains.

At that time, the Ouachitas extended across Texas. Today, the Texas portion of the old mountain range is entirely buried by younger rocks, and all that remains at the surface of the once-majestic Ouachita Mountain chain is exposed only in southeastern Oklahoma and southwestern Arkansas.

During the **Pennsylvanian Period**, however, the Ouachita Mountains bordered the eastern margin of shallow inland seas that covered most of West Texas. Rivers flowed westward from the mountains to the seas bringing sediment to form deltas along an ever-changing coastline.

The sediments were then reworked by the waves and currents of the inland sea. Today, these fluvial, delta and shallow marine deposits compose the late Paleozoic rocks that crop out and underlie the surface of North-Central Texas.

Broad marine shelves divided the West Texas seas into several sub-basins, or deeper areas, that received more sediments than accumulated on the limestone

shelves. Limestone reefs rimmed the deeper basins. Today, these reef limestones are important **oil reservoirs in West Texas**.

These seas gradually withdrew from Texas, and by the late **Permian Period**, all that was left in West Texas were shallow basins and wide tidal flats in which salt, gypsum and red muds accumulated in a hot, arid land. Strata deposited during the Permian Period are exposed today along the edge of the Panhandle, as far east as Wichita Falls and south to Concho County, and in the Trans-Pecos.

Mesozoic Era

Approximately 240 million years ago, the major geologic events in Texas shifted from West Texas to East and Southeast Texas. The European and African–South American plates, which had collided with the North American plate to form the Ouachita Mountains, began to separate from North America.

A series of faulted basins, or rifts, extending from Mexico to Nova Scotia were formed. These rifted basins received sediments from adjacent uplifts. As Europe and the southern continents continued to drift away from North America, the Texas basins were eventually buried beneath thick deposits of marine salt within the newly formed East Texas and Gulf Coast basins.

Jurassic and **Cretaceous** rocks in East and Southeast Texas document a sequence of broad limestone shelves at the edge of the developing Gulf of Mexico. From time to time, the shelves were buried beneath deltaic sandstones and shales, which built the northwestern margin of the widening Gulf of Mexico to the south and southeast.

As the underlying salt was buried more deeply by dense sediments, the salt became unstable and moved toward areas of least pressure. As the salt moved, it arched or pierced overlying sediments forming, in some cases, columns known as "**salt domes**." In some cases, these salt domes moved to the surface; others remain beneath a sedimentary overburden. This mobile salt formed numerous structures that would later serve to trap oil and natural gas.

By the early **Cretaceous** (approximately 140 million years ago), the shallow **Mesozoic seas** covered a large part of Texas, eventually extending west to the Trans-Pecos area and north almost to present-day state boundaries. Today, the limestone deposited in those seas are exposed in the walls of the magnificent **canyons of the Rio Grande** in the Big Bend National Park area and in the canyons and headwaters of streams that drain the Edwards Plateau, as well as in Central Texas from San Antonio to Dallas.

Animals of many types lived in the shallow Mesozoic seas, tidal pools and coastal swamps. Today these lower Cretaceous rocks are some of the most fossiliferous in the state. Tracks of **dinosaurs** occur in several places, and remains of **terrestrial**, **aquatic** and **flying reptiles** have been collected from Cretaceous rocks in many areas.

During most of the late Cretaceous, much of Texas lay beneath **marine waters** that were deeper than those of the early Cretaceous seas, except where rivers, deltas and shallow marine shelves existed. River delta and strandline sandstones are the reservoir rocks for the most prolific oil field in Texas. When discovered in 1930, this East Texas oil field contained recoverable reserves estimated at 5.6 billion barrels. The chalky rock that we now call the "**Austin Chalk**" was deposited when the Texas seas became deeper.

Today, the chalk (and other Upper Cretaceous rocks) crops out in a wide band that extends from near Eagle Pass on the Rio Grande, east to San Antonio, north to Dallas and east to the Texarkana area. The Austin Chalk and other upper Cretaceous rocks dip southeastward beneath the East Texas and Gulf Coast basins. The late Cretaceous was the time of the last major seaway across Texas, because mountains were forming in the western United States that influenced areas as far away as Texas.

A **chain of volcanoes** formed beneath the late Cretaceous seas in an area roughly parallel to and south and east of the old, buried Ouachita Mountains. The eruptions of these volcanoes were primarily on the sea floor and great clouds of steam and ash likely accompanied them. Between eruptions, invertebrate marine animals built reefs on the shallow volcanic cones. **Pilot Knob**, located southeast of Austin, is one of these old volcanoes that is now exposed at the surface.

Cenozoic Era

At the dawn of the Cenozoic Era, approximately 65 million years ago, deltas fed by rivers were in the northern and northwestern margins of the East Texas Basin. These streams flowed eastward, draining areas to the north and west. Although there were minor incursions of the seas, the Cenozoic rocks principally document extensive seaward building by broad deltas, marshy lagoons, sandy barrier islands and embayments.

Thick vegetation covered the levees and areas between the streams. Coastal plains were taking shape under the same processes still at work today.

The Mesozoic marine salt became buried by thick sediments in the coastal plain area. The salt began to form ridges and domes in the Houston and Rio Grande areas. The heavy load of sand, silt and mud deposited by the deltas eventually caused some areas of the coast to subside and form large fault systems, essentially parallel to the coast.

Many of these coastal faults moved slowly and probably generated little earthquake activity. However, movement along the Balcones and Luling-Mexia-Talco zones, a **complex system of faults** along the western and northern edge of the basins, likely generated large earthquakes millions of years ago.

Predecessors of modern animals roamed the Texas Cenozoic coastal plains and woodlands. Bones and teeth of **horses, camels, sloths, giant armadillos, mammoths, mastodons, bats, rats, large cats** and other modern or extinct mammals have been excavated from coastal plain deposits. Vegetation in the area included varieties of plants and trees both similar and dissimilar to modern ones. **Fossil palmwood**, the Texas "**state stone**," is found in sediments of early Cenozoic age.

The Cenozoic Era in Trans-Pecos Texas was entirely different. There, **extensive volcanic eruptions** formed great calderas and produced copious lava flows. These eruptions ejected great clouds of volcanic ash and rock particles into the air — many times the amount of material ejected by the 1980 eruption of Mount St. Helens.

Ash from the eruptions drifted eastward and is found in many of the sand-and-siltstones of the Gulf Coastal Plains. **Lava** flowed over older Paleozoic and Mesozoic rocks, and igneous intrusions melted their way upward into crustal rocks. These volcanic and intrusive igneous rocks are well exposed in arid areas of the Trans-Pecos today.

In the Texas Panhandle, streams originating in the recently elevated southern Rocky Mountains brought floods of gravel and sand into Texas. As the braided streams crisscrossed the area, they formed great **alluvial fans**.

These fans, which were deposited on the older **Paleozoic** and **Mesozoic** rocks, occur from northwestern Texas into Nebraska. Between 1 million and 2 million years ago, the streams of the Panhandle were isolated from their Rocky Mountain source, and the eastern edge of this sheet of alluvial material began to retreat westward, forming the **Caprock** of the modern High Plains.

Late in the Cenozoic Era, a great **Ice Age** descended on the northern North American continent. For more than 2 million years, there were successive advances and retreats of the thick sheets of glacial ice. Four periods of extensive glaciation were separated by warmer interglacial periods. Although the glaciers never reached as far south as Texas, the state's climate and sea level underwent major changes with each period of glacial advance and retreat.

Sea level during times of glacial advance was 300 to 450 feet lower than during the warmer interglacial periods because so much sea water was captured in the ice sheets. The climate was both more humid and cooler than today, and the major Texas rivers carried more water and more sand and gravel to the sea. These deposits underlie the outer 50 miles or more of the Gulf Coastal Plain.

Approximately 3,000 years ago, sea level reached its modern position. The rivers, deltas, lagoons, beaches and barrier islands that we know as coastal Texas today have formed since that time. ☆

Oil and natural gas, as well as nonfuel minerals, are important to the Texas economy. For a more detailed discussion, see pages 633–652.

Soils of Texas

Source: Natural Resources Conservation Service, U. S. Department of Agriculture, Temple, Texas; www.tx.nrcs.usda.gov/

Soil is one of Texas' most important natural resources. Texas soils are complex because of the wide diversity of climate, vegetation, geology and landscape. **More than 1,300 different kinds of soil** are recognized in Texas. Each has a specific set of properties that affect its use.

The location of each soil and information about use are in soil survey reports available for most counties. Contact the **Natural Resources Conservation Service** for more information: 101 S. Main St., Temple 76501-7602; phone: 254-742-9850. On the Web: **www.tx.nrcs.usda. gov**; click on "Information About: Soils."

The vast expanse of Texas soils encouraged wasteful use of soil and water throughout much of the state's history. About 21 percent of all land area in Texas has been classified as "prime farmland."

Settlers, attracted by these rich soils and the abundant water of the eastern half of the region, used them to build an agriculture and agribusiness of vast proportions, and then found their abuse had created critical problems.

Soil Conservation

In the 1930s, interest in soil and water conservation began to mount. In 1935, the Soil Conservation Service, now called the **Natural Resources Conservation Service**, was created in the U.S. Department of Agriculture. In 1939, the **Texas Soil Conservation Law** made it possible for landowners to organize local soil and water conservation districts.

As of July 2005, Texas had **216 conservation districts**, which manage conservation functions within the district. A subdivision of state government, each district is governed by a board of five elected landowners. Technical assistance in planning and applying conservation work is provided through the USDA, Natural Resources Conservation Service. State funds are administered through the **Texas State Soil and Water Conservation Board**.

The 1997 National Resources Inventory showed that **land use** in Texas consisted of about 57 percent rangeland, 16 percent cropland, 9 percent pastureland, 6 percent forestland, 5 percent developed land, 2 percent federal land, 2 percent land in the conservation reserve program (CRP), 1 percent miscellaneous land and 2 percent water.

Soil Subdivisions

Texas can be divided into 21 major subdivisions, called **Major Land Resource Areas**, that have similar or related soils, vegetation, topography, climate and land uses. Brief descriptions of these subdivisions follow.

Trans-Pecos Soils

The 18.7 million acres of the Trans-Pecos, mostly west of the Pecos River, are diverse plains and valleys intermixed with mountains. Surface drainage is slow to rapid. This arid region is used mainly as rangeland. A small amount of irrigated cropland is on the more fertile soils along the Rio Grande and the Pecos River. Vineyards are a more recent use of these soils, as is the disposal of large volumes of municipal wastes.

Upland soils are mostly well-drained, light reddish-brown to brown clay loams, clays and sands (some have a large amount of gypsum or other salts). Many areas have shallow soils and rock outcrops, and sizable areas have deep sands. Bottomland soils are deep, well-drained, dark grayish-brown to reddish-brown silt loams, loams, clay loams and clays. Lack of soil moisture and wind erosion are the major soil-management problems. Only irrigated crops can be grown on these soils, and most areas lack an adequate source of good water.

Upper Pecos, Canadian Valleys and Plains Soils

The Upper Pecos and Canadian Valleys and Plains area occupies a little over a half-million acres and is in the northwest part of Texas near the Texas-New Mexico border. It is characterized by broad rolling plains and tablelands broken by drainageways and tributaries of the Canadian River. It includes the Canadian Breaks, which are rough, steep lands below the adjacent High Plains. The average annual precipitation is about 15 inches, but it fluctuates widely from year to year. Surface drainage is slow to rapid.

The soils are well drained and alkaline. The mostly reddish-brown clay loams and sandy loams were formed mostly in material weathered from sandstone and shale. Depths range from shallow to very deep.

The area is used mainly as rangeland and wildlife habitat. Native vegetation is mid- to short-grass prairie species, such as hairy grama, sideoats grama, little bluestem, alkali sacaton, vine-mesquite, and galleta in the plains and tablelands. Juniper and mesquite grow on the relatively higher breaks. Soil management problems include low soil moisture and brush control.

High Plains Soils

The High Plains area comprises a vast high plateau of more than 19.4 million acres in northwestern Texas. It lies in the southern part of the Great Plains province that includes large similar areas in Oklahoma and New Mexico. The flat, nearly level treeless plain has few streams to cause local relief. However, several major rivers originate in the High Plains or cross the area. The largest is the Canadian River, which has cut a deep valley across the Panhandle section.

Playas, small intermittent lakes scattered through the area, lie up to 20 feet below the surrounding plains. A 1965 survey counted more than 19,000 playas in 44 counties occupying some 340,000 acres. Most runoff from rainfall is collected in the playas, but only 10 to 40 percent of this water percolates back to the Ogallala Aquifer. The aquifer is virtually the exclusive water source in this area

Upland soils are mostly well-drained, deep, neutral to alkaline clay loams and sandy loams in shades of brown or red. Sandy soils are in the southern part. Many soils have large amounts of lime at various depths and some are shallow over caliche. Soils of bottomlands are minor in extent.

The area is used mostly for cropland, but significant areas of rangeland are in the southwestern and extreme northern parts. Millions of cattle populate the many large feedlots in the area. The soils are moderately productive, and the flat surface encourages irrigation and mechanization. Limited soil moisture, constant danger of wind erosion and irrigation water management are the major soil-management problems, but the region is Texas' leading producer of three important crops: cotton, grain sorghums and wheat.

Rolling Plains Soils

The Rolling Plains include 21.7 million acres east of the High Plains in northwestern Texas. The area lies west of the North Central Prairies and extends from the edge of the Edwards Plateau in Tom Green County northward into Oklahoma. The landscape is nearly level to strongly rolling, and surface drainage is moderate to rapid. Outcrops of red beds, geologic materials and associated reddish soils led to use of the name "Red Plains" by some. Limestone underlies the soils in the southeastern part. The eastern part contains large areas of badlands.

Upland soils are mostly deep, pale-brown through reddish-brown to dark grayish-brown, neutral to alkaline sandy loams, clay loams and clays; some are deep sands.

Many soils have a large amount of lime in the lower part, and a few others are saline; some are shallow and stony. Bottomland soils are mostly reddish-brown and sandy to clayey; some are saline.

This area is used mostly for rangeland, but cotton, grain sorghums and wheat are important crops. The major soil-management problems are brush control, wind erosion, low fertility and lack of soil mosture. Salt spots are a concern in some areas.

Outcroppings in Devil's River State Natural Area in Val Verde County show the limestone and alluvial soils of the region. Robert Plocheck photo.

North Central Prairie Soils

The North Central Prairie occupies about 7 million acres in North Central Texas. Adjacent to this area on the north is the rather small (less than 1 million acres) Rolling Red Prairies area, which extends into Oklahoma and is included here because the soils and land use are similar. This area lies between the Western Cross Timbers and the Rolling Plains. It is dominantly grassland intermixed with small wooded areas. The landscape is undulating with slow to rapid surface drainage.

Upland soils are mostly deep, well-drained, brown or reddish-brown, slightly acid loams over neutral to alkaline, clayey subsoils. Some soils are shallow or moderately deep to shale. Bottomland soils are mostly well-drained, dark-brown or gray loams and clays.

This area is used mostly as rangeland, but wheat, grain sorghums and other crops are grown on the better soils. Brush control, wind and water erosion and limited soil moisture are the major soil-management concerns.

Edwards Plateau Soils

The 22.7 million acres of the Edwards Plateau are in southwest Texas east of the Trans-Pecos and west of the Blackland Prairie. Uplands are nearly level to undulating except near large stream valleys where the landscape is hilly with deep canyons and steep slopes. Surface drainage is rapid.

Upland soils are mostly shallow, stony or gravelly, dark alkaline clays and clay loams underlain by limestone. Lighter-colored soils are on steep sideslopes and deep, less-stony soils are in the valleys. Bottomland soils are mostly deep, dark-gray or brown, alkaline loams and clays.

Raising beef cattle is the main enterprise in this region, but it is also the center of Texas' and the nation's mohair and wool production. The area is a major deer habitat; hunting leases produce income. Cropland is mostly in the valleys on the deeper soils and is used mainly for growing forage crops and hay. The major soil-management concerns are brush control, large stones, low fertility, excess lime and limited soil moisture.

Central Basin Soils

The Central Basin, also known as the Llano Basin, occupies a relatively small area in Central Texas. It includes parts or all of Llano, Mason, Gillespie and adjoining counties. The total area is about 1.6 million acres of undulating to hilly landscape.

Upland soils are mostly shallow, reddish-brown to brown, mostly gravelly and stony, neutral to slightly acid sandy loams over granite, limestone, gneiss and schist bedrock. Large boulders are on the soil surface in some areas. Deeper, less stony sandy-loam soils are in the valleys. Bottomland soils are minor areas of deep, dark-gray or brown loams and clays.

Ranching is the main enterprise, with some farms producing peaches, grain sorghum and wheat. The area provides excellent deer habitat, and hunting leases are a major source of income. Brush control, large stones and limited soil moisture are soil-management concerns.

Northern Rio Grande Plain Soils

The Northern Rio Grande Plain comprises about 6.3 million acres in Southern Texas extending from Uvalde to Beeville. The landscape is nearly level to rolling, mostly brush-covered plains with slow to rapid surface drainage.

The major upland soils are deep, reddish-brown or dark grayish-brown, neutral to alkaline loams and clays. Bottomland soils are mostly dark-colored loams.

The area is mostly rangeland with significant areas of cropland. Grain sorghums, cotton, corn and small grains are the major crops. Crops are irrigated in the western part, especially in the Winter Garden area, where vegetables such as spinach, carrots and cabbage are grown. Much of the area is good deer and dove habitat; hunting leases are a major source of income. Brush control, soil fertility, and irrigation-water management are the major soil-management concerns.

Western Rio Grande Plain Soils

The Western Rio Grande Plain comprises about 5.3 million acres in an area of southwestern Texas from Del Rio to Rio Grande City. The landscape is nearly level to undulating except near the Rio Grande where it is hilly. Surface drainage is slow to rapid.

The major soils are mostly deep, brown or gray alkaline clays and loams. Some are saline.

Most of the soils are used for rangeland. Irrigated grain sorghums and vegetables are grown along the Rio Grande. Hunting leases are a major source of income. Brush control and limited soil moisture are the major soil-management problems.

Central Rio Grande Plain Soils

The Central Rio Grande Plain comprises about 5.9 million acres in an area of Southern Texas from Live Oak County to Hidalgo County. It Includes the South Texas Sand Sheet, an area of deep, sandy soils and active sand dunes. The landscape is nearly level to gently undulating. Surface drainage is slow to rapid. Upland soils are mostly deep, light-colored, neutral to alkaline sands and loams. Many are saline or sodic. Bottomland soils are of minor extent.

Most of the area is used for raising beef cattle. A few areas, mostly in the northeast part, are used for growing grain sorghums, cotton and small grains. Hunting leases are a major source of income. Brush control is the major soil-management problem on rangeland; wind erosion and limited soil moisture are major concerns on cropland.

Lower Rio Grande Valley Soils

The Lower Rio Grande Valley comprises about 2.1 million acres in extreme southern Texas. The landscape is level to gently sloping with slow surface drainage.

Upland soils are mostly deep, grayish-brown, neutral to alkaline loams; coastal areas are mostly gray, silty clay loam and silty clay; some are saline. Bottomland soils are minor in extent.

Most of the soils are used for growing irrigated vegetables and citrus, along with cotton, grain sorghums and sugar cane. Some areas are used for growing beef cattle. Irrigation water management and wind erosion are the major soil-management problems on cropland; brush control is the major problem on rangeland.

Western Cross Timbers Soils

The Western Cross Timbers area comprises about 2.6 million acres. It includes the wooded section west of the Grand Prairie and extends from the Red River southward to the north edge of Brown County. The landscape is undulating and is dissected by many drainageways including the Brazos and Red rivers. Surface drainage is rapid.

Upland soils are mostly deep, grayish-brown, slightly acid loams with loamy and clayey subsoils. Bottomland soils along the major rivers are deep, reddish-brown, neutral to alkaline silt loams and clays.

The area is used mostly for grazing beef and dairy cattle on native range and improved pastures. Crops are peanuts, grain sorghums, small grains, peaches, pecans and vegetables. The major soil-management problem on grazing lands is brush control. Waste management on dairy farms is a more recent concern. Wind and water erosion are the major problems on cropland.

Eastern Cross Timbers Soils

The Eastern Cross Timbers area comprises about 1 million acres in a long narrow strip of wooded land that separates the northern parts of the Blackland Prairie and Grand Prairie and extends from the Red River southward to the Hill County. The landscape is gently undulating to rolling and is dissected by many streams, including the Red and Trinity rivers. Sandstone-capped hills are prominent in some areas. Surface runoff is moderate to rapid.

The upland soils are mostly deep, light-colored, slightly acid sandy loams and loamy sands with reddish loamy or clayey subsoils. Bottomland soils are reddish-brown to dark gray, slightly acid to alkaline loams or gray clays.

Grassland consisting of native range and improved pastures is the major land use. Peanuts, grain sorghums, small grains, peaches, pecans and vegetables are grown in some areas. Brush control, water erosion and low fertility are the major concerns in soil management.

Grand Prairie Soils

The Grand Prairie comprises about 6.3 million acres in North Central Texas. It extends from the Red River to about the Colorado River. It lies between the Eastern and Western Cross Timbers in the northern part and just west of the Blackland Prairie in the southern part. The landscape is undulating to hilly and is dissected by many streams including the Red, Trinity and Brazos rivers. Surface drainage is rapid.

Upland soils are mostly dark-gray, alkaline clays; some are shallow over limestone and some are stony. Some areas have light-colored loamy soils over chalky limestone. Bottomland soils along the Red and Brazos rivers are reddish silt loams and clays. Other bottomlands have dark-gray loams and clays.

Land use is a mixture of rangeland, pastureland and cropland. The area is mainly used for growing beef cattle. Some small grain, grain sorghums, corn and hay are grown. Brush control and water erosion are the major management concerns.

Blackland Prairie Soils

The Blackland Prairies consist of about 12.6 million acres of east-central Texas extending southwesterly from the Red River to Bexar County. There are smaller areas to the southeast. The landscape is undulating with few scattered wooded areas that are mostly in the bottomlands. Surface drainage is moderate to rapid.

Both upland and bottomland soils are deep, dark-gray to black alkaline clays. Some soils in the western part are shallow to moderately deep over chalk. Some soils on the eastern edge are neutral to slightly acid, grayish clays and loams over mottled clay subsoils (sometimes called graylands). Blackland soils are known as "cracking clays" because of the large, deep cracks that form in dry weather. This high shrink-swell property can cause serious damage to foundations, highways and other structures and is a safety hazard in pits and trenches.

Land use is divided about equally between cropland and grassland. Cotton, grain sorghums, corn, wheat, oats and hay are grown. Grassland is mostly improved pastures, with native range on the shallower and steeper soils. Water erosion, cotton root rot, soil tilth and brush control are the major management problems.

Claypan Area Soils

The Claypan Area consists of about 6.1 million acres in east-central Texas just east of the Blackland Prairie. The landscape is a gently undulating to rolling, moderately dissected woodland also known as the Post Oak Belt or Post Oak Savannah. Surface drainage is moderate.

Upland soils commonly have a thin, light-colored, acid sandy loam surface layer over dense, mottled red, yellow and gray claypan subsoils. Some deep, sandy soils with less clayey subsoils exist. Bottomlands are deep, highly fertile, reddish-brown to dark-gray loamy to clayey soils.

Land use is mainly rangeland. Some areas are in improved pastures. Most cropland is in bottomlands that are protected from flooding. Major crops are cotton, grain sorghums, corn, hay and forage crops, most of which are irrigated. Brush control on rangeland and irrigation water management on cropland are the major management problems. Water erosion is a serious problem on the highly erosive claypan soils, especially where they are overgrazed.

East Texas Timberland Soils

The East Texas Timberlands area comprises about 16.1 million acres of the forested eastern part of the state. The land is gently undulating to hilly and well dissected by many streams. Surface drainage is moderate to rapid.

This area has many kinds of upland soils but most are deep, light-colored, acid sands and loams over loamy and clayey subsoils. Deep sands are in scattered areas and red clays are in areas of "redlands." Bottomland soils are mostly brown to dark-gray, acid loams and some clays.

The land is used mostly for growing commercial pine timber and for woodland grazing. Improved pastures are scattered throughout and are used for grazing beef and dairy cattle and for hay production. Some commercial hardwoods are in the bottomlands. Woodland management problems include seedling survival, invasion of hardwoods in pine stands, effects of logging on water quality and control of the southern pine beetle. Lime and fertilizers are necessary for productive cropland and pastures.

Coast Prairie Soils

The Coast Prairie includes about 8.7 million acres near the Gulf Coast in southeast Texas. It ranges from 30 miles to 80 miles in width and parallels the coast from the Sabine River in Orange County to Baffin Bay in Kleberg County. The landscape is level to gently undulating with slow surface drainage.

Upland soils are mostly deep, dark-gray, neutral to slightly acid clay loams and clays. Lighter-colored and more-sandy soils are in a strip on the northwestern edge; some soils in the southern part are alkaline; some are saline and sodic. Bottomland soils are mostly deep, dark-colored clays and loams along small streams but are greatly varied along the rivers.

Land use is mainly grazing lands and cropland. Some hardwood timber is in the bottomlands. Many areas are also managed for wetland wildlife habitat. The nearly level topography and productive soils encourage farming. Rice, grain sorghums, cotton, corn and hay are the main crops. Brush management on grasslands and removal of excess water on cropland are the major management concerns.

Coast Saline Prairies Soils

The Coast Saline Prairies area includes about 3.2 million acres along a narrow strip of wet lowlands adjacent to the coast; it includes the barrier islands that extend from Mexico to Louisiana. The surface is at or only a few feet above sea level with many areas of salt-water marsh. Surface drainage is very slow.

The soils are mostly deep, dark-colored clays and loams; many are saline and sodic. Light-colored sandy soils are on the barrier islands. The water table is at or near the surface of most soils.

Cattle grazing is the chief economic use of the various salt-tolerant cordgrasses and sedges. Many areas are managed for wetland wildlife. Recreation is popular on the barrier islands. Providing fresh water and access to grazing areas are the major management concerns.

Gulf Coast Marsh Soils

This 150,000-acre area lies in the extreme southeastern corner of Texas. The area can be subdivided into four parts: freshwater, intermediate, brackish, and saline (saltwater) marsh. The degree of salinity of this system grades landward from saltwater marshes along the coast to freshwater marshes inland. Surface drainage is very slow.

This area contains many lakes, bayous, tidal channels, and man-made canals. About one-half of the marsh is fresh, and one-half is salty. Most of the area is susceptible to flooding either by fresh water drained from lands adjacent to the marsh or by saltwater from the Gulf of Mexico. Most of the soils are very poorly drained, continuously saturated, soft and can carry little weight. In general, the organic soils have a thick layer of dark gray, relatively undecomposed organic material over a gray, clayey subsoil. The mineral soils have a surface of dark gray, highly decomposed organic material over a gray, clayey subsoil.

Most of the almost treeless and uninhabited area is in marsh vegetation, such as grasses, sedges and rushes. It is used mainly for wildlife habitat. Part of the fertile and productive estuarine complex that supports marine life of the Gulf of Mexico, it provides wintering ground for waterfowl and habitat for many fur-bearing animals and alligators. A significant acreage is firm enough to support livestock and is used for winter grazing of cattle. The major management problems are providing fresh water and access to grazing areas.

Flatwoods Soils

The Flatwoods area includes about 2.5 million acres of woodland in humid southeast Texas just north of the Coast Prairie and extending into Louisiana. The landscape is level to gently undulating. Surface drainage is slow.

Upland soils are mostly deep, light-colored, acid loams with gray, loamy or clayey subsoils. Bottomland soils are deep, dark-colored, acid clays and loams. The water table is near the surface at least part of the year.

The land is mainly used for forest, although cattle are grazed in some areas. Woodland management problems include seedling survival, invasion of hardwoods in pine stands, effects of logging on water quality and control of the southern pine beetle. ☆

Yuccas bloom in the coastal soils of Cameron County. Robert Plocheck photo.

Water Resources

Source: Texas Water Development Board; www.twdb.state.tx.us

Surface Water and Ground Water

In Texas, **water law has been historically different for surface water** and ground water. Surface water belongs to the state and, except for limited amounts of water for household and on-farm livestock use, requires permits for use.

In general, ground water is considered the property of the surface landowner by "right of capture," meaning the landowner may pump as much water from beneath his land as he can for any beneficial use. This right may be limited only through the creation of ground-water conservation districts, which may make rules to protect and conserve ground-water supplies within their boundaries.

The **Texas Commission on Environmental Quality** is responsible for permitting and adjudicating surface-water rights and uses. It is the primary regulator of surface water and polices contamination and pollution of both surface and ground water.

The **Texas Water Development Board** collects data on occurrence, availability and quality of water within the state; plans for future supply and use; and administers the state's funds for grants and loans to finance future water development and supply.

In January 2007, the Texas Water Development Board developed a comprehensive **statewide water plan**, which the 75th Texas Legislature in 1997 had required the board to do. The TWDB divided the state into 16 regional water-planning areas, and each area's Regional Water Planning Group is required to adopt a water plan that addresses conservation of water supplies, how to meet future water needs and how to respond to future droughts.

Ground-water Supplies and Use

Texas has historically relied on its wealth of fresh to slightly saline water that underlies more than 81 percent of the state. About 60 percent of the approximately 16 million acre-feet of water used yearly in Texas is derived from underground formations that make up 9 major and 21 minor aquifers.

Nearly 80 percent of the ground water produced in 2000 was used for irrigating crops, especially in the Panhandle region. Ground water also supplies about 36 percent of the state's municipal needs.

Major Aquifers of Texas

Ogallala

The Ogallala aquifer extends under 46 counties of the Texas Panhandle and is the southernmost extension of the largest aquifer (High Plains aquifer) in North America. The Ogallala Formation of late Miocene to early Pliocene age consists of heterogeneous sequences of coarse-grained sand and gravel in the lower part, grading upward into clay, silt and fine sand. In Texas, the Panhandle is the most extensive region irrigated with ground water. About 96 percent of the water pumped from the Ogallala is used for irrigation.

Water-level declines are occurring in part of the region because of extensive pumping that far exceeds recharge. Water-conservation measures by agricultural and municipal users are being promoted. Computer models of the northern and southern portions of the Ogallala aquifer were completed by the TWDB and its contractor. Several agencies are investigating playa recharge and agricultural re-use projects over the aquifer.

Gulf Coast Aquifer

The Gulf Coast aquifer forms an irregularly shaped belt that parallels the Texas coastline and extends through 54 counties from the Rio Grande northeastward to the Louisiana border. The **aquifer system** is composed of the water-bearing units of the Catahoula, Oakville, Fleming, Goliad, Willis, Lissie, Bentley, Montgomery and Beaumont formations.

This system has been divided into three major water-producing components referred to as the **Chicot, Evangeline**, and **Jasper** aquifers. Municipal uses account for about 53 percent and irrigation accounts for about 35 percent of the total pumpage from the aquifer.

Water quality is generally good northeast of the San Antonio River basin, but deteriorates to the southwest. Years of heavy pumpage have caused significant water-level declines in portions of the aquifer. Some of these declines have resulted in significant **land-surface subsidence**, particularly in the Houston-Galveston area. TWDB has developed computer models of the northern, central and southern portions of the aquifer.

Edwards (Balcones Fault Zone)

The Edwards (BFZ) aquifer forms a narrow belt extending through nine counties from a ground-water divide in Kinney County through the San Antonio area northeastward to the Leon River in Bell County. A poorly defined ground-water divide in Hays County hydrologically separates the aquifer into the San Antonio and Austin regions. Water in the aquifer occurs in fractures, honeycomb zones and solution channels in the Edwards and associated limestone formations of Cretaceous age.

More than 50 percent of aquifer pumpage is for municipal use, while irrigation is the principal use in the western segment. San Antonio is one of the largest cities in the world that relies solely on a single ground-water source for its municipal supply. The aquifer also feeds several well-known recreational springs and underlies some of the most environmentally sensitive areas in the state.

In 1993, the Edwards Aquifer Authority was created by the legislature to regulate aquifer pumpage to benefit all users from Uvalde County through a portion of Hays County. Barton Springs-Edwards Aquifer Conservation District provides aquifer management for the rest of Hays and southern Travis counties.

The EAA has an active program to educate the public on water conservation and also operates several active groundwater recharge sites. The San Antonio River Authority also has a number of flood-control structures that effectively recharge the aquifer.

Conservation districts are promoting more-efficient irrigation techniques, and market-based, voluntary transfers of unused agricultural water rights to municipal uses are more common. The EAA has developed a computer model of the San Antonio segment of the Edwards aquifer.

Carrizo-Wilcox

Extending from the Rio Grande in South Texas northeastward into Arkansas and Louisiana, the Carrizo-Wilcox aquifer provides water to all or parts of 60 counties. The Wilcox Group and overlying Carrizo Sand form a hydrologically connected system of sand locally interbedded with clay, silt, lignite and gravel.

Throughout most of its extent in Texas, the aquifer yields fresh to slightly saline water, which is used primarily for irrigation in the **Winter Garden District** of South Texas and for public supply and industrial use in Central and Northeast Texas.

Because of excessive pumping, the water level in the aquifer has been significantly lowered, particularly in the artesian portion of the Winter Garden District of Atascosa, Frio and Zavala counties and in municipal and industrial

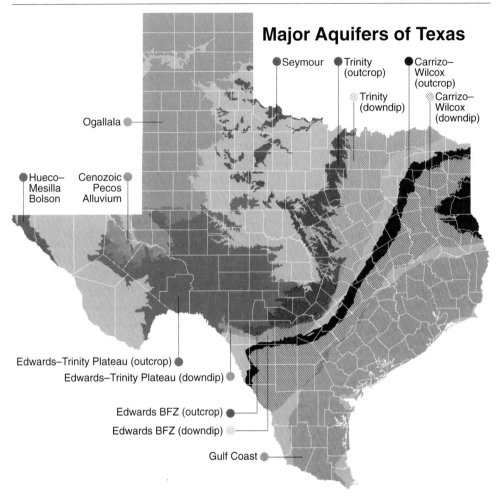

Major Aquifers of Texas

● Seymour   ● Trinity (outcrop)   ● Carrizo–Wilcox (outcrop)

Trinity (downdip)   Carrizo–Wilcox (downdip)

Ogallala ●

● Hueco–Mesilla Bolson   Cenozoic ● Pecos Alluvium

Edwards–Trinity Plateau (outcrop) ●
Edwards–Trinity Plateau (downdip) ●

Edwards BFZ (outcrop) ●
Edwards BFZ (downdip)

Gulf Coast ●

areas in Angelina and Smith counties. The TWDB has completed a computer model for much of the aquifer.

Trinity

The Trinity aquifer consists of basal Cretaceous-age Trinity Group formations extending from the Red River in North Texas to the Hill Country of Central Texas. Formations comprising the aquifer include the **Twin Mountains, Glen Rose** and **Paluxy**. Where the Glen Rose thins or is absent, the Twin Mountains and Paluxy formations coalesce to form the **Antlers Formation**. In the south, the Trinity includes the Glen Rose and underlying **Travis Peak** formations. Water from the Antlers portion is used mainly for irrigation in the outcrop area of North and Central Texas.

Elsewhere, water from the Trinity aquifer is used primarily for municipal and domestic supply. Extensive development of the Trinity aquifer in the Dallas-Fort Worth and Waco areas has historically resulted in water-level declines of several hundred feet. TWBD has completed a computer model of the Hill Country area and the northern portion of the aquifer.

Edwards-Trinity (Plateau)

This aquifer underlies the Edwards Plateau, extending from the Hill Country of Central Texas westward to the Trans-Pecos region. It consists of sandstone and limestone formations of the Trinity formations, and limestones

and dolomites of the Edwards and associated limestone formations. Ground-water movement is generally toward the southeast.

Near the plateau's edge, flow is toward the main streams, where the water issues from springs. Irrigation, mainly in the northwestern portion of the region, accounted for about 70 percent of total aquifer use in 2000 and has resulted in significant water-level declines in Glasscock and Reagan counties. Elsewhere, the aquifer supplies fresh but hard water for municipal, domestic and livestock use. The TWDB has developed a computer model of this aquifer.

Seymour

This aquifer consists of isolated areas of alluvium found in parts of 22 north-central and Panhandle counties in the upper Red River and Brazos River basins. Eastward-flowing streams during the Quaternary Period deposited discontinuous beds of poorly sorted gravel, sand, silt and clay that were later dissected by erosion, resulting in the isolated remnants of the formation. Individual accumulations vary greatly in thickness, but most of the Seymour is less than 100 feet.

The lower, more permeable part of the aquifer produces the greatest amount of ground water. Irrigation pumpage accounted for 93 percent of the total use from the aquifer in 1994. Water quality generally ranges from fresh to slightly saline. However, the salinity has increased in

The Rio Grande winds through the Bouquillas area of Big Bend National Park. Richard Kinler photo.

many heavily pumped areas to the point where the water has become unsuitable for domestic and municipal use. Natural salt pollution in the upper reaches of the Red and Brazos river basins precludes the full utilization of these water resources.

Hueco-Mesilla Bolson

These aquifers are located in El Paso and Hudspeth counties in far western Texas and occur in Quaternary basin-fill deposits that extend northward into New Mexico and westward into Mexico. The Hueco Bolson, located on the eastern side of the Franklin Mountains, consists of up to 9,000 feet of clay, silt, sand and gravel and is an important source of drinking water for both El Paso and Juarez, Mexico. Located west of the Franklin Mountains, the Mesilla Bolson reaches up to 2,000 feet in thickness and contains three separate water-producing zones. Ground-water depletion of the Hueco Bolson has become a serious problem.

Historical large-scale ground-water withdrawals, especially for the municipal uses of El Paso and Juarez, have caused major water-level declines and significantly changed the direction of flow, causing a deterioration of the chemical quality of the ground water in the aquifer. The USGS, along with El Paso Water Utilities, has developed a computer model of this aquifer.

Cenozoic Pecos Alluvium

Located in the upper Pecos River Valley of West Texas, this aquifer is the principal source of water for irrigation in Reeves and northwestern Pecos counties and for industrial uses, power supply and municipal use elsewhere. Consisting of up to 1,500 feet of alluvial fill, the aquifer occupies two hydrologically separate basins: the Pecos Trough in the west and the Monument Draw Trough in the east.

Water from the aquifer is generally hard and contains dissolved-solids concentrations ranging from less than 300 to more than 5,000 parts per million. Water-level declines in excess of 200 feet have historically occurred in Reeves and Pecos counties, but have moderated since the mid-1970s with the decrease in irrigation pumpage. TWDB has developed a computer model of the aquifer.

Major Rivers of Texas

Some **11,247 named Texas streams** are identified in the **U.S. Geological Survey Geographic Names Information System**. Their combined length is about 80,000 miles, and they drain 263,513 square miles within Texas. **Thirteen major rivers** are described below, starting with the southernmost and moving northward:

Rio Grande

The Pueblo Indians called this river **P'osoge**, which means the "river of great water." In 1582, **Antonio de Espejo** of Nueva Vizcaya, Mexico, followed the course of the **Río Conchos** to its confluence with a great river, which Espejo named **Río del Norte (River of the North)**. The name **Rio Grande** was first given the stream apparently by the explorer **Juan de Oñate**, who arrived on its banks near present-day El Paso in 1598.

Thereafter the names were often consolidated, as **Río Grande del Norte**. It was shown also on early Spanish maps as **Río San Buenaventura** and **Río Ganapetuan**. In its lower course it early acquired the name **Río Bravo**, which is its name on most Mexican maps. At times it has also been known as **Río Turbio**, probably because of its muddy appearance during its frequent rises. Some people erroneously call this watercourse the **Rio Grande River**. From source to mouth, the Rio Grande drops 12,000 feet to sea level as a snow-fed mountain torrent, desert stream and meandering coastal river. Along its banks and in its valley Indian civilizations developed, and Europeans established some of their first North American settlements.

This river rises in Colorado, flows the north-south length of New Mexico and **forms the boundary of Texas** and international U.S.-Mexican boundary for 889 to 1,254 river miles, depending upon method of measurement. (See **Texas Boundary Line**.) The length of the Rio Grande, as of other rivers, depends on method of measurement and varies yearly as its course changes. The latest **International Boundary and Water** Commission figure is 1,896 miles, which is considerably below the 2,200-mile figure often used. Depending upon methods of measurement, the Rio Grande is the fourth- or fifth-longest North American river, exceeded only by the Missouri-Mississippi, McKenzie-Peace, St. Lawrence and possibly Yukon. Since all of these except the Missouri-Mississippi are partly in Canada, the Rio Grande is the **second-longest river entirely within or bordering the United States**. It is **Texas' longest river**.

The snow-fed flow of the Rio Grande is used for irrigation in Colorado below the San Juan Mountains, where the river rises at the Continental Divide. Turning south, it flows through a canyon in northern New Mexico and again irrigates a broad valley of central New Mexico. This is the oldest irrigated area of the United States, where Spanish missionaries encouraged Indian irrigation in the 1600s.

Southern New Mexico impounds Rio Grande waters in Elephant Butte Reservoir for irrigation of 150 miles of valley above and below El Paso. Here is the **oldest irrigated**

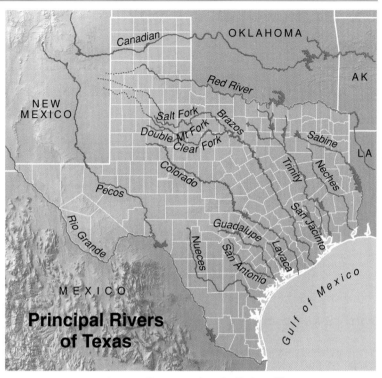

Principal Rivers of Texas

area in Texas and one of the oldest in the United States. Extensive irrigation practically exhausts the water supply. In this valley are situated **three of the oldest towns in Texas — Ysleta, Socorro** and **San Elizario**. At the lower end of the El Paso irrigated valley, the upper Rio Grande virtually ends except in seasons of above-normal flow.

It starts as a perennially flowing stream again where the Río Conchos of Mexico flows into it at Presidio-Ojinaga. Through the **Big Bend** the Rio Grande flows through three successive **canyons**, the **Santa Elena**, the **Mariscal** and the **Boquillas**. The Santa Elena has a river bed elevation of 2,145 feet and a canyon-rim elevation of 3,661. Corresponding figures for Mariscal are 1,925 and 3,625, and for Boquillas, 1,850 and 3,490.

The river here flows around the base of the **Chisos Mountains**. For about 100 miles the river is the southern boundary of **Big Bend National Park**. Below the Big Bend, the Rio Grande gradually emerges from mountains onto the Coastal Plains. A 191.2-mile strip on the American shore from Big Bend National Park downstream to the Terrell-Val Verde County line, has federal designation as the **Rio Grande Wild and Scenic River**.

At the confluence of the Rio Grande and the Devils River, the United States and Mexico have built **Amistad Dam**, to impound 3,505,400 acre-feet of water, of which Texas' share is 56.2 percent. **Falcon Reservoir**, also an international project, impounds 2,767,400 acre-feet of water, of which Texas' share in Zapata and Starr counties is 58.6 percent.

The Rio Grande, where it joins the Gulf of Mexico, has created a fertile delta called the **Lower Rio Grande Valley**, a major vegetable- and fruit-growing area. The Rio Grande drains 48,259 square miles of Texas. Principal tributaries flowing from the Texas side of the Rio Grande are the **Pecos** and **Devils** rivers. On the Mexican side are **Río Conchos, Río Salado** and **Río San Juan**. About three-fourths of the water running into the Rio Grande below El

Paso comes from the Mexican side.

Pecos River

The Pecos, one of the major tributaries of the Rio Grande, rises on the western slope of the Santa Fe mountain range in New Mexico. In Texas the river flows southeast, entering Val Verde County at its northwestern corner and angles across that county to its mouth on the Rio Grande in the Amistad Reservoir, between Comstock and Langtry northwest of Del Rio.

According to the Handbook of Texas the origins of the river's several names began with Antonio de Espejo, who called the river the Río de las Vacas ("river of the cows") because of the number of buffalo in the vicinity. Gaspar Castaño de Sosa, who followed the Pecos northward, called it the Río Salado because of its salty taste, which caused it to be shunned by men and animals alike.

It is believed that the name "Pecos" first appears in Juan de Oñate's reports concerning the Indian pueblo of Cicuye, now known as the Pecos Pueblo, and is of unknown origin. To Mexicans the river was long known as the Río Puerco ("dirty river").

Through most of its more than 900-mile-long course, the Pecos River parallels the Rio Grande. The total drainage area of the Pecos in New Mexico and Texas is about 44,000 square miles. Most of its tributaries flow from the west; these include the Delaware River, Toyah Creek, and Comanche Creek.

The topography of the river valley ranges from mountain pastures in the north, with an elevation of more than 13,000 feet above sea level, to grasslands, semiarid irrigated farmlands, desert with sparse vegetation, and, in the lowermost reaches of the river, deep canyons.

Nueces River

The Nueces River rises in Edwards County and flows 315 miles to Nueces Bay on the Gulf near Corpus Christi. Draining 16,950 square miles, it is a beautiful, **spring-fed stream** flowing through **canyons** until it issues from the

Balcones Escarpment onto the Coastal Plain in northern Uvalde County. **Alonso de León**, in 1689, gave it its name. (Nueces, plural of nuez, means nuts in Spanish.) Much earlier, Cabeza de Vaca had referred to a **Río de las Nueces** in this region, probably the same stream. Its original Indian name seems to have been **Chotilapacquen**. Crossing Texas in 1691, Terán de los Rios named the river **San Diego**. The Nueces was the boundary line between the Spanish provinces of Texas and Nuevo Santander.

After the Revolution of 1836, both Texas and Mexico claimed the territory between the Nueces and the Rio Grande, a dispute which was settled by the **Treaty of Guadalupe Hidalgo** in 1848, which fixed the international boundary at the Rio Grande. Average runoff of the Nueces is about 620,000 acre-feet a year in its lower course. Principal water conservation projects are **Lake Corpus Christi** and **Choke Canyon Reservoir**. Principal tributaries of the Nueces are the **Frio** and the **Atascosa**.

San Antonio River

The San Antonio River has its source in **large springs** within and near the city limits of San Antonio. It flows 180 miles across the Coastal Plain to a junction with the **Guadalupe** near the Gulf Coast. Its channel through San Antonio has been developed into a parkway known as the River Walk. Its principal tributaries are the **Medina River** and Cibolo Creek, both spring-fed streams and this, with its spring origin, gives it a remarkably steady flow of clear water. It was first named the **León** by Alonso de León in 1689; the name was not for himself, but he called it "lion" because its channel was filled with a rampaging flood.

Because of its limited and arid drainage area (4,180 square miles) the average runoff of the San Antonio River is relatively small, about 350,000 acre-feet annually near its mouth, but its flow, because of its springs, is one of the steadiest of Texas rivers.

Guadalupe River

The Guadalupe rises in its north and south prongs in the west-central part of Kerr County. A **spring-fed stream**, it flows eastward through the Hill Country until it issues from the **Balcones Escarpment** near New Braunfels. It then crosses the Coastal Plain to San Antonio Bay. Its total length is about 250 miles, and its drainage area is about 6,700 square miles. Its principal tributaries are the **San Marcos**, another spring-fed stream, which joins it in Gonzales County; the San Antonio, which joins it just above its mouth on San Antonio Bay; and the Comal, which joins it at New Braunfels.

The **Comal River** has its source in large springs within the city limits of New Braunfels and flows only about 2.5 miles to the Guadalupe. It is the **shortest river in Texas** and also the **shortest river in the United States** carrying an equivalent amount of water. There has been power development on the Guadalupe near Gonzales and Cuero for many years, and there is also power generation **at Canyon Lake.** Because of its springs, and its considerable drainage area, the Guadalupe has an average annual runoff of more than 1 million acre-feet in its lower course. The name Guadalupe is derived from **Nuestra Señora de Guadalupe**, the name given the stream by Alonso de León.

Lavaca River

The Lavaca is considered a primary stream in the Texas Basin because it flows directly into the Gulf through Lavaca Bay. Without a spring-water source and with only a small watershed, including that of its principal tributary, the **Navidad**, its flow is intermittent. The Spanish called it the Lavaca (cow) River because of the numerous bison they found near it. It is the principal stream running to the Gulf between the Guadalupe and the Colorado, and drains 2,309 square miles. The principal lake on the **Navidad** is **Lake Texana**. Runoff averages about 600,000 acre-feet yearly into the Gulf.

Colorado River

Measured by length, the Colorado is the **largest river wholly in Texas**. (Its drainage basin extends into New Mexico, as does that of the Brazos River.) Rising in Dawson County, the Colorado flows about 600 miles to Matagorda Bay on the Gulf. Its drainage area is 39,893 square miles. Its average annual runoff reaches a volume of more than 2 million acre-feet near the Gulf. Its name is a Spanish word meaning "**reddish**." There is evidence that Spanish explorers originally named the muddy Brazos "Colorado," but Spanish mapmakers later transposed the two names.

The river flows through a rolling, mostly prairie terrain to the vicinity of San Saba County, where it enters the rugged **Hill Country** and **Burnet-Llano Basin**. It passes through a picturesque series of **canyons** until it issues from the **Balcones Escarpment** at Austin and flows across the Coastal Plain to the Gulf.

In this area the **most remarkable series of reservoirs in Texas** has been built. The largest of these are **Lake Buchanan** in Burnet and Llano counties and **Lake Travis** in Travis County. Between the two in Burnet County are three smaller reservoirs: **Inks, Lyndon B. Johnson** (formerly **Granite Shoals**) and **Marble Falls,** built to aid power production from water running over the Buchanan Lake spillway. Below Lake Travis is the older **Lake Austin**, largely filled with silt, whose dam is used to produce power from waters flowing down from the lakes above. **Town Lake** is in the city of Austin. This area is known as the **Highland Lakes Country**.

As early as the 1820s, Anglo-Americans settled on the banks of the lower Colorado, and in 1839 the **Capital Commission of the Republic of Texas** chose the picturesque area where the river flows from the **Balcones Escarpment** as the site of a new capital of the Republic — now **Austin**, capital of the state. The early colonists encouraged navigation along the lower channel with some success, and boats occasionally ventured as far upstream as Austin. However, a **natural log "raft"** in the channel near the Gulf blocked river traffic. Conservation and utilization of the waters of the Colorado are under jurisdiction of three agencies created by the state Legislature, the **Lower, Central** and **Upper Colorado River Authorities**.

The principal tributaries of the Colorado River are the several prongs of the **Concho River** on its upper course, **Pecan Bayou (farthest west "bayou"** in the United States) and the **Llano**, **San Saba** and **Pedernales** rivers. All except Pecan Bayou flow into the Colorado from the **Edwards Plateau** and are spring-fed, perennially flowing. In the numerous mussels found along these streams, **pearls** occasionally have been found. On early Spanish maps, the Middle Concho was called **Río de las Perlas**.

Brazos River

The Brazos is the largest river between the Rio Grande and the Red River and is **third in size** of all rivers in Texas. It rises in three upper forks, the **Double Mountain, Salt** and **Clear forks** of the Brazos. The Brazos River proper is considered as beginning where the Double Mountain and Salt Forks flow together in Stonewall County. The Clear Fork joins this main stream in Young County, just above **Possum Kingdom Lake**. The Brazos crosses most of the main physiographic regions of Texas — High Plains, West Texas Lower Rolling Plains, Western Cross Timbers, Grand Prairie and Gulf Coastal Plain.

The total length from the source of its longest upper prong, the Double Mountain Fork, to the mouth of the main stream at the Gulf, was reported to be 923.2 miles in a 1970 study by the Army Corps of Engineers. The drainage area is about 43,000 square miles. It flows directly into the Gulf near Freeport. Its average annual runoff at places along its lower channel exceeds 5 million acre-feet.

The original name of this river was **Brazos de Dios,**

Campers relax along the Colorado River in Colorado Bend State Park. Ron Billings photo; Texas Forest Service.

meaning "Arms of God." There are several legends as to why. One is that the Coronado expedition, wandering on the trackless **Llano Estacado**, exhausted its water and was threatened with death from thirst. Arriving at the bank of the river, they gave it the name "Brazos de Dios" in thankfulness. Another is that a ship exhausted its water supply and its crew was saved when they found the mouth of the Brazos. Still another story is that miners on the San Saba were forced by drought to seek water near present-day Waco and in gratitude called it Brazos de Dios.

Much early Anglo-American colonization of Texas took place in the Brazos Valley. Along its channel were **San Felipe de Austin**, capital of Austin's colony; **Washington-on-the-Brazos**, where Texans declared independence; and other historic settlements. There was some navigation of the **lower channel** of the Brazos in this period. Near its mouth it intersects the **Gulf Intracoastal Waterway**, which provides connection with the commerce on the Mississippi.

Most of the Brazos Valley lies within the boundaries of the **Brazos River Authority**, which conducts a multipurpose program for development. A large reservoir on the Brazos is **Lake Whitney** (627,100 acre-feet capacity) on the main channel, where it is the boundary line between Hill and Bosque counties. Another large reservoir is **Possum Kingdom Lake** in Palo Pinto, Stephens, Young and Jack counties. **Lake Waco** on the Bosque and **Belton Lake** on the Leon are among the principal reservoirs on its tributaries. In addition to its three upper forks, other chief tributaries are the **Paluxy**, **Little** and **Navasota** rivers.

San Jacinto River

The San Jacinto is a short river with a drainage basin of 2,800 square miles and an average annual runoff of nearly 2 million acre-feet. It is formed by the junction of its East and West forks in northeastern Harris County and runs directly to the Gulf through Galveston Bay. Its total length, including the East Fork, is about 85 miles.

Lake Conroe is on the **West Fork**, and **Lake Houston** is located at the junction of the West Fork and the East Fork. The **Houston Ship Channel** runs through the lower course of the San Jacinto and its tributary, **Buffalo Bayou**, connecting the Port of Houston with the Gulf.

There are two stories of the origin of its name. One is that when early explorers discovered it, its channel was choked with hyacinth ("**jacinto**" is the Spanish word for hyacinth). The other is that it was discovered on Aug. 17, St. Hyacinth's Day. The **Battle of San Jacinto** was fought on the shore of this river on April 21, 1836, when Texas won its independence from Mexico. **San Jacinto State Park and monument** commemorate the battle.

Trinity River

The Trinity rises in its East Fork, Elm Fork, West Fork and Clear Fork in Grayson, Montague, Archer and Parker counties, respectively. The main stream begins with the junction of the Elm and West forks at Dallas. Its length is 550 river miles, and its drainage area is 17,969 square miles. Because of moderate to heavy rainfall over its drainage area, it has a average annual flow of 5.8 million acre-feet near its mouth on the Gulf, exceeded only by the Neches, Red and Sabine river basins.

The Trinity derives its name from the Spanish "**Trinidad**." Alonso de León named it **La Santísima Trinidad** (the Most Holy Trinity).

Navigation was developed along its lower course with several riverport towns, such as **Sebastopol** in Trinity County. For many years there has been a basin-wide movement for navigation, conservation and utilization of its water. The **Trinity River Authority** is a state agency and the **Trinity Improvement Association** is a publicly supported nonprofit organization advocating its development.

The Trinity has in its valley **more large cities, greater population and more industrial development** than any other river basin in Texas. On the Lower Coastal Plain there is large use of its waters for **rice irrigation**. Largest reservoir on the Elm Fork is **Lewisville Lake** (formerly **Garza-Little Elm** and **Lake Dallas**). There are four reservoirs above Fort Worth: **Lake Worth**, **Eagle Mountain** and **Bridgeport** on the West Fork and **Benbrook Lake** on the Clear Fork.

Lake Lavon in southeast Collin County and **Lake Ray Hubbard** in Collin, Dallas, Kaufman and Rockwall counties are on the East Fork. **Lake Livingston** is in Polk, San

Jacinto, Trinity and Walker counties. The three major reservoirs below the Dallas-Fort Worth area are **Cedar Creek Reservoir** and **Richland-Chambers Reservoir**.

Neches River

The Neches is in East Texas, with total length of about 416 miles and drainage area of 10,011 square miles. Abundant rainfall over its entire basin gives it an average annual flow near the Gulf of about 6 million acre-feet a year. The river takes its name from the **Neches Indians** that the early Spanish explorers found living along its banks. Principal tributary of the Neches, and comparable with the Neches in length and flow above their confluence, is the **Angelina River**, so named from **Angelina (Little Angel)**, a Hainai Indian girl who converted to Christianity and played an important role in the early development of this region.

Both the Neches and the Angelina run most of their courses in the **Piney Woods** and there was much settlement along them as early as the 1820s. **Sam Rayburn Reservoir**, near Jasper on the Angelina River, was completed and dedicated in 1965. Reservoirs located on the Neches River include **Lake Palestine** in the upper basin and **B. A. Steinhagen Lake** located at the junction of the Neches and the Angelina rivers.

Sabine River

The Sabine River is formed by three forks rising in Collin and Hunt counties. From its sources to its mouth on **Sabine Lake**, it flows approximately 360 miles and drains 7,426 square miles. Sabine comes from the **Spanish word** for cypress, as does the name of the **Sabinal River**, which flows into the Frio in Southwest Texas. The Sabine has the **largest average annual water discharge at its mouth of any Texas river**: 6.8 million acre-feet.

Throughout most of Texas history the lower Sabine has been the **eastern Texas boundary line**, though for a while there was doubt as to whether the Sabine or the Arroyo Hondo, east of the Sabine in Louisiana, was the boundary. For a number of years the outlaw-infested **neutral ground** lay between them. There was also a **boundary dispute** in which it was alleged that the Neches was really the Sabine and, therefore, the boundary.

Travelers over the part of the **Camino Real** known as the **Old San Antonio Road**, crossed the Sabine at the **Gaines Ferry**, and there were crossings for the **Atascosito Road** and other travel and trade routes of that day.

Two of Texas' largest man-made reservoirs have been created by dams on the Sabine River. The first of these is **Lake Tawakoni**, in Hunt, Rains and Van Zandt counties, with a capacity of 927,440 acre-feet. **Toledo Bend Reservoir** impounds 4,477,000 acre-feet of water on the Sabine in Newton, Panola, Sabine and Shelby counties. This is a joint project of Texas and Louisiana, through the **Sabine River Authority**.

Red River

The Red River (1,360 miles) is **exceeded in length only by the Rio Grande** among rivers associated with Texas. Its original source is water in Curry County, New Mexico, near the Texas boundary, forming a definite channel as it crosses Deaf Smith County, Texas, in tributaries that flow into **Prairie Dog Town Fork of the Red River**. These waters carve the spectacular **Palo Duro Canyon** of the High Plains before the Red River leaves the **Caprock Escarpment**, flowing eastward.

Where the Red River crosses the 100th meridian, the river becomes the **Texas-Oklahoma boundary** and is soon joined by the Salt Fork to form the main channel. Its length across the Panhandle is about 200 miles and, from the Panhandle east, it is the Texas-Oklahoma boundary line for 440 miles and thereafter the **Texas-Arkansas boundary** for 40 miles before it flows into Arkansas, where it swings south to flow through Louisiana.

The Red River, which drains 24,463 square miles, is a part of the **Mississippi drainage basin**, and at one time it emptied all of its water into the Mississippi. In recent years, however, part of its water, especially at flood stage, has flowed to the Gulf via the **Atchafalaya**.

The Red River takes its name from the red color of the current. This caused every explorer who came to its banks to call it "red" regardless of the language he spoke — Río **Rojo** or **Río Roxo** in Spanish, **Riviere Rouge** in French and **Red River** in English.

The Spanish and French names were often found on maps until the mid-19th century when English came to be generally accepted. At an early date, the river became the axis for French advance from Louisiana northwestward as far as present-day Montague County. There was consistent **early navigation** of the river from its mouth on the Mississippi to Shreveport, above which navigation was blocked by a **natural log raft**.

A number of important gateways into Texas from the North were established along the stream such as **Pecan Point** and **Jonesborough** in Red River County, **Colbert's Ferry** and **Preston** in Grayson County and, later, Doan's **Store Crossing** in Wilbarger County.

The river was a menace to the early traveler because of both its variable current and its **quicksands**, which brought disaster to many a trail-herd cow as well as ox team and covered wagon.

The largest water conservation project on the Red River is **Lake Texoma**, which is the **largest lake** lying wholly or partly in Texas and the **10th-largest reservoir (in capacity) in the United States**. Its total storage at the top of flood pool is 5,382,000 acre feet. Texas' share is 2,643,300.

Red River water's high content of salt and other minerals limits its usefulness along its upper reaches. Ten **salt springs** and tributaries in Texas and Oklahoma contribute most of these minerals.

The uppermost tributary of the Red River in Texas is **Tierra Blanca Creek**, which rises in Curry County, N.M., and flows easterly across Deaf Smith and Randall counties to become the **Prairie Dog Town Fork** a few miles east of Canyon. Other principal tributaries in Texas are the Pease and the **Wichita** in North Central Texas and the Sulphur in Northeast Texas, which flows into the Red River after it has crossed the boundary line into Arkansas.

The last major tributary in Northeast Texas is **Cypress Creek**, which flows into Louisiana before joining with the Red River. Major reservoirs on the Northeast Texas tributaries are **Wright Patman Lake, Lake O' the Pines** and **Caddo Lake**. From Oklahoma the principal tributary is the **Washita**. The **Ouachita**, a river with the same pronunciation of its name, though spelled differently, is the principal tributary to its lower course. The Red River boundary dispute, a long-standing feud between Oklahoma and Texas, was finally settled in 2000.

Canadian River

The Canadian River heads near **Raton Pass** in northern New Mexico near the Colorado boundary line and flows into Texas on the west line of Oldham County. It crosses the Texas Panhandle into Oklahoma and there flows into the Arkansas. It drains 12,700 square miles, and most of its course across the Panhandle is in a deep gorge.

A tributary dips into Texas' northern Panhandle and then flows to a confluence with the main channel in Oklahoma. One of several theories as to how the Canadian got its name is that some early explorers thought it flowed into Canada. **Lake Meredith**, formed by **Sanford Dam** on the Canadian, provides water for 11 Panhandle cities.

Because of the **deep gorge** and the **quicksand** that occurs in many places, the Canadian River has been a particularly difficult stream to bridge. It is known, especially in its lower course in Oklahoma, as outstanding among the streams of the country for the great amount of quicksand in its channel. ☆

Artificial Lakes and Reservoirs

Sources: U.S. Geological Survey, Texas Water Development Board, New Handbook of Texas, Texas Parks & Wildlife, U.S. Army Corps of Engineers, previous Texas Almanacs, various river basin authorities, Websites of owner of reservoirs.

The large increase in the number of reservoirs in Texas during the past half-century has greatly improved water conservation and supplies.

As late as 1913, Texas had only four major reservoirs with a total storage capacity of 277,600 acre-feet. Most of this capacity was in Medina Lake in southwest Texas, with 254,000 acre-feet* capacity, created by a dam completed in May 1913.

By January 2007, Texas had 196 major reservoirs (those with a normal capacity of 5,000 acre-feet or larger) existing, with a total conservation surface area of 1,666,856 acres and a conservation storage capacity of 37,179,139 acre-feet.

According to the U.S. Statistical Abstract of 2001, Texas has **4,959 square miles of inland water**, ranking it first in the 48 contiguous states, followed by Minnesota, with 4,780 sq. mi.; Florida, 4,683; and Louisiana, 4,153. There are about **6,736 reservoirs** in Texas with a normal storage capacity of 10 acre-feet or larger.

The following table lists reservoirs in Texas having more than 5,000 acre-feet capacity. With few exceptions, the listed reservoirs are those that were completed by Jan. 1, 2003. Reservoirs that are normally dry are in italics. Some industrial cooling reservoirs are not included.

Conservation storage capacity as of 2005 is used in the table below; the surface area used is that area at conservation elevation only. Because sediment deposition constantly reduces reservoir volumes over time, these are figures from the most recent surveys available. (Different methods of computing capacity area are used, and detailed information may be obtained from the **Texas Water Development Board**, Austin, from the **U.S. Army Corps of Engineers**, or from local sources.) It should be noted that boundary reservoir capacities include water designated for Texas use and non-Texas water, as well.

In the list below, information is in the following order: (1) Name of lake or reservoir; (2) year of first impounding of water; (3) county or counties in which located; (4) river or creek on which located; (5) location with respect to some city or town; (6) purpose of reservoir; (7) owner of reservoir.

Some of these items, when not listed, are not available. For the larger lakes and reservoirs, the dam impounding water to form the lake bears the same name, unless otherwise indicated. ☆

*An acre-foot is the amount of water necessary to cover an acre of surface area with water one foot deep.

The **years** *in the table below refer to first impounding of water.*

Caddo Lake— *In November 1873, the U.S. Army used nitroglycerin charges to remove the last portion of the Red River raft, a natural logjam. This resulted in the gradual depletion of Caddo water. In 1914, a dam was completed near Mooringsport, La. In 1971, a larger replacement dam was completed.*

Lake Austin — *In 1893, the first dam was completed. It broke in 1900. In 1915, a second dam was built but not completed. In 1939, the present Tom Miller Dam was completed.*

Other **double years** *refer to later, larger dams.*

Abbreviations in the list below are: L., lake; R., river; Co., county; Cr., creek; (C) conservation; (FC) flood control; (R) recreation; (P) power; (M) municipal; (D) domestic; (Ir.) irrigation; (In.) industry; (Mi.) mining, including oil production; (FH) fish hatchery; USAE, United States Army Corps of Engineers; WC&ID, Water Control and Improvement District; WID, Water Improvement District; USBR, United States Bureau of Reclamation; Auth., Authority; LCRA, Lower Colorado River Authority; USDA, United States Department of Agriculture; Imp., impounded.☆

Natural Lakes

There are many natural lakes in Texas, though none is of great size. The largest designated natural lake touching the border of Texas is Sabine Lake, into which the Sabine and Neches rivers discharge. It is more properly a bay of the Gulf of Mexico. Also near the coast, in Calhoun County, is Green Lake, which at about 10,000 acre-feet is one of the state's largest natural freshwater lakes.

Caddo Lake, on the Texas-Louisiana border, was a natural lake originally, but its present capacity and surface area are largely due to dams built to raise the surface of the original body of water. Natural Dam Lake, in Howard County, has a similar history.

In East Texas are many small natural lakes formed by "horse-shoe" bends that have been eliminated from the main channel of a river. There are also a number of these "horse-shoe" lakes along the Rio Grande in the lower valley, where they are called resacas.

On the South Plains and west of San Angelo are lakes, such as Big Lake in Reagan County, that are usually dry.

Fall colors shimmer at Raven Lake in Huntsville State Park in Walker County. Ron Billings photo; Texas Forest Service.

Lakes and Reservoirs, Date of Origin	Surface Area (Acres)	Storage Capacity (Acre-Ft.)
Abilene, L. — (1919) Taylor Co.; Elm Cr.; 6 mi. NW Tuscola; (M-In.-R); City of Abilene	595	7,900
Addicks Reservoir — *(1948) Harris Co.; South Mayde Cr.; 1 mi. E of Addicks; (FC only) USAE*.............	16,423	200,800
Alan Henry, L.— (1993) Garza Co.; Double Mountain Fork Brazos River; 10 mi. E Justiceburg; (M-In.-Ir.); City of Lubbock	2,741	94,808
Alcoa L. — (1952) Milam Co.; Sandy Cr.; 7 mi. SW Rockdale; (In.-R); Alcoa Aluminum (also called Sandow L.)	914	15,650
Amistad Reservoir, International — (1969) Val Verde Co.; Rio Grande; an international project of the U.S. and Mexico; 12 mi. NW Del Rio; (C-R-Ir.-P-FC); International Boundary and Water Com. (Texas'share of conservation capacity is 56.2 percent.) (Formerly Diablo R.).....................	64,900	3,150,267
Amon G. Carter, L. — (1961) Montague Co.; Big Sandy Cr.; 6 mi. S Bowie; (M-In.); City of Bowie..........	1,540	20,050
Anahuac, L. — (1936, 1954) Chambers Co.; Turtle Bayou; near Anahuac; (Ir.-In.-Mi.); Chambers-Liberty Counties Navigation District. (also called Turtle Bayou Reservoir)......................................	5,035	33,348
Anzalduas Channel Dam — Hidalgo Co.; Rio Grande; 11 mi. upstream from Hidalgo; (Ir.-FC); United States and Mexico...	1,472	13,910
Aquilla L. — (1983) Hill Co.; Aquilla Cr.; 10.2 mi. W of Hillsboro; (FC-M-Ir.-In.-R); USAE-Brazos R. Auth	3,020	45,319
Arlington, L. — (1957) Tarrant Co.; Village Cr.; 7 mi. W Arlington; (M-In.); City of Arlington	1,939	38,785
Arrowhead, L. — (1966) Clay-Archer counties.; Little Wichita R.; 13 mi. SE Wichita Falls; (M); City of Wichita Falls	14,969	235,997
Athens, L. — (1962) Henderson Co.; 8 mi. E Athens; (M-FC-R); Athens Mun. Water Authority (formerly Flat Creek Reservoir)	1,799	29,475
Austin, L. — (1893, 1915, 1939) Travis Co.; Colorado R.; W Austin city limits; (M-In.-P); City of Austin, leased to LCRA (Imp. by Tom Miller Dam)..	1,599	21,725
Ballinger/Moonen, L. — (1947) Runnels Co.; Valley Creek; 5 mi. W Ballinger; (M); City of Ballinger.......	500	6,850
Balmorhea, L. — (1917) Reeves Co.; Sandia Cr.; 3 mi. SE Balmorhea; (Ir.); Reeves Co. WID No. 1	573	6,350
Bardwell L. — (1965) Ellis Co.; Waxahachie Cr.; 3 mi. SE Bardwell; (FC-C-R); USAE.............................	3,138	46,472
Barker Reservoir — *(1945) Harris Co.; above Buffalo Bayou ; (FC only) USAE.*	16,739	209,000
Bastrop, L. — (1964) Bastrop Co.; Spicer Cr.; 3 mi. NE Bastrop; (In.); LCRA...	906	16,590
Baylor Creek L. — (1950) Childress Co.; 10 mi. NW Childress; (M-R); City of Childress	610	9,220
Belton L. — (1954) Bell-Coryell counties; Leon R.; 3 mi. N. Belton; (M-FC-In.-Ir.); USAE-Brazos R. Auth..	12,135	435,225
Benbrook L. — (1952) Tarrant Co.; Clear Fk. Trinity R.; 10 mi. SW Fort Worth; (FC-R); USAE 3,635......	3,635	85,648
Big Creek Reservoir — (1987) Delta Co; Big Creek; 1 mi. N Cooper; (M); City of Cooper....................	512	4,890
Bivins L. — (1927) Randall Co.; Palo Duro Cr.; 8 mi. NW Canyon; (M); Amarillo; City of Amarillo (also called Amarillo City Lake)...	379	5,120
Bob Sandlin, L. — (1977) Titus-Wood-Camp-Franklin counties; Big Cypress Cr.; 5 mi. SW Mount Pleasant; (In.-M-R); Titus Co. FWSD No. 1 (Imp. by Fort Sherman Dam)	9,004	204,678
Bonham, L. — (1969) Fannin Co.; Timber Cr.; 5 mi. NE Bonham; (M); Bonham Mun. Water Auth.	1,012	11,038
Brady Creek Reservoir — (1963) McCulloch Co.; Brady Cr.; 3 mi. W Brady; (M-In.); City of Brady........	2,020	30,430
Brandy Branch Reservoir — (1983) Harrison Co.; Brandy Br.; 10 mi. SW Marshall; (In.); AEP- Southwestern Electric Power Co..	1,242	29,513
Braunig L., Victor — (1962) Bexar Co.; Arroyo Seco; 15 mi. SE San Antonio; (In.); Pub. Svc. Bd./San Antonio..	1,350	26,500
Brazoria Reservoir — (1954) Brazoria Co.; off-channel reservoir; 1 mi. NE Brazoria; (In.); Dow Chemical Co...	1,865	21,970
Bridgeport, L. (1922) Wise-Jack counties; W. Fk. of Trinity R.; 4 mi. W Bridgeport; (M-In.-FC-R); Tarrant Regional Water Dist.	11,954	366,236
Brownwood, L. — (1933) Brown Co.; Pecan Bayou; 8 mi. N Brownwood; (M-In.-Ir.); Brown Co. WC&ID No. 1..	7,298	131,429
Bryan L. — (1977) Brazos Co.; unnamed stream; 6 mi. NW Bryan; (R-In.); City of Bryan	829	15,227
Buchanan, L. — (1937) Burnet-Llano-San Saba counties; Colorado R.; 13 mi. W Burnet; (M-Ir.-Mi-P); LCRA...	22,333	885,507
Buffalo Lake — (1938) Randall Co.; Tierra Blanca Cr.; 2 mi. S. Umbarger; (R); U.S. Fish and Wildlife Service; (Imp. by Umbarger Dam)	1,900	18,150
Caddo L. — (1873, 1914, 1971) Harrison-Marion counties, Texas and Caddo Parish, La. An original natural lake, whose surface and capacity were increased by construction of dams	26,800	129,000
Calaveras L. — (1969) Bexar Co.; Calaveras Cr.; 15 mi. SE San Antonio; (In.); Pub. Svc. Bd. of San Antonio..	3,624	63,200
Camp Creek L. — (1949) Robertson Co.; 13 mi. E Franklin; (R); Camp Creek Water Co.	750	7,000
Canyon L. — (1964) Comal Co.; Guadalupe R.; 12 mi. NW New Braunfels; (M-In.-P-FC); Guadalupe- Blanco R. Authority & USAE..	8,308	378,852
Casa Blanca L. — (1951) Webb Co.; Chacon Cr.; 3 mi. NE Laredo; (R); Webb Co.; (Imp. by Country Club Dam)...	1,680	20,000
Cedar Creek Reservoir — (1965) Henderson-Kaufman counties; Cedar Cr.; 3 mi. NE Trinidad; (M-R); Tarrant Regional Water Dist.; (also called Joe B. Hogsett, L.)...	32,873	640,415
Champion Creek Reservoir — (1959) Mitchell Co.; 7 mi. S. Colorado City; (M-In.); City of Colorado City..	1,560	42,500
Cherokee, L. — (1948) Gregg-Rusk counties; Cherokee Bayou; 12 mi. SE Longview; (M-In.-R); Cherokee Water Co...	3,467	43,737
Choke Canyon Reservoir — (1982) Live Oak-McMullen counties; Frio R.; 4 mi. W Three Rivers; (M-In.-R-FC); City of Corpus Christi-USBR	25,989	695,271
Cisco, L. — (1923) Eastland Co.; Sandy Cr.; 4 mi. N. Cisco; (M); City of Cisco (Imp. by Williamson Dam)..	445	8,800
Cleburne, L. Pat — (1964) Johnson Co.; Nolan R.; 4 mi. S. Cleburne; (M); City of Cleburne	1,558	25,730

Lakes and Reservoirs, Date of Origin	Surface Area (Acres)	Storage Capacity (Acre-Ft.)
Clyde, L. — (1970) Callahan Co.; N. Prong Pecan Bayou; 6 mi. S. Clyde; (M); City of Clyde and USDA Soil Conservation Service	449	5,748
Coffee Mill L. — (1939) Fannin Co.; Coffee Mill Cr.; 12 mi. NW Honey Grove; (R); U.S. Forest Service	650	8,000
Coleman, L. — (1966) Coleman Co.; Jim Ned Cr.; 14 mi. N. Coleman; (M-In.); City of Coleman	1,864	38,094
Coleto Creek Reservoir — (1980) Goliad–Victoria counties; Coleto Cr.; 12 mi. SW Victoria; (In); Guadalupe–Blanco River Auth.	3,100	31,040
Colorado City, L. — (1949) Mitchell Co.; Morgan Cr.; 4 mi. SW Colorado City; (M-In.-P); TXU	1,612	31,805
Conroe, L. — (1973) Montgomery-Walker counties; W. Fk. San Jacinto R.; 7 mi. NW Conroe; (M-In.-Mi.); San Jacinto River Authority, City of Houston and Texas Water Dev. Bd.	20,118	416,228
Cooper, L./Olney— (1953) Archer Co.; Mesquite Crk; 8 mi. E Megargel; (W-R); City of Olney; (see L. Olney)	446	6,650
Cooper Lake— (1991) Delta-Hopkins counties; Sulphur R.; 3 mi.SE Cooper; (FC-M-R); USAE; (also called Jim Chapman Lake)	19,305	310,312
Corpus Christi, L. — (1930) Live Oak-San Patricio-Jim Wells counties; Nueces R.; 4 mi. SW Mathis; (P-M-In.-Ir.-Mi.-R.); Lower Nueces River WSD (Imp. by Wesley E. Seale Dam)	18,256	257,463
Cox Creek Reservoir — Calhoun Co.; Cox Creek; 2 mi. E Point Comfort; (In); Alcoa Alumninum; (Also called Raw Water Lake and Recycle Lake)	541	5,034
Crook, L. — (1923) Lamar Co.; Pine Cr.; 5 Mi. N. Paris; (M); City of Paris	1,060	9,260
Cypress Springs, L. — (1970) Franklin Co.; Big Cypress Cr.; 8 mi. SE Mount Vernon; (In-M); Franklin Co. WD and Texas Water Development Board (formerly Franklin Co. L.); (Imp. by Franklin Co. Dam)	3,461	67,690
Daniel, L. — (1948) Stephens Co.; Gunsolus Cr.; 7 mi. S Breckenridge; (M-In.); City of Breckenridge; (Imp. by Gunsolus Creek Dam)	924	9,515
Davis, L. — Knox Co.; Double Dutchman Cr.; 5 mi. SE Benjamin; (Ir); League Ranch	585	5,454
Delta Lake Res. Units 1 and 2 — (1939) Hidalgo Co.; Rio Grande (off channel); 4 mi. N. Monte Alto; (Ir.); Hidalgo-Willacy counties WC&ID No. 1 (formerly Monte Alto Reservoir)	2,371	14,000
Diversion, L. — (1924) Archer-Baylor counties; Wichita R.; 14 mi. W Holliday; (M-In.); City of Wichita Falls and Wichita Co. WID No. 2	3,133	33,420
Dunlap, L. — (1928) Guadalupe Co.; Guadalupe R.; 9 mi. NW Seguin; (P); Guadalupe-Blanco R. Auth.; (Imp. by TP-1 Dam)	410	5,900
Eagle L. — (1900) Colorado Co.; Colorado R. (off channel; in Eagle Lake; (Ir.); Lakeside Irrigation Co.	1,200	9,600
Eagle Mountain Lake — (1934) Tarrant-Wise counties; W. Fk. Trinity R.; 14 mi. NW Fort Worth; (M-In.-Ir.); Tarrant Regional Water Dist.	8,702	182,505
Eagle Nest Lake — (1951) Brazoria Co.; off-channel Brazos R.; 12 mi. WNW Angleton; (Ir.); T.M. Smith, et al. (also called Manor Lake)	—	18,000
Eastman Lakes — 8 lakes; Harrison Co.; Sabine R. basin; NW of Longview; Texas Eastman Co.	—	8,135
Electra, L. — (1950) Wilbarger Co.; Camp Cr. and Beaver Cr.; 7 mi. SW Electra; (In.-M); City of Electra	731	5,626
Ellison Creek Reservoir — (1943) Morris Co.; Ellison Cr.; 8 mi. S. Daingerfield; (P-In.); Lone Star Steel	1,516	24,700
Fairfield L. — (1970) Freestone Co.; Big Brown Cr.; 11 mi. NE Fairfield; (In.); TXU; (formerly Big Brown Creek Reservoir)	2,159	44,169
Falcon Reservoir, International — (1954) Starr-Zapata counties; Rio Grande; (International— U.S.-Mexico); 3 mi. W Falcon Heights; (M-In.-Ir.-FC-P-R); International Boundary and Water Com.; (Texas' share of total conservation capacity is 58.6 per cent)	86,843	2,653,760
Fayette Co. Reservoir — (1958) Fayette Co.; Cedar Cr.; 8.5 mi. E. La Grange; (In.); LCRA (also called Cedar Creek Reservoir)	2,400	71,400
Forest Grove Reservoir — (1982) Henderson Co.; Caney Cr.; 7 mi. NW Athens; (In.); TXU, Agent	1,502	20,038
Fort Phantom Hill, Lake — (1938) Jones Co.; Elm Cr.; 5 mi. S. Nugent; (M-R); City of Abilene	4,213	70,036
Georgetown, L. — (1980) Williamson Co.; N. Fk. San Gabriel R.; 3.5 mi. W Georgetown; (FC-M-In.); USAE	1,287	36,904
Gibbons Creek Reservoir — (1981) Grimes Co.; Gibbons Cr.; 9.5 mi NW Anderson; (In.); Texas Mun. Power Agency	2,770	32,084
Gilmer Reservoir — (2001) Upshur Co.; Kelsey Creek; 15 mi. N of Longview; 4 mi. W of Gilmer; (M); City of Gilmer	1,010	12,720
Gladewater, L. — (1952) Upshur Co.; Glade Cr.; in Gladewater; (M-R); City of Gladewater	481	4,738
Gonzales, Lake — (1931) Gonzales Co.; Guadalupe R.; 4.5 mi. SE Belmont; (P); Guadalupe-Blanco R. Auth. (also called H-4 Reservoir)	696	6,500
Graham, L. — (1929) Young Co.; Flint and Salt Creeks; 2 mi. NW Graham; (M-In.); City of Graham	2,444	45,302
Granbury, L. — (1969) Hood Co.; Brazos R.; 8 mi. SE Granbury; (M-In.-Ir.-P); Brazos River Authority (Imp. by DeCordova Bend Dam)	7,945	129,011
Granger L. — (1980) Williamson Co.; San Gabriel R.; 10 mi. NE Taylor; (FC-M-In.); USAE (formerly Laneport L.)	4,064	52,525
Grapevine L. — (1952) Tarrant-Denton counties; Denton Cr.; 2 mi. NE Grapevine; (M-FC-In.-R.); USAE	6,893	164,703
Greenbelt L. — (1967) Donley Co.; Salt Fk. Red R.; 5 mi. N Clarendon; (M-In.); Greenbelt M&I Water Auth.	2,025	60,400
Greenville City Lakes — 6 lakes; Hunt Co.; Conleech Fork, Sabine R.; 2 mi. Greenville; (M-Other); City of Greenville	—	6,864
Halbert, L. — (1921) Navarro Co.; Elm Cr.; 4 mi. SE Corsicana; (M-In-R); City of Corsicana	603	6,033
Harris Reservoir, William — (1947) Brazoria Co.; off-channel between Brazos R. and Oyster Cr.; 8 mi. NW Angleton; (In.); Dow Chemical Co.	1,663	9,200
Hawkins, L. — (1962) Wood Co.; Little Sandy Cr.; 3 mi. NW Hawkins; (FC-R); Wood County; (Imp. by Wood Co. Dam No. 3)	800	11,890
Holbrook, L. — (1962) Wood Co.; Keys Cr.; 4 mi. NW Mineola; (FC-R); Wood County; (Imp. by Wood Co. Dam No. 2)	653	7,990
Hords Creek L. — (1948) Coleman Co.; Hords Cr.; 5 mi. NW Valera; (M-FC); City of Coleman and USAE	510	5,684

Lakes and Reservoirs, Date of Origin	Surface Area (Acres)	Storage Capacity (Acre-Ft.)
Houston, L. — (1954) Harris Co.; San Jacinto R.; 4 mi. N Sheldon; (M-In.-Ir.-Mi.-R); City of Houston	11,854	133,990
Houston County L. — (1966) Houston Co.; Little Elkhart Cr.; 10 mi. NW Crockett; (M-In.); Houston Co. WC&ID No. 1	1,330	17,665
Hubbard Creek Reservoir — (1962) Stephens Co.; 6 mi. NW Breckenridge; (M-In.-Mi.); West Central Texas Mun. Water Authority	14,992	324,983
Imperial Reservoir — (1912) Reeves-Pecos counties; Pecos R.; 35 mi. N Fort Stockton; (Ir.); Pecos County WC&ID No. 2	1,530	6,000
Inks L. — (1938) Burnet-Llano counties; Colorado R.; 12 mi. W Burnet; (M-Ir.-Mi.-P); LCRA	831	14,878
Jacksonville, L. — (1959) Cherokee Co.; Gum Cr.; 5 mi. SW Jacksonville; (M-R); City of Jacksonville; (Imp. by Buckner Dam)	1,164	25,732
J. B. Thomas, L. — (1952) Scurry-Borden counties; Colorado R.; 16 mi. SW Snyder; (M- In.-R); Colorado River Mun. Water Dist.; (Imp. by Colorado R. Dam)	7,282	200,604
J. D. Murphree Wildlife Management Area Impoundments — Jefferson Co.; off-channel reservoirs between Big Hill and Taylor bayous; at Port Acres; (FH-R); TP&WD (formerly Big Hill Reservoir)	6,881	32,000
Joe Pool Reservoir — (1986) Dallas-Tarrant-Ellis counties; Mountain Cr.; 14 mi. SW Dallas; (FC-M-R); USAE-Trinity River Auth. (formerly Lakeview Lake)	7,470	176,900
Johnson Creek Reservoir — (1961) Marion Co.; 13 mi. NW Jefferson; (In.); AEP-Southwestern Electric Power Co.	650	10,100
Kemp, L. — (1923) Baylor Co.; Wichita R.; 6 mi. N Mabelle; (M-P-Ir.); City of Wichita Falls; Wichita Co. WID 2	15,357	245,434
Kickapoo, L. — (1945) Archer Co.; N. Fk. Little Wichita R.; 10 mi. NW Archer City; (M); City of Wichita Falls	6,028	85,825
Kiowa, L. — (1967) Cooke Co.; Indian Cr.; 8 mi. SE Gainesville; (R); Lake Kiowa, Inc.	560	7,000
Kirby, L. — (1928) Taylor Co.; Cedar Cr.; 5 mi. S. Abilene; (M); City of Abilene	740	7,620
Kurth, L. — (1950) Angelina Co.; off-channel reservoir; 8 mi. N Lufkin; (In.); Abitibi Consolidated Industries.	726	14,769
Lake Creek L. — (1952) McLennan Co.; Manos Cr.; 4 mi. SW Riesel; (In.); TXU	550	8,400
Lake Fork Reservoir — (1980) Wood-Rains counties; Lake Fork Cr.; 5 mi. W Quitman; (M-In.); Sabine River Authority	27,264	636,133
Lake O' the Pines — (1959) Marion-Upshur-Morris counties; Cypress Cr.; 9 mi. W Jefferson; (FC-C-R-In.-M); USAE (Imp. by Ferrell's Bridge Dam)	17,677	241,081
Lavon, L. — (1953) Collin Co.; East Fk. Trinity R.; 2 mi. W Lavon; (M-FC-In.); USAE	21,400	456,526
Leon, Lake — (1954) Eastland Co.; Leon R.; 7 mi. S Ranger; (M-In.); Eastland Co. Water Supply Dist...	1,590	27,290
Lewis Creek Reservoir — Montgomery Co.; Lewis Cr.; 10 mi. NW Conroe; (In.); Gulf States Util. Co. ...	1,010	16,400
Lewisville L. — (1929, 1954) Denton Co.; Elm Fk. Trinity R.; 2 mi. NE Lewisville; (M-FC-In.-R); USAE; (also called Lake Dallas and Garza-Little Elm)	29,592	543,988
Limestone, L. — (1978) Leon-Limestone-Robertson cos.; Navasota R.; 7 mi. NW Marquez; (M-In.-Ir.); Brazos River Authority	12,553	208,017
Livingston, L. — (1969) Polk-San Jacinto-Trinity-Walker counties; Trinity R.; 6 mi. SW Livingston; (M-In.-Ir.); City of Houston and Trinity River Authority	83,277	1,741,867
Loma Alta Lake — Cameron Co.; off-channel Rio Grande; 8 mi. NE Brownsville; (M-In.); Brownsville Navigation Dist.	2,490	26,500
Lost Creek Reservoir — (1990) Jack Co.; Lost Cr.; 4 mi. NE Jacksboro; (M); City of Jacksboro	368	11,961
Lyndon B. Johnson, L. — (1951) Burnet-Llano counties; Colorado R.; 5 mi. SW Marble Falls; (P); LCRA; (Imp. by Alvin Wirtz Dam); (formerly Granite Shoals L.)	6,534	134,353
Mackenzie Reservoir — (1974) Briscoe Co.; Tule Cr.; 9 mi. NW Silverton; (M); Mackenzie Mun. Water Auth.	896	46,450
Marble Falls, L. — (1951) Burnet Co.; Colorado R.; 1.25 mi. SE Marble Falls; (P); LCRA; (Imp. by Max Starcke Dam)	611	6,420
Martin Creek L. — (1974) Rusk-Panola counties; Martin Cr.; 17 mi. NE Henderson; (P); TXU.	4,981	75,116
Medina L. — (1913) Medina-Bandera counties; Medina R.; 8 mi. W Rio Medina; (Ir.); Bexar- Medina-Atascosa Co. WID No. 1	6,066	254,843
Meredith, L. — (1965) Moore-Potter-Hutchinson counties; Canadian R.; 10 mi. NW Borger; (M-In.- FC-R); cooperative project for municipal water supply by Amarillo, Lubbock and other High Plains cities. Canadian R. Municipal Water Authority-USBR; (Imp. by Sanford Dam)	16,411	817,970
Millers Creek Reservoir — (1990) Baylor-Throckmorton counties.; Millers Cr.; 9 mi. SE Goree; (M); North Central Texas Mun. Water Auth. and Texas Water Development Board	2,268	29,171
Mineral Wells, L. — (1920) Parker Co.; Rock Cr.; 4 mi. E Mineral Wells; (M); Palo Pinto Co. Mun. WD No. 1	440	7,065
Mitchell County Reservoir — (1993) Mitchell Co.; branch of Beals Creek; (Mi.-In.); Colorado River MWD	1,463	27,266
Monticello Reservoir — (1972) Titus Co.; Blundell Cr.; 2.5 mi. E. Monticello; (In.); TXU	2,001	34,740
Moss L., Hubert H. — (1960) Cooke Co.; Fish Cr.; 10 mi. NW Gainesville; (M-In.); City of Gainesville....	1,140	24,155
Mountain Creek L. — (1937) Dallas Co.; Mountain Cr.; 4 mi. SE Grand Prairie; (In.); TXU.	2,170	22,840
Murvaul L. — (1958) Panola Co.; Murvaul Bayou; 10 mi. W Carthage; (M-In.-R); Panola Co. Fresh Water Supply Dist. No. 1	3,529	38,284
Mustang Lake East/West — Brazoria Co.; Mustang Bayou; 6 mi. S Alvin; (Ir.-In.-R); Chocolate Bayou Land & Water Co.	—	6,451
Nacogdoches, L. — (1976) Nacogdoches Co.; Bayo Loco Cr.; 10 mi. W Nacogdoches; (M); City of Nacogdoches	2,212	39,523
Nasworthy, L. — (1930) Tom Green Co.; S Concho R.; 6 mi. SW San Angelo; (M-In.-Ir); City of San Angelo	1,380	10,108
Natural Dam L. — (1957, 1989) Howard Co.; Sulphur Springs Draw; 8 mi. W Big Spring; An original natural lake, whose surface and capacity were increased by construction of dams; (FC); Wilkinson Ranch & Colorado River MWD	3,605	54,560

Lakes and Reservoirs, Date of Origin	Surface Area (Acres)	Storage Capacity (Acre-Ft.)
Navarro Mills L. — (1963) Navarro-Hill counties; Richland Cr.; 16 mi. SW Corsicana; (M-FC); USAE	5,070	55,817
Nocona, L.— (1960) Montague Co.; 8 mi. NE Nocona; (M-In.-Mi.); No. Montague County Water Supply District (also known as Farmers Creek Reservoir)	1,362	21,749
North Fk. Buffalo Creek Reservoir — (1964) Wichita Co.; 5 mi. NW Iowa Park; (M); Wichita Co. WC&ID No.3.	1,392	15,400
North L. — (1957) Dallas Co.; S. Fork Grapevine Cr.; 2 mi. SE Coppell; (In.); TXU	800	17,000
Oak Creek Reservoir — (1952) Coke Co.; 5 mi. SE Blackwell; (M-In.); City of Sweetwater	2,375	39,360
O. C. Fisher L. — (1952) Tom Green Co.; N. Concho R.; 3 mi. NW San Angelo; (M-FC-C- Ir.-R-In.-Mi); USAE —Upper Colo. River Auth. (formerly San Angelo L.)	5,440	79,483
O. H. Ivie Reservoir — (1990) Coleman-Concho-Runnels counties; 24 mi. SE Ballinger; (M-In.), Colorado R. Mun. Water Dist. (formerly Stacy Reservoir)	19,149	554,340
Olmos Reservoir — (1926) Bexar Co.; Olmos Cr.; in San Antonio; (FC only), City of San Antonio	1,050	15,500
Olney, L./Cooper— (1935) Archer Co.; Mesquite Crk; 8 mi. E Megargel; (W-R); City of Olney; (see L. Cooper)	446	6,650
Palestine, L. — (1962) Anderson-Cherokee-Henderson-Smith counties; Neches R.; 4 mi. E Frankston; (M-In.-R); Upper Neches R. MWA (Imp. by Blackburn Crossing Dam)	22,656	373,202
Palo Duro Reservoir — (1991) Hansford Co.; Palo Duro Cr.; 12 mi. N Spearman; (M-R); Palo DuroRiver Auth.	2,413	60,897
Palo Pinto, L. — (1964) Palo Pinto Co.; 15 mi. SW Mineral Wells; (M-In.); Palo Pinto Co. Muni. Water Dist. 1	2,498	27,650
Pat Mayse L. — (1967) Lamar Co.; Sanders Cr.; 2 mi. SW Arthur City; (M-In.-FC); USAE	5,940	118,110
Pinkston Reservoir — (1976) Shelby Co.; Sandy Cr.; 12.5 mi. SW Center; (M); City of Center; (formerly Sandy Creek Reservoir)	523	7,380
Possum Kingdom L. — (1941) Palo Pinto-Young-Stephens-Jack counties; Brazos R.; 11 mi. SW Graford; (M-In.-Ir.-Mi.-P-R); Brazos R. Authority; (Imp. by Morris Sheppard Dam)	16,716	540,340
Proctor L. — (1963) Comanche Co.; Leon R.; 9 mi. NE Comanche; (M-In.-Ir.-FC); USAE- Brazos River Auth.	4,537	55,457
Quitman, L. — (1962) Wood Co.; Dry Cr.; 4 mi. N Quitman; (FC-R); Wood County (Imp. by Wood Co. Dam No.1)	814	7,440
Randell L. — (1909) Grayson Co.; Shawnee Cr.; 4 mi. NW Denison; (M); City of Denison	280	6,290
Ray Hubbard, L. — (1968) Collin-Dallas-Kaufman-Rockwall counties; (formerly Forney Reservoir); E. Fk. Trinity R.; 15 mi. E Dallas; (M); City of Dallas	20,963	452,040
Ray Roberts, L. — (1987) Denton-Cooke-Grayson counties; Elm Fk. Trinity R.; 11 mi. NE Denton; (FC-M-D); City of Denton, Dallas, USAE; (also known as Aubrey Reservoir)	25,350	798,758
Red Bluff Reservoir — (1937) Loving-Reeves counties, Texas; and Eddy Co.; N.M.; Pecos R.; 5 mi. N Orla; (Ir.-P); Red Bluff Water Power Control District.	11,193	289,670
Red Draw Reservoir — (1985) Howard Co.; Red Draw; 5 mi. E Bi Spring; (Mi.-In.); Colorado River MWD	374	8,538
Richland-Chambers Reservoir — (1987) Freestone-Navarro counties; Richland Cr.; 20 mi. SE Corsicana; (M); Tarrant Regional Water Dist.	41,356	1,136,600
Rita Blanca, L. — (1940) Hartley Co.; Rita Blanca Cr.; 2 mi. S Dalhart; (R) City of Dalhart	524	12,100
River Crest L. — (1953) Red River Co.; off-channel reservoir; 7 mi. SE Bogata; (In.); TXU	555	7,000
Sam Rayburn Reservoir — (1965) Jasper-Angelina-Sabine-Nacogdoches-San Augustine counties; Angelina R.; (FC-P-M-In.-Ir.-R); USAE; (formerly McGee Bend Reservoir)	112,590	2,876,033
San Bernard Reservoirs #1, #2, #3 — Brazoria Co.; Off-Channel San Bernard R.; 3 mi. N Sweeney; (In.); ConocoPhillips	—	8,610
Santa Rosa L. — (1929) Wilbarger Co.; Beaver Cr.; 15 mi. S Vernon; (Mi.); W. T. Waggoner Estate	1,500	11,570
Sheldon Reservoir — (1943) Harris Co.; Carpenters Bayou; 2 mi. SW Sheldon; (R-FH); TP&WD	1,244	4,224
Smithers L. — (1957) Fort Bend Co.; Dry Creek; 10 mi. SE Richmond; (In.); Reliant Energy HL&P	2,480	18,700
Somerville L. — (1967) Burleson-Washington-Lee counties; Yegua Cr.; 2 mi. S Somerville; (M-In.-Ir.- FC); USAE-Brazos River Authority	11,555	147,104
South Texas Project Reservoir — (1983) Matagorda Co.; off-channel Colorado R.; 16 mi. S Bay City; (In.); Reliant Energy HL&P	7,000	202,600
Spence Reservoir, E. V. — (1969) Coke Co.; Colorado R.; 2 mi. W. Robert Lee; (M-In.-Mi); Colorado R. Mun. Water Dist.; (Imp. by Robert Lee Dam)	14,640	517,272
Squaw Creek Reservoir — (1983) Somervell-Hood counties; Squaw Cr.; 4.5 mi. N Glen Rose; (In.); TXU	3,297	151,418
Stamford, L. — (1953) Haskell Co.; Paint Cr.; 10 mi. SE Haskell; (M-In.); City of Stamford	5,124	51,573
Steinhagen L., B. A. — (1951) Tyler-Jasper counties; Neches R.; 1/2 mi. N Town Bluff; (FC-R-C); USAE (also called Town Bluff Reservoir and Dam B. Reservoir);(Imp. by Town Bluff Dam)	10,687	66,972
Stillhouse Hollow L. — (1968) Bell Co.; Lampasas R.; 5 mi. SW Belton; (M-In.-Ir.-FC); USAE- Brazos River Authority; (also called Lampasas Reservoir).	6,484	227,825
Striker Creek Reservoir — (1957) Rusk-Cherokee counties; Striker Cr.; 18 mi. SW Henderson; (M -In.); Angelina-Nacogdoches WC&ID No. 1.	1,920	22,865
Sulphur Springs, L. — (1950) Hopkins Co.; White Oak Cr.; 2 mi. N Sulphur Springs; (M); Sulphur Springs WD; (formerly called White Oak Creek Reservoir).	1,340	17,838
Sulphur Springs Draw Reservoir — (1992) Martin Co.; Sulphur Springs Draw; 12 mi. NE Stanton; (FC); Colorado River MWD.	970	7,997
Sweetwater, L. — (1930) Nolan Co.; Bitter Creek; 6 mi. SE Sweetwater (M-R); City of Sweetwater	630	11,900
Tawakoni, L. — (1960) Rains-Van Zandt-Hunt counties; Sabine R.; 9 mi. NE Wills Point; (M-In.-Ir-R); Sabine River Authority; (Imp. by Iron Bridge Dam)	37,879	888,140
Terrell City L. — (1955) Kaufman Co.; Muddy Cedar Cr.; 6 mi. E Terrell; (M-R); City of Terrell	830	8,594
Texana, L. — (1980) Jackson Co.; Navidad R. and Sandy Cr.; 6.8 mi. SE Edna; (M-Ir); USBR, Lavaca-Navidad R. Auth., Texas Water Dev. Bd.; (formerly Palmetto Bend Reservoir)	9,727	161,085

Ratcliff Lake in Davy Crockett National Forest. Ron Billings photo; Texas Forest Service.

Lakes and Reservoirs, Date of Origin	Surface Area (Acres)	Storage Capacity (Acre-Ft.)
Texoma, L. — (1943) Grayson-Cooke cos., Texas; Bryan-Marshall-Love cos., Okla.; (Imp. by Denison Dam) on Red R. below confluence of Red and Washita rivers; (P-FC-C-R); USAE	74,686	2,516,232
Toledo Bend Reservoir — (1967) Newton-Panola-Sabine-Shelby counties; Sabine R.; 14 mi. NE Burkeville; (M-In.-Ir.-PR); Sabine River Authority (Texas' share of capacity is half amount shown)	181,600	4,477,000
Town Lake — (1960) Travis Co.; Colorado R.; within Austin city limits; (R); City of Austin	477	6,248
Tradinghouse Creek Reservoir — (1968) McLennan Co.; Tradinghouse Cr.; 9 mi. E Waco; (In.); TXU..	2,010	37,800
Travis, L. — (1942) Travis-Burnet counties; Colorado R.; 13 mi. NW Austin; (M-In.-Ir.- Mi.-P-FC-R); LCRA: (Imp. by Mansfield Dam)	18,622	1,132,172
Trinidad L. — (1923) Henderson Co.; off-channel reservoir Trinity R.; 2 mi. S. Trinidad; (P); TXU.	740	6,200
Truscott Brine L. — (1987) Knox Co.; Bluff Cr.; 26 mi. NNW Knox City; (Chlorine Control); Red River Auth.	3,146	111,147
Twin Buttes Reservoir — (1963) Tom Green Co.; Concho R.; 8 mi. SW San Angelo; (M-In. -FC-Ir.-R.); City of San Angelo-USBR-Tom Green Co. WC&ID No. 1	9,080	186,200
Twin Oaks Reservoir — (1982) Robertson Co.; Duck Cr.; 12 mi. N. Franklin; (In) TXU	2,330	30,319
Tyler, L. /Lake Tyler East — (1949/1907) Smith Co.; Prairie and Mud Creeks.; 12 mi. SE Tyler; (M-In); City of Tyler; (Imp. by Whitehouse and Mud Creek dams)	4,800	80,198
Upper Nueces L. — (1926, 1948) Zavala Co.; Nueces R.; 6 mi. N Crystal City; (Ir.); Zavala-Dimmit Co. WID No. 1	316	5,200
Valley Acres Reservoir — (1956) Hidalgo Co.; off-channel Rio Grande; 7 mi. N Mercedes; (Ir-M-FC); Valley Acres Water Dist.	325	1,950
Valley L. — (1961) Fannin-Grayson counties; 2.5 mi. N Savoy; (P); TXU; (formerly Brushy Creek Reservoir)	1,080	16,400
Waco, L. — (1929) McLennan Co.; Bosque R.; 2 mi. W Waco; (M-FC-C-R); City of Waco-USAE Brazos River Authority	7,194	144,830
Walter E. Long, L. — (1967) Travis Co.; Decker Cr.; 9 mi. E Austin; (M-In.-R); City of Austin; (formerly Decker Lake)	1,269	33,940
Waxahachie, L. — (1956) Ellis Co.; S Prong Waxahachie Cr.; 4 mi. SE Waxahachie; (M-In); Ellis County WC&ID No. 1; (Imp. by S. Prong Dam)	656	11,386
Weatherford, L. — (1956) Parker Co.; Clear Fork Trinity River; 7 mi. E Weatherford; (M-In.); City of Weatherford	1,158	18,714
Welsh Reservoir — (1976) Titus Co.; Swauano Cr.; 11 mi. SE Mount Pleasant; (R-In.); AEP-Southwestern Electric Power Co.; (formerly Swauano Creek Reservoir)	1,269	20,242
White River L. — (1963) Crosby Co.; 16 mi. SE Crosbyton; (M-In.-Mi.); White River Municipal Water Dist.	1,642	31,846
White Rock L. — (1911) Dallas Co.; White Rock Cr.; within NE Dallas city limits; (R); City of Dallas	1,088	9,004
Whitney, L. — (1951) Hill-Bosque-Johnson counties; Brazos R.; 5.5 mi. SW Whitney; (FC-P); USAE	23,220	554,203
Wichita, L. — (1901) Wichita Co.; Holliday Cr.; 6 mi. SW Wichita Falls; (M-P-R); City of Wichita Falls	2,200	14,000
Winnsboro, L. — (1962) Wood Co.; Big Sandy Cr.; 6 mi. SW Winnsboro; (FC-R); Wood County; (Imp. by Wood Co. Dam No. 4)	806	8,100
Winters, L. — (1983) Runnels Co.; Elm Cr.; 4.5 mi. E Winters; (M); City of Winters (also known as Elm Creek Lake and New Lake Winters)	643	8,374
Worth, L. — (1914) Tarrant Co.; W. Fk. Trinity R.; in NW Fort Worth; (M); City of Fort Worth	3,458	33,495
Wright Patman L. — (1957) Bowie-Cass-Morris-Titus-Red River counties; Sulphur R.; 8 mi. SW Texarkana; (FC-M); USAE; (formerly Texarkana Lake)	18,994	110,099

Texas Plant Life

This article was updated for the Texas Almanac by Stephan L. Hatch, Director, S.M. Tracy Herbarium and Professor, Dept. of Rangeland Ecology and Management, Texas A&M University.

Vegetational Diversity

Variations in amount and frequency of rainfall, in soils and in frost-free days, gives Texas a great variety of vegetation. From the forests of East Texas to the deserts of West Texas, from the grassy plains of North Texas to the semi-arid brushlands of South Texas, plant species change continuously.

More than 100 million acres of Texas are devoted to providing grazing for domestic and wild animals. This is the **largest single use for land in the state**. More than 80 percent of the acreage is devoted to range in the Edwards Plateau, Cross Timbers and Prairies, South Texas Plains and Trans-Pecos Mountains and Basins.

Sideoats grama, which occurs on more different soils in Texas than any other native grass, was officially designated as the **state grass of Texas** by the Texas Legislature in 1971.

The 10 principal plant life areas of Texas, starting in the east, are:

1. Pineywoods

Most of this area of some 16 million acres ranges from about 50 to 700 feet above sea level and receives 40 to 56 inches of rain yearly. Many rivers, creeks and bayous drain the region. Nearly all of Texas' commercial timber comes from this area. There are three native species of pine, the principal timber: longleaf, shortleaf and loblolly. An introduced species, the **slash pine**, also is widely grown. Hardwoods include **oaks, elm, hickory, magnolia, sweet and black gum, tupelo** and others.

The area is interspersed with **native and improved grasslands**. Cattle are the primary grazing animals. Deer and **quail** are abundant in properly managed localities. Primary forage plants, under proper grazing management, include species of the **bluestems, rossettegrass, panicums, paspalums, blackseed needlegrass, Canada and Virginia wildryes, purpletop, broadleaf and spike woodoats, switchcane, lovegrasses, indiangrass** and numerous **legume** species.

Highly disturbed areas have understory and overstory of undesirable woody plants that suppress growth of pine and desirable grasses. The primary forage grasses have been reduced and the grasslands have been invaded by **threeawns, annual grasses, weeds, broomsedge bluestem, red lovegrass** and shrubby woody species.

2. Gulf Prairies and Marshes

The Gulf Prairies and Marshes cover approximately 10 million acres. There are two subunits: (a) The marsh and salt grasses immediately at tidewater, and (b) a little farther inland, a strip of bluestems and tall grasses, with some grains in the western part. Many of these grasses make excellent grazing.

Oaks, elm and other hardwoods grow to some extent, especially along streams, and the area has some post oak and brushy extensions along its borders. Much of the Gulf Prairies is fertile farmland. The area is well suited for cattle.

Principal grasses of the Gulf Prairies are **tall bunchgrasses**, including **big bluestem, little bluestem, seacoast bluestem, indiangrass, eastern gamagrass, Texas wintergrass, switchgrass** and **gulf cordgrass**. **Saltgrass** occurs on moist saline sites.

Heavy grazing has changed the native vegetation in many cases so the predominant grasses are the less desirable **broomsedge bluestem, smutgrass, threeawns, tumblegrass** and many other inferior grasses. Other

Loblolly pines are plentiful in the East Texas pineywoods. Ron Billings photo; Texas Forest Service.

plants that have invaded the productive grasslands include **oak underbrush, Macartney rose, huisache, mesquite, prickly pear, ragweed, bitter sneezeweed, broomweed** and others.

Vegetation of the Gulf Marshes consists primarily of **sedges, bullrush, flat-sedges, beakrush** and other rushes, **smooth cordgrass, marshhay cordgrass, marsh millet** and **maidencane**. The marshes are grazed best during winter.

3. Post Oak Savannah

This secondary forest area, also called the **Post Oak Belt**, covers some 7 million acres. It is immediately west of the primary forest region, with less annual rainfall and a little higher elevation. Principal trees are **post oak, blackjack oak** and **elm. Pecans, walnuts** and other kinds of water-demanding trees grow along streams. The southwestern extension of this belt is often poorly defined, with large areas of prairie.

The upland soils are **sandy and sandy loam**, while the bottomlands are **sandy loams and clays**.

The original vegetation consisted mainly of **little bluestem, big bluestem, indiangrass, switchgrass, purpletop, silver bluestem, Texas wintergrass, spike woodoats, longleaf woodoats, post oak** and **blackjack oak**. The area is still largely native or improved grasslands, with small farms located throughout. Intensive grazing has contributed to dense stands of a woody understory of **yaupon, greenbriar** and **oak** brush.

Mesquite has become a serious problem. Good forage plants have been replaced by such plants as **splitbeard bluestem, red lovegrass, broomsedge bluestem, broomweed, bullnettle** and **western ragweed**.

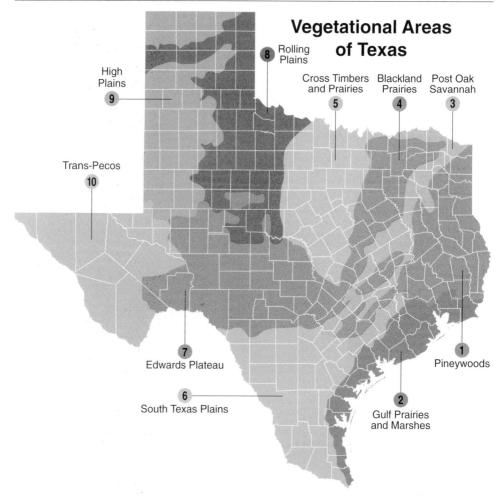

Vegetational Areas of Texas

8 Rolling Plains

High Plains 9

Cross Timbers and Prairies 5

Blackland Prairies 4

Post Oak Savannah 3

Trans-Pecos 10

Edwards Plateau 7

South Texas Plains 6

Pineywoods 1

Gulf Prairies and Marshes 2

4. Blackland Prairies

This area of about 12 million acres, while called a "prairie," has much timber along the streams, including a variety of **oaks, pecan, elm, horse-apple (bois d'arc)** and **mesquite**. In its native state it was largely a grassy plain — the first native grassland in the westward extension of the Southern Forest Region.

Most of this fertile area has been cultivated, and only small acreages of grassland remain in original vegetation. In heavily grazed pastures, the tall bunchgrass has been replaced by **buffalograss, Texas grama** and other less productive grasses. **Mesquite, lotebush** and other woody plants have invaded the grasslands.

The original grass vegetation includes **big** and **little bluestem, indiangrass, switchgrass, sideoats grama, hairy grama, tall dropseed, Texas wintergrass** and **buffalograss**. Non-grass vegetation is largely legumes and composites.

5. Cross Timbers and Prairies

Approximately 15 million acres of alternating woodlands and prairies, often called the **Western Cross Timbers**, constitute this region. Sharp changes in the vegetational cover are associated with different soils and topography, but the grass composition is rather uniform.

The prairie grasses are **big bluestem, little bluestem, indiangrass, switchgrass, Canada wildrye, sideoats grama, hairy grama, tall grama, tall dropseed, Texas wintergrass, blue grama** and **buffalograss**.

On the Cross Timbers soils, the vegetation is composed of **big bluestem, little bluestem, hooded windmillgrass, sand lovegrass, indiangrass, switchgrass** with many species of legumes. The woody vegetation includes **shinnery, blackjack, post** and **live oaks**.

The entire area has been invaded heavily by woody brush plants of oaks, mesquite, juniper and other unpalatable plants that furnish little forage for livestock.

6. South Texas Plains

South of San Antonio, between the coast and the Rio Grande, are some 21 million acres of subtropical dryland vegetation, consisting of small trees, shrubs, cactus, weeds and grasses. The area is noteworthy for extensive brushlands, known as the **brush country**, or the Spanish equivalents of **chaparral** or **monte**. Principal plants are **mesquite, small live oak, post oak, prickly pear (Opuntia) cactus, catclaw, blackbrush, whitebrush, guajillo, huisache, cenizo** and others which often grow very densely.

The original vegetation was mainly perennial warm-season **bunchgrasses** in **post oak, live oak** and **mesquite savannahs**. Other brush species form dense thickets on the ridges and along streams. Long-continued grazing has contributed to the dense cover of brush. Most of the desirable grasses have only persisted under the protection of brush and cacti.

There are distinct differences in the original plant communities on various soils. Dominant grasses on the sandy loam soils are **seacoast bluestem, bristlegrass, paspalum, windmillgrass, silver bluestem, big sandbur** and **tanglehead**. Dominant grasses on the clay and clay loams are **silver bluestem, Arizona cottontop, buffalograss, common curlymesquite, bristlegrass, pappusgrass, gramas, plains lovegrass, Texas cupgrass, vinemesquite**, other **panicums** and **Texas wintergrass**.

Low saline areas are characterized by **gulf cordgrass, saltgrass, alkali sacaton and switchgrass**. In the post oak and live oak savannahs, the grasses are mainly **seacoast bluestem, indiangrass, switchgrass, crinkleawn, paspalums** and **panicums**. Today much of the area has been reseeded to **buffelgrass**.

7. Edwards Plateau

These 25 million acres are rolling to mountainous, with woodlands in the eastern part and grassy prairies in the west. There is a good deal of brushy growth in the central and eastern parts. The combination of grasses, weeds and small trees is ideal for **cattle, sheep, goats, deer and wild turkey.**

This limestone-based area is characterized by the large number of **springfed, perennially flowing streams** which originate in its interior and flow across the Balcones **Escarpment**, which bounds it on the south and east. The soils are shallow, ranging from sands to clays and are calcareous in reaction. This area is predominantly rangeland, with cultivation confined to the deeper soils.

In the east-central portion is the well-marked **Central Basin** centering in Mason, Llano and Burnet counties, with a mixture of granitic and sandy soils. The western portion of the area comprises the semi-arid **Stockton Plateau**. Noteworthy is the growth of **cypress** along the perennially flowing streams. Separated by many miles from cypress growth of the moist Southern Forest Belt, they constitute one of Texas' several **"islands" of vegetation**. These trees, which grow to stately proportions, were commercialized in the past.

The principal grasses of the clay soils are **cane bluestem, silver bluestem, little bluestem, sideoats grama,** **hairy grama, indiangrass, common curlymesquite, buffalograss, fall witchgrass, plains lovegrass, wildryes** and **Texas wintergrass**.

The rocky areas support tall or mid-grasses with an overstory of **live oak, shinnery oak, juniper and mesquite**. The heavy clay soils have a mixture of **tobosagrass, buffalograss, sideoats grama and mesquite**.

Throughout the Edwards Plateau, **live oak, shinnery oak, mesquite** and **juniper** dominate the woody vegetation. Woody plants have invaded to the degree that they should be controlled before range forage plants can reestablish.

8. Rolling Plains

This is a region of approximately 24 million acres of alternating woodlands and prairies. The area is half **mesquite woodland** and half **prairie**. Mesquite trees have steadily invaded and increased in the grasslands for many years, despite constant control efforts.

Soils range from coarse sands along outwash terraces adjacent to streams to tight or compact clays on redbed clays and shales. Rough broken lands on steep slopes are found in the western portion. About two-thirds of the area is rangeland, but cultivation is important in certain localities.

The original vegetation includes **big, little, sand and silver bluestems, Texas wintergrass, indiangrass, switchgrass, sideoats and blue gramas, wildryes, tobosagrass** and **buffalograss** on the clay soils. The sandy soils support **tall bunchgrasses, mainly sand bluestem. Sand shinnery oak, sand sagebrush** and **mesquite** are the dominant woody plants.

Continued heavy grazing contributes to the increase in woody plants, low-value grasses such as **red grama, red lovegrass, tumblegrass, gummy lovegrass, Texas grama, sand dropseed and sandbur, with western ragweed, croton** and many other weedy forbs. **Yucca** is a problem plant on certain rangelands.

9. High Plains

The High Plains, some 19 million treeless acres, are an extension of the Great Plains to the north. The level nature and porous soils prevent drainage over wide areas.

Soils in Kendall County in the Hill Country support a large variety of trees and other vegetation. Robert Plocheck photo.

Wildflowers such as Indian Blanket grow along roadsides and in pastures in many parts of Texas. Natalie Caudill photo.

The relatively light rainfall flows into the numerous shallow **"playa" lakes** or sinks into the ground to feed the great **underground aquifer** that is the source of water for the countless wells that irrigate the surface of the plains. A large part of this area is under irrigated farming, but native grassland remains in about one-half of the High Plains.

Blue grama and **buffalograss** comprise the principal vegetation on the clay and clay loam "hardland" soils. Important grasses on the sandy loam "sandy land" soils are **little bluestem, western wheatgrass, indiangrass, switchgrass** and **sand reedgrass. Sand shinnery oak, sand sagebrush, mesquite** and **yucca** are conspicuous invading brushy plants.

10. Trans-Pecos, Mountains and Basins

With as little as eight inches of annual rainfall, long hot summers and usually cloudless skies to encourage evaporation, this 18-million-acre area produces only drought-resistant vegetation without irrigation. Grass is usually short and sparse.

The principal vegetation consists of **lechuguilla, ocotillo, yucca, cenizo, prickly pear** and other arid land plants. In the more arid areas, **gyp** and **chino grama**, and **tobosagrass** prevail. There is some **mesquite**. The vegetation includes **creosote-tarbush, desert shrub, grama grassland, yucca and juniper savannahs, pine oak forest and saline flats.**

The mountains are 3,000 to 8,751 feet in elevation and support **piñon pine, juniper** and some **ponderosa pine** and other forest vegetation on a few of the higher slopes. The grass vegetation, especially on the higher mountain slopes, includes many **southwestern and Rocky Mountain species** not present elsewhere in Texas. On the desert flats, black grama, burrograss and fluffgrass are frequent.

More productive sites have numerous species of **grama, muhly, Arizona cottontop, dropseed and perennial threeawn grasses**. At the higher elevations, plains **bristlegrass, little bluestem, Texas bluestem, sideoats grama, chino grama, blue grama, piñon ricegrass, wolftail** and several species of needlegrass are frequent.

The common invaders on all depleted ranges are **woody plants, burrograss, fluffgrass, hairy erioneuron, ear muhly, sand muhly, red grama, broom snakeweed, croton, cacti** and several poisonous plants. ☆

For Further Reading

Hatch, S.L., K.N. Gandhi and L.E. Brown, *Checklist of the Vascular Plants of Texas*; MP1655, Texas Agricultural Experiment Station, College Station, 1990.

Wildflowers grow near Round Top in Fayette County. Natalie Caudill photo.

Texas Forest Resources

Source: Texas Forest Service, The Texas A&M University System, Tarrow DR., Suite 364, College Station, TX 77840. On the Web: txforestservice.tamu.edu

Texas' forest resources are abundant and diverse. Forest land covers roughly 13 percent of the state's land area. The 21.5 million acres of forests and woodlands in Texas is an area larger than the states of Massachusetts, Connecticut, New Hampshire, Rhode Island and Vermont combined. **The principal forest and woodlands regions are:** the East Texas pine-hardwood region, often called the Piney Woods; the Post Oak Belt, which lies immediately west of the pine-hardwood forest; the Eastern and Western Cross Timbers areas of North Central Texas; the Cedar Brakes of Central Texas; the mountain forests of West Texas; and the coastal forests of the southern Gulf Coast.

East Texas Piney Woods

Although Texas' forests and woodlands are extensive, detailed forest resource data is available for only the 43-county East Texas timber region. The Piney Woods, which form the western edge of the southern pine region, extending from Bowie and Red River counties in northeast Texas to Jefferson, Harris and Waller counties in southeast Texas, contain 11.9 million acres of timberland and produce nearly all of the state's commercial timber. Following is a summary of the findings of the most recent Forest Inventory of East Texas, completed in 2006 by the Texas Forest Service in cooperation with the USDA Forest Service Southern Research Station.

Timberland Acreage and Ownership

Nearly all (11.9 million of 12.1 million acres) of the East Texas forest is classified as "timberland," which is suitable for production of timber products and not reserved as parks or wilderness areas. In contrast to the trends in several other Southern states, Texas timberland acreage increased by 1.3 percent between 1992 and 2006. The majority of the new timberland acres came from agricultural lands, such as idle farmland and pasture, which was either intentionally planted with trees or naturally reverted to forest.

Sixty-six percent of East Texas timberland is owned by approximately 210,000 private individuals, families, partnerships and non-wood-using corporations. Twenty-five percent is owned by forest-products companies and investment groups, and 9 percent is owned by the government. The following table shows acreage of timberland by ownership:

Ownership Class	Thous. Acres
Non-industrial Private	7,920.6
Forest Industry/Corporate	3,031.3
Public:	
National Forest	673.6
Misc. Federal	139.1
State	109.4
County & Municipal	53.7
Total	**11,927.7**

There are distinct regional differences in ownership patterns. Thirty-five percent of the timberland found south of Nacogdoches County is owned by forest industry and other corporations. North of Nacogdoches, the non-industrial private landowner predominates, owning 82 percent of the timberland, with industry owning a much smaller percent (13 percent).

Pine cones and seedlings in Davy Crocket National Forest. Ron Billings photo; Texas Forest Service.

Forest Types

Six major forest types are found in the East Texas Piney Woods. Two pine-forest types are most common. The loblolly-shortleaf and longleaf-slash forest types are dominated by the four species of southern yellow pine. In these forests, pine trees make up at least 50 percent of the trees.

Oak-hickory is the second most common forest type. These are upland hardwood forests in which oaks or hickories make up at least 50 percent of the trees, and pine species are less than 25 percent. Oak-pine is a mixed-forest type in which more than 50 percent of the trees are hardwoods, but pines make up 25–49 percent of the trees.

Two forest types, oak-gum-cypress and elm-ash-cottonwood, are bottomland types that are commonly found along creeks, river bottoms, swamps and other wet areas. The oak-gum-cypress forests are typically made up of many species including blackgum, sweetgum, oaks and southern cypress. The elm-ash-cottonwood bottomland forests are dominated by those trees but also contain many other species, such as willow, sycamore and maple. The following table shows the breakdown in acreage by forest type:

Forest Type Group	Thous. Acres
Southern Pine:	
Loblolly-shortleaf	4,756.6
Longleaf-slash	201.5
Oak-pine	1,582.2
Oak-hickory	3,040.9
Bottomland Hardwood:	
Oak-gum-cypress	1,324.9
Elm-ash-cottonwood	617.7
Other	403.9
Total	**11,927.7**

A loader gathers up logs in Angelina National Forest. Ron Billings photo; Texas Forest Service.

Southern pine plantations, established by tree planting and usually managed intensively to maximize timber production, are an increasingly important source of wood fiber. Texas forests include 2.3 million acres of pine plantations, 62 percent of which are on forest-industry-owned land, 34 percent on non-industrial private, and 4 percent on public land. Genetically superior tree seedlings, produced at industry and Texas Forest Service nurseries, are usually planted to improve survival and growth.

Timber Volume and Number of Trees

Texas timberland contains 15.9 billion cubic feet of timber "growing-stock" volume. One billion cubic feet of growing stock produces roughly enough lumber to build a 2,000 square foot home for one out of every three Texans. The inventory of softwood increased 15 percent from 8.1 billion cubic feet in 1992 to 9.2 billion cubic feet in 2006. The hardwood inventory increased to 6.67 billion cubic feet between 1992 and 2006.

There are an estimated 7.6 billion live trees in East Texas, according to the 2006 survey. This includes 2.2 billion softwoods and 5.4 billion hardwoods. The predominant species are loblolly and shortleaf pine; 2.1 billion pine trees are found in East Texas.

Timber Growth and Removals

Between 2003 and 2005, an annual average of 732.9 million cubic feet of growing stock timber was removed from the inventory either through harvest or land-use changes. Meanwhile, 1,022.8 million cubic feet of growing stock were added to the inventory through growth each year.

For pine, an average of 557.9 million cubic feet was removed during those years, while 665.6 million feet were added by growth. For hardwoods, 174.6 million feet were removed, while 346.4 million cubic feet were added by growth.

Other Tree Regions

Compared to commercially important East Texas, relatively little data are available for the other tree regions of Texas. However, these areas are environmentally important with benefits of wildlife habitat, improved water quality, recreation and aesthetics. A brief description of these areas (the Post Oak Belt, the Eastern and Western Cross Timbers, the Cedar Brakes, the Mountain Forests and the Coastal Forests) can be found in the descriptions of Texas' vegetation regions preceding this article.

The 2005 Timber Harvest

Total Removals

There was a 7.7 percent increase in total removal of growing stock in East Texas in 2005, including both pine and hardwood. The total volume removed from the 43-county region was 694.4 million cubic feet in 2005, compared to 644.8 million in 2004. Included in the total removal was timber harvested for industrial use and an estimate of logging residue and other timber removals.

By species group, the total removal comprised 555.3 million cubic feet of pine and 139.1 million cubic feet of hardwood. Pine removal was up 9.2 percent and hardwood removal was up 2.2 percent from 2004.

Industrial roundwood harvest in Texas, the portion of the total removal that was subsequently utilized in the manufacture of wood products, totaled 564.3 million cubic feet for pine and 137.2 million cubic feet for hardwood. The pine industrial roundwood harvest was up 9 percent and the hardwood roundwood harvest was up 2.8 percent from 2004. The combined harvest was up 7.7 percent to 701.4 million cubic feet. Top producing counties included Jasper, Polk, Hardin, Angelina, Cass and Newton.

Total Harvest Value

Stumpage value of the East Texas timber harvest in 2005 was $494.6 million, a 12.8-percent increase from 2004. The delivered value of timber was up 7.4 percent to $839.6 million. Pine timber accounted for 89.1 percent of the total stumpage value and 89.6 percent of the total delivered value.

The harvest of sawlogs for production of lumber was up by 8.6 percent in 2005 to 1.72 billion board feet. The pine sawlog cut totaled 1.47 billion board feet, up 13 percent, and the hardwood sawlog harvest decreased 11.6 percent to 250.7 million board feet. Cass, Jasper, Tyler, and Angelina counties were the top producers of sawlogs.

Timber cut for the production of structural panels, including both plywood and OSB and hardwood veneer, totaled 195.3 million cubic feet, a 7.4 percent increase from 2004. Polk, Tyler, Trinity, Panola, and Jasper counties were the top producers of veneer and panel roundwood.

Harvest of timber for manufacture of pulp and paper products rose 7.4 percent from 2004 to 2.78 million cords in 2005. Pine pulpwood made up 57.4 percent of the total pulpwood production in 2005. Jasper, Hardin, Cass, Polk, Newton and Liberty counties were the top producers of pulpwood.

Other roundwood harvest, including posts, poles and pilings, totaled 2.3 million cubic feet in 2005.

Import-Export Trends

Texas was a net exporter of timber products in 2005. The total import from other states was 63 million cubic feet while the total export was 87.9 million cubic feet. The net export was 3.5 percent of the total roundwood production in Texas.

Production of Forest Products

Lumber

Texas sawmills produced 1.96 billion board feet of lumber in 2005, an increase of 2.5 percent over 2004. Production of pine lumber rose 8.9 percent to 1.73 billion board feet in 2005 while hardwood lumber production dropped 29.1 percent, to 230.1 million board feet in 2005.

Texas Lumber Production, 1995–2005

Year	*Lumber Production	
	Pine	Hardwood
	(thousand board feet)	
1995	1,139,462	159,831
1996	1,248,627	175,570
1997	1,316,762	160,553
1998	1,293,432	191,165
1999	1,279,487	225,570
2000	1,410,999	184,172
2001	1,293,823	213,795
2002	1,425,613	223,932
2003	1,490,311	287,062
2004	1,591,109	324,663
2005	1,733,314	230,090

*Includes tie volumes.

Structural Panel Products

Production of structural panels, including plywood and OSB, increased to 2.85 billion square feet (3/8-inch basis) in 2004 and again to 3.24 billion square feet in 2005.

Texas Structural Panel Production, 1995–2005

Year	Pine (Thd. sq. ft.*)	Year	Pine (Thd. sq. ft.*)
1995	2,721,487	2001	2,732,940
1996	3,042,736	2002	2,818,356
1997	3,200,317	2003	2,723,225
1998	3,169,713	2004	2,859,012
1999	3,260,055	2005	3,249,558
2000	3,265,644	*3/8-inch basis	

Paper Products

Production of paperboard totaled 2.51 million tons in 2005, a 1.9 percent decline from 2004. There was no paper production due to the closure of a major paper mill by the end of 2002.

Texas Pulp, Paper and Paperboard Production, 1995–2005
(in short tons)

Year	Paper	Paperboard*	Total Paper Products
1995	1,159,677	2,317,212	3,476,889
1996	1,071,015	2,376,486	3,447,501
1997	1,116,018	2,052,153	3,168,171
1998	1,126,648	1,933,906	2,925,856
1999	1,079,397	1,979,592	3,058,989
2000	955,117	2,037,148	2,992,265
2001	599,902	2,083,326	2,683,228
2002	551,367	2,179,423	2,730,790
2003	255,462	2,170,185	2,425,647
2004	0	2,560,480	2,560,480
2005	0	2,512,262	2,512,262

*Includes fiberboard and miscellaneous products.

Treated Wood

There was a 24 percent decrease in the volume of wood processed by Texas wood treaters in 2005 from 2004. The total volume treated in 2005 was 41.0 million cubic feet. Among major treated products, lumber accounted for 47.4 percent of the total volume; crossties accounted for 28.8 percent; utility poles and switch ties each accounted for 8.1 percent and 9.6 percent, respectively.

Primary Mill Residue

Total mill residue, including chips, sawdust, shavings, and bark in primary mills such as sawmills, panel mills and chip mills in 2005 was 6.63 million short tons, a increase of 4.0 percent from 2004. Eighty-four percent of the residue was from pine species and 16 percent was from hardwood species. Chips accounted for 51.0 percent of mill residue, followed by bark (34.6 percent), sawdust (9.2 percent), and shavings (6.1 percent).

Reforestation

A total of 92,030 acres was planted during the winter 2005 and spring 2006 planting season, down 8 percent from 2004. Industrial landowners planted 64,457 acres in 2005, a 5,000-acre drop from 2004.

The non-industrial private forest (NIPF) landowners planted 26,710 acres in 2005, down 10 percent from 2004. Public landowners only planted 863 acres in 2005. The divestiture of industry lands into the non-industrial private sector will eventually lead to a sharp reduction in industry reforestation acreage. Non-industrial ownerships typically reforest less than industry.

A stand of slash pines in the E.O. Siecke State Forest in Newton County. Ron Billings photo; Texas Forest Service.

Fire Protection

After 515 days of wildfire response, Texas Forest Service closed the book Sept. 18, 2006, on the worst fire season on record for the state.

The rainfall that ended the fire season in Texas just prior to Sept 18 was the fifth consecutive front containing substantial rainfall to pass through the state. While they did not completely eliminate the threat of wildfires, the fronts served to moderate fire activity to a level well within local response capacity.

Prior to these rainfall events, the state of Texas experienced severe drought conditions requiring the Texas Forest Service to maintain large statewide fire response capabilities for most of 2005 and 2006. In addition to state and local resources, this included bringing in almost 4,000 out-of-state personnel and 500 pieces of equipment from all 50 states.

From Jan. 1, 2005, to Sept. 18, 2006, there were 29,141 wildfires that took 19 lives, burned 2,260,240 acres, consumed 734 homes and cost the citizens of Texas more than $628 million in losses. The vast majority (85 percent) of these wildfires occurred within two miles of a community, with numerous fires burning through subdivisions, small towns and large cities such as Amarillo, San Antonio and Arlington.

Due to the response efforts of local, state and national firefighters, nearly 22,000 homes were saved from the direct threat of wildfires. In total, an estimated $3.5 billion in homes and property were saved.

Wildfire response in Texas is coordinated by the Texas Forest Service under the Texas Wildfire Protection Plan (TWPP). The TWPP is a life-saving, cost-effective solution emphasizing prevention; reduction of risks and hazardous conditions; pre-positioning of resources based on fire risk; local fire department capacity-building; rapid initial attack to wild-land fires; and unified operations with local, state and national responders.

Forest Pests

The Texas Forest Service Forest Pest Management office headquartered in Lufkin has a staff of trained forest health specialists (three entomologists) to assist Texans with tree pest problems. The southern pine beetle is the most destructive insect pest in the 12 million acres of commercial forests in East Texas. Typically, this bark beetle kills more timber annually than forest fires.

Currently, this destructive insect is at very low levels in East Texas and has been for the past several years. The Texas Forest Service coordinates all southern pine beetle control activity on state and private forestlands in Texas. These activities include detecting infestations from the air, checking infestations on the ground to evaluate the need for control, and notifying landowners and providing technical assistance when control is warranted.

Recent efforts have focused on prevention of southern pine beetle infestations. Since 2003, the Texas Forest Service has offered federal cost shares to private forest landowners in East Texas as an incentive to thin the young pine stands that are most susceptible to bark beetles. Thinning dense forests to promote vigorous tree growth is the preferred long-run method to reduce tree losses caused by bark beetles.

Although southern pine beetle populations currently are at low levels, other forest and tree pests are always present and Forest Pest Management personnel monitor their activity.

Extensive mortality of live oaks in Central Texas (generally some 60 counties between Dallas and San Antonio) is causing considerable public concern. A vascular wilt disease, called oak wilt, is the major cause of the live oak mortality. A suppression project, administered by Texas Forest Service Forest Pest Management personnel, provides technical assistance and education for affected landowners.

Forest Pest Management personnel also administer the Western Gulf Forest Pest Management Cooperative. Through this coop, applied research and technical assistance are provided to members for a variety of forest pests including cone and seed insects, regeneration insects, pine bark beetles, and Texas leaf-cutting ants.

Forest Pest Management personnel also coordinate and conduct an aerial photography program in East Texas. Color infrared aerial photographs are taken, scanned at 0.5-meter resolution, geo-rectified, and placed in quarter-quad format. These photos can then be used with geographic information system computer software for forest management work, fire suppression activities, planning, forest health activities and other uses.

Urban Forests

Texas is an urban state with three of the nation's 10 largest cities. In fact, just 15 of our 254 counties hold 64 percent, or 13 million, of our population. In addition, Texas grew by over 22 percent by adding about 3.9 mil-

lion new residents between 1990 and 2000 — almost all to our cities. Because an estimated 86 percent of Texans now live in urban areas, urban trees and forests play an even more important role in the lives of Texans.

Trees reduce the urban heat island effect by shading and evaporative cooling. They also purify the air by absorbing pollutants, slowing the chemical reactions that produce harmful ozone, and filtering dust. Urban forests reduce storm water runoff and soil erosion and buffer against noise, glare and strong winds, while providing habitat for urban wildlife.

Environmental benefits from a single tree may be worth more than $275 each year. The value to real estate and the emotional and psychological benefits of urban trees raise the value of our urban trees even higher. ☆

Total Timber Production and Value by County in Texas, 2005

County	Pine	Hardwood	Total	Stumpage Value	Delivered Value
		Cubic feet		Thousand dollars	
Anderson	9,521,559	3,576,609	13,098,168	$ 9,698	$ 16,140
Angelina	29,861,187	3,977,390	33,838,577	25,888	43,394
Bowie	8,000,855	6,940,972	14,941,827	9,459	15,295
Camp	1,594,938	612,638	2,207,576	1,693	2,720
Cass	28,577,722	10,594,875	39,172,597	25,860	43,955
Chambers	6,795,423	2,863,052	9,658,475	3,941	8,410
Cherokee	12,723,012	5,067,731	17,790,743	12,251	21,058
Franklin	245,716	197,384	443,100	301	542
Gregg	1,983,376	1,655,022	3,638,398	2,603	4,433
Grimes	2,703,333	71,710	2,775,043	2,568	4,006
Hardin	29,785,502	7,246,909	37,032,411	18,288	36,919
Harris	4,636,431	1,300,993	5,937,424	5,733	8,448
Harrison	21,924,821	6,270,445	28,195,266	20,242	33,795
Henderson	739,290	2,339,949	3,079,239	1,612	2,770
Houston	17,457,525	3,888,380	21,345,905	15,545	26,003
Jasper	47,828,936	4,402,446	52,231,382	30,733	58,607
Jefferson	1,098,201	213,600	1,311,801	1,134	1,768
Leon	959,314	672,750	1,632,064	1,436	2,166
Liberty	16,620,112	8,248,833	24,868,945	16,673	28,170
Madison	220,225	86,596	306,821	223	353
Marion	8,030,992	5,361,883	13,392,875	9,830	15,639
Montgomery	14,361,175	1,156,165	15,517,340	16,724	24,385
Morris	3,497,992	2,171,268	5,669,260	3,888	6,214
Nacogdoches	23,727,126	5,483,115	29,210,241	22,507	37,150
Newton	29,183,081	2,050,645	31,233,726	21,243	38,049
Orange	2,752,114	1,229,889	3,982,003	3,479	5,255
Panola	22,985,778	3,948,781	26,934,559	17,639	31,419
Polk	49,194,971	4,698,749	53,893,720	32,549	60,733
Red River	8,367,214	5,563,394	13,930,608	5,355	11,500
Rusk	13,611,290	2,852,679	16,463,969	13,034	21,587
Sabine	14,214,461	2,096,577	16,311,038	10,804	19,118
San Augustine	13,817,535	4,240,890	18,058,425	12,500	20,979
San Jacinto	16,975,654	1,099,856	18,075,510	19,262	28,275
Shelby	17,007,673	2,003,803	19,011,476	14,587	24,356
Smith	5,044,726	3,050,055	8,094,781	6,239	9,996
Titus	919,791	3,592,018	4,511,809	2,361	3,755
Trinity	17,480,764	1,628,765	19,109,529	12,829	22,918
Tyler	27,891,012	4,245,054	32,136,066	26,635	42,549
Upshur	9,898,404	7,883,131	17,781,535	12,566	19,821
Van Zandt	187,616	243,830	431,446	405	629
Walker	18,259,311	248,996	18,508,307	21,333	30,689
Waller	223,052	5,159	228,211	227	345
Wood	2,364,789	1,469,797	3,834,586	1,906	3,556
Other Counties	993,660	622,250	1,615,910	861	1,706
Totals	**564,267,659**	**137,175,033**	**701,442,692**	**$494,644**	**$839,576**

National Forests and Grasslands in Texas

Source: U.S. Forest Service, Lufkin and Albuquerque, NM; www.fs.fed.us/r8/texas/

There are four national forests and all or part of five national grasslands in Texas. These federally owned lands are administered by the U.S. Department of Agriculture Forest Service and by district rangers. The national forests cover 637,472 acres in parts of 12 Texas counties. The national grasslands cover 117,394 acres in six Texas counties. Two of these grasslands extend into Oklahoma, as well.

Supervision of the East Texas forests and the two North Texas grasslands is by the Forest Supervisor of the division known as the National Forests and Grasslands in Texas (415 S. 1st St., Ste. 110, Lufkin 75901-3801; 936-639-8501).

The three West Texas grasslands (Black Kettle, McClellan Creek and Rita Blanca) are administered by the Forest Supervisor in Albuquerque, NM, as units of the Cibola National Forest. The following list gives the name of the forest or grassland, the administrative district(s) for each, the acreage in each county and the total acreage.

A turtle is at home in LBJ National Grasslands. File photo.

National Forests in Texas

Angelina National Forest — Angelina Ranger District (Zavalla); Angelina County, 58,520 acres; Jasper, 21,013; Nacogdoches, 9,238; San Augustine, 64,389. Total, 153,160 acres.

Davy Crockett National Forest — Davy Crockett District (Ratcliff); Houston County, 93,320 acres; Trinity, 67,323. Total, 160,643 acres.

Sabine National Forest — Sabine District (Hemphill); Jasper County, 64 acres; Newton, 1,781; Sabine, 95,456; San Augustine, 4,287; Shelby, 59,218. Total, 160,806 acres.

Sam Houston National Forest — Sam Houston District (New Waverly); Montgomery County, 47,801 acres; San Jacinto, 60,639; Walker, 54,597. Total, 163,037 acres.

National Grasslands in Texas

North Texas

Lyndon B. Johnson National Grassland and Caddo National Grassland — District Ranger at Decatur; Fannin County, 17,873 acres; Montague, 61; Wise, 20,252. Total, 38,186 acres.

A road disappears into the woods at Angelina National Forest. Ron Billings photo; Texas Forest Service.

West Texas

Black Kettle National Grassland — Lake Marvin District Ranger in Cheyenne, Okla.; Hemphill County, 576 acres; Roger Mills County, Okla., 30,724 acres. Total, 31,300 acres.

McClellan Creek National Grassland — District Ranger in Cheyenne, Okla.; Gray County, 1,449 acres. Total, 1,449 acres.

Rita Blanca National Grassland — District Ranger at Clayton, NM; Dallam County, 77,183 acres; Cimarron County, Okla., 15,639 acres. Total, 92,822 acres.

Establishment of National Forests and Grasslands

National forests in Texas were established by invitation of the Texas Legislature by an Act of 1933, authorizing the purchase of lands in Texas for the establishment of national forests. President Franklin D. Roosevelt proclaimed these purchases on Oct. 15, 1936.

The national grasslands were originally submarginal Dust Bowl project lands, purchased by the federal government primarily under the Bankhead-Jones Farm Tenant Act (1937). Today they are well covered with grasses and native shrubs.

Uses of National Forests and Grasslands

The national forests are managed under the ecosystem management concept. Ecosystem management is a means to achieve sustainable conditions and provide wildlife and fish habitat, outdoor recreation, wilderness, water, wood, minerals and forage for public use while retaining the esthetic, historic and spiritual qualities of the land.

In 1960, the Multiple Use-Sustained Yield Act put into law what had been practiced on the National Forests in Texas for almost 30 years. This act emphasized that resources on public lands will be managed so that they are used in ways that best meet the needs of the people, that the benefits obtained will exist indefinitely, and that each natural resource will be managed in balance with other resources.

Forest management plans outline direction under ecosystem management, but even the most carefully planned system of management cannot foresee environmental or natural factors that can cause drastic changes in a forest. Fire, storms, insects and disease, for example, can prompt managers to deviate from land management plans and can alter the way a forest is managed.

Timber Production

About 486,000 acres of the national forests in Texas are suitable for timber production. Sales of sawtimber, pulpwood and other forest products are initiated to implement forest plans and objectives. The estimated net growth is more than 200 million board feet per year and is valued at $40 million. A portion of this growth is normally removed by cutting.

Forests and Grasslands in Texas

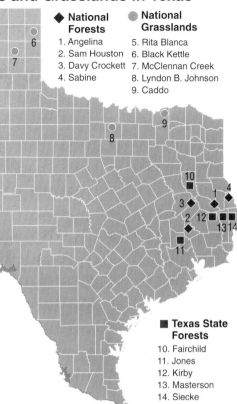

♦ **National Forests**
● **National Grasslands**

1. Angelina
2. Sam Houston
3. Davy Crockett
4. Sabine

5. Rita Blanca
6. Black Kettle
7. McClennan Creek
8. Lyndon B. Johnson
9. Caddo

■ **Texas State Forests**

10. Fairchild
11. Jones
12. Kirby
13. Masterson
14. Siecke

Cattle Grazing

Permits to graze cattle on national grasslands are granted to the public for an annual fee. About 600 head of cattle are grazed on the Caddo-Lyndon B. Johnson National Grasslands annually. On the Rita Blanca National Grasslands, 5,425 head of cattle are grazed each year, most of them in Texas.

Hunting and Fishing

State hunting and fishing laws and regulations apply to all national forest land. Game law enforcement is carried out by the Texas Parks and Wildlife. A wide variety of fishing opportunities are available on the Angelina, Sabine, Neches and San Jacinto rivers; the Sam Rayburn and Toledo Bend reservoirs; Lake Conroe; and many small streams. Hunting is not permitted on the McClellan Creek National Grassland nor at the Lake Marvin Unit of the Black Kettle National Grassland.

Recreational Facilities

An estimated 3 million people visit the recreational areas in the national forests and grasslands in Texas each year, primarily for picnicking, swimming, fishing, camping, boating and nature enjoyment.

The Sabine and Angelina National Forests are on the shores of Toledo Bend and Sam Rayburn Reservoirs, two large East Texas lakes featuring fishing and other water sports. Lake Conroe and Lake Livingston offer water-related outdoor recreation opportunities on and near the Sam Houston National Forest. These are listed in the Recreation section, beginning on page 170. ☆

Fog rises among loblolly pines in W. Goodrich Jones State Forest. Ron Billings photo; Texas Forest Service.

Texas State Forests

Source: Texas Forest Service, College Station, Texas; http://txforestservice.tamu.edu/

Texas has **five state forests**, all of which are used primarily for demonstration and research. Recreational opportunities, such as camping, hiking, bird-watching, and picnicking, are available in all but the Masterson forest.

I.D. Fairchild State Forest — Texas' largest forest is located west of Rusk in Cherokee County. This forest was transferred from the state prison system in 1925. Additional land was obtained in 1963 from the Texas State Hospitals and Special Schools for a total acreage of 2,740.

W. Goodrich Jones State Forest — Located south of Conroe in Montgomery County, it comprises 1,733 acres. It was purchased in 1926 and named for the founder of the Texas Forestry Association.

John Henry Kirby State Forest — This 600-acre forest in Tyler County was donated by lumberman John Henry Kirby in 1929, as well as later donors. Revenue from this forest is given to the Association of Former Students of Texas A&M University for student-loan purposes.

Paul N. Masterson Memorial Forest — Mrs. Leonora O'Neal Masterson of Beaumont donated this 519

Texas Forest Service personnel work at a TFS Command Center in Granbury in January 2006 during a wildfire outbreak. The center handles logistics to battle wildfires for two-thirds of the state. Brad Loper photo.

acres in Jasper County in 1984 in honor of her husband, who was a tree farmer and an active member of the Texas Forestry Association.

E.O. Siecke State Forest — The first state forest, it was purchased by the state in 1924. It contains 1,722 acres of pine land in Newton County. An additional 100 acres was obtained by a 99-year lease in 1946. ☆

Texas' Threatened and Endangered Species

Endangered species are those which the Texas Parks and Wildlife Department (TPWD) has named as being at risk of statewide extinction. Threatened species are those which are likely to become endangered in the future. The following species of Texas flora and fauna are either endangered or threatened as of July 15, 2007, according to the TPWD. This list varies slightly from the federal list. Any questions about protected species should be directed to the Endangered Resources Branch, Texas Parks and Wildlife, 4200 Smith School Road, Austin 78744; 1-800-792-1112; www.tpwd.state.tx.us/nature/endang/endang.htm

Endangered Species

Mammals
Bats: greater long-nosed and Mexican long-nosed bats. **Marine Mammels**: West Indian manatee; black right, blue, finback and sperm whales. **Carnivores**: black-footed ferret; jaguar; jaguarundi; ocelot; gray and red wolves.

Birds
Raptors: peregrine, American peregrine and northern aplomado falcons. **Shorebirds**: Eskimo curlew; interior least tern. **Upland Birds**: Attwater's greater prairie chicken. **Waterbirds**: Whooping crane; eastern brown pelican. **Woodpeckers**: ivory-billed and red-cockaded woodpeckers. **Songbirds**: southwestern willow flycatcher; black-capped vireo; Bachman's and golden-cheeked warblers.

The Texas horned lizard is a threatened species. Texas Parks & Wildlife photo.

Reptiles
Turtles: Atlantic hawksbill, leatherback and Kemp's ridley sea turtles.

Amphibians
Salamanders: Barton Springs and Texas blind salamanders. **Frogs & Toads**: Houston toad.

Fishes
Killifishes: Comanche Springs and Leon Springs pupfishes. **Livebearers**: Big Bend, Clear Creek, Pecos and San Marcos gambusias. **Minnows**: Rio Grande silvery minnow. **Perches**: Fountain darter.

Invertebrates
Crustaceans: Peck's cave amphipod. **Mollusks**: Ouachita rock pocketbook mussel.

Vascular Plants
Cacti: Black lace, Nellie Cory, Sneed pincushion, star and Tobusch fishhook cacti; Davis' green pitaya. **Grasses**: little aguja pondweed; Texas wild-rice. **Orchids**: Navasota ladies'-tresses. **Trees, Shrubs & Sub-shrubs**: Texas ayenia; Johnston's frankenia; Walker's manioc; Texas snowbells. **Wildflowers**: South Texas ambrosia; Zapata and white bladderpod; Terlingua Creek cat's-eye; ashy dogweed; Texas trailing phlox; Texas poppy-mallow; Texas prairie dawn; slender rush-pea; large-fruited sand verbena.

Threatened Species

Mammals
Bats: Rafinesque's big-eared, southern yellow, and spotted bats. **Carnivores**: black and Louisiana black bears; white-nosed coati; margay. **Marine Mammals**: Atlantic spotted and rough-toothed dolphins; dwarf sperm, false killer, Gervais' beaked, goose-beaked, killer, pygmy killer, pygmy sperm and short-finned pilot whales. **Rodents**: Palo Duro mouse; Coues' rice and Texas kangaroo rats.

Birds
Raptors: bald eagle; Arctic peregrine falcon; common black, gray, white-tailed and zone-tailed hawks; swallow-tailed kite; Mexican spotted owl; cactus ferruginous pygmy-owl. **Shorebirds**: piping plover; sooty tern. **Songbirds**: rose-throated becard; tropical parula; Bachman's, Texas Botteri's and Arizona Botteri's sparrows; northern beardless tyrannulet. **Waterbirds**: reddish egret; white-faced ibis; wood stork.

Reptiles
Lizards: reticulated gecko; mountain short-horned, reticulate collared and Texas horned lizards. **Snakes**: speckled racer; black-striped, Brazos water, Chihuahuan desert lyre, indigo, Louisiana pine, northern cat-eyed, smooth green, scarlet and Trans-Pecos black-headed snakes; timber (canebrake) rattlesnake. **Turtles**: loggerhead and green sea turtles; Texas tortoise; alligator snapping, Cagle's map and Chihuahuan mud turtles.

Amphibians
Salamanders: black-spotted newt; Blanco blind, Cascade Caverns, Comal blind and San Marcos salamanders; South Texas siren (large form). **Frogs & Toads**: sheep and white-lipped frogs; Mexican treefrog; Mexican burrowing toad.

Fishes
Catfishes: toothless blindcat and widemouth blindcat. **Coastal Fishes**: opossum pipefish; river and blackfin goby. **Large River Fish**: paddlefish and shovelnose sturgeon. **Livebearers**: blotched gambusia. Killifishes: Conchos and Pecos pupfishes. **Minnows**: Rio Grande chub; Devils River minnow; Arkansas River, bluehead, bluntnose, Chihuahua and proserpine shiners; Mexican stoneroller. **Perches**: blackside and Rio Grande darters. **Suckers**: blue sucker and creek chubsucker.

Vascular Plants
Cacti: Bunched cory, Chisos Mountains hedgehog and Lloyd's mariposa cacti. **Trees, Shrubs & Sub-shrubs**: Hinckley's oak. **Wildflowers**: Pecos Puzzle sunflower, tinytim. ☆

Texas Wildlife

Source: Texas Parks and Wildlife, Austin.

Texas has many native animals and birds, as well as introduced species. More than **540 species of birds** — about three fourths of all different species found in the United States — have been identified in Texas.

Some **142 species of animals**, including some that today are extremely rare, are found in Texas. A list of plant and animal species designated as threatened or endangered by state wildlife officials is found elsewhere in this chapter.

A few of the leading land mammals of Texas are described here. Those marked by an asterisk (*) are non-native species. Information was provided by the **Nongame and Urban Program**, Texas Parks and Wildlife, and updated using the online version of ***The Mammals of Texas*** by William B. Davis and David J. Schmidly: **www.nsrl.ttu.edu/tmot1/contents.htm**; the print version was published by Texas Parks and Wildlife Press, Austin, 1994. For additional wildlife information on the Web: **www.tpwd.state.tx.us/nature/wild/wild.htm**.

Mammals

Armadillo — The **nine-banded armadillo** *(Dasypus novemcinctus)* is one of Texas' most interesting mammals. It is found in most of the state except the western Trans-Pecos. It is now common as far north and east as Oklahoma and Mississippi.

Badger — The **badger** *(Taxidea taxus)* is found throughout the state, except the extreme eastern parts. It is a fierce fighter, and it is valuable in helping control the rodent population.

Bat — Thirty-two species of these winged mammals have been found in Texas, more than in any other state in the United States. Of these, 27 species are known residents, though they are seldom seen by the casual observer. The **Mexican**, or **Brazilian**, **free-tailed bat** *(Tadarida brasiliensis)* and the **cave myotis** *(Myotis velifer)* constitute most of the cave-dwelling bats of Southwest and West Texas. They have some economic value for their deposits of nitrogen-rich **guano**. Some commercial guano has been produced from **James River Bat Cave**, Mason County; **Beaver Creek Cavern**, Burnet County; and from large deposits in other caves including **Devil's Sinkhole** in Edwards County, **Blowout Cave** in Blanco County and **Bandera Bat Cave**, Bandera County. The largest concentration of bats in the world is found at **Bracken Cave** in Comal County, thought to hold between 20 and 40 million bats. The **big brown bat** *(Eptesicus fuscus)*, the **red bat** *(Lasiurus borealis)* and the **evening bat** *(Nycticeius humeralis)* are found in East and Southeast Texas. The evening and big brown bats are forest and woodland dwelling mammals.

Most of the rarer species of Texas bats have been found along the Rio Grande and in the Trans-Pecos. Bats can be observed at dusk near a water source, and many species may also be found foraging on insects attracted to street lights. Everywhere bats occur, they are the main predators of night-flying insects, including mosquitoes and many crop pests. On the Web: **www.batcon.org/**

Bear — The **black bear** *(Ursus americanus)*, formerly common throughout most of the state, is now surviving in remnant populations in portions of the Trans-Pecos.

Beaver — The **American beaver** *(Castor canadensis)* is found over most of the state except for the Llano Estacado and parts of the Trans-Pecos.

Bighorn — (See **Sheep**.)

Bison — The largest of native terrestrial wild mammals of North America, the **American bison** *(Bos bison)*, commonly called **buffalo**, was formerly found in the western two-thirds of the state. Today it is extirpated or confined on ranches. Deliberate slaughter of this majestic animal for hides and to eliminate the Plains Indians' main food source reached a peak about 1877-78, and the bison was almost eradicated by 1885. Estimates of the number of buffalo killed vary, but as many as 200,000 hides were sold in Fort Worth at a single two-day sale. Except for the interest of the late **Col. Charles Goodnight** and a few other foresighted men, the bison might be extinct.

Cat — The **jaguar** *(Felis onca)* is probably now extinct in Texas and, along with the **ocelot, jaguarundi** and **margay**, is listed as rare and endangered by both federal and state wildlife agencies. The **mountain lion** *(Felis concolor)*, also known as **cougar** and **puma**, was once found statewide. It is now found in the mountainous areas of the trans-Pecos and the dense Rio Grande Plain brushland. The **ocelot** *(Felis pardalis)*, also known as the **leopard cat**, is found usually along the border. The **red-and-gray cat**, or **jaguarundi** *(Felis yagouaroundi Geoffroy)* is found, rarely, in extreme South Texas. The **margay** *(Felis wiedii)* was reported in the 1850s near Eagle Pass. The **bobcat** *(Lynx rufus)* is found over the state in large numbers.

Chipmunk — The **gray-footed chipmunk** *(Tamias canipes)* is found at high altitudes in the Guadalupe and Sierra Diablo ranges of the Trans-Pecos (see also **Ground Squirrel**, with which it is often confused in public reference).

Coati — The **white-nosed coati** *(Nasua narica)*, a relative of the raccoon, is occasionally found in southern Texas from Brownsville to the Big Bend. It inhabits woodland areas and feeds both on the ground and in trees. The coati, which is on the list of threatened species, is also found occasionally in Big Bend National Park.

Coyote — The **coyote** *(Canis latrans)*, great in number, is the most destructive Texas predator of livestock. On the other hand, it is probably the most valuable predator in the balance of nature. It is a protection to crops and range lands by its control of rodents and rabbits. It is found throughout the state, but is most numerous in the brush country of southwest Texas. It is the second-most important fur-bearing animal in the state.

Deer — The **white-tailed deer** *(Odocoileus virginianus)*, found throughout the state in brushy or wooded areas, is the most important Texas game animal. Its numbers are estimated at more than 3 million. The **mule deer** *(Odocoileus heminous)* is found principally in the Trans-Pecos and Panhandle areas. It has increased in number in recent years. The little **Del Carmen deer** *(white-tailed subspecies)* is found in limited numbers in the high valleys of the Chisos Mountains in the Big Bend. The only native **elk** in Texas *(Cervus merriami)*, found in the southern Guadalupe Mountains, became extinct about the turn of the 20th century. The **wapiti** or **elk** *(Cervus elaphus)*, was introduced into the same area about 1928. There are currently several herds totalling several hundred individuals.

A number of exotic deer species have been introduced, mostly for hunting purposes. The **axis deer*** *(Cervus axis)* is the most numerous of the exotics. Native to India, it is found mostly in central and southern Texas, both free-ranging and confined on ranches. **Blackbuck*** *(Antilope cervicapra)*, also native to India, is the second-most numerous exotic deer in the state and is found on ranches in 86 counties. **Fallow deer*** *(Cervus dama)*, native to the Mediterranean, has been introduced to 93 counties, while the **nilgai*** *(Boselaphus tragocamelus)*, native of India and

The nine-banded armadillo is found across most of Texas except the western Trans-Pecos. It is now common as far north and east as Oklahoma and Mississippi. File photo.

Pakistan, is found mostly on ranches in Kenedy and Willacy counties. The **sika deer*** *(Cervus nippon)*, native of southern Siberia, Japan and China, has been introduced in 77 counties in central and southern Texas.

Ferret — The **black-footed ferret** *(Mustela nigripes)* was formerly found widely ranging through the West Texas country of the prairie dog on which it preyed. It is now considered extinct in Texas. It is of the same genus as the weasel and the mink.

Fox — The **common gray fox** *(Urocyon cinereoargenteus)* is found throughout most of the state, primarily in the woods of East Texas, in broken parts of the Edwards Plateau, and in the rough country at the foot of the Staked Plains. The **kit** or **Swift fox** *(Vulpes velox)* is found in the western one-third of the state. A second species of **kit fox** *(Vulpes macrotis)* is found in the Trans-Pecos and is fairly numerous in some localities. The **red fox*** *(Vulpes vulpes)*, which ranges across Central Texas, was introduced for sport.

Gopher — Nine species of pocket gopher occur in Texas. The **Botta's pocket gopher** *(Thomomys bottae)* is found from the Trans-Pecos eastward across the Edwards Plateau. The **plains pocket gopher** *(Geomys bursarius)* is found from Midland and Tom Green counties east and north to McLennan, Dallas and Grayson counties. The **desert pocket gopher** *(Geomys arenarius)* is found only in the Trans-Pecos, while the **yellow-faced pocket gopher** *(Cratogeomys castanops)* is found in the western one-third of the state, with occasional sightings along the Rio Grande in Maverick and Cameron counties. The **Texas pocket gopher** *(Geomys personatus)* is found in South Texas from San Patricio County to Val Verde County. **Attwater's pocket gopher** *(Geomys attwateri)* and **Baird's pocket gopher** *(Geomys breviceps)* are both found generally in East Texas from the Brazos River to the San Antonio River and south to Matagorda and San Patricio counties. **Jones' pocket gopher** *(Geomys knoxjonesi)*

is found only in far West Texas, while the **Llano pocket gopher** *(Geomys texensis)* is found only in two isolated areas of the Hill Country.

Ground Squirrel — Five or more species of ground squirrel live in Texas, mostly in the western part of the state. The **rock squirrel** *(Spermophilus variegatus)* is found throughout the Edwards Plateau and Trans-Pecos. The **Mexican ground squirrel** *(Spermophilus mexicanus)* is found in southern and western Texas. The **spotted ground squirrel** *(Spermophilus spilosoma)* is found generally in the western half of the state. The **thirteen-lined ground squirrel** *(Spermophilus tridecemlineatus)* is found in a narrow strip from Dallas and Tarrant counties to the Gulf. The **Texas antelope squirrel** *(Ammospermophilus interpres)* is found along the Rio Grande from El Paso to Val Verde County.

Hog, Feral — (see Pig, Feral)

Javelina — The **javelina** or **collared peccary** *(Tayassu tajacu)* is found in brushy semidesert where prickly pear, a favorite food, is found. The javelina was hunted commercially for its hide until 1939. They are harmless to livestock and to people, though they can defend themselves ferociously when attacked by hunting dogs.

Mink — The **mink** *(Mustela vison)* is found in the eastern half of the state, always near streams, lakes or other water sources. Although it is an economically important fur-bearing animal in the eastern United States, it ranked only 13th in numbers and 9th in economic value to trappers in Texas in 1988-89, according to a Texas Parks and Wildlife Department survey.

Mole — The **eastern mole** *(Scalopus aquaticus)* is found in the eastern two-thirds of the state.

Muskrat — The **common muskrat** *(Ondatra zibethica)*, occurs in aquatic habitats in the northern, southeastern and southwestern parts of the state. Although the muskrat was once economically valuable for its fur, its numbers have declined, mostly because of the loss of habitat.

Nutria* — This introduced species *(Myocastor coypus)*, native to South America, is found in the eastern two-thirds of the state. The fur is not highly valued and, since nutria are in competition with muskrats, their spread is discouraged. They have been used widely in Texas as a cure-all for ponds choked with vegetation, with spotty results.

Opossum — A **marsupial**, the **Virginia opossum** *(Didelphis virginiana)* is found in nearly all parts of the state. The opossum has economic value for its pelt, and its meat is considered a delicacy by some. It is one of the chief contributors to the Texas fur crop.

Otter — A few **river otter** *(Lutra canadensis)* are found in the eastern quarter of the state. It has probably been extirpated from the Panhandle, north-central and southern Texas.

Pig, Feral — Feral pigs, found in areas of the Rio Grande and coastal plains as well as the woods of East Texas, are descendants of escaped domestic hogs or of European wild hogs that were imported for sport.

Porcupine — The **yellow-haired porcupine** *(Erethizon dorsatum)* is found from the western half of the state east to Bosque County.

Prairie Dog — Until recent years probably no sight was so universal in West Texas as the **black-tailed prairie dog** *(Cynomys ludovicianus)*. Naturalists estimated its population in the hundreds of millions, and prairie-dog towns often covered many acres with thickly spaced burrows. Its destruction of range grasses and cultivated crops has caused farmers and ranchers to destroy many of them, and it is extirpated from much of its former range. It is being propagated in several public zoos, notably in the **prairie dog town in Mackenzie Park** at Lubbock. It has been honored in Texas by the naming of the **Prairie Dog Town Fork** of the Red River, along one segment of which is located the beautiful **Palo Duro Canyon**.

Pronghorn — The **Pronghorn** *(Antilocapra americana)* formerly was found in the western two-thirds of the state. It is currently found only in limited areas from the Panhandle to the Trans-Pecos. Despite management efforts, its numbers have been decreasing in recent years.

Rabbit — The **black-tailed jack rabbit** *(Lepus californicus)* is found throughout Texas except in the Big Thicket area of East Texas. It breeds rapidly, and its long hind legs make it one of the world's faster-running animals. The **Eastern cottontail** *(Sylvilagus floridanus)* is found mostly in the eastern three-quarters of the state. The **desert cottontail** *(Sylvilagus auduboni)* is found in the western half of the state, usually on the open range. The **swamp rabbit** *(Sylvilagus aquaticus)* is found in East Texas and the coastal area.

Raccoon — The **raccoon** *(Procyon lotor)* is found throughout Texas, especially along streams and in urban settings. It is the most important fur-bearing animal in the state.

Rats and Mice — There are 40 to 50 species of rats and mice in Texas of varying characteristics, habitats and economic destructiveness. The **Norway rat*** *(Rattus norvegicus)* and the **roof rat*** *(Rattus rattus)*, both non-native species, are probably the most common and the most destructive. They also are instrumental in the transmission of several dread diseases, including bubonic plague and typhus. The **common house mouse*** *(Mus musculus)* is estimated in the hundreds of millions annually. The **Mexican vole** *(Microtus mexicanus guadalupensis)*, also called the **Guadalupe Mountain vole**, is found only in the higher elevations of the Guadalupe Mountains National Park and just over the border into New Mexico.

Ringtail — The **ringtail** *(Bassariscus astutus)* is found statewide but is rare in the Lower Valley and the Coastal Plains.

Sheep — The **mountain sheep** *(Ovis canadensis)*, also called **desert bighorn**, formerly was found in isolated areas of the mountainous Trans-Pecos, but the last native sheep were seen in 1959. They have been recently introduced into the same areas. The **barbary sheep*** *(Ammotragus lervia)*, or **aoudad**, first introduced to the Palo Duro Canyon area in 1957–1958, has become firmly established. Private introductions have brought it into the Edwards Plateau, Trans-Pecos, South Texas, Rolling Plains and Post Oak Savannah regions.

Shrew — Four species are found in Texas: the **southern short-tailed shrew** *(Blarina Carolinensis)*, found in the eastern one-fourth of the state; the **least shrew** *(Cryptotis parva)*, in the eastern and central parts of the state; the **Elliot's short-tailed shrew** *(Blarina hylophaga)*, known only in Aransas, Montague and Bastrop counties); and the **desert shrew** *(Notiosorex crawfordi)*, found in the western two-thirds of the state.

Skunk — There are six species of skunk in Texas. The **Eastern spotted skunk** *(Spilogale putorius)* is found in the eastern half of the state and across north-central Texas to the Panhandle. A small skunk, it is often erroneously called civet cat. This skunk also is found in East Texas and the Gulf area. The **Western spotted skunk** *(Spilogale gracilis)* is found in the southwestern part of the state north to Garza and Howard counties and east to Bexar and Duval counties. The **striped skunk** *(Mephitis mephitis)* is found statewide, mostly in brush or wooded areas. The **hooded skunk** *(Mephitis macroura)* is found in limited numbers in the Big Bend and adjacent parts of the Trans-Pecos. The **eastern hog-nosed skunk** *(Conepatus leuconotus)*, found in the Gulf coastal plains, ranges southward into Mexico. The **common hog-nosed skunk** *(Conepatus mesoleucus)* is found in southwestern, central and southern Texas, north to Collin and Lubbock counties.

Squirrel — The **eastern fox squirrel** *(Sciurus niger)* is found in the eastern two-thirds of the state. The **eastern gray squirrel** *(Sciurus carolinensis)* is found generally in the eastern third of the state. The **flying squirrel** *(Glaucomys volans)* is found in wooded areas of East Texas.

Weasel — The **long-tailed weasel** *(Mustela frenata)*, akin to the mink, is found statewide, but is scarce in West Texas.

Wolf — The **red wolf** *(Canis rufus)* was once found throughout the eastern half of the state. It has now been extirpated from the wild, with the only known remnants of the population now in captive propagation. The **gray wolf** *(Canis lupus)* once had a wide range over the western two-thirds of the state. It is now considered extinct in Texas. The **red wolf** and **gray wolf** are on the federal and state rare and endangered species lists.

Reptiles and Arachnids

Most of the more than **100 species and subspecies of snakes** found in Texas are beneficial, as also are other reptiles. There are **16 poisonous species and subspecies.**

Poisonous reptiles include **three species of copperheads** *(southern, broad-banded and Trans-Pecos)*; one kind of **cottonmouth** *(western)*; **11 kinds of rattlesnakes** (canebrake, western massasauga, desert massasauga, western pigmy, western diamondback, timber, banded rock, mottled rock, northern blacktailed, Mojave and prairie); and the **Texas coral snake.**

Also noteworthy are the **horned lizard**, also called **horned toad**, which is on the list of threatened species; the **vinegarone**, a type of whip scorpion; **tarantula**, a hairy spider; and **alligator**. ☆

National Wildlife Refuges

Source: U.S. Fish and Wildlife Service, U.S. Department of the Interior.

Texas has more than 470,000 acres in **17 national wildlife refuges**. Their descriptions, with date of acquisition in parentheses, follow. Included in this acreage are two conservation easement refuges, which may be visited at different times of the year for bird watching and wildlife viewing, as well as hunting and fishing. Write or call before visiting to check on facilities and days and hours of operation. On the Web: **http://southwest.fws.gov/refuges/index.html**.

Anahuac (1963): The more than 34,000 acres of this refuge are located along the upper Gulf Coast in Chambers County. **Fresh and saltwater marshes** and miles of beautiful, sweeping **coastal prairie** provide wintering habitat for large flocks of waterfowl, including **geese, 27 species of ducks and six species of rails. Roseate spoonbills and white ibis** are among the other birds frequenting the refuge. Other species include **alligator, muskrat** and **bobcat**. Fishing, bird watching, auto tours and hunting are available. Office: Box 278, Anahuac 77514; 409-267-3337.

Aransas (1937): This refuge comprises 70,504 acres on Blackjack Peninsula and three satellite units in Aransas and Refugio counties. The three mainland units consist of **oak woodlands, fresh and saltwater marshes and coastal grasslands**. Besides providing wintering grounds for the endangered **whooping crane**, the refuge is home to many species of waterfowl and other migratory birds — more than 390 different bird species in all. Refuge is open daily, sunrise to sunset. Interpretive center is open daily, 8:30 a.m. to 4:30 p.m. Other facilities include a 40-foot observation tower, paved auto-tour loop and walking trails. Office: Box 100, Austwell 77950; 361-286-3559.

Attwater Prairie Chicken (1972): Established in 1972 in Colorado County to preserve habitat for the endangered **Attwater's prairie chicken**, the refuge comprises more than 10,000 acres of **native tallgrass prairie**, potholes, sandy knolls and some wooded areas. An auto-tour route is available year-round, and 350 acres of the refuge are accessible for watching the more than 250 species of birds that visit the refuge. Refuge open sunrise to sunset. Office: Box 519, Eagle Lake 77434; 979-234-3021.

Balcones Canyonlands (1992): This 25,000-acre refuge was dedicated in 1992. Located in Burnet, Travis and Williamson counties northwest of Austin, it was established to protect the nesting habitat of two endangered birds: **black-capped vireo** and **golden-cheeked warbler**. Eventually, the refuge will encompass 30,500 acres of **oak-juniper woodlands** and other habitats. An observation deck can be used for birdwatching. Hunting available. Office: 24518 FM-1431, Box 1, Marble Falls, 78654; 512-339-9432.

Big Boggy (1983): This refuge occupies 5,000 acres of **coastal prairie** and **salt marsh** along East Matagorda Bay for the benefit of wintering **waterfowl. The refuge** is generally closed, and visitors are encouraged to visit nearby **San Bernard or Brazoria refuges**. Waterfowl hunting is permitted in season. Office: 1212 N. Velasco, #200, Angleton 77515; 979-849-6062.

Brazoria (1966): The 43,388 acres of this refuge, located along the Gulf Coast in Brazoria County, serve as haven for wintering waterfowl and a wide variety of other migratory birds. The refuge also supports many **marsh** and **water birds**, from **roseate spoonbills** and **great blue**

A snowy egret wades at the Anahuac National Wildlife Refuge. Natalie Caudill photo.

herons to white ibis and sandhill cranes. Brazoria Refuge is within the **Freeport Christmas Bird Count** circle, which frequently achieves the highest number of species seen in a 24-hour period. Open daily sunrise to sunset. Hunting and fishing also available. Call for details. Office: 1212 N. Velasco, #200, Angleton 77515; 979-849-6062.

Buffalo Lake (1958): Comprising 7,664 acres in the **Central Flyway** in Randall County in the Panhandle; this refuge

A pied-billed grebe at Anahuac NWR. Natalie Caudill photo.

contains some of the best remaining **shortgrass prairie** in the United States. Buffalo Lake is now dry; a **marsh area** is artificially maintained for the numerous birds, reptiles and mammals. Available activities include picnicking, auto tour, birding, photography and hiking. Office: Box 179, Umbarger 79091; 806-499-3382.

Hagerman (1946): Hagerman National Wildlife Refuge lies on the Big Mineral arm of Texoma Lake in Grayson County. The 3,000 acres of **marsh** and water and 8,000 acres of **upland and farmland** provide a feeding and resting place for migrating **waterfowl**. Bird watching, fishing and hunting are available. Office: 6465 Refuge Road, Sherman 75092-5817; 903-786-2826.

Laguna Atascosa: Established in 1946 as southernmost waterfowl refuge in the **Central Flyway**, this refuge contains more than 45,000 acres fronting on the **Laguna Madre** in the Lower Rio Grande Valley in Cameron and Willacy counties. Open **lagoons, coastal prairies, salt flats and brushlands** support a wide diversity of wildlife. The United States' largest concentration of **redhead ducks** winters here, along with many other species of **waterfowl** and **shorebirds. White-tailed deer, javelina and armadillo** can be found, along with endangered **ocelot.** Bird watching and nature study are popular; auto-tour roads and nature trails are available. Camping and fishing are permitted within Adolph Thomae Jr. County Park. Hunting also available. Office: Box 450, Rio Hondo 78583; 956-748-3607.

Lower Rio Grande Valley (1979): The U.S. Fish and Wildlife Service has acquired about half the planned acreage in the Lower Rio Grande Valley for this refuge, which will eventually include 132,500 acres within Cameron, Hidalgo, Starr and Willacy counties. The refuge will include 11 different habitat types, including **sabal palm forest, tidal flats, coastal brushland, mid-delta thorn forest, woodland potholes and basins, upland thorn scrub, flood forest, barretal, riparian woodland** and **Chihuahuan thorn forest.** Nearly 500 species of birds and over 300 butterfly species have been found there, as well as four of the five cats that occur within the United States: **jaguarundi, ocelot, bobcat** and **mountain lion.** Office: Santa Ana/Lower Rio Grande Valley National Wildlife Refuges, Rt. 2, Box 202A, Alamo 78516; 956-784-2500.

Matagorda Island: Matagorda Island is **jointly owned and managed by the U.S. Fish and Wildlife Service and the State of Texas** under an agreement reached in 1983. Please check table of **Texas Wildlife Management Areas** on next page for facilities.

McFaddin (1980): Purchased in 1980, this refuge's

55,000 acres, in Jefferson and Chambers counties, are of great importance to wintering populations of **migratory waterfowl.** One of the densest populations of **alligators** in Texas is found here. Activities on the refuge include wildlife observation, hunting, fishing and crabbing. Access best by boat; limited roadways. Office: Box 609, Sabine Pass 77655; 409-971-2909.

Muleshoe (1935): Oldest of national refuges in Texas, Muleshoe provides winter habitat for **waterfowl** and the continent's largest wintering population of **sandhill cranes.** Comprising 5,809 acres in the High Plains of Bailey County, the refuge contains three **playa lakes, marsh areas, caliche outcroppings** and **native grasslands.** A nature trail, campground and picnic area are available. Office: Box 549, Muleshoe 79347; 806-946-3341.

San Bernard (1968): Located in Brazoria and Matagorda counties on the Gulf Coast near Freeport, this refuge's 27,414 acres attract **migrating waterfowl,** including thousands of **white-fronted and Canada geese and several duck species,** which spend the winter on the refuge. Habitats, consisting of **coastal prairies, salt/mud flats** and saltwater and freshwater ponds and potholes, also attract **yellow rails, roseate spoonbills, reddish egrets** and **American bitterns.** Visitors enjoy auto and hiking trails, photography, bird watching, fishing, and waterfowl hunting in season. Office: 1212 N. Velasco, #200, Angleton, 77515; 979-849-6062.

Santa Ana (1943): Santa Ana is located on the north bank of the Rio Grande in Hidalgo County. Santa Ana's 2,088 acres of **subtropical forest and native brushland are at an ecological crossroads** of subtropical, Gulf Coast, Great Plains and Chihuahuan desert habitats. Santa Ana attracts birders from across the United States who can view many species of **Mexican birds** as they reach the northern edge of their ranges in South Texas. Also found at Santa Ana are **ocelot** and **jaguarundi,** endangered members of the cat family. Visitors enjoy a tram or auto drive, bicycling and hiking trails. Office: Rt. 2, Box 202A, Alamo 78516; 956-784-7500.

Texas Point (1980): Texas Point's 8,900 acres are located in Jefferson County on the Upper Gulf Coast, 12 miles east of McFaddin NWR, where they serve a large wintering population of **waterfowl** as well as migratory birds. The endangered **southern bald eagle** and **peregrine falcon** may occasionally be seen during peak fall and spring migrations. **Alligators** are commonly observed during the spring, summer and fall months. Activities include wildlife observation, hunting, fishing and crabbing. Access to the refuge is by boat and on foot only. Office: Box 609, Sabine Pass 77655; 409-971-2909.

Trinity River (1994): Established to protect remnant **bottomland hardwood forests** and associated **wetlands,** this refuge, located in northern Liberty County off State Highway 787 approximately 15 miles east of Cleveland, provides habitat for **wintering, migrating and breeding waterfowl** and a variety of other wetland-dependent wildlife. Approximately 18,300 acres of the proposed 20,000-acre refuge have been purchased. Office: Box 10015, Liberty 77575; 936-336-9786. ☆

Texas Wildlife Management Areas

Source: Texas Parks and Wildlife Department; www.tpwd.state.tx.us/wma/index.htm.

Texas Parks and Wildlife Department is currently responsible for managing 51 wildlife management areas (WMAs) totaling approximately three quarters of a million acres. Of these, 32 WMAs are owned in fee title, while 19 are managed under license agreements with other agencies.

Wildlife management areas are used principally for hunting, but many are also used for research, fishing, wildlife viewing, hiking, camping, bicycling and horseback riding, when those activities are compatible with the primary goals for which the WMA was established.

Access to WMAs at times designated for public use is provided by various permits, depending on the activity performed.

Hunting permits include Special ($50 or $100), Regular daily ($10), or Annual ($40).

A Limited Public Use Permit ($10) allows access for such activities as birdwatching, hiking, camping or picnicking and on some WMAs under the Texas Conservation Passport (Gold $50, Silver $25). The Gold Passport also allows entry to state parks.

On most WMAs, restrooms and drinking water are not provided; check with the TPWD at the contacts above before you go.

For further information, contact the Texas Parks and Wildlife Department, 4200 Smith School Rd., Austin 78744; 1-800-792-1112, menu #5, selection #1. ☆

Texas Wildlife Management Areas

1. Candy Cain Abshier
2. Alabama Creek
3. Alazan Bayou
4. Angelina-Neches/Dam B
5. Aquilla
6. Atkinson Island
7. Bannister
8. Big Lake Bottom
9. Black Gap
10. Walter Buck
11. Caddo Lake State Park

12. Caddo National Grasslands
13. Cedar Creek Islands
14. Chaparral
15. Cooper
16. James E. Daughtrey
17. Elephant Mountain
18. Gus Engeling
19. Granger
20. Guadalupe Delta
21. Tony Houseman
22. Sam Houston National Forest

Gene Howe
23. Gene Howe Unit
24. W.A. Pat Murphy Unit
25. Keechi Creek
26. Kerr
Las Palomas
27. Lower Rio Grande Valley Units
28. Anacua Unit
29. Ocotillo Unit

30. Lower Neches
31. Mad Island
32. Mason Mountain
33. Matador
34. Matagorda Island
35. Pat Mayse
36. Moore Plantation
37. J.D. Murphree
38. The Nature Center
39. M.O. Neasloney
40. North Toledo Bend

41. Old Sabine Bottom
42. Old Tunnel
43. Peach Point
Playa Lakes
44. Taylor Lakes Unit
45. Dimmitt and Armstong Units
46. Redhead Pond
47. Richland Creek
48. Ray Roberts
49. Sierra Diablo

50. Somerville
51. Nannie M. Stringfellow
52. Tawakoni
53. Welder Flats
54. White Oak Creek
55. D.R. Wintermann

Texas Wildlife Management Areas

(Acreage)	County	Day Use Only	Hunting	Fishing	Camping	Wildlife Viewing	Hiking	Interpretive Trail	Auto Tour	Bicycling	Horseback Riding	Comments
Candy Cain Abshier (207)	CHAMBERS	★				★						Excellent birding spring and fall
Alabama Creek (14,561)	TRINITY		★	★	★	★	★		★	★	★	In Davy Crockett Nat. Forest
Alazan Bayou (2,063)	NACOGDOCHES		★	★	★	★				★		
Angelina-Neches/Dam B (12,636)	JASPER/TYLER		★	★	★	★	★		★			
Aquilla (9,826)	HILL	★	★	★		★	★		★			
Atkinson Island (150)	HARRIS	★		★		★						Boat access only
Bannister (25,695)	SAN AUGUSTINE		★	★	★	★	★			★	★	In Angelina National Forest
Big Lake Bottom (4,071)	ANDERSON	★	★	★		★						2,870 acres available to public
Black Gap (119,000)	BREWSTER		★	★	★	★	★		★	★		NW of Big Bend National Park
Walter Buck (2,155)	KIMBLE	★	★			★	★		★			Camping at adjacent state park
Caddo Lake WMA (8,129)	MARION/HARRISON		★	★	★	★	★			★	★	
Caddo National Grasslands (16,150)	FANNIN		★	★	★	★	★			★		
Cedar Creek Islands (160)	HENDERSON	★		★		★						Access by boat only
Chaparral (15,200)	LA SALLE/DIMMIT		★		★	★	★		★	★		
Cooper (14,160)	DELTA/HOPKINS	★	★	★		★	★					Camping at nearby state park
James E. Daughtrey (4,400)	LIVE OAK/MCMULLEN	★	★		★	★						Primitive camping for hunters
Elephant Mountain (23,147)	BREWSTER		★		★	★	★		★			Primitive camping only
Gus Engling (10,958)	ANDERSON		★	★	★	★	★		★	★	★	
Granger (11,116)	WILLIAMSON		★	★	★	★	★			★		Primitive camping only
Guadalupe Delta (6,594)	CALHOUN/REFUGIO	★	★	★		★	★			★		Freshwater Marsh
Tony Houseman (3,313)	ORANGE		★	★	★	★	★					
Sam Houston Natl Forest (161,508)	SAN JACINTO/WALKER		★	★	★	★	★		★	★	★	Also Montgomery County
Gene Howe (5,882)	HEMPHILL		★	★	★	★	★		★	★	★	Riding March–August only
Keechi Creek (1,500)	LEON		★									
Kerr (6,493)	KERR		★	★		★		★	★	★		On Guadalupe River
Las Palomas:												
Anacua Unit (222)	CAMERON		★			★						
Lower Rio Grande Valley Units (3,314)	CAMERON/HIDALGO	★	★			★	★					Also Starr & Willacy Counties
Ocotillo Unit (2,082)	PRESIDIO		★	★	★	★	★					
Lower Neches (7,998)	ORANGE	★	★	★		★	★					Coastal marsh
Mad Island (7,200)	MATAGORDA	★	★			★						Coastal wetlands
Mason Mountain (5,301)	MASON	★	★									Restricted access
Matador (28,183)	COTTLE		★	★	★	★	★	★	★	★	★	Primitive camping
Matagorda Island (43,900)	CALHOUN		★	★	★	★	★			★		Access by boat only
Pat Mayse (8,925)	LAMAR		★	★	★	★	★			★	★	
Moore Plantation (26,519)	SABINE/JASPER		★	★	★	★	★		★	★	★	In Sabine National Forest
J.D. Murphree (24,250)	JEFFERSON	★	★	★		★						Access by boat only
The Nature Center (82)	SMITH	★				★		★				Primarily for school groups
M.O. Neasloney (100)	GONZALES	★				★	★	★				Primarily for school groups
North Toldeo Bend (3,650)	SHELBY		★	★	★	★	★			★		Limited use of horses
Old Sabine Bottom (5,158)	SMITH		★	★	★	★	★			★	★	Canoeing
Old Tunnel (16)	KENDALL	★				★	★	★				Bat-viewing April–October
Peach Point (10,311)	BRAZORIA		★	★		★	★	★	★			On Texas Coastal Birding Trail
Playa Lakes (1,492 in 3 units)	CASTRO/DONLEY	★	★			★	★					Hunting only on Donley Co. unit
Redhead Pond (37)	NUECES	★				★						Freshwater wetland
Richland Creek (13,796)	FREESTONE/NAVARRO		★	★	★	★	★		★	★	★	Primitive camping only
Ray Roberts (40,920)	COOKE/DENTON	★	★	★		★	★					Also Grayson Co.
Sierra Diablo (11,625)	HUDSPETH/CULBERSON		★									Restricted acess
Somerville (3,180)	BURLESON/LEE	★	★	★		★	★			★		Camping at nearby state park
Nannie M. Stringfellow (3,644)	BRAZORIA		★									Open for special hunts only.
Tawakoni (2,335)	HUNT/VAN ZANDT		★	★	★	★	★				★	
Welder Flats (1,480)	CALHOUN	★		★		★						Boat access only
White Oak Creek (25,777)	BOWIE/CASS/MORRIS	★	★	★		★	★				★	Also Titus Co.
D.R. Wintermann (246)	WHARTON					★						Restricted access; bird refuge

Weather

This NOAA satellite image of Hurricane Rita was taken at 3:45 p.m. on Sept. 23, 2005, as the Category-3 storm made landfall near the Texas-Louisiana border.

Highlights 2005 & 2006

Monthly Summaries 2005 & 2006

Extremes 2005 & 2006

Temperatures & Precipitation 2005 & 2006

Destructive Weather 1766–2005

Tornado & Drought Records

Records by County

Weather

Source: Unless otherwise noted, this information is provided by John W. Nielsen-Gammon, Texas State Climatologist and graduate assistant Matt Mosier, Texas A&M University, College Station.

Weather Highlights 2005

March 25: In the evening of March 25, the most destructive hailstorm in 10 years struck the greater Austin area. The storm knocked out power to 5,000 homes in northwest Austin. Hail 2 inches in diameter was reported near the Travis County Exposition Center. Total damage was estimated at $100 million.

May was the first month in an extensive drought over North Central Texas that lasted until December 2006. The statewide drought losses were estimated at $4.1 billion.

June 9: An F-3 tornado affected the Petersburg area in southeast Hale County across to portions of southwest and south-central Floyd County. Total damage was estimated at $70 million.

Sept. 23: Hurricane Rita made landfall near the Texas-Louisiana border as a category-3 hurricane, with maximum sustained winds of 120 mph. Property damage was estimated at $2.1 billion.

2005 Weather Extremes

Lowest Temp.: Lipscomb, Lipscomb Co., Dec. 8...–8° F
Highest Temp.: Heath Canyon, Brewster Co.,
  July .... 117°F
24-hour Precip: Sam Rayburn Dam, Jasper Co.,
  Sept. 2... 14.00"
Monthly Precip.: Sam Rayburn Dam, Jasper Co.,
  September.. 15.12"
Least Annual Precip.: Heath Canyon, Brewster Co.
  .... 7.40"
Greatest Annual Precip.: Sam Rayburn Dam,
  Jasper Co. .... 54.83"

Monthly Summaries 2005

The beginning of 2005 was a roller coaster of record highs and freezing lows. **January** began with temperatures 15–20 degrees above normal across the state. Temperatures fell below normal on the 4th as a cold front passed over the state. A high pressure system followed, and temperatures again reached 15–20 degrees above normal. On the 12th, a line of heavy precipitation and severe weather developed ahead of a cold front. A slight warming occurred before a dry cold front arrived on the 22nd. Temperatures dropped about 15–20 degrees, and the rains continued as another low pressure system moved around state borders.

Most stations received above-normal rainfall. Austin (1.36 in.), Houston (1.22 in.), Port Arthur (1.33 in.), and San Antonio (1.57 in.) all had at least one day of heavy rainfall during the last week. Several other stations received at least 1 inch over

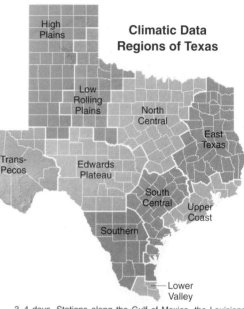

Climatic Data Regions of Texas

3–4 days. Stations along the Gulf of Mexico, the Louisiana border and in the middle of West Texas along I-20 did not receive their normal amount of rain.

The month of **February** was warmer and wetter than normal for most of Texas. A low pressure system moved across the state the first few days with showers and cooler-than-normal temperatures. Another system moved in from Mexico on the 5th, and showers and heavy clouds dominated. A high pressure system moved in on the 9th, drying out the state and raising average daily temperatures 10-20 degrees above normal.

A frontal system stalled over the state Feb. 22–24, and a low pressure system from the west collided with it to cause heavy rain for most of central and southeast Texas. Severe weather was also a result with 42 reports of hail, including reports of 4.25 inches in Taylor County, 3 inches in Kendall County and 2.75 inches in both Waller and Terrell counties. The month ended with partly to mostly cloudy skies across the state and light rain.

March began with temperatures slightly below normal, especially in eastern Texas, and little heavy rainfall. March

Average Temperatures 2005

	High Plains	Low Plains	North Central	East Texas	Trans-Pecos	Edwards Plateau	South Central	Upper Coast	South Texas	Lower Valley
Jan.	40.9	44.6	48.6	51.0	50.3	50.9	56.5	56.9	58.6	64.3
Feb.	43.6	46.8	50.2	52.5	49.5	50.8	57.4	58.4	59.6	64.8
Mar.	47.4	52.3	54.9	56.2	55.1	56.2	61.9	61.8	65.2	69.1
April	56.6	61.9	63.7	64.1	63.3	64.7	68.2	68.3	70.8	74.0
May	65.3	69.3	70.8	71.7	72.2	71.8	74.8	74.8	78.0	79.1
June	75.9	79.5	80.8	81.5	81.2	80.0	82.3	82.4	84.4	85.4
July	77.9	81.9	83.0	83.1	82.6	83.1	84.7	84.1	86.5	86.4
Aug.	75.8	79.7	83.1	84.4	78.5	80.7	85.2	84.7	86.9	86.9
Sep.	73.8	77.9	80.9	81.8	78.1	80.2	83.9	83.4	85.4	85.3
Oct.	60.1	64.3	66.4	66.5	65.1	65.9	71.3	71.4	73.4	76.6
Nov.	50.1	54.8	58.8	60.5	55.7	58.5	65.0	65.0	66.5	70.1
Dec.	38.7	42.6	45.1	46.8	47.6	46.5	52.8	53.3	55.4	60.2
Ann.	58.8	63.0	65.5	66.7	64.9	65.8	70.3	70.4	72.6	75.2

Precipitation 2005
(Inches)

	High Plains	Low Plains	North Central	East Texas	Trans-Pecos	Edwards Plateau	South Central	Upper Coast	South Texas	Lower Valley
Jan.	1.40	1.25	2.96	3.69	0.61	1.26	2.46	2.20	1.32	0.92
Feb.	0.99	1.75	2.52	4.47	1.51	2.32	3.32	5.05	2.38	1.32
Mar.	1.22	1.55	2.09	2.44	0.32	2.04	3.28	3.87	1.80	0.58
April	0.70	0.41	0.79	2.33	0.14	0.34	0.65	1.22	0.22	0.04
May	2.43	2.93	3.28	2.11	1.67	4.16	3.43	4.09	2.21	1.25
June	1.95	1.94	1.42	0.84	0.83	1.11	1.08	0.78	0.65	0.37
July	2.26	2.59	2.54	3.76	2.27	2.94	3.33	6.61	2.96	4.94
Aug.	4.04	6.04	4.09	3.51	2.98	4.03	1.50	2.55	0.46	1.06
Sep.	0.68	1.29	0.87	3.73	0.88	0.43	1.92	4.19	1.67	2.61
Oct.	1.76	2.35	0.92	0.41	2.88	3.70	2.29	2.44	2.92	2.30
Nov.	0.12	0.01	0.67	2.05	0.01	0.26	1.53	3.57	0.43	1.10
Dec.	0.06	0.08	0.28	1.19	0.17	0.13	0.61	2.35	0.31	0.98
Ann.	17.61	22.19	22.43	30.53	14.27	22.72	25.40	38.92	17.33	17.47

12 was the warmest day of the month for most first-order stations, but was followed by an abrupt cooling trend. The 16th had the lowest average temperature for the month across most of the state. Severe weather arrived on the 19th, and hail as large as 2 inches in diameter was reported in Caldwell and across Southeast Texas. The first tornado reports came on the 25th, with two reports in Travis County near Austin. Month's end saw temperatures much cooler than normal, with many stations reporting 10 degrees or more below average on 26–27. Generally, stations had temperatures just slightly below normal for March, with the exception of deep South Texas. The Edwards Plateau, South Central and Upper Coastal regions had above normal precipitation, while North Central and East Texas were drier than average.

April was dry throughout the state. The month was dominated by high pressure systems that brought clear skies and warm temperatures. The

Benny Salas rides his bike on a surf-covered pier in Galveston as Hurricane Rita approaches Sept. 23, 2005. Rick Wilking photo.

most significant cold front occurred on the 25th, and heavy showers for the northern half the state helped raise monthly rainfall totals. However, many stations received less than one-tenth of an inch of rainfall for the month. San Antonio had its driest April ever, while several other stations (Abilene, Brownsville, Dallas/Fort Worth, Del Rio, Midland, San Angelo and Wichita Falls) each had one of their 10 driest Aprils on record. Temperatures were just about average across most of the state. There were 6 tornadoes reported, 25 reports of high winds, and 167 hail reports.

May was another relatively dry month across most of Texas. The first week began cool, especially in the High Plains, where Amarillo turned wintry and received 4.7 inches of snow. On May 1, the Austin-Bergstrom station recorded its all-time low for May of 42 degrees. Severe weather was widespread on the 8th, with numerous reports of large hail, including 4.25-inch diameter hail in Mason County. The 9th saw 4.25-inch hail just one county east in Llano County. In the Panhandle, there were 12 tornado reports on the 12th and 4 more on the 13th. Temperatures turned hot between the 21st–22nd, reaching triple digits in numerous locations. Both Laredo and Wichita Falls reached 103 on the 22nd. After the mini-heat wave subsided, temperatures dipped below normal, especially in West Texas. The month went out with a bang with a severe weather outbreak in the High Plains, Low Rolling Plains and Edwards Plateau regions where there were 7 tornadoes, 20 reports of large hail and two reports of high wind (75 mph).

June was dry and had above normal temperatures. An upper-level disturbance on the 1st brought the bulk of monthly precipitation for many stations, especially across central and eastern Texas. For most stations, this was the first and only significant precipitation in June. Most of the precipitation was concentrated in the High Plains and Low Rolling Plains regions, and precipitation in these regions was also below normal for the month. Severe weather struck on the 5th, an active day across the West Texas plains, with 14 reports of tornadoes and 44 hail reports, including 4.25-in. diameter hail in Lynn County. June 9 saw 55 reports of hail and 10 tornado reports, including a multiple vortex tornado reportedly ¼- to ½-mile wide in Floyd County. There were 10 more reports of tornadoes the following day, with all the storms concentrated in a small area near Amarillo. The 2nd half of the month saw little severe weather. The lack of rainfall across eastern Texas was revealed in the Long Term Palmer Drought Severity Index, which classified the North Central, East and Upper Coast regions as being in a moderate drought and the Lower Valley in a severe drought.

July began extremely hot statewide, with triple-digit heat reported at most stations. However, the surge in temperature was tempered over the remainder of the month, with many

areas seeing below normal temperatures. In the Lower Valley and Southern regions, most of the precipitation was a result of the month's biggest weather story: Hurricane Emily. Although it came on shore well to the south of the Rio Grande, Emily brought substantial precipitation to the Lower Valley. McAllen saw 4.25 inches of rain, while isolated areas received in excess of 6 inches of rain on the 20th. Other areas of Texas remained dry. Hurricane Emily also brought tornadoes in its outer bands as 12 tornadoes struck extreme southern Texas on the 20th, though none caused any considerable damage.

August had its ups and downs, with the first half of the month was cooler and wetter than normal for most of the state, and the second half hot and dry. The Panhandle had a long stretch of below-average temperatures, including two days in Abilene of average temperatures more than 10 degrees below normal. On the 14th, the average temperature in Amarillo was 14 degrees below normal. From Aug. 13–16, Wichita Falls received 6.96 inches of rain, with one 24-hour total at 4.55 inches (normal monthly rainfall is 2.39 in.). Around the 16th, the state became hot and dry, with highs hovering near the century mark for many days and little rain reported. It was the hottest August on record for Corpus Christi, which received only 0.25 inches of rain and was 7.45 inches below its average annual total. Brownsville also had its hottest August on record and was 8.66 inches low on rainfall for the year.

In **September,** excessive heat and Hurricane Rita were the big stories for Texas. Average temperatures ranged between 3–6 degrees above normal. Many stations had the warmest September ever, including Austin, College Station, Dallas and Houston. Corpus Christi set or tied record highs for eight consecutive days from the 22nd–29th. College Station recorded a high of 105 degrees on the 26th, shattering the previous record high for that date by 7 degrees. On the same day, Austin Mabry recorded its highest ever autumn temperature of 107 degrees. The peak of the heat hit, especially in the eastern half of the state, after Hurricane Rita came ashore on Sept. 23 near the Texas-Louisiana border. Although Hurricane Rita was not a record-breaker, hurricane force winds and excessive rainfall took a toll on the Beaumont/Port Arthur area. On Sept. 23, Southeast Texas Regional Airport in Jefferson County reported a peak wind speed of 105 mph and 8.89 inches of rain.

Aside from Hurricane Rita, rainfall was sparse for the rest of the state. An exception was El Paso, which received almost twice its normal September precipitation. Marfa, in Presidio County, saw a remarkable 6.42 inches of rainfall on the 28th. Along with having its warmest September on record, College Station experienced its driest September on record with only a trace of rainfall for the month.

October was dominated by normal temperatures, although western Texas was slightly below normal due in part to greater

Average First Freeze

Nov. 1

Nov. 16

Dec. 1

Dec. 16

Rarely freezes

than average precipitation. Eastern Texas was drier than normal with slightly above-average temperatures. Del Rio recorded 7.59 inches of rain on the 13th, the fourth-highest single-day total in that city's recorded history. Dallas' high soared to 93 degrees on the 18th, tying a record high that was set in 2004. A cold front swept through the state on the 23rd, and the mercury plummeted in Amarillo to 26. On the 27th, two tornadoes touched down between Laredo and Corpus Christi. The day also saw nine reports of high winds and two reports of hail. A gloomy Halloween greeted trick-or-treaters on the 31st as a mass of rainfall pushed across the state.

November was warm and dry. All but three main stations (Brownsville, Corpus Christi and Galveston) reported below-average rainfall for the month. Only stations along the Gulf Coast received adequate rainfall. The High Plains, Low Rolling Plains, Edwards Plateau and Trans-Pecos regions received almost no rainfall, with only Amarillo (0.19 in.) and Midland (0.01 in.) receiving measurable amounts. The *U.S Drought Monitor* (http://www.drought.unl.edu/dm/monitor.htm) declared all but the Trans-Pecos to be in a drought, with severe conditions in Central Texas and abnormally dry conditions elsewhere.

The month began warm, with temperatures 10–15 degrees above normal from the 2nd–15th. Then a cold front lowered temperatures dramatically. The below-average temperatures continued until the 20th, when temperatures rose again to above-average levels.

December saw no drought relief, with only Houston and Brownsville recording above-average rainfall. In most locations, less than 30 percent of normal precipitation fell. The continued drought conditions heightened the threat of fires, which burned all over Texas, including a very serious fire in Eastland County. The "red flag" conditions persisted throughout the latter half of the month and a burn ban was in effect for the entire state. The month began with warm temperatures but a cold front moved through the state on the 8th, which dropped temperatures to minus-3 degrees in Amarillo on the 8th and 15 degrees in D-FW on the 9th. The second half of December proved to be very warm. On the 27th, highs of 85 degrees and 87 degrees were recorded in Waco and Corpus Christi, respectively.

Weather Highlights 2006

March 12–18: A wildfire now known as the Borger wildfire start 4 miles southwest of Borger. The wildfire burned 479,500 acres, seven people were killed and 28 structures were lost. Total property damage was $49.9 million and crop damage was $45.4 million. A second wildfire known as the Interstate-40 wildfire burned 427,696 acres. The Texas Forest Service named the two wildfires the East Amarillo Complex. In all, 12 people were killed, total property damage was $49.9 million and crop damage was $45.4 million.

April 20: Grapefruit-size hail as large at 4.25 inches in diameter was reported south of San Marcos. Damage from this storm was estimated at $100 million.

Aug. 1: Repeated thunderstorms over 4 days moved over the northwest third of El Paso County, concentrating near the Franklin Mountains. Rainfall reports varied from 4–6 inches within 15 hours, with an isolated report of 8 inches on the western slope. The rain and terrain effects of the mountains led to excessive runoff and flooding not seen in the area in more than 100 years. Property damage was estimated at $180 million.

2006 Weather Extremes

Lowest Temp.: Stratford, Sherman Co., Feb. 19......0° F
Highest Temp.: Greenville, Hunt Co., Aug. 20 ...... 115°F
24-hour Precip: Liberty, Liberty Co., June 19........11.79"
Monthly Precip.: Kountze, Hardin Co., October... 32.03"
Least Annual Precip.: Langtry, Val Verde Co. .... 7.61"
Greatest Annual Precip.: Kountze, Hardin Co..... 98.03"

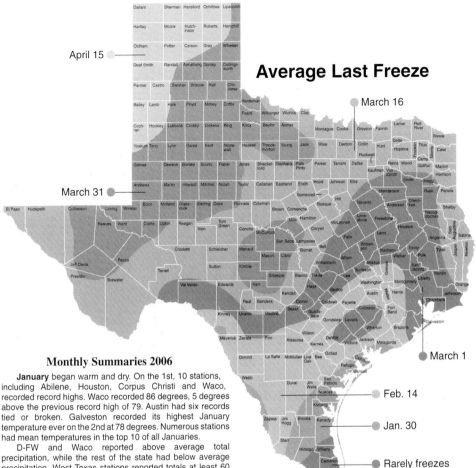

Average Last Freeze

April 15

March 31

March 16

March 1

Feb. 14

Jan. 30

Rarely freezes

Monthly Summaries 2006

January began warm and dry. On the 1st, 10 stations, including Abilene, Houston, Corpus Christi and Waco, recorded record highs. Waco recorded 86 degrees, 5 degrees above the previous record high of 79. Austin had six records tied or broken. Galveston recorded its highest January temperature ever on the 2nd at 78 degrees. Numerous stations had mean temperatures in the top 10 of all Januaries.

D-FW and Waco reported above average total precipitation, while the rest of the state had below average precipitation. West Texas stations reported totals at least 60 percent below average. However, D-FW and Waco set daily record rainfall totals on the 29th with 1.59 inches and 1.63 inches, respectively. College Station and Houston set record daily rainfall totals on the 23rd with totals of 1.66 inches and 1.02 inches, respectively. Despite these rainfall events, a drought continued to effect the entire state.

In **February**, Corpus Christi saw record highs of 93 degrees, 95 degrees and 82 degrees on the 2nd, 3rd and 5th, respectively. The 95-degree high on the 3rd topped the old record by 8 degrees. On the 16th, Abilene, San Angelo, Waco,

Austin, Houston, Dallas, Fort Worth and Midland broke or tied record high temperatures. A cold front passed through on the 17th–18th and brought some of the coldest air all winter. A record low of 19 degrees was set in Abilene on the 19th, only three days after a record high. Temperatures dropped to between 17 degrees and 23 degrees below normal.

Midland, Abilene, Dallas, Fort Worth, and College Station all recorded above average precipitation in February. College

Average Temperatures 2006

	High Plains	Low Plains	North Central	East Texas	Trans-Pecos	Edwards Plateau	South Central	Upper Coast	South Texas	Lower Valley
Jan.	44.8	50.7	53.1	53.5	50.0	52.5	58.3	58.9	60.2	64.9
Feb.	42.2	46.0	48.3	48.4	52.1	50.6	55.4	56.2	58.4	63.4
Mar.	51.5	57.4	60.8	61.1	61.1	62.4	67.4	66.3	71.7	73.8
April	63.1	68.5	70.4	70.6	71.1	71.7	75.3	73.2	78.9	79.4
May	70.6	74.3	74.6	74.0	77.0	76.2	78.5	76.6	81.6	81.8
June	78.3	81.0	80.7	79.4	81.6	81.2	81.6	80.6	84.3	83.9
July	80.7	85.3	85.2	83.4	81.8	83.5	83.6	82.3	85.0	85.3
Aug.	77.3	84.5	87.4	85.6	78.6	84.6	86.0	84.2	87.5	86.6
Sep.	66.5	72.2	76.4	77.0	73.1	75.9	78.9	79.8	81.4	82.2
Oct.	58.4	63.9	66.4	66.2	63.6	67.4	72.1	72.5	73.9	77.8
Nov.	49.6	54.6	57.3	57.5	56.7	59.2	64.2	63.9	66.6	70.4
Dec.	38.8	44.4	48.3	50.0	44.9	48.2	54.9	56.1	56.2	61.5
Ann.	60.2	65.2	67.4	67.2	66.0	67.8	71.4	70.9	73.8	75.9

Precipitation 2006
(Inches)

	High Plains	Low Plains	North Central	East Texas	Trans-Pecos	Edwards Plateau	South Central	Upper Coast	South Texas	Lower Valley
Jan.	0.07	0.23	2.10	4.16	0.05	0.50	0.85	2.04	0.17	0.18
Feb.	0.15	0.46	2.48	4.11	0.13	0.54	0.89	1.62	0.20	0.18
Mar.	1.41	2.00	4.34	4.92	0.34	1.59	1.67	1.73	0.51	0.44
April	0.57	1.56	2.71	2.85	0.23	1.76	1.24	2.15	0.54	0.05
May	1.60	2.97	2.54	2.21	0.27	1.96	3.43	5.32	2.34	1.74
June	1.48	1.24	2.00	2.50	0.65	1.48	3.47	7.50	1.45	1.70
July	1.64	0.59	0.93	3.38	1.47	1.07	4.39	10.75	3.80	3.21
Aug.	4.59	2.64	1.68	1.77	4.51	1.99	0.69	2.81	0.29	0.93
Sep.	3.35	3.47	2.56	2.30	1.84	2.56	5.25	4.81	6.38	7.19
Oct.	2.20	4.59	3.97	8.03	1.31	2.36	3.84	12.05	1.60	3.52
Nov.	0.21	0.45	1.77	2.82	0.01	0.16	0.52	0.87	0.07	0.26
Dec.	2.17	2.06	2.64	5.36	0.51	1.00	3.10	4.17	2.92	2.92
Ann.	19.44	22.26	29.72	44.41	11.32	16.99	29.34	55.82	20.27	22.32

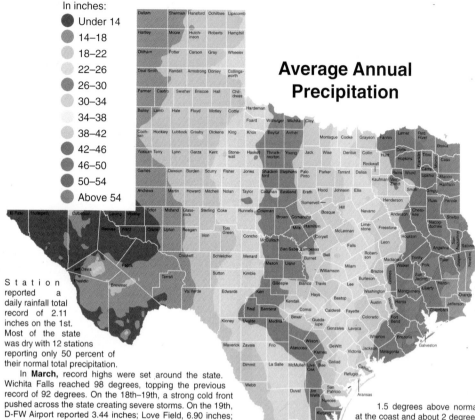

In inches:
- ● Under 14
- ● 14–18
- ● 18–22
- ● 22–26
- ● 26–30
- ● 30–34
- ● 34–38
- ● 38–42
- ● 42–46
- ● 46–50
- ● 50–54
- ● Above 54

Average Annual Precipitation

Station reported a daily rainfall total record of 2.11 inches on the 1st. Most of the state was dry with 12 stations reporting only 50 percent of their normal total precipitation.

In **March**, record highs were set around the state. Wichita Falls reached 98 degrees, topping the previous record of 92 degrees. On the 18th–19th, a strong cold front pushed across the state creating severe storms. On the 19th, D-FW Airport reported 3.44 inches; Love Field, 6.90 inches; and Arlington, 6.08 inches, causing widespread flooding. The front generated a squall line in West Texas that moved across the state, and the most severe weather occurred in the South Central and Edwards Plateau. A tornado was reported near Uvalde during the night of the 19th–20th. The cold air behind the front brought Amarillo low temperatures of 20 degrees, 19 degrees, and 22 degrees on the 21st, 22nd, and 23rd, respectively. Amarillo also reported 0.8 inches of snow on the 22nd. Houston reported a record low of 36 degrees on the 25th. Another weak front moved slowly across the state the 27th–28th, producing heavy rains on the 28th at Austin Mabry (3.26 inches) and College Station (2.87) and setting records for maximum daily rainfall at both locations.

April was warm and dry, and only one station, Abilene, reported above average precipitation. On the 15th–17th, Austin's 100 degrees broke a record of 90 degrees and D-FW's 101 degree high broke a record of 94 degrees. Most of the month's precipitation fell on three days. Strong storm systems moved through the state the 19th–21st and the 28th–29th. On the 20th, there were 2 tornado reports, 16 severe wind reports, and 56 hail reports. On the 25th, there were 2 tornado reports, 2 severe wind reports, and 37 hail reports. Large hail was reported in Coryell County. On the 28th–29th, there were 8 tornado reports (6 on the 29th alone), 40 severe wind reports and 65 hail reports. For the month there were 234 hail reports, 61 wind reports, and 13 tornado reports.

In **May,** storms and severe weather plagued the state for the first week. From the 1st–5th, there were 28 tornado reports, 68 strong wind reports and 286 hail reports. On the 5th alone, there were 82 hail reports, 20 severe wind reports, and 18 tornadoes. A strong bow-echo squall line moved on a northwest-southeast line from Lubbock through Waco and into College Station. Martin and Burnet counties reported four tornadoes each. An F-2 tornado touched down in Waco, producing damage to many businesses. McLennan County had a wind speed of 87 mph reported. Temperatures were

1.5 degrees above normal at the coast and about 2 degrees above normal Central Texas. West Texas was about 4 degrees above normal. Austin and San Antonio reported record highs of 97 degrees and 98 degrees, respectively, on the 27th. On the 29th, Houston reported 4.33 inches of rain and Victoria reported 5.39 inches, which were both record daily precipitation totals.

June provided very different weather for different areas of the state. Along the Gulf Coast, heavy rains led to flooding while the remainder of the state remained very dry, worsening the drought conditions. Dallas/Forth Worth received only 0.34 inches for the month, 11 percent of normal. Not all coastal stations reported above average rainfall; Brownsville only 0.24 inches, the lowest precipitation total statewide. The U.S. Drought Monitor placed most of South Texas under exceptional drought conditions, the most severe category it issues. Most of the coastal regions, however, received too much rainfall. Corpus Christi reported 8.62 inches on the 1st, and a three-day total for May 31st–June 2nd was a staggering 12.35 inches. The station reported total monthly precipitation of 11.19 inches, 3 times above the normal June total. Temperatures were above average across the state.

In **July,** coastal temperatures were cooler than normal and precipitation was well above average. Wichita Falls was the hottest part of the state, with an average high of 102 degrees, 4.8 degrees above normal. The average mean temperature was 88.4 degrees, which is 3.6 degrees above normal. Del Rio was the driest area, receiving only 0.01 inches for the month. The Dallas/Fort Worth had a mean temperature of 2.7 degrees above average, and an average high of 98.4 degrees, 3.0 degrees above normal. El Paso also reported 3.17 inches for the month, over twice its normal rainfall total. Statewide, there were 32 severe wind reports, 9 hail reports,

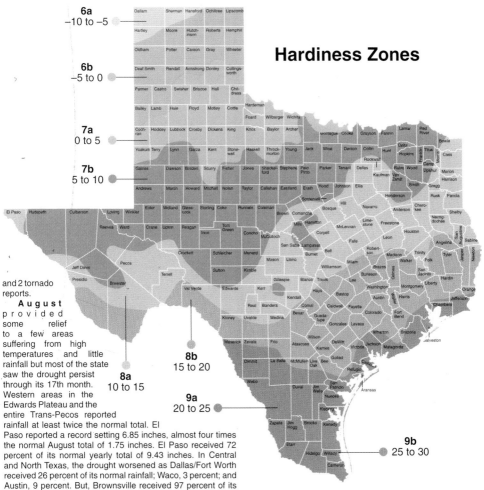

Hardiness Zones

6a
−10 to −5

6b
−5 to 0

7a
0 to 5

7b
5 to 10

8a
10 to 15

8b
15 to 20

9a
20 to 25

9b
25 to 30

and 2 tornado reports.

August provided some relief to a few areas suffering from high temperatures and little rainfall but most of the state saw the drought persist through its 17th month. Western areas in the Edwards Plateau and the entire Trans-Pecos reported rainfall at least twice the normal total. El Paso reported a record setting 6.85 inches, almost four times the normal August total of 1.75 inches. El Paso received 72 percent of its normal yearly total of 9.43 inches. In Central and North Texas, the drought worsened as Dallas/Fort Worth received 26 percent of its normal rainfall; Waco, 3 percent; and Austin, 9 percent. But, Brownsville received 97 percent of its monthly total, and Port Arthur, Houston and College Station all reported monthly rainfall totals of at least 89 percent of normal. Temperatures were above average for most of the state except for El Paso and Amarillo. The largest departure from normal was reported in Wichita Falls, which was 5.7 degrees above the normal monthly mean temperature. The average high for the entire month in Wichita Falls was 101.8.

September provided cooler temperatures and much needed rainfall. Although 9 stations reported above average precipitation totals, Central Texas, including Waco, Austin and College Station, reported below average precipitation totals. Temperatures across the state were mild compared to most Septembers. D-FW received 107 percent of normal rainfall. Wichita Falls received 112 percent in September. El Paso continued having high rainfall totals, with 4.99 inches reported this month, over three times the normal amount. However, most of Central and East Central areas reported below average rainfall totals.

October was a wet month for the eastern Texas. All stations east of I-35 received above normal precipitation. Port Arthur reported 14.72 inches, 315 percent of normal. The largest amount of this rainfall came on the 15th–16th when Houston International Airport reported 7.57 inches; Galveston, 6.07 inches; College Station, 5.36 inches; and Port Arthur, 7.73 inches. All of these precipitation totals were more than the normal average for the month. Most of the state, except the Panhandle, received copious rainfall on these two days. Temperatures were just about average in October. The statewide average temperature was 67.3 degrees, which is

1.0 degrees above normal. Some severe weather affected portions of the state on the 10th, 15th, and 18th. For the month there was a total of 18 severe wind reports, 10 hail reports, and 7 tornado reports.

In **November**, temperatures were well above average, while precipitation was well below average. Record highs were set in Abilene and San Angelo on the 9th with highs of 90 degrees and 91 degrees, respectively. Lubbock broke the all-time November high with 90 degrees on the 8th. This high broke a 90-year-old record set on November 7, 1916, when the high was 89 degrees. Rainfall was limited, and Dallas/Fort Worth was the only station to report at least average precipitation. The average total precipitation for the entire state was 0.81 inches.

Precipitation during **December** was above average for most stations except far West Texas and the upper Gulf coast. El Paso received 6 percent of its normal monthly rainfall while Midland reported 208 percent of normal monthly rainfall. The central areas received some much needed rain while the upper Gulf coast, including Victoria, Galveston, Houston and Port Arthur, reported below average totals. Temperatures statewide were above average except for El Paso, Galveston and Midland. On the 29th, a rare outbreak of winter storms affected the east and there were 27 reports of tornadoes, 8 reports of hail and 5 reports of severe wind. This tornado outbreak was the largest one-day total for December and also the largest monthly total for December. The average number of tornado reports in December is 3.☆

Extreme Weather Records in Texas

Temperature

Lowest — Tulia   Feb. 12, 1899   -23°F
         Seminole   Feb. 8, 1933   -23°F
Highest — Seymour   Aug. 12, 1936   120°F
         Monahans   June 28, 1994   120°F
Coldest Winter 1898–1899

Wind Velocity

Highest sustained wind

Matagorda   Sept. 11, 1961   SE, 145 mph
Port Lavaca   Sept. 11, 1961   NE, 145 mph

Highest peak gust

Aransas Pass   Aug. 3, 1970   SW, 180 mph
Robstown   Aug. 3, 1970   WSW, 180 mph

These velocities occurred during Hurricane Carla in 1961 and Hurricane Celia in 1970.

Tornadoes

Since 1950, there have been six tornadoes recorded of the F5 category, that is, with winds between 261-318 mph. They were:

Waco	May 11,	1953
Wichita Falls	April 3,	1964
Lubbock	May 11,	1970
Valley Mills (McLennan Co.)	May 6,	1973
Brownwood	April 19,	1976
Jarrell (Williamson Co.)	May 27,	1997

Rainfall

Wettest year statewide:	1941		42.62 in.
Driest year statewide:		1917	14.30 in.
Greatest annual:	Clarksville	1873	109.38 in.
Least annual:	Wink	1956	1.76 in.
†Greatest in 24 hours	Alvin	July 25–26, 1979	43.00 in.

†This is an unofficial estimate of rainfall that occurred during Tropical Storm Claudette. The greatest 24-hour rainfall ever recorded in Texas at an official observing site occurred at Albany, Shackelford County, on Aug. 4, 1978: 29.05 inches.

Hail

(Hailstones six inches or greater, since 1950)

Winkler County	May 31, 1960	8.00 in.
Young County	April 14, 1965	7.50 in.
Ward County	May 10, 1991	6.00 in.
Burleson County	Dec. 17, 1995	7.05 in.

Snowfall

Greatest seasonal
Romero* (Hartley Co.)   1923-1924   65.0 in.
Greatest monthly
Hale Center Feb. 1956   36.0 in.
Greatest single storm
Hale Center,   Feb. 2-5, 1956   33.0 in.
Greatest in 24 Hours
Plainview   Feb. 3-4, 1956   24.0 in.
Maximum depth on ground
Hale Center   Feb. 5, 1956   33in.
*Romero was in southwestern Hartley County but no longer exists.

Source: NOAA Environmental Data Service.

Meteorological Data

Source: Updated as of July 2007 by the National Climatic Data Center. Additional data for these locations are listed by county in the table of Texas temperature, freeze, growing season and precipitation records.

City	Temperature							Precipitation						Relative Humidity		Wind			Sun
	Record High	Month & Year	Record Low	Month & Year	No. Days Max. 90° and Above	No. Days Min. 32° and Below	Maximum in 24 Hours	Month & Year	Snowfall (Mean Annual)	Max. Snowfall in 24 Hours	Month & Year	6:00 a.m., CST	Noon, CST	Speed, MPH (Mean Annual)	Highest MPH	Month & Year	Percent Possible Sunshine
Abilene	110	7/1978	-9	1/1947	96	50	6.70	9/1961	4.6	9.3	4/1996	74	52	11.9	55	4/1998	70
Amarillo	108	6/1990	-14	2/1951	64	111	6.75	5/1951	16.2	20.6	0/1934	73	48	13.5	60	6/1994	74
Austin	112	9/2000	-2	1/1949	108	19	15.00	9/1921	0.9	9.7	11/1937	83	59	9.0	52	9/1987	60
Brownsville	106	3/1984	16	12/1989	121	2	12.19	9/1967	**	0.0	—	89	63	11.3	51	9/1996	59
Corpus Christi	109	9/2000	13	12/1989	106	5	8.92	8/1980	**	1.1	2/1973	89	65	12.0	56	5/1999	60
Dallas-Fort Worth	113	6/1980	-1	12/1989	97	37	5.91	10/1959	3.2	12.1	1/1964	81	58	10.7	73	8/1959	61
Del Rio	112	6/1988	10	12/1989	129	16	11.87	8/1998	0.9	8.6	1/1985	77	58	9.7	60	8/1970	84
El Paso	114	7/1994	-8	1/1962	108	60	2.63	7/1968	5.4	22.4	12/1987	56	28	8.8	64	1/1996	84
Galveston	104	9/2000	8	2/1999	12	3	14.35	7/2000	0.2	15.4	2/1895	83	72	11.0	*100	9/1900	59
†Houston	109	9/2000	7	12/1989	99	18	11.02	6/2001	0.4	2.0	1/1973	90	63	7.7	51	8/1983	72
Lubbock	114	6/1994	-16	1/1963	81	92	5.82	10/1983	10.1	16.3	1/1983	73	48	12.4	70	3/1952	72
Midland-Odessa	116	6/1994	-11	2/1985	100	63	5.99	7/1961	4.5	9.8	12/1998	73	45	11.1	67	2/1960	74
Prt. Arthur-Beaumont	108	8/2000	12	12/1989	83	14	17.76	7/1943	0.3	4.4	2/1960	91	66	9.6	55	6/1986	60
San Angelo	111	‡7/1960	-4	12/1989	109	52	6.25	9/1980	3.1	7.4	1/1978	77	52	10.3	75	4/1969	70
San Antonio	111	9/2000	0	1/1949	113	21	13.35	10/1998	0.7	13.2	1/1985	83	57	9.1	48	7/1979	60
Victoria	111	9/2000	9	12/1989	106	10	9.87	4/1991	0.1	2.1	1/1985	90	63	9.9	99	7/1963	49
Waco	112	8/1969	-5	1/1949	109	33	7.98	12/1997	1.4	7.0	1/1949	84	59	11.1	69	6/1961	59
Wichita Falls	117	6/1980	-8	2/1985	104	64	6.19	12/1980	5.8	9.8	1/1925	81	53	11.6	62	6/1954	60
§Shreveport, LA	109	‡8/2000	3	1/1962	90	35	12.44	7/1933	1.5	11	12/1929	87	61	8.3	63	5/2000	64

*100 mph recorded at 6:15 p.m., Sept. 8, 1900, just before the anemometer blew away. Maximum velocity was estimated to be 120 mph from the northeast between 7:30 p.m. and 8:30 p.m.
†The official Houston station was moved from near downtown to Intercontinental Airport, 12 miles north of the old station.
‡ Also recorded on earlier dates, months or years.
§Shreveport is included because it is near the boundary line and its data can be considered representative of Texas' east border.
**Trace, an amount too small to measure.

Texas Is Tornado Capital

An average of 132 tornadoes touch Texas soil each year. The annual total varies considerably, and certain areas are struck more often than others. Tornadoes occur with greatest frequency in the Red River Valley of North Texas.

Tornadoes may occur in any month and at any hour of the day, but they occur with greatest frequency during the late spring and early summer months, and between the hours of 4 p.m. and 8 p.m. In the period 1959–2006, nearly 63 percent of all Texas tornadoes occurred within the three-month period of April, May and June, with almost one-third of the total tornadoes occurring in May.

More tornadoes have been recorded in Texas than in any other state, which is partly due to the state's size. Between 1959 and 2006, 7,318 funnel clouds reached the ground, thus becoming tornadoes. Texas ranks 11th among the 50 states in the density of tornadoes, with an average of 5.7 tornadoes per 10,000 square miles per year during this period.

The greatest outbreak of tornadoes on record in Texas was associated with Hurricane Beulah in September 1967. Within a five-day period, Sept. 19–23, 115 known tornadoes, all in Texas, were spawned by this great hurricane. Sixty-seven occurred on Sept. 20, a Texas record for a single day.

In addition to Hurricane Beulah's 115 tornadoes, there were another 9 tornadoes in September for a total of 124, which is a Texas record for a single month. The greatest number of tornadoes in Texas in a single year is 232, also in 1967. The second-highest number in a single year is 1995, when 223 tornadoes occurred in Texas. In 1982, 123 tornadoes formed in May, making it the worst outbreak of spring tornadoes in Texas.

The accompanying table, compiled by the National Climatic Data Center, Environmental Data Service and the National Oceanic and Atmospheric Administration, lists tornado occurrences in Texas, by months, for the period 1951–2006. ☆

A funnel cloud touches down north of Jarrell in Williamson County on May 27, 1997. The twister was part of a violent storm system that ripped through four Central Texas counties and killed 27 people. Ted S. Warren photo.

Number of Tornadoes in Texas, 1959–2006
Source: Office of State Climatologist

Year	Jan.	Feb.	March	April	May	June	July	Aug.	Sept.	Oct.	Nov.	Dec.	Annual
1959	0	0	8	4	32	14	10	3	4	5	6	0	86
1960	4	1	0	8	29	14	3	4	2	11	1	0	77
1961	0	1	21	15	24	30	9	2	12	0	10	0	124
1962	0	4	12	9	25	56	12	15	7	2	0	1	143
1963	0	0	3	9	19	24	8	4	6	4	5	0	82
1964	0	1	6	22	15	11	9	7	3	1	3	0	78
1965	2	5	3	7	43	24	2	9	4	6	0	3	108
1966	0	4	1	21	22	15	3	8	3	0	0	0	77
1967	0	2	11	17	34	22	10	5	124	2	0	5	232
1968	2	1	3	13	47	21	4	8	5	8	11	16	139
1969	0	1	1	16	65	16	6	7	6	8	1	0	127
1970	1	3	5	23	23	9	5	20	9	20	0	3	121
1971	0	20	10	24	27	33	7	20	7	16	4	23	191
1972	1	0	19	13	43	12	19	13	8	9	7	0	144
1973	14	1	29	25	21	24	4	8	5	3	9	4	147
1974	2	1	8	19	18	26	3	9	6	22	2	0	116
1975	5	2	9	12	50	18	10	3	3	3	1	1	117
1976	1	1	8	53	63	11	16	6	13	4	0	0	176
1977	0	0	3	34	50	4	5	5	12	0	6	4	123
1978	0	0	0	34	65	10	13	6	6	1	2	0	137
1979	1	2	24	33	39	14	12	10	4	15	3	0	157
1980	0	2	7	26	44	21	2	34	10	5	0	2	153
1981	0	7	7	9	71	26	5	20	5	23	3	0	176
1982	0	0	6	27	123	36	4	0	3	0	3	1	203
1983	5	7	24	1	62	35	4	22	5	0	7	14	186
1984	0	13	9	18	19	19	0	4	1	5	2	5	95
1985	0	0	5	41	28	5	3	1	1	3	1	2	90
1986	0	12	4	21	50	24	3	5	4	7	1	0	131
1987	1	1	7	0	54	19	11	3	8	0	16	4	124
1988	0	0	0	11	7	7	6	2	42	4	10	0	89
1989	3	0	5	3	70	63	0	6	3	6	1	0	160
1990	3	3	4	56	62	20	5	2	3	0	0	0	158
1991	20	5	2	39	72	36	1	2	3	8	4	0	192
1992	0	5	13	22	43	66	4	4	4	7	21	0	189
1993	1	4	5	17	39	4	4	0	12	23	8	0	117
1994	0	1	1	48	88	2	1	4	3	9	8	0	165
1995	6	0	13	36	66	75	11	3	2	1	0	10	223
1996	7	1	2	21	33	9	3	8	33	8	4	1	130
1997	0	6	7	31	59	50	2	2	1	16	3	0	177
1998	24	15	4	9	11	6	3	5	3	28	1	0	109
1999	22	0	22	23	70	26	3	8	0	0	0	4	178
2000	0	7	49	33	23	8	3	0	0	10	20	1	154
2001	0	0	4	12	36	12	0	7	15	24	27	5	142
2002	0	0	44	25	61	5	1	4	13	8	0	22	183
2003	0	0	4	31	50	29	6	1	4	12	29	0	166
2004	1	1	27	25	29	34	1	5	0	4	55	2	184
2005	0	0	6	7	27	46	15	4	2	0	0	2	109
2006	0	1	4	20	43	7	3	3	0	9	0	27	117
Total	128	151	516	1153	2235	1177	300	357	439	382	311	169	7318

Destructive Weather

Source: This list of exceptionally destructive weather in Texas since 1766 was compiled from ESSA-Weather Bureau information.

Sept. 4, 1766: Hurricane. Galveston Bay. A Spanish mission destroyed.

Sept. 12, 1818: Hurricane. Galveston Island. Salt water flowed four feet deep. Only six buildings remained habitable. Of the six vessels and two barges in the harbor, even the two not seriously damaged were reduced to dismasted hulks. **Pirate Jean Lafitte** moved to one hulk so his **Red House** might serve as a hospital.

Aug. 6, 1844: Hurricane. Mouth of Rio Grande. All houses destroyed at the mouth of the river and at **Brazos Santiago**, eight miles north; 70 lives lost.

Sept. 19, 1854: Hurricane. It struck near **Matagorda**, and moved inland, northwestward over **Columbus**. Main impact fell in **Matagorda and Lavaca bays**. Almost all buildings in Matagorda were destroyed. Four lives were lost in town; more lives were lost on the peninsula.

Oct. 3, 1867: Hurricane. This hurricane moved inland **south of Galveston**, but raked the entire Texas coast **from the Rio Grande to the Sabine. Bagdad and Clarksville**, towns at the mouth of the Rio Grande, were destroyed. Much of Galveston was flooded and property damage there was estimated at $1 million.

Sept. 16, 1875: Hurricane. Struck **Indianola**, Calhoun County. Three-fourths of town swept away; 176 lives lost. Flooding from the bay caused nearly all destruction.

Aug. 13, 1880: Hurricane. Center struck **Matamoros, Mexico; lower Texas coast** affected.

Oct. 12–13, 1880: Hurricane. Brownsville. City nearly destroyed, many lives lost.

Aug. 23–24, 1882: Torrential rains caused **flooding** on the **North and South Concho and Bosque rivers** (South Concho reported 45 feet above normal level), destroying **Benficklen**, then county seat of Tom Green County, leaving only the courthouse and jail. More than 50 persons drowned in **Tom Green and Erath counties**, with property damage at $200,000 and 10,000 to 15,000 head of livestock lost.

Aug. 19–21, 1886: Hurricane. Indianola. Every house destroyed or damaged. Indianola was never rebuilt.

Oct. 12, 1886: Hurricane. Sabine, Jefferson County. Hurricane passed over Sabine. The inundation extended 20 miles inland and nearly every house in the vicinity was moved from its foundation; 150 persons were drowned.

April 28, 1893: Tornado. Cisco, Eastland County, 20 killed, 93 injured; damage $400,000.

May 15, 1896: Tornadoes, Sherman, Grayson County; **Justin**, Denton County; **Gribble Springs**, Cooke County; 76 killed; damage $225,000.

Sept. 12, 1897: Hurricane. Many houses in Port Arthur were demolished; 13 killed, damage $150,000.

May 1, 1898: Tornado. Mobeetie, Wheeler County. Four killed, several injured; damage $35,000.

June 27–July 1, 1899: Rainstorm. A storm, centered over **the Brazos River watershed**, precipitated an average of 17 inches over 7,000 square miles. At **Hearne**, the gage overflowed at 24 inches; estimated total rainfall was 30 inches. At **Turnersville**, Coryell County, 33 inches were recorded in three days. This rain caused the **worst Brazos River flood on record**. Between 30 and 35 lives were lost. Property damage was estimated at $9 million.

April 5–8, 1900: Rainstorm. This storm began in two centers, over **Val Verde County** on the Rio Grande, and over **Swisher County** on the High Plains, and converged in the vicinity of **Travis County**, causing disastrous floods in the **Colorado, Brazos and Guadalupe rivers**. McDonald Dam on the Colorado River at Austin crumbled suddenly. A wall of water swept through the city taking at least 23 lives. Damage was estimated at $1,250,000.

Sept. 8–9, 1900: Hurricane. Galveston. The Great Galveston Storm was the **worst natural disaster in U.S. history** in terms of human life. Loss of life at Galveston has been estimated at 6,000 to 8,000, but the exact number has never been exactly determined. The island was completely inundated; not a single structure escaped damage. Most of the loss of life was due to drowning by storm tides that reached 15 feet or more. The anemometer blew away when the wind reached 100 mph at 6:15 p.m. on the 8th. Wind reached an estimated maximum velocity of 120 mph between 7:30 and 8:30 p.m. Property damage has been estimated at $30 to $40 million.

May 18, 1902: Tornado. Goliad. This tornado cut a 250-yard-wide path through town, turning 150 buildings into rubble. Several churches were destroyed, one of which was holding services; all 40 worshippers were either killed or injured. This tornado killed 114, injured 230, and caused an estimated $200,000 in damages.

April 26, 1906: Tornado. Bellevue, Clay County, demolished; considerable damage done at Stoneburg, seven miles east; 17 killed, 20 injured; damage $300,000.

May 6, 1907: Tornado. North of Sulphur Springs, Hopkins County; five killed, 19 injured.

May 13, 1908: Tornado. Linden, Cass County. Four killed, seven injured; damage $75,000.

May 22–25, 1908: Rainstorm; unique because it originated on the Pacific Coast. It moved first into **North Texas** and southern Oklahoma and thence to **Central Texas**, precipitating as much as 10 inches. Heaviest floods were in the upper Trinity basin, but flooding was general as far south as the Nueces. Property damage exceeded $5 million and 11 lives were lost in the Dallas vicinity.

March 23, 1909: Tornado. Slidell, Wise County; 11 killed, 10 injured; damage $30,000.

May 30, 1909: Tornado. Zephyr, Brown County; 28 killed, many injured; damage $90,000.

July 21, 1909: Hurricane. Velasco, Brazoria County. One-half of town destroyed, 41 lives lost; damage $2,000,000.

Dec. 1–5, 1913: Rainstorm. This caused the **second major Brazos River flood**, and caused more deaths than the storm of 1899. It formed over **Central Texas** and spread both southwest and northeast with precipitation of 15 inches at **San Marcos** and 11 inches at **Kaufman**. Floods caused loss of 177 lives and $8,541,000 damage.

April 20–26, 1915: Rainstorm. Originated over Central Texas and spread into North and East Texas with precipitation up to 17 inches, causing floods in **Trinity, Brazos, Colorado, and Guadalupe rivers**. More than 40 lives lost and $2,330,000 damage.

Aug. 16–19, 1915: Hurricane. Galveston. Peak wind gusts of 120 miles recorded at Galveston; tide ranged 9.5 to 14.3 feet above mean sea level in the city, and up to 16.1 feet near the causeway. Business section flooded with 5 to 6 feet of water. At least 275 lives lost, damage $56 million. A new seawall prevented a repetition of the 1900 disaster.

Aug. 18, 1916: Hurricane. Corpus Christi. Maximum wind speed 100 mph. 20 Lives lost; damage $1,600,000.

Jan. 10–12, 1918: Blizzard. This was the most severe since that of February, 1899; it was accompanied by zero degree temperature in North Texas and temperatures from 7° to 12° below freezing along the lower coast.

April 9, 1919: Tornado. Leonard, Ector and Ravenna in Fannin County; 20 killed, 45 injured; damage $125,000.

April 9, 1919: Tornado. Henderson, Van Zandt, Wood, Camp, and Red River counties, 42 killed, 150 injured; damage $450,000.

May 7, 1919: Windstorms. Starr, Hidalgo, Willacy and Cameron counties. Violent thunderstorms with high winds, hail and rain occurred between **Rio Grande City** and the coast, killing 10 persons. Damage to property and crops was $500,000. Seven were killed at **Mission**.

Sept. 14, 1919: Hurricane. Near **Corpus Christi**. Center moved inland south of Corpus Christi; tides 16 feet above normal in that area and 8.8 feet above normal at **Galveston**. Extreme wind at Corpus Christi measured at 110 mph; 284 lives lost; damage $20,272,000.

April 13, 1921: Tornado. Melissa, Collin County, and **Petty**, Lamar County. Melissa was practically destroyed; 12 killed, 80 injured; damage $500,000.

April 15, 1921: Tornado. Wood, Cass and Bowie counties; 10 killed, 50 injured; damage $85,000.

Sept. 8–10, 1921: Rainstorm. Probably the **greatest rainstorm in Texas history**, it entered Mexico as a hurricane from the Gulf. Torrential rains fell as the storm moved northeasterly across Texas. **Record floods** occurred in **Bexar, Travis, Williamson, Bell and Milam counties**, killing 215 persons, with property losses over $19 million. Five to nine feet of water stood in downtown **San Antonio**. A total of 23.98 inches was measured at the U.S. Weather Bureau station at **Taylor** during a period of 35 hours, with a 24-hour maximum of 23.11 on September 9-10. The **greatest rainfall recorded in United States history during 18 consecutive hours** (measured at an unofficial weather-monitoring site) **fell at Thrall**, Williamson County, 36.40 inches fell on Sept. 9.

April 8, 1922: Tornado. Rowena, Runnels County. Seven killed, 52 injured; damage $55,000.

April 8, 1922: Tornado. Oplin, Callahan County. Five killed, 30 injured; damage $15,000.

April 23–24, 1922: Rainstorm. An exceptional storm entered Texas from the west and moved from the **Panhandle** to **North Central and East Texas**. Rains up to 12.6 inches over Parker, Tarrant and Dallas counties caused severe floods in the Upper Trinity at **Fort Worth**; 11 lives were lost; damage was estimated at $1 million.

May 4, 1922: Tornado. Austin, Travis County; 12 killed, 50 injured; damage $500,000.

May 14, 1922: Tornado. Howard and Mitchell counties; 23 killed, 100 injured; damage $50,000.

April 12, 1927: Tornado. Edwards, Real and Uvalde counties; 74 killed, 205 injured; damage $1,230,000. Most of damage was in Rocksprings where 72 deaths occurred and town was practically destroyed.

May 9, 1927: Tornado. Garland; eleven killed; damage $100,000.

May 9, 1927: Tornado. Nevada, Collin County; **Wolfe City**, Hunt County; and **Tigertown**, Lamar County; 28 killed, over 200 injured; damage $900,000.

Jan. 4, 1929: Tornado. Near **Bay City**, Matagorda County. Five killed, 14 injured.

April 24, 1929: Tornado. Slocum, Anderson County; seven killed, 20 injured; damage $200,000.

May 24–31, 1929: Rainstorm. Beginning over **Caldwell County**, a storm spread over much of **Central and Coastal Texas** with maximum rainfall of 12.9 inches, **causing floods in Colorado, Guadalupe, Brazos, Trinity, Neches and Sabine rivers.** Much damage at **Houston** from overflow of bayous. Damage estimated at $6 million.

May 6, 1930: Tornado. Bynum, Irene and Mertens in Hill County; **Ennis**, Ellis County; and **Frost**, Navarro County; 41 killed; damage $2,100,000.

May 6, 1930: Tornado. Kenedy and Runge in Karnes County; **Nordheim**, DeWitt County; 36 killed, 34 injured; damage $127,000.

June 30–July 2, 1932: Rainstorm. Torrential rains fell over the upper watersheds of the **Nueces and Guadalupe rivers**, causing destructive floods. Seven persons drowned; property losses exceeded $500,000.

Aug. 13, 1932: Hurricane. Near **Freeport**, Brazoria County. Wind speed at **East Columbia** estimated at 100 mph; 40 lives lost, 200 injured; damage $7,500,000.

March 30, 1933: Tornado. Angelina, Nacogdoches and San Augustine counties; 10 killed, 56 injured; damage $200,000.

April 26, 1933: Tornado. Bowie County near Texarkana. Five killed, 38 injured; damage $14,000.

July 22–25, 1933: Tropical Storm. One of the greatest U.S. storms in area and general rainfall. The storm reached the vicinity of **Freeport** late on July 22 and moved very slowly

overland across eastern Texas, July 22-25. The storm center moved into northern Louisiana on the 25th. Rainfall averaged 12.50 inches over an area of about 25,000 square miles. Twenty inches or more fell in a small area of eastern Texas and western Louisiana surrounding Logansport, La. The 4-day total at Logansport was 22.30 inches. Property damage was estimated at $1,114,790.

July 30, 1933: Tornado. Oak Cliff section of Dallas, Dallas County. Five killed, 30 injured; damage $500,000.

Sept. 4–5, 1933: Hurricane. Near **Brownsville**. Center passed inland a short distance north of Brownsville, where an extreme wind of 106 mph was measured before the anemometer blew away. Peak wind gusts were estimated at 120 to 125 mph. 40 known dead, 500 injured; damage $16,903,100. About 90 percent of the citrus crop in the **Lower Rio Grande Valley** was destroyed.

July 25, 1934: Hurricane. Near **Seadrift**, Calhoun County, 19 lives lost, many minor injuries; damage $4.5 million. About 85 percent of damage was in crops.

Sept. 15–18, 1936: Rainstorm. Excessive rains over the **North Concho and Middle Concho rivers** caused a sharp rise in the Concho River, which overflowed **San Angelo**. Much of the business district and 500 homes were flooded. Four persons drowned and property losses estimated at $5 million. Four-day storm rainfall at San Angelo measured 25.19 inches; 11.75 inches fell on the 15th.

June 10, 1938: Tornado. Clyde, Callahan County; 14 killed, 9 injured; damage $85,000.

Sept. 23, 1941: Hurricane. Near **Matagorda**. Center moved inland near Matagorda, and passed over **Houston** about midnight. Extremely high tides along coast in the **Matagorda to Galveston** area. Heaviest property and crop losses were in counties from Matagorda County to the Sabine River. Four lives lost. Damage was $6,503,300.

April 28, 1942: Tornado. Crowell, Foard County; 11 killed, 250 injured; damage $1,500,000.

Aug. 30, 1942: Hurricane. Matagorda Bay. Highest wind estimated 115 mph at **Seadrift**. Tide at **Matagorda**,14.7 feet. Storm moved west-north-westward and finally diminished over the **Edwards Plateau**; eight lives lost, property damage estimated at $11.5 million, and crop damage estimated at $15 million.

May 10, 1943: Tornado. Laird Hill, Rusk County, and **Kilgore**, Gregg County. Four killed, 25 injured; damage $1 million.

July 27, 1943: Hurricane. Near **Galveston**. Center moved inland across **Bolivar Peninsula and Trinity Bay**. A wind gust of 104 mph was recorded at **Texas City**; 19 lives lost; damage estimated at $16,550,000.

Aug. 26–27, 1945: Hurricane. Aransas-San Antonio Bay area. At **Port O'Connor**, the wind reached 105 mph when the cups were torn from the anemometer. Peak gusts of 135 mph were experienced at **Seadrift, Port O'Connor and Port Lavaca**; three killed, 25 injured; damage $20,133,000.

Jan. 4, 1946: Tornado. Near **Lufkin**, Angelina County and **Nacogdoches**, Nacogdoches County; 13 killed, 250 injured; damage $2,050,000.

Jan. 4, 1946: Tornado. Near **Palestine**, Anderson County; 15 killed, 60 injured; damage $500,000.

May 18, 1946: Tornado. Clay, Montague and Denton counties. Four killed, damage $112,000.

April 9, 1947: Tornado. White Deer, Carson County; **Glazier**, Hemphill County; and **Higgins**, Lipscomb County; 68 killed, 201 injured; damage $1,550,000. Glazier completely destroyed. **One of the largest tornadoes on record.** Width of path, 1 miles at Higgins; length of path, 221 miles across portions of Texas, Oklahoma and Kansas. This tornado also struck Woodward, Okla.

May 3, 1948: Tornado. McKinney, Collin County; three killed, 43 injured; $2 million damage.

May 15, 1949: Tornado. Amarillo and vicinity; six killed, 83 injured. Total damage from tornado, wind and hail, $5,310,000. Total destruction over one-block by three-block area in southern part of city; airport and 45 airplanes damaged; 28 railroad boxcars blown off track.

Sept. 8–10, 1952: Rainstorm. Heavy rains over the **Colorado and Guadalupe River watersheds** in southwestern Texas caused major flooding. From 23 to 26 inches fell between **Kerrville, Blanco and Boerne**. Highest stages ever known occurred in the **Pedernales River**; five lives lost, three injured; 17 homes destroyed, 454 damaged. Property loss several million dollars.

March 13, 1953: Tornado. Jud and O'Brien, Haskell County; and **Knox City**, Knox County; 17 killed, 25 injured; damage $600,000.

May 11, 1953: Tornado. Near **San Angelo**, Tom Green County; eleven killed, 159 injured; damage $3,239,000.

May 11, 1953: Tornado. Waco, McLennan County; 114 killed, 597 injured; damage $41,150,000. **One of two most disastrous tornadoes**; 150 homes destroyed, 900 homes damaged; 185 other buildings destroyed; 500 other buildings damaged.

High tides and winds from Hurricane Carla moved inland at Freeport on Sept. 10, 1961. Carla was the largest hurricane of record in Texas. File photo.

April 2, 1957: Tornado. Dallas, Dallas County; 10 killed, 200 injured; damage $4 million. Moving through Oak Cliff and West Dallas, it damaged 574 buildings, largely homes.

April–May, 1957: Torrential Rains. Excessive flooding occurred throughout the area **east of the Pecos River to the Sabine River** during the last 10 days of April; 17 lives were lost, and several hundred homes were destroyed. During May, more than 4,000 persons were evacuated from unprotected lowlands on the **West Fork of the Trinity above Fort Worth** and along creeks in Fort Worth. Twenty-nine houses at **Christoval** were damaged or destroyed and 83 houses at **San Angelo** were damaged. Five persons were drowned in floods in **South Central Texas**.

May 15, 1957: Tornado. Silverton, Briscoe County; 21 killed, 80 injured; damage $500,000.

June 27, 1957: Hurricane Audrey. Center crossed the Gulf coast near the Texas-Louisiana line. **Orange** was in the western portion of the eye between 9 and 10 a.m. In Texas, nine lives were lost, 450 persons injured; property damage was $8 million. Damage was extensive in **Jefferson and Orange counties**, with less in **Chambers and Galveston counties**. Maximum wind reported in Texas, 85 m.p.h. at **Sabine Pass**, with gusts to 100 m.p.h.

Oct. 28, 1960: Rainstorm. Rains of 7-10 inches fell in **South Central Texas**; 11 died from drowning in flash floods. In **Austin** about 300 families were driven from their homes. Damage in Austin was estimated at $2.5 million.

Sept. 8–14, 1961: Hurricane Carla. Port O'Connor; maximum wind gust at **Port Lavaca** estimated at 175 mph. Highest tide was 18.5 feet at Port Lavaca. Most damage was to **coastal counties between Corpus Christi and Port Arthur** and inland **Jackson, Harris and Wharton counties**. In Texas, 34 persons died; seven in a tornado that swept across **Galveston Island**; 465 persons were injured. Property and crop damage conservatively estimated at $300 million. The evacuation of an estimated 250,000 persons kept loss of life low. **Hurricane Carla was the largest hurricane of record.**

Sept. 7, 1962: Rainstorm. Fort Worth. Rains fell over the Big Fossil and Denton Creek watersheds ranging up to 11 inches of fall in three hours. Extensive damage from flash flooding occurred in **Richland Hills and Haltom City**.

Sept. 16–20, 1963: Hurricane Cindy. Rains of 15 to 23.5 inches fell in portions of **Jefferson, Newton and Orange counties** when Hurricane Cindy became stationary west of **Port Arthur**. Flooding from the excessive rainfall resulted in total property damage of $11,600,000 and agricultural losses of $500,000.

April 3, 1964: Tornado. Wichita Falls. Seven killed, 111 injured; damage $15 million; 225 homes destroyed, 50 with major damage, and 200 with minor damage. Sixteen other buildings received major damage.

Sept. 21–23, 1964: Rainstorm. Collin, Dallas and Tarrant counties. Rains of more than 12 inches fell during the first eight hours of the 21st. Flash flooding of tributaries of the Trinity River and smaller creeks and streams resulted in two drownings and an estimated $3 million property damage. Flooding of homes occurred in all sections of **McKinney**. In **Fort Worth**, there was considerable damage to residences along Big Fossil and White Rock creeks. Expensive homes in **North Dallas** were heavily damaged.

Jan. 25, 1965: Dust Storm. West Texas. The worst dust storm since February 1956 developed on the **southern High Plains**. Winds, gusting up to 75 mph at **Lubbock**, sent dust billowing to 31,000 feet in the area **from the Texas-New Mexico border eastward to a line from Tulia to Abilene**. Ground visibility was reduced to about 100 yards in many sections. The worst hit was the **Muleshoe, Seminole, Plains, Morton** area on the South Plains. The rain gage at Reese Air Force Base, Lubbock, contained 3 inches of fine sand.

June 2, 1965: Tornado. Hale Center, Hale County. Four killed, 76 injured; damage $8 million.

June 11, 1965: Rainstorm. Sanderson, Terrell County. Torrential rains of up to eight inches in two hours near Sanderson caused a major flash flood that swept through the town. As a result, 26 persons drowned and property losses were estimated at $2,715,000.

April 22–20, 1966: Flooding. Northeast Texas. Twenty to 26 inches of rain fell in portions of Wood, Smith, Morris, Upshur, Gregg, Marion and Harrison counties. Nineteen persons drowned in the rampaging rivers and creeks that swept away bridges, roads and dams, and caused an estimated $12 million damage.

April 28, 1966: Flash flooding. Dallas County. Flash flooding from torrential rains in Dallas County resulted in 14 persons drowned and property losses at $15 million.

Sept. 18–23, 1967: Hurricane Beulah. Near **Brownsville**. The **third largest hurricane of record**, Hurricane Beulah moved inland near the mouth of the Rio Grande on the 20th. Wind gusts of 136 mph were reported during Beulah's passage. Rains 10 to 20 inches over much of the area **south of San Antonio** resulted in record-breaking floods. An unofficial gaging station at **Falfurrias** registered the highest accumulated rainfall, 36 inches. The resultant stream overflow and surface runoff inundated 1.4 million acres. Beulah spawned 115 tornadoes, all in Texas, the **greatest number of tornadoes on record for any hurricane**. Hurricane Beulah caused 13 deaths and 37 injuries, of which five deaths and 34 injuries were attributed to tornadoes. Property losses were estimated at $100 million and crop losses at $50 million.

April 18, 1970: Tornado. Near **Clarendon**, Donley County. Seventeen killed, 42 injured; damage $2,100,000. Fourteen persons were killed at a resort community at Green Belt Reservoir, 7 miles north of Clarendon.

May 11, 1970: Tornado. Lubbock, Lubbock County.

Twenty-six killed, 500 injured; damage $135 million. Fifteen square miles, almost one-quarter of the city of Lubbock, suffered damage.

Aug. 3–5, 1970: Hurricane Celia. Corpus Christi. Hurricane Celia was a unique but severe storm. Measured in dollars, it was **the costliest in the state's history to that time**. Sustained wind speeds reached 130 mph, but it was great bursts of kinetic energy of short duration that appeared to cause the severe damage. Wind gusts of 161 mph were measured at the **Corpus Christi** National Weather Service Office. At **Aransas Pass**, peak wind gusts were estimated as high as 180 mph, after the wind equipment had been blown away. Celia caused 11 deaths in Texas, at least 466 injuries, and total property and crop damage in Texas estimated at $453,773,000. Hurricane Celia crossed the Texas coastline midway between Corpus Christi and Aransas Pass about 3:30 p.m. CST on Aug. 3. Hardest hit was the metropolitan area of **Corpus Christi**, including **Robstown, Aransas Pass, Port Aransas** and small towns on the north side of Corpus Christi Bay.

Feb. 20–22, 1971: Blizzard. Panhandle. Paralyzing blizzard, worst since March 22–25, 1957, storm transformed Panhandle into one vast snowfield as 6 to 26 inches of snow were whipped by 40 to 60 mph winds into drifts up to 12 feet high. At **Follett**, 3-day snowfall was 26 inches. Three persons killed; property and livestock losses were $3.1 million.

Sept. 9–13, 1971: Hurricane Fern. Coastal Bend. Ten to 26 inches of rain resulted in some of worst flooding since Hurricane Beulah in 1967. Two persons killed; losses were $30,231,000.

May 11–12, 1972: Rainstorm. South Central Texas. Seventeen drowned at **New Braunfels**, one at **McQueeney**. New Braunfels and **Seguin** hardest hit. Property damage $17.5 million.

June 12–13, 1973: Rainstorm. Southeastern Texas. Ten drowned. Over $50 million in property and crop damage. From 10-15 inches of rain recorded.

Nov. 23–24, 1974: Flash Flooding. Central Texas. Over $1 million in property damage. Thirteen people killed, ten in **Travis County**.

Jan. 31–Feb. 1, 1975: Flooding. Nacogdoches County. Widespread heavy rain caused flash flooding here, resulting in three deaths; damage over $5.5 million.

May 23, 1975: Rainstorm. Austin area. Heavy rains, high winds and hail resulted in over $5 million property damage; 40 people injured. Four deaths caused by drowning.

June 15, 1976: Rainstorm. Harris County. Rains in excess of 13 inches caused damage estimated at near $25 million. Eight deaths were storm-related, including three drownings.

Aug. 1–4, 1978: Heavy Rains, Flooding. Edwards Plateau, Low Rolling Plains. Remnants of **Tropical Storm Amelia** caused some of the worst flooding of this century. As much as 30 inches of rain fell near **Albany** in Shackelford County, where six drownings were reported. In **Bandera, Kerr, Kendall and Gillespie counties**, 27 people drowned and the damage total was at least $50 million.

Dec. 30–31, 1978: Ice Storm. North Central Texas. Possibly the **worst ice storm in 30 years** hit Dallas County particularly hard. Damage estimates reached $14 million, and six deaths were storm-related.

April 10, 1979: The worst single tornado in Texas' history hit **Wichita Falls**. Earlier on the same day, **several tornadoes** hit farther west. The destruction in Wichita Falls resulted in 42 dead, 1,740 injured, over 3,000 homes destroyed and damage of approximately $400 million. An estimated 20,000 persons were left homeless by this storm. In all, the tornadoes on April 10 killed 53 people, injured 1,812 and caused over $500 million damages.

May 3, 1979: Thunderstorms. Dallas County was hit by a wave of the most destructive thunderstorms in many years; 37 injuries and $5 million in damages resulted.

July 25–26, 1979: Tropical Storm Claudette caused over $750 million in property and crop damages, but fortunately only few injuries. Near **Alvin**, an estimated 43 inches of rain fell, a new state record for 24 hours.

Aug. 24, 1979: One of the worst **hailstorms** in **West Texas** in the past 100 years; $200 million in crops, mostly cotton, destroyed.

Sept. 18–20, 1979: Coastal flooding from heavy rain, 18 inches in 24 hours at **Aransas Pass**, and 13 inches at **Rockport**.

Aug. 9–11, 1980: Hurricane Allen hit **South Texas** and left three dead, causing $650 million-$750 million in property and crop damages. Over 250,000 coastal residents had to be evacuated. The worst damage occurred along **Padre Island** and in **Corpus Christi**. Over 20 inches of rain fell in **extreme South Texas**, and 29 tornadoes occurred; one of the worst hurricane-related outbreaks.

Summer 1980: One of the hottest summers in the history of the Lone Star State.

Sept. 5–8, 1980: Hurricane Danielle brought rain and flooding to Southeast and Central Texas. Seventeen inches of rain fell at Port Arthur, and 25 inches near Junction.

May 24–25, 1981: Severe flooding in **Austin** claimed 13 lives, injured about 100 and caused $40 million in damage. Up to 5.5 inches of rain fell in one hour west of the city.

Oct. 11–14, 1981: Record rains in North Central Texas caused by the remains of **Pacific Hurricane Norma**. Over 20 inches fell in some locations.

April 2, 1982: A tornado outbreak in Northeast Texas. The most severe tornado struck **Paris**; 10 people were killed, 170 injured and 1,000 left homeless. Over $50 million in damages resulted. A total of 7 tornadoes that day left 11 dead and 174 injured.

May, 1982: Texas recorded **123 tornadoes**, the most ever in May, and one less than the most recorded in any single month in the state. One death and 23 injuries occurred.

Dec. 1982: Heavy snow. El Paso recorded 18.2 inches of snow, the most in any month there.

Aug. 15–21, 1983: Hurricane Alicia was the first hurricane to make landfall in the continental U.S. in three years (Aug. 18), and **one of the costliest in Texas history** ($3 billion). Alicia caused widespread damage to a large section of **Southeast Texas**, including coastal areas near **Galveston** and the entire **Houston** area. Alicia spawned 22 tornadoes, and highest winds were estimated near 130 mph. In all, 18 people in South Texas were killed and 1,800 injured as a result of the tropical storm.

Jan. 12–13, 1985: A record-breaking snowstorm struck **West and South Central Texas** with up to 15 inches of snow that fell at many locations **between San Antonio and the Rio Grande**. San Antonio recorded 13.2 inches of snow for Jan. 12 (the greatest in a day) and 13.5 inches for the two-day total. **Eagle Pass** reported 14.5 inches of snow.

June 26, 1986: Hurricane Bonnie made landfall between **High Island and Sabine Pass** around 3:45 a.m. The highest wind measured in the area was a gust to 97 m.p.h., which was recorded at the **Sea Rim State Park**. As much as 13 inches of rain fell in **Ace** in southern Polk County. There were several reports of funnel clouds, but no confirmed tornadoes. While the storm caused no major structural damage, there was widespread minor damage. Numerous injuries were reported.

May 22, 1987: A strong, **multiple-vortex tornado** struck the town of **Saragosa**, Reeves Co.), essentially wiping it off the map. Of the town's 183 inhabitants, 30 were killed and 121 were injured. Eight-five percent of the town's structures were completely destroyed, while total damage topped $1.3 million.

Oct. 15–19, 1994: Extreme amounts of rainfall, up to 28.90 inches over a 4-day period, fell throughout southeastern part of the state. Seventeen lives were lost, most of them victims of flash flooding. Many rivers reached record flood levels. **Houston** was cut off from many other parts of the state, as numerous roads, including Interstate 10, were under water. Damage was estimated to be near $700 million; 26 counties were declared disaster areas.

May 5, 1995: A **thunderstorm** moved across the **Dallas/Fort Worth** area with 70 mph wind gusts and rainfall rates of almost three inches in 30 minutes (five inches in one hour). Twenty people lost their lives as a result of this storm, 109 people were injured by large hail and, with more than $2 billion in damage, the NOAA dubbed it the "costliest thunderstorm event in history."

May 28, 1995: A supercell thunderstorm produced extreme winds and giant hail in San Angelo, injuring at least 80 people and causing about $120 million in damage. Sixty-one homes were destroyed, and more than 9,000 were slightly damaged. In some areas, hail was six inches deep, with drifts to two feet.

Feb. 21, 1996: Anomalously high temperatures were reported over the entire state, breaking records in nearly every region of the state. Temperatures near 100°F shattered previous records by as many as 10°F as Texans experienced heat more characteristic of mid-summer than winter.

May 10, 1996: Hail up to five inches in diameter fell in Howard County, causing injuries to 48 people and $30 million worth of property damage.

May 27, 1997: A half-mile-wide F5 tornado struck Jarrell, Williamson Co., leveling the Double Creek subdisivion, claiming 27 lives, injuring 12 others, and causing more than $40 million in damage.

March–May, 1998: According to the Climate Prediction Center, this three-month period ranks as the seventh driest for a region including Texas, Oklahoma, Arkansas, Louisiana and Mississippi. May 1998 has been ranked as both the warmest and the driest May that this region has ever seen.

Aug. 22–25, 1998: Tropical Storm Charley brought torrential rains and flash floods to the Hill Country. Thirteen people lost their lives and more than 200 were injured.

Oct. 17–19, 1998: A massive, devastating flood set all-time records for rainfall and river levels, resulted in the deaths of 25 people, injured more than 2,000 others, and caused more than $500 million damage from the Hill Country to the counties surrounding San Antonio to the south and east.

Jan. 22, 1999: Golf ball- and softball-sized hail fell in the Bryan/College Station area, resulting in $10 million in damage to cars, homes and offices.

May 1999: Numerous severe weather outbreaks caused damaging winds, large hail, dangerous lightning, and numerous tornadoes. An F3 tornado moved through De Kalb's downtown area and high school on the 4th, injuring 22 people and causing $125 million to the community. On the same day, two F2 tornadoes roared through Kilgore simultaneously. On the 11th, an F4 tornado moved through parts of Loyal Valley, taking the life of one and injuring six. The 25th saw storms produce 2.5-inch hail in Levelland and Amarillo. The total cost of damages caused by May storms was more than $157 million.

August 1999: Excessive heat throughout the month resulted in 16 fatalities in the Dallas/Fort Worth area. The airport reported 26 consecutive days of 100°F or greater temperatures.

January–October 2000: A severe drought plagued most of Texas. Some regions experienced little to no rain for several months during the summer. Abilene saw no rain for 72 consecutive days, while Dallas had no rain for 84 consecutive days during the summer. During July, aquifers hit all-time lows, and lakes and streams fell to critical levels. Most regions had to cut back or stop agricultural activities because of the drought, which resulted in $515 million in agricultural loss, according to USDA figures.

March 28, 2000: A supercell over Fort Worth produced an F3 tornado, which injured 80 people and caused significant damage. Flooding claimed the lives of two people.

May 20, 2000: A flash flood in the Liberty and Dayton area was caused by 18.3 inches of rain's falling in five hours. Up to 80 people had to be rescued from the flood waters; property damage totalled an estimated $10 million.

July 2000: Excessive heat resulted from a high-pressure ridge, particularly from the 12th to the 21st. Dallas/Fort Worth airport reported a 10-day average of 103.3°F. College Station had 12 consecutive days of 100°F or greater temperatures. The heat caused 34 deaths in North and Southeast

Texas, primarily among the elderly.

Aug. 2, 2000: Lightning struck a tree at Astroworld in Houston injuring 17 teens.

Sept. 5, 2000: Excessive heat resulted in at least eight all-time high temperature records around the state, one of which was Possum Kingdom Lake, which reached 114°F. This day is being regarded as the hottest day ever in Texas, considering the state as a whole.

Dec. 13 and 24-25, 2000: Two major winter storms blanketed Northeast Texas with up to six inches of ice from each storm. Eight inches of snow fell in the Panhandle, while areas in North Texas received 12 inches. Thousands of motorists were stranded on Interstate 20 and had to be rescued by the National Guard; 235,000 people lost electric service from the first storm alone. Roads were treacherous, driving was halted in several counties, and the total cost of damages from both storms reached more than $156 million.

Jan. 1–31, 2001: The U.S. Department of Agriculture Farm Service Agency received a Presidential Disaster Declaration in December 2000 because of persistent drought conditions in deep Southern Texas; $125 million in damage was reported in the region.

May 2001: May is typically a month of extreme weather, and May 2001 was not exception, with numerous storms causing excessive damage. Four-inch hail caused nearly $150 million in damages in San Antonio on the 6th. On the 30th, supercell thunderstorms in the High Plains region produced winds over 100 mph and golf-ball- sized hail caused more than $186 million in damage. All told, storms caused 36 injuries and more than $358 million in damage to property and agriculture.

June–December 2001: Significant drought-like conditions occurred in Texas from early summer through December. After the yearly drought report was filed, it was determined that the total crop damage across the South Plains region was about $420 million. Consequential losses occurred to crops such as cotton, wheat, grain sorghum and corn.

June 5–10, 2001: Tropical Storm Allison hit the Houston area, which dumped large amounts of rain on the city. The storm made landfall on the western end of Galveston Island and over the next five days produced record rainfall. These amazing amounts of precipitation led to devastating flooding across southeastern Texas. Some weather stations in the Houston area reported more than 40 inches of rain total and more than 18 inches in a 24-hour period. Twenty-two deaths and $5.2 billion in damage resulted.

July–August 2001: Excessive heat plagued Texas during July and August, which resulted in 17 deaths in the Houston area.

Oct. 12, 2001: An F2 tornado in Hondo caused $20 million in damage. The tornado injured 25 people and damaged the Hondo Airport and the National Guard Armory. A large hangar and nearly two dozen aircraft were destroyed at the airport. The armory's roofs and concrete walls were damaged. Nearly 150 homes in Hondo and 50 on its outskirts were damaged, and nearly 100 mobile homes were damaged.

Nov. 15, 2001: Storms caused flash flooding and some weak tornadoes in the Edwards Plateau, South Central and southern portions of North Central regions. Flash flooding caused 8 deaths and 198 injuries.

March 2002: Several violent storms occurred, which produced hail, tornadoes and strong winds. Hail 1-3/4 inches in diameter caused $16 million in damage to San Angelo on the 19th, while 30 people where injured on the same day by an F2 tornado in Somerset that also caused $2 million in damage. For the month, there were three fatalities, 64 injuries and more than $37.5 million in damage.

June 30–July 7, 2002: Excessive rainfall occurred in the South Central and Edwards Plateau regions, with some areas reporting more than 30 inches of rain. In the South Central region alone nearly $250 million dollars worth of damage was reported from this significant weather event. In central Texas, 29 counties were devastated by the flooding and declared federal disaster areas by President George W. Bush. The total event damage was estimated at more than $2 billion.

Sept. 5–7, 2002: Tropical Storm Fay made landfall along the southeast Texas coast on the 6th. This system produced extremely heavy rainfall, strong damaging wind gusts and tornadoes. Ten to 20 inches of rain fell in eastern **Wharton County. Brazoria County** was hit the hardest from this system with about 1,500 homes flooded. Tropical Storm Fay produced five tornadoes, flooded many areas and caused significant wind damage. Damage of $4.5 million was reported.

Oct. 24, 2002: Severe **thunderstorms** in south Texas produced heavy rain, causing flooding and two tornadoes in **Corpus Christi**. The most extensive damage occurred across **Del Mar College**. The storm caused one death, 26 injuries and Total storm damages exceeded more then $85 million in damage.

Feb. 24–26, 2003: A severe cold front brought freezing rain, sleet and **snow** to the **North-Central region**. Snow accumulations were as high as **5 inches** resulting in $15 million in damages. Most schools and businesses were closed for this period.

April 8, 2003: A severe thunderstorm caused one of the **most destructive hail events in the history of Brownsville.** Hail exceeded 2.75 inches in diameter and caused $50 million in damages to the city. At least 5 injuries were reported.

July 14–16, 2003: Hurricane Claudette made landfall near Port O'Connor in the late morning hours of the 14th. At landfall, wind speeds were more than 90 mph. The system, which moved westward toward Big Bend and northern Mexico, caused 1 death and 2 injuries, and total damages were estimated at more than $100 million.

Sept. 2003: Persistent flooding during the month caused more than $2 million in damages. The remnants of **Tropical Storm Grace** caused flash flooding along the Upper Coast region near **Galveston** early in September, with rainfall estimates in Matagorda County ranging from 6 to 12 inches. During the second half of the month, deep south Texas was hit with a **deluge of rain caused by a tropical wave** combined with approaching cold fronts, and monthly rainfall totals ranged from 7 to 15 inches throughout the deep south.

June 1–9, 2004: Flash flooding due to an upper air disturbance and associated cold front caused damage to more than 1,000 homes through **North-Central Texas**. This was the first of many days in which heavy rains fell throughout the state. Estimated damages were more $7.5 million.

June 21, 2004: Severe weather kicked up just ahead of a frontal boundary causing damage to **Amarillo** and the surrounding area. Eight tornadoes were reported around the Panhandle, and there were many reports of hail, topping out at 4.25 inches in diameter in Potter County. Thousands of homes were damaged, and the total damage was estimated at more than **$150 million.**

July 28–29, 2004: A stationary front lead to **torrential rainfall in Dallas and Waco.** Hundreds of homes were damaged by flash flooding, as 24-hour rainfall totals for the two cities approached 5 inches. Outlying areas of the cities reported as much as 7 inches of rain in a 12-hour period on the 29th. Damage estimates topped $20 million.

Sept. 14, 2004: A **lightning strike** during football practice at **Grapeland High School** caused one death and injuries to 40 players and coaches.

Dec. 24–26, 2004: Large portions of **Southeast Texas** saw their **first white Christmas in recorded history**. A cold front past over the state a few days prior to Christmas Eve dropping

In 2004, South Texas got its first white Christmas in recorded history. Pictured is the 1900 Storm Memorial on Galveston Beach. Paul Joki photo.

temperatures below freezing. Another cold front brought snow, and it accumulated Christmas Eve night and into Christmas day. Galveston and Houston recorded 4 inches of snow, while areas even further south, such as **Victoria, had 12 inches**.

March 25, 2005: In the evening of March 25, the **most destructive hailstorm in 10 years** struck the greater Austin area. The storm knocked out power to 5,000 homes in northwest Austin. Hail of 2 inches in diameter was reported near the Travis County Exposition Center. Total damage was estimated at $100 million.

May 2005–December 2006: In May, portions of North-Central Texas were upgraded from moderate to **severe drought.** By the end of the May, the drought had made significant agricultural and hydrological impacts on the region. A lack of rainfall in June continued the drought that officially began in May. Burn bans were in place in 29 counties prior to the July 4th weekend. Some rainfall during August contributed to improved conditions during August, but most of the North Texas area was still under severe drought conditions. In November, many Central Texas counties were added to the drought. In December, an area of exceptional drought was introduced into a large area of North Texas, including the Dallas-Fort Worth Metroplex. Unseasonably warm temperatures and a lack of rainfall persisted, and the drought continued into 2006. Drought conditions began to improve with increased rainfall totals in March 2006, but rainfall deficits in June brought the area back into severe drought classification. The Texas Cooperative Extension estimated statewide drought losses at $4.1 billion, $1.9 billion in North Texas alone.

June 9, 2005: An **F-3 tornado** affected the Petersburg area in southeast Hale County across to portions of southwest and south-central Floyd County. Total damage was estimated at $70 million.

Sept. 23, 2005: The eye of **Hurricane Rita** moved ashore in extreme southwest Louisiana between Sabine Pass and Johnson's Bayou in Cameron Parish with maximum sustained winds of 120 mph, category-3 strength. On Sept. 22, Rita had strengthened to a peak intensity of 175 mph winds. In southeast Texas, Rita resulted in 3 fatalities, 3 injuries, and $159.5 million in property and crop damage. In far east Texas, including Hardin, Jasper, Jefferson, Newton, Orange and Tyler counties, one fatality was reported. Property damage was estimated at $2.1 billion.

Dec. 27, 2005: A **wildfire** in Callahan county caused $11 million in property damages. The fire started just west of Cross Plains and quickly moved east, fanned by winds gusting near 40 mph. The fire moved into Cross Plains quickly and two elderly people were unable to escape the flames; 16 firefighters were also injured while fighting this fire.

Jan. 1, 2006: Several **wildfires** exploded across North Texas due to low humidity, strong winds and the ongoing drought. Fires were reported in Montague, Eastland and Palo Pinto counties. Five injuries were reported as well as $10.8 million in property damage.

March 12–18, 2006: A wildfire now known as the **Borger wildfire** start four miles southwest of Borger. The wildfire burned a total of 479,500 acres. In all, seven people were killed and 28 structures were lost with total property damage at $49.9 million and crop damage at $45.4 million. A second wildfire known as the Interstate-40 wildfire burned 427,696 acres. The Texas Forest Service named the two wildfires the East Amarillo Complex. In all, 12 people were killed, total property damage was $49.9 million and crop damage was $45.4 million.

March 19, 2006: An **F-2 tornado** moved through the Uvalde area causing $1.5 million in property damage. It was the strongest tornado in South-Central Texas since Oct. 12, 2001.

April 11–13, 2006: A **wildfire** 10 miles north of Canadian burned 18,000 acres and destroyed crops. Two injuries were reported. Total crop damage was estimated at $90 million.

April 18, 2006: Hail as large as 2.5 inches in diameter destroyed windows in homes and car windshields between Harper and Doss in Gillespie County. The hail also damaged 70 percent of the area peach crop, an estimated loss of $5 million.

April 20, 2006: Hail as large at 4.25 inches in diameter (grapefruit-size) was reported south of San Marcos. Damage from this storm was estimated at $100 million with up to 10,000 vehicles damaged and another 7,000 vehicles at homes.

May 4, 2006: Lime-to-baseball-size **hail** fell across Snyder in Scurry County for a least 15 minutes. The hail was blown sideways at times by 60-to-70-mph winds. Total damage was estimated at $15 million.

May 5, 2006: A **tornado** was reported on Waco Drive overnight. Peak intensity was estimated at low F-2. Total damage was $3 million.

May 9, 2006: An **F-2 tornado** resulted in significant damage along a one-and-one-half mile path through the north side of Childress during the evening hours. An instrument at Childress High School measured a wind gust of 109 mph. Property damage was estimated at $5.7 million.

Aug. 1, 2006: Thunderstorms in a saturated atmosphere repeatedly developed and moved over mainly the northwest third of El Paso County, concentrating in an area near the Franklin Mountains. Rainfall reports varied from 4–6 inches within 15 hours, with an isolated report of about 8 inches on the western slope of the mountain range. Antecedent conditions from 4 days of heavy rains, combined with terrain effects of the mountains, led to excessive runoff and flooding not seen on such a large scale in the El Paso area in more than 100 years. Property damage was estimated at $180 million. ☆

Texas Droughts, 1892–2006

Year	High Plains	Low Rolling Plains	North Central	East Texas	Trans-Pecos	Edwards Plateau	South Central	Upper Coast	Southern	Lower Valley
1892	...	...	...	...	68	...	...	73	...	...
1893	...	...	67	70	...	49	56	64	53	59
1894	...	...	...	...	68	...	...	...	...	...
1897	...	...	...	...	...	...	73	...	72	...
1898	...	...	...	...	...	...	...	...	69	51
1901	...	71	70	...	...	60	62	70	44	...
1902	...	...	...	...	...	...	...	...	65	73
1907	...	...	...	...	...	...	...	...	...	65
1909	...	...	72	68	67	74	70	...	...	...
1910	59	59	64	69	43	65	69	74	59	...
1911	...	...	...	...	...	...	...	...	...	70
1916	...	73	...	74	70	...	73	69	...	...
1917	58	50	63	59	44	46	42	50	32	48
1920	...	...	...	...	...	...	...	...	...	71
1921	...	...	...	...	72	...	...	...	...	73
1922	...	...	...	...	68	...	...	...	...	...
1924	...	...	73	70	...	71	...	72	...	...
1925	...	...	72	...	...	...	72	...	...	...
1927	...	...	...	...	...	...	...	74	...	74
1933	72	...	...	...	62	68	...	...	...	...
1934	66	...	...	...	46	69	...	...	...	...
1937	...	...	...	...	...	...	...	72	...	...
1939	...	...	...	...	...	...	69	...	...	72
1943	...	...	72	...	...	...	...	...	...	...
1948	...	...	73	74	62	...	71	67	...	...
1950	...	...	...	...	...	...	68	...	74	64
1951	...	...	...	...	61	53	...	...	...	...
1952	68	66	...	...	73	...	...	...	56	70
1953	69	...	...	...	49	73	...	...	...	...
1954	70	71	68	73	...	50	50	57	71	...
1956	51	57	61	68	44	43	55	62	53	53
1962	...	...	...	...	...	68	...	...	67	65
1963	...	...	63	68	...	65	61	73	...	...
1964	74	...	...	...	69	...	...	...	...	63
1970	65	63	...	...	...	72	...	...	...	...
1988	...	...	...	...	...	67	62	67	68	...
1989	...	...	...	...	...	72	...	...	66	64
1990	...	...	...	...	...	...	...	...	...	73
1994	...	...	...	...	68	...	...	...	...	...
1996	...	...	...	...	...	...	71	...	60	70
1998	...	69	...	...	71	...	...	...	...	...
1999	...	...	73	...	...	67	69	69	...	...
2000	...	...	...	...	74	...	...	...	...	67
2001	...	...	...	...	56	...	...	...	...	...
2002	...	...	...	...	...	...	...	...	...	...
2003	65	71	...	...	...	...	...	...	...	...
2004	...	...	...	...	...	...	...	...	...	...
2005	...	...	68	66	...	...	...	...	...	72
2006	...	...	...	...	...	66	...	...	...	...

Normal Annual Rainfall by Region

Listed below is the normal annual rainfall in inches for five 30-year periods in each geographical area. Normals for each area are given in the same order as the divisions which appear in the table above.

Period	Normal Rainfall in Inches									
1931–1960	18.51	22.99	32.93	45.96	12.03	25.91	33.24	46.19	22.33	24.27
1941–1970	18.59	23.18	32.94	45.37	11.57	23.94	33.03	46.43	21.95	23.44
1951–1980	17.73	22.80	32.14	44.65	11.65	23.52	34.03	45.93	22.91	24.73
1961–1990	18.88	23.77	33.99	45.67	13.01	24.00	34.49	47.63	23.47	25.31
1971–2000	19.64	24.51	35.23	48.08	13.19	24.73	36.21	50.31	24.08	25.43

Drought Frequency

This table shows the number of years of drought and the number of separate droughts. For example, the High Plains has had 10 drought years, consisting of five 1-year droughts, one 2-year drought and one 3-year drought, a total of 7 droughts.

Years	High Plains	Low Rolling Plains	North Central	East Texas	Trans-Pecos	Edwards Plateau	South Central	Upper Coast	Southern	Lower Valley
1	5	8	10	7	7	9	13	10	10	15
2	1	1	2	2	5	5	2	2	3	2
3	1	...	...	...	1	...	...	...	...	...
Total Droughts	7	9	12	9	13	14	15	12	13	17
Dr'ght Yrs.	10	10	14	11	20	19	17	14	16	19

Texas Temperature, Freeze, Growing Season and Precipitation Records by County

Data in the table below are from the office of the Texas State Climatologist, Texas A&M University, College Station. Because of the small change in averages, data are revised only at intervals of 10 years. Data below are the latest compilations, as of Feb. 1, 2004, and reflect data compiled during 1971–2000. The table shows temperature, freeze, growing season and precipitation for each county in Texas. Data for counties where a National Weather Service Station has not been maintained long enough to establish a reliable mean are interpolated from isoline charts prepared from mean values from stations with long-established records. Mean maximum temperature for July is computed from the sum of the daily maxima. Mean minimum January is computed from the sum of the daily minima. Weather stations shown in italics do not measure all categories and some data are from the period 1961–1990. An asterisk (*) preceding a record high or low or rainfall extreme denotes a figure that also occurred on an earlier date.

COUNTY AND STATION	Mean Max July F.	Mean Min January F.	Record Highest F.	Year	Record Lowest F.	Year	Last in Spring Mo. Day	First in Fall Mo. Day	Growing Season Days	Jan In.	Feb In.	Mar In.	Apr In.	May In.	Jun In.	Jul In.	Aug In.	Sep In.	Oct In.	Nov In.	Dec In.	Annual In.	Highest Daily Rainfall In.	Mo.-Year
Anderson, Palestine	93.9	37.4	114	1954	-4	1930	Mar. 15	Nov. 18	247	3.60	3.34	3.87	3.80	4.51	4.53	2.55	3.23	3.45	4.90	4.44	4.16	46.38	9.10	08-1991
Andrews, Andrews	94.5	30.4	113	1994	-1	1985	Mar. 29	Nov. 10	226	0.48	0.51	0.52	0.85	1.78	2.12	2.25	1.77	2.21	1.43	0.64	0.59	15.15	7.60	07-1914
Angelina, Lufkin	93.5	37.9	*110	2000	*-2	1951	Mar. 13	Nov. 15	247	4.45	3.17	3.53	3.13	5.29	4.18	2.60	3.08	4.08	4.13	4.54	4.44	46.62	7.47	10-1994
Aransas, Rockport	90.1	44.9	105	2000	12	1983	Feb. 2	Dec. 20	318	2.40	2.18	2.36	2.07	3.66	3.50	2.60	3.13	5.53	4.23	2.56	1.91	35.96	8.15	09-1979
Archer, Archer City	97.0	26.7	114	1980	*-10	1989	Mar. 28	Nov. 9	225	1.13	1.75	2.05	2.46	4.33	3.46	1.79	2.66	3.11	3.39	1.90	1.75	29.78	7.95	10-1981
Armstrong, Claude	90.5	21.2	*108	1980	-16	1905	Apr. 19	Oct. 20	184	0.51	0.58	1.23	1.60	3.34	3.33	3.08	3.00	2.37	1.91	0.82	0.62	22.39	10.27	05-1982
Atascosa, Poteet	95.9	39.0	*110	2000	-1	1949	Feb. 25	Dec. 2	279	1.27	1.83	1.54	2.50	4.09	4.06	2.50	2.69	2.90	3.04	1.65	1.64	29.00	8.75	07-1949
Austin, Sealy	94.9	40.7	111	2000	0	1989	Feb. 18	Dec. 8	291	3.14	2.81	2.61	3.22	4.71	3.85	1.93	3.06	4.33	4.44	3.68	2.90	40.68	11.00	08-1945
Bailey, Muleshoe	91.9	20.2	*110	1944	-21	1933	Apr. 17	Oct. 21	186	0.43	0.50	0.64	1.01	2.04	2.49	2.09	3.07	2.34	1.50	0.67	0.59	17.37	5.25	05-1951
Bandera, Medina	93.9	33.3	109	1980	5	1989	Apr. 22	Nov. 10	233	1.72	1.91	2.27	2.69	4.35	4.29	2.55	3.08	3.66	4.14	2.84	2.28	35.78	9.86	08-1971
Bastrop, Smithville	95.4	36.7	*111	2000	5	1930	Mar. 4	Nov. 20	260	2.73	2.32	2.56	3.00	5.12	3.66	2.01	2.25	3.56	4.70	3.29	2.84	38.04	16.05	06-1940
Baylor, Seymour	96.5	27.7	120	1936	-14	1947	Mar. 30	Nov. 6	220	1.05	1.56	1.88	1.84	4.13	3.63	1.86	2.58	3.51	2.86	1.48	1.41	27.79	6.20	05-1989
Bee, Beeville	94.6	43.1	111	1939	8	1983	Feb. 14	Dec. 6	294	1.94	1.84	1.90	2.68	3.49	4.19	2.69	3.02	4.30	3.60	2.00	1.83	33.48	10.61	09-1967
Bell, Temple	95.0	34.6	112	1947	*-4	1989	Mar. 3	Nov. 22	264	1.91	1.75	2.70	2.81	4.56	3.71	1.82	2.20	4.00	3.73	3.04	2.68	35.81	9.62	10-1998
Bexar, San Antonio	94.6	38.6	111	2000	0	1949	Feb. 28	Nov. 25	270	1.66	1.75	1.89	2.60	4.72	4.30	2.03	2.57	3.00	3.86	2.58	1.79	32.92	11.26	10-1998
Blanco, Blanco	93.7	34.0	*110	2000	-6	1949	Mar. 20	Nov. 11	235	1.79	2.08	2.63	2.69	4.51	4.18	2.02	2.38	3.26	4.18	2.66	2.37	34.75	17.47	09-1952
Borden, Gail	94.6	29.8	116	1994	-7	1989	Mar. 27	Nov. 8	226	0.58	0.73	0.66	1.20	2.80	2.81	2.35	2.52	2.83	1.77	0.74	0.69	19.68	9.13	10-1960
Bosque, Lake Whitney	96.2	32.7	113	2000	*-3	1989	Mar. 15	Nov. 17	247	1.93	1.91	2.87	3.18	4.29	3.96	2.32	2.37	2.76	3.95	2.67	2.67	35.07	6.22	10-1971
Bowie, Texarkana	93.1	30.7	108	2000	*-6	1989	Mar. 14	Nov. 14	238	3.91	3.80	4.46	4.23	4.97	4.82	3.62	2.41	3.77	4.61	5.69	4.95	51.24	5.45	03-1989
Brazoria, Angleton	91.8	43.7	107	2000	*7	1989	Mar. 15	Dec. 5	290	4.76	3.50	3.76	3.74	5.20	4.24	4.24	4.83	7.49	4.25	4.86	4.17	57.24	14.36	07-1979
Brazos, College Station	95.6	39.0	112	2000	2	1989	Mar. 2	Nov. 29	271	3.32	2.38	2.84	3.20	5.05	3.74	1.92	2.63	3.91	4.22	3.23	3.18	39.67	6.23	05-1983
Brewster, Alpine	88.7	31.3	107	1972	-3	1983	Apr. 8	Nov. 1	207	0.45	0.50	0.34	0.58	1.25	2.18	3.04	2.92	3.23	1.58	0.45	0.67	17.19	3.13	06-1968
Brewster, Chisos Basin	84.2	36.1	103	1972	-3	1949	Mar. 16	Nov. 17	246	0.55	0.69	0.36	0.61	1.60	2.42	3.55	3.72	2.71	1.72	0.66	0.58	19.17	4.29	10-1966
Briscoe, Silverton	91.6	21.6	*109	1994	-9	1963	Apr. 14	Oct. 22	190	0.57	0.78	1.17	1.59	3.22	3.96	3.55	2.76	2.67	1.68	0.90	0.74	22.34	5.25	06-1979
Brooks, Falfurrias	97.0	43.9	115	1998	9	1962	Feb. 6	Dec. 13	311	1.12	1.56	0.86	1.48	2.95	3.25	1.84	2.91	3.84	3.22	1.31	1.08	25.42	10.00	09-1967
Brown, Brownwood	95.0	29.6	111	1964	-6	1989	Mar. 25	Nov. 11	231	1.28	2.09	2.07	2.45	3.62	3.75	1.80	2.28	2.67	3.01	1.62	1.68	28.32	*6.60	06-2000
Burleson, Somerville	96.7	36.4	114	2000	*-4	1989	Mar. 3	Nov. 23	264	2.93	2.53	2.62	2.92	4.39	4.09	1.78	2.43	3.59	4.33	3.63	3.14	38.50	15.25	10-1994
Burnet, Burnet	93.6	33.3	*114	1917	*-4	1989	Mar. 20	Nov. 12	237	1.61	2.04	2.33	2.48	4.58	4.09	2.04	2.06	3.15	3.46	2.15	2.30	32.43	9.80	09-1936
Caldwell, Luling	95.8	36.9	*110	2000	-3	1949	Mar. 7	Nov. 20	258	2.27	2.20	2.22	3.06	5.44	4.29	1.70	2.32	3.70	4.36	3.00	2.30	36.86	10.53	10-1998

County and Station	Mean Max. July (°F)	Mean Min. January (°F)	Record Highest (°F)	Year	Record Lowest (°F)	Year	Last in Spring	First in Fall	Growing Season Days	Jan.	Feb.	Mar.	Apr.	May	June	July	Aug.	Sept.	Oct.	Nov.	Dec.	Annual	Highest Daily Rainfall (In.)	Mo.-Year
Calhoun, Port O'Connor	88.2	47.9	105	2000	10	1989	Jan. 29	Dec. 31	338	3.07	2.20	1.73	1.55	3.70	2.77	3.05	2.94	4.97	4.45	2.53	1.82	34.78	12.50	07-1976
Callahan, Putnam	94.9	31.1	110	1964	-8	1989	Mar. 24	Nov. 13	234	1.17	1.55	1.76	1.80	3.13	3.25	1.97	2.02	2.79	3.03	1.64	1.41	25.52	5.00	08-1978
Cameron, Brownsville	92.4	50.5	106	1984	*15	1901	Dec. 25	Jan. 24	>365	1.36	1.18	0.93	1.96	2.48	2.93	1.77	2.99	5.31	3.78	1.75	1.11	27.55	12.09	09-1967
Camp, Pittsburg	94.0	32.0	109	1964	-3		Mar. 21	Nov. 14	238	3.40	3.40	4.40	3.70	4.60	3.90	3.30	2.10	3.30	4.80	4.80	3.90	45.10		
Carson, Panhandle	90.8	19.3	109	1964	*-10	1963	Apr. 18	Oct. 22	186	0.62	0.73	1.43	1.80	3.10	3.54	2.67	2.78	2.21	1.71	0.98	0.64	22.21	8.05	05-1951
Cass, Wright Patman Dam	94.0	31.0	103		8		Mar. 19	Nov. 11	237	3.70	3.60	4.40	4.00	4.50	4.50	3.00	2.60	3.50	4.30	5.30	4.80	48.20		
Castro, Dimmitt	90.1	20.4	111	1983	-9	1986	Apr. 25	Oct. 16	172	0.50	0.51	0.81	0.99	2.76	3.12	2.40	3.06	2.57	1.58	0.71	0.70	19.71	4.38	08-1998
Chambers, Anahuac	91.9	41.7	110	1943	-9	1989	Feb. 12	Dec. 9	299	4.84	2.83	3.33	3.56	5.22	5.88	4.59	4.74	6.42	4.06	4.31	4.30	54.08	15.87	08-1945
Cherokee, Rusk	92.8	36.8	110	2000	0	1982	Mar. 10	Nov. 21	255	4.41	3.64	4.12	3.86	4.69	4.34	2.95	2.38	4.01	4.94	4.63	4.53	48.50	10.00	06-2001
Childress, Childress	95.3	26.8	117	1994	-5	1989	Apr. 1	Nov. 6	218	0.57	0.95	1.41	2.01	3.46	3.51	2.05	2.19	2.51	2.07	1.06	0.86	22.65	5.32	10-1983
Clay, Henrietta	95.0	26.8	*110	1951	*-8	1989	Mar. 30	Nov. 5	220	1.53	1.45	2.45	2.71	4.39	3.52	1.74	2.40	3.35	2.51	1.77	2.17	31.66	6.07	06-1959
Cochran, Morton	91.4	23.1	*110	1994	-12	1963	Apr. 14	Oct. 24	193	0.50	0.58	0.64	0.89	1.92	2.52	2.61	2.97	2.66	1.64	0.62	0.62	18.34	4.69	07-1960
Coke, Robert Lee	96.4	29.0	114	2000	-2	1989	Mar. 26	Nov. 11	230	0.81	1.22	1.05	1.72	3.24	2.90	1.44	2.28	3.46	2.73	1.15	1.00	23.00	8.40	10-1957
Coleman, Coleman	93.7	30.1	114	1943	-5	1930	Mar. 23	Nov. 13	235	1.03	1.75	1.84	2.19	4.11	4.05	1.77	2.58	3.25	3.08	1.57	1.48	28.70	8.55	07-1932
Collin, McKinney	92.7	31.1	118	1936	-7	1930	Mar. 21	Nov. 11	235	2.43	2.91	3.37	3.65	5.68	4.11	2.36	2.16	3.15	4.24	3.71	3.24	41.01	12.10	09-1964
Collingsworth, Wellington	97.9	27.0	113	1994	-6	1989	Apr. 1	Nov. 4	216	0.62	0.73	1.47	2.07	3.88	3.47	2.25	1.85	2.58	2.37	0.89	0.62	22.80	9.50	10-1986
Colorado, Columbus	96.3	36.8	116	2000	*4	1989	Mar. 16	Nov. 16	250	3.61	2.84	2.93	3.57	5.75	5.03	2.64	3.07	3.92	4.16	3.99	3.21	44.72	10.00	06-1973
Comal, New Braunfels	94.7	35.5	118	2000	*2	1989	Mar. 4	Nov. 21	261	1.88	1.98	2.04	2.72	5.01	4.81	1.99	2.32	3.46	4.38	2.71	2.44	35.74	18.35	10-1998
Comanche, Proctor Reservoir	95.5	30.6	113	2000	-8	1989	Mar. 20	Nov. 15	238	1.34	2.30	2.13	2.81	4.75	3.70	1.70	2.22	3.01	3.32	2.07	1.77	31.12	8.37	06-1988
Concho, Paint Rock	97.4	31.9	111	1978	-8	1985	Mar. 31	Nov. 6	219	1.04	1.52	1.35	1.56	3.31	3.77	1.84	2.05	3.55	2.81	1.41	1.29	25.50	8.25	09-1980
Cooke, Gainesville	95.0	28.0	112				Mar. 27	Nov. 8	226	1.80	2.20	3.40	3.20	4.60	3.70	2.00	2.40	4.50	4.60	2.60	1.90	36.90		
Coryell, Gatesville	96.4	33.5	*112	2000	-6	1949	Mar. 24	Nov. 13	234	1.65	2.35	2.57	2.90	4.38	3.66	2.36	2.53	2.87	3.50	2.51	2.35	33.43	8.35	06-1964
Cottle, Paducah	96.8	26.2	118	1994	*-7	1989	Mar. 29	Nov. 5	221	0.82	1.11	1.31	1.92	3.85	3.67	1.72	2.63	2.96	2.06	1.08	0.98	24.11	6.65	06-1991
Crane, Crane	95.3	30.7	115	1994	*-7	1985	Mar. 23	Nov. 11	232	0.57	0.59	0.34	0.84	1.86	1.71	1.48	2.02	2.95	1.64	0.68	0.70	15.38	5.55	08-1986
Crockett, Ozona	93.0	27.7	109	1969	-8	1951	Apr. 2	Nov. 2	215	0.70	0.78	1.06	1.36	2.44	1.94	1.57	2.27	2.92	2.25	0.99	0.67	18.95	5.80	10-1959
Crosby, Crosbyton	92.5	25.3	113	1994	*-10	1930	Apr. 2	Nov. 1	212	0.68	0.96	1.03	1.87	3.05	3.10	2.05	3.05	3.46	1.91	0.95	0.84	22.95	5.78	06-1913
Culberson, Van Horn	91.7	27.8	112	1969	-7	1962	Apr. 4	Nov. 5	215	0.39	0.33	0.16	0.24	0.71	1.25	2.11	2.30	2.23	1.27	0.46	0.53	11.98	7.00	08-1966
Dallam, Dalhart	90.0	19.0	*107	1990	-21	1959	Apr. 23	Oct. 16	175	0.39	0.40	1.08	1.35	2.72	3.11	2.40	2.99	1.56	1.32	0.71	0.54	18.57	4.52	08-1985
Dallas, Dallas	96.1	36.4	115	1909	-8	1989	Mar. 3	Nov. 25	267	1.89	2.31	3.13	3.46	5.30	3.92	2.43	2.17	2.65	4.65	2.61	2.53	37.05	6.02	03-1977
Dawson, Lamesa	92.9	26.0	114	1994	-12	1933	Apr. 4	Nov. 5	214	0.57	0.77	0.73	0.88	2.35	2.81	2.19	2.00	3.42	1.76	0.82	0.77	19.07	6.24	10-1985
Deaf Smith, Hereford	91.6	21.1	110	1910	-17	1951	Apr. 19	Oct. 19	182	0.50	0.50	0.98	1.02	2.12	2.90	2.06	3.22	2.25	1.59	0.77	0.74	18.65	*5.30	08-1976
Delta, Cooper	94.0	30.0	110		-1		Mar. 25	Nov. 13	233	3.20	3.20	4.10	3.60	5.40	4.40	2.90	2.10	3.90	4.30	4.30	4.00	45.00		
Denton, Denton	94.1	32.0	*113	1954	*-3	1949	Mar. 18	Nov. 16	243	1.94	2.55	2.82	3.30	5.41	3.29	2.53	2.26	3.35	4.81	2.87	2.66	37.79	7.30	05-1982
DeWitt, Cuero	95.1	41.3	113	2000	7	1989	Feb. 28	Nov. 25	270	2.30	1.95	2.32	2.96	4.74	4.51	2.18	2.25	4.31	3.67	2.66	2.23	36.08	12.40	06-1940
Dickens, Spur	95.4	25.5	117	1994	-17	1933	Apr. 2	Nov. 4	215	0.55	0.70	0.84	1.53	3.18	2.78	1.74	2.12	2.17	2.66	0.82	0.69	18.68	4.70	08-1996
Dimmit, Carrizo Springs	98.3	39.6	114	1942	10	1989	Feb. 14	Dec. 4	292	1.00	0.94	0.89	1.47	2.96	2.78	1.26	2.33	1.95	2.66	1.10	0.87	20.21	8.78	07-1990
Donley, Clarendon	94.7	22.4	117	1936	*-11	1989	Apr. 11	Oct. 25	196	0.64	0.83	1.43	2.25	3.60	3.70	2.37	2.81	2.69	1.78	0.94	0.85	23.89	9.25	05-2001
Duval, Freer	97.3	42.5	116	1998	12	1963	Feb. 13	Dec. 8	297	1.15	1.31	1.58	1.69	3.63	3.68	1.54	2.25	3.06	2.92	1.54	1.05	25.40	7.85	09-1971

COUNTY AND STATION	TEMPERATURE Mean Max. July (F.)	Mean Min. January (F.)	Record Highest (F.)	Year	Record Lowest (F.)	Year	AVERAGE FREEZE DATES Last in Spring Mo.	Day	First in Fall Mo.	Day	Growing Season (Days)	MEAN PRECIPITATION January (In.)	February	March	April	May	June	July	August	September	October	November	December	Annual	EXTREMES Highest Daily Rainfall (In.)	Mo.-Year
Eastland, Eastland	94.9	26.7	*115	1943	*-6	1973	Apr.	1	Nov.	8	221	1.20	1.73	1.93	2.27	3.72	3.40	1.73	2.29	2.67	3.25	1.72	1.62	27.53	7.00	10-1957
Ector, Penwell	96.0	28.7	116	1994	-12	1985	Mar.	30	Nov.	7	222	0.42	0.58	0.42	0.61	2.11	1.56	1.30	1.46	2.35	1.24	0.63	0.61	13.29	4.53	04-1969
Edwards, Rocksprings	91.6	34.3	*108	1980	*3	1951	Mar.	18	Nov.	17	243	0.77	1.31	1.36	1.75	3.23	3.07	2.05	2.84	2.44	3.41	1.50	1.03	24.76	9.50	06-1935
Ellis, Waxahachie	96.0	35.0	115	1909	-4	1989	Mar.	14	Nov.	18	248	2.45	2.85	3.21	3.89	4.85	3.51	2.05	2.26	3.16	4.43	1.97	3.22	38.81	10.80	09-1958
El Paso, El Paso	96.0	32.9	114	1994	-8	1962	Mar.	22	Nov.	8	230	0.45	0.39	0.26	0.23	0.38	0.87	1.49	1.75	1.61	0.81	0.42	0.77	9.43	2.26	09-1974
Erath, Stephenville	93.6	30.0	111	1925	-8	1989	Mar.	22	Nov.	13	235	1.31	1.86	2.35	2.53	4.35	3.41	1.47	2.41	2.80	3.28	1.97	1.97	29.71	9.71	05-1956
Falls, Marlin	95.0	37.0	*112	1969	-5	1949	Mar.	10	Nov.	17	251	2.49	2.60	3.30	3.19	5.35	4.50	2.09	1.97	3.08	3.90	3.17	3.30	37.99	11.90	07-1903
Fannin, Bonham	92.6	30.2	115	1936	-7	1930	Mar.	27	Nov.	7	225	2.39	3.01	3.30	3.41	5.57	4.50	2.25	2.13	3.45	5.40	3.55	3.55	44.56	13.30	07-1903
Fayette, La Grange	95.9	41.4	110	2000	3	1989	Feb.	26	Nov.	23	269	3.05	2.88	2.55	2.99	4.82	4.41	1.92	2.81	3.68	4.47	3.36	3.04	40.31	9.41	06-1940
Fisher, Rotan	94.2	27.2	116	1994	-5	1989	Mar.	29	Nov.	9	225	0.80	1.35	1.30	1.72	3.68	2.74	1.92	2.76	3.45	2.30	1.13	1.07	24.22	6.85	08-1972
Floyd, Floydada	92.3	23.2	111	1994	-9	1963	Apr.	8	Oct.	30	205	0.45	0.72	0.98	1.58	3.01	3.74	2.50	2.50	2.88	1.62	0.84	0.63	20.95	6.51	09-1942
Foard, Crowell	97.0	24.0	114		-7		Apr.	2	Nov.	7	219	1.00	1.40	1.60	2.10	4.30	3.70	1.70	2.40	3.30	2.40	1.50	1.00	26.40	10.60	06-2001
Fort Bend, Sugar Land	93.7	41.6	108	2000	*6	1989	Feb.	15	Dec.	10	294	4.06	2.98	3.24	3.48	4.69	5.51	3.30	4.29	5.82	4.03	4.58	3.36	49.34	6.10	01-1990
Franklin, Mount Vernon	92.8	32.2	*108	2000	-1	1989	Mar.	22	Nov.	17	235	2.83	3.41	4.23	3.56	4.71	4.79	3.82	2.19	3.75	4.77	5.10	4.49	47.65	7.90	01-1999
Freestone, Fairfield	95.0	36.4	*110	2000	-2	1989	Mar.	19	Nov.	17	242	2.84	2.56	3.29	3.38	5.04	3.79	2.14	2.56	3.48	4.64	1.60	3.70	42.31	7.84	08-1946
Frio, Pearsall	97.5	37.9	113	2000	*7	1989	Feb.	22	Nov.	25	275	1.30	1.45	1.30	2.15	3.33	3.68	1.58	2.61	2.29	3.20	0.90	1.24	25.73	5.40	05-1999
Gaines, Seminole	94.1	26.7	114	1994	-9	1962	Apr.	2	Nov.	3	215	0.64	0.72	0.61	0.91	2.39	2.45	2.44	2.31	2.73	1.39	0.90	0.71	18.20	13.63	07-1900
Galveston, Galveston	88.7	49.7	102	1999	*14	1989	Jan.	19	Jan.	3	358	4.08	2.61	2.76	2.56	3.70	4.04	4.22	4.22	5.76	3.49	3.64	3.53	43.84	6.75	10-1926
Garza, Post	94.0	27.8	115	1994	*-1	1994	Mar.	30	Nov.	9	223	0.58	0.98	0.76	1.43	3.01	2.83	2.03	2.88	3.07	2.05	0.89	0.78	21.29	8.03	09-1952
Gillespie, Fredericksburg	93.1	36.1	*109	2000	-5	1949	Mar.	18	Nov.	12	238	1.36	1.91	1.86	2.40	4.29	3.97	2.00	2.74	3.07	3.72	2.19	2.14	31.65	8.75	07-1945
Glasscock, Garden City	94.0	26.7	114	1994	-3	1989	Apr.	3	Nov.	3	213	0.73	0.71	0.70	1.14	2.18	1.91	1.86	2.02	2.97	1.66	0.75	0.69	17.32	9.16	06-1967
Goliad, Goliad	95.5	43.3	*112	1998	7	1962	Feb.	25	Nov.	26	273	2.34	2.11	2.00	3.19	4.49	4.96	2.85	3.49	4.56	4.26	2.84	2.14	38.58	16.31	08-1981
Gonzales, Gonzales	93.9	38.7	111	2000	*4	1989	Feb.	26	Dec.	1	277	2.36	2.08	2.22	3.04	5.43	4.24	1.60	2.68	3.20	3.87	1.20	2.46	36.02	3.54	07-1982
Gray, Pampa	91.9	21.9	108	1980	-8	1989	Apr.	13	Oct.	25	195	0.57	0.83	1.50	1.95	3.37	3.52	2.85	2.38	2.29	1.58	1.20	0.70	22.74	8.40	04-1920
Grayson, Sherman	92.7	32.2	113	1936	*-2	1989	Mar.	22	Nov.	14	236	2.11	2.63	3.44	3.49	5.41	4.37	2.34	2.25	4.01	5.15	3.81	3.03	42.04	8.70	03-1989
Gregg, Longview	94.5	33.7	113	1936	-4	1930	Mar.	19	Nov.	15	240	3.79	3.93	4.11	4.19	4.79	5.03	2.83	2.71	3.81	4.34	4.75	4.78	49.06		
Grimes, Richards	96.0	40.0	108		4		Mar.	1	Dec.	4	278	4.10	3.00	3.30	3.40	5.20	3.90	2.20	2.60	4.20	3.50	4.10	4.30	44.70		
Guadalupe, New Braunfels	95.0	36.0	110		0		Mar.	6	Nov.	28	267	1.90	2.00	1.80	2.60	2.91	3.05	2.45	2.38	4.10	3.50	4.10	2.00	34.50	7.00	07-1960
Hale, Plainview	91.0	24.4	111	1994	-8	1933	Apr.	4	Oct.	31	209	0.59	0.63	0.80	1.52	3.93	3.51	1.88	2.25	2.28	1.72	0.84	0.73	19.90	8.80	06-1960
Hall, Memphis	95.7	25.5	*117	1944	-11	1930	Apr.	1	Nov.	4	217	0.57	0.88	1.52	2.04	3.70	3.71	1.53	1.57	2.45	1.77	0.96	0.75	22.51	8.20	10-1959
Hamilton, Hamilton	94.3	33.4	109	1964	-3	1930	Mar.	16	Nov.	15	243	1.64	1.76	2.61	2.72	3.70	2.97	2.77	2.38	2.85	2.90	2.00	1.60	28.59	5.80	05-1965
Hansford, Spearman	95.5	22.4	111	1936	-22	1959	Apr.	16	Oct.	23	189	0.53	0.62	1.52	1.58	2.83	2.77	2.42	2.57	2.08	1.35	1.01	0.66	30.30	8.03	08-1995
Hardeman, Quanah	96.5	24.6	*119	1994	-15	1989	Apr.	4	Nov.	2	211	0.96	1.17	1.65	2.08	3.86	3.73	2.42	2.38	3.43	2.37	1.40	1.12	26.76	9.95	10-1949
Hardin, Evadale	93.0	37.0	102		12		Mar.	31	Nov.	14	246	5.40	3.70	4.20	4.00	5.50	5.50	4.10	4.20	4.50	5.26	5.00	5.10	56.50		
Harris, Houston	93.6	45.2	108	2000	9	1989	Feb.	8	Dec.	2	308	4.25	3.01	3.19	3.46	5.11	6.84	2.59	4.54	5.62	5.36	4.54	3.78	53.96	8.58	03-1989
Harrison, Marshall	92.4	33.4	112	1909	-5	1930	Mar.	20	Nov.	12	236	4.38	4.07	4.33	4.35	5.07	5.23	3.02	2.68	3.89	4.66	4.59	4.95	51.22	3.80	12-1997
Hartley, Channing	90.9	20.0	*108	1981	-9	1979	Apr.	19	Oct.	19	182	0.35	0.45	0.76	1.10	1.88	2.30	2.59	3.50	1.66	1.33	0.61	0.67	17.20		
Haskell, Haskell	96.1	28.8	*115	1994	*-6	1989	Mar.	27	Nov.	12	229	0.96	1.47	1.46	1.99	3.32	3.26	1.61	2.74	2.96	2.53	1.26	1.37	24.93	14.29	08-1978

COUNTY AND STATION	TEMPERATURE						AVERAGE FREEZE DATES				Growing Season Days	MEAN PRECIPITATION													EXTREMES	
	Mean Max. July °F.	Mean Min. January °F.	Record Highest °F.	Year	Record Lowest °F.	Year	Last in Spring Mo. Day		First in Fall Mo. Day			January In.	February In.	March In.	April In.	May In.	June In.	July In.	August In.	September In.	October In.	November In.	December In.	Annual In.	Highest Daily Rainfall In.	Mo.-Year
Hays, San Marcos	95.1	38.6	*111	2000	–2	1949	Feb. 28		Nov. 24		268	2.05	2.21	2.09	2.85	5.31	4.84	2.12	2.65	3.46	4.03	3.17	2.41	37.19	15.78	10-1998
Hemphill, Canadian	93.9	18.8	*112	1994	*–14	1942	Apr. 10		Oct. 16		188	0.46	0.71	1.70	1.72	3.75	3.33	2.19	2.36	2.36	1.47	0.94	0.69	21.68	5.15	10-1985
Henderson, Athens	93.4	35.2	*109	2000	–6	1985	Mar. 19		Nov. 14		239	2.96	3.37	3.70	3.47	4.82	3.95	1.74	2.43	3.07	4.70	3.94	3.88	42.03	7.19	04-1986
Hidalgo, McAllen	95.5	48.2	109	1999	17	1962	Jan. 30				>365	1.20	1.37	0.95	1.36	2.51	2.49	1.70	2.31	4.00	2.76	0.95	1.01	22.61	7.81	08-1980
Hill, Hillsboro	95.2	35.2	113	1917	–6	1989	Mar. 19		Nov. 14		240	2.19	2.67	3.21	3.24	4.65	2.78	2.08	2.19	2.92	4.15	2.70	3.08	37.15	11.30	09-1936
Hockley, Levelland	92.7	23.7	115	1994	–16	1963	Apr. 08		Oct. 27		201	0.59	0.63	0.58	1.03	2.35	2.78	2.22	2.87	3.24	1.62	0.85	0.82	19.58	4.23	06-1999
Hood, Cresson	97.0	33.0	110				Mar. 26		Nov. 13		232	1.60	2.20	2.60	2.90	4.70	3.90	1.70	2.40	2.60	3.90	2.30	2.30	33.10		
Hopkins, Sulphur Springs	94.8	31.1	115	1969	–4	1989	Mar. 25		Nov. 12		232	2.88	3.20	4.27	4.34	5.00	3.90	3.22	2.35	3.35	5.21	4.46	4.46	47.69	8.11	07-1994
Houston, Crockett	93.3	35.9	114	1909	*0	1989	Mar. 10		Nov. 18		252	4.00	3.10	3.45	3.87	4.66	4.46	2.84	2.81	4.12	4.22	3.93	4.02	45.48	9.11	06-2001
Howard, Big Spring	94.3	29.6	114	1994	*–5	1985	Mar. 23		Nov. 13		235	0.72	0.81	0.73	1.34	3.05	2.58	1.78	2.38	3.51	1.78	0.77	0.67	20.12	4.84	05-1994
Hudspeth, Sierra Blanca	92.0	25.1	109	1994	–10	1989	Apr. 18		Oct. 29		193	0.49	0.41	0.26	0.29	0.53	1.11	2.11	2.29	2.19	1.15	0.44	0.66	11.93	3.32	09-1978
Hunt, Greenville	93.3	31.2	116	1936	–4	1930	Mar. 23		Nov. 13		235	2.51	3.16	3.67	3.79	5.47	4.03	2.96	2.18	3.56	4.91	3.98	3.48	43.70	6.95	09-1936
Hutchinson, Borger	92.6	23.4	*108	1998	–12	1951	Apr. 14		Oct. 25		193	0.65	0.69	1.56	1.77	3.08	3.20	2.69	3.16	2.00	1.60	0.88	0.70	21.98	3.79	05-1959
Irion, Funk Ranch	95.0	32.0	108		4		Mar. 27		Nov. 11		229	1.28	1.10	1.00	1.60	2.50	2.50	1.40	1.90	3.10	2.10	1.00	1.00	19.90		
Jack, Jacksboro	94.4	29.7	*113	1980	–7	1989	Mar. 21		Nov. 14		237	1.70	1.79	2.38	2.60	4.96	2.50	2.26	2.15	3.18	3.78	2.05	1.83	31.44	9.60	04-1957
Jackson, Edna	94.0	42.0	105		17		Feb. 19		Dec. 6		290	3.10	2.40	2.00	3.10	5.30	4.60	2.90	2.60	4.90	5.00	3.40	2.80	42.10		
Jasper, Sam Rayburn Dam	94.5	35.2	109	2000	7	1989	Feb. 17		Nov. 14		241	5.94	4.55	5.29	4.51	5.53	5.81	4.24	3.92	3.97	4.84	5.88	6.09	60.57	9.04	03-1999
Jeff Davis, Fort Davis	89.5	28.4	*107	1998	*0	1985	Apr. 9		Nov. 2		206	0.43	0.35	0.34	0.50	1.46	2.56	2.95	2.97	2.76	1.29	0.49	0.53	15.86	5.30	08-1932
Jeff Davis, Mount Locke	84.5	32.4	*104	1994	–10	1962	Apr. 17		Oct. 26		191	0.53	0.50	0.33	0.60	1.73	2.79	3.82	4.02	3.29	1.71	0.56	0.73	20.37	4.13	05-1984
Jefferson, Beaumont	91.6	42.9	108	2000	12	1989	Feb. 14		Dec. 6		295	5.69	3.35	3.75	3.84	5.83	6.58	5.23	4.85	6.10	4.67	4.75	5.25	59.89	12.09	09-1963
Jim Hogg, Hebbronville	97.5	43.8	111	1998	*12	1998	Feb. 11		Dec. 11		307	1.12	1.40	1.14	1.69	3.33	3.13	1.44	2.28	3.68	2.22	1.22	1.10	23.75	9.40	09-1971
Jim Wells, Alice	96.1	44.1	*111	1994	*12	1989	Jan. 29		Dec. 15		320	1.21	1.51	1.34	1.65	3.16	3.41	1.76	2.70	4.52	3.55	1.50	1.21	27.52	12.14	09-1971
Johnson, Cleburne	97.0	34.0	114	1939	–5	1989	Mar. 18		Nov. 13		240	1.90	2.29	3.07	3.53	5.11	3.90	2.18	2.36	2.88	3.92	2.54	2.57	36.25	9.02	05-1989
Jones, Anson	96.3	30.7	114	1994	–12	1989	Mar. 28		Nov. 12		228	1.03	1.51	1.21	1.94	3.20	3.13	2.04	2.94	3.93	2.55	1.22	1.30	26.00	5.60	09-1988
Karnes, Karnes City	95.0	41.0	112		7		Mar. 24		Dec. 2		281	1.50	1.70	1.50	2.50	3.40	3.13	1.90	2.40	3.40	3.00	1.90	1.50	28.40		
Kaufman, Kaufman	94.6	32.3	113	1936	*–3	1989	Mar. 19		Nov. 13		240	2.74	3.04	3.37	3.06	4.45	3.31	2.12	1.98	2.77	4.81	3.80	3.45	38.90	13.66	08-1908
Kendall, Boerne	91.9	34.3	112	1925	–4	1949	Mar. 20		Nov. 13		238	1.79	2.24	2.57	2.87	4.66	4.77	2.23	3.05	3.61	4.09	3.11	2.37	37.36	9.04	10-1913
Kenedy, Sarita	95.0	45.0	110		14		Feb. 2		Dec. 18		319	1.44	1.80	1.30	1.60	2.70	3.30	1.50	3.40	4.70	3.40	1.90	1.20	27.90		
Kent, Jayton	95.7	24.9	116	1994	–6	1985	Apr. 6		Nov. 7		218	0.91	1.40	1.12	1.73	3.35	3.21	1.59	2.81	3.04	2.17	0.97	0.90	22.94	6.50	06-1991
Kerr, Kerrville	92.0	32.0	110		–7		Apr. 6		Nov. 6		216	1.30	1.80	2.10	2.30	4.20	4.00	2.20	2.30	3.90	3.80	2.60	2.10	32.60		
Kimble, Junction	94.8	29.3	*111	1984	–11	1929	Apr. 2		Nov. 1		212	0.77	1.43	1.42	1.95	3.23	3.10	1.55	2.20	2.28	2.68	1.37	1.26	23.24	6.10	09-1980
King, Guthrie	96.7	23.9	119	1994	–10	1989	Apr. 6		Nov. 4		211	1.03	1.28	1.26	1.79	3.90	3.17	1.94	2.87	3.25	2.38	1.12	1.01	25.00	8.85	07-1986
Kinney, Brackettville	95.5	37.3	111	1988	4	1962	Mar. 5		Nov. 15		255	0.77	1.16	1.10	1.99	2.87	3.18	1.79	2.29	2.77	2.49	1.41	0.97	22.79	6.20	05-1900
Kleberg, Kingsville	95.5	43.4	*111	2000	10	1989	Feb. 10		Dec. 11		303	1.44	1.71	1.24	1.80	3.53	4.02	1.97	3.05	3.98	3.72	1.50	1.07	29.03	6.67	12-1991
Knox, Munday	96.5	28.1	*111	1994	*–9	1989	Mar. 28		Nov. 12		228	1.00	1.54	1.69	1.91	3.85	4.25	1.70	2.68	3.22	2.73	1.38	1.20	26.36	8.00	06-1930
Lamar, Paris	94.3	29.9	115	1936	*–5	1930	Mar. 18		Nov. 14		240	2.63	3.00	4.11	3.56	5.63	4.25	3.89	2.39	4.42	5.04	4.70	4.20	47.82	7.61	06-1928
Lamb, Littlefield	92.0	22.7	112	1994	–6	1979	Apr. 11		Oct. 25		196	0.55	0.52	0.75	1.11	2.24	3.04	2.44	2.80	2.26	1.52	0.77	0.69	18.69	5.10	06-1999
Lampasas, Lampasas	94.1	30.4	*112	1917	–12	1949	Apr. 1		Nov. 07		219	1.50	2.34	2.31	2.48	4.37	3.49	1.68	2.42	2.61	3.33	2.32	2.23	31.08	6.95	05-1957
La Salle, Fowlerton	98.9	39.1	113	1998	9	1962	Feb. 27		Nov. 26		271	0.93	1.08	1.46	1.84	2.73	2.61	1.53	2.19	2.71	3.15	1.22	1.11	22.56	9.50	10-1986

COUNTY AND STATION	TEMPERATURE						AVERAGE FREEZE DATES				MEAN PRECIPITATION													EXTREMES	
	Mean Max. July (F.)	Mean Min. January (F.)	Record Highest (F.)	Year	Record Lowest (F.)	Year	Last in Spring (Mo. Day)	First in Fall (Mo. Day)	Growing Season (Days)		January (In.)	February (In.)	March (In.)	April (In.)	May (In.)	June (In.)	July (In.)	August (In.)	September (In.)	October (In.)	November (In.)	December (In.)	Annual (In.)	Highest Daily Rainfall (In.)	Mo.-Year
Lavaca, Hallettsville	94.4	41.8	*111	1980	5	1989	Feb. 25	Nov. 29	277		2.91	2.50	2.46	3.44	5.75	5.02	2.28	2.95	4.49	4.07	3.53	2.83	42.23	11.30	07-1936
Lee, Lexington	93.6	37.3	111	2000	2	2000	Mar. 1	Nov. 22	265		2.60	2.13	2.54	2.48	4.82	3.78	1.63	2.06	3.26	4.69	3.25	2.78	36.02	10.13	10-1994
Leon, Centerville	94.7	34.3	*111	1954	-3	1949	Mar. 17	Nov. 14	242		3.40	3.18	3.51	3.29	4.77	4.12	2.48	2.62	3.50	4.79	3.82	3.60	43.08	8.50	10-1957
Liberty, Liberty	92.2	40.3	108	1913	7	1989	Feb. 18	Dec. 1	285		4.91	3.74	3.84	4.01	5.80	6.88	4.46	4.34	5.92	5.77	5.84	5.01	60.52	18.50	10-1994
Limestone, Mexia	95.8	33.7	112	1909	-5	1989	Mar. 6	Nov. 20	258		2.44	3.08	3.45	3.14	4.91	3.89	1.99	2.56	4.16	4.29	3.64	3.85	41.40	11.80	09-1932
Lipscomb, Lipscomb	94.2	16.2	114	1978	*-18	1974	Apr. 23	Oct. 11	170		0.54	0.81	1.91	2.00	3.85	3.28	2.30	2.52	1.97	1.46	1.12	0.81	22.57	6.62	05-1951
Live Oak, Choke Canyon Dam	97.0	42.0	109		12		Feb. 20	Dec. 6	289		1.20	1.10	1.80	2.40	2.80	2.70	1.60	1.40	2.10	2.00	1.70	1.20	22.00		
Llano, Llano	96.0	32.3	115	1933	-7	1929	Mar. 18	Nov. 12	238		1.80	1.80	1.90	2.19	3.94	3.40	1.84	2.03	2.14	2.88	2.23	1.90	27.33	12.53	09-1952
Loving, Mentone	96.0	28.0	114		-14		Apr. 3	Nov. 8	222		0.30	0.30	0.30	0.20	1.10	0.90	1.80	1.40	1.20	1.00	0.30	0.30	9.10		
Lubbock, Lubbock	91.9	24.4	114	1994	-17	1933	Apr. 3	Nov. 1	211		0.50	0.71	0.76	1.29	2.31	2.98	2.13	2.36	2.57	1.70	0.71	0.67	18.69	5.70	06-1967
Lynn, Tahoka	92.2	25.1	111	1994	-15	1933	Apr. 4	Nov. 4	213		0.66	0.79	0.71	1.48	2.74	3.22	2.62	2.23	2.65	1.73	0.86	0.79	20.48	8.32	10-1913
Madison, Madisonville	96.0	35.8	112	2000	-2	1949	Apr. 7	Nov. 18	255		3.81	2.83	3.24	3.26	4.60	4.00	2.72	2.95	4.20	4.41	4.01	3.62	44.00	8.00	08-1945
Marion, Jefferson	93.1	31.4	108	2000	-5	1989	Mar. 25	Nov. 6	225		4.13	3.96	4.41	4.07	4.60	4.84	2.89	2.93	3.40	4.64	4.68	4.71	49.26	9.10	04-1921
Martin, Lenorah	94.0	30.0	109		-8		Apr. 5	Nov. 6	215		0.70	0.70	0.70	2.05	2.40	2.50	2.00	1.60	3.10	1.80	0.80	0.70	18.20	7.45	09-1952
Mason, Mason	94.9	30.8	109	1962	*3	1985	Mar. 26	Nov. 9	227		0.91	1.97	1.74	2.05	3.31	4.00	2.00	2.52	3.10	3.01	2.07	1.37	27.95	8.95	09-1961
Matagorda, Bay City	92.4	45.7	*109	2000	*7	1989	Feb. 11	Dec. 13	306		3.89	2.97	3.00	3.18	4.90	4.68	3.89	3.48	5.61	5.13	3.97	3.33	48.03	15.60	06-1936
Maverick, Eagle Pass	98.1	40.1	*115	1944	-2	1962	Feb. 12	Dec. 5	295		0.80	0.94	0.72	1.75	2.95	3.49	2.03	2.01	2.57	2.33	1.08	0.81	21.48	6.51	07-1971
McCulloch, Brady	94.5	32.3	*110	1980	-2	1989	Mar. 21	Nov. 11	235		1.01	1.68	1.63	1.92	3.60	3.26	2.68	2.57	3.26	2.68	1.73	1.61	27.63	7.98	12-1997
McLennan, Waco	96.7	35.1	112	1969	-5	1949	Mar. 13	Nov. 19	250		1.15	1.27	1.33	1.95	3.10	3.08	2.23	1.85	2.88	2.14	2.61	2.76	33.34	6.93	09-1967
McMullen, Tilden	98.7	40.1	119	1910	5	1989	Feb. 21	Dec. 3	284		1.30	1.50	1.60	2.70	3.80	3.37	1.52	2.56	2.91	2.90	1.38	1.19	23.87		
Medina, Hondo	95.0	38.0	112		4		Mar. 6	Oct. 24	263		0.53	0.58	0.42	0.73	1.79	3.60	1.40	1.50	2.31	1.77	0.65	0.65	26.30	6.03	09-1936
Menard, Menard	94.8	30.7	114	1927	-6	1929	Apr. 7	Oct. 29	204		0.97	1.48	1.60	1.72	3.22	2.41	2.14	2.34	2.69	2.31	1.51	1.28	23.67	4.75	05-1968
Midland, Midland	94.3	29.6	116	1994	-11	1985	Mar. 30	Nov. 12	226		0.53	0.58	0.42	0.73	1.79	2.38	1.89	1.77	2.31	1.77	0.65	0.65	14.80	12.45	09-1921
Milam, Cameron	95.7	39.2	114	1917	-7	1930	Mar. 7	Nov. 22	260		2.29	2.53	2.45	2.88	5.01	3.22	1.94	1.95	3.54	3.73	3.12	2.86	35.52	7.20	10-1969
Mills, Goldthwaite	95.2	35.2	116	1964	-7	1947	Mar. 25	Nov. 15	239		1.26	2.10	2.04	2.28	3.85	3.81	1.76	1.95	2.79	3.11	2.05	1.78	28.78	8.65	04-1900
Mitchell, Colorado City	95.9	27.0	115	1907	-7	1947	Mar. 20	Nov. 7	236		0.44	0.89	1.07	1.33	2.49	3.42	1.23	2.29	3.09	2.22	0.90	0.64	19.43	10.25	05-1989
Montague, Bowie	94.7	28.3	115	1980	-11	1989	Mar. 21	Nov. 12	236		1.47	2.13	2.62	2.89	5.04	4.58	1.81	2.27	3.67	4.20	2.18	2.02	33.72	14.35	10-1994
Montgomery, Conroe	94.3	40.0	109	2000	3	1989	Feb. 27	Nov. 25	270		4.21	2.97	2.94	3.85	5.50	4.24	3.22	3.73	4.46	4.70	4.79	4.37	49.32	7.75	05-1989
Moore, Dumas	91.7	20.8	*100	1980	*-18	1959	Apr. 18	Oct. 22	186		0.47	0.58	1.13	1.31	2.74	3.60	2.42	2.47	1.95	1.77	0.66	0.50	17.75	4.10	05-1988
Morris, Daingerfield	95.0	33.7	112	1998	4	1962	Mar. 3	Nov. 22	263		3.54	3.35	4.64	4.32	4.43	4.10	2.98	2.39	3.29	4.35	4.84	4.39	46.76	7.48	04-1966
Motley, Matador	94.8	27.3	116	1994	-5	1989	Apr. 1	Nov. 8	221		0.67	0.90	1.21	1.81	3.16	3.53	2.10	2.41	3.11	2.09	0.99	0.85	22.90	5.30	10-1983
Nacogdoches, Nacogdoches	94.8	36.0	110		0		Mar. 16	Nov. 12	243		4.80	4.40	4.80	4.10	4.80	4.60	2.90	3.10	3.70	4.33	4.60	4.60	48.40	9.96	05-1968
Navarro, Corsicana	94.5	34.0	113	1954	-5	1949	Mar. 24	Nov. 23	259		3.90	3.90	4.20	4.10	4.95	4.10	1.89	2.37	3.04	4.10	3.33	3.60	39.48	8.28	09-1980
Newton, Toledo Bend Dam	94.0	35.0	107		7		Mar. 9	Nov. 10	228		5.70	4.40	4.80	4.00	4.90	5.00	3.60	3.40	3.90	4.10	5.00	6.10	54.90	7.92	10-1995
Nolan, Roscoe	93.8	28.9	113	1994	-11	1947	Mar. 31	Nov. 10	223		1.03	1.18	1.11	1.52	3.04	3.09	1.89	2.59	3.58	2.53	0.99	0.99	23.54		
Nueces, Corpus Christi	93.2	46.2	109	2000	13	1989	Feb. 3	Dec. 23	319		1.62	1.84	1.74	2.05	3.48	3.53	2.00	3.54	5.03	3.94	1.74	1.75	32.26		
Ochiltree, Perryton	91.4	18.4	111	1981	-17	1988	Apr. 25	Oct. 17	174		0.47	0.62	1.71	1.80	3.33	2.97	2.74	2.22	1.89	1.38	1.09	0.66	20.88	7.11	05-1989
Oldham, Boys Ranch	92.3	20.5	110	1982	-11	1983	Apr. 13	Oct. 16	186		0.49	0.28	0.89	1.13	2.47	2.18	2.96	3.20	1.94	1.48	0.66	0.50	18.18	4.50	09-1990

COUNTY AND STATION	Mean Max July °F	Mean Min January °F	Record Highest °F	Year	Record Lowest °F	Year	Last in Spring	First in Fall	Growing Season Days	Jan In.	Feb In.	Mar In.	Apr In.	May In.	June In.	July In.	Aug In.	Sept In.	Oct In.	Nov In.	Dec In.	Annual In.	Highest Daily Rainfall In.	Mo.-Year
Orange, Orange	91.0	41.0	104	1980	10		Mar. 16	Nov. 11	240	6.00	3.60	3.90	3.60	5.70	6.20	5.30	4.70	5.60	4.60	4.60	5.20	59.00	6.65	10-1981
Palo Pinto, Mineral Wells	97.3	33.4	*114	1980	-8	1989	Mar. 23	Nov. 13	233	1.42	1.99	2.69	2.75	4.59	3.25	2.25	2.34	2.80	3.81	2.16	1.74	31.79	9.25	04-1991
Panola, Carthage	93.7	33.9	*109	2000	*1	1989	Mar. 17	Nov. 14	242	4.76	3.88	4.00	4.36	5.05	4.95	3.25	2.92	3.75	4.65	4.93	5.01	51.51	7.05	07-1962
Parker, Weatherford	95.2	29.0	119	1980	*-10	1989	Mar. 29	Nov. 8	223	1.50	2.36	2.79	2.84	4.76	3.93	2.11	2.60	2.85	4.19	2.61	2.16	34.70	3.90	10-1998
Parmer, Friona	89.8	21.7	*108	1990	-15	1963	Apr. 19	Oct. 20	183	0.56	0.53	0.91	1.09	2.19	2.50	2.24	2.89	2.28	1.60	0.80	0.79	18.38	5.22	10-1986
Pecos, Fort Stockton	95.8	31.4	117	1994	-6	1985	Mar. 26	Nov. 12	230	0.50	0.47	0.38	0.72	1.59	1.70	1.34	1.95	2.75	1.45	0.61	0.60	14.06	10.47	10-1994
Polk, Livingston	94.1	35.8	*111	2000	*3	1989	Mar. 17	Nov. 13	241	4.64	3.47	3.89	3.92	5.20	5.20	3.55	3.41	4.73	3.82	4.76	4.92	51.85	4.92	06-1984
Potter, Amarillo	91.0	22.6	*108	1998	-14	1951	Apr. 18	Oct. 20	185	0.63	0.55	1.13	1.33	2.50	3.28	2.68	2.94	1.88	1.50	0.68	0.61	19.71	2.93	05-1984
Presidio, Marfa	88.9	23.9	*106	1994	-2	1972	Apr. 11	Oct. 30	201	0.41	0.47	0.24	0.67	1.33	1.80	2.83	2.70	2.88	1.48	0.39	0.59	15.79	3.30	04-1979
Presidio, Presidio	100.8	34.5	*117	1960	4	1962	Mar. 5	Nov. 20	260	0.31	0.36	0.15	0.38	0.66	1.51	2.01	1.82	1.69	0.99	0.37	0.51	10.76	5.65	06-1992
Rains, Emory	92.4	31.6	110	1964	-5	1960	Mar. 22	Nov. 12	234	3.04	3.34	3.88	3.72	5.31	4.19	2.33	2.23	2.98	4.66	3.89	3.93	43.50	7.87	08-1968
Randall, Canyon	92.6	23.7	*109	1981	-14	1951	Apr. 13	Oct. 22	191	0.46	0.52	0.99	1.08	2.89	2.96	2.39	2.84	1.97	1.78	0.69	0.62	19.19	4.85	07-1990
Reagan, Big Lake	93.4	29.1	110	1998	*1	1989	Apr. 1	Nov. 5	218	0.68	0.92	0.81	1.42	2.39	1.99	1.79	2.18	2.97	1.92	0.88	0.84	18.79	8.37	11-2001
Real, Camp Wood	94.2	33.1	*109	2000	*5	1989	Mar. 22	Nov. 11	233	1.11	1.44	1.55	2.41	3.16	3.68	2.09	3.07	2.87	3.46	1.77	1.38	27.99	8.30	05-1953
Red River, Clarksville	92.2	29.7	115	1936	-7	1930	Mar. 28	Nov. 9	226	2.65	3.17	4.50	4.02	5.43	4.00	3.23	2.07	3.83	4.51	5.43	4.51	47.83	4.13	07-1973
Reeves, Balmorhea	94.7	30.1	112	1939	-9	1933	Mar. 30	Nov. 9	223	0.58	0.56	0.24	0.63	1.45	1.24	1.78	2.29	3.08	1.19	0.54	0.61	14.19	4.38	05-1992
Reeves, Pecos	98.5	28.1	118	1968	-9	1962	Mar. 26	Nov. 7	223	0.47	0.45	0.34	0.47	1.25	1.24	1.35	1.62	3.00	1.10	0.47	0.61	11.61		
Refugio, Refugio	94.0	45.0	106		8		Feb. 14	Dec. 15	304	2.50	2.20	1.50	1.90	3.77	4.80	3.30	3.50	7.00	5.20	2.30	1.60	40.10		
Roberts, Miami	92.4	20.6	114	1917	*-15	1942	Apr. 15	Oct. 19	186	0.68	0.83	1.74	2.19	3.77	3.26	2.39	2.40	2.38	1.64	1.12	0.90	23.30	5.58	10-1985
Robertson, Franklin	95.1	38.2	112	2000	-1	1989	Mar. 9	Nov. 19	254	3.03	2.86	2.90	3.63	4.81	2.95	2.04	2.60	3.65	4.38	3.26	3.52	39.03	7.48	07-1979
Rockwall, Rockwall	96.0	33.0	118		-7		Mar. 23	Nov. 14	236	2.10	2.70	3.50	3.60	5.30	3.70	2.30	2.00	4.30	3.40	3.40	3.20	39.40		
Runnels, Ballinger	94.3	28.5	116	1907	-6	1949	Mar. 28	Nov. 9	225	0.94	1.32	1.27	1.80	3.38	3.15	1.39	2.40	3.08	2.52	1.31	1.20	23.76		
Rusk, Henderson	93.1	33.1	*111	2000	-1	1989	Mar. 20	Nov. 15	239	4.08	3.78	4.00	3.91	4.73	4.87	2.81	2.75	3.71	4.68	4.67	4.23	48.22	7.05	05-1946
Sabine, Hemphill	93.0	36.0	104		8		Mar. 21	Nov. 21	238	5.50	4.00	5.00	4.20	4.60	5.00	3.80	3.20	4.60	3.90	5.00	6.00	54.40	11.05	03-1989
San Augustine, Broaddus	93.0	35.0	106		9		Mar. 11	Nov. 22	255	5.30	4.10	5.00	3.40	5.40	4.50	3.00	3.90	3.60	3.60	4.40	5.70	51.10		
San Jacinto, Coldspring	93.8	37.5	110	1998	*3	1989	Feb. 7	Dec. 13	308	4.63	3.44	3.61	3.73	5.40	5.93	2.95	3.52	4.45	4.40	4.89	4.82	51.77	13.50	06-1973
San Patricio, Sinton	91.7	44.2	109	2000	10	1989	Mar. 14	Nov. 11	236	1.91	2.02	1.91	1.99	4.07	3.97	2.98	3.16	5.61	4.61	2.04	1.27	35.54	12.35	04-1930
San Saba, San Saba	95.8	34.2	112	1978	-1	1989	Mar. 28	Nov. 12	229	1.09	1.94	1.96	2.13	5.04	3.62	1.87	2.29	2.82	2.82	2.04	1.66	27.72	11.20	10-1969
Schleicher, Eldorado	93.0	28.0	107		3		Apr. 1	Nov. 7	219	0.70	0.90	0.70	1.70	2.50	1.90	1.60	2.10	3.10	2.10	1.00	0.60	19.00		
Scurry, Snyder	94.6	26.7	115	1936	-11	1947	Mar. 28	Nov. 6	222	0.69	1.03	1.09	1.69	3.01	3.06	2.04	2.55	3.30	2.34	0.91	0.80	22.51	5.26	07-1948
Shackelford, Albany	95.4	28.9	115	1972	-8	1947	Mar. 20	Nov. 10	234	1.01	1.65	1.95	2.34	3.76	3.45	1.91	3.04	3.17	3.00	1.55	1.62	28.45	5.80	07-1953
Shelby, Center	93.9	34.9	112	2000	0	1951	Apr. 26	Oct. 15	259	5.04	4.13	4.21	4.41	5.04	4.81	3.04	3.76	4.20	4.64	4.68	5.05	53.01	9.66	11-1940
Sherman, Stratford	91.1	18.5	*108	1953	*-20	1933	Apr. 20	Oct. 15	171	0.48	0.44	1.21	1.46	2.85	2.26	2.31	2.67	1.71	1.15	0.79	0.56	17.89	5.60	08-1992
Smith, Tyler	94.0	38.0	108		0		Mar. 7	Nov. 21	200	3.30	3.70	4.00	3.70	4.50	3.70	2.20	2.60	3.30	5.10	4.50	4.80	45.40	8.48	07-1995
Somervell, Glen Rose	97.3	28.9	115	1984	-15	1989	Apr. 11	Oct. 29	259	1.64	2.28	2.80	2.91	5.20	4.02	2.19	2.18	3.15	3.83	2.24	2.38	34.82	12.51	09-1967
Starr, Rio Grande City	99.1	44.5	116	1998	10	1962	Feb. 9	Dec. 14	309	0.97	1.10	0.74	1.22	2.42	2.94	1.27	1.97	4.68	2.48	0.90	0.92	21.61	15.70	10-1981
Stephens, Breckenridge	96.8	30.9	114	1936	-7	1989	Mar. 29	Dec. 10	226	1.30	1.39	2.05	2.17	3.53	3.12	1.86	2.06	2.93	3.44	1.56	1.63	27.04		
Sterling, Sterling City	94.7	27.4	112	1994	-13	1985	Apr. 4	Nov. 3	212	0.85	0.91	0.91	1.43	2.79	2.33	1.40	1.87	3.29	1.84	0.85	0.93	19.40	6.53	07-1948

Weather data by Texas county and station. Temperatures in °F; precipitation and rainfall in inches.

County and Station	Mean Max. July	Mean Min. January	Record Highest	Year	Record Lowest	Year	Last in Spring	First in Fall	Growing Season (Days)	Jan	Feb	Mar	Apr	May	June	July	Aug	Sep	Oct	Nov	Dec	Annual	Highest Daily Rainfall (In.)	Mo.-Year
Stonewall, Aspermont	97.4	27.2	117	1994	-10	1989	Mar. 30	Nov. 8	223	0.90	1.31	1.32	1.65	3.44	2.94	1.32	2.77	3.04	2.35	1.17	1.03	23.24	6.92	04-1930
Sutton, Sonora	94.7	27.2	109	1980	-8	1951	Apr. 4	Nov. 3	213	0.84	1.16	1.18	1.57	2.57	2.54	1.93	2.93	3.07	2.53	1.26	0.82	22.40	7.92	09-1976
Swisher, Tulia	91.1	22.2	*110	1994	*-10	1951	Apr. 14	Oct. 24	193	0.59	0.72	1.05	1.31	2.99	3.42	2.32	2.65	2.40	1.63	0.87	0.76	20.71	5.18	06-1985
Tarrant, Benbrook	96.6	31.4	111	1954	-6	1989	Apr. 15	Nov. 17	247	1.70	2.19	2.67	3.17	4.58	3.56	2.29	2.03	2.86	4.14	2.35	2.47	34.01	6.36	10-1991
Taylor, Abilene	94.8	31.8	110	1978	*-7	1989	Mar. 24	Nov. 12	232	0.97	1.13	1.41	1.67	2.83	3.06	1.70	2.63	2.91	2.90	1.30	1.27	23.78	6.30	08-1978
Terrell, Sanderson	91.9	30.5	110	1969	3	1989	Mar. 22	Nov. 10	233	0.39	0.59	0.40	0.86	1.74	2.09	1.52	1.87	2.41	1.75	0.81	0.51	14.94	5.35	06-1965
Terry, Brownfield	92.5	26.1	*111	1994	*-8	1963	Apr. 3	Nov. 3	213	0.54	0.68	0.64	0.95	1.90	3.00	2.31	2.15	2.78	1.50	0.79	0.65	18.89	5.05	10-1983
Throckmorton, Throckmorton	97.0	28.0	114		-11		Mar. 31	Nov. 6	220	1.00	1.50	1.60	2.10	3.30	3.50	1.80	2.60	3.30	2.90	1.50	1.50	26.60	8.06	11-1994
Titus, Mount Pleasant	94.2	29.3	118	1936	-12	1951	Mar. 29	Nov. 5	220	3.27	3.54	4.42	3.77	5.02	4.89	3.75	2.05	3.56	4.74	5.07	4.49	48.57	6.24	09-1980
Tom Green, San Angelo	95.0	31.8	111	1960	-4	1989	Feb. 28	Nov. 13	230	0.82	1.18	0.99	1.60	3.09	2.52	1.10	2.05	2.95	2.57	1.10	0.94	20.91	8.00	06-1941
Travis, Austin	95.0	40.0	112	2000	-2	1949	Feb. 17	Dec. 6	291	1.89	1.99	2.14	2.51	5.03	3.81	1.97	2.31	3.04	4.07	2.44	2.44	33.65	12.10	10-1994
Trinity, Groveton	92.1	37.1	111	2000	1	1989	Mar. 14	Nov. 14	244	4.17	3.21	3.67	3.13	5.11	5.01	3.48	3.25	4.10	4.07	4.49	4.41	48.10	7.50	09-1996
Tyler, Town Bluff Dam	93.4	38.3	109	2000	6	1989	Mar. 9	Nov. 19	255	5.08	4.02	4.56	4.41	5.61	5.74	3.46	3.42	3.84	4.01	5.08	5.56	54.79	7.88	04-1966
Upshur, Gilmer	93.4	31.4	*113	1994	*-4	1936	Mar. 29	Nov. 5	220	3.51	3.58	4.38	4.12	4.41	4.41	3.04	2.50	3.84	4.19	4.75	4.35	47.08	9.13	10-1986
Upton, McCamey	95.6	33.1	111		-2	1962	Mar. 20	Nov. 12	236	0.47	0.56	0.41	0.93	1.61	1.55	0.94	1.95	2.68	2.06	0.59	0.70	14.45		
Uvalde, Uvalde	96.0	37.0	111		6	1962	Mar. 10	Nov. 21	255	1.00	1.10	1.00	2.00	3.30	3.50	1.20	2.60	2.30	2.40	1.60	1.30	23.30	17.03	08-1998
Val Verde, Del Rio	96.3	39.7	112	1988	10	1989	Feb. 19	Dec. 1	284	0.57	0.96	0.96	1.71	2.31	2.34	2.02	2.16	2.06	2.00	0.96	0.75	18.80	10.38	10-1994
Van Zandt, Wills Point	93.3	31.4	115	1909	*-2	1909	Mar. 14	Nov. 18	248	3.10	3.22	3.74	3.68	4.74	4.45	2.16	2.26	3.39	4.78	4.23	3.93	44.15	7.08	06-1945
Victoria, Victoria	93.4	43.6	111	2000	9	1989	Feb. 9	Dec. 11	305	2.44	2.04	2.25	2.97	5.12	4.96	2.90	3.05	5.00	4.26	2.64	2.47	43.68	9.87	04-1991
Walker, Huntsville	93.8	39.0	108	2000	2	1989	Feb. 23	Nov. 30	279	4.28	3.14	3.47	3.50	5.08	4.66	2.67	3.69	4.73	4.32	4.87	4.10	48.51	10.21	10-1994
Waller, Hempstead	95.0	38.0	107		13		Feb. 28	Dec. 4	283	2.80	2.90	2.10	3.90	4.70	3.60	2.00	2.40	4.60	4.00	3.20	3.00			
Ward, Monahans	98.6	26.5	*118	1994	-9	1962	Apr. 1	Nov. 7	219	0.51	0.57	0.27	0.55	1.80	1.43	1.31	1.65	2.55	1.39	0.53	0.67	13.23	4.40	09-1980
Washington, Brenham	96.7	39.3	113	2000	*-2	1930	Feb. 20	Dec. 5	288	3.41	2.78	2.93	3.39	5.14	4.66	1.93	3.14	4.83	4.48	4.17	3.29	44.15	10.38	10-1994
Webb, Laredo	101.6	43.7	*114	1998	11	1983	Feb. 9	Dec. 5	290	0.76	0.94	0.92	1.55	2.99	2.99	1.79	2.42	2.73	2.46	1.13	0.85	21.53	6.65	07-1981
Wharton, Pierce	94.3	41.8	112	2000	11	1989	Feb. 19	Dec. 6	290	3.42	2.84	2.74	3.18	5.18	4.69	3.10	3.57	5.81	3.11	3.55	3.23	43.92	8.85	11-1943
Wheeler, Shamrock	93.3	22.9	113	1980	-13	1984	Apr. 6	Oct. 27	203	0.56	0.84	1.88	2.19	3.92	3.74	2.17	2.27	2.83	1.92	1.17	0.83	24.32	8.24	06-1995
Wichita, Wichita Falls	97.2	28.9	117	1980	-12	1947	Mar. 28	Nov. 9	225	1.12	1.58	2.27	2.62	4.11	3.69	1.58	2.39	3.19	2.92	1.68	1.68	28.83	6.19	09-1980
Wilbarger, Vernon	95.7	25.7	117	1943	-9	1943	Mar. 30	Nov. 9	223	1.04	1.34	1.98	2.36	3.82	3.82	1.94	3.07	3.54	2.70	1.48	1.12	28.55	14.82	08-1995
Willacy, Raymondville	95.3	47.5	109	1916	*14	1962	Jan. 19	Jan. 1	347	1.36	1.59	1.44	1.53	2.80	3.22	1.91	3.06	5.40	3.17	1.38	1.11	27.97	9.90	09-1975
Williamson, Taylor	95.3	35.8	*112	2000	-5	1949	Mar. 5	Nov. 20	259	2.09	2.38	2.63	2.68	5.19	3.78	1.62	2.09	3.30	3.83	2.95	2.57	35.11	*6.00	10-1958
Wilson, Floresville	95.7	38.4	111	2000	5	1985	Mar. 8	Nov. 21	257	1.58	1.60	1.65	2.53	3.69	3.69	1.60	2.54	2.14	2.75	2.24	1.57	27.60	9.25	09-1967
Winkler, Wink	96.1	27.8	117	1994	-14	1962	Apr. 2	Nov. 4	215	0.41	0.48	0.32	0.53	1.34	1.83	1.95	1.29	2.14	1.51	0.55	0.57	12.92	5.64	10-1940
Wise, Bridgeport	98.0	30.5	*115	1980	-8	1983	Mar. 30	Nov. 7	219	1.53	2.06	2.63	2.83	5.53	3.54	2.26	2.01	2.97	4.37	2.28	2.01	34.02	9.07	10-1919
Wood, Mineola	93.1	31.2	111	1994	*-12	1951	Apr. 1	Nov. 7	206	3.33	3.43	4.05	3.98	4.71	3.99	2.92	2.23	3.67	4.99	4.50	4.08	45.88	6.42	12-1982
Yoakum, Plains	91.7	21.7	111	1994	*-8	1989	Apr. 5	Oct. 29	219	0.46	0.72	0.60	1.15	2.38	2.35	2.34	2.75	2.67	1.47	0.75	0.77	18.41	6.11	07-1960
Young, Graham	96.6	27.1	117	1936	13	1911	Apr. 2	Nov. 6	217	1.16	1.79	2.22	2.45	4.52	3.60	2.17	2.32	3.64	3.79	1.88	1.81	31.35	8.22	10-1981
Zapata, Zapata	98.0	45.4	116	1998	13	1998	Jan. 24	Dec. 25	337	0.70	1.04	0.79	1.39	2.27	2.67	1.55	1.80	3.65	1.85	0.94	0.88	19.53	6.10	04-1966
Zavala, Crystal City	97.1	42.6	115	2000	*11	1989	Feb. 16	Dec. 6	292	0.93	1.08	1.08	1.75	2.41	3.25	1.67	2.03	2.10	2.44	1.12	0.84	20.70	6.83	10-1959

Calendar

McDonald Observatory on Mount Locke near Fort Davis. Tim Jones photo.

Seasons

Morning & Evening Stars

Eclipses

Major Meteor Showers

Chronological Eras & Cycles

Calendars for 2008 & 2009

Astronomical Calendar for 2008 and 2009

An Explanation of Texas Time

The subsequent calendars were calculated principally from data on the **U.S. Naval Observatory's Web site (http://aa.usno.navy.mil/data/),** and from its publication, **Astronomical Phenomena for 2008** and **Astronomical Phenomena for 2009.**

Times listed here are **Central Standard Time,** except for the period from 2:00 a.m. on the first Sunday in March until 2:00 a.m. on the first Sunday in November, when **Daylight Saving Time,** which is one hour later than Central Standard Time, is in effect.

All of Texas is in the Central Time Zone, except El Paso and Hudspeth counties and the northwest corner of Culberson County, which observe Mountain Time *(see map on page 150).* Mountain Time is one hour earlier than Central Time.

All times are calculated for the intersection of 99° 20' west longitude and 31° 08' north latitude, which is about 15 miles northeast of Brady, McCulloch County. This point is the **approximate geographical center of the state.**

To get the time of sunrise or sunset, moonrise or moonset for any point in Texas, apply the following rule: Add four minutes to the time given in this calendar for each degree of longitude that the place lies west of the 99th meridian; subtract four minutes for each degree of longitude the place lies east of the 99th meridian.

At times there will be considerable variation for distances north and south of the line of 31° 08' north latitude, but the rule for calculating it is complicated. The formula given above will get sufficiently close results.

The **accompanying map** shows the intersection for which all times given here are calculated, with some major Texas cities and their longitudes. These make it convenient to calculate time at any given point.

The Naval Observatory's Web site will allow you to determine more exactly the rise and set times of the Sun and the Moon at your location on a given date or for an entire year.

Planetary Configurations and Phenomena

The phenomena and planetary configurations of heavens for 2008 and 2009 are given in the center column of the calendar on pages 151–156. Below is an explanation of the symbols used in those tables:

⊙ The Sun	● The Earth	♅ Uranus
☾ The Moon	♂ Mars	♆ Neptune
☿ Mercury	♃ Jupiter	♇ Pluto
♀ Venus	♄ Saturn	

Aspects

☌ This symbol appearing between the symbols for heavenly bodies means they are "in conjunction," that is, having the same longitude as applies to the sky and appearing near each other.

☍ This symbol means that the two heavenly bodies are in "opposition," or differ by 180 degrees of longitude.

Common Astronomical Terms

★ **Aphelion** — Point at which a planet's orbit is farthest from the sun.

★ **Perihelion** — Point at which a planet's orbit is nearest the sun.

★ **Apogee** — That point of the moon's orbit farthest from the earth.

★ **Perigee** — That point of the moon's orbit nearest the earth.

The Seasons, 2008 and 2009

2008
The seasons of 2008 begin as follows: **Spring,** March 20, 12:48 a.m. (CDT); **Summer,** June 20, 6:59 p.m. (CDT); **Fall,** Sept. 22, 10:44 a.m. (CDT); **Winter,** Dec. 21, 6:04 a.m. (CST).

2009
The seasons of 2009 begin as follows: **Spring,** March 20, 6:44 a.m. (CDT); **Summer,** June 21, 12:46 a.m. (CDT); **Fall,** Sept. 22, 4:19 p.m. (CDT); **Winter,** Dec. 21, 11:47 a.m. (CST).

Morning & Evening Stars

Morning Stars 2008
Venus — Jan. 1 – May 3
Jupiter — Jan. 5 – July 9
Saturn — Jan. 1 – Feb. 24; Sept. 22 – Dec. 31

Evening Stars 2008
Venus — July 16 – Dec. 31
Mars — Jan. 1– Oct. 16
Jupiter — July 9 – Dec. 31
Saturn — Feb. 24 – Aug. 17

Morning Stars 2009
Venus — April 1 – Dec. 1
Mars — Feb. 1 – Dec. 31
Jupiter — Feb. 7 – Aug. 14
Saturn — Jan. 1 – March 8; Oct. 6 – Dec. 31

Evening Stars 2009
Venus — Jan. 1 – March 24
Jupiter — Jan. 1 – Jan. 11; Aug. 14 – Dec. 31
Saturn — March 8 – Aug. 31

Major Meteor Showers

These are approximate dates. Listen to local news/weather broadcasts several days beforehand to determine peak observation days and hours. Generally, viewing is best between midnight and dawn of the date listed.

Meteor shower dates are provided by Robert Hawkes, Mt. Allison University, Dept. of Physics, Sackville, New Brunswick, Canada.

Meteor Shower	Peak 2008	Peak 2009
Quadrantid	Jan. 4	Jan. 3
Lyrid	April 22	April 22
Perseid	Aug. 12	Aug. 12
Orionid	Oct. 21	Oct. 21
Leonid	Nov. 16	Nov. 17
Geminid	Dec. 13	Dec. 13

Eclipses

Eclipses 2008
Feb. 7 — Sun, annular eclipse, visible in most of Antarctica, New Zealand, southeastern Australia, Vanuatu, Fiji and Western Samoa.

Feb. 21 — Moon, total eclipse, visible in Arctic, western Russia, most of Arabia, Africa except Madagascar, Europe and the Americas.

Aug. 1 — Sun, total eclipse, visible in northern and eastern North America, Greenland, northern Europe and Asia except Japan.

Aug. 16 — Moon, partial eclipse, visible in Antarctica, Australasia except New Zealand, most of Asia, Europe, Africa and most of South America.

Eclipses 2009
Jan. 26—Sun, annular eclipse, visible in south Atlantic Ocean, southern Africa, Antarctica, southeast India, southeast Asia, Indonesia and Australia except Tasmania.

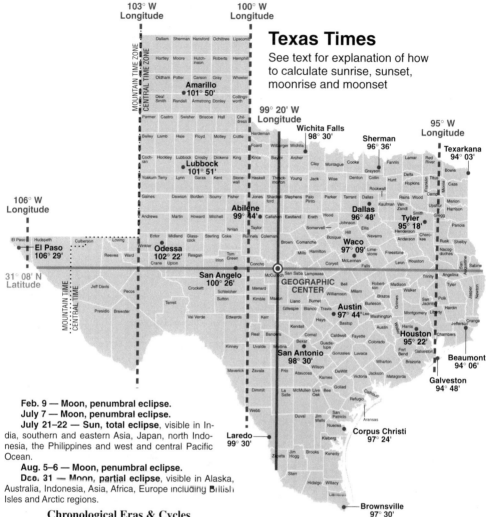

Texas Times

See text for explanation of how to calculate sunrise, sunset, moonrise and moonset

GEOGRAPHIC CENTER

Feb. 9 — **Moon, penumbral eclipse.**

July 7 — **Moon, penumbral eclipse.**

July 21–22 — **Sun, total eclipse**, visible in India, southern and eastern Asia, Japan, north Indonesia, the Philippines and west and central Pacific Ocean.

Aug. 5–6 — **Moon, penumbral eclipse.**

Dec. 31 — **Moon, partial eclipse**, visible in Alaska, Australia, Indonesia, Asia, Africa, Europe including British Isles and Arctic regions.

Chronological Eras & Cycles

Chronological Eras 2008

The year 2008 of the **Christian** era comprises the latter part of the 232nd and the beginning of the 233rd year of the independence of the United States of America, and corresponds to the year 6721 of the Julian period. All dates in the list below are given in terms of the Gregorian calendar, in which Jan. 14, 2008, corresponds to Jan. 1, 2008, Julian calendar.

Era	Year	Begins
Byzantine	7517	Sept. 14
Jewish (A.M.)*	5769	Sept. 29
Chinese (Bing-xu)	4645	Feb. 7
Roman (A.U.C.)	2761	Jan. 14
Nabonassar	2757	April 21
Japanese	2668	Jan. 1
Grecian (Seleucidae)	2320	Sept. 14 or Oct. 14
Indian (Saka)	1930	March 21
Diocletian	1725	Sept. 11
Islamic (Hegira)*	1429, 1430	Jan. 9, Dec. 29

Year begins at sunset.

Chronological Cycles 2008

Dominical Letter	FE	Julian Period	6721
Epact	22	Roman Indiction	1
Golden Number or Lunar Cycle	XIV	Solar Cycle	1

Chronological Eras 2009

The year 2009 of the **Christian** era comprises the latter part of the 233rd and the beginning of the 234th year of the independence of the United States of America, and corresponds to the year 6720 of the Julian period. All dates in the list below are given in terms of the Gregorian calendar, in which Jan. 14, 2009, corresponds to Jan. 1, 2009, of the Julian calendar:

Era	Year	Begins
Byzantine	7518	Sept. 14
Jewish (A.M.)*	5770	Sept. 18
Chinese (Ding-hai)	4646	Jan. 26
Roman (A.U.C.)	2762	Jan. 14
Nabonassar	2758	April 21
Japanese	2669	Jan. 1
Grecian (Seleucidae)	2321	Sept. 14 or Oct. 14
Indian (Saka)	1931	March 22
Diocletian	1726	Sept. 11
Islamic (Hegira)*	1431	Dec. 17

Year begins at sunset.

Chronological Cycles 2009

Dominical Letter	D	Julian Period	6722
Epact	3	Roman Indiction	2
Golden Number or Lunar Cycle	XV	Solar Cycle	2

Calendar for 2008

Times are **Central Standard Time,** except from March 9 to Nov. 2, during which **Daylight Saving Time** is observed. **Boldface times for moonrise and moonset** indicate p.m. Times are figured for the point **99° 20' West and 31° 08' North,** the approximate geographical center of the state. **See page 149 for explanation of how to get the approximate time at any other Texas point. (On the Web: http://aa.usno.navy.mil/data/)** Please note: Not all eclipses are visible in United States. For visibility, see listing beginning on page 149.

1st Month — January 2008 — 31 Days

Moon's Phases — *New*, Jan. 8, 5:37 a.m.; *First Qtr.*, Jan. 15, 1:46 p.m.; *Full*, Jan. 22, 7:35 a.m.; *Last Qtr.*, Jan. 29, 11:03 p.m.

Day of Year	Day of Month	Day of Week	Planetary Configurations and Phenomena	*Hour of Sunrise	Sunset	Moonrise	Moonset
1	1	Tu.		7:36	5:46	1:38	**12:51**
2	2	We.	● at perihelion	7:36	5:47	2:33	**1:21**
3	3	Th.	☾ at apogee	7:36	5:47	3:30	**1:55**
4	4	Fr.		7:36	5:48	4:27	**2:34**
5	5	Sa.	♀☌☾	7:37	5:49	5:24	**3:19**
6	6	Su.		7:37	5:50	6:20	**4:11**
7	7	Mo.		7:37	5:50	7:11	**5:08**
8	8	Tu.		7:37	5:51	7:58	**6:09**
9	9	We.		7:37	5:52	8:39	**7:11**
10	10	Th.	♆☌☾	7:37	5:53	9:15	**8:14**
11	11	Fr.		7:37	5:54	9:47	**9:15**
12	12	Sa.	♅☌☾	7:37	5:55	10:18	**10:17**
13	13	Su.		7:37	5:55	10:47	**11:19**
14	14	Mo.		7:37	5:56	11:17	
15	15	Tu.		7:36	5:57	11:49	12:23
16	16	We.		7:36	5:58	**12:25**	1:30
17	17	Th.		7:36	5:59	**1:08**	2:39
18	18	Fr.		7:36	6:00	**1:59**	3:50
19	19	Sa.	☾ at perigee; ♂☌☾	7:36	6:01	**2:58**	5:00
20	20	Su.		7:35	6:02	**4:05**	6:04
21	21	Mo.	☿ greatest elongation E	7:35	6:02	**5:15**	7:00
22	22	Tu.		7:35	6:03	**6:25**	7:47
23	23	We.		7:34	6:04	**7:31**	8:26
24	24	Th.		7:34	6:05	**8:34**	8:59
25	25	Fr.	♄☌☾	7:33	6:06	**9:33**	9:29
26	26	Sa.		7:33	6:07	**10:31**	9:56
27	27	Su.		7:33	6:08	**11:27**	10:23
28	28	Mo.	☿ stationary	7:32	6:09		10:51
29	29	Tu.		7:31	6:10	12:23	11:20
30	30	We.	♂ stationary; ☾ at apogee	7:31	6:11	1:19	11:52
31	31	Th.		7:30	6:11	2:17	12:29

2nd Month — February 2008 — 29 Days

Moon's Phases — *New*, Feb. 6, 9:44 p.m.; *First Qtr.*, Feb. 13, 9:33 p.m.; *Full*, Feb. 20, 9:30 p.m.; *Last Qtr.*, Feb. 28, 8:18 p.m.

Day of Year	Day of Month	Day of Week	Planetary Configurations and Phenomena	*Hour of Sunrise	Sunset	Moonrise	Moonset
32	1	Fr.	♀☌♃	7:30	6:12	3:14	**1:11**
33	2	Sa.		7:29	6:13	4:10	**2:00**
34	3	Su.		7:28	6:14	5:03	**2:55**
35	4	Mo.	♃☌☾; ♀☌☾	7:28	6:15	5:52	**3:55**
36	5	Tu.		7:27	6:16	6:35	**4:58**
37	6	We.	☿ inferior ☌	7:26	6:17	7:13	**6:02**
38	7	Th.	eclipse	7:26	6:18	7:48	**7:05**
39	8	Fr.		7:25	6:19	8:19	**8:08**
40	9	Sa.	♅☌☾	7:24	6:19	8:49	**9:12**
41	10	Su.	♆☌⊙	7:23	6:20	9:20	**10:16**
42	11	Mo.		7:22	6:21	9:51	**11:22**
43	12	Tu.		7:22	6:22	10:26	
44	13	We.	☾at perigee	7:21	6:23	11:07	12:31
45	14	Th.		7:20	6:24	11:54	1:41
46	15	Fr.		7:19	6:24	**12:49**	2:50
47	16	Sa.	♂☌☾	7:18	6:25	**1:52**	3:54
48	17	Su.		7:17	6:26	**2:59**	4:52
49	18	Mo.	☿ stationary	7:16	6:27	**4:07**	5:41
50	19	Tu.		7:15	6:28	**5:14**	6:22
51	20	We.		7:14	6:28	**6:18**	6:57
52	21	Th.	♄☌☾; eclipse	7:13	6:29	**7:18**	7:28
53	22	Fr.		7:12	6:30	**8:17**	7:56
54	23	Sa.		7:11	6:31	**9:14**	8:23
55	24	Su.	♄☍	7:10	6:32	**10:10**	8:50
56	25	Mo.	☿☌♀	7:09	6:32	**11:07**	9:19
57	26	Tu.		7:08	6:33		9:50
58	27	We.	☾at apogee	7:07	6:34	12:05	10:25
59	28	Th.		7:06	6:35	1:02	11:05
60	29	Fr.		7:05	6:35	1:59	11:51

*See text before January calendar for explanation.

3rd Month — March 2008 — 31 Days

Moon's Phases — *New*, March 7, 11:14 p.m; *First Qtr.*, March 14, 5:46 a.m.; *Full*, March 21, 1:40 p.m.; *Last Qtr.*, March 29, 4:47 p.m.

Day of Year	Day of Month	Day of Week	Planetary Configurations and Phenomena	*Hour of Sunrise	Sunset	Moonrise	Moonset
61	1	Sa.		7:03	6:36	2:53	**12:43**
62	2	Su.	♃☌☾	7:02	6:37	3:43	**1:40**
63	3	Mo.	☿ greatest elongation W	7:01	6:38	4:28	**2:41**
64	4	Tu.		7:00	6:38	5:08	**3:44**
65	5	We.	☿♀♆☌☾	6:59	6:39	5:44	**4:48**
66	6	Th.	♀☌♆	6:58	6:40	6:17	**5:52**
67	7	Fr.		6:56	6:40	6:49	**6:57**
68	8	Sa.	♅☌⊙; ☿☌♆	6:55	6:41	8:19	**8:02**
69	†9	Su.		7:54	7:42	8:51	**10:10**
70	10	Mo.	☾at perigee	7:53	7:42	9:26	**11:20**
71	11	Tu.		7:52	7:43	10:05	
72	12	We.		7:50	7:44	10:51	12:31
73	13	Th.		7:49	7:45	11:45	1:42
74	14	Fr.	♂☌☾	7:48	7:45	**12:45**	2:48
75	15	Sa.		7:47	7:46	**1:50**	3:48
76	16	Su.		7:46	7:47	**2:58**	4:38
77	17	Mo.		7:44	7:47	**4:03**	5:21
78	18	Tu.		7:43	7:48	**5:07**	5:57
79	19	We.	♄☌☾	7:42	7:49	**6:07**	6:29
80	20	Th.	**spring equinox**	7:41	7:49	**7:06**	6:57
81	21	Fr.		7:39	7:50	**8:03**	7:24
82	22	Sa.		7:38	7:51	**8:59**	7:51
83	23	Su.	☿☌♀	7:37	7:51	**9:56**	8:19
84	24	Mo.		7:36	7:52	**10:54**	8:50
85	25	Tu.		7:34	7:52	**11:51**	9:23
86	26	We.	☾at apogee	7:33	7:53		10:01
87	27	Th.		7:32	7:54	12:48	10:44
88	28	Fr.		7:31	7:54	1:43	11:34
89	29	Sa.		7:29	7:55	2:34	**12:28**
90	30	Su.	♃☌☾	7:28	7:56	3:21	**1:26**
91	31	Mo.		7:27	7:56	4:02	**2:27**

4th Month — April 2008 — 30 Days

Moon's Phases — *New*, April 5, 10:55 p.m.; *First Qtr.*, April 12, 1:32 p.m.; *Full*, April 20, 5:25 a.m.; *Last Qtr.*, April 28, 9:12 a.m.

Day of Year	Day of Month	Day of Week	Planetary Configurations and Phenomena	*Hour of Sunrise	Sunset	Moonrise	Moonset
92	1	Tu.		7:26	7:57	4:39	**3:29**
93	2	We.	♆☌☾ ; ♇ stationary	7:24	7:58	5:13	**4:32**
94	3	Th.		7:23	7:58	5:45	**5:36**
95	4	Fr.	♅☌☾; ♀☌☾	7:22	7:59	6:16	**6:42**
96	5	Sa.		7:21	8:00	6:47	**7:49**
97	6	Su.		7:19	8:00	7:22	**9:00**
98	7	Mo.	☾ at perigee	7:18	8:01	8:00	**10:13**
99	8	Tu.	♂☌☾	7:17	8:01	8:45	**11:27**
100	9	We.		7:16	8:02	9:37	
101	10	Th.		7:15	8:03	10:37	12:37
102	11	Fr.		7:13	8:03	11:43	1:41
103	12	Sa.		7:12	8:04	**12:50**	2:35
104	13	Su.		7:11	8:05	**1:57**	3:21
105	14	Mo.		7:10	8:05	**3:00**	3:59
106	15	Tu.	♄☌☾	7:09	8:06	**4:01**	4:31
107	16	We.	☿ superior ☌	7:08	8:07	**4:59**	5:00
108	17	Th.		7:07	8:07	**5:56**	5:28
109	18	Fr.		7:05	8:08	**6:52**	5:54
110	19	Sa.		7:04	8:09	**7:48**	6:22
111	20	Su.		7:03	8:09	**8:45**	6:51
112	21	Mo.		7:02	8:10	**9:42**	7:23
113	22	Tu.		7:01	8:11	**10:40**	8:00
114	23	We.	☾ at apogee	7:00	8:11	**11:35**	8:41
115	24	Th.		6:59	8:12		9:28
116	25	Fr.		6:58	8:13	12:28	10:20
117	26	Sa.		6:57	8:13	1:15	11:17
118	27	Su.	♃☌☾	6:56	8:14	1:58	**12:15**
119	28	Mo.		6:55	8:15	2:36	**1:16**
120	29	Tu.	♆☌☾	6:54	8:15	3:10	**2:16**
121	30	We.		6:53	8:16	3:42	**3:18**

† Daylight Saving Time begins at 2:00 a.m.

Calendar for 2008 (Cont'd.)

5th Month — May 2008 — 31 Days

Moon's Phases — *New*, May 5, 7:18 a.m.; *First Qtr.*, May 11, 10:47 p.m.; *Full*, May 19, 9:11 p.m.; *Last Qtr.*, May 27, 9:57 p.m.

Day of Year	Day of Month	Day of Week	Planetary Configurations and Phenomena	*Hour of Sunrise	Sunset	Moon-rise	Moon-set
122	1	Th.	⛢☌☾	6:52	8:17	4:12	**4:21**
123	2	Fr.	♄ stationary	6:51	8:17	4:43	**5:26**
124	3	Sa.		6:51	8:18	5:15	**6:35**
125	4	Su.		6:50	8:19	5:51	**7:47**
126	5	Mo.	☾ at perigee	6:49	8:20	6:33	**9:02**
127	6	Tu.	☿☌☾	6:48	8:20	7:23	**10:17**
128	7	We.		6:47	8:21	8:22	**11:26**
129	8	Th.		6:46	8:22	9:28	
130	9	Fr.	♃ stationary	6:46	8:22	10:38	12:27
131	10	Sa.	♂☌☾	6:45	8:23	11:47	1:17
132	11	Su.		6:44	8:24	**12:53**	1:58
133	12	Mo.	♄☌☾	6:43	8:24	**1:55**	2:33
134	13	Tu.	☿ greatest elongation E	6:43	8:25	**2:54**	3:03
135	14	We.		6:42	8:26	**3:51**	3:31
136	15	Th.		6:41	8:26	**4:47**	3:58
137	16	Fr.		6:41	8:27	**5:43**	4:25
138	17	Sa.		6:40	8:28	**6:39**	4:54
139	18	Su.		6:40	8:28	**7:36**	5:25
140	19	Mo.		6:39	8:29	**8:33**	6:00
141	20	Tu.	☾ at apogee	6:39	8:30	**9:29**	6:40
142	21	We.		6:38	8:30	**10:23**	7:25
143	22	Th.		6:38	8:31	**11:12**	8:16
144	23	Fr.		6:37	8:31	**11:56**	9:11
145	24	Sa.	♃☌☾	6:37	8:32		10:08
146	25	Su.		6:36	8:33	12:35	11:07
147	26	Mo.	☿, ♆ stationary; ♆☌☾	6:36	8:33	1:09	**12:07**
148	27	Tu.		6:35	8:34	1:41	**1:06**
149	28	We.		6:35	8:35	2:11	**2:07**
150	29	Th.	⛢☌☾	6:35	8:35	2:40	**3:08**
151	30	Fr.		6:35	8:36	3:11	**4:13**
152	31	Sa.		6:34	8:36	3:44	**5:22**

6th Month — June 2008 — 30 Days

Moon's Phases — *New*, June 3, 2:23 p.m.; *First Qtr.*, June 10, 10:04 a.m.; *Full*, June 18, 12:30 p.m.; *Last Qtr.*, June 16, 7:10 a.m.

Day of Year	Day of Month	Day of Week	Planetary Configurations and Phenomena	*Hour of Sunrise	Sunset	Moon-rise	Moon-set
153	1	Su.		6:34	8:37	4:22	**0:05**
154	2	Mo.		6:34	8:37	5:07	**7:50**
155	3	Tu.	☾ at perigee	6:34	8:38	6:02	**9:03**
156	4	We.		6:33	8:38	7:06	**10:09**
157	5	Th.		6:33	8:39	8:16	**11:06**
158	6	Fr.		6:33	8:39	9:28	**11:52**
159	7	Sa.	☿ inferior ☌; ♂☌☾	6:33	8:40	10:38	
160	8	Su.	♀ superior ☌	6:33	8:40	11:44	12:31
161	9	Mo.	♄☌☾	6:33	8:41	**12:46**	1:04
162	10	Tu.		6:33	8:41	**1:45**	1:33
163	11	We.		6:33	8:41	**2:42**	2:01
164	12	Th.		6:33	8:42	**3:37**	2:28
165	13	Fr.		6:33	8:42	**4:34**	2:56
166	14	Sa.		6:33	8:43	**5:30**	3:26
167	15	Su.		6:33	8:43	**6:27**	4:00
168	16	Mo.	☾ at apogee	6:33	8:43	**7:24**	4:38
169	17	Tu.		6:33	8:43	**8:18**	5:22
170	18	We.		6:34	8:44	**9:09**	6:11
171	19	Th.	☿ stationary	6:34	8:44	**9:55**	7:05
172	20	Fr.	♃☌☾; ♇☍; **sum. solstice**	6:34	8:44	**10:35**	8:03
173	21	Sa.		6:34	8:44	**11:11**	9:02
174	22	Su.		6:34	8:45	**11:43**	10:01
175	23	Mo.	♆☌☾	6:35	8:45		11:00
176	24	Tu.		6:35	8:45	12:13	11:59
177	25	We.	⛢☌☾	6:35	8:45	12:42	**12:59**
178	26	Th.		6:35	8:45	1:11	**2:01**
179	27	Fr.	⛢ stationary	6:36	8:45	1:42	**3:05**
180	28	Sa.		6:36	8:45	2:16	**4:14**
181	29	Su.		6:37	8:45	2:57	**5:26**
182	30	Mo.		6:37	8:45	3:46	**6:39**

*See text before January calendar for explanation.

7th Month — July 2008 — 31 Days

Moon's Phases — *New*, July 2, 9:19 p.m.; *First Qtr.*, July 9, 11:35 p.m.; *Full*, July 18, 2:59 a.m.; *Last Qtr.*, July 25, 1:42 p.m.

Day of Year	Day of Month	Day of Week	Planetary Configurations and Phenomena	*Hour of Sun-rise	Sunset	Moon-rise	Moon-set
183	1	Tu.	☿☌☾; ☾ at perigee	6:37	8:45	4:44	**7:48**
184	2	We.		6:38	8:45	5:51	**8:50**
185	3	Th.		6:38	8:45	7:03	**9:41**
186	4	Fr.	● at aphelion	6:39	8:45	8:16	**10:24**
187	5	Sa.		6:39	8:45	9:26	**11:01**
188	6	Su.	♂☌☾; ♄☌☾	6:40	8:45	10:31	**11:32**
189	7	Mo.		6:40	8:45	11:33	
190	8	Tu.		6:41	8:44	**12:32**	12:01
191	9	We.	♃☍	6:41	8:44	**1:29**	12:29
192	10	Th.		6:42	8:44	**2:26**	12:57
193	11	Fr.	♂☌☾	6:42	8:44	**3:23**	1:27
194	12	Sa.		6:43	8:43	**4:20**	2:00
195	13	Su.	☾ at apogee	6:43	8:43	**5:17**	2:37
196	14	Mo.		6:44	8:43	**6:13**	3:18
197	15	Tu.		6:44	8:42	**7:05**	4:06
198	16	We.		6:45	8:42	**7:52**	4:59
199	17	Th.	♃☌☾	6:45	8:41	**8:35**	5:56
200	18	Fr.		6:46	8:41	**9:12**	6:55
201	19	Sa.		6:47	8:40	**9:46**	7:55
202	20	Su.	♆☌☾	6:47	8:40	**10:16**	8:55
203	21	Mo.		6:48	8:39	**10:45**	9:54
204	22	Tu.	⛢☌☾	6:48	8:39	**11:14**	10:53
205	23	We.		6:49	8:38	**11:44**	11:54
206	24	Th.		6:50	8:38		**12:57**
207	25	Fr.		6:50	8:37	12:16	**2:02**
208	26	Sa.		6:51	8:36	12:53	**3:11**
209	27	Su.		6:51	8:36	1:37	**4:21**
210	28	Mo.		6:52	8:35	2:30	**5:30**
211	29	Tu.	☿ superior ☌; ☾ at perigee	6:53	8:34	3:31	**6:34**
212	30	We.		6:53	8:34	4:40	**7:29**
213	31	Th.		6:54	8:33	5:52	**8:16**

8th Month — August 2008 — 31 Days

Moon's Phases — *New*, Aug. 1, 5:13 a.m.; *First Qtr.*, Aug. 8, 3:20 p.m.; *Full*, Aug. 16, 4:16 p.m.; *Last Qtr.*, Aug. 23, 6:50 p.m.; *New*, Aug. 30, 2:58 p.m.

Day of Year	Day of Month	Day of Week	Planetary Configurations and Phenomena	*Hour of Sunrise	Sunset	Moon-rise	Moon-set
214	1	Fr.	eclipse	6:55	8:32	7:03	**8:55**
215	2	Sa.		6:55	8:31	8:12	**9:29**
216	3	Su.	♄☌☾	6:56	8:31	9:16	**10:00**
217	4	Mo.	♂☌☾	6:57	8:30	10:17	**10:29**
218	5	Tu.		6:57	8:29	11:17	**10:57**
219	6	We.		6:58	8:28	**12:15**	**11:27**
220	7	Th.		6:58	8:27	**1:13**	**11:58**
221	8	Fr.		6:59	8:26	**2:11**	
222	9	Sa.		7:00	8:25	**3:08**	12:34
223	10	Su.	☾ at apogee	7:00	8:24	**4:04**	1:14
224	11	Mo.		7:01	8:23	**4:58**	1:59
225	12	Tu.		7:02	8:22	**5:47**	2:50
226	13	We.	♃☌☾; ♀☌♄	7:02	8:21	**6:32**	3:46
227	14	Th.		7:03	8:20	**7:11**	4:45
228	15	Fr.	♆☍; ☿☌♄	7:03	8:19	**7:46**	5:45
229	16	Sa.	♆☌☾; eclipse	7:04	8:18	**8:18**	6:45
230	17	Su.		7:05	8:17	**8:48**	7:46
231	18	Mo.	⛢☌☾	7:05	8:16	**9:17**	8:46
232	19	Tu.		7:06	8:15	**9:47**	9:47
233	20	We.		7:07	8:14	**10:19**	10:50
234	21	Th.		7:07	8:13	**10:54**	11:55
235	22	Fr.		7:08	8:12	**11:35**	**1:02**
236	23	Sa.	☿☌♀	7:08	8:11		**2:12**
237	24	Su.		7:09	8:10	12:24	**3:20**
238	25	Mo.	☾ at perigee	7:10	8:08	1:21	**4:24**
239	26	Tu.		7:10	8:07	2:26	**5:21**
240	27	We.		7:11	8:06	3:35	**6:09**
241	28	Th.		7:11	8:05	4:45	**6:51**
242	29	Fr.		7:12	8:04	5:53	**7:26**
243	30	Sa.		7:13	8:02	6:58	**7:58**
244	31	Su.		7:13	8:01	8:01	**8:27**

Calendar for 2008 (Cont'd.)

9th Month — September 2008 — 30 Days

Moon's Phases — *First Qtr.*, Sept. 7, 9:04 a.m.; *Full*, Sept.15, 4:13 a.m.; *Last Qtr.*, Sept. 22, 12:04 a.m.; *New*, Sept. 29, 3:12 a.m.

Day of Year	Day of Month	Day of Week	Planetary Configurations and Phenomena	*Hour of Sunrise	*Hour of Sunset	*Hour of Moon-rise	*Hour of Moon-set
245	1	Mo.	♀☌☾; ☿☌☾	7:14	8:00	9:01	**8:56**
246	2	Tu.	♂☌☾	7:14	7:59	10:01	**9:26**
247	3	We.	♄☌☉	7:15	7:58	11:00	**9:57**
248	4	Th.		7:15	7:56	11:58	**10:31**
249	5	Fr.		7:16	7:55	**12:57**	**11:09**
250	6	Sa.		7:17	7:54	**1:54**	**11:53**
251	7	Su.	☾ at apogee; ♃ stationary	7:17	7:53	**2:49**	
252	8	Mo.		7:18	7:51	**3:39**	12:41
253	9	Tu.	♇ stationary; ♃☌☾	7:18	7:50	**4:26**	1:35
254	10	We.	☿ greatest elongation E	7:19	7:49	**5:07**	2:32
255	11	Th.	☿☌♀; ♀☌♂	7:19	7:47	**5:44**	3:31
256	12	Fr.	☿☌♂; ♆☌☾; ♅☍	7:20	7:46	**6:17**	4:32
257	13	Sa.		7:21	7:45	**6:48**	5:32
258	14	Su.		7:21	7:44	**7:18**	6:33
259	15	Mo.	♅☌☾	7:22	7:42	**7:48**	7:35
260	16	Tu.		7:22	7:41	**8:20**	8:39
261	17	We.		7:23	7:40	**8:55**	9:44
262	18	Th.		7:24	7:38	**9:35**	10:53
263	19	Fr.	☿☌♂; ☾ at perigee	7:24	7:37	**10:22**	**12:03**
264	20	Sa.		7:25	7:36	**11:16**	**1:12**
265	21	Su.		7:25	7:35		**2:18**
266	22	Mo.	**autumn equinox**	7:26	7:33	12:18	**3:16**
267	23	Tu.		7:26	7:32	1:25	**4:06**
268	24	We.	☿ stationary	7:27	7:31	2:34	**4:49**
269	25	Th.		7:28	7:29	3:41	**5:25**
270	26	Fr.		7:28	7:28	4:46	**5:58**
271	27	Sa.	♄☌☾	7:29	7:27	5:48	**6:28**
272	28	Su.		7:29	7:26	6:48	**6:56**
273	29	Mo.		7:30	7:24	7:48	**7:25**
274	30	Tu.		7:31	7:23	8:47	**7:56**

10th Month — October 2008 — 31 Days

Moon's Phases — *First Qtr.*, Oct. 7, 4:04 a.m.; *Full*, Oct. 14, 3:02 p.m.; *Last Qtr.*, Oct. 21, 6:55 a.m; *New*, Oct. 28, 6:14 p.m.

Day of Year	Day of Month	Day of Week	Planetary Configurations and Phenomena	*Hour of Sunrise	*Hour of Sunset	*Hour of Moon-rise	*Hour of Moon-set
275	1	We.	♂☌☾; ♀☌☾	7:31	7:22	9:46	**8:29**
276	2	Th.		7:32	7:21	10:44	**9:06**
277	3	Fr.		7:33	7:19	11:42	**9:47**
278	4	Sa.		7:33	7:18	**12:38**	**10:34**
279	5	Su.	☾ at apogee	7:34	7:17	**1:31**	**11:25**
280	6	Mo.	☿ inferior ☌	7:34	7:16	**2:19**	
281	7	Tu.	♃☌☾	7:35	7:14	**3:01**	12:20
282	8	We.		7:36	7:13	**3:39**	1:18
283	9	Th.		7:36	7:12	**4:14**	2:17
284	10	Fr.	♆☌☾	7:37	7:11	**4:45**	3:17
285	11	Sa.		7:38	7:10	**5:15**	4:17
286	12	Su.	♅☌☾	7:38	7:08	**5:45**	5:18
287	13	Mo.		7:39	7:07	**6:17**	6:21
288	14	Tu.		7:40	7:06	**6:51**	7:26
289	15	We.	☿ stationary	7:40	7:05	**7:30**	8:35
290	16	Th.		7:41	7:04	**8:16**	9:47
291	17	Fr.	☾ at perigee	7:42	7:03	**9:09**	10:59
292	18	Sa.		7:43	7:02	**10:11**	**12:08**
293	19	Su.		7:43	7:01	**11:18**	**1:10**
294	20	Mo.		7:44	7:00		**2:04**
295	21	Tu.		7:45	6:59	12:27	**2:49**
296	22	We.	☿ greatest elongation W	7:45	6:58	1:34	**3:27**
297	23	Th.		7:46	6:57	2:39	**4:00**
298	24	Fr.		7:47	6:56	3:41	**4:30**
299	25	Sa.	♄☌☾	7:48	6:55	4:41	**4:58**
300	26	Su.		7:48	6:54	5:39	**5:27**
301	27	Mo.	☿☌☾	7:49	6:53	6:37	**5:56**
302	28	Tu.		7:50	6:52	7:35	**6:28**
303	29	We.		6:51	6:51	8:34	**7:04**
304	30	Th.		6:52	6:50	9:32	**7:44**
305	31	Fr.		6:52	6:49	10:29	**8:28**

*See text before January calendar for explanation.

11th Month — November 2008 — 30 Days

Moon's Phases — *First Qtr.*, Nov. 5, 10:03 p.m.; *Full*, Nov. 13, 12:17 a.m.; *Last Qtr.*, Nov. 19, 3:31 p.m.; *New*, Nov. 27, 10:55 a.m.

Day of Year	Day of Month	Day of Week	Planetary Configurations and Phenomena	*Hour of Sunrise	*Hour of Sunset	*Hour of Moon-rise	*Hour of Moon-set
306	1	Sa.	♀☌☾; ☾ at apogee	7:53	5:48	10:23	**8:18**
307	†2	Su.	♆ stationary	6:54	5:47	11:12	**9:12**
308	3	Mo.	♃☌☾	6:55	5:47	11:57	**10:08**
309	4	Tu.		6:56	5:46	**12:36**	**11:05**
310	5	We.		6:56	5:45	**1:11**	
311	6	Th.	♆☌☾	6:57	5:44	**1:43**	12:03
312	7	Fr.		6:58	5:44	**2:12**	1:02
313	8	Sa.	♅☌☾	6:59	5:43	**2:42**	2:01
314	9	Su.		7:00	5:42	**3:12**	3:01
315	10	Mo.		7:01	5:42	**3:44**	4:04
316	11	Tu.		7:01	5:41	**4:21**	5:11
317	12	We.		7:02	5:40	**5:04**	6:22
318	13	Th.		7:03	5:40	**5:55**	7:36
319	14	Fr.	☾ at perigee	7:04	5:39	**6:55**	8:49
320	15	Sa.		7:05	5:39	**8:03**	9:57
321	16	Su.		7:06	5:38	**9:14**	10:56
322	17	Mo.		7:07	5:38	**10:25**	11:45
323	18	Tu.		7:07	5:38	**11:32**	**12:27**
324	19	We.		7:08	5:37		**1:02**
325	20	Th.		7:09	5:37	12:35	**1:33**
326	21	Fr.	♄☌☾	7:10	5:36	1:36	**2:02**
327	22	Sa.		7:11	5:36	2:34	**2:30**
328	23	Su.		7:12	5:36	3:31	**2:59**
329	24	Mo.		7:13	5:36	4:29	**3:30**
330	25	Tu.	☿ superior ☌	7:13	5:35	5:27	**4:04**
331	26	We.		7:14	5:35	6:25	**4:42**
332	27	Th.		7:15	5:35	7:22	**5:25**
333	28	Fr.		7:16	5:35	8:17	**6:13**
334	29	Sa.	☾ at apogee	7:17	5:35	9:08	**7:06**
335	30	Su.	♀☌♃	7:18	5:35	9:54	**8:01**

12th Month — December 2008 — 31 Days

Moon's Phases — *First Qtr.*, Dec. 5, 3:26 p.m.; *Full*, Dec. 12, 10:37 a.m.; *Last Qtr.*, Dec. 19, 4:29 a.m.; *New*, Dec. 27, 6:22 a.m.

Day of Year	Day of Month	Day of Week	Planetary Configurations and Phenomena	*Hour of Sunrise	*Hour of Sunset	*Hour of Moon-rise	*Hour of Moon-set
336	1	Mo.	♃☌☾; ♀☌☾	7:18	5:35	10:34	**8:58**
337	2	Tu.		7:19	5:35	11:10	**9:55**
338	3	We.	♆☌☾	7:20	5:35	11:42	**10:52**
339	4	Th.		7:21	5:35	**12:12**	**11:49**
340	5	Fr.	♂☌☉	7:22	5:35	**12:41**	
341	6	Sa.	♅☌☾	7:22	5:35	**1:09**	12:47
342	7	Su.		7:23	5:35	**1:39**	1:46
343	8	Mo.		7:24	5:35	**2:13**	2:49
344	9	Tu.		7:25	5:35	**2:51**	3:56
345	10	We.		7:25	5:35	**3:37**	5:07
346	11	Th.		7:26	5:36	**4:33**	6:21
347	12	Fr.	☾ at perigee	7:27	5:36	**5:38**	7:32
348	13	Sa.		7:27	5:36	**6:50**	8:38
349	14	Su.		7:28	5:37	**8:04**	9:34
350	15	Mo.		7:29	5:37	**9:16**	10:20
351	16	Tu.		7:29	5:37	**10:24**	10:59
352	17	We.		7:30	5:38	**11:27**	11:33
353	18	Th.	♄☌☾	7:30	5:38		**12:03**
354	19	Fr.		7:31	5:39	12:27	**12:32**
355	20	Sa.		7:31	5:39	1:26	**1:01**
356	21	Su.	**winter solstice**	7:32	5:40	2:24	**1:32**
357	22	Mo.	♇☌☉	7:32	5:40	3:21	**2:05**
358	23	Tu.		7:33	5:41	4:19	**2:41**
359	24	We.		7:33	5:41	5:16	**3:23**
360	25	Th.		7:34	5:42	6:12	**4:09**
361	26	Fr.	☾ at apogee; ♀☌♆	7:34	5:42	7:04	**5:01**
362	27	Sa.		7:35	5:43	7:51	**5:55**
363	28	Su.	☿☌☾	7:35	5:44	8:34	**6:52**
364	29	Mo.	♃☌☾	7:35	5:44	9:11	**7:50**
365	30	Tu.		7:35	5:45	9:44	**8:46**
366	31	We.	♆☌☾; ♀☌☾	7:36	5:46	10:14	**9:43**

† Daylight Saving Time ends at 2:00 a.m.

Calendar for 2009

Times are **Central Standard Time**, except from March 8 to Nov. 1, during which **Daylight Saving Time** is observed. **Boldface times for moonrise and moonset** indicate p.m. Times are figured for the point **99° 20' West and 31° 08' North**, the approximate geographical center of the state. **See page 149 for explanation of how to get the approximate time at any other Texas point. (On the Web: http://aa.usno.navy.mil/data/)** Please note: Not all **eclipses** are visible in United States. For visibility, see listing on p. 149

1st Month — January 2009 — 31 Days

Moon's Phases — *First Qtr.*, Jan. 4, 5:56 a.m.; *Full*, Jan. 10, 9:27 p.m.; *Last Qtr.*, Jan. 17, 8:46 p.m.; *New*, Jan. 26, 1:55 a.m.

Day of Year	Day of Month	Day of Week	Planetary Configurations and Phenomena	*Hour of Sunrise	*Hour of Sunset	*Hour of Moon-rise	*Hour of Moon-set
1	1	Th.	♄ stationary	7:36	5:46	10:43	**10:39**
2	2	Fr.	⛢☌☾	7:36	5:47	11:11	**11:37**
3	3	Sa.		7:36	5:48	11:39	
4	4	Su.	☿ gr elong E; ● at perihelion	7:36	5:49	**12:10**	12:36
5	5	Mo.		7:37	5:49	**12:44**	1:39
6	6	Tu.		7:37	5:50	**1:25**	2:45
7	7	We.		7:37	5:51	**2:14**	3:55
8	8	Th.		7:37	5:52	**3:13**	5:06
9	9	Fr.		7:37	5:53	**4:21**	6:14
10	10	Sa.	☾ at perigee	7:37	5:54	**5:35**	7:15
11	11	Su.	☿ stationary	7:37	5:54	**6:50**	8:07
12	12	Mo.		7:37	5:55	**8:01**	8:51
13	13	Tu.		7:37	5:56	**9:09**	9:28
14	14	We.	♀ greatest elongation E	7:36	5:57	**10:13**	10:01
15	15	Th.	♄☌☾	7:36	5:58	**11:15**	10:32
16	16	Fr.		7:36	5:59		11:02
17	17	Sa.		7:36	6:00	12:15	11:32
18	18	Su.		7:36	6:00	1:14	**12:05**
19	19	Mo.		7:35	6:01	2:12	**12:40**
20	20	Tu.	☿ inferior ☌	7:35	6:02	3:10	**1:20**
21	21	We.		7:35	6:03	4:06	**2:05**
22	22	Th.	☾ at apogee	7:34	6:04	4:59	**2:55**
23	23	Fr.	♀☌⛢	7:34	6:05	5:48	**3:49**
24	24	Sa.	♃☌☉	7:34	6:06	6:32	**4:45**
25	25	Su.		7:33	6:07	7:12	**5:43**
26	26	Mo.	eclipse	7:33	6:08	7:46	**6:41**
27	27	Tu.	♆☌☾	7:32	6:09	8:18	**7:38**
28	28	We.		7:32	6:09	8:47	**8:35**
29	29	Th.	⛢☌☾	7:31	6:10	9:15	**9:32**
30	30	Fr.	♀☌☾	7:30	6:11	9:43	**10:30**
31	31	Sa.	☿ stationary	7:30	6:12	10:12	**11:31**

2nd Month — February 2009 — 28 Days

Moon's Phases — *First Qtr.*, Feb. 2, 5:13 p.m.; *Full*, Feb. 9, 8:49 a.m.; *Last Qtr.*, Feb. 16, 3:37 p.m.; *New*, Feb. 24, 7:35 p.m.

Day of Year	Day of Month	Day of Week	Planetary Configurations and Phenomena	*Hour of Sunrise	*Hour of Sunset	*Hour of Moon-rise	*Hour of Moon-set
32	1	Su.		7:29	6:13	10:44	
33	2	Mo.		7:29	6:14	11:22	12:34
34	3	Tu.		7:28	6:15	**12:06**	1:41
35	4	We.		7:27	6:16	**12:58**	2:49
36	5	Th.		7:27	6:17	**2:00**	3:56
37	6	Fr.		7:26	6:17	**3:09**	4:58
38	7	Sa.	☾ at perigee	7:25	6:18	**4:22**	5:53
39	8	Su.		7:24	6:19	**5:35**	6:40
40	9	Mo.	penumbral eclipse	7:23	6:20	**6:45**	7:20
41	10	Tu.		7:23	6:21	**7:52**	7:56
42	11	We.	♄☌☾	7:22	6:22	**8:56**	8:28
43	12	Th.	♆☌☉	7:21	6:23	**9:59**	8:59
44	13	Fr.	☿ greatest elongation W	7:20	6:23	**11:00**	9:30
45	14	Sa.		7:19	6:24		10:03
46	15	Su.		7:18	6:25	12:00	10:38
47	16	Mo.		7:17	6:26	1:00	11:17
48	17	Tu.	♂☌♃	7:16	6:27	1:57	**12:00**
49	18	We.		7:15	6:27	2:52	**12:48**
50	19	Th.	☾ at apogee; ♀ gr. illum.	7:14	6:28	3:43	**1:41**
51	20	Fr.		7:13	6:29	4:29	**2:36**
52	21	Sa.		7:12	6:30	5:10	**3:34**
53	22	Su.	☿☌☾; ♃☌☾	7:11	6:31	5:46	**4:32**
54	23	Mo.	♂☌☾; ☿☌♃	7:10	6:31	6:19	**5:29**
55	24	Tu.		7:09	6:32	6:49	**7:25**
56	25	We.		7:08	6:33	7:18	**7:25**
57	26	Th.		7:07	6:34	7:46	**8:24**
58	27	Fr.	♀☌☾	7:06	6:34	8:15	**9:24**
59	28	Sa.		7:05	6:35	8:47	**10:27**

*See text before January calendar for explanation.

3rd Month — March 2009 — 31 Days

Moon's Phases — *First Qtr.*, March 4, 1:46 a.m.; *Full*, March 10, 9:38 p.m.; *Last Qtr.*, March 18, 12:47 p.m.; *New*, March 26, 11:06 a.m.

Day of Year	Day of Month	Day of Week	Planetary Configurations and Phenomena	*Hour of Sunrise	*Hour of Sunset	*Hour of Moon-rise	*Hour of Moon-set
60	1	Su.	☿☌♂	7:04	6:36	9:23	**11:33**
61	2	Mo.		7:03	6:37	10:04	
62	3	Tu.		7:01	6:37	10:53	12:40
63	4	We.	♀ stationary	7:00	6:38	11:50	1:46
64	5	Th.		6:59	6:39	**12:55**	2:48
65	6	Fr.		6:58	6:40	**2:04**	3:44
66	7	Sa.	☾ at perigee; ♂☌♆	6:57	6:40	**3:14**	4:33
67	†8	Su.	♄☍	7:56	7:41	**4:24**	5:14
68	9	Mo.		7:54	7:42	**6:31**	6:51
69	10	Tu.	♄☌☾	7:53	7:42	**7:36**	7:24
70	11	We.		7:52	7:43	**8:40**	7:56
71	12	Th.	⛢☌☉	7:51	7:44	**9:42**	8:27
72	13	Fr.		7:50	7:44	**10:44**	8:59
73	14	Sa.		7:48	7:45	**11:45**	9:34
74	15	Su.		7:47	7:46		10:12
75	16	Mo.		7:46	7:46	12:45	10:54
76	17	Tu.		7:45	7:47	1:42	11:41
77	18	We.		7:43	7:48	2:35	**12:32**
78	19	Th.	☾ at apogee	7:42	7:48	3:23	**1:26**
79	20	Fr.	**spring equinox**	7:41	7:49	4:06	**2:23**
80	21	Sa.		7:40	7:50	4:44	**3:20**
81	22	Su.	♃☌☾	7:38	7:50	5:18	**4:18**
82	23	Mo.	♆☌☾	7:37	7:51	5:49	**5:15**
83	24	Tu.	♂☌☾	7:36	7:52	6:18	**6:13**
84	25	We.		7:35	7:52	6:47	**7:13**
85	26	Th.		7:33	7:53	7:16	**8:13**
86	27	Fr.	♀ inferior ☌	7:32	7:54	7:48	**9:17**
87	28	Sa.		7:31	7:54	8:23	**10:23**
88	29	Su.		7:30	7:55	9:03	**11:31**
89	30	Mo.	☿ superior ☌	7:28	7:56	9:51	
90	31	Tu.		7:27	7:56	10:46	12:39

4th Month — April 2009 — 30 Days

Moon's Phases — *First Qtr.*, April 2, 9:34 a.m.; *Full*, April 9, 9:56 a.m.; *Last Qtr.*, April 17, 8:36 a.m; *New*, April 24, 10:23 p.m.

Day of Year	Day of Month	Day of Week	Planetary Configurations and Phenomena	*Hour of Sunrise	*Hour of Sunset	*Hour of Moon-rise	*Hour of Moon-set
91	1	We.	☾ at perigee	7:26	7:57	11:48	1:43
92	2	Th.		7:25	7:57	**12:55**	2:40
93	3	Fr.		7:23	7:58	**2:04**	3:30
94	4	Sa.	♇ stationary	7:22	7:59	**3:12**	4:13
95	5	Su.		7:21	7:59	**4:18**	4:50
96	6	Mo.		7:20	8:00	**5:22**	5:23
97	7	Tu.	♄☌☾	7:18	8:01	**6:25**	5:55
98	8	We.		7:17	8:01	**7:26**	6:25
99	9	Th.		7:16	8:02	**8:28**	6:57
100	10	Fr.		7:15	8:03	**9:30**	7:30
101	11	Sa.		7:14	8:03	**10:30**	8:07
102	12	Su.		7:13	8:04	**11:29**	8:48
103	13	Mo.		7:11	8:05		9:33
104	14	Tu.	♂☌⛢	7:10	8:05	12:25	10:23
105	15	We.	♀ stationary	7:09	8:06	1:15	11:17
106	16	Th.	☾ at apogee	7:08	8:07	2:00	**12:12**
107	17	Fr.		7:07	8:07	2:40	**1:09**
108	18	Sa.	♀☌♂	7:06	8:08	3:15	**2:06**
109	19	Su.	♃☌☾; ♆☌☾	7:05	8:09	3:47	**3:03**
110	20	Mo.		7:04	8:09	4:17	**4:00**
111	21	Tu.		7:02	8:10	4:45	**4:58**
112	22	We.	⛢☌☾	7:01	8:11	5:14	**5:58**
113	23	Th.		7:00	8:11	5:45	**6:00**
114	24	Fr.	♀☌☾; ♂☌☾	6:59	8:12	6:19	**7:06**
115	25	Sa.		6:58	8:13	6:58	**9:15**
116	26	Su.	☿ gr elong E; ☿☌☾	6:57	8:13	7:44	**10:25**
117	27	Mo.		6:56	8:14	8:38	**11:33**
118	28	Tu.	☾ at perigee	6:55	8:15	9:40	
119	29	We.		6:54	8:15	10:47	12:34
120	30	Th.		6:53	8:16	11:57	1:27

† Daylight Saving Time begins at 2:00 a.m.

Calendar for 2009 (Cont'd.)

5th Month — May 2009 — 31 Days

Moon's Phases — *First Qtr.*, May 1, 3:44 p.m.; *Full*, May 8, 11:01 p.m.; *Last Qtr.*, May 17, 2:26 a.m.; *New*, May 24, 7:11 a.m; *First Qtr.*, May 30, 10:22 p.m.

Day of Year	Day of Month	Day of Week	Planetary Configurations and Phenomena	*Hour of Sunrise	Sunset	Moon-rise	Moon-set
121	1	Fr.		6:53	8:17	**1:05**	2:12
122	2	Sa.	♀ greatest illumination	6:52	8:17	**2:11**	2:51
123	3	Su.		6:51	8:18	**3:15**	3:25
124	4	Mo.	♄☌☾	6:50	8:19	**4:16**	3:56
125	5	Tu.		6:49	8:19	**5:17**	4:27
126	6	We.		6:48	8:20	**6:17**	4:57
127	7	Th.	☿ stationary	6:47	8:21	**7:18**	5:29
128	8	Fr.		6:47	8:21	**8:19**	6:05
129	9	Sa.		6:46	8:22	**9:18**	6:44
130	10	Su.		6:45	8:23	**10:15**	7:27
131	11	Mo.		6:44	8:23	**11:07**	8:16
132	12	Tu.		6:44	8:24	**11:54**	9:08
133	13	We.	☾ at apogee	6:43	8:25		10:03
134	14	Th.		6:42	8:25	12:36	11:00
135	15	Fr.		6:42	8:26	1:13	11:56
136	16	Sa.		6:41	8:27	1:45	**12:52**
137	17	Su.	♃☌☾; ♆☌☾; ♄ stationary	6:40	8:27	2:15	**13:48**
138	18	Mo.	☿ inferior ☌	6:40	8:28	2:44	**14:44**
139	19	Tu.	⛢☌☾	6:39	8:29	3:12	**15:42**
140	20	We.		6:39	8:29	3:42	**16:42**
141	21	Th.	♀☌☾; ♂☌☾	6:38	8:30	4:14	**17:46**
142	22	Fr.		6:38	8:31	4:50	**18:54**
143	23	Sa.		6:37	8:31	5:33	**20:04**
144	24	Su.		6:37	8:32	6:24	**21:14**
145	25	Mo.	♃☌♆; ☾ at perigee	6:36	8:33	7:24	**22:20**
146	26	Tu.		6:36	8:33	8:32	**23:19**
147	27	We.		6:36	8:34	9:43	
148	28	Th.		6:35	8:34	10:54	12:08
149	29	Fr.	♆ stationary	6:35	8:35	**12:03**	12:50
150	30	Sa.	☿ stationary	6:35	8:35	**1:08**	1:26
151	31	Su.	♄☌☾	6:34	8:36	**2:11**	1:59

6th Month — June 2009 — 30 Days

Moon's Phases — *Full*, June 7, 1:12 p.m.; *Last Qtr.*, June 15, 5:15 p.m.; *New*, June 22, 2:35 p.m., *First Qtr.*, June 29, 6:29 a.m.

Day of Year	Day of Month	Day of Week	Planetary Configurations and Phenomena	*Hour of Sunrise	Sunset	Moon-rise	Moon-set
152	1	Mo.		6:34	8:37	**3:12**	2:29
153	2	Tu.		6:34	8:37	**4:11**	3:00
154	3	We.		6:34	8:38	**5:11**	3:31
155	4	Th.		6:33	8:38	**6:11**	4:05
156	5	Fr.	♀ greatest elongation W	6:33	8:39	**7:10**	4:42
157	6	Sa.		6:33	8:39	**8:08**	5:24
158	7	Su.		6:33	8:40	**9:01**	6:11
159	8	Mo.		6:33	8:40	**9:50**	7:02
160	9	Tu.		6:33	8:41	**10:34**	7:56
161	10	We.	☾ at apogee	6:33	8:41	**11:12**	8:52
162	11	Th.		6:33	8:41	**1:46**	9:48
163	12	Fr.		6:33	8:42		10:44
164	13	Sa.	☿ gr elong W; ♆☌☾; ♃☌☾	6:33	8:42	0:16	11:39
165	14	Su.		6:33	8:42	0:45	**12:34**
166	15	Mo.	♃ stationary	6:33	8:43	1:12	**1:30**
167	16	Tu.	⛢☌☾	6:33	8:43	1:41	**2:28**
168	17	We.		6:33	8:43	2:10	**3:28**
169	18	Th.		6:33	8:44	2:44	**4:32**
170	19	Fr.	♀☌♂; ♂☌☾; ♀☌☾	6:34	8:44	3:22	**5:40**
171	20	Sa.		6:34	8:44	4:08	**6:51**
172	21	Su.	**summer solstice;** ☿☌☾	6:34	8:44	5:04	**7:59**
173	22	Mo.		6:34	8:45	6:09	**9:03**
174	23	Tu.	♇☍; ☾ at perigee	6:35	8:45	7:20	**9:58**
175	24	We.		6:35	8:45	8:34	**10:44**
176	25	Th.		6:35	8:45	9:47	**11:24**
177	26	Fr.		6:35	8:45	10:56	**11:59**
178	27	Sa.	♄☌☾	6:36	8:45	**12:01**	
179	28	Su.		6:36	8:45	**1:04**	12:31
180	29	Mo.		6:36	8:45	**2:05**	1:02
181	30	Tu.		6:37	8:45	**3:06**	1:33

*See text before January calendar for explanation.

7th Month — July 2009 — 31 Days

Moon's Phases — *Full*, July 7, 4:21 a.m.; *Last Qtr.*, July 15, 4:53 a.m.; *New*, July 21, 9:35 p.m.; *First Qtr.*, July 28, 5:00 p.m.

Day of Year	Day of Month	Day of Week	Planetary Configurations and Phenomena	*Hour of Sunrise	Sunset	Moon-rise	Moon-set
182	1	We.	⛢ stationary	6:37	8:45	**4:05**	2:06
183	2	Th.		6:38	8:45	**5:05**	2:42
184	3	Fr.	● at aphelion	6:38	8:45	**6:02**	3:23
185	4	Sa.		6:38	8:45	**6:57**	4:07
186	5	Su.		6:39	8:45	**7:47**	4:57
187	6	Mo.		6:39	8:45	**8:32**	5:50
188	7	Tu.	penum eclipse; ☾ at apogee	6:40	8:45	**9:12**	6:46
189	8	We.		6:40	8:44	**9:47**	7:42
190	9	Th.		6:41	8:44	**10:19**	8:38
191	10	Fr.	♃☌☾; ♆☌☾	6:41	8:44	**10:48**	9:34
192	11	Sa.		6:42	8:44	**11:15**	10:29
193	12	Su.		6:42	8:43	**11:43**	11:23
194	13	Mo.	⛢☌☾; ♃☌♆; ☿ superior ☌	6:43	8:43		**12:19**
195	14	Tu.		6:44	8:43	0:11	**1:17**
196	15	We.		6:44	8:42	0:42	**2:18**
197	16	Th.		6:45	8:42	1:17	**3:22**
198	17	Fr.	♂☌☾	6:45	8:42	1:58	**4:30**
199	18	Sa.		6:46	8:41	2:48	**5:38**
200	19	Su.	♀☌☾	6:46	8:41	3:46	**6:43**
201	20	Mo.		6:47	8:40	4:54	**7:42**
202	21	Tu.	☾ at perigee	6:48	8:40	6:07	**8:33**
203	22	We.	eclipse	6:48	8:39	7:22	**9:16**
204	23	Th.		6:49	8:38	8:34	**9:54**
205	24	Fr.		6:49	8:38	9:44	**10:29**
206	25	Sa.	♄☌☾	6:50	8:37	10:50	**11:01**
207	26	Su.		6:51	8:37	11:54	**11:33**
208	27	Mo.		6:51	8:36	**12:56**	
209	28	Tu.		6:52	8:35	**1:57**	12:06
210	29	We.		6:53	8:35	**2:58**	12:42
211	30	Th.		6:53	8:34	**3:57**	1:21
212	31	Fr.		6:54	8:33	**4:52**	2:05

8th Month — August 2009 — 31 Days

Moon's Phases — *Full*, Aug. 5, 7:55 p.m.; *Last Qtr.*, Aug. 13, 1:55 p.m.; *New*, Aug. 20, 5:02 a.m.; *First Qtr.*, Aug. 27, 6:42 a.m.

Day of Year	Day of Month	Day of Week	Planetary Configurations and Phenomena	*Hour of Sunrise	Sunset	Moon-rise	Moon-set
213	1	Sa.		6:55	8:32	**5:44**	2:53
214	2	Su.		6:55	8:32	**6:31**	3:45
215	3	Mo.	☾ at apogee	6:56	8:31	**7:12**	4:40
216	4	Tu.		6:56	8:30	**7:49**	5:36
217	5	We.		6:57	8:29	**8:21**	6:33
218	6	Th.	penum eclipse; ♃☌☾; ♆☌☾	6:58	8:28	**8:51**	7:29
219	7	Fr.		6:58	8:27	**9:19**	8:24
220	8	Sa.		6:59	8:26	**9:47**	9:19
221	9	Su.	⛢☌☾	7:00	8:26	**10:15**	10:14
222	10	Mo.		7:00	8:25	**10:44**	11:11
223	11	Tu.		7:01	8:24	**11:17**	**12:10**
224	12	We.		7:01	8:23	**11:55**	**1:12**
225	13	Th.		7:02	8:22		**2:16**
226	14	Fr.	♃☍	7:03	8:21	0:40	**3:22**
227	15	Sa.	♂☌☾	7:03	8:20	1:32	**4:26**
228	16	Su.		7:04	8:19	2:34	**5:26**
229	17	Mo.	♆☍; ♀☌☾	7:05	8:18	3:43	**6:20**
230	18	Tu.	☿☌♄	7:05	8:17	4:56	**7:06**
231	19	We.	☾ at perigee	7:06	8:15	6:09	**7:47**
232	20	Th.		7:06	8:14	7:20	**8:23**
233	21	Fr.		7:07	8:13	8:29	**8:57**
234	22	Sa.	♄☌☾; ☿☌☾	7:08	8:12	9:35	**9:30**
235	23	Su.		7:08	8:11	10:40	**10:04**
236	24	Mo.	☿ greatest elongation E	7:09	8:10	11:44	**10:40**
237	25	Tu.		7:09	8:09	**12:46**	**11:18**
238	26	We.		7:10	8:08	**1:47**	
239	27	Th.		7:11	8:06	**2:45**	12:01
240	28	Fr.		7:11	8:05	**3:39**	12:48
241	29	Sa.		7:12	8:04	**4:27**	1:39
242	30	Su.	☾ at apogee	7:12	8:03	**5:11**	2:33
243	31	Mo.		7:13	8:02	**5:49**	3:29

Calendar for 2009 (Cont'd.)

9th Month — September 2009 — 30 Days

Moon's Phases — *Full*, Sept. 4, 11:04 a.m.; *Last Qtr.*, Sept. 11, 9:16 p.m.; *New*, Sept. 18, 1:44 p.m., *First Qtr.*, Sept. 25, 11:50 p.m.

Day of Year	Day of Month	Day of Week	Planetary Configurations and Phenomena	*Hour of Sunrise	*Hour of Sunset	*Hour of Moon-rise	*Hour of Moon-set
244	1	Tu.		7:14	8:00	**6:23**	4:26
245	2	We.	♃☌☾	7:14	7:59	**6:54**	5:22
246	3	Th.	♆☌☾	7:15	7:58	**7:23**	6:17
247	4	Fr.		7:15	7:57	**7:50**	7:13
248	5	Sa.	♅☌☾	7:16	7:55	**8:18**	8:09
249	6	Su.	☿ stationary	7:16	7:54	**8:48**	9:06
250	7	Mo.		7:17	7:53	**9:20**	10:04
251	8	Tu.		7:18	7:52	**9:56**	11:05
252	9	We.		7:18	7:50	**10:38**	**12:09**
253	10	Th.		7:19	7:49	**11:27**	**1:13**
254	11	Fr.	♇ stationary	7:19	7:48		**2:17**
255	12	Sa.		7:20	7:46	12:24	**3:17**
256	13	Su.	♂☌☾	7:21	7:45	1:29	**4:11**
257	14	Mo.		7:21	7:44	2:38	**4:59**
258	15	Tu.		7:22	7:43	3:48	**5:41**
259	16	We.	☾ at perigee; ♀☌☾	7:22	7:41	4:58	**6:18**
260	17	Th.	♅☍; ♄☌☉	7:23	7:40	6:07	**6:53**
261	18	Fr.		7:23	7:39	7:14	**7:26**
262	19	Sa.		7:24	7:37	8:20	**7:59**
263	20	Su.	☿ inferior ☌	7:25	7:36	9:25	**8:35**
264	21	Mo.		7:25	7:35	10:29	**9:13**
265	22	Tu.	**autumn equinox**	7:26	7:34	11:32	**9:55**
266	23	We.		7:26	7:32	**12:33**	**10:41**
267	24	Th.		7:27	7:31	**1:29**	**11:31**
268	25	Fr.		7:28	7:30	**2:21**	
269	26	Sa.		7:28	7:28	**3:06**	12:25
270	27	Su.	☾ at apogee	7:29	7:27	**3:46**	1:20
271	28	Mo.	☿ stationary	7:29	7:26	**4:22**	2:17
272	29	Tu.	♃☌☾	7:30	7:25	**4:54**	3:13
273	30	We.	♆☌☾	7:31	7:23	**5:24**	4:08

10th Month — October 2009 — 31 Days

Moon's Phases — *Full*, Oct. 4, 1:10 a.m.; *Last Qtr.*, Oct. 11, 3:56 a.m.; *New*, Oct. 18, 12:33 a.m.; *First Qtr.*, Oct. 25, 7:42 p.m.

Day of Year	Day of Month	Day of Week	Planetary Configurations and Phenomena	*Hour of Sunrise	*Hour of Sunset	*Hour of Moon-rise	*Hour of Moon-set
274	1	Th.		7:31	7:22	**5:52**	5:04
275	2	Fr.	♅☌☾	7:32	7:21	**6:20**	6:00
276	3	Sa.		7:32	7:20	**6:50**	6:57
277	4	Su.		7:33	7:18	**7:21**	7:56
278	5	Mo.	☿ greatest elongation W	7:34	7:17	**7:57**	8:57
279	6	Tu.		7:34	7:16	**8:37**	10:01
280	7	We.		7:35	7:15	**9:25**	11:06
281	8	Th.	☿☌♄	7:35	7:13	**10:20**	**12:10**
282	9	Fr.		7:36	7:12	**11:22**	**1:11**
283	10	Sa.		7:37	7:11		**2:07**
284	11	Su.	♂☌☾	7:38	7:10	12:28	**2:55**
285	12	Mo.		7:38	7:09	1:37	**3:38**
286	13	Tu.	♃ station.; ☾ perigee; ♀☌♄	7:39	7:08	2:45	**4:16**
287	14	We.		7:40	7:06	3:52	**4:50**
288	15	Th.		7:40	7:05	4:57	**5:23**
289	16	Fr.	♄☌☾; ♀☌☾	7:41	7:04	6:02	**5:56**
290	17	Sa.		7:42	7:03	7:06	**6:30**
291	18	Su.		7:42	7:02	8:11	**7:07**
292	19	Mo.		7:43	7:01	9:15	**7:47**
293	20	Tu.		7:44	7:00	10:17	**8:32**
294	21	We.		7:45	6:59	11:16	**8:22**
295	22	Th.		7:45	6:58	**12:11**	**10:15**
296	23	Fr.		7:46	6:57	**12:59**	**11:10**
297	24	Sa.		7:47	6:56	**1:42**	
298	25	Su.	☾ at apogee	7:48	6:55	**2:19**	12:06
299	26	Mo.		7:48	6:54	**2:52**	1:02
300	27	Tu.	♃☌☾; ♆☌☾	7:49	6:53	**3:23**	1:58
301	28	We.		7:50	6:52	**3:51**	2:53
302	29	Th.		7:51	6:51	**4:19**	3:48
303	30	Fr.	♅☌☾	7:51	6:50	**4:48**	4:44
304	31	Sa.		7:52	6:49	**5:19**	5:42

11th Month — November 2009 — 30 Days

Moon's Phases — *Full*, Nov. 2, 1:14 p.m.; *Last Qtr.*, Nov. 9, 9:56 a.m.; *New*, Nov. 16, 1:14 a.m; *First Qtr.*, Nov. 24, 3:59 p.m.

Day of Year	Day of Month	Day of Week	Planetary Configurations and Phenomena	*Hour of Sunrise	*Hour of Sunset	*Hour of Moon-rise	*Hour of Moon-set
305	†1	Su.		6:53	5:48	**5:54**	6:43
306	2	Mo.		6:54	5:48	**5:33**	6:47
307	3	Tu.		6:55	5:47	**6:19**	7:53
308	4	We.	♆ stationary	6:55	5:46	**7:13**	8:59
309	5	Th.	☿ superior ☌	6:56	5:45	**8:14**	10:03
310	6	Fr.		6:57	5:45	**9:21**	11:02
311	7	Sa.	☾ at perigee	6:58	5:44	**10:30**	11:53
312	8	Su.		6:59	5:43	**11:38**	**12:38**
313	9	Mo.	♂☌☾	7:00	5:42		**1:16**
314	10	Tu.		7:00	5:42	12:44	**1:51**
315	11	We.		7:01	5:41	1:49	**2:24**
316	12	Th.	♄☌☾	7:02	5:41	2:52	**2:56**
317	13	Fr.		7:03	5:40	3:54	**3:29**
318	14	Sa.		7:04	5:40	4:57	**4:04**
319	15	Su.		7:05	5:39	6:00	**4:42**
320	16	Mo.		7:06	5:39	7:03	**5:25**
321	17	Tu.		7:06	5:38	8:03	**6:13**
322	18	We.		7:07	5:38	9:00	**7:05**
323	19	Th.		7:08	5:37	9:51	**8:00**
324	20	Fr.		7:09	5:37	10:36	**8:56**
325	21	Sa.		7:10	5:37	11:16	**9:52**
326	22	Su.	☾ at apogee	7:11	5:36	11:50	**10:48**
327	23	Mo.	♃☌☾	7:12	5:36	**12:22**	**11:42**
328	24	Tu.	♆☌☾	7:12	5:36	**12:51**	
329	25	We.		7:13	5:35	**1:18**	12:37
330	26	Th.	♅☌☾	7:14	5:35	**1:46**	1:31
331	27	Fr.		7:15	5:35	**2:16**	2:27
332	28	Sa.		7:16	5:35	**2:48**	3:26
333	29	Su.		7:17	5:35	**3:25**	4:27
334	30	Mo.		7:17	5:35	**4:08**	5:32

12th Month — December 2009 — 31 Days

Moon's Phases — *Full*, Dec. 2, 1:30 a.m.; *Last Qtr.*, Dec. 8, 6:13 p.m.; *New*, Dec. 16, 6:02 a.m.; *First Qtr.*, Dec. 24, 11:36 a.m.; *Full*, Dec. 31, 1:13 p.m.

Day of Year	Day of Month	Day of Week	Planetary Configurations and Phenomena	*Hour of Sunrise	*Hour of Sunset	*Hour of Moon-rise	*Hour of Moon-set
335	1	Tu.	♅ stationary	7:18	5:35	**4:59**	6:40
336	2	We.		7:19	5:35	**5:59**	7:47
337	3	Th.		7:20	5:35	**7:06**	8:50
338	4	Fr.	☾ at perigee	7:21	5:35	**8:17**	9:46
339	5	Sa.		7:21	5:35	**9:27**	10:34
340	6	Su.	♂☌☾	7:22	5:35	**10:36**	11:16
341	7	Mo.		7:23	5:35	**11:42**	11:52
342	8	Tu.		7:24	5:35		**12:26**
343	9	We.		7:24	5:35	12:46	**12:58**
344	10	Th.	♄☌☾	7:25	5:35	1:48	**1:30**
345	11	Fr.		7:26	5:36	2:50	**2:04**
346	12	Sa.		7:26	5:36	3:52	**2:41**
347	13	Su.		7:27	5:36	4:53	**3:21**
348	14	Mo.		7:28	5:36	5:54	**4:07**
349	15	Tu.		7:28	5:37	6:51	**4:57**
350	16	We.		7:29	5:37	7:44	**5:50**
351	17	Th.		7:30	5:38	8:31	**6:47**
352	18	Fr.	☿☌☾; ☿ gr elongation E	7:30	5:38	9:13	**7:43**
353	19	Sa.	♃☌♆	7:31	5:38	9:49	**8:39**
354	20	Su.	☾ at apogee	7:31	5:39	10:22	**9:34**
355	21	Mo.	♃☌☾; ♆☌☾; **winter solstice**	7:32	5:39	10:51	**10:28**
356	22	Tu.		7:32	5:40	11:19	**11:21**
357	23	We.	♅☌☾	7:33	5:40	11:46	
358	24	Th.	♇☌☉	7:33	5:41	**12:14**	12:15
359	25	Fr.		7:34	5:42	**12:44**	1:11
360	26	Sa.	☿ stationary	7:34	5:42	**1:18**	2:10
361	27	Su.		7:34	5:43	**1:57**	3:12
362	28	Mo.		7:35	5:43	**2:43**	4:17
363	29	Tu.		7:35	5:44	**3:38**	5:23
364	30	We.		7:35	5:45	**4:42**	6:29
365	31	Th.	eclipse	7:36	5:46	**5:53**	7:30

† Daylight Saving Time ends at 2:00 a.m.

Recreation & Sports

Neches River float trip. Ron Billings photo; Texas Forest Service.

State Parks

National Parks & Landmarks

Birding, Fishing & Hunting

Fairs & Festivals

Baseball

Football

Basketball

Honored Sports Figures

Recreation

Information about recreational opportunities in state and national parks and forests and at U.S. Army Corps of Engineers Lakes, a representative list of festivals and celebrations in individual towns and communities across the state, as well as information on hunting and fishing opportunities and regulations is found in the following pages. Information about hunting, fishing and other recreation on National Wildlife Refuges and State Wildlife Management Areas can be found in the Environment section on pages 121–124. Recreation and special events in each county are also mentioned in the Counties section.

Texas State Parks

Texas' diverse system of state parks offers contrasting attractions — mountains and canyons, arid deserts and lush forests, spring-fed streams, sandy dunes, saltwater surf and fascinating historic sites.

The state park information below was provided by **Texas Parks and Wildlife** (TPW). Additional information and brochures on individual parks are available from the TPW's Austin headquarters, 4200 Smith School Rd., Austin 78744; 1-800-792-1112; **www.tpwd.state.tx.us/park/**.

The TPW's **Central Reservation Center** can take reservations for almost all parks that accept reservations. Exceptions are Indian Lodge, the Texas State Railroad and facilities not operated by the TPW. Call the center during usual business hours at 512-389-8900. The TDD line is 512-389-8915.

The **Texas State Parks Pass**, currently costing $60 per year, waives entrance fees for all members and all passengers in member's vehicle to all state parks when entrance fees are required, as well as other benefits. For further information, contact TPW 512-389-8900.

Texas State Parklands Passport is a windshield decal granting discounted entrance to state parks for Texas residents who are senior citizens or are collecting Social Security disability payments and free entrance for disabled U.S. veterans. Available at state parks with proper identification. Details can be obtained at numbers or addresses above.

The following information is a brief glimpse of what each park has to offer. Refer to the chart on pages 112-113 for a more complete list of available activities and facilities. Entrance fees to state parks range from $1 to $5 per person. There are also fees for tours and some activities. For up-to-date information, call the information number listed above before you go. Road abbreviations used in this list are: IH - interstate highway, US - U.S. Highway, TX - state highway, FM - farm-to-market road, RM - ranch-to-market road, PR - park road.

List of State Parks

Abilene State Park, 16 miles southwest of Abilene on FM 89 and PR 32 in Taylor County, consists of 529.4 acres that were deeded by the City of Abilene in 1933. A part of the **official Texas longhorn herd** and bison are located in the park. Large groves of pecan trees that once shaded bands of Comanches now shade visitors at picnic tables. Activities include camping, hiking, picnicking, nature study, biking, lake swimming and fishing. In addition to **Lake Abilene, Buffalo Gap**, the original Taylor County seat (1878) and one of the early frontier settlements, is nearby. Buffalo Gap was on the **Western**, or **Goodnight-Loving, Trail**, over which pioneer Texas cattlemen drove herds to railheads in Kansas.

Acton State Historic Site is a .01-acre cemetery plot in Hood County where **Davy Crockett's** second wife, Elizabeth, was buried in 1860. It is 4.5 miles east of Granbury on US 377 to FM 167 south, then 2.4 miles south to Acton. Nearby attractions include Cleburne, Dinosaur Valley and Lake Whitney state parks.

Admiral Nimitz Museum State Historic Site (see **National Museum of the Pacific War**).

Atlanta State Park is 1,475 acres located 11 miles northwest of Atlanta on FM 1154 in Cass County; adjacent to **Wright Patman Dam and Reservoir**. Land acquired from the U.S. Army in 1954 by license to 2004 with option to renew to 2054. Camping, biking and hiking in pine forests, as well as water activities, such as boating, fishing, lake swimming.

Nearby are historic town of **Jefferson and Caddo Lake and Daingerfield state parks**.

Balmorhea State Park is 45.9 acres four miles west of Balmorhea on TX 17 between Balmorhea and Toyahvale in Reeves County. Deeded in 1934-35 by private owners and Reeves Co. Water Imp. Dist. No. 1 and built by the Civilian Conservation Corps (CCC). Swimming pool (1-3/4 acres) fed by artesian **San Solomon Springs**; also provides water to **aquatic refuge** in park. Activities include swimming, picnicking, camping, scuba and skin diving. Motel rooms available at **San Solomon Springs Courts**. Nearby are city of Pecos, **Fort Davis National Historic Site, Davis Mountains State Park and McDonald Observatory**.

Barrington Living History Farm is the home of Anson Jones, the last president of the Republic of Texas. He and his family, along with five slaves, built the home in Washington (near Brazoria), and Jones retired there in 1846 after the annexation of Texas as the 28th state of the United States. The farm and its outbuildings function today as an interpretive center where farm life continues much as it did 150 years ago. Activities are guided by entries that Jones made in his daybook while living there. For further information, contact 916-878-2214 or link to Barrington.Farm@tpwd.state.tx.us.

Barton Warnock Environmental Education Center consists of 99.9 acres in Brewster County. Originally built by the Lajitas Foundation in 1982 as the Lajitas Museum Desert Gardens, the TPW purchased it in 1990 and renamed it for Texas botanist Dr. Barton Warnock. The center is also the eastern entrance station to **Big Bend Ranch State Park**. Self-guiding botanical and museum tours. On FM 170 one mile east of Lajitas.

Bastrop State Park is 3,503.7 acres one mile east of Bastrop on TX 21 or from TX 71. The park was acquired by deeds from the City of Bastrop and private owners in 1933-35; additional acreage acquired in 1979. Site of famous "**Lost Pines**," isolated region of loblolly pine and hardwoods. Swimming pool, cabins and lodge are among facilities. Fishing at Lake Bastrop, backpacking, picnicking, canoeing, bicycling, hiking. Golf course adjacent to park. **State capitol** at Austin 32 miles away; 13-mile drive through forest leads to **Buescher State Park**.

Battleship Texas State Historic Site (see **San Jacinto Battleground State Historic Site and Battleship Texas**)

Bentsen-Rio Grande Valley State Park, a scenic park, is along the Rio Grande five miles southwest of Mission off FM 2062 in Hidalgo County. The 760 acres of **subtropical resaca woodlands and brushlands** were acquired from private owners in 1944. Park is excellent base from which to tour **Lower Rio Grande Valley** of Texas and adjacent **Mexico**; most attractions within an hour's drive. Hiking trails provide chance to study unique plants and animals of park. Many birds unique to southern United States found here, including **pauraque, groove-billed ani, green kingfisher, rose-throated becard** and **tropical parula**. Birdwatching tours guided by park naturalists offered daily December –March. Park is one of last natural refuges in Texas for **ocelot** and **jaguarundi**. Trees include **cedar elm, anaqua, ebony** and **Mexican ash**. Camping, hiking, picnicking, boating, fishing also available. Nearby are **Santa Ana National Wildlife Refuge, Falcon State Park** and **Sabal Palm Sanctuary**.

Big Bend Ranch State Park, more than 299,008 acres of **Chihuahuan Desert wilderness** in Brewster and Presidio counties along the Rio Grande, was purchased from private

The Texas State Railroad runs through Fairchild State Forest between stations at Rusk and Palestine state parks. Ron Billings photo; Texas Forest Service.

owners in 1988. The purchase more than doubled the size of the state park system, which comprised at that time 220,000 acres. Eastern entrance at Barton Warnock Environmental Education Center one mile east of Lajitas on FM 170; western entrance is at **Fort Leaton State Historical Park** four miles east of Presidio on FM 170. The area includes **extinct volcanoes**, several **waterfalls**, two **mountain ranges**, at least **11 rare species of plants and animals**, and **90 major archaeological sites**. There is little development. Vehicular access limited; wilderness backpacking, hiking, scenic drive, picnicking, fishing and swimming. There are longhorns in the park, although they are not part of the official **state longhorn herd**.

Big Spring State Park is 382 acres located on FM 700 within the city limits of Big Spring in Howard County. Both city and park were named for a natural spring that was replaced by an artificial one. The park was deeded by the City of Big Spring in 1934 and 1935. Drive to top of **Scenic Mountain** provides panoramic view of surrounding country and look at **prairie dog colony**. The "big spring," nearby in a city park, provided watering place for herds of bison, antelope and wild horses. Used extensively also as campsite for early Indians, explorers and settlers.

Blanco State Park is 104.6 acres along the Blanco River four blocks south of Blanco's town square in Blanco County. The land was deeded by private owners in 1933. Park area was used as campsite by early explorers and settlers. Fishing, camping, swimming, picnicking, boating. **LBJ Ranch** and **LBJ State Historic Site, Pedernales Falls** and **Guadalupe River** state parks are nearby.

Boca Chica State Park is 1,054.92 acres of open beach located at the mouth of the Rio Grande in southeastern Cameron County. Park was acquired in May 1994. From US 77/83 at Olmito, take FM 511 12 miles to TX 4, then 17 miles east to park. Picnicking, wading, swimming, birding, camping, fishing allowed. No facilities provided.

Bonham State Park is a 261-acre park located two miles southeast of Bonham on TX 78, then two miles southeast on FM 271 in Fannin County. It includes a 65-acre lake, **rolling prairies** and **woodlands**. The land was acquired in 1933 from the city of Bonham. Swimming, camping, mountain-bike trail,

lighted fishing pier, boating. **Sam Rayburn Memorial Library** in Bonham. **Sam Rayburn Home** and **Valley Lake** nearby.

Brazos Bend State Park in Fort Bend County, seven miles west of Rosharon off FM 1462 on FM 762, approximately 28 miles south of Houston. The 4,897-acre park was purchased from private owners in 1976–77. **George Observatory** in park. **Observation platform** for spotting and photographing the **270 species of birds, 23 species of mammals, and 21 species of reptiles and amphibians, including American alligator**, that frequent the park. Interpretive and educational programs every weekend. Backpacking, camping, hiking, biking, fishing. Creekfield Lake Nature Trail.

Buescher State Park, a scenic area, is 1,016.7 acres 2 miles northwest of Smithville off TX 71 to FM 153 in Bastrop County. Acquired between 1933 and 1936, about one-third deeded by private owner; heirs donated a third; balance from City of Smithville. **El Camino Real** once ran near park, connecting **San Antonio de Béxar** with **Spanish missions in East Texas**. Parkland was part of **Stephen F. Austin's colonial grant**. Some **250 species of birds** can be seen. Camping, fishing, hiking, boating. Scenic park road connects with **Bastrop State Park** through **Lost Pines** area.

Caddo Lake State Park, north of Karnack one mile off TX 43 to FM 2198 in Harrison County, consists of 483.85 acres along **Cypress Bayou**, which runs into Caddo Lake. A scenic area, it was acquired from private owners in 1933. Nearby Karnack is childhood home of Mrs. Lyndon B. Johnson. Close by is old city of **Jefferson**, famous as commercial center of Northeast Texas during last half of 19th century. Caddo Indian legend attributes formation of Caddo Lake to **a huge flood**. Lake originally only natural lake of any size in state; dam added in 1914 for flood control; new dam replaced old one in 1971. **Cypress trees, American lotus** and **lily pads**, as well as **71 species of fish**, predominate in lake. **Nutria, beaver, mink, squirrel, armadillo, alligator** and **turtle** abound. Activities include camping, hiking, swimming, fishing, canoeing. Screened shelters, cabins.

Caddoan Mounds State Historic Site in Cherokee County six miles southwest of Alto on TX 21. Total of 93.8 acres acquired in 1975. Open for day visits only, park offers exhibits and interpretive trails through reconstructed **Caddo dwell-**

ings and ceremonial areas, including two temple mounds, a burial mound and a village area typical of people who lived in region for 500 years beginning about A.D. 800. Closed Tuesday and Wednesday. Nearby are **Jim Hogg State Historic Site, Mission Tejas State Historic Site** and **Texas State Railroad.**

Caprock Canyons State Park, 100 miles southeast of Amarillo and 3.5 miles north of Quitaque off FM 1065 and TX 86 in Briscoe, Floyd and Hall counties, has 15,313 acres. Purchased in 1975. Scenic escarpment's canyons provided camping areas for **Indians of Folsom culture** more than 10,000 years ago. **Mesquite** and **cacti** in the **badlands** give way to **tall grasses, cottonwood** and **plum thickets** in the bottomlands. Wildlife includes **aoudad sheep, coyote, bobcat, porcupine** and **fox.** Activities include scenic drive, camping, hiking, mountain-bike riding, horse riding and horse camping. A 64.25-mile trailway (hike, bike and equestrian trail) extends from South Plains to Estelline.

Casa Navarro State Historic Site, on .7 acre at corner of S. Laredo and W. Nueva streets in downtown San Antonio, was acquired by donation from San Antonio Conservation Society Foundation in 1975. Has furnished **Navarro House** three-building complex built about 1848, home of the statesman, rancher and Texas patriot **José Antonio Navarro.** Guided tours; exhibits. Open Wednesday through Sunday.

Cedar Hill State Park, an urban park on 1,826 acres 10 miles southwest of Dallas via US 67 and FM 1382 on **Joe Pool Reservoir,** was acquired by long-term lease from the Corp of Engineers in 1982. Camping mostly in wooded areas. Fishing from two lighted jetties and a perch pond for children. Swimming, boating, bicycling, birdwatching and picnicking. Vegetation includes several sections of **tall-grass prairie.** Penn Farm Agricultural History Center includes reconstructed buildings of the **19th-century Penn Farm** and exhibits; self-guided tours.

Choke Canyon State Park consists of two units, South Shore and Calliham, located on 26,000-acre **Choke Canyon Reservoir.** Park acquired in 1981 in a 50-year agreement among Bureau of Reclamation, City of Corpus Christi and Nueces River Authority. Thickets of **mesquite** and **black-brush acacia** predominate, supporting populations of **javelina, coyote, skunk** and **alligator,** as well as the **crested caracara.** The 385-acre South Shore Unit is located 3.5 miles west of Three Rivers on TX 72 in Live Oak County; the 1,100-acre Calliham Unit is located 12 miles west of Three Rivers, on TX 72, in McMullen County. Both units offer camping, picnicking, boating, fishing, lake swimming, and baseball and volleyball areas. The Calliham Unit also has a hiking trail, wildlife educational center, screened shelters, rentable **gym and kitchen. Sports complex** includes swimming pool and tennis, volleyball, shuffleboard and basketball courts. Across dam from South Shore is North Shore Equestrian and Camping Area; 18 miles of horseback riding trails.

Cleburne State Park is a 528-acre park located 10 miles southwest of Cleburne via US 67 and PR 21 in Johnson County with 116-acre spring-fed lake; acquired from the City of Cleburne and private owners in 1935 and 1936. **Oak, elm, mesquite, cedar** and **redbud** cover white rocky hills. Bluebonnets in spring. Activities include camping, picnicking, hiking, bicycling, canoeing, swimming, boating, fishing. Nearby are **Fossil Rim Wildlife Center** and **dinosaur tracks** in Paluxy River at **Dinosaur Valley State Park.**

Colorado Bend State Park, a 5,328.3-acre facility, is 28 miles west of Lampasas in Lampasas and San Saba counties.

The Texas State Bison Herd resides at Caprock Canyons State Park. They are the last genetically pure herd of southern bison in the world. Jim Mahoney photo.

Access is from Lampasas to Bend on FM 580 west, then follow signs (access road subject to flooding). Park site was purchased partly in 1984, with balance acquired in 1987. Primitive camping, fishing, swimming, hiking, biking and picnicking; guided tours to Gorman Falls. Rare and endangered species here include **golden-cheeked warbler, black-capped vireo** and **bald eagle.**

Confederate Reunion Grounds State Historic Site, located in Limestone County on the Navasota River, is 77.1 acres in size. Acquired 1983 by deed from Joseph E. Johnston Camp No. 94 CSA. Entrance is 6 miles south of Mexia on TX 14, then 2.5 miles west on FM 2705. **Historic buildings,** two **scenic footbridges** span creek; hiking trail. Nearby are **Fort Parker State Park** and **Old Fort Parker State Historic Site.**

Cooper Lake State Park, comprises 3,026 acres three miles southeast of Cooper in Delta and Hopkins counties acquired in 1991 by 25-year lease from Corps of Engineers. Two units, Doctors Creek and South Sulphur, adjoin 19,300-surface-acre Cooper Lake. Fishing, boating, camping, picnicking, swimming. Screened shelters and cabins. South Sulpher offers equestrian camping and horseback riding trails. Access to Doctors Creek Unit is via TX 24 east from Commerce to Cooper, then east on TX 154 to FM 1529 to park. To South Sulphur Unit, take IH 30 to Exit 122 west of Sulphur Springs to TX 19, then TX 71, then FM 3505.

Copano Bay State Fishing Pier, a 5.9-acre park, is located 5 miles north of Rockport on TX 35 in Aransas County. Acquired by transfer of jurisdiction from state highway department in 1967. Picnicking, saltwater fishing, boating and swimming. Operated by leased concession.

Copper Breaks State Park, 12 miles south of Quanah on TX 6 in Hardeman County, was acquired by purchase from private owner in 1970. Park features rugged scenic beauty on 1,898.8 acres, two lakes, **grass-covered mesas** and juniper breaks. Nearby **medicine mounds** were important ceremonial sites of Comanche Indians. Nearby **Pease River** was site of 1860 battle in which **Cynthia Ann Parker** was recovered from Comanches. Part of **state longhorn herd** lives at park. Abundant wildlife. Nature, hiking and equestrian trails; natural and historical exhibits; summer programs; horseback riding; camping, equestrian camping.

Texas State Parks, Sites and Piers

● PANHANDLE PLAINS
1. Palo Duro Canyon State Park (musical drama: *Texas!*)
2. Caprock Canyons State Park and Trailway
3. Copper Breaks State Park
4. Lake Arrowhead State Park
5. Fort Richardson State Historic Site & Lost Creek Reservoir Trailway
6. Possum Kingdom State Park
7. Fort Griffin State Park & Historic Site
8. Lake Brownwood State Park
9. Abilene State Park
10. Lake Colorado City State Park
11. Big Spring State Park
12. San Angelo State Park

● BIG BEND
13. Monahans Sandhills State Park
14. Fort Lancaster State Historic Site
15. Devils River State Natural Area (use by reservation only)
16. Seminole Canyon State Park & Historic Site (Indian pictographs)
17. Barton Warnock Environmental Education Center
18. Big Bend Ranch State Park Complex
19. Fort Leaton State Historic Site
20. Davis Mountains State Park (Indian Lodge)
21. Balmorhea State Park (San Solomon Springs Courts)
22. Wyler Aerial Tramway
23. Franklin Mountains State Park
24. Magoffin Home State Historic Site
25. Hueco Tanks State Historic Site (Indian pictographs)

● HILL COUNTRY
26. Fort McKavett State Historic Site
27. South Llano River State Park
28. Devil's Sinkhole State Natural Area
29. Kickapoo Cavern State Park (use by reservation only)
30. Garner State Park
31. Lost Maples State Natural Area

32. Hill Country State Natural Area
33. Landmark Inn State Historic Site (hotel rooms)
34. Colorado Bend State Park (cave tours)
35. Inks Lake State Park
36. Longhorn Cavern State Park (cavern tours)
37. Enchanted Rock State Natural Area
38. Admiral Nimitz State Historic Site & National Museum of the Pacific War
39. Lyndon B. Johnson State Park, Historic Site & Sauer-Beckmann Farmstead
40. Pedernales Falls State Park
41. Blanco State Park
42. Guadalupe River State Park/Honey Creek State Natural Area
43. McKinney Falls State Park
44. Government Canyon State Natural Area

● PRAIRIES AND LAKES
45. Eisenhower State Park (marina)
46. Eisenhower Birthplace State Historic Site
47. Ray Roberts Lake State Park, Johnson Unit
48. Ray Roberts Lake State Park, Isle du Bois Unit
49. Bonham State Park
50. Sam Bell Maxey House State Historic Site
51. Cooper Lake State Park, Doctors Creek Unit
52. Cooper Lake State Park, South Sulphur Unit
53. Lake Tawakoni State Park
54. Lake Mineral Wells State Park and Trailway
55. Cedar Hill State Park
56. Purtis Creek State Park
57. Acton State Historic Site (grave of Davy Crockett's wife)
58. Cleburne State Park
59. Dinosaur Valley State Park (dinosaur footprints)
60. Meridian State Park
61. Lake Whitney State Park (airstrip)
62. Fairfield Lake State Park
63. Confederate Reunion Grounds State Historic Site
64. Fort Parker State Park
65. Old Fort Parker (managed by City of Groesbeck)

66. Mother Neff State Park
67. Fort Boggy State Park
68. Fanthorp Inn State Historic Site
69. Washington-on-the-Brazos State Historic Site (Anson Jones Home & Barrington Living History Farm)
70. Lake Somerville State Park & Trailway, & Birch Creek Unit
71. Lake Somerville State Park & Trailway, Nails Creek Unit
72. Bastrop State Park
73. Buescher State Park
74. Monument Hill & Kreische Brewery State Historic Site
75. Stephen F. Austin State Park & San Felipe State Historic Site
76. Lockhart State Park
77. Palmetto State Park
78. Sebastopol State Historic Site

● PINEYWOODS
79. Atlanta State Park
80. Daingerfield State Park
81. Lake Bob Sandlin State Park
82. Governor Hogg Shrine Historic Site
83. Caddo Lake State Park
84. Starr Family State Historic Site
85. Martin Creek Lake State Park
86. Tyler State Park
87. Texas State Railroad State Park (contact park for schedule)
88. Rusk & Palestine State Parks (Texas State Railroad terminals)
89. Jim Hogg State Historic Site
90. Caddoan Mounds State Historic Site
91. Mission Tejas State Historic Site
92. Huntsville State Park
93. Lake Livingston State Park
94. Martin Dies Jr. State Park

GULF COAST

174. Lake Houston
175. *Addicks Reservoir*
176. Sheldon Reservoir
177. *Barker Reservoir*
178. Lake Anahuac
179. J.D. Murphree Wildlife Management Area Impoundments
180. Smithers Lake

181. William Harris Reservoir
182. Mustang Lake East/West
183. Eagle Nest Lake
184. Brazoria Reservoir
185. San Bernard Reservoirs 1, 2, 3
186. Lake Texana
187. South Texas Project Reservoir
188. Cox Creek Reservoir
189. Lake Corpus Christi
190. Loma Alta Lake

SOUTH TEXAS PLAINS

191. *Olmos Reservoir*
192. Calaveras Lake
193. Victor Braunig Lake
194. Upper Nueces Lake
195. Choke Canyon Reservoir
196. Coleto Creek Reservoir
197. Casa Blanca Lake
198. Falcon International Reservoir
199. Delta Lake Reservoir Units 1 and 2
200. Anzalduas Channel Dam
201. Valley Acres Reservoir

. Murvaul Lake
. Lake Tyler/ Lake Tyler East
. Lake Palestine
. Lake Jacksonville
. Striker Creek Reservoir
. Pinkston Reservoir
. Lake Nacogdoches
. Lake Kurth
. Houston County Lake
. Toledo Bend Reservoir
. Sam Rayburn Reservoir
. B.A. Steinhagen Lake
. Lake Livingston
. Lewis Creek Reservoir
. Lake Conroe

Texas Lakes

Bodies of water with a normal capacity of 5,000 acre-feet or larger. Italicized reservoirs usually dry.

● PANHANDLE PLAINS
1. Palo Duro Reservoir
2. Lake Rita Blanca
3. Lake Meredith
4. Bivins Lake
5. Buffalo Lake
6. Mackenzie Reservoir
7. Greenbelt Lake
8. Baylor Creek Lake
9. White River Lake
10. Lake Alan Henry
11. Lake J.B. Thomas
12. Sulphur Springs Draw Reservoir
13. Natural Dam Lake
14. Red Draw Reservoir
15. Lake Colorado City
16. Champion Creek Reservoir
17. Mitchell County Reservoir
18. Lake Sweetwater
19. E.V. Spence Reservoir
20. Oak Creek Reservoir
21. O.C. Fisher Lake
22. Twin Buttes Reservoir
23. Lake Nasworthy
24. Lake Ballinger/ Moonen
25. O.H. Ivie Reservoir
26. Hords Creek Lake
27. Lake Winters
28. Lake Abilene
29. Lake Coleman
30. Lake Brownwood
31. Lake Clyde
32. Lake Kirby
33. Lake Fort Phantom Hill
34. Lake Stamford
35. Lake Davis
36. Truscott Brine Lake
37. Santa Rosa Lake
38. Lake Electra
39. Lake Kemp
40. Lake Diversion
41. Lake Kickapoo
42. North Fork Buffalo Creek Reservoir
43. Lake Wichita
44. Lake Arrowhead
45. Millers Creek Reservoir
46. Lake Cooper/Olney
47. Lake Graham
48. Lost Creek Reservoir
49. Possum Kingdom Lake
50. Hubbard Creek Reservoir
51. Lake Daniel
52. Lake Cisco
53. Lake Palo Pinto
54. Lake Leon
55. Proctor Lake

● BIG BEND
56. Red Bluff Reservoir
57. Balmorhea Lake
58. Imperial Reservoir
59. Amistad International Reservoir

● HILL COUNTRY
60. Brady Creek Reservoir
61. Lake Buchanan
62. Inks Lake
63. Lake Lyndon B. Johnson
64. Lake Marble Falls
65. Lake Travis
66. Lake Austin
67. Town Lake
68. Lake Walter E. Long
69. Lake Georgetown
70. Granger Lake
71. Canyon Lake
72. Medina Lake

● PRAIRIES AND LAKES
73. Lake Nocona
74. Hubert H. Moss Lake
75. Lake Texoma
76. Randell Lake
77. Valley Lake
78. Lake Bonham
79. Coffee Mill Lake
80. Pat Mayse Lake
81. Lake Crook
82. River Crest Lake
83. Big Creek Reservoir
84. Cooper Lake
85. Lake Sulphur Springs
86. Lake Cypress Springs
87. Greenville City Lakes
88. Lake Tawakoni
89. Terrell City Lake
90. Lake Lavon
91. Lake Ray Hubbard
92. Lake Kiowa
93. Lake Ray Roberts
94. Lewisville Lake
95. Grapevine Lake
96. North Lake
97. White Rock Lake
98. Mountain Creek Lake
99. Joe Pool Reservoir
100. Lake Arlington
101. Lake Worth
102. Eagle Mountain Lake
103. Lake Weatherford
104. Lake Amon G. Carter
105. Lake Bridgeport
106. Lake Mineral Wells
107. Benbrook Lake
108. Lake Granbury
109. Squaw Creek Reservoir
110. Lake Pat Cleburne
111. Lake Waxahachie
112. Bardwell Lake
113. Cedar Creek Reservoir
114. Forest Grove Reservoir
115. Lake Athens
116. Trinidad Lake
117. Lake Halbert
118. Richland-Chambers Reservoir
119. Fairfield Lake
120. Navarro Mills Lake
121. Aquilla Lake
122. Lake Whitney
123. Lake Waco
124. Tradinghouse Creek Reservoir
125. Lake Creek Lake
126. Belton Lake
127. Stillhouse Hollow Lake
128. Alcoa Lake
129. Lake Limestone
130. Twin Oaks Reservoir
131. Camp Creek Lake
132. Bryan Lake
133. Gibbons Creek Reservoir
134. Somerville Lake
135. Lake Bastrop
136. Fayette County Reservoir
137. Lake Dunlap
138. Lake Gonzales
139. Eagle Lake

● PINEYWOODS
140. Wright Patman Lake
141. Monticello Reservoir
142. Lake Winnsboro
143. Lake Bob Sandlin
144. Welsh Reservoir
145. Ellison Creek Reservoir
146. Lake O' the Pines
147. Johnson Creek Reservoir
148. Caddo Lake
149. Lake Fork Reservoir
150. Lake Quitman
151. Lake Holbrook
152. Lake Hawkins
153. Gilmer Reservoir
154. Lake Gladewater
155. Eastman Lakes
156. Brandy Branch Reservoir
157. Lake Cherokee
158. Martin Creek Lake

Dallam | Sherman | H
Hartley ② | Moore | H i
③
Oldham | Potter | C
Deaf Smith | Randall | A
⑤
Parmer | Castro | Swisher
Bailey | Lamb | Hale
Cochran | Hockley | Lubbock
Yoakum | Terry | Lynn
Gaines | Dawson | Bo
Andrews | Martin | Ho
⑫ ⑬
Ector | Midland | Glasscock
El Paso | Hudspeth | Culberson | ㊶ Loving | Winkler
Reeves | Ward | Crane | Upton | Rea
㊿
Jeff Davis | Pecos | Crock
Presidio | Terrell
Brewster | Val
150
156
156
16
16
16
16
16
16
16
17
1
1

102. Galveston Island State Park (summer theater)
103. Brazos Bend State Park (George Observatory)
104. Varner-Hogg Plantation State Historic Site (guided tours)
105. Matagorda Island WMA (boat or air access only)
106. Lake Texana State Park
107. Copano Bay State Fishing Pier

108. Goose Island State Park
109. Fulton Mansion State Historic Site
110. Mustang Island State Park
111. Lake Corpus Christi State Park
112. Lipantitlan State Historic Site
113. Port Isabel Lighthouse State Historic Site

SOUTH TEXAS PLAINS
114. Casa Navarro State Historic Site
115. Fannin Battleground State Historic Site

95. Village Creek State Park

GULF COAST
96. Walter Umphrey State Park (managed by Jefferson County)
97. Sea Rim State Park
98. Sabine Pass Battleground State Historic Site
99. Sheldon Lake State Park
100. Battleship Texas Historic Site (at San Jacinto Battleground)
101. San Jacinto Battleground State Historic Site (Battleship Texas)

116. Goliad State Park & Mission Espiritu Santo State Historic Site
117. Zaragosa Birthplace State Historic Site
118. Mission Rosario State Historic Site
119. Choke Canyon State Park, Calliham Unit
120. Choke Canyon State Park, South Shore Unit
121. Lake Casa Blanca International State Park
122. Falcon State Park (airstrip)
123. Bentsen-Rio Grande Valley State Park
124. Estero Llano Grande State Park
125. Resaca de la Palma Park

Daingerfield State Park, off TX 49 and PR 17 southeast of Daingerfield in Morris County, is a 550.9-acre recreational area that includes an 80-surface-acre lake; deeded in 1935 by private owners. This area is center of iron industry in Texas; nearby is Lone Star Steel Co. In spring, **dogwood, redbuds** and **wisteria** bloom; in fall, brilliant foliage of **sweetgum, oaks** and **maples** contrast with dark green pines. Campsites, lodge and cabins.

Davis Mountains State Park is 2,709 acres in Jeff Davis County, 4 miles northwest of Fort Davis via TX 118 and PR 3. The scenic area was deeded in 1933-1937 by private owners. **First European, Antonio de Espejo**, came to area in 1583. Extremes of altitude produce both **plains grasslands** and **piñon-juniper-oak woodlands. Montezuma quail**, rare in Texas, visit park. Scenic drives, camping and hiking. **Indian Lodge**, built by the Civilian Conservation Corps during the early 1930s, has 39 rooms, restaurant and swimming pool (reservations: 432-426-3254). Four-mile hiking trail leads to **Fort Davis National Historic Site**. Other nearby points of interest include **McDonald Observatory** and 74-mile scenic loop through **Davis Mountains**. Nearby are scenic **Limpia, Madera, Musquiz** and **Keesey canyons; Camino del Rio;** ghost town of **Shafter; Big Bend National Park; Big Bend Ranch State Park; Fort Davis National Historic Site;** and **Fort Leaton State Historic Site**.

Devil's River State Natural Area comprises 19,988.6 acres in Val Verde County, 22 miles off US 277, about 65 miles north of Del Rio on graded road. It is an **ecological and archaeological crossroads**. Ecologically, it is in a **transitional area** between the **Edwards Plateau**, the **Trans-Pecos desert** and the **South Texas brush country**. Archaeological studies suggest occupation and/or use by cultures from both east and west. Camping, hiking and mountain biking. Canyon and pictograph-site tours by prearrangement only. Park accessible by reservation only. **Dolan Falls**, owned by The Nature Conservancy of Texas and open only to its members, is nearby.

Devil's Sinkhole State Natural Area, comprising 1,859.7 acres about 6 miles northeast of Rocksprings in Edwards County, is a **vertical cavern**. The sinkhole, discovered by Anglo settlers in 1867, is a registered **National Natural Landmark**; it was purchased in 1985 from private owners. The cavern opening is about 40 by 60 feet, with a vertical drop of about 140 feet. Access by prearranged tour with Devil's Sinkhole Society (830-683-BATS). Bats can be viewed in summer leaving cave at dusk; no access to cave itself. Access to the park is made by contacting **Kickapoo Cavern State Park** to arrange a tour.

Dinosaur Valley State Park, located off US 67 four miles west of Glen Rose in Somervell County, is a 1,524.72-acre scenic park. Land was acquired from private owners in 1968. **Dinosaur tracks** in bed of Paluxy River and two full-scale dinosaur models, originally created for New York World's Fair in 1964-65, on display. Part of state **longhorn herd** is in park. Camping, picnicking, hiking, mountain biking, swimming, fishing.

Eisenhower Birthplace State Historic Site is 6 acres off US 75 at 609 S. Lamar, Denison, Grayson County. The property was acquired in 1958 from the Eisenhower Birthplace Foundation. Restoration of home of Pres. Dwight David "Ike" Eisenhower includes furnishings of period and some personal effects of Gen. Eisenhower. Guided tour; call for schedule. Park open daily, except Christmas Day and New Year's Day; call for hours. Town of Denison established on **Butterfield Overland Mail** Route in 1858.

Eisenhower State Park, 423.1 acres five miles northwest of Denison via US 75 to TX 91N to FM 1310 on the shores of **Lake Texoma** in Grayson County, was acquired by an Army lease in 1954. Named for the **34th U.S. president, Dwight David Eisenhower**. First Anglo settlers came to area in 1835; **Fort Johnson** was established in area in 1840; **Colbert's Ferry** established on Red River in 1853 and operated until 1931. Areas of **tall-grass prairie** exist. Hiking, camping, picnicking, fishing, swimming.

Enchanted Rock State Natural Area is 1,643.5 acres on Big Sandy Creek 18 miles north of Fredericksburg on RM 965 on the line between Gillespie and Llano counties. Acquired in 1978 by The Nature Conservancy of Texas; state acquired from TNCT in 1984. Enchanted Rock is huge **pink granite boulder** rising 425 feet above ground and covering 640 acres. It is **second-largest batholith** (underground rock formation uncovered by erosion) in the United States. Indians believed **ghost fires** flickered at top and were awed by weird creaking and groaning, which geologists say resulted from rock's heating and expanding by day, cooling and contracting at night. Enchanted Rock is a **National Natural Landmark** and is on the **National Register of Historic Places**. Activities include hiking, geological study, camping, **rock climbing** and star gazing.

Fairfield Lake State Park is 1,460 acres adjacent to Lake Fairfield, 6 miles northeast of the city of Fairfield off FM 2570 and FM 3285 in Freestone County. It was leased from Texas Utilities in 1971-72. Surrounding woods offer sanctuary for many species of birds and wildlife. Camping, hiking, backpacking, nature study, water-related activities available. Extensive schedule of tours, seminars and other activities.

Falcon State Park is 572.6 acres located 15 miles north of Roma off US 83 and FM 2098 at southern end of Falcon Reservoir in Starr and Zapata counties. Park leased from International Boundary and Water Commission in 1949. Gently rolling hills covered by **mesquite, huisache, wild olive, ebony, cactus**. Excellent **birding** and **fishing**. Camping and water activities also. Nearby are **Mexico, Fort Ringgold** in Rio Grande City and historic city of **Roma. Bentsen-Rio Grande Valley State Park** is 65 miles away.

Fannin Battleground State Historic Site, 9 miles east of Goliad in Goliad County off US 59 to PR 27. The 13.6-acre park site was acquired by the state in 1914; transferred to TPW by legislative enactment in 1965. At this site on March 20, 1836, **Col. J. W. Fannin** surrendered to Mexican **Gen. José Urrea** after **Battle of Coleto**; 342 massacred and 28 escaped near what is now Goliad **State Historic Site**. Near Fannin site is **Gen. Zaragoza's Birthplace** and partially restored **Mission Nuestra Señora del Espíritu Santo de Zúñiga** (see also **Goliad State Historic Site** in this list).

Fanthorp Inn State Historic Site includes a historic double-pen cedar-log dogtrot house and 1.4 acres in Anderson, county seat of Grimes County, on TX 90. Acquired by purchase in 1977 from a Fanthorp descendant and opened to the public in 1987. Inn records report visits from many prominent civic and military leaders, including **Sam Houston, Anson Jones, Ulysses S. Grant** and generals **Robert E. Lee** and **Stonewall Jackson**. Originally built in 1834, it has been restored to its 1850 use as a family home and travelers' hotel. Tours available Friday, Saturday, Sunday. Call TPW for stagecoach-ride schedule. No dining or overnight facilities.

Fort Boggy State Park is 1,847 acres of wooded, rolling hills in Leon County near Boggy Creek, about 4 miles south of Centerville on TX 75. Land donated to TPWD in 1985 by Eileen Crain Sullivan. Area once home to Keechi and Kickapoo tribes. Log fort was built by settlers in 1840s; first settlement north of the Old San Antonio Road and between the Navasota and Trinity rivers. Swimming beach, fishing, picnicking, nature trails for hiking and mountain biking. Fifteen-acre lake open to small craft. Open-air group pavilion overlooking lake can be reserved ($50 per day). Nearby attractions include Rusk/Palestine State Park, Fort Parker State Park, Texas State Railroad, Old Fort Parker. Open Wed.–Sun. for day use only; entrance fee. For reservations, call 512-389-8900.

Fort Griffin State Historic Site is 506.2 acres 15 miles north of Albany off US 283 in Shackelford County. The state was deeded the land by the county in 1935. Portion of **state longhorn herd** resides in park. On bluff overlooking townsite of **Fort Griffin** and **Clear Fork of Brazos River** valley are partially restored ruins of **Old Fort Griffin**, restored bakery, replicas of enlisted men's huts. Fort constructed in 1867, deactivated 1881. Camping, equestrian camping, hiking. Nearby are **Albany** with restored courthouse square, **Abilene and Possum Kingdom State Park**. Albany annually holds "**Fandangle**" musical show in commemoration of frontier times.

Fort Lancaster State Historic Site, 81.6-acres located about 8 miles east of Sheffield on Interstate10 and US 290

Parks text continues on page 164.

☆ Texas State Parks ☆

Park / †Type of Park / Special Features	NEAREST TOWN	Day Use Only	Historic Site/Museum	Exhibit/Interpretive Center	Restrooms	Showers	Trailer Dump Stn.	††Camping	Screened Shelters	Cabins	Group Facilities	Nature Trail	Hiking Trail	Picnicking	Boat Ramp	Fishing	Swimming	Water Skiing	Miscellaneous
Abilene SP	BUFFALO GAP				★	★	★	15	★		BG	★		★		☆	★		L
Acton SHS (Grave of Davy Crockett's wife)	GRANBURY	★	★																
Atlanta SP	ATLANTA				★	★	★	14			DG	★	★	★	★	☆	☆	☆	
Balmorhea SP (San Solomon Springs Courts)	BALMORHEA			★	★	★	★	14			DG			★			★		I
Barton Warnock Environmental Education Ctr.	LAJITAS	★		★	★	★						★							
Bastrop SP	BASTROP				★	★	★	10		★	BG	★	★	★		☆	★		G
Battleship Texas HS (At San Jacinto Battleground)	DEER PARK	★	★	★															
Bentsen-Rio Grande Valley SP	MISSION				★	★		10			BG	★	★	★	★	☆			
Big Bend Ranch SP Complex	PRESIDIO			★	★	★		1			NG	★	★	★		☆	☆		B1, L, E
Big Spring SP	BIG SPRING			★	★			13			BG	★	★	★					
Blanco SP	BLANCO				★	★	★	16	★		DG	★		★		☆	☆		
Boca Chica Beach (Open Beach)	BROWNSVILLE							1								☆	☆		
Bonham SP	BONHAM				★	★	★	14			BG		★	★	★	★	☆		B1
Brazos Bend SP (George Observatory)	RICHMOND			★	★	★	★	4	★		BG	★	★	★		★			B1, B2
Buescher SP	SMITHVILLE				★	★	★	14	★		BG	★		★		★	☆		B2
Caddo Lake SP	KARNACK			★	★	★	★	15	★	★	BG	★	★	★	★	★	☆	☆	
Caddoan Mounds SHS	ALTO	★	★	★	★							★							
Caprock Canyons SP and Trailway	QUITAQUE				★	★	★	8			BG	★	★	★	★	★	☆		B1, E
Casa Navarro SHS	SAN ANTONIO	★	★	★	★														
Cedar Hill SP	CEDAR HILL				★	★	★	12			DG	★	★	★	★	★	☆	☆	B1
Choke Canyon SP, Calliham Unit	CALLIHAM				★	★	★	10	★		BG	★		★	★	★	☆	☆	
Choke Canyon SP, South Shore Unit	THREE RIVERS				★	★	★	8			DG			★	★	★	☆	☆	B1, E
Cleburne SP	CLEBURNE				★	★	★	16	★		BG	★	★	★	★	★	☆	☆	
Colorado Bend SP (Cave Tours)	BEND				★			1					★	★	★	★	☆		B1
Confederate Reunion Grounds SHS	MEXIA	★	★	★				1			BG	★		★		☆			
Cooper Lake SP (Doctors Creek Unit)	COOPER				★	★	★	4	★		DG	★	★	★	★	★	★	☆	
Cooper Lake SP (South Sulphur Unit)	SULPHUR SPRINGS				★	★	★	14	★	★	DG		★	★	★	★	★	☆	B1, E
Copano Bay SFP ▲	FULTON				★									★	★				
Copper Breaks SP	QUANAH			★	★	★	★	10			BG	★	★	★	★	★	☆		B1, E, L
Daingerfield SP	DAINGERFIELD				★	★	★	15		★	BG	★	★	★	★	★	☆		
Davis Mountains SP (Indian Lodge)	FORT DAVIS			★	★	★	★	11			DG	★	★						I, E
Devils River SNA (Use by reservation only)	DEL RIO							1			BG								B1, E
Devil's Sinkhole SNA	ROCKSPRINGS																		
Dinosaur Valley SP (Dinosaur Footprints)	GLEN ROSE			★	★	★	★	12			DG	★	★	★		☆	☆		B1, E, L
Eisenhower SP (Marina)	DENISON				★	★	★	15	★		BG	★	★	★	★	★	☆	☆	B1
Eisenhower Birthplace SHS	DENISON	★	★	★	★						DG								
Enchanted Rock SNA	FREDERICKSBURG			★	★	★		9			DG	★	★	★					R
Fairfield Lake SP	FAIRFIELD				★	★	★	11			DG		★	★	★	★	☆	☆	B1
Falcon SP (Airstrip)	ZAPATA				★	★	★	15	★		BG	★		★	★	☆	☆	☆	B1
Fannin Battleground SHS	GOLIAD	★	★	★	★						DG			★					
Fanthorp Inn SHS	ANDERSON	★	★	★	★									★					
Fort Boggy SP	CENTERVILLE	★									DG	★		★	★	☆	☆		
Fort Griffin SP & HS	ALBANY	★	★	★	★	★		10			BG	★	★	★		☆			I, F
Fort Lancaster SHS	OZONA	★	★	★	★									☆					
Fort Leaton SHS	PRESIDIO	★	★	★	★							★		★					
Fort McKavett SHS	FORT McKAVETT	★	★	★	★							★		★					
Fort Parker SP	MEXIA				★	★	★	14	★		BG	★	★	★	★	★	☆		B1
Fort Richardson SHS and Lost Creek Res. TW	JACKSBORO	★	★	★	★	★	★	10	★		DG	★	★	★		★	★		E
Franklin Mountains SP	EL PASO	★				★		6			DG	★	★						B1, E, R
Fulton Mansion SHS	FULTON	★	★	★	★									★					
Galveston Island SP (Summer Theater)	GALVESTON			★	★	★	★	4	★			★		★		☆	☆		B1
Garner SP	CONCAN				★	★	★	14	★	★	BG	★		★		☆	☆		B2
Goliad SHS	GOLIAD	★	★	★	★	★	★	11	★		DG	★	★	★		★			
Goose Island SP	ROCKPORT				★	★	★	14			BG			★	★	★			
Governor Hogg Shrine SHS	QUITMAN	★	★	★	★						DG	★		★					
Guadalupe River SP/Honey Creek SNA	BOERNE				★	★	★	13				★	★			☆	☆		E
Hill Country SNA	BANDERA							6			NG	★				☆	☆		B1, E
Hueco Tanks SHS (Indian Pictographs)	EL PASO	★	★	★	★	★		14			DG	★	★	★					R
Huntsville SP	HUNTSVILLE			★	★	★	★	14	★		DG	★	★	★	★	★	☆		B1, B2
Inks Lake SP	BURNET				★	★	★	10	★		BG		★	★	★	★	☆	☆	G
Jim Hogg SHS	RUSK	★	★	★	★							★		★					

Devil's Sinkhole SNA (ROCKSPRINGS): (No access to cavern. Tours of SNA by special request only.)

†Types of Parks

SP	State Park	SFP	State Fishing Pier
SHS	State Historic Site	TW	Trailway
SNA	State Natural Area		

††Type(s) of Camping

1-Primitive; 2-Walk-in tent; 3-Tent; 4-Water and Electric; 5-Water, Electric, Sewer; 6-1 & 2; 7-1, 2 & 4; 8-1, 2, 3 & 4; 9-1 & 3; 10-1, 3 & 4; 11-1, 3, 4 & 5; 12-1 & 4; 13-2, 3 & 4; 14- 3 & 4; 15-3, 4 & 5; 16-4 & 5; 17-1, 3 & 5.

☆ Texas State Parks ☆

Park / †Type of Park / Special Features	NEAREST TOWN	Day Use Only	Historic Site/Museum	Exhibit/Interpretive Center	Restrooms	Showers	Trailer Dump Stn.	††Camping	Screened Shelters	Cabins	Group Facilities	Nature Trail	Hiking Trail	Picnicking	Boat Ramp	Fishing	Swimming	Water Skiing	Miscellaneous
Kickapoo Cavern SP (Use by reservation only)	BRACKETTVILLE			★	★			6			NG	★	★						B1
Lake Arrowhead SP	WICHITA FALLS				★	★	★	10			DG	★	★	★	★	★	☆	☆	E
Lake Bob Sandlin SP	MOUNT PLEASANT				★	★	★	10	★		DG	★	★	★	★	★	☆	☆	B1
Lake Brownwood SP	BROWNWOOD				★	★	★	15	★	★	BG	★	★	★	★	★	☆	☆	B1
Lake Casa Blanca International SP	LAREDO				★	★	★	14			DG			★	★	☆	☆	☆	B1
Lake Colorado City SP	COLORADO CITY				★	★	★	14		★	BG	★	★	★	★	★	☆	☆	
Lake Corpus Christi SP	MATHIS				★	★	★	15	★		DG			★	★	★	☆	☆	
Lake Houston SP	NEW CANEY				★	★		9			BG	★	★	★		★			B1, E
Lake Livingston SP	LIVINGSTON				★	★	★	15	★		DG	★	★	★	★	★	☆	☆	B1, B2, E
Lake Mineral Wells SP and TW	MINERAL WELLS				★	★	★	10	★		DG	★	★	★	★	★	☆		B1, E, R
Lake Somerville SP and TW, Birch Creek Unit	SOMERVILLE			★	★	★	★	10			BG	★	★	★	★	★	☆		B1, E
Lake Somerville SP and TW, Nails Creek Unit	LEDBETTER			★	★	★	★	10			DG	★	★	★	★	★	☆	☆	B1, E
Lake Tawakoni SP	WILLS POINT				★	★	★	4				★	★	★	★	☆	☆	☆	
Lake Texana SP	EDNA			★	★	★	★	14			DG	★	★	★	★	★	☆	☆	B1
Lake Whitney SP (Airstrip)	WHITNEY				★	★	★	15	★		BG	★	★	★	★	☆	☆	☆	B1
Landmark Inn SHS (Hotel Rooms)	CASTROVILLE		★	★	★						DG	★		★		☆			I
Lipantitlan SHS	SAN PATRICIO	★										★		★					
Lockhart SP	LOCKHART				★	★		16			BG			★			★		G
Longhorn Cavern SP (Cavern Tours) ▲	BURNET	★	★	★	★							★	★	★					
Lost Maples SNA	VANDERPOOL				★	★	★	12				★	★	★		☆	☆		
Lyndon B. Johnson SHS	STONEWALL	★	★	★	★						DG	★		★		☆	★		L
Magoffin Home SHS	EL PASO	★	★	★	★														
Martin Creek Lake SP	TATUM				★	★	★	12	★	★	DG	★	★	★	★	★	☆	☆	B1
Martin Dies Jr. SP	JASPER				★	★	★	14	★		BG	★	★	★	★	★	☆	☆	B1
Matagorda Island SP (Boat or Air Access Only)	PORT O'CONNOR	★	★	★	★			1			NG	★	★			☆	☆		B1
McKinney Falls SP	AUSTIN	★		★	★	★	★	13	★		BG	★	★	★		☆	☆		B1, B2
Meridian SP	MERIDIAN				★	★	★	13	★		BG	★	★	★	★	★	☆		
Mission Tejas SHS	WECHES			★	★	★	★	15			BG	★	★	★		☆			
Monahans Sandhills SP	MONAHANS			★	★	★	★	14			DG	★		★					E
Monument Hill/Kreische Brewery SHS	LA GRANGE	★	★	★	★							★		★					
Mother Neff SP	MOODY				★	★	★	10			BG	★	★	★			☆		
Mustang Island SP	PORT ARANSAS				★	★	★	12						★		☆	☆		B1
National Museum of the Pacific War	FREDERICKSBURG	★	★	★	★							★							
Old Fort Parker SP (Managed by City of Groesbeck)	GROESBECK	★	★	★				1											E
Palmetto SP	LULING				★	★	★	15			BC	★	★	★		★	☆		
Palo Duro Canyon SP (Summer Drama: "Texas")	CANYON			★	★	★	★	8		★		★	★	★		★			B1, E, L
Pedernales Falls SP	JOHNSON CITY				★	★	★	9			NG	★	★	★		☆	☆		B1, E
Port Isabel Lighthouse SHS	PORT ISABEL	★	★																
Possum Kingdom SP	CADDO				★	★	★	10		★		★	★	★	★	★	☆	☆	
Purtis Creek SP	EUSTACE				★	★	★	10				★	★	★	★	★	☆		P
Ray Roberts Lake SP, Isle du Bois Unit	DENTON				★	★	★	13			DG	★	★	★	★	★	☆	☆	B1, B2, E
Ray Roberts Lake SP, Johnson Unit	DENTON				★	★	★	7			DG	★	★	★	★	★	☆	☆	B1, B2
Rusk/Palestine SP (Texas State RR Terminals)	RUSK/PALESTINE				★	★	★	15			DG	★		★		★			
Sabine Pass Battleground SHS	SABINE PASS		★	★	★			★	12						★	★	☆		
Sam Bell Maxey House SHS	PARIS	★	★	★	★														
San Angelo SP	SAN ANGELO				★	★	★	8		★	BG	★	★	★	★	★	☆	☆	B1, E, L
San Jacinto Battleground SHS (Battleship Texas)	HOUSTON	★	★	★	★						DG	★		★		☆			
Sea Rim SP	PORT ARTHUR				★	★	★	10				★		★	★	☆	★		B1
Sebastopol SHS	SEGUIN	★	★	★	★									★					
Seminole Canyon SHS (Indian Pictographs)	LANGTRY	★		★	★	★	★	14				★	★	★					B1
Sheldon Lake SP	HOUSTON	★			★							★	☆	★	★				
South Llano River SP	JUNCTION			★	★	★	★	10				★	★	★		☆	☆		B1
Starr Family SHS	MARSHALL	★	★	★	★														
Stephen F. Austin SHS	SAN FELIPE			★	★	★	★	15	★		BG	★	★	★		☆			G
Texas State Railroad SHS (Contact Park for Schedule)	PALESTINE/RUSK	★	★	★	★														
Tyler SP	TYLER				★	★	★	15	★		BG	★	★	★	★	★	☆		B1
Varner-Hogg Plantation SHS (Guided Tours)	WEST COLUMBIA	★	★	★	★							★		★		☆			
Village Creek SP	LUMBERTON				★	★	★	13			BG	★	★	★		☆	☆		B1
Walter Umphrey SP	PORT ARTHUR	*(Managed by Jefferson County)*																	
Washington-on-the-Brazos SHS (Anson Jones Home)	WASHINGTON	★	★	★	★						DG			★	★				
Wyler Aerial Tramway Franklin Mts. SP	EL PASO	★		★	★														

Facilities

▲ Facilities not operated by Parks & Wildlife.
★ Facilities or services available for activity.
☆ Permitted but facilities not provided.

Note: Contact individual parks for information on handicap facilities.

Miscellaneous Codes

B1	Mountain Biking	G	Golf
B2	Surfaced Bike Trail	I	Hotel-Type Facilities
BG	Both Day & Night Group Facilities	L	Texas Longhorn Herd
DG	Day-Use Group Facilities	NG	Overnight Group Facilities
E	Equestrian Trails	R	Rock Climbing

in Crockett County. Acquired in 1968 by deed from Crockett County; Henry Meadows donated 41 acres in 1975. **Fort Lancaster** established Aug. 20, 1855, to guard San Antonio-El Paso Road and protect movement of supplies and immigrants from Indian hostilities. Site of part of Camel Corps experiment. Fort abandoned March 19, 1861, after Texas seceded from Union. Exhibits on history, natural history and archaeology; nature trail, picnicking. Open daily; day use only.

Fort Leaton State Historic Site, 4 miles southeast of Presidio in Presidio County on FM 170, was acquired in 1967 from private owners. Consists of 23.4 acres, 5 of which are on site of **pioneer trading post**. In 1848, **Ben Leaton** built fortified adobe trading post known as Fort Leaton near present Presidio. Ben Leaton died in 1851. Guided tours; exhibits trace history, natural history and archaeological history of area. Serves as western entrance to **Big Bend Ranch State Park**. Day use only.

Fort McKavett State Historic Site, 79.5 acres acquired from 1967 through the mid-1970s from Fort McKavett Restoration, Inc., Menard County and private individuals, is located 23 miles west of Menard off US 190 and FM 864. Originally called **Camp San Saba**, the fort was built by War Department in 1852 to protect frontier settlers and travelers on Upper El Paso Road from Indians. Camp later renamed for **Capt. Henry McKavett**, killed at Battle of Monterrey, Sept. 21, 1846. A **Buffalo Soldier post**. Fort abandoned March 1859; reoccupied April 1868; abandoned again June 30, 1883. Once called by Gen. Wm. T. Sherman, "the prettiest post in Texas." More than 25 restored buildings, ruins of many others. Interpretive exhibits. Day use only.

Fort Parker State Park includes 1,458.8 acres, including 758.78 land acres and 700-acre lake between Mexia and Groesbeck off TX 14 in Limestone County. Named for the former private fort built near present park in 1836, the site was acquired from private owners and the City of Mexia 1935-1937. Camping, fishing, swimming, canoeing, picnicking. Nearby is **Old Fort Parker Historic Site**, which is operated by the City of Groesbeck.

Fort Richardson State Historic Site, located one-half mile south of Jacksboro off US 281 in Jack County, contains 454 acres. Acquired in 1968 from City of Jacksboro. Fort founded in 1867, northernmost of line of federal forts established after Civil War for protection from Indians; originally named **Fort Jacksboro**. In April 1867, fort was moved to its present location from 20 miles farther south; on Nov. 19, 1867, made permanent post at Jacksboro and named for **Israel Richardson**, who was fatally wounded at Battle of Antietam. Expeditions sent from Fort Richardson arrested Indians responsible for **Warren Wagon Train Massacre** in 1871 and fought Comanches in **Palo Duro Canyon**. Fort abandoned in May 1878. Park contains seven restored buildings and two replicas. Interpretive center, picnicking, camping, fishing; 10-mile trailway.

Franklin Mountains State Park, created by an act of the legislature in 1979 to protect the mountain range as a wilderness preserve and acquired by TPW in 1981, comprises 24,247.56 acres, all within El Paso city limits. **Largest urban park in the nation**. It includes virtually an entire **Chihuahuan Desert mountain range**, with an elevation of 7,192 feet at the summit. The park is habitat for many Chihuahuan Desert plants including **sotol, lechuguilla, ocotillo, cholla** and **barrel cactus**, and such animals as **mule deer, fox** and an occasional **cougar**. Camping, mountain biking, nature study, hiking, picnicking, rock-climbing.

Fulton Mansion State Historic Site is 3.5 miles north of Rockport off TX 35 in Aransas County. The 2.3 acre-property was acquired by purchase from private owner in 1976. Three-story wooden structure, built in 1874-1877, was home of **George W. Fulton**, prominent in South Texas for economic and commercial influence; mansion derives significance from its innovative construction and Victorian design. Call ahead for days and hours of guided tours; open Wednesday–Sunday; 800-792-1112.

Galveston Island State Park, on the west end of Galveston Island on FM 3005, is a 2,013.1-acre site acquired in 1969 from private owners. Camping, birding, nature study, swimming, bicycling and fishing amid **sand dunes and grassland**.

More Travel Information

Call the **Texas Department of Transportation**'s toll-free number: **1-800-888-8TEX** for:
- The **Texas State Travel Guide**, a free 288-page, full-color publication with a wealth of information about attractions, activities, history and historic sites.
- The official **Texas state highway map**. On the Internet: **www.traveltex.com**

Musical productions in **amphitheater** during summer.

Garner State Park is 1,419.8 acres of recreational facilities on US 83 on the Frio River in Uvalde County 9 miles south of Leakey. Named for **John Nance Garner**, U.S. Vice President, 1933-1941, the park was deeded in 1934-36 by private owners. Camping, hiking, picnicking, river recreation, miniature golf, biking, boat rentals. Cabins available. Nearby is **John Nance "Cactus Jack" Garner Museum** in Uvalde. Nearby also are ruins of historic **Mission Nuestra Señora de la Candelaria del Cañon**, founded in 1749; **Camp Sabinal** (a U.S. Cavalry post and later Texas Ranger camp) established 1856; **Fort Inge**, established 1849.

Goliad State Historic Site is 188.3 acres one-fourth mile south of Goliad on US 183 and 77A, along the San Antonio River in Goliad County. The land was deeded to state in 1931 by the City and County of Goliad; transferred to TPW 1949. Nearby are the sites of several battles in the Texas fight for independence from Mexico. The park includes a replica of **Mission Nuestra Señora del Espíritu Santo de Zúñiga**, originally established 1722 and settled at its present site in 1749. Park unit includes **Gen. Ignacio Zaragoza's Birthplace**, which is located near **Presidio la Bahía**. He was Mexican national hero who led troops against French at historic **Battle of Puebla** on May 5, 1862. Park also contains ruins of **Nuestra Señora del Rosario** mission, established 1754, located four miles west of Goliad on US 59. Camping, picnicking, historical exhibits, nature trail. Other nearby points of historical interest: restored **Nuestra Señora de Loreto de la Bahía** presidio, established 1721 and settled on site in 1749; it is located short distance south on US 183. Memorial shaft marking common burial site of **Fannin** and victims of Goliad massacre (1836) is near **Presidio la Bahía**. (See also **Fannin Battleground State Historic Site**.)

Goose Island State Park, 321.4 acres 10 miles northeast of Rockport on TX 35 and PR 13 on St. Charles and Aransas Bays in Aransas County, was deeded by private owners in 1931-1935 plus an additional seven acres donated in the early 1990s by Sun Oil Co. Located here is "Big Tree" estimated to be a 1,000-year-old **live oak**. Fishing, picnicking and camping, plus excellent birding; no swimming. Rare and endangered **whooping cranes** can be viewed during winter just across St. Charles Bay in **Aransas National Wildlife Refuge**.

Gov. Hogg Shrine State Historic Site is a 26.7-acre tract on TX 37 about six blocks south of the Wood County Courthouse in Quitman. Named for **James Stephen Hogg, first native-born governor of Texas**, the park includes museums housing items that belonged to the Hogg and Stinson families. Seventeen acres deeded by the Wood County Old Settlers Reunion Association in 1946; 4.74 acres gift of Miss Ima Hogg in 1970; 3 acres purchased. **Gov. James Stephen Hogg Memorial Shrine** created in 1941. Three museums: Gov. Hogg's wedding held in **Stinson Home; Honeymoon Cottage; Miss Ima Hogg Museum** houses both park headquarters and display of representative history of entire Northeast Texas area. Operated by City of Quitman.

Guadalupe River State Park comprises 1,938.7 acres on cypress-shaded Guadalupe River in Kendall and Comal counties, 13 miles east of Boerne on TX 46. Acquired by deed from private owners in 1974. Park has four miles of river frontage with several **white-water rapids** and is located in a stretch of **Guadalupe River** noted for canoeing, tubing. Picnicking,

Runners head down a trail at Huntsville State Park. Ron Billings photo; Texas Forest Service.

camping, hiking, nature study. Trees include **sycamore, elm, basswood, pecan, walnut, persimmon, willow** and **hackberry** (see also **Honey Creek State Natural Area**, below).

Hill Country State Natural Area in Bandera and Medina counties, 9 miles west of Bandera on RM 1077. The 5,369.8-acre site acquired by gift from Merrick Bar-O-Ranch and purchase in 1976. Park is located in typical Texas Hill Country on West Verde Creek and contains several **spring-fed streams**. Primitive and equestrian camping, hiking, horseback riding, mountain biking, fishing. Group lodge.

Honey Creek State Natural Area consists of 2,293.7 acres adjacent to **Guadalupe River State Park** (above); entrance is in the park. Acquired from The Nature Conservancy of Texas in 1985 with an addition from private individual in 1988. Diverse plant life includes **agarita, Texas persimmon** and Ashe juniper in hills, and cedar elm, Spanish oak, pecan, walnut and **Mexican buckeye** in bottomlands. Abundant wildlife includes **ringtail, leopard frog, green kingfisher, golden-cheeked warbler** and **canyon wren**. Schedule varies ; call 830-796-4413for details.

Hueco Tanks State Historic Site, located 32 miles northeast of El Paso in El Paso County on RM 2775 just north of US 62-180, was obtained from the county in 1969, with additional 121 acres purchased in 1970. Featured in this 860.3-acre park are large **natural rock basins** that provided water for archaic hunters, Plains Indians, Butterfield Overland Mail coach horses and passengers, and other travelers in this arid region. In park are **Indian pictographs, old ranch house** and relocated **ruins of stage station. Rock climbing**, picnicking, camping, hiking. Guided tours. Wildlife includes **gray fox, bobcat, prairie falcons, golden eagles.**

Huntsville State Park is 2,083.2-acre recreational area off IH 45 and PR 40 six miles south of Huntsville in Walker County, acquired by deeds from private owners in 1937. Heavily wooded park adjoins **Sam Houston National Forest** and encloses **Lake Raven**. Hiking, camping, fishing, biking, paddle boats, canoeing. At nearby Huntsville are **Sam Houston's old homestead (Steamboat House)**, containing some of his personal effects, and **his grave**. Approximately 50 miles away is **Alabama-Coushatta Indian Reservation** in Polk County.

Inks Lake State Park is 1,201 acres of recreational facilities along Inks Lake, 9 miles west of Burnet on the Colorado River off TX 29 on PR 4 in Burnet County. Acquired by deeds from the Lower Colorado River Authority and private owners in 1940. Camping, hiking, fishing, swimming, boating, golf. **Deer, turkey** and other wildlife abundant. Nearby are **Longhorn Cavern State Park, LBJ Ranch, LBJ State Historic Site, Pedernales Falls State Park** and **Enchanted Rock State Natural Area**. **Granite Mountain** quarry at nearby Marble

Falls furnished red granite for **Texas state capitol. Buchanan Dam**, largest multi-arch dam in world, located 4 miles from park.

Jim Hogg Historic Site is 178.4 acres of East Texas Pineywoods in Cherokee County, 2 miles east of Rusk off U.S. 84 E. and Fire Tower Road. Memorial to Texas' first native born governor, James Stephen Hogg, 1891–1895. Remnants of 1880s iron ore mining. Scale replica of Hogg birthplace. Picnicking, historical study, nature study, hiking and bird watching. Self-guided and guided museum tours and nature trail tours. Operated by the City of Rusk; 903-683-4850. Area attractions: Caddoan Mounds, Mission Tejas State Historic Sites, Rusk/Palestine State Park, Texas State Railroad, Tyler State Parks and historic Nacogdoches. Day use only; entrance fee.

Kickapoo Cavern State Park is located about 22 miles north of Brackettville on RM 674 on the Kinney/Edwards county line in the southern Edwards Plateau. The park (6,368.4 acres) contains **15 known caves**, two of which are large enough to be significant: Kickapoo Cavern, about 1/4 mile in length, has impressive formations, and **Green Cave**, slightly shorter, supports a nursery colony of **Brazilian freetail bats** in summer. Birds include rare species such as **black-capped vireo, varied bunting** and **Montezuma quail**. Reptiles and amphibians include barking frog, mottled rock rattlesnake and Texas alligator lizard. Tours of Kickapoo and observation of bats available only by special arrangement. Group lodge; primitive camping; hiking and mountain-biking trails. Open only by reservation.

Kreische Brewery State Historic Site (see Monument Hill and Kreische Brewery State Historic Sites).

Lake Arrowhead State Park consists of 524 acres in Clay County, about 14 miles south of Wichita Falls on US 281 to FM 1954, then 8 miles to park. Acquired in 1970 from the City of Wichita Falls. **Lake Arrowhead** is a reservoir on the Little Wichita River with 106 miles of shoreline. The land surrounding the lake is generally semiarid, gently rolling prairie, much of which has been invaded by mesquite in recent decades. Fishing, camping, lake swimming, picnicking, horseback-riding area.

Lake Bob Sandlin State Park, on the wooded shoreline of 9,400-acre Lake Bob Sandlin, is located 12 miles southwest of Mount Pleasant off FM 21 in Titus County. Activities in the 639.8-acre park include picnicking, camping, mountain biking, hiking, swimming, fishing and boating. **Oak, hickory, dogwood, redbud, maple** and **pine** produce spectacular fall color. Eagles can sometimes be spotted in winter months.

Lake Brownwood State Park in Brown County is 537.5 acres acquired from Brown County Water Improvement District No. 1 in 1934. Park reached from TX 279 to PR 15, 16 miles northwest of Brownwood on Lake Brownwood near **geographical center of Texas**. Water sports, hiking, camping. Cabins available.

Lake Casa Blanca International State Park, located one mile east of Laredo off US 59 on Loop 20, was formerly operated by the City of Laredo and Webb County and was acquired by TPW in 1990. Park includes 371 acres on Lake Casa Blanca. **Recreation hall** can be reserved. Camping, picnicking, fishing, ball fields, playgrounds, amphitheater, and tennis courts. County-operated golf course nearby.

Lake Colorado City State Park, 500 acres leased for 99 years from a utility company. It is located in Mitchell County 11 miles southwest of Colorado City off IH 20 on FM 2836. Water sports, picnicking, camping, hiking. Part of **state longhorn herd** can be seen in park.

Lake Corpus Christi State Park, a 14,112-acre park in San Patricio, Jim Wells and Live Oak counties. Located 35 miles northwest of Corpus Christi and four miles southwest of Mathis off TX 359 and Park Road 25. Was leased from City of Corpus Christi in 1934. Camping, picnicking, birding, water sports. Nearby are **Padre Island National Seashore; Mustang Island, Choke Canyon, Goliad and Goose Island** state parks; **Aransas National Wildlife Refuge, and Fulton Mansion State Historic Site**.

Lake Houston State Park is situated at the confluence of Caney Creek and the East Fork of the San Jacinto River. The 4,919.5-acre site, purchased from Champion Paper Company in 1981, is northeast of Houston in Harris and Montgomery counties. Camping, birding, hiking, biking, horseback riding.

Lake Livingston State Park, in Polk County, about one mile southwest of Livingston on FM 3126 and PR 65, contains 635.5 acres along Lake Livingston. Acquired by deed from private landowners in 1971. Near ghost town of **Swartwout**, steamboat landing on Trinity River in 1830s and 1850s. Camping, picnicking, swimming pool, fishing, mountain biking and stables.

Lake Mineral Wells State Park, located 4 miles east of Mineral Wells on US 180 in Parker County, consists of 3,282.5 acres encompassing Lake Mineral Wells. In 1975, the City of Mineral Wells donated 1,095 land acres and the lake to TPW; the U.S. Government transferred additional land from Fort Wolters army post. Popular for **rock-climbing/rappelling**. Swimming, fishing, boating, camping; **Lake Mineral Wells State Trailway** (hiking, bicycling, equestrian trail).

Lake Somerville State Park, northwest of Brenham in Lee and Burleson counties, was leased from the federal government in 1969. **Birch Creek Unit** (2,365 acres reached from TX 60 and PR 57) and **Nails Creek Unit** (3,155 acres

Acoustics make for great concerts at Longhorn Cavern State Park. Texas Parks & Wildlife photo.

reached from US 290 and FM 180), are connected by a **13-mile trailway system**, with **equestrian and primitive camp sites**, rest benches, shelters and drinking water. Also camping, birding, picnicking, volleyball and water sports. **Somerville Wildlife Management Area**, 3,180 acres is nearby.

Lake Tawakoni State Park is a 376.3-acre park in Hunt County along the shore of its namesake reservoir. It was acquired in 1984 through a 50-year lease agreement with the Sabine River Authority and opened in 2001. Includes a swimming beach, half-mile trail, picnic sites, boat ramp and campsites. A **40-acre tallgrass prairie** will be managed and enhanced in the post-oak woodlands. The park is reached from IH 20 on TX 47 north to FM 2475 about 20 miles past Wills Point.

Lake Texana State Park is 575 acres, 6.5 miles east of Edna on TX 111, half-way between Houston and Corpus Christi in Jackson County, with camping, boating, fishing and picnicking facilities. It was acquired by a 50-year lease agreement with the Bureau of Reclamation in 1977. Good birding in the **oak/pecan woodlands**. **Alligators** are often found in park coves.

Lake Whitney State Park is 1,280.7 acres along the east shore of Lake Whitney west of Hillsboro via TX 22 and FM 1244 in Hill County. Acquired in 1954 by a Department of the Army lease, effective through 2003. Located near ruins of **Towash**, early Texas settlement inundated by the lake.

Towash Village named for chief of Hainai Indians. Park noted for **bluebonnets** in spring. Camping, hiking, birding, picnicking, water activities.

Landmark Inn State Historic Site, 4.7 acres in Castroville, Medina County, about 15 miles west of San Antonio, was acquired through donation by Miss Ruth Lawler in 1974. Castroville, settled in the 1840s by Alsatian farmers, is called **Little Alsace of Texas**. Landmark Inn built about 1844 as residence and store for **Cesar Monod**, mayor of Castroville 1851-1864. Special workshops, tours and events held at inn; grounds may be rented for receptions, family reunions and weddings. **Overnight lodging**; no phones; all rooms air-conditioned and nonsmoking.

Lipantitlan State Historic Site is 5 acres 9 miles east of Orange Grove in Nueces County off Texas 359, FM 624 and FM 70. The property was deeded by private owners in 1937. Fort constructed here in 1833 by Mexican government fell to Texas forces in 1835. Only facilities are picnic tables. **Lake Corpus Christi State Park** is nearby.

Lockhart State Park is 263.7 acres 4 miles south of Lockhart via US 183, FM 20 and PR 10 in Caldwell County. The land was deeded by private owners between 1934 and 1937. Camping, picnicking, hiking, fishing, **9-hole golf course**. After Comanche raid at Linnville, **Battle of Plum Creek** (1840) was fought in area.

Longhorn Cavern State Park, off US 281 and PR 4 about 6 miles west and 6 miles south of Burnet in Burnet

County, is 645.62 acres dedicated as a natural landmark in 1971. It was acquired in 1932-1937 from private owners. The cave has been used as a shelter since prehistoric times. Among legends about the cave is that the outlaw **Sam Bass** hid stolen money there. Confederates made gunpowder in the cave during the Civil War. **Nature trail; guided tours** of cave; picnicking, hiking. Cavern operated by concession agreement. **Inks Lake State Park** and **Lyndon B. Johnson Ranch** located nearby.

Lost Maples State Natural Area consists of 2,174.2 scenic acres on the Sabinal River in Bandera and Real counties, 5 miles north of Vanderpool on RM 187. Acquired by purchase from private owners in 1973-1974. Outstanding example of Edwards Plateau flora and fauna, features isolated stand of uncommon **Uvalde bigtooth maple. Rare golden-cheeked warbler, black-capped vireo** and **green kingfisher** nest and feed in park. Fall foliage can be spectacular (late Oct. through early Nov.). Hiking trails, camping, fishing, picnicking, birding.

Lyndon B. Johnson State Historic Site, off US 290 in Gillespie County 14 miles west of Johnson City near Stonewall, contains 717.9 acres. Acquired in 1965 with private donations. **Home of Lyndon B. Johnson** located north bank of **Pedernales River** across Ranch Road 1 from park; portion of **official Texas longhorn herd** maintained at park. Wildlife exhibit includes **turkey, deer** and **bison. Living-history demonstrations** at restored **Sauer-Beckmann house**. Reconstruction of **Johnson birthplace** is open to public. Historic structures, swimming pool, tennis courts, baseball field, picnicking. Day use only. Nearby is family cemetery where former president and relatives are buried. In Johnson City is **boyhood home of President Johnson**. (See also **National Parks**.)

Magoffin Home State Historic Site, in El Paso, is a 19-room territorial-style adobe on a 1.5-acre site. Purchased by the state and City of El Paso in 1976, it is operated by TPW. Home was built in 1875 by pioneer El Pasoan **Joseph Magoffin**. Furnished with original family artifacts. Guided tours; call for schedule. Day use only.

Martin Creek Lake State Park, 286.9 acres, is located 4 miles south of Tatum off TX 43 and CR 2183 in Rusk County. It was deeded to the TPW by Texas Utilities in 1976. Water activities; also cabins, camping, picnicking. Roadbed of **Trammel's Trace**, old Indian trail that became major route for settlers moving to Texas from Arkansas, can be seen. **Hardwood and pine** forest shelters abundant wildlife including **swamp rabbits, gophers, nutria** and numerous species of land birds and waterfowl.

Martin Dies Jr. State Park, until 1965 the **Dam B State Park**, is 705 acres in Jasper and Tyler counties on B. A. Steinhagen Reservoir between Woodville and Jasper via US 190. Land leased for 50 years from Corps of Engineers in 1964. Located at edge of **Big Thicket**. Plant and animal life varied and abundant. Winter **bald eagle census** conducted at nearby Sam Rayburn Reservoir. Camping, hiking, mountain biking, water activities. Wildscape/herb garden. Park is approximately 30 miles from **Alabama and Coushatta Indian Reservation**.

Matagorda Island State Park and Wildlife Management Area is separated from the mainland by San Antonio and Espíritu Santo bays. Matagorda Island is one of the **barrier islands** that border the Gulf and protect the mainland from the great tides and strong wave action of the open ocean. About 43,893 acres of park and WMA are managed by the TPW. The park occupies about 7,325 acres of the total. **La Salle** had a camp on the island in 1684. The first Matagorda Island **lighthouse** was constructed in 1852; the present cast-iron structure was a replacement built in 1873. It is listed on the National Register of Historic Places. Nineteen endangered or threatened species are found here, including **whooping crane, peregrine falcon, brown pelican** and **Ridley sea turtle**. More than **300 species of birds** use island during spring and fall migrations. Camping, birding, water activities, scheduled tours. Access only by boat; passenger **ferry** operates from Port O'Connor Friday–Sunday.

McKinney Falls State Park is 744.4 acres 13 miles southeast of the state capitol in Austin off US 183. Acquired in 1970 by gift from private owners. Named for Thomas F. McK-

inney, **one of Stephen F. Austin's first 300 colonists**, who built his home here in the mid-1800s on Onion Creek. Ruins of his homestead can be viewed. Swimming, hiking, biking, camping, picnicking, fishing, guided tours.

Meridian State Park in Bosque County is a 505.4-acre park. The heavily wooded land, on TX 22 three miles southwest of Meridian, was acquired from private owners in 1933-1935. **Texas-Santa Fe expedition** of 1841 passed through Bosque County near present site of park on Bee Creek. **Endangered golden-cheeked warbler** nests here. Camping, picnicking, hiking, fishing, lake swimming, birding, bicycling.

Mission Tejas State Historic Site is a 363.5-acre park in Houston County. Situated 12 miles west of Alto via TX 21 and PR 44, the park was acquired from the Texas Forest Service in 1957. In the park is a replica of **Mission San Francisco de los Tejas**, the first mission in East Texas (1690). It was abandoned, then re-established 1716; abandoned again 1719; re-established again 1721; abandoned for last time in 1730 and moved to San Antonio. Also in park is restored **Rice Family Log Home**, built about 1828. Camping, hiking, fishing, picnicking.

Monahans Sandhills State Park consists of 3,840 acres of sand dunes, some up to 70 feet high, in Ward and Winkler counties 5 miles northeast of Monahans on IH 20 to PR 41. Land leased by state from private foundation until 2056. Dunes used as meeting place by raiding Indians. Camping, hiking, picnicking, sand-surfing. Scheduled tours. **Odessa meteor crater** is nearby, as is **Balmorhea State Park**.

Monument Hill State Historic Site and **Kreische Brewery State Historic Site** are operated as one park unit. Monument Hill consists of 40.4 acres one mile south of La Grange on US 77 to Spur Road 92 in Fayette County. Monument and tomb area acquired by state in 1907; additional acreage acquired from the Archbishop of San Antonio in 1956. Brewery and home purchased from private owners in 1977. Monument is dedicated to **Capt. Nicholas Dawson** and his men, who fought at **Salado Creek** in 1842, in Mexican **Gen. Woll's** invasion of Texas, and to the men of the "**black bean lottery**" (1843) of the **Mier Expedition**. Remains were brought to **Monument Hill** for reburial in 1848. Kreische Complex, on 36 acres, is linked to Monument Hill through interpretive trail. **Kreische Brewery State Historic Site** includes Kreische Brewery and stone-and-wood house built between 1850-1855 on Colorado River. One of **first commercial breweries** in state, it closed in 1884. Smokehouse and barn also in complex. Guided tours of brewery and house; call for schedule. Also picnicking, nature study.

Mother Neff State Park was the **first official state park** in Texas. It originated with 6 acres donated by Mrs. I. E. Neff, mother of **Pat M. Neff**, Governor of Texas from 1921 to 1925. Gov. Neff and Frank Smith donated remainder in 1934. The park, located 8 miles west of Moody on FM 107 and TX 236, now contains 259 acres along the Leon River in Coryell County. Heavily wooded. Camping, picnicking, fishing, hiking.

Mustang Island State Park, 3,954 acres on Gulf of Mexico in Nueces County, 14 miles south of Port Aransas on TX 361, was acquired from private owners in 1972. Mustang Island is a barrier island with a complicated ecosystem, dependent upon the sand dune. The foundation plants of the dunes are **sea oats, beach panic grass** and **soilbind morning glory**. Beach camping, picnicking; sun, sand and water activities. Excellent birding. **Padre Island National Seashore** 14 miles south.

National Museum of the Pacific War (formerly Admiral Nimitz Museum and Historical Center) is on 7 acres in downtown Fredericksburg. First established as a state agency in 1969 by Texas Legislature; transferred to TPW in 1981. George Bush Gallery opened in 1999. Named for **Adm. Chester W. Nimitz** of World War II fame, it includes the **Pacific War Museum** in the **Nimitz Steamboat Hotel**; the **Japanese Garden of Peace**, donated by the people of Japan; the **History Walk of the Pacific War**, featuring planes, boats and other equipment from World War II; and other special exhibits. Nearby is **Kerrville State Park**.

Old Fort Parker is a 37.5-acre park 4 miles north of Groesbeck on TX 14 in Limestone County. Deeded by private owners in 1936 and originally constructed by the Civilian Conservation Corps (CCC); rebuilt in 1967. Reconstructed fort is pioneer memorial and site of Cynthia Ann Parker abduction on May 19, 1836, by Comanche Indians. Nearby Fort Parker Cemetery has graves of those killed at the Fort in the 1836 raid. Historical study and picnicking. Living History events throughout year. Primitive skills classes/campouts by appointment. Groups welcome. Operated by the City of Groesbeck, 254-729-5253.

Palmetto State Park, a scenic park, is 270.3 acres 8 miles southeast of Luling on US 183 and PR 11 along the San Marcos River in Gonzales County. Land deeded in 1934-1936 by private owners and City of Gonzales. Named for **tropical dwarf palmetto** found there. Diverse plant and animal life; excellent birding. Also picnicking, fishing, hiking, pedal boats, swimming. Nearby **Gonzales** and **Ottine** important in early Texas history. Gonzales settled 1825 as center of **Green DeWitt's colonies**.

Palo Duro Canyon State Park consists of 16,402 acres 12 miles east of Canyon on TX 217 in Armstrong and Randall counties. The land was deeded by private owners in 1933 and is the scene of the annual summer production of the musical drama, "**Texas**." Spectacular one-million-year-old **scenic canyon** exposes rocks spanning about 200 million years of geological time. **Coronado** may have visited canyon in 1541. Canyon officially discovered by **Capt. R. B. Marcy** in 1852. Scene of decisive battle in 1874 between Comanche and Kiowa Indians and U.S. Army troops under **Gen. Ranald Mackenzie**. Also scene of ranching enterprise started by **Charles Goodnight** in 1876. Part of **state longhorn herd** is kept here. Camping, mountain biking, scenic drives, horseback and hiking trails, horse rentals.

Pedernales Falls State Park, 5,211.7 acres in Blanco County about 9 miles east of Johnson City on FM 2766 along Pedernales River, was acquired from private owners in 1970. Typical **Edwards Plateau** terrain, with **live oaks, deer, turkey** and **stone hills**. Camping, picnicking, hiking, swimming, tubing. Falls main scenic attraction.

Port Isabel Lighthouse State Historic Site consists of 0.9 acre in Port Isabel, Cameron County. Acquired by purchase from private owners in 1950, site includes **lighthouse** constructed in 1852; visitors can climb to top. Park is near sites of Civil War battle of **Palmito Ranch** (1865), and Mexican War battles of **Palo Alto** and **Resaca de la Palma (1846)**. Operated by City of Port Isabel.

Port Lavaca State Fishing Pier, a 10.8-acre recreational area on Lavaca Bay in Calhoun County, was acquired by transfer of authority from state highway department in 1963. The 24-hour, lighted, 3,200-foot-long fishing pier was created from former causeway. **Port Lavaca City Park**, at base of pier, offers a boat ramp and picnicking facilities. Operated by City of Port Lavaca.

Possum Kingdom State Park, west of Mineral Wells via US 180 and PR 33 in Palo Pinto County, is 1,528.7 acres adjacent to **Possum Kingdom Lake**, in **Palo Pinto Mountains** and **Brazos River Valley**. Rugged canyons home to **deer**, other wildlife. Acquired from the Brazos River Authority in 1940. Camping, picnicking, swimming, fishing, boating. Cabins available.

Purtis Creek State Park is 1,582.4 acres in Henderson and Van Zandt counties 3.5 miles north of Eustace on FM 316. Acquired in 1977 from private owners. Fishing, camping, hiking, picnicking, paddle boats and canoes.

Ray Roberts Lake State Park (Isle du Bois Unit), consists of 2,263 acres on the south side of Ray Roberts Lake on FM 455 in Denton County. **Johnson Branch Unit** contains 1,514 acres on north side of lake in Denton and Cooke counties 7 miles east of IH 30 on FM 3002. There are also six satellite parks. Land acquired in 1984 by lease from secretary of Army. Abundant and varied plant and animal life. Fishing, camping, picnicking, swimming, hiking, biking; tours of 19-century farm buildings at Johnson Branch. Includes Lantana Ridge Lodge on the east side of the lake. It is a full-service lodging facility with restaurant.

Rusk/Palestine State Park, a total of 136 acres, includes Rusk unit, adjacent to **Texas State Railroad Rusk Depot** off US 84 in Cherokee County, and Palestine unit, off US 84 adjacent to Texas State Railroad Palestine Depot. Fishing,

picnicking, camping, tennis courts, playground. **Train rides** in restored passenger cars (see also **Texas State Railroad State Historic Site**).

Sabine Pass Battleground State Historic Site in Jefferson County 1.5 miles south of Sabine Pass on Dick Dowling Road, contains 57.6 acres acquired from Kountze County Trust in 1972. **Lt. Richard W. Dowling**, with small Confederate force, repelled an attempted 1863 invasion of Texas by Union gunboats. **Monument, World War II ammunition bunkers**. Fishing, picnicking, camping.

Sam Bell Maxey House State Historic Site, at the corner of So. Church and Washington streets in Paris, Lamar County, was donated by City of Paris in 1976. Consists of .4 acre with 1868 Victorian Italianate-style frame house, plus outbuildings. Most of furnishings accumulated by Maxey family. Maxey served in Mexican and Civil wars and was two-term U.S. Senator. House is on the **National Register of Historic Places**. Open for tours Friday through Sunday.

San Angelo State Park, on **O.C. Fisher Reservoir** adjacent to the city of San Angelo in Tom Green County, contains 7,677 acres of land, most of which will remain undeveloped. Leased from U.S. Corps of Engineers in 1995. Access is from US 87 or 67, then FM 2288. Highly diversified plant and animal life. Activities include boating, water activities, hiking, mountain biking, horseback riding, camping, picnicking. Part of **state longhorn herd** is here. Nearby is **Fort Concho**.

San Jacinto Battleground State Historic Site and **Battleship Texas State Historic Site** are located 20 miles east of downtown Houston off TX 225 east to TX 134 to PR 1836 in east Harris County. The park is 1,200 acres with 570-foot-tall monument erected in 1936-1939 in honor of Texans who defeated Mexican **Gen. Antonio López de Santa Anna** on April 21, 1836, to win Texas' independence from Mexico. The park is original site of Texans' camp acquired in 1883. Subsequent acquisitions made in 1897, 1899 and 1985. Park transferred to TPW in 1965. Park registered as **National Historic Landmark**. Elevator ride to observation tower near top of monument; museum. Monument known as **tallest free-standing concrete structure in the world** at the time it was erected. Interpretive trail around battleground. Adjacent to park is the **U.S.S. Texas**, commissioned in 1914. The battleship, the only survivor of the dreadnought class and the only surviving veteran of two world wars, was donated to people of Texas by U.S. Navy. Ship was moored in the Houston Ship Channel at the **San Jacinto Battleground** on San Jacinto Day, 1948. Extensive repairs were done 1988-1990. Some renovation is on-going, but ship is open for tours. Ship closed Christmas Eve and Christmas Day.

Sea Rim State Park in Jefferson County, 20 miles south of Port Arthur, off TX 87, contains 4,141 acres of marshland and 5.2 miles of **Gulf beach shoreline**, acquired from private owners in 1972. It is prime wintering area for **waterfowl**. Wetlands also shelter such wildlife as river otter, nutria, alligator, mink, muskrat. Camping, fishing, swimming; wildlife observation; nature trail; boating. **Airboat tours of marsh**. Near McFaddin National Wildlife Refuge.

Sebastopol State Historic Site at 704 Zorn Street in Seguin, Guadalupe County, was acquired by purchase in 1976 from Seguin Conservation Society; approximately 2.2 acres. Built about 1856 by **Col. Joshua W. Young** of **limecrete**, concrete made from local gravel and lime, the Greek Revival-style house, which was restored to its 1880 appearance by the TPW, is on National Register of Historic Places. Tours available Friday and Sunday. Also of interest in the area is historic **Seguin**, founded 1838.

Seminole Canyon State Historic Site in Val Verde County, 9 miles west of Comstock off US 90, contains 2,172.5 acres; acquired by purchase from private owners 1973-1977. **Fate Bell Shelter** in canyon contains several important **prehistoric Indian pictographs**. Historic interpretive center. Tours of rock-art sites Wednesday-Sunday; also hiking, mountain biking, camping.

Sheldon Lake State Park & Wildlife Management Area, 2,800 acres in Harris County on Garrett Road 20 miles east of Beltway 8. Acquired by purchase in 1952 from the City of Houston. Freshwater marsh habitat. Activities include nature study, birding, fishing. Wildscape gardens of native plants.

Fall foliage in Tyler State Park. John Crawley photo.

South Llano River State Park, 5 miles south of Junction in Kimble County off US 377, is a 524-acre site. Land donated to the TPW by private owner in 1977. Wooded bottomland along the winding South Llano River is **largest and oldest winter roosting site for the Rio Grande turkey** in Central Texas. Roosting area closed to visitors October-March. Other animals include **wood ducks, javelina, fox, beaver, bobcat** and **armadillo**. Camping, picnicking, tubing, swimming and fishing, hiking, mountain biking.

Starr Family State Historic Site, 3.1 acres at 407 W. Travis in Marshall, Harrison County. Greek Revival-style mansion, **Maplecroft**, built 1870-1871, was home to four generations of Starr family, powerful and economically influential Texans. Two other family homes also in park. Acquired by gift in 1976; additional land donated in 1982. Maplecroft is on National Register of Historic Places. Tours Friday–Sunday or by appointment. Special events during year.

Stephen F. Austin State Historic Site is 663.3 acres along the Brazos River in San Felipe, Austin County, named for the **"Father of Texas."** The area was deeded by the San Felipe de Austin Corporation and the **San Felipe** Park Association in 1940. Site of township of San Felipe was seat of government where conventions of 1832 and 1833 and Consultation of 1835 held. These led to **Texas Declaration of Independence**. San Felipe was home of **Stephen F. Austin** and other famous early Texans; home of **Texas' first Anglo newspaper (the Texas Gazette)** founded in 1829; postal system of Texas originated here. Area called **"Cradle of Texas**

Liberty." Museum. Camping, picnicking, golf, fishing, hiking.

Texas State Railroad State Historic Site, in Anderson and Cherokee counties between the cities of Palestine and Rusk, adjacent to US 84, contains 499 acres. Acquired by Legislative Act in 1971. Trains run seasonal schedules on 25.5 miles of track. Call for information and reservations: In Texas 1-800-442-8951; outside 903-683-2561. Railroad built by the State of Texas to support the **state-owned iron works** at Rusk. Begun in 1893, and built largely by inmates from the state prison system, the railroad was gradually extended until it reached Palestine in 1909 and established regular rail service between the towns. (See also **Rusk/Palestine State Park**.)

Tyler State Park is 985.5 acres 2 miles north of IH 20 on FM 14 north of Tyler in Smith County. Includes 64-acre lake. The land was deeded by private owners in 1934–1935. Heavily wooded. Camping, hiking, fishing, boating, lake swimming. Nearby Tyler called **rose capital of world, with Tyler Rose Garden and annual Tyler Rose Festival**. Also in Tyler are **Caldwell Children's Zoo** and **Goodman Museum**.

Varner-Hogg Plantation State Historic Site is 66 acres in Brazoria County two miles north of West Columbia on FM 2852. Land originally owned by Martin Varner, a member of Stephen F. Austin's **"Old Three Hundred"** colony; later was home of Texas governor **James Stephen Hogg**. Property was deeded to the state in 1957 by Miss Ima Hogg, Gov. Hogg's daughter. **First rum distillery** in Texas established in 1829 by Varner. Mansion tours Tuesday through Saturday. Also picnicking, fishing.

Village Creek State Park, comprising 1,004 heavily forested acres, is located in Lumberton, Hardin County, 10 miles north of Beaumont off US 69 and FM 3513. Purchased in 1979 from private owner, the park contains abundant flora and fauna typical of the Big Thicket area. The **200 species of birds** found here include wood ducks, egrets and herons. Activities include fishing, camping, canoeing, swimming, hiking and picnicking. Nearby is the **Big Thicket National Preserve**.

Walter Umphrey State Park is operated by Jefferson County. For RV site reservations, contact SGS Causeway Bait & Tackle, 409-985-4811.

Washington-on-the-Brazos State Historic Site consists of 293.1 acres 7 miles southwest of Navasota in Washington County on TX 105 and FM 1155. Land acquired by deed from private owners in 1916, 1976 and 1996. Park includes the site of the signing on March 2, 1836, of the **Texas Declaration of Independence** from Mexico, as well as the site of the later **signing of the Constitution of the Republic of Texas**. In 1842 and 1845, the land included the **capitol of the Republic**. Daily tours of Barrington, restored **home of Anson Jones, last president of the Republic of Texas. Star of the Republic Museum**. Activities include picnicking and birding.

Wyler Aerial Tramway Franklin Mountains State Park features an aerial cable-car tramway on 195 acres of rugged mountain on east side of Franklin Mountains in El Paso. Purchase tickets at tramway station on McKinley Avenue to ride in Swiss-made gondola to 5,632-foot Ranger Peak. Passengers view cacti, rock formations, wildlife and 7,000 square miles of Texas, New Mexico and Mexico. Accessible ramps and paved grounds at top lead to observation deck with 360-degree view. Check with park for fees and hours; 915-566-6622. Other area attractions include Franklin Mountains State Park, Hueco Tanks State Historic Site and Magoffin Home State Historic Site. ☆

National Parks, Historical Sites, Recreation Areas in Texas

Below are listed the facilities in and the activities that can be enjoyed at the two national parks, a national seashore, a biological preserve, several historic sites, memorials and recreation areas in Texas. They are under supervision of the **U.S. Department of Interior**. On the Web: **www.nps.gov/parks/search.htm**; under "Select State," choose "Texas." In addition, the recreational opportunities in the national forests and national grasslands in Texas, under the jurisdiction of the **U.S. Department of Agriculture**, are listed at the end of the article.

Alibates Flint Quarries National Monument consists of 1,371 acres in Potter County. For more than 10,000 years, **pre-Columbian Indians** dug **agatized limestone** from the quarries to make projectile points, knives, scrapers and other tools. The area is presently undeveloped. You may visit the flint quarries on **guided walking tours** with a park ranger. Tours are at 10:00 a.m. and 2:00 p.m. from Memorial Day to Labor Day. Off-season tours can be arranged by writing to Lake Meredith National Recreation Area, Box 1460, Fritch 79036, or by calling 806-857-3151.

Amistad National Recreation Area is located on the U.S. side of **Amistad Reservoir**, an international reservoir on the Texas-Mexico border. The 57,292-acre park's attractions include **boating, water skiing, swimming, fishing, camping** and archaeological sites. If lake level is normal, visitors can see **4000-year-old prehistoric pictographs** in Panther and Parida caves, which are accessible only by boat. Check with park before visiting. The area is **one of the densest concentrations of Archaic rock art in North America** — more than 300 sites. Commercial campgrounds, motels and restaurants nearby. Marinas located at Diablo East and Rough Canyon. Open year round. NPS Administration, 4121 Hwy. 90 W, Del Rio 78840; 830-775-7491.

Big Bend National Park, established in 1944, has spectacular **mountain and desert scenery** and a variety of unusual **geological structures**. It is the **nation's largest** protected area of **Chihuahuan Desert**. Located in the great bend of the Rio Grande, the 801,000-acre park, which is part of the **international boundary** between the United States and Mexico, was designated a **U.S. Biosphere Reserve** in 1976. **Hiking, birding and float trips** are popular. Numerous campsites are located in park, and the **Chisos Mountain Lodge** has accommodations for approximately 345 guests. Write for reservations to National Park Concessions, Inc., Big Bend National Park, Texas 79834; 915-477-2291; www.chisosmountainslodge.com. Park open year round; facilities most crowded during spring break. PO Box 129, Big Bend National Park 79834; 915-477-2251.

Big Thicket National Preserve, established in 1974, consists of 13 separate units totalling 97,000 acres of diverse flora and fauna, often nicknamed the **"biological crossroads of North America."** The preserve, which includes parts of seven East Texas counties, has been designated an **"International Biosphere Reserve"** by the United Nations Educational, Scientific and Cultural Organization (UNESCO).

A park ranger canoes on the Rio Grande through Santa Elena Canyon in Big Bend National Park. Erich Schlegel photo.

The preserve includes **four different ecological systems**: southeastern swamps, eastern forests, central plains and southwestern deserts. The visitor information station is located on FM 420, seven miles north of Kountze; phone 409-951-6725. Open daily from 9 a.m. to 5 p.m. Naturalist activities are available by reservation only; reservations are made through the station. **Nine trails**, ranging in length from one-half mile to 18 miles, visit a variety of forest communities. The two shortest trails are handicapped accessible. Trails are open year round, but flooding may occur after heavy rains. Horses permitted on the **Big Sandy Horse Trail** only. Boating and canoeing are popular on preserve corridor units. Park headquarters are at 3785 Milam, Beaumont 77701; 409-246-2337.

Chamizal National Memorial, established in 1963 and opened to the public in 1973, stands as a monument to Mexican-American friendship and goodwill. The memorial, on 52 acres in El Paso, commemorates the peaceful settlement on Aug. 29, 1963, of a **99-year-old boundary dispute between the United States and Mexico**. Chamizal uses the visual and performing arts as a medium of interchange, helping people better understand not only other cultures but their own, as well. It hosts a variety of programs throughout the year, including: the fall **Chamizal Festival** musical event; the **Siglo de Oro** drama festival (early March); the **Oñate Historical Festival** celebrating the First Thanksgiving (April); and **Music Under the Stars** (Sundays, June-August). The park has a 1.8-mile walking trail and picnic areas. Phone: 915-532-7273.

Fort Davis National Historic Site in Jeff Davis County was a key post in the West Texas defense system, guarding immigrants and tradesmen on the San Antonio-El Paso road from 1854 to 1891. At one time, Fort Davis was manned by black troops, called **"Buffalo Soldiers"** (because of their curly hair) who fought with great distinction in the Indian Wars. **Henry O. Flipper, the first black graduate of West Point**, served at Fort Davis in the early 1880s. The 474-acre historic site is located on the north edge of the town of Fort Davis in the **Davis Mountains**, the second-highest mountain range in the state. The site includes a museum, an auditorium with daily audio-visual programs, restored and refurnished buildings, picnic area and hiking trails. Open year round except Christmas Day. PO Box 1379, Fort Davis 79734; 915-426-3224.

Guadalupe Mountains National Park, established in 1972, includes 86,416 acres in Hudspeth and Culberson counties. The Park contains one of the most **extensive fos-**

Cypress trees show their fall colors in the Big Thicket National Preserve. Ron Billings photo; Texas Forest Service.

sil **reefs** on record. Deep **canyons** cut through this reef and provide a rare opportunity for geological study. Special points of interest are **McKittrick Canyon**, a fragile riparian environment, and **Guadalupe Peak**, the highest in Texas. Camping, hiking on 80 miles of trails, Frijole Ranch Museum, summer amphitheater programs. Orientation, free information and natural history exhibits available at Visitor Center. Open year round. Lodging at Van Horn, Texas, and White's City or Carlsbad, NM. HC 60, Box 400, Salt Flat 79847; 915-828-3251.

Lake Meredith National Recreation Area, 30 miles northeast of Amarillo, centers on a reservoir on the Canadian River, in Moore, Hutchinson and Potter counties. The 50,000-acre recreational area is popular for water-based activities. Boat ramps, picnic areas, unimproved campsites. Commercial lodging and trailer hookups available in nearby towns. Open year round. PO Box 1460, Fritch 79036; 806-857-3151.

Lyndon B. Johnson National Historic Site includes two separate districts 14 miles apart. The **Johnson City District** comprises the **boyhood home of the 36th President of United States** and the **Johnson Settlement**, where his grandparents resided during the late 1800s. The **LBJ Ranch District** can be visited only by taking the National Park Service bus tour starting at the LBJ State Historic Site. The tour includes the reconstructed **LBJ Birthplace**, old school, family cemetery, show barn and a view of the **Texas White House**. Site in Blanco and Gillespie counties was established in 1969, and contains 1,570 acres, 674 of which are federal. Open year round except Thanksgiving, Christmas Day and New Year's Day. No camping on site; commercial campgrounds, motels in area. PO Box 329, Johnson City 78636; 830-868-7128.

Padre Island National Seashore consists of a 67.5-mile stretch of a barrier island along the Gulf Coast; noted for white-sand beaches, excellent fishing and abundant bird and marine life. Contains 133,000 acres in Kleberg, Willacy and Kenedy counties. Open year round. One paved campground (fee charged) located north of Malaquite Beach; unpaved (primitive) campground area south on beach. Five miles of beach are accessible by regular vehicles; 55 miles are accessible only by 4x4 vehicles. Off-road vehicles prohibited. Camping permitted in two designated areas. Commercial lodging avail-

able on the island outside the National Seashore boundaries. PO Box 181300, Corpus Christi 78480; 361-949-8068.

Palo Alto Battlefield National Historic Site, Brownsville, preserves the site of the **first major battle in the Mexican-American War**. Fought on May 8, 1846, it is recognized for the innovative use of light or "flying" artillery. Participating in the battle were three future presidents: **General Zachary Taylor and Ulysses S. Grant** on the U.S. side, and **Gen. Mariano Arista** on the Mexican. Historical markers are located at the junction of Farm-to-Market roads 1847 and 511. Access to the 3,400-acre site is currently limited. Exhibits at the park's interim visitor center, at 1623 Central Blvd., Ste. 213 in Brownsville (78520), interpret the battle as well as the causes and consequences of the war. Phone 956-541-2785.

Rio Grande Wild and Scenic River is a 196-mile strip on the U.S. shore of the Rio Grande in the **Chihuahuan Desert**, beginning in Big Bend National Park and continuing downstream to the Terrell-Val Verde County line. There are federal facilities in Big Bend National Park only. Contact Big Bend National Park for more information.

San Antonio Missions National Historic Site preserves four Spanish Colonial Missions — **Concepción, San José, San Juan and Espada** — as well as the Espada dam and aqueduct, which are two of the best-preserved remains in the United States of the **Spanish Colonial irrigation system**, and Rancho de las Cabras, the colonial ranch of Mission Espada. All were crucial elements to Spanish settlement on the Texas frontier. When Franciscan attempts to establish a chain of missions in East Texas in the late 1600s failed, the Spanish Crown ordered three missions transferred to the San Antonio River valley in 1731.

The missions are located within the city limits of **San Antonio**, while **Rancho de las Cabras** is located 25 miles south in Wilson County near **Floresville**. The four missions, which are still in use as active parishes, are open to the public from 9 a.m. to 5 p.m. daily except Thanksgiving, Christmas and New Year's. Public roadways connect the sites; a hike-bike trail is being developed. The visitor center for the mission complex is at San José. For more information, write to 2202 Roosevelt Ave., San Antonio 78210; 210-534-8833 or 210-

932-1001. For more information about the missions, see the story, "Franciscan Missionaries in Texas before 1690" at www. texasalmanac.com/history/highlights/.

Recreation in the National Forests

For general information about the National Forests and National Grasslands, see page 103 in the Environment section.

An estimated 3 million people visit the National Forests in Texas for recreation annually. These visitors use established recreation areas primarily for hiking, picnicking, swimming, fishing, camping, boating and nature enjoyment. In the following list of some of these areas, Forest Service Road is abbreviated FSR:

Angelina NF

Bouton Lake, 7 miles southeast of Zavalla off Texas 63 and FSR 303, has a 9-acre natural lake with primitive facilities for camping, picnicking and fishing. Boykin Springs, 11 miles southeast of Zavalla, has a 6-acre lake and facilities for hiking, swimming, picnicking, fishing and camping.

Caney Creek on Sam Rayburn Reservoir, 10 miles southeast of Zavalla off FM 2743, offers fishing, boating and picnicking. Sandy Creek, 15.5 miles east of Zavalla on Sam Rayburn, offers fishing, boating and picnicking.

The Sawmill Hiking Trail is 5.5 miles long and winds from Bouton Lake to Boykin Springs Recreation Area.

Davy Crockett NF

Ratcliff Lake, 25 miles west of Lufkin on Texas 7, includes

Recreational Facilities,
Corps of Engineers Lakes, 2006

Source: Southwestern Division, Corps of Engineers, Dallas

Reservoir	Swim Areas	Boat Ramps	Picnic Sites	Camp Sites	Rental Units	Visitor Hours, 2006
Aquilla	0	3	0	0	0	237,700
Bardwell	3	6	47	155	0	677,200
Belton	4	21	368	278	0	16,407,200
Benbrook	2	16	109	186	0	2,934,700
Buffalo Bayou*	0	0	848	0	0	12,165,800
Canyon	5	18	189	497	24	2,016,900
Cooper	2	5	110	329	14	2,572,700
Georgetown	1	3	100	224	0	2,000,800
Granger	2	5	129	143	0	1,498,600
Grapevine	1	12	139	161	0	7,492,500
Hords Creek	3	9	8	136	0	3,306,900
Joe Pool	3	7	315	556	0	6,137,000
Lake O' the Pines	7	33	148	495	0	9,050,200
Lavon	3	22	209	280	0	4,315,700
Lewsville	7	24	349	615	5	19,974,200
Navarro Mills	3	6	26	255	0	4,087,300
O.C. Fisher	0	13	75	61	0	637,100
Pat Mayse**	3	9	0	216	0	1,425,100
Proctor	5	6	39	216	0	2,590,200
Ray Roberts	2	11	291	371	30	21,491,300
Sam Rayburn	4	36	21	737	61	18,312,600
Somerville	2	12	150	949	21	15,028,800
Stillhouse Hollow	3	5	75	67	0	4,136,500
Texoma**†	3	25	110	669	370	90,236,100
Town Bluff	2	13	81	370	1	3,654,700
Waco	3	12	143	281	0	4,425,200
Wallisville*	0	2	10	0	0	231,500
Whitney	3	26	47	764	0	4,242,400
Wright Patman	4	22	203	578	0	11,050,000
Totals	80	382	4,348	9,589	526	273,270,000

All above lakes managed by the Fort Worth District, U.S. Army Corps of Engineers, with the following exceptions:
* Includes both Addicks and Barker Dams; managed by Galveston District, USACE.
**Managed by Tulsa District, USACE.
†Figures for facilities on Texas side of lake. Visitation is for entire lake.

a 45-acre lake and facilities for picnicking, hiking, swimming, boating, fishing and camping. There is also an amphitheater. The 20-mile-long 4C National Recreation Trail connects Ratcliff Recreation Area to the Neches Bluff overlook. The Piney Creek Horse Trail, 54 miles long, can be entered approximately 5.5 miles south of Kennard off FSR 514. There are two horse camps along the trail.

Sabine NF

Indian Mounds Recreation Area, accessible via FM 83 3.5 miles east of Hemphill, has camping facilities and a boat-launch ramp. Lakeview, on Toledo Bend Reservoir 20 miles from Pineland, offers camping, hiking, boating and fishing and can be reached via Texas 87, FM 2928 and FSR 120.

Ragtown, 21 miles southeast of Center and accessible by Texas 87 and Texas 139, County Road 3184 and FSR 132, is also on Toledo Bend and has facilities for hiking, camping and boating. Red Hill Lake, 3 miles north of Milam on Texas 87, has facilities for hiking, fishing, swimming, camping and picnicking. Willow Oak Recreation Area, on Toledo Bend 11 miles south of Hemphill off Texas 87, offers fishing, picnicking, camping and boating.

Trail Between the Lakes is 28 miles long from Lakeview Recreation Area on Toledo Bend to U.S. 96 near Sam Rayburn Reservoir.

Sam Houston NF

Cagle Recreation Area is located on the shores of Lake Conroe, 50 miles north of Houston and 5 miles west of I-45 at FM 1375. Cagle offers camping, fishing, hiking, birding and other recreational opportunities in a forested lakeside setting. Double Lake, 3 miles south of Coldspring on FM 2025, has facilities for picnicking, hiking, camping, swimming and fishing. Stubblefield Lake, 15 miles west-northwest of New Waverly off Texas 1375 on the shores of Lake Conroe, has facilities for camping, hiking, picnicking and fishing.

The Lone Star Hiking Trail, approximately 128 miles long, is located in Sam Houston National Forest in Montgomery, Walker and San Jacinto counties.

Recreation on the National Grasslands

North Texas

Lake Davy Crockett Recreation Area, 12 miles north of Honey Grove on FM 409, just off FM 100, has a boat-launch ramp and camping sites on a 450-acre lake.

Coffee Mill Lake Recreation Area has camping and picnicking facilities on a 650-acre lake. This area is 4 miles west of Lake Davy Crockett Recreation Area.

The Caddo Multi-Use Trail system, also 4 miles west of Lake Davy Crockett, offers camping, hiking and horseback riding on 35 miles of trails.

Black Creek Lake Recreation Area is 8 miles north of Decatur and has camping, picnic facilities and a boat-launch ramp on a 35-acre lake.

Cottonwood Lake, 13 miles north of Decatur, is around 40 acres and offers hiking, boating and fishing.

The Cottonwood-Black Creek Hiking Trail is 4 miles long and connects the two lakes. It is rated moderately difficult. There are nearly 75 miles of multipurpose trails which run in the Cottonwood Lake vicinity.

TADRA Horse Trail, 10 miles north of Decatur, has camping and 35 miles of horse trails. Restrooms and and parking facilities are available.

West Texas

Lake McClellan in Gray County and Lake Marvin, which is part of the Black Kettle National Grassland in Hemphill County, receive more than 28,000 recreation visitors annually. These areas provide camping, picnicking, fishing, birdwatching and boating facilities. Concessionaires operate facilities at Lake McClellan, and a nominal fee is charged for use of the areas. Thompson Grove Picnic Area is 14 miles northeast of Texline.

At the Rita Blanca National Grassland, about 4,500 visitors a year enjoy picnicking and hunting. ☆

National Natural Landmarks in Texas

Nineteen Texas natural areas have been listed on the **National Registry of Natural Landmarks**.

The registry was established by the Secretary of the Interior in 1962 to identify and encourage the preservation of geological and ecological features that represent nationally significant examples of the nation's natural heritage.

The registry currently lists a total of 587 national natural landmarks. Texas areas on the list, as of August 2001, and their characteristics, are these (dates of listing in parentheses):

Attwater Prairie Chicken Preserve, Colorado County, 55 miles west of Houston in the national wildlife refuge, is rejuvenated Gulf Coastal Prairie, which is habitat for Attwater's prairie chickens. (April 1968)

Bayside Resaca Area, Cameron County, Laguna Atascosa National Wildlife Refuge, 28 miles north of Brownsville. Excellent example of a resaca, supporting coastal salt-marsh vegetation and rare birds. (Aug. 1980)

Catfish Creek, Anderson County, 20 miles northwest of Palestine, is undisturbed riparian habitat. (June 1983)

Caverns of Sonora, Sutton County, 16 miles southwest of Sonora, has unusual geological formations. (Oct. 1965)

Devil's Sink Hole, Edwards County, 9 miles northeast of Rocksprings, Is a deep, bell-shaped, collapsed limestone sink with cave passages extending below the regional water table. (Oct. 1972)

Dinosaur Valley, Somervell County, in Dinosaur Valley State Park, four miles west of Glen Rose, contains fossil footprints exposed in bed of Paluxy River. (Oct. 1968)

Enchanted Rock, Gillespie and Llano counties, 12 miles southwest of Oxford, is a classic batholith, composed of coarse-grained pink granite. (Oct. 1971)

Ezell's Cave, Hays County, within the city limits of San Marcos, houses at least 36 species of cave creatures. (Oct. 1971)

Fort Worth Nature Center and Refuge, Tarrant County, within the Fort Worth city limits. Contains remnants of the Grand Prairie and a portion of the Cross Timbers, with limestone ledges and marshes. Refuge for migratory birds and other wildlife, and home to 11 buffalo raised by the center's staff. Educational programs offered for youth and adults. Self-guided hiking. (Nov. 1980)

Greenwood Canyon, Montague County, along a tributary of Braden Branch, is a rich source of Cretaceous fossils. (May 1975)

High Plains Natural Area, Randall County, Buffalo Lake National Wildlife Refuge, 26 miles southwest of Amarillo, is a grama-buffalo shortgrass area. (Aug. 1980)

Little Blanco River Bluff, Blanco County, comprises an Edwards Plateau limestone-bluff plant community. (May 1982)

Longhorn Cavern, Burnet County, 11 miles southwest of Burnet. Formed at least 450 million years ago, cave contains several unusual geologic features. (Oct. 1971)

Lost Maples State Natural Area, Bandera and Real

Lost Maples State Natural Area is a National Natural Landmark and is known for brilliant fall foliage. Texas Parks & Wildlife photo.

counties, 61 miles northwest of San Antonio, contains Edwards Plateau fauna and flora, including unusual bigtooth maple. Largest known nesting population of golden-cheeked warbler. (Feb. 1980)

Muleshoe National Wildlife Refuge, Bailey County, 59 miles northwest of Lubbock, contains playa lakes and typical High Plains shortgrass grama grasslands. (Aug. 1980)

Natural Bridge Caverns, Comal County, 16 miles west of new Braunfels, is a multilevel cavern system, with beautiful and unusual geological formations. (Oct. 1971)

Odessa Meteor Crater, Ector County, 10 miles southwest of Odessa, is one of only two known meteor sites in the country. (April 1965)

Palo Duro Canyon State Park, Armstrong and Randall counties, 22 miles south-southwest of Amarillo. Cut by waters of the Red River, it contains cross-sectional views of sedimentary rocks representing four geological periods. (May 1976)

Santa Ana National Wildlife Refuge, Hidalgo County, 7 miles south of Alamo, is a lowland forested area with jungle-like vegetation. It is habitat for more than 300 species of birds and some rare mammals. (Oct. 1966) ☆

Birding in Texas

World Birding Center

The World Birding Center comprises nine birding education centers and observation sites in the Lower Rio Grande Valley designed to protect wildlife habitat and offer visitors a view of more than 500 species of birds. The center has partnered with the Texas Parks and Wildlife Department, the U.S. Fish and Wildlife Service and nine communities to turn 10,000 acres back into natural areas for birds, butterflies and other wildlife.

This area in Cameron, Hidalgo and Starr counties is a natural migratory path for millions of birds that move between the Americas. The nine WBC sites are situated along the border with Mexico:

Bentsen-Rio Grande Valley State Park

This is the World Birding Center Headquarters and comprises the 760-acre Bentsen-RGV State Park and1,700 acres of adjoining federal refuge land near **Mission.** The site offers: daily tram service; 4 nature trails ranging in length from 1/4 mile to 2 miles; 2-story high Hawk Observation Tower with a 210-foot-long handicapped access ramp; 2 observation decks; 2 accessible bird blinds; primitive camping sites (by reservation); rest areas; picnic sites with tables; exhibit hall; park store; coffee bar; meeting room (available for rental); catering kitchen; bike rentals (1 and 2 seat bikes). Access within the park is by foot, bike and tram only; (956) 585-1107. **Hours:** 6 a.m. to 10 p.m., seven days a week.

Edinburg Scenic Wetlands

This 40-acre wetlands in **Edinburg** is an oasis for water-loving birds, butterflies and other wildlife. The site is currently offering:walking trails, nature tours and classes; (956) 381-9922. **Hours:** 8 a.m. – 5 p.m., Monday through Wednesday; 8 a.m.–6 p.m., Thursday through Saturday. Closed Sunday.

Estero Llano Grande State Park

This 176-acre refuge in **Weslaco** attracts a wide array of South Texas wildlife with its varied landscape of shallow lake, woodlands and thorn forest; 956-565-3919. **Hours:** 8 a.m.–5 p.m., Monday through Friday; 8 a.m.–7:30 p.m., Saturday and Sunday through August.

Harlingen Arroyo Colorado

This site in **Harlingen** is connected by an arroyo waterway, as well as hike-and-bike trails meandering through the city, Hugh Ramsey Nature Park to the east and the Harlingen Thicket to the west; (956) 427-8873. **Hours:** Office, 8 a.m.–5:00 p.m., Monday through Friday. Nature trails are open seven days a week, sunrise to sunset.

Old Hidalgo Pumphouse

Visitors to this museum in **Hidalgo** on the Rio Grande can learn about the steam-driven irrigation pumps that transformed Hidalgo County into a year-round farming area. The museum's grounds feature hummingbird gardens, walking trails and historic tours; (956) 843-8686. **Hours:** 10 a.m.–5 p.m., Monday through Friday; 1 p.m.–5 p.m., Sunday. Closed Saturday.

Quinta Mazatlan

This 1930s country estate in **McAllen** is a historic Spanish Revival adobe hacienda surrounded by lush tropical landscaping and native woodland. It is also an urban oasis, where quiet trails wind through more than 15 acres of birding habitat; (956) 688-3370. **Hours:** 8 a.m.–5 p.m., Tuesday through Saturday. Open until sunset on Thursdays. Closed Mondays and holidays.

Resaca de la Palma State Park

More than 1,700 acres of newly opened wilderness near **Brownsville,** this site comprises the largest tract of native habitat in the World Birding Center network. The park offers birding tours and natural history tours. Admission is by

Visitors enjoy the sites at the Bentsen-Rio Grande Valley State Park. Texas Parks & Wildlife photo.

appointment and reservation only; (956) 565-3919.

Roma Bluffs

History and nature meet on scenic bluffs above the Rio Grande, where the World Birding Center in **Roma** is located on the old plaza of a once-thriving steamboat port. Part of a national historic district, the WBC Roma Bluffs includes a riverside nature area of three acres in Starr County. The site offers: walking trails, canoe trips, birding tours, natural history tours and classes; (956) 849-4930. **Hours:** 8 a.m.–4:00 p.m. Tuesday through Saturday, although trails are open seven days a week and are free to the public.

South Padre Island Birding and Nature Center

At the southern tip of the world's longest barrier island, **South Padre Island** Birding and Nature Center is a slender thread of land between the shallow Laguna Madre and the Gulf of Mexico. This site offers: a nature trail boardwalk and birding tours; 1-800-SOPADRE. **Hours:** 9 a.m.–5 p.m., seven days a week.

Great Texas Coastal Birding Trail

The Great Texas Coastal Birding Trail winds its way through 43 Texas counties along the entire Texas coast. The trail, completed in April 2000, is divided into upper, central and lower coastal regions. It includes 308 wildlife-viewing sites and such amenities as boardwalks, parking pullouts, kiosks, observation platforms and landscaping to attract native wildlife.

Color-coded maps are available, and signs mark each site. Trail maps contain information about the birds and habitats likely to be found at each site, the best season to visit, and food and lodging.

For information, contact: Nature Tourism Coordinator, Texas Parks and Wildlife, 4200 Smith School Road, Austin, TX 78744; 512-389-4396. On the Web at www.tpwd.state. tx.us/huntwild/wild/wildlife_trails/. ☆

Freshwater and Saltwater Fish and Fishing

Source: Texas Parks and Wildlife Department.

Freshwater Fish and Fishing

In Texas, **247 species of freshwater fish** are found. This includes 78 species that inhabit areas with low salinity and can be found in rivers entering the Gulf of Mexico. Also included in that total are 18 species that are not native, but were introduced into the state.

The estimated **number of freshwater recreational anglers** is 1.84 million, with annual expenditures of $1.49 billion annually. Catch-and-release fishing has emerged on the Texas scene as the conservation theme of anglers who desire continued quality fishing.

The **most popular fish** for recreational fishing are largemouth bass; catfish; crappie; and striped, white and hybrid striped bass.

The **Texas Parks and Wildlife Department** (TPWD) operates field stations, fish hatcheries and research facilities to support the conservation and management of fishery resources.

TPWD has continued its programs of stocking fish in public waters to increase angling opportunities. The hatcheries operated by TPWD raise largemouth and smallmouth bass, as well as catfish, striped and hybrid striped bass and sunfish.

An angler on the Pedernales River fly fishes for white bass at the Milton Reimers Ranch Park. Eric Schlegel photo.

Texas Freshwater Fisheries Center

The Texas Freshwater Fisheries Center in Athens, about 75 miles southeast of Dallas, is an $18 million hatchery, aquarium and educational center, where visitors can learn about the underwater life in Texas' freshwater streams, ponds and lakes.

The 24,000-square-foot hatchery and research facility concentrates on genetic research and the production of Florida largemouth bass for restocking Texas reservoirs and rivers.

The interactive Cox Visitors Center includes aquarium displays of fish in their natural environment. Visitors get an "eye-to-eye" view of three authentically designed Texas freshwater habitats: a Hill Country stream, an East Texas pond and a reservoir. A marsh exhibit features live American alligators.

Through touch-screen computer exhibits, visitors can learn more about fish habitats, life cycles and the importance of catch-and-release fishing. Daily dive shows featuring hand-feeding of fish are followed by tram tours of the hatchery.

A casting pond stocked with rainbow trout in the winter and catfish in the summer provides a place for visitors to learn how to bait a hook, cast a line and land a fish. A 0.8 mile self-guided wetlands trail explains how land and water create special habitats for plants, birds and other living things. The center has conference facilities, hosts school and tour groups by appointment and holds special events throughout the year. See the calendar at http://www.tpwd.state.tx.us/spdest/visitorcenters/tffc/.

The center is a cooperative effort of Texas Parks and Wildlife Department, the U.S. Fish and Wildlife Service, the City of Athens and private organizations.

The Texas Freshwater Fisheries Center is open Tuesday through Saturday, 9 a.m. to 4 p.m., and Sunday, 1 to 4 p.m. It is closed on Monday. Admission is charged.

The Center is located four-and-a-half miles east of Athens on FM 2495 at Lake Athens. Address: 5550 Flat Creek Road, Athens 75751, or call 903-676-2277.

Saltwater Fish and Fishing

There are about 1 million saltwater anglers in Texas (6 years old and older) who have a $1.328 billion economic im-

pact annually. Catch averaged 2,321,100 fish annually in the 10 years between 1993–2003 for both Texas bays and the Gulf of Mexico off Texas combined.

The most popular saltwater sport fish in Texas bays are spotted seatrout, sand seatrout, Atlantic croaker, red drum, southern flounder, black drum, sheepshead and gafftopsail catfish. Offshore, some of the fish anglers target are red snapper, king mackerel, dolphin (fish), spotted seatrout, tarpon and yellowfin tuna.

Commercial Fisheries

Total coastwide landings in 2003 were more than 52 million pounds, valued at more than $125 million. Shrimp accounted for 68 percent of the weight and 77 percent of the value of all seafood landed during 2003. The approximately *4,800 licensed saltwater commercial fishermen in Texas in 2003 made an economic impact of more than $529 million. ☆

Commercial Landings, 2003		
Finfish	**Pounds**	**Value**
Drum, Black	1,676,700	$1,365,100
Flounder	158,500	335,900
Sheepshead	67,600	26,100
Snapper	1,807,100	4,122,700
Other	1,391,900	3,110,200
Total Finfish	5,101,800	$8,960,000
Shellfish		
Shrimp (Heads On):		
Brown and Pink	24,430,600	$72,979,100
White	8,019,000	21,907,500
Other	714,400	1,340,700
Crabs, Blue	4,811,300	3,157,000
Oyster, Eastern	6,833,400	16,537,700
Other	94,200	143,700
Total Shellfish	**46,902,900**	**$116,065,700**
Grand Total	**52,004,700**	**$125,025,700**

* Deck hands and other crew members no longer need a license to work on commercial boats, so total number of commercial fishermen will vary from previous years.
Source: Trends in Texas Commercial Fishery Landings, 1972–2003, Texas Parks and Wildlife Department Coastal Fisheries Div., Management Data Series, Austin, 2004.

Sea Center Texas

Sea Center Texas is a marine aquarium, fish hatchery and nature center operated by the Texas Parks and Wildlife Department to educate and entertain visitors. The visitor center opened in 1996 and has interpretive displays, a "touch tank" and native Texas habitat exhibits depicting a salt marsh, jetty, reef and open Gulf waters. The aquarium features "Gordon," a 300-pound grouper, and sharks. The "Coastal Kids" educational program offers students on field trips hands-on learning activities.

Touted as the world's largest redfish hatchery, the facility is one of three marine hatcheries on the Texas coast that produces juvenile red drum and spotted speckled trout for enhancing natural populations in Texas bays. The hatchery has the capability to produce 20 million juvenile fish yearly. It also serves as a testing ground for production of other marine species, such as flounder and tarpon.

A half-acre youth fishing pond introduces youngsters to saltwater fishing through scheduled activities. The pond is handicap accessible and stocked with a variety of marine fish.

The center's wetland area is part of the Great Texas Coastal Birding Trail, where more than 150 species of birds have been identified. The wetland consists of a one-acre salt marsh and a three-acre freshwater marsh. Damselflies, dragonflies, butterflies and frogs are frequently sighted off the boardwalk. A small outdoor pavilion provides a quiet resting place for lunch adjacent to the butterfly and hummingbird gardens.

Sea Center Texas is operated in partnership with The Dow Chemical Company and the Coastal Conservation Association. It is located in Lake Jackson, 50 miles south of Houston off of Texas 288. Admission and parking are free. Open 9 a.m. to 4 p.m. Tuesday through Friday; 10 a.m. to 5 p.m. Saturday, and 1 p.m. to 4 p.m. Sunday. Closed Monday and some holidays. Reservations are required for some group tours, nature tours and hatchery tours. For more information call 979-292-0100. On the web: www.tpwd.state.tx.us/fish. ☆

Hunting and Fishing Licenses

A **hunting license** is required of Texas residents and nonresidents of Texas who hunt any bird or animal. Hunting licenses and stamp endorsements are valid during the period Sept. 1 through the following Aug. 31 of each year, except lifetime licenses and licenses issued for a specific number of days.

A hunting license (except the nonresident special hunting license and non-resident 5-day special hunting license) is valid for taking all legal species of wildlife in Texas including **deer, turkey, javelina, antelope, aoudad (sheep)** and all **small game and migratory game birds.**

Special licenses and tags are required for taking **alligators,** and a **trapper's license** is required to hunt **fur-bearing animals.**

In addition to a valid hunting license, an Upland Game Bird Stamp Endorsement is required to hunt **turkey, pheasant, quail, lesser prairie chicken** or **chachalaca.** Non-residents who purchase the non-resident spring turkey license are exempt from this stamp endorsement requirement. To hunt any migratory game birds (including **waterfowl, coot, rail, gallinule, snipe, dove, sandhill crane** and **woodcock**), a Migratory Game Bird Stamp Endorsement is required, in addition to a valid hunting license. A valid Federal Duck Stamp and HIP Certification are also required of waterfowl hunters age 16 or older.

All fishing licenses and stamp endorsements are valid only during the period Sept. 1 through Aug. 31, except lifetime licenses and licenses issued for a specific number of days. If you own any valid freshwater fishing package, you will be able to purchase a saltwater stamp, and, if you own any valid saltwater fishing package, you will be able to purchase a freshwater stamp. An all-water

Jim Clay bagged a gobbler during spring turkey hunting in Kerr County. Ray Sasser photo.

fishing package is also available.

Detailed information concerning licenses, stamps, seasons, regulations and related information can be obtained from **Texas Parks and Wildlife, 4200 Smith School Road, Austin 78744; (800) 792-1112 or 512-389-4800.**

On the Web, information from TPW on hunting: **www.tpwd.state.tx.us/hunt/hunt.htm;** on fishing: **www.tpwd.state.tx.us/fish/fish.htm.**

Texas Parks and Wildlife Department reported that for the year ending **August 31, 2005,** there were 1,082,062 paid **hunting-license holders** and 1,603,873 **sport or recreation fishing-license holders.** These licenses, plus stamps, tags or permits, resulted in revenue to the state of $32,423,934 from hunting and $44,954,075 from fishing.

For the year ending **August 31, 2006,** there were 1,087,602 paid **hunting-license holders** and 1,571,158 paid **sport or recreation fishing-license holders.** These licenses, plus stamps, tags or permits, resulted in revenue to the state of $33,244,169 from hunting and $43,473,700 from fishing.

During the 2004–2005 license year, hunters harvested 434,387 **white-tailed deer;** 32,729 **wild turkey** in the fall and 30,979 in the spring; 4,729 **mule deer;** and 15,829 **javelina.** In addition, 581,709 **rabbits;** 657,135 **squirrels;** 8,592,970 **mourning dove;** and 2,315,437 **bobwhite quail** were harvested.

During the 2005–2006 license year, hunters harvested 464,378 **white-tailed deer;** 26,116 **wild turkey** in the fall and 26,671 in the spring; 6,476 **mule deer;** and 22,109 **javelina.** In addition, 6,361,779 **mourning dove;** and 1,944,636 **bobwhite quail** were harvested. Harvest of rabbits and squirrels are no longer surveyed.☆

Fairs, Festivals and Special Events

Fairs, festivals and other special events provide year-round recreation in Texas. Some are of national interest, while many attract visitors from across the state. In addition to those listed here, the recreational paragraphs in the Counties section list numerous events. Information was furnished by the event sponsors. You can find more events on the Web at: www.traveltex.com/ActivitiesAndEvents.aspx.

Abilene — West Texas Fair & Rodeo; September; 1700 Hwy. 36, 79602; www.taylorcountyexpocenter.com. *Since 1897.*

Albany — Fort Griffin Fandangle; June; PO Box 155, 76430; www.fortgriffinfandangle.org. *Since 1938.*

Alvarado — Johnson County Pioneers & Old Settlers Reunion; August; PO Box 217, 76009. *Since 1893.*

Amarillo — Tri-State Fair; September; PO Box 31087, 79120.

Anderson — Grimes County Fair; June; PO Box 435, 77830.

Angleton — Brazoria County Fair; October; PO Box 818, 77516; www.bcfa.org. *Since 1939.*

Aransas Pass — Shrimporee; June, 130 W. Goodnight, 78336; www.aransaspass.org. *Since 1949.*

Arlington — Texas Scottish Festival; June; PO Box 511, 76634; www.texasscottishfestival.com. *Since 1986.*

Athens — Texas Fiddlers' Asso. Reunion; May (last Fri.); PO Box 1441, 75751. *Since 1932.*

Austin — Star of Texas Fair & Rodeo; March; 9100 Decker Lake Rd. 78724; www.rodeoaustin.com. *Since 1937.*

Austin — Austin Fine Arts Festival; April; PO Box 5705, 78763; www.austinfineartsfestival.org.

Bay City — Matagorda County Fair & Livestock Show; February; PO Box 1803, 77404; www.matagordacounty fair.com. *Since 1945.*

Bay City — Bay City Rice Festival; October; PO Box 867; 77404; www.baycitylions.org.

Beaumont — South Texas State Fair; October; 7250 Wespark Cr., 77705; www.ymbl.org. *Since 1943.*

Bellville — Austin County Fair; October; PO Box 141, 77418; www.austincountyfair.com.

Belton — 4th of July Celebration & PRCA Rodeo; July; PO Box 659, 76513; www.beltonchamber.com.

Belton — Central Texas State Fair; Aug.-Sept.; PO Box 206, 76513; www.centraltexasstatefair.com.

Big Spring — Howard County Fair; September; PO Box 2356, 79721. *Since 1973*

Boerne — Boerne Berges Fest; June; PO Box 748, 78006; www.bergesfest.com.

Boerne — Kendall County Fair; September (Labor Day Wknd.); PO Box 954, 78006; www.kcfa.org. *Since 1906.*

Brackettville — Gunfighter Competition; July; PO Box 528, 78832; www.alamovillage.com.

Brackettville — Western Horse Races & BBQ; September (Labor Day); PO Box 528, 78832; www.alamovillage.com.

Brenham — Washington County Fair; September; 1305 E. Blue Bell Rd., 77833; www.washingtoncofair.com. *Since 1870.*

Brownsville — Charro Days Fiesta; February; PO Box 3247, 78523-3247; www.charrodaysfiesta.com. *Since 1938.*

Burnet — Burnet Bluebonnet Festival; April; 229 S. Pierce; 78611. 222.burnetchamber.org. *Since 1986.*

Burton — Cotton Gin Festival; April (3rd wknd.); PO Box 98; 77835; www.cottonginmuseum.org. *Since 1990.*

Caldwell — Burleson County Fair; September; PO Box 634, 77836.

Canyon — TEXAS! Musical Drama; June–August; 1514 5th Ave., 79015; www.texas-show.com. *Since 1966.*

Clifton — Norse Smorgasbord; November; 152 Cnty. Rd. 4145, 76634; http://clifton.centraltx.com/heritage.htm.

TEXAS! Musical Drama runs from June through August in Canyon. Justin Cook photo.

Clute — Great Texas Mosquito Festival; July; PO Box 997, 77531; www.mosquitofestival.com. *Since 1981.*

Columbus — Colorado County Fair; September; PO Box 506, 78933; www.coloradocountyfair.org.

Conroe — Montgomery County Fair; March–April; PO Box 869, 77305-0869; www.mcfa.org. *Since 1957.*

Corpus Christi — Bayfest; September–October; PO Box 1858, 78403-1858; www.bayfesttexas.com.

Corpus Christi — Buc Days; April–May; PO Box 30404, 78463; www.bucdays.com.

Corsicana — Derrick Days; April; 120 N. 12th St., 75110; www.corsicana.org. *Since 1976.*

Crowell — Cynthia Ann Parker Festival; May; PO Box 452, 79227; www.crowelltex.com/CAP/cappage1.html.

Dalhart — XIT Rodeo & Reunion; August (1st full wknd.); PO Box 967, 79022. *Since 1936.*

Dallas — State Fair of Texas; September–October; PO Box 150009, 75315; www.bigtex.com. *Since 1886.*

Decatur — Wise County Old Settlers Reunion; July (last full week); PO Box 203, 76234.

De Leon — De Leon Peach & Melon Festival; August; PO Box 44, 76444-0044; www.cctc.net/~pmdeleon/index.htm. *Since 1917.*

Denton — North Texas State Fair & Rodeo; August; PO Box 1695, 76202; www.ntfair.com. *Since 1929.*

Edna — Jackson County Youth Fair; October; PO Box 457, 77957; www.jcyf.org. *Since 1949.*

Ennis — National Polka Festival; May; PO Box 1177, 75120-1237; www.visitennis.org/festivals.html.

Fairfield — Freestone County Fair; June; PO Box 196; 75840.

Flatonia — Czhilispiel; October (4th full wknd.); PO Box 610, 78941; www.flatoniachamber.com. *Since 1973.*

Fort Worth — Pioneer Days; September; 131 E. Exchange Ave., Ste 100B, 76106; www.fortworthstockyards.org.

Fort Worth — Southwestern Exposition & Livestock Show; January-February; PO Box 150, 76101; www.fwssr.com. *Since 1897.*

Fredericksburg — Night in Old Fredericksburg; July; 302 E. Austin, 78624; www.fredericksburg-texas.com. *Since 1963.*

Fredericksburg — Oktoberfest; October (1st wknd.); PO Box 222, 78624; www.Oktoberfestinfbg.com.

Freer — Freer Rattlesnake Roundup; May; PO Box 717, 78357; www.freerrattlesnake.com. *Since 1966.*

Galveston — Dickens on The Strand; December; 502 20th St., 77550; www.dickensonthestrand.org. *Since 1973.*

Galveston — Galveston Historic Homes Tour; May; 502 20th St., 77550-2014; www.galvestonhistory.org. *Since 1974.*

Gilmer — East Texas Yamboree; October; PO Box 854, 75644; www.yamboree.com. *Since 1937.*

Glen Flora — Wharton County Youth Fair; April; PO Box 167, 77443; www.whartoncountyyouthfair.org. *Since 1976.*

Graham — Art Splash on the Square; May; PO Box 1684, 76450; www.art-splash.com.

Graham — Red, White & You Parade & Festivities; July; PO Box 299; 76450; www.visitgraham.com.

Granbury — Annual July 4th Celebration; July; 116 W. Bridge St., 76048; www.granburychamber.com.

Granbury — Harvest Moon Festival; October; 116 W. Bridge St., 76048; www.hgma.com. *Since 1977.*

Grand Prairie — National Championship Pow-Wow; September; 2602 Mayfield Rd, 75052; www.tradersvillage.com. *Since 1963.*

Greenville — Hunt County Fair; June; PO Box 1071, 75403; www.huntcountyfair.com. *Since 1970.*

Groesbeck — Limestone County Fair; March–April; PO Box 965, 76642.

Hallettsville — Hallettsville Kolache Fest; September; PO Box 313, 77964; www.hallettsville.com. *Since 1995.*

Helotes — Helotes Cornyval; May (1st wknd.); PO Box 376, 78023; www.cornyval.com. *Since 1967.*

Hempstead — Waller County Fair; September–October; PO Box 911, 77445. www.wallercountyfair.com. *Since 1946.*

Hico — Hico Old Settler Reunion; July; PO Box 93, 76457; www.hico-tx.com. *Since 1887.*

Hidalgo — BorderFest; March; PO Box 722; 78557; www.borderfest.com.

Hondo — Medina County Fair; September (3rd wknd.); PO Box 4, 78861. *Since 1980.*

Houston — Harris County Fair; October; 1 Abercrombie Dr, 77084-4233; www.harriscountyfair.net. *Since 1977.*

Houston — Houston International Festival; April–May; 1111 Bagby St., Ste. 2550, 77002; www.ifest.org.

Houston — Houston Livestock Show and Rodeo; March; PO Box 20070; 77225-0070; www.hlsr.com.

Hughes Springs — Wildflower Trails of Texas; April; PO Box 805, 75656. *Since 1970.*

Huntsville — Walker County Fair & Rodeo; March–April; PO Box 1817, 77342; www.walkercountyfair.com. *Since 1979.*

Jefferson — Historical Pilgrimage and Spring Festival; May (1st wknd.); PO Box 301, 75657-0301; www.the-excelsiorhouse.com. *Since 1947.*

Johnson City — Blanco County Fair; August; PO Box 261, 78636-0261; www.lbjcountry.com/

Kenedy — Bluebonnet Days; April; 205 South 2nd St., 78119-2729.

Kerrville — Kerr County Fair; October; PO Box 290842, 78029; www.kerrcountyfair.com. *Since 1980.*

Kerrville — Kerrville Folk Festival; May–June; PO Box 291466, 78029; www.kerrvillefolkfestival.com. *Since 1972.*

Kerrville — The Official Texas State Arts & Crafts Fair; May (Memorial wknd.); 4000 Riverside Dr., 78028, www.tacef.org. *Since 1972.*

Kerrville — Kerrville Wine and Music Festival; September (Labor Day wknd.); PO Box 291466; 78029; www.kerrvillefolkfestival.com. *Since 1991.*

LaGrange — Fayette County Fair; September (Labor Day wknd.); PO Box 544, 78945; www.fayettecounty.fair.net. *Since 1926.*

Laredo — Border Olympics; January–March; PO Box 450037, 78044-0037; http://borderolympics.net. *Since 1947.*

Laredo — Laredo International Fair & Expo; March; PO Box 1770, 78043; www.laredofair.com. *Since 1963.*

Laredo — Washington's Birthday Celebration; January–February; 1819 E. Hillside Rd., 78041-3383; www.wbcalaredo.com. *Since 1898.*

Longview — Gregg County Fair & Exposition; September; 1511 Judson Rd., Ste. F, 75601; www.greggcountyfair.com. *Since 1951.*

Lubbock — 4th on Broadway Festival; July; PO Box 1643, 79408; www.broadwayfestivals.com. *Since 1991.*

Lubbock — Lights on Broadway Celebration; December; PO Box 1643, 79408; www.broadwayfestivals.com.

Lubbock — Panhandle-South Plains Fair; September; PO Box 208, 79408; www.southplainsfair.com. *Since 1914.*

Lufkin — Texas Forest Festival; September; 1615 S. Chestnut St., 75901; www.texasforestfestival.com. *Since 1984.*

Luling — Luling Watermelon Thump; June (last full wknd); PO Box 710, 78648-0710; www.watermelonthump.com. *Since 1953.*

Marshall — Fire Ant Festival; October; PO Box 520, 75671; www.marshall-chamber.com. *Since 1984.*

Marshall — Stagecoach Days Festival; May; PO Box 520, 75671; www.marshall-chamber.com. Since 1973.

Marshall — Wonderland of Lights; November–December;

The Parker County Peach Festival takes place the second Saturday in July. Photo courtesy of the Weatherfold Chamber of Commerce.

PO Box 520, 75671; www.marshalltxchamber.com.

Mercedes — Rio Grande Valley Livestock Show; March; 1000 N. Texas; www.rgvlivestockshow.com. *Since 1940.*

Mesquite — Mesquite Championship Rodeo; April–September (each Fri. & Sat.); 1818 Rodeo Dr, 75149-3800; www.mesquiterodeo.com. *Since 1958.*

Monahans — Butterfield-Overland Stage Coach and Wagon Festival; July; 401 S. Dwight Ave., 79756 www.butterfield.ws/. *Since 1994.*

Mount Pleasant — Titus County Fair; September; PO Box 1232, 75456-1232; www.tituscountyfair.com.

Nacogdoches — Piney Woods Fair; October; 3805 NW Stallings Dr., 75964; www.nacexpo.net. *Since 1978.*

Nederland — Nederland Heritage Festival; March; PO Box 1176, 77627; www.nederlandhf.org. *Since 1973.*

New Braunfels — Comal County Fair; September; PO Box 310223, 78131-0223; www.comalcountyfair.org. *Since 1894.*

New Braunfels — Wurstfest; October–November; PO Box 310309, 78131-0309; www.wurstfest.com.

Odessa — Permian Basin Fair & Expo; September; 218 W. 46th St., 79764; www.permianbasinfair.com.

Palestine — Dogwood Trails Festival; March–April; PO Box 2828, 75802-2828; www.visitpalestine.com.

Paris — Red River Valley Fair; August–September; 570 E. Center St., 75460; www.rrvfair.org. *Since 1911.*

Pasadena — Pasadena Livestock Show & Rodeo; September–October; 7601 Red Bluff Rd., 77507-1035; www.pasadenarodeo.com.

Plantersville — Texas Renaissance Festival; October–November (8 weekends); 21778 FM 1774, 77363; www.texrenfest.com. *Since 1975.*

Port Arthur — CalOILcade; October; PO Box 2336, 77643; www.portarthur.com/cavoilcade. *Since 1953.*

Port Lavaca — Calhoun County Fair; October (3rd wknd.); PO Box 42, 77979-0042. *Since 1963.*

Poteet — Poteet Strawberry Festival; April; PO Box 227, 78065; www.strawberryfestival.com. *Since 1948.*

Refugio — Refugio County Fair & Rodeo & Livestock Show; March; PO Box 88, 78377. *Since 1961.*

Rio Grande City — Starr County Fair; March (1st full wknd.); PO Box 841, 78582. *Since 1961.*

Rosenberg — Fort Bend County Fair; September–October; PO Box 428, 77471; www.fbcfa.org. *Since 1937.*

Salado — Salado Scottish Games and Competitions; November (2nd wknd.); PO Box 36, 76571-0036; www.ctam-salado.org.

San Angelo — San Angelo Stock Show & Rodeo; February; 200 W 43rd St., 76903; www.sanangelorodeo.

com. *Since 1932.*

San Antonio — Fiesta San Antonio; April; 2611 Broadway St.; 78215; www.fiesta-sa.org. *Since 1891.*

San Antonio — Texas Folklife Festival; June; 801 S. Bowie, 78205; www.texasfolklifefestival.org. *Since 1972.*

Sanderson — Cinco de Mayo Celebration; May (1st Sat.); PO Box 598, 79848.

Sanderson — 4th of July Celebration; July; PO Box 4810, 79848-4810; www.sanderson-tx.info. *Since 1908.*

Sanderson — Prickly Pear Pachanga; October; PO Box 410, 79848; www.sandersontx.info. *Since 2001.*

Santa Fe — Galveston County Fair & Rodeo; April; PO Box 889, 77510; www.galvestoncountyfair.com.

Schulenburg — Schulenburg Festival; August (1st full wknd.); PO Box 115; 78956; www.schulenburgfestival.com. *Since 1976.*

Seguin — Guadalupe Agricultural & Livestock Fair; October (2nd wknd); PO Box 334, 78155; www.guadalupecountyfairandrodeo.com. *Since 1885.*

Shamrock — St. Patrick's Day Celebration; March; PO Box 588, 79079. www.shamrocktx.net/site/index-2.html. *Since 1947.*

Stamford — Texas Cowboy Reunion; July; PO Box 948, 79553; www.tcrrodeo.com. *Since 1933.*

Sulphur Springs — Hopkins County Fall Festival; September (3rd Sat.); PO Box 177, 75483. *Since. 1970.*

Sweetwater — Rattlesnake Roundup; March; PO Box 416, 79556-0416; www.rattlesnakeroundup.net. *Since 1958.*

Terlingua — Terlingua International Chili Championship; November; PO Box 39, 79852; www.chili.org. *Since 1947.*

Texarkana — Four States Fair; September; 3700 E. 50th St., Texarkana AR, 75504; www.fourstatesfair.com.

Tyler — East Texas State Fair; September; 2112 W. Front St., 75702; www.etstatefair.com. *Since 1914.*

Tyler — Texas Rose Festival; Ocober (3rd wknd.); PO Box 8224, 75711; www.texasrosefestival.com. *Since 1933.*

Waco — Heart O' Texas Fair & Rodeo; October; 4601 Bosque Blvd.; 76710; www.hotfair.com. *Since 1954.*

Waxahachie — Gingerbread Trail Tour of Homes; June (1st full wknd); PO Box 706, 75168; www.-rootsweb.com/~txecm/ginger.htm. *Since 1969.*

Waxahachie — Scarborough Renaissance Festival; April–May; PO Box 538, 75168-0538; www.scarboroughrenfest.com. *Since 1980.*

Weatherford — Parker County Peach Festival; July (2nd Sat.); PO Box 310, 76086; www.weatherfod-chamber.com. *Since 1983.*

Weatherford — Christmas on the Square; December; PO Box 310, 76086; www.weatherfod-chamber.com. *Since 1986.*

West — Westfest; September (Labor Day wknd.); PO Box 123, 76691; www.westfest.com. *Since 1976.*

Winnsboro — Autumn Trails Festival; October (every wkend.); PO Box 464; 75494.

Woodville — Tyler County Dogwood Festival; March–April; PO Box 2151, 75979-2151; www.tylercountydogwoodfestival.org. Since 1944.

Yorktown — Yorktown's Fiesta En La Calle Festival; April (1st Sat.); PO Box 488, 78164-0488; www.yorktowntx.com.

Yorktown — Yorktown's Annual Western Days Celebration; October (3rd full wknd.); PO Box 488, 78164-0488; www.yorktowntx.com. *Since 1959.* ☆

PROFESSIONAL BASEBALL HAD AN EARLY START IN SMALL TOWNS

By Mark Presswood

Sports teams have for many years cast a magical spell over Texas cities and towns, giving citizens a pride in the community while providing a social gathering for otherwise distant neighbors. High school football currently provides this excitement, and stadiums are full during Friday night home games under the lights.

Not so long ago, it was professional minor league baseball that entertained fans throughout Texas. Over

100 communities in Texas have hosted a professional baseball team. The Texas League, established in 1888, has been the most well-known and continuous circuit for the larger cities of San Antonio, Houston, Fort Worth, Dallas, Beaumont, El Paso, Waco, Wichita Falls and Midland. Round Rock, Corpus Christi and Frisco are new additions to the Texas League family of franchises, but 50 years ago, fans sat in dimly lit ballparks rooting

The Texas League of Professional Baseball Clubs was first organized in 1888, the year this photo was taken of an amateur baseball team in Odessa. The Presswood Collection.

This photo of the 1895 Fort Worth Panthers was taken the year they won the Texas League Championship. In those early years, the Texas League was struggling to stay organized and turn a profit. The Presswood Collection.

Branch Rickey is credited with starting the affiliation of major league teams with minor league programs when, as general manager of the St. Louis Cardinals, he purchased the Houston Buffalos and other teams. The concept quickly caught on and by the 1940s, all major league teams began building their minor league systems. File photo.

for the Paris Red Peppers, the Plainview Ponies and the Vernon Dusters.

In its early years, the Texas League, like any new business, was struggling to stay organized and turn a profit. The Spanish-American War stopped operations in 1898, as would other wars in later years. From 1899 through 1902, only the southern teams survived under another league designation, and the northern cities, except for a one-year run by Dallas, struggled to find organization. Travel was a major concern as new railroad tracks were still to be laid and a wagon trip between cities was an all-day or two-day excursion. The Texas League was a split league from 1902 through the 1906 season, with the northern cities keeping the Texas League name and the southern cities using the South Texas League moniker. During those years, Sherman-Denison, Corsicana and Paris all experienced their brief Texas League histories.

During this early era, all minor league baseball teams were independent clubs with talent being bought and sold throughout the country. There was little governance or rules about players leaving teams and finding higher pay. In 1901, the National Association of Professional Baseball Leagues was formed to give the minor league a structure and rules between leagues. This led to the classification system of leagues but affiliation with major league teams was still 30 to 40 years away. Branch Rickey is credited with starting the affiliation of major league teams with minor league programs when, as general manager of the St. Louis Cardinals, he purchased the Houston Buffalos and other teams. The idea was to control costs of purchasing players from independent teams and to teach the same techniques at all levels as the players progressed. The concept quickly caught on

Hall of Fame second baseman Rogers Hornsby, third from left, and some of his players participate in a War Bond promotion during World War II. Hornsby grew up in Fort Worth and after retiring from the major leagues returned to manage the Fort Worth Cats in 1942. The Presswood Collection.

and by the 1940s, all major league teams began building their minor league systems.

The Texas League eventually earned a high ranking of Class AA baseball but many of the smaller leagues carried a Class B, C or D classification. This was by no means an indication of the talent; most circuits had an alumnus who found his way onto a major league roster.

There have been minor leagues in Texas every decade of the last century. Professional baseball has been played from the mountains of El Paso to the Louisiana border in Texarkana and from the plains of Amarillo to the tip of Texas in Brownsville. Economic prosperity, competitive spirit and a love of the game has allowed baseball to entertain fans for almost 125 years. *See list of teams and towns in the table on pages 189–191.*

West Texas

The Panhandle region of Texas witnessed professional baseball starting in the early 1920s. The West Texas League, West Texas/New Mexico League, Longhorn League and Sophomore League all provided organization to baseball in the wide-open plains of West Texas. These leagues also included many towns in southeastern New Mexico and introduced professional baseball to Roswell, Artesia, Hobbs, Carlsbad and Clovis. The dry, arid and windy conditions of West Texas gave enormous flight to home runs, and many big hitters took advantage of those prevailing winds. Pitchers hated seeing fly balls rocket out of parks, but it became a big favorite of fans to root for their big sluggers. Joe Baumann of the Roswell Rockets broke longstanding home run records when

he belted 72 round-trippers in 1954. In 1947, a small shortstop named Bill Serena led all of baseball with 57 homers and led the league in RBIs (190) and runs (183) playing for the Lubbock Hubbers.

The first western Texas circuit, the West Texas League (1920–1922 and 1928–1929) was a short-lived affair in the oil towns of Cisco, Eastland, Gorman, Coleman, Winters, Abilene, Sweetwater and San Angelo. The nicknames for several teams reflected the oil industry impact, such as the Nitros in Ranger and the Gassers in Amarillo. The area's western heritage was also represented by the Midland Colts; the Big Spring Cowboys; the Coleman Bobcats; and the Colts, Bronchos and Sheep Herders of San Angelo. The Resorters of Mineral Wells gave recognition to the mineral water baths of the Crazy Water area, and the Hubbers in Lubbock recognized the "Hub City" nickname. The oil prosperity also gave rise to other opportunities, such as Conrad Hilton's purchase of his first hotel in the home of the Cisco Scouts.

The West Texas/New Mexico League was by far the most stable of the West Texas organizations and reigned from 1937 through the 1955 season, with the exception, as with many leagues, of the war years (1943–1945). Abilene, Pampa, Amarillo, Lubbock, Borger and Lamesa were stable throughout the league's tenure, but El Paso and Plainview replace Borger and Lamesa, respectively, near the league's end. El Paso spent many years in the Arizona/Texas League as the lone Texas representative.

After helping to establish the Abilene franchise in the WT/NM League, Abilene sports reporter How-

When Joe Baumann played for the Roswell Rockets of the Longhorn League in 1954, he broke longstanding home run records when he belted 72 round-trippers in one season, which stood as professional baseball's single-season record until Barry Bonds hit 73 homers in 2001. File photo.

ard Green became the youngest president of a minor league. He accomplished this in 1947 when he began a nine-year run as president of the Longhorn League. The Longhorn League provided a framework for teams in the southern part of the Panhandle and offered fans in Midland, Odessa, Big Spring, Sweetwater, Vernon, San Angelo and Ballinger a chance to root for their hometown team. The Midland Indians, Odessa Oilers and Big Spring Broncs were all former members of the WT/NM League before moving to the Longhorn League, as were

Driller Park in Kilgore is shown in this 1947 photo. Kilgore hosted teams in both the East Texas and Lone Star leagues from 1931–1948. The Presswood Collection.

The 1958 Alpine Cowboys played in the Sophomore League. Team owner, Herbert L. Kokernot Jr. (wearing a tie), built Kokernot Stadium for the Cowboys. Today it is home to the Sul Ross State University baseball team. Much of the rock used in the statium was quarried off Kokernot's 06 Ranch. Photo courtesy of the Archives of the Big Bend, Bryan Wildenthal Memorial Library, Sul Ross State University.

several of the southern New Mexico teams.

The Blue Sox of Abilene played in Blue Sox Stadium on the northeast corner of Barrow and South 114th streets, currently home to an H-E-B grocery store. Plainview showcased the Ponies at Jaycee Park, and Kokernot Field in Alpine still serves as home to the Sul Ross State University baseball team after having hosted the Alpine Cowboys for several years. The Lubbock Hubbers played at Rosenthal Field near the railroad tracks and Vernon Avenue and Midland built Christensen Stadium in 1952 before moving to the new First American Bank Ballpark in 2002.

East Texas

Oil also had an impact on the eastern part of the state and made boom towns of Kilgore, Marshall and Henderson. Oil brought in millions of dollars to local coffers and, more importantly for professional baseball, it brought in oilfield workers who needed the escape an evening of minor league baseball could offer.

The East Texas League name was used six times to organize the cities of East Texas. Twice the league changed its name to the Lone Star League, and in one stretch during the Great Depression, it became the Dixie and West Dixie leagues.

The prosperity of oil gave fans the Cannibals of Longview; the Oilers of Henderson; the Rangers, Boomers and Drillers of Kilgore; the Jax of Jacksonville; the Indians, Tigers and Browns of Marshall; and the Trojans, Tigers and East Texans of Tyler. Other teams that were brief members of the East

Clyde Liedtke played briefly for Tyler in the East Texas League in 1950. Liedtke also played for minor league teams in the Alabama-Florida League and the Georgia League. The Presswood Collection.

The Big State League

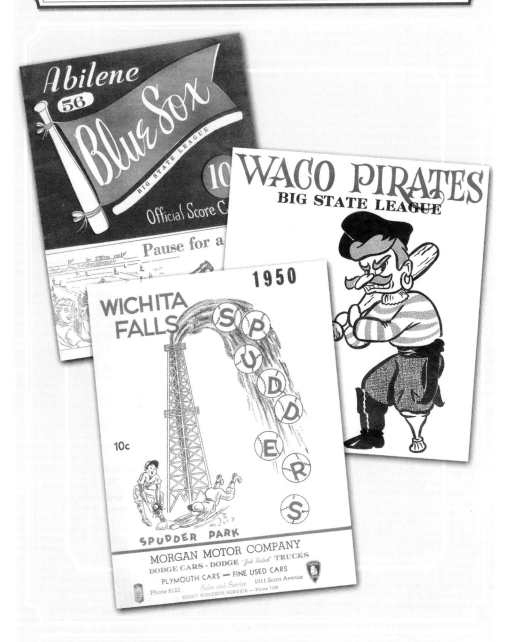

A 1956 program for the Abilene Blue Sox, a 1954 program for the Waco Pirates, and a 1950 program for the Wichita Falls Spudders, all of which were in the Big State League. The Presswood Collection.

Texas Leagues at different stages include the Gladewater Bears; the Paris Bearcats, Panthers and Red Peppers; the Palestine Pals; the Sulphur Springs Lions, Saints and Spartans; the Lufkin Foresters; and the Texarkana Liners and Bears.

Driller Park in Kilgore is still a jewel supporting local high school and community college baseball teams. Built in 1947 from oilfield materials, the park hosted a 2006 exhibition game between the Fort Worth Cats and Shreveport Sports where nearly 2,000 fans witnessed professional baseball for the first time in many years. The remains of Henderson Park in Henderson can still be seen behind the old middle school at Fair Park and South High streets. The Jacksonville Jax played at the current rodeo arena on the corner of Mulberry and Bridge streets, with home plate in the northwest corner of the lot.

The 1947 Paris Red Peppers played in the Big State League. Paris has a long history of minor league baseball, beginning in 1896 and running through1953. At various times, the town had teams in 10 different leagues. The Presswood Collection.

Big State

One of the more successful and longest running leagues borrowed a reference for the state of Texas and called itself the Big State League. This effort began in 1947 and continued through the 1957 season. Wichita Falls, Waco, Greenville, Gainesville, Temple, Austin, Texarkana and Sherman-Dennison were the heart of the league. In later years when financial circumstances caused a movement among teams, Bryan, Paris, Galveston, Beaumont, Port Arthur, Tyler and Corpus Christi were members when needed. Rated a Class B league for much of its history, the circuit also featured some of the most famous executives in Texas baseball lore. J. Walter Morris served as president from 1947–1950, Howard Green replaced Morris through the 1955 season, and Howard Sayles led the league until its demise in 1957.

The Pioneers in Austin played at Disch Field, currently an empty pasture behind the Convention Center south of downtown, and the Gainesville Owls played

The 1947 Waco Dons played in the Big State League. Waco fielded minor league teams beginning in 1889. The Presswood Collection.

These trading cards of the 1953 Galvestion White Caps were compliments of Coca-Cola Bottling Co. The players are (top row, from left) Mike Conovan, Bob Miller and Tom Moore; (bottom row, from left) Bob Pugatch, Bob Ramsey and Hank Robinson. The Presswood Collection.

at Locke Field on Interstate 35 in Gainesville. All that remains of Majors Field in Greenville are the bricked archways marking the entrance to the stadium on Lee Street. Travis Field in Bryan is still playable, and the Brazos Valley Bombers began calling the park home for the 2007 season of the Texas Collegiate League.

Katy Park, formerly at the corner of Eighth and Webster streets in Waco, was the first ballpark to host a night game in 1933 when the Texas League Waco Cubs hosted the Fort Worth Cats. Train tracks ran to the park's west side, and then–General Manager Buster Chatham constantly complained about the trains being parked so close to the front entrance of the ballpark. In May 1953, a tornado ripped through Waco destroying much of Katy Park, but Chatham found refuge in a large engine car and never again complained about the trains.

The precursor to the Big State League was the Central Texas and Texas Association leagues of the late 1910s and early 1920s. The Texas Association featured the Marlin Bathers, the Mexia Gushers, the Terrell Ter-

rors and the Palestine Pals. It also included teams from Austin, Corsicana, Sherman, Temple and Waco.

Gulf Coast

The Gulf Coast region of Texas has been home to several leagues whose founders believed the good weather, close proximity of cities and a love of baseball would signal good fortunes in the ticket office. The first organized leagues fielded teams in 1910, 1911 and 1931 but a more successful post-WWII Rio Grande Valley League had a two-year run before being morphed into the Gulf Coast League. The Galveston White Caps, Texas City Texans, Brownsville Charros, Port Arthur Sea Hawks, Laredo Apaches, Harlingen Capitols, McAllen Giants and Palms, and the Corpus Christi Aces and Seahawks all competed for Gulf Coast supremacy.

In 1976 and 1977, a brief attempt at independent baseball was organized to bring baseball to a new generation of fans. Mr. Baseball, Bobby Bragan, with help

Activities at a Fort Worth Cats game at LaGrave Field in 2006 show that minor league baseball is having a resurgence as the national pastime. Photo courtesy of the Fort Worth Cats.

from several others including Bill Wood, Dick King and Howard Green, found support for new franchises in Beeville, Seguin, Baton Rouge, Victoria, Corpus Christi and Harlingen (Rio Grande Valley). The Gulf States League changed names the following year to the Lone Star League and was unceremoniously blown away at the end of 1977 when a hurricane pelted Cabiness Field in Corpus Christi resulting in a cancelled championship series and an abrupt end to the attempt.

Robinson Park served as home to the Texas City Stars, Fairgrounds Park hosted the Seguin Toros, and Joe Hunter Field on the campus of Bee County Junior College was home to the Beeville Bees and Blazers.

Many cities experienced only brief flirtations with professional baseball, either as members of a single season forgotten league or a mid-season replacement for troubled franchises. Brenham, Bay City, Corsicana, Crockett, Donna-Weslaco, Del Rio, Ennis, Hamlin, Kaufman, Hillsboro, Mission, Nacogdoches, Rusk, Waxahachie and Winters are but a few of the cities and towns that entertained fans with the "National Pastime," though for a fleeting moment.

Recently, independent baseball has again revived professional minor league teams for many smaller markets. The defunct Texas Louisiana/Central Baseball League had teams in Tyler, Lubbock and Abilene. Former members Fort Worth and Coastal Bend (Robstown) are now part of the Independent American Association, and Amarillo, San Angelo, Laredo, Edinburg and Rio Grande Valley (Harlingen) are now having a resurgence in the United League of Professional Baseball. ☆

Mark Presswood is the senior vice president and baseball historian for the Fort Worth Cats Baseball Club. He is coauthor, with Chris Holaday, of Baseball in Fort Worth: Images of Baseball *and* Baseball in Dallas: Images of Baseball *published by Arcadia Publishing. He is also an avid collector of Texas Professional Minor League memorabilia. Mark is host of "This Week in Cats Baseball" on Community Cable Television in Tarrant County.*

See list of minor league teams and towns in the table on pages 189–191.

Sources

Holaday, Chris, and Mark Presswood. Baseball in Dallas. *Arcadia Publishing, Charleston, SC, 2004.*

Johnson, Lloyd, and Miles Wolff, editors. The Encyclopedia of Minor League Baseball. *Baseball America, Inc., Durham, NC, 1997.*

Presswood, Mark, and Chris Holaday. Baseball in Fort Worth. *Arcadia Publishing, Charleston, SC, 2004.*

Town	League	Years
Abilene	West Texas	1920-21, 1928-29
	West Texas-New Mexico	1939, 1946-55
	Big State	1956-57
	Texas-Louisiana	1995-99
Alpine	Sophomore	1959-61
Amarillo	West Texas	1922
	Panhandle-Pecos Valley	1923
	Western	1927-28, 1956-58
	West Texas-New Mexico	1939-42, 1946-55
	Texas	1959-63, 1965-74, 1976-82
	Texas-Louisiana	1994-2000
	Central	2001-04
	United	2006-
Austin	Texas	1888-90, 1895-99, 1905, 1907-08, 1911-14, 1956-67
	South Texas	1905-06
	Middle Texas	1915
	Texas Association	1923-26
	Big State	1947-55
Ballinger	Texas-Oklahoma	1921
	West Texas	1921-29
	Longhorn	1947-50
	Southwestern	1956-57
(see also Winters)		
Bartlett	Middle Texas	1914-15
Bay City	Southwest Texas	1910-11
Beaumont	South Texas	1903-06
	Gulf Coast	1908
	Texas	1912-17, 1919-55, 1983-86
	Big State	1956-57
	Texas-Louisiana	1994
Beeville	Southwest Texas	1910-11
	Gulf Coast	1926
	Gulf States	1976
	Lone Star	1977
Belton	Middle Texas	1914-15
Big Spring	West Texas	1928-29
	West Texas-New Mexico	1938-42
	Longhorn	1947-55
Bonham	Texas-Oklahoma	1911-14, 1921-22
Borger	West Texas-New Mexico	1939, 1942, 1946-54
Brenham	South Texas	1905
	Middle Texas	1914-15
Brownsville	Southwest Texas	1910-11
	Texas Valley	1938
	Rio Grande Valley	1949-50
	Gulf Coast	1951-53
Bryan	Lone Star	1947-48
	East Texas	1949-50
	Big State	1953-54
Cleburne	Texas	1906
	Texas-Oklahoma	1911, 1921-22
	South Central	1912
Cisco	West Texas	1920-21
Coleman	West Texas	1928-29

Town	League	Years
Corpus Christi	Southwest Texas	1910-11
	Gulf Coast	1926, 1951-53
	Texas Valley	1927, 1938
	Rio Grande Valley	1931, 1949-50
	Big State	1954-57
	Texas	1958-59, 2005-
	Gulf States	1976
	Lone Star	1977
	Texas-Louisiana	1994-95
Corsicana	Texas	1902-05
	North Texas State	1907
	Central Texas	1914-15, 1917
	Texas-Oklahoma	1922
	Texas Association	1923-26
	Lone Star	1927-28
Crockett	East Texas	1916
Dallas	Texas	1888-90, 1892, 1895-98, 1902-58
	American Association	1959
	Pacific Coast	1964
Dallas/Fort Worth	American Association	1960-62
	Pacific Coast	1963
	Texas	1965-71
Del Rio	Longhorn	1948
	Rio Grande Valley	1949-50
	Big State	1954
Denison	Texas-Oklahoma	1912-14
	Western Association	1915-17
(see also Sherman)		
Donna	Rio Grande Valley	1949-50
(aka Donna-Weslaco)		
Eastland	West Texas	1920
Edinburg	Gulf Coast	1926
	Texas Valley	1927
	Texas-Louisiana	2001
	Central	2002-05
	United	2006-
El Paso	Rio Grande Valley Assn.	1915
	Arizona State	1930
	Arizona-Texas	1931-32, 1937-41, 1947-50, 1952-54
	Mexican National	1946
	Southwest International	1951
	West Texas-New Mexico	1955
	Southwestern	1956-57
	Sophomore	1961
	Texas	1962-70, 1972-2004
	Central	2005
	American Association	2006-
Ennis	Central Texas	1914-17
Fort Worth	Texas	1888-90, 1892, 1895-98, 1902-58, 1964
	American Association	1959
	All-American Association	2001
	Central	2002-05
	American Association	2006-
Frisco	Texas	2003-
Gainesville	Texas-Oklahoma	1911
	Big State	1947-51
	Sooner State	1953-55

Town	League	Years
Galveston	Texas	1888-90, 1892, 1895-99, 1907-17, 1919-24, 1931-37
	South Texas	1903-06
	Gulf Coast	1950-53
	Big State	1954-55
George-town	Middle Texas	1914
Gladewater	West Dixie	1935
	East Texas	1936, 1949-50
	Lone Star	1948
Gorman	West Texas	1920
Graham	Texas-Oklahoma	1921
Greenville	North Texas State	1907
	Texas-Oklahoma	1912, 1922
	East Texas	1923-26, 1946
	Big State	1947-50, 1953
	Sooner State	1957
Hamlin	West Texas	1928
Harlingen (aka Rio Grande Valley)	Rio Grande Valley	1931, 1950
	Texas Valley	1938
	Gulf Coast	1951-53
	Big State	1954-55
	Texas	1960-61
	Gulf States	1976
	Lone Star	1977
	Texas-Louisiana	1994-2001
	Central	2002-03
	United	2006-
Henderson	East Texas	1931, 1936-40, 1946, 1949-50
	Dixie	1933
	West Dixie	1934-35
	Lone Star	1947-48
Hillsboro	Central Texas	1914
Houston	Texas	1888-90, 1892, 1895-98, 1907-58
	South Texas	1903-06
	American Association	1959-61
Italy	Central Texas	1914
Jacksonville	West Dixie	1934-35
	East Texas	1936-40, 1946
	Lone Star	1947
	Gulf Coast	1950
Kaufman	Central Texas	1915
Kilgore	East Texas	1931, 1936-40, 1949-50
	Lone Star	1947-48
La Feria	Rio Grande Valley	1931
Lamesa	West Texas-New Mexico	1939-42, 1946-52
	Longhorn	1953
	Southwest	1957
Lampasas	Middle Texas	1914
Laredo	Southwest Texas	1910-11
	Gulf Coast	1926, 1951-53
	Texas Valley	1927
	Rio Grande Valley	1949-50
	Texas-Louisiana	1995
	United	2006-

Town	League	Years
Longview	South Central	1912
	East Texas	1923-26, 1931, 1936-40, 1949-50
	Lone Star	1927, 1947-48
	Texas	1932
	Dixie	1933
	West Dixie	1934-35
	Big State	1952-53
Lubbock	West Texas	1922, 1928
	Panhandle-Pecos Valley	1923
	West Texas-New Mexico	1938-42, 1946-55
	Big State	1956
Lufkin	East Texas	1916, 1946
	West Dixie	1934
	Lone Star	1947-48
	Gulf Coast	1950
Marlin	Central Texas	1916-17
	Texas Association	1923-24
Marshall	South Central	1912
	East Texas	1923-26, 1936-40, 1949-50
	Lone Star	1927, 1947-48
	Cotton States	1941
McAllen	Gulf Coast	1926
	Texas Valley	1938
	Rio Grande Valley	1931, 1949-50
	Lone Star	1977
McKinney	Texas-Oklahoma	1912
Mexia	Central Texas	1915-17
	Texas-Oklahoma	1922
	Texas Association	1923-26
	Lone Star	1927-28
Midland	West Texas	1928-29
	West Texas-New Mexico	1937-40
	Longhorn	1947-55
	Southwestern	1956-57
	Sophomore	1958-59
	Texas	1972-
Mineral Wells	West Texas	1920
	Texas-Oklahoma	1921
Mission	Gulf Coast	1926
	Texas Valley	1927
Monahans	West Texas-New Mexico	1937
Mount Pleasant	East Texas	1923-25
Nacog-doches	East Texas	1916
Odessa	West Texas-New Mexico	1937, 1940
	Longhorn	1947-55
	Sophomore	1959-60
Orange	Gulf Coast	1907-08
Palestine	East Texas	1916, 1936-40
	Texas Association	1925-26
	Lone Star	1927-29
	West Dixie	1934-35
Pampa	West Texas-New Mexico	1939-42, 1946-55
	Southwestern	1956-57

Town	League	Years
Paris	Texas	1896-97, 1902-04
	North Texas State	1907
	South Central	1912
	Texas-Oklahoma	1913-14, 1921-22
	Western Association	1915-17
	Central Texas	1917
	East Texas	1923-26, 1931, 1946, 1949-50
	Lone Star	1927-29
	West Dixie	1934
	Big State	1947-48, 1952-53
Plainview	West Texas-New Mexico	1953-55
	Southwest	1956-57
	Sophomore	1958-59
Port Arthur	Cotton States	1932
	Evangeline	1940-42, 1954
	Gulf Coast	1950-53
	Big State	1955-57
Ranger	West Texas	1920-22
Refugio	Texas Valley	1938
Rio Grande Valley (see Harlingen)		
Robstown	Rio Grande Valley	1949-50
	Central	2003-05
	American Association	2006-
(aka Coastal Bend)		
Round Rock	Texas	2000-2004
	Pacific Coast	2005-
Rusk	East Texas	1916
San Angelo	West Texas	1921-22, 1928-29
	Longhorn	1948-55
	Southwestern	1956-57
	Sophomore	1958-59
	Texas-Louisiana	2000-01
	Central	2002-05
	United	2006-
San Antonio	Texas	1888, 1892, 1895-99, 1907-42, 1946-64, 1967-
	South Texas	1903-06
San Benito	Rio Grande Valley	1931
Schulen-burg	Middle Texas	1915
Seguin	Gulf States	1976
Sherman	Texas	1895-96
	Texas-Oklahoma	1912-14, 1921-22
	Western Association	1915-17
	Texas Association	1923
	Lone Star	1929
	East Texas	1946
	Sooner State	1952
Sherman-Denison	Texas	1902
	Big State	1947-51
	Sooner	1953
Stamford	West Texas	1922
Sulphur Springs	East Texas	1923-25
Sweetwater	West Texas	1920-22
	Longhorn	1947-52, 1954
Taft	Texas Valley	1938

Town	League	Years
Taylor	Middle Texas	1915
Temple	Texas	1905-07
	Middle Texas	1914-15
	Central Texas	1916-17
	Texas Association	1924-26
	Big State	1949-54, 1957
Terrell	North Texas State	1907
	Central Texas	1915-16
	Texas Associaiton	1925-26
Texarkana	Texas	1902
	Arkansas-Texas	1906
	South Central	1912
	Texas-Oklahoma	1913-14
	East Texas	1924-26, 1937-40, 1946
	Lone Star	1927-29
	Cotton States	1941
	Big State	1947-53
Texas City	Gulf Coast	1951-53
	Evangeline	1954
	Big State	1955-56
	Lone Star	1977
Tyler	South Central	1912
	East Texas	1924-26, 1931, 1936-40, 1946, 1949-50
	Lone Star	1927-29, 1947-48
	Texas	1932
	Dixie	1933
	West Dixie	1934-35
	Big State	1951-55
	Texas-Louisiana	1994-97
	All-American Association	2001
Vernon	Longhorn	1947-52
Victoria	Southwest Texas	1910-11
	Gulf Coast	1926
	Big State	1956-57
	Texas	1958-61, 1974
	Gulf States	1976
	Lone Star	1977
Waco	Texas	1889-90, 1892, 1897, 1902-03, 1905-19, 1925-30
	Texas Association	1923-24
	Dixie	1933
	Big State	1947-56
Waxa-hachie	Central Texas	1914-16
Weslaco (see Donna)		
West	Central Texas	1914
Wichita Falls	Texas-Oklahoma	1911-13
	Texas	1920-32
	West Texas-New Mexico	1941-42
	Big State	1947-53, 1956-57
	Longhorn	1954
Wink	West Texas-New Mexico	1937-38
Winters-Ballinger	Longhorn	1953

Black Professional Baseball in Texas

Negro Leagues Gave Many Players Opportunities Before Baseball's Integration

By Mark Presswood

Though much has been written and researched about the Negro National and American professional leagues, little is known about black minor league and semiprofessional baseball in Texas. Unfortunately, the major newspapers of the day, whose archives are readily available, carried little information about black ballgames or their organization, and the black newspapers have little or no archives chronicling the early years of organized black baseball.

Dr. Layton Revel, of the Center for Negro League Baseball Research in Dallas, and the Negro Leagues Baseball Museum in Kansas City have done a very credible job of gathering interviews and researching what archives exist but still much is not known. What we do know is the great impact Texas-born black baseball stars had not only in Texas but across the nation as they founded and shaped the black baseball leagues.

Rube Foster, who was born and raised in Calvert, is credited with the formation of the Negro National League in 1920. Foster started playing for amateur and semiprofessional teams in the late 1800s and early 1900s, primarily with teams from Waco and Fort Worth. His skill as a pitcher soon earned him recognition on a national scale, and barnstorming teams throughout the country were securing his services. Barnstorming was a common occurrence in the early part of the 1900s, as all-star teams would organize, travel around the country,

Rube Foster was born and raised in Calvert and is credited with the formation of the Negro National League in 1920. Photo courtesy of the National Baseball Hall of Fame Library.

The Fort Worth Wonders were a barnstorming team that was formed in 1905. This photo was taken in the 1930s.

In the 1950s, many amateur baseball teams were still segregated. The Fort Worth Giants were sponsored by Jaxx Beer. The Presswood Collection.

and play local amateur, semiprofessional or professional teams. Professional baseball players were paid specifically to play baseball and were held to that team by contract or team agreement. Semiprofessional players were paid only if the gate receipts exceeded the cost of the event and a profit for the promoter.

Early black baseball teams in Texas were primarily barnstorming semiprofessionals but included some of the best baseball in the nation. The Fort Worth Wonders formed in 1905 and featured at different times George "Dibo" Johnson and Louis "Big Bertha" Santop from Tyler, who both would find recognition as some of the

The 1956 Amarillo Gold Sox of the Western League in the early years of integrated baseball. The Presswood Collection.

The Texas League was integrated when Dave Hoskins was signed to play for the Dallas Eagles. In this circa 1952 photo, Hoskins signs autographs for his fans. Photo courtesy of the Dallas Public Library History and Archives Division.

greatest black baseball stars of the era.

Several times during this period attempts were made to form professional leagues in Texas. One of those was a circuit started in 1916 called the Colored Texas League. Fort Worth native Hiram McGar served as league president and also manager of the Fort Worth Black Panthers. Other cities in the league included Cleburne (Yellow Jackets), Dallas, Waco, Houston, San Antonio, Beaumont and Galveston. The teams played a 142-game schedule but travel was difficult and expensive, and it is unknown whether the league finished the season.

In 1920, another attempt at organization led to the formation of the Texas Negro League. McGar again was a leader in the organization and was assisted by A.S. Wells of Dallas. Wichita Falls (Black Spudders), San Antonio (Black Indians), Beaumont, Houston (Black Buffalos), Dallas (Black Giants) and Fort Worth formed the nucleus of teams the first year. Austin (Black Senators), Abilene (Eagles), Paris (Giants), San Angelo and Waco also would field teams in later years. This organization lasted through the 1927 season, when poor economics and other circumstances led to its disbanding.

The next attempt at forming a professional black league happened in 1929. Quincy Gilmore, a former secretary of the Negro National League, called several black community leaders and met at the Pythian Temple in Dallas. Shreveport, Dallas, Houston, Tulsa, San Antonio, Oklahoma City, Wichita Falls and Fort Worth

Maury Wills signed in 1955 as the first black player with the Fort Worth Cats. He broke into the majors in 1959, where he played for the Los Angeles Dodgers, Pittsburgh Pirates and Montreal Expos. In 2005, the Cats retired Wills' jersey number 6. The Presswood Collection.

were all represented and all agreed to form teams. These teams, as had been done in former leagues, would play in the ballparks of the white Texas League teams when they were on the road and would usually adopt their nickname, though prefaced with the word black.

It was recorded that one game in Dallas between the Black Giants and the Fort Worth Black Panthers drew almost 6,000 fans. William Tresivant of Fort Worth served as the league's first commissioner, and the league lasted through the 1932 season. The Great Depression caused too many financial difficulties for the league to survive, as was the case with many other minor leagues, both black and white.

The Depression did not deter black ballplayers from playing the game they loved but caused them to return to barnstorming and amateur organizations. The Fort Worth Black Cats, the Mineola Black Spiders, the Waco Tigers, the Jasper Steers and the Dallas Brown Bombers played all over Texas and as far north as Canada. These teams and a few others were recognized as having some of the greatest black baseball talent not in the Negro National or American leagues, and many of these players went on to play in those leagues.

When integration of Major League Baseball occurred in 1947, many of the great stars of the Negro professional leagues turned their attention to playing in the major leagues. This led to an economic decline of professional black leagues, but it was also the only time a Texas city was part of the Negro American League. In 1949, the Newark Eagles were sold and moved to Houston. The Houston Eagles had a two-year run before being sold and moved to New Orleans, but manager "Red" Parnell and Bill "Fireball" Beverly led the team to a competitive finish.

Integration for the Texas League happened shortly thereafter when Dave Hoskins was signed to play for the Dallas Eagles. Maury Wills and Eddie Moore signed with the Fort Worth Cats in 1955, and many other teams followed suit. Shreveport was the lone holdout in the Texas League, and teams visiting Shreveport were given roster exemptions to add white ballplayers to their teams because black players were still not allowed to play in Shreveport. Although integration removed the need to organize professional black leagues, black semiprofessional leagues still offered opportunities not yet offered to all.

Jerry Craft, who currently is the mayor of Jacksboro, became the first white player in an all-black league when he pitched for the Wichita Falls All Stars in the West Texas Colored League. Randy Eli Grothe photo.

The South Texas Negro League and the West Texas Colored League were two examples of strong semiprofessional competition throughout Texas. For many years, a Texas "colored" team championship was held in Waco but was moved to Fort Worth when a tornado tore through Waco's Katy Park. These segregated leagues also led to an unexpected story when Jerry Craft, who currently is the mayor of Jacksboro, became the first white player in an all-black league. His story is being chronicled by author Kathleen Sullivan in her tentatively titled book *Our White Boy,* due to be printed by the Southern Methodist University Press Sports Series.

Today the black community is challenged with reintroducing baseball to the black youth. Football and basketball have a stronghold with many in these communities; however, Major League Baseball's RBI program and other efforts have been formed to spur renewed interest in baseball. ☆

Major League Baseball in Texas

Major league baseball came to Texas when the National League awarded two franchises in 1961, one to New York (Mets) and the other to Houston and Roy Hofheinz, who named the team the Colt .45s.

The team played in the temporary Colt Stadium until the completion next door of the Astrodome. With the 1965 move to the world's first domed stadium, the team became the Astros.

In 2000, the Astros moved to the new downtown ballpark now called Minute Maid Park. The Astros have been in the playoffs nine times, including the World Series in 2005.

Houston Colt .45s (National League)

Year	Win	Loss	%	Finish
1962	64	96	.400	8th in league
1963	66	96	.407	9th in league
1964	66	96	.407	9th in league

Houston Astros

Year	Win	Loss	%	Finish
1965	65	97	.407	9th in league
1966	72	90	.444	8th in league
1967	69	93	.426	9th in league
1968	72	90	.444	10th in league

Craig Biggio stands in the Astrodome in September 1999 before one of the last major league games ever played there. AP photo.

National League split into divisions with Houston in the **West** Division

Year	Win	Loss	%	Finish
1969	81	81	.500	5th in division
1970	79	83	.488	4th in division
1971	79	83	.488	tied for 4th
1972	84	69	.549	tied for 2nd
1973	82	80	.506	4th in division
1974	81	81	.500	4th in division
1975	64	97	.398	6th in division
1976	80	82	.494	3rd in division
1977	81	81	.500	3rd in division
1978	74	88	.457	5th in division
1979	89	73	.549	2nd in division
1980	93	70	.571	1st in division; lost NLCS to Philadelphia Phillies 3-2
1981	61	49	.555	3rd in division; lost NLDS to Los Angeles Dodgers 3-2
1982	77	85	.475	5th in division
1983	85	77	.525	3rd in division
1984	80	82	.494	tied for 2nd in division
1985	83	79	.512	tied for 3rd in division
1986	96	66	.593	1st in division; lost NLCS to New York Mets 4-2
1987	76	86	.469	3rd in division
1988	82	80	.506	5th in division
1989	86	76	.531	3rd in division
1990	75	87	.463	tied for 4th in division
1991	65	97	.401	6th in division
1992	81	81	.500	4th in division
1993	85	77	.525	3rd in division

Realignment to **Central** Division

Year	Win	Loss	%	Finish
1994	66	49	.574	2nd in division; (baseball strike, no playoffs)

Year	Win	Loss	%	Finish
1995	76	68	.528	2nd in division
1996	82	80	.506	2nd in division
1997	84	78	.519	1st in division; lost NLDS to Atlanta Braves 3-0
1998	102	60	.630	1st in division; lost NLDS to San Diego Padres 3-1
1999	97	65	.599	1st in division; lost NLDS to Altanta Braves 3-1
2000	72	90	.444	4th in division
2001	93	69	.574	1st in division; lost NLDS to Atlanta Braves 3-0
2002	84	78	.519	2nd in division
2003	87	75	.537	2nd in division
2004	92	70	.568	1st in division; lost NLCS to St. Louis Cardinals 4-3
2005	89	73	.549	1st in division; lost **World Series** to Chicago White Sox 4-0
2006	82	80	.506	2nd in division

Texas Rangers (American League)

The Texas Rangers began play in Arlington in 1972 after Washington Senators owner Bob Short got permission to move his team to the Dallas-Fort Worth area. The Senators were a 1961 expansion franchise. (The original Washington Senators had moved to Minneapolis-St. Paul to become the Minnesota Twins.)

The Rangers played in Arlington Stadium until 1994 when they moved next door to the new Ballpark in Arlington. Oil executive Eddie Chiles bought the team in 1980 and sold it in 1989 to a group of investors that included future President George W. Bush. In 1998, Dallas businessman Tom Hicks bought the team.

The Rangers have made the postseason playoffs three times.

Texas Rangers fans line up at the Ballpark in Arlington for tickets for the playoffs in 1996. Erich Schlegel photo.

Year	Win	Loss	%	Finish
-1971 played as the Washington Senators				
1972	54	100	.351	6th in **AL West** Division
1973	57	105	.352	6th in division
1974	84	76	.525	2nd in division
1975	79	83	.488	3rd in division
1976	76	86	.469	4th in division
1977	94	68	.580	2nd in division

Year	Win	Loss	%	Finish
1978	87	75	.537	2nd in division
1979	83	79	.512	3rd in division
1980	76	85	.472	4th in division
1981	57	48	.543	3rd in division
1982	64	98	.395	6th in division
1983	77	85	.475	3rd in division
1984	69	92	.429	7th in division
1985	62	99	.385	7th in division
1986	87	75	.537	2nd in division
1987	75	87	.463	6th in division
1988	70	91	.435	6th in division
1989	83	79	.512	4th in division
1990	83	79	.512	3rd in division
1991	85	77	.525	3rd in division
1992	77	85	.475	4th in division
1993	86	76	.531	2nd in divsion
1994	52	62	.546	1st in division; no postseason due to players' strike
1995	74	70	.514	3rd in division
1996	90	72	.556	1st in division; lost ALDS to New York Yankees 3-1
1997	77	85	.475	3rd in division
1998	88	74	.543	1st in division; lost ALDS to New York Yankees 3-0
1999	95	67	.586	1st in division; lost ALDS to New York Yankees 3-0
2000	71	91	.438	4th in division
2001	73	89	.451	4th in division
2002	72	90	.444	4th in division
2003	71	91	.438	4th in division
2004	89	73	.549	3rd in division
2005	79	83	.488	3rd in division
2006	80	82	.494	3rd in division

Sources: MLB Websites, The Dallas Morning News, *and other sources.*

The Silver Boot

The trophy that the Houston Astros and Tex-as Rangers have competed for each year, the Silver Boot, honors the major league team with the most wins each year over the state opponent.

In 2007, the Rangers won the trophy, win-ning four of the six games between the two teams.

The total for the Silver Boot series, since in-terleague play began in 2001 through 2007, is 22 wins for Houston and 20 for Texas.

Tom Fox photo.

Texas Olympic Medalists

This is a list of athletes with Texas connections who have won medals in Olympic Games. This includes those born in Texas and those living in Texas at the time they competed.

Information included is: the athlete's name, the sport and the year, as well as the types of medals (G-Gold, S-Silver, B-Bronze). If the athlete won more than one of the same kind of medal in any one Games, the number is noted before the letter code; i.e., 2G indicates that the athlete won two gold medals in the games indicated.

The symbol (†) following the medal code indicates that the athlete participated in preliminary contests only; the medal was awarded because of membership on a winning team. Years in which the athlete participated in the Games but did not win a medal are not included.

Track indicates all track and field events except those noted separately.

Source: United States Olympic Committee

Olympian	Sport	Year	Medal
Abdallah, Nia Nicole	Taekwondo	2004	S
Allen, Chad	Baseball	1996	B
Armstrong, Lance	Cycling	2000	B
Arnette, Jay Hoyland	Basketball	1960	G
Austin, Charles	Track	1996	G
Baker, Walter Thane	Track	1956	G,S,B
Baker, Walter Thane	Track	1952	S
Baptiste, Kirk	Track	1984	S
Bassham, Lanny Robert	Shooting	1976	G
Bassham, Lanny Robert	Shooting	1972	S
Bates, Michael D.	Track	1992	B
Beck, Robert Lee	Pentathlon	1960	2B
Berube, Ryan Thomas	Swimming	1996	G
Brew, Derrick K.	Track	2004	G, B
Brown, Earlene Dennis	Track	1960	B
Buckner, William Quinn	Basketball	1976	G
Buford-Bailey, Tonja	Track	1996	B
Burrell, Leroy Russel	Track	1992	G
Carlisle, Daniel T.	Shooting	1984	B
Carter, Michael D.	Shotput	1984	S
Clay, Bryan Ezra	Decathlon	2004	S
Cline, Nancy Lieberman	Basketball	1976	S
Corbelli, Laurie Flachmeier	Volleyball	1984	S
Cotton, John	Baseball	2000	G
Cross-Battle, Tara	Volleyball	1992	B
Davis, Clarissa G.	Basketball	1992	B
Davis, Jack Wells	Track	1956	S
Davis, Jack Wells	Track	1952	S

Olympian	Sport	Year	Medal
Davis, Josh Clark	Swimming	2000	2S
Davis, Josh Clark	Swimming	1996	2S
Davis, W.F. (Buddy)	High Jump	1952	G
Didrikson, Mildred (Babe)	Track	1932	2G, S
Donie, Scott R.	Diving	1992	S
Drexler, Clyde	Basketball	1992	G
Ethridge, Mary (Kamie)	Basketball	1988	G
Farmer-Patrick, Sandra	Track	1992	S
Finn-Burrell, Michelle Bonae	Track	1992	G
Forbes, James Ricardo	Basketball	1972	S
Ford, Gilbert (Gib)	Basketball	1956	G
Foreman, George	Boxing	1968	G
Fortenberry, Joe Cephis	Basketball	1936	G
George, Chris	Baseball	2000	G
Glenesk, Dean William	Pentathlon	1984	S
Gonzáles, Paul G. Jr.	Boxing	1984	G
Guidry, Carlette D.	Track	1996	G†
Guidry, Carlette D.	Track	1992	G
Harkrider, Kiplan P.	Baseball	1996	B
Hartwell, Erin Wesley	Cycling	1996	S
Hartwell, Erin Wesley	Cycling	1992	B
Hays, Todd	Bobsled	2002	S
Heath S, Michael Steward	Swimming	1984	2G, S
Hedgepeth, Whitney L.	Swimming	1996	G, 2S
Henry, James Edward	Diving	1968	B

LEFT, Carl Lewis of Houston celebrates after finishing the 4X100m relay and winning the Olympic Gold Medal in Barcelona in 1992. AP photo.
ABOVE, Lance Armstrong of Austin and Plano, left, races with an American teammate George Hincapie in Sydney in 2000. Erich Schlegel photo.

Olympian	Sport	Year	Medal
	Track	1992	S
Hill, Denean E.	Track	1988	S
	Track	1984	G
Hill, Grant Henry	Basketball	1996	G
Homfeld, Conrad E.	Equestrian	1984	G, S
Hooper, Clarence D.	Shotput	1952	S
Howard, Sherri Francis	Track	1988	S
	Track	1984	G
Jackson, Lucious Brown	Basketball	1964	G
Jackson, Zina Garrison	Tennis	1988	G, B
	Track	2000	2G
Johnson, Michael	Track	1996	2G
	Track	1992	G
Johnson, Rafer Lewis	Decathlon	1960	G
	Decathlon	1956	S
Jones, John Wesley(Lamb)	Track	1976	G
Juarez, Ricardo Rocky	Boxing	2000	S
Julich, Robert William	Cycling	2004	B
Keeler, Kathryn Elliott	Rowing	1984	G
Kern, Douglas James	Sailing	1992	S
King, Judith Brown	Track	1984	S
Kleine, Megan	Swimming	1992	G†
Kolius, John Waldrip	Sailing	1976	S
Langkop, Dorothy Franey	Speed Skating	1932	B
Leetch, Brian Joseph	Ice Hockey	2002	S
	Track	1996	G
Lewis, Fred (Carl) Carlton L	Track	1992	2G
	Track	1988	2G, S
	Track	1984	4G
Lienhard, William Barner	Basketball	1952	G
Lipinski, Tara K.	Figure Skating	1998	G
Losey, Robert G. (Greg)	Pentathlon	1984	S
Lowe, Sara Elizabeth	Swimming	2004	B
Magers, Rose Mary	Volleyball	1984	S
Marsh, Michael L.	Track	1996	S
	Track	1992	2G
Matson, James Randel	Shotput	1968	G
	Shotput	1964	G
Matson, Ollie G.	Track	1952	S, B
McFalls, Jennifer Yvonne	Softball	2000	G
McKenzie, Kim	Track	1984	B
Mills, Ronald P.	Swimming	1968	B
Moceanu, Dominique H.	Gymnastics	1996	G
Montgomery, James P.	Swimming	1976	3G, B
Moore, James Warren	Pentathlon	1964	S
Morrow, Bobby Joe	Track	1956	3G
Neilson-Bell, Sandy	Swimming	1972	3G
Nelson, Lianne Bennion	Rowing	2004	S
Newhouse, Frederick V.	Track	1976	G, S
Nott/Cunningham, Tara Lee	Weightlifting	2004	G
Okafor, Emeka	Basketball	2004	B
Olajuwon, Hakeem	Basketball	1996	G
Osterman, Catherine	Softball	2004	G
Paddock, Charles W.	Track	1924	S
	Track	1920	2G, S
Patton, Davis	Track	2004	S

Olympian	Sport	Year	Medal
Perry, Nanceen L.	Track	2000	B
Pesthy, Paul Karoly	Fencing	1964	S
Postma, Joan Spillane	Swimming	1960	G
Potter, Cynthia Ann	Diving	1976	B
Rambo, John Barnett	Track	1964	B
	Track	1956	G
Richards, Robert E.	Track	1952	G
	Track	1948	B
Ritter, Louise Dorothy	Track	1988	G
Robertson, Alvin Cyrrale	Basketball	1984	G
	Basketball	1996	G
Robinson, David M.	Basketball	1992	G
	Basketball	1988	B
Robinson, Robert J.	Basketball	1948	G
Robinzine, Kevin B.	Track	1988	G
Roe, Frederick	Polo	1924	S
Russell, Douglas Albert	Swimming	1968	2G
Russell, John William	Equestrian	1952	B
Schneider, Marcus B.	Rowing	1996	B
Slay, Brandon Douglas	Wrestling	2000	G
Smith, Dean	Track	1952	G
Smith, Lamont	Track	1996	G
Smith, Owen Guinn	Track	1948	G
Smith, Tommie C.	Track	1968	G
Southern, Silas Edward	Track	1956	S
Sterkle, Jill Ann	Swimming	1988	2B
	Swimming	1976	G
Stevenson, Toby	Pole Vault	2004	S
Stulce, Michael S.	Shotput	1992	G
	Basketball	2004	G
Swoopes, Sheryl Denise	Basketball	2000	G
	Basketball	1996	G
Tisdale, Wayman L.	Basketball	1984	G
Valdez, Jesse	Boxing	1972	B
Van, Allen	Ice Hockey	1952	S
Vollmer, Dana	Swimming	2004	G
Walker, Laura Anne	Swimming	1988	B
Wariner, Jeremy	Track	2004	2G
Weatherspoon, Teresa G.	Basketball	1992	B
	Basketball	1988	G
Wells, Rhoshii S.	Boxing	1996	B
Wells, Wayne A.	Wrestling	1972	G
Whitfield, Malvin G.	Track	1952	G, S
	Track	1948	G, S
Wilkinson, Laura A.	Diving	2000	G
Williams, Christa L.	Softball	2000	G
	Softball	1996	G
Williamson, Darold	Track	2004	G
Wilson, Craig Martin	Water Polo	1988	S
	Water Polo	1984	S
Wolfe, Rowland (Flip)	Gymnastics	1932	G
Wrightson, Bernard C.	Diving	1968	G
Wylie, Paul Stanton	Figure Skating	1992	S
Young, Earl Verdelle	Track	1960	2G
Zmeskal, Kim	Gymnastics	1992	B

Texas Sports Hall of Fame

The Texas Sports Hall of Fame was organized in 1951 by the Texas Sports Writers Association. Each year the honorees are inducted into the Hall of Fame at a gala dinner.

(The second such fete in 1952 was headlined by, "That filmland athlete, Ronald Reagan, and his actress wife, Nancy Davis," *The Dallas Morning News*, June 9, 1952.)

The hall was originally in Grand Prairie in the Dallas-Fort Worth area.

The Hall of Fame was closed in 1986 for financial reasons, but in 1991 it was reopened in Waco.

In addition to memorabilia, the new location also houses archives.

Under the current selection process, dues-paying

Zina Garrison, 2005.

Rafer Johnson, 2006.

Mary Lou Retton, 2004.

members of the Texas Sports Hall of Fame can nominate any number of individuals. (Anyone can become a member.)

The selection committee, chaired by Dave Campbell, founder of *Texas Football Magazine*, reviews all nominees and creates the "Official Voting Membership" ballot.

Ballots are then mailed to the voting membership, former Texas Sports Hall of Fame inductees and the media selection committee.

The results of the balloting are announced in the fall with the induction banquet following in the winter.

The hall of fame web site is at www.tshof.org.

Year	Inductee	Sport	Texas connection, career
			From the Texas Sports Hall of Fame, The Handbook of Texas, The Dallas Morning News and other sources.
2006	DeLoss Dodds	Athletics	UT athletic director, 1981-
	Mia Hamm	Soccer	Wichita Falls, college/national/Olympics 1989-2004
	Rafer Johnson	Olympics	Olympic decathlon 1956, 1960, Hillsboro native
	Jerry Jones	Football	Dallas Cowboys owner, 1989-
	Roosevelt Leaks	Football	UT running back 1972-74, Brenham
	Warren Moon	Football	Houston Oilers quarterback, 1984-93
	Don Perkins	Football	Dallas Cowboys running back, 1961-68
	Billy Sims	Football	Oklahoma, Heisman 1978, Hooks native
2005	Bobby Bragan	Baseball	Fort Worth Cats manager, Houston Colt .45s coach
	Tim Brown	Football	Notre Dame, Heisman, NFL 1988-04, from Dallas
	Augie Garrido	Baseball	UT coach, 1997-
	Zina Garrison	Tennis	Houston, Olympics 1988, pro 1982-96
	Bela Karolyi	Gymnastics	Trainer, Olympics coach, Houston resident
	Martha Karolyi	Gymnastics	Trainer, Olympics coach, Houston resident
	James Segrest	Track	Coach, Odessa College 1973-94
	R.C. Slocum	Football	A&M coach, 1989-2003
	Emmitt Smith	Football	Dallas Cowboys running back, 1990-2002
2004	Jeff Bagwell	Baseball	Houston Astros, 1991-2004
	Craig Biggio	Baseball	Houston Astros, 1988-
	Wayne Graham	Baseball	Coach, San Jacinto Jr. College, Rice 1992-
	Harley Redin	Basketball	Coach, Wayland Baptist 1946-73, U.S. national teams
	Mary Lou Retton	Gymnastics	Olympics 1984, Houston resident
	Rayfield Wright	Football	Dallas Cowboys tackle, 1967-79
2003	Elvin Bethea	Football	Houston Oilers lineman, 1968-83
	Carroll Dawson	Basketball	Alba, coach Baylor 1973-77, Houston Rockets exec.
	Bob Hayes	Football	Dallas Cowboys receiver 1965-74
	Robert Hughes	Basketball	Winningest coach 1958- 2005, Ft. Worth high schools
	Rudy Tomjanovich	Basketball	Player, coach, Houston Rockets beginning 1970
	Stanley Williams	Football	Cisco, Baylor 1949-51, All America
	Bill Yeoman	Football	Coach, University of Houston, 1962-86

Earl Campbell, 1996.

Ty Murray, 1999.

Jerry Jones, 2006, and Bum Phillips, 1999.

Year	Inductee	Sport	Texas connection, career
2002	Michael Carter	Football	Dallas, SMU 1979-83, San Francisco 49ers 1984-92
	Bobby Joe Conrad	Football	Clifton, A&M 1955-57, St. Louis Cardinals 1958-68
	Eddie Reese	Swimming	UT coach since 1978
	Joe Washington Jr.	Football	Port Arthur, Oklahoma 1972-75, NFL 1976-85
2001	Troy Aikman	Football	Dallas Cowboys quarterback, 1989-2000
	Norm Cash	Baseball	Justiceburg, Detroit Tigers 1960-74
	Bobby Labonte	Auto racing	Corpus Christi, NASCAR 1991-
	Terry Labonte	Auto racing	Corpus Christi, NASCAR 1978-2006
	Dick Lane	Football	Austin, 'Night Train,' NFL 1952-65
	Bruce Matthews	Football	NFL lineman, Houston/Tennessee 1983-2001
	Mike Munchak	Football	Houston Oilers lineman, 1982-93
2000	Charles Coody	Golf	Stamford, TCU, PGA 1960-2006
	Darrell Green	Football	Houston native, Washington Redskins 1983-2002
	Clyde Hart	Track	Coach, Baylor 1963-2005
	Larry Isbell	Football	Baylor quarterback 1949-51, Canadian football
	Jimmy Johnson	Football	Dallas Cowboys coach, 1984-89, Port Arthur native
	Payne Stewart	Golf	SMU All-American, PGA 1982-1999
	James Street	Football	UT quarterback 1968-69, Longview native
	Gene Upshaw	Football	Robstown native, Oakland Raiders 1967-81
1999	Red Cashion	Football	College Station, referee, 1952-1997
	Eric Dickerson	Football	Sealy, SMU 1979-82, NFL 1983-93
	Jim Hall	Auto racing	Abilene, road racing driver 1960-63, constructor
	Ty Murray	Rodeo	Stephenville, Odessa College, pro career 1989-2002
	Bum Phillips	Football	Orange, Houston Oilers coach, 1975-80
	Mel Renfro	Football	Dallas Cowboys defensive back, 1964-1977
	David Robertson	Basketball	San Antonio Spurs, 1989-2003
	Marsha Sharp	Basketball	Tulia, Lockney, Texas Tech coach 1982-
	Sheryl Swoopes	Basketball	Brownfield, Texas Tech, Houston Comets 1997-
1998	Roger Clemens	Baseball	San Jacinto College, UT, Houston Astros 2004-
	Larry Dierker	Baseball	Houston Astros, player 1964-76, manager 1997-01
	Clyde Drexler	Basketball	U of H, Olympics, Houston Rockets 1995-98
	Bill Foster	Baseball	Calvert, Negro League pitcher 1923-37
	Rube Foster	Baseball	Calvert, black pitcher 1897, a founder Negro League
	Sandra Meadows	Basketball	Duncanville coach 1968-94
	Hakeem Olajuwon	Basketball	U of H 1980-84 , Houston Rockets 1984-2001
	Judy Rankin	Golf	Midland resident, LPGA 1965-79
1997	Lee Ballanfant	Baseball	Waco, minor/major league umpire 1926-1958
	Jody Conradt	Basketball	Goldwaite, Baylor, coach UT 1976-
	Tex Coulter	Football	Fort Worth, Army, NY Giants tackle 1946-52
	Hayden Fry	Football	Odessa, coach SMU 1962-72, North Texas 1973-78
	Michael Johnson	Track	Dallas native, Olympics 1996

Year	Inductee	Sport	Texas connection, career
	Louise Ritter	Track	Texas Woman's 1977-79, Olympics 1980, '84,'88
1996	Miller Barber	Golf	Sherman, PGA 1958-89
	Don Baylor	Baseball	Austin, MLB 1970-88, manager Rockies, Cubs
	Earl Campbell	Football	Tyler, UT, Heisman, Houston Oilers 1978-84
	Bobby Dillon	Football	Temple, UT, Green Bay Packers 1952-59
	Don Gay	Rodeo	Mesquite, bull-riding titles 1974-84
	George Gervin	Basketball	San Antonio Spurs 1974-85
	Joe Morgan	Baseball	Bonham native, Houston Colt .45s/Astros 1962-72
	Gene Stallings	Football	Powderly, A&M player 1954-56, coach 1965-71
	Billy Welu	Bowling	Houston, pro career 1954-
	Randy White	Football	Dallas Cowboys 1975-88
1995	Tut Bartzen	Tennis	San Angelo, player 1953-74, TCU coach 1974-99
	Emory Bellard	Football	Breckenridge, coach A&M 1972-78
	Ben Crenshaw	Golf	Austin, UT, PGA 1973-
	Sandra Haynie	Golf	Fort Worth, LPGA 1963-89
	Tom Kite	Golf	Austin, UT, PGA 1972-
	Jerry LeVias	Football	Beaumont, SMU 1965-68, Houston Oilers 1969-70
	Carl Lewis	Track	U of H, Olympics 1984-96
	Toots Mansfield	Rodeo	Bandera, Big Spring, roping 1939-50
	Ray Renfro	Football	North Texas All-America 1951, NFL Browns 1952-63
	Tex Schramm	Football	Dallas Cowboys general manager 1960-88
	Mike Singletary	Football	Houston, Baylor 1978-80, Chicago Bears 1981-92
	Grant Teaff	Football	Snyder, Baylor coach 1972-92
1994	J. Alvin Gardner	Baseball	Texas League executive 1920-53
	Claude Gilstrap	Football	UT-Arlington coach-athletic director 1952-75
	Cliff Gustafson	Baseball	UT coach 1968-96
	Ken Hall	Football	Sugar Land 1950-53 state records, A&M, AFL, NFL
	Jim Hines	Track	Texas Southern, Olympics 1968
	Ken Houston	Football	Lufkin, Prairie View, Houston Oilers 1967-72
	Malcolm Kutner	Football	Dallas, UT All-America 1941, Chicago Cardinals
	Yale Lary	Football	Fort Worth, A&M, Detroit Lions 1952-1964
	Guy Lewis	Basketball	U of H coach 1956-86
	Shelby Metcalf	Basketball	A&M coach 1963-90
	Allie White	Football	TCU player 1936-38, assistant coach 1950-70
	1988-1993		No inductions
1987	Bill Glass	Football	Baylor All-America 1956, NFL Detroit, Cleveland
	Don Haskins	Basketball	Texas Western/UTEP coach 1961-99
	Jerry Heidenreich	Swimming	Dallas, SMU, Olympics 1972
	Tex Hughson	Baseball	Buda, UT, Boston Red Sox 1941-49
	Darrell Lester	Football	Jacksboro, TCU All-America 1934-35, Green Bay
	Jack Pardee	Football	Christoval, A&M, Houston Oilers coach 1990-94
	Y.A. Tittle	Football	Marshall native, LSU, NFL 1948-64
1986	George Foreman	Boxing	Marshall native, Olympics 1968, pro 1969-97
	Forrest Gregg	Football	Sulphur Springs, SMU, NFL player/coach 1956-87
	Elvin Hayes	Basketball	U of H 1965-68, Houston Rockets
	Ernie Koy Sr.	Baseball	Sealy native, UT, MLB 1938-42
	Odus Mitchell	Football	Coach 42 years, North Texas 1946-66
	Chuck Moser	Football	Coach 1946-59, McAllen and Abilene
	J. Curtis Sanford	Football	Dallas, began Cotton Bowl 1936
	Field Scovell	Football	Dallas, A&M, executive Cotton Bowl
	Carroll Shelby	Auto racing	Driver 1954-60, designer, Leesburg native
1985	Eck Curtis	Football	Vernon, Abilene Christian, high school coach 1925-45

John David Crow, 1982.

Nolan Ryan, 1985.
At right, Don Meredith, 1977,
and Bobby Layne, 1960.

Year	Inductee	Sport	Texas connection, career
1985	Joe Greene	Football	Temple, North Texas, Pittsburgh Steelers 1969-81
	I.B. Hale	Football	Dallas, TCU All-America tackle 1936-39
	Ted Lyons	Baseball	Baylor, Chicago White Sox 1923-46
	Bob Neyland	Football	Greenville native, Army, coach Tennessee 1926-52
	Dick O'Neal	Basketball	TCU All-America 1955-57
	Harvey Penick	Golf	Austin, pro golfer/instructor beginning in 1920s
	Nolan Ryan	Baseball	Alvin, MLB 1966-93, Astros 1980-88/Rangers 89-93
	Dean Smith	Track	UT 1952-54, Olympics 1952
	James Williams	Football	Waco, All-America Rice end/kicker 1946-49
1984	Donny Anderson	Football	Stinnett, Texas Tech 1963-65, Green Bay Packers
	Emmett Brunson	Track	Rice athlete/coach 1928-70
	Curtis Cokes	Boxing	Dallas, pro 1966-73
	Lamar Hunt	Sports	Entrepreneur, a founder AFL 1960, Dallas Texans
	Bob Kinney	Basketball	San Antonio, Rice All-America 1940-42, NBA
	Buddy Parker	Football	Kemp, coach Cardinals/Detroit/Pittsburgh 1943-64
	Harley Sewell	Football	St. Jo, UT 1950-52, Detroit Lions/LA Rams
	Charley Taylor	Football	Grand Prairie, Washington Redskins 1964-77
	Joe Utay	Football	A&M 1905-07, a founder Southwest Conference
1983	Tonto Coleman	Football	Roscoe, coach for 37 years, Abilene Christian 1942-50
	Don Maynard	Football	Crosbyton, Texas Western, AFL-NFL 1958-73
	Bud McFadin	Football	Iraan, UT 1949-50, NFL-AFL 1952-65
	James St Clair	Basketball	Coach North Texas 1915, SMU 1925-37
	Roger Staubach	Football	Dallas Cowboys quarterback 1969-79
	Pinky Whitney	Baseball	San Antonio, major leagues 1928-39, All-Star
	Dave Williams	Golf	U of H coach 1952-87
	Gordon Wood	Football	HS coach 43 years, 26 at Brownwood, retired 1985
	Pep Youngs	Baseball	San Antonio, NY Giants 1917-27
1982	John David Crow	Football	A&M, Heisman 1957, Cardinals/49ers 1958-68
	E.J. Holub	Football	Schulenburg, Texas Tech, Texans/Chiefs 1962-70
	Fred Marberry	Baseball	Streetman, majors 1923-36, first relief pitcher
	Johnny Rutherford	Auto racing	Fort Worth, driver 1963-1994
	Pete Runnels	Baseball	Lufkin, majors 1951-Houston Colt .45s 1963-64
	Kathy Whitworth	Golf	Monahans, LPGA 1965-85
1981			No inductions
1980	Fred Cobb	Golf	North Texas coach 1946-54
	Dick Maegle	Football	Rice 1952-54, All America, NFL 1955-1961
	Gus Mancuso	Baseball	Galveston, major-league catcher 1928-45
	Tommy Nobis	Football	San Antonio, UT 1963-65, Atlanta Falcons 1966-76

Year	Inductee	Sport	Texas connection, career
1980	Jack Patterson	Track	Merkel, Rice, coach 1950-71 U of H, Baylor, UT
1979	Bruce Barnes	Tennis	Dallas, UT 1929-31, pro 1932-43
	Darrow Hooper	Track	Fort Worth, A&M 1949-53, Olympics 1952
	Don January	Golf	Plainview, Dallas, North Texas, PGA 1952-87
	Catfish Smith	Football	Coach 1936-58, Carey, Mt. Vernon, East Texas State
	Al Vincent	Baseball	Texas League manager 1946-50, majors coach
	Floyd Wagstaff	Basketball	Coach, Tyler Junior College 1946-75
1978	Jackie Burke Jr.	Golf	Galveston, PGA 1949-63
	Spec Goldman	Golf	Dallas, won 165 amateur tournaments 1930s-50s
	Oliver Jackson	Track	Coach, Abilene Christian 1948-63
	Tom Landry	Football	Mission, UT, Dallas Cowboys coach 1960-88
	Polly Riley	Golf	Fort Worth, 1947-62
	Bill Wallace	Football	Eagle Lake, Rice 1933-35, All-America
1977	Don Meredith	Football	Mt. Vernon, SMU, Dallas Cowboys 1960-1968
	J.V. Sikes	Football	A&M 1920s, coach A&M, East Texas State
	Gil Steinke	Football	Ganado, Texas A&I player/coach, NFL 1945-48
	Jim Swink	Football	TCU 1954-56, All-America
	Warren Woodson	Football	College coach 1927-66, Trinity, Hardin-Simmons
1976	Bill Henderson	Basketball	Baylor coach 1942-61
	Jim Krebs	Basketball	SMU, NBA 1957-64
	Darrell Royal	Football	UT coach 1957-76
	Harrison Stafford	Football	Wharton, UT halfback 1930-32
	Jerry Thompson	Track	Dallas, UT runner 1940s
1975	Frank Anderson	Track	A&M coach 1920-57
	Red Barr	Swimming	SMU coach 1946-71
	Bob Lilly	Football	Throckmorton, TCU, Dallas Cowboys 1961-74
	Johnny Vaught	Football	Olney, TCU 1930-32, coach Ole Miss for 25 years
1974	Raymond Berry	Football	Corpus Christi, SMU, Baltimore Colts 1955-67
	Bill Henderson	Football	Houston, A&M 1940-42, lettered in four sports
	Randy Matson	Track	Pampa, A&M, Olympics 1964, '68
	Lee Trevino	Golf	Dallas, PGA 1967-2000
1973	Dusty Boggess	Baseball	Waco, Texas League player, MLB umpire 1944-62
	Frank Bridges	Football	Baylor coach 1920-25
	James Conley	Baseball	Texas League pitcher 1916-27
	Albert Curtis	Football	Fort Worth, UT 1922-24, SWC official
	Lew Jenkins	Boxing	Milburn, Sweetwater, pro 1940-50
	John Drew Johnson	Football	Waco 1920-22, Baylor
1972	E.O. (Doc) Hayes	Basketball	Coach 1927-67, Pilot Point, Dallas, SMU
	Bill Lillard	Bowling	Houston, pro 1955-71

Lee Trevino, 1974.

A.J. Foyt, 1967.

Ernie Banks, 1970.

Year	Inductee	Sport	Texas connection, career
1972	Abe Martin	Football	Jacksboro, TCU player 1929-32, coach 1953-66
	Joe Pate	Baseball	Alice, Texas League pitcher 1920s, Athletics 1926-27
1971	Jack Johnson	Boxing	Galveston, pro 1897-1915
	Bubba Reynolds	Baseball	Southwestern U., MLB 1927-39
	Rusty Russell	Football	Coach 1927-52, Fort Worth, Dallas, SMU
	Pete Shotwell	Football	Coach 1916-52, Abilene, Breckenridge, Longview
	W.J. Wisdom	Basketball	Coach 1922-42, Tarleton Jr./State
1970	Ernie Banks	Baseball	Dallas, Chicago Cubs 1953-71
	Buster Brannon	Basketball	Athens, coach Van, Rice 1940-42, TCU 1948-67
	Max Hirsch Sr.	Horse Races	Fredericksburg, trainer 1920s-50s
	Jess Neely	Football	Rice coach 1940-66
1969	Weldon Humble	Football	Nixon, San Antonio, Rice 1940-47, Cleveland Browns
	Clarence Kraft	Baseball	Fort Worth, Texas League 1918-24
	Eddie Southern	Track	Dallas, UT 1954-59, Olympics 1956
	Bobby Wilson	Football	Brenham, SMU 1933-35, pro Brooklyn 1936-37
1968	Ralph Guldahl	Golf	Dallas, PGA 1931-40
	Betty Jameson	Golf	UT, pro 1945, a founder LPGA
	Homer Norton	Football	A&M coach 1934-47
	Dick Todd	Football	Crowell, A&M, Washington Redskins 1939-51
1967	A.J. Foyt	Auto racing	Houston, 1957-92
	Howard Grubbs	Sports	Kaufman, TCU, commissioner SWC 1950-73
	Fred Hansen	Track	Rice, Olympics 1964
	Barton Koch	Football	Temple, Baylor 1928-30, All-America
1966	Wesley Bradshaw	Football	Athens, Baylor, NFL 1924-26
	Blair Cherry	Football	Kerens, coach 1930-50, Amarillo, UT
	Eddie Dyer	Baseball	Houston, Rice, St. Louis player/manager 1922-50
	Lloyd Mangrum	Golf	Trenton, PGA 1940-56
	J. Walter Morris	Baseball	Rockwall, Texas League player/executive 1902-28
	Jackie Robinson	Basketball	Fort Worth, Baylor, Olympics 1948
	Ad Toepperwein	Shooting	Leon Springs, touring marksman beginning in 1901
1965	Ben Lee Boynton	Football	Waco, 1917 1st Texan All-America, Williams College
	Pinky Higgins	Baseball	Red Oak, UT, MLB player, Red Sox manager 1955-62
	Ray Matthews	Football	Fort Worth, TCU 1926-28, All-America
	Willie Shoemaker	Horse Races	Fabens, Abilene, jockey 1949-90
1964	Walt Davis	Track	Beaumont, A&M, Olympics 1952, NBA 1952-57
	Jack Gray	Basketball	Edom, UT 1932-35 player, coach 1937-51
	Slater Martin	Basketball	Houston, UT, NBA 1949-60
	Tex Rickard	Boxing	Henrietta, promoter 1906-29, started NHL Rangers
1963	Jake Atz	Baseball	Majors 1902-09, Texas League manager 1914-39
	Wilson Elkins	Football	San Antonio, UT 1929-32, Texas Western president
	Earl Meadows	Track	Fort Worth, USC, Olympics 1936
	Ray Morrison	Football	SMU coach 1915-16, '22-34, Austin College 1949-52
1962	David Browning	Diving	Corpus Christi, UT, Olympics 1952
	Cecil Grigg	Football	NFL 1920-27, coach Austin College, asst. coach Rice
	Gerald Mann	Football	Sulphur Springs, SMU 1925-27, All-America
	John J. McCloskey	Baseball	Father of Texas League 1888
	D.A. Penick	Tennis	UT coach 1908-57, SWC president 1922-34
	Kyle Rote	Football	San Antonio, SMU, NY Giants 1951-61
1961	Pete Cawthon	Football	Coach 1919-40, Beaumont, Austin Col., Texas Tech
	Bibb Falk	Baseball	Austin, UT, MLB 1920-31, UT coach 1942-67
	Monty Stratton	Baseball	Wagner, MLB 1934-38, 1948 film Stratton Story
	Clyde Turner	Football	Sweetwater, Hardin-Simmons, NFL 1940-52

Year	Inductee	Sport	Texas connection, career
1960	Charles Aldrich	Football	Temple, TCU, Cardinals/Redskins 1939-47
	Matty Bell	Football	Coach 1923-49, TCU, A&M, SMU
	Bobby Layne	Football	Santa Anna, Dallas, UT, NFL 1948-62
	Bobby Morrow	Track	San Benito, Abilene Christian, Olympics 1956
1959	Dana X. Bible	Football	Coach 1913-46, A&M, UT
	Paul Richards	Baseball	Waxahachie, MLB 1932-86, Colt .45s/Rangers exec.
	Doak Walker	Football	Dallas, SMU 1947-49, Heisman, Detroit Lions
1958	Joel Hunt	Football	Teague, A&M quarterback 1925-27
	John Kimbrough	Football	Haskell, A&M 1938-40, All America, pro 1946-48
	Clyde Littlefield	Track	Beaumont, UT 1912-16 athlete, coach 1920-61
	Fred Wolcott	Track	Rice 1938-40, world records running
1957	Wilmer Allison	Tennis	San Antonio, UT 1925-29 player, coach 1957-73
	Jimmy Demaret	Golf	Houston, PGA 1938-57
	Dutch Meyer	Football	Ellinger, TCU 1917-20 player, coach 1934-52
1956	Jimmy Kitts	Basketball	Coach 1929-39, Athens (national title), Rice
	Davey O'Brien	Football	Dallas, TCU quarterback, Heisman, NFL 1939-40
	Cecil Smith	Polo	Oxford (Llano Co.), international competitor 1938-62
1955	Rogers Hornsby	Baseball	Winters, Fort Worth, MLB player/manager 1915-53
	Byron Nelson	Golf	Long Branch, Fort Worth, PGA 1935-51
	Paul Tyson	Football	Coach, Waco 1913-31
1954	Sammy Baugh	Football	Sweetwater, TCU 1934-36, Redskins 1937-52
	William Disch	Baseball	UT coach 1911-39
	Bo McMillin	Football	Fort Worth, college coach 1922-1947, NFL 1948-50
	Babe Didrikson Zaharias	Golf	Port Arthur, Olympic athlete 1932, a founder LPGA
1953			No inductees
1952	Ben Hogan	Golf	Dublin, Fort Worth, PGA 1931 67
	Joe Routt	Football	Chappell Hill, A&M All America 1936-37
1951	Tris Speaker	Baseball	Hubbard, MLB 1907-28, manager of world champion Cleveland Indians 1920
END			

Rogers Hornsby, 1955.

Babe Didrikson Zaharias, 1954.

At left, Kyle Rote, 1962.

At right, the University of Houston's coach Guy Lewis, 1994, and star player Hakeem Olajuwon, 1998.

STATE: High School Football Championships

The University Interscholastic League, which governs literary and athletic competition among schools in Texas, was organized in 1910 as a division of the University of Texas extension service. Initially, it sponsored forensic competition.

By 1920, the UIL organized the structure of the high school football game. Town teams had begun competing in Texas in the 1890s, and the sport gained popularity in the 20th century.

From 1920 until 1947, the UIL named only one state high school football champion for the larger schools. Smaller schools were limited to regional titles.

The Strawn 6-Man team celebrates their 2003 state championship victory. File photo.

Beginning in 1948, champions were named by divisions based on school enrollment, with the introduction of City, AA and A divisions.

Over the years, other adjustments have been made in determining the divisions, so that today the divisions range from 6-Man competition for the smaller schools to the largest 5A schools.

In the 1990s, subdivisions were added within 2A-5A divisions, with the larger schools included in the Division I. Subdivisions were added to the two other divisions for the season competition in 2006.

Following are listed the champions by UIL division, along with the runner up, and the points scored by each team in the championship game. Included in years 1940-68 are the teams competing in the Prairie View Interscholastic League (PVIL, first called the Interscholastic League of Colored Schools). Between 1965 and 1968, the schools were integrated into the UIL. (OT refers to overtime.) *Source: The University Interscholastic League at* www.uil.utexas.edu.

2006

6-Man Division I
Richland Springs 78
Rule 58
6-Man Division II
Vernon Northside 60
Jayton 41
A Division I
Alto 42
McCamey 13
A Division II
Chilton 20
Windthorst 10
AA Division I
Tatum 32
Littlefield 14
AA Division II
Mart 23
Cisco 13
AAA Division I
Texarkana
Liberty-Eylau 35
Robinson 34
AAA Division II
Liberty Hill 22
Celina 19
AAAA Division I
Alamo Heights 40
Copperas Cove 28
AAAA Division II
La Marque 34
Waco 14
AAAAA Division I
Southlake Carroll 43
Austin Westlake 29
AAAAA Division II

Cedar Hill 51
Cypress Falls 17

2005

6-Man
Throckmorton 68
Turkey Valley 22
A
Stratford 21
Big Sandy 20
AA Division I
Newton 28
Argyle 20
AA Division II
Celina 28
Omaha Paul Pewitt 12
AAA Division I
Wimberley 21
Gainsville 7
AAA Division II
Tatum 38
Hutto 34
AAAA Division I
Highland Park (Dallas) 59
Marshall 0
AAAA Division II
Lewisville Hebron 28
Calallen (Corpus Christi) 0
AAAAA Division I
Euless Trinity 28
Converse Judson 14
AAAAA Division II
Southlake Carroll 34
Katy 20

2004

6-Man
Richland Springs 58

Turkey Valley 38
A
Shiner 33
Stratford 19
AA Division I
Boyd 17
Newton 14
AA Division II
Crawford 28
Troup 14
AAA Division I
Wylie (Abilene) 17
Cuero 14
AAA Division II
Gilmer 49
Jasper 47
AAAA Division I
Ennis 23
Marshall 21
AAAA Division II
(OT2)   Kilgore 33
Dallas Lincoln 27
AAAAA Division I
Tyler Lee 28
Spring Westfield 21
AAAAA Division II
Southlake Carroll 27
Smithson Valley 24

2003

6-Man
Strawn 67
Fort Davis 62
A
Windthorst 28
Shiner 27
AA Division I

San Augustine 28
Tuscola Jim Ned 7
AA Division II
Garrison 27
Bangs 0
AAA Division I
Gainsville 35
Burnet 24
AAA Division II
Atlanta 34
Marlin 0
AAAA Division I
North Crowley 20
Bay City 6
AAAA Division II
(OT 3)   La Marque 43
Denton Ryan 35
AAAAA Division I
Galena Park
North Shore 23
Conroe The Woodlands 7
AAAAA Division II
Katy 16
Southlake Carroll 15

2002

6-Man
Calvert 51
Sanderson 46
A
Petrolia 39
Celeste 18
AA Division I
Corrigan-Camden 33
Bangs 14
AA Division II
Rosebud-Lott 34

Cisco 0
AAA Division I
Everman 35
Burnet 14
AAA Division II
(OT 2) Bandera 27
Greenwood 24
AAAA Division I
Texarkana 42
New Braunfels 11
AAAA Division II
Denton Ryan 38
Brenham 8
AAAAA Division I
Converse Judson 33
Midland 32
AAAAA Division II
Southlake Carroll 45
Smithson Valley 14

2001
6-Man
Whitharral 27
Richland Springs 20
A
Burkeville 27
Celeste 8
AA Division I
Blanco 16
Van Alstyne 0
AA Division II
Celina 41
Garrison 35
AAA Division I
Everman 25
Sinton 14
AAA Division II
Commerce 14
La Grange 11
AAAA Division I
(OT) Denton Ryan 42
Smithson Valley 35
AAAA Division II
Ennis 21
Bay City 0
AAAAA Division I
Mesquite 14
San Antonio Taft 13
AAAAA Division II
Lufkin 38
Westlake (Austin) 24

2000
6-Man
Panther Creek 42
Highland 36
A
Stratford 49
Burkeville 14
AA Division I
Sonora 27
Blanco 24
AA Division II
Celina 21
Mart 17
AAA Division I
Gatesville 14
Wylie (Abilene) 10
AAA Division II
La Grange 20

Forney 17
AAAA Division I
Bay City 24
Denton Ryan 2
AAAA Division II
Ennis 38
West Orange-Stark 24
AAAAA Division I
Midland Lee 33
Westlake (Austin) 21
AAAAA Division II
Katy 35
Tyler John Tyler 20

1999
6-Man
Gordon 54
Groom 34
A
Bartlett 35
Aspermont 6
AA Division I
Mart 40
Boyd 7
AA Division II
Celina 38
Elysian Fields 7
AAA Division I
Liberty Eylau 49
Mathis 6
AAA Division II
Commerce 17
Sealy 10
AAAA Division I
Texas City 27
Hereford 14
AAAA Division I
Stephenville 28
Port Neches-Groves 18
AAAAA Division I
Midland Lee 42
Aldine Eisenhower 21
AAAAA Division II
Garland 37
Katy 25

1998
6-Man
Trinidad 62
Borden County 16
A
Tenaha 20
Wheeler 13
AA Division I
Omaha Paul Pewitt 28
Brookshire-Royal 26
AA Division II
Celina 21
Elysian Fields 0
AAA Division I
Aledo 14
Cuero 7
AAA Division II
Newton 21
Daingerfield 0
AAAA Division I
Grapevine 22
Bay City 0
AAAA Division II
Stephenville 34

La Marque 7
AAAAA Division I
Duncanville 24
Converse Judson 21
AAAAA Division II
Midland Lee 54
San Antonio MacArthur 0

1997
6-Man
Borden County 48
Panther Creek 16
A
Granger 40
Wheeler 0
AA
Stanton 33
Rogers 7
AAA
Sealy 28
Commerce 21
AAAA Division I
Texas City 37
Corsicana 34
AAAA Division II
La Marque 17
Denison 0
AAAAA Division I
Katy 24
Longview 3
AAAAA Division II
Flower Mound Marcus 59
Alief Hastings 20

1996
6-Man
Gordon 51
Whitharral 50
A
Windthorst 41
Tenaha 12
AA
Iraan 14
Groveton 7
AAA
Sealy 36
Tatum 27
AAAA Division I
Grapevine 34
Hays Consolidated 19
AAAA Division II
La Marque 34
Denison 3
AAAAA Division I
Lewisville 58
Converse Judson 34
AAAAA Division II
Westlake (Austin) 55
Abilene Cooper 15

1995
6-Man
Amherst 78
Milford 42
A
Thorndale 14
Roscoe 7
AA
Celina 32
Alto 28
AAA

Sealy 21
Commerce 20
AAAA
La Marque 31
Denison 8
AAAAA Division I
Converse Judson 31
Odessa Permian 28
AAAAA Division II
San Antonio Roosevelt 17
Flower Mound Marcus 10

1994
6-Man
Amherst 30
Milford 20
A
Thorndale 36
Crawford 13
AA
Goldthwaite 20
Schulenburg 16
AAA
Sealy 36
Atlanta 15
AAAA
Stephenville 32
La Marque 17
AAAAA Division I
Plano 28
Katy 7
AAAAA Division II
Tyler John Tyler 35
Westlake (Austin) 24

1993
6-Man
Panther Creek 56
Dell City 28
A
Sudan 54
Bremond 0
AA
Goldthwaite 21
Omaha Paul Pewitt 8
AAA
Southlake Carroll 14
Cuero 6
AAAA
Stephenville 26
La Marque 13
AAAAA Division I
Converse Judson 36
Plano 13
AAAAA Division II
Lewisville 43
Aldine MacArthur 37

1992
6-Man
Panther Creek 54
Fort Hancock 26
A
Bartlett 33
Sudan 26
AA
Schulenburg 35
Goldthwaite 20
AAA
Southlake Carroll 48
Coldspring 0

AAAA
    Waxahachie 28
A&M Consolidated 24
AAAAA Division I
    Converse Judson 52
    Euless Trinity 0
AAAAA Division II
    Temple 38
    Houston Yates 20

1991

6-Man
    Fort Hancock 64
    Christoval 14
A
    Memphis 21
    Oakwood 14
AA
    Schulenburg 21
    Albany 0
AAA
    Groesbeck 7
    Burnet 0
AAAA
    A&M Consolidated 35
    Carthage 16
AAAAA Division I
    Killeen 14
    Sugar Land Dulles 10
AAAAA Division II
    Odessa Permian 27
    San Antonio Marshall 14

1990

6-Man
    Fort Hancock 66
    Christoval 17
A
    Bartlett 36
    Munday 28
AA
    Groveton 25
    De Leon 19
AAA
    Vernon 41
    Crockett 20
AAAA
    Wilmer-Hutchins 19
    Westlake (Austin) 7
AAAAA Division I
    Marshall 21
    Converse Judson 19
AAAAA Division II
    Aldine 27
    Arlington Lamar 10

1989

6-Man
    Fort Hancock 48
    Jayton-Girard 24
A
    Thorndale 42
    Sudan 24
AA
    Groveton 20
    Lorena 13
AAA
    Mexia 22
    Vernon 21
AAAA
    Chapel Hill (Tyler) 14

    A&M Consolidated 0
AAAAA
    Odessa Permian 28
    Aldine 14

1988

6-Man
    Fort Hancock 76
    Zephyr 30
A
    White Deer 14
    Flatonia 13
AA
    Corrigan-Camden 35
    Quanah 14
AAA
    Southlake Carroll 42
    Navasota 8
AAAA
    Paris 31
    West Orange-Stark 13
AAAAA
    Converse Judson 1
    Dallas Carter 0
    (On-field score:
Dallas Carter 31, Converse
Judson 14. Dallas Carter
stripped of title.)

1987

6-Man
    Lohn 58
    Wellman 30
A
    Wheeler 23
    Bremond 21
AA
    Lorena 8
    Refugio 7
AAA
    Cuero 14
    McGregor 6
AAAA
    West Orange-Stark 17
    Rockwall 7
AAAAA
    Plano 28
    Houston Stratford 21

1986

6-Man
    Fort Hancock 50
    Christoval 36
A
    Burkeville 33
    Throckmorton 7
AA
    Shiner 18
    Mart 0
AAA
    Jefferson 24
    Cuero 0
AAAA
    West Orange-Stark 21
    McKinney 9
AAAAA
    Plano 24
    La Marque 7

1985

6-Man
    Jayton 64

    Christoval 14
A
    Goldthwaite 24
    Runge 7
AA
    Electra 29
    Groveton 13
AAA
    Daingerfield 47
    Cuero 22
AAAA
    Sweetwater 17
    Tomball 7
AAAAA
    Houston Yates 37
    Odessa Permian 0

1984

6-Man
    Jayton 44
    May 28
A
    Munday 13
    Union Hill 0
AA
    Groveton 38
    Panhandle 7
AAA
    Medina Valley 21
    Daingerfield 13
AAAA
    Denison 27
    Tomball 13
AAAAA Co-Champions
    Odessa Permian 21
    Beaumont French 21

1983

6-Man
    Highland 67
    Mozella 50
A
    Knox City 27
    Bremond 20
AA
    Boyd 16
    Groveton 0
AAA
    Daingerfield 42
    Sweeny 0
AAAA
    Bay City 30
    Lubbock Estacado 0
AAAAA
    Converse Judson 25
    Midland Lee 21

1982

6-Man
    Highland 60
    Mullin 13
A
    Union Hill 13
    Roscoe 0
AA
    Eastland 28
    East Bernard 6
AAA
    Refugio 22
    Littlefield 21
AAAA

    Sugar Land Willowridge 22
    Corsicana 17
AAAAA
    Beaumont West Brook 21
    Hurst Bell 10

1981

6-Man
    Whitharral 56
    Mullin 36
A
    Bremond 12
    Wink 9
AA
    Pilot Point 32
    Garrison 0
AAA
    Cameron 26
    Gilmer 3
AAAA
    Brownwood 24
    Sugar Land Willowridge 9
AAAAA
    Richardson
    Lake Highlands 19
    Houston Yates 6

1980

6-Man
    Milford 36
    Highland 16
A
    Valley View 7
    Rankin 6
AA Co-Champions
    Pilot Point 0
    Tidehaven 0
AAA
    Pittsburg 13
    Van Vleck 2
AAAA
    Huntsville 19
    Paris 0
AAAAA
    Odessa Permian 28
    Port Arthur Jefferson 19

1979

6-Man
    Milford 53
    Cotton Center 34
A
    Wheeler 33
    High Island 21
AA
    Hull-Daisetta 28
    China Spring 18
AAA
    Van 25
    McGregor 0
AAAA
    McKinney 20
    Bay City 7
AAAAA
    Temple 28
    Houston Memorial 6

1978

6-Man
    Cherokee 29
    Cotton Center 27

A
Union Hill 14
Wheeler 7
AA
China Spring 42
Lexington 3
AAA
Sealy 42
Wylie 20
AAAA
Brownwood 21
Gainesville 12
AAAAA
Houston Stratford 29
Plano 13

1977

6-Man
May 42
Marathon 35
B
Wheeler 35
Lone Oak 13
A
East Bernard 27
Seagraves 10
AA
Wylie 22
Bellville 14
AAA
Dickinson 40
Brownwood 28
AAAA
Plano 13
Port Neches-Groves 10

1976

6-Man
Marathon 62
May 16
B
Gorman 18
Ben Bolt 6
A
Barbers Hill 17
De Leon 8
AA
Rockdale 23
Childress 6
AAA
Beaumont Hebert 35
Gainesville 7
AAAA
San Antonio Churchill 10
Temple 0

1975

6-Man
Cherokee 40
Marathon 26
8-Man
Leakey 32
Follett 14
B
Big Sandy 26
Groom 2
A
De Leon 28
Schulenburg 15
AA
La Grange 27
Childress 6
AAA
Ennis 13
Cuero 10
AAAA
Port Neches-Groves 20
Odessa Permian 10

1974

6-Man
Marathon 60
Cherokee 58
8-Man
Follett 28
La Pryor 22
B
Big Sandy 0
Celina 0
A
Grapeland 19
Aledo 18
AA
Newton 56
Spearman 26
AAA
Cuero 19
Gainsville 7
AAAA
Brazoswood (Clute) 22
Mesquite 12

1973

6-Man
Cherokee 43
Marathon 12
8-Man
Goree 52
La Pryor 22
B
Big Sandy 25
Rule 0
A
Troup 28
Vega 7
AA
Friendswood 28
Hooks 15
AAA
Cuero 21
Mount Pleasant 7
AAAA
Tyler John Tyler 21
Austin Reagan 14

1972

6-Man
O'Brien 60
Jarrell 14
8-Man
Goree 28
Harold 24
B
Chilton 6
Windthorst 0
A
Schulenburg 14
Clarendon 10
AA
Boling 20
Rockwall 0
AAA
Uvalde 33
Lewisville 27
AAAA
Odessa Permian 37
Baytown Sterling 7

1971

A Co-Champions
Barbers Hill 3
Sonora 3
AA
Jacksboro 20
Rosebud-Lott 14
AAA
Plano 21
Gregory-Portland 20
AAAA
San Antonio Lee 28
Wichita Falls 27

1970

A
Sonora 45
Pflugerville 6
AA Co-Champions
Refugio 7
Iowa Park 7
AAA
Brownwood 14
Cuero 0
AAAA
Austin Reagan 21
Odessa Permian 14

1969

A
Mart 28
Sonora 0
AA
Iowa Park 31
Klein 14
AAA
Brownwood 34
West Columbia 16
AAAA
Wichita Falls 28
San Antonio Lee 20

1968

A
Sonora 9
Poth 0
AA
Daingerfield 7
Lufkin Dunbar 6
AAA
Lubbock Estacado 14
Refugio 0
AAAA
Austin Reagan 17
Odessa Permian 11
PVIL AAA
Corsicana Jackson 31
Galdewater Weldon 6

1967

A
Tidehaven 7
Clifton 6
AA
Plano 27
San Antonio Randolph 8
AAA
Brownwood 36
El Campo 12
AAAA
Austin Reagan 20
Abilene Cooper 19
PVIL AA
Jasper Rowe 55
Hallsville Gallilee 12
PVIL AAA
Lufkin Dunbar 44
Texarkana Dunbar 24

1966

A
Sonora 40
Schulenburg 14
AA
Sweeny 29
Granbury 7
AAA
Bridge City 30
McKinney 6
AAAA
San Angelo Central 21
Spring Branch 14
PVIL AA
Bay City Hilliard 42
Denton Moore 0
PVIL AAA
Lufkin Dunbar 14
Wichita Falls Washington 7
PVIL AAAA
Beaumont Hebert 14
Dallas Madison 3

1965

A
Wills Point 14
White Deer 0
AA
Plano 20
Edna 17
AAA
Brownwood 14
Bridge City 0
AAAA
Odessa Permian 11
San Antonio Lee 6
PVIL A
Sweeny Carver 21
Cameron Price 14
PVIL AA
Conroe Washington 33
Sherman Douglas 12
PVIL AAA
Wichita Falls
Washington 31
Nacogdoches Campbell 0
PVIL AAAA
Houston Yates 18
Fort Worth Terrell 0

1964

A
Archer City 13
Ingleside 6
AA
Palacios 12
Marlin 0

AAA
Palestine 24
San Marcos 15

AAAA
Garland 26
Galena Park 21

PVIL A
Bartlett Washington 8
Garland Carver 6

PVIL AA
Sherman Douglas 32
Conroe Washington 18

PVIL AAA
Lufkin Dunbar 20
Marlin Washington 7

PVIL AAAA
Waco Moore 16
Houston Yates 14

1963

A
Petersburg 20
George West 12

AA
Rockwall 7
Sugar Land Dulles 6

AAA
Corsicana 7
Pharr-San Juan-Alamo 0

AAAA
Garland 17
Corpus Christi Miller 0

PVIL A
Smithville Brown 38
Mineola McFarland 6

PVIL AA
Lubbock Dunbar 19
Conroe Washington 14

PVIL AAA
Fort Worth Kirkpatrick 46
Gladewater Weldon 14

PVIL AAAA
Galveston Central 34
Dallas Madison 14

1962

A
Rotan 39
Ingleside 6

AA
Jacksboro 52
Rockdale 0

AAA
Dumas 14
Pharr-San Juan-Alamo 3

AAAA
San Antonio Brackenridge 30
Borger 26

PVIL A
Taylor Price 42
Dayton Colbert 6

PVIL AA
Wharton Training 40
Lubbock Dunbar 6

PVIL AAA
Fort Worth Kirkpatrick 6
Houston Fidelity Manor 0

PVIL AAAA
Houston Yates 18

Fort Worth Dunbar 15

1961

A
Albany 18
Hull-Daisetta 12

AA
Donna 28
Quanah 21

AAA
Dumas 6
Nederland 0

AAAA
Wichita Falls 21
Galena Park 14

PVIL A
Richardson Hamilton Park 24
Sweeny Carver 0

PVIL AA
Midland Carver 42
Conroe Washington 16

PVIL AAA
Baytown Carver 21
Fort Worth Kirkpatrick 6

PVIL AAAA
Austin Anderson 20
Houston Yates 13

1960

A
Albany 20
Crosby 0

AA
Denver City 26
Bellville 21

AAA
Brownwood 26
Port Lavaca 6

AAAA
Corpus Christi Miller 13
Wichita Falls 6

PVIL A
Freeport Lanier 28
West Dunbar 24

PVIL AA
Conroe Washington 16
Midland Carver 6

PVIL AAA
Corpus Christi Coles 38
Wichita Falls Washington 21

PVIL AAAA Co-Champions
Houston Washington 6
Waco Moore 6

1959

A
Katy 16
Sundown 6

AA
Brady 1
Stamford 0
(On-field score: Stamford 19, Brady 14. Stamford stripped of title.)

AAA Co-Champions
Breckenridge 20
Cleburne 20

AAAA
Corpus Christi Ray 20

Wichita Falls 6

PVIL A
West Dunbar 42
Livingston Dunbar 12

PVIL AA
Bay City Hilliard 22
Fort Worth Kirkpatrick 14

PVIL AAA
Beaumount Hebert 37
Dallas Lincoln 0

1958

A
White Deer 44
Elgin 22

AA
Stamford 23
Angleton 0

AAA
Breckenridge 42
Kingsville 14

AAAA
Wichita Falls 48
Pasadena 6

PVIL A
Livingston Dunbar 26
Grand Prairie Dal-Worth 24

PVIL AA
Baytown Carver 17
Denton Moore 14

PVIL AAA
Dallas Washington 35
Houston Washington 0

1957

A
Mart 7
White Oak 7

AA
Terrell 41
Brady 6

AAA
Nederland 20
Sweetwater 7

AAAA
Highland Park (Dallas) 21
Port Arthur 9

PVIL A
Galena Park Fidelity Manor 29
Vernon Washington 6

PVIL AA
Corsicana Jackson 46
Denton Moore 0

PVIL AAA
Austin Anderson 22
Dallas Washington 14

1956

A
Stinnett 35
Hondo 13

AA
Stamford 26
Brady 13

AAA
Garland 3
Nederland 0

AAAA
Abilene 14
Corpus Christi Ray 0

PVIL A
Sealy County Austin 19
Kaufman Pyle 18

PVIL AA
Corsicana Jackson 18
Denton Moore 0

PVIL AAA
Austin Anderson 26
Dallas Washington 7

1955

A
Deer Park 7
Stinnett 0

AA
Stamford 34
Hillsboro 7

AAA
Port Neches 20
Garland 14

AAAA
Abilene 33
Tyler 13

PVIL A
Rockdale Aycock 21
West Dunbar 7

PVIL AA
Baytown Carver 33
Gladewater Weldon 13

PVIL AAA
Port Arthur Lincoln 9
Dallas Lincoln 6

1954

A
Deer Park 26
Albany 6

AA
Phillips 21
Killeen 13

AAA
Breckenridge 20
Port Neches 7

AAAA
Abilene 14
Houston S.F. Austin 7

PVIL A
Livingston Dunbar 26
College Station Lincoln 20

PVIL AA
Orange Wallace 39
Greenville Carver 0

PVIL AAA
Houston Wheatley 13
Waco Moore 0

1953

A
Ranger 34
Luling 21

AA
Huntsville 40
Ballinger 6

AAA
Port Neches 24
Big Spring 13

AAAA
Houston Lamar 33
Odessa 7

PVIL A
Livingston Dunbar (winner)

West Columbia Brown
(No Score Available.)
PVIL AA
Corsicana Jackson 19
Abilene Woodson 0
PVIL AAA
Port Arthur Lincoln 38
Dallas Washington 7

1952
A
Wink 26
Deer Park 20
AA
Terrell 61
Yoakum 13
AAA
Breckenridge 28
Temple 20
AAAA
Lubbock 12
Baytown Lee 7
PVIL A
Arp Industrial (winner)
Lockhart Carver
(No Score Available.)
PVIL AA
Amarillo Carver 7
Palestine Lincoln 0
PVIL AAA
Waco Moore 14
Corpus Christi Coles 0

1951
A
Giddings 25
Newcastle 9
AA
Arlington 7
La Vega (Waco) 0
AAA
Breckenridge 20
Temple 14
AAAA
Lubbock 14
Baytown Lee 12
PVIL A
Huntsville Sam Houston 7
Hillsboro Peabody 6
PVIL AA Co-Champions
Houston Yates 6
Waco Moore 6

1950
A
Wharton 13
Kermit 9
AA
Wichita Falls 14
Austin 13

City
Dallas Sunset 14
Houston Reagan 6
PVIL A
San Angelo Blackshear 32
Huntsville Sam Houston 0
PVIL AA
Dallas Washington 24
Houston Yates 21

1949
A
Littlefield 13
Mexia 0
AA
Wichita Falls 34
Austin 13
City
San Antonio Jefferson 31
Dallas Sunset 13
PVIL A
Orange Wallace 34
Victoria Gross 13
PVIL AA Co-Champions
Dallas Lincoln 13
Port Arthur Lincoln 13

1948
A
Monahans 14
New Braunfels 0
AA
Waco 21
Amarillo 0
City
Fort Worth
Arlington Heights 20
Houston Lamar 0
PVIL A
Denison Terrell 13
Orange Wallace 0
PVIL AA
Corpus Christi Coles 6
Dallas Washington 0

1947
San Antonio
Brackenridge 22
Highland Park (Dallas) 13
PVIL A Co-Champions
Denison Terrell 6
Taylor Price 6
PVIL AA
Fort Worth Terrell 13
Corpus Christi Coles 6

1946
Odessa 21
San Antonio Jefferson 14
PVIL Co-Champions
Dallas Washington 19

Galveston Central 19

1945
Co-Champions
Highland Park (Dallas) 7
Waco 7
PVIL
Wichita Falls
Washington 12
Austin Anderson 2

1944
Port Arthur 20
Highland Park (Dallas) 7
PVIL
Houston Wheatley 7
Fort Worth Terrell 6

1943
San Angelo 26
Lufkin 13
PVIL
Wichita Falls Washington 7
Houston Yates 7

1942
Austin 20
Dallas Sunset 7
PVIL
Austin Anderson 20
Paris Gibbons 0

1941
Wichita Falls 13
Temple 0
PVIL
Dallas Washington 12
Houston Wheatley 0

1940
Amarillo 20
Temple 7
PVIL
Fort Worth Terrell 26
Austin Anderson 0

1939
Lubbock 20
Waco 14

1938
Corpus Christi 20
Lubbock 6

1937
Longview 19
Wichita Falls 12

1936
Amarillo 10
Kerrville 6

1935
Amarillo 13
Greenville 7

1934
Amarillo 48
Corpus Christi 0

1933
Greenville 21
Dallas Tech 0

1932
Corsicana 0
Fort Worth
Masonic Home 0
(Corsicana awarded title on penetrations, 3-0.)

1931
Abilene 13
Beaumont 0

1930
Tyler 25
Amarillo 13

1929
Co-Champions
Port Arthur 0
Breckenridge 0

1928
Abilene 38
Port Arthur 0

1927
Waco 21
Abilene 14

1926
Waco 20
Dallas Oak Cliff 7

1925
Waco 20
Dallas Forest Avenue 7

1924
Dallas Oak Cliff 31
Waco 0

1923
Abilene 3
Waco 0

1922
Waco 13
Abilene 10

1921
Bryan 35
Dallas Oak Cliff 13

1920
Co-Champions
Houston Heights 0
Cleburne 0

Boys High School Basketball Champions

The University Inter-scholastic League basket-ball championships began in 1921 when El Paso High School, coached by Luther Coblentz, won over the Brackenridge team from San Antonio.

The Prairie View Inter-scholastic League began basketball championships in 1940 when Houston Yates defeated Houston Wheatley.

The PVIL began to merge with the UIL at the start of the 1967-68 school year and disbanded at the end of the 1969-70 school year.

Today, the UIL has di-visions determined by the school size from 1A to 5A.

Girls basketball cham-pionships have been award-ed by the UIL since 1951.

Dallas South Oak Cliff players hold their trophy after defeating Beaumont Ozen in the state 4A basketball championship in March 2007. Bob Pearson photo.

Following are listed the champions by UIL division, along with the runner up, and the points scored by each team in the championship game. Included in years 1940-70 are the teams competing in the Prairie View Interscholastic League (PVIL, first called the Interscholastic League of Colored Schools). (OT refers to overtime.) *Sources: The University Interscholastic League at* www.uil.utexas.edu, *and The Dallas Morning News.*

2007

A Division I

Thorndale	39
Martins Mill	37

A Division II

Nazareth	52
Laneville	43

AA

Kountze	71
Shallowater	57

AAA

Sour Lake Hardin-Jefferson	56
Wylie (Abilene)	44

AAAA

Dallas South Oak Cliff	54
Beaumont Ozen	42

AAAAA

Duncanville	60
Humble Kingwood	46

2006

A Division I

Bogata Rivercrest	57
Gruver	49

A Division II

Nazareth	53
Lipan	48

AA

Arp	65

Ponder	49

AAA

Dallas Roosevelt	61
Carrollton Ranchview	46

AAAA

Dallas South Oak Cliff	64
San Antonio Houston	43

AAAAA

(OT)	Plano	60
Humble Kingwood		58

2005

A (Texas Cup)

Morton	69
Lipan	53

AA

Kountze	77
Tuscola Jim Ned	64

AAA

Van	62
Graham	41

AAAA

Dallas South Oak Cliff	76
Fort Worth Dunbar	58

AAAAA

Humble Kingwood	54
DeSoto	52

2004

A (Texas Cup)

Normangee	50
Lenorah Grady	37

AA

(OT)	Shallowater	47
	Argyle	45

AAA

Kountze	73
Greenwood (Midland)	54

AAAA

Houston Jones	63
Dallas Lincoln	61

AAAAA

Houston Milby	72
Cedar Hill	67

2003

A (Texas Cup)

Nazareth	51
Tenaha	47

AA

Brock	81
Hitchcock	52

AAA

Everman	72
Tatum	44

AAAA

Fort Worth Dunbar	66
Beaumont Ozen	54

AAAAA

DeSoto	94
Corpus Christi Ray	73

2002

A (Texas Cup)

Brock	70

Nazareth	50

AA

Little River-Academy	49
Frankston	48

AAA

Gainesville	79
Kountze	62

AAAA

Dallas Lincoln	71
Beaumount Ozen	51

AAAAA

San Antonio Jay	54
Dallas Kimball	53

2001

A (Texas Cup)

Evadale	66
Goodrich	60

AA

Ponder	50
Danbury	49

AAA

Mexia	74
Corpus Christi West Oso	49

AAAA

Beaumount Ozen	58
San Antonio Lanier	42

AAAAA

Sugar Land Willowridge	65
Bryan	58

2000

A
Brookeland 63
Moulton 53

AA
Peaster 67
Van Vleck 58

AAA
Waco La Vega 60
Gainesville 47

AAAA
Denton Ryan 80
Madison 69

AAAAA
Sugar Land Willowridge 59
Klein Forest 52

1999

A
Moulton 54
Brookeland 49

AA
(OT) Peaster 66
Wellington 62

AAA
(OT) Mexia 77
Seminole 71

AAAA
Crowley 60
Port Arthur Lincoln 51

AAAAA
Duncanville 78
Dallas Kimball 61

1998

A
Moulton 67
Goodrich 44

AA
Krum 64
Little River-Academy 52

AAA
Clarksville 90
Crockett 83

AAAA
Houston Waltrip 67
Highland Park (Dallas) 60

AAAAA
Midland 63
San Antonio Taft 51

1997

A
Wortham 50
Nazareth 42

AA
Italy 71
Vanderbilt Industrial 63

AAA
Dallas Madison 64
Tulia 58

AAAA
San Antonio Fox Tech 68
Dallas Lincoln 59

AAAAA
Dallas Kimball 64
Galena Park North Shore 53

1996

A
Avinger 51

Anderson-Shiro 48

AA
Krum 53
Winnie East Chambers 39

AAA
Sinton 66
Graham 59

AAAA
Pampa Arthur 82
Dallas Madison 68

AAAAA
Dallas Kimball 72
Euless Trinity 64

1995

A
Sudan 74
Calvert 71

AA
Larue La Poynor 60
Maypearl 56

AAA
Clarksville 87
Madisonville 69

AAAA
Port Arthur Lincoln 57
Austin Anderson 56

AAAAA
San Antonio East Central 108
Dallas Carter 86

1994

A
Lipan 62
Nazareth 60

AA
Krum 56
Troup 45

AAA
Ferris 84
Littlefield 66

AAAA
Plainview 54
Austin Anderson 52

AAAAA
Suger Land Willowridge 50
Plano East 44

1993

A
Laneville 77
Brock 68

AA
Troup 69
Amarillo Highland Park 49

AAA
Southlake Carroll 66
Ferris 56

AAAA
Dallas Lincoln 46
Port Arthur Lincoln 45

AAAAA
Fort Worth Dunbar 74
Converse Judson 64

1992

A
Laneville 51
Petersburg 49

AA
Troup 60

Krum 40

AAA
Stafford 73
Groesbeck 72

AAAA
Dallas South Oak Cliff 73
Georgetown 60

AAAAA
(OT) Longview 71
Victoria 67

1991

A
Moulton 53
Bronte 44

AA
Abernathy 55
Troup 46

AAA
Sour Lake
Hardin-Jefferson 75
Clarksville 68

AAAA
Port Arthur Lincoln 77
SA Alamo Heights 68

AAAAA
Duncanville 65
San Antonio Jay 38

1990

A
Santo 67
Moulton 64

AA
Ingram Moore 73
Troup 72

AAA
Navasota 71
Lamesa 54

AAAA
Dallas Lincoln 87
Boerne 77

AAAAA
Dallas Kimball 59
League City Clear Lake 56

1989

A
Ladonia Fannindel 75
Moulton 58

AA
Edgewood 48
Tidehaven 46

AAA
San Antonio Cole 66
Clarksville 60

AAAA
Port Arthur Lincoln 86
Austin Travis 72

AAAAA
League City Clear Lake 86
San Antonio Jay 69

1988

A
Paducah 99
Dallardsville Big Sandy 61

AA
Archer City 80
Liberty Hill 69

AAA
Sweeny 59
Corpus Christi West Oso 50

AAAA
Port Arthur Lincoln 66
Wichita Falls Hirschi 59

AAAAA
Houston Sam Houston 73
Fort Worth Dunbar 68

1987

A
Paducah 71
Bronte 39

AA
Morton 84
Liberty Hill 72

AAA
Sweeny 66
Hughes Springs 64

AAAA
Dallas Hillcrest 54
Cleburne 42

AAAAA
La Porte 64
San Antonio Holmes 58

1986

A
Nazareth 53
Archer City 49

AA
Morton 73
Dripping Springs 59

AAA
Cleveland 57
Dimmitt 56

AAAA
Port Arthur Lincoln 55
Mansfield 39

AAAAA
Amarillo 68
Dallas Kimball 63

1985

A
Larue La Poynor 47
Nazareth 41

AA
Grapeland 63
Morton 56

AAA
Sweeny 55
Brownsboro 43

AAAA
Bay City 65
Lamesa 63

AAAAA
Houston Madison 86
Conroe 69

1984

A
Snook 39
Nazareth 30

AA
Shelbyville 73
Somerville 67

AAA
New Boston 76
Sour Lake
Hardin-Jefferson 65

AAAA
Port Arthur Lincoln 61
Flour Bluff (Corpus Christi) 52
AAAAA
Bryan 68
Houston Memorial 56

1983
A
Snook 76
Nacogdoches Central Heights 40
AA
Morton 91
Bartlett 69
AAA
Dimmitt 81
Van Vleck 54
AAAA
Waxahachie 79
Borger 66
AAAAA
Bryan 71
Fort Worth Paschal 54

1982
A
Snook 52
Greenwood (Midland) 45
AA
Shelbyville 46
Nixon 39
AAA
Dimmitt 60
Linden Kildare 59
AAAA
Beaumont Hebert 76
Waxahachie 71
AAAAA
San Antonio Churchill 75
Galveston Ball 74

1981
A
Snook 41
Henrietta Midway 33
AA
Liberty City Sabine 62
Shallowater 42
AAA
Altair Rice 56
Paris North Lamar 52
AAAA
Beaumont Hebert 59
Canyon 57
AAAAA
Port Arthur Lincoln 92
San Antonio Marshall 84

1980
B
Snook 59
Petty West Lamar 58
A
Liberty City Sabine 69
Bartlett 68
AA
Abernathy 64
Boling 58

AAA
Beaumont Hebert 88
Snyder 53
AAAA
Houston Kashmere 70
Plano 69

1979
B
Snook 57
Krum 56
A
Vega 52
Larue La Poynor 44
AA
Seminole 47
Altair Rice 42
AAA
Huntsville 48
Mineral Wells 45
AAAA
Lufkin 75
Fort Worth Dunbar 74

1978
B
Krum 69
Avinger 68
A
Snook 63
Coppell 62
AA
Whitehouse 60
Dimmitt 59
AAA
Huntsville 55
Mineral Wells 49
AAAA
Houston Wheatley 84
San Antonio Fox Tech 83

1977
B
Avinger 68
Hedley 62
A
Broaddus 84
Whitewright 71
AA
Morton 63
Kountze 60
AAA
Daingerfield 72
Borger 68
AAAA
Dallas South Oak Cliff 78
Fort Worth Dunbar 71

1976
B
Richards 57
Brookeland 47
A
Broaddus 57
Crowell 46
AA
Mart 57
Moulton 52
AAA
Odessa Ector 78
Waxahachie 75

AAAA
El Paso Eastwood 74
Tyler 62

1975
B
Larue La Poynor 52
Spade 42
A
Brookshire Royal 62
Whitewright 57
AA
Dimmitt 49
Van Vleck 43
AAA
Lamesa 59
South Grand Prairie 55
AAAA
Houston Kashmere 60
Fort Worth Paschal 58

1974
B
Huckabay 49
Larue La Poynor 48
A
Huntington 41
Snook 39
AA
Bowie 76
Friona 66
AAA
Gonzales 77
Crosby 62
AAAA
Houston Kashmere 91
Dallas South Oak Cliff 87

1973
B
Larue La Poynor 72
Brock 52
A
Kennard 77
Petrolia 67
AA
San Augustine 60
Grand Saline 58
AAA
Longview Pine Tree 45
Lamesa 38
AAAA
Houston Wheatley 84
Midland 78

1972
B
Larue La Poynor 53
Snook 44
A
Pottsboro 61
Garrison 60
AA
Morton 62
Whitehouse 59
AAA
Odessa Ector 71
Henderson 64
AAAA
Dallas Roosevelt 68
San Antonio Jefferson 63

1971
B
Krum 52
Snook 51
A
Van Horn 68
Pottsboro 67
AA
Hughes Spring 64
Friendswood 60
AAA
Dumas 65
Fort Worth Como 59
AAAA
Cypress-Fairbanks 70
Houston Wheatley 58

1970
B
Chester 75
Henrietta Midway 53
A
Kennard 72
Clarendon 64
AA
Kountze 75
Taft 73
AAA
Kerrville Tivy 81
Cypress-Fairbanks 68
AAAA
Houston Wheatley 108
Carrollton R.L. Turner 80
PVIL AAA
Jacksonville Douglass 88
Kilgore Dansby 69

1969
B
Snook 50
Brookeland 41
A
Friendswood 51
Pineland West Sabine 49
AA
Fort Worth Kirkpatrick 63
Spring Klein 54
AAA
Kerrville Tivy 55
Perryton 54
AAAA
Houston Wheatley 52
Houston Memorial 47
PVIL A
Carverdale Houston 78
Madisonville Marion 66
PVIL AAA
Jacksonville Douglass 69
Crockett Bunch 45

1968
B
Kennard 64
Friendswood 49
A
Aspermont 52
Louise 50

AA
Kirbyville 57
Mexia 52

AAA
Richardson Lake Highlands 51
Lubbock Dunbar 49

AAAA
Houston Wheatley 85
Dallas Jefferson 80

PVIL A
East Liberty Center 67
Mount Enterprise Concord 56

PVIL AA
Crockett Bunch 67
Texarkana Macedonia 62

PVIL AAA
Tyler Emmett 114
Carthage Turner 90

1967

B
Kennard 51
Krum 47

A
Brownsboro 68
Archer City 59

AA
Sour Lake Hardin-Jefferson 59
Dimmitt 51

AAA
Lamesa 60
South San Antonio 56

AAAA
San Antonio Lee 70
Houston Memorial 69

PVIL A
Mount Enterprise Concord 61
West Kirbyville 39

PVIL AA
San Augustine Lincoln 87
Mexia Dunbar 77

PVIL AAA
Fort Worth Kirkpatrick 68
Galena Park Fidelity Manor 66

PVIL AAAA
Fort Worth Terrell 92
Houston Yates 67

1966

B
Snook 64
Channing 40

A
Gruver 63
Honey Grove 62

AA
FW Lake Worth 60
Crane 42

AAA
San Antonio Marshall 64
League City Clear Creek 60

AAAA
Houston Memorial 73
Dallas Samuell 68

PVIL A
Center Daniels (winner)
Taylor Hughes
(No Score Available.)

PVIL AA
Cypress-Fairbanks Carverdale 70
Gilmer Valley View 67

PVIL AAA
Galena Park Fidelity Manor 61
Bryan Kemp 45

PVIL AAAA
Houston Wheatley 87
Fort Worth Terrell 74

1965

B
Snook 48
Deweyville 44

A
Pineland West Sabine 51
Woodsboro 48

AA
FW Lake Worth 60
Port Arthur Austin 49

AAA
San Marcos 87
Waxahachie 63

AAAA
Houston Jones 64
Dallas Jefferson 59

PVIL A
Arp Industrial 63
Sweeny Carver 38

PVIL AA
Cypress-Fairbanks Carverdale 75
Grand Prairie Dal-Worth 72

PVIL AAA
Lubbock Dunbar 82
Carthage Turner 66

PVIL AAAA
Fort Worth Terrell 81
Houston Worthing 80

1964

B
McAdoo 66
Hutto 65

A
Talco 75
Henrietta 60

AA
Canyon 52
Lancaster 51

AAA
Graham 60
League City Cleark Creek 50

AAAA
Houston Austin 50
Dallas Adamson 42

PVIL A
Commerce Norris 51
Larue Central 46

PVIL AA
Daingerfield Rhoads 57
Midland Carver 55

PVIL AAA
Fort Worth Kirkpatrick 65
Galena Park Fidelity Manor 61

PVIL AAAA
Beaumont Pollard 58
Houston Kashmere 55

1963

B
McAdoo 53
Nocona Prairie Valley 35

A
Pineland West Sabine 66
Woodsboro 51

AA
Buna 47
Canyon 41

AAA
League City Clear Creek 62
Seminole 57

AAAA
San Angelo 62
Houston Spring Branch 49

PVIL A
West Kirbyville 64
Smithville Brown 45

PVIL AA
Midland Carver 47
Fairfield Dogan 36

PVIL AAA
Carthage Turner 68
Bryan Kemp 48

PVIL AAAA
(OT2) Ft. Worth Terrell 87
Galveston Central 83

1962

B
Huntington 60
Roxton 56

A
White Deer 59
Woodsboro 39

AA
Buna 49
Jacksboro 30

AAA
Dumas 58
Waxahachie 38

AAAA
Dallas Jefferson 69
Houston Jeff Davis 46

PVIL A
Colorado City Wallace 70
Brucesville Sunset 56

PVIL AA
Lubbock Dunbar 63
Galena Park Fidelity Manor 52

PVIL AAA
Fort Worth Como 75
Carthage Turner 56

PVIL AAAA
(OT) Houston Worthing 62
Dallas Madison 56

1961

B
Frankston 60
Hutto 44

A
Simms Bowie 53
Brownsboro 52

AA
Buna 60
Dimmitt 36

AAA
South San Antonio 67
League City Clear Creek 54

AAAA
Houston Austin 68
Amarillo Palo Duro 60

PVIL A
Prairie View 75
Neches Clemons 48

PVIL AA
Galena Park Fidelity Manor 63
Daingerfield Rhoads 48

PVIL AAA
Fort Worth Kirkpatrick 67
Corpus Christi Coles 45

PVIL AAAA
Houston Wheatley 98
Dallas Madison 48

1960

B
McAdoo 58
Henrietta Midway 42

A
Huntington 61
Sunray 46

AA
Linden-Kildare 52
Dimmitt 44

AAA
Lamesa 56
South San Antonio 54

AAAA
Beaumont South Park 41
Austin S.F. Austin 36

PVIL A
College Station Lincoln 69
Ladonia Clark 56

PVIL AAA
Lubbock Dunbar 74
Houston Elmore 71

PVIL AAAA Co-Champions
Houston Kashmere
Dallas Madison
(Game called off.)

1959

B
Henrietta Midway 65
Kyle 58

A
Huntington 63
Plains 43

AA
Buna 53
Bowie 48

AAA
Houston Smiley 58
Hereford 42

AAAA
Pampa 65
Dallas Jefferson 52

PVIL A
Center Daniels (winner)
Linden Fairview
(No Score Available.)

PVIL AAA
Navasota Carver 66
Amarillo Carver 58

PVIL AAAA
Houston Wheatley 70
Dallas Madison 55

1958

B
Blossom 67
Dallardsville Big Sandy 61

A
Simms Bowie 48
Brownsboro 47

AA
Belton 58
New London 56

AAA
Waxahachie 77
South San Antonio 63

AAAA
Pampa 48
Port Arthur 47

PVIL A
Woodville Scott 67
Fairfield Dogan 40

PVIL AAA
Temple Dunbar 66
Aldine Carver 45

PVIL AAAA
Houston Wheatley 63
Beaumont Hebert 39

1957

B
Dallardsville Big Sandy 80
Meadows 59

A
White Oak 66
McGregor 51

AA
Buna 74
Seminole 45

AAA
Houston Smiley 52
Pecos 35

AAAA
Port Arthur 67
Pampa 51

PVIL A
Woodville Scott 75
Fairfield Dogan 54

PVIL AAA
Lubbock Dunbar 98
Baytown Carver 79

PVIL AAAA
Fort Worth Terrell 73
Houston Wheatley 69

1956

B
Pollok Central 74
Krum 68

A
Buna 52
Troup 42

AA
Jacksonville 70
Phillips 68

AAA
Amarillo Palo Duro 59
Beaumont French 51

AAAA
Laredo 65
North Dallas 54

PVIL A
Rockdale Aycock 53
Daingerfield Rhoads 51

PVIL AAA
Orange Wallace 49
Lufkin Dunbar 46

PVIL AAAA
Port Arthur Lincoln 76
Galveston Central 64

1955

B
Avoca 47
Dallardsville Big Sandy 41

A
Buna 58
Dickinson 49

AA
Seminole 50
San Marcos 49

AAA
Victoria 60
Beaumont French 51

AAAA
Dallas Crozier Tech 59
Waco 57

PVIL A
Palestine Green Bay 64
Daingerfield Rhoads 48

PVIL AAA
Victoria Goss 71
Odessa Blackshear 48

PVIL AAAA
Houston Wheatley 58
Houston Yates 45

1954

B
Cayuga 79
Dallardsville Big Sandy 54

A
Sweeny 92
Sundown 67

AA
Bowie 70
Houston Spring Branch 40

AAA
SA Alamo Heights 67
Galena Park 60

AAAA
Pampa 47
Dallas Crozier Tech 44

PVIL A
Palestine Green Bay 80
Tyler Stanton 48

PVIL AAA
Paris Gibbons 62
Odessa Blackshear 60

PVIL AAAA
Houston Wheatley 63
Beaumont Charlton 47

1953

B
Cayuga 66
Dallardsville Big Sandy 50

A
White Oak 69
Denver City 53

AA
Bowie 81
Dumas 44

AAA
Beaumont South Park 83
San Antonio Edison 54

AAAA
Pampa 61
Austin 47

PVIL A
Center Daniels 55
Palestine Green Bay 33

PVIL AAA
Lubbock Dunbar 67
Odessa Blackshear 55

PVIL AAAA
Houston Wheatley 62
Fort Worth Terrell 43

1952

B
Dallardsville Big Sandy 62
Laneville 41

A
Dimmitt 62
Plano 40

AA
Bowie 65
Levelland 59

AAA
SA Alamo Heights 49
Gladewater 45

AAAA
Fort Worth Polytechnic 56
Borger 51

Division I (4A vs. 3A)
SA Alamo Heights 54
Fort Worth Polytechnic 46

Division II (2A vs 1A)
Dimmitt 59
Bowie 54

PVIL A
West Columbia Brown (winner)
Livingston Dunbar
(No Score Available.)

PVIL AAAA
Houston Wheatley 56
Houston Washington 50

1951

B
Cayuga 44
Dallardsville Big Sandy 38

A
Bowie 54
Brenham 34

AA
Lubbock 44
Austin 43

City
Houston Lamar 78
SA Alamo Heights 52

PVIL A
Huntsville Sam Houston 58
Atlanta Pruitt 56

PVIL AAAA
Houston Wheatley 61
Austin Anderson 51

1950

B
Gruver 43
Waelder 34

A
Canyon 49
South San Antonio 25

AA
Corpus Christi 40
Vernon 34

City
Houston Milby 40
Dallas Crozier Tech 39

PVIL A
West Columbia Brown 72
Hallsville Galilee 34

PVIL AAAA
Houston Wheatley 54
Houston Yates 47

1949

B
Martin's Mill 39
Dallardsville Big Sandy 33

A
Memphis 27
Beaumont French 25

AA
Texas City 30
Brownwood 28

City
Fort Worth Paschal 41
Houston Milby 40

PVIL A
Arp Industrial 59
Wharton 38

PVIL AAAA
Houston Yates (winner)
San Antonio Wheatley
(No Score Available.)

1948

B
Maydelle 35
Johnson City 22

A
Mount Vernon 44
East Mountain 43

AA
Dallas Crozier Tech 29
Lufkin 28

PVIL A
West Columbia Brown 65
Hallsville Galilee 42

PVIL AAAA
Houston Wheatley 46
Dallas Lincoln 26

1947
B
- Johnson City 16
- Marfa 14

A
- East Mountain 35
- Bowie 22

AA
- El Paso 27
- San Antonio Jefferson 22

PVIL AAAA
- Houston Yates 40
- Beaumont Hebert 33

1946
B
- Stratford 29
- Perrin 18

A
- Pasadena 50
- Levelland 35

AA
- Dallas Crozier Tech 32
- Houston Jeff Davis 28

PVIL AAAA
- Houston Washington 40
- Galveston Central 31

1945
B
- Prairie Lea 35
- Mount Enterprise 33

A
- San Antonio Lanier 30
- Quitman 24

AA
- Fort Worth Paschal 43
- Lufkin 29

PVIL AAAA
- Houston Yates 42
- Beaumont Hebert 16

1944
B
- Prairie Lea 30
- Blossom 26

A
- Nocona 33
- Mount Vernon 22

AA
- Sunset 29
- Childress 20

PVIL AAAA
- Galveston Central 40
- Dallas Lincoln 29

1943
B
- Slidell 36
- Sidney 23

A
- San Antonio Lanier 30
- Beaumont French 18

AA
- Houston Jeff Davis 40
- Austin 27

PVIL AAAA
- Houston Yates 35
- Beaumont Hebert 15

1942
B
- Slidell 32
- Fayetteville 22

A
- Van 35
- Nederland 27

AA
- Houston Jeff Davis 55
- Lufkin 35

PVIL AAAA
- Houston Wheatley 31
- Houston Yates 30

1941
- El Paso 27
- Abilene 20

PVIL AAAA
- Dallas Washington 26
- Houston Wheatley 25

1940
- San Marcos 22
- El Paso 21

PVIL AAAA
- Houston Yates 32
- Houston Wheatley 19

1939
- Livingston 37
- San Antonio Lanier 35

1938
- Dallas Wilson 41
- Abilene 27

1937
- Carey 26
- Gober 18

1936
- Cushing 33
- El Paso 29

1935
- Denton 38
- Lamesa 23

1934
- Athens 28
- Lamesa 22

1933
- Athens 36
- Houston Davis 20

1932
- Temple 30
- Houston San Jacinto 23

1931
- Athens 25
- Houston San Jacinto 22

1930
- Denton 30
- Estelline 11

1929
- Athens 22
- Denton 11

1928
- Austin 33
- Temple 13

(Austin disqualified.)

1927
- Athens 23
- Denton 14

1926
- San Antonio Brackenridge 29
- Corsicana 23

1925
- Beaumont 14
- San Antonio 12

1924
- Dallas Oak Cliff 29
- El Paso 18

1923
- Dallas Oak Cliff 17
- El Paso 15

1922
- Lindale 27
- El Paso 15

(Lindale disqualified.)

1921
- El Paso 25
- San Antonio Brackenridge 11

Girls High School Basketball Champions

Following are listed the champions by UIL division, along with the runner up, and the points scored by each team in the championship game. (OT refers to overtime.) *Sources: The University Interscholastic League at* www.uil.utexas.edu, *and The Dallas Morning News.*

2007
A Division I
- Lindsay 43
- Sundown 36

A Division II
- Nazareth 61
- Garden City 31

AA
- (OT2) Poth 72
- Winnsboro 70

AAA
- Canyon 53
- Crockett 38

AAAA
- Forth Worth Dunbar 62
- Dickinson 51

AAAAA
- (OT) Rockwall 59
- Cypress-Fairbanks 54

2006
A Division I
- Martin's Mill 61
- Elkhart Slocum 30

A Division II
- Kennard 44
- Springlake-Earth 26

AA
- Argyle 51
- Wall 33

AAA
- China Spring 57
- Wylie (Abilene) 54

AAAA
- Waxahachie 52
- Kerrville Tivy 48

AAAAA
- Plano West 54
- Rockwall 47

2005
A (Texas Cup)
- Seagraves 56
- Nazareth 51

AA
- Brock 64
- Canadian 30

AAA
- Canyon 66
- Cleveland 46

AAAA
- Fort Worth Dunbar 56
- Angleton 50

AAAAA
- Arlington Bowie 69
- Humble 62

2004
A (Texas Cup)
- Archer City 59
- Fayetteville 47

AA
- Shallowater 44
- Aubrey 37

AAA
- Canyon 63
- Winnsboro 33

AAAA
- Dallas Lincoln 57
- Plainview 35

AAAAA
- Spring Westfield 66

Duncanville 49

2003
A (Texas Cup)
Priddy 66
La Poynor 63
AA
Brock 55
Shallowater 36
AAA
Canyon 76
Kountze 45
AAAA
Plainview 50
Dallas Lincoln 42
AAAAA
Duncanville 47
Georgetown 27

2002
A Division I
Brock 58
Larue La Poynor 26
A Division II
Nazareth 67
Dodd City 42
AA
Buffalo 48
Abernathy 43
AAA
Llano 67
Texarkana Liberty-Eylau 51
AAAA
Plainview 68
Dallas Lincoln 40
AAAAA
Mansfield 47
San Antonio Taft 42

2001
A
Nazareth 61
Kennard 44
AA
Nacogdoches Central Heights 57
Boyd 56
AAA
Winnsboro 51
Wylie (Abilene) 48
AAAA
Plainview 51
Dallas Lincoln 40
AAAAA
Mansfield 62
Spring Westfield 49

2000
A
Nazareth 72
Valley View 56
AA
Farwell 47
Brock 35
AAA
Winnsboro 54
Smithville 51
AAAA
Canyon 74
Waxahachie 54

AAAAA
Mansfield 69
Plano 43

1999
A
Vega 70
Valley View 64
AA
Hughes Springs 61
Salado 33
AAA
Winnsboro 56
Lufkin Hudson 48
AAAA
Dallas Lincoln 52
Canyon 49
AAAAA
Mansfield 65
Corpus Christi Carroll 46

1998
A
Karnack 69
Nazareth 45
AA
Hamilton 54
Ozona 45
AAA
Comanche 65
Winnsboro 56
AAAA
Canyon Randall 52
Bay City 23
AAAAA
Alief Elsik 58
Amarillo Palo Duro 38

1997
A
Whiteface 59
Celeste 39
AA
Poth 54
Shallowater 50
∧∧∧
Barbers Hill 66
Dripping Springs 45
AAAA
Levelland 36
Cedar Hill 33
AAAAA
Duncanville 44
Alief Elsik 33

1996
A
Nazareth 43
Celeste 30
AA
Ozona 45
Gunter 39
AAA
Groesbeck 63
Slaton 61
AAAA
Canyon 60
Cedar Hill 34
AAAAA
(OT2) Westlake (Austin) 64
Alief Elsik 60

1995
A
Sudan 66
Alvord 42
AA
Ozona 61
Cooper 47
AAA
Bowie 65
Dripping Springs 50
AAAA
Cleburne 55
Silsbee 50
AAAAA
(OT) Westlake (Austin) 59
Duncanville 56

1994
A
Sudan 40
Jayton 36
AA
Tuscola Jim Ned 31
Hemphill 29
AAA
Dripping Springs 64
Waco La Vega 56
AAAA
Waco Midway 52
Dallas Lincoln 40
AAAAA
Amarillo 62
Conroe 46

1993
A
Celeste 63
Muenster 38
AA
Marion 69
Hamilton 63
AAA
Dimmitt 59
Dripping Springs 51
AAAA
Westlake (Austin) 40
Levelland 40
AAAAA
Amarillo 68
Corpus Christi King 65

1992
A
Celeste 70
Brock 57
AA
Panhandle 52
Marion 49
AAA
Canyon 49
Winnsboro 29
AAAA
Canyon Randall 43
Georgetown 42
AAAAA
San Marcos 45
Duncanville 43

1991
A
Nazareth 50

Moulton 30
AA
Abernathy 37
Honey Grove 32
AAA
Tulia 58
Winnsboro 39
AAAA
Levelland 51
Lincoln 30
AAAAA
Amarillo Tascosa 54
Victoria 41

1990
A
Nazareth 53
Moulton 34
AA
Tatum 61
Marion 50
AAA
Wylie (Abilene) 51
Edna 37
AAAA
Corpus Chrisit Calallen 46
Waco Midway 39
AAAAA
Duncanville 74
Houston Yates 51

1989
A
Nazareth 57
La Poynor 33
AA
Grapeland 54
Abernathy 47
AAA
Hardin-Jefferson 46
Canyon 44
AAAA
Levelland 45
West Orange-Stark 24
AAAAA
Duncanville 42
Victoria 38

1988
A
Nazareth 64
La Poynor 28
AA
Godley 60
Grapeland 58
AAA
Brownfield 49
Hardin-Jefferson 40
AAAA
Levelland 38
Corpus Christi Calallen 35
AAAAA
Duncanville 60
North Mesquite 46

1987
A
Sudan 55
Moulton 26
AA
Morton 68
Paris 53

AAA
Slaton 43
Sweeny 40
AAAA
Levelland 41
Corpus Christi Calallen 30
AAAAA
Plainview 59
Austin Lanier 47

1986
A
Snook 36
Nazareth 33
AA
Abernathy 51
Rogers 42
AAA
Hardin-Jefferson 72
Ingleside 53
AAAA
Levelland 44
A&M Consolidated 43
AAAAA
Victoria 57
Tyler Lee 44

1985
A
Nazareth 56
Priddy 48
AA
Troy 80
Abernathy 72
AAA
Vernon 52
Sweeny 51
AAAA
Waco Richfield 44
Sweetwater 35
AAAAA
Dallas Sout Oak Cliff 60
Victoria 46

1984
A
Nazareth 64
Petty West Lamar 32
AA
Pollock Central 37
Hale Center 36
AAA
Abernathy 67
Groesbeck 57
AAAA
Waco Richfield 56
Levelland 43
AAAAA
Longview 72
Houston Yates 52

1983
A
Sudan 46
La Poynor 34
AA
Hardin 41
Hale Center 39
AAA
Barbers Hill 86
Sweeny 81

AAAA
Levelland 41
Corpus Christi Calallen 28
AAAAA
Houston Yates 58
Victoria 56

1982
A
Nazareth 64
Dime Box 37
AA
Hardin 69
Phillips 61
AAA
Barbers Hill 68
Sweeny 53
AAAA
Del Valle (Austin) 76
Carthage 64
AAAAA
Victoria 46
Dallas South Oak Cliff 45

1981
A
Nazareth 84
Colmesneil 39
AA
Hardin 61
New Deal 46
AAA
Abernathy 61
Sweeny 59
AAAA
Canyon 64
Bay City 53
AAAAA
Lubbock Monterey 71
Duncanville 70

1980
B
Nazareth 56
Brock 50
A
Bogata Rivercrest 68
Panhandle 41
AA
Slaton 75
Kyle Hays 44
AAA
Duman 53
Flour Bluff (Corpus Christi) 43
AAAA
Dallas South Oak Cliff 74
Lubbock Monterey 49

1979
B
Nazareth 46
Brock 43
A
Hale Center 46
Bogata Rivercrest 29
AA
Slaton 68
Pflugerville 54
AAA

Georgetown 41
Sweeny 49
AAAA
Victoria 43
Dallas South Oak Cliff 41

1978
B
Nazareth 47
Graford 39
A
Robert Lee 44
Cushing 41
AA
Slaton 55
Granbury 45
AAA
Canyon 59
Corpus Christi Tuloso Midway 37
AAAA
Dallas South Oak Cliff 70
Victoria 62

1977
B
Nazareth 73
May 54
A
Cooper 85
Deweyville 69
AA
Spearman 61
Waco Robinson 58
AAA
Canyon 58
Waco Midway 54
AAAA
Dallas South Oak Cliff 79
Schertz Clemens 65

1976
B
Neches 53
Crawford 49
A
Stratford 60
Archer City 57
AA
Phillips 83
Bellville 69
AAA
Waco Midway 64
Canyon 59
AAAA
Duncanville 70
Victoria 69

1975
B
Crawford 45
Neches 44
A
Southlake Carroll 50
Vega 48
AA
George West 52
Bellville 51
AAA
Waco Midway 60
Canyon 52

1974
B
Poolville 60
Lamesa Klondike 54
A
Grandview 52
Shiner 36
AA
Slaton 51
Comanche 45
AAA
Canyon 65
Conroe 41

1973
B
Neches 49
Poolville 45
A
Grandview 39
Turkey Valley 37
AA
Waco Midway 65
Comanche 46
AAA
Angleton 57
Canyon 55

1972
B
Round Top-Carmine 54
Huckabay 48
A
Claude 57
Southlake Carroll 55
AA
Spearman 50
Waco Robinson 49
AAA
Canyon 59
Rockdale 36

1971
B
Round Top-Carmine 48
Grandview 33
A
Claude 46
Glen Rose 33
AA
Spearman 52
Buna 47
AAA
Victoria 55
Canyon 51

1970
B
Follett 59
Trent 50
A
Wylie (Abilene) 80
Grandview 57
AA
Waco Robinson 57
Spearman 49
AAA
Corpus Christi Tuloso Midway 66
Canyon 54

1969

B
Lamesa Klondike 62
High Island 48

A
Stratford 42
Deweyville 37

AA
Waco Midway 66
Spearman 55

AAA
Canyon 59
Angleton 42

1968

B
High Island 53
Lamesa Klondike 40

A
Springlake-Earth 75
George West 65

AA
Bogata Rivercrest 56
Gregory-Portland 54

AAA
Stephenville 39
West Orange 27

1967

B
High Island 48
Quitaque 39

A
Springlake-Earth 105
Cross Plains 52

AA
Little Cypress
(Orange) 52
Spearman 43

AAA
Tulia 70
Victoria 57

1966

B
Round Top-Carmine 67
Deport 32

A
Jourdanton 79
Springlake-Earth 74

AA
Spearman 50
Little Cypress
(Orange) 46

AAA
Tulia 76
Victoria 75

1965

B
Trent 69
Round Top-Carmine 65

A
Lubbock Roosevelt 77
Jourdanton 71

AA
Edna 60
Friona 57

AAA
Victoria 63
Weslaco 46

1964

B
Trent 76
Burkeville 27

A
Baird 85
Jourdanton 68

AA
Friona 50
Clear Creek 45

1963

B
Slidell 71
Wells 65

A
Sundown 51
Moulton 48

AA
West 49
Little Cypress (Orange) 42

1962

B
Claude 55
Wells 41

A
Sundown 51
Ladonia
Fannindel 46

AA
Devine 38
Tulia 37

1961

B
Henrietta Midway 54
Claude 48

A
Sundown 50
Moulton 46

AA
Buna 66
Spearman 47

1960

B
North Hopkins
(Sulphur Springs) 42
Claude 38

A
Cooper 60
Moulton 51

AA
Buna 66
Friona 63

1959

B
North Hopkins 64
Bovina 47

A
Pollok Central 58
Sudan 57

AA
Abernathy 59
Buna 57

1958

B
North Hopkins
(Sulphur Springs) 86

Collinsville 28

A
Cooper 59
Moulton 53

AA
Abernathy 64
Fort Worth Brewer 53

1957

B
Lubbock
Roosevelt 56
Hawley 40

A
Ropesville 64
Cooper 51

AA
Buna 69
Seagoville 31

1956

B
Collinsville 83
North Hopkins
(Sulphur Springs) 75

A
Buna 54
New Deal 44

AA
Angleton 51
Seagoville 48

1955

B
Waco Midway 58
Cotton Center 50

A
Dimmitt 62

Granbury 44

AA
Bowie 54
Angleton 52

1954

B
Winnie East Chambers 46
Claude 45

A
Dimmitt 66
Granbury 60

1953

B
New Deal 58
Whitesboro 44

A
Claude 40
Bryson 30

1952

B
Claude 47
Duncanville 42

A
Hamilton 27
Morton 19

1951

B
Claude 42
Clyde
Denton Valley 40

A
Comanche 50
McLean 49

Kennard guard Jesse Skinner, left, wrestles the ball from Nazareth guard Stephanie Thiel, right, during the 2001 championship game in Austin. Harry Cabluck photo.

Counties

The Mason County Courthouse in Mason. Robert Plocheck photo.

History

Maps

Vital Statistics

Recreation

Population

Cities and Towns

Climate

Counties of Texas

These pages describe Texas' 254 counties and hundreds of towns. Descriptions are based on reports from chambers of commerce, the Texas Cooperative Extension, federal and state agencies, the *New Handbook of Texas* and other sources. Consult the index for other county information.

County maps are based on those of the Texas Department of Transportation and are copyrighted, 2007, as are the entire contents.

Physical Features: Descriptions are from U.S. Geological Survey and local sources.

Economy: From information provided by local chambers of commerce and county extension agents.

History: From Texas statutes, *Fulmore's History and Geography of Texas as Told in County Names*, WPA Historical Records Survey, Texas Centennial Commission Report and the *New Handbook of Texas*.

Ethnicity: Percentages from the 2000 Census of Population, U.S. Bureau of the Census, as compiled by the Texas State Data Center, University of Texas at San Antonio. **Anglo** refers to non-Hispanic whites; **Black** refers to non-Hispanic blacks; **Hispanic** refers to Hispanics of all races; **Other** is composed of persons from all other racial groups who are non-Hispanic.

Vital Statistics, 2004: From the Texas Department of State Health Services Annual Report, 2004.

Recreation: From information provided by local chambers of commerce and county extension agents. Attempts were made to note activities unique to the area or that point to ethnic or cultural heritage.

Minerals: From county extension agents.

Agriculture: Condensed from information provided to the Texas Almanac by county extension agents in 2006. Market value (total cash receipts) of agricultural products sold is from the **2002 Census of Agriculture** of the U.S. Department of Agriculture for that year.

Cities: The county seat, incorporated cities and towns with post offices are listed. Population figures for incorporated towns are estimates from the State Data Center that were published Jan. 1, 2006. (NA) means a population count is not available. When figures for a small part of a city are given, such as **part [45,155] of Dallas** in Collin County, they are from the 2000 U.S. census because more recent estimates are not available.

Sources of DATA LISTS

Population: The county population estimate as of July 1, 2006, U.S. Census Bureau. The line following gives the percentage of increase or decrease from the 2000 U.S. census count.

Area: Total area in square miles, including water surfaces, as determined in the 2000 U.S. census.

Land Area: The land area in square miles as determined by the U.S. Census Bureau in 2000.

Altitude (ft.): Principally from the U.S. Geological Survey. Not all of the surface of Texas has been precisely surveyed for elevation; in some cases data are from the Texas Railroad Commission or the Texas Department of Transportation.

Climate: Provided by the National Oceanic and Atmospheric Administration state climatologist, College Station. Data are revised at 10-year intervals. Listed are the latest compilations, as of Jan. 1, 2003, and pertain to a particular site within the county (usually the county seat). The data include: **Rainfall** (annual mean in inches); **Temperature** (in degrees Fahrenheit); January mean minimum and July mean maximum.

Workforce/Wages: Prepared by the Texas Workforce Commission, Austin, in cooperation with the Bureau of Labor Statistics of the U.S. Department of Labor. The data are computed from reports by all establishments subject to the Texas Unemployment Compensation Act.

(Agricultural employers are subject to the act if they employ as many as three workers for 20 weeks or pay cash wages of $6,250 in a quarter. Employers who pay $1,000 in wages in a quarter for domestic services are subject also. Still not mandatorily covered are self-employed, unpaid family workers, and those employed by churches and some small nonprofit organizations.)

The work/wage data include (state total, lowest county and highest county included here):

Civilian labor force as of December 2006. Texas, 11,616,514; Loving County, 35; Harris County, 1,934,335.

Unemployed: The unemployment rate (percentage of workforce) as of December 2006. Texas, 4.1; Gillespie, Hemphill, Reagan and Sutton counties, 2.1; Maverick County, 13.5.

Total Wages paid in the third quarter, 2006. Texas, $101,617,058,674; Loving County $302,691; Harris County, $24,044,183,268.

Average Weekly Wage as of the third quarter of 2006. Texas, $785.35; Hall County, $391.29; Carson County, $1,243.43.

Property Values: Appraised gross market value of real and personal property in each county appraisal district in 2005 as reported to the State Property Tax Board.

Retail Sales: Figures for 2005 as reported to the state Comptroller of Public Accounts.

Railroad Abbreviations

AAT	Austin Area Terminal Railroad
AGC	Alamo Gulf Coast Railway
ATK	AMTRAK
ANR	Angelina & Neches River Railroad
ATCX	Austin & Texas Central Railroad
BLR	Blacklands Railroad
BNSF	BNSF Railroad
BOP	Border Pacific Railroad
BRG	Brownsville & Rio Grande Int'l Railroad
CMC	CMC Railroad
DART	Dallas Area Rapid Transit
DGNO	Dallas, Garland & Northeastern Railroad
FWWR	Fort Worth & Western Railroad/Tarantula
GCSR	Gulf, Colorado & San Saba RailwayCorp.
GRR	Georgetown Railroad
GVSR	Galveston Railroad
KCS	Kansas City Southern Railway
KRR	Kiamichi Railroad Company
MCSA	Moscow, Camden & San Augustine RR
PCN	Point Comfort & Northern Railway
PNR	Panhandle Northern Railroad Company
PTRA	Port Terminal Railroad Association
PVS	Pecos Valley Southern Railway
RSS	Rockdale, Sandow & Southern Railroad
RVSC	Rio Valley Switching
SAW	South Plains Switching LTD
SRN	Sabine River & Northern Railroad Company
SSC	Southern Switching (Lone Star Railroad)
SW	Southwestern Shortline Railroad
TCT	Texas City Terminal Railway
TIBR	Timber Rock Railroad
TM	The Texas Mexican Railway Company
TN	Texas & Northern Railway
TNER	Texas Northeastern Railroad
TNMR	Texas & New Mexico Railroad
TNW	Texas North Western Railway
TP	Texas Pacifico Transportation
TSE	Texas South-Eastern Railroad Company
TXGN	Texas, Gonzales & Northern Railway
TXR	Texas Rock Crusher Railway
TSSR	Texas State Railroad
UP	Union Pacific Railroad Company
WTJR	Wichita, Tillman & Jackson Railway
WTLR	West Texas & Lubbock Railroad

Anderson County

Physical Features: Forested, hilly East Texas county, slopes to Trinity and Neches rivers; sandy, clay, black soils; pines, hardwoods.

Economy: Manufacturing, distribution, agribusiness, tourism; hunting and fishing leases; prison units.

History: Comanche, Waco, other tribes. Anglo-American settlers arrived in 1830s. Antebellum slaveholding area. County created from Houston County in 1846; named for K.L. Anderson, last vice president of the Republic of Texas.

Race/Ethnicity, 2000: (In percent) Anglo, 63.45; Black, 23.60; Hispanic, 12.17; Other, 0.78.

Vital Statistics, 2004: Births, 670; deaths, 597; marriages, 400; divorces, 228.

Recreation: Fishing, hunting, streams, lakes; dogwood trails; historic sites; railroad park; museum. Tourist information at 1890 depot.

Minerals: Oil and gas.

Agriculture: Cattle, hay, truck vegetables, melons, pecans, peaches. Market value $23.1 million. Timber sold.

PALESTINE (17,667), county seat; clothing, metal, wood products; transportation and agribusiness center; scientific balloon station; historic bakery; library; vocational-technical facilities; hospitals; community college; dulcimer festival in March, hot pepper festival in October.

Other towns include: **Cayuga** (137); **Elkhart** (1,273); **Frankston** (1,280); **Montalba** (110); **Neches** (175); and **Tennessee Colony** (300) site of state prisons.

Population	57,064
Change fm 2000	3.5
Area (sq. mi.)	1,077.95
Land Area (sq. mi.)	1,070.79
Altitude (ft.)	198-725
Rainfall (in.)	46.38
Jan. mean min.	37.4
July mean max.	93.9
Civ. Labor	20,257
Unemployed	5.2
Wages	$136,712,058
Av. Weekly Wage	$609.91
Prop. Value	$2,693,210,632
Retail Sales	$3,222,666,147

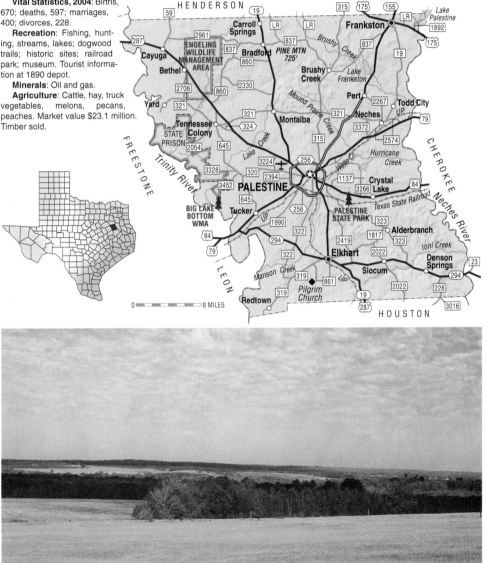

The fields and rolling hills of northern Anderson County along FM 2961. Robert Plocheck photo.

Andrews County

Population	12,952
Change fm 2000	-0.4
Area (sq. mi.)	1,500.99
Land Area (sq. mi.)	1,500.64
Altitude (ft.)	2,900-3,500
Rainfall (in.)	15.15
Jan. mean min.	30.4
July mean max.	94.5
Civ. Labor	6,803
Unemployed	3.2
Wages	$49,670,179
Av. Weekly Wage	$700.55
Prop. Value	$2,633,489,751
Retail Sales	$109,860,612

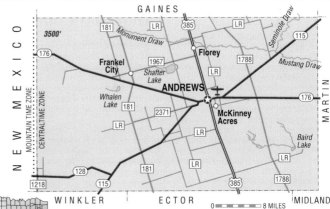

Physical Features: South Plains, drain to playas; grass, mesquite, shin oak; red clay, sandy soils.

Economy: Natural resources/mining; manufacturing; trade, construction; government/services; agribusiness.

History: Apache, Comanche area until U.S. Army campaigns of 1875. Ranching developed around 1900. Oil boom in 1940s. County created 1876 from Bexar Territory; organized 1910; named for Texas Revolutionary soldier Richard Andrews.

Race/Ethnicity, 2000: (In percent) Anglo, 57.07; Black, 1.62; Hispanic, 40.00; Other, 1.31.

Vital Statistics, 2004: Births, 211; deaths, 110; marriages, 108; divorces, 49.

Recreation: Prairie dog town, wetlands, bird viewing; museum; camper facilities; Fall Fiesta in September.

Minerals: Oil and gas.

Agriculture: Beef cattle, cotton, sorghums, grains, corn, hay; significant irrigation. Market value $8.7 million.

ANDREWS (9,322) county seat; trade center, amphitheatre, hospital.

Angelina County

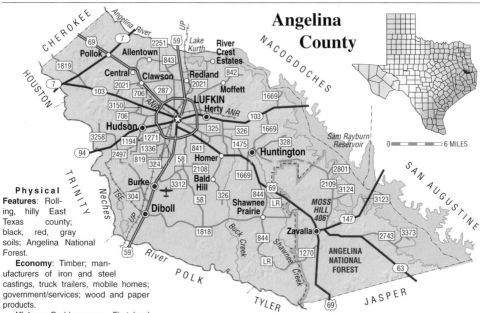

Physical Features: Rolling, hilly East Texas county; black, red, gray soils; Angelina National Forest.

Economy: Timber; manufacturers of iron and steel castings, truck trailers, mobile homes; government/services; wood and paper products.

History: Caddoan area. First land deed to Vicente Micheli 1801. Anglo-American setters arrived in 1820s. County created 1846 from Nacogdoches County; named for legendary Indian maiden Angelina.

Race/Ethnicity, 2000: (In percent) Anglo, 69.87; Black, 14.78; Hispanic, 14.35; Other, 1.00.

Vital Statistics, 2004: Births, 1,296; deaths, 773; marriages, 730; divorces, 460.

Recreation: Sam Rayburn Reservoir; national, state forests, parks; locomotive exhibit; Forest Festival, bike ride in fall.

Minerals: Limited output of natural gas and oil.

Agriculture: Poultry, beef, landscape horticulture, limited fruits and vegetables. Market value $18.4 million. A leading timber-producing county.

LUFKIN (33,307) county seat; manufacturing; Angelina College; hospitals; U.S., Texas Forest centers; zoo; Expo Center and Texas Forestry Museum.

Other towns include: **Burke** (302); **Diboll** (5,875); **Hudson** (4,193); **Huntington** (2,156); **Pollok** (300); **Zavalla** (642).

Population	82,524
Change from 2000	3.0
Area (sq. mi.)	864.45
Land Area (sq. mi.)	801.56
Altitude (ft.)	139-406
Rainfall (in.)	46.62
Jan. mean min.	37.9
July mean max.	93.5
Civ. Labor	39,484
Unemployed	4.3
Wages	$284,170,184
Av. Weekly Wage	$589.74
Prop. Value	$3,702,122,107
Retail Sales	$942,245,961

Aransas County

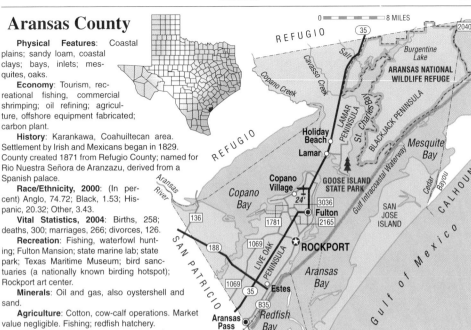

Physical Features: Coastal plains; sandy loam, coastal clays; bays, inlets; mesquites, oaks.

Economy: Tourism, recreational fishing, commercial shrimping; oil refining; agriculture, offshore equipment fabricated; carbon plant.

History: Karankawa, Coahuiltecan area. Settlement by Irish and Mexicans began in 1829. County created 1871 from Refugio County; named for Rio Nuestra Señora de Aranzazu, derived from a Spanish palace.

Race/Ethnicity, 2000: (In percent) Anglo, 74.72; Black, 1.53; Hispanic, 20.32; Other, 3.43.

Vital Statistics, 2004: Births, 258; deaths, 300; marriages, 266; divorces, 126.

Recreation: Fishing, waterfowl hunting; Fulton Mansion; state marine lab; state park; Texas Maritime Museum; bird sanctuaries (a nationally known birding hotspot); Rockport art center.

Minerals: Oil and gas, also oystershell and sand.

Agriculture: Cotton, cow-calf operations. Market value negligible. Fishing; redfish hatchery.

ROCKPORT (8,705) county seat; tourism, commercial oyster and shrimp harvesting, sport fishing; commuting to Corpus Christi and Victoria, retirement residences; Festival of Wines in May.

Fulton (1,682) tourism, oyster and shrimp harvesting, Oysterfest in March.

Part [867] of **Aransas Pass**.

Population	**24,831**
Change fm 2000	10.4
Area (sq. mi.)	527.95
Land Area (sq. mi.)	251.86
Altitude (ft.)	sea level-24

Rainfall (in.)	35.96
Jan. mean min.	44.9
July mean max.	90.1
Civ. Labor	11,114
Unemployed	4.1
Wages	$37,274,473
Av. Weekly Wage	$509.83

Prop. Value	$1,903,313,739
Retail Sales	$258,121,197

For explanation of sources, abbreviations and symbols, see p. 224 and foldout map.

Relaxing in the harbor of Rockport-Fulton. Robert Plocheck photo.

Archer County

Physical Features: North Central county, rolling to hilly, drained by Wichita, Trinity River forks; black, red loams, sandy soils; mesquites, post oaks.

Economy: Cattle; milk production, oil, hunting leases. Part of Wichita Falls metropolitan area.

History: Caddo, Comanche, Kiowas and other tribes in area until 1875; Anglo-American settlement developed soon afterward. County created from Fannin Land District, 1858; organized 1880. Named for Dr. B.T. Archer, Republic commissioner to United States.

Race/Ethnicity, 2000: (In percent) Anglo, 94.19; Black, 0.15; Hispanic, 4.87; Other, 0.79.

Vital Statistics, 2004: Births, 120; deaths, 66; marriages, 47; divorces, 38.

Recreation: Hunting of deer, turkey, dove, feral hog, coyote; fishing in area lakes, rodeo in June.

Minerals: Oil and natural gas.

Agriculture: Beef cow/calf, stocker cattle, dairy, wheat, swine, hay and silage. Market value $58 million.

ARCHER CITY (1,837) county seat; cattle, oil field service center; museum; book center; Royal Theatre productions; some manufacturing.

Other towns include: **Holliday** (1,688) Mayfest in spring; **Lakeside City** (1,010); **Megargel** (244); **Scotland** (445); **Windthorst** (478), biannual German sausage festival (also in Scotland).

Population		9,266
Change fm 2000		4.7
Area (sq. mi.)		925.78
Land Area (sq. mi.)		909.70
Altitude (ft.)		900–1,286
Rainfall (in.)		29.78
Jan. mean min.		26.7
July mean max.		97.0
Civ. Labor		5,558
Unemployed		3.1
Wages		$15,940,124
Av. Weekly Wage		$539.84
Prop. Value		$697,015,428
Retail Sales		$64,335,097

Armstrong County

Physical Features: Partly on High Plains, broken by Palo Duro Canyon. Chocolate loam, gray soils.

Economy: Agribusiness, tourism.

History: Apache, then Comanche territory until U.S. Army campaigns of 1874-75. Anglo-Americans began ranching soon afterward. County created from Bexar District, 1876; organized 1890; name honors pioneer Texas family.

Race/Ethnicity, 2000: (In percent) Anglo, 94.00; Black, 0.23; Hispanic, 5.40; Other, 0.37.

Vital Statistics, 2004: Births, 24; deaths, 31; marriages, 13; divorces, 0.

Recreation: Caprock Roundup in July, state park; Goodnight Ranch Home.

Minerals: Sand, gravel.

Agriculture: Stocker cattle, cow-calf operations; wheat, sorghum, cotton and hay; some irrigation. Market value $26.6 million.

CLAUDE (1,333) county seat; farm, ranch supplies; glass company; medical center; Caprock Roundup.

Population		2,120
Change fm 2000		-1.3
Area (sq. mi.)		913.81
Land Area (sq. mi.)		913.63
Altitude (ft.)		2,300-3,512
Rainfall (in.)		22.39
Jan. mean min.		21.2
July mean max.		90.5
Civ. Labor		1,190
Unemployed		2.9
Wages		$2,994,546
Av. Weekly Wage		$567.36
Prop. Value		$160,381,090
Retail Sales		$5,683,146

For explanation of sources, abbreviations and symbols, see p. 224 and foldout map.

Atascosa County

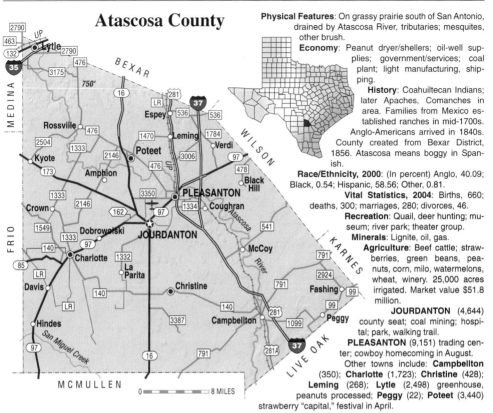

Physical Features: On grassy prairie south of San Antonio, drained by Atascosa River, tributaries; mesquites, other brush.

Economy: Peanut dryer/shellers; oil-well supplies; government/services; coal plant; light manufacturing, shipping.

History: Coahuiltecan Indians; later Apaches, Comanches in area. Families from Mexico established ranches in mid-1700s. Anglo-Americans arrived in 1840s. County created from Bexar District, 1856. Atascosa means boggy in Spanish.

Race/Ethnicity, 2000: (In percent) Anglo, 40.09; Black, 0.54; Hispanic, 58.56; Other, 0.81.

Vital Statistics, 2004: Births, 660; deaths, 300; marriages, 280; divorces, 46.

Recreation: Quail, deer hunting; museum; river park; theater group.

Minerals: Lignite, oil, gas.

Agriculture: Beef cattle; strawberries, green beans, peanuts, corn, milo, watermelons, wheat, winery. 25,000 acres irrigated. Market value $51.8 million.

JOURDANTON (4,644) county seat; coal mining; hospital; park, walking trail.

PLEASANTON (9,151) trading center; cowboy homecoming in August.

Other towns include: **Campbellton** (350); **Charlotte** (1,723); **Christine** (428); **Leming** (268); **Lytle** (2,498) greenhouse, peanuts processed; **Peggy** (22); **Poteet** (3,440) strawberry "capital," festival in April.

Population **43,876**	Rainfall (in.) 29.00	Unemployed 3.6
Change frm 2000 .... 13.6	Jan. mean min. 39.0	Wages $68,206,439
Area (sq. mi.) 1,235.61	July mean max. 95.9	Av. Weekly Wage $577.40
Land Area (sq. mi.) 1,232.12	Civ. Labor 19,802	Prop. Value $2,141,905,111
Altitude (ft.) 200-750		Retail Sales $358,,104,173

Farm tractors in the fields near Charlotte in Atascosa County. Robert Plocheck photo.

Austin County

Physical Features: Southeast county; level to hilly, drained by San Bernard, Brazos rivers; black prairie to sandy upland soils.

Economy: Agribusiness; tourism, government/services; metal, other manufacturing; commuting to Houston.

History: Tonkawa Indians; reduced by diseases. Birthplace of Anglo-American colonization, 1821, and German mother colony at Industry, 1831. County created 1837; named for Stephen F. Austin, father of Texas.

Race/Ethnicity, 2000: (In percent) Anglo, 72.39; Black, 10.81; Hispanic, 16.13; Other, 0.67.

Vital Statistics, 2004: Births, 344; deaths, 310; marriages, 197; divorces, 98.

Recreation: Fishing, hunting; state park, Pioneer Trail; Bellville Country Livin' festival in April; Lone Star Raceway Park.

Minerals: Oil and natural gas.

Agriculture: Beef production and hay. Also rice, corn, sorghum, nursery crops, grapes, pecans. Market value $24.0 million.

BELLVILLE (4,435) county seat; varied manufacturing; hospital; oil.

SEALY (6,664) oil-field and military vehicle manufacturing, varied industries; Blinn College branch; polka fest in March.

Other towns include: **Bleiblerville** (125); **Brazos Country** (283); **Cat Spring** (200); **Frydek** (900) Grotto celebration in April; **Industry** (322); **Kenney** (957); **New Ulm** (974) retail, art festival in April; **San Felipe** (907) colonial capital of Texas; **Wallis** (1,285).

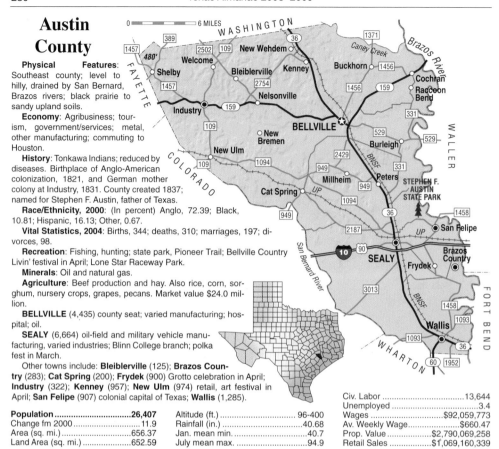

Population	26,407
Change fm 2000	11.9
Area (sq. mi.)	656.37
Land Area (sq. mi.)	652.59
Altitude (ft.)	96-400
Rainfall (in.)	40.68
Jan. mean min.	40.7
July mean max.	94.9
Civ. Labor	13,644
Unemployed	3.4
Wages	$92,059,773
Av. Weekly Wage	$660.47
Prop. Value	$2,790,069,258
Retail Sales	$1,069,160,339

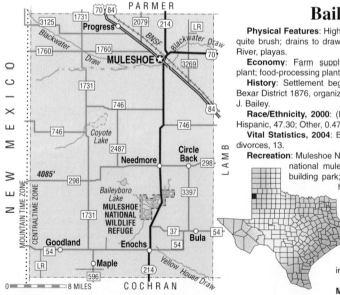

Bailey County

Physical Features: High Plains county, sandy loam soils; mesquite brush; drains to draws forming upper watershed of Brazos River, playas.

Economy: Farm supply manufacturing; electric generating plant; food-processing plants; muffler manufacturing.

History: Settlement began after 1900. County created from Bexar District 1876, organized 1917. Named for Alamo hero Peter J. Bailey.

Race/Ethnicity, 2000: (In percent) Anglo, 50.94; Black, 1.29; Hispanic, 47.30; Other, 0.47.

Vital Statistics, 2004: Births, 128; deaths, 68; marriages, 62; divorces, 13.

Recreation: Muleshoe National Wildlife Refuge; "Old Pete," the national mule memorial; outdoor drama; historical building park; museum; motorcycle rally; pheasant hunting.

Minerals: Insignificant.

Agriculture: Feedlot, dairy cattle; cotton, wheat, sorghum, corn, vegetables; 100,000 acres irrigated. Market value $127.8 million.

MULESHOE (4,620) county seat; agribusiness center; feed-corn milling; hospital; livestock show.

Other towns include: **Enochs** (80); **Maple** (75).

Population	6,597
Change fm 2000	0.0
Area (sq. mi.)	827.38
Land Area (sq. mi.)	826.69
Altitude (ft.)	3,700-4,085
Rainfall (in.)	17.37
Jan. mean min.	20.2
July mean max.	91.9
Civ. Labor	3,261
Unemployed	4.7
Wages	$17,885,093
Av. Weekly Wage	$512.39
Prop. Value	$318,119,705
Retail Sales	$72,078,254

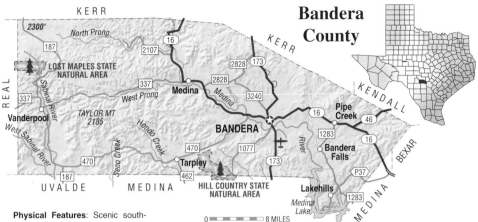

Bandera County

Physical Features: Scenic southwestern county of cedar-covered hills on the Edwards Plateau; Medina, Sabinal Rivers; limestone, sandy soils; species of oaks, walnuts, native cherry and Uvalde maple.

Economy: Tourism, hunting, fishing, ranching supplies, forest products.

History: Apache, then Comanche territory. White settlement began in early 1850s, including Mormons and Poles. County created from Bexar, Uvalde counties, 1856; named for Bandera (flag) Mountains.

Race/Ethnicity, 2000: (In percent) Anglo, 85.03; Black, 0.35; Hispanic, 13.51; Other, 1.11.

Vital Statistics, 2004: Births, 194; deaths, 141; marriages, 150; divorces, 69.

Recreation: RV parks, resort ranches; Lost Maples and Hill Country State Natural Areas; rodeo on Memorial Day weekend; Medina Lake.

Agriculture: Beef cattle, sheep, goats, horses, apples. Market value $7 million. Hunting and nature tourism important.

BANDERA (1,075) county seat; "cowboy capital of the world"; tourism, ranching, furniture making; Frontier Times Museum.

Other towns include: **Medina** (850) apple growing; **Pipe Creek** (NA); **Tarpley** (30); **Vanderpool** (20). Also, the community of **Lakehills** (5,185) on Medina Lake, Cajun Fest in September.

Population	20,203
Change fm 2000	14.5
Area (sq. mi.)	797.54
Land Area (sq. mi.)	791.73
Altitude (ft.)	1,064-2,300
Rainfall (in.)	35.78
Jan. mean min.	33.3
July mean max.	93.9
Civ. Labor	10,138
Unemployed	3.4
Wages	$17,873,283
Av. Weekly Wage	$452.16
Prop. Value	$1,767,201,349
Retail Sales	$96,213,833

For explanation of sources, abbreviations and symbols, see p. 224 and foldout map.

Hikers in Lost Maples State Natural Area in Bandera County. Robert Plocheck photo.

Physical Features: Rolling; alluvial, sandy, loam soils; varied timber, Lost Pines; bisected by Colorado River.

Economy: Government/services; tourism; agribusiness; bio-technology research; computer-related industries; commuters to Austin.

History: Tonkawa Indian area; Comanches also present. Spanish fort established 1804. County created 1836; named for Baron de Bastrop, who aided Moses and Stephen F. Austin in establishing colony in 1820s.

Race/Ethnicity, 2000: (In percent) Anglo, 66.12; Black, 8.85; Hispanic, 23.98; Other, 1.05.

Vital Statistics, 2004: Births, 871; deaths, 486; marriages, 389; divorces, 229.

Recreation: Fishing, hunting; state parks; Lake Bastrop; historic sites; museum; railroad park; natural science center; nature trails.

Minerals: Clay, oil, gas and lignite.

Agriculture: Hay; beef cattle; horses, goats; pecans. Market value $27.8 million. Pine for lumber, oak for firewood.

BASTROP (8,053) county seat; government/services, tourism, hospitals; University of Texas cancer research center; federal prison; riverwalk; River of Lights in December.

Elgin (8,394) sausage plants, brick plant; horse, cattle breeding; medical research; library; Western Days in June, Hogeye festival in October.

Smithville (4,282) rail maintenance, light manufacturing, environmental science park; hospital; model recycling center; jamboree on weekend after Easter.

Other towns: **Cedar Creek** (NA); **Circle D-KC Estates** (2,162); **McDade** (345) watermelon festival in July; **Paige** (275); **Red Rock** (100); **Rosanky** (210) automotive museum; **Wyldwood** (2,564). Also, **Camp Swift** (5,267).

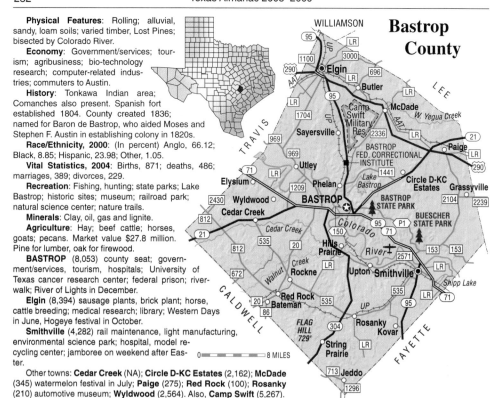

Bastrop County

Population	71,684	
Change fm 2000	24.2	
Area (sq. mi.)	895.92	
Land Area (sq. mi.)	888.35	
Altitude (ft.)	300-729	
Rainfall (in.)	38.04	
Jan. mean min.	36.7	
July mean max.	95.4	
Civ. Labor	35,665	
Unemployed	3.4	
Wages	$90,364,538	
Av. Weekly Wage	$554.04	
Prop. Value	$4,658,786,027	
Retail Sales	$648,529,681	

Baylor County

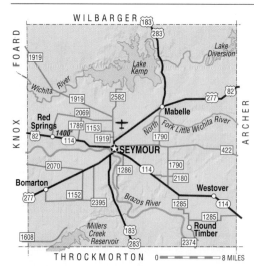

Physical Features: North Central county; level to hilly; drains to Brazos, Wichita rivers; sandy, loam, red soils; grassy, mesquites, cedars.

Economy: Agribusiness; retail/service; health services.

History: Comanches, with Wichitas and other tribes; removed in 1874-75. Anglo-Americans settled in the 1870s. County created from Fannin County 1858; organized 1879. Named for H.W. Baylor, Texas Ranger surgeon.

Race/Ethnicity, 2000: (In percent) Anglo, 86.22; Black, 3.40; Hispanic, 9.33; Other, 1.05.

Vital Statistics, 2004: Births, 47; deaths, 66; marriages, 30; divorces, 24.

Recreation: Lakes; hunting; settlers reunion, fish day in spring, autumn leaves festival.

Minerals: Oil, gas produced.

Agriculture: Cattle, cow-calf operations; wheat, cotton, grain sorghum, hay. Market value $42.6 million.

SEYMOUR (2,845) county seat; agribusiness; hospital; dove hunters' breakfast in September.

Population	3,805	
Change fm 2000	-7.0	
Area (sq. mi.)	901.01	
Land Area (sq. mi.)	870.77	
Altitude (ft.)	1,053-1,400	
Rainfall (in.)	27.79	
Jan. mean min.	27.7	
July mean max.	96.5	
Civ. Labor	1,799	
Unemployed	3.9	
Wages	$6,869,195	
Av. Weekly Wage	$426.24	
Prop. Value	$339,976,670	
Retail Sales	$32,191,187	

Bee County

Physical Features: South Coastal Plain, level to rolling; black clay, sandy, loam soils; brushy.

Economy: Agriculture, government/services; hunting leases; oil and gas business.

History: Karankawa, Apache, Pawnee territory. First Spanish land grant, 1789. Irish settlers arrived 1826-29. County created from Karnes, Live Oak, Goliad, Refugio, San Patricio, 1857; organized 1858; named for Gen. Barnard Bee.

Race/Ethnicity, 2000: (In percent) Anglo, 35.53; Black, 9.79; Hispanic, 53.93; Other, 0.75.

Vital Statistics, 2004: Births, 370; deaths, 222; marriages, 170; divorces, 91.

Recreation: Hunting, camping; historical sites, antiques; rodeo/roping events.

Minerals: Oil, gas produced.

Agriculture: Beef cattle, corn, cotton and grain sorghum. Market value $19.5 million. Hunting leases.

BEEVILLE (14,186) county seat; retail center; prison units, training academy; Costal Bend College; hospital, art museum; Diez y Seis festival in September.

Other towns and places include: **Blue Berry Hill** (940); **Mineral** (65); **Normanna** (183); **Pawnee** (280); **Pettus** (809); **Skidmore** (1,212); **Tuleta** (391); **Tynan** (300).

For explanation of sources, abbreviations and symbols, see p. 224 and foldout map.

Population	33,176
Change fm 2000	2.5
Area (sq. mi.)	880.31
Land Area (sq. mi.)	880.14
Altitude (ft.)	87-500
Rainfall (in.)	33.48
Jan. mean min.	43.1
July mean max.	94.6
Civ. Labor	10,800
Unemployed	5.9
Wages	$59,017,983
Av. Weekly Wage	$537.64
Prop. Value	$1,379,802,126
Retail Sales	$179,380,633

Trail riders from the Rio Grande Valley take a rest along U.S. 59 between Beeville and Goliad on their way to the Houston Livestock Show and Rodeo. Robert Plocheck photo.

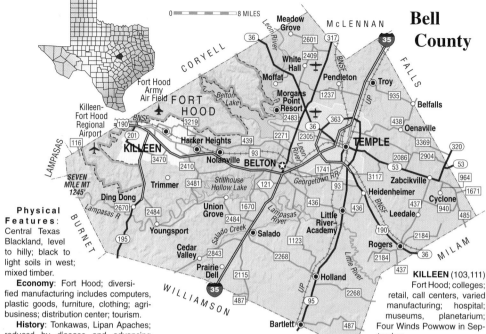

Bell County

Physical Features: Central Texas Blackland, level to hilly; black to light soils in west; mixed timber.

Economy: Fort Hood; diversified manufacturing includes computers, plastic goods, furniture, clothing; agribusiness; distribution center; tourism.

History: Tonkawas, Lipan Apaches; reduced by disease and advancing frontier by 1840s. Comanches raided into 1870s. Settled in 1830s as part of Robertson's colony. A few slaveholders in 1850s. County created from Milam County in 1850; named for Gov. P.H. Bell.

Population	257,897
Change fm 2000	8.4
Area (sq. mi.)	1,087.93
Land Area (sq. mi.)	1,059.72
Altitude (ft.)	400-1,245
Rainfall (in.)	35.81
Jan. mean min.	34.9
July mean max.	95.0
Civ. Labor	117,629
Unemployed	4.5
Wages	$759,239,424
Av. Weekly Wage	$611.02
Prop. Value	$10,606,142,008
Retail Sales	$4,158,706,336

Race/Ethnicity, 2000: (In percent) Anglo, 58.38; Black, 20.93; Hispanic, 16.68; Other, 4.01.

Vital Statistics, 2004: Births, 4,916; deaths, 1,653; marriages, 3,447; divorces, 1,724.

Recreation: Fishing, hunting; lakes; historic sites; exposition center; Salado gathering of Scottish clans in November.

Minerals: Gravel.

Agriculture: Beef, corn, sorghum, wheat, cotton. Market value $40.8 million.

BELTON (16,156) county seat; University of Mary Hardin-Baylor; manufactures include school and office furniture, roofing felt, athletic equipment; museum, nature center.

KILLEEN (103,111) Fort Hood; colleges; retail, call centers, varied manufacturing; hospital; museums, planetarium; Four Winds Powwow in September.

TEMPLE (57,216) Major medical center with two hospitals and VA hospital; diversified industries; rail, wholesale distribution center; retail center; Temple College; Czech museum, early-day tractor, engine show in October.

Other towns include: **Harker Heights** (20,692) Founder's Day in October; **Heidenheimer** (224); **Holland** (1,095) corn festival in June; **Little River-Academy** (1,696); **Morgan's Point Resort** (3,940); **Nolanville** (2,485); **Pendelton** (369); **Rogers** (1,162); **Salado** (3,663) tourism, civic center, amphitheathre; art fair in August; **Troy** (1,346). Also, part of **Bartlett** (1,843) is in Bell County.

Fort Hood has a population of 32,259.

San Jose Mission, above, was established in San Antonio in 1720. Robert Plocheck photo.

Bexar County

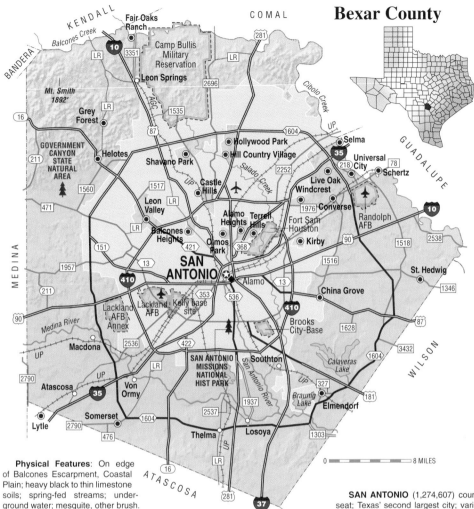

Physical Features: On edge of Balcones Escarpment, Coastal Plain; heavy black to thin limestone soils; spring-fed streams; underground water; mesquite, other brush.

Economy: Medical/biomedical research and services; government center with large federal payroll, military bases; tourism; education center with 14 colleges.

History: Coahuiltecan Indian area; also Lipan Apaches and Tonkawas present. Mission San Antonio de Valero (Alamo) founded in 1718. Canary Islanders arrived in 1731. Anglo-American settlers began arriving in late 1820s. County created 1836 from Spanish municipality named for Duke de Bexar, a colonial capital of Texas.

Race/Ethnicity, 2000: (In percent) Anglo, 36.33; Black, 7.20; Hispanic, 54.35; Other, 2.12.

Vital Statistics, 2004: Births, 25,398; deaths, 10,426; marriages, 12,570; divorces, 4,858.

Recreation: Historic sites include the Alamo, other missions, Casa Navarro, La Villita; Riverwalk; El Mercado (market); Tower of the Americas; Brackenridge Park; zoo; Seaworld; symphony orchestra; HemisFair Plaza; Fiesta in

Population	1,555,592
Change fm 2000	11.7
Area (sq. mi.)	1,256.66
Land Area (sq. mi.)	1,246.82
Altitude (ft.)	486-1,892
Rainfall (in.)	32.92
Jan. mean min.	38.6
July mean max.	94.6
Civ. Labor	744,087
Unemployed	3.8
Wages	$6,337,333,558
Av. Weekly Wage	$695.06
Fed. Wages	$347,876,629
Prop. Value	$72,215,772,000
Retail Sales	$21,638,067,781

April; Institute of Texan Cultures; Folklife Festival in June; parks, museums; hunting, fishing; NBA Spurs.

Minerals: Gravel, sand, limestone.

Agriculture: Nursery crops, beef cattle, corn, horses. Market value $80.7 million. Hunting important.

Education: Fourteen colleges including Our Lady of the Lake, St. Mary's University, Trinity University and the University of Texas at San Antonio.

SAN ANTONIO (1,274,607) county seat; Texas' second largest city; varied manufacturing with emphasis on high-tech industries; other products include construction equipment, concrete and dairy products; industrial warehousing. **Leon Springs** is now part of San Antonio.

Other towns include: **Alamo Heights** (7,280); **Balcones Heights** (2,952); **Castle Hills** (3,881); **China Grove** (1,299); **Converse** (13,801); **Elmendorf** (796); **Fair Oaks Ranch** (5,663); **Grey Forest** (425) **Helotes** (6,405); **Hill Country Village** (1,062); **Hollywood Park** (3,170).

Also, **Kirby** (8,632); **Leon Valley** (9,604); **Live Oak** (11,267); **Macdona** (297); **Olmos Park** (2,333); **St. Hedwig** (2,139); **Selma** (2,092, parts in Guadalupe and Comal counties); **Shavano Park** (2,946); **Somerset** (1,727); **Terrell Hills** (4,881); **Universal City** (17,318); **Windcrest** (4,955).

Part [1,045] of **Schertz** (28,180).

For explanation of sources, abbreviations and symbols, see p. 224 and foldout page.

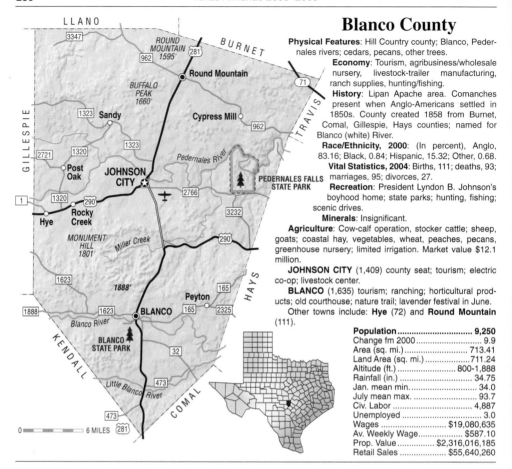

Blanco County

Physical Features: Hill Country county; Blanco, Pedernales rivers; cedars, pecans, other trees.

Economy: Tourism, agribusiness/wholesale nursery, livestock-trailer manufacturing, ranch supplies, hunting/fishing.

History: Lipan Apache area. Comanches present when Anglo-Americans settled in 1850s. County created 1858 from Burnet, Comal, Gillespie, Hays counties; named for Blanco (white) River.

Race/Ethnicity, 2000: (In percent), Anglo, 83.16; Black, 0.84; Hispanic, 15.32; Other, 0.68.

Vital Statistics, 2004: Births, 111; deaths, 93; marriages, 95; divorces, 27.

Recreation: President Lyndon B. Johnson's boyhood home; state parks; hunting, fishing; scenic drives.

Minerals: Insignificant.

Agriculture: Cow-calf operation, stocker cattle; sheep, goats; coastal hay, vegetables, wheat, peaches, pecans, greenhouse nursery; limited irrigation. Market value $12.1 million.

JOHNSON CITY (1,409) county seat; tourism; electric co-op; livestock center.

BLANCO (1,635) tourism; ranching; horticultural products; old courthouse; nature trail; lavender festival in June.

Other towns include: **Hye** (72) and **Round Mountain** (111).

Population	**9,250**
Change fm 2000	9.9
Area (sq. mi.)	713.41
Land Area (sq. mi.)	711.24
Altitude (ft.)	800-1,888
Rainfall (in.)	34.75
Jan. mean min.	34.0
July mean max.	93.7
Civ. Labor	4,887
Unemployed	3.0
Wages	$19,080,635
Av. Weekly Wage	$587.10
Prop. Value	$2,316,016,185
Retail Sales	$55,640,260

Borden County

Physical Features: West Texas county of rolling surface, broken by Caprock Escarpment; drains to Colorado River; sandy loam, clay soils.

Economy: Agriculture and hunting leases; oil; wind turbines.

History: Comanche area. Anglo-Americans settled in 1870s. County created 1876 from Bexar District, organized 1891; named for Gail Borden, patriot, inventor, editor.

Race/Ethnicity, 2000: (In percent) Anglo, 87.52; Black, 0.14; Hispanic, 11.93; Other, 0.41.

Vital Statistics, 2004: Births, 2; deaths, 1; marriages, 1; divorce, 0.

Recreation: Fishing and quail, deer hunting; Lake J.B. Thomas; museum; Coyote Opry in September; junior livestock show in January, ranch horse competition in September.

Minerals: Oil, gas, caliche, sand, gravel.

Agriculture: Beef cattle, cotton, wheat, hay, pecans, oats; some irrigation. Market value $7.8 million.

GAIL (200) county seat; museum; antique shop, ambulance service; "star" construction atop Gail Mountain.

Population	648	Jan. mean min.	29.8
Change fm 2000	-11.1	July mean max.	94.6
Area (sq. mi.)	906.04	Civ. Labor	484
Land Area (sq. mi.)	898.80	Unemployed	3.3
Altitude (ft.)	2,258-3,000	Wages	$1,093,580
Rainfall (in.)	19.68	Av. Weekly Wage	$576.17

Prop. Value	$594,623,063
Retail Sales	$168,623

For explanation of sources, abbreviations and symbols, see p. 224 and foldout page.

Bosque County

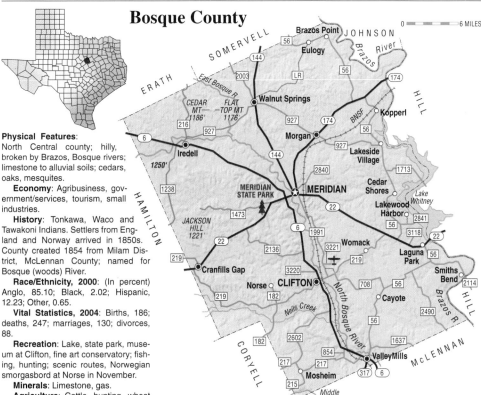

Physical Features:
North Central county; hilly, broken by Brazos, Bosque rivers; limestone to alluvial soils; cedars, oaks, mesquites.

Economy: Agribusiness, government/services, tourism, small industries.

History: Tonkawa, Waco and Tawakoni Indians. Settlers from England and Norway arrived in 1850s. County created 1854 from Milam District, McLennan County; named for Bosque (woods) River.

Race/Ethnicity, 2000: (In percent) Anglo, 85.10; Black, 2.02; Hispanic, 12.23; Other, 0.65.

Vital Statistics, 2004: Births, 186; deaths, 247; marriages, 130; divorces, 88.

Recreation: Lake, state park, museum at Clifton, fine art conservatory; fishing, hunting; scenic routes, Norwegian smorgasbord at Norse in November.

Minerals: Limestone, gas.

Agriculture: Cattle, hunting, wheat and oats, forages, turkeys, feed grains, horses. Market value $38 million.

MERIDIAN (1,535) county seat; distribution center; varied manufacturing; national championship barbecue cookoff in August.

CLIFTON (3,705) retirement/health care; limestone sales; light manufacturing; hospital; library; Norwegian historic district; Oktoberfest in November.

Other towns include: **Cranfills Gap** (358) Lutefisk dinner in December; **Iredell** (387); **Kopperl** (225); **Laguna Park** (550); **Morgan** (539); **Valley Mills** (1,174); **Walnut Springs** (819).

Population	**18,058**
Change fm 2000	5.0
Area (sq. mi.)	1,002.63
Land Area (sq. mi.)	989.18

Altitude (ft.)	450-1,250
Rainfall (in.)	35.07
Jan. mean min.	32.7
July mean max.	96.2
Civ. Labor	8,627
Unemployed	4.0
Wages	$24,508,032
Av. Weekly Wage	$514.20
Prop. Value	$1,884,848,769
Retail Sales	$81,967,490

A Caprock mesa along FM 669 north of Gail. Robert Plocheck photo.

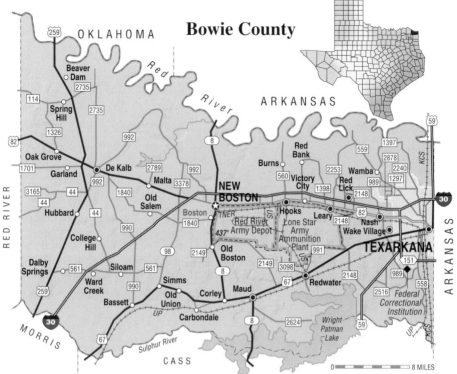

Bowie County

Physical Features: Forested hills at northeast corner of state; clay, sandy, alluvial soils; drained by Red and Sulphur rivers.

Economy: Government/services, lumber, manufacturing, agribusiness.

History: Caddo area, abandoned in 1790s after trouble with Osage tribe. Anglo-Americans began arriving 1815-20. County created 1840 from Red River County; named for Alamo hero James Bowie.

Race/Ethnicity, 2000: (In percent) Anglo, 70.83; Black, 23.58; Hispanic, 4.47; Other, 1.12.

Vital Statistics, 2004: Births, 1,127; deaths, 962; marriages, 637; divorces, 360.

Recreation: Lakes, Crystal Springs beach; hunting, fishing, historic sites; Four-States Fair in September, Octoberfest.

Minerals: Oil, gas, sand, gravel.

Agriculture: Beef cattle, pecans, hay, corn, poultry, soybeans, dairy, nurseries, wheat, rice, horses, milo. Market value $37.3 million. Pine timber, hardwoods, pulpwood harvested.

NEW BOSTON (4,657) site of county courthouse; steel manufactured; agribusiness; lumber mill; hospital; state prison; Pioneer Days in August.

The area of **Boston**, officially designated as the county seat, has been annexed by New Boston.

TEXARKANA (36,045 in Texas, 35,037 in Arkansas) army depot, rubber company, paper manufacturing, distribution; hospitals; tourism; colleges; federal prison; Quadrangle Festival in September, Perot Theatre.

Other towns include: **De Kalb** (1,627) agriculture, government/services, commuting to Texarkana, Oktoberfest; **Hooks** (3,071); **Leary** (578); **Maud** (1,016); **Nash** (2,346); **Red Lick** (874); **Redwater** (876); **Simms** (240); **Wake Village** (5,446).

Population	**91,455**
Change fm 2000	2.4
Area (sq. mi.)	922.77
Land Area (sq. mi.)	887.87
Altitude (ft.)	200-437
Rainfall (in.)	51.24
Jan. mean min.	30.7
July mean max.	93.1
Civ. Labor	44,311
Unemployed	4.9
Wages	$339,786,392
Av. Weekly Wage	$630.84
Prop. Value	$ 4,357,534,116
Retail Sales	$1,275,584,258

The Federal Courthouse in Texarkana is located on the state line; half in Texas and half in Arkansas. Robert Plocheck photo.

Brazoria County

Physical Features: Flat Coastal Plain, coastal soils, drained by Brazos and San Bernard rivers.

Economy: Petroleum and chemical industry; fishing; tourism; agribusiness. Part of Houston metropolitan area.

History: Karankawa area. Part of Austin's "Old Three Hundred" colony of families arriving in early 1820s. County created 1836 from Municipality of Brazoria; name derived from Brazos River.

Race/Ethnicity, 2000: (In percent) Anglo, 66.09; Black, 8.58; Hispanic, 22.78; Other, 2.55.

Vital Statistics, 2004: Births, 4,288; deaths, 1,680; marriages, 1,522; divorces, 1,363.

Recreation: Beaches, water sports; fishing, hunting; wildlife refuges, historic sites; state and county parks; replica of the first capitol of the Republic of Texas at West Columbia.

Minerals: Oil, gas, sand, gravel.

Agriculture: Cattle, hay, rice, soybeans, sorghum, nursery, corn, cotton, aquaculture. 20,000 acres of rice irrigated. Market value $47.4 million.

ANGLETON (18,868) county seat; banking, distribution center for oil, chemical, agricultural area; fish-processing plant; hospital.

BRAZOSPORT (59,759) is a community of eight cities; chemical complex; deepwater seaport; commercial fishing; tourism; college; hospital; Brazosport cities include: **Clute** (11,092) mosquito festival in July, **Freeport** (13,038) blues festival in August, **Jones Creek** (2,167), **Lake Jackson** (27,874) museum, sea center, Gulf Coast Bird Observatory, **Oyster Creek** (1,359), **Quintana** (34), Neotropical Bird Sanctuary, **Richwood** (3,338), **Surfside Beach** (857).

ALVIN (23,031) petrochemical processing; agribusiness; rail, trucking; junior college; hospital; Crawfest and Shrimp Boil in April.

PEARLAND (59,994, partly in Harris County) rail, trucking, oilfield, chemical production; commuting to Houston, NASA; community college.

Other towns include: **Bailey's Prairie** (747); **Bonney** (406); **Brazoria** (2,958) library; No-Name Festival in June, Santa Anna Ball in July; **Brookside Village** (2,092).

Also, **Damon** (551); **Danbury** (1,740); **Danciger** (357); **Hillcrest Village** (738); **Holiday Lakes** (1,148); **Iowa Colony** (879); **Liverpool**

(435); **Manvel** (3,885); **Old Ocean** (915); **Rosharon** (NA); **Sandy Point** (250); **Sweeny** (3,743) petrochemicals, agriculture, grass farming, hospital, library, Pride Day in May, Levi Jordan Plantation; **West Columbia** (4,274) chemical, construction companies; cattle, rice farming; museum, historic sites, plantation; San Jacinto Festival in April, Stephen F. Austin funeral procession reeactment in October.

Population	**287,898**
Change fm 2000	19.1
Area (sq. mi.)	1,597.44
Land Area (sq. mi.)	1,386.40
Altitude (ft.)	sea level-146
Rainfall (in.)	57.24
Jan. mean min.	43.7
July mean max.	91.8
Civ. Labor	139,621
Unemployed	4.1
Wages	$796,790,789
Av. Weekly Wage	$749.45
Prop. Value	$21,154,308,305
Retail Sales	$2,838,726,097

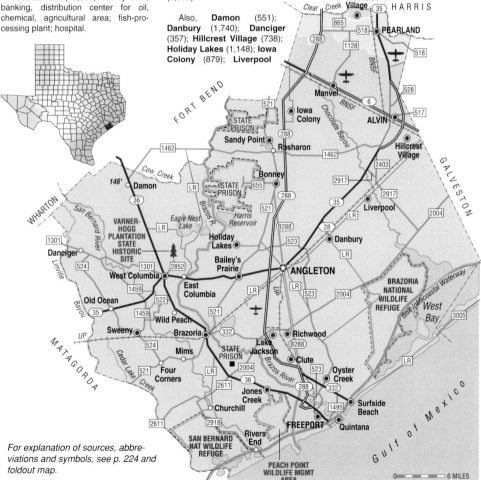

For explanation of sources, abbreviations and symbols, see p. 224 and foldout map.

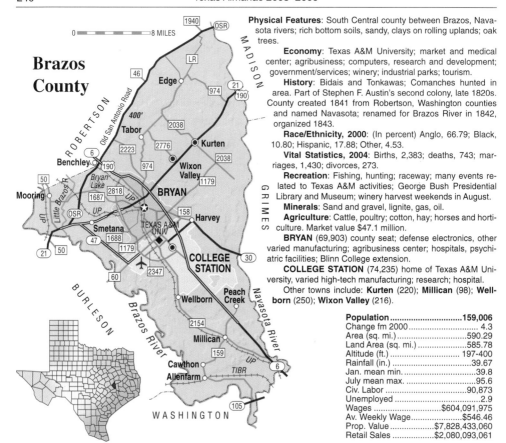

Brazos County

0 ████ 8 MILES

Physical Features: South Central county between Brazos, Navasota rivers; rich bottom soils, sandy, clays on rolling uplands; oak trees.

Economy: Texas A&M University; market and medical center; agribusiness; computers, research and development; government/services; winery; industrial parks; tourism.

History: Bidais and Tonkawas; Comanches hunted in area. Part of Stephen F. Austin's second colony, late 1820s. County created 1841 from Robertson, Washington counties and named Navasota; renamed for Brazos River in 1842, organized 1843.

Race/Ethnicity, 2000: (In percent) Anglo, 66.79; Black, 10.80; Hispanic, 17.88; Other, 4.53.

Vital Statistics, 2004: Births, 2,383; deaths, 743; marriages, 1,430; divorces, 273.

Recreation: Fishing, hunting; raceway; many events related to Texas A&M activities; George Bush Presidential Library and Museum; winery harvest weekends in August.

Minerals: Sand and gravel, lignite, gas, oil.

Agriculture: Cattle, poultry; cotton, hay; horses and horticulture. Market value $47.1 million.

BRYAN (69,903) county seat; defense electronics, other varied manufacturing; agribusiness center; hospitals, psychiatric facilities; Blinn College extension.

COLLEGE STATION (74,235) home of Texas A&M University, varied high-tech manufacturing; research; hospital.

Other towns include: **Kurten** (220); **Millican** (98); **Wellborn** (250); **Wixon Valley** (216).

Population	159,006
Change fm 2000	4.3
Area (sq. mi.)	590.29
Land Area (sq. mi.)	585.78
Altitude (ft.)	197-400
Rainfall (in.)	39.67
Jan. mean min.	39.8
July mean max.	95.6
Civ. Labor	90,873
Unemployed	2.9
Wages	$604,091,975
Av. Weekly Wage	$546.46
Prop. Value	$7,828,433,060
Retail Sales	$2,080,093,061

A chapel beneath the mountains in Mexico across from FM 2627 in Brewster County. Robert Plocheck photo.

Brewster County

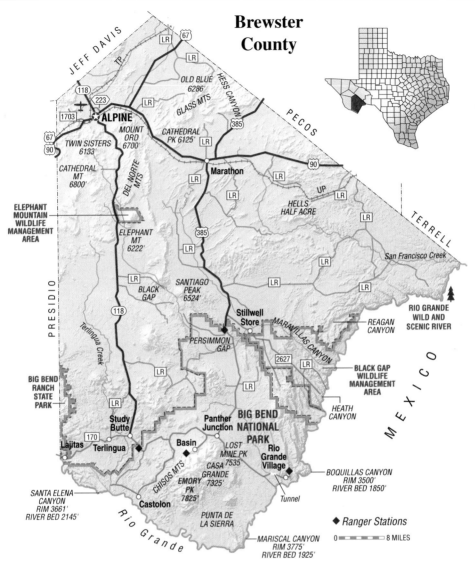

JEFF DAVIS

TP

118

223

1703

ALPINE

67
90

TWIN SISTERS
6133'

CATHEDRAL
MT
6800'

MOUNT
ORD
6700'

DEL NORTE MTS

67

LR

LR

OLD BLUE
6286'

GLASS MTS

HESS CANYON

385

CATHEDRAL
PK 6125'   LR

Marathon

LR

LR

PECOS

90

LR

UP

LR

LR

HELLS
HALF ACRE

LR

TERRELL

ELEPHANT
MOUNTAIN
WILDLIFE
MANAGEMENT
AREA

ELEPHANT
MT
6222'

385

LR

PRESIDIO

118

Terlingua Creek

LR

BLACK
GAP

SANTIAGO
PEAK
6524'

LR

Stillwell
Store

San Francisco Creek

LR

LR

MARAVILLAS CANYON

REAGAN
CANYON

RIO GRANDE
WILD AND
SCENIC RIVER

MEXICO

PERSIMMON
GAP

2627

LR

BLACK GAP
WILDLIFE
MANAGEMENT
AREA

BIG BEND
RANCH
STATE
PARK

LR

LR

LR

Study
Butte

Panther
Junction

BIG BEND
NATIONAL
PARK

HEATH
CANYON

170

Lajitas   Terlingua

Basin

LOST
MINE PK
7535'

Rio
Grande
Village

BOQUILLAS CANYON
RIM 3500'
RIVER BED 1850'

SANTA ELENA
CANYON
RIM 3661'
RIVER BED 2145'

CHISOS MTS

CASA
GRANDE
7325'

EMORY
PK
7825'

Castolon

Tunnel

Rio Grande

PUNTA DE
LA SIERRA

MARISCAL CANYON
RIM 3775'
RIVER BED 1925'

◆ Ranger Stations

0 ▬▬▬▬ 8 MILES

Physical Features: Largest county, with area slightly less than that of Connecticut plus Rhode Island; mountains, canyons, distinctive geology, plant life, animals.

Economy: Tourism, ranching, Sul Ross State University; government/services; retirement developments; hunting leases.

History: Pueblo culture had begun when Spanish explored in 1500s. Mescalero Apaches in Chisos; Comanches raided in area. Ranching developed in northern part 1880s; Mexican agricultural communities along river. County created 1887 from Presidio County; named for Henry P. Brewster, Republic secretary of war.

Race/Ethnicity, 2000: (In percent) Anglo, 54.08; Black, 1.12; Hispanic, 43.62; Other, 1.18.

Vital Statistics, 2004: Births, 120; deaths, 81; marriages, 60; divorces, 0.

Recreation: Big Bend National Park; Big Bend Ranch State Park; Rio Grande Wild and Scenic River; ghost towns; scenic drives; museum; rockhound areas; November chili cookoff at Terlingua; cavalry post, Barton Warnock Environmental Education Center at Lajitas; hunting.

Minerals: Bentonite.

Agriculture: Beef cattle, horses, pecans. Market value $5.2 million.

ALPINE (6,147) county seat; ranch trade center; tourism; Sul Ross State University; hospital; varied manufacturing.

Marathon (449) tourism, ranching center, Gage Hotel, Marathon Basin quilt show in October. Also, **Basin** (22) and **Study Butte-Terlingua** (275).

Population	9,048
Change fm 2000	2.1
Area (sq. mi.)	6,192.78
Land Area (sq. mi.)	6,192.61
Altitude (ft.)	1,700-7,825
Rainfall (in.) Alpine	17.19
Rainfall (in.) Big Bend	19.17
Jan. mean min. Alpine	31.3
Jan. mean min. Big Bend	36.1
July mean max. Alpine	88.7
July mean max. Big Bend	84.2
Civ. Labor	5,415
Unemployed	2.9
Wages	$33,951,160
Av. Weekly Wage	$546.63
Prop. Value	$615,224,832
Retail Sales	$89,406,017

For explanation of sources, abbreviations and symbols, see p. 224 and foldout map.

Briscoe County

Physical Features: Partly on High Plains, broken by Caprock Escarpment, fork of Red River; sandy, loam soils.

Economy: Agribusiness, government/services, banking.

History: Apaches, displaced by Comanches around 1700. Ranchers settled in 1880s. County created from Bexar District, 1876, organized 1892; named for Andrew Briscoe, Republic of Texas soldier.

Race/Ethnicity, 2000: (In percent) Anglo, 74.58; Black, 2.40; Hispanic, 22.74; Other, 0.28.

Vital Statistics, 2004: Births, 17; deaths, 14; marriages, 6; divorces, 9.

Recreation: Hunting, fishing; scenic drives; museum; state park, trailway, Clarity tunnel, Mackenzie Reservoir.

Minerals: Insignificant.

Agriculture: Cotton, cow-calf, stocker cattle, sorghum, wheat, hay. Some 32,000 acres irrigated. Market value $14.6 million.

SILVERTON (740) county seat; agribusiness center; irrigation supplies manufactured; clinics.

Quitaque (383) trade center, agribusiness, nature tourism.

Population	1,598
Change fm 2000	-10.7
Area (sq. mi.)	901.59
Land Area (sq. mi.)	900.25
Altitude (ft.)	2,100-3,350
Rainfall (in.)	22.34
Jan. mean min.	21.6
July mean max.	90.9
Civ. Labor	696
Unemployed	3.9
Wages	$2,122,277
Av. Weekly Wage	$429.99
Prop. Value	$155,450,733
Retail Sales	$7,024,518

Brooks County

Physical Features: On Rio Grande plain; level to rolling; brushy; light to dark sandy loam soils.

Economy: Oil, gas, hunting leases, cattle, watermelons and hay.

History: Coahuiltecan Indians. Spanish land grants date to around 1800. County created from Hidalgo, Starr, Zapata counties, 1911. Named for J.A. Brooks, Texas Ranger and legislator.

Race/Ethnicity, 2000: (In percent) Anglo, 8.04; Black, 0.06; Hispanic, 91.57; Other, 0.33.

Vital Statistics, 2004: Births, 139; deaths, 47; marriages, 64; divorces, 17.

Recreation: Hunting, fishing; Heritage Museum, Don Pedrito Shrine; fiestas, May and October.

Minerals: Oil, gas production.

Agriculture: Beef cow-calf operations, stocker crops include hay, squash, watermelons, habanero peppers. Market value $7.6 million.

FALFURRIAS (5,010) county seat; agricultural market center, government/services.

Other towns include: **Encino** (172).

Population	7,731
Change fm 2000	- 3.1
Area (sq. mi.)	943.61
Land Area (sq. mi.)	943.28
Altitude (ft.)	46-400
Rainfall (in.)	25.42
Jan. mean min.	43.9
July mean max.	97.0
Civ. Labor	3,092
Unemployed	5.3
Wages	$16,087,426
Av. Weekly Wage	$535.09
Prop. Value	$1,069,571,901
Retail Sales	$64,696,285

For explanation of sources, abbreviations and symbols, see p. 224 and foldout map.

Brown County

Physical Features: Rolling, hilly; drains to Colorado River; varied soils, timber.

Economy: Manufacturing plants, distribution center; government/services; agribusiness.

History: Apaches; displaced by Comanches who were removed by U.S. Army in 1874-75. Anglo-Americans first settled in mid-1850s. County created 1856 from Comanche, Travis counties, organized in 1857. Named for frontiersman Henry S. Brown.

Race/Ethnicity, 2000: (In percent) Anglo, 79.66; Black, 4.11; Hispanic, 15.38; Other, 0.85.

Vital Statistics, 2004: Births, 490; deaths, 472; marriages, 335; divorces, 85.

Recreation: State park; museum; fishing, hunting; wildflowers, walking trails; wine and chocolate festival in May.

Minerals: Oil, gas, paving materials, gravel, clays.

Agriculture: Cattle, hay, peanuts, pecans, meat goats, wheat, hogs. Market value $25.7 million.

BROWNWOOD (19,694) county seat; manufacturing, retail trade; distribution center; Howard Payne University, MacArthur Academy of Freedom; state substance abuse treatment center; state 4-H Club center; hospital; bluegrass festival in June.

Early (2,689) varied manufacturing, government/services, agribusiness; Memorial Day rib burn-off.

Other towns include: **Bangs** (1,608); **Blanket** (415); **Brookesmith** (61); **May** (270); **Zephyr** (201). **Lake Brownwood** area has 1,747.

Population	38,970
Change fm 2000	3.4
Area (sq. mi.)	956.94

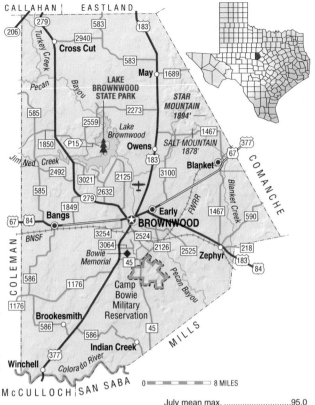

Land Area (sq. mi.)	943.85
Altitude (ft.)	1,300-1,894
Rainfall (in.)	28.32
Jan. mean min.	29.6
July mean max.	95.0
Civ. Labor	18,986
Unemployed	4.5
Wages	$113,741,266
Av. Weekly Wage	$557.26
Prop. Value	$2,167,169,044
Retail Sales	$447,220,394

Caprock Canyons State Park in Briscoe County. Robert Plocheck photo.

Physical Features: Rolling to hilly; drains to Brazos, Yegua Creek, Somerville Lake; loam and heavy bottom soils; oaks, other trees.

Economy: Oil and gas; tourism; commuters to Texas A&M University; agribusiness.

History: Tonkawas and Caddoes roamed the area. Mexicans and Anglo-Americans settled around fort in 1830. Black freedmen migration increased until 1910. Germans, Czechs, Italians migrated in 1870s-80s. County created 1846 from Milam, Washington counties; named for Edward Burleson, a hero of the Texas Revolution.

Race/Ethnicity, 2000: (In percent) Anglo, 69.68; Black, 15.06; Hispanic, 14.64; Other, 0.62.

Vital Statistics, 2004: Births, 231; deaths, 150; marriages, 88; divorces, 89.

Recreation: Fishing, hunting; lake recreation; historic sites; Czech heritage museum; Kolache Festival in September.

Minerals: Oil, gas, sand, gravel.

Agriculture: Cattle, cotton, corn, hay, sorghum, broiler production, soybeans; some irrigation. Market value $36.2 million.

CALDWELL (3,720) county seat; agribusiness, oil and gas; manufacturing; distribution center; tourism; hospital, civic center, museum.

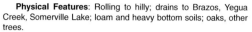

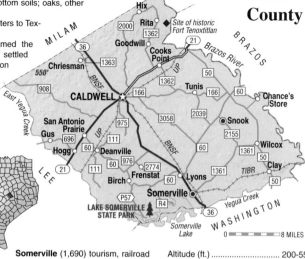

Burleson County

Somerville (1,690) tourism, railroad center, some manufacturing.

Other towns include: **Chriesman** (30); **Deanville** (130); **Lyons** (360); **Snook** (561) Snookfest in June.

Population	**16,932**
Change fm 2000	2.8
Area (sq. mi.)	677.78
Land Area (sq. mi.)	665.54
Altitude (ft.)	200-550
Rainfall (in.)	38.50
Jan. mean min.	36.4
July mean max.	96.7
Civ. Labor	8,986
Unemployed	3.4
Wages	$28,108,357
Av. Weekly Wage	$584.90
Prop. Value	$1,350,652,411
Retail Sales	$119,664,681

Burnet County

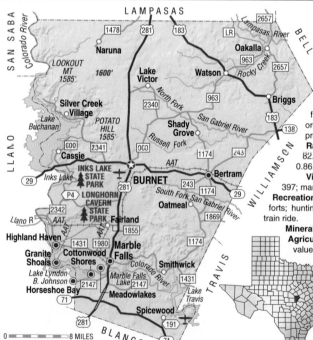

Physical Features: Scenic Hill Country county with lakes; caves; sandy, red, black waxy soils; cedars, other trees.

Economy: Tourism, manufacturing, stone processing, hunting leases.

History: Tonkawas, Lipan Apaches. Comanches raided in area. Frontier settlers arrived in the late 1840s. County created from Bell, Travis, Williamson counties, 1852; organized 1854; named for David G. Burnet, provisional president of the Republic.

Race/Ethnicity, 2000: (In percent) Anglo, 82.76; Black, 1.61; Hispanic, 14.77; Other, 0.86.

Vital Statistics, 2004: Births, 485; deaths, 397; marriages, 287; divorces, 210.

Recreation: Water sports on lakes; sites of historic forts; hunting; state parks; wildflowers; birding; scenic train ride.

Minerals: Granite capital of Texas, limestone.

Agriculture: Hay, cattle, goats, horses. Market value $10.3 million. Deer, wild hog and turkey hunting leases.

BURNET (5,470) county seat; tourism; government/services; ranching; varied industries; hospital; museums; vineyards; Bluebonnet festival in April.

Marble Falls (6,471) tourism; ranching; varied manufacturing; stone quarry; August drag boat race.

Other towns include: **Bertram** (1,318) Oatmeal festival on Labor Day; **Briggs** (172); **Cottonwood Shores** (1,051); **Granite Shoals** (2,346); **Highland Haven** (464); **Meadowlakes** (1,659); **Spicewood** (2,000). Also, part of **Horseshoe Bay** (3,359).

Population	**42,896**
Change fm 2000	25.7
Area (sq. mi.)	1,020.96
Land Area (sq. mi.)	996.04
Altitude (ft.)	700-1,600
Rainfall (in.)	32.43
Jan. mean min.	33.3
July mean max.	93.6
Civ. Labor	20,560
Unemployed	3.0
Wages	$92,997,442
Av. Weekly Wage	$590.46
Prop. Value	$4,405,911,980
Retail Sales	$528,200,716

Caldwell County

Physical Features: Varied soils ranging from black clay to waxy; level, draining to San Marcos River.

Economy: Petroleum, varied manufacturing; government/services; part of Austin metro area, also near San Antonio.

History: Tonkawa area. Part of the DeWitt colony, Anglo-Americans settled in the 1830s. Mexican migration increased after 1890. County created from Bastrop, Gonzales counties, 1848; named for frontiersman Mathew Caldwell.

Race/Ethnicity, 2000: (In percent) Anglo, 50.15; Black, 8.58; Hispanic, 40.44; Other, 0.83.

Vital Statistics, 2004: Births, 575; deaths, 276; marriages, 204; divorces, 135.

Recreation: Fishing; state park; Luling Watermelon Thump and Lockhart Chisholm Trail roundup in June; museums; nature trails; rodeo.

Minerals: Oil, gas, sand, gravel.

Agriculture: Eggs, beef cattle, broilers; hay, nurseries, cotton. Market value $35.1 million.

LOCKHART (12,978) county seat, petroleum, agribusiness center, tourism; light manufacturing; prison.

Luling (5,704) oil-industry center, oil museum; hospital, barbecue cook-off in April.

Other towns include: **Dale** (500); **Fentress** (291); **Martindale** (1,163); **Maxwell** (500); part of **Mustang Ridge** (953, mostly in Travis County), and **Prairie Lea** (255).

Also, part of **Niederwald** (416), part of **Uhland** (425) and a small part of **San Marcos** (47,005), all mostly in Hays County.

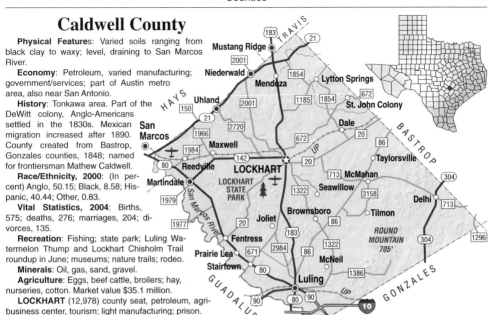

Population	36,720
Change fm 2000	14.1
Area (sq. mi.)	547.41
Land Area (sq. mi.)	545.73
Altitude (ft.)	350-705
Rainfall (in.)	36.86

Jan. mean min.	36.9
July mean max.	95.8
Civ. Labor	17,231
Unemployed	3.7
Wages	$43,202,689
Av. Weekly Wage	$514.92
Prop. Value	$1,808,296,760
Retail Sales	$266,817,753

Lavaca Bay at Magnolia Beach in Calhoun County. Robert Plocheck photo.

Calhoun County

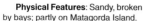

Physical Features: Sandy, broken by bays; partly on Matagorda Island.

Economy: Aluminum manufacturing, plastics plant, marine construction, agribusinesses; petroleum; tourism; fish processing.

History: Karankawa area. Empresario Martín De León brought 41 families in 1825. County created from Jackson, Matagorda, Victoria counties, 1846. Named for John C. Calhoun, U.S. statesman.

Race/Ethnicity, 2000: (In percent) Anglo, 52.29; Black, 2.67; Hispanic, 40.92; Other, 3.72.

Vital Statistics, 2004: Births, 291; deaths, 173; marriages, 162; divorces, 52.

Recreation: Beaches, fishing, water sports, duck, goose hunting; historic sites, county park; La Salle Days in April.

Minerals: Oil, gas.

Agriculture: Cotton, cattle, corn, grain sorghum. Market value $18.9 million. Commercial fishing.

PORT LAVACA (11,883) county seat; commercial seafood operations; offshore drilling operations; tourist center; some manufacturing; convention center; hospital.

Other towns include: **Long Mott** (76); **Point Comfort** (713) aluminum, plastic plants, deepwater port; **Port O'Connor** (1,184) tourist center; seafood processing; manufacturing; lighted boat parade in December; **Seadrift** (1,384) commercial fishing, processing plants; Bayfront Park; Shrimpfest in June.

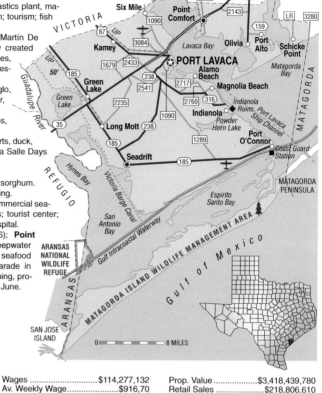

Population	**20,705**
Change fm 2000	0.3
Area (sq. mi.)	1,032.16
Land Area (sq. mi.)	512.31
Altitude (ft.)	sea level-50
Rainfall (in.)	34.78
Jan. mean min.	47.9
July mean max.	88.2
Civ. Labor	9,746
Unemployed	4.0

Wages	$114,277,132
Av. Weekly Wage	$916,70
Prop. Value	$3,418,439,780
Retail Sales	$218,806,610

Callahan County

Physical Features: West Texas county on divide between Brazos, Colorado rivers; level to rolling.

Economy: Manufacturing; feed and fertilizer business; many residents commute to Abilene; 200,000 acres in hunting leases.

History: Comanche territory until 1870s. Anglo-American settlement began around 1860. County created 1858 from Bexar, Bosque, Travis counties; organized 1877. Named for Texas Ranger J.H. Callahan.

Race/Ethnicity, 2000: (In percent) Anglo, 92.31; Black, 0.32; Hispanic, 6.29; Other, 1.08.

Vital Statistics, 2004: Births, 133; deaths, 150; marriages, 62; divorces, 82.

Recreation: Hunting; museums; lake; Hunters' Supper at deer season.

Minerals: Oil and gas.

Agriculture: Cattle; wheat, dairy, hay, peanuts, sorghum; goats, horses. Market value $16.9 million.

BAIRD (1,576) county seat; ranching trade center; antiques shops; some manufacturing; shipping; historic sites.

Clyde (3,740) steel water systems manufacturing; government/services; library; Pecan Festival in October.

Other towns include: **Cross Plains** (1,071) government/services, agriculture, home of creator of Conan the Barbarian; **Putnam** (85).

Population	13,491
Change fm 2000	4.5
Area (sq. mi.)	901.26
Land Area (sq. mi.)	898.62
Altitude (ft.)	1,400-2,204
Rainfall (in.)	25.52
Jan. mean min.	31.1

July mean max.	94.9
Civ. Labor	7,187
Unemployed	3.2
Wages	$14,311,957
Av. Weekly Wage	$518.98
Prop. Value	$937,949,274
Retail Sales	$49,148,389

Physical Features: Southernmost county in rich Rio Grande Valley soils; flat landscape; semitropical climate.

Economy: Agribusiness; tourism; seafood processing; shipping, manufacturing; government/services.

History: Coahuiltecan Indian area. Spanish land grants date to 1781. County created from Nueces County, 1848; named for Capt. Ewen Cameron of Mier Expedition.

Race/Ethnicity, 2000: (In percent) Anglo, 14.73; Black, 0.30; Hispanic, 84.34; Other, 0.63.

Vital Statistics, 2004: Births, 8,665; deaths, 1,930; marriages, 2,722; divorces, 973.

Recreation: South Padre Island: year-round resort; fishing, hunting, water sports; historical sites, Palo Alto visitors center; gateway to Mexico, state parks; wildlife refuge; recreational vehicle center; Birding Festival in February.

Minerals: Natural gas, oil.

Agriculture: Cotton top crop with grain sorghums, vegetables, and sugar cane raised; wholesale nursery plants raised; small feedlot and cow-calf operations; 200,000 acres irrigated, mostly cotton and grain sorghums. Market value $74.6 million.

Cameron County

BROWNSVILLE (167,448) county seat; international trade, varied industries, shipping, tourism; college, hospitals, crippled children health center; Gladys Porter Zoo, historic Fort Brown; University of Texas at Brownsville.

Harlingen (66,459) government/services; hospitals; garment, apparel industries; agribusiness, college; Riofest in April.

San Benito (25,574) varied manufacturing, bottling; tourism; hospital; recreation facilities.

Other towns include: **Bayview** (408); **Bluetown-Iglesia Antigua** (701); **Cameron Park** (6,422); **Combes** (2,751);

Encantada- **Ranchito El Calaboz** (2,255); **Indian Lake** (541); **La Feria** (6,958); **Laguna Heights** (2,115); **Laguna Vista** (2,848); **Laureles** (3,389); **Los Fresnos** (5,454) Little Graceland Museum, Butterfly Farm, library; **Los Indios** (1,297); **Olmito** (1,248); **Palm Valley** (1,228).

Also, **Port Isabel** (5,117) tourist center, fishing, Shrimp Cook-Off in November, museums, old lighthouse; **Primera** (3,653); **Rancho Viejo** (1,881); **Rangerville** (198); **Rio Hondo** (2,172); **Santa Maria** (872); **Santa Rosa** (3,382); **South Padre Island** (2,751) beaches, tourism/convention center, Coast Guard station, Sand Castle Days in October.

Population	387,717
Change fm 2000	15.7
Area (sq. mi.)	1,276.33
Land Area (sq. mi.)	905.76
Altitude (ft.)	sea level-67
Rainfall (in.)	27.55
Jan. mean min.	50.5
July mean max.	92.4
Civ. Labor	146,494
Unemployed	5.7
Wages	$776,483,076
Av. Weekly Wage	$494.23
Prop. Value	$12,677,151,789
Retail Sales	$3,351,136,725

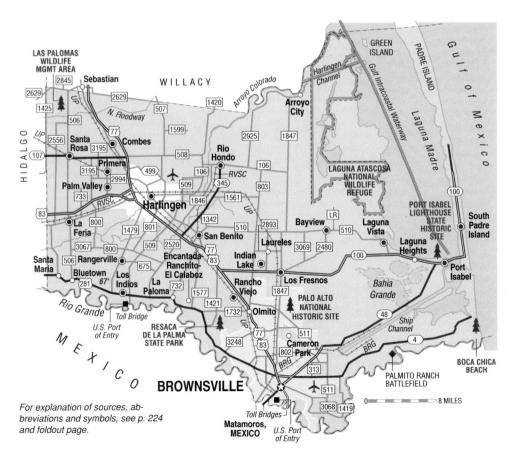

For explanation of sources, abbreviations and symbols, see p. 224 and foldout page.

Camp County

Population	12,410
Change fm 2000	7.5
Area (sq. mi.)	203.20
Land Area (sq. mi.)	197.51
Altitude (ft.)	277-538
Rainfall (in.)	45.10
Jan. mean min.	32.0
July mean max.	94.0
Civ. Labor	5,286
Unemployed	4.7
Wages	$28,110,403
Av. Weekly Wage	$506.76
Prop. Value	$752,082,120
Retail Sales	$119,173,052

Physical Features: East Texas county with forested hills; drains to Cypress Creek on north; Lake O' the Pines, Lake Bob Sandlin; third smallest county in Texas.

Economy: Agribusiness, chicken processing; timber industries; light manufacturing; retirement center.

History: Caddo area. Anglo-American settlers arrived in late 1830s. Antebellum slaveholding area. County created from Upshur County 1874; named for jurist J.L. Camp.

Race/Ethnicity, 2000: (In percent) Anglo, 65.45; Black, 19.24; Hispanic, 14.78; Other, 0.53.

Vital Statistics, 2004: Births, 193; deaths, 134; marriages, 98; divorces, 31.

Recreation: Water sports, fishing on lakes; farmstead and airship museum; Chickfest in September, Pittsburg hot links.

Minerals: Oil, gas, clays, coal.

Agriculture: Poultry and products important; beef, dairy cattle, horses; peaches, hay, blueberries, vegetables. Market value $81.7 million. Forestry.

PITTSBURG (4,626) county seat; agribusiness; timber; tourism; food processing; light manufacturing; hospital; community college; Prayer Tower.

Other towns include: **Leesburg** (128) and **Rocky Mound** (101).

Carson County

Physical Features: In center of Panhandle on level, some broken land; loam soils.

Economy: Pantex nuclear weapons assembly/disassembly facility (U.S. Department of Energy), commuting to Amarillo, petrochemical plants; agribusiness.

History: Apaches, displaced by Comanches. Anglo-American ranchers settled in 1880s. German, Polish farmers arrived around 1910. County created from Bexar District, 1876; organized 1888. Named for Republic secretary of state S.P. Carson.

Race/Ethnicity, 2000: (In percent) Anglo, 91.22; Black, 0.81; Hispanic, 7.03; Other, 0.94.

Vital Statistics, 2004: Births, 76; deaths, 54; marriages, 48; divorces, 34.

Recreation: Museum, Square House Barbecue in fall; The Cross at Groom.

Minerals: Oil, gas production.

Agriculture: Cattle, cotton, wheat, sorghum, corn, hay, soybeans. Market value $44.1 million.

PANHANDLE (2,666) county seat; government/services; agribusiness, petroleum center, commuters; Veterans Day celebration, car show in June.

Other towns include: **Groom** (581) farming center, government/services, Groom Day festival in August, **Skellytown** (595), **White Deer** (1,036) Polish Sausage festival in November.

Population	6,595
Change fm 2000	1.2
Area (sq. mi.)	924.10
Land Area (sq. mi.)	923.19
Altitude (ft.)	3,000-3,573
Rainfall (in.)	22.21
Jan. mean min.	19.3
July mean max.	90.8
Civ. Labor	3,646
Unemployed	2.8
Wages	$77,417,464
Av. Weekly Wage	$1,243.43
Prop. Value	$920,797,930
Retail Sales	$39,028,508

For explanation of sources, abbreviations and symbols, see p. 224 and foldout page.

Cass County

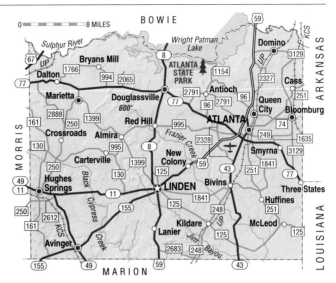

Physical Features: Forested Northeast county rolling to hilly; drained by Cypress Bayou, Sulphur River.

Economy: Timber, paper industries; varied manufacturing; agribusiness; government/services.

History: Caddoes, displaced by other tribes in 1790s. Anglo-Americans arrived in 1830s. Antebellum slaveholding area. County created 1846 from Bowie County; named for U.S. Sen. Lewis Cass.

Race/Ethnicity, 2000: (In percent) Anglo, 77.89; Black, 19.71; Hispanic, 1.73; Other, 0.67.

Vital Statistics, 2004: Births, 338; deaths, 378; marriages, 212; divorces, 162.

Recreation: Fishing, hunting, water sports; state, county parks; lake, wildflower trails.

Minerals: Oil, iron ore.

Agriculture: Poultry, cattle; nursery; forage; watermelons. Market value $32.3 million. Timber important.

LINDEN (2,133) county seat, timber, agribusiness, tourism; oldest courthouse still in use as courthouse, hospital; Rock and Roll Hall of Fame.

ATLANTA (5,686) Paper and timber industries, government/services, varied manufacturing, hospital, library; Forest Festival in August.

Other towns include: **Avinger** (457) timber, paper industry, steel plant, early cemetery, Glory Days celebration in October; **Bivins** (215); **Bloomburg** (383); **Domino** (68); **Douglassville** (174); **Hughes Springs** (1,837) varied manufacturing, warehousing; trucking school; Pumpkin Glow in October; **Kildare** (104); **Marietta** (111); **McLeod** (600); **Queen City** (1,616) paper industry, commuters to Texarkana, government/services, historic sites.

Population	**29,955**
Change fm 2000	-1.6
Area (sq. mi.)	960.35
Land Area (sq. mi.)	937.35
Altitude (ft.)	200-600
Rainfall (in.)	48.20
Jan. mean min.	31.0
July mean max.	94.0
Civ. Labor	13,435
Unemployed	5.3
Wages	$58,198,019
Av. Weekly Wage	$570.19
Prop. Value	$1,748,955,300
Retail Sales	$208,425,447

The bridge connects Port Isabel, foreground, with South Padre Island in Cameron County. Robert Plocheck photo.

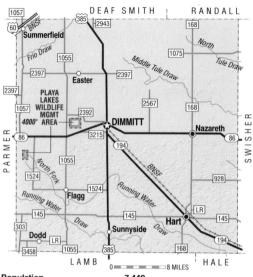

Castro County

Physical Features: Flat northwest county, drains to creeks, draws and playas; underground water.

Economy: Agribusiness.

History: Apaches, displaced by Comanches in 1720s. Anglo-American ranchers began settling in 1880s. Germans settled after 1900. Mexican migration increased after 1950. County created 1876 from Bexar District, organized 1891. Named for Henri Castro, Texas colonizer.

Race/Ethnicity, 2000: (In percent) Anglo, 45.58; Black, 2.37; Hispanic, 51.65; Other, 0.40.

Vital Statistics, 2004: Births, 142; deaths, 59; marriages, 43; divorces, 9.

Recreation: Pheasant hunting; Dimmitt Harvest Days celebrated in August; Italian POW camp site.

Minerals: Not significant.

Agriculture: beef cattle, dairies, corn, cotton, wheat, sheep. Market value $592.6 million; third in state.

DIMMITT (4,056) county seat; agribusiness center; library, hospital; quilt festival in April.

Other towns include: **Hart** (1,123) and **Nazareth** (356).

Population	**7,449**
Change fm 2000	-10.1
Area (sq. mi.)	899.32
Land Area (sq. mi.)	898.31
Altitude (ft.)	3,600-4,000
Rainfall (in.)	19.71
Jan. mean min.	20.4
July mean max.	90.1
Civ. Labor	3,210
Unemployed	4.1
Wages	$13,979,010
Av. Weekly Wage	$482.56
Prop. Value	$471,453,540
Retail Sales	$63,985,678

Chambers County

Physical Features: Gulf coastal plain, coastal soils; some forests.

Economy: Chemical plants; agribusinesses; fish and oyster processing; varied manufacturing.

History: Karankawa and other coastal tribes. Nuestra Señora de la Luz Mission established near present Wallisville in 1756. County created 1858 from Liberty, Jefferson counties. Named for Gen. T. J. Chambers, surveyor.

Race/Ethnicity, 2000: (In percent) Anglo, 78.14; Black, 9.88; Hispanic, 10.79; Other, 1.19.

Vital Statistics, 2004: Births, 360; deaths, 198; marriages, 138; divorces, 171.

Recreation: Fishing, hunting; water sports; camping; county parks; wildlife refuge; historic sites; Wallisville Heritage Museum; Texas Rice Festival and Texas Gatorfest in September.

Minerals: Oil, gas.

Agriculture: Rice, cattle and forage, soybeans, aquaculture, corn, grain sorghum, sugar cane; significant irrigation. Market value $13.4 million.

ANAHUAC (2,524) county seat; canal connects with Houston Ship Channel; agribusiness; hospital; library.

Winnie (3,314) fertilizer manufacturing; wholesale greenhouse; hospital; depot museum.

Other towns include: **Beach City** (2,043), **Cove** (345), **Hankamer** (226), **Mont Belvieu** (2,741), **Old River-Winfree** (1,620), **Stowell** (1,741) and **Wallisville** (452).

Population	**28,779**
Change fm 2000	10.6
Area (sq. mi.)	871.99
Land Area (sq. mi.)	599.31
Altitude (ft.)	sea level-73
Rainfall (in.)	54.08
Jan. mean min.	41.7
July mean max.	91.9
Civ. Labor	14,899
Unemployed	4.4
Wages	$94,412,034
Av. Weekly Wage	$803.73
Prop. Value	$5,677,206,490
Retail Sales	$924,340,010

For explanation of sources, abbreviations and symbols, see p. 224 and foldout map.

Cherokee County

Physical Features: East Texas county; hilly, partly forested; drains to Angelina, Neches rivers; many streams, lakes; sandy, clay soils.

Economy: Nurseries, timber production; government/services; varied manufacturing; agriculture; tourism.

History: Caddo tribes attracted Spanish missionaries around 1720. Cherokees began settling area around 1820, and soon afterward Anglo-Americans began to arrive. Cherokees forced to Indian Territory 1839. Named for Indian tribe; created 1846 from Nacogdoches County.

Race/Ethnicity, 2000: (In percent) Anglo, 69.80; Black, 16.17; Hispanic, 13.24; Other, 0.79.

Vital Statistics, 2004: Births, 695; deaths, 548; marriages, 383; divorces, 205.

Recreation: Water sports; fishing, hunting; historic sites and parks; Texas State Railroad; nature trails through forests; lakes.

Minerals: Gas, oil.

Agriculture: Nurseries, beef cattle, dairies, hay, poultry. Market value $123.2 million. Timber, hunting income significant.

RUSK (5,145) county seat; agribusiness; tourism, state mental hospital; prison unit; Indian Summer festival.

JACKSONVILLE (14,531) varied manufacturing, plastics, agribusiness, tourism, retail center; hospitals, junior colleges; Love's Lookout; Tomato Fest in June.

Other towns include: **Alto** (1,271); **Cuney** (147); **Gallatin** (390); **Maydelle** (250); **New Summerfield** (1,124); **Reklaw** (356, partly in Rusk County); **Wells** (746). Part [53] of **Bullard** and part [40] of **Troup**.

Population	48,513	
Change fm 2000	4.0	
Area (sq. mi.)	1,061.93	
Land Area (sq. mi.)	1,052.22	
Altitude (ft.)	200-708	

Rainfall (in.)	48.50
Jan. mean min.	36.8
uly mean max.	92.8
Civ. Labor	20,718
Unemployed	4.8

Wages	$101,776,450
Av. Weekly Wage	$507,62
Prop. Value	$2,430,514,433
Retail Sales	$376,658,210

A stucco ranch house on the rolling prairies of northern Clay County. Robert Plocheck photo.

Childress County

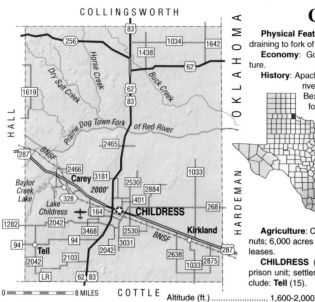

Physical Features: Rolling prairie, at corner of Panhandle, draining to fork of Red River; mixed soils.

Economy: Government/services; trade; tourism, agriculture.

History: Apaches, displaced by Comanches. Ranchers arrived around 1880. County created 1876 from Bexar, Young districts; organized 1887; named for author of Texas Declaration of Independence, George C. Childress.

Race/Ethnicity, 2000: (In percent) Anglo, 64.50; Black, 14.30; Hispanic, 20.47; Other, 0.73.

Vital Statistics, 2004: Births, 81; deaths, 60; marriages, 58; divorces, 24.

Recreation: Recreation on lakes and creek, fishing, hunting of deer, turkey, wild hog, quail, dove; parks; county museum.

Agriculture: Cotton, beef cattle, wheat, hay, sorghum, peanuts; 6,000 acres irrigated. Market value $13.6 million. Hunting leases.

CHILDRESS (6,706) county seat; agribusiness, hospital, prison unit; settlers reunion and rodeo in July. Other towns include: **Tell** (15).

Population	7,717
Change fm 2000	0.4
Area (sq. mi.)	713.61
Land Area (sq. mi.)	710.34
Altitude (ft.)	1,600-2,000
Rainfall (in.)	22.65
Jan. mean min.	26.8
July mean max.	95.3
Civ. Labor	3,057
Unemployed	4.8
Wages	$14,832,029
Av. Weekly Wage	$477.11
Prop. Value	$320,064,530
Retail Sales	$65,532,910

Clay County

Physical Features: Hilly, rolling; north central county drains to Red, Trinity rivers, lake; sandy loam, chocolate soils; mesquites, post oaks.

Economy: Oil; agribusiness; varied manufacturing.

History: Wichitas arrived from north-central plains in mid-1700s, followed by Apaches and Comanches. Ranching attempts began in 1850s. County created from Cooke County, 1857; Indians forced disorganization, 1862; reorganized, 1873; named for Henry Clay, U.S. statesman.

Race/Ethnicity, 2000: (In percent) Anglo, 94.81; Black, 0.41; Hispanic, 3.67; Other, 1.11.

Vital Statistics, 2004: Births, 100; deaths, 100; marriages, 60; divorces, 45.

Recreation: Fishing, water sports; state park; pioneer reunion.

Minerals: Oil and gas, stone.

Agriculture: Beef and dairy cattle, horses raised; wheat, cotton, pecan, peaches. Market value $39.2 million. Oaks, cedar, elms sold to nurseries, mesquite cut for firewood.

HENRIETTA (3,354) county seat; agribusiness center; hospital.

Other towns include: **Bellevue** (396), **Bluegrove** (135), **Byers** (498), **Dean** (346), **Jolly** (181), **Petrolia** (769).

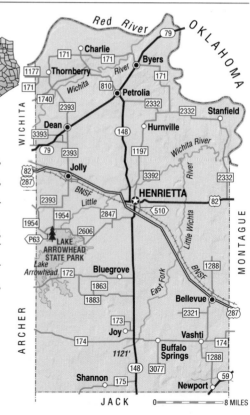

Population	11,104
Change fm 2000	0.9
Area (sq. mi.)	1,116.17
Land Area (sq. mi.)	1,097.82
Altitude (ft.)	800-1,121
Rainfall (in.)	31.66
Jan. mean min.	26.8
July mean max.	95.0
Civ. Labor	6,621
Unemployed	3.1
Wages	$11,432,395
Av. Weekly Wage	$502.43
Prop. Value	$942,021,226
Retail Sales	$71,990,875

For explanation of sources, abbreviations and symbols, see p. 224 and foldout page.

Cochran County

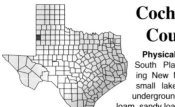

Physical Features: South Plains bordering New Mexico with small lakes (playas); underground water; loam, sandy loam soils.

Economy: Cotton, government/services.

History: Hunting area for various Indian tribes. Ranches operated in 1880s but population in 1900 was still only 25. Farming began in 1920s. County created from Bexar, Young districts, 1876; organized 1924; named for Robert Cochran, who died at the Alamo.

Race/Ethnicity 2000: (In percent) Anglo, 50.18; Black, 4.91; Hispanic, 44.13; Other, 0.78.

Vital Statistics, 2004: Births, 67; deaths, 39; marriages, 21; divorces, 12.

Recreation: Rodeo; Last Frontier Trail Drive and Buffalo Soldier Day in June; museum.

Minerals: Oil, gas.

Agriculture: Cotton production. Crops 60 percent irrigated. Market value $39.5 million.

MORTON (2,175) county seat; oil, farm center, meat packing; light manufacture; hospital.

Other towns include: **Bledsoe** (126), **Whiteface** (457).

Population		3,214
Change fm 2000		-13.8
Area (sq. mi.)		775.31
Land Area (sq. mi.)		775.22
Altitude (ft.)		3,600-4,000
Rainfall (in.)		18.34
Jan. temp. min.		23.1
July temp. max.		91.4
Civ. Labor		1,543
Unemployed		4.7
Wages		$5,888,821
Av. Weekly Wage		$510.89
Prop. Value		$556,575,290
Retail Sales		$31,173,406

Coke County

Physical Features: West Texas prairie, hills, Colorado River valley; sandy loam, red soils; reservoir.

Economy: Oil and gas, government/services, agriculture.

History: From 1700 to 1870s, Comanches roamed the area. Ranches began operating after the Civil War. County created 1889 from Tom Green County; named for Gov. Richard Coke.

Race/Ethnicity, 2000: (In percent) Anglo, 80.18; Black, 1.99; Hispanic, 16.90; Other, 0.93.

Vital Statistics, 2004: Births, 30; deaths, 54; marriages, 9; divorces, 9.

Recreation: Hunting, fishing, Caliche Loop birdwatching trail; lakes; historic sites, Fort Chadbourne, county museum; Ole Coke County Pageant, July 4.

Minerals: Oil, gas.

Agriculture: Beef cattle, small grains, sheep and goats, hay. Market value $12.7 million.

ROBERT LEE (1,159) county seat; ranching, oil and gas, government/services; old jail; Midnight Madness softball tournament in July.

Bronte (1,129) ranching, oil.

Other towns include: **Silver** (34) and **Tennyson** (46). Also, a small part of **Blackwell** (345).

Population		3,623
Change fm 2000		-6.2
Area (sq. mi.)		927.97
Land Area (sq. mi.)		898.81
Altitude (ft.)		1,700-2,608
Rainfall (in.)		23.00
Jan. mean min.		29.0
July mean max.		96.4
Civ. Labor		1,300
Unemployed		4.1
Wages		$5,014,560
Av. Weekly Wage		$456.67
Prop. Value		$517,925,130
Retail Sales		$21,320,415

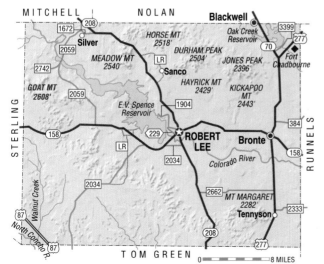

For explanation of sources, abbreviations and symbols, see p. 224 and foldout page.

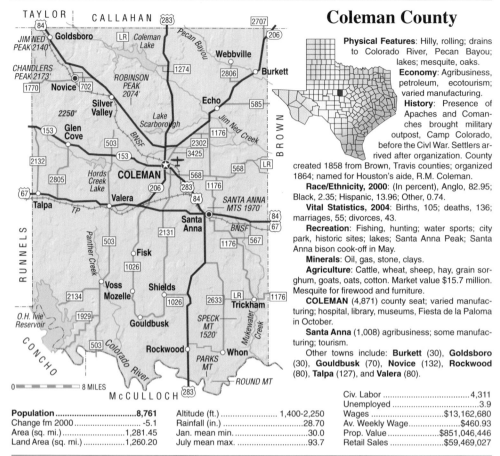

Coleman County

Physical Features: Hilly, rolling; drains to Colorado River, Pecan Bayou; lakes; mesquite, oaks.

Economy: Agribusiness, petroleum, ecotourism; varied manufacturing.

History: Presence of Apaches and Comanches brought military outpost, Camp Colorado, before the Civl War. Settlers arrived after organization. County created 1858 from Brown, Travis counties; organized 1864; named for Houston's aide, R.M. Coleman.

Race/Ethnicity, 2000: (In percent), Anglo, 82.95; Black, 2.35; Hispanic, 13.96; Other, 0.74.

Vital Statistics, 2004: Births, 105; deaths, 136; marriages, 55; divorces, 43.

Recreation: Fishing, hunting; water sports; city park, historic sites; lakes; Santa Anna Peak; Santa Anna bison cook-off in May.

Minerals: Oil, gas, stone, clays.

Agriculture: Cattle, wheat, sheep, hay, grain sorghum, goats, oats, cotton. Market value $15.7 million. Mesquite for firewood and furniture.

COLEMAN (4,871) county seat; varied manufacturing; hospital, library, museums, Fiesta de la Paloma in October.

Santa Anna (1,008) agribusiness; some manufacturing; tourism.

Other towns include: **Burkett** (30), **Goldsboro** (30), **Gouldbusk** (70), **Novice** (132), **Rockwood** (80), **Talpa** (127), and **Valera** (80).

Population	**8,761**
Change fm 2000	-5.1
Area (sq. mi.)	1,281.45
Land Area (sq. mi.)	1,260.20
Altitude (ft.)	1,400-2,250
Rainfall (in.)	28.70
Jan. mean min.	30.0
July mean max.	93.7
Civ. Labor	4,311
Unemployed	3.9
Wages	$13,162,680
Av. Weekly Wage	$460.93
Prop. Value	$851,046,446
Retail Sales	$59,469,027

DART rail trains link Plano, above, in Collin County, with downtown Dallas. Juan Garcia photo.

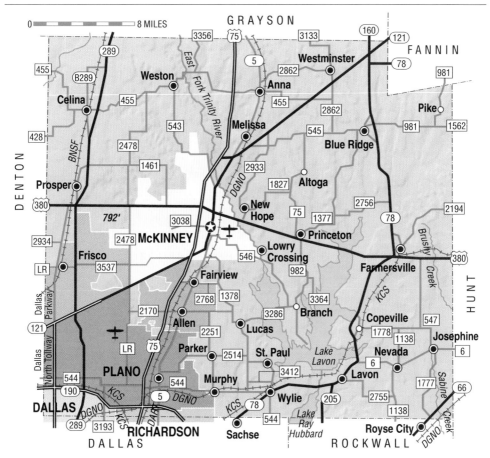

Collin County

Physical Features: North Texas county with heavy, black clay soil; level to rolling; drains to Trinity, Lake Lavon.

Economy: Government/services; manufacturing plants, retail and wholesale center; many residents work in Dallas.

History: Caddo area until 1850s. Settlers of Peters colony arrived in early 1840s. County created from Fannin County 1846. Named for pioneer settler Collin McKinney.

Race/Ethnicity, 2000: (In percent) Anglo, 77.11; Black, 4.98; Hispanic, 10.27; Other, 7.64.

Vital Statistics, 2004: Births, 10,415; deaths, 2,239; marriages, 4,658; divorces, 2,544.

Recreation: Fishing, water sports; historic sites; old homes restoration, tours; natural science museum.

Minerals: Stone production.

Agriculture: Landscape nurseries, cattle, corn, wheat, horses. Market value $38.1 million.

McKINNEY (101,224) county seat; agribusiness, trade center; varied industry; hospital, community college; museums.

PLANO (255,593) telecommunications; manufacturing; newspaper printing; medical services, research center; community college; commercial and financial center; hospitals; balloon festival in September.

Frisco (73,804) technical, areospace industry, hospital, community college.

Other towns include: **Allen** (69,110) telecommunications, hospital, conservatory, natatorium, historic dam, Cinco de Mayo celebration; **Anna** (2,025); **Blue Ridge** (870); **Celina** (3,693) museum, historic town square, Fun Day in September; **Copeville** (243); **Fairview** (6,113) government/services, retail center, commuters, museum, old mill site; **Farmersville** (3,136) agriculture, light industries, Audie Murphy Day in June.

Also, **Josephine** (805); **Lavon** (500); **Lowry Crossing** (1,720); **Lucas** (3,798); **Melissa** (2,735); **Murphy** (11,452); **Nevada** (805); **New Hope** (647); **Parker** (2,085); **Princeton** (4,491) manufacturing, commuters, Spring Onion festival in April; **Prosper** (4,686); **St. Paul** (800); **Westminster** (397); **Weston** (578); **Wylie** (29,868) hospital.

Also, part [45,155] of **Dallas**, part [20,873] of **Richardson** and part [1,660] of **Sachse**.

Population	698,851
Change fm 2000	42.1
Area (sq. mi.)	885.85
Land Area (sq. mi.)	847.56
Altitude (ft.)	434-792
Rainfall (in.)	41.01
Jan. mean min.	31.1
July mean max.	92.7
Civ. Labor	375,730
Unemployed	3.2
Wages	$3,201,361,505
Av. Weekly Wage	$914.48
Prop. Value	$68,869,976,071
Retail Sales	$10,010,773,908

For explanation of sources, abbreviations and symbols, see p. 224 and foldout map.

Collingsworth County

Physical Features: Panhandle county of rolling, broken terrain, draining to Red River forks; sandy and loam soils.

Economy: Agribusiness.

History: Apaches, displaced by Comanches. Ranchers from England arrived in late 1870s. County created 1876, from Bexar and Young districts, organized 1890. Named for Republic of Texas' first chief justice, James Collinsworth (name misspelled in law).

Race/Ethnicity, 2000: (In percent) Anglo, 72.46; Black, 5.33; Hispanic, 20.43; Other, 1.78.

Vital Statistics, 2004: Births, 44; deaths, 51; marriages, 50; divorces, 11.

Recreation: Deer, quail hunting; children's camp, county museum, peanut festival; pioneer park.

Minerals: Gas, oil production.

Agriculture: Peanuts (second in acreage), cotton; cow-calf operations, stocker cattle; alfalfa, wheat; 22,000 acres irrigated. Market value $34.2 million.

WELLINGTON (2,220) county seat; peanut-processing plants, varied manufacturing; agriculture; hospital, library.

Other towns include: **Dodson** (111), **Quail** (37), **Samnorwood** (40).

Population	2,930	July mean max.	97.9
Change fm 2000	-8.6	Civ. Labor	1,618
Area (sq. mi.)	919.44	Unemployed	3.2
Land Area (sq. mi.)	918.80	Wages	$5,497,438
Altitude (ft.)	1,789-2,600	Av. Weekly Wage	$440.96
Rainfall (in.)	22.80	Prop. Value	$279,262,480
Jan. mean min.	27.0	Retail Sales	$12,316,425

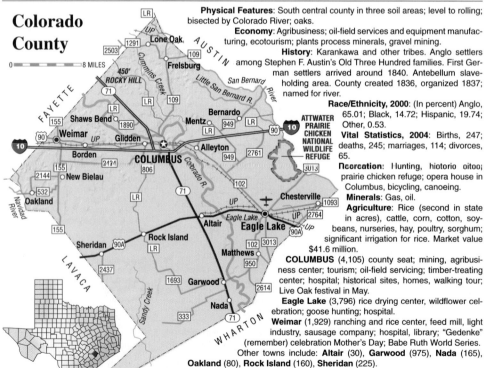

Colorado County

Physical Features: South central county in three soil areas; level to rolling; bisected by Colorado River; oaks.

Economy: Agribusiness; oil-field services and equipment manufacturing, ecotourism; plants process minerals, gravel mining.

History: Karankawa and other tribes. Anglo settlers among Stephen F. Austin's Old Three Hundred families. First German settlers arrived around 1840. Antebellum slave-holding area. County created 1836, organized 1837; named for river.

Race/Ethnicity, 2000: (In percent) Anglo, 65.01; Black, 14.72; Hispanic, 19.74; Other, 0.53.

Vital Statistics, 2004: Births, 247; deaths, 245; marriages, 114; divorces, 65.

Recreation: Hunting, historic sites; prairie chicken refuge; opera house in Columbus, bicycling, canoeing.

Minerals: Gas, oil.

Agriculture: Rice (second in state in acres), cattle, corn, cotton, soybeans, nurseries, hay, poultry, sorghum; significant irrigation for rice. Market value $41.6 million.

COLUMBUS (4,105) county seat; mining, agribusiness center; tourism; oil-field servicing; timber-treating center; hospital; historical sites, homes, walking tour; Live Oak festival in May.

Eagle Lake (3,796) rice drying center, wildflower celebration; goose hunting; hospital.

Weimar (1,929) ranching and rice center, feed mill, light industry, sausage company; hospital, library; "Gedenke" (remember) celebration Mother's Day; Babe Ruth World Series.

Other towns include: **Altair** (30), **Garwood** (975), **Nada** (165), **Oakland** (80), **Rock Island** (160), **Sheridan** (225).

Population	20,824	July mean max.	96.3
Change fm 2000	2.1	Civ. Labor	10,510
Area (sq. mi.)	973.59	Unemployed	3.5
Land Area (sq. mi.)	962.95	Wages	$50,968,368
Altitude (ft.)	150-450	Av. Weekly Wage	$576.06
Rainfall (in.)	44.72	Prop. Value	$2,428,328,962
Jan. mean min.	36.8	Retail Sales	$249,473,878

For explanation of sources, abbreviations and symbols, see p. 224 and foldout map.

Comal County

Population 101,181
Change fm 2000 ....29.7
Area (sq. mi.) 574.59
Land Area (sq. mi.) 561.45
Altitude (ft.) 600-1,473
Rainfall (in.) 35.74
Jan. mean min. 35.5
July mean max. 94.7
Civ. Labor 49,463
Unemployed 3.3
Wages $282,029,994
Av. Weekly Wage.....................$596.09
Prop. Value $9,952,173,106
Retail Sales $3,215,399,342

Physical Features: Scenic Southwest county of hills. Eighty percent above Balcones Escarpment. Spring-fed streams; 2.5-mile-long Comal River, Guadalupe River; Canyon Lake.

Economy: Varied manufacturing; tourism; government/services; agriculture; county in San Antonio metropolitan area.

History: Tonkawa, Waco Indians. A pioneer German settlement 1845. Mexican migration peaked during Mexican Revolution. County created from Bexar, Gonzales, Travis counties and organized in 1846; named for river, a name for Spanish earthenware or metal pan used for cooking tortillas.

Race/Ethnicity, 2000: (In percent) Anglo, 75.46; Black, 1.01; Hispanic, 22.57; Other, 0.96.

Vital Statistics, 2004: Births, 1,144; deaths, 766; marriages, 846; divorces, 326.

Recreation: Fishing, hunting; historic sites, Hummel museum; scenic drives; lake facilities; Prince Solms Park, other county parks; Landa Park with 76 species of trees; Gruene historic area; caverns; river resorts; river tubing; Schlitterbahn water park; Wurstfest in November.

Minerals: Stone, lime, sand and gravel.

Agriculture: Cattle, goats, sheep, hogs, horses; nursery, hay, corn, sorghum, wheat. Market value $5.6 million.

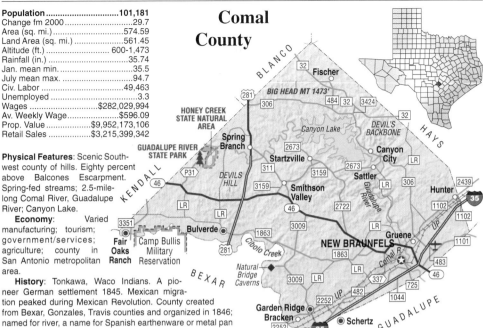

NEW BRAUNFELS (48,148) county seat; manufacturing, call centers; retail, distribution; one of the most picturesque cities in Texas, making it a tourist center; Conservation Plaza; rose garden; hospital; library; mental health and retardation center. **Gruene** is now part of New Braunfels.

Other towns include: **Bulverde** (4,014), **Garden Ridge** (2,502), and the retirement and recreation community around **Canyon Lake** (18,281), which includes **Startzville, Sattler, Smithson Valley, Canyon City, Fischer** and **Spring Branch**.

Also in the county, parts of **Fair Oaks Ranch** (5,663), **Selma** (2,092) and **Schertz** (28,180).

The tube chute at Prince Solms Park in New Braunfels. Randy Eli Grothe photo.

Comanche County

Physical Features: West central county with rolling, hilly terrain; sandy, loam, waxy soils; drains to Leon River, Proctor Lake; pecans, oaks, mesquites, cedars.

Economy: Dairies, other agribusiness; peanut- and pecan-shelling plants; food processing; manufacturing.

History: Comanche area. Anglo-American settlers arrived in 1854 on land granted earlier to Stephen F. Austin and Samuel May Williams. County created 1856 from Bosque, Coryell counties; named for Indian tribe.

Race/Ethnicity, 2000: (In percent) Anglo, 78.10; Black, 0.49; Hispanic, 20.88; Other, 0.53.

Vital Statistics, 2004: Births, 200; deaths, 159; marriages, 89; divorces, 39.

Recreation: Hunting, fishing, water sports, nature tourism; parks, community center, museums; Comanche Pow-Wow in September, rodeo in July.

Minerals: Limited gas, oil, stone, clay.

Agriculture: Dairies, beef cattle, hay, pecans, wildlife, melons. Market value $102.5 million.

COMANCHE (4,525) county seat; plants process feed, food; varied manufacturing; agribusiness, winery; hospital; Ranger College branch; library; state's oldest courthouse, "Old Cora," on display on town square.

De Leon (2,420) peanuts, pecans; hospital; car museum, Peach and Melon Festival in August.

Other towns include: **Energy** (70), **Gustine** (457), **Proctor** (228) and **Sidney** (148).

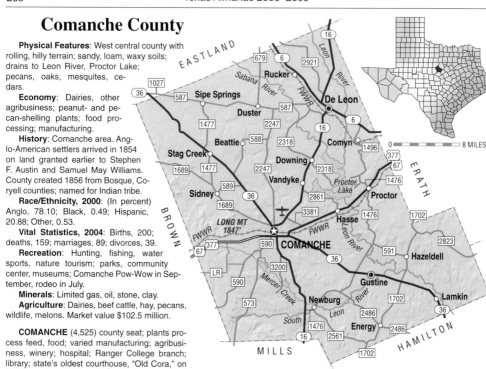

Population 13,837	July mean max. 95.5
Change fm 2000 .... -1.3	Civ. Labor 6,207
Area (sq. mi.) 947.67	Unemployed 4.1
Land Area (sq. mi.) 937.69	Wages $23,480,715
Altitude (ft.) 1,056-1,847	Av. Weekly Wage.............. $482.60
Rainfall (in.) 31.12	Prop. Value $1,136,987,179
Jan. mean min. 30.6	Retail Sales $105,418,418

Concho County

Physical Features: West central county on Edwards Plateau, rough, broken to south; level in north, sandy, loam and dark soils; drains to creeks and Colorado River.

Economy: Agribusiness, manufacturing.

History: Athabascan-speaking Plains Indians, then Jumanos in 1600s, absorbed by Lipan Apaches 1700s. Comanches raided after 1800. Anglo-Americans began ranching around 1850; farming after the Civil War. Mexican-Americans employed on sheep ranches 1920s-30s. County created from Bexar District, 1858, organized 1879; named for river.

Race/Ethnicity, 2000: (In percent) Anglo, 57.39; Black, 0.98; Hispanic, 41.33; Other, 0.30.

Vital Statistics, 2004: Births, 36; deaths, 29; marriages, 11; divorces, 10.

Recreation: Famed for 1,500 Indian pictographs; reservoir.

Minerals: Oil, gas, stone.

Agriculture: A leading sheep-raising county; cattle, goats; wheat, feed grains; 10,000 acres irrigated for cotton. Market value $14.3 million.

PAINT ROCK (313) county seat; named for Indian pictographs nearby; farming, ranching center.

EDEN (2,451) steel fabrication, detention center; hospital; fall fest.

Other towns include: **Eola** (215), **Lowake** (40) and **Millersview** (80).

Population 3,654	July mean max. 97.4
Change fm 2000 .... -7.9	Civ. Labor 1,425
Area (sq. mi.) 993.69	Unemployed 4.3
Land Area (sq. mi.) 991.45	Wages $5,937,961
Altitude (ft.) 1,500-2,400	Av. Weekly Wage.................. $500.84
Rainfall (in.) 25.50	Prop. Value $451,604,400
Jan. mean min. 31.9	Retail Sales $21,587,862

Cooke County

Physical Features: North central county; drains to Red, Trinity rivers, lakes; sandy, red, loam soils.

Economy: Oil, agribusiness, tourism, varied manufacturing.

History: Frontier between Caddoes and Comanches. Anglo-Americans arrived in late 1840s. Germans settled western part around 1890. County created 1848 from Fannin County; named for Capt. W.G. Cooke of the Texas Revolution.

Race/Ethnicity, 2000: (In percent) Anglo, 85.55; Black, 3.19; Hispanic, 9.97; Other, 1.29.

Vital Statistics, 2004: Births, 544; deaths, 382; marriages, 758; divorces, 141.

Recreation: Water sports; hunting, fishing; zoo; museum; park, Depot Day/car show in October.

Minerals: Oil, sand, gravel.

Agriculture: Beef, horses, dairies, wheat, grain sorghum, corn, pecans. Market value $46.2 million. Hunting leases.

GAINESVILLE (16,432) county seat; tourism, plastics, agribusiness; aircraft, steel fabrication; Victorian homes, walking tours; hospital; community college, juvenile correction unit; Camp Sweeney for diabetic children.

Muenster (1,585) oil, food processing, tourism, varied manufacturing; hospital, Germanfest in April.

Other towns include: **Callisburg** (374), **Era** (150), **Lindsay** (918), **Myra** (150), **Oak Ridge** (245), **Rosston** (75), **Valley View** (814) and the residential community around **Lake Kiowa** (1,766).

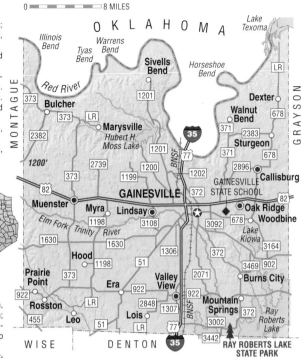

Population	38,946
Change fm 2000	7.1
Area (sq. mi.)	898.81
Land Area (sq. mi.)	873.64
Altitude (ft.)	617-1,200
Rainfall (in.)	36.90
Jan. mean min.	28.0
July mean max.	95.0
Civ. Labor	20,631
Unemployed	3.1
Wages	$115,373,637
Av. Weekly Wage	$605.08
Prop. Value	$3,036,837,465
Retail Sales	$548,362,836

The Fischer's Meat Market and Grocery in Muenster reflects its German heritage. Robert Plocheck photo.

Physical Features: Leon Valley in center, remainder rolling, hilly.

Economy: Fort Hood, state prisons, agribusiness, plastics and other manufacturing.

History: Tonkawa area, later various other tribes. Anglo-Americans settled around Fort Gates in late 1840s. Permanent establishment of Fort Hood in 1950 changed cultural geography. County created from Bell County 1854; named for local pioneer James Coryell.

Race/Ethnicity, 2000: (In percent) Anglo, 61.74; Black, 22.30; Hispanic, 12.57; Other, 3.39.

Vital Statistics, 2004: Births, 796; deaths, 358; marriages, 469; divorces, 148.

Recreation: state park; deer hunting; fishing; nearby lakes and Leon River, bluebonnet area. Historic homes; log jail; Shivaree in June.

Minerals: Oil and gas.

Agriculture: Beef, forages, wildlife, row crops. Market value $34.7 million. Hunting leases, timber.

GATESVILLE (15,945) county seat; prisons; varied manufacturing; hospital; refurbished courthouse; museum; branch Central Texas College.

COPPERAS COVE (31,425) business center for Fort Hood; industrial filters, other manufacturing; hospital, library; Central Texas College; Spurfest in September.

Other towns include: **Evant** (398, partly in Hamilton County), **Flat** (210), **Jonesboro** (125), **Mound** (125), **Oglesby** (445), **Purmela** (50), **South Mountain** (407). Part [16,429] of **Fort Hood**.

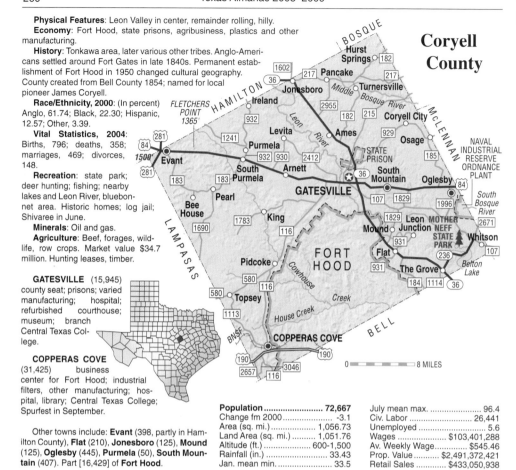

Coryell County

Population	72,667
Change fm 2000	-3.1
Area (sq. mi.)	1,056.73
Land Area (sq. mi.)	1,051.76
Altitude (ft.)	600-1,500
Rainfall (in.)	33.43
Jan. mean min.	33.5
July mean max.	96.4
Civ. Labor	26,441
Unemployed	5.6
Wages	$103,401,288
Av. Weekly Wage	$545.46
Prop. Value	$2,491,372,421
Retail Sales	$433,050,938

The Coryell County Courthouse in Gatesville was built in 1897. Robert Plocheck photo.

Cottle County

Physical Features: Western county below Caprock, rough in west, level in east; gray, black, sandy and loam soils; drains to Pease River.

Economy: Agribusiness, government/services.

History: Around 1700, Apaches were displaced by Comanches, who in turn were driven out by U.S. Army 1870s. Anglo-American settlers arrived in 1880s. County created 1876 from Fannin County; organized 1892; named for George W. Cottle, Alamo hero.

Race/Ethnicity, 2000: (In percent) Anglo, 71.42; Black, 9.30; Hispanic, 18.91; Other, 0.37.

Vital Statistics, 2004: Births, 14; deaths, 10; marriages, 0; divorces, 0.

Recreation: Hunting of quail, dove, wild hogs, deer; wildlife management area; museum, Fiesta Patria, horse and colt show in April.

Minerals: Oil, natural gas.

Agriculture: Beef cattle, cotton, peanuts, wheat. 3,000 acres irrigated. Market value $13 million.

PADUCAH (1,301) county seat; government/services, library.

Other towns include: **Cee Vee** (45).

Population 1,679	Rainfall (in.) 24.11	Wages $3,585,798
Change fm 2000 ....-11.8	Jan. mean min...............................26.2	Av. Weekly Wage....................$564.84
Area (sq. mi.) 901.59	July mean max. 96.8	Prop. Value $192,935,520
Land Area (sq. mi.) 901.18	Civ. Labor 833	Retail Sales $12,802,464
Altitude (ft.) 1,600-2,200	Unemployed 4.3	

Physical Features: Rolling prairie, Pecos Valley, some hills; sandy, loam soils; Juan Cordona Lake (intermittent).

Economy: Oil and gas; agriculture; government/services.

History: Lipan Apache area. Ranching developed in 1890s. Oil discovered in 1926. County created from Tom Green County 1887, organized 1927; named for Baylor University president W. C. Crane.

Race/Ethnicity, 2000: (In percent) Anglo, 52.42; Black, 2.98; Hispanic, 43.87; Other, 0.73.

Vital Statistics, 2004: Births, 61; deaths, 43; marriages, 29; divorces, 0.

Recreation: Sites of pioneer trails and historic Horsehead Crossing on Pecos River; hunting of mule deer, quail; county stock show in January; camping park.

Minerals: Oil, gas production.

Agriculture: Cattle ranching, goats. Market value $1.3 million.

CRANE (3,033) county seat; oil-well servicing, production; foundry; steel, surfboard manufacturing; hospital.

Population 3,845
Change fm 2000 ....-3.8
Area (sq. mi.) 785.59
Land Area (sq. mi.) 785.56
Altitude (ft.) 2,300-2,902
Rainfall (in.) 15.38
Jan. mean min. 30.6
July mean max. 95.3
Civ. Labor 1,569
Unemployed 4.3
Wages $18,534,183
Av. Weekly Wage....................$921.40
Prop. Value $1,436,978,890
Retail Sales $34,352,776

Crane County

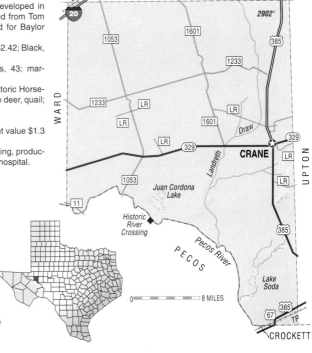

For explanation of sources, abbreviations and symbols, see p. 224 and foldout map.

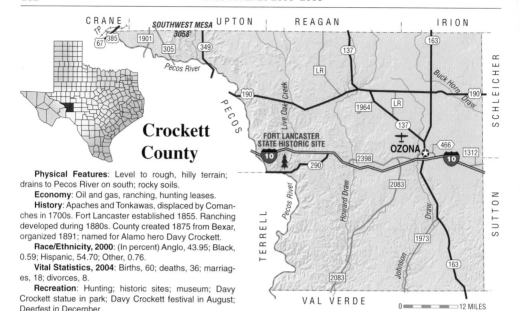

Crockett County

Physical Features: Level to rough, hilly terrain; drains to Pecos River on south; rocky soils.

Economy: Oil and gas, ranching, hunting leases.

History: Apaches and Tonkawas, displaced by Comanches in 1700s. Fort Lancaster established 1855. Ranching developed during 1880s. County created 1875 from Bexar, organized 1891; named for Alamo hero Davy Crockett.

Race/Ethnicity, 2000: (In percent) Anglo, 43.95; Black, 0.59; Hispanic, 54.70; Other, 0.76.

Vital Statistics, 2004: Births, 60; deaths, 36; marriages, 18; divorces, 8.

Recreation: Hunting; historic sites; museum; Davy Crockett statue in park; Davy Crockett festival in August; Deerfest in December.

Minerals: Oil, gas production.

Agriculture: Sheep, goats; beef cattle. Market value $10.2 million.

OZONA (3,449) county seat; trade center for ranching; hunting leases; tourism.

Population	**3,879**
Change fm 2000	-5.4
Area (sq. mi.)	2,807.43
Land Area (sq. mi.)	2,807.42
Altitude (ft.)	1,700-3,058
Rainfall (in.)	18.95
Jan. mean min.	27.7
July mean max.	93.0
Civ. Labor	2,077
Unemployed	3.2
Wages	$8,747,569
Av. Weekly Wage	$475.32
Prop. Value	$1,841,737,390
Retail Sales	$39,157,052

Crosby County

Physical Features: Flat, rich soil above Caprock, broken below; drains into Brazos River forks and playas.

Economy: Agribusiness, tourism, commuters to Lubbock.

History: Comanches, driven out by U.S. Army in 1870s; ranching developed soon afterward. Quaker colony founded in 1879. County created from Bexar District 1876, organized 1886; named for Texas Land Commissioner Stephen Crosby.

Race/Ethnicity, 2000: (In percent) Anglo, 46.93; Black, 3.83; Hispanic, 48.93; Other, 0.31.

Vital Statistics, 2004: Births, 115; deaths, 86; marriages, 28; divorces, 20.

Recreation: White River Lake; Silver Falls Park; hunting.

Minerals: Sand, gravel, oil, gas.

Agriculture: Cotton, beef cattle; sorghum; about 200,000 acres irrigated. Market value $39.5 million.

CROSBYTON (1,734) county seat; agribusiness center; hospital, Pioneer Museum, Prairie Ladies Multi-Cultural Center, library; Cowboy Gathering in October.

Other towns include: **Lorenzo** (1,334). **Ralls** (2,154) government/services, agribusiness; museums; Cotton Boll Fest in September.

Population	**6,549**
Change fm 2000	-7.4
Area (sq. mi.)	901.69
Land Area (sq. mi.)	899.51
Altitude (ft.)	2,300-3,200
Rainfall (in.)	22.95
Jan. mean min.	25.3
July mean max.	92.5
Civ. Labor	3,006
Unemployed	4.4
Wages	$9,520,759
Av. Weekly Wage	$460.41
Prop. Value	$354,232,880
Retail Sales	$119,044,091

For explanation of sources, abbreviations and symbols, see p. 224 and foldout map.

A Texas madrone tree in Guadalupe Mountains National Park. Robert Plocheck photo.

Culberson County

Physical Features: Contains Texas' highest mountain; slopes toward Pecos Valley on east, Diablo Bolson on west; salt lakes; unique vegetation in canyons.

Economy: Tourism; government/services; talc mining, processing; agribusiness.

History: Apaches arrived about 600 years ago. U.S. military frontier after Civil War. Ranching developed after 1880. Mexican migration increased after 1920. County created from El Paso County 1911, organized 1912; named for D.B. Culberson, Texas congressman.

Race/Ethnicity, 2000: (In percent) Anglo, 25.98; Black, 0.64; Hispanic, 72.24; Other, 1.14.

Vital Statistics, 2004: Births, 25; deaths, 27; marriages, 0; divorces, 2.

Recreation: National park; Guadalupe and El Capitan, twin peaks; scenic canyons and mountains; classic car museum, antique saloon bar; frontier days in June, big buck tournament.

Minerals: Sulfur, talc, marble, oil.

Agriculture: Beef cattle; crops include cotton, vegetables, melons, pecans; 4,000 acres in irrigation. Market value $7.5 million.

VAN HORN (2,197) county seat; agribusiness; tourism; rock crushing; government/services; hospital.

Other towns: **Kent** (60).

Population	2,525
Change fm 2000	-15.1
Area (sq. mi.)	3,812.71
Land Area (sq. mi.)	3,812.46
Altitude (ft.)	3,000-8,749
Rainfall (in.)	11.98
Jan. mean min.	27.8
July mean max.	91.7
Civ. Labor	1,659
Unemployed	3.4
Wages	$6,231,746
Av. Weekly Wage	$432.38
Prop. Value	$305,437,100
Retail Sales	$100,078,012

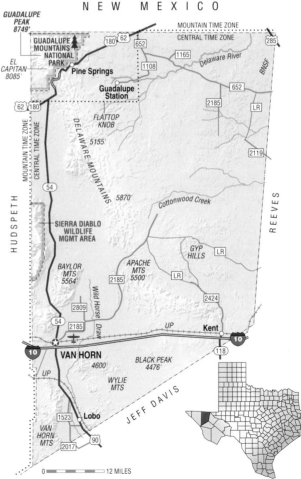

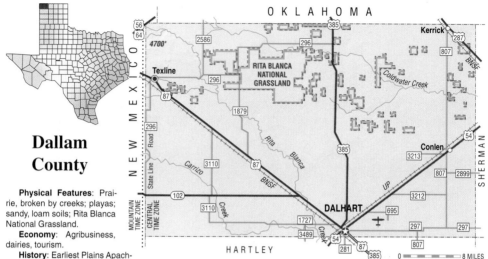

Dallam County

Physical Features: Prairie, broken by creeks; playas; sandy, loam soils; Rita Blanca National Grassland.

Economy: Agribusiness, dairies, tourism.

History: Earliest Plains Apaches; displaced by Comanches and Kiowas. Ranching developed in late 19th century. Farming began after 1900. County created from Bexar District, 1876, organized 1891. Named for lawyer-editor James W. Dallam.

Race/Ethnicity, 2000: (In percent) Anglo, 68.95; Black, 1.69; Hispanic, 28.38; Other, 0.98.

Vital Statistics, 2004: Births, 107; deaths, 48; marriages, 68; divorces, 36.

Recreation: XIT Museum; XIT Rodeo in August; hunting, wildlife; grasslands.

Minerals: Petroleum.

Agriculture: A leader in production of grain (corn, wheat, sorghum). Cattle and hogs raised, dairies; potatoes, sunflowers, beans; substantial irrigation. Market value $369.7 million.

DALHART (7,273, partly in Hartley County) county seat; government/services; agribusiness center for parts of Texas, New Mexico, Oklahoma; railroad; cheese plant; grain operations; hospital; prison.

Other towns include: **Kerrick** (35) and **Texline** (525).

Population	6,143
Change fm 2000	-1.3
Area (sq. mi.)	1,505.26
Land Area (sq. mi.)	1,504.69
Altitude (ft.)	3,700-4,700
Rainfall (in.)	18.57
Jan. mean min.	19.0
July mean max.	90.0
Civ. Labor	3,049
Unemployed	3.1
Wages	$24,937,803
Av. Weekly Wage	$553.19
Prop. Value	$753,269,270
Retail Sales	$100,489,862

Dallas County

Physical Features: Mostly flat, heavy blackland soils, sandy clays in west; drains to Trinity River.

Economy: A national center for telecommunications, transportation, electronics manufacturing, data processing, conventions and trade shows; foreign-trade zone located at D/FW International Airport, U.S. Customs port of entry; government/services.

History: Caddoan area. Anglo-Americans began arriving in 1840. Antebellum slaveholding area. County created 1846 from Nacogdoches, Robertson counties; named for U.S. Vice President George Mifflin Dallas.

Race/Ethnicity, 2000: (In percent) Anglo, 44.99; Black, 20.47; Hispanic, 29.87; Other, 4.67.

Population	2,345,815
Change fm 2000	5.7
Area (sq. mi.)	908.56
Land Area (sq. mi.)	879.60
Altitude (ft.)	382-870
Rainfall (in.)	37.05
Jan. mean min.	36.4
July mean max.	96.1
Civ. Labor	1,222,715
Unemployed	4.4
Wages	$18,267,313,796
Av. Weekly Wage	$959.64
Prop. Value	$188,778,393,600
Retail Sales	$56,215,441,342

Vital Statistics, 2004: Births, 42,524; deaths, 13,741; marriages, 15,481; divorces, 8,710.

Recreation: One of the state's top tourist destinations and one of the nation's most popular convention centers; State Fair, museums, zoo, West End shopping and tourist district, historical sites, including Sixth Floor museum in the old Texas School Book Depository, site of the assassination of President Kennedy.

Other important attractions include the Morton H. Meyerson Symphony Center; performing arts; professional sports; Texas broadcast museum; lakes; theme and amusement parks.

Minerals: Sand, gravel.

Agriculture: Horticultural crops; wheat, hay, corn; horses. Market value $19 million.

Education: Southern Methodist University, University of Dallas, Dallas Baptist University, University of Texas at Dallas, University of Texas Southwestern Medical Center and many other education centers.

DALLAS (1,224,397) county seat; center of state's largest consolidated metropolitan area and second-largest city in Texas; D/FW International Airport is one of the world's busiest; headquarters for the U.S. Army and Air Force Exchange Service; Federal Reserve Bank; a leader in fashions and in computer operations; hospitals; Infomart, a large computer-sales complex; many hotels in downtown area offer adequate accommodations for most conventions.

Garland (218,303) varied manufacturing, community college branch, hospitals, performing arts center.

Irving (194,842) Texas Stadium, home of the Dallas Cowboys; telecommunications; varied light manufacturing, food processing; distribution center; Boy Scout headquarters and museum; North Lake College; hospitals.

Other cities include: **Addison**

(14,777) general aviation airport; **Balch Springs** (20,770); part [49,822] of **Carrollton** (122,005 total) residential community, distribution center, hospital; **Cedar Hill** (41,340) residential, light manufacturing, retail, Northwood University, Country Day on the Hill in October; **Cockrell Hill** (4,364); **Coppell** (39,063) distribution, varied manufacturing; office center; **DeSoto** (45,075) residential community, light industry and distribution, hospitals; Toad Holler Creekfest in June.

Also, **Duncanville** (34,809) varied manufacturing, many commuters to Dallas; Sandra Meadows Classic girls basketball tournament in December; **Farmers Branch** (27,091) distribution center, varied manufacturing, Brookhaven College, hospital; **Glenn Heights** (9,940, partly in Ellis County); most [99,760] of **Grand Prairie** (148,992 total) wholesale trade, aerospace, entertainment; hospital, library, Joe Pool Reservoir, Indian pow-wow

Largest U.S. Media Markets

Rank	Homes
1. New York	7.37 million
2. Los Angeles	5.61 million
3. Chicago	3.46 million
4. Philadelphia	2.94 million
5. San Francisco	2.38 million
6. Dallas/Fort Worth	2.38 million
7. Boston	2.37 million
8. Washington	2.27 million
9. Atlanta	2.21 million
10. Houston	1.98 million

Source: Nielsen Media Research, 2007.

in September, Lone Star horse-racing track; **Highland Park** (8,305); **Hutchins** (2,846) varied manufacturing; **Lancaster** (32,342) residential, industrial, distribution center, Cedar Valley College, Commemorative Air Force museum, hospital, park, depot, historic town square; Musicfests

monthly in the spring.

Also, **Mesquite** (129,383) varied industries; hospitals; championship rodeo, rodeo parade in spring; community college, historical parks; most [70,929] of **Richardson** (98,857 total) telecommunications, software development, financial services, hospital; Wildflower Music Festival in May; **Rowlett** (54,786) residential, manufacturing, government/services, hospital, library, park, hike and bike trails; **Sachse** (17,346, partly in Collin County) commuting to Dallas, government/services, Fallfest in October; **Seagoville** (11,218) rural/suburban setting, federal prison, Seagofest in October; **Sunnyvale** (4,065); **University Park** (23,233); **Wilmer** (3,690).

Part of **Combine** (2,058) and part of **Ovilla** (3,747).

For explanation of sources, abbreviations and symbols, see p. 224 and foldout map.

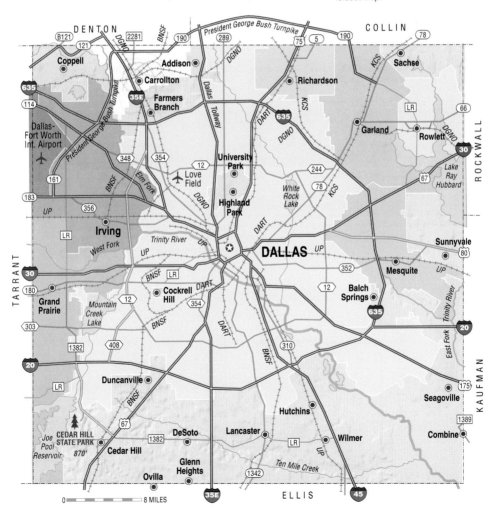

Dawson County

Physical Features: South High Plains county in West Texas, broken on the east; loam and sandy soils.

Economy: Agriculture; farm, gin equipment manufacturing; peanut plant; government/services.

History: Comanche, Kiowa area. Ranching developed in 1880s. Farming began after 1900. Hispanic population increased after 1940. County created from Bexar District, 1876, organized 1905; named for Nicholas M. Dawson, San Jacinto veteran.

Race/Ethnicity, 2000: (In percent) Anglo, 42.65; Black, 8.69; Hispanic, 48.19; Other, 0.47.

Vital Statistics, 2004: Births, 186; deaths, 151; marriages, 91; divorces, 40.

Recreation: Parks; museum; campground; May Fun Fest; July 4 celebration.

Minerals: Oil, natural gas.

Agriculture: A major cotton-producing county; peanuts, sorghums, watermelons, alfalfa, grapes. 70,000 acres irrigated. Market value $55.4 million.

LAMESA (9,534) county seat; agribusiness; food processing, oil-field services; some manufacturing; computerized cotton-classing office; hospital; campus of Howard College; prison unit.

Other towns include: **Ackerly** (244, partly in Martin County), **Los Ybañez** (32) and **Welch** (95). Also, **O'Donnell** (962, mostly in Lynn County).

Population	**14,174**
Change fm 2000	-5.4
Area (sq. mi.)	902.12
Land Area (sq. mi.)	902.06
Altitude (ft.)	2,600-3,100
Rainfall (in.)	19.07
Jan. mean min.	26.0
July mean max.	92.9
Civ. Labor	5,116
Unemployed	5.5
Wages	$28,798,541
Av. Weekly Wage	$502.67
Prop. Value	$1,11,995,870
Retail Sales	$119,277,668

Population	**18,623**
Change fm 2000	0.3
Area (sq. mi.)	1,498.26
Land Area (sq. mi.)	1,497.34
Altitude (ft.)	3,700-4,400
Rainfall (in.)	18.65
Jan. mean min.	21.1
July mean max.	91.6
Civ. Labor	8,754
Unemployed	3.8
Wages	$45,092,215
Av. Weekly Wage	$534.24
Prop. Value	$954,855,236
Retail Sales	$164,433,372

Deaf Smith County

Physical Features: Panhandle High Plains county, partly broken; chocolate and sandy loam soils; drains to Palo Duro and Tierra Blanca creeks.

Economy: Agriculture, varied industries, meat packing, offset printing.

History: Apaches, displaced by Comanches, Kiowas. Ranching developed after U.S. Army drove out Indians 1874-75.

Farming began after 1900. Hispanic settlement increased after 1950. County created 1876, from Bexar District; organized 1890. Named for famed scout in Texas Revolution, Erastus (Deaf) Smith.

Race/Ethnicity, 2000: (In percent) Anglo, 40.60; Black, 1.40; Hispanic, 57.40; Other, 0.60.

Vital Statistics, 2004: Births, 355; deaths, 156; marriages, 131; divorces, 39.

Recreation: Museum, tours, POW camp chapel; Cinco de Mayo, Pioneer Days in May.

Minerals: Not significant.

Agriculture: Leading agricultural county, dairies, feedlot operations, cotton, wheat, sorghum, corn; 50 percent irrigated. Market value $841.8 million, first in state.

HEREFORD (14,757) county seat; agribusinesses, food processing; ethanol production, varied manufacturing; trucking; hospital, aquatic center. Other towns include: **Dawn** (52).

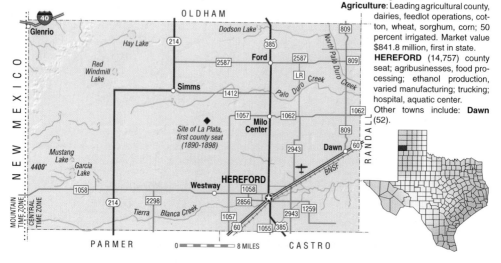

Delta County

Physical Features: Northeast county between two forks of Sulphur River; Cooper Lake (also designated Jim Chapman Lake); black, sandy loam soils.

Economy: Agriculture; government/services; retirement location.

History: Caddo area, but disease, other tribes caused displacement around 1790. Anglo-Americans arrived in 1820s. County created from Lamar, Hopkins counties 1870. Greek letter delta origin of name, because of shape of the county.

Race/Ethnicity, 2000: (In percent) Anglo, 87.55; Black, 8.62; Hispanic, 3.10; Other, 0.73.

Vital Statistics, 2004: Births, 50; deaths, 55; marriages, 36; divorces, 4.

Recreation: Fishing, hunting; lake, state park; Cooper Chiggerfest in October.

Minerals: Not significant.

Agriculture: Beef; hay, soybeans, wheat, corn, sorghum, cotton. Market value $10.7 million.

COOPER (2,096) county seat; industrial park, some manufacturing; agribusiness; museum.

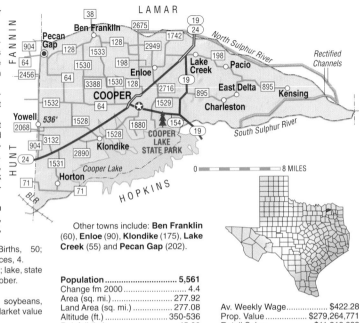

Other towns include: **Ben Franklin** (60), **Enloe** (90), **Klondike** (175), **Lake Creek** (55) and **Pecan Gap** (202).

Population	**5,561**
Change fm 2000	4.4
Area (sq. mi.)	277.92
Land Area (sq. mi.)	277.08
Altitude (ft.)	350-536
Rainfall (in.)	45.00
Jan. mean min.	30.0
July mean max.	94.0
Civ. Labor	2,603
Unemployed	4.1
Wages	$5,648,836

Av. Weekly Wage	$422.28
Prop. Value	$279,264,771
Retail Sales	$11,919,933

For explanation of sources, abbreviations and symbols, see p. 224 and foldout map.

An autumn morning on Cooper Lake. Robert Plocheck photo.

Denton County

Physical Features: North Texas county; partly hilly, draining to Elm Fork of Trinity River, lakes; Blackland and Grand Prairie soils and terrain.

Economy: Varied industries; colleges; horse industry; tourism; government/services; part of Dallas-Fort Worth metropolitan area.

History: Land grant from Texas Congress 1841 for Peters colony. County created out of Fannin County 1846; named for John B. Denton, pioneer Methodist minister.

Race/Ethnicity, 2000: (In percent) Anglo, 76.93; Black, 6.07; Hispanic, 12.15; Other, 4.85.

Vital Statistics, 2004: Births, 8,854; deaths, 1,967; marriages, 3,740; divorces, 2,201.

Recreation: Water sports at Lewisville, Grapevine lakes, seven U.S. Corps of Engineers parks; Ray Roberts lake; universities' cultural, athletic activities, including "Texas Women; A Celebration of History'" exhibit at TWU library; Texas Motor Speedway; State D.A.R. Museum "First Ladies of Texas" collection of gowns and memorabilia; Little Chapel in the Woods; Denton Jazzfest in April. Minerals: Natural gas.

Education: University of North Texas and Texas Woman's University.

Agriculture: Important horse-raising area. Eggs, nurseries, turf, cattle; also, hay, sorghum, wheat, peanuts grown. Market value $49.1 million.

DENTON (104,728) county seat; universities; Denton State School; manufacturers of trucks (Peterbilt), bricks; milling; hospitals; Blues Festival in September, storytelling festival in spring.

LEWISVILLE (92,847) commuting to Dallas and Fort Worth, retail center, electronics and varied industries including missile manufacturing; Lewisville Lake, hospital, library; Celtic Feis & Scottish Highland Games in March.

Flower Mound (64,041) residential community, library, mound of native grasses, bike classic in spring.

Carrollton (122,005, also in Dallas County), hospital.

Other towns include: **The Colony** (35,558) on eastern shore of Lewisville Lake, tourism, IBM offices, chili cook-off in June, Las Vegas Night in April.

Also, **Argyle** (2,890); **Aubrey** (2,202) horse farms/training, cabinet construction, peanut festival in October;

Bartonville (1,245); **Copper Canyon** (1,260); **Corinth** (17,147); **Corral City** (103); **Cross Roads** (724); **Dish** (362); **Double Oak** (2,769); **Hackberry** (601); **Hebron** (162); **Hickory Creek** (3,040); **Highland Village** (14,816); **Justin** (3,412); **Krugerville** (1,434); **Krum** (3,237) commuters, old grain mill; **Lake Dallas** (7,328) light manufacturing, marina, historic downtown.

Also, **Lakewood Village** (446); **Lincoln Park** (601); **Little Elm** (19,472) light manufacturing, lake activities, library, Cinco de Mayo; **Marshall Creek** (530); **Northlake** (1,432); **Oak Point** (2,230); **Pilot Point** (4,159) light manufacturing, horse ranches, Fireman's Fest in April; **Ponder** (837); **Roanoke** (3,777); **Sanger** (6,398) lake recreation enterprises; **Shady Shores** (1,986); **Trophy Club** (7,608).

Population	**584,238**
Change fm 2000	34.9
Area (sq. mi.)	957.88
Land Area (sq. mi.)	888.54
Altitude (ft.)	450-950
Rainfall (in.)	37.79
Jan. mean min.	32.0
July mean max.	94.1
Civ. Labor	323,201
Unemployed	3.3
Wages	$1,393,702,098
Av. Weekly Wage	$695.00
Prop. Value	$51,002,577,292
Retail Sales	$8,290,512,989

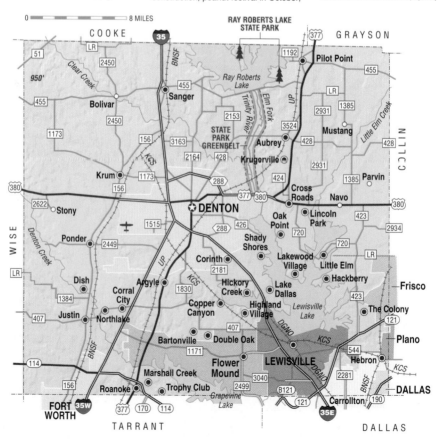

DeWitt County

Physical Features: South central county drained by Guadalupe and tributaries; rolling to level; waxy, loam, sandy soils.

Economy: Wood, furniture plants, textile mill; varied manufacturing; agri-businesses; prison unit.

History: Coahuiltecan area, then Karankawas and other tribes, finally the Comanches. Mexican and Anglo-American settlers arrived in 1820s. County created from Gonzales, Goliad, Victoria counties 1846; named for Green De-Witt, colonizer.

Race/Ethnicity, 2000: (In percent) Anglo, 61.22; Black, 10.94; Hispanic, 27.24; Other, 0.60.

Vital Statistics, 2004: Births, 218; deaths, 228; marriages, 91; divorces, 86.

Recreation: Hunting, fishing; historic homes, museums; wildflowers.

Minerals: Oil and natural gas.

Agriculture: Cattle, dairy products, poultry, swine; corn, sorghum, cotton, hay, pecans. Market value $29.5 million.

CUERO (6,954) county seat; agribusiness, leather products; food processing; hospital, Turkeyfest in October.

Yorktown (2,297) agribusiness, oil-well servicing; library, museum, park;

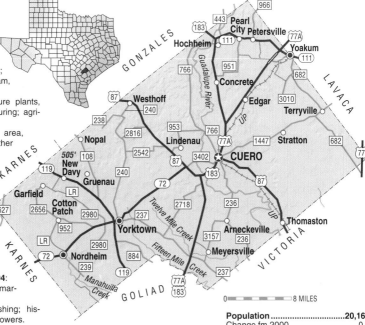

Western Days in October.

Other towns include: **Hochheim** (70), **Meyersville** (110), **Nordheim** (324), **Thomaston** (45), **Westhoff** (410). Part [2,137] of **Yoakum** (5,831 total) cattle, leather; hospital; museum; Land of Leather in February.

For explanation of sources, abbreviations and symbols, see p. 224 and foldout map.

Population	**20,167**
Change fm 2000	0.8
Area (sq. mi.)	910.47
Land Area (sq. mi.)	909.18
Altitude (ft.)	100-505
Rainfall (in.)	36.08
Jan. mean min.	41.3
July mean max.	95.1
Civ. Labor	9,312
Unemployed	3.7
Wages	$46,712,085
Av. Weekly Wage	$505.09
Prop. Value	$1,505,463,455
Retail Sales	$146,624,350

A field of grain near the Denton-Cooke county line. Robert Plocheck photo.

Dickens County

Physical Features: West Texas county; broken land, Caprock in northwest; sandy, chocolate, red soils; drains to Croton, Duck creeks.

Economy: Services/prison unit, agribusiness, hunting leases.

History: Comanches driven out by U.S. Army 1874-75. Ranching and some farming began in late 1880s. County created 1876, from Bexar District; organized 1891; named for Alamo hero who is variously listed as James R. Demkins or Dimpkins and J. Dickens.

Race/Ethnicity, 2000: (In percent) Anglo, 67.67; Black, 8.07; Hispanic, 23.90; Other, 0.36.

Vital Statistics, 2004: Births, 25; deaths, 30; marriages, 21; divorces, 7.

Recreation: Hunting, fishing; Soldiers Mound site, Dickens Springs; downtown Spur.

Agriculture: Cattle, cotton, forages, small grains, horses. Some irrigation. Market value $11.8 million. Hunting leases important.

Minerals: Oil, gas.

DICKENS (349) county seat, market for ranching country.

SPUR (1,119) agribusiness and shipping center, oil and gas, homecoming in October; state prison.

Other towns include: **Afton** (15) and **McAdoo** (75).

Population	2,596	July mean max.	95.4
Change fm 2000	-6.0	Civ. Labor	1,013
Area (sq. mi.)	905.21	Unemployed	4.9
Land Area (sq. mi.)	904.21	Wages	$4,037,120
Altitude (ft.)	1,800-3,000	Av. Weekly Wage	$505.50
Rainfall (in.)	18.68	Prop. Value	$285,365,020
Jan. mean min.	25.5	Retail Sales	$11,754,463

Population	10,385
Change fm 2000	1.3
Area (sq. mi.)	1,334.48
Land Area (sq. mi.)	1,330.91
Altitude (ft.)	400-871
Rainfall (in.)	20.21
Jan. mean min.	39.6
July mean max.	98.3
Civ. Labor	3,838
Unemployed	8.0
Wages	$17,859,508
Av. Weekly Wage	$520.59
Prop. Value	$942,328,343
Retail Sales	$68,243,062

Dimmit County

Physical Features: Southwest county; level to rolling; much brush; sandy, loam, red soils; drained by Nueces River.

Economy: Government/services; agribusiness; petroleum products; tourism.

History: Coahuiltecan area, later Comanches. John Townsend, a black man from Nacogdoches, led first attempt at settlement before the Civil War. Texas Rangers forced out Indians in 1877. Mexican migration increased after 1910. County created 1858 from Bexar, Maverick, Uvalde, Webb counties; organized 1880. Named for Philip Dimitt of Texas Revolution; law misspelled name.

Race/Ethnicity, 2000: (In percent) Anglo, 13.39; Black, 0.74; Hispanic, 84.97; Other, 0.90.

Vital Statistics, 2004: Births, 190; deaths, 70; marriages, 51; divorces, 7.

Recreation: Hunting, fishing, campsites, wildlife area; winter haven for tourists.

Minerals: Oil, natural gas.

Agriculture: Onions, pecans, cantaloupes, olives, tomatoes, tangerines; cattle, goats, horses, hay. Market value $27.5 million.

CARRIZO SPRINGS (5,568) county seat; agribusiness center, feedlot, food processing; oil, gas processing; hunting center; hospital; historic Baptist church; Brush Country Day in October.

Other towns include: **Asherton** (1,271), **Big Wells** (685) Cinco de Mayo, and **Catarina** (130) Camino Real festival in April.

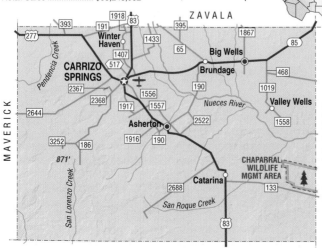

For explanation of sources, abbreviations and symbols, see p. 224 and foldout map.

Donley County

Physical Features: Northwest county bisected by Red River Salt Fork; rolling to level; clay, loam, sandy soils.

Economy: Agribusiness; government/services; tourism.

History: Apaches displaced by Kiowas and Comanches, who were driven out in 1874-75 by U.S. Army. Methodist colony from New York settled in 1878. County created in 1876, organized 1882, out of Bexar District; named for Texas Supreme Court Justice S.P. Donley.

Race/Ethnicity, 2000: (In percent) Anglo, 88.43; Black, 4.36; Hispanic, 6.35; Other, 0.86.

Vital Statistics, 2004: Births, 31; deaths, 55; marriages, 35; divorces, 15.

Recreation: Lake, hunting, fishing, camping, water sports; Col. Goodnight Chuckwagon cook-off in September.

Minerals: Small amount of natural gas.

Agriculture: Cattle top revenue source; cotton, peanuts, alfalfa, wheat, hay, melons; 11,000 acres irrigated. Market value $73.6 million.

CLARENDON (2,042) county seat; junior college; Saints Roost museum; library; agribusiness; tourism; medical center.

Other towns include: **Hedley** (365) cotton festival in October, **Howardwick** (448) and **Lelia Lake** (71).

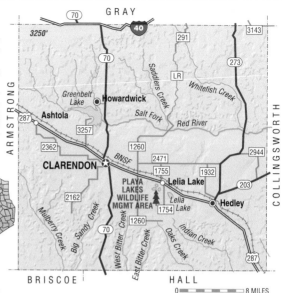

Population	3,848
Change fm 2000	0.5
Area (sq. mi.)	933.05
Land Area (sq. mi.)	929.77
Altitude (ft.)	2,200-3,250
Rainfall (in.)	23.89
Jan. mean min.	22.4
July mean max.	94.7
Civ. Labor	1,852
Unemployed	3.4
Wages	$5,713,367
Av. Weekly Wage	$459.08
Prop. Value	$329,669,078
Retail Sales	$17,648,279

The old hotel on U.S. 83 in Catarina in Dimmit County. Robert Plocheck photo.

Duval County

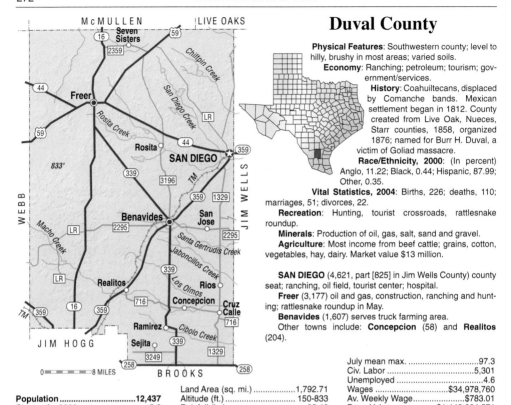

Physical Features: Southwestern county; level to hilly, brushy in most areas; varied soils.

Economy: Ranching; petroleum; tourism; government/services.

History: Coahuiltecans, displaced by Comanche bands. Mexican settlement began in 1812. County created from Live Oak, Nueces, Starr counties, 1858, organized 1876; named for Burr H. Duval, a victim of Goliad massacre.

Race/Ethnicity, 2000: (In percent) Anglo, 11.22; Black, 0.44; Hispanic, 87.99; Other, 0.35.

Vital Statistics, 2004: Births, 226; deaths, 110; marriages, 51; divorces, 22.

Recreation: Hunting, tourist crossroads, rattlesnake roundup.

Minerals: Production of oil, gas, salt, sand and gravel.

Agriculture: Most income from beef cattle; grains, cotton, vegetables, hay, dairy. Market value $13 million.

SAN DIEGO (4,621, part [825] in Jim Wells County) county seat; ranching, oil field, tourist center; hospital.

Freer (3,177) oil and gas, construction, ranching and hunting; rattlesnake roundup in May.

Benavides (1,607) serves truck farming area.

Other towns include: **Concepcion** (58) and **Realitos** (204).

Population	12,437
Change fm 2000	-5.2
Area (sq. mi.)	1,795.67
Land Area (sq. mi.)	1,792.71
Altitude (ft.)	150-833
Rainfall (in.)	25.40
Jan. mean min.	42.5
July mean max.	97.3
Civ. Labor	5,301
Unemployed	4.6
Wages	$34,978,760
Av. Weekly Wage	$783.01
Prop. Value	$1,449,904,571
Retail Sales	$39,361,681

The campus of Benavides High School in Duval County. Robert Plocheck photo.

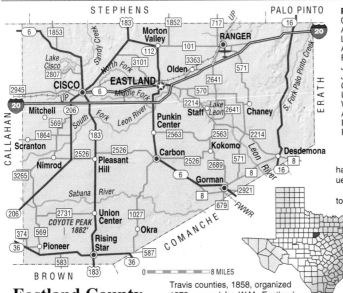

Eastland County

Physical Features: West central county; hilly, rolling; sandy, loam soils; drains to Leon River forks.

Economy: Agribusinesses; education; petroleum industries; varied manufacturing.

History: Plains Indian area. Frank Sánchez among first settlers in 1850s. County created from Bosque, Coryell, Travis counties, 1858, organized 1873; named for W.M. Eastland, Mier Expedition casualty.

Race/Ethnicity, 2000: (In percent) Anglo, 86.26; Black, 2.30; Hispanic, 10.80; Other, 0.64.

Vital Statistics, 2004: Births, 227; deaths, 319; marriages, 141; divorces, 59.

Recreation: Lakes, water sports; fishing, hunting; museums; historic sites and displays.

Population	18,293
Change fm 2000	0.0
Area (sq. mi.)	931.90
Land Area (sq. mi.)	926.01
Altitude (ft.)	1,000-1,882
Rainfall (in.)	27.53
Jan. mean min.	26.7
July mean max.	94.9
Civ. Labor	8,396
Unemployed	3.8
Wages	$48,770,956
Av. Weekly Wage	$549.04
Prop. Value	$1,091,866,240
Retail Sales	$271,773,590

Minerals: Oil, gas.

Agriculture: Beef cattle, forage and hay. 20,000 acres irrigated. Market value $30.4 million.

EASTLAND (4,004) county seat; tourism; government/services, petroleum industries, varied manufacturing; hospital, library; Old Ripfest in September.

CISCO (3,910) manufacturing, oilfield services; Conrad Hilton's first hotel restored, museums; junior college; folklife festival in April.

RANGER (2,519) oil center, varied manufacturing, junior college.

Other towns include: **Carbon** (233) livestock equipment manufacturing; **Desdemona** (180), **Gorman** (1,242) peanut processing, agribusiness, hospital; **Olden** (113), and **Rising Star** (839) cap manufacturing, plant nursery; Octoberfest.

Ector County

Physical Features: West Texas county; level to rolling, some sand dunes; meteor crater; desert vegetation.

Economy: Center for Permian Basin oil field operations; plastics; electric generation plants.

History: First settlers in late 1880s. Oil boom in 1926. County created from Tom Green County, 1887; organized 1891; named for jurist M.D. Ector.

Race/Ethnicity, 2000: (In percent) Anglo, 51.87; Black, 4.60; Hispanic, 42.36; Other, 1.17.

Vital Statistics, 2004: Births, 2,312; deaths, 1,112; marriages, 1,000; divorces, 674.

Recreation: Globe Theatre replica; presidential museum and Bush childhood home; art institute; second-largest U.S. meteor crater; Stonehenge replica.

Minerals: More than 2 billion barrels of oil produced since 1926; gas, cement, stone.

Agriculture: Beef cattle, horses are chief producers; pecans, hay raised; poultry; minor irrigation. Market value $1.9 million.

Education: University of Texas of Permian Basin; Texas Tech University Health Sciences Center; Odessa (junior) College.

ODESSA (94,089, part [1,042] in Midland County) county seat; oil field services; petrochemical complex; retail center; hospitals; cultural center; Permian Basin Fair and Expo in September.

Other towns include: **Gardendale** (1,239), **Goldsmith** (246), **Notrees** (20), **Penwell** (41), and **West Odessa** (18,480).

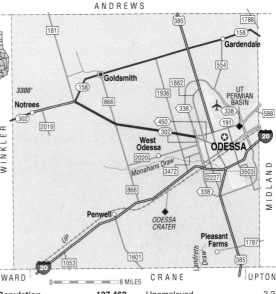

Population	127,462
Change fm 2000	5.2
Area (sq. mi.)	901.68
Land Area (sq. mi.)	901.06
Altitude (ft.)	2,800-3,300
Rainfall (in.)	13.29
Jan. mean min.	28.7
July mean max.	96.0
Civ. Labor	65,921
Unemployed	3.2
Wages	$512,063,284
Av. Weekly Wage	$687.74
Prop. Value	$6,734,447,644
Retail Sales	$2,009,778,795

For explanation of sources, abbreviations and symbols, see p. 224 and foldout map.

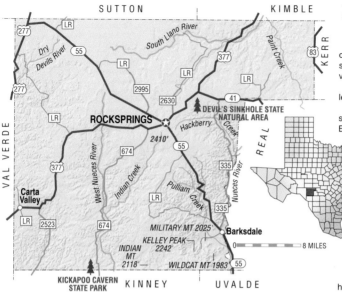

Edwards County

Physical Features: Rolling, hilly; caves; spring-fed streams; rocky, thin soils; drained by Llano, Nueces rivers; varied timber.

Economy: Ranching; hunting leases; tourism; oil, gas production.

History: Apache area. First land sold in 1876. County created from Bexar District, 1858; organized 1883; named for Nacogdoches empresario Hayden Edwards.

Race/Ethnicity, 2000: (In percent) Anglo, 54.25; Black, 0.14; Hispanic, 45.05; Other, 0.56.

Vital Statistics, 2004: Births, 28; deaths, 17; marriages, 16; divorces, 4.

Recreation: Hunting, fishing; scenic drives; state park.

Minerals: Gas.

Agriculture: Center for mohair-wool production; Angora goats, sheep, cattle; some pecans. Market value $7.5 million. Cedar for oil.

ROCKSPRINGS (1,313) county seat; ranching, tourism, Top of the World Festival, July 4.

Other towns include: **Barksdale** (100).

Population..................................... **1,935**	July mean max. 91.6
Change fm 2000............................ -10.5	Civ. Labor 987
Area (sq. mi.) 2,119.95	Unemployed 4.0
Land Area (sq. mi.) 2,119.75	Wages $2,717,810
Altitude (ft.) 1,507-2,410	Av. Weekly Wage...................... $494.63
Rainfall (in.) 24.76	Prop. Value $722,914,638
Jan. mean min. 34.3	Retail Sales $11,568,420

Joe Pool Reservoir, which is in Dallas, Tarrant and Ellis counties. Robert Plocheck photo.

Ellis County

Physical Features: North Texas Blackland soils; level to rolling; Chambers Creek, Trinity River.

Economy: Cement, steel production; warehousing and distribution; government/services; many residents work in Dallas.

History: Tonkawa area. Part of Peters colony settled in 1843. County created 1849, organized 1850, from Navarro County. Named for Richard Ellis, president of convention that declared Texas' independence.

Race/Ethnicity, 2000: (In percent) Anglo, 71.94; Black, 8.73; Hispanic, 18.42; Other, 0.91.

Vital Statistics, 2004: Births, 1,996; deaths, 963; marriages, 1,141; divorces, 177.

Recreation: Medieval-theme Scarborough Faire; Waxahachie Gingerbread Trail homes tour, fall festival; lakes, fishing, hunting.

Minerals: Cement, gas.

Agriculture: Cattle, cotton, corn, hay, nursery crops. Market value $43.4 million.

WAXAHACHIE (24,754) county seat; manufacturing; transportation; steel, aluminum; tourism; hospital; colleges; museum; hike and bike trail; Crape Myrtle festival in July.

Ennis (19,565) agribusiness; manufacturing; bluebonnet trails, National Polka Festival; tourism; hospital.

Midlothian (12,995) cement plants, steel plant; distribution center, manufacturing; heritage park, cabin; Scarecrow fall festival in October.

Other towns include: **Alma** (326); **Avalon** (400); **Bardwell** (615); **Ferris** (2,185); **Forreston** (400); **Garrett** (501); **Howard** (60); **Italy** (2,175); **Maypearl** (933); **Milford** (749); **Oak Leaf** (1,275); **Ovilla** (3,747); **Palmer** (2,018); **Pecan Hill** (689); and **Red Oak** (7,986) manufacturing, Founders Day in September.

Also, **Glenn Heights** (9,940, mostly in Dallas County).

And part of **Grand Prairie**.

Population	**139,300**
Change fm 2000	25.1
Area (sq. mi.)	951.66
Land Area (sq. mi.)	939.91
Altitude (ft.)	300-850
Rainfall (in.)	38.81
Jan. mean min.	35.0
July mean max.	96.0
Civ. Labor	68,588
Unemployed	3.8
Wages	$316,868,860
Av. Weekly Wage	$654.95
Prop. Value	$9,991,117,602
Retail Sales	$1,180,374,873

For explanation of sources, abbreviations and symbols, see p. 224 and foldout map.

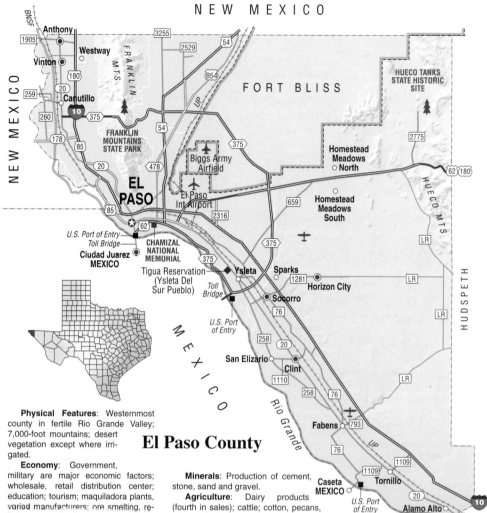

El Paso County

Physical Features: Westernmost county in fertile Rio Grande Valley; 7,000-foot mountains; desert vegetation except where irrigated.

Economy: Government, military are major economic factors; wholesale, retail distribution center; education; tourism; maquiladora plants, varied manufacturers; ore smelting, refining, cotton, food processing.

History: Various Indian tribes inhabited the valley before Spanish civilization arrived in late 1650s. Agriculture in area dates to at least 100 A.D. Spanish and Tigua and Piro tribes fleeing Santa Fe uprising of 1680 sought refuge at Ysleta and Socorro. County created from Bexar District, 1849; organized 1850; named for historic pass (Paso del Norte), lowest all-weather pass through Rocky Mountains.

Race/Ethnicity, 2000: (In percent) Anglo, 17.41; Black, 2.93; Hispanic, 78.23; Other, 1.43.

Vital Statistics, 2004: Births, 14,414; deaths, 4,143; marriages, 6,088; divorces, 200.

Recreation: Gateway to Mexico; Chamizal Museum; major tourist center; December Sun Carnival with football game; state parks, mountain tramway, missions and other historic sites.

For explanation of sources, abbreviations and symbols, see p. 224 and foldout map.

Minerals: Production of cement, stone, sand and gravel.

Agriculture: Dairy products (fourth in sales); cattle; cotton, pecans, onions, forage, peppers also raised; 50,000 acres irrigated, mostly cotton. Market value $67.9 million.

Education: University of Texas at El Paso; UT School of Nursing at El Paso; Texas Tech University Health Sciences Center; El Paso Community College.

EL PASO (602,112) county seat; fifth-largest Texas city, largest U.S. city on Mexican border.

A center for government operations. Federal installations include Fort Bliss, William Beaumont General Hospital, La Tuna federal prison, and headquarters of the U.S. Army Air Defense Command.

Manufactured products include clothing, electronics, auto equipment, plastics, trade and distribution; refining; processing of ore, oil, food, cotton and other farm products.

Hospitals; museums; convention center; theater; symphony orchestra.

Other towns include: **Anthony** (12,011, partly in New Mexico); **Ca-** nutillo (5,365); **Clint** (1,028); **Fabens** (8,622); **Homestead Meadows North** (4,147); **Homestead Meadows South** (6,884); **Horizon City** (7,744); **Prado Verde** (201); **San Elizario** (11,958); **Socorro** (30,672); **Sparks** (3,168); **Tornillo** (1,698); **Vinton** (2,120); **Westway** (4,078), and **Ysleta** (now within El Paso) settled in 1680, called the oldest town in Texas.

And, **Fort Bliss** (7,962).

Population 736,310
Change fm 2000 ....8.3
Area (sq. mi.)........................1,014.68
Land Area (sq. mi.) 1,013.11
Altitude (ft.) 3,582-7,192
Rainfall (in.) 9.43
Jan. mean min. 32.9
July mean max. 94.5
Civ. Labor 303,152
Unemployed 6.0
Wages $1,925,240,173
Av. Weekly Wage....................$570.23
Prop. Value $25,671,567,178
Retail Sales $7,985,143,434

Erath County

Physical Features: West central county on Rolling Plains; clay loam, sandy soils; drains to Bosque, Paluxy rivers.

Economy: Agricultural, industrial and educational enterprises.

History: Caddo and Anadarko Indians moved to Oklahoma in 1860. Anglo-American settlement began 1854-55. County created from Bosque, Coryell counties 1856; named for George B. Erath, Texas Revolution figure.

Race/Ethnicity, 2000: (In percent) Anglo, 83.21; Black, 0.88; Hispanic, 15.03; Other, 0.88.

Vital Statistics, 2004: Births, 405; deaths, 349; marriages, 353; divorces, 160.

Recreation: Old courthouse; log cabins; museums; nearby lakes, hunting, Bosque River Park; university fine arts center; Dairy Fest in June.

Minerals: Gas, oil.

Agriculture: Dairies; beef cattle; horticulture industry; horses raised. Market value $207.7 million.

STEPHENVILLE (15,978) county seat; Tarleton State University; various manufacturing plants; hospital, mental health center; Texas A&M research and extension center.

Dublin (3,579) dairies/ dairy support; food processing; varied manufacturing; tourism; library; St. Patrick's celebration; old Dr Pepper plant.

Other towns include: **Bluff Dale** (123); **Lingleville** (100); **Morgan Mill** (206); **Thurber** (8) former coal-mining town; Gordon Center for Industrial History of Texas.

Population.............................34,289
Change fm 2000 ....3.9
Area (sq. mi.) 1,089.80
Land Area (sq. mi.) 1,086.33
Altitude (ft.) 900-1,650

Rainfall (in.) 29.71
Jan. mean min. 30.0
July mean max. 93.6
Civ. Labor 17,837
Unemployed 3.1
Wages $89,752,679
Av. Weekly Wage..................$480.16
Prop. Value $2,662,244,262
Retail Sales $475,294,856

A fiesta at San Elizario, south of El Paso. Robert Plocheck photo.

Physical Features: East central county on rolling prairie; bisected by Brazos; blackland, red, sandy loam soils; mineral springs.

Economy: Government/services, agribusiness, varied manufacturing.

History: Wacos, Tawokanis, Anadarkos in conflict with Comanches. Cherokees alone in area 1830 until 1835 when Anglo-American settlement began. County created 1850 from Limestone, Milam counties; named for Brazos River falls.

Race/Ethnicity, 2000: (In percent) Anglo, 56.27; Black, 27.42; Hispanic, 15.83; Other, 0.48.

Vital Statistics, 2004: Births, 208; deaths, 225; marriages, 89; divorces, 43.

Recreation: Fishing, hunting, camping; Highland Mansion and Falls on the Brazos.

Minerals: Gravel, sand, oil.

Agriculture: Stocker cattle, cow-calf operations; corn, grain sorghum, soybeans, cotton; wheat, oats; goats, sheep, horses raised. Some cotton irrigated. Market value $68 million.

MARLIN (6,431) county seat; veterans hospital, prison, hospital; agribusiness, small industries; mineral water; tourism; library.

Other towns include: **Chilton** (274); **Golinda** (451); **Lott** (691); **Reagan** (208); **Rosebud** (1,390) feed, fertilizer processing, clothing manufactured; **Satin** (86). Part of **Bruceville-Eddy** (1,568).

Falls County

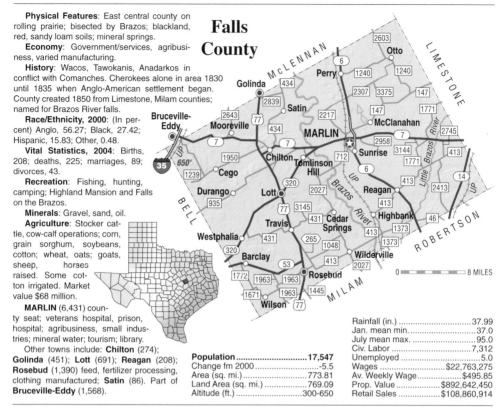

Population	17,547
Change fm 2000	-5.5
Area (sq. mi.)	773.81
Land Area (sq. mi.)	769.09
Altitude (ft.)	300-650

Rainfall (in.)	37.99
Jan. mean min.	37.0
July mean max.	95.0
Civ. Labor	7,312
Unemployed	5.0
Wages	$22,763,275
Av. Weekly Wage	$495.85
Prop. Value	$892,642,450
Retail Sales	$108,860,914

Lake Crockett in the Caddo National Grassland in Fannin County. Robert Plocheck photo.

Fannin County

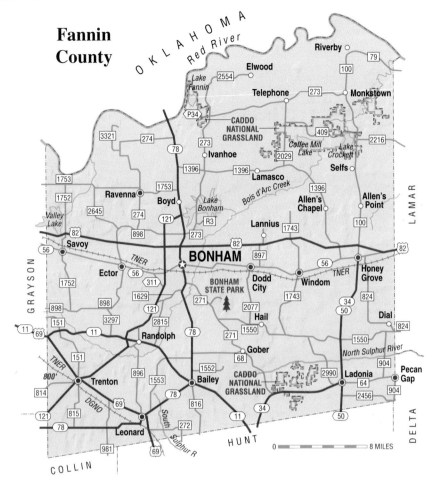

Physical Features: North Texas county of rolling prairie, drained by Red River, Bois d'Arc Creek; mostly blackland soils; national grassland.

Economy: Communications; agriculture; government/services, prisons; petroleum distribution, tourism; varied manufacturing.

History: Caddoes who joined with Cherokees. Anglo-American settlement began in 1836. County created from Red River County, 1837, organized 1838; named for James W. Fannin, a victim of Goliad massacre.

Race/Ethnicity, 2000: (In percent) Anglo, 85.12; Black, 8.12; Hispanic, 5.61; Other, 1.15.

Vital Statistics, 2004: Births, 409; deaths, 413; marriages, 244; divorces, 130.

Recreation: Water activities on lakes; hunting; state park, fossil beds; winery; Sam Rayburn home, memorial library; Bois D'Arc festival in May.

Minerals: Not significant; some sand produced.

Agriculture: Beef cattle, wheat, corn, grain sorghum, hay, horses, pecans. Market value $57.4 million.

BONHAM (10,813) county seat; varied manufacturing; veterans hospital and private hospital; state jail; Sam Rayburn birthday celebration in January.

Other towns include: **Bailey** (230); **Dodd City** (459); **Ector** (661); **Gober** (146); **Honey Grove** (1,788) agribusiness center, varied manufacturing, tourism, historic buildings, library, Davy Crockett Day in October; **Ivanhoe** (110).

Also, **Ladonia** (680) restored historical downtown, tourism; varied manufacturing, commuters, rodeo; **Leonard** (1,990) varied manufacturing, museum, library; **Randolph** (70); **Ravenna** (236); **Savoy** (845); **Telephone** (210); **Trenton** (711); **Windom** (247).

Also, part of **Pecan Gap** (202).

Population	**33,337**
Change fm 2000	6.7
Area (sq. mi.)	899.16
Land Area (sq. mi.)	891.45
Altitude (ft.)	450-800
Rainfall (in.)	44.56
Jan. mean min.	30.2
July mean max.	92.6
Civ. Labor	14,019
Unemployed	4.7
Wages	$54,372,847
Av. Weekly Wage	$610.23
Prop. Value	$1,586,015,981
Retail Sales	$196,330,357

For explanation of sources, abbreviations and symbols, see p. 224 and foldout map.

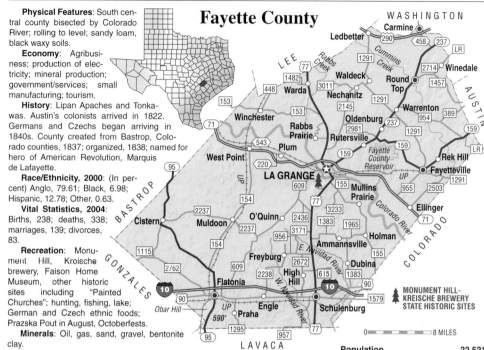

Fayette County

Physical Features: South central county bisected by Colorado River; rolling to level; sandy loam, black waxy soils.

Economy: Agribusiness; production of electricity; mineral production; government/services; small manufacturing; tourism.

History: Lipan Apaches and Tonkawas. Austin's colonists arrived in 1822. Germans and Czechs began arriving in 1840s. County created from Bastrop, Colorado counties, 1837; organized, 1838; named for hero of American Revolution, Marquis de Lafayette.

Race/Ethnicity, 2000: (In percent) Anglo, 79.61; Black, 6.98; Hispanic, 12.78; Other, 0.63.

Vital Statistics, 2004: Births, 238; deaths, 338; marriages, 139; divorces, 83.

Recreation: Monument Hill, Kroesche brewery, Faison Home Museum, other historic sites including "Painted Churches"; hunting, fishing, lake; German and Czech ethnic foods; Prazska Pout in August, Octoberfests.

Minerals: Oil, gas, sand, gravel, bentonite clay.

Agriculture: Beef cattle; corn, sorghum, peanuts, hay, pecans. Market value $51.7 million. Firewood sold.

LA GRANGE (4,650) county seat; electric-power generation; varied manufacturing; food processing; retail trade center; tourism; hospital, library, museum, archives; Czech heritage center; Texas Independence Day observance.

Schulenburg (2,586) varied manufacturing; food processing; Bluebonnet Festival.

Round Top (80) music center, International Festival Institute, July-August; museums, tourism, old Bethlehem Lutheran church, Schuetzenfest in September, and **Winedale** (67), historic restorations including Winedale Inn.

Other towns include: **Carmine** (232); **Ellinger** (386) Tomato Festival in May; **Fayetteville** (264) tourism, antiques shops, old precinct courthouse, Lickskillet festival in October; **Flatonia** (1,339) farm market, varied manufacturing, antiques, Czhilispiel in October; **Ledbetter** (83); **Muldoon** (95); **Plum** (145); **Warda** (121); **Warrenton** (186); **West Point** (213), and **Winchester** (232).

Population	22,521
Change fm 2000	3.3
Area (sq. mi.)	959.84
Land Area (sq. mi.)	950.03
Altitude (ft.)	200-590
Rainfall (in.)	40.31
Jan. mean min.	41.4
July mean max.	95.9
Civ. Labor	12,110
Unemployed	2.8
Wages	$66,376,942
Av. Weekly Wage	$601.03
Prop. Value	$2,993,150,027
Retail Sales	$313,034,507

For explanation of sources, abbreviations and symbols, see p. 224 and foldout map.

The Caprock Escarpment in northeastern Floyd County. Robert Plocheck photo.

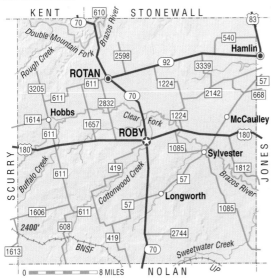

Fisher County

Physical Features: West central county on rolling prairie; mesquite; red, sandy loam soils; drains to forks of Brazos River.

Economy: Agribusiness, hunting, gypsum.

History: Lipan Apaches, disrupted by Comanches and other tribes around 1700. Ranching began in 1876. County created from Bexar District, 1876; organized 1886; named for S.R. Fisher, Republic of Texas secretary of navy.

Race/Ethnicity, 2000: (In percent) Anglo, 75.30; Black, 2.72; Hispanic, 21.36; Other, 0.62.

Vital Statistics, 2004: Births, 32; deaths, 65; marriages, 20; divorces, 6.

Recreation: Quail, dove, turkey hunting; wildlife viewing; county fair, rodeo in August in Roby.

Minerals: Gypsum, oil.

Agriculture: Cattle, cotton, hay, wheat, sorghum, horses, sheep, goats. Irrigation for cotton and alfalfa. Market value $19 million.

ROBY (677) county seat; agribusiness, cotton gin; hospital between Roby and Rotan.

ROTAN (1,573) gypsum plant; oil mill; agribusinesses.

Other towns include: **McCaulley** (96) and **Sylvester** (79). Part of **Hamlin** (2,114).

Population	**4,027**
Change fm 2000	-7.3
Area (sq. mi.)	901.74
Land Area (sq. mi.)	901.16
Altitude (ft.)	1,723-2,400
Rainfall (in.)	24.22
Jan. mean min.	27.2
July mean max.	94.2
Civ. Labor	1,922
Unemployed	4.0
Wages	$6,258,285
Av. Weekly Wage	$554.62
Prop. Value	$303,151,513
Retail Sales	$11,724,206

Floyd County

Physical Features: Flat High Plains, broken by Caprock on east, by White River on south; many playas; red, black loam soils.

Economy: Cotton; livestock feedlots; varied manufacturing; government/services.

History: Plains Apaches and later Comanches. First white settlers arrived in 1884. County created from Bexar District, 1876; organized 1890. Named for Dolphin Ward Floyd, who died at Alamo.

Race/Ethnicity, 2000: (In percent) Anglo, 50.05; Black, 3.35; Hispanic, 45.93; Other, 0.67.

Vital Statistics, 2004: Births, 114; deaths, 77; marriages, 39; divorces, 37.

Recreation: Hunting, fishing; Blanco Canyon; Floydada Punkin Day in October; museum.

Minerals: Not significant.

Agriculture: Cotton, wheat, sorghum; beef cattle, sunflowers, pumpkins; 260,000 acres irrigated. Market value $158.8 million.

FLOYDADA (3,358) county seat; some manufacturing; meat, vegetable processing; distribution center; Old Settlers Reunion; Texas A&M engineering extension.

Lockney (1,859) agriculture center; manufacturing; hospital.

Other towns include: **Aiken** (52), **Dougherty** (91), and **South Plains** (67).

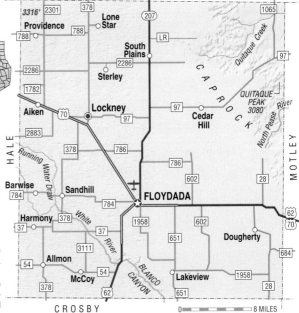

Population	**7,053**
Change fm 2000	-9.2
Area (sq. mi.)	992.51
Land Area (sq. mi.)	992.19
Altitude (ft.)	2,574-3,316
Rainfall (in.)	20.95
Jan. mean min.	23.2
July mean max.	92.3
Civ. Labor	3,233
Unemployed	5.0
Wages	$11,414,375
Av. Weekly Wage	$444.12
Prop. Value	$346,931,930
Retail Sales	$37,492,828

For explanation of sources, abbreviations and symbols, see p. 224 and foldout map.

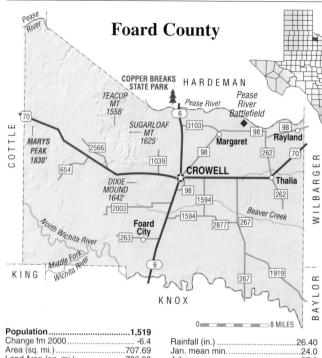

Foard County

Physical Features: Northwest county drains to North Wichita, Pease rivers; sandy, loam soils, rolling surface.

Economy: Agribusiness, clothes manufacturing, government/service.

History: Comanches, Kiowas ranged the area until driven away in 1870s. Ranching began in 1880. County created out of Cottle, Hardeman, King, Knox counties, 1891; named for Maj. Robert L. Foard of Confederate army.

Race/Ethnicity, 2000: (In percent) Anglo, 79.53; Black, 3.39; Hispanic, 16.34; Other, 0.74

Vital Statistics, 2004: Births, 13; deaths, 9; marriages, 0; divorces, 0.

Recreation: Three museums; hunting; wild hog cook-off in November; astronomy and ecotourism foundation.

Minerals: Natural gas, some oil.

Agriculture: Wheat, cattle, alfalfa, cotton, sorghum, dairies. Market value $9.5 million. Hunting leases important.

CROWELL (1,107) county seat; retail center; clothing manufacturing, library.

Population	1,519
Change fm 2000	-6.4
Area (sq. mi.)	707.69
Land Area (sq. mi.)	706.68
Altitude (ft.)	1,300-1,830
Rainfall (in.)	26.40
Jan. mean min.	24.0
July mean max.	97.0
Civ. Labor	608
Unemployed	3.9
Wages	$1,832,939
Av. Weekly Wage	$404.00
Prop. Value	$128,178,472
Retail Sales	$5,985,090

Red grasses and cedars surround the small lake at Copper Breaks State Park near the Pease River, which separates Hardeman and Foard counties. Robert Plocheck photo.

Physical Features: On Gulf Coastal Plain; drained by Brazos, San Bernard rivers; level to rolling; rich alluvial soils.

Economy: Agribusiness, petrochemicals, technology, government/ services; many residents work in Houston.

History: Karankawas retreated to Mexico by 1850s. Named for river bend where some of Austin's colonists settled 1824. Antebellum plantations made it one of six Texas counties with black majority in 1850. County created 1837 from Austin County; organized 1838.

Race/Ethnicity, 2000: (In percent) Anglo, 47.05; Black, 19.98; Hispanic, 21.12; Other, 11.85.

Vital Statistics, 2004: Births, 6,158; deaths, 1,672; marriages, 2,074; divorces, 1,341.

Recreation: Many historic sites, museums, memorials; George Ranch historical park; state park with George Observatory; fishing, waterfowl hunting.

Minerals: Oil, gas, sulphur, salt, clays, sand and gravel.

Fort Bend County

Agriculture: Nursery crops, cotton, sorghum, corn, hay, cattle, horses; irrigation for rice. Market value $49.9 million.

RICHMOND (13,796) county seat; foundry, Richmond State School (for mentally retarded), hospital.

SUGAR LAND (85,101) government/services, prisons; commuting to Houston; hospitals; Museum of Southern History.

MISSOURI CITY (70,763, part [5,494] in Harris County) hospital.

ROSENBERG (31,003) varied industry; annual Czech fest in May; Wharton County Junior College campus.

Other towns include: **Arcola** (1,293); **Beasley** (613); **Cinco Ranch** (12,658); **Fairchilds** (791); **Fresno** (8,318); **Fulshear** (950); **Guy** (239); **Katy** (14,441, mostly in Harris County)

Population **493,187**
Change fm 2000 .... 39.1
Area (sq. mi.) 886.05
Land Area (sq. mi.) 874.64
Altitude (ft.) 46-140
Rainfall (in.) 49.34
Jan. mean min. 41.6
July mean max. 93.7
Civ. Labor 240,596
Unemployed 3.4
Wages $1,228,947,146
Av. Weekly Wage................... $811.30
Prop. Value $33,277,934,955
Retail Sales $4,687,946,930

hospital; **Kendleton** (539); **Meadows Place** (6,237); **Mission Bend** (34,887).

Also, **Needville** (3,365); **New Territory** (16,286); **Orchard** (492); **Pecan Grove** (16,473); **Pleak** (1,151); **Simonton** (862); **Stafford** (20,510, partly in Harris County); **Thompsons** (283).

Also, part [33,384] of **Houston**.

For explanation of sources, abbreviations and symbols, see p. 224 and foldout map.

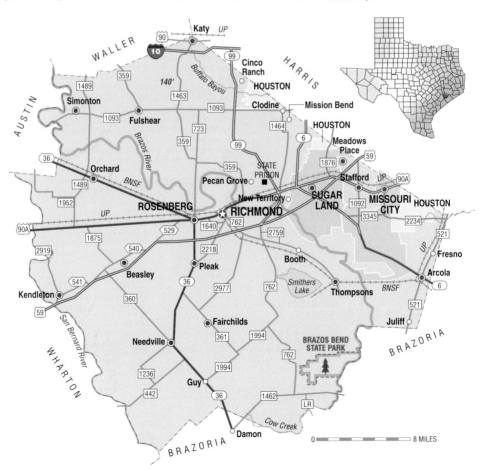

Physical Features: Small Northeast county with many wooded hills; drained by numerous streams; alluvial to sandy clay soils; two lakes.

Economy: Agribusiness, government/services, retirement center, distribution.

History: Caddoes abandoned the area in 1790s because of disease and other tribes. First white settlers arrived around 1818. County created 1875 from Titus County; named for jurist B.C. Franklin.

Race/Ethnicity, 2000: (In percent) Anglo, 86.40; Black, 3.96; Hispanic, 8.90; Other, 0.74.

Vital Statistics, 2004: Births, 123; deaths, 92; marriages, 86; divorces, 45.

Franklin County

Population	10,367
Change fm 2000	9.6
Area (sq. mi.)	294.77
Land Area (sq. mi.)	285.66
Altitude (ft.)	300-600
Rainfall (in.)	47.65
Jan. mean min.	32.2
July mean max.	92.8
Civ. Labor	5,244
Unemployed	3.9
Wages	$23,014,207
Av. Weekly Wage	$561.71
Prop. Value	$970,941,210
Retail Sales	$71,268,524

Recreation: Fishing, water sports; Countryfest/stew cook-off in October; historic homes; wild hog hunting, horse stables.

Minerals: Lignite coal, oil and gas.

Agriculture: Beef cattle, milk production, poultry, hay. Market value $63.9 million. Timber marketed.

MOUNT VERNON (2,440) county seat; distribution center, manufacturing; tourism, antiques, hospital, museum with Don Meredith exhibit; Labor Day rodeo.

Other towns include: **Scroggins** (150), and **Winnsboro** (3,603, mostly in Wood County) commercial center, Autumn Trails.

Freestone County

Physical Features: East central county bounded by the Trinity River; rolling Blackland, sandy, loam soils.

Economy: Natural gas, mining, electricity generating plants, agriculture.

History: Caddo and Tawakoni area. David G. Burnet received land grant in 1825. Seven Mexican citizens received grants in 1833. In 1860, more than half population was black. County created 1850 from Limestone County; organized 1851. Named for indigenous stone.

Race/Ethnicity, 2000: (In percent) Anglo, 72.16; Black, 18.98; Hispanic, 8.20; Other, 0.66.

Vital Statistics, 2004: Births, 213; deaths, 227; marriages, 135; divorces, 74.

Recreation: Fishing, hunting; lakes; historic sites; state park.

Minerals: Natural gas, oil and lignite coal.

Agriculture: Beef cattle, peaches, hay, blueberries, horticulture. Market value $32.6 million. Hunting leases.

FAIRFIELD (3,625) county seat; lignite mining; government/services; trade center; hospital, museum; wild game supper in July.

TEAGUE (5,049) government/services, prison; varied manufacturing, oil, ranching; library, railroad terminal, museum; Guadalupe celebration in December, M.L. King Jr. celebration in January, rodeo July 4.

Other towns include: **Donie** (250), **Kirvin** (131), **Streetman** (209), **Wortham** (1,132) agribusiness, blues festival in September; Blind Lemon Jefferson gravesite.

Population	18,803
Change fm 2000	5.2
Area (sq. mi.)	892.13
Land Area (sq. mi.)	877.43
Altitude (ft.)	209-608
Rainfall (in.)	42.31
Jan. mean min.	36.4
July mean max.	95.0
Civ. Labor	10,242
Unemployed	3.3
Wages	$47,601,440
Av. Weekly Wage	$596.88
Prop. Value	$4,470,608,210
Retail Sales	$566,530,320

For explanation of sources, abbreviations and symbols, see p. 224 and foldout map.

Frio County

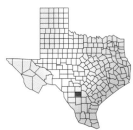

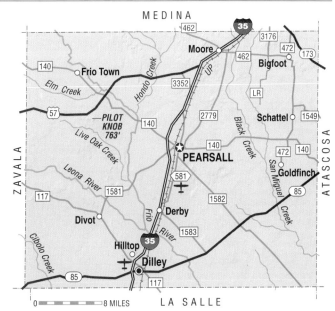

Physical Features: South Texas county of rolling terrain with much brush; bisected by Frio River; sandy, red sandy loam soils.

Economy: Agribusiness; oil-field services; hunting leases.

History: Coahuiltecans; many taken into San Antonio missions. Comanche hunters kept settlers out until after the Civil War. Mexican citizens recruited for labor after 1900. County created 1858 from Atascosa, Bexar, Uvalde counties, organized in 1871; named for Frio (cold) River.

Race/Ethnicity, 2000: (In percent) Anglo, 20.79; Black, 4.79; Hispanic, 73.76; Other, 0.66.

Vital Statistics, 2004: Births, 233; deaths, 119; marriages, 95; divorces, 15.

Recreation: Hunting; Big Foot Wallace Museum; Winter Garden area; Pearsall potato fest in May.

Minerals: Oil, natural gas, stone.

Agriculture: Peanuts, potatoes, sorghum, cotton, corn, spinach, cucumbers, watermelons. Market value $71 million. Hunting leases.

PEARSALL (7,645) county seat; agriculture center; oil, gas; food processing, shipping; old jail museum; hospital; Pioneer days in April.

Dilley (3,923) shipping center for melons, peanuts, hospital.

Other towns include: **Bigfoot** (308), **Hilltop** (299); **Moore** (638); **North Pearsall** (569) and **West Pearsall** (344).

Population	16,336
Change fm 2000	0.5
Area (sq. mi.)	1,134.28
Land Area (sq. mi.)	1,133.02
Altitude (ft.)	400-763
Rainfall (in.)	25.73
Jan. mean min.	37.9
July mean max.	97.5
Civ. Labor	6,523
Unemployed	4.8
Wages	$26,309,409
Av. Weekly Wage	$483.55
Prop. Value	$977,348,340
Retail Sales	$89,870,177

A tree in Bigfoot grows in the middle of FM 472 in Frio County. Robert Plocheck photo.

Gaines County

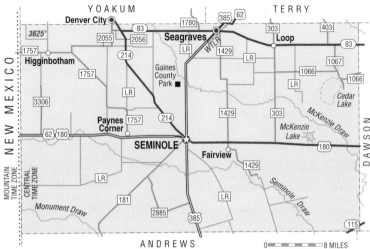

Physical Features: On South Plains, drains to draws; playas; underground water.

Economy: Oil and gas production, cotton and peanut farming.

History: Comanche country until U.S. Army campaigns of 1875. Ranchers arrived in 1880s; farming began around 1900. County created from Bexar District, 1876; organized 1905; named for James Gaines, signer of Texas Declaration of Independence.

Race/Ethnicity, 2000: (In percent) Anglo, 61.48; Black, 2.19; Hispanic, 35.77; Other, 0.56.

Vital Statistics, 2004: Births, 312; deaths, 104; marriages, 109; divorces, 14.

Recreation: Cedar Lake one of largest alkali lakes on Texas plains.

Minerals: One of leading oil-producing counties; gas.

Agriculture: Cotton, peanuts (a leader in acreage), small grains, pecans, paprika, rosemary; cattle, sheep, hogs; substantial irrigation. Market value $144.6 million.

SEMINOLE (6,047) county seat; oil and gas, market center, biodiesel fuel plant; hospital, library; county airport; Ag and Oil Day in September.

Seagraves (2,446) market for three-

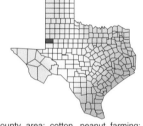

county area; cotton, peanut farming; library, museum; Celebrate Seagraves in July.

Other towns include: **Loop** (315). Also, part of **Denver City** (3,887).

Population	**15,008**
Change fm 2000	3.7
Area (sq. mi.)	1,502.84
Land Area (sq. mi.)	1,502.35
Altitude (ft.)	3,000-3,625
Rainfall (in.)	18.20
Jan. mean min.	26.7
July mean max.	94.1
Civ. Labor	6,662
Unemployed	3.5
Wages	$35,935,682
Av. Weekly Wage	$565.45
Prop. Value	$3,284,076,300
Retail Sales	$193,787,944

For explanation of sources, abbreviations and symbols, see p. 224 and foldout map.

A sportsman at sunset fishes the surf along the seawall in Galveston. Lamberto Alvarez photo.

Galveston County

Physical Features: Partly island, partly coastal; flat, artificial drainage; sandy, loam, clay soils; broken by bays.

Economy: Port activities dominate economy; insurance and finance center; petrochemical plants; varied manufacturing; tourism; medical education center; oceanographic research center; ship building; commercial fishing.

History: Karankawa and other tribes roamed the area until 1850. French, Spanish and American settlement began in 1815 and reached 1,000 by 1817. County created from Brazoria County 1838; organized 1839; named for Spanish governor of Louisiana Count Bernardo de Gálvez.

Race/Ethnicity, 2000: (In percent) Anglo, 63.80; Black, 15.54; Hispanic, 17.96; Other, 2.70.

Vital Statistics, 2004: Births, 3,957; deaths, 2,261; marriages, 2,093; divorces, 1,021.

Recreation: One of Texas' most historic cities; popular tourist and convention center; fishing, surfing, boating, sailing and other water sports; state park; historic homes tour in spring, Moody Gardens; Mardi Gras celebration; Rosenberg Library; museums; restored sailing ship, "Elissa," railroad museum; Dickens on the Strand in early December.

Minerals: Production of oil, gas, clays, sand and gravel.

Agriculture: Cattle, aquaculture, nursery crops, rice, hay, horses, soybeans, grain sorghum. Market value $5.7 million.

GALVESTON (56,983) county seat; tourist center; shipyard; other industries; insurance; port container facility; University of Texas Medical Branch; National Maritime Research Center; Texas A&M University at Galveston; Galveston College; hospitals.

League City (62,622) residential community, commuters to Houston, hospital.

Texas City (43,330) refining, petrochemical plants; port, rail shipping; College of the Mainland; hospital, library; dike; Cinco de Mayo, Shrimp Boil in August.

Bolivar Peninsula (3,733) includes: **Port Bolivar** (900) lighthouse, free ferry; **Crystal Beach** (1,500) seafood industry; sport fishing; tourism, Fort Travis Seashore Park, shorebird sanctuary; Crab Festival in May; **Gilchrist** (800) and **High Island** (500).

Other towns include: **Bacliff** (7,515); **Bayou Vista** (1,743); **Clear Lake Shores** (1,275).

Also, **Dickinson** (19,481) manufacturing, commuters; strawberry festival in May; **Friendswood** (32,566, partly [7,800] in Harris County); **Hitchcock** (7,161) residential community, tourism, fishing and shrimping, Good Ole Days in August, WWII blimp base, museum.

Also, **Jamaica Beach** (1,136); **Kemah** (2,586) tourism, boating, commuters, museum, Blessing of Fleet in August; **La Marque** (13,805) refining, greyhound racing, farming; hospital, library; Gulf Coast Grill-off in October; **San Leon** (4,633); **Santa Fe** (10,629); **Tiki Island** (1,148).

Population	283,551
Change fm 2000	13.3
Area (sq. mi.)	872.93
Land Area (sq. mi.)	398.47
Altitude (ft.)	sea level-35
Rainfall (in.)	43.84
Jan. mean min.	49.7
July mean max.	88.7
Civ. Labor	145,029
Unemployed	4.2
Wages	$883,068,371
Av. Weekly Wage	$719.57
Prop. Value	$28,146,824,906
Retail Sales	$2,577,035,216

For explanation of sources, abbreviations and symbols, see p. 224 and foldout map.

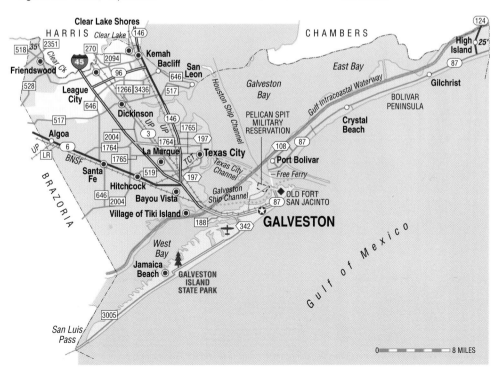

Garza County

Physical Features: On edge of Caprock; rough, broken land, with playas, gullies, canyons, Brazos River forks, lake; sandy, loam, clay soils.

Economy: Agriculture, oil & gas, trade, government/services, hunting leases.

History: Kiowas and Comanches yielded to U.S. Army in 1875. Ranching began in 1870s, farming in the 1890s. C.W. Post, the cereal millionaire, established enterprises in 1906. County created from Bexar District, 1876; organized 1907; named for early Texas family.

Race/Ethnicity, 2000: (In percent) Anglo, 57.44; Black, 4.86; Hispanic, 37.15; Other, 0.55.

Vital Statistics, 2004: Births, 64; deaths, 46; marriages, 40; divorces, 17.

Recreation: Founders Day in September, scenic areas; lake activities; Post-Garza Museum.

Minerals: Oil, gas, sand, gravel.

Agriculture: Cotton, beef cattle, hay; 12,800 acres irrigated. Market value $9.7 million. Hunting leases.

POST (3,709) county seat; founded by C.W. Post; agriculture, tourism, government/services, prisons; Garza Theatre.

For explanation of sources, abbreviations and symbols, see p. 224 and foldout map.

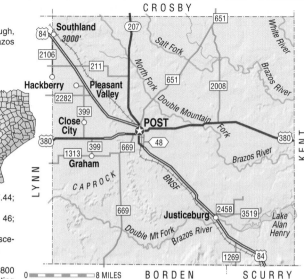

Population **4,877**	July mean max. 94.0
Change fm 2000 .... 0.1	Civ. Labor 2,470
Area (sq. mi.) 896.19	Unemployed 3.4
Land Area (sq. mi.) 895.56	Wages $13,055,125
Altitude (ft.) 2,176-3,000	Av. Weekly Wage.............. $554.11
Rainfall (in.) 21.29	Prop. Value $600,916,000
Jan. mean min. 27.8	Retail Sales $33,875,174

Lange's Mill, northeast of Doss in Gillespie County, dates from 1849. Robert Plocheck photo.

Gillespie County

Physical Features: Picturesque Edwards Plateau area with hills, broken by spring-fed streams.

Economy: Tourism; government/services; agriculture; wine/specialty foods; hunting leases.

History: German settlement founded 1846 in heart of Comanche country. County created 1848 from Bexar, Travis counties; named for Texas Ranger Capt. R.A. Gillespie. Birthplace of President Lyndon B. Johnson and Fleet Admiral Chester W. Nimitz.

Race/Ethnicity, 2000: (In percent) Anglo, 83.39; Black, 0.17; Hispanic, 15.90; Other, 0.54.

Vital Statistics, 2004: Births, 249; deaths, 279; marriages, 191; divorces, 83.

Recreation: Among leading deer-hunting areas; numerous historic sites and tourist attractions include LBJ Ranch, Nimitz Hotel and Pacific war museum; Pioneer Museum Complex, Enchanted Rock.

Minerals: Sand, gravel, gypsum, limestone rock.

Agriculture: Beef cattle, a leading peach-producing county, grapes, sheep and goats, hay, grain sorghum, oats, wheat. Market value $24 million. Hunting leases.

FREDERICKSBURG (10,370) county seat; agribusiness, tourism, wineries, food processing; museum; tourist attractions; hospital; Easter Fires, Oktoberfest.

Other towns include: **Doss** (100); **Harper** (1,127) ranching, deer hunting; Dachshund Hounds Downs race and Trades Day in October; **Luckenbach** (25); **Stonewall** (525) agribusiness, wineries, tourism, hunting, Peach Jamboree in June, and **Willow City** (22).

Population	**23,527**
Change fm 2000	13.0
Area (sq. mi.)	1,061.48
Land Area (sq. mi.)	1,061.06
Altitude (ft.)	1,400-2,244
Rainfall (in.)	31.65
Jan. mean min.	36.1
July mean max.	93.1
Civ. Labor	13,551
Unemployed	2.1
Wages	$58,039,944
Av. Weekly Wage	$507.98
Prop. Value	$4,593,382,994
Retail Sales	$354,816,204

Glasscock County

Physical Features: Western county on rolling plains, broken by small streams; sandy, loam soils.

Economy: Farming, ranching, hunting leases, oil and gas; quarries.

History: Hunting area for Kickapoos and Lipan Apaches. Anglo-American sheep ranchers and Mexican-American shepherds or pastores moved into the area in 1880s. County created 1887, from Tom Green County; organized, 1893; named for Texas pioneer George W. Glasscock.

Race/Ethnicity, 2000: (In percent) Anglo, 69.56; Black, 0.50; Hispanic, 29.87; Other, 0.07.

Vital Statistics, 2004: Births, 7; deaths, 5; marriages, 3; divorces, 3.

Recreation: Hunting of deer, quail, turkey, fox, bobcat, coyote; St. Lawrence Fall Festival in October.

Minerals: Oil, gas, stone/rock.

Agriculture: Cotton, watermelons, wheat, sorghum, hay. 60,000 acres irrigated. Cattle, goats, sheep, hogs raised. Market value $13.6 million.

GARDEN CITY (293), county seat; serves sparsely settled ranching, oil area.

Population	**1,248**
Change fm 2000	-11.2

Area (sq. mi.)	900.93
Land Area (sq. mi.)	900.75
Altitude (ft.)	2,495-2,727
Rainfall (in.)	17.32
Jan. mean min.	26.7
July mean max.	94.0

Civ. Labor	631
Unemployed	3.8
Wages	$2,206,773
Av. Weekly Wage	$453.07
Prop. Value	$702,242,660
Retail Sales	$2,830,067

Physical Features: South Texas county; rolling, brushy; bisected by San Antonio River; sandy, loam, alluvial soils.

Economy: Government/services; oil/gas; agriculture, electricity-generating plant.

History: Karankawas, Comanches and other tribes in area in historic period. La Bahía presidio/mission established 1749. County created 1836 from Spanish municipality; organized 1837; name is anagram of (H)idalgo. Birthplace of Gen. Ignacio Zaragoza, hero of Battle of Puebla (Mexico).

Race/Ethnicity, 2000: (In percent) Anglo, 59.75; Black, 4.69; Hispanic, 35.20; Other, 0.36.

Vital Statistics, 2004: Births, 72; deaths, 76; marriages, 47; divorces, 25.

Recreation: Missions, restored Presidio La Bahía, Fannin Battleground; Old Market House museum; lake, fishing, hunting (deer, quail, dove, hogs), camping, canoeing, birding.

Minerals: Production of oil, gas.

Agriculture: Beef cattle, stocker operations and fed cattle are top revenue producers; corn, grain sorghum, cotton, hay; minor irrigation for pasture. Market value $17 million. Hunting leases.

GOLIAD (1,887) county seat; one of state's oldest towns; oil, gas center; agriculture; tourism; library; Goliad Massacre re-enactment in March; Zaragoza Birthplace State Historic Site, statue.

Other towns include: **Berclair** (253), **Fannin** (359) and **Weesatche** (411).

Goliad County

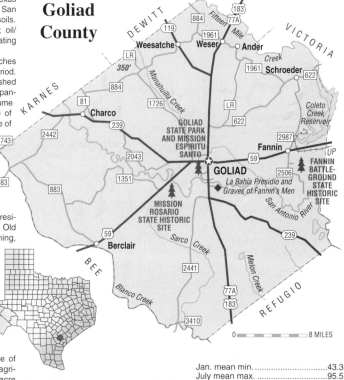

Population	7,192
Change fm 2000	3.8
Area (sq. mi.)	859.35
Land Area (sq. mi.)	853.52
Altitude (ft.)	50-350
Rainfall (in.)	38.58

Jan. mean min.	43.3
July mean max.	95.5
Civ. Labor	3,571
Unemployed	3.5
Wages	$11,169,822
Av. Weekly Wage	$633.95
Prop. Value	$1,195,753,633
Retail Sales	$36,578,725

The chapel of La Bahía Presidio in Goliad was built in 1749. Robert Plocheck photo.

Gonzales County

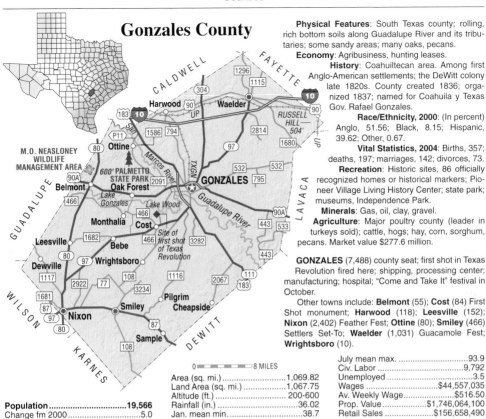

Physical Features: South Texas county; rolling, rich bottom soils along Guadalupe River and its tributaries; some sandy areas; many oaks, pecans.

Economy: Agribusiness, hunting leases.

History: Coahuiltecan area. Among first Anglo-American settlements; the DeWitt colony late 1820s. County created 1836; organized 1837; named for Coahuila y Texas Gov. Rafael Gonzales.

Race/Ethnicity, 2000: (In percent) Anglo, 51.56; Black, 8.15; Hispanic, 39.62; Other, 0.67.

Vital Statistics, 2004: Births, 357; deaths, 197; marriages, 142; divorces, 73.

Recreation: Historic sites, 86 officially recognized homes or historical markers; Pioneer Village Living History Center; state park; museums, Independence Park.

Minerals: Gas, oil, clay, gravel.

Agriculture: Major poultry county (leader in turkeys sold); cattle, hogs; hay, corn, sorghum, pecans. Market value $277.6 million.

GONZALES (7,488) county seat; first shot in Texas Revolution fired here; shipping, processing center; manufacturing; hospital; "Come and Take It" festival in October.

Other towns include: **Belmont** (55); **Cost** (84) First Shot monument; **Harwood** (118); **Leesville** (152); **Nixon** (2,402) Feather Fest; **Ottine** (80); **Smiley** (466) Settlers Set-To; **Waelder** (1,031) Guacamole Fest; **Wrightsboro** (10).

Population	**19,566**
Change fm 2000	5.0

Area (sq. mi.)	1,069.82
Land Area (sq. mi.)	1,067.75
Altitude (ft.)	200-600
Rainfall (in.)	36.02
Jan. mean min.	38.7

July mean max.	93.9
Civ. Labor	9,792
Unemployed	3.5
Wages	$44,557,035
Av. Weekly Wage	$516.50
Prop. Value	$1,746,064,100
Retail Sales	$156,658,490

Gray County

Physical Features: Panhandle High Plains, broken by Red River forks, tributaries; sandy loam, waxy soils.

Economy: Petroleum, agriculture, feedlot operations, chemical plant, other manufacturing.

History: Apaches, displaced by Comanches and Kiowas. Ranching began in late 1870s. Farmers arrived around 1900. Oil discovered 1926. County created 1876, from Bexar District; organized 1902; named for Peter W. Gray, member of first Legislature.

Race/Ethnicity, 2000: (In percent) Anglo, 79.61; Black, 6.03; Hispanic, 13.01; Other, 1.35.

Vital Statistics, 2004: Births, 289; deaths, 270; marriages, 187; divorces, 122.

Recreation: Water sports, Lake McClellan and grassland; White Deer Land Museum; barbed-wire museum, Chautauqua in September.

Minerals: Production of oil, gas.

Agriculture: Cattle, wheat, cotton, sorghum, corn, hay, soybeans, silage. Market value $94.9 million.

PAMPA (17,282) county seat; petroleum and agriculture; chemical plant; hospital; college; prison unit; Woody Guthrie museum.

Other towns include: **Alanreed** (48); **Lefors** (530); **McLean** (784) commercial center for southern part of county.

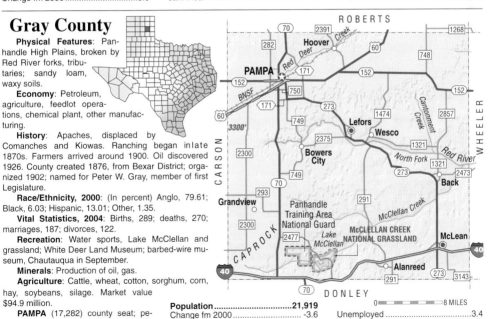

Population	**21,919**
Change fm 2000	-3.6
Area (sq. mi.)	929.25
Land Area (sq. mi.)	928.28
Altitude (ft.)	2,500-3,300
Rainfall (in.)	22.74
Jan. mean min.	21.9
July mean max.	92.0
Civ. Labor	11,132

Unemployed	3.4
Wages	$75,219,334
Av. Weekly Wage	$693.58
Prop. Value	$1,325,904,335
Retail Sales	$565,076,436

For explanation of sources, abbreviations and symbols, see p. 224.

Grayson County

Physical Features: North Texas county; level, some low hills; sandy loam, blackland soils; drains to Red River and tributaries of Trinity River.

Economy: A manufacturing, distribution and trade center for northern Texas and southern Oklahoma; nature tourism; mineral production; prisons.

History: Caddo and Tonkawa area. Preston Bend trading post established 1836-37. Peters colony settlers arrived in 1840s. County created 1846 from Fannin County; named for Republic Atty. Gen. Peter W. Grayson.

Race/Ethnicity, 2000: (In percent) Anglo, 85.10; Black, 6.14; Hispanic, 6.80; Other, 1.96.

Vital Statistics, 2004: Births, 1,659; deaths, 1,223; marriages, 1,119; divorces, 605.

Recreation: Lakes; fishing; pheasant hunting; water sports; state park; cultural activities; wildlife refuge; Pioneer Village; railroad museum.

Minerals: Oil, gas, sand, gravel.

Agriculture: Beef cattle, corn, wheat, hay, sorghum. Market value $41.9 million.

Education: Austin College in Sherman and Grayson County College located between Sherman and Denison.

SHERMAN (39,256) county seat; varied manufacturing; processors, distributors for major companies; Austin College; hospital.

DENISON (24,178) food processing, tourism, hospital, transportation center; Eisenhower birthplace; Main Street Fall festival.

Other towns include: **Bells** (1,292); **Collinsville** (1,603); **Dorchester** (108); **Gordonville** (165); **Gunter** (1,634); **Howe** (3,073) distribution; varied manufacturing; museum, Founders' Day in May; **Knollwood** (387); **Pottsboro** (2,251); **Sadler** (425); **Southmayd** (1,011); **Tioga** (917) Gene Autry museum, festival in September; **Tom Bean**

(1,069); **Van Alstyne** (2,754) window screen, electronics, saddle, tack manufacturing; **Whitesboro** (4,416) agribusiness, tourism, manufacturing, library, Peanut Festival in October; **Whitewright** (2,038) varied manufacturing, government/services.

Population	118,478
Change fm 2000	7.1
Area (sq. mi.)	979.19
Land Area (sq. mi.)	933.51
Altitude (ft.)	500-890
Rainfall (in.)	42.04
Jan. mean min.	32.2
July mean max.	92.7
Civ. Labor	58,956
Unemployed	3.8
Wages	$351,589,862
Av. Weekly Wage	$622.64
Prop. Value	$6,826,898,512
Retail Sales	$1,479,888,013

For explanation of sources, abbreviations and symbols, see p. 224 and foldout map.

Physical Features: A populous, leading petroleum county, heart of the famed East Texas oil field; bisected by the Sabine River; hilly, timbered; with sandy, clay, alluvial soils.

Economy: Oil but with significant other manufacturing; tourism, conventions; agribusiness and lignite coal production.

History: Caddoes; later Cherokees, who were driven out in 1838 by President Lamar. First land grants issued in 1835 by Republic of Mexico. County created and organized in 1873 from Rusk, Upshur counties; named for Confederate Gen. John Gregg. In U.S. censuses 1880-1910, blacks were more numerous than whites. Oil discovered in 1931.

Race/Ethnicity, 2000: (In percent) Anglo, 69.59; Black, 20.07; Hispanic, 9.14; Other, 1.20.

Vital Statistics, 2004: Births, 1,879; deaths, 1,184; marriages, 1,342; divorces, 335.

Recreation: Water activities on lakes; hunting; varied cultural events; the East Texas Oil Museum in Kilgore.

Minerals: Leading oil-producing county with more than 3 billion barrels produced since 1931; also, sand, gravel and natural gas.

Agriculture: Cattle, horses, hay, nursery crops. Market value $2.4 million. Timber sales.

LONGVIEW (75,132, small part [1,598] in Harrison County) county seat; chemical manufacturing, oil industry, distribution and retail center; hospitals; Le-Tourneau University, UT-Tyler Longview center; convention center; balloon race in July.

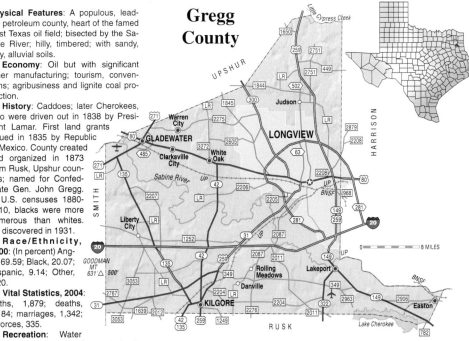

Gregg County

Kilgore (12,021, part [2,580] in Rusk County), oil center; manufacturing; hospital; Kilgore College (junior college); East Texas Treatment Center; Shakespeare festival in summer, Celtic Heritage festival in April.

Gladewater (6,155, part [2,454] in Upshur County) oil, manufacturing, tourism and antiques center, agriculture; library; airport; Gusher Days in April; daffodil gardens in Febuary-March.

Other towns include: **Clarksville City** (855); **Easton** (561, partly in Rusk County); **Judson** (1,057); **Lakeport** (913); **Liberty City** (1,973) oil, tourism, government/services; Honor America Night in November; **Warren City** (368);

White Oak (5,974) petroleum, government/services, commuting to Longview; Roughneck Days in April.

Population	117,090
Change fm 2000	5.1
Area (sq. mi.)	276.37
Land Area (sq. mi.)	274.03
Altitude (ft.)	280-500
Rainfall (in.)	49.06
Jan. mean min.	33.7
July mean max.	94.5
Civ. Labor	63,337
Unemployed	3.7
Wages	$605,446,495
Av. Weekly Wage	$663.11
Prop. Value	$7,711,326,703
Retail Sales	$2,377,989,892

A pickup truck heads toward Lake Texoma in the Hagerman National Wildlife Refuge. Robert Plocheck photo.

Grimes County

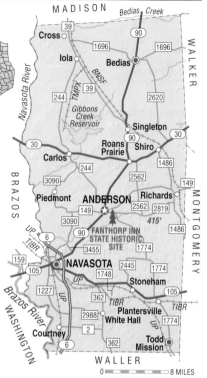

Physical Features: Rich bottom soils along Brazos, Navasota rivers; remainder hilly, partly forested.

Economy: Varied manufacturing; agribusiness; tourism.

History: Bidais (customs similar to the Caddoes) lived peacefully with Anglo-American settlers who arrived in 1820s, but tribe was removed to Indian Territory. Planter agriculture reflected in 1860 census, which listed 77 persons owning 20 or more slaves. County created from Montgomery County 1846; named for Jesse Grimes, who signed Texas Declaration of Independence.

Race/Ethnicity, 2000: (In percent) Anglo, 63.28; Black, 20.02; Hispanic,16.08; Other, 0.62.

Vital Statistics, 2004: Births, 343; deaths, 229; marriages, 129; divorces, 49.

Recreation: Hunting, fishing; Gibbons Creek Reservoir; historic sites; fall Renaissance Festival at Plantersville.

Minerals: Lignite coal, natural gas.

Agriculture: Cattle, forage, horses, poultry; berries, pecans, honey sales significant. Market value $31.8 million. Some timber sold, Christmas tree farms.

ANDERSON (271) county seat; rural center; Fanthorp Inn historic site; Go-Texan weekend in February.

NAVASOTA (7,192) agribusiness center for parts of three counties; varied manufacturing; food, wood processing; hospital; prisons; La Salle statue; Blues Fest in August.

Other towns include: **Bedias** (400); **Iola** (350); **Plantersville** (260); **Richards** (300); **Roans Prairie** (64); **Shiro** (210); **Todd Mission** (161).

Population **25,552**	July mean max. 96.0
Change fm 2000 .... 8.5	Civ. Labor 10,468
Area (sq. mi.) 801.16	Unemployed 4.4
Land Area (sq. mi.) 793.60	Wages $59,368,833
Altitude (ft.) 150-415	Av. Weekly Wage............. $683.49
Rainfall (in.) 44.70	Prop. Value $2,292,425,126
Jan. mean min. 40.0	Retail Sales $405,526,840

For explanation of sources, abbreviations and symbols, see p. 224 and foldout map.

The Grimes County Courthouse in Anderson. Robert Plocheck photo.

Guadalupe County

Physical Features: South central county bisected by Guadalupe River; level to rolling surface; sandy, loam, blackland soils.

Economy: Varied manufacturing; many residents work in San Antonio; agribusiness, tourism.

History: Karankawas, Comanches, other tribes until 1850s. Spanish land grant in 1806 to José de la Baume. DeWitt colonists arrived in 1827. County created 1846 from Bexar, Gonzales counties; named for river.

Race/Ethnicity, 2000: (In percent) Anglo, 60.21; Black, 5.10; Hispanic, 33.21; Other, 1.48.

Vital Statistics, 2004: Births, 1,352; deaths, 665; marriages, 521; divorces, 395.

Recreation: Fishing, hunting, river floating; Sebastopol historic site, other historic sites; river drive, Freedom Fiesta in July, Diez y Seis.

Minerals: Oil, gas, gravel, clays.

Agriculture: Nursery crops, cattle, hay, row crops. Market value $37.2 million.

SEGUIN (24,783) county seat; electronics, steel, other manufacturing; government/services; hospital, museums; Texas Lutheran University.
Other towns include: **Cibolo** (8,129), **Geronimo** (578), **Kingsbury** (894), **Marion** (1,228), **McQueeney** (2,958), **New Berlin** (505), **Northcliff** (1,813); **Redwood** (3,810); **Santa Clara** (922); **Schertz** (28,180, parts in Bexar and Comal counties), **Staples** (396).

Population	**108,410**
Change fm 2000	21.8
Area (sq. mi.)	714.17
Land Area (sq. mi.)	711.14
Altitude (ft.)	350-850

Rainfall (in.)	34.50
Jan. mean min.	35.5
July mean max.	94.7
Civ. Labor	53,035
Unemployed	3.5
Wages	$218,626,029
Av. Weekly Wage	$611.50
Prop. Value	$7,370,107,820
Retail Sales	$798,686,770

Hale County

Physical Features: High Plains; fertile sandy, loam soils; many playas; large underground water supply.

Economy: Agribusiness, food-processing plants, distribution; manufacturing; government/services.

History: Comanche hunters driven out by U.S. Army in 1875. Ranching began in 1880s. First motor-driven irrigation well drilled in 1911. County created from Bexar District, 1876; organized 1888; named for Lt. J.C. Hale, who died at San Jacinto.

Race/Ethnicity, 2000: (In percent) Anglo, 45.54; Black, 5.77; Hispanic, 47.90; Other, 0.79.

Vital Statistics, 2004: Births, 628; deaths, 305; marriages, 287; divorces, 92.

Recreation: Llano Estacado Museum; art gallery, antiques stores; pheasant hunting; Plainview Cattle Drive in September.

Minerals: Some oil.

Agriculture: Cotton, fed beef, sorghum, dairies, corn, vegetables, wheat. Market value $225.2 million. Irrigation of 448,000 acres.

PLAINVIEW (21,887) county seat; distribution center; food processing, other industries; Wayland Baptist University; hospital, library, mental health center; state prisons.

Hale Center (2,204) farming trade center; farm museum, library, parks, murals, cacti gardens.

Abernathy (2,798, part [708] in Lubbock County) government/services, farm supplies, textile plant, gins.

Other towns include: **Cotton Center** (300), **Edmonson** (128), **Petersburg** (1,214), **Seth Ward** (2,001).

Population	**36,317**
Change fm 2000	-0.8
Area (sq. mi.)	1,004.77
Land Area (sq. mi.)	1,004.65
Altitude (ft.)	3,315-3,600
Rainfall (in.)	19.90
Jan. mean min.	24.4

July mean max.	91.0
Civ. Labor	16,745
Unemployed	4.2
Wages	$96,126,928
Av. Weekly Wage	$513.31
Prop. Value	$1,775,369,495
Retail Sales	$2,216,232,568

Hall County

Physical Features: Rolling to hilly, broken by Red River forks, tributaries; red and black sandy loam.

Economy: Agriculture, farm, ranch supplies, marketing for large rural area.

History: Apaches displaced by Comanches, who were removed to Indian Territory in 1875. Ranching began in 1880s. Farming expanded after 1910. County created 1876 from Bexar, Young districts; organized 1890; named for Republic of Texas secretary of war W.D.C. Hall.

Race/Ethnicity, 2000: (In percent) Anglo, 63.88; Black, 8.12; Hispanic, 27.50; Other, 0.50.

Vital Statistics, 2004: Births, 41; deaths, 53; marriages, 18; divorces, 11.

Recreation: Hunting of deer, wild hog, turkey, quail, dove; Rails to Trails system; Bob Wills museum; Memphis Old Settlers reunion in September.

Minerals: None.

Agriculture: Cotton, cattle, peanuts, wheat sorghum, alfalfa hay. Market value $20.6 million. Hunting leases.

MEMPHIS (2,465) county seat; cotton gins; peanut processing, historic buildings.

Other towns include: **Estelline** (160), motorcyle rally/chili cookoff in August, **Lakeview** (150), **Turkey** (482) Bob Wills Day in April.

Population	3,668
Change fm 2000	-3.0
Area (sq. mi.)	904.08
Land Area (sq. mi.)	903.09
Altitude (ft.)	1,799-2,400
Rainfall (in.)	22.51
Jan. mean min.	25.5
July mean max.	95.7
Civ. Labor	1,587
Unemployed	4.7
Wages	$4,827,331
Av. Weekly Wage	$391.29
Prop. Value	$288,265,690
Retail Sales	$24,754,317

Hamilton County

Physical Features: Hilly north central county broken by scenic valleys; loam soils.

Economy: Varied manufacturing; agribusiness; hunting leases; tourism.

History: Waco and Tawakoni Indian area. Anglo-American settlers arrived in mid-1850s. County created, organized 1858, from Bosque, Comanche, Lampasas counties; named for South Carolina Gov. James Hamilton, who aided Texas Revolution and Republic.

Race/Ethnicity, 2000: (In percent) Anglo, 91.68; Black, 0.16; Hispanic, 7.41; Other, 0.75.

Vital Statistics, 2004: Births, 76; deaths, 143; marriages, 66; divorces, 49.

Recreation: Deer, quail, duck hunting; dove festival on Labor Day; Linear Pecan Creek park in Hamilton.

Minerals: Limited oil, gas.

Agriculture: Dairies, beef cattle top revenue sources. Hay, wheat, oats, sorghum. Also, pecans, sheep, horses. Market value $41.6 million.

HAMILTON (2,986) county seat; varied manufacturing; hospital; Central Texas College branch; historical homes.

Hico (1,365) tourism, agriculture; Billy the Kid museum; steak cookoff in May.

Other towns include: **Carlton** (75), **Evant** (398, partly in Coryell County), **Jonesboro** (125, partly in Coryell County); **Pottsville** (105).

For explanation of sources, abbreviations and symbols, see p. 224 and foldout map.

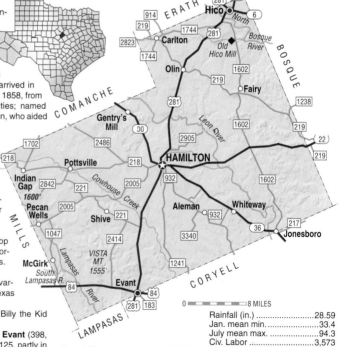

Population	8,186
Change fm 2000	-0.5
Area (sq. mi.)	836.38
Land Area (sq. mi.)	835.71
Altitude (ft.)	900-1,600
Rainfall (in.)	28.59
Jan. mean min.	33.4
July mean max.	94.3
Civ. Labor	3,573
Unemployed	3.7
Wages	$16,976,770
Av. Weekly Wage	$506.03
Prop. Value	$1,011,885,024
Retail Sales	$73,962,872

Hansford County

Physical Features: High Plains, many playas, creeks, draws; sandy, loam, black soils; underground water.

Economy: Agribusinesses; oil, gas operations.

History: Apaches, pushed out by Comanches around 1700. U.S. Army removed Comanches in 1874-75 and ranching began soon afterward. Farmers, including some from Norway, moved in around 1900. County created 1876, from Bexar, Young districts; organized 1889; named for jurist J.M. Hansford.

Race/Ethnicity, 2000: (In percent) Anglo, 67.64; Black, 0.17; Hispanic, 31.48; Other, 0.71.

Vital Statistics, 2004: Births, 112; deaths, 61; marriages, 47; divorces, 12.

Recreation: Stationmasters House Museum; hunting; lake activities; ecotourism.

Minerals: Production of gas, oil.

Agriculture: Large cattle-feeding operations; corn, wheat, sorghum; hogs. Substantial irrigation. Market value $366.9 million.

SPEARMAN (2,976) county seat; farming, cattle production, oil and gas; wind energy, biofuels; hospital, library, windmill collection; Heritage Days in June.

Other towns include: **Gruver** (1,167) farm-ranch market, natural gas production; Fourth of July barbecue; **Morse** (176).

Population	5,237
Change fm 2000	-2.5
Area (sq. mi.)	920.40
Land Area (sq. mi.)	919.80
Altitude (ft.)	2,800-3,360
Rainfall (in.)	20.30
Jan. mean min.	22.4
July mean max.	95.5

Civ. Labor	2,327
Unemployed	3.4
Wages	$14,324,811
Av. Weekly Wage	$605.33
Prop. Value	$875,688,532
Retail Sales	$42,431,363

Hardeman County

Physical Features: Rolling, broken area on divide between Pease, Red rivers' forks; sandy loam soils.

Economy: Mineral production, agribusiness.

History: Apaches, later the semi-sedentary Wichitas and Comanche hunters. Ranching began in late 1870s. Farming expanded after 1900. County created 1858 from Fannin County; re-created 1876, organized 1884; named for pioneer brothers Bailey and T.J. Hardeman.

Race/Ethnicity, 2000: (In percent) Anglo, 79.64; Black, 4.97; Hispanic, 14.50; Other, 0.89.

Vital Statistics, 2004: Births, 62; deaths, 43; marriages, 37; divorces, 23.

Recreation: state park; lake activities; Medicine Mound aborigine gathering site; Quanah Parker monument; old railroad depot.

Minerals: Gypsum, oil.

Agriculture: Cattle, wheat, cotton. Market value $16.8 million. Hunting leases.

QUANAH (2,846) county seat; agribusiness; cotton oil mill; manufacturing; hospital; historical sites; Fall Festival in September.

Other towns include: **Chillicothe** (780) farm market center, hospital.

Av. Weekly Wage	$537.39
Prop. Value	$435,588,100
Retail Sales	$22,764,853

For explanation of sources, abbreviations and symbols, see p. 224 and foldout map.

Population	4,250
Change fm 2000	-10.0
Area (sq. mi.)	697.00
Land Area (sq. mi.)	695.38
Altitude (ft.)	1,287-1,749
Rainfall (in.)	26.76

Jan. mean min.	24.6
July mean max.	96.5
Civ. Labor	2,282
Unemployed	3.8
Wages	$8,958,405

Hardin County

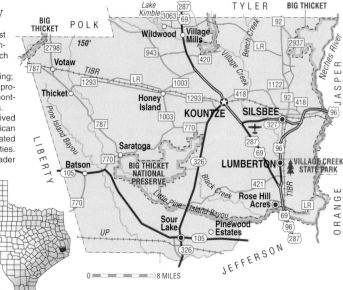

Physical Features: Southeast county; timbered; many streams; sandy, loam soils; Big Thicket covers much of area.

Economy: Paper manufacturing; wood processing; minerals; food processing; oil, gas; county in Beaumont-Port Arthur-Orange metropolitan area.

History: Lorenzo de Zavala received first land grant in 1829. Anglo-American settlers arrived in 1830. County created 1858 from Jefferson, Liberty counties. Named for Texas Revolutionary leader William Hardin.

Race/Ethnicity, 2000: (In percent) Anglo, 89.93; Black, 6.95; Hispanic, 2.54; Other, 0.58.

Vital Statistics, 2004: Births, 705; deaths, 501; marriages, 420; divorces, 319.

Recreation: Big Thicket with rare plant, animal life; national preserve; Red Cloud Water Park in Silsbee; hunting, fishing; state park; Cajun Country Music Festival in October in Kountze.

Minerals: Oil, gas, sand, gravel.

Agriculture: Beef cattle, hay, blueberries and rice; market value negligible. Timber provides most income; more than 85 percent of county forested. Hunting leases.

KOUNTZE (2,141) county seat; government/services, retail center, commuting to Beaumont; library, museum.

SILSBEE (6,416) forest products, rail center, oil and gas; library, Ice House museum; Dulcimer Festival in September.

LUMBERTON (10,324) construction company; government/services; tourism, library, Village Creek Festival in April.

Other towns and places include: **Batson** (140); **Pinewood Estates** (1,698); **Rose Hill Acres** (471); **Saratoga** (1,000); Big Thicket Museum; **Sour Lake** (1,785) oil, lumbering; Old Timer's Day in September; **Thicket** (306); **Village Mills** (1,700); **Votaw** (160).

Population	**51,483**
Change fm 2000	7.1
Area (sq. mi.)	897.37
Land Area (sq. mi.)	894.33
Altitude (ft.)	25-150
Rainfall (in.)	56.50
July mean max.	93.0
Jan. mean min.	37.0
Civ. Labor	24,189
Unemployed	4.7
Wages	$96,764,291
Av. Weekly Wage	$601.65
Prop. Value	$2,611,625,220
Retail Sales	$517,780,080

The Fred Hartman Bridge and the Baytown marina in Harris County. Robert Plocheck photo.

TEXAS A&M UNIVERSITY PRESS

HISTORIC HOTELS OF TEXAS
A Traveler's Guide
Liz Carmack
69 color photos. $23.00 flexbound with flaps

New, updated edition
THE COURTHOUSES
OF TEXAS
A Travel Guide
Mavis P. Kelsey Sr. and Donald H. Dyal
Photographs contributed
by Frank Thrower
254 color photos. $22.95 flexbound with flaps

CLAYTIE
The Roller-Coaster Life of a Texas Wildcatter
Mike Cochran
72 b&w photos. $24.95 cloth

TEXAS ALMANAC 2008–2009
64th Edition
Edited by Elizabeth Cruce Alvarez and
Robert Plocheck
More than 245 color photos and 285 color maps. $23.95 cloth;
$16.95 paper

DOUG WELSH'S
TEXAS GARDEN ALMANAC
Doug Welsh
Ilustrated by Aletha St. Romain
More than 170 color illustrations. 50 black and white
drawings. $24.95 flexbound with flaps

HUMMINGBIRDS OF TEXAS
Clifford E. Shackelford, Madge M. Lindsay,
and C. Mark Klym
87 color photos and 48 color illustrations. $24.95 cloth

FRESHWATER FISHES
OF TEXAS
A Field Guide
Chad Thomas, Timothy H. Bonner, and
Bobby G. Whiteside
215 color photos and 162 maps. $23.00 flexbound with flaps

New in paperback
FROM A WATERY GRAVE
The Discovery and Excavation of La Salle's
Shipwreck, La Belle
James E. Bruseth and Toni S. Turner
Foreword by T. R. Fehrenbach
126 color and 13 black and white photos.
$39.95 cloth; $24.95 paper

College Station, Texas • Orders: 800-826-8911 • Fax: 888-617-2421
www.tamu.edu/upress

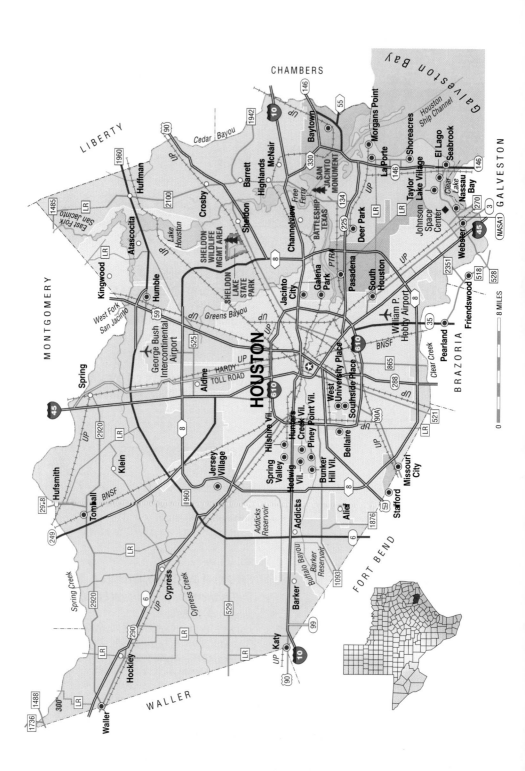

Physical Features: Largest county in eastern half of state; level; typically coastal surface and soils; many bayous, lakes, canals for artificial drainage; partly forested.

Economy: Highly industrialized county with largest population; more than 80 foreign governments maintain offices in Houston; corporate management center; nation's largest concentration of petrochemical plants; largest U.S wheat-exporting port, among top U.S. ports in the value of foreign trade and total tonnage.

Petroleum refining, chemicals, food, fabricated metal products, non-electrical machinery, primary metals, scientific instruments; paper and allied products, printing and publishing; center for energy, space and medical research; center of international business.

History: Orcoquiza villages visited by Spanish authorities in 1746. Pioneer settlers arrived by boat from Louisiana in 1822. Antebellum planters brought black slaves. Mexican migration increased after Mexican Revolution. County created 1836, organized 1837; named for John R. Harris, founder of Harrisburg (now part of Houston) in 1824.

Race/Ethnicity, 2000: (In percent) Anglo, 42.84; Black, 18.53; Hispanic, 32.93; Other, 5.70.

Vital Statistics, 2004: Births, 67,131; deaths, 20,195; marriages, 30,382; divorces, 14,338.

Recreation: Professional baseball, basketball, football, soccer; rodeo and livestock show; Jones Hall for the Performing Arts; Nina Vance Alley Theatre; Convention Center; Toyota Center, a 19,000-seat sports and entertainment center; Astroworld and WaterWorld amusement parks, Reliant Stadium and downtown ballpark.

Sam Houston Park, with restored early Houston homes, church, stores; Museum of Fine Arts, Contemporary Arts Museum, Rice Museum; Wortham Theater; Hobby Center for Performing Arts; museum of natural science, planetarium, zoo in Hermann Park.

San Jacinto Battleground, Battleship Texas; Johnson Space Center.

Fishing, boating, other freshwater and saltwater activities.

Minerals: Among leading oil, gas, petrochemical areas; production of petroleum, cement, natural gas, liquids, salt, lime, sulfur, sand and gravel, clays, stone.

Agriculture: Nursery crops, cattle, hay, horses, vegetables, Christmas trees, goats, rice, corn. Market value $52.9 million. Substantial income from forest products.

Education: Houston is a major center of higher education, with more than 188,000 students enrolled in 28 colleges and universities in the county. Among these are Rice University, the University

Harris County

The San Jacinto Monument stands along the Houston Ship Channel. Robert Plocheck photo.

of Houston, Texas Southern University, University of St. Thomas, Houston Baptist University.

Medical schools include Houston Baptist University School of Nursing, University of Texas Health Science Center, Baylor College of Medicine, Institute of Religion and Human Development, Texas Chiropractic College, Texas Woman's University-Houston Center.

HOUSTON (2,085,737) county seat; largest Texas city; fourth-largest in nation.

A leading center for manufacture of petroleum equipment, agricultural chemicals, fertilizers, pesticides, oil and gas pipeline transmission; a leading scientific center; manufacture of machinery, fabricated metals; a major distribution, shipping center; engineering and research center; food processing; hospitals.

Plants make apparel, lumber and wood products; furniture, paper, chemical, petroleum and coal products; publishing center; one of the nation's largest public school systems; prominent corporate center; Go Texan Days (rodeo) in February, international festival in April.

Pasadena (147,926) residential city with large industrial area manufacturing petrochemicals and other petroleum-related products; civic center; San Jacinto College, Texas Chiropractic College; hospitals; historical museum; Strawberry Festival in May.

Baytown (68,858) refining, petrochemical center; commuters to Houston; Lee College; hospital, museum, library; historical homes; Chili When It's Chilly cookoff in January.

Bellaire (15,798) residential city with several major office buildings.

The **Clear Lake Area** — which includes **El Lago** (2,894); **Nassau Bay** (3,981); **Seabrook** (11,133); **Taylor Lake Village** (5,807); **Webster** (9,184) — tourism, Johnson Space Center, University of Houston-Clear Lake, commuting to Houston; Bayport Industrial Complex includes Port of Bayport; 12 major marinas; hospitals; Christmas lighted boat parade.

Other towns include: **Aldine** (14,424); **Atascocita** (35,174); **Barrett** (2,702); **Bunker Hill Village** (3,489); **Channelview** (30,291) hospital; **Crosby** (1,804); **Deer Park** (29,046) ship-channel industries, Totally Texas celebration in April; **Galena Park** (10,423); **Hedwig Village** (2,148); **Highlands** (7,022), heritage museum, Jamboree in October; **Hilshire Village** (692); **Hockley** (NA); **Huffman** (15,000); **Humble** (16,196) oil-field equipment manufactured, retail center, hospital; **Hunters Creek Village** (4,187); **Jacinto City** (10,429); **Jersey Village** (7,143).

Also, **Katy** (14,441, partly in Fort Bend, Waller counties) corporate headquarters, distribution center, hospitals; museums, urban park; Rice Harvest festival in October; **Klein** (45,000); **La Porte** (32,985) petrochemical industry; Sylvan Beach Festival in April; Galveston Bay; **Morgan's Point** (325); **Piney Point Village** (3,298); **Sheldon** (1,820); **Shoreacres** (1,557); **South Houston** (16,294).

Also, **Southside Place** (1,596); **Spring** (37,285); **Spring Valley** (3,457); **Tomball** (10,625) computers, oil equipment, retail center; antiques; hospital, sports medical center; museum, junior college, parks; Germanfest in March; **West University Place** (14,408).

Parts of **Friendswood, Missouri City, Pearland, Stafford** and **Waller**.

Addicks, Alief and **Kingwood** are now within the city limits of Houston.

Population	**3,886,207**
Change fm 2000	14.3
Area (sq. mi.)	1,777.69
Land Area (sq. mi.)	1,728.83
Altitude (ft.)	sea level-300
Rainfall (in.)	53.96
Jan. mean min.	45.2
July mean max.	93.6
Civ. Labor	1,934,335
Unemployed	4.1
Wages	$24,044,183,268
Av. Weekly Wage	$948.84
Prop. Value	$254,817,697,471
Retail Sales	$56,238,451,858

For explanation of sources, abbreviations and symbols, see p. 224 and foldout map.

Harrison County

Physical Features: East Texas county; hilly, rolling; over half forested; Sabine River; Caddo Lake.

Economy: Oil, gas processing; lumbering; pottery, other varied manufacturing.

History: Agriculturist Caddo Indians whose numbers were reduced by disease. Anglo-Americans arrived in 1830s. In 1850, the county had more slaves than any other in the state. County created 1839 from Shelby County; organized 1842. Named for eloquent advocate of Texas Revolution, Jonas Harrison.

Race/Ethnicity, 2000: (In percent) Anglo, 69.81; Black, 24.13; Hispanic, 5.34; Other, 0.72.

Vital Statistics, 2004: Births, 807; deaths, 585; marriages, 503; divorces, 119.

Recreation: Fishing, other water activities on Caddo and other lakes; hunting; plantation homes, historic sites; Stagecoach Days in May; Old Courthouse Museum; Old World Store; state park, performing arts; Fire Ant festival in October.

Minerals: Oil, gas, lignite coal, clays, sand and gravel.

Agriculture: Cattle, hay. Also, poultry, nursery plants, horses, vegetables, watermelons. Market value $12.3 million. Hunting leases important. Substantial timber industry.

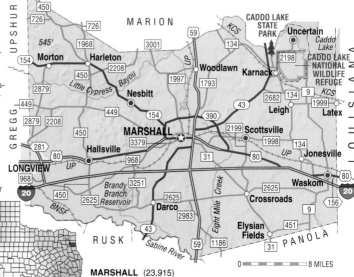

MARSHALL (23,915) county seat; petroleum, lumber processing; varied manufacturing; Wonderland of Lights in December; civic center; historic sites, including Starr Family State Historic Site; hospital; Wiley College; East Texas Baptist University.

Other towns include: **Elysian Fields** (300); **Hallsville** (3,050) Western Days in October, museum; **Harleton** (260); **Jonesville** (28); **Karnack** (775); **Nesbitt** (310); **Scottsville** (257); **Uncertain** (148) tourism, fishing, hunting, Mayhaw Festival in May; **Waskom** (2,157) oil, gas; ranching; Armadillo Daze in April;

Woodlawn (370). Also, part [1,598] of **Longview**.

Population	63,819
Change fm 2000	2.8
Area (sq. mi.)	915.09
Land Area (sq. mi.)	898.71
Altitude (ft.)	168-545
Rainfall (in.)	51.22
Jan. mean min.	33.4
July mean max.	92.4
Civ. Labor	31,654
Unemployed	4.3
Wages	$182,142,656
Av. Weekly Wage	$625.08
Prop. Value	$5,395,214,690
Retail Sales	$640,807,928

A foggy day on Caddo Lake. John Winn photo.

Hartley County

Physical Features: Panhandle High Plains; drains to Canadian River tributaries, playas; sandy, loam, chocolate soils; lake.

Economy: Agriculture, dairies, gas production.

History: Apaches, pushed out by Comanches around 1700. U.S. Army removed Indians in 1875. Pastores (Hispanic sheepmen) in area until 1880s. Cattle ranching began in 1880s. Farming expanded after 1900. County created 1876 from Bexar, Young districts; organized 1891; named for Texas pioneers O.C. and R.K. Hartley.

Race/Ethnicity, 2000: (In percent) Anglo, 77.59; Black, 8.11; Hispanic, 13.69; Other, 0.61.

Vital Statistics, 2004: Births, 65; deaths, 54; marriages, 9; divorces, 17.

Recreation: Rita Blanca Lake activities; ranch museum; local events; XIT Rodeo and Reunion at Dalhart.

Minerals: Sand, gravel, natural gas.

Agriculture: Cattle, corn, wheat, hay, dairy cows, vegetables. 110,000 acres irrigated. Market value $447.3 million. Hunting leases.

CHANNING (366) county seat, Roundup.

DALHART (7,273, mostly in Dallam County), feedlots; feed, meat processing, cheese plant; other industries; hospital. Also, **Hartley** (439).

Population	**5,335**
Change fm 2000	-3.6
Area (sq. mi.)	1,463.20
Land Area (sq. mi.)	1,462.25
Altitude (ft.)	3,400-4,470
Rainfall (in.)	17.20
Jan. mean min.	20.0
July mean max.	90.9
Civ. Labor	2,241
Unemployed	3.6
Wages	$6,226,662
Av. Weekly Wage	$473.45
Prop. Value	$802,585,764
Retail Sales	$18,440,382

Haskell County

Physical Features: West central county; rolling; broken areas; drained by Brazos tributaries; lake; sandy loam, gray, black soils.

Economy: Agribusiness, oil-field operations.

History: Apaches until 1700, then Comanche area. Ranching began in late 1870s after Indians removed. Farming expanded after 1900. County created 1858, from Milam, Fannin counties; re-created 1876; organized 1885; named for Goliad victim C.R. Haskell.

Race/Ethnicity, 2000: (In percent) Anglo, 76.02; Black, 2.86; Hispanic, 20.50; Other, 0.62.

Vital Statistics, 2004: Births, 65; deaths, 103; marriages, 28; divorces, 24.

Recreation: Lake Stamford activities; bass tournament, arts & crafts show; hunting of deer, geese, wild hog.

Minerals: Oil and gas.

Agriculture: Wheat, cotton, peanuts; 28,000 acres irrigated. Beef cattle raised. Market value $40.8 million.

HASKELL (2,851) county seat; farming center; hospital; city park; Wild Horse Prairie Days in June.

Other towns include: **O'Brien** (116), **Rochester** (334), **Rule** (618), **Weinert** (198). Also, **Stamford** (3,489, mostly in Jones County).

Population	5,438
Change fm 2000	-10.8
Area (sq. mi.)	910.25
Land Area (sq. mi.)	902.97
Altitude (ft.)	1,400-1,681
Rainfall (in.)	24.93
Jan. mean min.	28.8
July mean max.	96.1
Civ. Labor	3,294
Unemployed	3.1
Wages	$8,894,078
Av. Weekly Wage	$403.32
Prop. Value	$341,788,380
Retail Sales	$30,814,364

For explanation of sources, abbreviations and symbols, see p. 224 and foldout map.

Physical Features: Hilly in west, blackland in east; on edge of Balcones Escarpment.

Economy: Education, tourism, retirement area, some manufacturing; part of Austin metropolitan area.

History: Tonkawa area, also Apache and Comanche presence. Spanish authorities attempted first permanent settlement in 1807. Mexican land grants in early 1830s to Juan Martín Veramendi, Juan Vicente Campos and Thomas Jefferson Chambers. County created 1843 from Travis County; named for Capt. Jack Hays, famous Texas Ranger.

Race/Ethnicity, 2000: (In percent) Anglo, 65.26; Black, 3.74; Hispanic, 29.57; Other, 1.43.

Vital Statistics, 2004: Births, 1,700; deaths, 563; marriages, 807; divorces, 366.

Recreation: Fishing, hunting; college cultural, athletic events; African-American museum, LBJ museum; Cypress Creek and Blanco River resorts; guest ranches, Wonder World park.

Minerals: Sand and gravel, cement produced.

Agriculture: Beef cattle, goats, exotic wildlife; greenhouse nurseries; hay, corn, sorghum, wheat and cotton. Market value $14.6 million.

SAN MARCOS (47,005) county seat; Texas State University, San Marcos Baptist Academy, Gary Job Corps Training Center; government/services; distribution center; outlet centers; hospital, sports medicine, physical therapy center; Scheib Center for mentally handicapped; Cinco de Mayo festival.

Other towns include: **Bear Creek** (381); **Buda** (4,424); **Driftwood** (NA); **Dripping Springs** (1,839); **Hays** (235); **Kyle** (19,335); **Mountain City** (773); **Niederwald** (416, partly in Caldwell County); **Uhland** (425, partly in Caldwell County); **Wimberley** (4,111) tourism, retirement community, artists, concert series; Country Pie Social and Fair in April; **Woodcreek** (1,380).

Hays County

Population	130,325
Change fm 2000	33.6
Area (sq. mi.)	679.79
Land Area (sq. mi.)	677.87
Altitude (ft.)	550-1,501
Rainfall (in.)	37.19
Jan. mean min.	38.6
July mean max.	95.1
Civ. Labor	69,580
Unemployed	3.0
Wages	$319,550,101
Av. Weekly Wage	$556.60
Prop. Value	$9,454,586,312
Retail Sales	$1,604,242,759

Hemphill County

Physical Features: Panhandle county; sloping surface, broken by Canadian, Washita rivers; sandy, red, dark soils.

Economy: Oil and gas, agriculture, tourism/hunting, government/services.

History: Apaches, who were pushed out by Comanches, Kiowas. Tribes removed to Indian Territory in 1875. Ranching began in late 1870s. Farmers began to arrive after 1900. County created from Bexar, Young districts, 1876; organized 1887; named for Republic of Texas Justice John Hemphill.

Race/Ethnicity, 2000: Anglo, 81.42; Black, 1.55; Hispanic, 15.58; Other, 1.13.

Vital Statistics, 2004: Births, 47; deaths, 39; marriages, 50; divorces, 9.

Recreation: Lake Marvin activities; fall foliage tour; hunting, fishing; Buffalo Wallow Indian Battleground, wildlife management area; 4th of July rodeo.

Minerals: Oil, natural gas, caliche.

Agriculture: Beef cattle, wheat, horses, hay, alfalfa; some irrigation. Market value $92.5 million. Hunting leases, nature tourism.

CANADIAN (2,352) county seat; oil, gas production; feedlot; hospital.

Population	3,412
Change fm 2000	1.8
Area (sq. mi.)	912.06
Land Area (sq. mi.)	909.68
Altitude (ft.)	2,185-3,000
Rainfall (in.)	21.68
Jan. mean min.	18.8
July mean max.	93.9
Civ. Labor	2,444
Unemployed	2.1
Wages	$15,702,957
Av. Weekly Wage	$645.14
Prop. Value	$1,517,855,890
Retail Sales	$32,784,148

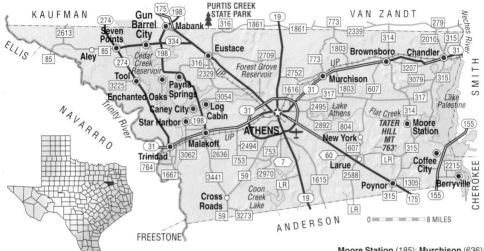

Henderson County

Physical Features: East Texas county bounded by Neches, Trinity rivers; hilly, rolling; one-third forested; sandy, loam, clay soils; commercial timber; Cedar Creek, other lakes.

Economy: Agribusiness, retail trade; varied manufacturing; minerals; recreation; tourism.

History: Caddo area. Cherokee, other tribes migrated into the area in 1819-20 ahead of white settlement. Cherokees forced into Indian Territory in 1839. Anglo-American settlers arrived in 1840s. County created 1846 from Nacogdoches, Houston counties and named for Gov. J. Pinckney Henderson.

Race/Ethnicity, 2000: (In percent) Anglo, 85.49; Black, 6.72; Hispanic, 6.92; Other, 0.87.

Vital Statistics, 2004: Births, 938; deaths, 889; marriages, 609; divorces, 225.

Recreation: Cedar Creek Reservoir, Lake Palestine, and other lakes; Purtis

Creek State Park; hunting, fishing, birdwatching; East Texas Arboretum.

Minerals: Oil, gas, clays, lignite, sulfur, sand and gravel.

Agriculture: Nurseries, cattle, hay, horses. Market value $43.2 million. Hunting leases and fishing.

ATHENS (12,430) county seat; agribusiness center; varied manufacturing; tourism; state fish hatchery and museum; hospital, mental health center; Trinity Valley Community College; Texas Fiddlers' Contest in May.

Gun Barrel City (5,765) recreation, retirement, retail center.

Malakoff (2,356) brick factory, varied industry, tourism, library, Cornbread Festival in April.

Other towns include: **Berryville** (960); **Brownsboro** (909); **Caney City** (261); **Chandler** (2,384); **Coffee City** (195); **Enchanted Oaks** (373); **Eustace** (922); **Larue** (250); **Log Cabin** (813);

Moore Station (185); **Murchison** (636); **Payne Springs** (716); **Poynor** (339); **Seven Points** (1,262) agribusiness, retail trade, recreation, Monte Carlo celebration in November; **Star Harbor** (415); **Tool** (2,412), and **Trinidad** (1,142).

Also, **Mabank** (2,693, mostly in Kaufman County).

Population	**80,222**
Change fm 2000	9.5
Area (sq. mi.)	949.00
Land Area (sq. mi.)	874.24
Altitude (ft.)	256-763
Rainfall (in.)	42.03
Jan. mean min.	35.2
July mean max.	93.4
Civ. Labor	34,762
Unemployed	4.3
Wages	$103,700,496
Av. Weekly Wage	$500.44
Prop. Value	$5,364,683,540
Retail Sales	$701,941,128

For explanation of sources, abbreviations and symbols, see p. 224 and foldout map.

U.S. 60 southwest of Canadian. Robert Plocheck photo.

Hidalgo County

Physical Features: Rich alluvial soils along Rio Grande; sandy, loam soils in north; semitropical vegetation.

Economy: Food processing, shipping; other agribusinesses; tourism; mineral operations.

History: Coahuiltecan and Karankawa area. Comanches forced Apaches southward into valley in 1700s; Comanches arrived in valley in 1800s. Spanish settlement occurred 1750-1800. County created 1852 from Cameron, Starr counties; named for leader of Mexico's independence movement, Father Miguel Hidalgo y Costilla.

Race/Ethnicity, 2000: (In percent) Anglo, 10.59; Black, 0.36; Hispanic, 88.35; Other, 0.70.

Vital Statistics, 2004: Births, 16,540; deaths, 3,050; marriages, 4,628; divorces, 19.

Recreation: Winter resort, retirement area; fishing, hunting; gateway to Mexico; historical sites; Bentsen-Rio Grande Valley State Park; museums; All-Valley Winter Vegetable Show at Pharr.

Minerals: Oil, gas, stone, sand and gravel.

Agriculture: Ninety percent of farm cash receipts from crops, principally from sugar cane, grain, vegetables, citrus, cotton; livestock includes cattle; 270,000 acres irrigated. Market value $202.1 million.

EDINBURG (64,604) county seat; vegetable processing, packing; petroleum operations; clothing; tourism, planetarium; the University of Texas-Pan American; hospitals; mental health center; museum; Fiesta Hidalgo in February.

Population	**700,634**
Change fm 2000	23.0
Area (sq. mi.)	1,582.66
Land Area (sq. mi.)	1,569.75
Altitude (ft.)	28-376
Rainfall (in.)	22.61
Jan. mean min.	48.2
July mean max.	95.5
Civ. Labor	281,444
Unemployed	6.6
Wages	$1,334,200,133
Av. Weekly Wage	$513.42
Prop. Value	$21,384,963,691
Retail Sales	$6,925,731,957

McALLEN (123,055) government/services; food processing, shipping; varied manufacturing; tourism; community college; hospitals; Palmfest in October.

Mission (63,775) citrus groves, with Citrus Fiesta in January; agricultural processing and distribution; hospital; community college; international butterfly park.

Pharr (60,560) agriculture, trading center; trucking; tourism; old clock, juke box museums; folklife festival in February.

Other towns include: **Abram-Perezville** (5,664); **Alamo** (17,576) live steam museum; **Alton** (8,698); **Alton North** (5,264); **Doffing** (4,466); **Donna** (17,046) citrus center, varied manufacturing; lamb, sheep show; **Edcouch** (4,040); **Elsa** (6,196); **Granjeno** (317); **Hargill** (1,349); **Hidalgo** (10,884) trade zone, shipping; winter resort, agribusiness, historical sites, library; Borderfest in March; **La Blanca** (2,498); **La Homa** (11,401); **La Joya** (4,197); **Los Ebanos** (419); **La Villa** (1,376).

Also, **Mercedes** (15,053) "boot capital," citrus, vegetable center; food processing; tourism; recreation vehicle show in January, Hispanic Fest July 4; **Mila Doce** (5,360); **Monte Alto** (1,678); **North Alamo** (2,122); **Nurillo** (5,285); **Palmhurst** (5,348); **Palmview** (4,889); **Palmview South** (6,402); **Peñitas** (1,309); **Progreso** (5,739); **Progreso Lakes** (258); **San Carlos** (2,759); **San Juan** (32,747) retirement area, trucking, Shrine of Our Lady of San Juan, Spring Fiesta in February; **San Manuel-Linn** (951); **South Alamo** (3,233); **Sullivan City** (4,469); **Weslaco** (31,177) agriculture, nature tourism, South Texas College, hospital, Dragonfly Days in May.

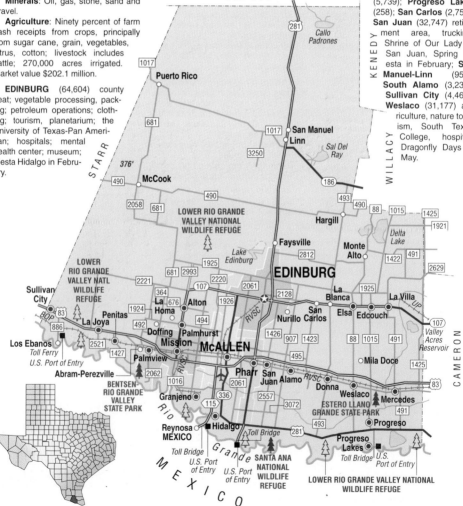

Hill County

Physical Features: North central county; level to rolling; blackland soils, some sandy loams; drains to Brazos; lakes.

Economy: Agribusiness, tourism, varied manufacturing.

History: Waco and Tawakoni area, later Comanches. Believed to be Indian "council spot," a place of safe passage without evidence of raids. Anglo-Americans of the Robertson colony arrived in early 1830s. Fort Graham established in 1849. County created from Navarro County 1853; named for G.W. Hill, Republic of Texas official.

Race/Ethnicity, 2000: (In percent) Anglo, 78.40; Black, 7.51; Hispanic, 13.49; Other, 0.60.

Vital Statistics, 2004: Births, 453; deaths, 401; marriages, 301; divorces, 191.

Recreation: Lake activities; excursion boat on Lake Whitney; Texas Heritage Museum including Confederate and Audie Murphy exhibits, historic structures, rebuilt frontier fort barracks; motorcycle track.

Minerals: Gas, limestone.

Agriculture: Corn, cattle, sorghum, wheat, cotton, dairies. Market value $54 million. Some firewood marketed.

HILLSBORO (8,899) county seat; agribusiness, varied manufacturing, retail, outlet center; tourism, antique malls; Hill College; hospital; Cotton Pickin Fair in September; Cell Block museum, restored courthouse.

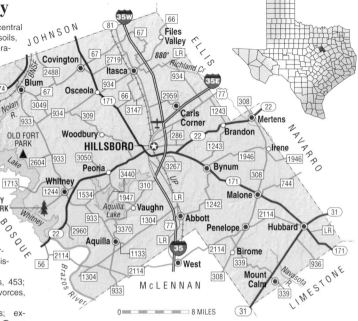

Whitney (1,984) tourist center; hospital, varied manufacturing.

Other towns include: **Abbott** (303); **Aquilla** (145); **Blum** (434); **Brandon** (75); **Bynum** (240); **Carl's Corner** (147); **Covington** (299); **Hubbard** (1,596) agriculture, antiques shops, museums, Magnolias & Mistletoe Victorian Christmas celebration; **Irene** (170); **Itasca** (1,547); **Malone** (276); **Mertens** (155); **Mount Calm** (325); **Penelope** (217).

Population	35,806
Change fm 2000	10.8
Area (sq. mi.)	985.65
Land Area (sq. mi.)	962.36
Altitude (ft.)	450-880
Rainfall (in.)	37.15
Jan. mean min.	35.2
July mean max.	95.2
Civ. Labor	15,467
Unemployed	4.5
Wages	$555,533,122
Av. Weekly Wage	$491.48
Prop. Value	$1,984,630,225
Retail Sales	$423,223,820

For explanation of sources, abbreviations and symbols, see p. 224 and foldout map.

Palm trees line the orange groves of Hidalgo County. Robert Plocheck photo.

Hockley County

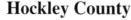

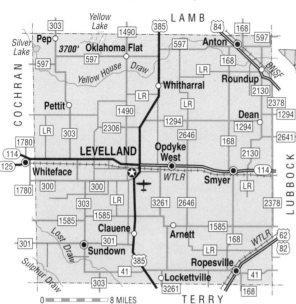

Physical Features: West Texas High Plains, numerous playas, drains to Yellow House Draw; loam, sandy loam soils.

Economy: Extensive oil, gas production and services; manufacturing; varied agribusiness.

History: Comanches displaced Apaches in early 1700s. Large ranches of 1880s brought few residents. Homesteaders arrived after 1900. County created 1876, from Bexar, Young districts; organized 1921. Named for Republic of Texas secretary of war Gen. G.W. Hockley.

Race/Ethnicity, 2000: Anglo, 58.37; Black, 3.79; Hispanic, 37.24; Other, 0.60.

Vital Statistics, 2004: Births, 363; deaths, 211; marriages, 168; divorces, 83.

Recreation: Early Settlers' Day in July; Marigolds Arts, Crafts Festival in November.

Minerals: Oil, gas, stone; one of leading oil counties with more than 1 billion barrels produced.

Agriculture: Cotton, grain sorghum; cattle, hogs raised; substantial irrigation. Market value $90.2 million.

LEVELLAND (12,658) county seat; oil, cotton, cattle center; government/services; hospital; South Plains College; Hot Burrito & Bluegrass Music Festival in July.

Other towns include: **Anton** (1,186); **Opdyke West** (206); **Pep** (3); **Ropesville** (539); **Smyer** (490); **Sundown** (1,488); **Whitharral** (158).

Population	22,609
Change fm 2000	-0.5
Area (sq. mi.)	908.55
Land Area (sq. mi.)	908.28
Altitude (ft.)	3,300-3,700
Rainfall (in.)	19.58
Jan. mean min.	23.7
July mean max.	92.7
Civ. Labor	10,752
Unemployed	3.7
Wages	$64,555,497
Av. Weekly Wage	$610.25
Prop. Value	$2,833,969,795
Retail Sales	$248,801,572

Hood County

Physical Features: Hilly; broken by Paluxy, Brazos rivers; sandy loam soils.

Economy: Tourism; commuting to Fort Worth; nuclear power plant; agriculture.

History: Lipan Apache and Comanche area. Anglo-American settlers arrived in late 1840s. County created 1866 from Johnson and Erath counties; named for Confederate Gen. John B. Hood.

Race/Ethnicity, 2000: (In percent) Anglo, 91.22; Black, 0.36; Hispanic, 7.24; Other, 1.18.

Vital Statistics, 2004: Births, 537; deaths, 528; marriages, 387; divorces, 200.

Recreation: Lakes, fishing, scenic areas; summer theater; Gen. Granbury's Bean & Rib cookoff in March; Acton historic site.

Minerals: Oil, gas, stone.

Agriculture: Hay, turfgrass, beef cattle, nursery crops, pecans, peaches; some irrigation. Market value $21.7 million.

GRANBURY (7,148) county seat; tourism; real estate; power plants; historic downtown area; opera house; hospital; library; Civil War reenactment in October.

Other towns include: **Acton** (1,129) grave of Elizabeth Crockett, wife of Davy; **Brazos Bend** (250); **Cresson** (443); **DeCordova** (3,032); **Lipan** (618); **Oak Trail Shores** (2,549); **Paluxy** (76); **Pecan Plantation** (3,306); **Tolar** (615).

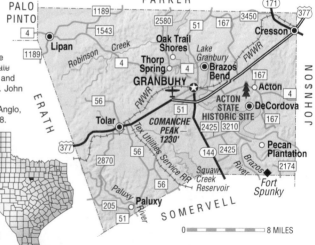

Population	49,238
Change fm 2000	19.8
Area (sq. mi.)	436.80
Land Area (sq. mi.)	421.61
Altitude (ft.)	600-1,230
Rainfall (in.)	33.10
Jan. mean min.	33.0
July mean max.	97.0
Civ. Labor	22,716
Unemployed	3.9
Wages	$81,380,677
Av. Weekly Wage	$556.56
Prop. Value	$3,711,563,980
Retail Sales	$503,982,182

For explanation of sources, abbreviations and symbols, see p. 224 and foldout map.

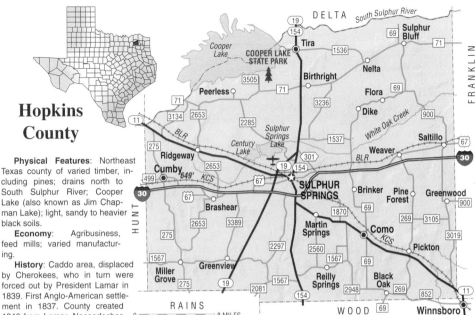

Hopkins County

Physical Features: Northeast Texas county of varied timber, including pines; drains north to South Sulphur River; Cooper Lake (also known as Jim Chapman Lake); light, sandy to heavier black soils.

Economy: Agribusiness, feed mills; varied manufacturing.

History: Caddo area, displaced by Cherokees, who in turn were forced out by President Lamar in 1839. First Anglo-American settlement in 1837. County created 1846 from Lamar, Nacogdoches counties; named for pioneer Hopkins family.

Race/Ethnicity, 2000: (In percent) Anglo, 81.74; Black, 8.07; Hispanic, 9.28; Other, 0.91.

Vital Statistics, 2004: Births, 431; deaths, 461; marriages, 317; divorces, 190.

Recreation: Fishing, hunting; lake activities; stew contest in September; dairy museum; dairy festival in June.

Minerals: Lignite coal.

Agriculture: Dairies, beef cattle; forage, horses, poultry. Market value $134.2 million. Firewood and hardwood lumber marketed.

SULPHUR SPRINGS (15,128) county seat; dairy farming; equine center; food processing, distribution; varied manufacturing; tourism; hospital; library; heritage park; music box gallery; civic center.

Other towns include: **Brashear** (280), **Como** (661), **Cumby** (637), **Dike** (170), **Pickton** (300), **Saltillo** (200), **Sulphur Bluff** (280), **Tira** (247).

Population	33,496
Change fm 2000	4.8
Area (sq. mi.)	792.74
Land Area (sq. mi.)	782.40
Altitude (ft.)	350-649
Rainfall (in.)	47.69
Jan. mean min.	31.1
July mean max.	94.8
Civ. Labor	18,023
Unemployed	3.5
Wages	$81,587,954
Av. Weekly Wage	$535.13
Prop. Value	$1,854,493,510
Retail Sales	$435,024,029

Autumn in northern Hopkins County. Robert Plocheck photo.

Houston County

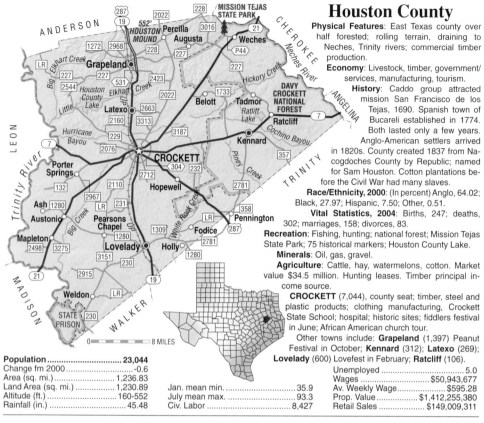

Physical Features: East Texas county over half forested; rolling terrain, draining to Neches, Trinity rivers; commercial timber production.

Economy: Livestock, timber, government/services, manufacturing, tourism.

History: Caddo group attracted mission San Francisco de los Tejas, 1690. Spanish town of Bucareli established in 1774. Both lasted only a few years. Anglo-American settlers arrived in 1820s. County created 1837 from Nacogdoches County by Republic; named for Sam Houston. Cotton plantations before the Civil War had many slaves.

Race/Ethnicity, 2000: (In percent) Anglo, 64.02; Black, 27.97; Hispanic, 7.50; Other, 0.51.

Vital Statistics, 2004: Births, 247; deaths, 302; marriages, 158; divorces, 83.

Recreation: Fishing, hunting; national forest; Mission Tejas State Park; 75 historical markers; Houston County Lake.

Minerals: Oil, gas, gravel.

Agriculture: Cattle, hay, watermelons, cotton. Market value $34.5 million. Hunting leases. Timber principal income source.

CROCKETT (7,044), county seat; timber, steel and plastic products; clothing manufacturing, Crockett State School; hospital; historic sites; fiddlers festival in June; African American church tour.

Other towns include: **Grapeland** (1,397) Peanut Festival in October; **Kennard** (312); **Latexo** (269); **Lovelady** (600) Lovefest in February; **Ratcliff** (106).

Population	23,044
Change fm 2000	-0.6
Area (sq. mi.)	1,236.83
Land Area (sq. mi.)	1,230.89
Altitude (ft.)	160-552
Rainfall (in.)	45.48
Jan. mean min.	35.9
July mean max.	93.3
Civ. Labor	8,427
Unemployed	5.0
Wages	$50,943,677
Av. Weekly Wage	$595.28
Prop. Value	$1,412,255,380
Retail Sales	$149,009,311

Howard County

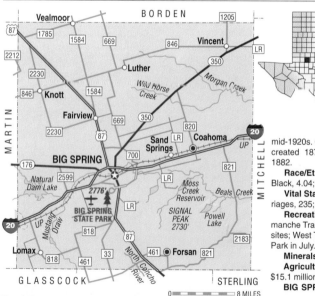

Physical Features: On edge of Llano Estacado; sandy loam soils.

Economy: Government/services; agribusiness; oil, gas; varied manufacturing, including clothing.

History: Pawnee and Comanche area. Anglo-American settlement began in 1870. Oil boom in mid-1920s. County named for V.E. Howard, legislator; created 1876 from Bexar, Young districts; organized 1882.

Race/Ethnicity, 2000: (In percent) Anglo, 57.47; Black, 4.04; Hispanic, 37.46; Other, 1.03.

Vital Statistics, 2004: Births, 465; deaths, 378; marriages, 235; divorces, 44.

Recreation: Lakes; state park; campground in Comanche Trail Park; Native Plant Trail; museum; historical sites; West Texas agricultural expo in March; Pops in the Park in July.

Minerals: Oil, gas, sand, gravel and stone.

Agriculture: Cotton, beef, hay, beans. Market value $15.1 million.

BIG SPRING (25,179) county seat; agriculture, petrochemicals produced; hospitals, including a state institution and Veterans Administration hospital; federal prison; varied manufacturing; Howard College; railroad plaza.

Other towns include: **Coahoma** (860), **Forsan** (211), **Knott** (200).

Population	32,463
Change fm 2000	-3.5
Area (sq. mi.)	904.19
Land Area (sq. mi.)	902.84
Altitude (ft.)	2,200-2,776
Rainfall (in.)	20.12
Jan. mean min.	29.6
July mean max.	94.3
Civ. Labor	12,896
Unemployed	4.3
Wages	$97,648,806
Av. Weekly Wage	$622.55
Prop. Value	$1,466,019,476
Retail Sales	$342,625,886

The irrigated fields along the Rio Grande off Texas 20 north of Fort Hancock. Robert Plocheck photo.

Hudspeth County

Physical Features: Plateau, basin terrain, draining to salt lakes; Rio Grande; mostly rocky, alkaline, clay soils and sandy loam soils, except alluvial along Rio Grande; desert, mountain vegetation. Fertile agricultural valleys.

Economy: Agribusiness, mining, tourism, hunting leases.

History: Mescalero Apache area. Fort Quitman established in 1858 to protect routes to west. Railroad in 1881 brought Anglo-American settlers. Political turmoil in Mexico (1912-29) brought more settlers from Mexico. County named for Texas political leader Claude B. Hudspeth; created 1917 from El Paso County.

Race/Ethnicity, 2000: (In percent) Anglo, 23.50; Black, 0.21; Hispanic, 75.03; Other, 1.26.

Vital Statistics, 2004: Births, 51; deaths, 18; marriages, 10; divorces, 0.

Recreation: Scenic drives; fort ruins; hot springs; salt basin; white sands; hunting; birding; part of Guadalupe Mountains National Park, containing unique plant life, canyons.

Minerals: Talc, stone, gypsum.

Agriculture: Most income from cotton, vegetables, hay, alfalfa; beef cattle raised; 35,000 acres irrigated. Market value $27.2 million.

SIERRA BLANCA (572) county seat; ranching center; tourist stop on interstate highway; adobe courthouse; 4th of July fair, livestock show in January.

Other towns include: **Dell City** (423) feedlots; vegetable packing; gypsum processing; clinic; trade center; airport; some of largest water wells in state, Wild West Chili Fest in September, and **Fort Hancock** (1,839).

Map labels:
NEW MEXICO
GUADALUPE MTS NATIONAL PARK
EL PASO
CORNUDAS MTS 5500'
5500'
LR
2249
Dell City
1576 Salt Basin
1437
SIERRA TINAJA PINTA 5303'
62
180
Cornudas
2317
Eight Mile Draw
Salt Flat
62
180
LR
Antelope Draw
South Well Draw
BLACK MTS 5561'
APACHE CANYON
MOUNTAIN TIME ZONE
CENTRAL TIME ZONE
RIM ROCK
1111
SIERRA DIABLO WILDLIFE MANAGEMENT AREA
10
20
Acala
Fort Hancock
SIERRA BLANCA 6950'
LR
SIERRA DIABLO MTS
CULBERSON
FORT HANCOCK SITE
McNary
1088
UP
LR
U.S. Port of Entry
SIERRA BLANCA
UP
LR
2217
Esperanza
34
1111
Allamoore
FORT QUITMAN SITE
192
LR
5683'
DEVIL RIDGE
UP
10
QUITMAN MTS
Red Light Draw
LR
MEXICO
Rio Grande
INDIAN HOT SPRINGS
EAGLE PEAK 7484'
Green River
0   12 MILES
JEFF DAVIS

Population	3,320
Change fm 2000	.... -0.7
Area (sq. mi.)	............................4,571.93
Land Area (sq. mi.)	.................4,571.00
Altitude (ft.)	 3,200-7,484
Rainfall (in.)	..................................11.93
Jan. mean min.	..............................25.1

July mean max.	..............................92.0
Civ. Labor	1,405
Unemployed	......................................5.8
Wages	................................$7,546,284
Av. Weekly Wage	.....................$597.62

Prop. Value	....................$343,408,585
Retail Sales	......................$12,007,680

For explanation of sources, abbreviations and symbols, see p. 224 and foldout map.

Hunt County

Physical Features: North Texas county; level to rolling surface; Sabine, Sulphur rivers; Lake Tawakoni; mostly heavy Blackland soil, some loam, sandy loams.

Economy: Education, varied manufacturing, agribusiness; several Fortune 500 companies in county; many residents employed in Dallas area.

History: Caddo Indians gone by 1790s. Kiowa bands in the area when Anglo-American settlers arrived in 1839. County named for Memucan Hunt, Republic secretary of navy; created 1846 from Fannin, Nacogdoches counties.

Race/Ethnicity, 2000: (In percent) Anglo, 80.61; Black, 9.67; Hispanic, 8.31; Other, 1.41.

Vital Statistics, 2004: Births, 1,053; deaths, 734; marriages, 638; divorces, 312.

Recreation: Lake sports; Texas A&M University-Commerce events; museum; Audie Murphy exhibit.

Minerals: Sand and white rock, gas, oil.

Agriculture: Cattle, forage, greenhouse crops, top revenue sources; horses, wheat, oats, cotton, grain sorghum. Market value $28.1 million. Some firewood sold.

GREENVILLE (25,347) county seat; varied manufacturing, government/services, commuters to Dallas; hospital; branch of Paris Junior College; Native American Pow-wow in January, cotton museum.

Commerce (9,005) Texas A&M University-Commerce; varied manufacturing; tourism, children's museum; Bois d'Arc Bash in September; hospital.

Other towns include: **Caddo Mills** (1,203); **Campbell** (774); **Celeste** (867); **Hawk Cove** (472); **Lone Oak** (552); **Merit** (225); **Neylandville** (60); **Quinlan** (1,460); **West Tawakoni** (1,632) tourist center, light industry, catfish tournament, Lakefest; **Wolfe City** (1,576) light manufacturing, antiques shops.

Population	83,338
Change fm 2000	8.8
Area (sq. mi.)	882.02
Land Area (sq. mi.)	841.16
Altitude (ft.)	437-692
Rainfall (in.)	43.70
Jan. mean min.	31.2
July mean max.	93.3
Civ. Labor	41,108
Unemployed	4.4
Wages	$247,173,854
Av. Weekly Wage	$680,56
Prop. Value	$3,835,918,509
Retail Sales	$912,437,363

The science building on the campus of Texas A&M University–Commerce. Robert Plocheck photo.

Hutchinson County

Physical Features: High Plain, broken by Canadian River and tributaries, Lake Meredith; fertile valleys along streams.

Economy: Oil, gas, petrochemicals; agribusiness; varied manufacturing; tourism.

History: Antelope Creek Indian area. Later Comanches were driven out in U.S. cavalry campaigns of 1874-75. Adobe Walls site of two Indian attacks, 1864 and 1874. Ranching began in late 1870s. Oil boom in early 1920s. County created 1876 from Bexar Territory; organized 1901; named for pioneer jurist Anderson Hutchinson.

Race/Ethnicity, 2000: (In percent) Anglo, 81.15; Black, 2.47; Hispanic, 14.70; Other, 1.68.

Vital Statistics, 2004: Births, 316; deaths, 251; marriages, 175; divorces, 110.

Recreation: Lake activities; fishing, camping; Adobe Walls, historic Indian battle site.

Minerals: Gas, oil, sand, gravel.

Agriculture: Cattle, corn, wheat, grain sorghum; about 45,000 acres irrigated. Market value $29.3 million.

STINNETT (1,853) county seat; petroleum refining; farm center.

BORGER (13,189) petroleum refining, petrochemicals, carbon-black production, oil-field servicing; varied manufacturing; retail center; Frank Phillips College; museum; hospital; downtown beach bash in June.

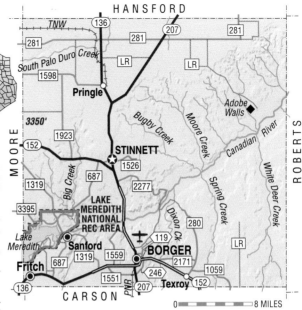

Other cities include: **Fritch** (2,073), **Sanford** (197).

Population	22,460
Change fm 2000	-5.9
Area (sq. mi.)	894.95
Land Area (sq. mi.)	887.37
Altitude (ft.)	2,700-3,350
Rainfall (in.)	21.98
Jan. mean min.	23.4
July mean max.	92.6
Civ. Labor	9,596
Unemployed	4.8
Wages	$77,983,067
Av. Weekly Wage	$717.23
Prop. Value	$1,928,820,780
Retail Sales	$161,347,360

Irion County

Physical Features: West Texas county with hilly surface, broken by Middle Concho, tributaries; clay, sandy soils.

Economy: Ranching; oil, gas production, wildlife recreation, commuters.

History: Tonkawa Indian area. Anglo-American settlement began in late 1870s. County named for Republic leader R.A. Irion; created 1889 from Tom Green County.

Race/Ethnicity, 2000: (In percent) Anglo, 74.81; Black, 0.23; Hispanic, 24.62; Other, 0.34.

Vital Statistics, 2004: Births 9; deaths, 14; marriages, 12; divorces, 3.

Recreation: Hunting; historic sites, including Dove Creek battlefield and stagecoach stops, old Sherwood courthouse built 1900; hunters appreciation dinner in November.

Minerals: Oil, gas.

Agriculture: Beef cattle, sheep, goats; wheat, cotton, hay. Market value $3.5 million.

MERTZON (820) county seat; farm center; wool warehouse.

Other towns include: **Barnhart** (110).

Population	1,814
Change fm 2000	2.4
Area (sq. mi.)	1,051.59
Land Area (sq. mi.)	1,051.48
Altitude (ft.)	2,000-2,725
Rainfall (in.)	19.90
Jan. mean min.	32.0
July mean max.	95.0
Civ. Labor	953
Unemployed	2.4
Wages	$5,052,858
Av. Weekly Wage	$790.54
Prop. Value	$413,627,310
Retail Sales	$4,587,535

For explanatiion of sources, abbreviations and symbols, see p. 224 and foldout map.

Jack County

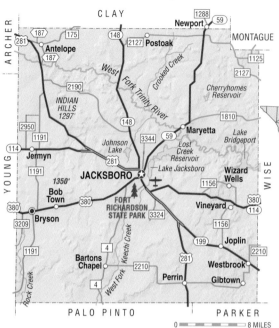

Physical Features: Rolling Cross Timbers, broken by West Fork of the Trinity, other streams; sandy, dark brown, loam soils; lakes.

Economy: Petroleum production, oil-field services, livestock, manufacturing, tourism.

History: Caddo and Comanche borderland. Anglo-American settlers arrived in 1855, part of Peters Colony. County named for brothers P.C. and W.H. Jack, leaders in Texas' independence effort; created 1856 from Cooke County; organized 1857 with Mesquiteville (orginal name of Jacksboro) as county seat.

Race/Ethnicity, 2000: (In percent) Anglo, 85.75; Black, 5.50; Hispanic, 7.89; Other, 0.86.

Vital Statistics, 2004: Births, 90; deaths, 81; marriages, 67; divorces, 38.

Recreation: Hunting, wildlife leases; fishing; lake activities; Fort Richardson, museum, other historic sites; Lost Creek Reservoir State Trailway; rattlesnake roundup in March.

Minerals: Oil, gas.

Agriculture: Cattle, hay, wheat, goats, sheep. Market value $15.6 million. Firewood sold.

JACKSBORO (4,534) county seat; agribusiness; manufacturing; tourism; petroleum production and services; hospital; hospice; library; Old Mesquiteville Festival in fall.

Other towns include: **Bryson** (512), **Jermyn** (75), **Perrin** (300).

Population	9,110
Change fm 2000	4.0
Area (sq. mi.)	920.11
Land Area (sq. mi.)	916.61
Altitude (ft.)	836–1,350

Rainfall (in.)	31.44
Jan. mean min.	29.7
July mean max.	94.4
Civ. Labor	4,010
Unemployed	3.7

Wages	$20,044,710
Av. Weekly Wage	$692.16
Prop. Value	$1,220,160,871
Retail Sales	$48,661,335

Workers make repairs to Half Moon Reef Lighthouse, which now sits on the shore of Lavaca Bay on Texas 35. Constructed in 1858, it was originally in Matagorda Bay and was in use there until 1943. Robert Plocheck photo.

Jackson County

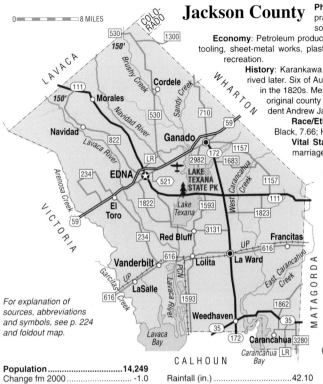

0 ▪▪▪▪▪▪▪ 8 MILES

Physical Features: South coastal county of prairie and motts of trees; loam, clay, black soils; drains to creeks, rivers, bays.

Economy: Petroleum production and operation; metal fabrication and tooling, sheet-metal works, plastics manufacturing; agribusinesses; lake recreation.

History: Karankawa area. Lipan Apaches and Tonkawas arrived later. Six of Austin's Old Three Hundred families settled in the 1820s. Mexican municipality, created 1835, became original county the following year; named for U.S. President Andrew Jackson. Oil discovered in 1934.

Race/Ethnicity, 2000: (In percent) Anglo, 66.82; Black, 7.66; Hispanic, 24.68; Other, 0.84.

Vital Statistics, 2004: Births, 194; deaths, 147; marriages, 87; divorces, 56.

Recreation: Hunting, fishing, birding (southern bald eagle in area); historic sites; Texana Museum; Lake Texana, Brackenridge Plantation campground, state park; county fair, rodeo in April.

Minerals: Oil and natural gas.

Agriculture: Cotton, cattle, corn, rice; also, sorghums, soybeans; 13,000 acres of rice irrigated. Market value $41.9 million.

EDNA (6,036) county seat; plastic manufacturing; agriculture; tourism; oil and gas; hospital, library, museums; Chili Spill/Go Texan Day in November.

Other towns include: **Francitas** (125); **Ganado** (1,987) oil and gas, agriculture, historic movie theater; **LaSalle** (110); **La Ward** (214); **Lolita** (549); **Vanderbilt** (411).

For explanation of sources, abbreviations and symbols, see p. 224 and foldout map.

Population **14,249**	Rainfall (in.) 42.10	Unemployed 3.8
Change fm 2000 ....-1.0	Jan. mean min. 42.0	Wages $35,239,501
Area (sq. mi.) 857.03	July mean max. 94.0	Av. Weekly Wage....................$569.92
Land Area (sq. mi.) 829.49	Civ. Labor 6,523	Prop. Value $1,416,741,983
Altitude (ft.) ....sea level-150		Retail Sales $165,486,906

Jasper County

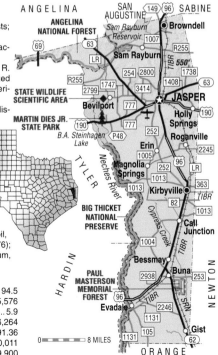

0 ▪▪▪▪▪▪▪ 8 MILES

Physical Features: East Texas county; hilly to level; national forests; lakes; Neches River.

Economy: Timber industries; oil; tourism; fishing; aircraft manufacturer; agriculture.

History: Caddo and Atakapa Indian area. Land grants to John R. Bevil and Lorenzo de Zavala in 1829. County created 1836, organized 1837, from Mexican municipality; named for Sgt. William Jasper of American Revolution.

Race/Ethnicity, 2000: (In percent) Anglo, 77.38; Black, 17.94; Hispanic, 3.89; Other, 0.79.

Vital Statistics, 2004: Births, 489; deaths, 421; marriages, 314; divorces, 241.

Recreation: Lake activities; hunting, fishing; state park, Big Thicket.

Minerals: Oil, gas produced.

Agriculture: Cattle, hogs, major revenue source; vegetables, fruit, pecans. Market value $4.8 million. Timber is major income producer.

JASPER (7,661) county seat; timber; government/services; manufacturing; hospitals; prison; Azalea Festival in April.

Other towns include: **Browndell** (226); **Buna** (2,246) timber, oil, agriculture, polka dot house, redbud festival in March; **Evadale** (1,376); **Kirbyville** (2,085) government/services, retail, commuters, museum, Calaboose museum, Magnolia Festival in April; **Sam Rayburn** (600).

Population **35,293**	July mean max. 94.5
Change fm 2000 ....-0.9	Civ. Labor 15,576
Area (sq. mi.) 969.62	Unemployed 5.9
Land Area (sq. mi.) 937.40	Wages $85,066,264
Altitude (ft.) 25-550	Av. Weekly Wage............$591.36
Rainfall (in.) 60.57	Prop. Value $1,969,720,011
Jan. mean min. 35.2	Retail Sales $335,939,900

The Davis Mountains in Jeff Davis County. Robert Plocheck photo.

Physical Features: Highest average elevation in Texas; peaks (Mt. Livermore, 8,378 ft.), canyons, plateaus; intermountain wash, clay, loam soils; cedars, oaks in highlands.

Economy: Tourism, ranching, greenhouse/nurseries.

History: Mescalero Apaches in area when Antonio de Espejo explored in 1583. U.S. Army established Fort Davis in 1854 to protect routes to west. Civilian settlers followed, including Manuel Músquiz, a political refugee from Mexico. County named for Jefferson Davis, U.S. war secretary, Confederate president; created 1887 from Presidio County.

Race/Ethnicity, 2000: (In percent) Anglo, 63.20; Black, 0.82; Hispanic, 35.48; Other, 0.50.

Vital Statistics, 2004: Births, 21; deaths, 23; marriages, 1; divorces, 0.

Recreation: Scenic drives including scenic loop along Limpia Creek, Mt.

Jeff Davis County

Livermore, Blue Mountain; hunting; Fort Davis National Historic Site; state park; McDonald Observatory on Mt. Locke; solar power park; Chihuahuan Desert Research Institute; hummingbird festival in August.

Minerals: Bentonite.

Agriculture: Greenhouse nurseries, beef cattle, apples, grapes, pecans. Market value $6.4 million.

FORT DAVIS (1,468), county seat; ranch center; trade, tourism; government/services; library; "Coolest July 4th in Texas".

Other town: **Valentine** (240).

Population	**2,315**
Change fm 2000	4.9
Area (sq. mi.)	2,264.60
Land Area (sq. mi.)	2,264.43
Altitude (ft.)	3,500-8,378
Rainfall (in.) Fort Davis	15.86
Rainfall (in.) Mt. Locke	20.37
Jan. mean min. Fort Davis	28.4
Jan. mean min. Mt. Locke	32.4
July mean max. Fort Davis	89.5
July mean max. Mt. Locke	84.5
Civ. Labor	1,022
Unemployed	3.6
Wages	$6,176,302
Av. Weekly Wage	$498.88
Prop. Value	$318,839,306
Retail Sales	$9,311,234

For explanation of sources, abbreviations and symbols, see p. 224 and foldout map.

0 ▰▰▰▰▰ 12 MILES

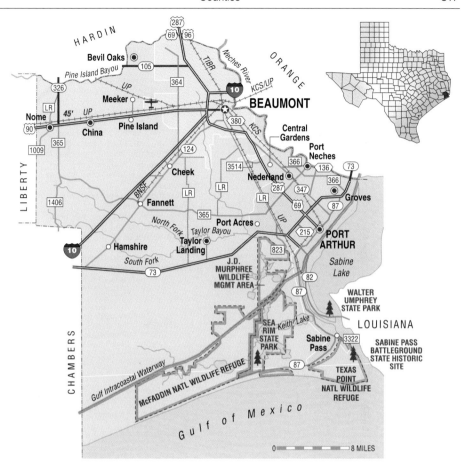

Jefferson County

Physical Features: Gulf Coast grassy plain, with timber in northwest; beach sands, sandy loams, black clay soils; drains to Neches River, Gulf of Mexico.

Economy: Government/services; petrochemical, other chemical plants; shipbuilding; steel mill; port activity; oilfield supplies; .

History: Atakapas and Orcoquizas, whose numbers were reduced by epidemics or migration before Anglo-American settlers arrived in 1820s. Cajuns arrived in 1840s; Europeans in 1850s. Antebellum slaveholding area. County created 1836 from Mexican municipality; organized 1837; named for U.S. President Thomas Jefferson.

Race/Ethnicity, 2000: (In percent) Anglo, 52.27; Black, 33.83; Hispanic, 10.53; Other, 3.37.

Vital Statistics, 2004: Births, 3,447; deaths, 2,518; marriages, 2,196; divorces, 1,152.

Recreation: Beaches, fresh and saltwater fishing; duck, goose hunting; water activities; Dick Dowling Monument and Park; Spindletop site, museums; saltwater lake; wildlife refuge; Lamar University events; historic sites; South Texas Fair in October.

Minerals: Large producer of oil, gas, sulfur, salt, sand and gravel.

Agriculture: Rice, soybeans; crawfish; beef cattle; hay; considerable rice irrigated. Market value $16.9 million. Timber sales significant.

BEAUMONT (111,174) county seat; petrochemical production; shipbuilding; port activities; rice milling; government/services; Lamar University; hospitals; entertainment district; Neches River Festival in April.

PORT ARTHUR (55,574) oil, chemical activities; shrimping and crawfishing; shipping; offshore marine; tourism; hospitals; museum; prison. Asian New Year Tet, Janis Joplin Birthday Bash in January. **Sabine Pass** and **Port Acres** are now within the city limits of Port Arthur.

Other towns include: **Bevil Oaks** (1,284); **Central Gardens** (3,935); **China** (1,052); **Fannett** (1,877); **Groves** (14,654) retail center, some manufacturing, government/services, tourism;

hospital, pecan festival in September; **Hamshire** (759).

Also, **Nederland** (17,052) manufacturing, transportation, petrochemical refining; Windmill and French museum; hospital; Tex Ritter memorial and park, heritage festival in March (city founded by Dutch immigrants in 1898); **Nome** (514); **Port Neches** (13,118) chemical and synthetic rubber industry, manufacturing, library, river-front park with La Maison Beausoleil; RiverFest in May; **Taylor Landing** (250).

Population	243,914
Change fm 2000	-3.2
Area (sq. mi.)	1,111.26
Land Area (sq. mi.)	903.55
Altitude (ft.)	sea level-45
Rainfall (in.)	59.89
Jan. mean min.	42.9
July mean max.	91.6
Civ. Labor	111,010
Unemployed	5.6
Wages	$1,220,523,977
Av. Weekly Wage	$780.46
Prop. Value	$18,242,457,560
Retail Sales	$3,307,184,270

For explanation of sources, symbols and abbreviations, see p. 224 and foldout map.

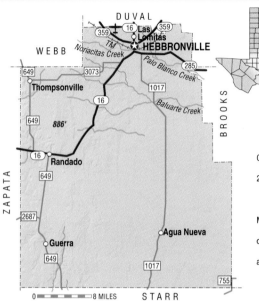

Jim Hogg County

Physical Features: South Texas county on rolling plain, with heavy brush cover; white blow sand and sandy loam; hilly, broken.

Economy: Oil, cattle operations.

History: Coahuiltecan area, then Lipan Apache. Spanish land grant in 1805 to Xavier Vela. County named for Gov. James Stephen Hogg; created, organized 1913 from Brooks, Duval counties.

Race/Ethnicity, 2000: (In percent) Anglo, 9.07; Black, 0.42; Hispanic, 89.98; Other, 0.53.

Vital Statistics, 2004: Births, 84; deaths, 46; marriages, 26; divorces, 1.

Recreation: White-tailed deer and bobwhite hunting.

Minerals: Oil and gas.

Agriculture: Cattle, hay, milk goats; some irrigation. Market value $7 million.

HEBBRONVILLE (4,236) county seat; ranching, oil-field center.

Other towns include: **Guerra** (12), **Las Lomitas** (256) and **South Fork Estates** (47).

Population	5,027
Change fm 2000	-4.8
Area (sq. mi.)	1,136.16
Land Area (sq. mi.)	1,136.11
Altitude (ft.)	249-886
Rainfall (in.)	23.75
Jan. mean min.	43.8
July mean max.	97.5
Civ. Labor	2,725
Unemployed	3.6
Wages	$10,711,189
Av. Weekly Wage	$447.47
Prop. Value	$603,407,561
Retail Sales	$38,117,057

Jim Wells County

Physical Features: South Coastal Plains; level to rolling; sandy to dark soils; grassy with mesquite brush.

Economy: Oil and gas production, agriculture, nature tourism.

History: Coahuiltecans, driven out by Lipan Apaches in 1775. Tomás Sánchez established settlement in 1754. Anglo-American settlement in 1878. County created 1911 from Nueces County; organized 1912; named for developer J.B. Wells Jr.

Race/Ethnicity, 2000: (In percent) Anglo, 23.10; Black, 0.48; Hispanic, 75.71; Other, 0.71.

Vital Statistics, 2004: Births, 665; deaths, 305; marriages, 271; divorces, 76.

Recreation: Hunting; fiestas; Tejano Roots hall of fame; South Texas museum.

Minerals: Oil, gas, caliche.

Agriculture: Cattle, sorghum, corn, cotton, dairies, goats, wheat, watermelons, sunflowers, peas, hay. Market value $47.3 million.

ALICE (19,626) county seat; oil-field service center; agribusiness; government/services; hospital; Fiesta Bandana (from original name of city) in May; Bee County College extension.

Other towns include: **Alfred-South La Paloma** (465); **Ben Bolt** (1,600); **Orange Grove** (1,423); **Pernitas Point** (280, partly in Live Oak County); **Premont** (2,789) wildflower tour, youth rodeo; **Rancho Alegre** (1,835); **Sandia** (461).

Also, a small part of **San Diego** (4,621).

Population	41,131
Change fm 2000	4.6
Area (sq. mi.)	868.22
Land Area (sq. mi.)	864.52
Altitude (ft.)	50-400
Rainfall (in.)	27.52
Jan. mean min.	44.1
July mean max.	96.1
Civ. Labor	20,442
Unemployed	4.2
Wages	$128,912,931
Av. Weekly Wage	$594.96
Prop. Value	$1,531,730,242
Retail Sales	$400,925,078

For explanation of sources, symbols and abbreviations, see p. 224 and foldout map.

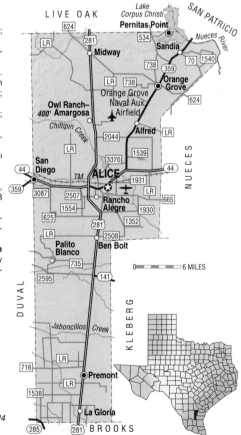

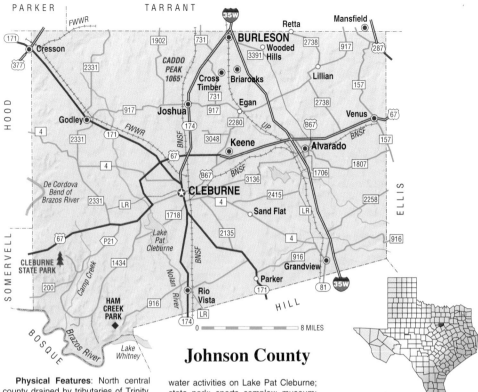

Johnson County

Physical Features: North central county drained by tributaries of Trinity, Brazos rivers; lake; hilly, rolling, many soil types.

Economy: Agribusiness; railroad shops; manufacturing; distribution; lake activities; many residents employed in Fort Worth; part of Fort Worth-Arlington metropolitan area.

History: No permanent Indian villages existed in area. Anglo-American settlers arrived in 1840s. County named for Col. M.T. Johnson of Mexican War, Confederacy; created, organized 1854. Formed from McLennan, Hill, Navarro counties.

Race/Ethnicity, 2000: (In percent) Anglo, 83.91; Black, 2.58; Hispanic, 12.12; Other, 1.39.

Vital Statistics, 2004: Births, 2,057; deaths, 1,043; marriages, 1,145; divorces, 530.

Recreation: Bird, deer hunting; water activities on Lake Pat Cleburne; state park; sports complex; museum; Chisholm Trail; Goatneck bike ride in July.

Minerals: Limestone, sand and gravel.

Agriculture: A leading dairy county, cattle, hay, horses (a leader in number sold), cotton, sorghum, wheat, oats, hogs. Market value $43.6 million.

CLEBURNE (28,496) county seat; varied manufacturing, oil and gas; hospital, library, museum; Hill College county campus; Whistle Stop Christmas.

BURLESON (31,207, part [3,462] in Tarrant County) agriculture, retail center; hospital.

Other towns include: **Alvarado** (3,919) County Pioneer Days; **Briaroaks** (488); **Cresson** (443); **Cross Timber** (297); **Godley** (1,040); **Grandview** (1,454); **Joshua** (5,231) many residents work in Fort Worth; **Keene** (6,089) Southwestern Adventist University; **Lillian** (1,160); **Rio Vista** (759), and **Venus** (2,164).

Also, part of **Mansfield** (37,213 total, mostly in Tarrant County).

Population	**149,016**
Change fm 2000	17.5
Area (sq. mi.)	734.46
Land Area (sq. mi.)	729.42
Altitude (ft.)	600-1,065
Rainfall (in.)	36.25
Jan. mean min.	34.0
July mean max.	97.0
Civ. Labor	75,078
Unemployed	3.7
Wages	$297,031,772
Av. Weekly Wage	$605.96
Prop. Value	$7,826,140,715
Retail Sales	$2,260,657,005

Riders on the Six O Ranch in southwest Johnson County. Mei-Chun Jau photo.

Jones County

Physical Features: West Texas Rolling Plains; drained by Brazos River fork, tributaries; Lake Fort Phantom Hill.

Economy: Agribusiness; government/services; varied manufacturing.

History: Comanches and other tribes hunted in area. Military presence began in 1851. Ranching established in 1870s. County named for the last president of the Republic, Anson Jones; created 1858 from Bexar, Bosque counties; re-created 1876; organized 1881.

Race/Ethnicity, 2000: (In percent) Anglo, 66.67; Black, 11.53; Hispanic, 20.91; Other, 0.89.

Vital Statistics, 2004: Births, 191; deaths, 184; marriages, 91; divorces, 63.

Recreation: Lake activities, hunting; Fort Phantom Hill, Cowboys Christmas Ball; Cowboy Reunion July 4 weekend; old courthouse, opera house, museums, art show.

Minerals: Oil, gas, sand and gravel, stone.

Agriculture: Cotton, wheat, sesame and peanuts; cattle. Some 10,000 acres irrigated for peanuts and hay. Market value $39.2 million.

ANSON (2,522) county seat; farming center; government/services; trailer and ranch furniture manufacturing; hospital; historic buildings; Mesquite Daze festivals in April and October.

STAMFORD (3,489) trade center for three counties, hospital, historic homes, cowboy museum.

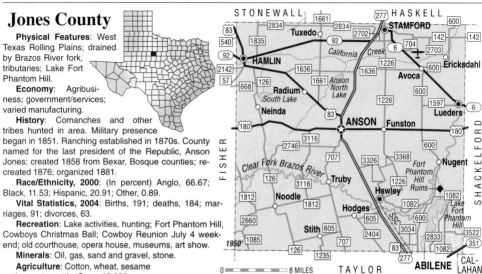

HAMLIN (2,114) farm and ranching, feed mill, oil and gas; electricity/steam plant using mesquite trees; hospital; museums; dove cookoff in October.

Other towns include: **Hawley** (648), **Lueders** (285) limestone quarries.

Part [5,488] of **Abilene**.

Population 19,645
Change fm 2000 .... -5.5
Area (sq. mi.) 937.13

Land Area (sq. mi.) 930.99
Altitude (ft.) 1,500-1,950
Rainfall (in.) 26.00
Jan. mean min. 30.7
July mean max. 96.3
Civ. Labor 8,346
Unemployed 4.3
Wages $37,885,766
Av. Weekly Wage $577.81
Prop. Value $654,490,958
Retail Sales $182,734,789

Karnes County

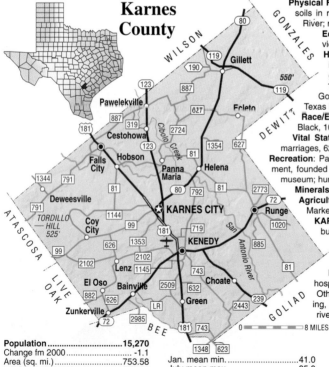

Physical Features: Sandy loam, dark clay, alluvial soils in rolling terrain; traversed by San Antonio River; mesquite, oak trees.

Economy: Agribusiness; government/services.

History: Coahuiltecan Indian area. Spanish ranching began around 1750. Anglo-Americans arrived in 1840s; Polish in 1850s. County created 1854 from Bexar, Goliad, San Patricio counties; named for Texas Revolutionary figure Henry W. Karnes.

Race/Ethnicity, 2000: (In percent) Anglo, 41.20; Black, 10.53; Hispanic, 47.42; Other, 0.76.

Vital Statistics, 2004: Births, 170; deaths, 147; marriages, 62; divorces, 21.

Recreation: Panna Maria, nation's oldest Polish settlement, founded 1854; Old Helena restored courthouse, museum; hunting, nature tourism, guest ranches.

Minerals: Oil, gas.

Agriculture: Beef cattle, feed grain, hay, cotton. Market value $18.2 million.

KARNES CITY (3,486) county seat; agribusiness; tourism; processing center; oilfield servicing; manufacturing; library; Lonesome Dove Fest in September.

KENEDY (3,421) farm and oil center, library, dove/quail hunting leases, prison, hospital; Bluebonnet Days in April.

Other towns include: **Falls City** (644) ranching, sausage making, library, city park on river; **Gillett** (120); **Hobson** (135); **Panna Maria** (45); **Runge** (1,003) oil and gas services, farming, museum, library; cowboy breakfast in December.

Population 15,270
Change fm 2000 .... -1.1
Area (sq. mi.) 753.58
Land Area (sq. mi.) 750.32
Altitude (ft.) 180-550
Rainfall (in.) 28.40

Jan. mean min. 41.0
July mean max. 95.0
Civ. Labor 5,489
Unemployed 5.0

Wages $24,494,142
Av. Weekly Wage $491.65
Prop. Value $874,236,501
Retail Sales $93,649,890

Kaufman County

Physical Features: North Blackland prairie, draining to Trinity River, Cedar Creek and Lake.

Economy: varied manufacturing; trade center; government/services; antique center; commuting to Dallas.

History: Caddo and Cherokee Indians; removed by 1840 when Anglo-American settlement began. County created from Henderson County and organized, 1848; named for member of Texas and U.S. congresses D.S. Kaufman.

Race/Ethnicity, 2000: (In percent) Anglo, 76.97; Black, 10.76; Hispanic, 11.11; Other, 1.16.

Vital Statistics, 2004: Births, 1,257; deaths, 716; marriages, 712; divorces, 374.

Recreation: Lake activities; Porter Farm near Terrell is site of origin of U.S.-Texas Agricultural Extension program; antique centers near Forney; historic homes at Terrell.

Minerals: Oil, gas, stone, sand.

Agriculture: Nursery crops; beef cattle, horses, goats, hogs, sheep; wheat, hay, sorghum, oats, cotton, peaches. Market value $30 million.

KAUFMAN (8,222) county seat; government/services, manufacturing and distribution; commuters to Dallas; hospital; Caboodle Fest in October.

TERRELL (17,149) agribusiness, varied manufacturing; outlet center; private hospital, state hospital; community college, Southwestern Christian College.

Other towns include: **Combine** (2,058, partly in Dallas County); **Cottonwood** (220); **Crandall** (3,265); **Elmo** (90); **Forney** (10,929) important antiques center, light manufacturing, historic homes, Jackrabbit Stampede bike race in September; **Grays Prairie** (340); **Kemp** (1,157); **Lawrence** (279); **Mabank** (2,693, partly in Henderson County) varied manufacturing, tourism, retail trade, Western Week in June; **Oak Grove** (817); **Oak Ridge** (450); **Post Oak Bend** (580); **Rosser** (415); **Scurry** (629); **Talty** (1,280).

For explanation of sources, abbreviations and symbols, see p. 224 and foldout map.

Population	93,241
Change fm 2000	30.8
Area (sq. mi.)	806.81
Land Area (sq. mi.)	786.04
Altitude (ft.)	300-550
Rainfall (in.)	38.90
Jan. mean min.	32.3
July mean max.	94.6
Civ. Labor	44,311
Unemployed	4.2
Wages	$203,706,995
Av. Weekly Wage	$588.00
Prop. Value	$5,874,960,010
Retail Sales	$1,465,199,963

Panna Maria in Karnes County is the oldest Polish community in the nation. Robert Plocheck photo.

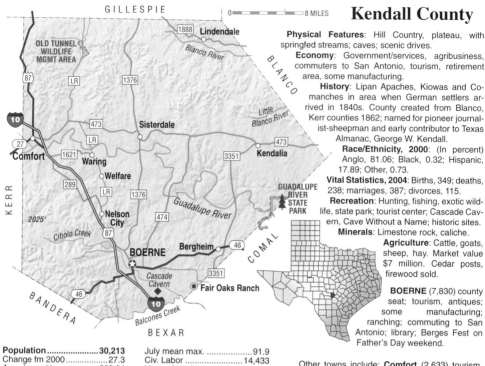

Kendall County

Physical Features: Hill Country, plateau, with springfed streams; caves; scenic drives.

Economy: Government/services, agribusiness, commuters to San Antonio, tourism, retirement area, some manufacturing.

History: Lipan Apaches, Kiowas and Comanches in area when German settlers arrived in 1840s. County created from Blanco, Kerr counties 1862; named for pioneer journalist-sheepman and early contributor to Texas Almanac, George W. Kendall.

Race/Ethnicity, 2000: (In percent) Anglo, 81.06; Black, 0.32; Hispanic, 17.89; Other, 0.73.

Vital Statistics, 2004: Births, 349; deaths, 238; marriages, 387; divorces, 115.

Recreation: Hunting, fishing, exotic wildlife, state park; tourist center; Cascade Cavern, Cave Without a Name; historic sites.

Minerals: Limestone rock, caliche.

Agriculture: Cattle, goats, sheep, hay. Market value $7 million. Cedar posts, firewood sold.

BOERNE (7,830) county seat; tourism, antiques; some manufacturing; ranching; commuting to San Antonio; library; Berges Fest on Father's Day weekend.

Other towns include: **Comfort** (2,633) tourism, ranching, Civil War monument honoring Unionists, library, mountain bike trail; **Kendalia** (149); **Sisterdale** (110); **Waring** (73). Part of **Fair Oaks Ranch** (5,663).

Population......................**30,213**	July mean max. 91.9
Change fm 2000.................27.3	Civ. Labor 14,433
Area (sq. mi.)...................663.04	Unemployed 3.0
Land Area (sq. mi.)..........662.44	Wages $96,173,898
Altitude (ft.)..............1,000-2,025	Av. Weekly Wage...........$748.71
Rainfall (in.) 37.36	Prop. Value $4,901,398,485
Jan. mean min. 34.3	Retail Sales $650,387,174

The Guadalupe River in Kendall County. Robert Plocheck photo.

Kenedy County

Physical Features: Gulf coastal county; flat, sandy terrain, some loam soils; motts of live oaks.

Economy: Oil, ranching; hunting leases/eco-tourism.

History: Coahuiltecan Indians who assimilated or were driven out by Lipan Apaches. Spanish ranching began in 1790s. Anglo-Americans arrived after Mexican War. Among last counties created, organized 1921, from Cameron, Hidalgo, Willacy counties; named for pioneer steamboat operator and cattleman, Capt. Mifflin Kenedy.

Race/Ethnicity, 2000: (In percent) Anglo, 20.29; Black, 0.00; Hispanic, 78.99; Other, 0.72.

Vital Statistics, 2004: Births, 3; deaths, 2; marriages, 4; divorces, 0.

Recreation: Hunting; fishing; bird watching.

Minerals: Oil, gas.

Agriculture: Beef cattle. Market value $9 million. Hunting leases.

SARITA (185) county seat; cattle-shipping point; ranch headquarters; gas processing; one of state's least populous counties.

Also, **Armstrong** (4).

Population	**402**
Change fm 2000	-2.9

Area (sq. mi.)	1,945.60	Civ. Labor	266
Land Area (sq. mi.)	1,456.77	Unemployed	3.0
Altitude (ft.)	sea level-118	Wages	$4,091,477
Rainfall (in.)	27.90	Av. Weekly Wage	$705.67
Jan. mean min.	45.0	Prop. Value	$627,202,572
July mean max.	95.0	Retail Sales	$204,037

Kent County

Physical Features: West central county of rolling, broken terrain; lake; drains to Salt and Double Mountain forks of Brazos River; sandy, loam soils.

Economy: Agribusiness, oil-field operations, hunting leases.

History: Comanches driven out by U.S. Army in 1870s. Ranching developed in 1880s. County created 1876 from Bexar, Young territories; organized 1892. Name honors Andrew Kent, one of 32 volunteers from Gonzales who died at the Alamo.

Race/Ethnicity, 2000: (In percent) Anglo, 90.57; Black, 0.23; Hispanic, 9.08; Other, 0.12.

Vital Statistics, 2004: Births, 5; deaths, 20; marriages, 4; divorces, 4.

Recreation: Hunting, fishing; scenic croton breaks and salt flat; wildlife festival in November.

Minerals: Oil, gas.

Agriculture: Cattle, cotton, wheat, sorghum. Market value $5.3 million.

JAYTON (455) county seat; oil-field services; farming center; fun fest in August.

Other towns include: **Girard** (59).

Population	**734**
Change fm 2000	-14.6
Area (sq. mi.)	902.91
Land Area (sq. mi.)	902.33
Altitude (ft.)	1,823-2,830

Rainfall (in.)	22.94	Av. Weekly Wage	$423.07
Jan. mean min.	24.9	Prop. Value	$528,722,097
July mean max.	95.7	Retail Sales	$12,388,576
Civ. Labor	449		
Unemployed	3.8		
Wages	$1,429,987		

For explanation of symbols, sources and abbreviations, see p. 224 and foldout map.

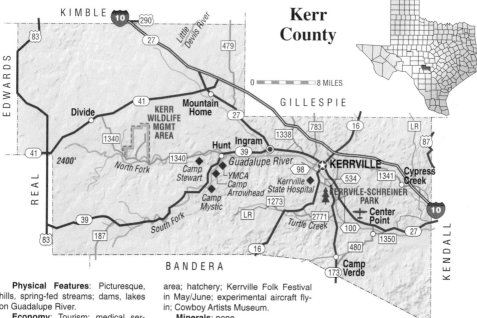

Kerr County

Physical Features: Picturesque, hills, spring-fed streams; dams, lakes on Guadalupe River.

Economy: Tourism; medical services; retirement area; agribusiness; manufacturing; hunting leases.

History: Lipan Apaches, Kiowas and Comanches in area. Anglo-American settlers arrived in late 1840s. County created 1856 from Bexar County; named for member of Austin's Colony, James Kerr.

Race/Ethnicity, 2000: (In percent) Anglo, 78.11; Black, 1.78; Hispanic, 19.13; Other, 0.98.

Vital Statistics, 2004: Births, 514; deaths, 653; marriages, 413; divorces, 259.

Recreation: Popular area for tourists, hunters, fishermen; private and youth camps; dude ranches; park; Point theater; wildlife management area; hatchery; Kerrville Folk Festival in May/June; experimental aircraft fly-in; Cowboy Artists Museum.

Minerals: none.

Agriculture: Cattle, sheep, goats for wool, mohair; meat and breeding goats on increase; crops include hay, pecans. Market value $12 million.

KERRVILLE (21,929) county seat; tourist center; youth camps; agribusiness; aircraft and parts and varied manufacturing; Schreiner University; state hospital, veterans hospital, private hospital; retirement center; retail trade; state arts, crafts show in May-June; experimental aircraft fly-in during October.

Other towns include: **Camp Verde** (41); **Center Point** (800); **Hunt** (708) youth camps; hospital; **Ingram** (1,023) camps, cabins; **Mountain Home** (96).

Population	47,254
Change fm 2000	8.3
Area (sq. mi.)	1,107.66
Land Area (sq. mi.)	1,106.12
Altitude (ft.)	1,450-2,400
Rainfall (in.)	32.60
Jan. mean min.	32.0
July mean max.	92.0
Civ. Labor	24,156
Unemployed	2.8
Wages	$134,924,409
Av. Weekly Wage	$594.63
Prop. Value	$3,797,063,680
Retail Sales	$704,790,397

For explanation of symbols, sources and abbreviations, see p. 224 and foldout map.

A delivery truck makes its way on Texas 16 through the Hill Country south of Kerrville. Robert Plocheck photo.

Kimble County

Population **4,570**
Change fm 2000 .... 2.3
Area (sq. mi.) 1,250.92
Land Area (sq. mi.) 1,250.70
Altitude (ft.) 1,500-2,400
Rainfall (in.) 23.24
Jan. mean min. 29.3
July mean max. 94.8
Civ. Labor 2,333
Unemployed 2.9
Wages $9,286,674
Av. Weekly Wage $462.67
Prop. Value $1,096,648,417
Retail Sales $63,576,367

Physical Features: Picturesque southwestern county; rugged, broken by numerous streams; drains to Llano River; sandy, gray, chocolate loam soils.

Economy: Livestock production, market; tourism, cedar oil and wood products sold; metal building materials manufactured.

History: Apache, Kiowas and Comanche stronghold until 1870s. Military outposts protected first Anglo-American settlers in 1850s. County created from Bexar County 1858; organized 1876. Named for George C. Kimble, a Gonzales volunteer who died at the Alamo.

Race/Ethnicity, 2000: (In percent) Anglo, 78.37; Black, 0.09; Hispanic, 20.73; Other, 0.81.

Vital Statistics, 2004: Births, 42; deaths, 61; marriages, 37; divorces, 30.

Recreation: Hunting, fishing in spring-fed streams, nature tourism; among leading deer counties; state park; Kimble Kounty Kow Kick on Labor Day, Wild Game dinner on Thanksgiving Saturday.

Minerals: gravel.

Agriculture: Cattle, meat goats, sheep, Angora goats, pecans. Market value $7.4 million. Hunting leases important. Firewood, cedar sold.

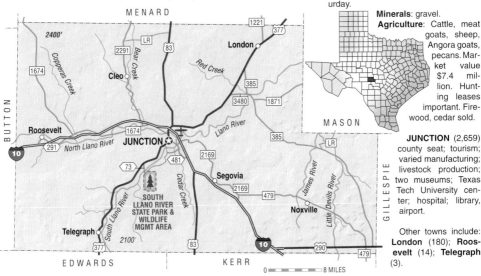

JUNCTION (2,659) county seat; tourism; varied manufacturing; livestock production; two museums; Texas Tech University center; hospital; library; airport.

Other towns include: **London** (180); **Roosevelt** (14); **Telegraph** (3).

King County

Physical Features: Hilly, broken by Wichita, Brazos tributaries; extensive grassland; dark loam to red soils.

Economy: Oil and gas, ranching, government/services, horse sales, hunting leases, .

History: Apache area until Comanches moved in about 1700. Comanches removed by U.S. Army in 1874-75 after which ranching began. County created 1876 from Bexar District; organized 1891; named for William P. King, a volunteer from Gonzales who died at the Alamo.

Race/Ethnicity, 2000: (In percent) Anglo, 89.33; Black, 0.00; Hispanic, 9.55; Other, 1.12.

Vital Statistics, 2004: Births, 1; deaths, 3; marriages, 2; divorces, 0.

Recreation: Large ranches (6666, Pitchfork, Tongue River) offer tours, visits, hunting; roping and ranch horse competitions.

Minerals: Oil, gas.

Agriculture: Cattle, horses, cotton, hay, wheat. Market value $11.8 million. Hunting leases important.

GUTHRIE (125) county seat; ranch-supply center; government/services; community center complex; library; Thanksgiving community supper.

Population **287**
Change fm 2000 .... -19.4
Area (sq. mi.) 913.33
Land Area (sq. mi.) 912.29
Altitude (ft.) 1,500-2,100
Rainfall (in.) 25.00
Jan. mean min. 23.9
July mean max. 96.7
Civ. Labor 151
Unemployed 6.6
Wages $1,108,920
Av. Weekly Wage $496.90
Prop. Value $276,420,098
Retail Sales $1,638,371

Kinney County

Physical Features: Hilly, broken by Rio Grande tributaries; Anacacho Mountains; Nueces Canyon.

Economy: Agribusiness, government/services, hunting leases.

History: Coahuiltecans, Apaches, Comanches in area. Spanish Franciscans established settlement in late 1700s. English empresarios John Beales and James Grant established English-speaking colony in 1834. Black Seminoles served as army scouts in 1870s. County created from Bexar County 1850; organized 1874; named for H.L. Kinney, founder of Corpus Christi.

Race/Ethnicity, 2000: (In percent) Anglo, 47.79; Black, 1.39; Hispanic, 50.52; Other, 0.30.

Vital Statistics, 2004: Births, 33; deaths, 34; marriages, 26; divorces, 3.

Recreation: Hunting; replica of Alamo; old Fort Clark Springs; state park; Cinco de Mayo, Juneteenth.

Minerals: Not significant.

Agriculture: Cattle, goats, hay, grain sorghum, cotton, corn, oats, wheat. Market value $4.7 million.

BRACKETTVILLE (1,859) county seat; agriculture, tourism; museum; cowboy cauldron.

Other towns include: **Fort Clark Springs** (1,300); **Spofford** (72).

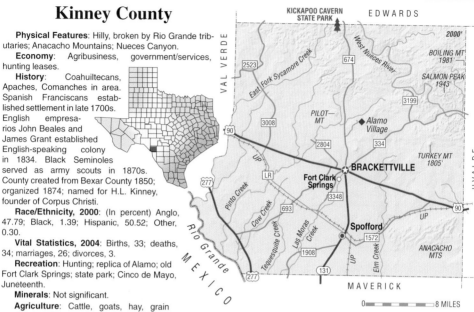

Population	3,342
Change fm 2000	-1.1
Area (sq. mi.)	1,365.31
Land Area (sq. mi.)	1,363.44
Altitude (ft.)	850-2,000
Rainfall (in.)	22.79
Jan. mean min.	37.3

July mean max.	95.5
Civ. Labor	1,446
Unemployed	4.6
Wages	$5,173,523
Av. Weekly Wage	$579.28
Prop. Value	$610,023,511
Retail Sales	$10,960,920

Kleberg County

Physical Features: Coastal plain, broken by bays; sandy, loam, clay soils; tree motts.

Economy: Oil and gas; Naval air station; chemicals and plastics; agriculture; Texas A&M University-Kingsville.

History: Coahuiltecan and Karankawa area. Spanish land grants date to 1750s. In 1853 Richard King purchased Santa Gertrudis land grant. County created 1913 from Nueces County; named for San Jacinto veteran and rancher Robert Kleberg.

Race/Ethnicity, 2000: (In percent) Anglo, 29.03; Black, 3.59; Hispanic, 65.41; Other, 1.97.

Vital Statistics, 2004: Births, 495; deaths, 249; marriages, 236; divorces, 110.

Recreation: Fishing, hunting, water sports, park on Baffin Bay; wildlife sanctuary; winter bird watching; university events, museum; King Ranch headquarters, tours; La Posada celebration in November.

Minerals: Oil, gas.

Agriculture: Cotton, beef cattle, grain sorghum. Market value $57.8 million. Hunting leases/eco-tourism.

KINGSVILLE (24,227) county seat; government/services; oil, gas; agribusiness; tourism; chemical plant; university, Coastal Bend College branch; hospital; ranching heritage festival in February.

Other towns include: **Riviera** (1,064).

Population	30,353
Change fm 2000	-3.8
Area (sq. mi.)	1,090.29
Land Area (sq. mi.)	870.97
Altitude (ft.)	sea level-151
Rainfall (in.)	29.03
Jan. mean min.	43.4
July mean max.	95.5

Civ. Labor	17,934
Unemployed	3.9
Wages	$83,804,489
Av. Weekly Wage	$514.96
Prop. Value	$1,566,921,020
Retail Sales	$381,524,433

Knox County

Physical Features: Eroded breaks on West Texas Rolling Plains; Brazos, Wichita rivers; sandy, loam soils.

Economy: Oil, agriculture, government/services.

History: Indian conscripts used during Spanish period to mine copper deposits along the Brazos. Ranching, farming developed in 1880s. German colony settled in 1895. County created from Bexar, Young territories 1858; re-created 1876; organized 1886; named for U.S. Secretary of War Henry Knox.

Race/Ethnicity, 2000: (In percent) Anglo, 67.06; Black, 7.24; Hispanic, 25.09; Other, 0.61.

Vital Statistics, 2004: Births, 46; deaths, 58; marriages, 9; divorces, 10.

Recreation: Lake activities, fishing; hunting; Knox City seedless watermelon festival in July.

Minerals: Oil, gas.

Agriculture: Cattle, cotton. Some cotton irrigated. Market value $46.2 million.

BENJAMIN (263) county seat; ranching, farm center.

MUNDAY (1,432) portable buildings, other manufacturing; Texas A&M Vegetable Research Station; vegetable festival.

KNOX CITY (1,129) agribusiness, petroleum center; USDA Plant Materials Research Center; veterans memorial; hospital.

Other towns include: **Goree** (307); **Rhine-**

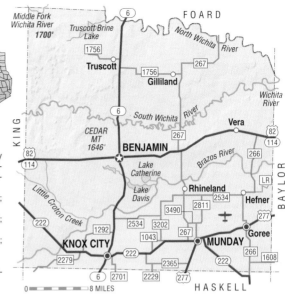

land (120) old church established by German immigrants.

Population **3,702**
Change fm 2000 .... -13.0
Area (sq. mi.) 855.43
Land Area (sq. mi.) 849.00
Altitude (ft.) 1,300-1,700
Rainfall (in.) 26.36
Jan. mean min. 28.1
July mean max. 96.5

Civ. Labor 1,732
Unemployed 3.8
Wages $9,396,966
Av. Weekly Wage..............$562.09
Prop. Value $290,916,305
Retail Sales $33,984,512

For explanation of sources, symbols and abbreviations, see p. 224 and foldout map.

The farming community of Rhineland in Knox County. Robert Plocheck photo.

Lamar County

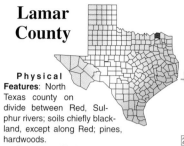

Physical Features: North Texas county on divide between Red, Sulphur rivers; soils chiefly blackland, except along Red; pines, hardwoods.

Economy: Varied manufacturing; agribusiness; medical, government/services.

History: Caddo Indian area. First Anglo-American settlers arrived about 1815. County created 1840 from Red River County; organized 1841; named for second president of Republic, Mirabeau B. Lamar.

Race/Ethnicity, 2000: (In percent) Anglo, 81.43; Black, 13.72; Hispanic, 3.33; Other, 1.52.

Vital Statistics, 2004: Births, 688; deaths, 584; marriages, 487; divorces, 330.

Recreation: Lake activities; Gambill goose refuge; hunting, fishing; state park; Trail de Paris rail-to-trail; Sam Bell Maxey Home; State Sen. A.M. Aikin Archives, other museums.

Minerals: Negligible.

Agriculture: Beef, hay, dairy, soybeans, wheat, corn, sorghum, cotton. Market value $39 million.

PARIS (26,474) county seat; varied manufacturing; food processing; government/services; hospitals; junior college; museums; Tour de Paris bicycle rally in July; archery pro-am tournament in March.

Other towns include: **Arthur City** (180), **Blossom** (1,449), **Brookston** (130), **Chicota** (150), **Cunningham** (110), **Deport** (690, partly in Red River County), **Patton-**

ville (180), **Petty** (130), **Powderly** (185), **Reno** (3,046), **Roxton** (714), **Sumner** (95), **Sun Valley** (54), **Toco** (83).

Population	**49,863**
Change fm 2000	2.8
Area (sq. mi.)	932.47
Land Area (sq. mi.)	916.81
Altitude (ft.)	350-650
Rainfall (in.)	47.82
Jan. mean min.	29.9

July mean max.	94.3
Civ. Labor	22,928
Unemployed	4.9
Wages	$151,329,612
Av. Weekly Wage	$571.28
Prop. Value	$2,847,793,661
Retail Sales	$592,548,685

For explanation of sources, symbols and abbreviations, see p. 224 and foldout map.

A farm pond along FM 196 in Lamar County. Robert Plocheck photo.

Lamb County

Physical Features: Rich, red, brown soils on West Texas High Plains; some hills; drains to upper Brazos River tributaries; numerous playas.

Economy: Agribusiness; distribution center; denim textiles.

History: Apaches, displaced by Comanches around 1700. U.S. Army pushed Comanches into Indian Territory in 1875. Ranching began in 1880s; farming after 1900. County created 1876 from Bexar District; organized 1908; named for Lt. G.A. Lamb, who died in battle of San Jacinto.

Race/Ethnicity, 2000: (In percent) Anglo, 51.71; Black, 4.32; Hispanic, 43.46; Other, 0.51.

Vital Statistics, 2004: Births, 248; deaths, 142; marriages, 101; divorces, 46.

Recreation: Caprock Soaring glider competition.

Minerals: Oil, stone, gas.

Agriculture: Fed cattle; cotton, corn, wheat, grain sorghum, vegetables, soybeans, hay; sheep. 385,000 acres irrigated. Market value $260.2 million.

LITTLEFIELD (6,360) county seat; agribusiness; varied manufacturing; hospital; prison.

Olton (2,389) agribusiness, commercial center for northeast part of county; pheasant hunt in winter; Sandhills Celebration in summer.

Other towns include: **Amherst** (811); **Earth** (1,139) farming center, manufacturing, feed lot, supplies; **Fieldton** (20); **Spade** (99); **Springlake** (134); **Sudan** (1,042) farming center, government/services, Homecoming Day in fall.

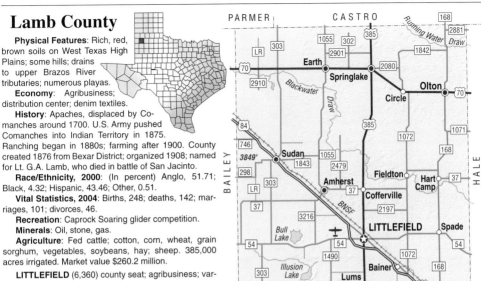

Population	14,244
Change fm 2000	-3.2
Area (sq. mi.)	1,017.73
Land Area (sq. mi.)	1,016.21
Altitude (ft.)	3,400-3,849
Rainfall (in.)	18.69
Jan. mean min.	22.7
July mean max.	92.0
Civ. Labor	7,192
Unemployed	3.7
Wages	$31,357,754
Av. Weekly Wage	$475.95
Prop. Value	$699,129,182
Retail Sales	$72,629,881

Lampasas County

Physical Features: Central Texas on edge of Hill Country; Colorado, Lampasas rivers; cedars, oaks, pecans.

Economy: Many employed at Fort Hood; several industrial plants; agribusinesses; tourism.

History: Mineral springs attracted first Anglo-Americans in 1853. Frontier confrontations between settlers, Comanches continued into 1870s. County created 1856 from Bell, Travis counties. Named for river. Some have speculated that an early expedition named river for city of Lampazos in Mexico.

Race/Ethnicity, 2000: (In percent) Anglo, 80.40; Black, 3.12; Hispanic, 15.07; Other, 1.41.

Vital Statistics, 2004: Births, 239; deaths, 189; marriages, 164; divorces, 81.

Recreation: Scenic drives; state park; deer hunting, fishing in streams.

Minerals: Sand and gravel, building stone.

Agriculture: Beef cattle, hay, goats, exotic animals. Market value $13.4 million. Hunting leases, ecotourism.

LAMPASAS (7,568) county seat; varied manufacturing; government/services; ranching, hunting center; historic downtown; hospital; Spring Ho in July.

Other towns include: **Bend** (115, partly in San Saba County); **Izoro** (17); **Kempner** (1,084); **Lometa** (894) market and shipping point; Diamondback Jubilee in March.

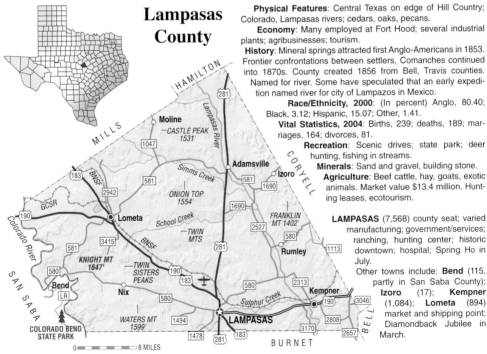

Population	20,758
Change fm 2000	16.9
Area (sq. mi.)	713.96
Land Area (sq. mi.)	712.04
Altitude (ft.)	800-1,647
Rainfall (in.)	31.08
Jan. mean min.	30.4
July mean max.	94.1
Civ. Labor	10,931
Unemployed	3.0
Wages	$32,556,925
Av. Weekly Wage	$520.23
Prop. Value	$1,493,579,380
Retail Sales	$161,948,866

La Salle County

Physical Features: South Texas county on brushy plain, broken by Nueces, Frio rivers and their tributaries; chocolate, dark gray, sandy loam soils.

Economy: Agribusiness, hunting leases; tourism; government services.

History: Coahuiltecans, squeezed out by migrating Apaches. U.S. military outpost in 1850s; settlers of Mexican descent established nearby village. Anglo-American ranching developed in 1870s. County created from Bexar District 1858; organized 1880; named for Robert Cavelier Sieur de La Salle, French explorer who died in Texas.

Race/Ethnicity, 2000: (In percent) Anglo, 19.15; Black, 3.29; Hispanic, 77.12; Other, 0.44.

Vital Statistics, 2004: Births, 85; deaths, 44; marriages, 32; divorces, 3.

Recreation: Nature trails; Cotulla school where Lyndon B. Johnson taught; wildlife management area; deer, bird, javelina hunting; wild hog cookoff in March; fishing.

Minerals: Oil, gas.

Agriculture: Beef cattle, peanuts, watermelons, grain sorghum. Market value $23.2 million.

COTULLA (3,561) county seat; livestock, state prison; hunting center; Brush Country museum; Cinco de Mayo celebration.

Other towns include: **Encinal** (671), **Fowlerton** (51).

Population	5,969
Change fm 2000	1.8
Area (sq. mi.)	1,494.23
Land Area (sq. mi.)	1,488.85
Altitude (ft.)	250-600
Rainfall (in.)	22.56
Jan. mean min.	39.1
July mean max.	98.9
Civ. Labor	2,968
Unemployed	4.4
Wages	$16,429,370
Av. Weekly Wage	$ 733.34
Prop. Value	$566,984,294
Retail Sales	$58,572,848

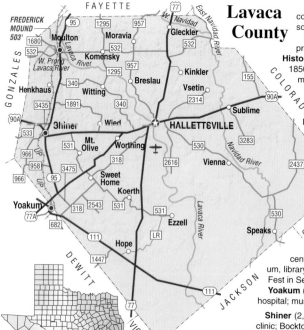

Lavaca County

Physical Features: Southern Coastal Plains county; north rolling; sandy loam, black waxy soils; drains to Lavaca, Navidad rivers.

Economy: Varied manufacturing; oil and gas production; agribusinesses; tourism.

History: Coahuiltecan area; later Comanches until 1850s. Anglo-Americans first settled in 1831. Germans and Czechs arrived 1880-1900. County created 1846 from Colorado, Jackson, Gonzales, Victoria counties. Name is Spanish word for cow, la vaca, from name of river.

Race/Ethnicity, 2000: (In percent) Anglo, 81.37; Black, 6.85; Hispanic, 11.36; Other, 0.42.

Vital Statistics, 2004: Births, 234; deaths, 268; marriages, 123; divorces, 61.

Recreation: Deer, other hunting, fishing; wildflower trails, Hallettsville fiddlers frolic in April; historic sites, churches.

Minerals: Some oil, gas.

Agriculture: Cattle, forage, poultry, rice, corn, sorghum. Market value $45.7 million. Hunting leases.

HALLETTSVILLE (2,494) county seat; retail center; varied manufacturing; agribusiness; museum, library, hospital; domino, "42" tournaments; Kolache Fest in September.

Yoakum (5,831, partly in DeWitt County); cattle, leather; hospital; museum; Land of Leather in February.

Shiner (2,028) brewery, varied manufacturing; museum; clinic; Bocktoberfest.

Other towns include: **Moulton** (914) agribusiness, Town & Country Jamboree in July; **Sublime** (75); **Sweet Home** (360).

Land Area (sq. mi.)	969.90
Altitude (ft.)	100-503
Rainfall (in.)	42.23
Jan. mean min.	41.8
July mean max.	94.4
Civ. Labor	10,706
Unemployed	2.8

Population	18,970
Change fm 2000	-1.2
Area (sq. mi.)	970.35

Total Wages	$38,851,327
Av. Weekly Wage	$479.42
Prop. Value	$2,335,053,537
Retail Sales	$176,987,788

Physical Features: South central county; rolling terrain, broken by Yegua and its tributaries; red to black soils, sandy to heavy loams.

Economy: Varied manufacturing; agribusiness; lignite coal operations; government/services.

History: Tonkawas; removed in 1855 to Brazos Reservation. Most Anglo-American settlement occurred after Texas Revolution. Slaveholding area. Germans, Wends, other Europeans began arriving in 1850s. County created from Bastrop, Burleson, Fayette, Washington counties and organized in 1874; named for Confederate Gen. Robert E. Lee.

Race/Ethnicity, 2000: (In percent) Anglo, 68.96; Black, 12.15; Hispanic, 18.19; Other, 0.70.

Vital Statistics, 2004: Births, 200; deaths, 130; marriages, 136; divorces, 47.

Recreation: Fishing, hunting; state park; pioneer village; Giddings Geburtstag celebration; historic sites.

Minerals: Lignite coal, iron ore, gravel.

Agriculture: Beef cattle, hay, nurseries, poultry, peanuts, goats, horses, aquaculture, corn; 25,000 acres irrigated. Market value $23 million. Firewood.

GIDDINGS (5,474) county seat; agriculture, oilfield services, light manufacturing, hospital.

Other towns include: **Dime Box** (381); **Lexington** (1,279) livestock-marketing center; **Lincoln** (336); **Serbin** (109) Wendish museum.

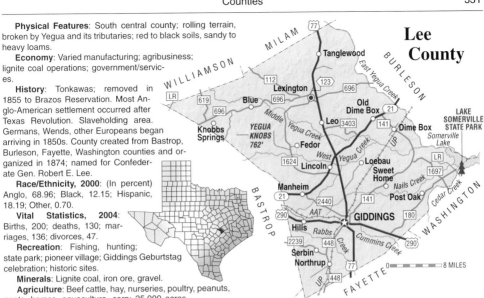

Lee County

Population	16,573	July mean max	93.6
Change fm 2000	5.9	Civ. Labor	8,838
Area (sq. mi.)	634.03	Unemployed	3.1
Land Area (sq. mi.)	628.50	Wages	$41,872,616
Altitude (ft.)	238-762	Av. Weekly Wage	$597.07
Rainfall (in.)	36.02	Prop. Value	$1,689,877,471
Jan. mean min.	37.3	Retail Sales	$188,150,816

Physical Features: East central county; hilly, rolling, almost half covered by timber; drains to Navasota, Trinity rivers and tributaries; sandy, dark, alluvial soils.

Economy: Oil, gas production; agribusiness.

History: Bidais band, absorbed into Kickapoos and other groups. Permanent settlement by Anglo-Americans occurred after Texas Revolution; Germans in 1870s. County created 1846 from Robertson County; named for founder of Victoria, Martín de León.

Race/Ethnicity, 2000: (In percent) Anglo, 81.04; Black, 10.41; Hispanic, 7.91; Other, 0.64.

Vital Statistics, 2004: Births, 198; deaths, 206; marriages, 98; divorces, 61.

Recreation: Hilltop Lakes resort area; sites of Camino Real, Fort Boggy State Park; deer hunting.

Minerals: Oil, gas, iron ore, lignite.

Agriculture: A leading county in cow-calf production; hogs, poultry raised; hay, watermelons, vegetables, small grains; Christmas trees. Market value $51.3 million. Hardwoods, pine marketed.

CENTERVILLE (934) county seat; farm center; hunting; tourism; oil, gas; timber.

BUFFALO (1,926) agriculture, oil and gas; clinic, library; Spring Fest with fiddlers' contest.

Other towns include: **Concord** (28); **Flynn** (81); **Hilltop Lakes** (300) resort, retirement center; **Jewett** (949) electricity-generating plant, steel mill, strip mining, civic center, museum, library, Classic Coon Hunt in January; **Leona** (188) candle factory; **Marquez** (233); **Normangee** (767, partly in Madison County) farming, tourism; library, museum, city park; **Oakwood** (481).

For explanation of sources, symbols and abbreviations, see p. 224 and foldout map.

Leon County

Population	16,538	Rainfall (in.)	43.08
Change fm 2000	7.8	Jan. mean min.	34.3
Area (sq. mi.)	1,080.38	July mean max.	94.7
Land Area (sq. mi.)	1,072.04	Civ. Labor	7,593
Altitude (ft.)	150-600	Unemployed	4.1
		Wages	$47,957,156
		Av. Weekly Wage	$699.83
		Prop. Value	$2,209,965,828
		Retail Sales	$142,720,366

Liberty County

Physical Features: Coastal Plain county east of Houston; 60 percent in pine, hardwood timber; bisected by Trinity River; sandy, loam, black soils; Big Thicket.

Economy: Agribusiness; chemical plants; varied manufacturing; tourism; forest industries; prisons; many residents work in Houston; part of Houston metropolitan area.

History: Karankawa area until 1740s. Spanish established Atascosito settlement in 1756. Settlers from Louisiana began arriving in 1810s. County named for Spanish municipality, Libertad; created 1836, organized 1837.

Race/Ethnicity, 2000: (In percent) Anglo, 75.17; Black, 12.99; Hispanic, 10.92; Other, 0.92.

Vital Statistics, 2004: Births, 1,098; deaths, 671; marriages, 673; divorces, 296.

Recreation: Big Thicket; hunting, fishing; historic sites; Trinity Valley exposition; Liberty Opry.

Minerals: Oil, gas.

Agriculture: Beef cattle; rice is principal crop. Also nursery crops, corn, hay, sorghum. Market value $21 million. Some lumbering.

LIBERTY (8,281) county seat; petroleum-related industry; agribusiness; library; museum; regional historical resource depository; Liberty Bell; hospital; Jubilee in March.

Cleveland (7,874) forest products processed, shipped; tourism; library; museum; hospital.

Dayton (6,862) rice, oil center.

Other towns include: **Ames** (1,086);

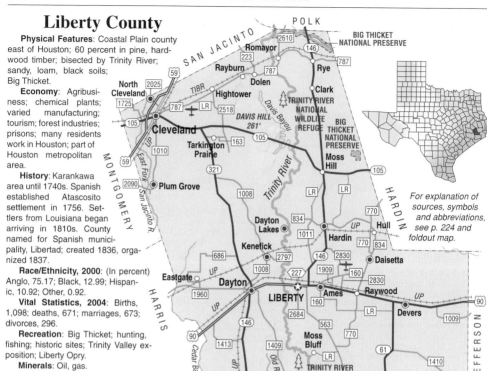

Daisetta (1,042); **Dayton Lakes** (95); **Devers** (429); **Hardin** (795); **Hull** (800); **Kenefick** (703); **North Cleveland** (258); **Plum Grove** (990); **Raywood** (231); **Romayor** (135); **Rye** (150).

Population	**75,685**
Change fm 2000	7.9
Area (sq. mi.)	1,176.22

Land Area (sq. mi.)	1,159.68
Altitude (ft.)	23-261
Rainfall (in.)	60.52
Jan. mean min.	40.3
July mean max.	92.2
Civ. Labor	33,314
Unemployed	4.8
Wages	$126,884,460
Av. Weekly Wage	$576.26
Prop. Value	$4,367,039,565
Retail Sales	$646,451,220

The old saloon in Lipscomb, a town of only 42 people and the county seat of Lipscomb County. Robert Plocheck photo.

Limestone County

Physical Features: East central county on divide between Brazos and Trinity rivers; borders Blacklands, level to rolling; drained by Navasota and tributaries.

Economy: Agribusiness; rock quarry, oil and gas.

History: Tawakoni (Tehuacana) and Waco area, later Comanche raiders. First Anglo-Americans arrived in 1833. Antebellum slaveholding area. County created from Robertson County and organized 1846; named for indigenous rock.

Race/Ethnicity, 2000: (In percent) Anglo, 67.20; Black, 19.33; Hispanic, 12.97; Other, 0.50.

Vital Statistics, 2004: Births, 270; deaths, 290; marriages, 165; divorces, 70.

Recreation: Fishing, lake activities; Fort Parker; Confederate Reunion Grounds; historic sites; museum; hunting; Christmas at the Fort.

Minerals: Oil, gas, lignite, crushed rock.

Agriculture: Cow-calf, stocker cattle, hay, corn, cotton, horses, goats, sheep, wheat, ornamental fruit, pecans. Market value $32.8 million.

GROESBECK (4,593) county seat, agribusiness, tourism, hunting, mining, prison, power generating, hospital.

MEXIA (7,071) agribusiness, grocery distribution, state school, hospital.

Other towns include: **Coolidge** (911), **Kosse** (508), **Prairie Hill** (150), **Tehuacana** (316), **Thornton** (544).

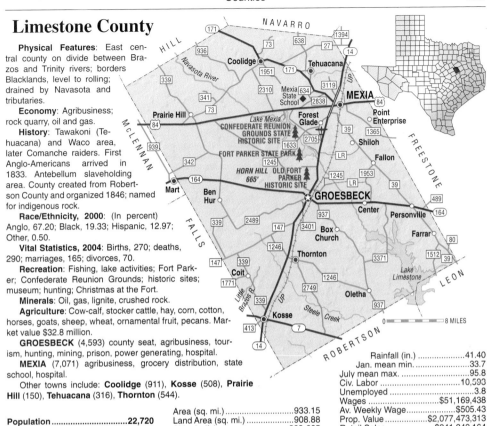

Population	22,720
Change fm 2000	3.0

Area (sq. mi.)	933.15
Land Area (sq. mi.)	908.88
Altitude (ft.)	363-665

Rainfall (in.)	41.40
Jan. mean min.	33.7
July mean max.	95.8
Civ. Labor	10,593
Unemployed	3.8
Wages	$51,169,438
Av. Weekly Wage	$505.43
Prop. Value	$2,077,473,313
Retail Sales	$241,842,164

Lipscomb County

Physical Features: High Plains, broken in east; drains to tributaries of Canadian, Wolf Creek; sandy loam, black soils.

Economy: Oil, gas operations; agribusinesses; government/services.

History: Apaches, later Kiowas and Comanches who were driven into Indian Territory in 1875. Ranching began in late 1870s. County created 1876 from Bexar District; organized 1887; named for A.S. Lipscomb, Republic of Texas leader.

Race/Ethnicity, 2000: (In percent) Anglo, 77.46; Black, 0.46; Hispanic, 20.71; Other, 1.37.

Vital Statistics, 2004: Births, 41; deaths, 39; marriages, 60; divorces, 11.

Recreation: Hunting; Wolf Creek museum.

Minerals: Oil, natural gas.

Agriculture: Cattle, silage, hogs, wheat, dairies, corn, hay. Some 19,000 acres irrigated. Market value $42.3 million.

LIPSCOMB (42), county seat; livestock center.

BOOKER (1,365, partly in Ochiltree County) trade center, library.

Other towns include: **Darrouzett** (293) Deutsches Fest in July; **Follett** (406); **Higgins** (406) library, Will Rogers Day in August .

Population	3,114
Change fm 2000	1.9
Area (sq. mi.)	932.22
Land Area (sq. mi.)	932.11
Altitude (ft.)	2,300-2,837
Rainfall (in.)	22.57
Jan. mean min.	16.2

July mean max.	94.2
Civ. Labor	1,727
Unemployed	2.9
Wages	$11,900,751
Av. Weekly Wage	$659.22
Prop. Value	$767,012,579
Retail Sales	$17,470,336

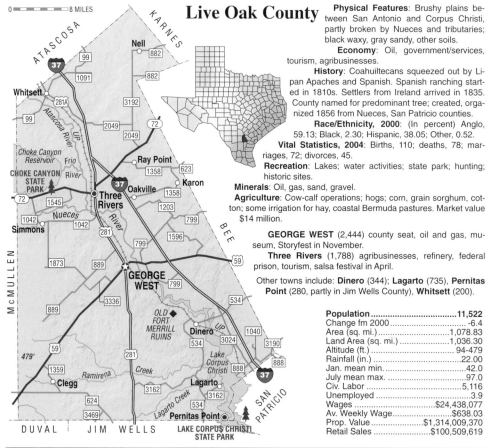

Live Oak County

0 ▭▬▬▬▬▭ 8 MILES

Physical Features: Brushy plains between San Antonio and Corpus Christi, partly broken by Nueces and tributaries; black waxy, gray sandy, other soils.

Economy: Oil, government/services, tourism, agribusinesses.

History: Coahuiltecans squeezed out by Lipan Apaches and Spanish. Spanish ranching started in 1810s. Settlers from Ireland arrived in 1835. County named for predominant tree; created, organized 1856 from Nueces, San Patricio counties.

Race/Ethnicity, 2000: (In percent) Anglo, 59.13; Black, 2.30; Hispanic, 38.05; Other, 0.52.

Vital Statistics, 2004: Births, 110; deaths, 78; marriages, 72; divorces, 45.

Recreation: Lakes; water activities; state park; hunting; historic sites.

Minerals: Oil, gas, sand, gravel.

Agriculture: Cow-calf operations; hogs; corn, grain sorghum, cotton; some irrigation for hay, coastal Bermuda pastures. Market value $14 million.

GEORGE WEST (2,444) county seat, oil and gas, museum, Storyfest in November.

Three Rivers (1,788) agribusinesses, refinery, federal prison, tourism, salsa festival in April.

Other towns include: **Dinero** (344); **Lagarto** (735), **Pernitas Point** (280, partly in Jim Wells County), **Whitsett** (200).

Population	11,522
Change fm 2000	-6.4
Area (sq. mi.)	1,078.83
Land Area (sq. mi.)	1,036.30
Altitude (ft.)	94-479
Rainfall (in.)	22.00
Jan. mean min.	42.0
July mean max.	97.0
Civ. Labor	5,116
Unemployed	3.9
Wages	$24,438,077
Av. Weekly Wage	$638.03
Prop. Value	$1,314,009,370
Retail Sales	$100,509,619

The road into Mentone in Loving County, Texas' least populous county. Robert Plocheck photo.

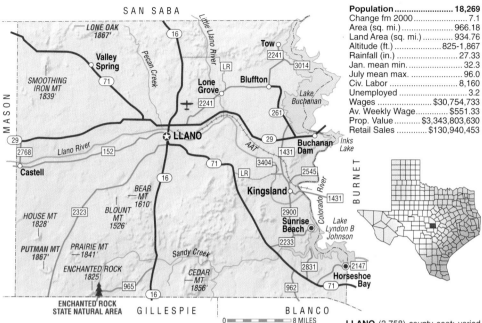

Population **18,269**
Change fm 2000 .... 7.1
Area (sq. mi.) 966.18
Land Area (sq. mi.) 934.76
Altitude (ft.) 825-1,867
Rainfall (in.) 27.33
Jan. mean min. 32.3
July mean max. 96.0
Civ. Labor 8,160
Unemployed 3.2
Wages $30,754,733
Av. Weekly Wage............. $551.33
Prop. Value $3,343,803,630
Retail Sales $130,940,453

Llano County

Physical Features: Central county drains to Colorado, Llano rivers; rolling to hilly; Highland lakes.

Economy: Tourism, retirement, ranch trading center, vineyards.

History: Tonkawas, later Comanches. Anglo-American and German settlers arrived in 1840s. County name is Spanish for plains; created, organized 1856 from Bexar District, Gillespie County.

Race/Ethnicity, 2000: (In percent) Anglo, 93.74; Black, 0.34; Hispanic, 5.13; Other, 0.79.

Vital Statistics, 2004: Births, 144; deaths, 273; marriages, 103; divorces, 95.

Recreation: Leading deer-hunting county; fishing; lake activities; major tourist area; Enchanted Rock; bluebonnet festival; Hill Country Wine Trail in spring.

Minerals: Granite, vermiculite, llanite.

Agriculture: Beef cattle, sheep, goats. Market value $11.8 million. Deer-hunting, wildlife leases.

LLANO (3,758) county seat; varied manufacturing; hunting center; government/services; livestock trading; hospital; historic district; museum; Heritage Day festival in October.

Kingsland (4,605) tourism, retirement community, fishing and water sports; metal fabrication; wood work; library; AquaBoom on July 4.

Other towns include: **Bluffton** (75); **Buchanan Dam** (1,729) hydroelectric industry, tourism; **Castell** (72); **Horseshoe Bay** (3,359, partly in Burnet County); **Sunrise Beach** (751); **Tow** (305); **Valley Spring** (50).

Loving County

Physical Features: Western county of dry, rolling prairies; slopes to Pecos River; Red Bluff Reservoir; sandy, loam, clay soils.

Economy: Petroleum operations; cattle.

History: Land developers began operations in late 19th century. Oil discovered in 1925. County created 1887 from Tom Green County; organized 1931, last county organized. Named for Oliver Loving, trail driver. Loving is Texas' least populous county.

Race/Ethnicity, 2000: (In percent) Anglo, 89.55; Black, 0.00; Hispanic, 10.45; Other, 0.00.

Vital Statistics, 2004: Births, 0; deaths, 0; marriages, 4; divorces, 0.

Recreation: NA.

Minerals: Oil, gas.

Agriculture: Some cattle. Market value $523,000.

MENTONE (20) county seat, oil-field supply center; only town.

For explanation of sources, abbreviations and symbols, see p. 224 and foldout map.

Population **60**
Change fm 2000 .... -10.4
Area (sq. mi.) 676.85
Land Area (sq. mi.) 673.08
Altitude (ft.) 2,685-3,311
Rainfall (in.) 9.10
Jan. mean min. 28.0
July mean max. 96.0
Civ. Labor 35
Unemployed 11.4
Wages $302,691
Av. Weekly Wage......... $831.57
Prop. Value $333,798,100
Retail Sales $0

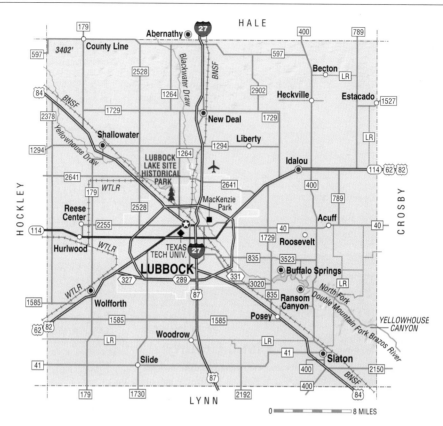

Lubbock County

Physical Features: High Plains of West Texas, broken by 1,500 playas, upper Brazos River tributaries; rich soils with underground water.

Economy: Among world's largest cottonseed processing centers; a leading agribusiness center; cattle feedlots; manufacturing; higher education center; medical center; government/services.

History: Evidence of human habitation for 12,000 years. In historic period, Apache Indians, followed by Comanche hunters. Sheep raisers from Midwest arrived in late 1870s. Cotton farms brought in Mexican laborers in 1940s-60s. County named for Col. Tom S. Lubbock, an organizer of Confederate Terry's Rangers; county created 1876 from Bexar District; organized 1891.

Race/Ethnicity, 2000: (In percent) Anglo, 63.06; Black, 7.71; Hispanic, 27.45; Other, 1.78.

Vital Statistics, 2004: Births, 4,049; deaths, 1,898; marriages, 2,160; divorces, 1,127.

Recreation: Lubbock Lake archaeological site; Texas Tech events;

civic center; Buddy Holly statue, Walk of Fame, festival in September; planetarium; Ranching Heritage Center; Panhandle-South Plains Fair; wine festivals; Buffalo Springs Lake.

Minerals: Oil, gas, stone, sand and gravel.

Agriculture: A leading cotton-producing county. Fed beef, cow-calf operations; poultry, eggs; hogs. Other crops, nursery, grain sorghum, wheat, sunflowers, soybeans, hay, vegetables; more than 230,000 acres irrigated, mostly cotton. Market value $143.6 million.

Education: Texas Tech University with law and medical schools; Lubbock Christian University; South Plains College branch; Wayland Baptist University off-campus center.

LUBBOCK (209,972) county seat; center for large agricultural area; manufacturing includes electronics, earth-moving equipment, food containers, fire-protection equipment, clothing, other products; distribution

center for South Plains; feedlots; museum; government/services; hospitals, psychiatric hospital; state school for retarded; wind power center.

Other towns include: **Buffalo Springs** (475); **Idalou** (2,135); **New Deal** (784); **Ransom Canyon** (1,074); **Shallowater** (2,279); **Slaton** (5,918) agribusiness, government/services, varied manufacturing, railroad, Harvey House museum, sausagefest in October; **Wolfforth** (3,073) retail, government/services, harvest festival in September.

Also, part of **Abernathy** (2,798).

Population	254,862
Change fm 2000	5.0
Area (sq. mi.)	900.70
Land Area (sq. mi.)	899.49
Altitude (ft.)	2,900-3,402
Rainfall (in.)	18.69
Jan. mean min.	24.4
July mean max.	91.9
Civ. Labor	141,383
Unemployed	3.1
Wages	$938,128,767
Av. Weekly Wage	$592.04
Prop. Value	$11,845,589,905
Retail Sales	$5,268,311,025

For explanation of sources, abbreviations and symbols, see p. 224 and foldout map.

Lynn County

Physical Features: South High Plains, broken by Caprock Escarpment, playas, draws; sandy loam, black, gray soils.

Economy: Agribusiness.

History: Apaches, ousted by Comanches who were removed to Indian Territory in 1875. Ranching began in 1880s. Farming developed after 1900. County created 1876 from Bexar District; organized 1903; named for Alamo victim W. Lynn.

Race/Ethnicity,2000: (In percent) Anglo, 51.95; Black, 2.63; Hispanic, 44.63; Other, 0.79.

Vital Statistics, 2004: Births, 86; deaths, 51; marriages, 37; divorces, 19.

Recreation: Pioneer museum in Tahoka; Dan Blocker museum in O'Donnell; sandhill crane migration in winter.

Minerals: Oil, natural gas, stone.

Agriculture: Cotton produces largest income; 77,000 acres irrigated. Market value $48.9 million.

TAHOKA (2,794) county seat; agricultural center; electric/telephone cooperatives; hospital; museum; Harvest Festival in the fall.

O'Donnell (962, partly in Dawson County) commercial center.

Other towns include: **New Home** (356); **Wilson** (507).

Population **6,212**	July mean max. 92.2
Change fm 2000 .... -5.2	Civ. Labor 2,719
Area (sq. mi.) 893.46	Unemployed 4.8
Land Area (sq. mi.) 891.88	Wages $8,626,413
Altitude (ft.) 2,800-3,300	Av. Weekly Wage............. $477.39
Rainfall (in.) 20.48	Prop. Value $416,371,060
Jan. mean min. 25.1	Retail Sales $19,303,308

The Ranching Heritage Center in Lubbock. Sophia Dembling photo.

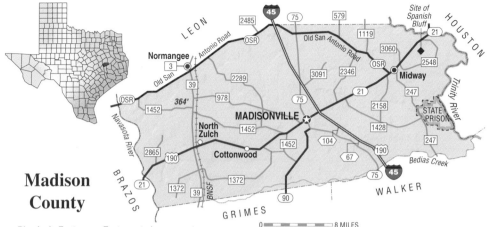

Madison County

Physical Features: East central county; hilly, draining to Trinity, Navasota rivers, Bedias Creek; one-fifth of area timbered; alluvial, loam, sandy soils.

Economy: Prison; government/services; varied manufacturing; agribusinesses; oil production.

History: Caddo and Bidai Indian area; Kickapoos migrated from east. Spanish settlements established in 1774 and 1805. Anglo-Americans arrived in 1829. Census of 1860 showed 30 percent of population was black. County named for U.S. President James Madison; created from Grimes, Leon, Walker counties 1853; organized 1854.

Race/Ethnicity, 2000: (In percent) Anglo, 60.72; Black, 22.76; Hispanic, 15.78; Other, 0.74.

Vital Statistics, 2004: Births, 145; deaths, 142; marriages, 89; divorces, 33.

Recreation: Fishing, hunting; Spanish Bluff where survivors of the Gutíerrez-Magee expedition were executed in 1813; other historic sites.

Minerals: sand, oil.

Agriculture: Nursery crops, cattle, horses, poultry raised; forage for livestock. Market value $60.6 million.

MADISONVILLE (4,393) county seat; farm-trade center; varied manufacturing; hospital; library; Spring Fling in April.

Other towns, **Midway** (291); **Normangee** (767, mostly in Leon County); **North Zulch** (150).

Population	13,310
Change fm 2000	2.9
Area (sq. mi.)	472.44
Land Area (sq. mi.)	469.65
Altitude (ft.)	150-364
Rainfall (in.)	44.00
Jan. mean min.	35.8
July mean max.	96.0
Civ. Labor	4,908
Unemployed	4.5
Wages	$26,588,266
Av. Weekly Wage	$522.73
Prop. Value	$871,065,511
Retail Sales	$157,628,580

For explanation of sources, symbols and abbreviations, see p. 224 and foldout map.

The Excelsior Hotel in Jefferson. Marion County Chamber of Commerce photo.

Marion County

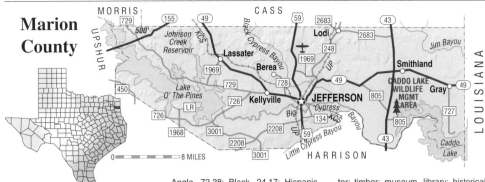

Physical Features: Northeastern county; hilly, three-quarters forested with pines, hardwoods; drains to Caddo Lake, Lake O' the Pines, Cypress Bayou.

Economy: Forestry, tourism, food processing.

History: Caddoes forced out in 1790s. Kickapoo in area when settlers arrived from Deep South around 1840. Antebellum slaveholding area. County created 1860 from Cass County; named for Gen. Francis Marion of American Revolution.

Race/Ethnicity, 2000: (In percent) Anglo, 72.38; Black, 24.17; Hispanic, 2.40; Other, 1.05.

Vital Statistics, 2004: Births, 121; deaths, 127; marriages, 90; divorces, 50.

Recreation: Lake activities; hunting; Excelsior Hotel; 84 medallions on historic sites including Jay Gould railroad car; museum; Mardi Gras; historical homes tour in May with Civil War reenactment.

Minerals: Iron ore.

Agriculture: Hay, cattle. Market value $4.1 million. Forestry is most important industry.

JEFFERSON (1,984) county seat; tourism; board plant; agriculture center; timber; museum, library; historical sites.

Other towns include: **Lodi** (175).

Population	10,970
Change fm 2000	0.3
Area (sq. mi.)	420.36
Land Area (sq. mi.)	381.21
Altitude (ft.)	168-500
Rainfall (in.)	49.26
Jan. mean min.	31.4
July mean max.	93.1
Civ. Labor	5,157
Unemployed	4.3
Wages	$12,863,354
Av. Weekly Wage	$521.33
Prop. Value	$635,981,850
Retail Sales	$74,485,761

Martin County

Physical Features: Western county on South Plains; sandy, loam soils, broken by playas, creeks.

Economy: Petroleum production, agribusiness.

History: Apaches, ousted by Comanches who in turn were forced out by U.S. Army 1875. Farming began in 1881. County created from Bexar District 1876; organized 1884; named for Wylie Martin, senator of Republic of Texas.

Race/Ethnicity, 2000: (In percent) Anglo, 57.37; Black, 1.73; Hispanic, 40.56; Other, 0.34.

Vital Statistics, 2004: Births, 66; deaths, 57; marriages, 32; divorces, 12.

Recreation: Museum, settlers reunion, restored monastery.

Minerals: Oil, gas.

Agriculture: Cotton, milo, wheat; beef cattle, horses, meat goats, sheep raised. Market value $14.1 million.

STANTON (2,500) county seat; farm, ranch, oil center; varied manufacturing; electric co-op; communting to Midland, Big Spring; hospital, restored convent, other historic buildings; Old Sorehead trade days April, June, October.

Other towns include: **Ackerly** (244, partly in Dawson County); **Lenorah** (83); **Tarzan** (30). A small part of **Midland**.

Population	4,441
Change fm 2000	-6.4
Area (sq. mi.)	915.62
Land Area (sq. mi.)	914.78
Altitude (ft.)	2,500-2,900
Rainfall (in.)	18.20
Jan. mean min.	30.0
July mean max.	94.0
Civ. Labor	2,106
Unemployed	3.5
Wages	$9,795,512
Av. Weekly Wage	$589.13
Prop. Value	$907,481,366
Retail Sales	$37,375,047

The Brandenberger Ranch, one of many stone houses in Mason County. Robert Plocheck photo.

Mason County

Physical Features: Central county; hilly, draining to Llano and San Saba rivers and their tributaries; limestone, red soils; varied timber.

Economy: Nature tourism, agriculture.

History: Lipan Apaches, driven south by Comanches around 1790. German settlers arrived in mid-1840s, followed by Anglo-Americans. Mexican immigration increased after 1930. County created from Bexar, Gillespie counties 1858; named for Mexican War victim U.S. Army Lt. G.T. Mason.

Race/Ethnicity, 2000: (In percent) Anglo, 78.25; Black, 0.16; Hispanic, 20.95; Other, 0.64.

Vital Statistics, 2004: Births, 33; deaths, 53; marriages, 21; divorces, 20.

Recreation: Hunting of deer, turkey, hogs, dove; river fishing; camping; historic homes of stone; Fort Mason, where Robert E. Lee served; wildflower drives in spring.

Minerals: Topaz, sand.

Agriculture: Cattle, goats, hay, sheep. Market value $44.8 million. Hunting leases important.

MASON (2,230) county seat; ranching center; camping; tourism; museum; historical district, homes, rock fences built by German settlers; wild game dinner in November.

Other towns include: **Art** (14), **Fredonia** (55), **Pontotoc** (125).

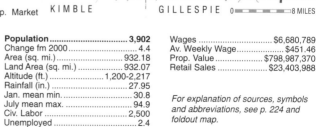

Population	3,902
Change fm 2000	4.4
Area (sq. mi.)	932.18
Land Area (sq. mi.)	932.07
Altitude (ft.)	1,200-2,217
Rainfall (in.)	27.95
Jan. mean min.	30.8
July mean max.	94.9
Civ. Labor	2,500
Unemployed	2.4

Wages	$6,680,789
Av. Weekly Wage	$451.46
Prop. Value	$798,987,370
Retail Sales	$23,403,988

For explanation of sources, symbols and abbreviations, see p. 224 and foldout map.

Matagorda County

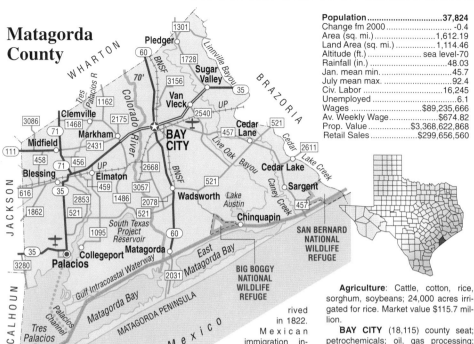

Pledger

WHARTON
BRAZORIA
JACKSON
CALHOUN

1301
60
1728
Sugar Valley
3156
Van Vleck
1162
Clemville
1468
3086
Markham
71
Midfield
2431
111
458
456
Blessing
71
616
35
1862
521
2853
1486
521
1095
Collegeport
Palacios
3280
2175
UP
Elmaton
459
2078
South Texas Project Reservoir
Matagorda
60
2031
East Matagorda Bay

35
2540
Cedar Lane
521
457
BAY CITY
2611
Live Oak Bayou
Cedar Lake
Caney Creek
Sargent
457
Wadsworth Lake Austin
Chinquapin
2668
3057
521

Tres Palacios R
Colorado River
70'
UP
BNSF
Linnville Bayou
Cedar Lake Creek
BNSF
Lake Creek

SAN BERNARD NATIONAL WILDLIFE REFUGE

Gulf Intracoastal Waterway
Palacios Channel
Tres Palacios Bay
Matagorda Bay
MATAGORDA PENINSULA
Port Lavaca Ship Channel
Gulf of Mexico

BIG BOGGY NATIONAL WILDLIFE REFUGE

0 ——— 8 MILES

Population	37,824
Change fm 2000	-0.4
Area (sq. mi.)	1,612.19
Land Area (sq. mi.)	1,114.46
Altitude (ft.)	sea level-70
Rainfall (in.)	48.03
Jan. mean min.	45.7
July mean max.	92.4
Civ. Labor	16,245
Unemployed	6.1
Wages	$89,235,666
Av. Weekly Wage	$674.82
Prop. Value	$3,368,622,868
Retail Sales	$299,656,560

Physical Features: Gulf Coast county; flat, broken by bays; contains part of Matagorda Island; many different soils; drains to Colorado River, creeks, coast.

Economy: Nuclear power plant, petrochemicals, agribusiness.

History: Karankawa Indian area, Tonkawas later. Anglo-Americans arrived in 1822. Mexican immigration increased after 1920. An original county, created 1836 from Spanish municipality, named for canebrake; organized 1837; settled by Austin colonists.

Race/Ethnicity, 2000: (In percent) Anglo, 53.00; Black, 12.84; Hispanic, 31.35; Other, 2.81.

Vital Statistics, 2004: Births, 587; deaths, 316; marriages, 284; divorces, 150.

Recreation: Fishing, water sports, hunting, birding; historic sites, museums; Bay City rice festival in October.

Minerals: Oil and gas.

Agriculture: Cattle, cotton, rice, sorghum, soybeans; 24,000 acres irrigated for rice. Market value $115.7 million.

BAY CITY (18,115) county seat; petrochemicals; oil, gas processing; nuclear power plant; commercial fishing; hospital.

Palacios (5,242) tourism; seafood industry; hospital; Marine Education Center; Bay Festival Labor Day; public fishing piers.

Other towns include: **Blessing** (835) historic sites; **Cedar Lane** (300); **Collegeport** (80); **Elmaton** (160); **Markham** (1,080); **Matagorda** (710); **Midfield** (305); **Pledger** (265); **Sargent** (900) retirement community, fishing, birding, commercial fishing; **Van Vleck** (1,342); **Wadsworth** (160).

Boaters on Caney Creek in Sargent. Robert Plocheck photo.

Maverick County

Physical Features: Southwestern county on Rio Grande; broken, rolling surface, with dense brush; clay, sandy, alluvial soils.

Economy: Oil, government/services, agribusiness, tourism.

History: Coahuiltecan Indian area; later Comanches in area. Spanish ranching began in 1760s. First Anglo-Americans arrived in 1834. County named for Sam A. Maverick, whose name is now a synonym for unbranded cattle; created 1856 from Kinney County; organized 1871.

Race/Ethnicity, 2000: (In percent) Anglo, 3.54; Black, 0.12; Hispanic, 95.01; Other, 1.33.

Vital Statistics, 2004: Births, 1,093; deaths, 241; marriages, 522; divorces, 84.

Recreation: Tourist gateway to Mexico; white-tailed deer, bird hunting; fishing; historic sites, Fort Duncan museum.

Minerals: Oil, gas, sand, gravel.

Agriculture: Cattle feedlots; pecans, vegetables, sorghum, wheat; goats, sheep. Some irrigation from Rio Grande. Market value $34.7 million.

EAGLE PASS (25,440) county seat; government/services; retail center; tourism; hospital, junior college, Sul Ross college campus; entry point to Piedras Negras, Mex., Nacho Festival in Piedras Negras in October.

Other communities include: **Eidson Road** (9,861), **El Indio** (277), **Las Quintas Fronterizas** (2,141), **Rosita North** (3,591); **Rosita South** (2,709), all immediately south of Eagle Pass.

Also, **Elm Creek** (2,045) and **Quemado** (260).

Population	**52,298**
Change fm 2000	10.6
Area (sq. mi.)	1,291.74
Land Area (sq. mi.)	1,280.08
Altitude (ft.)	600-958
Rainfall (in.)	21.48
Jan. mean min.	40.1
July mean max.	98.1
Civ. Labor	20,116
Unemployed	13.5
Wages	$83,785,283
Av. Weekly Wage	$459.58
Prop. Value	$1,843,269,048
Retail Sales	$500,818,963

McCulloch County

Physical Features: Central county; hilly and rolling; drains to Colorado, Brady Creek and Lake, San Saba River; black loams to sandy soils.

Economy: Agribusiness; manufacturing; tourism; hunting leases.

History: Apache area. First Anglo-American settlers arrived in late 1850s, but Comanche raids delayed further settlement until 1870s. County created from Bexar District 1856; organized 1876; named for San Jacinto veteran Gen. Ben McCulloch.

Race/Ethnicity, 2000: (In percent) Anglo, 70.93; Black, 1.52; Hispanic, 27.04; Other, 0.51.

Vital Statistics, 2004: Births, 93; deaths, 118; marriages, 61; divorces, 17

Recreation: Hunting; lake activities; museum, restored Santa Fe depot, goat cookoff on Labor Day, muzzle-loading rifle association state championship; rodeos; golf, tennis tournaments.

Minerals: Sand, gravel, gas and oil.

Agriculture: Beef cattle provide most income; wheat, sheep, goats, hay, cotton, sorghum, hogs, dairy cattle; some irrigation for peanuts. Market value $13 million.

BRADY (5,514) county seat; silica sand, oil-field equipment, ranching, tourism, other manufacturing; hospital; Heart of Texas car show in April, Cinco de Mayo.

Other towns: **Doole** (74), **Lohn** (149), **Melvin** (148), **Mercury** (166), **Rochelle** (163) and **Voca** (56).

Population	**8,016**
Change fm 2000	-2.3
Area (sq. mi.)	1,073.35
Land Area (sq. mi.)	1,069.31
Altitude (ft.)	1,300-2,021
Rainfall (in.)	27.63
Jan. mean min.	32.3
July mean max.	94.5
Civ. Labor	3,825
Unemployed	3.6
Wages	$19,201,199
Av. Weekly Wage	$529.33
Prop. Value	$764,985,000
Retail Sales	$127,417,619

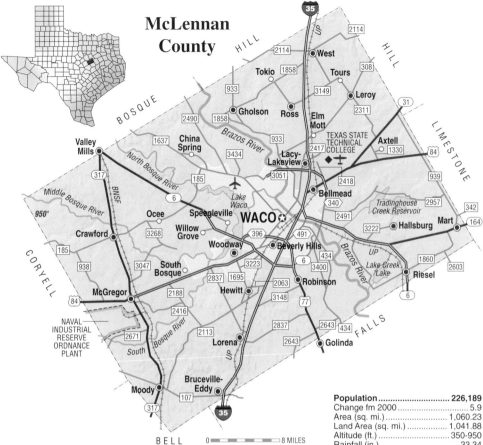

McLennan County

Population 226,189
Change fm 2000 .... 5.9
Area (sq. mi.) 1,060.23
Land Area (sq. mi.) 1,041.88
Altitude (ft.) 350-950
Rainfall (in.) 33.34
Jan. mean min. 35.1
July mean max. 96.7
Civ. Labor 116,240
Unemployed 3.7
Wages $842,917,916
Av. Weekly Wage.................... $632.11
Prop. Value $10,799,530,805
Retail Sales $2,847,867,847

Physical Features: Central Texas county of mostly Blackland prairie, but rolling hills in west; drains to Bosque, Brazos rivers and Lake Waco; heavy, loam, sandy soils.

Economy: A leading distribution, government center for Central Texas; diversified manufacturing; agribusiness; education; health care.

History: Tonkawas, Wichitas and Wacos in area. Anglo-American settlers arrived in 1840s. Indians removed to Brazos reservations in 1854. County created from Milam County in 1850; named for settler, Neil McLennan Sr.

Race/Ethnicity, 2000: (In percent) Anglo, 65.19; Black, 15.33; Hispanic, 17.91; Other, 1.57.

Vital Statistics, 2004: Births, 3,264; deaths, 1,956; marriages, 2,032; divorces, 987.

Recreation: Varied metropolitan activies; Texas Ranger Hall of Fame; Texas Sports Hall of Fame; Dr Pepper Museum; Cameron Park; drag boat races April and May; zoo; historic sites, homes; museums; libraries, art center; symphony; civic theater; Baylor University events; Heart o' Texas Fair in October.

Minerals: Sand and gravel, limestone, oil, gas.

Agriculture: Poultry, beef cattle, corn, wheat, hay, grain sorghum, soybeans, dairy cattle. Market value $61.1 million.

Education: Baylor University; community college; Texas State Technical College.

WACO (119,641) county seat; education, government/services; varied manufacturing; hospitals; riverside park, zoo.

Hewitt (12,686) iron works, other manufacturing; hamburger cookoff.

West (2,672) famous for Czech foods; varied manufacturing; Westfest Labor Day weekend.

Other towns include: **Axtell** (300); **Bellmead** (9,291); **Beverly Hills** (2,055); **Bruceville-Eddy** (1,568, partly in Falls County); **China Spring** (1,000); **Crawford** (749); **Elm Mott** (300); **Gholson** (958); **Hallsburg** (526); **Lacy-Lakeview** (5,914); **Leroy** (336); **Lorena** (1,621); **Mart** (2,402) agricultural center, some manufacturing, museum, juvenile correction facility; **McGregor** (4,836) agriculture, manufacturing, distribution; private telephone museum; Frontier Founders Day in September; **Moody** (1,430) agriculture, commuting to Waco, Temple; library; Cotton Harvest fest in September; **Riesel** (1,007); **Robinson** (8,611); **Ross** (235); **Woodway** (8,532).

Part of **Golinda** (451, mostly in Falls County) and part of **Valley Mills** (1,174, mostly in Bosque County).

For explanation of sources, abbreviations and symbols, see p. 224 and foldout map.

McMullen County

Physical Features: Southern county of brushy plain, sloping to Frio, Nueces rivers and tributaries; saline clay soils.

Economy: Livestock, hunting leases, oil and gas, government/services.

History: Coahuiltecans, squeezed out by Lipan Apaches and other tribes. Anglo-American settlers arrived in 1858. Sheep ranching of 1870s attracted Mexican laborers. County created from Atascosa, Bexar, Live Oak counties 1858; organized 1862, reorganized 1877; named for Nueces River pioneer-empresario John McMullen.

Race/Ethnicity, 2000: (In percent) Anglo, 65.44; Black, 1.18; Hispanic, 33.14; Other, 0.24.

Vital Statistics, 2004: Births, 7; deaths, 6; marriages, 1; divorces, 2.

Recreation: Hunting, wildlife viewing; lake activities, state park; Labor Day rodeo; Dogtown Days festival in October.

Minerals: Gas, oil, lignite coal, zeolite-kaline.

Agriculture: Beef cattle, hay, grain sorghum. Market value $6.4 million. Wildlife enterprises important.

TILDEN (300), county seat; oil, gas, lignite mining; ranch center; government/services. Other towns include: **Calliham** (100).

Population	913
Change fm 2000	7.3
Area (sq. mi.)	1,142.60
Land Area (sq. mi.)	1,113.00
Altitude (ft.)	200-642
Rainfall (in.)	23.87
Jan. mean min.	40.1
July mean max.	98.7
Civ. Labor	370
Unemployed	4.3
Wages	$1,592,769
Av. Weekly Wage	$619.83
Prop. Value	$748,381,613
Retail Sales	$5,030,660

Medina County

Physical Features: Southwestern county with scenic hills in north; south has fertile valleys, rolling surface; Medina River, Lake.

Economy: Agribusinesses; tourism; varied manufacturing; commuters to San Antonio; government/services.

History: Lipan Apaches and Comanches. Settled by Alsatians led by Henri Castro in 1844. Mexican immigration increased after 1900. County created 1848 from Bexar; named for river, probably for Spanish engineer Pedro Medina.

Race/Ethnicity, 2000: (In percent) Anglo, 51.44; Black, 2.13; Hispanic, 45.47; Other, 0.96.

Vital Statistics, 2004: Births, 574; deaths, 341; marriages, 235; divorces, 115.

Recreation: A leading deer area; scenic drives; camping, fishing; historic buildings, museum; market trail days most months.

Minerals: Oil, gas, clay, sand, gravel.

Agriculture: Most income from cattle; crops include corn, grains, peanuts, hay, vegetables; 40,000 acres irrigated. Market value $60.7 million.

HONDO (8,988) county seat; Air Force screening center; aerospace industry; agribusiness; varied manufacturing; hunting leases; hospital; prisons.

Castroville (2,863) farm, ranch center; tourism; government/services; commuting to San Antonio; Landmark Inn; St. Louis Day celebration in August.

Devine (4,248) commuters, shipping for truck crop-livestock; fall festival in October.

Other towns: **D'Hanis** (575), **La Coste** (1,368), **Natalia** (1,895), **Riomedina** (60), **Yancey** (209). Also, **Lytle** (2,498, mostly in Atascosa County).

Population	43,913
Change fm 2000	11.7
Area (sq. mi.)	1,334.53
Land Area (sq. mi.)	1,327.76
Altitude (ft.)	635-1,995
Rainfall (in.)	26.30
Jan. mean min.	38.0
July mean max.	95.0
Civ. Labor	20,219
Unemployed	3.7
Wages	$52,562,130
Av. Weekly Wage	$487.80
Prop. Value	$2,671,707,026
Retail Sales	$383,058,284

Menard County

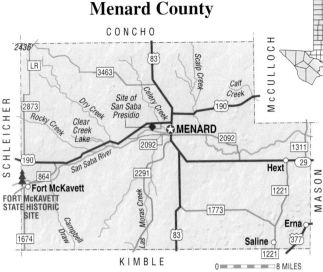

CONCHO

CO N C H O

SCHLEICHER

McCULLOCH

MASON

KIMBLE

2436

LR

3463

2873

Rocky Creek

Dry Creek

Clear Creek Lake

Site of San Saba Presidio

Celery Creek

Scalp Creek

Calf Creek

83

190

★ MENARD

2092

2092

2092

1311

Hext

29

864

190

San Saba River

Fort McKavett

FORT McKAVETT STATE HISTORIC SITE

2291

Moras Creek

1221

1773

Erna

1674

Campbell Draw

Las

83

Saline

1221

377

0 ▬▬▬▬ 8 MILES

Physical Features: West central county of rolling topography, draining to San Saba River and tributaries; limestone soils.

Economy: Agribusiness; tourism; oil, gas production.

History: Apaches, followed by Comanches in 18th century. Mission Santa Cruz de San Sabá established in 1757. A few Anglo-American and German settlers arrived in 1840s. County created from Bexar County in 1858, organized 1871; named for Galveston's founder, Michel B. Menard.

Race/Ethnicity, 2000: (In percent) Anglo, 66.83; Black, 0.42; Hispanic, 31.69; Other, 1.06.

Vital Statistics, 2004: Births, 26; deaths, 31; marriages, 7; divorces, 6.

Recreation: Hunting, fishing; historic sites, including Spanish presidio, mission, irrigation ditches; U.S. fort; museum; Jim Bowie days in September.

Minerals: Oil, gas.

Agriculture: Sheep, goats, cattle, pecans, wheat, alfalfa. Market value $7.4 million.

Population	**2,210**
Change fm 2000	-6.4
Area (sq. mi.)	902.25
Land Area (sq. mi.)	901.91
Altitude (ft.)	1,690-2,436
Rainfall (in.)	24.90
Jan. mean min.	30.7
July mean max.	94.8
Civ. Labor	1,132

Unemployed	3.5
Wages	$2,758,712
Av. Weekly Wage	$404.72
Prop. Value	$483,546,820
Retail Sales	$12,117,107

For explanation of sources, symbols and abbreviations, see p. 224 and foldout map.

MENARD (1,611) county seat; ranching center, tourism. Other towns include: **Fort McKavett** (50); **Hext** (75).

Prickly pear cactus in the brush country of McMullen County in South Texas. Robert Plocheck photo.

Midland County

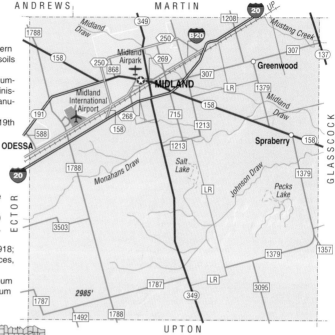

Physical Features: Flat western county, broken by draws; sandy, loam soils with native grasses.

Economy: Among leading petroleum-producing counties; distribution, administrative center for oil industry; varied manufacturing; government/services.

History: Comanches in area in 19th century. Sheep ranching developed in 1880s. Permian Basin oil boom began in 1920s. County created from Tom Green County 1885; name came from midway location on railroad between El Paso and Fort Worth. Chihuahua Trail and Emigrant Road were pioneer trails that crossed county.

Race/Ethnicity, 2000: (In percent) Anglo, 62.54; Black, 7.05; Hispanic, 29.03; Other, 1.38.

Vital Statistics, 2004: Births, 1,918; deaths, 905; marriages, 939; divorces, 527.

Recreation: Permian Basin Petroleum Museum, Library, Hall of Fame; Museum of Southwest; Commemorative Air Force and Museum; community theater; metropolitan events; homes of Presidents Bush.

Minerals: Oil, natural gas.

Agriculture: Beef cattle, horses, sheep and goats; cotton, hay, pecans; 20,000 acres irrigated. Market value $7.4 million.

MIDLAND (100,193) county seat; petroleum, petrochemical center; varied manufacturing; livestock sale center; hospitals; cultural activities; community college; Celebration of the Arts in May; polo club, Texas League baseball.

Part [1,042] of **Odessa**.

Population 124,380
Change fm 2000 .... 7.2
Area (sq. mi.) 901.97
Land Area (sq. mi.) 900.25
Altitude (ft.) 2,600-2,985
Rainfall (in.) 14.80

Jan. mean min. 29.6
July mean max. 94.3
Civ. Labor 71,390
Unemployed 2.7
Wages $625,392,688
Av. Weekly Wage $765.77
Prop. Value $6,901,536,840
Retail Sales $2,217,121,707

For explanation of sources, symbols and abbreviations, see p. 224 and foldout map.

Oil tanks in the Permian Basin fields northwest of Midland. Smiley N. Pool photo.

Milam County

Physical Features: East central county of partly level Blackland; southeast rolling to Post Oak Belt; Brazos, Little rivers.

Economy: Aluminum manufacturing; other varied manufacturing; lignite mining; agribusiness.

History: Lipan Apaches, Tonkawas and Comanches in area. Mission San Francisco Xavier established in 1745-48. Anglo-American settlers arrived in 1834. County created 1836 from municipality named for Ben Milam, a leader who died at the battle for San Antonio in December 1835; organized 1837.

Race/Ethnicity, 2000: (In percent) Anglo, 69.64; Black, 11.01; Hispanic 18.63; Other, 0.72.

Vital Statistics, 2004: Births, 396; deaths, 283; marriages, 173; divorces, 89.

Recreation: Fishing, hunting; historic sites include Fort Sullivan, Indian battlegrounds, mission sites; museum in old jail at Cameron.

Minerals: Large lignite deposits; limited oil, natural gas production.

Agriculture: Cattle, poultry, hay, corn, sorghum, cotton. Market value $72.4 million.

CAMERON (5,823) county seat; government/services; manufacturing; hospital; library; restored courthouse; dewberry festival in April.

ROCKDALE (5,688) aluminum plant, government/services; hospital; juvenile detention center.

Other towns include: **Buckholts** (426); **Burlington** (100); **Davilla** (191); **Gause** (425); **Milano** (421); **Thorndale** (1,426) market center.

Population 25,286
Change fm 2000 ....4.3

Area (sq. mi.)......................1,021.67
Land Area (sq. mi.) 1,016.71
Altitude (ft.) 250-648
Rainfall (in.) 35.52
Jan. mean min. 39.2
July mean max. 95.7
Civ. Labor 12,278
Unemployed 3.6
Wages $69,126,608
Av. Weekly Wage................$762.39
Prop. Value $1,809,161,491
Retail Sales $166,588,051

Mills County

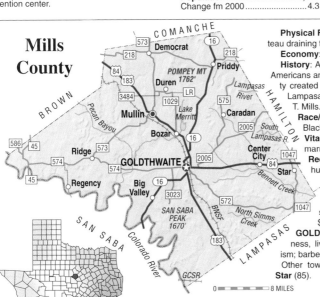

Physical Features: West central county of hills, plateau draining to Colorado River; sandy, loam soils.

Economy: Agribusiness, hunting leases.

History: Apache-Comanche area of conflict. Anglo-Americans and a few Germans settled in 1850s. County created 1887 from Brown, Comanche, Hamilton, Lampasas counties; named for pioneer jurist John T. Mills.

Race/Ethnicity, 2000: (In percent) Anglo, 85.32; Black, 1.30; Hispanic, 13.03; Other, 0.35.

Vital Statistics, 2004: Births, 54; deaths, 57; marriages, 37; divorces, 6.

Recreation: Fishing; deer, dove and turkey hunting; Regency suspension bridge; rangeland recreation.

Minerals: Not significant.

Agriculture: Beef cattle, goats, sheep; some irrigation for pecans. Market value $22 million.

GOLDTHWAITE (1,851) county seat; agribusiness, livestock center; light manufacturing, tourism; barbecue & goat cook-off in April.

Other towns include: **Mullin** (180); **Priddy** (215); **Star** (85).

Population 5,184
Change fm 2000 ....0.6
Area (sq. mi.).....................749.89
Land Area (sq. mi.) 748.11
Altitude (ft.) 1,200-1,762
Rainfall (in.) 28.78
Jan. mean min. 35.2
July mean max. 92.0
Civ. Labor 2,645
Unemployed 3.1
Wages $9,661,573
Av. Weekly Wage............$486.07
Prop. Value $757,693,270
Retail Sales $56,772,341

For explanation of sources, abbreviations and symbols, see p. 224 and foldout map.

Mitchell County

Physical Features: Rolling, draining to Colorado and tributaries; sandy, red, dark soils; Lake Colorado City and Champion Creek Reservoir.

Economy: Government/services; agribusiness, oil, some manufacturing.

History: Jumano Indians in area; Comanches arrived about 1780. Anglo-American settlers arrived in late 1870s after Comanches were forced into Indian Territory. County created 1876 from Bexar District; organized 1881; named for pioneer brothers Asa and Eli Mitchell.

Race/Ethnicity, 2000: (In percent) Anglo, 55.39; Black, 12.79; Hispanic, 31.03; Other, 0.79.

Vital Statistics, 2004: Births, 96; deaths, 107; marriages, 50; divorces, 26.

Recreation: Lake activities; state park; museums, hunting; railhead arts, crafts show, Colorado City playhouse.

Minerals: Oil.

Agriculture: Cotton principal crop, grains also produced. Cattle, sheep, goats, hogs raised. Market value $12.3 million.

COLORADO CITY (4,151) county seat; prisons; varied manufacturing; tourism; electric service center; hospital; bluegrass festival.

Other towns include: **Loraine** (639) and **Westbrook** (201), trade centers.

Population	9,327
Change fm 2000	-3.8
Area (sq. mi.)	915.90
Land Area (sq. mi.)	910.04
Altitude (ft.)	2,000-2,574
Rainfall (in.)	19.43
Jan. mean min.	27.0
July mean max.	95.9
Civ. Labor	3,289
Unemployed	4.6
Wages	$16,967,089
Av. Weekly Wage	$563.38
Prop. Value	$654,245,027
Retail Sales	$38,770,951

Montague County

Physical Features: Rolling, draining to tributaries of Trinity, Red rivers; sandy loams, red, black soils; Lake Nocona, Lake Amon G. Carter.

Economy: Agribusiness; oil production; varied manufacturing, government/services

History: Kiowas and Wichitas who allied with Comanches. Anglo-American settlements developed in 1850s. County created from Cooke County 1857, organized 1858; named for pioneer Daniel Montague.

Race/Ethnicity, 2000: (In percent) Anglo, 93.42; Black, 0.17; Hispanic, 5.41; Other, 1.00.

Vital Statistics, 2004: Births, 253; deaths, 270; marriages, 146; divorces, 85.

Recreation: Lake activities; quail, turkey, deer hunting; scenic drives; museums; historical sites.

Minerals: Oil, rock, limestone.

Agriculture: Beef, hay, wheat, dairies, pecans, peaches, melons. Market value $31.9 million.

MONTAGUE (400) county seat.

BOWIE (5,526) varied manufacturing, livestock, hospital, library; Jim Bowie Days in June.

NOCONA (3,299) athletic goods, boot manufacturing; hospital; Fun Day each May, Chisholm Trail rodeo in September.

Other towns include: **Forestburg** (50); **Ringgold** (100); **Saint Jo** (988) farm center; Pioneer Days on last weekend in May, saloon; **Sunset** (349).

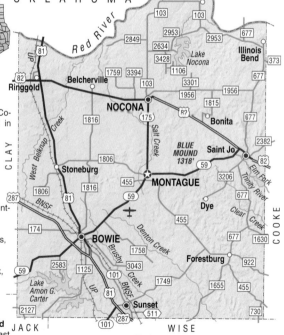

Population	19,810
Change fm 2000	3.6
Area (sq. mi.)	938.44
Land Area (sq. mi.)	930.66
Altitude (ft.)	750-1,318
Rainfall (in.)	33.72
Jan. mean min.	28.3
July mean max.	94.7
Civ. Labor	10,085
Unemployed	3.3
Wages	$32,269,827
Av. Weekly Wage	$521.97
Prop. Value	$1,679,374,200
Retail Sales	$197,397,384

Montgomery County

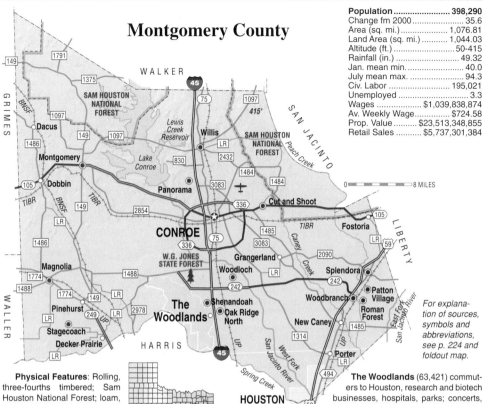

For explanation of sources, symbols and abbreviations, see p. 224 and foldout map.

Population	398,290
Change fm 2000	35.6
Area (sq. mi.)	1,076.81
Land Area (sq. mi.)	1,044.03
Altitude (ft.)	50-415
Rainfall (in.)	49.32
Jan. mean min.	40.0
July mean max.	94.3
Civ. Labor	195,021
Unemployed	3.3
Wages	$1,039,838,874
Av. Weekly Wage	$724.58
Prop. Value	$23,513,348,855
Retail Sales	$5,737,301,384

Physical Features: Rolling, three-fourths timbered; Sam Houston National Forest; loam, sandy, alluvial soils.

Economy: Many residents work in Houston; lumber, oil production; government/services; part of Houston metropolitan area.

History: Orcoquisacs and Bidais, removed from area by 1850s. Anglo-Americans arrived in 1820s as part of Austin's colony. County created 1837 from Washington County; named for Richard Montgomery, American Revolution general.

Race/Ethnicity, 2000: (In percent) Anglo, 82.09; Black, 3.57; Hispanic, 12.65; Other, 1.69.

Vital Statistics, 2004: Births, 5,169; deaths, 2,170; marriages, 2,678; divorces, 1,522.

Recreation: Hunting, fishing; Lake Conroe activities; national and state forests; hiking, boating, horseback riding; historic sites.

Minerals: Natural gas.

Agriculture: Greenhouse crops, forage, beef cattle, horses. Also, Christmas trees and blueberries. Market value $20.1 million. Timber is primary industry.

CONROE (49,230) county seat; retail/wholesale center; government/services; manufacturing; commuters to Houston; hospitals; community college; museum; Cajun Catfish festival in October.

The Woodlands (63,421) commuters to Houston, research and biotech businesses, hospitals, parks; concerts, festivals at Mitchell Pavilion.

Other towns include: **Cut and Shoot** (1,307); **Dobbin** (310); **Grangerland** (NA); **Magnolia** (1,824); **Montgomery** (845) commuters to Houston and Conroe, historic buildings, antiques stores, pioneer museum, Montgomery Trek historic homes tour in April; **New Caney** (6,800); **Oak Ridge North** (3,460); **Panorama** (2,210); **Patton Village** (1,573); **Pinehurst** (4,937); **Porter** (4,200); **Porter Heights** (1,598); **Roman Forest** (3,121); **Shenandoah** (2,337); **Splendora** (1,576); **Stagecoach** (537); **Willis** (4,692) commuters to Conroe and Houston; **Woodbranch** (1,391); **Woodloch** (259).

Also, part [458] of **Houston** [Kingwood], hospital.

Pasture land near Spanish Fort in Montague County. Robert Plocheck photo.

Moore County

Physical Features: Northern Panhandle county; flat to rolling, broken by creeks; sandy loams; lake.

Economy: Varied agribusiness, petroleum, natural gas.

History: Comanches, removed to Indian Territory in 1874-75; ranching began soon afterward. Farming developed after 1910. Oil boom in 1920s. County created 1876 from Bexar District; organized 1892; named for Republic of Texas navy commander E.W. Moore.

Race/Ethnicity, 2000: (In percent) Anglo, 50.54; Black, 0.48; Hispanic, 47.50; Other, 1.48.

Vital Statistics, 2004: Births, 437; deaths, 122; marriages, 158; divorces, 108.

Recreation: Lake Meredith activities; pheasant, deer, quail hunting; historical museum; arts center; free overnight RV park; Dogie Days in June.

Minerals: Oil and gas.

Agriculture: Fed beef, corn, wheat, stocker cattle, sorghum, cotton, soybeans, sunflowers. Market value $303.3 million. Irrigation of 162,000 acres.

DUMAS (13,427) county seat; tourist, retail trade center; varied agribusiness; hospital, hospice, retirement complex.

Other towns include: **Cactus** (2,822), **Sunray** (1,902). Small part of **Fritch**.

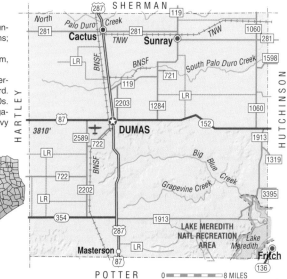

Population	20,591
Change fm 2000	2.3
Area (sq. mi.)	909.61
Land Area (sq. mi.)	899.66
Altitude (ft.)	2,900-3,810
Rainfall (in.)	17.75
Jan. mean min.	20.8
July mean max.	91.7
Civ. Labor	10,336
Unemployed	3.1
Wages	$74,642,545
Av. Weekly Wage	$625.28
Prop. Value	$2,233,978,950
Retail Sales	$141,810,631

For explanation of sources, symbols and abbreviations, see p. 224 and foldout map.

Lake Meredith covers more than 16,000 acres in three counties, including Moore County. Robert Plocheck photo.

Morris County

Physical Features: East Texas county of forested hills; drains to streams, lakes.

Economy: Steel manufacturing, agriculture, timber, government/services.

History: Caddo Indians until 1790s. Kickapoo and other tribes in area 1820s-30s. Anglo-American settlement began in mid-1830s. Antebellum slaveholding area. County named for legislator-jurist W.W. Morris; created from Titus County and organized in 1875.

Race/Ethnicity, 2000: (In percent) Anglo, 71.26; Black, 24.26; Hispanic, 3.66; Other, 0.82.

Vital Statistics, 2004: Births, 162; deaths, 160; marriages, 124; divorces, 50.

Recreation: Activities on Lake O' the Pines, small lakes; fishing, hunting; state park.

Minerals: Iron ore.

Agriculture: Beef cattle, broiler production; hay. Market value $20.1 million. Timber industry significant.

DAINGERFIELD (2,419) county seat; varied manufacturing; library, city park; Northeast Texas Community College; Captain Daingerfield Day in October.

Other towns include: **Cason** (173); **Lone Star** (1,580) oil-field equipment manufactured, catfish farming, Starfest in September; **Naples** (1,349) trailer manufacturing, livestock, watermelon festival in July; **Omaha** (979), retail center, government/services, commuters.

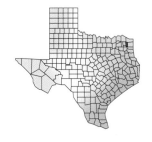

For explanation of sources, symbols and abbreviations, see p. 224 and foldout map.

Population	**13,002**
Change fm 2000	-0.4
Area (sq. mi.)	258.64
Land Area (sq. mi.)	254.51
Altitude (ft.)	228-598
Rainfall (in.)	46.76
Jan. mean min.	33.7
July mean max.	95.0
Civ. Labor	6,365
Unemployed	4.8
Wages	$47,199,147
Av. Weekly Wage	$754.20
Prop. Value	$734,008,950
Retail Sales	$77,131,443

Motley County

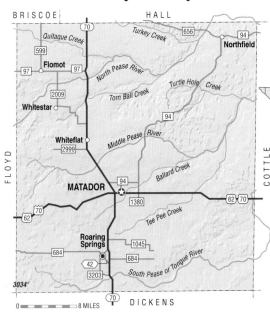

Physical Features: Western county just below Caprock; rough terrain, broken by Pease tributaries; sandy to red clay soils.

Economy: Government/services; ranching; cotton; light manufacturing; hunting.

History: Comanches, removed to Indian Territory by U.S. Army in 1874-75. Ranching began in late 1870s. County created out of Bexar District 1876; organized 1891; named for Dr. J.W. Mottley, signer of Texas Declaration of Independence (name misspelled in statute).

Race/Ethnicity, 2000: (In percent) Anglo, 83.17; Black, 4.00; Hispanic, 12.13; Other, 0.70.

Vital Statistics, 2004: Births, 12; deaths, 18; marriages, 8; divorces, 4.

Recreation: Quail, dove, turkey, deer hunting; Matador Ranch headquarters; spring-fed pool at Roaring Springs; camp grounds; Motley-Dickens settlers reunion in August at Roaring Springs.

Minerals: Minimal.

Agriculture: Beef cattle, cotton, peanuts, hunting leases. Also vegetables, wheat, hay produced. Some irrigation. Market value $9.9 million.

MATADOR (691) county seat; farm trade center; museum; historic oil-derrick gas station; motorcycle race in March.

Other towns include: **Flomot** (181) and **Roaring Springs** (247).

Population	1,276	
Change fm 2000	-10.5	
Area (sq. mi.)	989.81	
Land Area (sq. mi.)	989.38	
Altitude (ft.)	1,900-3,034	
Rainfall (in.)	22.90	
Jan. mean min.	27.3	
July mean max.	94.8	
Civ. Labor	707	
Unemployed	3.4	
Wages	$1,831,909	
Av. Weekly Wage	$409.24	
Prop. Value	$183,505,407	
Retail Sales	$4,756,188	

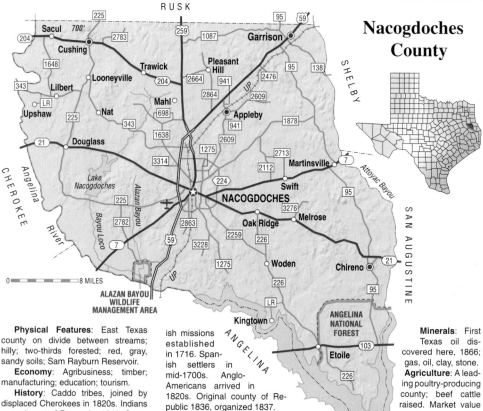

Nacogdoches County

Physical Features: East Texas county on divide between streams; hilly; two-thirds forested; red, gray, sandy soils; Sam Rayburn Reservoir.

Economy: Agribusiness; timber; manufacturing; education; tourism.

History: Caddo tribes, joined by displaced Cherokees in 1820s. Indians moved west of Brazos by 1840. Spanish missions established in 1716. Spanish settlers in mid-1700s. Anglo-Americans arrived in 1820s. Original county of Republic 1836, organized 1837.

Race/Ethnicity, 2000: (In percent) Anglo, 70.83; Black, 16.80; Hispanic, 11.25; Other, 1.12.

Vital Statistics, 2004: Births, 993; deaths, 574; marriages, 571; divorces, 104.

Recreation: Lake, river activities; Stephen F. Austin State University events; Angelina National Forest; historic sites; tourist attractions include the Old Stone Fort, pioneer homes, museums, Millard's Crossing Historic Village; Piney Woods Fair, Blueberry Festival in June.

Population	61,079
Change fm 2000	3.2
Area (sq. mi.)	981.33
Land Area (sq. mi.)	946.77
Altitude (ft.)	164-700
Rainfall (in.)	48.40
Jan. mean min.	36.0
July mean max.	94.0
Civ. Labor	30,927
Unemployed	3.8
Wages	$157,990,025
Av. Weekly Wage	$533.66
Prop. Value	$3,507,010,980
Retail Sales	$655,843,417

Minerals: First Texas oil discovered here, 1866; gas, oil, clay, stone.

Agriculture: A leading poultry-producing county; beef cattle raised. Market value $198 million. Substantial timber sold.

NACOGDOCHES (30,414) county seat; varied manufacturing; lumber mills, wood products; trade center; hospitals; Stephen F. Austin State University; Nine Flags Festival in December.

Other towns include: Appleby (442), Chireno (404), Cushing (649), Douglass (380), Etoile (700), Garrison (864), Martinsville (350), Sacul (150), Woden (400).

Historic downtown Nacogdoches, a city that dates to the 1700s. Robert Plocheck photo.

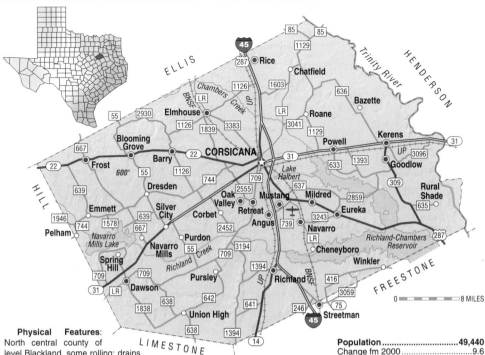

Navarro County

Physical Features:
North central county of level Blackland, some rolling; drains to creeks, Trinity River; Navarro Mills Lake, Richland-Chambers Reservoir.

Economy: Diversified manufacturing; agribusinesses; oil-field operations, distribution.

History: Kickapoo and Comanche area. Anglo-Americans settled in late 1830s. Antebellum slaveholding area. County created from Robertson County, organized in 1846; named for Republic of Texas leader José Antonio Navarro.

Race/Ethnicity, 2000: (In percent) Anglo, 66.12; Black, 16.96; Hispanic, 15.76; Other, 1.16.

Vital Statistics, 2004: Births, 619; deaths, 500; marriages, 368; divorces, 236.

Recreation: Lake activities; Pioneer Village; historic buildings; youth exposition, Derrick Days in April.

Minerals: Longest continuous Texas oil flow; more than 200 million barrels produced since 1895; natural gas, sand and gravel also produced.

Agriculture: Beef cattle, cotton, sorghum, corn, wheat, herbs, horses, dairies. Market value $36.5 million.

CORSICANA (25,972) county seat; major distribution center, pecans, candy, fruitcakes; varied manufacturing; agribusiness; hospital; Navarro College; Texas Youth Commission facility.

Other towns include: **Angus** (387); **Barry** (229); **Blooming Grove** (875); **Chatfield** (40); **Dawson** (876); **Emhouse** (169); **Eureka** (330); **Frost** (704); **Goodlow** (273).

Also, **Kerens** (1,880) some manufacturing, nature tourism; **Mildred** (397); **Mustang** (54); **Navarro** (203); **Oak Valley** (442); **Powell** (110); **Purdon** (133); **Retreat** (357); **Rice** (929); **Richland** (308).

Population	49,440
Change fm 2000	9.6
Area (sq. mi.)	1,086.17
Land Area (sq. mi.)	1,070.66
Altitude (ft.)	250-600
Rainfall (in.)	39.48
Jan. mean min.	34.0
July mean max.	94.5
Civ. Labor	21,923
Unemployed	4.3
Wages	$113,542,497
Av. Weekly Wage	$548.57
Prop. Value	$2,267,294,579
Retail Sales	$487,790,096

For explanation of sources, symbols and abbreviations, see p. 224 and foldout map.

A statue of José Antonio Navarro in front of the county courthouse in Corsicana. Elizabeth Alvarez photo.

Newton County

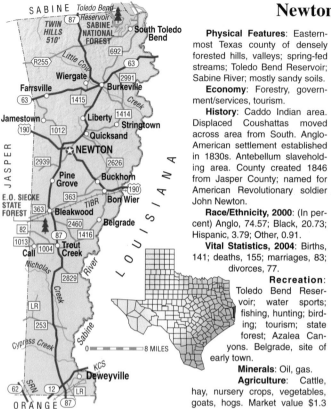

Physical Features: Easternmost Texas county of densely forested hills, valleys; spring-fed streams; Toledo Bend Reservoir; Sabine River; mostly sandy soils.

Economy: Forestry, government/services, tourism.

History: Caddo Indian area. Displaced Coushattas moved across area from South. Anglo-American settlement established in 1830s. Antebellum slaveholding area. County created 1846 from Jasper County; named for American Revolutionary soldier John Newton.

Race/Ethnicity, 2000: (In percent) Anglo, 74.57; Black, 20.73; Hispanic, 3.79; Other, 0.91.

Vital Statistics, 2004: Births, 141; deaths, 155; marriages, 83; divorces, 77.

Recreation: Toledo Bend Reservoir; water sports; fishing, hunting; birding; tourism; state forest; Azalea Canyons. Belgrade, site of early town.

Minerals: Oil, gas.

Agriculture: Cattle, hay, nursery crops, vegetables, goats, hogs. Market value $1.3 million. Hunting leases. Major forestry area.

NEWTON (2,576) county seat; lumber manufacturing; plywood mill; private prison unit; tourist center; genealogical library, museum; Wild Azalea festival in March.

Deweyville (1,099) power plant; commercial center for forestry, farming area.

Other towns include: **Bon Wier** (475); **Burkeville** (515); **Call** (170); **South Toledo Bend** (486); **Wiergate** (461).

Population	**14,090**
Change fm 2000	-6.5
Area (sq. mi.)	939.51
Land Area (sq. mi.)	932.69
Altitude (ft.)	23-510
Rainfall (in.)	54.90
Jan. mean min.	35.0
July mean max.	94.0
Civ. Labor	5,619
Unemployed	7.5
Wages	$11,776,332
Av. Weekly Wage	$487.81
Prop. Value	$1,086,041,691
Retail Sales	$38,247,316

For explanation of sources, symbols and abbreviations, see p. 224 and foldout map.

Nolan County

Physical Features: On divide between Brazos, Colorado watersheds; mostly red sandy loams, some wavy, sandy soils; lakes.

Economy: Farming and ranching; oil and gas; wind energy; government/services.

History: Anglo-American settlement began in late 1870s. County created from Bexar, Young districts 1876; organized 1881; named for adventurer Philip Nolan, who was killed near Waco.

Race/Ethnicity, 2000: (In percent) Anglo, 66.64; Black, 4.85; Hispanic, 28.04; Other, 0.47.

Vital Statistics, 2004: Births, 227; deaths, 209; marriages, 132; divorces, 90.

Recreation: Lakes; hunting; rattlesnake roundup in March; pioneer museum; Soap Box Derby in June.

Minerals: Oil, gas.

Agriculture: Beef cattle, cotton, grain sorghum. Market value $13.4 million. Twenty percent irrigated.

SWEETWATER (10,971) county seat; wind energy, varied manufacturing, gypsum; hospital; Texas State Technical College; WWII museum.

Other towns include: **Blackwell** (345, partly in Coke County), Oak Creek Reservoir to south; **Maryneal** (61); **Nolan** (47); **Roscoe** (1,306).

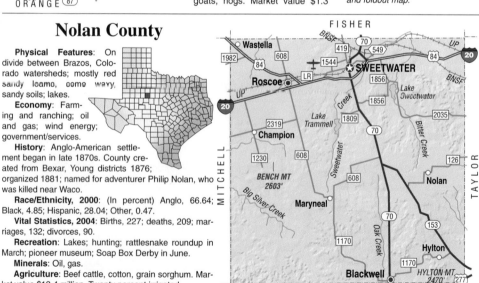

Population	**14,812**
Change fm 2000	-6.3
Area (sq. mi.)	913.93
Land Area (sq. mi.)	911.98
Altitude (ft.)	1,990-2,603
Rainfall (in.)	23.54
Jan. mean min.	28.9
July mean max.	93.8
Civ. Labor	7,521
Unemployed	3.9
Wages	$40,250,200
Av. Weekly Wage	$520.92
Prop. Value	$1,071,217,691
Retail Sales	$175,306,427

Youngsters on bikes and boards at the skate park along Corpus Christi Bay. Robert Plocheck photo.

Nueces County

Population **321,457**
Change fm 2000 .... 2.5
Area (sq. mi.) 1,166.42
Land Area (sq. mi.) 835.82
Altitude (ft.) .... sea level-129
Rainfall (in.) 32.26
Jan. mean min. 46.2
July mean max. 93.2
Civ. Labor 162,152
Unemployed 4.4
Wages $1,300,358,139
Av. Weekly Wage.................... $671.09
Prop. Value $16,055,569,933
Retail Sales $3,851,459,645

Physical Features: Southern Gulf Coast county; flat, rich soils, broken by bays, Nueces River, Petronila Creek; includes Mustang Island, north tip of Padre Island.

Economy: Diversified economy includes petroleum processing and production; deepwater port facilities; agriculture; tourism, conventions; coastal shipping; manufacturing; military complex.

History: Coahuiltecan, Karankawa and other tribes who succumbed to disease or fled by 1840s.

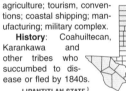

LIPANTITLAN STATE
HISTORIC SITE

Spanish settlers arrived in 1760s. Settlers from Ireland arrived around 1830. County name is Spanish for nuts; county named for river; created 1846 out of San Patricio County.

Race/Ethnicity, 2000: (In percent) Anglo, 38.32; Black, 4.24; Hispanic, 55.78; Other, 1.66.

Vital Statistics, 2004: Births, 5,023; deaths, 2,407; marriages, 2,005; divorces, 1,449.

Recreation: Major resort area; fishing, water sports, birding; Padre Island National Seashore; Mustang Island State Park; Lipantitlan State Historic Site; Art Museum of South Texas, Corpus Christi Museum of Science and History; Texas State Aquarium; various metropolitan events; greyhound race track.

Minerals: Sand and gravel, oil and gas.

Agriculture: Grain sorghum (a leader in sales, acreage); cotton, corn, hay, sunflowers, canola, beef cattle. Market value $62.6 million.

CORPUS CHRISTI (283,384) county seat; seaport, naval bas-

es; varied manufacturing; petroleum processing; tourism; hospitals; museums; Army depot; Texas A&M University-Corpus Christi; Del Mar College; Buccaneer Days in late April; replicas of Columbus' ships on display, USS Lexington museum.

Port Aransas (3,398) deepwater port, tourism, Coast Guard base, fishing industry; University of Texas Marine Science Institute; Celebration of Whooping Cranes in Febuary; Texas Sand Fest in April.

Robstown (13,195) market center for oil, farm area; regional fairgrounds; Cottonfest in November; Fiesta Mexicana in March.

Other towns include: **Agua Dulce** (701); **Banquete** (582); **Bishop** (3,362) petrochemicals, agriculture, pharmaceuticals, plastics; nature trail; Old Tyme Faire in April; **Chapman Ranch** (100); **Driscoll** (830); **La Paloma-Lost Creek** (259); **North San Pedro** (791); **Petronila** (78); **Rancho Banquete** (431); **Sandy Hollow-Escondidas** (354); **Spring Garden-Tierra Verde** (602); **Tierra Grande** (352).

Annaville, Calallen and **Flour Bluff** are now part of Corpus Christi.

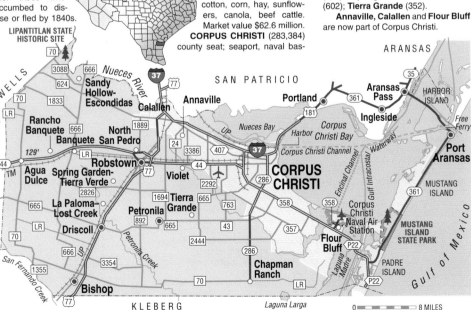

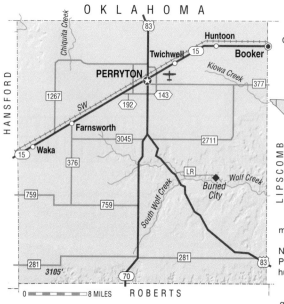

Ochiltree County

Physical Features: Panhandle county bordering Oklahoma; level, broken by creeks; deep loam, clay soils.

Economy: Oil and gas; agribusiness, center of large feedlot and swine operations.

History: Apaches, pushed out by Comanches in late 1700s. Comanches removed to Indian Territory in 1874-75. Ranching developed in 1880s; farming after 1900. Created from Bexar District 1876, organized 1889; named for Republic of Texas leader W.B. Ochiltree.

Race/Ethnicity, 2000: (In percent) Anglo, 66.95; Black, 0.11; Hispanic, 31.79; Other, 1.15.

Vital Statistics, 2004: Births, 182; deaths, 54; marriages, 108; divorces, 42.

Recreation: Wolf Creek park; Wheatheart of the Nation celebration in August; Museum of the Plains; Prehistoric settlement site of "Buried City"; pheasant hunting, also deer and dove.

Minerals: Oil, natural gas, caliche.

Agriculture: Cattle, swine, wheat, corn, grain sorghum, cotton; 80,000 acres irrigated. Market value $241.9 million.

PERRYTON (8,007) county seat; oil and gas, cattle feeding; grain center; hospital; college; convention center.

Other towns include: **Farnsworth** (130); **Waka** (65). Also, **Booker** (1,365, mostly in Lipscomb County).

Population	9,550
Change fm 2000	6.0
Area (sq. mi.)	918.07
Land Area (sq. mi.)	917.56
Altitude (ft.)	2,642-3,105
Rainfall (in.)	20.88
Jan. mean min.	18.4
July mean max.	91.4
Civ. Labor	5,327
Unemployed	2.5
Wages	$39,068,255
Av. Weekly Wage	$688.33
Prop. Value	$821,456,329
Retail Sales	$114,052,302

Oldham County

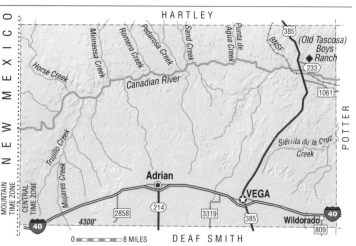

Physical Features: Northwestern Panhandle county; level, broken by Canadian River and tributaries.

Economy: Agriculture, wind energy, sand and gravel.

History: Apaches; followed later by Comanches, Kiowas. U.S. Army removed Indians in 1875. Anglo ranchers and Spanish pastores (sheep men) from New Mexico were in area in 1870s. County created 1876 from Bexar District; organized 1880; named for editor-Confederate senator W.S. Oldham.

Race/Ethnicity, 2000: (In percent) Anglo, 85.13; Black, 2.24; Hispanic, 11.03; Other, 1.60.

Vital Statistics, 2004: Births, 34; deaths, 19; marriages, 13; divorces, 11.

Recreation: Old Tascosa with Boot Hill Cemetery nearby, pioneer town; County Roundup in August; youth cowboy poetry gathering in June; midway point on old Route 66.

Minerals: Sand and gravel, oil, natural gas, stone.

Agriculture: Beef cattle; crops include wheat, grain sorghum. Market value $65.9 million.

VEGA (953) county seat; ranch trade center; museums.

Other towns: **Adrian** (149); **Wildorado** (210). Also, Cal Farley's **Boys Ranch** (470).

Population	2,133
Change fm 2000	-2.4
Area (sq. mi.)	1,501.42
Land Area (sq. mi.)	1,500.63
Altitude (ft.)	3,200-4,300
Rainfall (in.)	18.18
Jan. mean min.	20.5
July mean max.	92.3
Civ. Labor	1,004
Unemployed	4.0
Wages	$5,652,158
Av. Weekly Wage	$526.79
Prop. Value	$336,242,348
Retail Sales	$11,604,015

Orange County

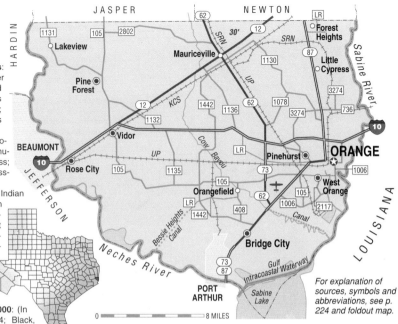

JASPER

NEWTON

HARDIN

JEFFERSON

LOUISIANA

1131 105 2802 Lakeview Pine Forest 12 1132 Vidor BEAUMONT 10 Rose City 105 1135 30' SRN Mauriceville KCS 1442 1136 62 1078 3274 Cow Bayou LR UP Pinehurst 73 105 Orangefield 62 105 LR 1442 408 1006 Bessie Heights Canal Bridge City 73 87 Neches River Gulf Intracoastal Waterway PORT ARTHUR Sabine Lake 12 SRN 1130 87 Forest Heights Little Cypress Sabine River 3274 736 10 ORANGE 1006 West Orange 2117 Canal

0 ———— 8 MILES

For explanation of sources, symbols and abbreviations, see p. 224 and foldout map.

Physical Features: In southeastern corner of the state; bounded by Sabine, Neches rivers, Sabine Lake; coastal soils; two-thirds timbered.

Economy: Petrochemicals; varied manufacturing; agribusiness; tourism; lumber processing.

History: Atakapan Indian area. French traders in area by 1720. Anglo-American settlement began in 1820s. County created from Jefferson County in 1852; named for early orange grove.

Race/Ethnicity, 2000: (In percent) Anglo, 86.54; Black, 8.50; Hispanic, 3.62; Other, 1.34.

Vital Statistics, 2004: Births, 1,079; deaths, 870; marriages, 650; divorces, 316.

Recreation: Fishing, hunting; water sports; birding; county park; museums; historical homes; crawfish and crab festivals in spring.

Minerals: Salt, oil, gas, clays, sand and gravel.

Agriculture: Cattle, hay, Christmas trees and rice are top revenue sources; honey a significant revenue producer; fruits, berries, vegetables. Also, crawfishing. Market value $3.8 million. Hunting leases. Timber important.

ORANGE (17,557) county seat; seaport; petrochemical plants; varied manufacturing; food, timber processing; shipping; hospital, theater, museums; Lamar State College-Orange; Mardi Gras/gumbo festival in February.

Bridge City (8,681) varied manufacturing; ship repair yard; steel fabrication; fish farming; government/services; library; tall bridge and newer suspension bridge over Neches; stop for Monarch butterfly in fall during its migration to Mexico.

Vidor (11,354) steel processing; railroad-car refinishing; library; barbecue festival in April.

Other towns include: **Mauriceville** (2,791); **Orangefield** (725); **Pine Forest** (584); **Pinehurst** (2,041); **Rose City** (497); **West Orange** (3,826).

Population	**84,243**
Change fm 2000	-0.9
Area (sq. mi.)	379.54
Land Area (sq. mi.)	356.40
Altitude (ft.)	sea level-30
Rainfall (in.)	59.00
Jan. mean min.	41.0
July mean max.	91.0
Civ. Labor	40,224
Unemployed	5.4
Wages	$196,550,123
Av. Weekly Wage	$683.21
Prop. Value	$4,973,191,159
Retail Sales	$790,970,805

The coastal prairie along Sabine Lake stretches out to the refineries of Port Arthur. Robert Plocheck photo.

Palo Pinto County

Physical Features: North central county west of Fort Worth; broken, hilly, wooded in parts; Possum Kingdom Lake, Lake Palo Pinto; sandy, gray, black soils.

Economy: Varied manufacturing; tourism; petroleum; agribusiness.

History: Anglo-American ranchers arrived in 1850s. Conflicts between settlers and numerous Indian tribes who had sought refuge on Brazos resulted in Texas Rangers removing Indians in 1856. County created 1856 from Bosque, Navarro counties; organized 1857; named for creek (in Spanish name means painted stick).

Race/Ethnicity, 2000: (In percent) Anglo, 82.77; Black, 2.51; Hispanic, 13.57; Other, 1.15.

Vital Statistics, 2004: Births, 388; deaths, 331; marriages, 237; divorces, 136.

Recreation: Lake activities; hunting, fishing, water sports; state park; Rails to Trails conversion for hiking, biking.

Minerals: Oil, gas, clays.

Agriculture: Cattle, dairy products, nursery crops, hay, wheat. Market value $15.3 million. Cedar fence posts marketed.

PALO PINTO (411) county seat; old settlers reunion; government center.

MINERAL WELLS (17,174, part [2,176] in Parker County) varied manufacturing; tourism; agriculture; hospital, prison; Weatherford College extension; Crazy Water Festival in October; state park east of city in Parker County.

Other towns include: **Gordon** (446); **Graford** (601) retirement and recreation area, Possum Fest in October; **Mingus** (251); **Santo** (445), and **Strawn** (749).

Population.............................27,797	July mean max. 97.3
Change fm 2000..........................2.9	Civ. Labor 14,619
Area (sq. mi.) 985.50	Unemployed 3.7
Land Area (sq. mi.) 952.93	Wages $71,440,333
Altitude (ft.) 782-1,470	Av. Weekly Wage..................$586.34
Rainfall (in.) 31.79	Prop. Value $2,222,840,650
Jan. mean min. 33.4	Retail Sales $264,645,528

Panola County

Physical Features: East Texas county; sixty percent forested, rolling plain; broken by Sabine, Murvaul Creek and Lake, Toledo Bend Reservoir.

Economy: Gas processing; oil-field operation; agribusinesses; food processing.

History: Caddo area. Anglo-American settlement established in 1833. Antebellum slaveholding area. County name is Indian word for cotton; created from Harrison, Shelby counties 1846.

Race/Ethnicity, 2000: (In percent) Anglo, 77.97; Black, 17.85; Hispanic, 3.51; Other, 0.67.

Vital Statistics, 2004: Births, 286; deaths, 276; marriages, 201; divorces, 54.

Recreation: Lake fishing, other water activities; hunting; scenic drives; Jim Reeves memorial, Tex Ritter museum and Texas Country Music Hall of Fame; historic sites, homes.

Minerals: Oil, gas.

Agriculture: Broilers; beef cattle, forages; market value $46.2 million. Timber sales significant.

CARTHAGE (6,808) county seat; petroleum processing; poultry; sawmills; hospital; junior college; Oil & Gas Blast in October.

Other towns include: **Beckville** (752), **Clayton** (125), **DeBerry** (200), **Gary** (310), **Long Branch** (150), **Panola** (305). Also, **Tatum** (1,169, mostly in Rusk County).

Population 22,989	
Change fm 2000..................................1.0	
Area (sq. mi.) 821.34	
Land Area (sq. mi.) 800.92	
Altitude (ft.) 172-481	
Rainfall (in.) 51.51	
Jan. mean min. 33.9	
July mean max. 93.7	
Civ. Labor 12,010	
Unemployed 3.9	
Wages $64,169,706	
Av. Weekly Wage......................$631.60	
Prop. Value $3,789,053,505	
Retail Sales $216,186,644	

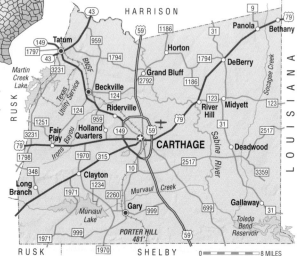

Parker County

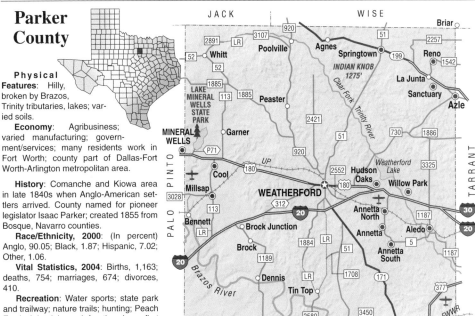

Physical Features: Hilly, broken by Brazos, Trinity tributaries, lakes; varied soils.

Economy: Agribusiness; varied manufacturing; government/services; many residents work in Fort Worth; county part of Dallas-Fort Worth-Arlington metropolitan area.

History: Comanche and Kiowa area in late 1840s when Anglo-American settlers arrived. County named for pioneer legislator Isaac Parker; created 1855 from Bosque, Navarro counties.

Race/Ethnicity, 2000: (In percent) Anglo, 90.05; Black, 1.87; Hispanic, 7.02; Other, 1.06.

Vital Statistics, 2004: Births, 1,163; deaths, 754; marriages, 674; divorces, 410.

Recreation: Water sports; state park and trailway; nature trails; hunting; Peach Festival in July and frontier days; first Monday trade days monthly.

Minerals: Natural gas, oil, stone, sand and gravel, clays.

Agriculture: Cattle, horticultural plants, hay, horses, dairies, peaches, peanuts, pecans. Market value $47.6 million.

WEATHERFORD (22,445) county seat; communting to Fort Worth and Arlington; retail center; varied manufacturing; government/services; equine industry; hospital; Weatherford College.

Other towns include: **Aledo** (2,360); **Annetta** (1,248), **Annetta North** (495) and **Annetta South** (623); **Cool** (167); **Dennis** (300); **Hudson Oaks** (1,770); **Millsap** (362); **Peaster** (102); **Poolville** (520); **Reno** (2,613); **Sanctuary** (589); **Springtown** (2,468) commuters, government/services, Wild West Festival in September; **Whitt** (38); **Willow Park** (3,295).

Also, part of **Azle** (10,217) and **Briar**, (5,651), both mostly in Tarrant County, and part [2,176] of **Mineral Wells**.

Population	106,266
Change fm 2000	20.1
Area (sq. mi.)	910.09
Land Area (sq. mi.)	903.51
Altitude (ft.)	700-1,275
Rainfall (in.)	34.70
Jan. mean min.	29.0
July mean max.	95.2
Civ. Labor	52,622
Unemployed	3.7
Wages	$169,554,569
Av. Weekly Wage	$587.43
Prop. Value	$7,795,215,640
Retail Sales	$1,368,002,866

The state trailway between Weatherford and Mineral Wells. Robert Plocheck photo.

Workers cut pumpkins from vines in a field near Farwell. Eric Kluth photo.

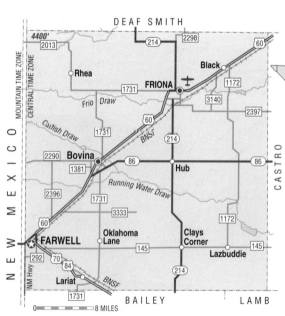

Parmer County

Physical Features: Western High Plains, broken by draws, playas; sandy, clay, loam soils.

Economy: Cattle feeding; grain elevators; meat-packing plant; other agribusiness.

History: Apaches, pushed out in late 1700s by Comanches, Kiowas. U.S. Army removed Indians in 1874-75. Anglo-Americans arrived in 1880s. Mexican migration increased after 1950. County named for Republic figure Martin Parmer; created from Bexar District 1876, organized 1907.

Race/Ethnicity, 2000: (In percent) Anglo, 49.17; Black, 1.01; Hispanic, 49.19; Other, 0.63.

Vital Statistics, 2004: Births, 198; deaths, 73; marriages, 43; divorces, 28.

Recreation: Hunting, Border Town Days in July.

Minerals: Not significant.

Agriculture: Among leading counties in total farm income. Beef cattle, dairies; crops include wheat, corn, cotton, grain sorghum, alfalfa; apples and potatoes also raised; 190,000 acres irrigated. Market value $603.9 million, second in state.

FARWELL (1,316) county seat; agribusiness center; grain storage; plants make farm equipment.

FRIONA (3,895) feedlots, grain elevators, meat packing; hospital; museum; Cheeseburger Festival in July.

Other towns include: **Bovina** (1,917) farm trade center; **Lazbuddie** (248).

Population	**9,714**
Change fm 2000	-3.0
Area (sq. mi.)	885.17
Land Area (sq. mi.)	881.66
Altitude (ft.)	3,850-4,400
Rainfall (in.)	18.38
Jan. mean min.	21.7
July mean max.	89.8
Civ. Labor	4,548
Unemployed	3.2

Wages	$34,991,336
Av. Weekly Wage	$560.80
Prop. Value	$610,985,554
Retail Sales	$45,144,352

For explanation of sources, symbols and abbreviations, see p. 224 and foldout map.

Pecos County

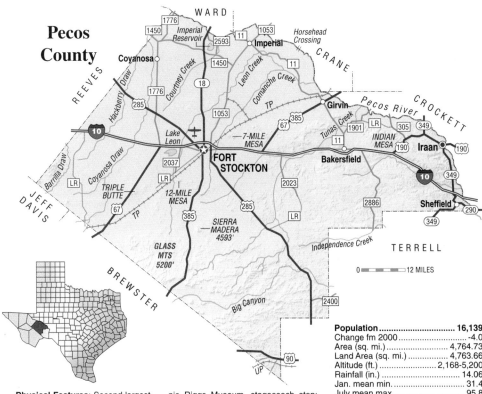

Physical Features: Second largest county; high, broken plateau in West Texas; draining to Pecos and tributaries; sandy, clay, loam soils.

Economy: Oil, gas; agriculture; government/services; wind turbines.

History: Comanches in area when military outpost established in 1859. Settlement began after Civil War. Created from Presidio County 1871; organized 1872; named for Pecos River, name origin uncertain.

Race/Ethnicity, 2000: (In percent) Anglo, 33.98; Black, 4.21; Hispanic, 61.05; Other, 0.76.

Vital Statistics, 2004: Births, 269; deaths, 120; marriages, 88; divorces, 23.

Recreation: Old Fort Stockton, Annie Riggs Museum, stagecoach stop; scenic drives; Dinosaur Track Roadside Park; cattle-trail sites; archaeological museum with oil, ranch-heritage collections; Comanche Springs Water Carnival in summer.

Minerals: Natural gas, oil, gravel, caliche.

Agriculture: Cattle, alfalfa, pecans, sheep, goats, onions, peppers, melons. Market value $38.2 million. Aquaculture firm producing shrimp. Hunting leases.

FORT STOCKTON (7,442) county seat, distribution center for petroleum industry, government/services, agriculture, tourism, varied manufacturing, winery, hospital, historical tours, prison units, spaceport launching small satellites.

Population	16,139
Change fm 2000	-4.0
Area (sq. mi.)	4,764.73
Land Area (sq. mi.)	4,763.66
Altitude (ft.)	2,168-5,200
Rainfall (in.)	14.06
Jan. mean min.	31.4
July mean max.	95.8
Civ. Labor	6,409
Unemployed	4.1
Wages	$33,572,453
Av. Weekly Wage	$553.71
Prop. Value	$2,941,269,910
Retail Sales	$119,402,693

Iraan (1,153) oil, gas center, tourism; ranching, meat processing, hospital, Alley Oop park.

Other towns include: **Coyanosa** (135); **Girvin** (20); **Imperial** (399) center for irrigated farming; **Sheffield** (322) oil, gas center.

For explanation of sources, symbols and abbreviations, see p. 224 and foldout map.

Wind turbines in the Pecos River Valley north of Iraan. Robert Plocheck photo.

Polk County

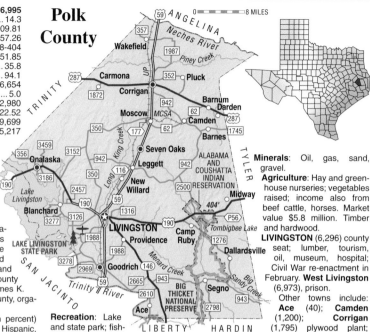

Population **46,995**
Change fm 2000 .... 14.3
Area (sq. mi.) 1,109.81
Land Area (sq. mi.) 1,057.26
Altitude (ft.) 68-404
Rainfall (in.) 51.85
Jan. mean min. 35.8
July mean max. 94.1
Civ. Labor 16,654
Unemployed 5.0
Wages $70,702,980
Av. Weekly Wage $522.52
Prop. Value $2,488,059,699
Retail Sales $393,505,217

Physical Features: Rolling; densely forested, with Big Thicket, unique plant, animal life; Neches, Trinity rivers, tributaries.

Economy: Timber; lumber production; tourism; manufacturing.

History: Caddo area; Alabama and Coushatta Indians arrived from Louisiana in late 1700s. Anglo-American and Hispanic families received land grants in early 1830s. County named for U.S. President James K. Polk; created from Liberty County, organized 1846.

Race/Ethnicity, 2000: (In percent) Anglo, 75.37; Black, 13.18; Hispanic, 9.39; Other, 2.06.

Vital Statistics, 2004: Births, 508; deaths, 592; marriages, 362; divorces, 115.

Recreation: Lake and state park; fishing, other water activities; hunting; Alabama-Coushatta Reservation, museum; Big Thicket; woodland trails, champion trees; historic homes.

Minerals: Oil, gas, sand, gravel.

Agriculture: Hay and greenhouse nurseries; vegetables raised; income also from beef cattle, horses. Market value $5.8 million. Timber and hardwood.

LIVINGSTON (6,296) county seat; lumber, tourism, oil, museum, hospital; Civil War re-enactment in February. **West Livingston** (6,973), prison.

Other towns include: **Ace** (40); **Camden** (1,200); **Corrigan** (1,795) plywood plant; **Dallardsville** (350); **Goodrich** (280); **Leggett** (500); **Moscow** (170) historic sites; **Onalaska** (1,423); **Seven Oaks** (132).

Potter County

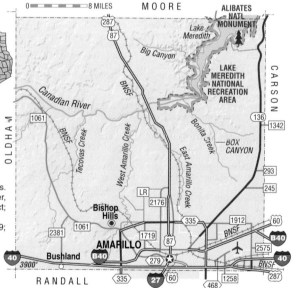

Physical Features: Panhandle county; mostly level, part rolling; broken by Canadian River and tributaries; sandy, sandy loam, chocolate loam, clay soils; Lake Meredith.

Economy: Transportation, distribution hub for large area; manufacturing; agribusinesses; tourism; government/services; petrochemicals; gas processing; .

History: Apaches, pushed out by Comanches in 1700s. Comanches removed to Indian Territory in 1874-75. Ranching began in late 1870s. Oil boom in 1920s. County named for Robert Potter, Republic leader; created 1876 from Bexar District; organized 1887.

Race/Ethnicity, 2000: (In percent) Anglo, 58.49; Black, 10.15; Hispanic, 28.11; Other, 3.25.

Vital Statistics, 2004: Births, 2,406; deaths, 1,164; marriages, 1,648; divorces, 440.

Recreation: Metropolitan activities, events; lake activities; Alibates Flint Quarries National Monument; hunting, fishing; Wildcat Bluff nature center; Cadillac Ranch; Tri-State Fair in September.

Minerals: Natural gas, oil, helium.

Agriculture: Beef cattle production and processing; wheat, sorghum, cotton. Market value $19.5 million.

AMARILLO (185,745 total, part [73,794] in Randall County) county seat; hub for northern Panhandle oil and ranching; distribution, marketing center; tourism; varied manufacturing; food processing; hospitals; prison; museum; varied cultural, recreational events; junior college, Texas Tech University medical, engineering schools; Texas State Technical College branch; Quarter Horse Heritage Center.

Other towns include: **Bishop Hills** (213) and **Bushland** (1,485).

Population **121,328**
Change fm 2000 .... 6.9
Area (sq. mi.) 921.98
Land Area (sq. mi.) 909.24
Altitude (ft.) 2,915-3,900
Rainfall (in.) 19.71
Jan. mean min. 22.6
July mean max. 91.0
Civ. Labor 59,437
Unemployed 3.6
Wages $618,162,792
Av. Weekly Wage $642.88
Prop. Value $5,511,006,889
Retail Sales $2,623,794,887

The rugged country along the Rio Grande and Texas 170 south of Presidio. Robert Plocheck photo.

Presidio County

Physical Features: Rugged, some of Texas' tallest mountains; scenic drives; clays, loams, sandy loams on uplands; intermountain wash; timber sparse; Capote Falls, state's highest.

Economy: Government/services; ranching; hunting leases; tourism.

History: Presidio area has been cultivated farmland since at least 1200 A.D. Spanish explorers of 1500s encountered villages along Rio Grande. Jumanos, Apaches and Comanches in area when Spanish missions began in 1680s. Anglo-Americans arrived in 1840s. County created 1850 from Bexar District; organized 1875; named for Spanish Presidio del Norte (fort of the north).

Race/Ethnicity, 2000: (In percent) Anglo, 15.03; Black, 0.21; Hispanic, 84.36; Other, 0.40.

Vital Statistics, 2004: Births, 159; deaths, 37; marriages, 54; divorces, 0.

Recreation: Mild climate and scenic surroundings; hunting; scenic drives along Rio Grande, in mountains; ghost towns, mysterious Marfa Lights; Fort D.A. Russell; Big Bend Ranch State Park; hot springs; Cibolo Creek Ranch Resort; Chinati Foundation art festival in fall. (Chinati Mountains State Natural Area not yet open to public.)

Minerals: Sand, gravel, silver, zeolite.

Agriculture: Cattle, tomatoes, hay, onions, melons. 5,500 acres irrigated near Rio Grande. Market value $51.2million.

MARFA (2,053) county seat; ranching supply, Border Patrol headquarters; tourist, art center; gateway to mountainous area; Paisano Hotel, headquarters for movie, *Giant*; Old Timers Roping on Memorial Day weekend.

PRESIDIO (4,985) international bridge to Ojinaga, Mex., gateway to Mexico's West Coast by rail; Fort Leaton historic site; asado cook-off in February.

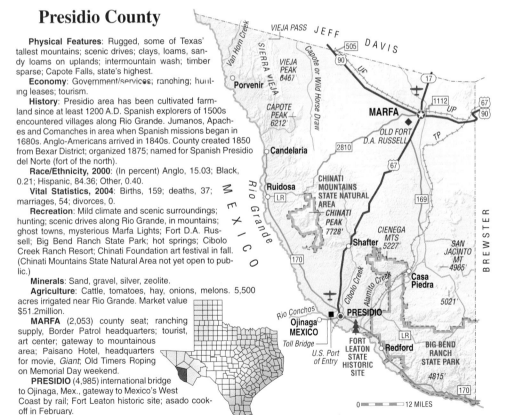

Population 7,713	
Change fm 2000 .... 5.6	
Area (sq. mi.) 3,856.26	
Land Area (sq. mi.) 3,855.51	
Altitude (ft.) 2,400-7,728	
Rainfall (in.) Marfa 15.79	
Rainfall (in.) Presidio 10.76	

Jan. mean min. Marfa 23.9	
Jan. mean min. Presidio 34.5	
July mean max. Marfa 88.9	
July mean max. Presidio 100.8	
Civ. Labor 3,091	
Unemployed 9.9	
Wages $13,170,969	

Av. Weekly Wage $502.22
Prop. Value $329,892,014
Retail Sales $41,191,940

For explanation of sources, symbols and abbreviations, see p. 224 and foldout map.

Rains County

Physical Features: Northeastern county; rolling; partly Blackland, sandy loams, sandy soils; Sabine River, Lake Tawakoni.

Economy: Agribusiness, some manufacturing.

History: Caddo area. In 1700s, Tawakoni Indians entered the area. Anglo-Americans arrived in 1840s. County, county seat named for Emory Rains, Republic leader; created 1870 from Hopkins, Hunt and Wood counties; birthplace of National Farmers Union, 1902.

Race/Ethnicity, 2000: (In percent) Anglo, 90.25; Black, 2.98; Hispanic, 5.53; Other, 1.24.

Vital Statistics, 2004: Births, 115; deaths, 119; marriages, 70; divorces, 56.

Recreation: Lake Tawakoni and Lake Fork Reservoir activities; birding, Eagle Fest in February.

Minerals: Gas, oil.

Agriculture: Beef, forages, dairies, vegetables, fruits, nurseries. Market value $11.8 million.

EMORY (1,249) county seat; local trade; tourism; government/services; commuting to Greenville, Dallas; African-American museum. Other towns include: **East Tawakoni** (890) and **Point** (969), manufacturing, tourism, tamale fest on July 4. Part of **Alba** (440), mostly in Wood County.

Population	11,514
Change fm 2000	26.0
Area (sq. mi.)	258.87
Land Area (sq. mi.)	232.05
Altitude (ft.)	345-570
Rainfall (in.)	43.50
Jan. mean min.	31.6
July mean max.	92.4
Civ. Labor	5,030
Unemployed	3.5
Wages	$9,892,906
Av. Weekly Wage	$435.35
Prop. Value	$544,572,357
Retail Sales	$96,274,826

Randall County

Randal (name misspelled in statute).

Physical Features: Panhandle county; level, but broken by scenic Palo Duro Canyon, Buffalo Lake; silty clay, loam soils.

Economy: Agribusinesses; education; tourism; part of Amarillo metropolitan area.

History: Comanche Indians removed in mid-1870s; ranching began soon afterward. County created 1876 from Bexar District; organized 1889; named for Confederate Gen. Horace

Race/Ethnicity, 2000: (In percent) Anglo, 86.48; Black, 1.60; Hispanic, 10.27; Other, 1.65.

Vital Statistics, 2004: Births, 1,365; deaths, 736; marriages, 361; divorces, 465.

Recreation: Palo Duro Canyon State Park, with *Texas* outdoor musical drama a tourist attraction each summer; Panhandle-Plains Historical Museum; West Texas A&M University events; aoudad sheep, migratory waterfowl hunting in season; Buffalo Lake National Wildlife Refuge; cowboy breakfasts at ranches.

Minerals: Not significant.

Agriculture: Beef cattle, wheat, sorghum, silage, cotton, dairies, hay. Market value $261.1 million.

CANYON (13,399) county seat; West Texas A&M University; tourism; commuting to Amarillo; ranching, farm center; light manufacturing; gateway to state park.

AMARILLO (185,745 total, mostly [111,851] in Potter County) hub for northern Panhandle oil and ranching; distribution, marketing center; varied manufacturing; hospitals; varied cultural, recreational events.

Other towns include: **Lake Tanglewood** (756); **Palisades** (352); **Timbercreek Canyon** (437); **Umbarger** (327) German sausage festival in November. Part of **Happy** (634, mostly in Swisher County).

Population	111,472
Change fm 2000	6.9
Area (sq. mi.)	922.42
Land Area (sq. mi.)	914.43
Altitude (ft.)	2,700-3,900
Rainfall (in.)	19.19
Jan. mean min.	23.7
July mean max.	92.6
Civ. Labor	69,081
Unemployed	2.6
Wages	$194,641,051
Av. Weekly Wage	$539.08
Prop. Value	$5,657,922,397
Retail Sales	$907,768,240

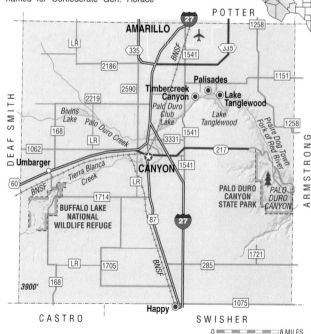

Reagan County

Physical Features: Western county; level to hilly, broken by draws, Big Lake (intermittent); sandy, loam, clay soils.

Economy: Oil production; natural gas; ranching.

History: Comanches in area until mid-1870s. Ranching began in 1880s. Hispanic migration increased after 1950. County named for Sen. John H. Reagan, first chairman, Texas Railroad Commission; county created 1903 from Tom Green County.

Race/Ethnicity, 2000: (In percent) Anglo, 46.84; Black, 3.04; Hispanic, 49.49; Other, 0.63.

Vital Statistics, 2004: Births, 47; deaths, 20; marriages, 17; divorces, 15.

Recreation: Texon reunion; rodeo; site of 1923 discovery well Santa Rita No. 1 on University of Texas land.

Minerals: Gas, oil.

Agriculture: Cotton, cattle, sheep, goats; cotton, grains principal crops; 36,000 acres irrigated. Market value $6.6 million.

BIG LAKE (2,677) county seat; center for oil activities, farming, ranching; hospital; Spring Bluegrass Festival.

Population		**3,022**
Change fm 2000		-9.1
Area (sq. mi.)		1,175.98
Land Area (sq. mi.)		1,175.30
Altitude (ft.)		2,400-2,953
Rainfall (in.)		18.79
Jan. mean min.		29.1
July mean max.		93.4
Civ. Labor		2,524
Unemployed		2.1
Wages		$17,825,889
Av. Weekly Wage		$784.00
Prop. Value		$906,351,390
Retail Sales		$24,082,158

For explanation of sources, abbreviations and symbols, see p. 224 and foldout map.

Biking in Palo Duro Canyon State Park. Robert Plocheck photo.

Real County

Physical Features: Hill Country, spring-fed streams, scenic canyons; Frio, Nueces rivers; cedars, pecans, walnuts, many live oaks.

Economy: Ranching; tourism, government/ services; cedar cutting.

History: Tonkawa area; Lipan Apaches arrived in early 1700s; later, Comanche hunters in area. Spanish mission established 1762. Anglo-Americans arrived in 1850s. County created 1913 from Bandera, Edwards, Kerr counties; named for legislator-ranchman Julius Real.

Race/Ethnicity, 2000: (In percent) Anglo, 76.53; Black, 0.23; Hispanic, 22.58; Other, 0.66.

Vital Statistics, 2004: Births, 34; deaths, 52; marriages, 29; divorces, 9.

Recreation: Tourist and hunting center; birding, fishing, camping; scenic drives; state natural area.

Minerals: Not significant.

Agriculture: Goats, sheep, beef cattle produce most income. Market value $2.7 million. Cedar posts processed.

LEAKEY (395) county seat; tourism, ranching; museums; July Jubilee.

CAMP WOOD (910) San Lorenzo de la Santa Cruz mission site; museum; settlers reunion in August; a tourist, ranching hub for parts of three counties.

Other towns include: **Rio Frio** (50).

Population	3,061
Change fm 2000	0.3
Area (sq. mi.)	700.04
Land Area (sq. mi.)	699.91
Altitude (ft.)	1,450-2,381
Rainfall (in.)	27.99
Jan. mean min.	33.1
July mean max.	94.2
Civ. Labor	1,042
Unemployed	4.7
Wages	$3,332,683
Av. Weekly Wage	$405.85
Prop. Value	$546,099,932
Retail Sales	$12,192,305

Red River County

Physical Features: On Red-Sulphur rivers' divide; 39 different soil types; half timbered.

Economy: Agribusinesses; lumbering; manufacturing.

History: Caddo Indians abandoned area in 1790s. One of the oldest counties; settlers were moving in from the United States in 1810s. Kickapoo and other tribes arrived in 1820s. Antebellum slaveholding area. County created 1836 as original county of the Republic; organized 1837; named for Red River, its northern boundary.

Race/Ethnicity, 2000: (In percent) Anglo, 76.65; Black, 17.93; Hispanic, 4.67; Other, 0.75.

Vital Statistics, 2004: Births, 145; deaths, 216; marriages, 83; divorces, 52.

Recreation: Historical sites include pioneer homes, birthplace of John Nance Garner; water activities; hunting of deer, turkey, duck, small game.

Minerals: Small oil flow.

Agriculture: Beef cattle, hay, corn. Market value $30.9 million. Timber sales substantial. Hunting leases important.

CLARKSVILLE (3,612) county seat; varied manufacturing; hospital; library; century-old courthouse; Historical Society bazaar in October.

Other towns include: **Annona** (260); **Avery** (462); **Bagwell** (150); **Bogata** (1,377); **Detroit** (787) commercial center in west. Part of **Deport** (690).

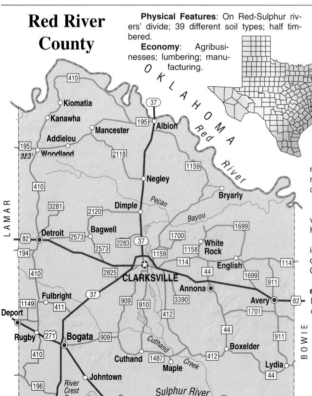

Population	13,440
Change fm 2000	-6.1
Area (sq. mi.)	1,057.61
Land Area (sq. mi.)	1,050.18
Altitude (ft.)	287-525
Rainfall (in.)	47.83
Jan. mean min.	29.7
July mean max.	92.2
Civ. Labor	6,336
Unemployed	5.1
Wages	$18,531,971
Av. Weekly Wage	$449.03
Prop. Value	$946,438,360
Retail Sales	$57,439,541

Reeves County

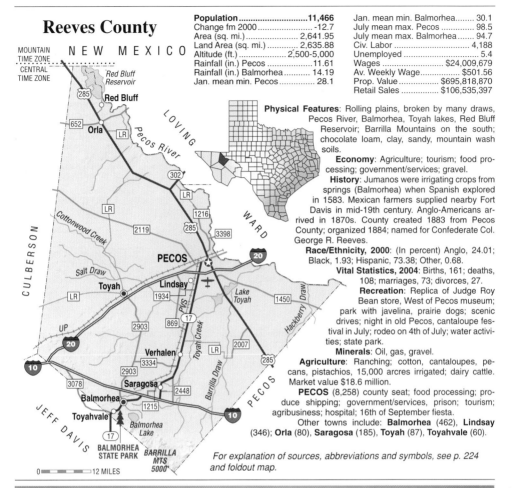

MOUNTAIN TIME ZONE

CENTRAL TIME ZONE

NEW MEXICO

Red Bluff Reservoir

285 Red Bluff

652 Orla LR

LOVING

Pecos River

302

LR

LR

1216

2119 285 3398

WARD

CULBERSON

Cottonwood Creek

Salt Draw

PECOS

20

Toyah LR

Lindsay

1934

PVS

Lake Toyah

1450

Hackberry Draw

UP

20

2903 869 17

Toyah Creek

2007

10

Verhalen LR 285

3334

2903 Barrilla Draw

PECOS

3078 Saragosa

2448

Balmorhea

1215

10

JEFF DAVIS

Toyahvale

17 Balmorhea Lake

BALMORHEA STATE PARK

BARRILLA MTS 5000'

0 ████ 12 MILES

Population............................**11,466**
Change fm 2000......................-12.7
Area (sq. mi.).....................2,641.95
Land Area (sq. mi.)............2,635.88
Altitude (ft.)....................2,500-5,000
Rainfall (in.) Pecos...................11.61
Rainfall (in.) Balmorhea...........14.19
Jan. mean min. Pecos...............28.1

Jan. mean min. Balmorhea........30.1
July mean max. Pecos..............98.5
July mean max. Balmorhea.......94.7
Civ. Labor.................................4,188
Unemployed................................5.4
Wages.........................$24,009,679
Av. Weekly Wage.................$501.56
Prop. Value.................$695,818,870
Retail Sales................$106,535,397

Physical Features: Rolling plains, broken by many draws, Pecos River, Balmorhea, Toyah lakes, Red Bluff Reservoir; Barrilla Mountains on the south; chocolate loam, clay, sandy, mountain wash soils.

Economy: Agriculture; tourism; food processing; government/services; gravel.

History: Jumanos were irrigating crops from springs (Balmorhea) when Spanish explored in 1583. Mexican farmers supplied nearby Fort Davis in mid-19th century. Anglo-Americans arrived in 1870s. County created 1883 from Pecos County; organized 1884; named for Confederate Col. George R. Reeves.

Race/Ethnicity, 2000: (In percent) Anglo, 24.01; Black, 1.93; Hispanic, 73.38; Other, 0.68.

Vital Statistics, 2004: Births, 161; deaths, 108; marriages, 73; divorces, 27.

Recreation: Replica of Judge Roy Bean store, West of Pecos museum; park with javelina, prairie dogs; scenic drives; night in old Pecos, cantaloupe festival in July; rodeo on 4th of July; water activities; state park.

Minerals: Oil, gas, gravel.

Agriculture: Ranching; cotton, cantaloupes, pecans, pistachios, 15,000 arcres irrigated; dairy cattle. Market value $18.6 million.

PECOS (8,258) county seat; food processing; produce shipping; government/services, prison; tourism; agribusiness; hospital; 16th of September fiesta.

Other towns include: **Balmorhea** (462), **Lindsay** (346); **Orla** (80), **Saragosa** (185), **Toyah** (87), **Toyahvale** (60).

For explanation of sources, abbreviations and symbols, see p. 224 and foldout map.

Autumn in northern Red River County. Robert Plocheck photo.

Refugio County

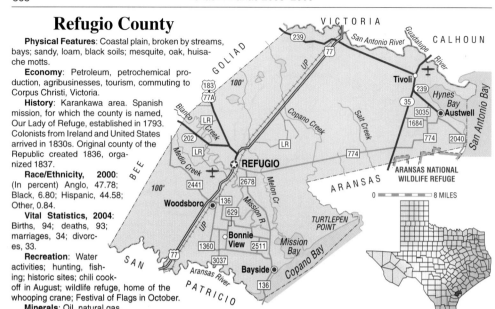

Physical Features: Coastal plain, broken by streams, bays; sandy, loam, black soils; mesquite, oak, huisache motts.

Economy: Petroleum, petrochemical production, agribusinesses, tourism, commuting to Corpus Christi, Victoria.

History: Karankawa area. Spanish mission, for which the county is named, Our Lady of Refuge, established in 1793. Colonists from Ireland and United States arrived in 1830s. Original county of the Republic created 1836, organized 1837.

Race/Ethnicity, 2000: (In percent) Anglo, 47.78; Black, 6.80; Hispanic, 44.58; Other, 0.84.

Vital Statistics, 2004: Births, 94; deaths, 93; marriages, 34; divorces, 33.

Recreation: Water activities; hunting, fishing; historic sites; chili cookoff in August; wildlife refuge, home of the whooping crane; Festival of Flags in October.

Minerals: Oil, natural gas.

Agriculture: Cotton, beef cattle, sorghum, corn, soybeans, horses. Market value $21.4 million. Hunting leases.

REFUGIO (2,780) county seat; petroleum, agribusiness center; hospital; museum, historic homes.

Other towns include: **Austwell** (179); **Bayside** (340) resorts; **Tivoli** (550); **Woodsboro** (1,619) commercial center.

Population	7,596
Change fm 2000	-3.0
Area (sq. mi.)	818.64
Land Area (sq. mi.)	770.21
Altitude (ft.)	sea level-100
Rainfall (in.)	40.10
Jan. mean min.	45.0
July mean max.	94.0
Civ. Labor	3,912
Unemployed	4.0
Wages	$13,711,227
Av. Weekly Wage	$521.96
Prop. Value	$1,186,974,220
Retail Sales	$69,693,806

Roberts County

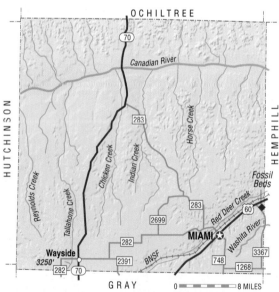

Physical Features: Rolling, broken by Canadian and tributaries; Red Deer Creek; black, sandy loam, alluvial soils.

Economy: Oil-field operations; agribusiness.

History: Apaches; pushed out by Comanches who were removed in 1874-75 by U.S. Army. Ranching began in late 1870s. County created 1876 from Bexar District; organized 1889; named for Texas leaders John S. Roberts and Gov. O.M. Roberts.

Race/Ethnicity, 2000: (In percent) Anglo, 96.39; Black, 0.34; Hispanic, 3.16; Other, 0.11.

Vital Statistics, 2004: Births, 9; deaths, 10; marriages, 9; divorces, 2.

Recreation: National cow-calling contest in June; scenic drives; hunting; museum.

Minerals: Production of gas, oil.

Agriculture: Beef cattle; wheat, sorghum, corn, soybeans, hay; 10,000 acres irrigated. Market value $13.2 million.

MIAMI (573) county seat; ranching, oil center; some manufacturing.

Population	835
Change fm 2000	-5.9
Area (sq. mi.)	924.19
Land Area (sq. mi.)	924.09
Altitude (ft.)	2,400-3,250
Rainfall (in.)	23.30
Jan. mean min.	20.6
July mean max.	92.4
Civ. Labor	598
Unemployed	2.2
Wages	$1,768.365
Av. Weekly Wage	$555.22
Prop. Value	$504,985,266
Retail Sales	$933,823

For explanation of sources, abbreviations and symbols, see p. 224 and foldout map.

Robertson County

Physical Features: Rolling in north and east, draining to bottoms along Brazos, Navasota rivers; sandy soils, heavy in bottoms.

Economy: Agribusiness; government/services; oil and gas.

History: Tawakoni, Waco, Comanche and other tribes. Anglo-Americans arrived in 1820s. Antebellum slaveholding area. County created 1837, organized 1838, subdivided into many others later; named for pioneer Sterling Clack Robertson.

Race/Ethnicity, 2000: (In percent) Anglo, 60.55; Black, 24.11; Hispanic, 14.74; Other, 0.60.

Vital Statistics, 2004: Births, 216; deaths, 192; marriages, 85; divorces, 49.

Recreation: Hunting, fishing; historic sites; historic-homes tour; dogwood trails, wildlife preserves.

Minerals: Gas, oil, lignite coal.

Agriculture: Most revenue from beef cattle, cotton, hay, corn; 20,000 acres of cropland irrigated. Market value $74.7 million.

FRANKLIN (1,513) county seat; farm-trade center, power plants, feed mill, library.

HEARNE (4,759) agribusiness; varied manufacturing; depot museum; music festival in October.

Other towns include: **Bremond** (858) power plant, coal mining, Polish Days in June; **Calvert** (1,440) agriculture, tourism, antiques, Maypole festival, tour of homes; **Mumford** (170); **New Baden** (150); **Wheelock** (225).

Population		16,214
Change fm 2000		1.4
Area (sq. mi.)		865.67
Land Area (sq. mi.)		854.56
Altitude (ft.)		250-550
Rainfall (in.)		39.03
Jan. mean min.		38.2
July mean max.		95.1
Civ. Labor		7,919
Unemployed		4.0
Wages		$26,565,745
Av. Weekly Wage		$560.48
Prop. Value		$1,816,740,110
Retail Sales		$88,945,601

Morning in Austwell on Hynes Bay in Refugio County. Robert Plocheck photo.

Rockwall County

Physical Features: Rolling prairie, mostly Blackland soil; Lake Ray Hubbard. Texas' smallest county.

Economy: Industrial employment in local plants and in Dallas; in Dallas metropolitan area; residential development around Lake Ray Hubbard.

History: Caddo area. Cherokees arrived in 1820s. Anglo-American settlers arrived in 1840s. County created 1873 from Kaufman; named for wall-like rock formation.

Race/Ethnicity, 2000: (In percent) Anglo, 83.77; Black, 3.32; Hispanic, 11.07; Other, 1.84.

Vital Statistics, 2004: Births, 855; deaths, 357; marriages, 1,477; divorces, 255.

Recreation: Lake activities; proximity to Dallas; unusual rock outcrop.

Minerals: Not significant.

Agriculture: Small grains, cattle, horticulture, horses. Market value $3 million.

ROCKWALL (29,198) county seat; commuters, varied manufacturing; hospital; harbor retail/entertainment district; Founders Day in April.

Other towns include: **Fate** (3,000); **Heath** (6,188); **McLendon-Chisholm** (1,054) chili cookoff in October; **Mobile City** (231); **Royse City** (6,542) varied manufacturing, agribusiness, Funfest in April, North Texas Speedway. Part [7,041] of **Rowlett**, hospital, and a small part [315] of **Wylie**.

Population		69,155
Change fm 2000		60.5
Area (sq. mi.)		148.70
Land Area (sq. mi.)		128.79
Altitude (ft.)		450-624
Rainfall (in.)		39.40
Jan. mean min.		33.0
July mean max.		96.0
Civ. Labor		32,196
Unemployed		3.3
Wages		$138,182,748
Av. Weekly Wage		$587.76
Prop. Value		$5,593,505,382
Retail Sales		$913,385,579

For explanation of sources, abbreviations and symbols, see p. 224 and foldout map.

Runnels County

Physical Features: West central county; level to rolling; bisected by Colorado and tributaries; sandy loam, black waxy soils.

Economy: Agribusiness; oil activity; government/services; manufacturing.

History: Spanish explorers found Jumanos in area in 1650s; later, Apaches and Comanches driven out in 1870s by U.S. military. First Anglo-Americans arrived in 1850s; Germans, Czechs around 1900. County named for planter-legislator H.G. Runnels; created 1858 from Bexar, Travis counties; organized 1880.

Race/Ethnicity, 2000: (In percent) Anglo, 68.32; Black, 1.57; Hispanic, 29.33; Other, 0.78.

Vital Statistics, 2004: Births, 145; deaths, 139; marriages, 66; divorces, 31.

Recreation: Deer, dove and turkey hunting; O.H. Ivie Reservoir; fishing; antique car museum; historical markers in county.

Minerals: Oil, gas, sand.

Agriculture: Cattle, cotton, wheat, sorghum, dairy products, sheep and goats. Market value $27.4 million.

BALLINGER (4,084) county seat; varied manufacturing; oil-field services; meat processing; Carnegie Library; hospital; Western Texas College extension; the Cross, 100-ft. tall atop hill south of city; Festival of Ethnic Cultures in April.

Other towns include: **Miles** (854); **Norton** (50); **Rowena** (349); **Wingate** (100); **Winters** (2,851) manufacturing, museum; hospital.

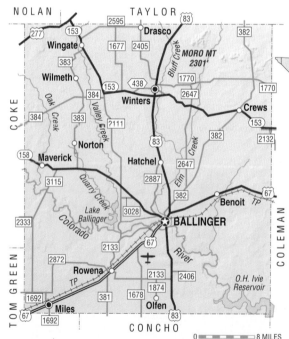

Population		10,724
Change fm 2000		-6.7
Area (sq. mi.)		1,057.13
Land Area (sq. mi.)		1,050.73
Altitude (ft.)		1,600-2,301
Rainfall (in.)		23.76
Jan. mean min.		28.5
July mean max.		94.3
Civ. Labor		4,480
Unemployed		4.5
Wages		$19,324,668
Av. Weekly Wage		$519.58
Prop. Value		$775,647,515
Retail Sales		$64,245,369

Rusk County

Physical Features: East Texas county on Sabine-Angelina divide; varied deep, sandy soils; over half in pines, hardwoods; lakes.

Economy: Lignite mining, electricity generation, oil and gas, lumbering, brick production, agribusiness, government/services.

History: Caddo area. Cherokees settled in 1820s; removed in 1839. First Anglo-Americans arrived in 1829. Antebellum slaveholding area. County named for Republic, state leader Thomas J. Rusk; created from Nacogdoches County 1843.

Race/Ethnicity, 2000: (In percent) Anglo, 71.61; Black, 19.31; Hispanic, 8.44; Other, 0.64.

Vital Statistics, 2004: Births, 618; deaths, 503; marriages, 312; divorces, 274.

Recreation: Water sports, state park; historic homes, sites; scenic drives; marked site of East Texas Field discovery oil well; syrup festival in November.

Minerals: Oil, natural gas, lignite, clays.

Agriculture: Beef cattle, hay, broilers, nursery plants. Market value $39.3 million. Timber income substantial.

HENDERSON (11,012) county seat; center for agribusiness, oil activities; manufacturing; hospital; museum; state jails.

Other towns include: **Joinerville** (140); **Laird Hill** (300); **Laneville** (169); **Minden** (150); **Mount Enterprise** (521); **New London** (973) site of 1937 school explosion that killed 293 students and faculty; **Overton** (2,268, partly in Smith County) oil, lumbering center, petroleum processing, A&M research center, blue grass festival in July, prison; **Price** (275); **Tatum** (1,169, partly in Panola County); **Turnertown-Selman City** (271).

Also, part of **Easton** (561, mostly in Gregg County), part of **Reklaw** (356, mostly in Cherokee County) and part [2,580] of **Kilgore** (12,021 total).

Population..................... **48,354**	July mean max. 93.1
Change fm 2000.................. 2.1	Civ. Labor 22,903
Area (sq. mi.)............... 938.62	Unemployed 4.1
Land Area (sq. mi.) 923.55	Wages $111,466,950
Altitude (ft.) 280-662	Av. Weekly Wage......... $657.36
Rainfall (in.) 48.22	Prop. Value $4,401,607,040
Jan. mean min. 33.1	Retail Sales $387,976,731

The Kilgore Rangerettes of Kilgore College perform at the 2006 Cotton Bowl. Michael Mulvey photo.

Sabine County

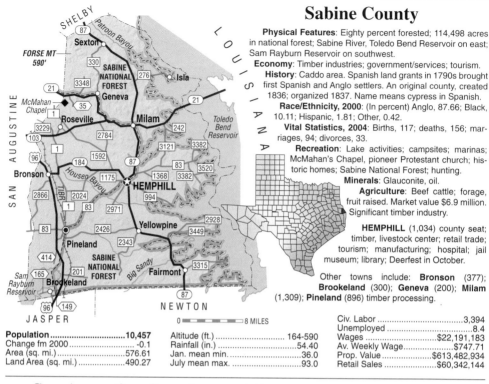

Physical Features: Eighty percent forested; 114,498 acres in national forest; Sabine River, Toledo Bend Reservoir on east; Sam Rayburn Reservoir on southwest.

Economy: Timber industries; government/services; tourism.

History: Caddo area. Spanish land grants in 1790s brought first Spanish and Anglo settlers. An original county, created 1836; organized 1837. Name means cypress in Spanish.

Race/Ethnicity, 2000: (In percent) Anglo, 87.66; Black, 10.11; Hispanic, 1.81; Other, 0.42.

Vital Statistics, 2004: Births, 117; deaths, 156; marriages, 94; divorces, 33.

Recreation: Lake activities; campsites; marinas; McMahan's Chapel, pioneer Protestant church; historic homes; Sabine National Forest; hunting.

Minerals: Glauconite, oil.

Agriculture: Beef cattle; forage, fruit raised. Market value $6.9 million. Significant timber industry.

HEMPHILL (1,034) county seat; timber, livestock center; retail trade; tourism; manufacturing; hospital; jail museum; library; Deerfest in October.

Other towns include: **Bronson** (377); **Brookeland** (300); **Geneva** (200); **Milam** (1,309); **Pineland** (896) timber processing.

Population	10,457
Change fm 2000	-0.1
Area (sq. mi.)	576.61
Land Area (sq. mi.)	490.27
Altitude (ft.)	164-590
Rainfall (in.)	54.40
Jan. mean min.	36.0
July mean max.	93.0
Civ. Labor	3,394
Unemployed	8.4
Wages	$22,191,183
Av. Weekly Wage	$747.71
Prop. Value	$613,482,934
Retail Sales	$60,342,144

San Augustine County

Physical Features: Hilly East Texas county, 80 percent forested with 66,799 acres in Angelina National Forest, 4,317 in Sabine National Forest; Sam Rayburn Reservoir; varied soils, sandy to black alluvial.

Economy: Lumbering; poultry; varied manufacturing.

History: Presence of Ais Indians attracted Spanish mission in 1717. First Anglos and Indians from U.S. southern states arrived around 1800. Antebellum slaveholding area. County created and named for Mexican municipality in 1836; an original county; organized 1837.

Race/Ethnicity, 2000: (In percent) Anglo, 68.13; Black, 27.93; Hispanic, 3.58; Other, 0.36.

Vital Statistics, 2004: Births, 106; deaths, 140; marriages, 67; divorces, 2.

Recreation: Lake activities; sassafras festival in October; many historic homes; tourist facilities in national forests.

Minerals: Small amount of oil.

Agriculture: Poultry, cattle, horses; watermelons, peas, corn, truck crops. Market value $25 million. Timber sales significant.

SAN AUGUSTINE (2,496) county seat; poultry, timber, livestock center; Deep East Texas Electric Cooperative; hospital; Mission Dolores museum.

Other towns include: **Broaddus** (187).

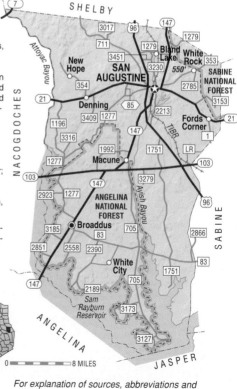

Population	8,888
Change fm 2000	-0.6
Area (sq. mi.)	592.21
Land Area (sq. mi.)	527.87
Altitude (ft.)	164-550
Rainfall (in.)	51.10
Jan. mean min.	35.0
July mean max.	93.0
Civ. Labor	3,637
Unemployed	5.5
Wages	$10,413,791
Av. Weekly Wage	$469.10
Prop. Value	$446,450,342
Retail Sales	$77,843,035

For explanation of sources, abbreviations and symbols, see p. 224 and foldout map.

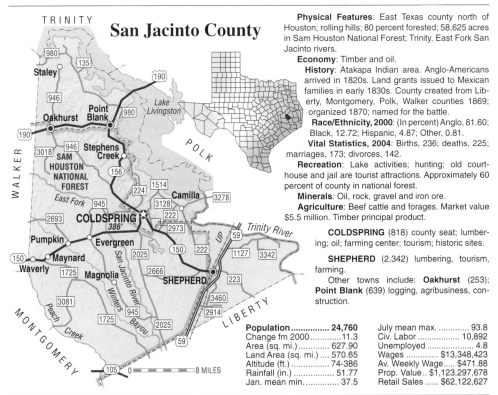

San Jacinto County

Physical Features: East Texas county north of Houston; rolling hills; 80 percent forested; 58,625 acres in Sam Houston National Forest; Trinity, East Fork San Jacinto rivers.

Economy: Timber and oil.

History: Atakapa Indian area. Anglo-Americans arrived in 1820s. Land grants issued to Mexican families in early 1830s. County created from Liberty, Montgomery, Polk, Walker counties 1869; organized 1870; named for the battle.

Race/Ethnicity, 2000: (In percent) Anglo, 81.60; Black, 12.72; Hispanic, 4.87; Other, 0.81.

Vital Statistics, 2004: Births, 236; deaths, 225; marriages, 173; divorces, 142.

Recreation: Lake activities; hunting; old courthouse and jail are tourist attractions. Approximately 60 percent of county in national forest.

Minerals: Oil, rock, gravel and iron ore.

Agriculture: Beef cattle and forages. Market value $5.5 million. Timber principal product.

COLDSPRING (818) county seat; lumbering; oil; farming center; tourism; historic sites.

SHEPHERD (2,342) lumbering, tourism, farming.

Other towns include: **Oakhurst** (253); **Point Blank** (639) logging, agribusiness, construction.

Population		**24,760**
Change fm 2000		11.3
Area (sq. mi.)		627.90
Land Area (sq. mi.)		570.65
Altitude (ft.)		74-386
Rainfall (in.)		51.77
Jan. mean min.		37.5
July mean max.		93.8
Civ. Labor		10,892
Unemployed		4.8
Wages		$13,348,423
Av. Weekly Wage		$471.88
Prop. Value		$1,123,297,678
Retail Sales		$62,122,627

Toledo Bend Reservoir, above, covers 181,600 acres in East Texas and Louisiana. Robert Plocheck photo.

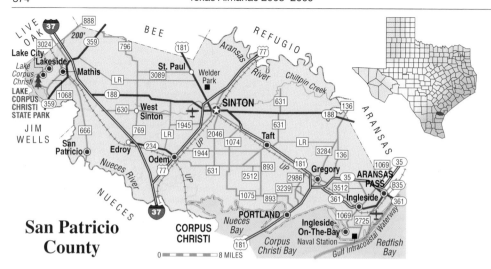

San Patricio County

0 ▬▬▬▬▬ 8 MILES

Physical Features: Grassy, coastal prairie draining to Aransas, Nueces rivers and to bays; sandy loam, clay, black loam soils; lake.

Economy: Oil, petrochemicals; agribusiness; manufacturing; tourism, naval base; in Corpus Christi metropolitan area.

History: Karankawa area. Mexican sheep herders in area before colonization. Settled by Irish families in 1830 (name is Spanish for St. Patrick). Created, named for municipality 1836; organized 1837, reorganized 1847.

Race/Ethnicity, 2000: (In percent) Anglo, 46.48; Black, 2.84; Hispanic, 49.42; Other, 1.26.

Vital Statistics, 2004: Births, 1,215; deaths, 519; marriages, 326; divorces, 288.

Recreation: Water activities; hunting; Corpus Christi Bay; state park; Welder Wildlife Foundation and Park; birdwatching.

Minerals: Production of oil, gas, gravel, caliche.

Agriculture: Cotton, grain sorghum, beef cattle, corn. Market value $68.9 million. Fisheries income significant.

SINTON (5,514) county seat; oil, agribusiness; tourism; Go Texan Days in October.

ARANSAS PASS (8,704, part in Aransas County) deepwater port, shrimping, tourist center; offshore oilwell servicing; aluminum, chemical plants; hospital; Shrimporee in May.

PORTLAND (16,100) retail center; petrochemicals; many residents work in Corpus Christi, naval base; Indian Point pier; Windfest in April.

Other towns include: **Edroy** (413); **Gregory** (2,250); **Ingleside** (9,575) naval base, chemical and manufacturing plants, ship repair, birding, Round Up Days in May; **Ingleside-on-the-Bay** (685); **Lake City** (519); **Lakeside** (324);

Population	69,522
Change fm 2000	3.6
Area (sq. mi.)	707.06
Land Area (sq. mi.)	691.65
Altitude (ft.)	sea level-200
Rainfall (in.)	35.54
Jan. mean min.	44.2
July mean max.	91.7
Civ. Labor	30,108
Unemployed	5.0
Wages	$143,371,562
Av. Weekly Wage	$659.21
Prop. Value	$3,773,128,164
Retail Sales	$576,822,142

Mathis (5,166); **Odem** (2,534); **St. Paul** (526); **San Patricio** (303); **Taft** (3,441) manufacturing, processing; drug rehabilitation center, hospital; blackland museum; **Taft Southwest** (1,586).

For explanation of sources, abbreviations and symbols, see p. 224 and foldout map.

A ship docks near the Naval Station at Ingleside. Robert Plocheck photo.

San Saba County

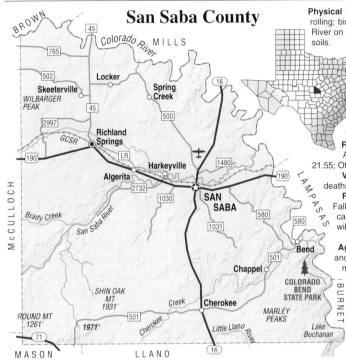

Physical Features: West central county; hilly, rolling; bisected by San Saba River; Colorado River on east; black, gray sandy loam, alluvial soils.

Economy: Government/services; retail pecan industry; tourism, hunting leases.

History: Apaches and Comanches in area when Spanish explored. Anglo-American settlers arrived in 1850s. County created from Bexar District 1856; named for river.

Race/Ethnicity, 2000: (In percent) Anglo, 75.19; Black, 2.63; Hispanic, 21.55; Other, 0.63.

Vital Statistics, 2004: Births, 58; deaths, 72; marriages, 31; divorces, 14.

Recreation: State park with Gorman Falls; deer hunting; historic sites; log cabin museum; fishing; scenic drives; wildflower trail.

Minerals: Limestone, rock quarry.

Agriculture: Cattle, pecans, hay, sheep and goats, wheat. Market value $22.9 million. Hunting, wildlife leases.

SAN SABA (2,577) county seat; claims title "Pecan Capital of the World"; stone processing; varied manufacturing; state prison; Cow Camp cookoff in May.

Other towns include: **Bend** (115, partly in Lampasas County); **Cherokee** (175); **Richland Springs** (345).

Population...................................5,993	Rainfall (in.) 27.72	Wages $11,570,711
Change fm 2000 ....-3.1	Jan. mean min. 33.4	Av. Weekly Wage....................$471.68
Area (sq. mi.)......................1,138.25	July mean max. 95.8	Fed. Wages $193,542
Land Area (sq. mi.) 1,134.47	Civ. Labor 2,607	Prop. Value $1,013,293,671
Altitude (ft.) 1,100-1,971	Unemployed 4.1	Retail Sales $31,590,638

Schleicher County

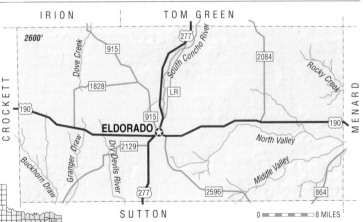

Physical Features: West central county on edge of Edwards Plateau, broken by Devils, Concho, San Saba tributaries; part hilly; black soils.

Economy: Oil, ranching; hunting.

History: Jumanos in area in 1630s. Later, Apaches and Comanches; removed in 1870s. Ranching began in 1870s. Census of 1890 showed third of population from Mexico. County named for Gustav Schleicher, founder of German colony; county created from Crockett County 1887, organized 1901.

Race/Ethnicity, 2000: (In percent) Anglo, 54.59; Black, 1.26; Hispanic, 43.54; Other, 0.61.

Vital Statistics, 2004: Births, 39; deaths, 36; marriages, 14; divorces, 15.

Recreation: Hunting; livestock show in January, youth, open rodeos; mountain bike events; playhouse "Way off Broadway".

Minerals: Oil, natural gas.

Agriculture: Beef cattle, goats, sheep; crops include cotton, milo, hay, small grains. Market value $9.2 million. Hunting leases important.

ELDORADO (1,897) county seat; oil activities; center for livestock, mohair marketing, woolen mill; government/services, hospital.

Population................................ 2,776
Change fm 2000 ....-5.4
Area (sq. mi.) 1,310.65
Land Area (sq. mi.) 1,310.61
Altitude (ft.) 2,100-2,600
Rainfall (in.) 19.00
Jan. mean min. 28.0
July mean max. 93.0
Civ. Labor 1,354
Unemployed 3.6
Wages $5,605,257
Av. Weekly Wage................... $552.31
Prop. Value $578,390,147
Retail Sales $10,647,539

Scurry County

Physical Features: Plains county below Caprock, some hills; drained by Colorado, Brazos tributaries; lake; sandy, loam soils.

Economy: Oil production; government/services; agribusinesses, manufacturing.

History: Apaches; displaced later by Comanches who were relocated to Indian Territory in 1875. Ranching began in late 1870s. County created from Bexar District 1876; organized 1884; named for Confederate Gen. W.R. Scurry.

Race/Ethnicity, 2000: (In percent) Anglo, 65.55; Black, 6.14; Hispanic, 27.77; Other, 0.54.

Vital Statistics, 2004: Births, 219; deaths, 166; marriages, 127; divorces, 67.

Recreation: Lake J.B. Thomas water recreation; Towle Memorial Park; museums, community theater, White Buffalo Days and Bikefest in October.

Minerals: Oil, gas.

Agriculture: Cotton, wheat, cattle, hay. Market value $23 million.

SNYDER (10,493) county seat; textiles, brick plant, cotton, oil center; Western Texas (Jr.) College; hospital; prison; walking trail; Western Swing days in July.

Other towns include: **Dunn** (75); **Fluvanna** (180); **Hermleigh** (398); **Ira** (250).

Population	16,202
Change fm 2000	-1.0
Area (sq. mi.)	907.53
Land Area (sq. mi.)	902.50
Altitude (ft.)	2,000-2,822
Rainfall (in.)	22.51
Jan. mean min.	26.7
July mean max.	94.6
Civ. Labor	7,036
Unemployed	3.6
Wages	$50,752,877
Av. Weekly Wage	$672.46
Prop. Value	$1,904,575,278
Retail Sales	$174,050,423

Shackelford County

Physical Features: Rolling, hilly, drained by tributaries of Brazos; sandy and chocolate loam soils; lake.

Economy: Oil and ranching; some manufacturing; hunting leases.

History: Apaches; driven out by Comanches. First Anglo-American settlers arrived soon after establishment of military outpost in 1850s. County created from Bosque County 1858; organized 1874; named for Dr. Jack Shackelford (sometimes referred to as John), Texas Revolutionary hero.

Race/Ethnicity, 2000: (In percent) Anglo, 91.68; Black, 0.33; Hispanic, 7.60; Other, 0.39.

Vital Statistics, 2004: Births, 35; deaths, 48; marriages, 31; divorces, 23.

Recreation: Fort Griffin State Park, June Fandangle musical about area history; courthouse historical district; hunting, lake, outdoor activities.

Minerals: Oil, natural gas.

Agriculture: Beef cattle, wheat, hay, cotton. Market value $15.1 million. Hunting leases.

ALBANY (1,828) county seat; tourism; hunting; oil; ranching; historical district, Old Jail art center.

Other town: **Moran** (226).

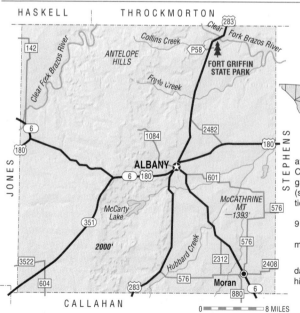

Population	3,194
Change fm 2000	-3.3
Area (sq. mi.)	915.54
Land Area (sq. mi.)	913.95
Altitude (ft.)	1,200-2,000
Rainfall (in.)	28.45
Jan. mean min.	28.4
July mean max.	95.4
Civ. Labor	1,963
Unemployed	2.8
Wages	$7,960,361
Av. Weekly Wage	$569.26
Prop. Value	$460,165,673
Retail Sales	$13,843,545

Shelby County

Physical Features: East Texas county; partly hills, much bottomland; well-timbered, 67,762 acres in national forest; Attoyac Bayou and Toledo Bend, other streams; sandy, clay, alluvial soils.

Economy: Broiler, egg production; timber; cattle; tourism.

History: Caddo Indian area. First Anglo-Americans settled in 1810s. Antebellum slaveholding area. Original county of Republic, created 1836; organized 1837; named for Isaac Shelby of American Revolution.

Race/Ethnicity, 2000: (In percent) Anglo, 69.95; Black, 19.53; Hispanic, 9.87; Other, 0.65.

Vital Statistics, 2004: Births, 406; deaths, 310; marriages, 204; divorces, 114.

Recreation: Toledo Bend Reservoir activities; Sabine National Forest; hunting, fishing; camping; historic sites; restored 1885 courthouse.

Minerals: Natural gas, oil.

Agriculture: A leader in broiler and egg production; cattle; hay, vegetables, watermelons. Market value $240.6 million. Timber sales significant.

CENTER (5,762) county seat; poultry, lumber processing; tourism; hospital; Shelby College Center; Poultry festival in October.

Other towns: **Huxley** (309); **Joaquin** (959); **Shelbyville** (600); **Tenaha** (1,012); **Timpson** (1,082) livestock, timber, farming, commuters; genealogy library; So-So Festival in fall.

For explanation of sources, abbreviations and symbols, see p. 224 and foldout map.

Population	26,575
Change fm 2000	5.4
Area (sq. mi.)	834.53
Land Area (sq. mi.)	794.11
Altitude (ft.)	174-630
Rainfall (in.)	53.01
Jan. mean min.	34.9
July mean max.	93.9
Civ. Labor	11,642
Unemployed	4.2
Wages	$53,169,293
Av. Weekly Wage	$523.35
Prop. Value	$1,409,532,238
Retail Sales	$244,530,921

The Shackelford County Courthouse in Albany. Robert Plocheck photo.

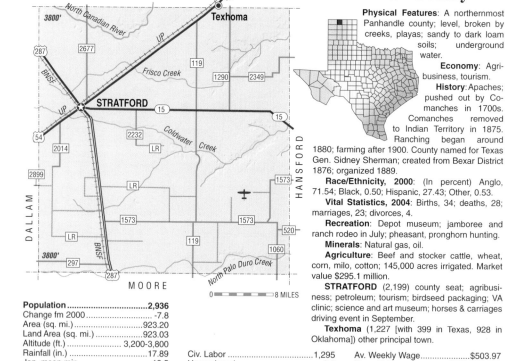

Sherman County

Physical Features: A northernmost Panhandle county; level, broken by creeks, playas; sandy to dark loam soils; underground water.

Economy: Agribusiness, tourism.

History: Apaches; pushed out by Comanches in 1700s. Comanches removed to Indian Territory in 1875. Ranching began around 1880; farming after 1900. County named for Texas Gen. Sidney Sherman; created from Bexar District 1876; organized 1889.

Race/Ethnicity, 2000: (In percent) Anglo, 71.54; Black, 0.50; Hispanic, 27.43; Other, 0.53.

Vital Statistics, 2004: Births, 34; deaths, 28; marriages, 23; divorces, 4.

Recreation: Depot museum; jamboree and ranch rodeo in July; pheasant, pronghorn hunting.

Minerals: Natural gas, oil.

Agriculture: Beef and stocker cattle, wheat, corn, milo, cotton; 145,000 acres irrigated. Market value $295.1 million.

STRATFORD (2,199) county seat; agribusiness; petroleum; tourism; birdseed packaging; VA clinic; science and art museum; horses & carriages driving event in September.

Texhoma (1,227 [with 399 in Texas, 928 in Oklahoma]) other principal town.

Population	**2,936**
Change fm 2000	-7.8
Area (sq. mi.)	923.20
Land Area (sq. mi.)	923.03
Altitude (ft.)	3,200-3,800
Rainfall (in.)	17.89
Jan. mean min.	18.5
July mean max.	91.1

Civ. Labor	1,295	Av. Weekly Wage	$503.97
Unemployed	3.8	Prop. Value	$756,525,189
Wages	$5,385,452	Retail Sales	$10,026,687

The Riter Bell Tower on the campus of the University of Texas at Tyler. Robert Plocheck photo.

Smith County

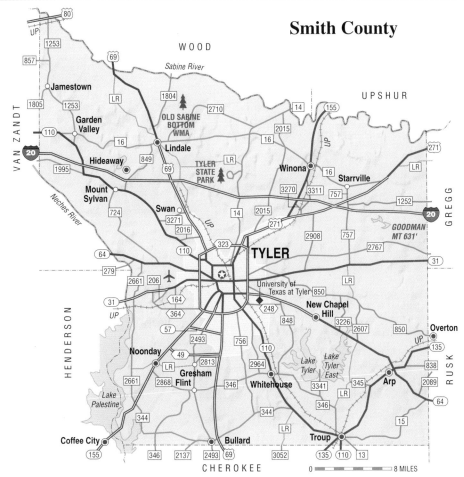

Physical Features: Populous East Texas county of rolling hills, many timbered; Sabine, Neches, other streams; Tyler, Palestine lakes; alluvial, gray, sandy loam, clay soils.

Economy: Medical facilities, education, government/services; agribusiness; petroleum production; manufacturing, distribution center; tourism.

History: Caddoes of area reduced by disease and other tribes in 1790s. Cherokees settled in 1820s; removed in 1839. In late 1820s, first Anglo-American settlers arrived. Antebellum slaveholding area. County named for Texas Revolutionary Gen. James Smith; county created 1846 from Nacogdoches County.

Race/Ethnicity, 2000: (In percent) Anglo, 68.40; Black, 19.24; Hispanic, 11.17; Other, 1.19

Vital Statistics, 2004: Births, 2,876; deaths, 1,575; marriages, 1,803; divorces, 546.

Recreation: Activities on Palestine, Tyler lakes and others; famed Rose Garden; Texas Rose Festival in October; Azalea Trail; state park; Goodman Museum; Juneteenth celebration, East

Texas Fair in Sept./Oct.; Caldwell Zoo; collegiate events.

Minerals: Oil, gas.

Agriculture: Horticultural crops and nurseries, beef cattle, forages, fruits and vegetables, horses. Market value $63.5 million. Timber sales substantial.

TYLER (92,987) county seat; claims title, "Rose Capital of the Nation"; administrative center for oil production; varied manufacturing; University of Texas at Tyler, Tyler Junior College; Texas College, University of Texas Health Center; hospitals, nursing school.

Other towns include: **Arp** (995) Strawberry Festival in April; **Bullard**

(1,696, part in Cherokee County); **Flint** (NA); **Hideaway** (2,860); **Lindale** (4,234) distribution center, foundry, varied manufacturing, Country Fest in October; **New Chapel Hill** (587); **Noonday** (544) Sweet Onion festival in June; **Troup** (2,104, part in Cherokee County); **Whitehouse** (7,118) commuters to Tyler, government/services, Yesteryear festival in June; **Winona** (620).

Part of **Overton** (2,268, mostly in Rusk County).

Population	**194,635**
Change fm 2000	11.4
Area (sq. mi.)	949.45
Land Area (sq. mi.)	928.38
Altitude (ft.)	300-631
Rainfall (in.)	45.40
Jan. mean min.	38.0
July mean max.	94.0
Civ. Labor	98,685
Unemployed	5.0
Wages	$817,191,882
Av. Weekly Wage	$692.49
Prop. Value	$12,194,627,864
Retail Sales	$2,909,934,840

For explanation of sources, symbols and abbreviations, see p. 224 and foldout map.

Somervell County

Physical Features: Hilly terrain southwest of Fort Worth; Brazos, Paluxy rivers; gray, dark, alluvial soils; second-smallest county.

Economy: Tourism, nuclear power plant, agribusiness, government/services.

History: Wichita, Tonkawa area; Comanches later. Anglo-Americans arrived in 1850s. County created as Somerville County 1875 from Hood County. Spelling was changed 1876; named for Republic of Texas Gen. Alexander Somervell.

Race/Ethnicity, 2000: (In percent) Anglo, 85.29; Black, 0.32; Hispanic, 13.44; Other, 0.95.

Vital Statistics, 2004: Births, 93; deaths, 61; marriages, 62; divorces, 27.

Recreation: Fishing, hunting; unique geological formations; dinosaur tracks in state park; Glen Rose Big Rocks Park; Fossil Rim Wildlife Center; nature trails, museums; exposition center; Paluxy Pedal bicycle ride in October.

Minerals: Sand, gravel, silica, natural gas.

Agriculture: Cattle, hay, horses, nuseries. Market value $2 million. Hunting leases important.

GLEN ROSE (2,589) county seat; nuclear power plant, tourism, farm trade center; hospital; Hill College branch.

Other towns include: **Nemo** (56); **Rainbow** (121).

Population	**7,773**
Change fm 2000	14.2
Area (sq. mi.)	191.90
Land Area (sq. mi.)	187.17
Altitude (ft.)	600-1,200
Rainfall (in.)	34.82
Jan. mean min.	28.9
July mean max.	97.3
Civ. Labor	3,778
Unemployed	4.3
Wages	$35,460,000
Av. Weekly Wage	$798.58
Prop. Value	$2,105,156,506
Retail Sales	$49,963,263

Starr County

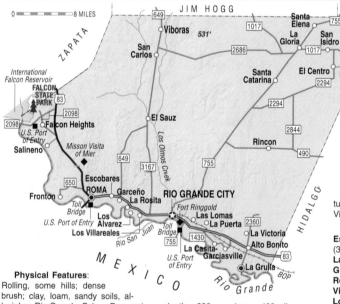

Physical Features: Rolling, some hills; dense brush; clay, loam, sandy soils, alluvial on Rio Grande; Falcon Reservoir.

Economy: Vegetable packing, shipping, other agribusiness; oil processing; tourism; government/services.

History: Coahuiltecan Indian area. Settlers from Spanish villages that were established in 1749 on south bank began to move across river soon afterward. Fort Ringgold established in 1848. County named for Dr. J.H. Starr, secretary of treasury of the Republic; county created from Nueces 1848.

Race/Ethnicity, 2000: (In percent) Anglo, 2.08; Black, 0.01; Hispanic, 97.54; Other, 0.37.

Vital Statistics, 2004: Births, 1,492; deaths, 283; marriages, 433; divorces, 63.

Recreation: Falcon Reservoir activities; deer, white-wing dove hunting; access to Mexico; historic houses, Lee House at Fort Ringgold; grotto at Rio Grande City; Roma Fest in November.

Minerals: Oil, gas, sand, gravel.

Agriculture: Beef and fed cattle; vegetables, cotton, sorghum; 18,000 acres irrigated for vegetables. Market value $66.7 million.

RIO GRANDE CITY (14,044) county seat; government/services; tourism; agriculture; hospital; college branches; trolley tours; Vaquero Days in February.

ROMA-Los Caenz (11,492) agriculture center; La Purísima Concepción Visita.

Other towns include: **Delmita** (50); **Escobares** (1,986); **Falcon Heights** (356); **Fronton** (629); **Garceño** (1,519); **La Casita-Garciasville** (2,419); **La Grulla** (1,637); **La Puerta** (1,724); **La Rosita** (1,812); **Las Lomas** (2,832); **La Victoria** (1,773); **Los Alvarez** (1,504); **Los Villareales** (976); **North Escobares** (1,787); **Salineño** (324); **San Isidro** (277); **Santa Elena** (64).

Population	**61,780**
Change fm 2000	15.3
Area (sq. mi.)	1,229.28
Land Area (sq. mi.)	1,223.02
Altitude (ft.)	125-531
Rainfall (in.)	21.61
Jan. mean min.	44.5
July mean max.	99.1
Civ. Labor	21,950
Unemployed	12.5
Wages	$68,850,275
Av. Weekly Wage	$414.00
Prop. Value	$2,189,636,710
Retail Sales	$401,202,892

Stephens County

Physical Features: West central county; broken, hilly; Hubbard Creek Reservoir, Possum Kingdom, Daniel lakes; Brazos River; loam, sandy soils.

Economy: Oil, agribusinesses, recreation, some manufacturing.

History: Comanches, Tonkawas in area when Anglo-American settlement began in 1850s. County created as Buchanan 1858 from Bosque; renamed 1861 for Confederate Vice President Alexander H. Stephens; organized 1876.

Race/Ethnicity, 2000: (In percent) Anglo, 81.76; Black, 3.04; Hispanic, 14.66; Other, 0.54.

Vital Statistics, 2004: Births, 123; deaths, 99; marriages, 83; divorces, 59.

Recreation: Lakes activities; hunting; campsites; historical points; Swenson Museum; Sandefer Oil Museum; aviation museum; Fabulous Fifties and car show in September.

Minerals: Oil, natural gas, stone.

Agriculture: Beef cattle, hogs, goats, sheep; wheat, oats, hay, peanuts, grain sorghums, cotton, pecans. Market value $8.8 million.

BRECKENRIDGE (5,787) county seat; oil; agriculture center; oilfield equipment, aircraft parts manufacturing; hospital; prison unit; Texas State Technical College branch, library.

Other towns include: **Caddo** (40) gateway to Possum Kingdom State Park.

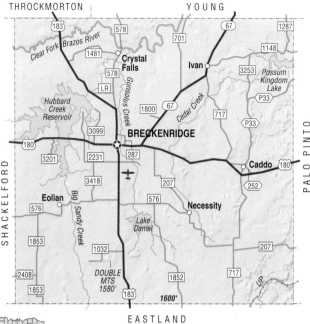

Population	9,610
Change fm 2000	-0.7
Area (sq. mi.)	921.48
Land Area (sq. mi.)	894.64
Altitude (ft.)	995-1,600
Rainfall (in.)	27.04
Jan. mean min.	30.9
July mean max.	96.8
Civ. Labor	4,250
Unemployed	3.7

Wages	$21,444,012
Av. Weekly Wage	$524.33
Prop. Value	$769,765,204
Retail Sales	$84,828,116

For explanation of sources, symbols and abbreviations, see p. 224 and foldout map.

The grotto in Rio Grande City is built to resemble the shrine of Lourdes, France. Robert Plocheck photo.

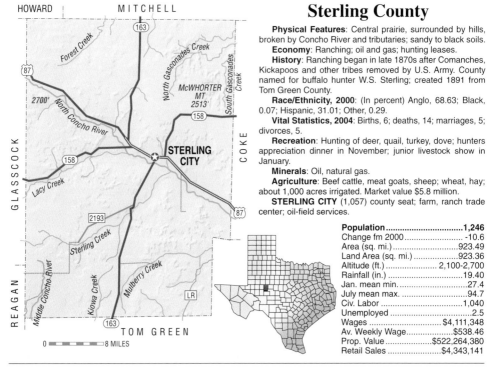

Sterling County

Physical Features: Central prairie, surrounded by hills, broken by Concho River and tributaries; sandy to black soils.

Economy: Ranching; oil and gas; hunting leases.

History: Ranching began in late 1870s after Comanches, Kickapoos and other tribes removed by U.S. Army. County named for buffalo hunter W.S. Sterling; created 1891 from Tom Green County.

Race/Ethnicity, 2000: (In percent) Anglo, 68.63; Black, 0.07; Hispanic, 31.01; Other, 0.29.

Vital Statistics, 2004: Births, 6; deaths, 14; marriages, 5; divorces, 5.

Recreation: Hunting of deer, quail, turkey, dove; hunters appreciation dinner in November; junior livestock show in January.

Minerals: Oil, natural gas.

Agriculture: Beef cattle, meat goats, sheep; wheat, hay; about 1,000 acres irrigated. Market value $5.8 million.

STERLING CITY (1,057) county seat; farm, ranch trade center; oil-field services.

Population	1,246
Change fm 2000	-10.6
Area (sq. mi.)	923.49
Land Area (sq. mi.)	923.36
Altitude (ft.)	2,100-2,700
Rainfall (in.)	19.40
Jan. mean min.	27.4
July mean max.	94.7
Civ. Labor	1,040
Unemployed	2.5
Wages	$4,111,348
Av. Weekly Wage	$538.46
Prop. Value	$522,264,380
Retail Sales	$4,343,141

Physical Features: Western county on rolling plains below Caprock, bisected by Brazos forks; sandy loam, sandy, other soils; some hills.

Economy: Agribusiness, light fabrication, government/services.

History: Anglo-American ranchers arrived in 1870s after Comanches and other tribes removed by U.S. Army. German farmers settled after 1900. County named for Confederate Gen. T.J. (Stonewall) Jackson; created from Bexar District 1876, organized 1888.

Race/Ethnicity, 2000: (In percent) Anglo, 84.17; Black, 3.37; Hispanic, 11.75; Other, 0.71.

Vital Statistics, 2004: Births, 17; deaths, 16; marriages, 7; divorces, 4.

Recreation: Deer, quail, feral hog, turkey hunting; rodeos in June, September; livestock show.

Minerals: Gypsum, gravel, oil.

Agriculture: Beef cattle, wheat, cotton, peanuts, hay. Also, grain sorghum, meat goats and swine. Market value $9 million.

ASPERMONT (873) county seat; oil field, ranching center; light fabrication; hospital; springfest; livestock show in February.

Other towns include: **Old Glory** (100) farming center.

For explanation of sources, symbols and abbreviations, see p. 224 and foldout map.

Stonewall County

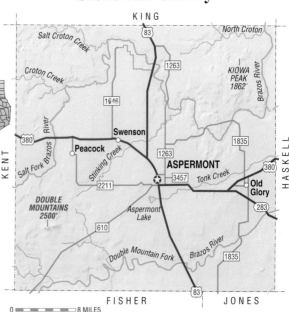

Population	1,402	July mean max.	97.4
Change fm 2000	-17.2	Civ. Labor	854
Area (sq. mi.)	920.23	Unemployed	3.0
Land Area (sq. mi.)	918.67	Wages	$3,766,186
Altitude (ft.)	1,500-2,500	Av. Weekly Wage	$465.77
Rainfall (in.)	23.24	Prop. Value	$197,104,611
Jan. mean min.	27.2	Retail Sales	$9,159,164

Sutton County

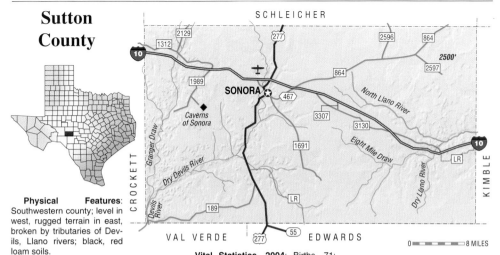

Physical Features: Southwestern county; level in west, rugged terrain in east, broken by tributaries of Devils, Llano rivers; black, red loam soils.

Economy: Oil and gas; agribusiness; hunting; tourism.

History: Lipan Apaches drove out Tonkawas in 1600s. Comanches, military outpost and disease forced Apaches south. Anglo-Americans settled in 1870s. Mexican immigration increased after 1890. County created from Crockett 1887; organized 1890; named for Confederate officer Col. John S. Sutton.

Race/Ethnicity, 2000: (In percent) Anglo, 47.51; Black, 0.29; Hispanic, 51.66; Other, 0.54.

Vital Statistics, 2004: Births, 71; deaths, 35; marriages, 29; divorces, 18.

Recreation: Hunting; Meirs Museum; Caverns of Sonora; goat cookoff; Diez y Seis in September.

Minerals: Oil, natural gas.

Agriculture: Meat goats, sheep, cattle, Angora goats. Exotic wildlife. Wheat and oats raised for grazing, hay; minor irrigation. Market value $6.4 million. Hunting leases important.

SONORA (3,067) county seat; oil, gas production; ranching; tourism; hospital; wool, mohair show in June.

Population	**4,281**
Change fm 2000	5.0
Area (sq. mi.)	1,454.40
Land Area (sq. mi.)	1,453.76
Altitude (ft.)	1,900-2,500
Rainfall (in.)	22.40
Jan. mean min.	27.2
July mean max.	94.7
Civ. Labor	3,017
Unemployed	2.1
Wages	$25,171,896
Av. Weekly Wage	$839.68
Prop. Value	$1,458,265,535
Retail Sales	$42,136,701

Swisher County

Physical Features: High Plains county; level, broken by Tule Canyon and Creek; playas; large underground water supply; rich soils.

Economy: Feedlots, grain storage, other agribusinesses; varied manufacturing; tourism; prison unit.

History: Apaches; displaced by Comanches around 1700. U.S. Army removed Comanches in 1874. Ranching began in late 1870s. Farming developed after 1900. County named for J.G. Swisher of Texas Revolution; county created from Bexar, Young territories 1876; organized 1890.

Race/Ethnicity, 2000: (In percent) Anglo, 58.37; Black, 5.91; Hispanic, 35.22; Other, 0.50.

Vital Statistics, 2004: Births, 141; deaths, 72; marriages, 38; divorces, 19.

Recreation: Mackenzie battle site; museum; county picnic in July; "Rogue of the Railways" melodrama in March.

Minerals: Not significant.

Agriculture: A major agricultural county. Stocker cattle, feed lots. Cotton, corn, wheat, sorghum raised. Some 400,000 acres irrigated. Market value $296.3 million.

TULIA (4,918) county seat; farming center; government/services; food processing; hospital; library, museum; prison; Tule Creek bluegrass festival in July.

Other towns include: **Happy** (634, partly in Randall County); **Kress** (819); **Vigo Park** (36).

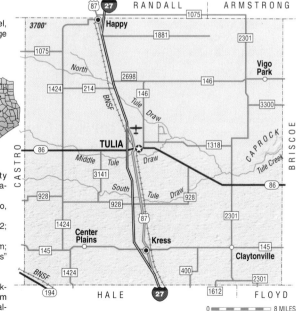

Population	**7,830**
Change fm 2000	-6.5
Area (sq. mi.)	900.68
Land Area (sq. mi.)	900.43
Altitude (ft.)	3,100-3,700
Rainfall (in.)	20.71
Jan. mean min.	22.2
July mean max.	91.1
Civ. Labor	3,698
Unemployed	4.1
Wages	$13,813,403
Av. Weekly Wage	$480.80
Prop. Value	$411,433,081
Retail Sales	$37,018,515

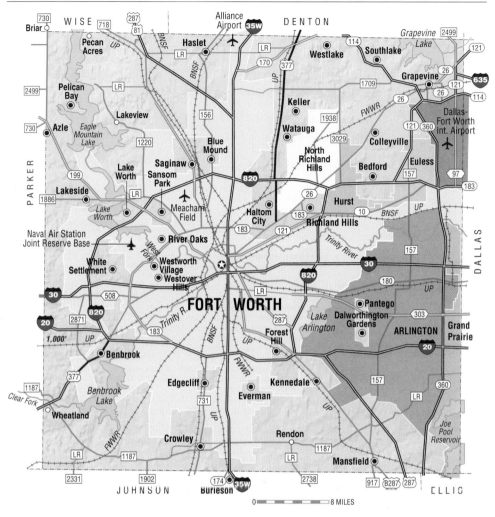

Tarrant County

Physical Features: Part Blackland, level to rolling; drains to Trinity; Worth, Grapevine, Eagle Mountain, Benbrook lakes.

Economy: Tourism; planes, helicopters, foods, mobile homes, electronic equipment, chemicals, plastics among products of more than 1,000 factories; large federal expenditure; D/FW International Airport; economy closely associated with Dallas urban area.

History: Caddoes in area. Comanches, other tribes arrived about 1700. Anglo-Americans settled in 1840s. Named for Gen. Edward H. Tarrant, who helped drive Indians from area. County created 1849 from Navarro County; organized 1850.

Race/Ethnicity, 2000: (In percent) Anglo, 62.79; Black, 13.01; Hispanic, 19.73; Other, 4.47.

Vital Statistics, 2004: Births, 27,592; deaths, 9,670; marriages, 12,514; divorces, 7,347.

Recreation: Scott Theatre; Amon G. Carter Museum; Kimbell Art Museum; Modern Art Museum; Museum of Science and History; Casa Manana; Botanic Gardens; Fort Worth Zoo; Log Cabin Village, all in Fort Worth.

Also, Six Flags Over Texas at Arlington; Southwestern Exposition, Stock Show; Convention Center; Stockyards Historical District; Texas Rangers major-league baseball at Arlington, other athletic events.

Minerals: Production of cement, sand, gravel, stone, gas.

Agriculture: Hay, beef cattle, wheat, horses, horticulture. Market value $29.1 million. Firewood marketed.

Education: Texas Christian University, University of Texas at Arlington, Texas Wesleyan University, Southwestern Baptist Theological Seminary and several other academic centers including a junior college system (three campuses).

FORT WORTH (638,102) county seat; a major mercantile, commercial and financial center; airplane, helicopter and other plants.

A cultural center with renowned art museums, Bass Performance Hall; many conventions held in downtown center; agribusiness center for wide area with grain-storage and feed-mill operations; adjacent to D/FW International Airport; hospitals.

ARLINGTON (365,723) tourist center with Six Flags Over Texas, the Texas Rangers baseball team, numerous restaurants, retail; educational facilities; industrial and distribution center for automobiles, food products, electronic components, aircraft and parts, rubber and plastic products; hospitals. Scottish Highland games in June.

Other towns include: **Hurst** (37,406); **Euless** (51,562); **Bedford** (48,270) helicopter plant, hospital, Celtic festival in fall; **North Richland Hills** (60,723) hospital.

Azle (10,217, partly in Parker County) government/services, varied industries, natural gas, hospital, commuters to Fort Worth, Jumpin' Jack Jamboree in September; **Benbrook** (21,377) varied manufacturing; hospitals; **Blue Mound** (2,495); **Briar** (5,651, parts in Wise and Parker counties).

Also, **Colleyville** (22,242) major residential development, some retail, manufacturing; **Crowley** (9,115) varied manufacturing, government/services; hospital; **Dalworthington Gardens** (2,373); **Edgecliff** (2,423); **Everman** (5,929); **Forest Hill** (13,668).

Also, **Grapevine** (47,271) varied manufacturing, distribution; near the D/FW International Airport; tourist center; hospital; Grapefest in September; **Haltom City** (41,721)

light manufacturing, food processing, medical center; library; **Haslet** (1,408); **Keller** (34,986) Bear Creek Park, Wild West Fest.

Also, **Kennedale** (6,625) printing, manufacturing, library, custom car show in April, drag strip; **Lakeside** (1,137); **Lake Worth** (4,641) retail, government/services, Bullfrog festival in April; **Mansfield** (37,213, partly in Johnson County) varied manufacturing; hospital; hometown celebration in September; **Pantego** (2,270); **Pelican Bay** (1,734); **Rendon** (9,436); **Richland Hills** (7,967).

Also, **River Oaks** (6,917); **Saginaw** (16,652) grain milling, manufacturing, distribution; North Texas Western Days in July; library; **Sansom Park** (4,326); **Southlake**

(24,943) technology, financial, retail center, hospital, parks, Oktoberfest; **Watauga** (22,693); **Westlake** (249); **West-over Hills** (640); **Westworth Village** (2,653); **White Settlement** (15,262) aircraft manufacturing, drilling equipment, technological services; museums, parks, historical sites; industrial park; White Settlement Day parade in fall.

Also, part [3,462] of **Burleson** (31,207); part [27,621] of **Grand Prairie** (148,992), and part of **Pecan Acres** (2,396).

Population	**1,671,295**
Change fm 2000	15.6
Area (sq. mi.)	897.48
Land Area (sq. mi.)	863.42
Altitude (ft.)	450-1,000
Rainfall (in.)	34.01
Jan. mean min.	31.4
July mean max.	96.6
Civ. Labor	879,606
Unemployed	4.0
Wages	$7,811,197,592
Av. Weekly Wage	$811.37
Prop. Value	$129,952,827,697
Retail Sales	$24,985,303,860

For explanation of sources, abbreviations and symbols, see p. 224 and foldout map.

Kids scream as they rotate on a ride at Six Flags Over Texas in Arlington. Nathan Hunsinger photo.

Taylor County

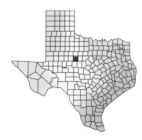

Physical Features: Prairies, with Callahan Divide, draining to Colorado tributaries, Brazos forks; Lakes Abilene, Kirby; mostly loam soils.

Economy: Agribusiness, oil and gas, education, Dyess Air Force Base.

History: Comanches in area about 1700. Anglo-American settlers arrived in 1870s. Named for Alamo heroes Edward, James and George Taylor, brothers; county created from Bexar, Travis counties 1858; organized 1878.

Race/Ethnicity, 2000: (In percent) Anglo, 73.54; Black, 6.95; Hispanic, 17.64; Other, 1.87.

Vital Statistics, 2004: Births, 2,055; deaths, 1,203; marriages, 1,469; divorces, 752.

Recreation: Abilene State Park; lake activities; Nelson Park Zoo; Texas Cowboy Reunion, West Texas Fair in September; Buffalo Gap historical tour and art festival; rodeo, college events.

Minerals: Oil, natural gas.

Agriculture: Beef cattle, small grain, cotton, milo. Market value $55.4 million.

Education: Abilene Christian University, Hardin-Simmons University, McMurry University, Cisco Junior College branch.

ABILENE (115,745, a small part in Jones County) county seat; distribution center; plants make a variety of products; meat, dairy processing; oil-field service center; hospitals; Abilene State School; West Texas Rehabilitation Center; Fort Phantom Hill (in Jones County). **Wylie** is now part of Abilene.

Other communities include: **Buffalo Gap** (443) historic sites; **Impact** (43); **Lawn** (345); **Merkel** (2,669) agribusiness center, clothing manufacturing, oil-field services; **Ovalo** (225); **Potosi** (1,700); **Trent** (310); **Tuscola** (776); **Tye** (1,171).

Population	124,927
Change fm 2000	-1.3
Area (sq. mi.)	919.25
Land Area (sq. mi.)	915.63
Altitude (ft.)	1,670-2,500
Rainfall (in.)	23.78
Jan. mean min.	31.8
July mean max.	94.8
Civ. Labor	68,120
Unemployed	3.2
Wages	$419,308,202
Av. Weekly Wage	$580.39
Prop. Value	$5,528,474,586
Retail Sales	$1,839,654,581

For explanation of sources, abbreviations and symbols, see p. 224 and foldout map.

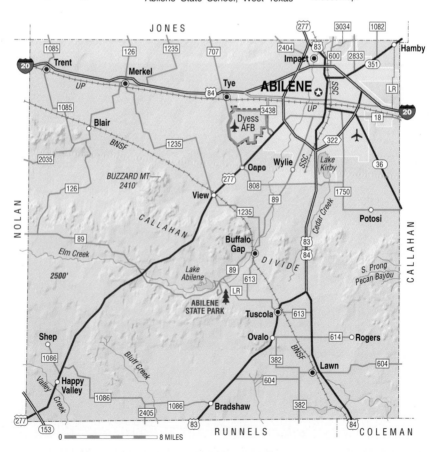

Terrell County

Physical Features: Trans-Pecos southwestern county; semi-mountainous, many canyons; rocky, limestone soils.

Economy: Ranching, hunting leases; oil and gas exploration; tourism.

History: Coahuiltecans, Jumanos and other tribes left many pictographs in area caves. Sheep ranching began in 1880s. Named for Confederate Gen. A.W. Terrell; county created 1905 from Pecos County.

Race/Ethnicity, 2000: (In percent) Anglo, 49.02; Black, 0.00; Hispanic, 48.57; Other, 2.41.

Vital Statistics, 2004: Births, 11; deaths, 13; marriages, 10; divorces, 0.

Recreation: Nature tourism, hunting, especially white-tailed, mule deer, Rio Grande Wild and Scenic River, varied wildlife; Cinco de Mayo, Prickly Pear Pachanga in October.

Minerals: Gas, oil, limestone.

Agriculture: Goats (meat, Angora); sheep (meat, wool); some beef cattle. Market value $3.9 million. Wildlife leases important.

SANDERSON (818) county seat; ranching, petroleum center; tourism; museum; motorcycle Buzzard Rally in spring. Other town: **Dryden** (13).

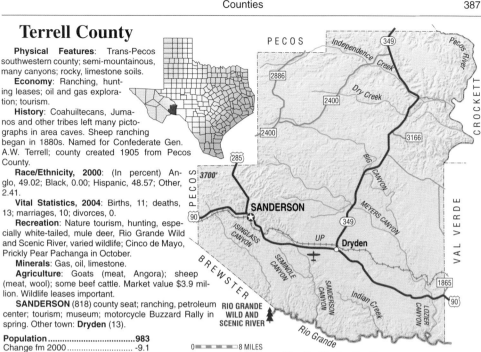

Population	983
Change fm 2000	-9.1
Area (sq. mi.)	2,357.75
Land Area (sq. mi.)	2,357.72
Altitude (ft.)	1,400-3,700
Rainfall (in.)	14.94
Jan. mean min.	30.5
July mean max.	91.9

Civ. Labor	353
Unemployed	5.7
Wages	$2,152,548

Av. Weekly Wage	$560.66
Prop. Value	$648,606,780
Retail Sales	$2,458,644

The Trans-Pecos terrain near the Rio Grande at the Terrell-Val Verde county line. Robert Plocheck photo.

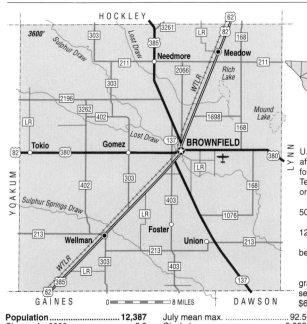

Terry County

Physical Features: Western county on South Plains, broken by draws, playas; sandy, sandy loam, loam soils.

Economy: Agribusiness, government/services, trade, commuting to Lubbock.

History: Comanches removed in 1870s by U.S. Army. Ranching developed in 1890s; farming after 1900. Oil discovered in 1940. County named for head of famed Texas Ranger troop, Col. B.F. Terry. County created from Bexar District 1876; organized 1904.

Race/Ethnicity, 2000: (In percent), Anglo, 50.32; Black, 5.02; Hispanic, 44.09; Other, 0.57.

Vital Statistics, 2004: Births, 182; deaths, 122; marriages, 90; divorces, 44.

Recreation: Museum; harvest festival in October; Brisket and Bean cook-off in April.

Minerals: Oil, gas, salt mining.

Agriculture: Cotton is principal crop; peanuts, grain sorghum, guar, wheat, melons, cucumbers, sesame. 170,000 acres irrigated. Market value $63.4 million.

BROWNFIELD (9,347) county seat; oil-field services; agribusiness; minerals processed; peanut processing; hospital; prison.

Other towns include: **Meadow** (679); **Tokio** (5); **Wellman** (188).

Population		12,387
Change fm 2000		-2.9
Area (sq. mi.)		890.93
Land Area (sq. mi.)		889.88
Altitude (ft.)		3,100-3,600
Rainfall (in.)		18.89
Jan. mean min.		26.1
July mean max.		92.5
Civ. Labor		5,833
Unemployed		4.1
Wages		$29,526,060
Av. Weekly Wage		$565.36
Prop. Value		$817,206,430
Retail Sales		$107,439,732

Throckmorton County

Physical Features: North Central county southwest of Wichita Falls; rolling, between Brazos forks; red to black soils.

Economy: Oil, agribusiness, hunting leases.

History: Site of Comanche Indian Reservation 1854-59. Ranching developed after Civil War. County named for Dr. W.E. Throckmorton, father of Gov. J.W. Throckmorton; county created from Fannin 1858; organized 1879.

Race/Ethnicity, 2000: (In percent) Anglo, 90.11; Black, 0.05; Hispanic, 9.35; Other, 0.49.

Vital Statistics, 2004: Births, 14; deaths, 25; marriages, 9; divorces, 3.

Recreation: Hunting, fishing; historic sites include Camp Cooper, site of former Comanche reservation; restored ranch home, Millers Creek Reservoir; wild game dinner in January.

Minerals: Natural gas, oil.

Agriculture: Beef cattle, horses, wheat, hay. Market value $16.4 million. Mesquite firewood sold. Hunting leases important.

THROCKMORTON (719) county seat; varied manufacturing; oil-field services; hospital; Old Jail museum.

Other towns include: **Elbert** (52), **Woodson** (275).

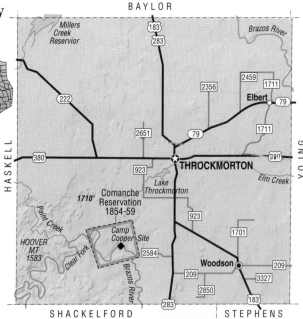

Population		1,678
Change fm 2000		-9.3
Area (sq. mi.)		915.47
Land Area (sq. mi.)		912.34
Altitude (ft.)		1,140-1,710
Rainfall (in.)		26.60
Jan. mean min.		28.0
July mean max.		97.0
Civ. Labor		935
Unemployed		3.3
Wages		$2,778,440
Av. Weekly Wage		$445.88
Prop. Value		$355,898,806
Retail Sales		$5,452,247

Titus County

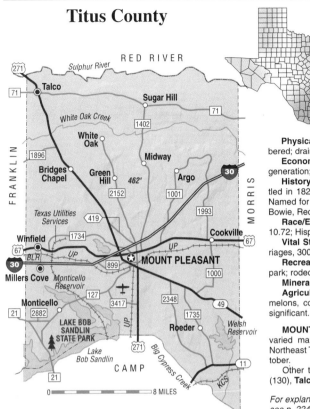

Population	**30,306**
Change fm 2000	7.8
Area (sq. mi.)	425.69
Land Area (sq. mi.)	410.54
Altitude (ft.)	300-462
Rainfall (in.)	48.57
Jan. mean min.	29.3
July mean max.	94.2
Civ. Labor	15,182
Unemployed	3.6
Wages	$126,000,641
Av. Weekly Wage	$563.74
Prop. Value	$2,715,419,772
Retail Sales	$526,627,494

Physical Features: Northeast Texas county; hilly, timbered; drains to Big Cypress Creek, Sulphur River.

Economy: Agribusinesses; lignite mining and power generation; trailer manufacturing.

History: Caddo area. Cherokees and other tribes settled in 1820s. Anglo-American settlers arrived in 1840s. Named for pioneer settler A.J. Titus; county created from Bowie, Red River counties 1846.

Race/Ethnicity, 2000: (In percent) Anglo, 60.03; Black, 10.72; Hispanic, 28.31; Other, 0.94.

Vital Statistics, 2004: Births, 588; deaths, 248; marriages, 300; divorces, 54.

Recreation: Fishing, hunting; lake activities; state park; rodeo; railroad museum; riverboat; flower gardens.

Minerals: Lignite coal, oil, gas.

Agriculture: Poultry, beef cattle, hay, horses, watermelons, corn. Market value $56.4 million. Timber sales significant.

MOUNT PLEASANT (14,796) county seat; tourism; varied manufacturing; food-processing plants; hospital; Northeast Texas Community College; WranglerFest in October.

Other towns include: **Cookville** (105), **Millers Cove** (130), **Talco** (578), **Winfield** (562).

For explanation of sources, symbols and abbreviations, see p. 224 and foldout map.

Fall foliage in Northeast Texas, here in Red River County. Robert Plocheck photo.

Tom Green County

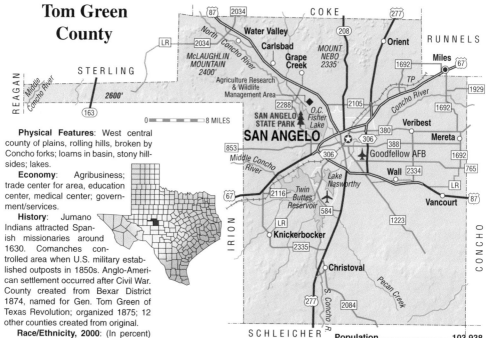

Physical Features: West central county of plains, rolling hills, broken by Concho forks; loams in basin, stony hillsides; lakes.

Economy: Agribusiness; trade center for area, education center, medical center; government/services.

History: Jumano Indians attracted Spanish missionaries around 1630. Comanches controlled area when U.S. military established outposts in 1850s. Anglo-American settlement occurred after Civil War. County created from Bexar District 1874, named for Gen. Tom Green of Texas Revolution; organized 1875; 12 other counties created from original.

Race/Ethnicity, 2000: (In percent) Anglo, 63.65; Black, 4.22; Hispanic, 30.71; Other, 1.42.

Vital Statistics, 2004: Births, 1,590; deaths, 1,000; marriages, 1,128; divorces, 545.

Recreation: Water sports; hunting; Fort Concho museum; urban, collegiate activities; symphony; Christmas at Old Fort Concho; February rodeo; minor league hockey, baseball teams.

Minerals: Oil, natural gas.

Agriculture: Cotton, cattle, goats, sheep, small grains, milo. About 30,000 acres irrigated. Market value $97.2 million.

SAN ANGELO (87,212) county seat; government/services, retail center, transportation; airbase; riverwalk; hospitals; Angelo State University, A&M extension center; Museum of Fine Arts; Feast of Santa Angela in January; Wool Capital triathalon in August.

Other towns include: **Carlsbad** (236); **Christoval** (404); **Grape Creek** (3,007); **Knickerbocker** (94); **Mereta** (131); **Vancourt** (131); **Veribest** (115); **Wall** (329); **Water Valley** (203).

Population	**103,938**
Change fm 2000	-0.1
Area (sq. mi.)	1,540.54
Land Area (sq. mi.)	1,522.10
Altitude (ft.)	1,700-2,600
Rainfall (in.)	20.91
Jan. mean min.	31.8
July mean max.	94.4
Civ. Labor	52,416
Unemployed	3.5
Wages	$321,062,451
Av. Weekly Wage	$558.94
Prop. Value	$4,226,620,466
Retail Sales	$1,395,676,784

For explanation of sources, symbols and abbreviations, see p. 224 and foldout map.

A parade up Austin's Congress Ave. to the State Capitol. David Woo photo.

Travis County

Physical Features: Central county of scenic hills, broken by Colorado River and lakes; cedars, pecans, other trees; diverse soils, mineral deposits.

Economy: Government/services, education, technology, research and industry.

History: Tonkawa and Lipan Apache area; Comanches, Kiowas arrived about 1700. Spanish missions from East Texas temporarily relocated near Barton Springs in 1730 before removing to San Antonio. Anglo-Americans arrived in early 1830s. County created 1840, when Austin became Republic's capital, from Bastrop County; organized 1843; named for Alamo commander Col. William B. Travis; many other counties created from its original area.

Race/Ethnicity, 2000: (In percent) Anglo, 57.28; Black, 9.38; Hispanic, 28.20; Other, 5.14.

Vital Statistics, 2004: Births, 14,930; deaths, 3,982; marriages, 7,289; divorces, 2,692.

Recreation: Colorado River lakes; hunting, fishing; McKinney Falls State Park; Lady Bird Johnson Wildflower Center; South by Southwest film,

0	8 MILES

Population	921,006
Change fm 2000	13.4
Area (sq. mi.)	1,022.06
Land Area (sq. mi.)	989.30
Altitude (ft.)	400-1,421
Rainfall (in.)	33.65
Jan. mean min.	40.0
July mean max.	95.0
Civ. Labor	533,638
Unemployed	3.3
Wages	$6,297,239,531
Av. Weekly Wage	$890.53
Prop. Value	$78,046,715,006
Retail Sales	$15,281,565,947

music festival in March; collegiate, metropolitan, governmental events; official buildings and historic sites; museums; Sixth St. restoration area; scenic drives; many city parks.

Minerals: Production of lime, stone, sand, gravel, oil and gas.

Agriculture: Cattle, nursery crops, hogs; sorghum, corn, cotton, small grains, pecans. Market value $17.1 million.

Education: University of Texas main campus; St. Edward's University, Concordia Lutheran University, Huston-Tillotson College, Austin Community College, Episcopal and Presbyterian seminaries; state schools and institutions for blind, deaf, mental illnesses.

AUSTIN (705,611, part [11,810] in Williamson County) county seat and state capital; state and federal payrolls; IRS center; tourism; Lyndon B. Johnson Library; research, high-tech industries; hospitals, including state institutions; popular retirement area. **Del Valle** is now part of Austin.

Other towns include: **Bee Cave** (1,695) retail, tourism; **Briarcliff** (834); **Creedmoor** (225); **Garfield** (1,633); **Jonestown** (1,935); **Lago Vista** (5,761); **Lakeway** (8,682) tourism, retail; **Manchaca** (2,259); **Manor** (2,044); **McNeil** (NA); **Mustang Ridge** (953, partly in Caldwell County).

Also, **Pflugerville** (28,520) high-tech industries, agriculture, government/services, Deutchenfest in May; **Point Venture** (470); **Rollingwood** (1,283); **San Leanna** (522); **Sunset Valley** (459); **The Hills** (1,838) residential community; **Volente** (450); **Webberville** (299); **Wells Branch** (10,512); **West Lake Hills** (3,056).

Also, part of **Anderson Mill**, part of **Cedar Park**, part of **Jollyville** and part of **Round Rock**, all mostly in Williamson County.

Trinity County

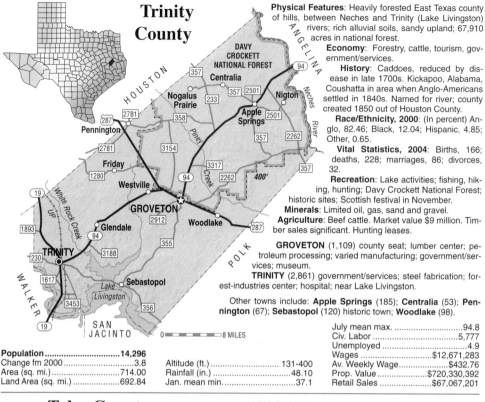

Physical Features: Heavily forested East Texas county of hills, between Neches and Trinity (Lake Livingston) rivers; rich alluvial soils, sandy upland; 67,910 acres in national forest.

Economy: Forestry, cattle, tourism, government/services.

History: Caddoes, reduced by disease in late 1700s. Kickapoo, Alabama, Coushatta in area when Anglo-Americans settled in 1840s. Named for river; county created 1850 out of Houston County.

Race/Ethnicity, 2000: (In percent) Anglo, 82.46; Black, 12.04; Hispanic, 4.85; Other, 0.65.

Vital Statistics, 2004: Births, 166; deaths, 228; marriages, 86; divorces, 32.

Recreation: Lake activities; fishing, hiking, hunting; Davy Crockett National Forest; historic sites; Scottish festival in November.

Minerals: Limited oil, gas, sand and gravel.

Agriculture: Beef cattle. Market value $9 million. Timber sales significant. Hunting leases.

GROVETON (1,109) county seat; lumber center; petroleum processing; varied manufacturing; government/services; museum.

TRINITY (2,861) government/services; steel fabrication; forest-industries center; hospital; near Lake Livingston.

Other towns include: **Apple Springs** (185); **Centralia** (53); **Pennington** (67); **Sebastopol** (120) historic town; **Woodlake** (98).

Population	14,296
Change fm 2000	3.8
Area (sq. mi.)	714.00
Land Area (sq. mi.)	692.84

Altitude (ft.)	131-400
Rainfall (in.)	48.10
Jan. mean min.	37.1

July mean max.	94.8
Civ. Labor	5,777
Unemployed	4.9
Wages	$12,671,283
Av. Weekly Wage	$432.76
Prop. Value	$720,330,392
Retail Sales	$67,067,201

Tyler County

Physical Features: Hilly East Texas county; densely timbered; drains to Neches River; B.A. Steinhagen Lake; Big Thicket is unique plant and animal area.

Economy: Lumbering; government/services, some manufacturing; tourism, hunting leases.

History: Caddoan area. Cherokees, Alabama and Coushatta pushed into area from U.S. South in 1820s. Anglo-Americans settled in 1830s. Named for U.S. President John Tyler; county created 1846 from Liberty County.

Race/Ethnicity, 2000: (In percent) Anglo, 83.49; Black, 12.16; Hispanic, 3.56; Other, 0.79.

Vital Statistics, 2004: Births, 253; deaths, 279; marriages, 161; divorces, 127.

Recreation: Big Thicket National Preserve; Heritage Village; lake activities; Allan Shivers Museum; state forest; historic sites; dogwood festival; rodeo, frontier frolics in September; gospel music fest in June.

Minerals: Oil, natural gas.

Agriculture: Cattle, hay, nursery crops, blueberries, horses. Market value $4.7 million. Timber sales significant.

WOODVILLE (2,346) county seat; lumber, cattle market; varied manufacturing; tourism; hospital; prison.

Other towns include: **Chester** (257) **Colmesneil** (654), **Doucette** (160), **Fred** (299), **Hillister** (250), **Spurger** (590), **Warren** (310).

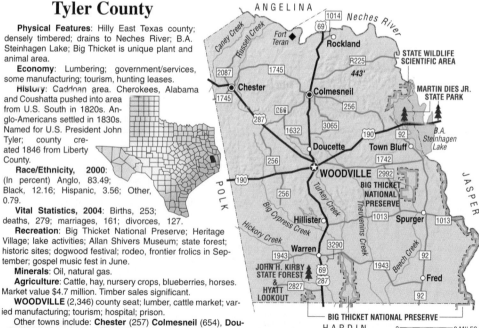

Population	20,557
Change fm 2000	-1.5
Area (sq. mi.)	935.71
Land Area (sq. mi.)	922.90
Altitude (ft.)	50-443

Rainfall (in.)	54.79
Jan. mean min.	38.3
July mean max.	92.1
Civ. Labor	8,302

Unemployed	5.4
Wages	$25,782,803
Av. Weekly Wage	$497.23
Prop. Value	$1,169,304,780
Retail Sales	$105,446,245

Upshur County

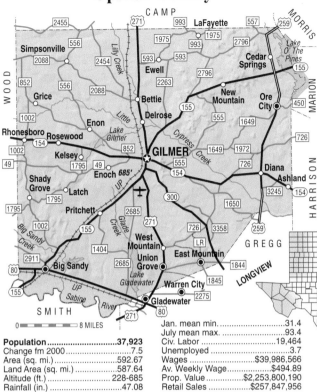

Physical Features: East Texas county; rolling to hilly, over half forested; drains to Sabine River, Little Cypress Creek, Lake O' the Pines, Lake Gilmer, Lake Gladewater.

Economy: Manufacturing, petroleum products, agribusiness, timber products.

History: Caddoes; reduced by epidemics in 1700s. Cherokees in area in 1820s. Anglo-American settlement in mid-1830s. County created from Harrison, Nacogdoches counties 1846; named for U.S. Secretary of State A.P. Upshur.

Race/Ethnicity, 2000: (In percent) Anglo, 84.82; Black, 10.31; Hispanic, 3.95; Other, 0.92.

Vital Statistics, 2004: Births, 457; deaths, 386; marriages, 276; divorces, 208.

Recreation: Scenic trails; hunting, fishing; Fall Foliage, East Texas Yamboree in October.

Minerals: Oil, gas, sand, gravel.

Agriculture: Poultry (among leading broiler counties), dairies, beef cattle; vegetable crops, hay, peaches raised. Market value $40.8 million. Timber a major product.

GILMER (5,038) county seat; varied manufacturing; timber, ceramics produced; vegetable processing; hospital; museums; civic center.

Other towns include: **Big Sandy** (1,344); **Diana** (585); **East Mountain** (589); **Ore City** (1,227); **Union Grove** (375). Part [2,454] of **Gladewater** (6,155).

Jan. mean min.	31.4
July mean max.	93.4
Civ. Labor	19,464
Unemployed	3.7
Wages	$39,986,566
Av. Weekly Wage	$494.89
Prop. Value	$2,253,800,190
Retail Sales	$257,847,956

Population	37,923
Change fm 2000	7.5
Area (sq. mi.)	592.67
Land Area (sq. mi.)	587.64
Altitude (ft.)	228-685
Rainfall (in.)	47.08

Upton County

Physical Features: Western county; north flat, south rolling, hilly; limestone, sandy loam soils, drains to creeks.

Economy: Oil, wind turbines, farming, ranching.

History: Apache and Comanche area until tribes removed by U.S. Army in 1870s. Sheep and cattle ranching developed in 1880s. Oil discovered in 1925. County created in 1887 from Tom Green County; organized 1910; name honors brothers John and William Upton, Confederate colonels.

Race/Ethnicity, 2000: (In percent) Anglo, 54.93; Black, 1.62; Hispanic, 42.57; Other, 0.88.

Vital Statistics, 2004: Births, 51; deaths, 18; marriages, 26; divorces, 17.

Recreation: Historic sites, Mendoza Trail Museum; scenic areas; chili cookoff in October, pecan show in November, Christmas bazaar.

Minerals: Oil, natural gas.

Agriculture: Cotton, sheep, goats, cattle, watermelons, pecans. Extensive irrigation. Market value $4.8 million.

RANKIN (698) county seat, oil, ranching, farming; hospital; Barbados cookoff in May, All Kid rodeo in June.

McCAMEY (1,634) oil, gas, wind; hospital; Wind Energy bluegrass festival in September. Other town: **Midkiff** (182).

Population	3,134
Change fm 2000	-7.9
Area (sq. mi.)	1,241.83
Land Area (sq. mi.)	1,241.68

Altitude (ft.)	2,400-3,141
Rainfall (in.)	14.45
Jan. mean min.	33.1
July mean max.	95.6
Civ. Labor	1,700

Unemployed	3.0
Wages	$11,891,957
Av. Weekly Wage	$743.71
Prop. Value	$1,736,454,800
Retail Sales	$12,306,703

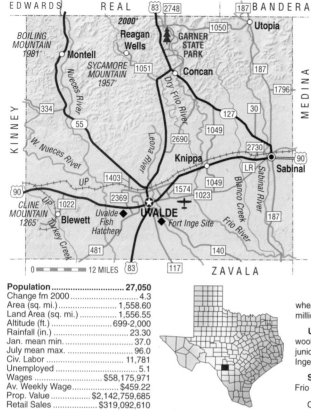

Uvalde County

Physical Features: Edwards Plateau, rolling hills below escarpment; spring-fed Sabinal, Frio, Leona, Nueces rivers; cypress, cedar, other trees; unique maple groves.

Economy: Agribusinesses; hunting leases; light manufacturing; tourism.

History: Spanish mission Nuestra Señora de la Candelaria founded in 1762 for Lipan Apaches near present-day Montell; Comanches harassed mission. U.S. military outpost established in 1849. County created from Bexar 1850; re-created, organized 1856; named for 1778 governor of Coahuila, Juan de Ugalde, with name Anglicized.

Race/Ethnicity, 2000: (In percent) Anglo, 33.08; Black, 0.34; Hispanic, 65.91; Other, 0.67.

Vital Statistics, 2004: Births, 471; deaths, 228; marriages, 160; divorces, 68.

Recreation: Deer, turkey hunting area; Garner State Park; water activities on rivers; John Nance Garner Museum; Uvalde Memorial Park; scenic trails; historic sites; recreational homes.

Minerals: Asphalt, stone, sand and gravel.

Agriculture: Beef cattle, vegetables, corn, cotton, grain sorghum; sheep, goats; hay, wheat. Substantial irrigation. Market value $69 million.

UVALDE (16,529) county seat; vegetable, wool, mohair processing; tourism, opera house; junior college; A&M research center; hospital; Fort Inge Day in April.

Sabinal (1,804) farm, ranch center; gateway to Frio and Sabinal canyons; tourist, retirement area.

Other towns include: **Concan** (225); **Knippa** (769); **Utopia** (306) resort; **Uvalde Estates** (1,893).

Population **27,050**
Change fm 2000 .... 4.3
Area (sq. mi.) 1,558.60
Land Area (sq. mi.) 1,556.55
Altitude (ft.) 699-2,000
Rainfall (in.) 23.30
Jan. mean min. 37.0
July mean max. 96.0
Civ. Labor 11,781
Unemployed 5.1
Wages $58,175,971
Av. Weekly Wage................... $459.22
Prop. Value $2,142,759,685
Retail Sales $319,092,610

For explanation of sources, symbols and abbreviations, see p. 224.

Yuccas in bloom along Texas 55 northwest of Uvalde. Robert Plocheck photo.

The high bridge over the Pecos River on U.S. 90 north of Del Rio. Robert Plocheck photo.

Val Verde County

Physical Features: Southwestern county bordering Mexico, rolling, hilly; brushy; Devils, Pecos rivers, Amistad Reservoir; limestone, alluvial soils.

Economy: Agribusiness; tourism; area trade center; large military, Border Patrol; hunting leases, fishing.

History: Apaches, Coahuiltecans, Jumanos present when Spanish explored area 1535. Comanches arrived later. U.S. military outposts established in 1850s to protect settlers. Only county named for Civil War battle; Val Verde means green valley. Created 1885 from Crockett, Kinney, Pecos counties.

Race/Ethnicity, 2000: (In percent) Anglo, 22.11; Black, 1.46; Hispanic, 75.46; Other, 0.97.

Vital Statistics, 2004: Births, 998; deaths, 281; marriages, 418; divorces, 158.

Recreation: Gateway to Mexico; deer hunting, fishing; Amistad lake activities; two state parks; Langtry restoration of Judge Roy Bean's saloon; ancient pictographs; San Felipe Springs; winery.

Minerals: Production sand and gravel, gas, oil.

Agriculture: Major sheep-raising county, Angora goats, cattle, meat goats; minor irrigation. Market value $10.9 million.

DEL RIO (36,019) county seat; tourism and trade with Mexico; government/services, including federal agencies and military; varied manufacturing, winery; hospital; extension colleges; Fiesta de Amistad in October.

Laughlin Air Force Base (2,248).

Other towns and places include: **Cienegas Terrace** (2,991); **Comstock** (344); **Langtry** (30); **Val Verde Park** (2,013).

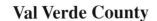

Population	48,145
Change fm 2000	7.3
Area (sq. mi.)	3,232.40
Land Area (sq. mi.)	3,170.38
Altitude (ft.)	900-2,300
Rainfall (in.)	18.80
Jan. mean min.	39.7
July mean max.	96.2
Civ. Labor	20,423
Unemployed	5.4
Wages	$116,340,705
Av. Weekly Wage	$539.59
Prop. Value	$1,626,133,127
Retail Sales	$497,547,824

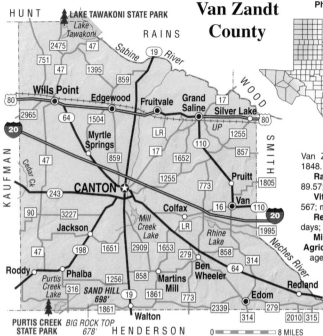

Van Zandt County

Physical Features: Eastern county in three soil belts; level to rolling; Sabine, Neches rivers; Lake Tawakoni; partly forested.

Economy: Agriculture, goverment/services, commuters to Dallas and Tyler.

History: Caddo tribes, reduced by epidemics before settlers arrived. Cherokees settled in 1820s; removed in 1839 under policies of Republic President Lamar; Anglo-American settlement followed. County named for Republic leader Isaac Van Zandt; created from Henderson County 1848.

Race/Ethnicity, 2000: (In percent) Anglo, 89.57; Black, 3.05; Hispanic, 6.65; Other, 0.73.

Vital Statistics, 2004: Births, 598; deaths, 567; marriages, 348; divorces, 261.

Recreation: Canton First Monday trades days; lake activities; state parks; historic sites.

Minerals: Oil, gas.

Agriculture: Nurseries, beef cattle, dairies, forage, vegatables. Market value $73 million.

CANTON (3,353) county seat; tourism; agribusiness; commuters to Dallas, Tyler; museums, bluegrass festival in June.

Wills Point (3,703) government/services, some manufacturing, retail center, Bluebird festival in April.

Other towns include: **Ben Wheeler** (504); **Edgewood** (1,337) commuters to Dallas; heritage park, antiques; **Edom** (325) arts and crafts; **Fruitvale** (438); **Grand Saline** (3,088) salt plant, hospital, Salt Palace museum, birding, Bloomin' Festival in March; **Van** (2,438) oil center, hay, cattle; oil festival in October.

Population	52,916
Change fm 2000	9.9
Area (sq. mi.)	859.48
Land Area (sq. mi.)	848.64
Altitude (ft.)	400-698
Rainfall (in.)	43.68
Jan. mean min.	31.4
July mean max.	93.3
Civ. Labor	25,966
Unemployed	3.7

Wages	$67,519,551
Av. Weekly Wage	$503.31
Prop. Value	$3,260,757,420
Retail Sales	$393,860,090

For explanation of sources, symbols and abbreviations, see p. 224 and foldout map.

Van Zandt County landscape on FM 1861 near Big Rock Top. Robert Plocheck photo.

Victoria County

Physical Features: South Central county of rolling prairies, intersected by many streams; sandy loams, clays, alluvial soils.

Economy: Petrochemical plants, government services, oil, manufacturing, agribusiness, tourism.

History: Karankawas, other tribes in area when Spanish explored in 1528. Comanches, Tawakonis arrived later. French Fort St. Louis on Garcitas Creek 1685-87. Spanish ranching developed in 1750s. Anglo-Americans arrived after 1836. An original county, created 1836 from Mexican municipality named for President Guadalupe Victoria of Mexico.

Race/Ethnicity, 2000: (In percent) Anglo, 53.38; Black, 6.33; Hispanic, 39.20; Other, 1.09.

Vital Statistics, 2004: Births, 1,409; deaths, 692; marriages, 711; divorces, 357.

Recreation: Fishing, hunting, saltwater activities; historic homes, sites; riverside park, Coleto Creek Reservoir

Population	86,191
Change fm 2000	2.5
Area (sq. mi.)	888.73
Land Area (sq. mi.)	882.50
Altitude (ft.)	sea level-205
Rainfall (in.)	40.10

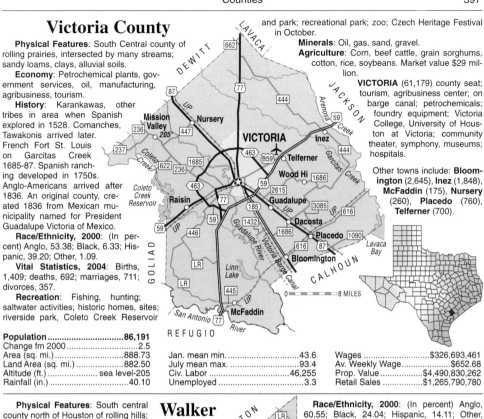

and park; recreational park; zoo; Czech Heritage Festival in October.

Minerals: Oil, gas, sand, gravel.

Agriculture: Corn, beef cattle, grain sorghums, cotton, rice, soybeans. Market value $29 million.

VICTORIA (61,179) county seat; tourism, agribusiness center; on barge canal; petrochemicals; foundry equipment; Victoria College, University of Houston at Victoria; community theater, symphony, museums; hospitals.

Other towns include: **Bloomington** (2,645), **Inez** (1,848), **McFaddin** (175), **Nursery** (260), **Placedo** (760), **Telferner** (700).

Jan. mean min.	43.6	Wages	$326,693,461
July mean max.	93.4	Av. Weekly Wage	$652.68
Civ. Labor	46,255	Prop. Value	$4,490,830,262
Unemployed	3.3	Retail Sales	$1,265,790,780

Walker County

Physical Features: South central county north of Houston of rolling hills; more than 70 percent forested; national forest; San Jacinto, Trinity rivers.

Economy: State employment in prison system, education.

History: Coahuiltecans, Bidais in area when Spanish explored around 1690. Later, area became trading ground for many Indian tribes. Anglo-Americans settled in 1830s. Antebellum slaveholding area. County created 1846 from Montgomery County; first named for U.S. Secretary of Treasury R.J. Walker; renamed 1863 for Texas Ranger Capt. S.H. Walker.

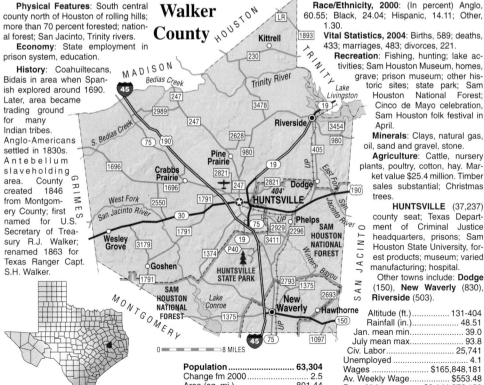

Race/Ethnicity, 2000: (In percent) Anglo, 60.55; Black, 24.04; Hispanic, 14.11; Other, 1.30.

Vital Statistics, 2004: Births, 589; deaths, 433; marriages, 483; divorces, 221.

Recreation: Fishing, hunting; lake activities; Sam Houston Museum, homes, grave; prison museum; other historic sites; state park; Sam Houston National Forest; Cinco de Mayo celebration; Sam Houston folk festival in April.

Minerals: Clays, natural gas, oil, sand and gravel, stone.

Agriculture: Cattle, nursery plants, poultry, cotton, hay. Market value $25.4 million. Timber sales substantial; Christmas trees.

HUNTSVILLE (37,237) county seat; Texas Department of Criminal Justice headquarters, prisons; Sam Houston State University, forest products; museum; varied manufacturing; hospital.

Other towns include: **Dodge** (150), **New Waverly** (830), **Riverside** (503).

Altitude (ft.)	131-404
Rainfall (in.)	48.51
Jan. mean min.	39.0
July mean max.	93.8
Civ. Labor	25,741
Unemployed	4.1
Wages	$165,848,181
Av. Weekly Wage	$553.48
Prop. Value	$2,144,876,159
Retail Sales	$686,262,611

Population	63,304
Change fm 2000	2.5
Area (sq. mi.)	801.44
Land Area (sq. mi.)	787.45

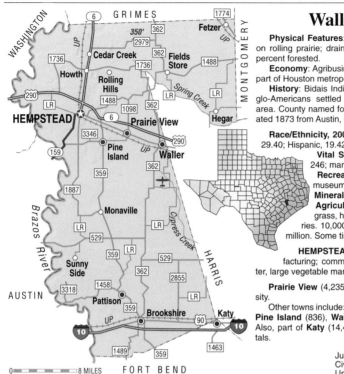

Waller County

Physical Features: South central county near Houston on rolling prairie; drains to Brazos; alluvial soils; about 20 percent forested.

Economy: Agribusiness, construction, education, county part of Houston metropolitan area.

History: Bidais Indians reduced to about 100 when Anglo-Americans settled in 1820s. Antebellum slaveholding area. County named for Edwin Waller, Republic leader; created 1873 from Austin, Grimes counties.

Race/Ethnicity, 2000: (In percent), Anglo, 50.36; Black, 29.40; Hispanic, 19.42; Other, 0.82.

Vital Statistics, 2004: Births, 527; deaths, 246; marriages, 287; divorces, 145.

Recreation: Fishing, hunting; historic sites; museum.

Minerals: Oil, gas.

Agriculture: Cattle, hay, nurseries, rice, turf grass, horses, corn, watermelons, goats, berries. 10,000 acres irrigated. Market value $37.9 million. Some timber marketed.

HEMPSTEAD (6,201) county seat; varied manufacturing; commuting to Houston; agribusiness center, large vegetable market; watermelon fest in July.

Prairie View (4,235) home of Prairie View A&M University.

Other towns include: **Brookshire** (4,136), **Pattison** (476), **Pine Island** (836), **Waller** (2,183, partly in Harris County). Also, part of **Katy** (14,441, mostly in Harris County) hospitals.

Population	35,185
Change fm 2000	7.7
Area (sq. mi.)	518.49
Land Area (sq. mi.)	513.63
Altitude (ft.)	100-350
Rainfall (in.)	38.20
Jan. mean min.	38.0
July mean max.	95.0
Civ. Labor	17,006
Unemployed	4.0
Wages	$102,450,529
Av. Weekly Wage	$646.14
Prop. Value	$16,968,493,161
Retail Sales	$591,394,092

Ward County

Physical Features: Western county on Pecos River; plain covered by grass, brush; sandy, loam soils.

Economy: Oil, gas; sand and gravel produced; agriculture; some light manufacturing.

History: Jumano Indians in area when Spanish explored in 1580s. Comanches arrived later. Railroad stations established in 1880s. Oil discovered in 1920s. County named for Republic leader Thomas W. Ward; county created from Tom Green 1887; organized 1892.

Race/Ethnicity, 2000: (In percent) Anglo, 52.72; Black, 4.50; Hispanic, 41.98; Other, 0.80.

Vital Statistics, 2004: Births, 156; deaths, 109; marriages, 61; divorces, 34.

Recreation: Sandhills state park, camel treks; Million Barrel museum; county park; Butterfield stagecoach festival in July.

Minerals: Oil, gas, caliche, sand, gravel.

Agriculture: Beef cattle, goats, horses, cotton, alfalfa, pecans, forages. Some irrigation for cotton. Market value $1.7 million.

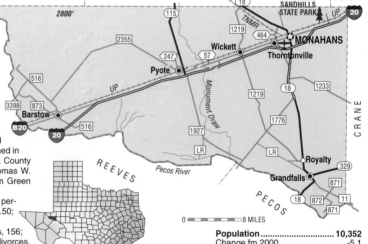

MONAHANS (6,490) county seat; oil and gas; ranching; tourism; hospital; Cinco de Mayo.

Other towns: **Barstow** (370); **Grandfalls** (372); **Pyote** (148) West Texas Children's Home, Rattlesnake bomber base museum; **Thorntonville** (406); **Wickett** (439).

Population	10,352
Change fm 2000	-5.1
Area (sq. mi.)	835.74
Land Area (sq. mi.)	835.49
Altitude (ft.)	2,400-2,800
Rainfall (in.)	13.23
Jan. mean min.	26.5
July mean max.	98.6
Civ. Labor	4,590
Unemployed	4.0
Wages	$30,868,542
Av. Weekly Wage	$677.27
Prop. Value	$1,276,484,378
Retail Sales	$79,623,311

Washington County

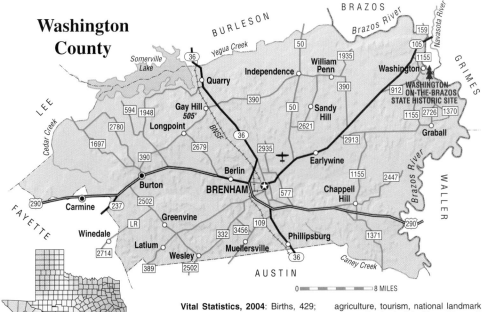

Physical Features: South central county in Brazos valley; rolling prairie of sandy loam, alluvial soils.

Economy: Agribusinesses, oil, tourism, manufacturing; government/services.

History: Coahuiltecan tribes and Tonkawas in area when Anglo-American settlers arrived in 1821. Antebellum slaveholding area. Germans arrived around 1870. County named for George Washington; an original county, created 1836, organized 1837.

Race/Ethnicity, 2000: (In percent), Anglo, 71.15; Black, 18.67; Hispanic, 8.71; Other, 1.47.

Vital Statistics, 2004: Births, 429; deaths, 344; marriages, 237; divorces, 96.

Recreation: Many historic sites; Washington-on-the-Brazos; Texas Baptist Historical Museum; Star of Republic Museum; Somerville Lake; fishing, hunting; antique rose nursery, miniature horse farm.

Minerals: Oil, gas and stone.

Agriculture: Beef cattle, poultry, dairy products, hogs, horses; hay, corn, sorghum, cotton, small grains, nursery crops. Market value $36.7 million.

BRENHAM (14,504) county seat; cotton processing; varied manufacturing including ceramics, mattresses, computers, Blue Bell creamery; wholesale distribution center; tourism; hospital; Blinn College, Brenham State School; Maifest.

Other towns include: **Burton** (403)

agriculture, tourism, national landmark cotton gin, festival in May; **Chappell Hill** (750) historic homes; **Washington** (265) site of signing of Texas Declaration of Independence.

Population	**31,912**
Change fm 2000	5.1
Area (sq. mi.)	621.35
Land Area (sq. mi.)	609.22
Altitude (ft.)	150-505
Rainfall (in.)	44.15
Jan. mean min.	39.3
July mean max.	96.7
Civ. Labor	16,536
Unemployed	3.2
Wages	$102,200,936
Av. Weekly Wage	$562.90
Prop. Value	$3,071,101,060
Retail Sales	$396,999,704

For explanation of sources, abbreviations and symbols, see p. 224 and foldout map.

Largest Counties by Population 2006

Rank	County (Major city)	Population
1.	Harris County (Houston)	3,886,207
2.	Dallas County (Dallas)	2,345,815
3.	Tarrant County (Fort Worth)	1,671,295
4.	Bexar County (San Antonio)	1,555,592
5.	Travis County (Austin)	921,006
6.	El Paso County (El Paso)	736,310
7.	Hidalgo County (McAllen)	700,634
8.	Collin County (Plano)	698,851
9.	Denton County (Denton)	584,238
10.	Fort Bend County (Sugar Land)	493,187
11.	Montgomery County (Woodlands)	398,290
12.	Cameron County (Brownsville)	387,717
13.	Williamson County (Round Rock)	353,830
14.	Nueces County (Corpus Christi)	321,457
15.	Brazoria County (Brazosport)	287,898
16.	Galveston County (Galveston)	283,551
17.	Bell County (Killeen-Temple)	257,897
18.	Lubbock County (Lubbock)	254,862
19.	Jefferson County (Beaumont)	243,914
20.	Webb County (Laredo)	231,470
21.	McLennan County (Waco)	226,189
22.	Smith County (Tyler)	194,635
23.	Brazos County (Bryan-Coll.Station)	159,006
24.	Johnson County (Cleburne)	149,016
25.	Ellis County (Waxahachie)	139,300
26.	Hays County (San Marcos)	130,325
27.	Ector County (Odessa)	127,462
28.	Wichita County (Wichita Falls)	125,158
29.	Taylor County (Abilene)	124,927
30.	Midland County (Midland)	124,380
	Source: Estimates from the U.S. Census Bureau	

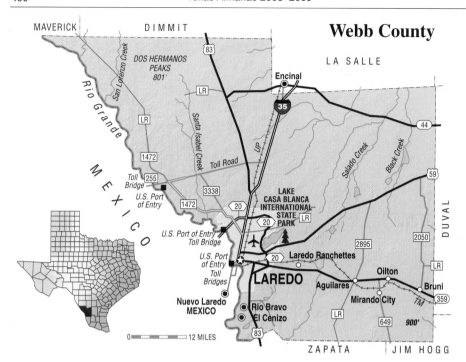

Webb County

Physical Features: Southwestern county on Rio Grande: rolling, some hills; much brush; sandy, gray soils; alluvial along river.

Economy: International trade, manufacturing, tourism, government/services, natural gas, oil.

History: Coahuiltecan groups squeezed out by Comanches, Apaches and Spanish settlers. Laredo founded in 1755 by Tomás Sánchez. County named for Republic leader James Webb; created 1848 from Nueces and Bexar counties.

Race/Ethnicity, 2000: (In percent) Anglo, 5.02; Black, 0.17; Hispanic, 94.28; Other, 0.53.

Vital Statistics, 2004: Births, 6,035; deaths, 946; marriages, 1,732; divorces, 303.

Recreation: Major tourist gateway to Mexico; top hunting, fishing; Lake Casa Blanca park, water recreation; art festival; Washington's Birthday celebration; historic sites; Museum of the Republic of the Rio Grande; Fort McIntosh; minor league baseball and hockey.

Minerals: Natural gas, oil, coal.

Agriculture: Onions, melons, nursery crops, cattle, horses, goats. About 4,500 acres irrigated. Market value $23.6 million. Mesquite sold. Hunting leases important.

LAREDO (213,915) county seat; international trade, government/services, retail center; rail, highway gateway to Mexico; junior college, Texas A&M International University; hospitals; entertainment/sports arena; "El Grito" on Sept. 15; Jalapeño festival in February.

Other towns and places include:

Bruni (461); **El Cenizo** (3,781); **Laredo Ranchettes** (1,800); **Mirando City** (587); **Oilton** (376); **Rio Bravo** (5,955).

Population	231,470
Change fm 2000	19.9
Area (sq. mi.)	3,375.53
Land Area (sq. mi.)	3,356.83
Altitude (ft.)	300-900
Rainfall (in.)	21.53
Jan. mean min.	43.7
July mean max.	101.6
Civ. Labor	93,205
Unemployed	4.2
Wages	$577,492,664
Av. Weekly Wage	$519.38
Prop. Value	$11,059,779,281
Retail Sales	$3,004,717,681

For explanation of sources, abbreviations and symbols, see p. 224 and foldout map.

Business and residential developments in booming Laredo expand to Lake Casa Blanca. Robert Plocheck photo.

Wharton County

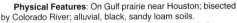

Physical Features: On Gulf prairie near Houston; bisected by Colorado River; alluvial, black, sandy loam soils.

Economy: Oil; agribusiness, hunting leases, varied manufacturing; government/services.

History: Karankawas in area until 1840s. Anglo-American colonists settled in 1823. Czechs, Germans arrived in 1880s. Mexican migration increased after 1950. County named for John A. and William H. Wharton, brothers active in the Texas Revolution; created 1846 from Jackson, Matagorda counties.

Race/Ethnicity, 2000: (In percent) Anglo, 53.29; Black, 14.84; Hispanic, 31.29; Other, 0.58.

Vital Statistics, 2004: Births, 663; deaths, 451; marriages, 246; divorces, 174.

Recreation: Waterfowl hunting, fishing, big-game, birding; art and historical museums; river-front park in Wharton; historic sites; Fiesta Hispano Americana in September.

Minerals: Oil, gas.

Agriculture: Top rice-producing county; other crops are cotton, milo, corn, grain sorghum, soybeans; about 130,000 acres irrigated, mostly rice. Also, eggs, turfgrass, beef cattle, aquaculture. Market value $146.4 million.

WHARTON (9,357) county seat; regional medical center/hospital; plastics manufacturing; government/services; Wharton County Junior College; Riverfront park; Hidden Garden tour in April.

EL CAMPO (11,187) rice processing, storage; plastic, styrofoam processing; wholesale nursery; hospital; Polka Expo in November.

Other towns include: **Boling-Iago** (1,326); **Danevang** (61); **East Bernard** (2,228) agribusiness, varied manufacturing; **Egypt** (26); **Glen Flora** (210); **Hungerford** (652); **Lane City** (111); **Lissie** (72); **Louise** (985); **Pierce** (51).

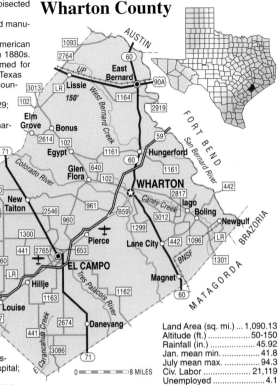

Population 41,475
Change fm 2000 .... 0.7
Area (sq. mi.) 1,094.43

Land Area (sq. mi.) ... 1,090.13
Altitude (ft.) 50-150
Rainfall (in.) 45.92
Jan. mean min. 41.8
July mean max. 94.3
Civ. Labor 21,119
Unemployed 4.1
Wages $109,307,096
Av. Weekly Wage $551.01
Prop. Value $2,651,668,721
Retail Sales $481,763,989

Wheeler County

Physical Features: Panhandle county adjoining Oklahoma. Plain, on edge of Caprock; Red River, Sweetwater Creek; some canyons; red sandy loam, black clay soils.

Economy: Oil and gas, agribusinesses, tourism.

History: Apaches, displaced by Kiowas, Comanches around 1700. Military outpost established in 1875 after Indians forced into Oklahoma. Ranching began in late 1870s. Oil boom in 1920s. County named for pioneer jurist R.T. Wheeler; county created from Bexar, Young districts 1876; organized 1879.

Race/Ethnicity, 2000: (In percent) Anglo, 83.55; Black, 2.63; Hispanic, 12.57; Other, 1.25.

Vital Statistics, 2004: Births, 61; deaths, 71; marriages, 145; divorces, 4.

Recreation: Pioneer West museum at Shamrock; historic sites; Old Mobeetie jail, trading post, Fort Elliott; ostrich depot.

Minerals: Oil, natural gas.

Agriculture: Fed beef, cow-calf and stocker cattle, swine, horses; crops include wheat, grain sorghum, cotton. Market value $94 million.

WHEELER (1,289) county seat; agribusiness; petroleum center; tourism; slaughter plant; hospital; library.

SHAMROCK (1,966) tourism; agribusiness; hospital; library; St. Patrick's Day event; old Route 66 sites.

Other towns include: **Allison** (135); **Briscoe** (135); **Mobeetie** (104).

Population **4,854**
Change fm 2000 .... -8.1
Area (sq. mi.) 915.34
Land Area (sq. mi.) 914.26
Altitude (ft.) 2,000-3,000
Rainfall (in.) 24.32
Jan. mean min. 22.9
July mean max. 93.3
Civ. Labor 2,623
Unemployed 3.0
Wages $11,696,793
Av. Weekly Wage $475.89
Prop. Value $1,352,689,698
Retail Sales $37,530,262

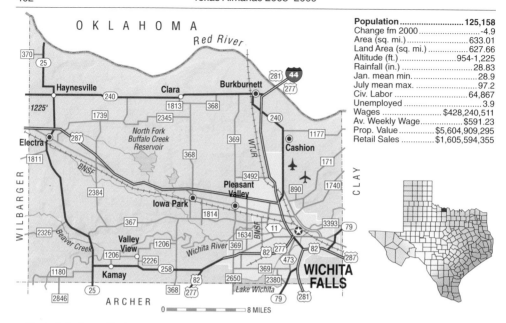

Population **125,158**
Change fm 2000 .... -4.9
Area (sq. mi.) 633.01
Land Area (sq. mi.) 627.66
Altitude (ft.) 954-1,225
Rainfall (in.) 28.83
Jan. mean min. 28.9
July mean max. 97.2
Civ. Labor 64,867
Unemployed 3.9
Wages $428,240,511
Av. Weekly Wage................. $591.23
Prop. Value $5,604,909,295
Retail Sales $1,605,594,355

Wichita County

Physical Features: North central county in prairie bordering Oklahoma; drained by Red, Wichita rivers; lakes; sandy, loam soils.

Economy: Manufacturing; retail trade center for large area; air base; government/services and agriculture.

History: Wichitas and other Caddoan tribes in area in 1700s; Comanches, Apaches also present until 1850s. Anglo-American settlement increased after 1870. County named for Indian tribe; created from Young Territory 1858; organized 1882.

Race/Ethnicity, 2000: (In percent) Anglo, 74.34; Black, 10.57; Hispanic, 12.23; Other, 2.86.

Vital Statistics, 2004: Births, 1,961; deaths, 1,286; marriages, 2,436; divorces, 719.

Recreation: Metropolitan events; museums; historic sites; Texas-Oklahoma High School Oil Bowl football game; collegiate activities; water sports on lakes; Fiestas Patrias parade; Ranch Round-up in August.

Minerals: Oil.

Agriculture: Beef cattle, horticulture, wheat, hay. Seventy-five percent of hay irrigated; 10 percent of wheat/cotton. Market value $15.8 million.

WICHITA FALLS (101,852) county seat; distribution center for large area in Texas, Oklahoma; government/services; varied manufacturing; oil-field services; hospitals; Midwestern State University, vocational-technical training center; North Texas State Hospital; hiking trails, Hotter'n Hell bicycle race in August; **Sheppard Air Force Base**.

Other cities include: **Burkburnett** (10,750) some manufacturing, Trails and Tales of Boomtown USA display and tours; **Cashion** (326); **Electra** (3,009) oil, agriculture, manufacturing, commuters to Wichita Falls; hospital; goat barbecue in May; **Iowa Park** (6,372) some manufacturing, prison, Whoop-t-do homecoming in September; **Kamay** (640); **Pleasant Valley** (382).

For explanation of sources, abbreviations and symbols, see p. 224 and foldout map.

Electra sunrise, Wichita County. Robert Plocheck photo.

Wilbarger County

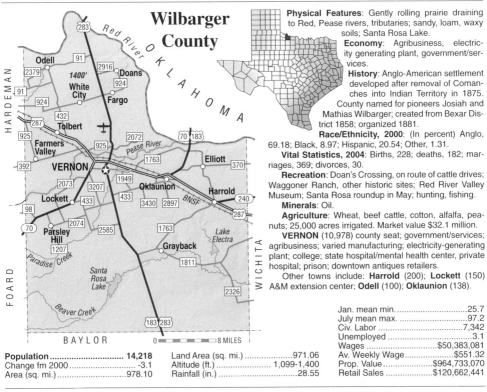

Physical Features: Gently rolling prairie draining to Red, Pease rivers, tributaries; sandy, loam, waxy soils; Santa Rosa Lake.

Economy: Agribusiness, electricity generating plant, government/services.

History: Anglo-American settlement developed after removal of Comanches into Indian Territory in 1875. County named for pioneers Josiah and Mathias Wilbarger; created from Bexar District 1858; organized 1881.

Race/Ethnicity, 2000: (In percent) Anglo, 69.18; Black, 8.97; Hispanic, 20.54; Other, 1.31.

Vital Statistics, 2004: Births, 228; deaths, 182; marriages, 369; divorces, 30.

Recreation: Doan's Crossing, on route of cattle drives; Waggoner Ranch, other historic sites; Red River Valley Museum; Santa Rosa roundup in May; hunting, fishing.

Minerals: Oil.

Agriculture: Wheat, beef cattle, cotton, alfalfa, peanuts; 25,000 acres irrigated. Market value $32.1 million.

VERNON (10,978) county seat; government/services; agribusiness; varied manufacturing; electricity-generating plant; college; state hospital/mental health center, private hospital; prison; downtown antiques retailers.

Other towns include: **Harrold** (200); **Lockett** (150) A&M extension center; **Odell** (100); **Oklaunion** (138).

Jan. mean min.	25.7
July mean max.	97.2
Civ. Labor	7,342
Unemployed	3.1
Wages	$50,383,081
Av. Weekly Wage	$551.32
Prop. Value	$964,733,070
Retail Sales	$120,662,441

Population		14,218
Change fm 2000		-3.1
Area (sq. mi.)		978.10
Land Area (sq. mi.)		971.06
Altitude (ft.)		1,099-1,400
Rainfall (in.)		28.55

Willacy County

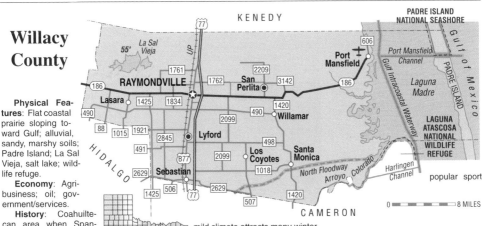

Physical Features: Flat coastal prairie sloping toward Gulf; alluvial, sandy, marshy soils; Padre Island; La Sal Vieja, salt lake; wildlife refuge.

Economy: Agribusiness; oil; government/services.

History: Coahuiltecan area when Spanish explored in 1500s. Spanish ranching began in 1790s. County named for Texas legislator John G. Willacy; created 1911 from Cameron, Hidalgo counties; reorganized 1921.

Race/Ethnicity, 2000: (In percent) Anglo, 11.98; Black, 2.02; Hispanic, 85.69; Other, 0.31.

Vital Statistics, 2004: Births, 411; deaths, 117; marriages, 126; divorces, 27.

Recreation: Fresh and saltwater fishing, hunting of deer, turkey, dove; mild climate attracts many winter tourists; Port Mansfield fishing tournament.

Minerals: Oil, natural gas.

Agriculture: Cotton, sorghum, corn, vegetables, sugar cane; 20 percent of cropland irrigated. Livestock includes cattle, horses, goats, hogs. Market value $18.9 million.

RAYMONDVILLE (9,683) county seat; agribusiness, oil center; food processing, shipping; tourist center; museum; enterprise zone; prison unit; Boot Fest in October.

Other towns include: **Lasara** (1,017); **Lyford** (2,349); **Port Mansfield** (392) fishing port; tourism; fishing tournament in late July; **San Perlita** (713); **Sebastian** (1,861).

Population	20,645
Change fm 2000	2.8
Area (sq. mi.)	784.23
Land Area (sq. mi.)	596.68
Altitude (ft.)	sea level-55
Rainfall (in.)	27.97
Jan. mean min.	47.5
July mean max.	95.3
Civ. Labor	7,912
Unemployed	7.8
Wages	$23,462,035
Av. Weekly Wage	$492.26
Prop. Value	$812,274,903
Retail Sales	$77,254,220

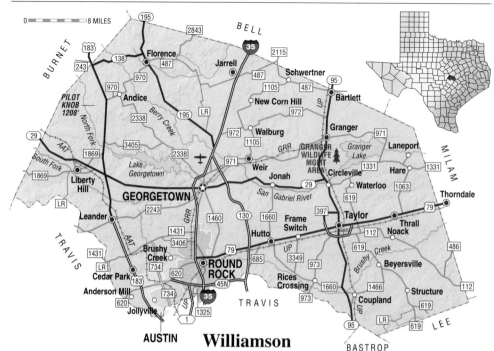

Williamson County

Physical Features: Central county near Austin. Level to rolling; mostly Blackland soil, some loam, sand; drained by San Gabriel River and tributaries.

Economy: Agribusinesses, varied manufacturing, education center, government/services; the county is part of Austin metropolitan area.

History: Tonkawa area; later, other tribes. Comanches raided until 1860s. Anglo-American settlement began in late 1830s. County named for Robert M. Williamson, pioneer leader; created from Milam and organized in 1848.

Race/Ethnicity, 2000: (In percent) Anglo, 74.33; Black, 5.27; Hispanic, 17.20; Other, 3.20.

Vital Statistics, 2004: Births, 5,409; deaths, 1,410; marriages, 1,889; divorces, 1,046.

Recreation: Lake recreation; Inner Space Cavern; historic sites; deer hunting, fishing; Gov. Dan Moody Museum at Taylor; San Gabriel Park; old settlers park; walking tours, rattlesnake sacking, barbecue cookoff, frontier days in summer; Round Rock minor league baseball.

Minerals: Building stone, sand and gravel.

Agriculture: Corn, cattle, grain sorghum, cotton, wheat, meat goats. Market value $46.4 million.

GEORGETOWN (39,787) county seat; agribusiness, manufacturing, education, tourism, mining; hospital; Southwestern University; Mayfair; Christmas Stroll.

ROUND ROCK (89,865, part [1,076] in Travis County) semiconductor, varied manufacturing; tourism and distribution center; hospital; Texas Baptist Children's Home.

Taylor (14,872) agribusiness, publishing center; varied manufacturing including cottonseed and meat processing; hospital; movie location.

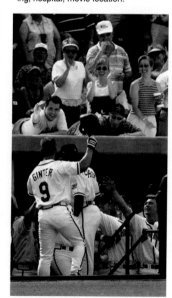

Fans at Dell Diamond cheer on the Round Rock Express. Michael Ainsworth photo.

Other towns include: **Andice** (300); **Bartlett** (1,843, partly in Bell County) cotton, corn production; commuters; prison; first rural electrification in nation in 1933; clinic; library; Friendship Fest in September; **Brushy Creek** (19,014); **Cedar Park** (45,222, partly in Travis County) oil production/services; varied manufacturing, commuting to Austin; hospital, steam-engine train; **Coupland** (280); **Florence** (1,312).

Also, **Granger** (1,495); **Hutto** (7,977) agriculture, manufacturing, government/services; commuters to Austin; museum; Olde Tyme Days in October; **Jarrell** (1,408); **Jollyville** (17,098, partly in Travis County); **Leander** (16,822); **Liberty Hill** (1,487) artisans center; **Schwertner** (175); **Thrall** (891); **Walburg** (277); **Weir** (737).

Also, the residential community of **Anderson Mill** (9,855), which extends into Travis County, and part [11,810] of **Austin**.

Population	**353,830**
Change fm 2000	41.5
Area (sq. mi.)	1,134.74
Land Area (sq. mi.)	1,122.77
Altitude (ft.)	400-1,208
Rainfall (in.)	35.11
Jan. mean min.	35.8
July mean max.	95.3
Civ. Labor	184,985
Unemployed	2.9
Wages	$1,032,048,196
Av. Weekly Wage	$746.51
Prop. Value	$ 34,492,974,636
Retail Sales	$ 4,459,917,822

For explanation of sources, abbreviations and symbols, see p. 224 and foldout map.

Wilson County

0 ▭▬▬▬▬▬▬ 8 MILES

Physical Features: South central county on rolling plains; mostly sandy soils, some heavier; San Antonio River, Cibolo Creek.

Economy: Agribusiness; some residents employed in San Antonio; part of San Antonio metropolitan area.

History: Coahuiltecan Indians in area when Spanish began ranching around 1750. Anglo-American settlers arrived in 1840s. German, Polish settled in 1850s. County created from Bexar, Karnes counties 1860; named for James C. Wilson, member of the Mier Expedition.

Race/Ethnicity, 2000: (In percent) Anglo, 61.51; Black, 1.21; Hispanic, 36.52; Other, 0.76.

Vital Statistics, 2004: Births, 459; deaths, 301; marriages, 225; divorces, 93.

Recreation: Mission ranch ruins, historic homes; Stockdale watermelon jubilee in June; Floresville peanut festival in October.

Minerals: Oil, gas, clays.

Agriculture: Cattle, dairy products, hogs, poultry; peanuts, sorghum, corn, small grains, vegetables, watermelons, fruit. Market value $42.7 million.

FLORESVILLE (6,827) county seat; agribusiness center; hospital; veterans home; Heritage Days in spring; annual Pony Express ride.

Other towns include: **La Vernia** (1,239); **Pandora** (125); **Poth** (2,125) agriculture, commuting to San Antonio; Mayfest; **Stockdale** (1,567) agriculture, commuting to San Antonio, nature center; **Sutherland Springs** (362). Part of **Nixon** (2,402, mostly in Gonzales County).

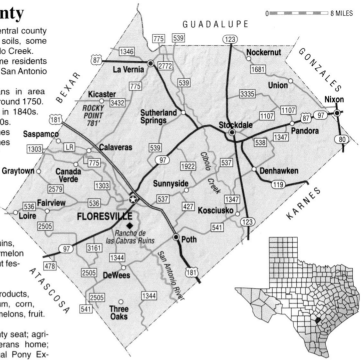

Population	38,829
Change fm 2000	19.8
Area (sq. mi.)	808.57
Land Area (sq. mi.)	806.99
Altitude (ft.)	300-781
Rainfall (in.)	27.60
Jan. mean min.	38.4

July mean max.	95.7
Civ. Labor	18,345
Unemployed	3.6
Wages	$37,626,749
Av. Weekly Wage	$468.93
Prop. Value	$2,146,829,436
Retail Sales	$178,197,575

Winkler County

Physical Features: Western county adjoining New Mexico on plains, partly sandy hills.

Economy: Oil, natural gas; ranching; prison; farming.

History: Apache area until arrival of Comanches in 1700s. Anglo-Americans began ranching in 1880s. Oil discovered 1926. Mexican migration increased after 1960. County named for Confederate Col. C.M. Winkler; created from Tom Green County 1887; organized 1910.

Race/Ethnicity, 2000: (In percent) Anglo, 53.60; Black, 1.87; Hispanic, 44.00; Other, 0.53.

Vital Statistics, 2004: Births, 101; deaths, 85; marriages, 51; divorces, 6.

Recreation: Sandhills Park; museum; zoo; wooden oil derrick; Roy Orbison festival in June at Wink; Wink Sink, large sinkhole.

Minerals: Oil, gas.

Agriculture: Major producer of chip potatoes; meat goats, beef cattle. Market value $1.9 million.

KERMIT (5,219) county seat; hospital.

Wink (837) oil, gas, ranching.

Population	6,609
Change fm 2000	-7.9
Area (sq. mi.)	841.24
Land Area (sq. mi.)	841.05
Altitude (ft.)	2,671-3,368
Rainfall (in.)	12.92

Jan. mean min.	27.8
July mean max.	96.1
Civ. Labor	3,040
Unemployed	4.0
Wages	$23,033,979
Av. Weekly Wage	$762.85

Prop. Value	$1,267,383,085
Retail Sales	$45,732,336

Wise County

Physical Features: North central county of rolling prairie, some oaks; clay, loam, sandy soils; lakes.

Economy: Petroleum; sand and gravel; agribusiness; many residents work in Fort Worth.

History: Caddo Indian groups. Delaware tribe present when Anglo-Americans arrived in 1850s. County created 1856 from Cooke County; named for Virginian, U.S. Sen. Henry A. Wise, who favored annexation of Texas.

Race/Ethnicity, 2000: (In percent) Anglo, 86.88; Black, 1.33; Hispanic, 10.76; Other, 1.03.

Vital Statistics, 2004: Births, 684; deaths, 431; marriages, 440; divorces, 286.

Recreation: Lake activities; hunting; exotic deer preserve; historical sites; Lyndon B. Johnson National Grassland; Chisholm trail days in June, antique auto swap meet; Butterfield stage days in July; heritage museum, old courthouse.

Minerals: Gas, oil, sand, gravel.

Agriculture: Beef cattle, hay, dairies, horses, wheat, goats. Market value $33.3 million.

DECATUR (5,707) county seat; petroleum center; dairying; cattle marketing; some manufacturing; hospital.

BRIDGEPORT (5,507) trade center for lake resort; oil, gas production; time-share housing; artistic community; manufacturing; prison release facility.

Other towns include: **Alvord** (1,220); **Aurora** (970) sand and gravel, manufacturing, equestrian center, "alien crash" site; **Boyd** (1,238) chili cookoff in May; **Briar** (5,651, mostly in Tarrant County); **Chico** (1,045); **Greenwood** (76); **Lake Bridgeport** (405); **Newark** (1,022); **New Fairview** (1,214); **Paradise** (512); **Pecan Acres** (2,396, partly in Tarrant County); **Rhome** (928); **Runaway Bay** (1,261); **Slidell** (175).

Population 57,891
Change fm 2000 .... 18.6
Area (sq. mi.) 922.77

Land Area (sq. mi.) 904.61
Altitude (ft.) 649-1,180
Rainfall (in.) 34.02
Jan. mean min. 30.5
July mean max. 98.0
Civ. Labor 28,687
Unemployed 3.3
Wages $167.057,830
Av. Weekly Wage.................... $700.36
Prop. Value $6,248,715,580
Retail Sales $576,068,054

For explanation of sources, abbreviations and symbols, see p. 224 and foldout map.

The Lyndon B. Johnson National Grassland. Kim Ritzenthaler photo.

Wood County

Physical Features: Hilly northeastern county almost half forested; sandy to alluvial soils; drained by Sabine and tributaries; many lakes.

Economy: Agribusiness, oil and gas; tourism.

History: Caddo Indians; reduced by disease. Anglo-American settlement developed in 1840s. County created from Van Zandt County 1850; named for Gov. George T. Wood.

Race/Ethnicity, 2000: (In percent) Anglo, 87.23; Black, 6.27; Hispanic, 5.72; Other, 0.78.

Vital Statistics, 2004: Births, 453; deaths, 495; marriages, 297; divorces, 158.

Recreation: Autumn trails; lake activities; hunting, birding; Gov. Hogg shrine and museum; historic sites; scenic drives; Mineola Choo Choo, Chili & Bean Fest in May; autumn trails.

Minerals: Natural gas, oil, sand, gravel.

Agriculture: Poultry, beef cattle, dairies, forages. Market value $57.8 million. Timber production significant.

QUITMAN (2,065) county seat; tourism; food processing; some manufacturing; hospital; Light Crust Doughboy museum; Dogwood Fiesta.

MINEOLA (4,774) agribusiness, some manufacturing; railroad center, antiques shops; museum, library; nature preserve; Ironhorse Fall Fest.

Winnsboro (3,603, partly in Franklin County) chicken-raising, dairies, distribution; hospital; prison.

Other towns include: **Alba** (440, partly in Rains County); **Golden** (398) Sweet Potato festival; **Hawkins** (1,542) petroleum, water bottling, Jarvis Christian College; oil festival in October; **Yantis** (320).

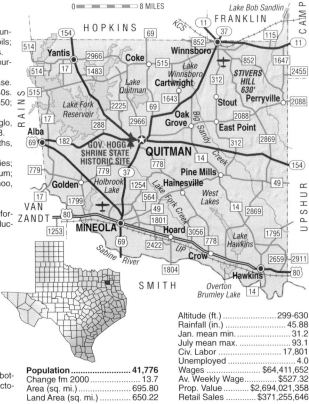

Population	41,776
Change fm 2000	13.7
Area (sq. mi.)	695.80
Land Area (sq. mi.)	650.22

Altitude (ft.)	299-630
Rainfall (in.)	45.88
Jan. mean min.	31.2
July mean max.	93.1
Civ. Labor	17,801
Unemployed	4.0
Wages	$64,411,652
Av. Weekly Wage	$527.32
Prop. Value	$2,694,021,358
Retail Sales	$371,255,646

Yoakum County

Physical Features: Western county is level to rolling; playas, draws; sandy, loam, chocolate soils.

Economy: Oil and gas, cotton.

History: Comanche hunting area. Anglo-Americans began ranching in 1890s. Oil discovered 1936. Mexican migration increased in 1950s. County named for Henderson Yoakum, pioneer historian; created from Bexar District 1876; organized 1907.

Race/Ethnicity, 2000: (In percent) Anglo, 52.14; Black, 1.26; Hispanic, 45.93; Other, 0.67.

Vital Statistics, 2004: Births, 138; deaths, 50; marriages, 55; divorces, 18.

Recreation: Tsa Mo Ga Museum at Plains; Roughneck rodeo and farmboy jamboree in May; settlers reunion in August; watermelon roundup on Labor Day weekend.

Minerals: Oil, natural gas.

Agriculture: Cotton, peanuts, sorghum, watermelons, wheat, cattle. 100,000 acres irrigated. Market value $49.9 million.

PLAINS (1,477) county seat; oil, agribusiness center.

DENVER CITY (3,887) center for oil, agriculture activities in two counties; hospital, library, museum.

Population	7,438
Change fm 2000	1.6
Area (sq. mi.)	799.76
Land Area (sq. mi.)	799.75
Altitude (ft.)	3,490-3,891
Rainfall (in.)	18.41
Jan. mean min.	25.1

July mean max.	91.7
Civ. Labor	3,355
Unemployed	3.5
Wages	$28,337,294
Av. Weekly Wage	$730.66
Prop. Value	$2,649,591,816
Retail Sales	$66,251,975

Young County

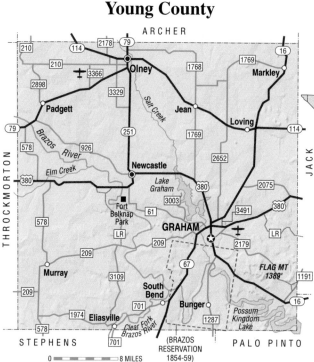

Economy: Oil, agribusiness, tourism; hunting leases.

History: U.S. military outpost established 1851. Site of Brazos Indian Reservation 1854-59 with Caddoes, Wacos, other tribes. Anglo-American settlers arrived in 1850s. County named for early Texan, Col. W.C. Young; created 1856 from Bosque, Fannin counties; reorganized 1874.

Race/Ethnicity, 2000: (In percent) Anglo, 87.25; Black, 1.32; Hispanic, 10.62; Other, 0.81.

Vital Statistics, 2004: Births, 213; deaths, 255; marriages, 142; divorces, 87.

Recreation: Lake activities; hunting; Fort Belknap; marker at oak tree in Graham where ranchers formed forerunner of Texas and Southwestern Cattle Raisers Association.

Minerals: Oil, gas, sand, gravel.

Agriculture: Beef cattle; wheat chief crop, also hay, cotton, pecans, nursery plants. Market value $23.9 million.

GRAHAM (8,532) county seat; oil, agribusiness, manufacturing, tourism, hunting; hospital; old post office museum/art center; art festival in May.

Other towns include: **Loving** (300); **Newcastle** (595); **Olney** (3,278) aluminum, varied manufacturing, hospital; One-Arm Dove Hunt in September; **South Bend** (140).

Population	18,021
Change fm 2000	0.4
Area (sq. mi.)	930.84
Land Area (sq. mi.)	922.33
Altitude (ft.)	995-1,389
Rainfall (in.)	31.35
Jan. mean min.	27.1
July mean max.	96.6
Civ. Labor	9,587
Unemployed	3.1
Wages	$52,816,560
Av. Weekly Wage	$584.58
Prop. Value	$1,179,738,670
Retail Sales	$190,308,149

The plaza and Nuestra Senora del Refugio Church in San Ygnacio in Zapata County. Robert Plocheck photo.

Zapata County

Physical Features: Southern county of rolling, brushy topography; broken by tributaries of Rio Grande; Falcon Reservoir.

Economy: Natural gas, oil; ranching, Falcon Reservoir activities, government/services.

History: Coahuiltecan Indians in area when the ranch settlement of Nuestra Señora de los Dolores was established in 1750. Anglo-American migration increased after 1980. County named for Col. Antonio Zapata, pioneer rancher; created 1858 from Starr, Webb counties.

Race/Ethnicity, 2000: (In percent) Anglo, 14.78; Black, 0.18; Hispanic, 84.78; Other, 0.26.

Vital Statistics, 2004: Births, 297; deaths, 66; marriages, 27; divorces, 1.

Recreation: Lake; state park; historic sites; Nuestra Señora de los Dolores Hacienda site; winter tourist center; rock hunting; hang gliding encampment in June/July.

Minerals: Natural gas, oil, caliche.

Agriculture: Beef cattle; onions, cantaloupes and melons; goats. Market value $9.8 million. Hunting/wildlife leases.

ZAPATA (5,521) county seat; tourism, agribusiness, oil center; retirement, winter tourist center; clinic; Fajita Cook-off in November.

Other towns and places include: **Falcon** (203); **Lopeño** (163); **Medina** (3,369), and **San Ygnacio** (961) historic buildings, museum.

Population	**13,615**
Change fm 2000	11.8
Area (sq. mi.)	1,058.10
Land Area (sq. mi.)	996.76
Altitude (ft.)	301-800
Rainfall (in.)	19.53
Jan. mean min.	45.4
July mean max.	98.0
Civ. Labor	5,289
Unemployed	4.7
Wages	$30,576,383
Av. Weekly Wage	$706.53
Prop. Value	$2,650,204,113
Retail Sales	$76,777,812

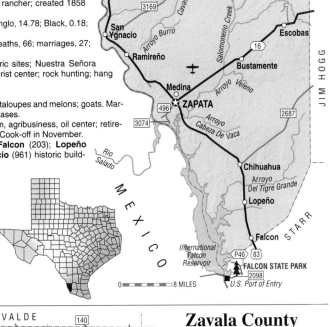

Zavala County

Physical Features: Southwestern county near Mexican border of rolling plains broken by much brush; Nueces, Leona, other streams.

Economy: Agribusiness, food packaging, leading county in Winter Garden truck-farming area; government/services.

History: Coahuiltecan area; Apaches, Comanches arrived later. Ranching developed in late 1860s. County created from Maverick, Uvalde counties 1858; organized 1884; named for Texas Revolutionary leader Lorenzo de Zavala.

Race/Ethnicity, 2000: (In percent) Anglo, 8.15; Black, 0.40; Hispanic, 91.22; Other, 0.23.

Vital Statistics, 2004: Births, 241; deaths, 76; marriages, 42; divorces, 0.

Recreation: Hunting, fishing; spinach festival in November.

Minerals: Oil, natural gas.

Agriculture: Cattle, grains, vegetables, cotton, pecans. About 50,000 acres irrigated. Market value $48.7 million. Hunting leases important.

CRYSTAL CITY (7,259) county seat; agribusiness; food processing; oil-field services; site of Japanese detention center. Home of Popeye statue.

Other towns include: **Batesville** (1,240) and **La Pryor** (1,524).

For explanation of sources, abbreviations and symbols, see p. 224 and foldout map.

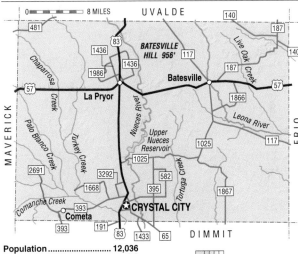

Population	**12,036**
Change fm 2000	3.8
Area (sq. mi.)	1,301.72
Land Area (sq. mi.)	1,298.48
Altitude (ft.)	540-956
Rainfall (in.)	20.70
Jan. mean min.	42.6
July mean max.	97.1
Civ. Labor	4,076
Unemployed	11.8
Wages	$13,842,420
Av. Weekly Wage	$397.61
Prop. Value	$863,745,950
Retail Sales	$32,243,034

Population

Shoppers in downtown Brownsville. Robert Plocheck photo.

2006 Estimates

2000 Census

Growth Analysis

Metro Areas

Zapata, above, and Zapata County are booming, with an 11.8 percent population rise since 2000. The Texas border from Laredo to Brownsville is one of four areas in the state where growth has been concentrated. Robert Plocheck photo.

Texas Population: A Hurricane and Immigration

By Steve H. Murdock, Md. Nazrul Hoque, Beverly Pecotte and Jeff Jordan, of the Institute for Demographic and Socioeconomic Research, the University of Texas at San Antonio.

Impacted by an influx of persons entering Texas as a result of Hurricane Katrina, Texas' population growth edged by that in California to make Texas the fastest growing state (in numerical terms) in the nation from 2000 to 2006.

Texas increased its population from 20,851,820 in 2000 to 23,507,783 as of July 1, 2006. This was an increase of 2,655,963 or 12.7 percent. By comparison, California increased from 33,871,648 in 2000 to 36,457,549 in 2006, an increase of 2,585,901 or 7.6

Population change, 1850–2006

Year	Total Population		Percent change	
	Texas	U.S.	Texas	U.S.
1850	212,592	23,191,876	...	...
1860	604,215	31,443,321	184.2	35.6
1870	818,579	39,181,449	35.5	26.6
1880	1,591,749	50,155,783	94.5	26.0
1890	2,235,527	62,947,714	40.4	25.5
1900	3,048,710	75,994,575	36.4	20.7
1910	3,896,542	91,972,266	27.8	21.0
1920	4,663,228	105,710,620	19.7	14.9
1930	5,824,715	122,775,046	24.9	16.1
1940	6,414,824	131,669,275	10.1	7.2
1950	7,711,194	150,697,361	20.2	14.5
1960	9,579,677	179,323,175	24.2	19.0
1970	11,196,730	203,302,031	16.9	13.4
1980	14,229,191	226,545,805	27.1	11.4
1990	16,986,510	248,709,873	19.4	9.8
2000	20,851,820	281,421,906	22.8	13.2
2006	**23,507,783**	**299,398,484**	**12.7**	**6.4**

Source: U.S. Bureau of the Census, compiled by the Texas State Data Center, University of Texas at San Antonio.

percent. Both states showed a faster rate of increase than the 6.4 percent changed in the nation from 2000 to 2006, from 281,421,906 in 2000 to 299,398,484 on July 1, 2006.

Although it is impossible to know exactly how many persons migrated to Texas from Louisiana as a result of Hurricane Katrina, Texas' average annual population increase of approximately 400,000 per year in the years from 2000 to 2005 increased to 579,000 from 2005 to 2006, with an increase in the number of domestic migrants (migrants coming to Texas from other states) from roughly 60,000 from 2004 to 2005, to nearly 218,000 from 2005 to 2006.

Texas domestic migration has been increasing after reaching a low of only about 36,000 from 2003 to 2004 but even allowing for a likely increase in domestic migration from other sources, the Office of the State Demographer estimates that Texas received between 120,000 and 160,000 persons from Louisiana from 2005 to 2006.

Texas' percentage rate of growth from 2000 to 2006 was the seventh fastest among the states and was exceeded by only Florida and Georgia among the large states.

Florida's estimated 2006 population was 18.1 million, an increase of 13.2 percent. Georgia's estimated 2006 population was 8.9 million, an increase of 14.4 percent.

Texas' 23.5 million people in 2006 was greater than that in all other states except California and substantially greater than the next largest states of New York (with a 2006 population of 19.3 million) and Florida, and more than 10 million larger than the next two largest states, Illinois with 12.8 million and Pennsylvania with 12.4 million. Whether viewed historically or comparatively, Texas' population is showing substantial growth.

Changing Sources of Growth

What also remains evident, however, is that Texas' growth in the post-2000 period is not necessarily identical in source to that of the 1990s.

In the 1990s, Texas' population increase of approximately 3.9 million was about 50 percent due to natural increase (the excess of births relative to deaths), about 30 percent was due to domestic migration, and 20 percent was a result of international immigration.

Of the nearly 2.7 million person increase in the population of Texas from 2000 to 2006, roughly 52 percent was from natural increase, 18 percent from domestic migration, and international immigration accounted for roughly 30 percent.

Assuming that growth levels due to Katrina do not continue and that there is little net out-migration of these persons from Texas, present trends if continued from the remainder of the 2000 to 2010 period would result in an increase of roughly 744,000 domestic migrants and nearly 1.3 million international immigrants.

These patterns would be the opposite of those in the 1990s when there were some 1.2 million domestic migrants and 777,000 international immigrants.

Rural Areas Struggling

It is also evident that post-2000 population growth has become increasingly concentrated in the central cities and suburbs of Texas while many rural areas are losing population.

Thus, growth in the 2000-2006 period was concentrated in four regions of Texas: Dallas-Fort Worth, Houston-Galveston, Austin-San Antonio, and the Texas border from Laredo to Brownsville.

But, whereas 68 counties lost population from 1990 to 2000, 103 lost population from 2000 to 2006.

What some have called the Texas Triangle (Dallas-Fort Worth to San Antonio to Houston) continues to grow substantially while many counties in the Panhandle and West Texas are struggling to maintain their populations.

In all, 47 counties increased their populations by more than 10 percent from 2000 to 2006, with Rockwall, Collin, Williamson, Fort Bend, Montgomery, Denton, Hays and Kaufman all increasing by more than 30 percent.

On the other hand, 18 counties, mostly located in the Panhandle and West Texas, decreased by more than 10 percent with the largest decreases in King, Stonewall, Culberson, Kent, Cochran and Knox. ☆

Counties of Significant Population Change: 2000 to 2006

Fastest Growing by Percent Gain			Fastest Growing by Most Persons Gained		
Rank, County	Largest cities	Percent	Rank, County	Largest cities	Number
1. Rockwall	Rockwall	60.5	1. Harris	Houston	485,653
2. Collin	Plano-McKinney-Frisco	42.1	2. Tarrant	Fort Worth-Arlington	225,121
3. Williamson	Round Rock-Georgetown	41.5	3. Collin	Plano-McKinney-Frisco	207,079
4. Fort Bend	Sugar Land-Missouri City	39.1	4. Bexar	San Antonio	162,661
5. Montgomery	The Woodlands-Conroe	35.6	5. Denton	Denton-Lewisville	151,272
6. Denton	Denton-Lewisville	34.9	6. Fort Bend	Sugar Land-Missouri City	138,716
7. Hays	San Marcos	33.6	7. Hidalgo	McAllen-Edinburg-Mission	131,171
8. Kaufman	Terrell-Kaufman	30.8	8. Dallas	Dallas	126,972
9. Comal	New Braunfels	29.7	9. Travis	Austin	108,707
10. Kendall	Boerne	27.3	10. Montgomery	The Woodlands-Conroe	104,522

Chart shows Rockwall County increased in population by 60.5 percent since 2000, while Harris County (Houston) gained 485,653 people, etc. Source: U.S. Bureau of the Census.

Fastest Declining by Percent Loss			Fasting Declining by Most Persons Lost		
Rank, County	Largest towns	Percent	Rank, County	Largest cities	Number
1. King	Guthrie	-19.4	1. Jefferson	Beaumont-Port Arthur	-8,137
2. Stonewall	Aspermont	-17.2	2. Wichita	Wichita	-6,506
3. Culberson	Van Horn	-15.1	3. Coryell	Gatesville	-2,311
4. Kent	Jayton	-14.6	4. Reeves	Pecos-Balmorhea	-1,671
5. Cochran	Morton-Whiteface	-13.8	5. Taylor	Abilene	-1,624
6. Knox	Munday-Knox City	-13.0	6. Hutchinson	Borger-Stinnett	-1,397
7. Reeves	Pecos-Balmorhea	-12.7	7. Kleberg	Kingsville	-1,196
8. Cottle	Paducah	-11.8	8. Howard	Big Spring	-1,164
9. Glasscock	Garden City	-11.2	9. Jones	Anson-Stamford	-1,140
10. Borden	Gail	-11.1	10. Falls	Marlin-Rosebud	-1,029

Chart shows King County declined in population by 19.4 percent since the 2000 census according to state estimates, while Jefferson County lost 8,137 people, etc. Source: U.S. Bureau of the Census.

The federal government in 1949 began defining geographic units as standard metropolitan areas for the gathering of statistics.

Now called **Metropolitan Statistical Areas** (MSAs), these may be composed of one or more counties. Metropolitan Divisions (MD) are sub-units of a larger MSA classification.

Following are the 25 Texas metro areas listed in descending order by population. The MSAs are based on the 2005 designations of the federal Office of Management and Budget.

Population estimates are from the U.S. Census Bureau for July 2006.

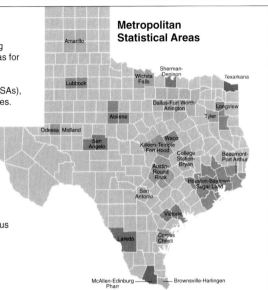

Metropolitan Statistical Areas

Metropolitan Statistical Areas	2006 Population estimate	Percent change 2000-2006
1. **Dallas-Fort Worth-Arlington** (Dallas-Plano-Irving MD and Fort Worth-Arlington MD) Dallas-Plano-Irving MD (Collin, Dallas, Delta, Denton, Ellis, Hunt, Kaufman, Rockwall counties) Fort Worth-Arlington MD (Johnson, Parker, Tarrant, Wise counties)	6,003,967	16.3
2. **Houston-Baytown-Sugar Land** (Austin, Brazoria, Chambers, Fort Bend, Galveston, Harris, Liberty, Montgomery, San Jacinto, Waller counties)	5,539,949	17.5
3. **San Antonio** (Atascosa, Bandera, Bexar, Comal, Guadalupe, Kendall, Medina, Wilson counties)	1,942,217	13.5
4. **Austin-Round Rock** (Bastrop, Caldwell, Hays, Travis, Williamson counties)	1,513,565	21.1
5. **El Paso** (El Paso County)	736,310	8.3
6. **McAllen-Edinburg-Pharr** (Hidalgo County)	700,634	23.0
7. **Corpus Christi** (Aransas, Nueces, San Patricio counties)	415,810	3.1
8. **Brownsville-Harlingen** (Cameron County)	387,717	15.7
9. **Beaumont-Port Arthur** (Hardin, Jefferson, Orange counties)	379,640	-1.4
10. **Killeen-Temple-Fort Hood** (Bell, Coryell, Lampasas counties)	351,322	6.2
11. **Lubbock** (Crosby, Lubbock counties)	261,411	4.7
12. **Amarillo** (Armstrong, Carson, Potter, Randall counties)	241,515	6.6
13. **Laredo** (Webb County)	231,470	19.9
14. **Waco** (McLennan County)	226,189	5.9
15. **Longview** (Gregg, Rusk, Upshur counties)	203,367	4.8
16. **Tyler** (Smith County)	194,635	11.4
17. **Bryan-College Station** (Brazos, Burleson, Robertson counties)	192,152	3.9
18. **Abilene** (Callahan, Jones, Taylor counties)	158,063	-1.4
19. **Wichita Falls** (Archer, Clay, Wichita counties)	145,528	-4.0
20. **Texarkana** (Bowie County, TX, and Miller County, AR)	134,510	3.7
21. **Odessa** (Ector County)	127,462	5.2
22. **Midland** (Midland County)	124,380	7.2
23. **Sherman-Denison** (Grayson County)	118,478	7.1
24. **Victoria** (Calhoun, Goliad, Victoria counties)	114,088	2.2
25. **San Angelo** (Irion, Tom Green counties)	105,752	0.0

Population 2000 and 2006

Population: Numbers in parentheses are from the 2000 U.S. census. The Census Bureau counts only incorporated cities and a few unincorporated towns called Census Designated Places.

Population figures at the far right for incorporated cities are Texas State Data Center estimates as of Jan. 1, 2006. Names of the incorporated cities are in capital letters, e.g., "ABBOTT".

The population figure given for all other towns is an estimate received from local officials through a Texas Almanac survey.

In some cases, when no population estimate could be obtained, these places show "NA" (Not Available) in place of a population figure.

Location: The county in which the town is located follows the name of town. If more than one county is listed, the town is principally in the first-named county, e.g., "ABERNATHY, Hale-Lubbock".

Businesses: For incorporated cities, the number following the county name indicates the number of business in the city as of January 2006 as reported by the state comptroller. For unincorporated towns, it is the number of businesses within the postal zip code as reported by the U.S. Economic Census 2002.

For example, "ABBOTT, Hill, 24" means that Abbott in Hill County had 24 businesses.

Post Offices: Places with post offices, as of Nov. 2006, are marked with an asterisk (*), e.g., "*Afton".

Town, County ....Pop. 2006	Town, County ....Pop. 2006	Town, County ....Pop. 2006
*ABBOTT, Hill, 24, (300)................303	(132)......................................125	Almira, Cass 30
Aberfoyle, Hunt,.............................35	Airville, Bell....................................65	*ALPINE, Brewster, 365,
*ABERNATHY, Hale-Lubbock,	Alabama-Coushatta, Polk, (480) 480	(5,786)...............................6,147
82, (2,839),............................2,798	*ALAMO, Hidalgo, 434,	Alsa, Van Zandt 30
*ABILENE, Taylor-Jones, 4,115,	(14,760) 17,576	*Altair, Colorado, 6...........................30
(115,930) 115,745	Alamo Alto, El Paso 19	*ALTO, Cherokee, 74, (1,190).....1,271
Ables Springs, Kaufman.................NA	Alamo Beach, Calhoun..................100	Alto Bonito, Starr, (569) 607
Abner, Kaufman..............................75	ALAMO HEIGHTS, Bexar, 364,	Altoga, Collin 137
Abram-Perezville, Hidalgo,	(7,319)................................7,280	*ALTON, Hidalgo, 315,
(5,444)................................5,664	*Alanreed, Gray, 5 48	(4,384)................................8,698
*ACADEMY [Little River-], Bell,	Alazan, Nacogdoches....................100	Alton North, Hidalgo,
26, (1,645)..........................1,696	*ALBA, Wood-Rains, 70,	(5,051)................................5,264
Acala, Hudspeth 25	(430)...................................440	Alum Creek, Bastrop ....NA
*Ace, Polk, 3...................................40	*ALBANY, Shackelford, 129,	*ALVARADO, Johnson, 260,
*ACKERLY, Dawson-Martin, 16,	(1,921)................................1,828	(3,288)................................3,919
(245)...................................244	Albert, Gillespie, 2 25	*ALVIN, Brazoria, 1,051,
Acme, Hardeman............................14	Albion, Red River............................52	(21,413)..............................23,031
Acton, Hood...............................1,129	Alderbranch, Anderson.....................5	*ALVORD, Wise, 52, (1,007).......1,220
Acuff, Lubbock..............................152	Aldine, Harris, (13,979).............14,424	Amargosa [Owl Ranch-],
Acworth, Red River..........................50	*ALEDO, Parker, 243,	Jim Wells, (527)......................549
Adams Gardens, Cameron............200	(1,726)................................2,360	*AMARILLO, Potter-Randall,
Adams Store, Panola.....................NA	Aleman, Hamilton 50	6,939, (173,627)..............185,745
Adamsville, Lampasas....................41	Alexander, Erath 40	Ambia, Lamar 16
Addicks, Harris ....[part of Houston]	Aley, Henderson 45	Ambrose, Grayson..........................90
Addielou, Red River........................31	Alfred-South La Paloma,	Ames, Coryell 10
*ADDISON, Dallas, 1,966,	Jim Wells, (451)......................465	AMES, Liberty, 9, (1,079) 1,086
(14,166) 14,777	Algerita, San Saba..........................48	Amherst, Lamar 125
Addran, Hopkins ....NA	Algoa, Galveston 135	*AMHERST, Lamb, 17, (791)........811
Adell, Parker..................................NA	*ALICE, Jim Wells, 832,	Amistad [Box Canyon-], Val Verde,
*Adkins, Bexar, 95 ....NA	(19,010) 19,626	(76)......................................77
Admiral, Callahan 18	Alice Acres, Jim Wells,	Ammannsville, Fayette 137
Adobes, Presidio............................NA	(491)...................................521	Amphion, Atascosa.........................26
*ADRIAN, Oldham, 14, (159).........149	*Alief, Harris, 19.........[part of Houston]	Amsterdam, Brazoria.....................193
Advance, Parker.............................NA	Allamoore, Hudspeth 25	Anadarko, Rusk...............................30
*Afton, Dickens, 1 15	*ALLEN, Collin, 2,363,	*ANAHUAC, Chambers, 89,
Agnes, Parker.................................NA	(43,554) 69,110	(2,210)................................2,524
*AGUA DULCE, Nueces, 32,	Allenfarm, Brazos 35	*ANDERSON, Grimes, 55,
(737)...................................701	Allenhurst, Matagorda 72	(257)...................................271
Agua Dulce, El Paso, (738)...........749	Allen's Chapel, Fannin....................41	Anderson Mill, Williamson-Travis,
Agua Nueva, Jim Hogg.....................5	Allen's Point, Fannin.......................76	(8,953)................................9,855
Aguilares, Webb 37	Allentown, Angelina 110	Ander-Weser-Kilgore, Goliad.........322
*Aiken, Floyd, 1 52	Alleyton, Colorado, 20 165	*Andice, Williamson, 9..................300
Aiken, Shelby................................150	*Allison, Wheeler, 2 135	*ANDREWS, Andrews, 394,
Aikin Grove, Red River...................15	Allmon, Floyd..................................24	(9,652)................................9,322
Airport City, Bexar........................106	Allred, Yoakum...............................90	*ANGLETON, Brazoria, 643,
Airport Road Addition, Brooks,	ALMA, Ellis, 12, (302)...................326	(18,130) 19,031

Town, County ....Pop. 2006	Town, County ....Pop. 2006	Town, County ....Pop. 2006

ANGUS, Navarro, 19,
   (334) 387
*ANNA, Collin, 159, (1,225).........2,025
Annaville, Nueces
   ....[part of Corpus Christi]
ANNETTA, Parker, 28,
   (1,108) 1,248
ANNETTA NORTH, Parker, 17,
   (467) 495
ANNETTA SOUTH, Parker, 8,
   (555) 623
*ANNONA, Red River, 10,
   (282) 260
*ANSON, Jones, 99,
   (2,556) 2,522
Antelope, Jack................................65
*ANTHONY, El Paso-
   (Dona Ana Co., NM) 141,
   (11,754) 12,011
Antioch, Cass 45
Antioch, Delta 10
Antioch, Madison 15
Antioch, Smith ....NA
Antioch Colony, Hays 25
*ANTON, Hockley, 21,
   (1,200) 1,186
APPLEBY, Nacogdoches,
   (444) 442
*Apple Springs, Trinity, 14 185
*AQUILLA, Hill, 7, (136).................145
*ARANSAS PASS, San Patricio-
   Aransas, 399, (8,138)...........8,704
Arbala, Hopkins 41
Arcadia, Shelby 35
*ARCHER CITY, Archer, 82,
   (1,848) 1,837
ARCOLA, Fort Bend, 47,
   (1,048) 1,293
Arden, Irion 1
Argo, Titus 200
*ARGYLE, Denton, 231,
   (2,365) 2,890
*ARLINGTON, Tarrant, 11,432,
   (332,969) 365,723
Armstrong, Bell...............................25
*Armstrong, Kenedy, 1.......................4
Arneckeville, DeWitt 50
Arnett, Coryell.................................15
Arnett, Hockley 5
*ARP, Smith, 57, (901)....................995
Arroyo Alto, Cameron, (320)...........325
Arroyo City, Cameron 250
Arroyo Colorado Estates,
   Cameron, (755) 773
Arroyo Gardens-La Tina Ranch,
   Cameron, (732) 737
*Art, Mason, 1 14
Artesia Wells, La Salle, 2................35
*Arthur City, Lamar, 12 180
Arvana, Dawson 25
Asa, McLennan................................46
Ash, Houston 19
Ashby, Matagorda............................60
*ASHERTON, Dimmit, 15,
   (1,342) 1,271
Ashland, Upshur 45
Ashtola, Donley 25
Ashwood, Matagorda.....................132
Asia, Polk...83
*ASPERMONT, Stonewall, 73,
   (1,021) 873
Atascocita, Harris, (35,757).......35,174

*Atascosa, Bexar, 37 ....NA
Ater, Coryell....................................12
*ATHENS, Henderson, 662,
   (11,297) 12,430
*ATLANTA, Cass, 277,
   (5,745) 5,686
Atlas, Lamar 28
Atoy, Cherokee 50
*AUBREY, Denton, 167,
   (1,500) 2,202
Augusta, Houston 40
AURORA, Wise, 18, (853)..............970
*AUSTIN, Travis-Williamson,
   31,625, (656,562) 705,611
Austonio, Houston, 10 37
*AUSTWELL, Refugio, 2,
   (192) 179
Authon, Parker.................................15
*Avalon, Ellis, 7.............................400
*AVERY, Red River, 24, (462)........462
*AVINGER, Cass, 22, (464)...........457
*Avoca, Jones, 5.............................121
*Axtell, McLennan, 24....................300
*AZLE, Tarrant-Parker, 558,
   (9,600) 10,217

B

Back, Gray...6
*Bacliff, Galveston, 80,
   (6,962) 7,515

*Bagwell, Red River, 3...................150
*BAILEY, Fannin, 9, (213)..............230
BAILEY'S PRAIRIE, Brazoria, 16,
   (694) 747
Baileyville, Milam 32
Bainer, Lamb 10
Bainville, Karnes................................8
*BAIRD, Callahan, 76,
   (1,623) 1,576
Baker, Floyd.....................................28
Bakersfield, Pecos...........................11
*BALCH SPRINGS, Dallas, 491,
   (19,375) 20,770
BALCONES HEIGHTS, Bexar,
   153, (3,016)........................2,952
Bald Hill, Angelina.........................100
Bald Prairie, Robertson 40
*BALLINGER, Runnels, 222,
   (4,243) 4,084
*BALMORHEA, Reeves, 17,
   (527) 462
Balsora, Wise 50
*BANDERA, Bandera, 295,
   (957) 1,075
Bandera Falls, Bandera..................NA
*BANGS, Brown, 49, (1,620).......1,608
*Banquete, Nueces, 15..................582
Barbarosa, Guadalupe 46
Barclay, Falls 58

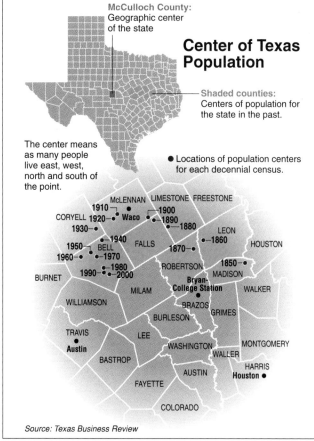

McCulloch County:
Geographic center
of the state

Center of Texas Population

Shaded counties:
Centers of population for
the state in the past.

The center means
as many people
live east, west,
north and south of
the point.

● Locations of population centers
for each decennial census.

McLENNAN LIMESTONE FREESTONE
1910 ● ●1900
CORYELL 1920 ● Waco ●1890
1930 ● ●1880
●1940 LEON ●1860
1950 ● BELL FALLS 1870 ● HOUSTON
1960 ● ●1970
●1980 ROBERTSON 1850 ●
1990 ●●2000 MADISON
BURNET Bryan- WALKER
College Station
WILLIAMSON MILAM BRAZOS GRIMES
BURLESON
TRAVIS LEE
Austin WASHINGTON MONTGOMERY
BASTROP WALLER
AUSTIN HARRIS
FAYETTE Houston ●
COLORADO

Source: Texas Business Review

Town, County ....Pop. 2006	Town, County ....Pop. 2006	Town, County ....Pop. 2006
*BARDWELL, Ellis, 10,	*BELLAIRE, Harris, 885,	Biry, Medina.....................................24
(583)................................615	(15,642).............................15,798	*BISHOP, Nueces, 69,
*Barker, Harris, 14 2,500	Bell Branch, Ellis.........................125	(3,305)..............................3,362
*Barksdale, Edwards, 7 100	*BELLEVUE, Clay, 21, (386).........396	BISHOP HILLS, Potter, 0,
Barnes, Polk 75	*BELLMEAD, McLennan, 255,	(210)................................213
*Barnhart, Irion, 6 110	(9,214)...............................9,291	*Bivins, Cass, 19 215
Barnum, Polk 50	*BELLS, Grayson, 53,	Bixby, Cameron, (356)..................361
*Barrett, Harris, (2,872) 2,702	(1,190)...............................1,292	Black, Parmer..............................100
*BARRY, Navarro, 29,	*BELLVILLE, Austin, 340,	Blackfoot, Anderson.......................33
(209)................................229	(3,794)...............................4,435	Black Hill, Atascosa.......................60
*BARSTOW, Ward, 1,	Belmena, Milam..............................15	Black Hills, Navarro.......................80
(406)................................370	*Belmont, Gonzales, 2....................55	Black Jack, Cherokee.....................47
*BARTLETT, Williamson-Bell, 65,	Belott, Houston 101	Black Jack, Robertson....................45
(1,675).............................1,843	*BELTON, Bell, 656,	Blackjack, Smith............................NA
Barton Corners, Lipscomb.................4	(14,623)...........................16,156	Black Oak, Hopkins......................150
Barton Creek, Travis, (1,589) 1,538	Ben Arnold, Milam 100	*BLACKWELL, Nolan-Coke, 14,
Bartons Chapel, Jack ....NA	*BENAVIDES, Duval, 29,	(360)................................345
BARTONVILLE, Denton, 78,	(1,686).............................1,607	Blair, Taylor...................................25
(1,093).............................1,245	*Ben Bolt, Jim Wells, 3 1,600	Blanchard, Polk............................NA
Barwise, Floyd................................16	*BENBROOK, Tarrant, 766,	*BLANCO, Blanco, 215,
Bascom, Smith ....NA	(20,208)...........................21,377	(1,505).............................1,635
*Basin, Brewster, 5 22	Benchley, Robertson 110	Blanconia, Bee...............................40
Bassett, Bowie..............................373	*Bend, San Saba-Lampasas, 3 115	Bland Lake, San Augustine 25
*BASTROP, Bastrop, 603,	*Ben Franklin, Delta........................60	*BLANKET, Brown, 26, (402).........415
(5,340).............................8,053	Ben Hur, Limestone.......................100	Blanton, Hill.....................................5
Bateman, Bastrop...........................NA	*BENJAMIN, Knox, 12, (264) 263	Bleakwood, Newton......................300
Batesville, Red River 14	Bennett, Parker..............................40	*Bledsoe, Cochran, 3....................126
*Batesville, Zavala, 10,	Benoit, Runnels 10	*Bleiblerville, Austin, 5 125
(1,298).............................1,240	Bentonville, Jim Wells.....................15	*Blessing, Matagorda, 24,
*Batson, Hardin, 12 140	*Ben Wheeler, Van Zandt, 57 504	(861)................................835
Battle, McLennan...........................100	*Berclair, Goliad, 2.........................253	Blevins, Falls..................................36
Bausell-Ellis, Willacy, (112)............109	Berea, Houston...............................41	Blewett, Uvalde..............................10
Baxter, Henderson.........................150	Berea, Marion 200	Blodgett, Titus...............................60
*BAY CITY, Matagorda, 628,	Bergheim, Kendall, 14 1,213	*BLOOMBURG, Cass, 11,
(18,667)...........................18,115	Berlin, Washington..........................NA	(375)................................383
Baylor Lake, Childress.....................27	Bernardo, Colorado 155	*BLOOMING GROVE, Navarro,
BAYOU VISTA, Galveston, 33,	BERRYVILLE, Henderson, 10,	21, (833)...........................875
(1,644).............................1,743	(891)................................960	*Bloomington, Victoria, 8,
*BAYSIDE, Refugio, 11, (360) 340	*BERTRAM, Burnet, 95,	(2,562)..............................2,645
*BAYTOWN, Harris, 2,063,	(1,122).............................1,318	*BLOSSOM, Lamar, 51,
(66,430)...........................68,858	Bessmay, Jasper ....NA	(1,439).............................1,449
BAYVIEW, Cameron, 11,	Best, Reagan................................... 2	Blue, Lee.......................................75
(323)................................408	Bethany, Panola 50	Blue Berry Hill, Bee, (982)............940
Bazette, Navarro.............................30	Bethel, Anderson.............................50	*Bluegrove, Clay, 1 135
BEACH CITY, Chambers, 0,	Bethel, Ellis...................................100	BLUE MOUND, Tarrant, 51,
(1,645).............................2,043	Bethel, Henderson.........................125	(2,388)..............................2,495
Beans, Jasper................................NA	Bethel, Runnels 20	*BLUE RIDGE, Collin, 37,
Bear Creek, Dallas 1,000	Bethlehem, Upshur..........................75	(672)................................870
BEAR CREEK, Hays, 0, (360)........381	Bettie, Upshur...............................110	Bluetown-Iglesia Antigua, Cameron,
*BEASLEY, Fort Bend, 13,	Beulah, Limestone...........................12	(692)................................701
(590)................................613	BEVERLY HILLS, McLennan, 107,	*Bluff Dale, Erath, 14 123
Beattie, Comanche..........................48	(2,113)..............................2,055	Bluff Springs, Travis......................NA
*BEAUMONT, Jefferson, 4,350,	BEVIL OAKS, Jefferson, 23,	*Bluffton, Llano, 3 75
(113,866)........................ 111,174	(1,346)..............................1,284	*BLUM, Hill, 19, (399)....................434
Beaver Dam, Bowie.........................55	Bevilport, Jasper.............................NA	Bluntzer, Nueces 150
Bebe, Gonzales 42	Beyersville, Williamson....................80	Bob Town, Jack ....NA
Becker, Kaufman 300	Biardstown, Lamar...........................75	*BOERNE, Kendall, 1,223,
*BECKVILLE, Panola, 37,	*Bigfoot, Frio, 2, (304) 308	(6,178)..............................7,830
(752)................................752	Big Hill, Limestone............................9	*BOGATA, Red River, 43,
Becton, Lubbock..............................62	*BIG LAKE, Reagan, 138,	(1,396).............................1,377
*BEDFORD, Tarrant, 1,739,	(2,885)..............................2,677	Bois d'Arc, Anderson 10
(47,152)...........................48,270	*BIG SANDY, Upshur, 113,	Bois d'Arc, Rains 10
*BEDIAS, Grimes, 58, (nc) 400	(1,288).............................1,344	Bold Springs, Polk 100
BEE CAVE, Travis, 157,	*BIG SPRING, Howard, 701,	Boldtville, Bexar.............................20
(656).............................1,695	(25,233)...........................25,179	*Boling-Iago, Wharton, 27,
Bee House, Coryell..........................15	Big Valley, Mills..............................35	(1,271).............................1,326
*BEEVILLE, Bee, 492,	*BIG WELLS, Dimmit, 16,	Bolivar, Denton 40
(13,129)...........................14,186	(704)................................685	Bolivar Peninsula, Galveston,
Belcherville, Montague 25	Biloxi, Newton................................NA	(3,853)..............................3,733
Belfalls, Bell...................................30	Birch, Burleson 200	Bomarton, Baylor............................15
Belgrade, Newton ....NA	Birome, Hill.....................................30	Bon Ami, Jasper ....NA
Belk, Lamar 58	Birthright, Hopkins 40	Bonanza, Hopkins 26

Town, County ....Pop. 2006	Town, County ....Pop. 2006	Town, County ....Pop. 2006
*BONHAM, Fannin, 392 (9,990) 10,813	Bradford, Anderson..........................30 Bradshaw, Taylor 61	*BROADDUS, San Augustine, 31, (189) 187
Bonita, Montague 25	*BRADY, McCulloch, 271, (5,523) 5,514	Broadway, Lamar...............................25
Bonnerville, Freestone....................NA		Brock, Parker..............................2,000
BONNEY, Brazoria, (384) 406	Branch, Collin 530	Brock Junction, Parker 100
Bonnie View, Refugio 97	Branchville, Milam 127	Bronco, Yoakum...............................30
Bonus, Wharton................................44	*Brandon, Hill, 1.............................75	*Bronson, Sabine, 6........................377
*Bon Wier, Newton, 9 475	*Brashear, Hopkins, 6....................280	*BRONTE, Coke, 43, (1,076) 1,129
*BOOKER, Lipscomb-Ochiltree, 48, (1,315) 1,365	*BRAZORIA, Brazoria, 235, (2,787) 2,958	*Brookeland, Sabine, 26................300
Boonsville, Wise 52	Brazos, Palo Pinto 97	*Brookesmith, Brown, 1 61
Booth, Fort Bend 118	BRAZOS BEND, Hood, (nc) 250	Brooks, Panola 40
Borden, Colorado 60	BRAZOS COUNTRY, Austin, 3,	Brookshier, Runnels 15
*BORGER, Hutchinson, 487, (14,302) 13,189	(nc) 283	*BROOKSHIRE, Waller, 178, (3,450) 4,136
Bosqueville, McLennan 200	Brazos Point, Bosque ....NA	
Boston, Bowie..... [part of New Boston]	Brazosport, Brazoria, (59,440) 59,759	BROOKSIDE VILLAGE, Brazoria, 35, (1,960) 2,092
Botines, Webb, (132).....................138	*BRECKENRIDGE, Stephens, 343, (5,868) 5,787	*Brookston, Lamar, 13...................130
*BOVINA, Parmer, 28, (1,874) 1,917	*BREMOND, Robertson, 49, (876) 858	Broom City, Anderson......................20
Bowers City, Gray............................26		Brown College, Washington ....NA
*BOWIE, Montague, 362, (5,219) 5,526	*BRENHAM, Washington, 964, (13,507) 14,504	BROWNDELL, Jasper, 1, (219) 226
Bowman, Archer, ...200	Breslau, Lavaca................................65	*BROWNFIELD, Terry, 289, (9,488) 9,347
Bowser, San Saba............................20	Briar, Tarrant-Wise-Parker, (5,350) 5,651	Browning, Smith 25
Box Canyon-Amistad, Val Verde, (76) 77	BRIARCLIFF, Travis, 41, (895) 834	Brownsboro, Caldwell......................50 *BROWNSBORO, Henderson, 56, (796) 909
Box Church, Limestone 45	BRIAROAKS, Johnson, 5, (493) 488	*BROWNSVILLE, Cameron, 4,383, (139,722) 167,448
Boxelder, Red River.......................100	Brice, Hall 20	*BROWNWOOD, Brown, 756, (18,813) 19,694
Boxwood, Upshur 20	*BRIDGE CITY, Orange, 269, (8,651) 8,681	Broyles Chapel, Anderson 40
Boyce, Ellis 125		
Boyd, Fannin 40	*BRIDGEPORT, Wise, 277, (4,309) 5,507	*BRUCEVILLE-EDDY, McLennan-Falls, 30, (1,490) 1,568
*BOYD, Wise, 134, (1,099) 1,238	Bridges Chapel, Titus 90	Brumley, Upshur 75
*Boys Ranch, Oldham, 4 470	*Briggs, Burnet, 7 172	Brundage, Dimmit, (31) 32
Bozar, Mills 9	Bright Star, Rains..........................592	*Bruni, Webb, 7, (412)...................461
Brachfield, Rusk 40	Brinker, Hopkins 100	Brushie Prairie, Navarro 35
Bracken, Comal................................76	*Briscoe, Wheeler, 5 135	Brushy Creek, Anderson..................50
*BRACKETTVILLE, Kinney, 82, (1,876) 1,859	Bristol, Ellis 250	Brushy Creek, Brazos.....................NA
Brad, Palo Pinto...............................16		

The McCulloch County Courthouse in Brady. Robert Plocheck photo.

Town, County	Pop. 2006

Brushy Creek, Williamson,
(15,371) 19,014
*BRYAN, Brazos, 2,416,
(65,660) 69,903
Bryans Mill, Cass............................150
Bryarly, Red River...............................3
Bryce, Rusk.......................................15
*BRYSON, Jack, 17, (528) 512
*Buchanan Dam, Llano, 36,
(1,688) 1,729
Buchel, DeWitt..................................45
Buckeye, Matagorda.........................16
*BUCKHOLTS, Milam, 27,
(387) 426
Buckhorn, Austin...............................50
Buckhorn, Newton ....NA
Buckner, Parker ....NA
*BUDA, Hays, 415,
(2,404) 4,424
*BUFFALO, Leon, 163,
(1,804) 1,926
*BUFFALO GAP, Taylor, 51,
(463) 443
Buffalo Mop, Limestone....................21
Buffalo Springs, Clay 45
BUFFALO SPRINGS, Lubbock,
0, (493) 475
Buford, Mitchell.................................30
Bula, Bailey.......................................35
Bulcher, Cooke....................................3
*BULLARD, Smith-Cherokee,
179, (1,150) 1,696
Bull Run, Newton ....NA
*BULVERDE, Comal, 409,
(3,761) 4,014
*Buna, Jasper, 91, (2,269)...........2,246
Buncombe, Panola, ...95
Bunger, Young 40
Bunker Hill, Jasper ....NA
BUNKER HILL VILLAGE, Harris,
55, (3,654) 3,489
Bunyan, Erath 20
*BURKBURNETT, Wichita, 259,
(10,927) 10,750
BURKE, Angelina, 0, (315).............002
*Burkett, Coleman, 2 30
*Burkeville, Newton, 19 515
Burleigh, Austin...............................150
*BURLESON, Johnson-Tarrant,
1,277, (20,976) 31,207
*Burlington, Milam, 6 100
*BURNET, Burnet, 370,
(4,735) 5,470
Burns, Bowie....................................400
Burns City, Cooke 45
Burrantown, Houston.........................70
Burrow, Hunt....................................NA
*BURTON, Washington, 59,
(359) 403
*Bushland, Potter, 12.....................1,485
Bustamante, Zapata 15
Busterville, Hockley 6
Butler, Bastrop ....NA
Butler, Freestone 67
Butterfield, El Paso, (61)..................64
*BYERS, Clay, 22, (517).................498
*BYNUM, Hill, 11, (225) 240
Byrd, Ellis..30
Byrdtown, Lamar 22

C

*CACTUS, Moore, 36,
(2,538) 2,822

*Caddo, Stephens, 2 40
*CADDO MILLS, Hunt, 104,
(1,149) 1,203
Cade Chapel, Navarro......................25
Cadiz, Bee 15
Calallen, Nueces
.................[part of Corpus Christi]
Calaveras, Wilson...........................100
*CALDWELL, Burleson, 300,
(3,449) 3,720
Caledonia, Rusk 75
Calf Creek, McCulloch.......................23
Calina, Limestone.............................10
*Call, Newton, 3..............................170
*Calliham, McMullen, 3...................100
CALLISBURG, Cooke, (365)..........374
Call Junction, Jasper 50
*CALVERT, Robertson, 82,
(1,426) 1,440
*Camden, Polk, 1.........................1,200
*CAMERON, Milam, 230,
(5,634) 5,823
Cameron Park, Cameron,
(5,961) 6,422
Camilla, San Jacinto.......................200
Camp Air, Mason 12
*CAMPBELL, Hunt, 42,
(734) 774
*Campbellton, Atascosa, 8 350
Camp Creek Lake, Robertson 350
Campo Alto, Hidalgo.......................NA
Camp Ruby, Polk 35
Camp San Saba, McCulloch 36
Camp Seale, Polk 53
Camp Springs, Scurry 10
Camp Swift, Bastrop, (4,731) 5,267
Camp Switch, Gregg 70
Campti, Shelby 25
*Camp Verde, Kerr 41
*CAMP WOOD, Real, 52,
(822) 910
Camp Worth, San Augustine ....NA
Canada Verde, Wilson......................23
*CANADIAN, Hemphill, 138,
(2,233) 2,352
Candelaria, Presidio 55
CANEY CITY, Henderson, 13,
(236) 261
Cannon, Grayson 50
*CANTON, Van Zandt, 925,
(3,292) 3,353
Cantu Addition, Brooks,
(217) 218
*Canutillo, El Paso, 110,
(5,129) 5,365
*CANYON, Randall, 416,
(12,875) 13,399
Canyon City, Comal........................NA
*Canyon Lake, Comal,
(16,870) 18,281
Caplen, Galveston 60
Capps Corner, Montague 30
Cap Rock, Crosby 6
Caps, Taylor....................................300
Caradan, Mills 20
Carancahua, Jackson 375
*CARBON, Eastland, 9,
(224) 233
Carbondale, Bowie 30
Carey, Childress 15
Carl, Travis ....NA
Carlisle, Trinity 68

Carlos, Grimes..................................60
*Carlsbad, Tom Green, 10 236
CARL'S CORNER, Hill, 2, (134)....147
Carlson, Travis ....NA
*Carlton, Hamilton, 1 75
*CARMINE, Fayette, 44,
(228) 232
Carmona, Polk 50
Caro, Nacogdoches...........................70
Carricitos, Cameron........................147
Carrizo Hill, Dimmit, (548) 550
*CARRIZO SPRINGS, Dimmit,
137, (5,655) 5,568
Carroll, Smith....................................60
Carroll Springs, Anderson.................20
*CARROLLTON, Dallas-Denton,
5,240, (109,576) 122,005
Carson, Fannin 22
Carta Valley, Edwards.......................12
Carterville, Cass 39
*CARTHAGE, Panola, 357,
(6,664) 6,808
Cartwright, Wood 144
Carver, Leon ....NA
Casa Piedra, Presidio 21
Cash, Hunt...56
CASHION, Wichita, 0,
(346) 326
*Cason, Morris, 3............................173
Cass, Cass 100
Cassie, Burnet 496
Cassin, Bexar ....NA
*Castell, Llano 72
CASTLE HILLS, Bexar, 361,
(4,202) 3,881
Castolon, Brewster 8
*CASTROVILLE, Medina, 251,
(2,664) 2,863
*Catarina, Dimmit, 5,
(135) 130
*Cat Spring, Austin, 15 200
Cavazos, Cameron..........................282
Caviness, Lamar 90
Cawthon, Brazos 75
Cayote, Bosque 75
*Cayuga, Anderson, 4.....................137
*Cedar Bayou, Harris....................1,555
*Cedar Creek, Bastrop, 87 ....NA
Cedar Creek, Waller ....NA
*CEDAR HILL, Dallas-Ellis,
1,202, (32,093) 41,340
Cedar Hill, Floyd...............................24
Cedar Lake, Matagorda...................160
*Cedar Lane, Matagorda, 3 300
*CEDAR PARK, Williamson-Travis,
1,550, (26,049) 45,222
Cedar Shores, Bosque 170
Cedar Springs, Falls 90
Cedar Springs, Upshur....................100
Cedarvale, Kaufman..........................50
Cedar Valley, Bell.............................14
*Cee Vee, Cottle, 1 45
Cego, Falls 42
Cele, Travis ....NA
*CELESTE, Hunt, 42, (817)............867
*CELINA, Collin, 169,
(1,861) 3,693
Center, Limestone 76
*CENTER, Shelby, 345,
(5,678) 5,762
Center City, Mills..............................15
Center Grove, Houston....................39

Town, County .... Pop. 2006	Town, County .... Pop. 2006	Town, County .... Pop. 2006
Center Grove, Titus 65	Chita, Trinity....................................81	Clinton, Hunt....................................NA
Center Hill, Houston 105	Choate, Karnes................................20	Clodine, Fort Bend............................51
Center Plains, Swisher 20	Chocolate Bayou, Brazoria...............60	Close City, Garza..............................94
Center Point, Camp 41	Choice, Shelby.................................35	Cloverleaf, Harris, (23,508) 24,407
*Center Point, Kerr, 43....................800	*Chriesman, Burleson......................30	*CLUTE, Brazoria, 380,
Center Point, Panola ....NA	*CHRISTINE, Atascosa, 0,	(10,424) 11,092
Center Point, Upshur 50	(436) 428	*CLYDE, Callahan, 177,
Centerview, Leon..............................NA	*Christoval, Tom Green, 47,	(3,345) 3,740
*CENTERVILLE, Leon, 98,	(422) 404	*COAHOMA, Howard, 26,
(903) 934	Chula Vista-Orason, Cameron,	(932) 860
Centerville, Trinity 60	(394) 405	Cobb, Kaufman................................NA
Central, Angelina 200	Chula Vista-River Spur, Zavala,	Coble, Hockley 11
Central Gardens, Jefferson,	(400) 357	Cochran, Austin 200
(4,106) 3,935	Church Hill, Rusk..............................20	COCKRELL HILL, Dallas, 88,
Central High, Cherokee 30	Churchill, Brazoria ....NA	(4,443) 4,364
*Centralia, Trinity 53	*CIBOLO, Guadalupe, 276,	COFFEE CITY, Henderson, 14,
Cesar Chavez, Hidalgo, (1,469) ..1,469	(3,035) 8,129	(193) 195
Cestohowa, Karnes 110	Cienegas Terrace, Val Verde,	Coffeeville, Upshur 50
Chalk, Cottle 17	(2,878) 2,991	Cofferville, Lamb.................................4
Chalk Hill, Rusk 200	Cinco Ranch, Fort Bend-Harris,	Coit, Limestone.................................25
Chalk Mountain, Erath 25	(11,196) 12,658	Coke, Wood......................................53
Chambersville, Collin......................103	Cipres, Hidalgo................................20	*COLDSPRING, San Jacinto, 137,
Chambliss, Collin..............................29	Circle, Lamb.......................................6	(691) 818
Champion, Nolan................................8	Circle Back, Bailey...........................10	*COLEMAN, Coleman, 237,
Champions, Harris....................21,250	Circle D-KC Estates, Bastrop,	(5,127) 4,871
Chances Store, Burleson.................15	(2,010) 2,162	Colfax, Van Zandt.............................44
*CHANDLER, Henderson, 157,	Circleville, Williamson......................50	Colita, Polk.......................................50
(2,099) 2,384	*CISCO, Eastland, 159,	College Hill, Bowie..........................116
Chaney, Eastland 35	(3,851) 3,910	College Mound, Kaufman 500
*Channelview, Harris, 371,	Cistern, Fayette..............................137	*Collegeport, Matagorda, 1..............80
(29,685) 30,291	Citrus City, Hidalgo, (941).............989	*COLLEGE STATION, Brazos,
*CHANNING, Hartley, 12,	Citrus Grove, Matagorda 30	1,689, (67,890) 74,235
(356) 366	Clairemont, Kent..............................12	*COLLEYVILLE, Tarrant, 1,077,
Chapman, Rusk.................................20	Clairette, Erath.................................55	(19,636) 22,242
*Chapman Ranch, Nueces, 5.........100	Clara, Wichita.................................100	*COLLINSVILLE, Grayson, 61,
Chappel, San Saba 25	Clardy, Lamar 160	(1,235) 1,603
*Chappell Hill, Washington, 34 750	*CLARENDON, Donley, 106,	*COLMESNEIL, Tyler, 52,
Charco, Goliad..................................96	(1,974) 2,042	(638) 654
Charleston, Delta............................150	Clareville, Bee 25	Colony, Rains 70
Charlie, Clay......................................70	Clark, Liberty 75	*COLORADO CITY, Mitchell, 190,
*CHARLOTTE, Atascosa, 30,	Clarkson, Milam................................10	(4,281) 4,151
(1,637) 1,723	*CLARKSVILLE, Red River, 148,	Colquitt, Kaufman............................NA
*Chatfield, Navarro, 2 40	(3,883) 3,612	Coltharp, Houston.............................40
Cheapside, Gonzales 5	CLARKSVILLE CITY, Gregg, 21,	Colton, Travis....................................50
Cheek, Jefferson 1,096	(806) 855	*COLUMBUS, Colorado, 325,
Cheneyboro, Navarro 100	*CLAUDE, Armstrong, 50,	(3,916) 4,105
*Cherokee, San Saba, 17...............175	(1,313) 1,333	*COMANCHE, Comanche, 220,
Cherry Spring, Gillespie...................75	Clauene, Hockley 10	(4,482) 4,525
*CHESTER, Tyler, 24, (265) 257	Clawson, Angelina..........................195	*COMBES, Cameron, 33,
Chesterville, Colorado 50	Clay, Burleson..................................61	(2,553) 2,751
*CHICO, Wise, 67, (947) 1,045	Clays Corner, Parmer 15	COMBINE, Kaufman-Dallas, 54,
*Chicota, Lamar, 1 150	*Clayton, Panola, 6........................125	(1,788) 2,058
Chihuahua, Hidalgo........................NA	Claytonville, Swisher 85	Cometa, Zavala 10
Chihuahua, Zapata.........................105	Clear Creek, Burnet..........................78	*Comfort, Kendall, 122,
*CHILDRESS, Childress, 216,	CLEAR LAKE SHORES, Galveston,	(2,358) 2,633
(6,778) 6,706	99, (1,205) 1,275	*COMMERCE, Hunt, 241,
*CHILLICOTHE, Hardeman, 18,	Clear Spring, Guadalupe................280	(7,669) 9,005
(798) 780	*CLEBURNE, Johnson, 1,221,	*COMO, Hopkins, 30,
*Chilton, Falls, 13 274	(26,005) 28,496	(621) 661
*CHINA, Jefferson, 43,	Clegg, Live Oak..............................125	*Comstock, Val Verde, 3................344
(1,112) 1,052	Clemons, Waller ....NA	Comyn, Comanche...........................30
CHINA GROVE, Bexar, 40,	Clemville, Matagorda.......................25	*Concan, Uvalde, 22.......................225
(1,247) 1,299	Cleo, Kimble.......................................3	*Concepcion, Duval, 2, (61)..............58
China Grove, Scurry 15	Cleveland, Austin............................125	Concord, Cherokee 50
*China Spring, McLennan, 171....1,000	*CLEVELAND, Liberty, 497,	Concord, Hunt 30
Chinati, Presidio ....NA	(7,605) 7,874	*Concord, Leon, 2.............................28
Chinquapin, Matagorda 6	Cliffside, Potter 206	Concord, Madison 50
Chinquapin, San Augustine ....NA	*CLIFTON, Bosque, 222,	Concord, Rusk..................................23
*CHIRENO, Nacogdoches, 29,	(3,542) 3,705	Concrete, DeWitt..............................46
(405) 404	Climax, Collin...................................82	Cone, Crosby....................................50
CHISHOLM [McLendon-],	Cline, Uvalde 15	Conlen, Dallam 14
Rockwall, 3, (914)..................1,054	*CLINT, El Paso, 72, (980) 1,028	Connor, Madison 20

Town, County ....Pop. 2006	Town, County ....Pop. 2006	Town, County ....Pop. 2006
*CONROE, Montgomery, 2,524, (36,811) 49,230	Cotton Gin, Freestone 28	Crescent Heights, Henderson 180
Content, Bell....................................25	Cotton Patch, DeWitt.......................11	*CRESSON, Hood-Johnson-Parker,
*CONVERSE, Bexar, 448, (11,508) 13,801	Cottonwood, Brazos ....NA	47, (nc) 443
Conway, Carson 20	Cottonwood, Callahan 65	Crews, Runnels 30
Cooks Point, Burleson.....................60	COTTONWOOD, Kaufman,	Crisp, Ellis.....................................115
*Cookville, Titus, 15 105	(181) 220	*CROCKETT, Houston, 325,
COOL, Parker, 11, (162)................167	Cottonwood, Madison......................40	(7,141) 7,044
*COOLIDGE, Limestone, 17, (848) 911	Cottonwood, McLennan.................150	*Crosby, Harris, 321, (1,714).......1,804
*COOPER, Delta, 66, (2,150)......2,096	Cottonwood, Somervell-Erath.......... 24	*CROSBYTON, Crosby, 64,
Cooper, Houston..............................27	COTTONWOOD SHORES,	(1,874)....................................1,734
Copano Village, Aransas 210	Burnet, 29, (877) 1,051	Cross, Grimes.................................53
Copeland, Smith ....NA	*COTULLA, La Salle, 115,	Cross, McMullen..............................25
*Copeville, Collin, 6 243	(3,614) 3,561	Cross Cut, Brown 22
*COPPELL, Dallas-Denton, 1,421, (35,958) 39,063	Couch, Karnes.................................10	Cross Mountain, Bexar, (1,524)...1,566
*COPPERAS COVE, Coryell, 633, (29,592) 31,425	Coughran, Atascosa 20	*CROSS PLAINS, Callahan, 67, (1,068) 1,071
COPPER CANYON, Denton, 49, (1,216) 1,260	County Acres [Falman-], San Patricio, (289)...................282	Crossroads, Cass............................60
Corbet, Navarro 80	County Line, Lubbock.......................59	Crossroads, Delta............................20
Cordele, Jackson.............................51	County Line, Rains 40	CROSS ROADS, Denton, 42,
CORINTH, Denton, 530, (11,325) 17,147	*Coupland, Williamson, 20 280	(603) 724
Corinth, Jones 10	Courtney, Grimes.............................60	Crossroads, Harrison.....................100
Corinth, Leon ....NA	COVE, Chambers, 18, (323) 345	Cross Roads, Henderson 160
Corley, Bowie...................................35	Cove Springs, Cherokee 40	Crossroads, Hopkins.......................50
Cornersville, Hopkins....................200	*COVINGTON, Hill, 18, (282) 299	Cross Roads, Madison 75
Cornett, Cass...................................30	Cox, Upshur.....................................30	Cross Roads, Milam 35
Cornudas, Hudspeth........................19	*Coyanosa, Pecos, 4, (138)............135	CROSS TIMBER, Johnson,
*CORPUS CHRISTI, Nueces, 9,966, (277,454) 283,384	Coy City, Karnes..............................30	(277) 297
CORRAL CITY, Denton, 2, (89) 103	Coyote Acres, Jim Wells, (389) 410	Croton, Dickens.................................7
*CORRIGAN, Polk, 69, (1,721) 1,795	Crabbs Prairie, Walker...................240	Crow, Wood....................................178
*CORSICANA, Navarro, 996, (24,485) 25,972	Craft, Cherokee 21	*CROWELL, Foard, 48, (1,141) 1,017
Coryell City, Coryell 70	Crafton, Wise...................................20	*CROWLEY, Tarrant, 357, (7,467) 9,115
*Cost, Gonzales, 5...........................84	*CRANDALL, Kaufman, 106, (2,774) 3,265	Crown, Atascosa..............................10
Cotton Center, Fannin 5	*CRANE, Crane, 103, (3,191) 3,033	Cruz Calle, Duval............................NA
*Cotton Center, Hale, 6..................300	*CRANFILLS GAP, Bosque, 19, (335) 358	Cryer Creek, Navarro 15
Cottondale, Wise ....NA	*CRAWFORD, McLennan, 52, (705) 749	Crystal Beach, Galveston 1,500
	Creath, Houston 20	*CRYSTAL CITY, Zavala, 121, (7,190) 7,259
	Crecy, Trinity...................................15	Crystal Falls, Stephens....................10
	CREEDMOOR, Travis, 21, (211) 225	Crystal Lake, Anderson 20
		Cuadrilla, El Paso............................67
		*CUERO, DeWitt, 323, (6,571) 6,954
		Cuevitas, Hidalgo, (07)....................07

The skyline of Cisco in Eastland County. Robert Plocheck photo.

Town, County ....Pop. 2006	Town, County ....Pop. 2006	Town, County ....Pop. 2006

*CUMBY, Hopkins, 46,
   (616) 637
Cumings, Fort Bend, (683) 808
Cundiff, Jack..45
*CUNEY, Cherokee, 9, (145) 147
*Cunningham, Lamar.....................110
Currie, Navarro 25
Curtis, Jasper ....NA
*CUSHING, Nacogdoches, 54,
   (637)...649
Cusseta, Cass 30
*CUT AND SHOOT, Montgomery,
   56, (1,158)..............................1,307
Cuthand, Red River 116
Cyclone, Bell......................................47
Cypress, Franklin..............................20
Cypress Creek, Kerr 200
*Cypress [-Fairbanks] , Harris,
   832 27,000
Cypress Mill, Blanco 200

D

Dacosta, Victoria 89
Dacus, Montgomery 190
Daffan, Travis ....NA
*DAINGERFIELD, Morris, 123,
   (2,517)......................................2,419
*DAISETTA, Liberty, 11,
   (1,034)......................................1,042
Dalby Springs, Bowie 141
*Dale, Caldwell, 30 500
*DALHART, Dallam-Hartley, 299,
   (7,237)......................................7,273
*Dallardsville, Polk, 1 350
*DALLAS, Dallas-Collin-Denton,
   45,980, (1,188,580) 1,224,397
Dalton, Cass 50
DALWORTHINGTON GARDENS,
   Tarrant, 135, (2,186).............2,373
*Damon, Brazoria, 21,
   (535) 551
*DANBURY, Brazoria, 33,
   (1,611)......................................1,740
*Danciger, Brazoria..........................357
*Danevang, Wharton, 8 61
Daniels, Panola 75
Danville, Gregg 200
Darby Hill, San Jacinto 50
Darco, Harrison 85
Darden, Polk.....................................320
*DARROUZETT, Lipscomb, 18,
   (303) 293
Datura, Limestone 2
*Davilla, Milam, 1 191
Davis, Atascosa 8
Davis Prairie, Limestone....................17
*Dawn, Deaf Smith, 2 52
*DAWSON, Navarro, 28, (852).......876
*DAYTON, Liberty, 365,
   (5,709)......................................6,862
DAYTON LAKES, Liberty, 0,
   (101)..95
Deadwood, Panola 106
DEAN, Clay, 3, (341) 346
Dean, Hockley 20
*Deanville, Burleson, 6 130
*DeBerry, Panola, 25 200
*DECATUR, Wise, 477,
   (5,201)......................................5,707
Decker Prairie, Montgomery............NA
DeCORDOVA, Hood, (nc) 3,032
*DEER PARK, Harris, 1,067,
   (28,520) 29,046

*DE KALB, Bowie, 98,
   (1,769) 1,627
*DE LEON, Comanche, 110,
   (2,433).....................................2,420
Delhi, Caldwell.................................300
Delia, Limestone................................20
*DELL CITY, Hudspeth, 21,
   (413) 423
Del Mar Heights, Cameron, (259)...262
*Delmita, Starr, 2 50
Delray, Panola 45
*DEL RIO, Val Verde, 983,
   (33,867) 36,019
Delrose, Upshur.................................35
Del Sol-Loma Linda, San Patricio,
   (726)..716
*Del Valle, 74 ....[part of Austin]
Delwin, Cottle.....................................12
Democrat, Mills....................................8
Denhawken, Wilson...........................46
*DENISON, Grayson, 1,058,
   (22,773) 24,178
Denning, San Augustine 361
*Dennis, Parker, 3...........................300
Denson Springs, Anderson............100
Denton, Callahan..................................6
*DENTON, Denton, 3,463,
   (80,537) 104,728
*DENVER CITY, Yoakum, 178,
   (3,985).....................................3,887
*DEPORT, Lamar-Red River, 19,
   (718)..690
Derby, Frio 50
*Desdemona, Eastland, 6..............180
Desert, Collin......................................35
*DESOTO, Dallas, 964,
   (37,646) 45,075
Dessau, Travis...................................NA
*DETROIT, Red River, 30,
   (776)..787
*DEVERS, Liberty, 20, (416) 429
*DEVINE, Medina, 227,
   (4,140).....................................4,248
Dew, Freestone 71
DeWees, Wilson 35
Deweesville, Karnes..........................12
*Deweyville, Newton, 17,
   (1,190)......................................1,099
Dewville, Gonzales 30
Dexter, Cooke 12
*D'Hanis, Medina, 18.......................575
Dial, Fannin 76
Dialville, Cherokee...........................200
*Diana, Upshur, 33 585
*DIBOLL, Angelina, 147,
   (5,470).....................................5,875
Dicey, Parker ....NA
*DICKENS, Dickens, 13, (332).......349
*DICKINSON, Galveston, 648,
   (17,093) 19,481
*Dike, Hopkins, 3 170
*DILLEY, Frio, 75, (3,674)...........3,923
Dilworth, Gonzales 18
Dilworth, Red River...........................22
*Dime Box, Lee, 21.........................381
*DIMMITT, Castro, 149,
   (4,375).....................................4,056
Dimple, Red River 60
*Dinero, Live Oak 344
Ding Dong, Bell................................301
Direct, Lamar......................................85
Dirgin, Rusk 50

DISH, Denton, (nc) 362
Divide, Hopkins................................NA
Divide, Kerr......................................250
Divot, Frio 9
Dixie, Grayson 17
Dixon, Hunt...31
Dixon-Hopewell, Houston 10
Doak Springs, Lee.............................50
Doans, Wilbarger...............................20
*Dobbin, Montgomery, 4 310
Dobrowolski, Atascosa 10
Dodd, Castro 12
*DODD CITY, Fannin, 17, (419) 459
*Dodge, Walker, 2............................150
*DODSON, Collingsworth, (115)..... 111
Dodson Prairie, Palo Pinto 18
Doffing, Hidalgo, (4,256)............4,466
Dog Ridge, Bell................................215
Dogwood City, Smith 800
Dolen, Liberty 75
DOMINO, Cass, 3, (52) 68
*Donie, Freestone, 7.......................250
*DONNA, Hidalgo, 447,
   (14,768) 17,046
*Doole, McCulloch.............................74
Doolittle, Hidalgo, (2,358) 2,467
DORCHESTER, Grayson, (109) 108
Dorras, Stonewall..............................20
Doss, Cass 15
*Doss, Gillespie, 7 100
Dot, Falls 17
Dothan, Eastland 20
Dotson, Panola 35
Double Bayou, Chambers 400
DOUBLE OAK, Denton, 105,
   (2,179).....................................2,769
*Doucette, Tyler, 6 160
*Dougherty, Floyd, 7 91
Dougherty, Rains 342
Douglas, Smith ....NA
*Douglass, Nacogdoches, 15 380
*DOUGLASSVILLE, Cass, 9,
   (175)..174
Downing, Comanche 30
Downsville, McLennan.....................150
Doyle, Limestone................................50
Doyle, San Patricio, (285)..............275
Dozier, Collingsworth..........................4
Drane, Navarro 16
Drasco, Runnels 15
Draw, Lynn 18
Dreka, Shelby.....................................30
Dresden, Navarro 25
Dreyer, Gonzales 20
*Driftwood, Hays, 41 ....NA
*DRIPPING SPRINGS, Hays,
   178, (1,548) 1,839
*DRISCOLL, Nueces, 18,
   (825)..830
*Dryden, Terrell, 2............................13
Dubina, Fayette 272
*DUBLIN, Erath, 160, (3,754)......3,579
Dudley, Callahan 25
Duffau, Erath 76
*DUMAS, Moore, 425,
   (13,747) 13,427
Dumont, King......................................19
Dunbar, Rains 40
*DUNCANVILLE, Dallas, 1,373,
   (36,081) 34,809
Dundee, Archer...................................12
Dunlap, Cottle....................................10

The approach to Dell City in Hudspeth County. Robert Plocheck photo.

Town, County ....Pop. 2006	Town, County ....Pop. 2006	Town, County ....Pop. 2006
Dunlap, Travis.....................80	Ecleto, Karnes 22	Elevation, Milam 12
Dunlay, Medina................145	*ECTOR, Fannin, 20, (600) 661	El Gato, Hidalgo ....NA
*Dunn, Scurry 75	*EDCOUCH, Hidalgo, 45,	*ELGIN, Bastrop, 378,
Duplex, Fannin 25	(3,342)............................4,040	(5,700).........................8,394
Durango, Falls 54	*EDDY [Bruceville-], McLennan-Falls,	Eliasville, Young, 7............150
Duren, Mills.......................15	30, (1,490) 1,568	*El Indio, Maverick, 1, (263) 277
Duster, Comanche..............25	*EDEN, Concho, 52, (2,561) 2,451	Elk, McLennan 150
Dye, Montague...................30	Eden, Nacogdoches 100	*ELKHART, Anderson, 72,
E	Edgar, DeWitt 8	(1,215).........................1,273
Eagle, Chambers...............50	Edge, Brazos 100	EL LAGO, Harris, 74, (3,075) 2,894
*EAGLE LAKE, Colorado, 147,	EDGECLIFF, Tarrant,	*Ellinger, Fayette, 6 386
(3,664) 3,796	(2,550)............................2,423	Elliott, Robertson 55
Eagle Mountain, Tarrant,	Edgewater-Paisano, San Patricio,	Elliott, Wilbarger 50
(6,599) 6,770	(182)............................182	Ellis [Bausell-], Willacy, (112)..........109
*EAGLE PASS, Maverick, 831,	*EDGEWOOD, Van Zandt, 91,	*Elmaton, Matagorda, 3.................160
(22,413)........................25,440	(1,348)............................1,337	Elm Creek, Maverick, (1,928) ..2,045
*EARLY, Brown, 174, (2,588).......2,689	Edgeworth, Bell 15	*ELMENDORF, Bexar, 72,
Earlywine, Washington ....NA	Edhube, Fannin 25	(664).............................796
*EARTH, Lamb, 22, (1,109).........1,139	*EDINBURG, Hidalgo, 1,458,	Elm Grove, Cherokee.......................50
East Afton, Dickens 13	(48,465).........................64,604	Elm Grove, San Saba.......................15
*EAST BERNARD, Wharton, 114,	*EDMONSON, Hale, 4, (123) 128	Elm Grove, Wharton 76
(1,729) 2,228	*EDNA, Jackson, 266,	Elm Grove Camp, Guadalupe 88
East Caney, Hopkins 100	(5,899) 6,036	*Elm Mott, McLennan, 67 300
East Columbia, Brazoria..................95	Edna Hill, Erath..............32	*Elmo, Kaufman, 4.......................90
East Delta, Delta..............60	EDOM, Van Zandt, 12, (322) 325	Elmont, Grayson 15
East Direct, Lamar...........................48	*Edroy, San Patricio, 3, (420) 413	Elm Ridge, Milam 25
Easter, Castro..............26	Egan, Johnson...............21	Elmwood, Anderson........................25
Easterly, Robertson 61	*Egypt, Wharton, 3 26	Eloise, Falls 29
Eastgate, Liberty..............NA	Eidson Road, Maverick, (9,348) ..9,861	El Oso, Karnes 35
East Hamilton, Shelby 25	Elam Springs, Upshur.....................50	*EL PASO, El Paso, 16,044,
*EASTLAND, Eastland, 266,	El Arroyo, Starr 500	(563,662) 602,112
(3,769) 4,004	Elbert, Throckmorton, (56)...............52	El Refugio, Starr, (221) 234
EAST MOUNTAIN, Upshur, 9,	El Camino Angosto, Cameron,	Elroy, Travis...................125
(580) 589	(254) 259	*ELSA, Hidalgo, 112, (5,549).......6,196
*EASTON, Gregg-Rusk, 7,	*EL CAMPO, Wharton, 563,	El Sauz, Starr 50
(524) 561	(10,945) 11,187	El Tacalote, Jim Wells...................100
East Point, Wood..............40	EL CENIZO, Webb, 25, (3,545) ...3,781	Elton, Dickens 4
East Sweden, McCulloch.................40	El Centro, Starr................................10	El Toro, Jackson 136
EAST TAWAKONI, Rains, 14,	*ELDORADO, Schleicher, 82,	El Venadito, Cameron....................207
(775) 890	(1,951) 1,897	Elwood, Fannin 31
East Tempe, Polk..............NA	Eldorado Center, Navarro................20	Elwood, Madison 50
Ebenezer, Camp..............55	Eldridge, Colorado..........................20	*Elysian Fields, Harrison, 6 300
Ebenezer, Jasper..............NA	*ELECTRA, Wichita, 82,	Elysium, Bastrop.............................NA
Echo, Coleman 16	(3,168) 3,009	Emberson, Lamar.............80

Town, County ....Pop. 2006	Town, County ....Pop. 2006	Town, County ....Pop. 2006
Emblem, Hopkins 52	FAIRVIEW, Collin, 122,	*FLORENCE, Williamson, 80,
Emerald Bay, Smith 616	(2,644) 6,113	(1,054) 1,312
EMHOUSE, Navarro, 1, (159) 169	Fairview, Gaines 160	*FLORESVILLE, Wilson, 334,
Emmett, Navarro 100	Fairview, Hockley............................10	(5,868) 6,827
*EMORY, Rains, 173, (1,021)......1,249	Fairview, Hood................................30	Florey, Andrews...............................25
Encantada-Ranchito El Calaboz,	Fairview, Howard...............................5	Flour Bluff, Nueces
Cameron, (2,100) 2,255	Fairview, Wilson..............................322	................[part of Corpus Christi]
ENCHANTED OAKS, Henderson, 0,	Fairy, Hamilton................................40	Flowella, Brooks, (134)...................126
(357)....................................373	Falcon, Zapata, (184)......................203	Flower Hill, Colorado 20
*ENCINAL, La Salle, 17, (629) 671	*Falcon Heights, Starr, 1, (335) 356	*FLOWER MOUND, Denton,
*Encino, Brooks, 6, (177)...............172	Falcon Lake Estates, Zapata,	2,262, (50,702) 64,041
*Energy, Comanche, 1.....................70	(830) 919	Floyd, Hunt 220
Engle, Fayette 141	Falcon Mesa, Zapata, (506) 530	*FLOYDADA, Floyd, 103,
English, Red River..........................100	Falcon Village, Starr, (78)................81	(3,676) 3,358
*Enloe, Delta, 4................................90	*FALFURRIAS, Brooks, 170,	*Fluvanna, Scurry, 3 180
*ENNIS, Ellis, 731,	(5,297) 5,010	*Flynn, Leon, 3 81
(16,045) 19,565	Fallon, Limestone 100	Foard City, Foard............................10
Enoch, Upshur.................................25	*FALLS CITY, Karnes, 32,	Fodice, Houston 49
*Enochs, Bailey 80	(591) 644	*FOLLETT, Lipscomb, 24,
Enon, Upshur.................................204	Falman-County Acres, San Patricio,	(412) 406
*Eola, Concho, 5.............................215	(289) 282	Folsom, Shelby................................30
Eolian, Stephens 9	Famuliner, Cochran 5	Ford, Deaf Smith..............................25
*Era, Cooke, 7 150	Fannett, Jefferson........................1,877	Fords Corner, San Augustine 30
Ericksdahl, Jones 35	*Fannin, Goliad, 8..........................359	Fordtran, Victoria 18
Erin, Jasper 40	Fargo, Wilbarger............................169	Forest, Cherokee..............................85
Erna, Menard 27	Farmers Academy, Titus 75	*Forestburg, Montague, 6................50
Erwin, Grimes..................................52	*FARMERS BRANCH, Dallas,	Forest Chapel, Lamar....................105
Escobares, Starr, (1,954).............1,986	1,751, (27,508) 27,091	Forest Glade, Limestone 340
Escobas, Zapata................................3	Farmers Valley, Wilbarger...............30	Forest Grove, Milam.........................60
Escondidas [Sandy Hollow-],	*FARMERSVILLE, Collin, 181,	Forest Heights, Orange 250
Nueces, (433).........................354	(3,118) 3,136	Forest Hill, Lamar 50
Esperanza, Hudspeth......................75	Farmington, Grayson.......................38	FOREST HILL, Tarrant, 365,
Espey, Atascosa...............................55	*Farnsworth, Ochiltree, 6...............130	(12,949) 13,668
Estacado, Lubbock-Crosby 32	Farrar, Limestone............................51	Forest Hill, Wood.............................30
*ESTELLINE, Hall, 4, (168) 160	Farrsville, Newton..........................150	*FORNEY, Kaufman, 615,
Estes, Aransas.................................50	*FARWELL, Parmer, 55,	(5,588) 10,929
Ethel, Grayson.................................40	(1,364) 1,316	*Forreston, Ellis, 4 400
*Etoile, Nacogdoches, 9 700	Fashing, Atascosa 35	*FORSAN, Howard, 9, (226) 211
Eula, Callahan 125	*FATE, Rockwall, 68, (497)..........3,000	Fort Bliss, El Paso, (8,264)..........7,962
*EULESS, Tarrant, 1,493,	Faught, Lamar 25	Fort Clark Springs, Kinney..........1,300
(46,005) 51,562	Faulkner, Lamar...............................48	*Fort Davis, Jeff Davis, 55,
Eulogy, Bosque................................45	Fawil, Newton ....NA	(1,050)..............................1,468
Eunice, Leon..................................NA	*FAYETTEVILLE, Fayette, 66,	*Fort Hancock, Hudspeth, 16,
Eureka, Franklin 18	(261) 264	(1,713)..............................1,839
EUREKA, Navarro, 14,	Faysville, Hidalgo, (348) 354	Fort Hood, Bell-Coryell,
(340)....................................330	Fedor, Lee 92	(33,711) 32,259
*EUSTACE, Henderson, 60,	*Fentress, Caldwell, 7....................291	*Fort McKavett, Menard, 1...............50
(798)....................................922	*FERRIS, Ellis, 89, (2,175)..........2,185	Fort Parker, Limestone 2
*Evadale, Jasper, 17, (1,430)......1,376	Fetzer, Waller................................NA	Fort Parker State Park, Limestone ...30
*EVANT, Coryell-Hamilton, 32,	Fields Store, Waller ....NA	Fort Spunky, Hood...........................15
(393)....................................398	*Fieldton, Lamb, 2 20	*FORT STOCKTON, Pecos, 320,
Evergreen, San Jacinto 150	Fife, McCulloch................................32	(7,846)..............................7,422
EVERMAN, Tarrant, 145,	Fifth Street, Fort Bend, (2,059)....2,319	*FORT WORTH, Tarrant, 19,523,
(5,836) 5,929	Files Valley, Hill..............................60	(534,694) 638,102
Ewell, Upshur 20	Fincastle, Henderson.......................75	Foster, Terry......................................6
Ezzell, Lavaca 55	Finney, Hale 18	Fostoria, Montgomery....................NA
F	*Fischer, Comal, 10 ....NA	Fouke, Wood....................................30
*Fabens, El Paso, 78,	Fisk, Coleman..................................40	Four Corners, Brazoria ....NA
(8,043) 8,622	Five Points, Ellis 25	Four Corners, Chambers.................18
FAIRCHILDS, Fort Bend, (678) 791	Flaccus, Karnes 15	Four Corners, Fort Bend,
*FAIRFIELD, Freestone, 233,	Flagg, Castro 26	(2,954)..............................3,464
(3,094) 3,625	*Flat, Coryell, 1 210	Four Corners, Montgomery ....NA
Fairland, Burnet.............................340	Flat Fork, Shelby 10	*Fowlerton, La Salle, 2, (62)............51
Fairlie, Hunt.....................................80	*FLATONIA, Fayette, 107,	Frame Switch, Williamson 25
Fairmount, Sabine 1,500	(1,377)..............................1,339	*Francitas, Jackson 125
Fair Oaks, Limestone 15	Flat Prairie, Trinity...........................33	Frankel City, Andrews........................2
*FAIR OAKS RANCH, Bexar-Comal-	Flats, Rains 646	Frankell, Stephens.........................NA
Kendall, 102, (4,695) 5,663	Flat Top, Stonewall 5	*FRANKLIN, Robertson, 95,
Fair Play, Panola 80	*Flint, Smith, 131 ....NA	(1,470)..............................1,513
Fairview, Armstrong..........................75	Flo, Leon...20	*FRANKSTON, Anderson, 117,
Fairview, Brazos ....NA	*Flomot, Motley, 3..........................181	(1,209)..............................1,280
Fairview, Cass 20	Flora, Hopkins ....NA	*Fred, Tyler, 7 299

Town, County	Pop. 2006

*FREDERICKSBURG, Gillespie,
798, (8,911) 10,370
*Fredonia, Mason, 3 55
Freedom, Rains.................................60
*FREEPORT, Brazoria, 366,
(12,708) 13,038
*FREER, Duval, 106, (3,241) 3,177
Freestone, Freestone 100
Frelsburg, Colorado........................75
Frenstat, Burleson..........................50
Fresno, Collingsworth.....................10
*Fresno, Fort Bend, 65,
(6,603) 8,318
Freyburg, Fayette 148
Friday, Trinity..................................99
Friendship, Dawson...........................5
Friendship, Leon..............................NA
Friendship, Smith...........................200
Friendship, Upshur 25
Friendship Village, Bowie 200
*FRIENDSWOOD, Galveston-Harris,
1,273, (29,037) 32,566
Frio Town, Frio...................................9
*FRIONA, Parmer, 103,
(3,854) 3,895
*FRISCO, Collin-Denton, 2,855,
(33,714) 73,804
*FRITCH, Hutchinson-Moore, 101,
(2,235) 2,073
Frog, Kaufman..................................NA
Front, Panola...................................NA
Fronton, Starr, (599) 629
*FROST, Navarro, 27, (648) 704
Fruitland, Montague.........................20
*FRUITVALE, Van Zandt, 8,
(418) 438
Frydek, Austin.................................900
Fulbright, Red River........................150
*FULSHEAR, Fort Bend, 101,
(716) 950
*FULTON, Aransas, 97,
(1,553) 1,682
Funston, Jones 26
Furrh, Panola....................................40

G

Gadston, Lamar.................................35
Gafford, Hopkins..............................NA
*Gail, Borden, 2 200
*GAINESVILLE, Cooke, 870,
(15,538) 16,432
Galena, Smith...................................NA
*GALENA PARK, Harris, 200,
(10,592) 10,423
Galilee, Smith 150
*GALLATIN, Cherokee, 3, (378) 390
Galloway, Panola..............................71
*GALVESTON, Galveston, 1,861,
(57,247) 56,983
*GANADO, Jackson, 103,
(1,915) 1,987
Garceño, Starr, (1,438)................1,519
*Garciasville [La Casita-], Starr, 6,
(2,177) 2,419
*Garden City, Glasscock, 15...........293
*Gardendale, Ector, 17,
(1,197) 1,239
Gardendale, La Salle........................40
GARDEN RIDGE, Comal, 110,
(1,882) 2,502
Garden Valley, Smith 150
Garfield, DeWitt 16
Garfield, Travis, (1,660)...............1,633

Garland, Bowie 125
*GARLAND, Dallas, 7,236,
(215,768) 218,303
Garner, Parker 196
Garner State Park, Uvalde 50
GARRETT, Ellis, 4, (448)................501
Garretts Bluff, Lamar 25
*GARRISON, Nacogdoches, 40,
(844) 864
*Garwood, Colorado, 65 975
*GARY, Panola, 20,
(303) 310
Gastonia, Kaufman...........................30
*GATESVILLE, Coryell, 403,
(15,591) 15,945
*Gause, Milam, 17 425
Gay Hill, Washington 145
*Geneva, Sabine 200
Geneview, Stonewall 3
Gentry's Mill, Hamilton....................20
George's Creek, Somervell 43
*GEORGETOWN, Williamson,
1,793, (28,339) 39,787
*GEORGE WEST, Live Oak, 158,
(2,524) 2,444
Georgia, Lamar.................................55
Germany, Houston...........................23
*Geronimo, Guadalupe, 8, (619) 578
GHOLSON, McLennan, 20,
(922) 958
Gibtown, Jack..................................NA
*GIDDINGS, Lee, 343,
(5,105) 5,474
*Gilchrist, Galveston, 10 800
*Gillett, Karnes, 3..........................120
Gilliland, Knox..................................20
*GILMER, Upshur, 427,
(4,799) 5,038
Gilpin, Dickens...................................2
Ginger, Rains....................................96
*Girard, Kent, (62) 59
Girlstown USA, Cochran...................98
*Girvin, Pecos, 1..............................20
Gist, Jasper ....NA
Givens, Lamar.................................135
*GLADEWATER, Gregg-Upshur,
389, (6,078).......................6,155
Glaze City, Gonzales 10
Glazier, Hemphill 48
Glecker, Lavaca................................78
Glen Cove, Coleman 40
Glendale, Trinity.............................175
Glenfawn, Rusk 100
*Glen Flora, Wharton, 4................210
Glenn, Dickens...................................4
GLENN HEIGHTS, Dallas-Ellis,
138, (7,224) 9,940
Glenrio, Deaf Smith 5
*GLEN ROSE, Somervell, 203,
(2,122) 2,589
Glenwood, Upshur 150
Glidden, Colorado, 1.......................255
Globe, Lamar....................................60
Glory, Lamar.....................................30
*Gober, Fannin 146
*GODLEY, Johnson, 56,
(879) 1,040
*Golden, Wood, 7 398
Goldfinch, Frio 35
*Goldsboro, Coleman 30
*GOLDSMITH, Ector, 24,
(253) 246

*GOLDTHWAITE, Mills, 105,
(1,802) 1,851
*GOLIAD, Goliad, 147,
(1,975) 1,887
GOLINDA, Falls-McLennan, 7,
(423) 451
Golly, DeWitt.....................................41
Gomez, Terry 6
*GONZALES, Gonzales, 381,
(7,202) 7,488
Goober Hill, Shelby..........................30
Goodland, Bailey 10
Goodlett, Hardeman 80
GOODLOW, Navarro, 4, (264) 273
Good Neighbor, Hopkins ....NA
Goodnight, Armstrong......................18
Goodnight, Navarro..........................25
*GOODRICH, Polk, 22, (243).........280
Goodsprings, Rusk 40
Goodwill, Burleson...........................12
Goodwin, San Augustine ....NA
*GORDON, Palo Pinto, 26,
(451) 446
*Gordonville, Grayson, 19 165
*GOREE, Knox, 6, (321)................307
*GORMAN, Eastland, 45,
(1,236) 1,242
Goshen, Walker...............................250
Gould, Cherokee 20
*Gouldbusk, Coleman, 1...................70
Graball, Washington ....NA
Graceton, Upshur 100
*GRAFORD, Palo Pinto, 41,
(578) 601
Graham, Garza 139
*GRAHAM, Young, 642,
(8,716) 8,532
*GRANBURY, Hood, 1,149,
(5,718) 7,148
Grand Acres, Cameron, (203) 204
Grand Bluff, Panola 115
*GRANDFALLS, Ward, 8,
(391) 372
*GRAND PRAIRIE, Dallas-Tarrant,
4,343, (127,427) 148,992
*GRAND SALINE, Van Zandt,
155, (3,028),.......................3,088
Grandview, Dawson.........................12
Grandview, Gray...............................13
*GRANDVIEW, Johnson, 98,
(1,358) 1,454
*GRANGER, Williamson, 52,
(1,299) 1,495
Grangerland, Montgomery..............NA
*GRANITE SHOALS, Burnet, 56,
(2,040) 2,346
GRANJENO, Hidalgo, 1,
(313) 317
Grape Creek, Tom Green,
(3,138) 3,007
*GRAPELAND, Houston, 94,
(1,451) 1,397
*GRAPEVINE, Tarrant, 2,613,
(42,059) 47,271
Grassland, Lynn 40
Grassyville, Bastrop.........................50
Gray, Marion ....NA
Grayback, Wilbarger........................10
GRAYS PRAIRIE, Kaufman, 4,
(296) 340
Graytown, Wilson 64
Greatwood, Fort Bend, (6,640)....7,758

Town, County	Pop. 2006	Town, County	Pop. 2006	Town, County	Pop. 2006

Green, Karnes 35
Green Hill, Titus..........................150
Green Lake, Calhoun 51
Greenpond, Hopkins......................150
Green's Creek, Erath......................75
Green Valley Farms, Cameron,
  (720)..741
Greenview, Hopkins......................NA
*GREENVILLE, Hunt, 1,018,
  (23,960) 25,347
Greenvine, Washington 35
Greenwood, Hopkins 100
Greenwood, Midland 2,000
Greenwood, Red River....................20
*Greenwood, Wise, 2......................76
*GREGORY, San Patricio, 38,
  (2,318) 2,250
Gresham, Smith............................NA
GREY FOREST, Bexar, 19,
  (418)..425
Grice, Upshur 20
Griffith, Cochran 12
Grigsby, Shelby 15
Grit, Mason....................................15
*GROESBECK, Limestone, 169,
  (4,291) 4,593
*GROOM, Carson, 36, (587) 581
*GROVES, Jefferson, 427,
  (15,733) 14,654
*GROVETON, Trinity, 50,
  (1,107) 1,109
Grow, King......................................9
Gruenau, DeWitt............................18
Gruene, Comal
  ....[part of New Braunfels]
Grulla, Starr ....(see La Grulla)
*GRUVER, Hansford, 43,
  (1,162) 1,167
Guadalupe, Victoria......................106
Guadalupe Station, Culberson 80
*Guerra, Jim Hogg, (8) 12
Gum Springs, Cass........................50
*GUN BARREL CITY, Henderson,
  249, (5,145) 5,765
Gunsight, Stephens..........................6
*GUNTER, Grayson, 53,
  (1,230) 1,634
Gus, Burleson................................50
*GUSTINE, Comanche, 17,
  (457) 457
*Guthrie, King, 1 125
*Guy, Fort Bend, 5 239
Guys Store, Leon..........................NA

H

Haciendito, Presidio......................NA
Hackberry, Cottle 30
HACKBERRY, Denton, 2,
  (544)..601
Hackberry, Edwards 3
Hackberry, Garza............................5
Hackberry, Lavaca..........................40
Hagansport, Franklin......................40
Hagerville, Houston........................70
Hail, Fannin 30
Hainesville, Wood..........................95
*HALE CENTER, Hale, 42,
  (2,263) 2,204
Halfway, Hale................................165
Hall, San Saba..............................15
*HALLETTSVILLE, Lavaca, 214,
  (2,345) 2,494
Hall's Bluff, Houston 67

HALLSBURG, McLennan, 5,
  (518)..526
Halls Store, Panola........................NA
*HALLSVILLE, Harrison, 123,
  (2,772) 3,050
*HALTOM CITY, Tarrant, 1,497,
  (39,018) 41,721
Hamby, Taylor..............................100
*HAMILTON, Hamilton, 207,
  (2,977) 2,986
*HAMLIN, Jones-Fisher, 83,
  (2,248) 2,114
Hammond, Robertson 44
Hamon, Gonzales............................20
*Hamshire, Jefferson, 16 759
Hancock, Comal ....NA
Hancock, Dawson............................30
*Hankamer, Chambers, 7 226
Hannibal, Erath..............................NA
Hanover, Milam..............................25
*HAPPY, Swisher-Randall, 24,
  (647) 634
Happy Union, Hale 25
Happy Valley, Taylor 10
Harbin, Erath..................................21
*HARDIN, Liberty, 15, (755) 795
Hare, Williamson............................60
*Hargill, Hidalgo, 4......................1,349
*HARKER HEIGHTS, Bell, 392,
  (17,308) 20,692
Harkeyville, San Saba 12
*Harleton, Harrison, 22 260
*HARLINGEN, Cameron, 2,116,
  (57,564) 66,459
Harmon, Lamar..............................12
Harmony, Floyd..............................42
Harmony, Grimes............................12
Harmony, Kent................................10
Harmony, Nacogdoches....................50
*Harper, Gillespie, 39,
  (1,006) 1,127
Harpersville, Stephens ....NA
Harrison, McLennan......................100
*Harrold, Wilbarger, 4 200
*HART, Castro, 38, (1,198)..........1,123
Hartburg, Newton 275
Hart Camp, Lamb............................4
*Hartley, Hartley, 15, (441)..........439
Harvard, Camp................................48
Harvey, Brazos............................310
Harwell Point, Burnet....................138
*Harwood, Gonzales, 7................118
*HASKELL, Haskell, 153,
  (3,106) 2,851
Haslam, Shelby............................100
*HASLET, Tarrant, 172,
  (1,134) 1,408
Hasse, Comanche............................50
Hatchel, Runnels..............................6
Hatchetville, Hopkins......................NA
Havana, Hidalgo, (452)..................468
HAWK COVE, Hunt, 3,
  (457) 472
*HAWKINS, Wood, 111,
  (1,331) 1,542
*HAWLEY, Jones, 39, (646)..........648
Hawthorne, Walker........................100
Haynesville, Wichita 65
HAYS, Hays, 3, (233) 235
Hazeldell, Comanche 12
*HEARNE, Robertson, 167,
  (4,690) 4,759

HEATH, Rockwall, 209,
  (4,149)....................................6,188
*Hebbronville, Jim Hogg, 95,
  (4,498)....................................4,236
HEBRON, Denton, 21, (874) 162
Heckville, Lubbock..........................91
*HEDLEY, Donley, 9, (379)............365
Hedwigs Hill, Mason 12
HEDWIG VILLAGE, Harris, 242,
  (2,334)....................................2,148
Hefner, Knox....................................3
Hegar, Waller................................NA
Heidelberg, Hidalgo, (1,586)........1,632
*Heidenheimer, Bell, 9................224
Helena, Karnes................................35
Helmic, Trinity..............................86
*HELOTES, Bexar, 445,
  (4,285)....................................6,405
*HEMPHILL, Sabine, 130,
  (1,106)....................................1,034
*HEMPSTEAD, Waller, 248,
  (4,691)....................................6,201
*HENDERSON, Rusk, 585,
  (11,273) 11,012
Hendricks, Hunt............................NA
Henkhaus, Lavaca............................88
Henly, Hays................................140
*HENRIETTA, Clay, 140,
  (3,264)....................................3,354
Henry's Chapel, Cherokee 75
*HEREFORD, Deaf Smith, 470,
  (14,597) 14,757
Hermits Cove, Rains......................40
*Hermleigh, Scurry, 8, (393) 398
Herty, Angelina............................605
Hester, Navarro 35
*HEWITT, McLennan, 396,
  (11,085) 12,686
*Hext, Menard................................75
HICKORY CREEK, Denton, 91,
  (2,078)....................................3,040
Hickory Creek, Houston..................31
Hickory Creek, Hunt 40
*HICO, Hamilton, 135,
  (1,341)....................................1,365
*HIDALGO, Hidalgo, 416,
  (7,322)..................................10,884
Hidden Acres [Lakeshore Gardens-],
  San Patricio, (720)..................687
HIDEAWAY, Smith, 0, (2,619)......2,860
Higginbotham, Gaines....................21
*HIGGINS, Lipscomb, 18,
  (425) 406
High, Lamar....................................14
Highbank, Falls..............................68
High Hill, Fayette 176
*High Island, Galveston, 2 500
Highland, Erath..............................60
HIGHLAND HAVEN, Burnet, 0,
  (450) 464
HIGHLAND PARK, Dallas, 412,
  (8,842)....................................8,305
*Highlands, Harris, 117,
  (7,089)....................................7,022
HIGHLAND VILLAGE, Denton,
  403, (12,173)........................14,816
Hightower, Liberty........................225
HILL COUNTRY VILLAGE, Bexar,
  105, (1,028)............................1,062
Hillcrest, Colorado 25
HILLCREST VILLAGE, Brazoria,
  (722) 738

The town of Groom in Carson County in the Panhandle. Robert Plocheck photo.

Town, County .... Pop. 2006

*Hillister, Tyler, 12 250
Hillje, Wharton 51
Hills, Lee 20
*HILLSBORO, Hill, 448,
　(8,232) 8,899
Hills Prairie, Bastrop 50
Hilltop, Frio, (300) 299
*Hilltop Lakes, Leon 300
HILSHIRE VILLAGE, Harris, 17,
　(720) 692
Hinckley, Lamar 40
Hindes, Atascosa 14
Hinkles Ferry, Brazoria 35
Hiram, Kaufman 75
*HITCHCOCK, Galveston, 179,
　(6,386) 7,161
Hitchland, Hansford 15
Hix, Burleson 35
Hoard, Wood 45
Hobbs, Fisher 02
*Hobson, Karnes, 9 135
*Hochheim, DeWitt 70
*Hockley, Harris, 84 .... NA
Hodges, Jones 150
Hogansville, Rains 200
Hogg, Burleson 20
Holiday Beach, Aransas 1,000
HOLIDAY LAKES, Brazoria, 7,
　(1,095) 1,148
*HOLLAND, Bell, 42,
　(1,102) 1,095
Holland Quarters, Panola 40
*HOLLIDAY, Archer, 75,
　(1,632) 1,688
Holly, Houston 95
Holly Grove, Polk 20
Holly Springs, Jasper 50
HOLLYWOOD PARK, Bexar, 118,
　(2,983) 3,170
Holman, Fayette 101
Homer, Angelina 360
Homestead Meadows North, El Paso,
　(4,232) 4,147
Homestead Meadows South, El Paso,
　(6,807) 6,884
*HONDO, Medina, 295,
　(7,897) 8,988

*HONEY GROVE, Fannin, 81,
　(1,746) 1,788
Honey Island, Hardin 401
Hood, Cooke 13
Hooker Ridge, Rains 250
*HOOKS, Bowie, 66, (2,973) 3,071
Hoover, Gray 5
Hoover, Lamar 20
Hope, Lavaca 45
Hopewell, Franklin 50
Hopewell, Houston 22
Hopewell [Dixon-], Houston 10
Hopewell, Red River 152
HORIZON CITY, El Paso, 148,
　(5,233) 7,744
Hornsby Bend, Travis .... NA
HORSESHOE BAY, Llano-Burnet,
　74, (3,337) 3,359
Hortense, Polk 20
Horton, Delta 40
Horton, Panola 200
*HOUSTON, Harris-Fort Bend-
　Montgomery, 86,710,
　(1,953,631) 2,085,737
Howard, Ellis 60
HOWARDWICK, Donley, 10,
　(437) 448
*HOWE, Grayson, 86,
　(2,478) 3,073
Howland, Lamar 65
Howth, Waller 65
Hoxie, Williamson 60
Hoyte, Milam 20
Hub, Parmer 25
Hubbard, Bowie 269
*HUBBARD, Hill, 78,
　(1,586) 1,596
Huber, Shelby 15
Huckabay, Erath 150
HUDSON, Angelina, 85,
　(3,792) 4,193
Hudson Bend, Travis, (2,369) 2,217
HUDSON OAKS, Parker, 107,
　(1,637) 1,770
Huffines, Cass 140
*Huffman, Harris, 116 15,000
Hufsmith, Harris 500

*HUGHES SPRINGS, Cass, 67,
　(1,856) 1,837
*Hull, Liberty, 14 800
*HUMBLE, Harris, 2,394,
　(14,579) 16,196
*Hungerford, Wharton, 16,
　(645) 652
*Hunt, Kerr, 40 708
Hunter, Comal 30
HUNTERS CREEK VILLAGE,
　Harris, 106, (4,374) 4,187
*HUNTINGTON, Angelina, 110,
　(2,068) 2,156
Huntoon, Ochiltree 21
*HUNTSVILLE, Walker, 1,105,
　(35,078) 37,237
Hurley, Wood 30
Hurlwood, Lubbock 115
Hurnville, Clay 10
*HURST, Tarrant, 1,860,
　(36,273) 37,406
Hurstown, Shelby 20
Hurst Springs, Coryell 10
*HUTCHINS, Dallas, 104,
　(2,805) 2,846
*HUTTO, Williamson, 268,
　(1,250) 7,977
HUXLEY, Shelby, 6, (298) 309
*Hye, Blanco, 3 72
Hylton, Nolan 6

I

*Iago [Boling-], Wharton, 27,
　(1,271) 1,326
Ida, Grayson 30
*IDALOU, Lubbock, 78,
　(2,157) 2,135
Iglesia Antigua [Bluetown-],
　Cameron, (692) 701
Ike, Ellis 50
Illinois Bend, Montague 40
IMPACT, Taylor, (39) 43
*Imperial, Pecos, 3, (428) 399
Inadale, Scurry 8
Independence, Washington 140
India, Ellis 30
Indian Creek, Brown 28
Indian Creek, Smith 300

Town, County .... Pop. 2006	Town, County .... Pop. 2006	Town, County .... Pop. 2006
Indian Gap, Hamilton 35	*JOAQUIN, Shelby, 33,	Kelton, Wheeler 20
Indian Hill, Newton ....NA	(925) 959	*KEMAH, Galveston, 289,
Indian Hills, Hidalgo,	Joe Lee, Bell 8	(2,330) 2,586
(2,036) 2,128	*JOHNSON CITY, Blanco, 152,	*KEMP, Kaufman, 132,
INDIAN LAKE, Cameron, (541) 541	(1,191) 1,409	(1,133) 1,157
Indianola, Calhoun 200	Johnsville, Erath 25	Kemper City, Victoria 16
Indian Rock, Upshur 45	Johntown, Red River 175	*KEMPNER, Lampasas, 98,
Indian Springs, Polk 250	*Joinerville, Rusk 140	(1,004) 1,084
Indio, Presidio ....NA	Joliet, Caldwell 192	*Kendalia, Kendall, 9 149
*INDUSTRY, Austin, 34, (304) 322	JOLLY, Clay, 8, (188) 181	*KENDLETON, Fort Bend, 4,
*Inez, Victoria, 28, (1,787) 1,848	Jollyville, Williamson-Travis,	(466) 539
*INGLESIDE, San Patricio, 236,	(15,813) 17,098	*KENEDY, Karnes, 139,
(9,388) 9,575	Jonah, Williamson 60	(3,487) 3,421
INGLESIDE-ON-THE-BAY,	*Jonesboro, Coryell-Hamilton,	KENEFICK, Liberty, 10,
San Patricio, 11, (659) 685	10 125	(667) 703
*INGRAM, Kerr, 178,	JONES CREEK, Brazoria, 28,	*KENNARD, Houston, 14,
(1,740) 1,923	(2,130) 2,167	(317) 312
*Iola, Grimes, 15 350	Jones Prairie, Milam 20	*KENNEDALE, Tarrant, 325,
IOWA COLONY, Brazoria, 15,	JONESTOWN, Travis, 89,	(5,850) 6,625
(804) 879	(1,681) 1,935	*Kenney, Austin, 1 957
*IOWA PARK, Wichita, 216,	*Jonesville, Harrison, 5 28	Kenser, Hunt 100
(6,431) 6,372	Joplin, Jack ....NA	Kensing, Delta 30
*Ira, Scurry, 12 250	Joppa, Burnet 84	Kent, Culberson 60
*IRAAN, Pecos, 63, (1,238) 1,153	Jordans Store, Shelby 20	Kentucky Town, Grayson 20
*IREDELL, Bosque, 20,	*JOSEPHINE, Collin, 15,	*KERENS, Navarro, 68,
(360) 387	(594) 805	(1,681) 1,880
Ireland, Coryell 60	*JOSHUA, Johnson, 259,	*KERMIT, Winkler, 192,
*Irene, Hill 170	(4,528) 5,231	(5,714) 5,219
Ironton, Cherokee 110	Josserand, Trinity 29	*Kerrick, Dallam, 1 35
*IRVING, Dallas, 6,988,	Jot-Em-Down, Delta 8	*KERRVILLE, Kerr, 1,559,
(191,615) 194,842	*JOURDANTON, Atascosa, 134,	(20,425) 21,929
Isla, Sabine 350	(3,732) 4,644	Kerrville South, Kerr 6,600
Israel, Polk 25	Joy, Clay 110	Key, Dawson 20
*ITALY, Ellis, 61, (1,993) 2,175	Juarez [Las Palmas-], Cameron,	Kiam, Polk 24
*ITASCA, Hill, 61, (1,503) 1,547	(1,666) 1,695	Kicaster, Wilson 100
Ivan, Stephens 15	Jud, Haskell 60	*Kildare, Cass, 1 104
*Ivanhoe, Fannin, 7 110	*Judson, Gregg, 10 1,057	Kilgore, Goliad .... (see Ander)
Izoro, Lampasas 17	Juliff, Fort Bend 250	*KILGORE, Gregg-Rusk, 797,
J	Jumbo, Panola 60	(11,301) 12,021
*JACINTO CITY, Harris, 220,	*JUNCTION, Kimble, 158,	*KILLEEN, Bell, 2,283,
(10,302) 10,429	(2,618) 2,659	(86,911) 103,111
*JACKSBORO, Jack, 199,	Justiceburg, Garza, 2 76	King, Coryell 30
(4,533) 4,534	*JUSTIN, Denton, 176,	King Ranch Headquarters,
Jackson, Shelby 50	(1,891) 3,412	Kleberg 191
Jackson, Van Zandt 25	**K**	*Kingsbury, Guadalupe, 17,
Jackson, Smith ....NA	Kalgary, Crosby 2	(652) 894
*JACKSONVILLE, Cherokee,	*Kamay, Wichita, 7 640	*Kingsland, Llano, 137,
729, (13,868) 14,531	Kamey, Calhoun 25	(4,584) 4,605
Jacobia, Hunt 60	Kanawha, Red River 90	Kingston, Hunt 140
Jakes Colony, Guadalupe 95	*Karnack, Harrison, 31 775	*KINGSVILLE, Kleberg, 676,
JAMAICA BEACH, Galveston,	*KARNES CITY, Karnes, 102,	(25,575) 24,277
44, (1,075) 1,136	(3,457) 3,486	Kingtown, Nacogdoches 300
James, Shelby 75	Karon, Live Oak 25	Kingwood, Harris .... [part of Houston]
Jamestown, Newton 70	Katemcy, Mason 80	Kinkler, Lavaca 75
Jamestown, Smith 75	*KATY, Harris-Waller-Fort Bend,	Kiomatia, Red River 50
Jardin, Hunt 22	2,159, (11,775) 14,441	KIRBY, Bexar, 146, (8,673) 8,632
*JARRELL, Williamson, 62,	*KAUFMAN, Kaufman, 358,	*KIRBYVILLE, Jasper, 142,
(1,319) 1,408	(6,490) 8,222	(2,085) 2,085
*JASPER, Jasper, 486,	K-Bar Ranch, Jim Wells,	Kirk, Limestone 10
(7,657) 7,661	(350) 363	Kirkland, Childress-Hardeman 25
*JAYTON, Kent, 25, (513) 455	Keechi, Leon 67	Kirtley, Fayette 93
Jean, Young 110	*KEENE, Johnson, 123,	*KIRVIN, Freestone, 6, (122) 131
Jeddo, Bastrop 75	(5,003) 6,089	Kittrell, Walker 126
*JEFFERSON, Marion, 259,	Keeter, Wise ....NA	Klein, Harris 45,000
(2,024) 1,984	Keith, Grimes 50	Klondike, Dawson 50
Jenkins, Morris 350	*KELLER, Tarrant, 1,586,	*Klondike, Delta, 4 175
Jennings, Lamar 85	(27,345) 34,986	Klump, Washington ....NA
*Jermyn, Jack, 3 75	Kellers Corner, Cameron 123	Knapp, Scurry 10
JERSEY VILLAGE, Harris, 242,	Kellerville, Wheeler 50	*Knickerbocker, Tom Green 94
(6,880) 7,143	Kellogg, Hunt 20	*Knippa, Uvalde, 12,
*JEWETT, Leon, 85, (861) 949	Kellyville, Marion 75	(739) 769
Jiba, Kaufman 50	Kelsey, Upshur 50	Knobbs Springs, Lee 20

Town, County ....Pop. 2006	Town, County ....Pop. 2006	Town, County ....Pop. 2006
KNOLLWOOD, Grayson, 4, (375) 387	Lake Brownwood, Brown, (1,694) 1,747	La Puerta, Starr, (1,636) 1,724
*Knott, Howard, 1 200	Lake Cisco, Eastland......................105	*LAREDO, Webb, 5,652, (176,576) 213,915
*KNOX CITY, Knox, 59, (1,219) 1,129	LAKE CITY, San Patricio, (526) 519	Laredo Ranchettes, Webb, (1,845) 1,800
Koerth, Lavaca 45	*Lake Creek, Delta, 2 55	La Reforma, Starr 45
Kokomo, Eastland 25	*LAKE DALLAS, Denton, 277, (6,166) 7,328	Larga Vista, Webb, (742)................755
Komensky, Lavaca 75	Lake Dunlap, Guadalupe.............1,370	Lariat, Parmer................................100
Kopernik Shores, Cameron 34	Lakehills, Bandera, (4,668)..........5,185	La Rosa, Nueces 20
*Kopperl, Bosque, 12......................225	*LAKE JACKSON, Brazoria, 824, (26,386)..................27,874	La Rosita, Starr, (1,729) 1,812
Kosciusko, Wilson 390	Lake Kiowa, Cooke, (1,883) 1,766	*Larue, Henderson, 22 250
*KOSSE, Limestone, 19, (497).......508	Lake Leon, Eastland.......................75	*LaSalle, Jackson 110
*KOUNTZE, Hardin, 138, (2,115) 2,141	Lake Nueces, Uvalde 60	Lasana, Cameron, (135)................137
Kovar, Bastrop ....NA	LAKEPORT, Gregg, 17, (861) 913	*Lasara, Willacy, 1, (1,024)..........1,017
*KRESS, Swisher, 21, (826)..........819	Lakeshore Gardens-Hidden Acres, San Patricio, (720)................687	Las Colonias, Zavala, (283)...........247
KRUGERVILLE, Denton, 34, (903) 1,434	LAKESIDE, San Patricio, (333) 324	Las Escobas, Starr 10
*KRUM, Denton, 136, (1,979) 3,237	LAKESIDE, Tarrant, 46, (1,040) 1,137	Las Lomas, Starr, (2,684) 2,832
*KURTEN, Brazos, 4, (227)............220	LAKESIDE CITY, Archer, 22, (984) 1,010	Las Lomitas, Jim Hogg, (267) 256
*KYLE, Hays, 483, (5,314) 19,335	Lakeside Village, Bosque 226	Las Palmas-Juarez, Cameron, (1,666) 1,695
Kyote, Atascosa..............................34	LAKE TANGLEWOOD, Randall, 9, (825) 756	Las Quintas Fronterizas, Maverick, (2,030) 2,141
L	Lake Victor, Burnet 265	Las Rusias, Cameron 225
*La Blanca, Hidalgo, 11, (2,351) 2,498	Lakeview, Floyd................................39	Las Yescas, Cameron......................221
La Casa, Stephens ....NA	*LAKEVIEW, Hall, 4, (152) 150	Latch, Upshur 50
La Casita-Garciasville, Starr, 6, (2,177) 2,419	Lakeview, Lynn................................15	Latex, Harrison 75
Laceola, Madison 10	Lakeview, Orange.............................75	*LATEXO, Houston, 4, (272) 269
Lackland Air Force Base, Bexar, (7,123) 6,797	Lake View, Val Verde, (167) 167	La Tina Ranch [Arroyo Gardens-], Cameron, (732) 737
*LA COSTE, Medina, 60, (1,255) 1,368	LAKEVIEW [Lacy-], McLennan, 123, (5,764) 5,914	Latium, Washington..........................30
Lacy, Trinity...................................44	*LAKEWAY, Travis, 512, (8,002) 8,682	Laughlin Air Force Base, Val Verde, (2,225) 2,248
LACY-LAKEVIEW, McLennan, 123, (5,764) 5,914	Lakewood Harbor, Bosque ....NA	Laurel, Newton 125
*LADONIA, Fannin, 29, (667) 680	LAKEWOOD VILLAGE, Denton, (342) 446	Laureles, Cameron, (3,285).........3,389
LaFayette, Upshur...........................80	*LAKE WORTH, Tarrant, 242, (4,618) 4,641	Lavender, Limestone 30
*LA FERIA, Cameron, 196, (6,115) 6,958	Lamar, Aransas............................1,600	*LA VERNIA, Wilson, 172, (931) 1,239
La Feria North, Cameron, (168) 168	*LA MARQUE, Galveston, 419, (13,682) 13,805	La Victoria, Starr, (1,683)..............1,773
Lagarto, Live Oak 735	Lamasco, Fannin 32	*LA VILLA, Hidalgo, 7, (1,305) 1,376
La Gloria, Jim Wells........................70	*LAMESA, Dawson, 351, (9,952) 9,534	*LAVON, Collin, 75, (387)..............500
La Gloria, Starr 102	Lamkin, Comanche..........................87	Law, Brazos ....NA
Lago, Cameron, (246) 249	*LAMPASAS, Lampasas, 423, (6,786) 7,568	*LA WARD, Jackson, 17, (200) 214
*LAGO VISTA, Travis, 286, (4,507) 5,761	Lanark, Cass 30	*LAWN, Taylor, 19, (353) 316
*LA GRANGE, Fayette, 435, (4,478) 4,650	*LANCASTER, Dallas, 742, (25,894) 32,342	Lawrence, Kaufman........................259
*LA GRULLA, Starr, 8, (1,211) 1,637	Landrum Station, Cameron 125	*Lazbuddie, Parmer, 8...................248
Laguna, Uvalde 20	*Lane City, Wharton, 2....................111	*LEAGUE CITY, Galveston-Harris, 1,922, (45,444)..................62,622
Laguna Heights, Cameron, (1,990) 2,115	Lanely, Freestone 27	Leagueville, Henderson....................50
*Laguna Park, Bosque....................550	Laneport, Williamson........................40	*LEAKEY, Real, 63, (387)..............395
Laguna Seca, Hidalgo, (251).........256	*Laneville, Rusk, 10........................169	*LEANDER, Williamson, 713, (7,596) 16,822
Laguna Vista, Burnet.......................94	*Langtry, Val Verde...........................30	LEARY, Bowie, 10, (555).................578
LAGUNA VISTA, Cameron, 55, (1,658) 2,848	Lanier, Cass...................................80	*Ledbetter, Fayette, 16 83
La Homa, Hidalgo, (10,433) 11,401	Lannius, Fannin 79	Leedale, Bell...................................24
*Laird Hill, Rusk, 4........................300	Lantana, Cameron..........................137	*Leesburg, Camp, 18.....................128
La Isla, El Paso...............................27	La Paloma, Cameron, (354)...........358	Lee Spring, Smith ....NA
Lajitas, Brewster.............................75	La Paloma-Lost Creek, Nueces, (323) 259	*Leesville, Gonzales, 2 152
*LA JOYA, Hidalgo, 62, (3,303) 4,197	La Parita, Atascosa..........................48	*LEFORS, Gray, 17, (559)..............530
La Junta, Parker ....NA	*LA PORTE, Harris, 1,017, (31,880) 32,985	*Leggett, Polk, 6 500
Lake Arrowhead, Clay 250	La Presa, Webb, (508) 553	Lehman, Cochran 6
LAKE BRIDGEPORT, Wise, 8, (372) 405	*La Pryor, Zavala, 13, (1,491) 1,524	Leigh, Harrison 100
		Lela, Wheeler.................................135
		*Lelia Lake, Donley, 4.......................71
		*Leming, Atascosa, 7.......................268
		*Lenorah, Martin, 4............................83
		Lenz, Karnes...................................20
		Leo, Cooke..20
		Leo, Lee..10

Town, County ....Pop. 2006	Town, County ....Pop. 2006	Town, County ....Pop. 2006
*LEONA, Leon, 11, (181)...............188	*LIPAN, Hood, 38, (425).................618	*LOMETA, Lampasas, 48,
*LEONARD, Fannin, 95,	*Lipscomb, Lipscomb, 2, (44)..........42	(782).......................................894
(1,846)...................................1,990	*Lissie, Wharton, 4 72	*London, Kimble, 3 180
Leona Schroder, Nueces.................40	Littig, Travis 37	Lone Camp, Palo Pinto..................110
Leon Junction, Coryell......................50	Little Cypress, Orange................1,050	Lone Cedar, Ellis 18
Leon Springs, Bexar	*LITTLE ELM, Denton, 431,	Lone Grove, Llano..........................50
....................[part of San Antonio]	(3,646)................................19,472	Lone Oak, Colorado 50
*LEON VALLEY, Bexar, 533,	*LITTLEFIELD, Lamb, 225,	Lone Oak, Erath ....NA
(9,239) 9,604	(6,507) 6,360	*LONE OAK, Hunt, 47,
*LEROY, McLennan, 6,	Little Hope, Wood 25	(521).......................................552
(335) 336	Little Midland, Burnet.......................82	Lone Pine, Houston 81
Lesley, Hall 25	Little New York, Gonzales................15	Lone Star, Cherokee........................20
*LEVELLAND, Hockley, 476,	*LITTLE RIVER-ACADEMY, Bell,	Lone Star, Floyd 42
(12,866) 12,658	26, (1,645) 1,696	Lone Star, Lamar 35
Leverett's Chapel, Rusk 400	Lively, Kaufman ....NA	*LONE STAR, Morris, 50,
Levi, McLennan 50	LIVE OAK, Bexar, 371,	(1,631) 1,580
Levita, Coryell...................................70	(9,156) 11,267	*Long Branch, Panola, 3.................150
*LEWISVILLE, Denton, 3,661,	*LIVERPOOL, Brazoria, 21,	Long Hollow, Leon..........................NA
(77,737) 92,847	(404) 435	Long Lake, Anderson.......................15
*LEXINGTON, Lee, 89,	*LIVINGSTON, Polk, 649,	Long Mott, Calhoun 76
(1,178) 1,279	(5,433) 6,296	Longpoint, Washington.....................80
Liberty, Hopkins ....NA	*LLANO, Llano, 286,	*LONGVIEW, Gregg-Harrison,
*LIBERTY, Liberty, 417,	(3,325) 3,758	3,865, (73,344) 75,132
(8,033) 8,281	Llano Grande, Hidalgo, (3,333) ...3,378	Longworth, Fisher............................47
Liberty, Lubbock 228	Lobo, Culberson 15	Looneyville, Nacogdoches...............50
Liberty, Milam 40	Locker, San Saba 16	*Loop, Gaines, 6.............................315
Liberty, Newton...............................NA	Lockett, Wilbarger.........................150	*Lopeno, Zapata, 3, (140)..............163
Liberty City, Gregg, (1,935) 1,973	Lockettville, Hockley.......................20	Lopezville, Hidalgo, (4,476).........4,876
Liberty Hill, Houston 73	*LOCKHART, Caldwell, 419,	*LORAINE, Mitchell, 15,
Liberty Hill, Milam 25	(11,615) 12,978	(656) 639
*LIBERTY HILL, Williamson,	*LOCKNEY, Floyd, 65,	*LORENA, McLennan, 148,
273, (1,409) 1,487	(2,056) 1,859	(1,433) 1,621
Lilbert, Nacogdoches.....................100	Locust, Grayson 118	*LORENZO, Crosby, 20,
*Lillian, Johnson, 11....................1,160	Lodi, Marion 175	(1,372) 1,334
*Lincoln, Lee, 12............................336	Loebau, Lee......................................35	Los Alvarez, Starr, (1,434)...........1,504
LINCOLN PARK, Denton, 4,	Logan, Panola 40	Los Angeles, La Salle 20
(517) 601	LOG CABIN, Henderson, 4,	Los Angeles Subdivision, Willacy,
*LINDALE, Smith, 376,	(733).......................................813	(86)..85
(2,954) 4,234	*Lohn, McCulloch, 3 149	Los Barreras, Starr 75
*LINDEN, Cass, 95, (2,256) 2,133	Loire, Wilson 50	Los Coyotes, Willacy 4
Lindenau, DeWitt.............................50	Lois, Cooke......................................10	*Los Ebanos, Hidalgo, 1, (403).......419
Lindendale, Kendall.........................70	*Lolita, Jackson, 8, (548)...............549	Los Escondidos, Burnet....................80
*LINDSAY, Cooke, 19, (788)...........918	Loma Alta, McMullen 25	*LOS FRESNOS, Cameron, 149,
Lindsay, Reeves, (394)...................346	Loma Alta, Val Verde 30	(4,512) 5,454
*Lingleville, Erath, 1 100	Loma Linda [Del Sol-], San Patricio,	*LOS INDIOS, Cameron, 11,
Linn Flat, Nacogdoches...................60	(726) 716	(1,149) 1,297
*Linn [San Manuel-], Hidalgo,	Loma Linda East, Jim Wells,	Losoya, Bexar.................................322
11, (958)................................951	(214) 224	LOS SAENZ [Roma-], Starr, 265,
Linwood, Cherokee..........................40	Lomax, Howard 25	(9,617) 11,492

Lindsay, settled by Germans, lies in the Trinity River valley in Cooke County. Robert Plocheck photo.

Town, County .... Pop. 2006	Town, County .... Pop. 2006	Town, County .... Pop. 2006
Lost Creek, Travis, (4,729) 4,616	Malvern, Leon..................................NA	Mayfield, Hale...............................26
Lost Creek [La Paloma-], Nueces,	Mambrino, Hood...............................74	Mayfield, Hill.................................25
(323) 259	*Manchaca, Travis, 93.................2,259	Mayflower, Newton......................100
Lost Prairie, Limestone......................2	Manchester, Red River..................185	Maynard, San Jacinto....................150
Los Villareales, Starr, (930) 976	Mangum, Eastland.............................15	*MAYPEARL, Ellis, 27, (746).....933
LOS YBANEZ, Dawson, 2, (32).......32	Manheim, Lee....................................50	Maysfield, Milam...........................140
*LOTT, Falls, 68, (724) 691	Mankin, Henderson...........................30	*McAdoo, Dickens, 3.......................75
*Louise, Wharton, 34, (977)............985	Mankins, Archer................................10	*McALLEN, Hidalgo, 5,073,
Lovelace, Hill...................................30	*MANOR, Travis, 183,	(106,414) 123,055
*LOVELADY, Houston, 42,	(1,204)..2,044	*McCAMEY, Upton, 57,
(608), ...600	*MANSFIELD, Tarrant-Johnson,	(1,805)..1,634
*Loving, Young, 2............................300	1,713, (28,031) 37,213	*McCaulley, Fisher, 1 96
*Lowake, Concho, 1 40	*MANVEL, Brazoria, 243,	McClanahan, Falls............................42
LOWRY CROSSING, Collin, 35,	(3,046)..3,885	McCook, Hidalgo..............................91
(1,229)..1,720	*Maple, Bailey, 1 75	McCoy, Atascosa.............................30
Loyal Valley, Mason.........................52	Maple, Red River..............................30	McCoy, Floyd..................................20
Loyola Beach, Kleberg 195	Maple Springs, Titus........................25	McCoy, Kaufman.............................20
*Lozano, Cameron, 2, (324) 333	Mapleton, Houston...........................32	McCoy, Panola.................................30
*LUBBOCK, Lubbock, 7,852,	*Marathon, Brewster, 16,	McCoy, Red River..........................175
(199,564) 209,972	(455)..449	*McDade, Bastrop, 17 345
LUCAS, Collin, 127, (2,890) 3,798	*MARBLE FALLS, Burnet, 678,	*McFaddin, Victoria, 1 175
Luckenbach, Gillespie 25	(4,959)..6,471	McGirk, Hamilton...............................9
*LUEDERS, Jones, 12,	*MARFA, Presidio, 108,	*McGREGOR, McLennan, 140,
(300) 285	(2,121)..2,053	(4,727)...4,836
Luella, Grayson 639	Margaret, Foard...............................50	*McKINNEY, Collin, 1,054,
*LUFKIN, Angelina, 1,822,	Marie, Runnels.................................10	(54,369)...................................101,224
(32,709) 33,307	*MARIETTA, Cass, 4, (112)........... 111	McKinney Acres, Andrews.............197
*LULING, Caldwell, 254,	*MARION, Guadalupe, 97,	*McLEAN, Gray, 40, (830).............784
(5,080) 5,704	(1,099)..1,228	McLENDON-CHISHOLM,
Lull, Hidalgo..................................999	*Markham, Matagorda, 13,	Rockwall, 3, (914)...................1,054
*LUMBERTON, Hardin, 414,	(1,138)..1,080	*McLeod, Cass, 4 600
(8,731) 10,324	Markley, Young................................50	McMahan, Caldwell 125
Lums Chapel, Lamb 6	*MARLIN, Falls, 195, (6,628).......6,431	McMillan, San Saba........................15
Luther, Howard.................................3	Marlow, Milam.................................45	McNair, Harris............................2,039
Lutie, Collingsworth 10	*MARQUEZ, Leon, 35, (220).........233	McNary, Hudspeth.........................250
Lydia, Red River.............................109	Mars, Van Zandt..............................20	McNeil, Caldwell...........................200
*LYFORD, Willacy, 36,	*MARSHALL, Harrison, 996,	McNeil, Travis..................................NA
(1,973)..2,349	(23,935).................................23,915	*McQueeney, Guadalupe, 32,
Lyford South, Willacy, (172)...........169	MARSHALL CREEK, Denton, 3,	(2,527)...2,958
Lynn Grove, Grimes.........................25	(431)..530	*MEADOW, Terry, 15, (658)...........679
*Lyons, Burleson, 7 360	Marshall Northeast, Harrison.......1,500	Meadow Grove, Bell 20
*LYTLE, Atascosa-Medina-Bexar,	Marston, Polk...................................25	MEADOWLAKES, Burnet, 20,
158, (2,383)...............................2,498	*MART, McLennan, 74,	(1,293)...1,659
Lytton Springs, Caldwell 500	(2,273)..2,402	MEADOWS PLACE, Fort Bend,
M	*MARTINDALE, Caldwell, 46,	97, (4,912)...............................6,237
*MABANK, Kaufman-Henderson,	(953)...1,163	Mecca, Madison................................40
254, (2,151)...............................2,693	Martins Mill, Van Zandt...................158	Medicine Mound, Hardeman 50
Mabelle, Baylor..................................9	Martin Springs, Hopkins 200	Medill, Lamar..................................50
Mabry, Red River.............................60	*Martinsville, Nacogdoches, 3 350	*Medina, Bandera, 30.....................850
*Macdona, Bexar, 2 297	Marvin, Lamar.................................48	Medina, Zapata, (2,960) 3,369
Macey, Brazos ....NA	Maryetta, Jack....................................7	Meeker, Jefferson........................2,280
Macon, Franklin 21	*Maryneal, Nolan, 3..........................61	Meeks, Bell..6
Macune, San Augustine.................100	Marysville, Cooke 12	*MEGARGEL, Archer, 13,
Madero, Hidalgo.............................720	*MASON, Mason, 199,	(248)..244
*MADISONVILLE, Madison,	(2,134)..2,230	*MELISSA, Collin, 99,
218, (4,159)...............................4,393	Massey Lake, Anderson 30	(1,350)...2,735
Madras, Red River............................61	Masterson, Moore, 1..........................2	Melrose, Nacogdoches...................400
Magnet, Wharton..............................42	*MATADOR, Motley, 37,	*MELVIN, McCulloch, 5, (155)........148
*MAGNOLIA, Montgomery, 482,	(740)..691	*MEMPHIS, Hall, 83,
(1,111)..1,824	*Matagorda, Matagorda, 21...........710	(2,479)...2,465
Magnolia, San Jacinto 330	*MATHIS, San Patricio, 144,	-*MENARD, Menard, 75,
Magnolia Beach, Calhoun 250	(5,034)..5,166	(1,653)...1,611
Magnolia Springs, Jasper 80	Matthews, Colorado.........................25	Mendoza, Caldwell 100
Maha, Travis.....................................NA	*MAUD, Bowie, 41, (1,028) 1,016	Menlow, Hill...................................12
Mahl, Nacogdoches........................150	*Mauriceville, Orange, 26,	*Mentone, Loving, 2..........................20
Mahomet, Burnet..............................97	(2,743)..2,791	Mentz, Colorado............................100
Majors, Franklin 13	Maverick, Runnels............................35	*MERCEDES, Hidalgo, 384,
*MALAKOFF, Henderson, 124,	Maxdale, Bell....................................25	(13,649)..................................15,053
(2,257) 2,356	Maxey, Lamar...................................70	Mercury, McCulloch.......................166
Mallard, Montague...........................12	*Maxwell, Caldwell, 28...................500	*Mereta, Tom Green, 5 131
*MALONE, Hill, 15, (278)................276	*May, Brown, 12 270	*MERIDIAN, Bosque, 83,
Malta, Bowie..................................297	*Maydelle, Cherokee, 1 250	(1,491)...1,535

Town, County ....Pop. 2006	Town, County ....Pop. 2006	Town, County ....Pop. 2006
*Merit, Hunt, 3................................225	*MINGUS, Palo Pinto, 16,	*MOULTON, Lavaca, 78,
*MERKEL, Taylor, 124,	(246)...251	(944).......................................914
(2,637)...................................2,669	Minter, Lamar...................................78	*Mound, Coryell, 3.........................125
Merle, Burleson 10	*Mirando City, Webb, 11, (493).......587	Mound City, Anderson-Houston........60
Merriman, Eastland 14	*MISSION, Hidalgo, 1,673,	MOUNTAIN CITY, Hays, (671) 773
*MERTZON, Hill, 3, (146) 155	(45,408)................................63,775	*Mountain Home, Kerr, 15 96
*MERTZON, Irion, 68,	Mission Bend, Fort Bend-Harris,	Mountain Peak, Ellis......................300
(839)..820	(30,831) 34,887	Mountain Springs, Cooke 600
*MESQUITE, Dallas, 3,879,	Mission Valley, Victoria 225	Mountain Top, Eastland....................22
(124,523)............................129,383	*MISSOURI CITY, Fort Bend-Harris,	Mount Bethel, Panola 65
Metcalf Gap, Palo Pinto.....................6	1,782, (52,913)...................70,763	*MOUNT CALM, Hill, 29,
*MEXIA, Limestone, 320,	Mitchell, Eastland 46	(310) 325
(6,563)...................................7,071	Mixon, Cherokee..............................50	*MOUNT ENTERPRISE, Rusk,
*Meyersville, DeWitt, 9 110	*MOBEETIE, Wheeler, 8,	36, (525)................................521
*MIAMI, Roberts, 33,	(107) 104	Mount Haven, Cherokee...................30
(588).......................................573	MOBILE CITY, Rockwall, 2,	Mount Hermon, Shelby.....................80
Mico, Medina 107	(196).......................................231	Mount Olive, Lavaca 50
Midcity, Lamar 50	Moffat, Bell..................................1,406	*MOUNT PLEASANT, Titus, 559,
Middleton, Leon 26	Moffett, Angelina 100	(13,935) 14,796
*Midfield, Matagorda, 4...................305	Moline, Lampasas 12	Mount Rose, Falls............................26
*Midkiff, Upton, 7 182	*MONAHANS, Ward, 235,	Mount Selman, Cherokee................325
*MIDLAND, Midland-Martin,	(6,821) 6,490	Mount Sylvan, Smith.......................181
4,394, (94,996)................100,193	Monaville, Waller 160	*MOUNT VERNON, Franklin, 138,
*MIDLOTHIAN, Ellis, 638,	Monkstown, Fannin 35	(2,286)...................................2,440
(7,480) 12,995	Monroe, Rusk...................................96	Mount Vernon, Houston....................43
Midway, Bell...................................140	Monroe City, Chambers 11	Mozelle, Coleman ....NA
Midway, Dawson...............................20	Mont, Lavaca...................................30	Muellersville, Washington.................20
Midway, Fannin...................................7	*Montague, Montague, 16 400	*MUENSTER, Cooke, 135,
Midway, Jim Wells 24	*Montalba, Anderson, 15 110	(1,556)...................................1,585
Midway, Limestone.............................9	*MONT BELVIEU, Chambers,	Mulberry, Fannin...............................17
*MIDWAY, Madison, 20, (288) 291	156, (2,324)...........................2,741	*Muldoon, Fayette, 5 95
Midway, Red River............................40	Monte Alto, Hidalgo, (1,611) 1,678	*MULESHOE, Bailey, 216,
Midway, Smith ....NA	Monte Grande, Cameron...................97	(4,530)...................................4,620
Midway, Titus 110	Montell, Uvalde................................20	*MULLIN, Mills, 11, (175)...............180
Midway, Upshur................................20	*MONTGOMERY, Montgomery,	Mullins Prairie, Fayette...................107
Midway, Van Zandt 31	353, (489)...............................845	*Mumford, Robertson, 1 170
Midway, Polk...................................525	Monthalia, Gonzales.........................32	*MUNDAY, Knox, 43,
Midway North, Hidalgo, (3,946)...4,108	Monticello, Titus...............................20	(1,527)...................................1,432
Midway South, Hidalgo, (1,711)...1,773	*MOODY, McLennan, 75,	Munger, Limestone.............................5
Midyett, Panola..............................150	(1,400)...................................1,430	Mungerville, Dawson 25
Mikeska, Live Oak 10	Moore, Brazos................................NA	Muniz, Hidalgo, (1,106) 1,162
Mila Doce, Hidalgo, (4,907).........5,360	*Moore, Frio, 9, (644) 638	*MURCHISON, Henderson, 53,
*Milam, Sabine, 9, (1,329).............1,309	Moore Hill, Polk ....NA	(592).......................................636
*MILANO, Milam, 33, (400) 421	Moore's Crossing, Travis 25	MURPHY, Collin, 357,
Milburn, McCulloch 8	MOORE STATION, Henderson,	(3,099) 11,452
MILDRED, Navarro, 2,	0, (184)...................................185	Murray, Young..................................45
(405)..397	Mooreville, Falls...............................96	Murvaul, Panola 150
*MILES, Runnels, 50,	Mooring, Brazos 80	Mustang, Denton ....NA
(850).......................................854	Morales, Jackson..............................72	MUSTANG, Navarro, 1, (47)............54
*MILFORD, Ellis, 19, (685) 749	*MORAN, Shackelford, 13,	Mustang Mott, DeWitt.......................20
Mill Creek, Washington.....................40	(233).......................................226	MUSTANG RIDGE, Travis-Caldwell,
Miller Grove, Hopkins 115	Moravia, Lavaca 165	17, (785)................................953
MILLERS COVE, Titus, 4,	*MORGAN, Bosque, 14, (485) 539	*Myra, Cooke, 3.............................150
(120).......................................130	Morgan Creek, Burnet 126	Myrtle Springs, Van Zandt 165
*Millersview, Concho, 2 80	Morgan Farm Area, San Patricio,	**N**
Millett, La Salle 40	(484).......................................479	*NACOGDOCHES, Nacogdoches,
Millheim, Austin..............................170	*Morgan Mill, Erath, 4 206	1,415, (29,914)...................30,414
*Millican, Brazos, 6,	MORGAN'S POINT, Harris, 16,	*Nada, Colorado, 9.........................165
(108)...98	(336).......................................325	*NAPLES, Morris, 58,
*MILLSAP, Parker, 40, (353)...........362	MORGAN'S POINT RESORT, Bell,	(1,410)...................................1,349
Milo Center, Deaf Smith.....................5	53, (2,989)............................3,940	Naruna, Burnet.................................95
Milton, Lamar...................................50	Morning Glory, El Paso, (627) 636	*NASH, Bowie, 75, (2,169)...........2,346
Mims, Brazoria...............................NA	*Morse, Hansford, 3, (172)............176	Nash, Ellis..40
Mims Chapel, Marion......................NA	*MORTON, Cochran, 49,	NASSAU BAY, Harris, 201,
*Minden, Rusk, 4 150	(2,249)...................................2,175	(4,170) 3,981
*MINEOLA, Wood, 449,	Morton, Harrison...............................75	Nat, Nacogdoches.............................50
(4,550)...................................4,774	Morton Valley, Eastland 46	*NATALIA, Medina, 78,
Mineral, Bee 65	*Moscow, Polk, 8 170	(1,663)...................................1,895
*MINERAL WELLS, Palo Pinto-	Mosheim, Bosque.............................75	NAVARRO, Navarro, 1, (191).........203
Parker, 635, (16,946)..........17,174	Moss Bluff, Liberty 65	Navarro Mills, Navarro......................50
Minerva, Milam 100	Moss Hill, Liberty 180	*NAVASOTA, Grimes, 362,
Mings Chapel, Upshur......................50	Mostyn, Montgomery.........................90	(6,789) 7,192

Town, County .... Pop. 2006	Town, County .... Pop. 2006	Town, County .... Pop. 2006
Navidad, Jackson 227	New Salem, Rusk 55	*Nursery, Victoria, 5........................260
Navo, Denton.....................................35	Newsome, Camp 113	**O**
*NAZARETH, Castro, 17,	*NEW SUMMERFIELD, Cherokee,	Oakalla, Burnet..................................99
(356) 356	26, (998) 1,124	Oakdale, Hopkins ....NA
Necessity, Stephens 10	New Sweden, Travis 60	Oakdale, Polk 25
Nechanitz, Fayette............................57	New Taiton, Wharton 10	Oak Forest, Gonzales........................24
*Neches, Anderson, 6....................175	New Territory, Fort Bend,	Oak Grove, Bowie 294
*NEDERLAND, Jefferson, 779,	(13,861) 16,286	Oak Grove, Colorado.........................40
(17,422) 17,052	*NEWTON, Newton, 74,	Oak Grove, Hopkins ....NA
Needmore, Bailey 45	(2,459) 2,576	OAK GROVE, Kaufman,
Needmore, Terry 7	*New Ulm, Austin, 92....................974	0, (710)..817
*NEEDVILLE, Fort Bend,	*NEW WAVERLY, Walker, 100,	Oak Grove, Wood.............................140
135, (2,609) 3,365	(950) 830	Oak Hill, Hood 247
Negley, Red River...........................136	New Wehdem, Austin 414	Oak Hill, Rusk..................................200
Neinda, Jones....................................21	New Willard, Polk 160	*Oakhurst, San Jacinto, 8,
Nell, Live Oak 60	New York, Henderson........................60	(230) 253
Nelson City, Kendall 50	NEYLANDVILLE, Hunt, 2, (56).........60	Oak Island, Chambers....................255
Nelsonville, Austin 200	NIEDERWALD, Hays-Caldwell,	Oakland, Cherokee............................50
Nelta, Hopkins 36	17, (584)......................................416	*Oakland, Colorado 80
*Nemo, Somervell, 8........................56	Nigton, Trinity....................................87	Oakland, Van Zandt..........................26
Nesbitt, Harrison, (302) 310	Nimrod, Eastland...............................85	OAK LEAF, Ellis, 27, (1,209) 1,275
Neuville, Shelby.................................65	Nineveh, Leon..................................101	OAK POINT, Denton, 94,
*NEVADA, Collin, 48, (563) 805	Nix, Lampasas 6	(1,747)......................................2,230
*NEWARK, Wise, 56,	*NIXON, Gonzales-Wilson, 65,	OAK RIDGE, Cooke, (224)............245
(887) 1,022	(2,186) 2,402	Oak Ridge, Grayson 161
*New Baden, Robertson, 5...........150	Noack, Williamson 70	OAK RIDGE, Kaufman, 9,
NEW BERLIN, Guadalupe, 10,	Nobility, Fannin 21	(400) 450
(467) 505	Noble, Lamar 14	Oak Ridge, Nacogdoches................225
New Bielau, Colorado.......................75	Nockernut, Wilson 10	OAK RIDGE NORTH, Montgomery,
New Birthright, Hopkins ....NA	*NOCONA, Montague, 156,	194, (2,991) 3,460
New Blox, Jasper.............................NA	(3,198) 3,299	Oak Trail Shores, Hood,
*NEW BOSTON, Bowie, 204,	Nogalus Prairie, Trinity 109	(2,475)......................................2,549
(4,808) 4,657	*Nolan, Nolan, 1 47	OAK VALLEY, Navarro, 3,
*NEW BRAUNFELS, Comal-	*NOLANVILLE, Bell, 47,	(401) 442
Guadalupe, 2,498,	(2,150) 2,485	Oakville, Live Oak, 2........................260
(36,494) 48,148	*NOME, Jefferson, 31, (515) 514	*OAKWOOD, Leon, 25, (471)........481
New Bremen, Austin 125	Noodle, Jones....................................40	Oatmeal, Burnet 74
Newburg, Comanche.........................32	NOONDAY, Smith, 51, (515)...........544	*O'BRIEN, Haskell, 1, (132) 116
Newby, Leon.....................................40	Nopal, DeWitt 25	Ocee, McLennan 84
*New Caney, Montgomery,	*NORDHEIM, DeWitt, 21,	Odds, Limestone 24
205 6,800	(323) 324	*Odell, Wilbarger 100
*NEWCASTLE, Young, 22,	Norman, Williamson 40	*ODEM, San Patricio, 67,
(575) 595	Normandy, Maverick 114	(2,499)......................................2,534
NEW CHAPEL HILL, Smith, 11,	*NORMANGEE, Leon-Madison,	*ODESSA, Ector-Midland,
(553) 597	63, (719) 767	3,823, (90,943) 94,089
New Colony, Bell 12	*Normanna, Bee, 1, (121)..............183	*O'DONNELL, Lynn-Dawson,
New Colony, Cass 65	Norse, Bosque.................................110	18, (1,011) 962
New Corn Hill, Williamson 475	North Alamo, Hidalgo, (2,601) 2,122	Oenaville, Bell 108
New Davy, DeWitt..............................20	NORTH CLEVELAND, Liberty, 2,	O'Farrell, Cass..................................20
*NEW DEAL, Lubbock, 14,	(263) 258	Ogburn, Wood 10
(708) 784	Northcliff, Guadalupe, (1,819) 1,813	*OGLESBY, Coryell, 21,
NEW FAIRVIEW, Wise, 12,	North Escobares, Starr,	(458) 445
(877) 1,214	(1,692) 1,787	*Oilton, Webb, (310) 376
Newgulf, Wharton 10	Northfield, Motley................................15	Oklahoma, Montgomery ....NA
New Harmony, Shelby 40	North Hopkins, Hopkins...................NA	Oklahoma Flat, Hockley 4
New Harmony, Smith 350	NORTHLAKE, Denton, 17,	Oklahoma Lane, Parmer....................25
*NEW HOME, Lynn, 9, (320).........356	(921) 1,432	*Oklaunion, Wilbarger, 4................138
New Hope, Cherokee 50	North Pearsall, Frio, (561) 569	Okra, Eastland 20
NEW HOPE, Collin, 25,	*NORTH RICHLAND HILLS,	Ola, Kaufman.....................................65
(662) 647	Tarrant, 1,757, (55,635)......60,723	Old Boston, Bowie 100
New Hope, Jones 9	Northrup, Lee.....................................86	Old Bowling, Leon 20
New Hope, San Augustine................75	North San Pedro, Nueces, (920) 791	Old Center, Panola 83
New Hope, Smith...............................75	North Star, Archer 10	Old Dime Box, Lee 225
New Hope, Wood...............................15	*North Zulch, Madison, 14..............150	*Olden, Eastland, 6.........................113
Newlin, Hall..27	*Norton, Runnels, 1 50	Oldenburg, Fayette............................92
*NEW LONDON, Rusk, 14,	*Notrees, Ector, 2 20	*Old Glory, Stonewall, 1.................100
(987) 973	*NOVICE, Coleman, 5, (142)..........132	Old Midway, Leon............................NA
New Lynn, Lynn 4	Novice, Lamar 35	*Old Ocean, Brazoria, 10................915
New Moore, Lynn...............................10	Noxville, Kimble 3	OLD RIVER-WINFREE, Chambers,
New Mountain, Upshur 20	Nugent, Jones 41	17, (1,364) 1,620
Newport, Clay-Jack 75	Nunelee, Fannin 25	Old Salem, Bowie 50
New Salem, Palo Pinto 89	Nurillo, Hidalgo, (5,056) 5,285	Old Union, Bowie.............................238

Town, County	Pop. 2006
Old Union, Limestone	25
Oletha, Limestone	53
Olfen, Runnels	35
Olin, Hamilton	15
Olivarez, Hidalgo, (2,445)	2,545
Olivia, Calhoun	215
Ollie, Polk	5
*Olmito, Cameron, 46, (1,198)	1,248
Olmos, Guadalupe	65
OLMOS PARK, Bexar, 115, (2,343)	2,333
*OLNEY, Young, 140, (3,396)	3,278
*OLTON, Lamb, 59, (2,288)	2,389
*OMAHA, Morris, 31, (999)	979
Omen, Smith	150
*ONALASKA, Polk, 136, (1,174)	1,423
Onion Creek, Travis, (2,116)	1,969
Opdyke, Hockley	20
OPDYKE WEST, Hockley, 3, (188)	206
Oplin, Callahan	75
O'Quinn, Fayette	191
Oran, Palo Pinto	61
*ORANGE, Orange, 790, (18,643)	17,557
Orangedale, Bee	40
*Orangefield, Orange, 8	725
*ORANGE GROVE, Jim Wells, 99, (1,288)	1,423
Oranson [Chula Vista-], Cameron, (394)	405
*ORCHARD, Fort Bend, 20, (408)	492
*ORE CITY, Upshur, 64, (1,106)	1,227

Town, County	Pop. 2006
Orient, Tom Green	57
*Orla, Reeves, 2	80
Osage, Colorado	50
Osage, Coryell	30
Oscar, Bell	58
Osceola, Hill	95
Otey, Brazoria	318
*Ottine, Gonzales, 1	80
Otto, Falls	48
*Ovalo, Taylor, 2	225
*OVERTON, Rusk-Smith, 121, (2,350)	2,268
*OVILLA, Ellis-Dallas, 114, (3,405)	3,747
Owens, Brown	16
Owens, Crosby	4
Owentown, Smith	100
Owl Creek, Bell	130
Owl Ranch-Amargosa, Jim Wells, (527)	549
OYSTER CREEK, Brazoria, 39, (1,192)	1,359
*Ozona, Crockett, 122, (3,436)	3,449

P

Pacio, Delta	35
Padgett, Young	28
*PADUCAH, Cottle, 57, (1,498)	1,301
*Paige, Bastrop, 17	275
Paint Creek, Haskell	150
*PAINT ROCK, Concho, 11, (320)	313
Paisano [Edgewater-], San Patricio, (182)	182
*PALACIOS, Matagorda, 158, (5,153)	5,242
*PALESTINE, Anderson, 834, (17,598)	17,667

Town, County	Pop. 2006
PALISADES, Randall, 0, (352)	352
Palito Blanco, Jim Wells	750
*PALMER, Ellis, 79, (1,774)	2,018
PALMHURST, Hidalgo, 49, (4,872)	5,348
PALM VALLEY, Cameron, 19, (1,298)	1,228
PALMVIEW, Hidalgo, 196, (4,107)	4,889
Palmview South, Hidalgo, (6,219)	6,313
Palo Alto, Nueces	15
Paloduro, Armstrong	10
*Palo Pinto, Palo Pinto, 17	411
*Paluxy, Hood	76
*PAMPA, Gray, 678, (17,887)	17,282
Pancake, Coryell	11
Pandale, Val Verde	25
*Pandora, Wilson	125
*PANHANDLE, Carson, 79, (2,589)	2,666
*Panna Maria, Karnes, 4	45
*Panola, Panola, 6	305
PANORAMA, Montgomery, 29, (1,965)	2,210
*PANTEGO, Tarrant, 441, (2,318)	2,270
Panther Junction, Brewster	112
Papalote, Bee	75
*PARADISE, Wise, 58, (459)	512
*PARIS, Lamar, 1,215, (25,898)	26,474
Parita, Bexar	NA
Park, Fayette	25
PARKER, Collin, 64, (1,379)	2,085

Downtown Odell in Wilbarger County consists of a post office and grocery. Robert Plocheck photo.

Town, County ....Pop. 2006	Town, County ....Pop. 2006	Town, County ....Pop. 2006
Parker, Johnson................................21	Perryville, Wood 35	Placid, McCulloch 32
Park Springs, Wise ....NA	Personville, Limestone 50	Plain, Houston 30
Parsley Hill, Wilbarger 25	Pert, Anderson..................................20	*PLAINS, Yoakum, 46,
Parvin, Denton..................................44	Peters, Austin 150	(1,450) 1,477
*PASADENA, Harris, 3,480,	*PETERSBURG, Hale, 39,	*PLAINVIEW, Hale, 832,
(141,674) 147,926	(1,262) 1,214	(22,336) 21,887
Patillo, Erath 10	Peter's Prairie, Red River................40	*PLANO, Collin-Denton, 10,986,
Patman Switch, Cass 40	Petersville, DeWitt 38	(222,030) 255,593
Patonia, Polk 15	*PETROLIA, Clay, 17, (782) 769	*Plantersville, Grimes, 32 260
Patricia, Dawson..............................40	PETRONILA, Nueces, 5, (83)..........78	Plaska, Hall......................................20
Patroon, Shelby 25	Petteway, Robertson 25	PLEAK, Fort Bend, 24,
*PATTISON, Waller, 27,	Pettibone, Milam..............................25	(947) 1,151
(447) 476	Pettit, Hockley..................................15	Pleasant Farms, Ector 800
Pattonfield, Upshur 20	*Pettus, Bee, 12, (608) 809	Pleasant Grove, Bastrop ....NA
PATTON VILLAGE, Montgomery,	*Petty, Lamar, 2 130	Pleasant Grove, Falls 35
16, (1,391) 1,572	Petty, Lynn..8	Pleasant Grove, Hopkins ....NA
*Pattonville, Lamar, 6....................180	Peyton, Blanco 30	Pleasant Grove, Limestone 20
Pawelekville, Karnes 105	*PFLUGERVILLE, Travis, 1,090,	Pleasant Grove, Upshur 35
*Pawnee, Bee, 3, (201) 280	(16,335) 28,520	Pleasant Grove, Wood 30
Paxton, Shelby 50	Phalba, Van Zandt............................73	Pleasant Hill, Eastland....................15
Paynes Corner, Gaines 18	*PHARR, Hidalgo, 1,384,	Pleasant Hill, Nacogdoches..........250
PAYNE SPRINGS, Henderson,	(46,660) 60,560	Pleasant Hill, Yoakum....................40
17, (683) 716	Phelan, Bastrop ....NA	*PLEASANTON, Atascosa, 427,
Peach Creek, Brazos......................150	Phelps, Walker..................................98	(8,266) 9,151
Peacock, Stonewall 100	Phillipsburg, Washington 75	Pleasant Ridge, Leon ....NA
Peadenville, Palo Pinto..................15	Pickens, Henderson 20	Pleasant Springs, Leon ....NA
Pearl, Coryell..................................50	Pickett, Navarro................................30	Pleasant Valley, Garza....................5
*PEARLAND, Brazoria-Harris,	*Pickton, Hopkins, 5 300	PLEASANT VALLEY, Wichita,
2,450, (37,640) 59,994	Pidcoke, Coryell..............................50	0, (408) 382
Pearl City, DeWitt 4	Piedmont, Grimes............................50	*Pledger, Matagorda......................265
*PEARSALL, Frio, 202,	Piedmont, Upshur............................20	Pluck, Polk..53
(7,157) 7,645	*Pierce, Wharton, 3 51	*Plum, Fayette, 7 145
Pearson, Medina 24	Pike, Collin..47	Plum Creek, Freestone..................NA
Pearsons Chapel, Houston..............95	Pilgrim, Gonzales 22	PLUM GROVE, Liberty, 3,
Pear Valley, McCulloch....................37	Pilgrim Rest, Rains 72	(930) 990
*Peaster, Parker, 3..........................102	Pilot Grove, Grayson 48	Pluto, Ellis..30
Pecan Acres, Tarrant-Wise,	Pilot Knob, Travis............................NA	Poetry, Kaufman ....NA
(2,289) 2,396	*PILOT POINT, Denton, 186,	*POINT, Rains, 47, (792) 969
*PECAN GAP, Delta-Fannin, 9,	(3,538) 4,159	*POINT BLANK, San Jacinto, 9,
(214) 202	Pine, Camp..78	(559) 639
Pecan Grove, Fort Bend,	Pine Branch, Red River....................40	*POINT COMFORT, Calhoun, 50,
(13,551) 16,473	Pine Forest, Hopkins 100	(781) 713
PECAN HILL, Ellis, 6,	PINE FOREST, Orange, 11,	Point Enterprise, Limestone 200
(672) 689	(632) 584	POINT VENTURE, Travis, 6,
Pecan Plantation, Hood,	Pine Grove, Cherokee 30	(nc) 470
(3,544) 3,306	Pine Grove, Newton 160	Polar, Kent..15
Pecan Wells, Hamilton 6	Pinehill, Rusk....................................70	*Pollok, Angelina, 25......................300
*PECOS, Reeves, 257,	*Pinehurst, Montgomery, 94,	*PONDER, Denton, 55, (607) 837
(9,501) 8,258	(4,266) 4,937	Ponta, Cherokee..............................50
Peeltown, Kaufman ....NA	PINEHURST, Orange, 185,	*Pontotoc, Mason, 4 125
Peerless, Hopkins............................NA	(2,274) 2,041	Poole, Rains......................................50
*Peggy, Atascosa, 2..........................22	Pine Island, Jefferson 350	*Poolville, Parker, 15 520
Pelham, Navarro..............................75	PINE ISLAND, Waller, 0,	Port Acres, Jefferson
PELICAN BAY, Tarrant, 5,	(849) 836	......................[part of Port Arthur]
(1,505) 1,734	*PINELAND, Sabine, 34,	Port Alto, Calhoun............................45
*Pendleton, Bell, 1 369	(980) 896	*PORT ARANSAS, Nueces, 363,
*PENELOPE, Hill, 5, (211)..............217	Pine Mills, Wood..............................75	(3,370) 3,398
*PEÑITAS, Hidalgo, 78,	Pine Prairie, Walker ....NA	*PORT ARTHUR, Jefferson,
(1,167) 1,309	Pine Springs, Culberson 20	1,230, (57,755) 55,574
*Pennington, Trinity-Houston, 4........67	Pine Springs, Smith 150	*Port Bolivar, Galveston, 73..........900
*Penwell, Ector, 5 41	Pineview, Wood................................10	*Porter, Montgomery, 271 4,200
Peoria, Hill 105	Pinewood Estates, Hardin,	Porter Heights, Montgomery,
*Pep, Hockley....................................3	(1,633) 1,698	(1,490) 1,598
Percilla, Houston 95	Piney, Austin....................................60	Porter Springs, Houston 50
Perezville [Abram-], Hidalgo,	PINEY POINT VILLAGE, Harris,	*PORT ISABEL, Cameron, 236,
(5,444) 5,664	55, (3,380) 3,298	(4,865) 5,117
PERNITAS POINT, Live Oak-Jim	Pioneer, Eastland 40	*PORTLAND, San Patricio, 468,
Wells, 0, (269) 280	*Pipe Creek, Bandera, 270..............NA	(14,827) 16,100
*Perrin, Jack, 8 300	Pitner Junction, Rusk......................20	*PORT LAVACA, Calhoun, 485,
Perry, Falls..76	*PITTSBURG, Camp, 246,	(12,035) 11,883
*PERRYTON, Ochiltree, 377,	(4,347) 4,626	*Port Mansfield, Willacy, 10,
(7,774) 8,007	*Placedo, Victoria, 5 760	(415) 392

Town, County ....Pop. 2006	Town, County ....Pop. 2006	Town, County ....Pop. 2006
*PORT NECHES, Jefferson, 383, (13,601) 13,118	Punkin Center, Dawson 30	Rattan, Delta.....................................10
*Port O'Connor , Calhoun, 43......1,184	Punkin Center, Eastland 12	*RAVENNA, Fannin, 11, (215)........236
Port Sullivan, Milam.........................15	*Purdon, Navarro, 10....................133	Rayburn, Liberty 60
Porvenir, Presidio ....NA	Purley, Franklin 100	Rayland, Foard 30
Posey, Hopkins...............................NA	*Purmela, Coryell, 4..........................50	*RAYMONDVILLE, Willacy, 197, (9,733)..9,683
Posey, Lubbock 225	Pursley, Navarro 40	Ray Point, Live Oak.........................200
*POST, Garza, 248, (3,708) 3,709	Purves, Erath 50	*Raywood, Liberty, 11 231
Post Oak, Blanco.............................10	*PUTNAM, Callahan, 5, (88) 85	Razor, Lamar 20
Postoak, Jack 79	*PYOTE, Ward, 4, (131) 148	*Reagan, Falls, 2............................208
Postoak, Lamar 65	**Q**	Reagan Wells, Uvalde 20
Post Oak, Lee..................................100	*Quail, Collingsworth, 1, (33)............37	Reagor Springs, Ellis 250
POST OAK BEND, Kaufman, 7, (404) 580	*QUANAH, Hardeman, 107, (3,022) 2,846	*Realitos, Duval, 1, (209)...............204
Post Oak Point, Austin......................60	Quarry, Washington ....NA	Red Bank, Bowie 125
*POTEET, Atascosa, 123, (3,305) 3,440	Quarterway, Hale..............................24	Red Bluff, Jackson............................45
*POTH, Wilson, 63, (1,850) 2,125	*QUEEN CITY, Cass, 77, (1,613) 1,616	Red Bluff, Reeves.............................40
Potosi, Taylor, (1,664) 1,700	*Quemado, Maverick, 13, (243) 260	Red Branch, Leon ....NA
*POTTSBORO, Grayson, 150, (1,579) 2,251	Quicksand, Newton ....NA	Red Cut Heights, Bowie 563
*Pottsville, Hamilton.......................105	Quihi, Medina 125	*Redford, Presidio, (132)...............129
*Powderly, Lamar, 44......................185	*QUINLAN, Hunt, 205, (1,370) 1,460	Red Gate, Hidalgo ....NA
*POWELL, Navarro, 10, (105) 110	QUINTANA, Brazoria, 3, (38) 34	Red Hill, Cass 28
*POYNOR, Henderson, 21, (314) 339	*QUITAQUE, Briscoe, 19, (432) 383	Red Hill, Limestone 20
Prado Verde, El Paso, (200)...........201	*QUITMAN, Wood, 205, (2,030) 2,065	Red Lake, Freestone ....NA
Praesel, Milam................................115	**R**	Redland, Angelina 250
Praha, Fayette 90	Rabb, Nueces 20	Redland, Leon 35
Prairie Chapel, McLennan 35	Rabbs Prairie, Fayette......................79	Redland, Van Zandt...........................45
Prairie Dell, Bell 34	Raccoon Bend, Austin 775	RED LICK, Bowie, (853).................874
*Prairie Hill, Limestone, 3 150	Rachal, Brooks 36	*RED OAK, Ellis, 424, (4,301) 7,986
Prairie Hill, Washington ....NA	Radar Base, Maverick, (162)...........168	Red Ranger, Bell 30
*Prairie Lea, Caldwell, 8 255	Radium, Jones 10	*Red Rock, Bastrop, 19..................100
Prairie Point, Cooke..........................22	Ragtown, Lamar 30	Red Springs, Baylor..........................42
*PRAIRIE VIEW, Waller, 29, (4,410) 4,235	*Rainbow, Somervell, 9 121	Red Springs, Smith..........................350
Prairieville, Kaufman.........................50	Raisin, Victoria 50	Redtown, Anderson 30
*PREMONT, Jim Wells, 84, (2,772) 2,789	Raleigh, Navarro 40	Redtown, Angelina 50
*PRESIDIO, Presidio, 101, (4,167) 4,985	*RALLS, Crosby, 52, (2,252) 2,154	*REDWATER, Bowie, 20, (872) 876
Preston, Grayson.............................325	Ramireno, Zapata..............................25	Redwood, Guadalupe, (3,586) 3,810
*Price, Rusk, 4................................275	Ramirez, Duval 40	Reeds Settlement, Red River 50
*Priddy, Mills, 11 215	Ranchette Estates, Willacy, (133)...136	Reedville, Caldwell 432
PRIMERA, Cameron, 20, (2,723) 3,653	Ranchito El Calaboz [Encantada-], Cameron, (2,100) 2,255	Reese, Cherokee...............................75
Primrose, Van Zandt.........................26	Ranchitos Las Lomas, Webb, (334) 364	Reese Center, Lubbock, (42)...........42
*PRINCETON, Collin, 174, (3,477) 4,491	Rancho Alegre, Jim Wells, (1,775) 1,835	Refuge, Houston...............................20
Pringle, Hutchinson 20	Rancho Banquete, Nueces, (469) 431	*REFUGIO, Refugio, 136, (2,941) 2,780
Pritchett, Upshur.............................125	Rancho Chico, San Patricio, (309) 303	Regency, Mills 25
*Proctor, Comanche, 3 228	Rancho Penitas West, Webb, (520) 513	Rehburg, Washington ....NA
*PROGRESO, Hidalgo, 51, (4,851) 5,739	RANCHO VIEJO, Cameron, 47, (1,754) 1,881	Reid Hope King, Cameron, (802) 815
PROGRESO LAKES, Hidalgo, 13, (234) 258	Rand, Kaufman..................................70	Reilly Springs, Hopkins....................75
Progress, Bailey 49	Randado, Jim Hogg............................6	Rek Hill, Fayette 168
Prospect, Rains 40	*Randolph, Fannin, 1........................70	*REKLAW, Cherokee-Rusk, 11, (327) 356
*PROSPER, Collin, 183, (2,097) 4,686	*RANGER, Eastland, 103, (2,584) 2,519	Relampago, Hidalgo, (104).............108
Providence, Floyd.............................78	RANGERVILLE, Cameron, 0, (203) 198	Rendon, Tarrant, (9,022) 9,436
Providence, Polk.............................350	Rankin, Ellis 10	*RENO, Lamar, 4, (2,767) 3,046
Pruitt, Cass 25	*RANKIN, Upton, 38, (800)............698	RENO, Parker, 4, (2,441) 2,613
Pruitt, Van Zandt...............................45	RANSOM CANYON, Lubbock, 0, (1,011) 1,074	Retreat, Grimes 25
Puerto Rico, Hidalgo.........................91	Ratamosa, Cameron, (218)............217	RETREAT, Navarro, 0, (339) 357
Pullman, Potter 31	*Ratcliff, Houston, 3........................106	Retta, Tarrant-Johnson 780
Pumphrey, Runnels 15	Ratibor, Bell 22	Reynard, Houston.............................75
Pumpkin, San Jacinto....................150		Rhea, Parmer 98
Pumpville, Val Verde.........................25		Rhea Mills, Collin.............................25
		Rhineland, Knox 120
		*RHOME, Wise, 80, (551) 928
		Rhonesboro, Upshur 40
		Ricardo, Kleberg...........................1,641
		*RICE, Navarro, 39, (798) 929
		Rice's Crossing, Williamson 130
		*Richards, Grimes, 8 300

Autumn in Roxton in Lamar County. Robert Plocheck photo.

Town, County .... Pop. 2006	Town, County .... Pop. 2006	Town, County .... Pop. 2006
*RICHARDSON, Dallas-Collin, 5,422, (91,802) 98,857	Rivers End, Brazoria......................NA	*Rockwood, Coleman, 2 80
*RICHLAND, Navarro, 7, (291) 308	*RIVERSIDE, Walker, 33, (425) 503	Rocky Branch, Morris 135
Richland, Rains 100	River Spur [Chula Vista-], Zavala, (400) 357	Rocky Creek, Blanco 20
*RICHLAND HILLS, Tarrant, 325, (8,132) 7,967	*Riviera, Kleberg, 29...................1,064	ROCKY MOUND, Camp, 0, (93) 101
*RICHLAND SPRINGS, San Saba, 5, (350) 345	Riviera Beach, Kleberg..................155	Rocky Point, Burnet.......................152
*RICHMOND, Fort Bend, 720, (11,081) 13,796	Roach, Cass.....................................50	Roddy, Van Zandt............................29
RICHWOOD, Brazoria, 81, (3,012) 3,338	Roane, Navarro 120	Rodney, Navarro..............................15
Riderville, Panola..............................50	*ROANOKE, Denton, 390, (2,810) 3,777	Roeder, Titus 110
Ridge, Mills 25	*Roans Prairie, Grimes, 3................64	Roganville, Jasper..........................100
Ridge, Robertson.............................67	*ROARING SPRINGS, Motley, 17, (265) 247	*ROGERS, Bell, 43, (1,117) 1,162
Ridgeway, Hopkins 54	Robbins, Leon 20	Rogers, Taylor 151
Ridings, Fannin................................10	*ROBERT LEE, Coke, 51, (1,171) 1,159	Rolling Hills, Potter 1,000
*RIESEL, McLennan, 47, (973) 1,007	Robertson, Crosby...........................10	Rolling Hills, Waller........................NA
Rincon, Starr.....................................5	ROBINSON, McLennan, 346, (7,845) 8,611	Rolling Meadows, Gregg 362
*Ringgold, Montague, 1 100	*ROBSTOWN, Nueces, 401, (12,727) 13,195	ROLLINGWOOD, Travis, 127, (1,403) 1,283
RIO BRAVO, Webb, 50, (5,553) 5,955	*ROBY, Fisher, 24, (673) 677	*ROMA-Los Saenz, Starr, 265, (9,617) 11,492
*Rio Frio, Real, 2 50	*Rochelle, McCulloch, 6 163	Roma Creek, Starr, (610) 646
*RIO GRANDE CITY, Starr, 369, (11,923) 14,044	*ROCHESTER, Haskell, 14, (378) 334	ROMAN FOREST, Montgomery, 0, (1,279) 3,121
Rio Grande Village, Brewster 9	Rock Bluff, Burnet............................90	*Romayor, Liberty, 6 135
*RIO HONDO, Cameron, 52, (1,942) 2,172	Rock Creek, Somervell......................70	Romney, Eastland 12
*Riomedina, Medina, 7 60	*ROCKDALE, Milam, 272, (5,439) 5,688	*Roosevelt, Kimble, 2 14
Rios, Duval 75	Rockett, Ellis.................................300	Roosevelt, Lubbock 362
*RIO VISTA, Johnson, 49, (656) 759	Rockford, Lamar 30	*ROPESVILLE, Hockley, 14, (517) 539
*RISING STAR, Eastland, 48, (835) 839	Rockhouse, Austin 100	Rosalie, Red River..........................100
Rita, Burleson..................................50	*Rock Island, Colorado, 1..............160	*Rosanky, Bastrop, 8 210
Riverby, Fannin................................15	Rockland, Tyler................................98	*ROSCOE, Nolan, 30, (1,378) 1,306
River Crest Estates, Angelina.........250	Rockne, Bastrop 400	*ROSEBUD, Falls, 79, (1,493) 1,390
River Hill, Panola...........................125	*ROCKPORT, Aransas, 597, (7,385) 8,705	ROSE CITY, Orange, 28, (519) 497
RIVER OAKS, Tarrant, 158, (6,985) 6,917	*ROCKSPRINGS, Edwards, 48, (1,285) 1,313	Rose Hill, Harris...........................3,500
	*ROCKWALL, Rockwall, 1,580, (17,976) 29,198	Rose Hill, San Jacinto 30
		ROSE HILL ACRES, Hardin, 0, (480) 471
		*ROSENBERG, Fort Bend, 906, (24,043) 31,003

Town, County ....Pop. 2006	Town, County ....Pop. 2006	Town, County ....Pop. 2006
Rosevine, Sabine 50	*SAINT JO, Montague, 42,	*San Isidro, Starr, 8,
Rosewood, Upshur.......................100	(977) 988	(270) 277
*Rosharon, Brazoria, 89 ....NA	St. John Colony, Caldwell..............150	San Jose, Duval 15
Rosita, Duval 25	St. Lawrence, Glasscock.................35	*SAN JUAN, Hidalgo, 523,
Rosita North, Maverick,	St. Mary's Colony, Bastrop ....NA	(26,229) 32,747
(3,400) 3,591	ST. PAUL, Collin, 38, (630)............800	SAN LEANNA, Travis, 0,
Rosita South, Maverick, (2,574) ..2,709	St. Paul, San Patricio,	(384) 522
*ROSS, McLennan, 10,	(542) 526	San Leon, Galveston,
(228) 235	*SALADO, Bell, 323,	(4,365) 4,633
*ROSSER, Kaufman, 5,	(3,475) 3,663	*San Manuel-Linn, Hidalgo, 11,
(379) 415	Salem, Cherokee............................20	(958) 951
*Rosston, Cooke, 2...........................75	Salem, Grimes................................54	*SAN MARCOS, Hays-Caldwell,
Rossville, Atascosa.......................200	Salem, Newton................................85	1,717, (34,733) 47,005
*ROTAN, Fisher, 58, (1,611)........1,573	Salesville, Palo Pinto......................88	SAN PATRICIO, San Patricio,
Rough Creek, San Saba...................15	Saline, Menard 70	0, (318) 303
Round House, Navarro.....................40	*Salineño, Starr, (304) 324	San Pedro, Cameron, (668) 681
*ROUND MOUNTAIN, Blanco, 4,	Salmon, Anderson 20	*SAN PERLITA, Willacy, 1,
(111) 111	*Salt Flat, Hudspeth, 1...................35	(680) 713
Round Mountain, Travis...................59	Salt Gap, McCulloch........................25	San Roman, Starr.............................5
Round Prairie, Navarro....................40	*Saltillo, Hopkins, 6.......................200	*SAN SABA, San Saba, 156,
*ROUND ROCK, Williamson-Travis,	Samaria, Navarro 90	(2,637) 2,577
3,191, (61,136).................89,865	*Samnorwood, Collingsworth,	SANSOM PARK, Tarrant, 89,
Round Timber, Baylor........................2	(39) 40	(4,181) 4,326
*ROUND TOP, Fayette, 67,	Sample, Gonzales 16	*SANTA ANNA, Coleman, 55,
(77) 80	Sam Rayburn, Jasper.....................600	(1,081) 1,008
Roundup, Hockley 20	*SAN ANGELO, Tom Green,	Santa Anna, Starr 20
Rowden, Callahan 30	3,562, (88,439) 87,212	Santa Catarina, Starr.......................15
*Rowena, Runnels, 12....................349	*SAN ANTONIO, Bexar, 41,360,	SANTA CLARA, Guadalupe, 18,
*ROWLETT, Dallas-Rockwall,	(1,144,646) 1,274,607	(889) 922
1,737, (44,503)..................54,786	San Antonio Prairie, Burleson..........20	Santa Cruz, Starr, (630)................668
*ROXTON, Lamar, 16,	*SAN AUGUSTINE, San Augustine,	*Santa Elena, Starr, 1 64
(694) 714	112, (2,475) 2,496	*SANTA FE, Galveston, 410,
Royalty, Ward 27	*SAN BENITO, Cameron, 612,	(9,548) 10,629
*ROYSE CITY, Rockwall-Collin,	(23,444) 25,574	*Santa Maria, Cameron, 1,
312, (2,957) 6,542	San Carlos, Hidalgo, (2,650) 2,759	(846) 872
Rucker, Comanche 28	San Carlos, Starr 10	Santa Monica, Willacy, (78).............76
Rucker's Bridge, Lamar.....................20	Sanco, Coke 15	*SANTA ROSA, Cameron, 43,
Rugby, Red River 24	SANCTUARY, Parker, 30,	(2,833) 3,382
Ruidosa, Presidio 18	(256) 589	*Santo, Palo Pinto, 22 445
*RULE, Haskell, 19, (698) 618	Sandbranch, Dallas 400	*San Ygnacio, Zapata, 2,
Rumley, Lampasas 8	*Sanderson, Terrell, 17,	(853) 961
RUNAWAY BAY, Wise, 25,	(861) 818	*Saragosa, Reeves, 1....................185
(1,104) 1,261	Sand Flat, Johnson..........................NA	*Saratoga, Hardin, 8 1,000
*RUNGE, Karnes, 30,	Sand Flat, Rains 100	Sardis, Ellis....................................60
(1,080) 1,003	Sand Flat, Smith 100	Sargent, Matagorda.......................900
Runn, Hidalgo.................................NA	Sand Flat, Leon 32	*Sarita, Kenedy, 5.........................185
Rural Shade, Navarro.......................30	Sandhill, Floyd 33	Saron, Trinity...................................5
Rushing, Navarro.............................10	Sand Hill, Upshur.............................75	Saspamco, Wilson.........................443
*RUSK, Cherokee, 180,	*Sandia, Jim Wells, 28,	*Satin, Falls, 1 86
(5,085) 5,145	(431) 461	Sattler, Comal.................................NA
Russell, Leon 27	*SAN DIEGO, Duval-Jim Wells,	Saturn, Gonzales.............................15
Rutersville, Fayette........................137	110, (4,753) 4,621	*SAVOY, Fannin, 41, (850) 845
Ruth Springs, Henderson 120	Sandlin, Stonewall 3	Sayers, Bexar ....NA
*Rye, Liberty, 8 150	Sandoval, Williamson.......................60	Sayersville, Bastrop........................NA
	Sand Springs, Howard.................1,000	Scatter Branch, Hunt ....NA
S	Sandusky, Grayson 15	Scenic Oaks, Bexar, (3,279).......3,209
Sabanno, Eastland 12	Sandy, Blanco................................150	Schattel, Frio 30
*SABINAL, Uvalde, 67,	Sandy, Limestone 5	*SCHERTZ, Guadalupe-Comal-
(1,586) 1,804	Sandy Harbor, Llano........................85	Bexar, 796, (18,694)..........28,180
*Sabine Pass, Jefferson, 24	Sandy Hill, Washington....................50	Schicke Point, Calhoun 70
.....................[part of Port Arthur]	Sandy Hollow-Escondidas, Nueces,	Schroeder, Goliad.........................347
*SACHSE, Dallas, Collin, 446,	(433) 354	*SCHULENBURG, Fayette, 240,
(9,751) 17,346	SANDY POINT, Brazoria, (nc) 250	(2,699) 2,586
*Sacul, Nacogdoches, 2 150	*San Elizario, El Paso, 36,	Schumansville, Guadalupe............678
*SADLER, Grayson, 20,	(11,046) 11,958	Schwab City, Polk.........................120
(404) 425	*SAN FELIPE, Austin, 17,	*Schwertner, Williamson, 3.............175
Sagerton, Haskell 171	(868) 907	Science Hall, Jasper.......................NA
*SAGINAW, Tarrant, 508,	*SANFORD, Hutchinson, 12,	Scissors, Hidalgo, (2,805) 3,050
(12,374) 16,652	(203) 197	*SCOTLAND, Archer, 12,
St. Elmo, Freestone........................NA	San Gabriel, Milam 70	(438) 445
St. Francis, Potter............................39	*SANGER, Denton, 285,	*SCOTTSVILLE, Harrison, 8,
*ST. HEDWIG, Bexar, 92,	(4,534) 6,398	(263) 257
(1,875) 2,139		

Town, County .... Pop. 2006	Town, County .... Pop. 2006	Town, County .... Pop. 2006
Scranton, Eastland 40	Seven Sisters, Duval 60	Shiloh, Bastrop ....NA
*Scroggins, Franklin, 20 150	Sexton, Sabine 29	Shiloh, Leon.....................................NA
*SCURRY, Kaufman, 110,	*SEYMOUR, Baylor, 157,	Shiloh, Limestone 250
(nc) 629	(2,908) 2,845	*SHINER, Lavaca, 144,
*SEABROOK, Harris, 523,	Shady Grove , Burnet...................114	(2,070) 2,028
(9,443) 11,133	Shady Grove, Cherokee 30	Shirley, Hopkins...............................NA
*SEADRIFT, Calhoun, 65,	Shady Grove, Houston 83	*Shiro, Grimes, 4 210
(1,352) 1,384	Shady Grove, Panola 45	Shive, Hamilton 60
*SEAGOVILLE, Dallas, 388,	Shady Grove, Smith 250	SHOREACRES, Harris,
(10,823) 11,218	Shady Grove, Upshur 40	(1,488) 1,557
*SEAGRAVES, Gaines, 61,	Shady Hollow, Travis, (5,140)......4,922	Short, Shelby.....................................15
(2,334) 2,446	Shady Oaks, Henderson 300	Shovel Mountain, Burnet 148
Seale, Robertson..............................60	SHADY SHORES, Denton,	*Sidney, Comanche, 3 148
*SEALY, Austin, 347,	77, (1,461) 1,986	Sienna Plantation, Fort Bend,
(5,248) 6,664	Shafter, Presidio 57	(1,896) 2,237
Seaton, Bell 60	*SHALLOWATER, Lubbock,	*Sierra Blanca, Hudspeth, 12,
Seawillow, Caldwell 100	98, (2,086) 2,279	(533) 572
*Sebastian, Willacy, 19,	*SHAMROCK, Wheeler, 110,	Siesta Shores, Zapata, (890).......1,001
(1,864) 1,861	(2,029) 1,966	Silas, Shelby.....................................75
Sebastopol, Trinity 120	Shangri La, Burnet.........................108	Siloam, Bowie...................................50
Seco Mines, Maverick 692	Shankleville, Newton ....NA	*SILSBEE, Hardin, 343,
Security, Montgomery.....................200	Shannon, Clay 20	(6,393) 6,416
Sedalia, Collin...................................24	Sharp, Milam 52	*Silver, Coke, 2 34
Segno, Polk.......................................80	SHAVANO PARK, Bexar, 97,	Silver City, Milam 25
Segovia, Kimble................................12	(1,754) 2,946	Silver City, Navarro 100
*SEGUIN, Guadalupe, 1,196,	Shawnee Prairie, Angelina 20	Silver City, Red River........................25
(22,011) 24,783	Shaws Bend, Colorado...................100	Silver Creek Village, Burnet...........300
Sejita, Duval 22	*Sheffield, Pecos, 11 322	Silver Lake, Van Zandt 42
Selden, Erath.......................................7	Shelby, Austin 300	*SILVERTON, Briscoe, 37,
Selfs, Fannin......................................30	*Shelbyville, Shelby, 25 600	(771) 740
SELMA, Bexar-Guadalupe-	Sheldon, Harris, (1,831) 1,820	Silver Valley, Coleman 20
Comal, 219, (788).................2,092	SHENANDOAH, Montgomery,	Simmons, Live Oak 65
*Selman City [Turnertown-], Rusk,	174, (1,503) 2,337	*Simms, Bowie, 10 240
7 271	Shep, Taylor......................................60	Simms, Deaf Smith............................10
*SEMINOLE, Gaines, 238,	*SHEPHERD, San Jacinto, 111,	*SIMONTON, Fort Bend, 45,
(5,910) 6,047	(2,029) 2,342	(718) 862
Sempronius, Austin...........................25	*Sheridan, Colorado, 13 225	Simpsonville, Matagorda 6
Senior, Bexar.....................................NA	*SHERMAN, Grayson, 1,719,	Simpsonville, Upshur.......................100
Serbin, Lee 109	(35,082) 39,256	Sims, Brazos ....NA
Serenada, Williamson, (1,847) 1,800	Sherry, Red River 15	Sinclair City, Smith...........................NA
Seth Ward, Hale, (1,926).............2,001	Sherwood, Irion 170	Singleton, Grimes 47
SEVEN OAKS, Polk, 7, (131).........132	Sherwood Shores, Bell...................774	*SINTON, San Patricio, 219,
Seven Pines, Gregg-Upshur.............50	Sherwood Shores, Burnet 920	(5,676) 5,514
*SEVEN POINTS, Henderson,	Sherwood Shores, Grayson 1,590	Sipe Springs, Comanche...................70
113, (1,145) 1,262	Shields, Coleman 13	Sisterdale, Kendall..........................110

The old Route 66 through Shamrock with the landmark art deco gas station. Robert Plocheck photo.

CITIES & TOWNS

Town, County ....Pop. 2006	Town, County ....Pop. 2006	Town, County ....Pop. 2006
Sivells Bend, Cooke 36	South Toledo Bend, Newton,	*STERLING CITY, Sterling, 38,
Six Mile, Calhoun............................300	(576) 486	(1,081) 1,057
Skeeterville, San Saba 10	Southton, Bexar............................113	Stewards Mill, Freestone 22
*SKELLYTOWN, Carson, 11,	*Spade, Lamb, 4, (100) 99	Stewart, Rusk 15
(610) 595	Spanish Fort, Montague 50	Stiles, Reagan 4
*Skidmore, Bee, 11, (1,013) 1,212	Sparenberg, Dawson.......................20	Stillwell Store, Brewster.....................2
Slate Shoals, Lamar 10	Sparks, Bell 40	*STINNETT, Hutchinson, 51,
*SLATON, Lubbock, 184,	Sparks, El Paso, (2,974).............3,168	(1,936) 1,853
(6,109) 5,918	Speaks, Lavaca................................60	Stith, Jones.......................................50
Slayden, Gonzales 10	*SPEARMAN, Hansford, 123,	*STOCKDALE, Wilson, 77,
Slide, Lubbock................................245	(3,021) 2,976	(1,398) 1,567
*Slidell, Wise, 4..............................175	Specht Store, Bexar 20	Stockholm, Hidalgo..........................50
Sloan, San Saba...............................30	Speegleville, McLennan 1,655	Stockman, Shelby 55
Slocum, Anderson 250	*Spicewood, Burnet, 161 2,000	Stoneburg, Montague 51
Smetana, Brazos 80	Spider Mountain, Burnet..................92	Stone City, Brazos ....NA
*SMILEY, Gonzales, 17, (453)........466	Spiller's Store, Leon ....NA	Stoneham, Grimes.............................15
Smithland, Marion...........................179	*SPLENDORA, Montgomery, 132,	*Stonewall, Gillespie, 29, (469) 525
Smith Point, Chambers....................180	(1,275) 1,576	Stony, Denton....................................25
Smiths Bend, Bosque ....NA	SPOFFORD, Kinney, 0, (75) 72	Stout, Wood.....................................302
Smithson Valley, Comal ....NA	Spraberry, Midland 46	*Stowell, Chambers, 13,
*SMITHVILLE, Bastrop, 276,	*Spring, Harris, 2,230,	(1,572) 1,741
(3,901) 4,282	(36,385) 37,285	Stranger, Falls 27
Smithwick, Burnet...........................102	*Spring Branch, Comal, 171 ....NA	*STRATFORD, Sherman, 76,
*SMYER, Hockley, 6, (480) 490	Spring Creek, Hutchinson...............139	(1,991) 2,199
Smyrna, Cass 215	Spring Creek, San Saba...................20	Stratton, DeWitt 25
Smyrna, Rains 25	Springdale, Cass..............................55	*STRAWN, Palo Pinto, 35,
*SNOOK, Burleson, 22, (568).........561	Springfield, Anderson 30	(739) 749
Snow Hill, Collin...............................23	Spring Garden-Tierra Verde, Nueces,	Streeter, Mason 85
Snow Hill, Upshur.............................75	(693) 602	*STREETMAN, Freestone, 21,
*SNYDER, Scurry, 471,	Spring Hill, Bowie 209	(203) 209
(10,783) 10,493	Spring Hill, Navarro 60	String Prairie, Bastrop 125
*SOCORRO, El Paso, 508,	Spring Hill, San Jacinto 38	Stringtown, Newton ....NA
(27,152)................................30,672	*SPRINGLAKE, Lamb, 11,	Structure, Williamson.......................50
Soldier Mound, Dickens....................10	(135) 134	Stuart Place, Cameron 990
Solis, Cameron, (545)....................551	*SPRINGTOWN, Parker, 290,	Stubblefield, Houston 15
*SOMERSET, Bexar, 75,	(2,062) 2,468	Stubbs, Kaufman ....NA
(1,550) 1,727	SPRING VALLEY, Harris, 112,	*Study Butte-Terlingua, Brewster,
*SOMERVILLE, Burleson, 89,	(3,611) 3,457	33, (267) 275
(1,704) 1,690	Spring Valley, McLennan 400	Sturgeon, Cooke...............................10
Sommer's Mill, Bell 27	Sprinkle, Travis ....NA	Styx, Kaufman ....NA
*SONORA, Sutton, 183,	*SPUR, Dickens, 51,	*Sublime, Lavaca..............................75
(2,924) 3,067	(1,088) 1,119	*SUDAN, Lamb, 25,
*SOUR LAKE, Hardin, 113,	*Spurger, Tyler, 12 590	(1,039) 1,042
(1,667) 1,785	Stacy, McCulloch 20	Sugar Hill, Titus 150
South Alamo, Hidalgo, (3,101)....3,233	Staff, Eastland 65	*SUGAR LAND, Fort Bend,
*South Bend, Young, 3 140	*STAFFORD, Fort Bend-Harris,	3,274, (63,328) 85,101
South Bosque, McLennan 1,523	1,492, (15,681) 20,510	Sugar Valley, Matagorda..................47
South Brice, Hall..............................10	Stag Creek, Comanche 45	*SULLIVAN CITY, Hidalgo, 65,
South Fork Estates, Jim Hogg,	STAGECOACH, Montgomery, 12,	(3,998) 4,469
(47) 47	(455) 537	*Sulphur Bluff, Hopkins, 4..............280
*SOUTH HOUSTON, Harris, 711,	Stairtown, Caldwell 35	*SULPHUR SPRINGS, Hopkins,
(15,833) 16,294	Staley, San Jacinto 55	633, (14,551) 15,128
*SOUTHLAKE, Tarrant-Denton,	*STAMFORD, Jones-Haskell,	Summerfield, Castro, 1....................48
1,423, (21,519) 24,943	131, (3,636) 3,489	Summerville, Gonzales.....................45
Southland, Garza............................157	Stampede, Bell 6	*Sumner, Lamar, 25.........................95
South La Paloma [Alfred-], Jim Wells,	Stamps, Upshur................................45	*SUNDOWN, Hockley, 49,
(451) 465	Stanfield, Clay 10	(1,505) 1,488
*SOUTHMAYD, Grayson, 22,	*STANTON, Martin, 90,	Sunnyside, Castro 64
(992) 1,011	(2,556) 2,500	Sunny Side, Waller 120
SOUTH MOUNTAIN, Coryell,	*Staples, Guadalupe, 5....................396	Sunnyside, Wilson 300
0, (412) 407	*Star, Mills, 1....................................85	SUNNYVALE, Dallas, 224,
*SOUTH PADRE ISLAND, Cameron,	STAR HARBOR, Henderson, 3,	(2,693) 4,065
309, (2,422) 2,751	(416) 415	*SUNRAY, Moore, 52,
*South Plains, Floyd 67	Star Route, Cochran.........................15	(1,950) 1,902
South Point, Cameron,	Starrville, Smith 75	Sunrise, Falls 845
(1,118) 1,151	Startzville, Comal............................NA	*SUNRISE BEACH, Llano, 32,
South Purmela, Coryell....................10	Steele Hill, Dickens............................4	(704) 751
South Shore, Bell..............................80	Steep Creek, San Augustine ....NA	*SUNSET, Montague, 21,
SOUTHSIDE PLACE, Harris, 51,	Stephens Creek, San Jacinto 385	(339) 349
(1,547) 1,596	*STEPHENVILLE, Erath, 751,	Sunset Oaks, Burnet 198
South Sulphur, Hunt 60	(14,921) 15,978	SUNSET VALLEY, Travis, 108,
South Texarkana, Bowie................370	Sterley, Floyd....................................31	(365) 459

Town, County .... Pop. 2006	Town, County .... Pop. 2006	Town, County .... Pop. 2006
SUN VALLEY, Lamar, 3, (51)............54	Terry Chapel, Falls............................30	*TOLAR, Hood, 39, (504) 615
SURFSIDE BEACH, Brazoria,	Terryville, DeWitt.............................40	Tolbert, Wilbarger 15
22, (763) 857	*TEXARKANA, Bowie- (Miller Co.,	Tolette, Lamar.................................40
*Sutherland Springs, Wilson, 5.......362	Ark.), 2,672, (61,230) 71,330	Tolosa, Kaufman.............................58
Swamp City, Gregg.............................8	*TEXAS CITY, Galveston, 1,049,	*TOMBALL, Harris, 1,367,
Swan, Smith 150	(41,512) 43,330	(9,089) 10,625
*SWEENY, Brazoria, 110,	TEXHOMA, Sherman- (Texas Co.,	*TOM BEAN, Grayson, 30,
(3,624) 3,743	Okla.), (1,306) 1,227	(941) 1,069
Sweet Home, Guadalupe 294	*TEXLINE, Dallam, 27, (511).........525	Tomlinson Hill, Falls..........................64
*Sweet Home, Lavaca, 7................360	Texroy, Hutchinson 30	TOOL, Henderson, 35,
Sweet Home, Lee 30	Thalia, Foard 50	(2,275) 2,412
Sweet Union, Cherokee....................40	*THE COLONY, Denton, 924,	Topsey, Coryell 35
*SWEETWATER, Nolan, 447,	(26,531) 35,558	*Tornillo, El Paso, 17,
(11,415) 10,971	Thedford, Smith 65	(1,609) 1,698
Swenson, Stonewall 80	The Grove, Coryell 100	Tours, McLennan 130
Swift, Nacogdoches.......................210	THE HILLS, Travis, 0, (1,492) 1,838	*Tow, Llano, 12 305
Swiss Alp, Fayette 17	Thelma, Bexar 45	Town Bluff, Tyler.............................429
Sylvan, Lamar...................................68	Thelma, Limestone 20	*TOYAH, Reeves, 7,
*Sylvester, Fisher, 1 79	Theon, Williamson 30	(100) 87
T	Thermo, Hopkins 56	*Toyahvale, Reeves, 1.......................60
Tabor, Brazos.................................150	*The Woodlands, Montgomery,	Tradewinds, San Patricio, (163) 163
Tadmor, Houston 67	51, (55,649) 63,421	Travis, Falls 48
*TAFT, San Patricio, 93,	*Thicket, Hardin, 4 306	Trawick, Nacogdoches 375
(3,396) 3,441	*Thomaston, DeWitt, 3 45	*TRENT, Taylor, 6, (318)................310
Taft Southwest, San Patricio,	*THOMPSONS, Fort Bend, 3,	*TRENTON, Fannin, 54,
(1,721) 1,586	(236) 283	(662) 711
*TAHOKA, Lynn, 72,	Thompsonville, Gonzales 30	Trickham, Coleman............................12
(2,910) 2,794	Thompsonville, Jim Hogg 55	Trimmer, Bell..................................390
*TALCO, Titus, 22, (570) 578	Thornberry, Clay 75	*TRINIDAD, Henderson, 44,
*Talpa, Coleman, 2 127	*THORNDALE, Milam, 56,	(1,091) 1,142
TALTY, Kaufman, 20,	(1,278) 1,426	*TRINITY, Trinity, 174,
(1,028) 1,280	*THORNTON, Limestone, 21,	(2,721) 2,861
Tamina, Montgomery 900	(525) 544	TROPHY CLUB, Denton,
Tanglewood, Lee 60	THORNTONVILLE, Ward, 6,	227, (6,350) 7,608
Tarkington Prairie, Liberty...............NA	(442) 406	*TROUP, Smith-Cherokee, 124,
*Tarpley, Bandera, 5 30	Thorp Spring, Hood 222	(1,949) 2,104
*Tarzan, Martin, 4 30	*THRALL, Williamson, 27,	Trout Creek, Newton.......................NA
Tascosa Hills, Potter........................90	(710) 891	*TROY, Bell, 85, (1,378) 1,346
*TATUM, Rusk-Panola, 55,	Three Oaks, Wilson 150	Truby, Jones 26
(1,175) 1,169	*THREE RIVERS, Live Oak, 107,	Trumbull, Ellis 100
*TAYLOR, Williamson, 495,	(1,878) 1,788	Truscott, Knox 50
(13,575) 14,872	Three States, Cass...........................45	Tucker, Anderson...........................304
TAYLOR LAKE VILLAGE, Harris,	*THROCKMORTON, Throckmorton,	*Tuleta, Bee, 6, (292) 391
68, (3,694) 5,807	52, (905) 719	*TULIA, Swisher, 150,
TAYLOR LANDING, Jefferson	Thurber, Erath....................................8	(5,117) 4,918
(nc) 250	Tidwell, Hunt....................................50	Tulip, Fannin 10
Taylorsville, Caldwell 20	Tierra Bonita, Cameron,	Tulsita, Bee, (20) 26
Taylor Town, Lamar 40	(160) 162	Tundra, Van Zandt............................04
Tazewell, Hopkins...........................NA	Tierra Grande, Nueces, (362).........352	Tunis, Burleson...............................150
*TEAGUE, Freestone, 119,	Tierra Verde [Spring Garden-],	*TURKEY, Hall, 26, (494) 482
(4,557) 5,049	Nueces, (693)...........................602	Turlington, Freestone........................27
Teaselville, Smith...........................150	Tigertown, Lamar............................400	Turnersville, Coryell 125
*TEHUACANA, Limestone, 2,	TIKI ISLAND VILLAGE, Galveston,	Turnersville, Travis............................90
(307) 316	39, (1,016)............................1,148	*Turnertown-Selman City, Rusk,
*Telegraph, Kimble, 2 3	*Tilden, McMullen, 12 300	7 271
*Telephone, Fannin, 7.....................210	Tilmon, Caldwell 117	Turtle Bayou, Chambers....................42
*Telferner, Victoria, 12 700	TIMBERCREEK CANYON, Randall,	*TUSCOLA, Taylor, 57,
Telico, Ellis.....................................115	0, (406) 437	(714) 776
*Tell, Childress, 2............................15	Timberwood, Bexar, (5,889) 6,136	Tuxedo, Jones 42
*TEMPLE, Bell, 2,072,	Timesville, Leon..............................NA	Twichell, Ochiltree 22
(54,514) 57,216	*TIMPSON, Shelby, 53,	Twitty, Wheeler 12
*TENAHA, Shelby, 44, (1,046) 1,012	(1,094) 1,082	*TYE, Taylor, 38, (1,158) 1,171
Tenmile, Dawson 30	Tin Top, Parker 500	*TYLER, Smith, 4,768,
*Tennessee Colony, Anderson,	*TIOGA, Grayson, 50, (754)...........917	(83,650) 92,987
9 300	TIRA, Hopkins, (248) 247	*Tynan, Bee, 4, (301)......................300
*Tennyson, Coke, 1 46	*Tivoli, Refugio, 7...........................550	Type, Williamson 40
*Terlingua [Study Butte-], Brewster,	TOCO, Lamar, 2, (89).......................83	**U**
33, (267) 275	Todd City, Anderson.........................10	UHLAND, Hays-Caldwell, 16,
*TERRELL, Kaufman, 800,	TODD MISSION, Grimes, 64,	(386) 425
(13,606) 17,149	(146) 161	*Umbarger, Randall, 4 327
TERRELL HILLS, Bexar, 106,	Tokio, McLennan 250	UNCERTAIN, Harrison, 14,
(5,019) 4,881	*Tokio, Terry......................................5	(150) 148

Town, County ....Pop. 2006	Town, County ....Pop. 2006	Town, County ....Pop. 2006
Westcott, San Jacinto 25	Whitman, Washington....................25	*Woden, Nacogdoches, 3..............400
Westdale, Jim Wells,	*WHITNEY, Hill, 237,	*WOLFE CITY, Hunt, 95,
(295) 310	(1,833) 1,984	(1,566) 1,576
*Westhoff, DeWitt, 6 410	*Whitsett, Live Oak, 3 200	*WOLFFORTH, Lubbock, 199,
WESTLAKE, Tarrant-Denton, 46,	Whitson, Coryell 50	(2,554) 3,073
(207) 249	*Whitt, Parker 38	Womack, Bosque 25
*WEST LAKE HILLS, Travis, 346,	Whon, Coleman..............................15	Woodbine, Cooke 250
(3,116)......................................3,056	*WICHITA FALLS, Wichita, 3,312,	WOODBRANCH, Montgomery,
West Livingston, Polk,	(104,197)...............................101,852	(1,305) 1,391
(6,612) 6,973	*WICKETT, Ward, 22, (455)...........439	Woodbury, Hill................................45
West Mineola, Wood 20	Wied, Lavaca.................................65	WOODCREEK, Hays, 43,
*Westminster, Collin, 3, (390) 379	Wiedeville, Washington ....NA	(1,274) 1,380
West Mountain, Upshur 325	Wieland, Hunt...............................NA	Wooded Hills, Johnson 580
West Odessa, Ector,	*Wiergate, Newton, 2.....................461	Wood Hi, Victoria 35
(17,799) 18,480	Wigginsville, Montgomery..............100	*Woodlake, Trinity, 1 98
*WESTON, Collin, 18,	Wilcox, Burleson............................39	Woodland, Red River 128
(635) 578	Wilderville, Falls 45	*Woodlawn, Harrison, 4.................370
WEST ORANGE, Orange, 85,	*Wildorado, Oldham, 8 210	WOODLOCH, Montgomery,
(4,111)......................................3,826	Wild Peach, Brazoria,	(247) 259
Westover, Baylor 18	(2,498) 2,523	Woodrow, Lubbock 2,034
WESTOVER HILLS, Tarrant,	Wildwood, Hardin 499	Woods, Panola 65
(658) 640	Wilkins, Upshur...............................75	*WOODSBORO, Refugio, 67,
West Pearsall, Frio, (349)...............344	Willamar, Willacy, (15) 18	(1,685) 1,619
Westphalia, Falls 186	William Penn, Washington..............100	*WOODSON, Throckmorton,
*West Point, Fayette, 5...................213	*WILLIS, Montgomery, 317,	23, (296).....................................275
West Sharyland, Hidalgo,	(3,985) 4,692	Wood Springs, Smith.....................200
(2,947) 3,077	*Willow City, Gillespie, 2 22	Woodville, Cherokee 20
West Sinton, San Patricio..............318	Willow Grove, McLennan...............100	*WOODVILLE, Tyler, 326,
WEST TAWAKONI, Hunt, 63,	WILLOW PARK, Parker, 119,	(2,415) 2,346
(1,462) 1,632	(2,849) 3,295	Woodward, La Salle 10
WEST UNIVERSITY PLACE,	Willow Springs, Fayette 74	WOODWAY, McLennan, 312,
Harris, 313, (14,211)...........14,408	Willow Springs, Rains.....................50	(8,733) 8,532
Westville, Trinity..............................46	*WILLS POINT, Van Zandt, 416,	Woosley, Rains...............................47
Westway, Deaf Smith.......................15	(3,496) 3,703	*WORTHAM, Freestone, 46,
Westway, El Paso, (3,829)...........4,078	*WILMER, Dallas, 71,	(1,082) 1,132
WESTWORTH VILLAGE,	(3,393) 3,690	Worthing, Lavaca............................55
Tarrant, 31, (2,124)...............2,653	Wilmeth, Runnels 15	Wright City, Smith 172
*WHARTON, Wharton, 396,	Wilson, Falls 42	*Wrightsboro, Gonzales...................10
(9,237) 9,357	*WILSON, Lynn, 44,	Wyldwood, Bastrop, (2,310) 2,564
Wheatland, Tarrant 175	(532) 507	*WYLIE, Collin-Rockwall-Dallas,
*WHEELER, Wheeler, 62,	*WIMBERLEY, Hays, 819,	1,094, (15,132) 29,868
(1,378) 1,289	(3,797) 4,111	Wylie, Taylor ....[part of Abilene]
Wheeler Springs, Houston...............89	Winchell, Brown..............................20	**Y**
*Wheelock, Robertson, 7...............225	Winchester, Fayette......................232	*Yancey, Medina, 5.......................209
White City, San Augustine 20	WINDCREST, Bexar, 110,	*YANTIS, Wood, 62, (321)..............320
White City, Wilbarger 40	(5,105) 4,955	Yard, Anderson 18
*WHITE DEER, Carson, 50,	Windemere, Travis, (6,868) 6,395	Yarrellton, Milam............................35
(1,060) 1,036	*WINDOM, Fannin, 18,	Yellowpine, Sabine 97
*WHITEFACE, Cochran, 17,	(245) 247	*YOAKUM, Lavaca-DeWitt, 264,
(465) 457	*WINDTHORST, Archer, 72,	(5,731) 5,831
Whiteflat, Motley 4	(440) 478	*YORKTOWN, DeWitt, 136,
White Hall, Bell 262	Winedale, Fayette...........................67	(2,271) 2,297
White Hall, Grimes...........................30	*WINFIELD, Titus, 20, (499).........562	Young, Freestone 27
*WHITEHOUSE, Smith, 321,	WINFREE [Old River-], Chambers,	Youngsport, Bell 49
(5,346) 7,118	17, (1,364)..............................1,620	Yowell, Delta-Hunt 30
*WHITE OAK, Gregg, 254,	*Wingate, Runnels, 4.....................100	*Ysleta del Sur Pueblo, El Paso 421
(5,624) 5,974	*WINK, Winkler, 21,	Yznaga, Cameron, (103) 101
White Oak, Titus 100	(919) 837	**Z**
White River Lake, Crosby.................83	Winkler, Navarro-Freestone............26	Zabcikville, Bell 79
White Rock, Hunt.............................80	*Winnie, Chambers, 138,	*Zapata, Zapata, 142,
White Rock, Red River 90	(2,914) 3,314	(4,856) 5,521
White Rock, Robertson.....................80	*WINNSBORO, Wood-Franklin,	Zapata Ranch, Willacy, (88) 85
White Rock, San Augustine 60	505, (3,584) 3,603	*ZAVALLA, Angelina, 35,
*WHITESBORO, Grayson, 178,	*WINONA, Smith, 105,	(647) 642
(3,760) 4,416	(582) 620	*Zephyr, Brown, 11 201
*WHITE SETTLEMENT, Tarrant,	Winter Haven, Dimmit....................123	Zimmerscheidt, Colorado 50
296, (14,831) 15,262	*WINTERS, Runnels, 160,	Zion Hill, Guadalupe 595
White Star, Motley 6	(2,880) 2,851	Zipperlandville, Falls........................22
Whiteway, Hamilton 8	Witting, Lavaca...............................90	Zorn, Guadalupe...........................287
*WHITEWRIGHT, Grayson-Fannin,	WIXON VALLEY, Brazos, 3,	Zuehl, Guadalupe, (346)................352
101, (1,740) 2,038	(235) 216	Zunkerville, Karnes 15
*Whitharral, Hockley 158	Wizard Wells, Jack 69	

Elections

Texas gubernatorial candidates debate during the 2006 campaign. Smiley N. Pool photo.

2006 General Election

2006 Primaries

Marriage Constitutional Amendment

Party Leaders

Political Analysis

Colorful Cast in Race for Governor

By Carolyn Barta

Texas reinforced its reputation for lively political theater with the 2006 gubernatorial election.

A colorful cast included two independents trying to derail Republican Gov. Rick Perry's re-election. Independents Carole "Grandma" Strayhorn and cowboy musician-humorist Kinky Friedman attracted national attention, but Perry pulled out a plurality win in the field that included Democrat Chris Bell.

Perry's 39 percent election positioned him to be the longest-serving governor in Texas history. He first assumed the governorship automatically, as lieutenant governor when George W. Bush was elected president in 2000. He was elected in 2002, and his 2006 re-election guaranteed him 10 years in office, if he served out his term.

Bell, a former one-term congressman and Houston city councilman, finished second with 29 percent in the five-way race that included a Libertarian. The two independents together only mustered about 30 percent, splitting the vote among those dissatisfied with Gov. Perry and the major parties. Still, they provided marquee value.

Offbeat candidate Friedman and Comptroller Strayhorn, who was elected to statewide office as a Republican, mounted impressive campaigns to gather more than the 45,000 signatures required to get on the ballot. But they failed to crack Sam Houston's record as the last independent elected governor in 1856.

Ms. Strayhorn, who started her career as a Democrat and mayor of Austin, hoped to put together a Democrat-Republican coalition. Much of her funding came from disgruntled Democrats who wanted to oust Perry but feared their party wouldn't muster a strong campaign in the GOP-dominated state.

She garnered national attention as the mother of two former Bush administration officials– White House press secretary Scott McClellan and Mark McClellan, director of the Food and Drug Administration and Medicare Commissioner.

Her slogan was "One Tough Grandma" and she spent much of her time challenging a Secretary of State ruling that she couldn't be listed on the ballot as "Grandma." Friedman was on the ballot as Kinky.

Richard "Kinky" Friedman found notoriety in the 1970s in a country rock band called Kinky Friedman and the Texas Jewboys, mixing social commentary with humor in songs such as "They Ain't Making Jews Like Jesus Anymore."

In the 1980s, he turned to writing detective novels. In the campaign for governor, he was part politician, part humorist.

President Bush campaigned for Gov. Rick Perry in Texas where the president remained popular. Here he thanks the crowd at Reunion Area in Dallas the night before the general election. With him, from left, are First Lady Laura Bush, Texas First Lady Anita Perry, and Gov. Perry. Erich Schlegel photo.

His slogans were "How hard could it be?" and "Why the hell not? When campaigning, Friedman wore a trademark black cowboy hat, black frock coat, boots and jeans, and clutched an ever-present unlit cigar. He built a grass roots organization and funded his campaign with online memorabilia.

Much of his appeal was on college campuses. He hoped to motivate usual non-voters, saying: "Politics is the only field in which the more experience you have, the worse you get." Friedman wanted Texas "to be No. 1 in something other than executions, toll roads and property taxes."

He had the help of former Minnesota Gov. Jesse Ventura, a successful independent, and Ventura's chief campaign strategist, and the support of singers Willie Nelson and Jimmy Buffett. But he never made the transition from wisecracking candidate to serious contender.

Ms. Strayhorn spent most of the campaign criticizing the governor's record on public education and immigration and his plans for a vast foreign-built superhighway network that farmers and ranchers said would gobble up rural land. But she had difficulting appeasing conflicting interests between Democrats and Republicans.

Bell, therefore, emerged as the main opposition to Perry, turning the election into a traditional choice between the Republican and Democrat party structures.

In the U.S. Senate election, incumbent Kay Bailey Hutchison -- after dropping her designs on the governor's office -- cruised to election over her opponent, Houston lawyer Barbara Ann Radnofsky.

Hutchison, well respected as a Senate leader who reached across both sides of the aisle and who paid attention to folks at home, won almost 62 percent of the vote. She remained a potential candidate for governor in 2010.

The most closely-watched 2006 congressional election was to replace congressman Tom DeLay, R-Sugar Land, the former House Majority Leader. DeLay resigned his seat and decided not seek re-election after he was indicted for conspiring to violate campaign finance laws in funding Texas legislative candidates.

His support had helped Republicans take control of the Texas House before the 2003 legislative session, when he served as the architect of a new congressional redistricting plan.

Democrat Nick Lampson, who lost his district in the DeLay-engineered redistricting, won DeLay's old U.S. House seat in the 22nd District in the general election, although Shelley Sekula-Gibbs won a special election to finish the last two months of DeLay's term.

After the redistricting, the U.S. Supreme Court ruled that the 23rd District was unconstitutional because it diluted minority votes by splitting Laredo, an almost all-Hispanic city, into two districts.

A three-judge panel added more Hispanics to the district, and it was captured in a runoff by former U.S. Rep. Ciro Rodriguez, a Democrat, over seven-term Republican incumbent Henry Bonilla. The two new Democrats joined the Democratic majority that took over the U.S. House in 2006. though the Texas congressional delegation had 19 Republicans and 13 Democrats.

While President George W. Bush was faltering in national polls, largely the result of dissatisfaction with the war in Iraq, the Texas Republican remained popular in his home state, where the GOP maintained superiority over a depressed and hardly competitive Democratic party.

Republicans swept all statewide offices in 2006, re-electing Lt. Gov. David Dewhurst, Attorney General Greg Abbott, and Land Commissioner Jerry Patterson. Texas Railroad Commissioner Elizabeth Ames Jones, who had been appointed by Gov. Perry, was elected for a full term. Susan Combs moved from agriculture commissioner to comptroller, and Republican Todd Staples, a state senator from East Texas, was elected agriculture commissioner. Republicans also held onto all eight state judicial offices on the ballot.

Carolyn Barta, a retired staff writer for The Dallas Morning News, *is a senior lecturer in journalism at Southern Methodist University.*

Texas Election Turnout by Voting Age Population

Year	2004	2000	1996	1992	1988	1984	1980	1976	1972
Major Candidates	Bush Kerry	Bush Gore	Clinton Dole	Clinton Bush Perot	Bush Dukakis	Reagan Mondale	Reagan Carter	Carter Ford	Nixon McGovern
Percent of VAP that voted	46.1	44.3	41.0	47.6	44.3	47.6	45.6	46.1	44.9
Percent of registered voters that voted	56.6	51.8	53.2	72.9	66.2	68.3	68.4	64.8	89.6

The **voting age population (VAP)** refers to the total number of persons of voting age regardless of citizenship, military status, felony conviction or mental state. The Bureau of the Census is the source for the VAP estimates.

Since the National Voter Registration Act of 1993, non-voters cannot be removed from registration rolls of a county until two federal elections have been held. So, for instance, if a person moved in December 2004 from one county to another, that person could be counted as a non-voter in the previous county of residence through the general election of November 2008.

These are called "suspense voters" on county rolls and have affected the statistical reports of the percentage of registered voters participating in elections.

In the early 1970s, various election reforms were enacted by the Legislature, including eliminating the requirement for an annual registration and allowing for a continuing voter registration system.

The presidential elections have a larger voter turnout than off-year and state elections. — RP

Sources: Federal Election Commission and the Texas Secretary of State office.

2006 Gubernatorial Election Results by County

Below are the official results by county in the race for governor. The leading candidates were Rick Perry, Republican; Chris Bell, Democrat; Carole Keeton Strayhorn, Independent; and Kinky Friedman, Independent.

The total number of votes, **4,399,116**, was 33.64 percent of the registered voters. The voting age population was estimated at 16,636,742.

The statewide turnout in the previous gubernatorial election in 2002 was 36.24 percent of registered voters. *Source: Texas Secretary of State.*

County	Registered Voters	Turnout %	GOVERNORS RACE (votes and percentage of total vote)							
			Perry	%	Bell	%	Strayhorn	%	Friedman	%
Statewide	**13,074,279**	**33.64**	**1,716,792**	**39.02**	**1,310,337**	**29.78**	**796,851**	**18.11**	**547,674**	**12.44**
Anderson	27,719	38.4	4,305	40.5	2,496	23.5	2,751	25.9	1,035	9.7
Andrews	8,264	31.6	1,282	49.1	352	13.5	685	26.2	284	10.9
Angelina	47,567	46.1	8,788	40.1	6,618	30.5	4,170	19.0	2,228	10.2
Aransas	16,109	42.2	3,051	44.9	1,349	19.8	1,140	16.8	1,223	18.0
Archer	6,477	45.3	1,335	45.5	419	14.3	853	29.1	315	10.7
Armstrong	1,398	48.9	324	47.4	71	10.4	132	19.3	151	22.1
Atascosa	25,038	31.0	2,423	31.3	2,040	26.3	1,934	24.9	1,314	17.0
Austin	17,550	45.4	2,908	36.5	1,377	17.3	2,284	28.7	1,354	17.0
Bailey	3,893	39.1	692	45.4	284	18.6	331	21.7	202	13.3
Bandera	14,246	46.2	2,595	39.5	881	13.4	1,192	18.1	1,853	28.2
Bastrop	39,006	43.8	5,216	30.5	5,709	33.4	2,962	17.3	3,057	17.9
Baylor	2,791	35.2	396	40.3	202	20.6	283	28.8	98	10.0
Bee	16,377	42.9	2,300	32.7	2,489	35.4	1,430	20.3	774	11.0
Bell	152,130	28.5	17,633	40.7	10,404	24.0	10,717	24.8	4,276	9.9
Bexar	898,687	30.5	92,387	33.7	86,906	31.7	57,150	20.9	35,596	13.0
Blanco	6,716	49.9	1,411	42.1	709	21.2	598	17.8	612	18.3
Borden	446	57.4	118	46.1	48	18.8	56	21.9	34	13.3
Bosque	11,902	47.4	2,099	37.2	1,162	20.6	1,559	27.6	810	14.3
Bowie	57,400	32.1	7,936	43.1	5,851	31.8	3,019	16.4	1,529	8.3
Brazoria	163,532	35.7	22,543	38.6	13,661	23.4	10,650	18.2	11,250	19.6
Brazos	87,838	34.6	15,590	51.3	6,449	21.2	4,325	14.2	3,772	12.4
Brewster	5,637	43.3	749	30.7	722	29.6	385	15.8	559	22.9
Briscoe	1,272	44.0	220	39.3	130	23.2	133	23.8	74	13.2
Brooks	6,312	18.4	224	19.3	662	57.0	181	15.6	93	8.0
Brown	24,685	35.9	4,147	46.7	1,647	18.6	1,896	21.4	1,118	12.6
Burleson	11,230	40.1	1,837	40.8	1,178	26.2	912	20.3	544	12.1
Burnet	26,291	42.7	5,246	46.7	2,330	20.7	2,013	17.9	1,537	13.7
Caldwell	21,837	35.6	2,502	32.2	2,478	31.9	1,520	19.5	1,207	15.5
Calhoun	13,136	33.6	1,435	32.5	1,496	33.9	958	21.7	505	11.4
Callahan	8,979	36.7	1,385	42.0	574	17.4	420	12.7	900	27.3
Cameron	167,636	24.5	14,407	35.1	14,327	34.9	9,400	23.0	2,581	6.3
Camp	7,572	40.0	1,254	41.4	953	31.5	561	18.5	256	8.4
Carson	4,748	43.2	965	47.1	287	14.0	463	22.6	327	16.0
Cass	18,388	40.5	2,758	37.0	2,544	34.1	1,550	20.8	575	7.7
Castro	4,600	38.6	723	40.7	471	26.5	302	17.0	274	15.4
Chambers	21,858	35.6	3,142	40.4	1,577	20.3	1,427	18.6	1,587	20.4
Cherokee	28,208	39.8	4,847	43.2	2,436	21.7	2,823	25.2	1,061	9.5
Childress	3,560	34.8	533	44.0	249	20.6	253	20.9	170	14.0
Clay	7,696	45.9	1,530	43.3	613	17.4	939	26.6	438	12.4
Cochran	2,052	43.7	356	39.7	174	19.4	220	24.5	137	15.3
Coke	2,543	44.8	522	45.9	182	16.0	260	22.8	163	14.3
Coleman	6,267	36.8	939	40.7	430	18.6	598	25.9	324	14.1
Collin	381,821	36.2	67,813	49.1	32,457	23.5	21,467	15.5	15,340	11.1
Collingsworth	2,303	46.7	486	45.2	201	18.7	261	24.3	121	11.3
Colorado	13,600	41.3	1,803	32.1	1,213	21.6	1,743	31.0	832	14.8
Comal	67,871	42.0	13,551	47.6	4,616	16.2	5,491	19.3	4,570	16.0
Comanche	9,182	38.7	1,408	39.6	1,000	28.1	668	18.8	458	12.9
Concho	1,827	45.7	373	44.7	169	20.2	124	14.9	167	20.0
Cooke	24,445	41.1	3,297	32.8	1,817	18.1	3,908	38.9	977	9.7
Coryell	38,030	25.5	4,279	44.1	2,030	20.9	2,243	23.1	1,096	11.3
Cottle	1,295	49.1	209	32.9	166	26.1	129	20.3	126	19.8
Crane	2,619	41.6	488	44.8	182	16.7	286	26.5	123	11.3

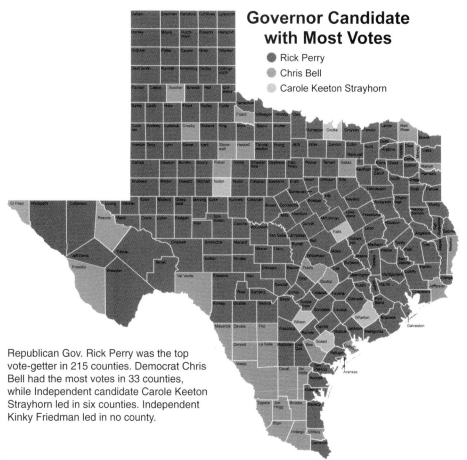

Governor Candidate with Most Votes

- ● Rick Perry
- ◐ Chris Bell
- ○ Carole Keeton Strayhorn

Republican Gov. Rick Perry was the top vote-getter in 215 counties. Democrat Chris Bell had the most votes in 33 counties, while Independent candidate Carole Keeton Strayhorn led in six counties. Independent Kinky Friedman led in no county.

County	Registered Voters	Turnout %	GOVERNORS RACE (votes and percentage of total vote)							
			Perry	%	Bell	%	Strayhorn	%	Friedman	%
Crockett	2,880	36.3	502	48.0	220	21.1	143	13.7	173	16.6
Crosby	4,210	33.1	447	32.0	467	33.5	294	21.1	178	12.8
Culberson	1,912	22.3	170	39.8	122	28.6	63	14.8	68	15.9
Dallam	3,216	26.9	439	50.7	97	11.2	152	17.6	177	20.4
Dallas	1,197,921	33.9	143,132	35.2	161,886	39.9	57,581	14.2	41,330	10.2
Dawson	8,457	37.6	1,397	44.0	767	24.1	625	19.7	362	11.4
Deaf Smith	9,737	28.0	1,237	45.3	525	19.2	635	23.5	327	12.0
Delta	3,470	44.0	577	37.8	433	28.4	335	21.9	176	11.5
Denton	333,351	32.6	50,888	46.9	25,156	23.2	18,300	16.9	13,536	12.5
DeWitt	12,198	33.5	1,449	35.5	795	19.5	1,243	30.5	580	14.2
Dickens	1,466	41.7	230	37.6	151	24.7	128	20.9	96	15.7
Dimmit	7,619	24.1	433	24.1	900	49.0	324	17.7	158	8.6
Donley	2,607	48.4	538	42.6	170	13.5	292	23.1	258	20.4
Duval	9,825	33.0	526	16.2	2,087	64.4	221	6.8	395	12.2
Eastland	10,576	44.5	2,073	44.1	898	19.1	1,230	26.1	481	10.2
Ector	69,063	25.7	8,843	49.9	2,748	15.5	4,003	22.6	2,031	11.5
Edwards	1,500	49.5	346	46.6	116	15.6	173	23.3	100	13.5
Ellis	80,229	36.6	12,738	43.4	5,833	19.9	6,799	23.2	3,810	13.0
El Paso	375,425	24.2	29,989	33.1	32,854	36.2	17,973	19.8	9,386	10.3
Erath	20,547	37.7	3,372	43.5	1,676	21.6	1,762	22.7	892	11.5
Falls	9,730	37.6	853	23.3	982	26.8	1,508	41.2	299	8.2
Fannin	18,822	39.9	2,819	37.5	2,261	30.1	1,531	20.4	862	11.5
Fayette	15,087	51.6	2,492	32.0	1,801	23.1	2,242	28.8	1,212	15.6

County	Registered Voters	Turnout %	GOVERNORS RACE (votes and percentage of total vote)							
			Perry	%	Bell	%	Strayhorn	%	Friedman	%
Fisher	2,896	41.4	317	26.4	455	37.9	331	27.6	93	7.8
Floyd	4,489	46.5	877	42.0	530	25.4	455	21.8	217	10.4
Foard	1,036	36.7	87	22.9	166	43.7	97	25.5	28	7.4
Fort Bend	267,754	36.8	39,819	40.5	33,241	33.8	14,454	14.7	10,414	10.6
Franklin	6,571	47.6	1,447	46.2	649	20.7	700	22.4	312	10.0
Freestone	11,406	38.7	1,933	43.8	976	22.1	1,054	23.9	429	9.7
Frio	10,062	21.0	530	25.1	729	34.5	587	27.8	255	12.1
Gaines	7,190	34.3	1,202	48.7	475	19.2	472	19.1	306	12.4
Galveston	189,780	34.4	21,072	32.3	19,926	30.5	10,417	16.0	13,522	20.7
Garza	2,970	39.1	522	44.9	200	17.2	277	23.8	153	13.2
Gillespie	16,816	50.0	4,375	52.1	1,170	13.9	1,385	16.5	1,404	16.7
Glasscock	728	45.6	169	50.9	27	8.1	86	25.9	50	15.1
Goliad	5,675	42.3	657	27.4	659	27.5	678	28.3	396	16.5
Gonzales	12,098	34.6	1,494	35.7	899	21.5	1,246	29.8	531	12.7
Gray	14,838	36.3	3,104	57.7	550	10.2	998	18.5	709	13.2
Grayson	74,345	35.1	11,945	45.7	6,852	26.2	4,304	16.5	2,865	11.0
Gregg	72,307	31.2	10,834	48.1	4,851	21.5	5,349	23.7	1,404	6.2
Grimes	13,409	40.4	1,766	32.6	1,361	25.1	1,345	24.8	903	16.7
Guadalupe	68,015	36.5	10,324	41.6	5,094	20.5	5,658	22.8	3,561	14.3
Hale	21,015	30.1	2,678	42.3	1,674	26.5	1,267	20.0	678	10.7
Hall	2,176	42.6	335	36.1	227	24.5	204	22.0	158	17.0
Hamilton	5,626	50.7	1,093	38.3	636	22.3	688	24.1	427	15.0
Hansford	3,236	44.3	782	54.6	125	8.7	292	20.4	221	15.4
Hardeman	2,971	48.1	553	38.7	325	22.8	345	24.2	194	13.6
Hardin	33,680	30.6	5,244	50.8	2,100	20.4	1,659	16.1	1,283	12.4
Harris	1,918,652	30.7	215,150	36.5	203,102	34.5	86,890	14.7	80,808	13.7
Harrison	42,638	35.1	6,244	41.7	3,857	25.7	3,928	26.2	912	6.1
Hartley	2,909	43.2	665	52.9	161	12.8	213	16.9	217	17.5
Haskell	3,833	45.2	539	31.1	572	33.0	465	26.8	150	8.7
Hays	85,601	36.5	10,591	33.9	9,845	31.5	4,955	15.9	5,457	17.5
Hemphill	2,278	52.0	532	44.9	131	11.1	289	24.4	227	19.2
Henderson	49,371	36.8	7,715	42.5	3,942	21.7	4,118	22.7	2,332	12.8
Hidalgo	279,979	17.1	16,029	33.5	20,404	42.7	8,403	17.6	2,644	5.5
Hill	22,321	41.4	3,192	34.5	2,130	23.0	2,767	29.9	1,101	11.9
Hockley	14,014	32.9	2,081	45.2	871	18.9	920	20.0	710	15.4
Hood	33,269	42.3	6,770	48.1	2,988	21.2	2,564	18.2	1,670	11.9
Hopkins	21,717	39.0	3,379	39.9	2,361	27.9	1,764	20.8	939	11.1
Houston	15,261	39.1	2,050	44.4	1,452	24.4	1,264	21.2	573	9.6
Howard	17,975	37.8	2,652	39.1	1,424	21.0	2,000	29.6	650	9.6
Hudspeth	1,648	32.8	269	47.4	83	14.6	109	19.2	100	17.6
Hunt	49,688	35.6	7,731	43.7	3,899	22.0	3,781	21.4	2,228	12.6
Hutchinson	15,785	34.6	2,904	53.2	730	13.4	1,047	19.2	745	13.7
Irion	1,269	41.0	240	46.2	105	20.2	62	11.9	109	21.0
Jack	5,078	43.1	979	44.8	378	17.3	571	26.1	244	11.2
Jackson	9,555	35.2	1,058	31.5	862	25.7	1,016	30.2	405	12.1
Jasper	20,826	36.0	3,341	44.6	2,147	28.6	1,317	17.6	666	8.9
Jeff Davis	1,861	57.3	378	35.4	293	27.5	178	16.7	208	19.5
Jefferson	159,927	29.2	17,110	36.6	18,519	39.6	6,600	14.1	4,373	9.3
Jim Hogg	3,924	23.9	310	33.0	466	49.6	111	11.8	46	4.9
Jim Wells	26,646	28.3	2,122	28.2	3,705	49.2	1,072	14.2	605	8.0
Johnson	80,834	37.1	12,989	43.3	6,399	21.3	6,450	21.5	4,038	13.5
Jones	10,450	36.5	1,298	34.0	964	25.3	1,126	29.5	398	10.4
Karnes	8,319	38.4	1,013	31.7	851	26.7	818	25.6	482	15.1
Kaufman	53,900	35.4	7,910	41.5	4,375	23.0	4,344	22.8	2,342	12.3
Kendall	22,126	46.8	5,120	49.5	1,346	13.0	1,966	19.0	1,827	17.7
Kenedy	349	41.3	68	47.2	42	29.2	25	17.4	8	5.6
Kent	722	40.3	105	36.1	85	29.2	51	17.5	50	17.2
Kerr	33,531	46.5	7,711	49.4	2,325	14.9	2,437	15.6	3,035	19.5
Kimble	2,920	47.9	647	47.1	222	16.2	256	18.6	243	17.7
King	196	43.4	38	44.7	12	14.1	22	25.9	13	15.3

County	Registered Voters	Turnout %	GOVERNORS RACE (votes and percentage of total vote)							
			Perry	%	Bell	%	Strayhorn	%	Friedman	%
Kinney	2,411	45.5	441	40.2	279	25.5	197	18.0	172	15.7
Kleberg	18,742	26.6	1,806	36.2	1,674	33.6	948	19.0	539	10.8
Knox	2,510	35.9	336	37.3	237	26.3	212	23.6	113	12.6
Lamar	29,773	38.8	4,600	39.8	3,498	30.3	2,259	19.6	1,140	9.9
Lamb	9,338	28.8	1,179	43.2	610	22.4	598	21.9	330	12.1
Lampasas	12,404	40.7	2,490	49.3	905	17.9	1,042	20.6	575	11.4
La Salle	4,380	25.3	304	25.4	433	36.1	323	26.9	134	11.2
Lavaca	14,065	35.7	1,864	37.1	1,118	22.3	1,228	24.5	775	15.4
Lee	8,932	47.7	1,380	32.4	1,316	30.9	933	21.9	599	14.1
Leon	11,402	38.1	2,279	52.5	771	17.7	836	19.2	431	9.9
Liberty	46,510	31.4	5,134	35.1	3,306	22.6	3,085	21.1	3,037	20.8
Limestone	14,179	38.0	1,994	37.0	1,503	27.9	1,347	25.0	510	9.5
Lipscomb	1,953	38.9	401	52.8	103	13.6	178	23.5	74	9.7
Live Oak	7,507	37.6	1,210	42.9	538	19.1	573	20.3	476	16.9
Llano	14,035	51.2	3,489	48.6	1,303	18.1	1,414	19.7	933	13.0
Loving	136	66.2	45	50.0	9	10.0	22	24.4	11	12.2
Lubbock	158,399	33.8	24,030	44.9	11,484	21.4	9,778	18.3	7,963	14.9
Lynn	4,158	34.8	530	36.6	394	27.2	303	20.9	219	15.1
Madison	7,081	40.8	1,267	43.9	704	24.4	610	21.1	290	10.0
Marion	8,088	28.2	759	33.3	794	34.8	507	22.2	206	9.0
Martin	2,857	33.9	394	40.7	115	11.9	337	34.8	118	12.2
Mason	2,935	45.7	589	44.0	269	20.1	299	22.3	164	12.2
Matagorda	21,152	37.1	2,637	33.6	2,083	26.5	1,841	23.5	1,253	16.0
Maverick	25,528	15.5	1,109	28.0	1,888	47.7	690	17.4	244	6.2
McCulloch	5,527	37.8	924	44.7	392	19.0	465	22.5	273	13.2
McLennan	134,067	39.6	19,451	36.6	14,577	27.4	14,283	26.9	4,644	8.7
McMullen	694	62.1	142	32.9	55	12.8	120	27.8	109	25.3
Medina	24,982	39.4	3,895	39.6	1,908	19.4	2,464	25.0	1,515	15.4
Menard	1,893	47.1	422	47.4	148	16.6	120	13.5	181	20.3
Midland	72,839	34.9	14,394	56.6	2,922	11.5	5,184	20.4	2,773	10.9
Milam	14,548	38.1	1,707	30.8	1,646	29.7	1,477	26.6	685	12.3
Mills	3,273	45.6	593	39.7	331	22.2	381	25.5	177	11.9
Mitchell	5,222	27.3	499	35.0	290	20.3	493	34.5	137	9.6
Montague	12,961	41.1	2,353	44.2	1,036	19.5	1,238	23.3	663	12.5
Montgomery	227,026	35.6	41,066	50.8	11,700	14.5	13,786	17.1	13,805	17.1
Moore	9,916	30.8	1,698	55.5	402	13.1	504	16.5	440	14.4
Morris	9,003	32.1	886	30.6	1,181	40.8	637	22.0	174	6.0
Motley	904	44.6	205	50.9	75	18.6	71	17.6	46	11.4
Nacogdoches	31,164	40.1	5,425	43.4	3,109	24.9	2,219	17.7	1,703	13.6
Navarro	28,293	39.1	4,296	38.9	2,794	25.9	2,571	23.3	1,340	12.1
Newton	9,319	31.1	1,072	37.0	1,153	39.8	409	14.1	253	8.7
Nolan	9,400	33.7	981	30.9	731	23.0	1,078	33.9	378	11.9
Nueces	197,596	34.2	25,066	37.1	20,931	31.0	11,870	17.5	9,423	13.9
Ochiltree	5,045	34.0	1,114	65.0	114	6.7	253	14.8	221	12.9
Oldham	1,485	36.8	269	49.2	62	11.3	118	21.6	97	17.7
Orange	52,936	32.7	7,377	42.6	5,484	31.7	2,658	15.6	1,744	10.1
Palo Pinto	17,188	37.6	2,432	37.7	1,577	24.4	1,410	21.8	1,000	15.5
Panola	16,357	35.6	2,586	44.3	1,497	25.7	1,449	24.8	283	4.9
Parker	67,774	39.9	12,877	47.7	5,178	19.2	5,483	20.3	3,344	12.4
Parmer	5,003	36.3	944	52.0	251	13.8	400	22.0	209	11.5
Pecos	7,920	40.4	1,288	40.2	833	26.0	766	23.9	291	9.1
Polk	38,400	31.2	4,653	38.8	2,938	24.5	2,238	18.7	2,075	17.3
Potter	56,762	30.4	7,326	42.4	3,395	19.7	3,367	19.5	3,044	17.6
Presidio	5,425	17.4	209	22.1	419	44.3	163	17.2	147	15.6
Rains	6,509	43.8	1,128	39.5	627	22.0	699	24.5	396	13.9
Randall	76,220	40.8	15,486	49.8	4,232	13.6	6,687	21.5	4,552	14.6
Reagan	1,929	33.0	254	39.9	107	16.8	168	26.4	103	16.2
Real	2,516	44.1	534	48.1	168	15.1	212	19.1	191	17.2
Red River	8,186	41.0	1,145	34.1	1,198	35.7	705	21.0	291	8.7
Reeves	6,656	31.8	712	33.6	737	34.8	487	23.0	166	7.8

County	Registered Voters	Turnout %	GOVERNORS RACE (votes and percentage of total vote)							
			Perry	%	Bell	%	Strayhorn	%	Friedman	%
Refugio	5,567	35.3	705	35.9	522	26.6	424	21.6	305	15.5
Roberts	736	41.7	173	56.4	12	3.9	60	19.5	61	19.9
Robertson	11,921	41.9	1,791	35.9	1,778	35.6	982	19.7	406	8.1
Rockwall	40,137	38.9	8,390	53.7	2,757	17.6	2,782	17.8	1,631	10.4
Runnels	7,027	34.5	1,016	41.9	408	16.8	601	24.8	388	16.0
Rusk	31,253	38.0	5,555	46.8	2,536	21.34	2,741	23.1	978	8.2
Sabine	7,373	41.2	1,323	43.6	763	25.1	602	19.8	331	10.9
San Augustine	6,633	36.7	929	38.2	871	35.8	401	16.5	216	8.9
San Jacinto	16,346	39.8	2,246	34.5	1,742	26.8	1,345	20.7	1,141	17.5
San Patricio	46,814	28.0	5,057	38.6	4,208	32.1	2,217	16.9	1,565	11.9
San Saba	3,749	40.6	757	49.8	265	17.4	333	21.9	159	10.5
Schleicher	1,863	37.5	336	48.1	171	24.5	91	13.0	97	13.9
Scurry	10,872	25.7	1,331	47.6	494	17.6	659	23.6	290	10.4
Shackelford	2,500	37.8	451	47.7	133	14.1	243	25.7	115	12.2
Shelby	14,905	39.9	2,783	46.8	1,563	26.3	1,132	19.0	452	7.6
Sherman	1,393	44.4	294	47.5	72	11.6	151	24.4	99	16.0
Smith	119,192	36.3	23,701	54.8	8,477	19.6	6,973	16.1	3,966	9.2
Somervell	5,761	44.0	1,067	42.1	536	21.2	553	21.8	364	14.4
Starr	27,908	22.9	1,283	20.1	4,215	66.0	611	9.6	216	3.4
Stephens	5,814	36.3	897	42.5	408	19.3	547	25.9	248	11.8
Sterling	877	34.8	158	51.8	42	13.8	60	19.7	45	14.8
Stonewall	1,134	47.6	136	25.2	192	35.6	149	27.6	62	11.5
Sutton	2,707	41.0	537	48.3	264	23.8	153	13.8	150	13.5
Swisher	4,964	33.5	463	27.9	520	31.3	383	23.1	279	16.8
Tarrant	924,321	35.3	130,513	40.0	101,402	31.1	56,084	17.2	36,770	11.3
Taylor	80,087	35.4	12,280	43.3	5,127	18.1	7,989	28.2	2,793	9.9
Terrell	811	63.7	186	36.0	179	34.6	70	13.5	74	14.3
Terry	7,615	32.8	1,015	40.6	681	27.3	446	17.9	338	13.5
Throckmorton	1,230	40.0	187	38.0	87	17.7	154	31.3	63	12.8
Titus	15,410	37.9	2,242	38.4	1,851	31.7	1,235	21.2	484	8.3
Tom Green	64,936	33.2	10,987	50.9	4,296	19.9	2,740	12.7	3,423	15.9
Travis	566,140	40.0	59,794	26.4	101,989	45.1	31,090	13.7	30,519	13.5
Trinity	11,096	38.6	1,296	30.2	1,259	29.4	1,031	24.0	681	15.9
Tyler	13,568	38.7	2,043	38.9	1,494	28.5	1,053	20.1	634	12.1
Upshur	24,684	38.6	4,221	44.3	2,230	23.4	2,102	22.1	938	9.8
Upton	2,050	31.0	292	46.0	94	14.8	185	29.1	63	9.9
Uvalde	16,211	33.4	1,981	36.6	1,582	29.2	984	18.2	846	15.6
Val Verde	26,521	27.4	2,651	36.4	2,736	37.6	1,184	16.3	661	9.1
Van Zandt	32,827	37.8	5,695	45.9	2,525	20.4	2,629	21.2	1,513	12.2
Victoria	54,430	34.4	7,757	41.4	4,743	25.3	4,152	22.1	1,042	10.4
Walker	29,248	37.9	4,012	36.2	2,600	23.4	2,520	22.7	1,882	17.0
Waller	26,062	31.1	2,389	29.5	2,161	26.7	2,382	29.4	1,129	13.9
Ward	6,578	31.8	828	39.6	361	17.3	685	32.8	205	9.8
Washington	20,974	44.9	3,867	41.1	1,774	18.9	1,882	20.0	1,831	19.5
Webb	101,455	18.1	4,641	25.2	9,254	50.3	3,172	17.2	1,222	6.6
Wharton	24,812	35.3	2,278	26.0	2,396	27.3	2,797	31.9	1,256	14.3
Wheeler	3,638	36.1	671	51.1	194	14.8	239	18.2	201	15.3
Wichita	78,202	35.1	12,475	45.4	5,211	19.0	6,824	24.8	2,820	10.3
Wilbarger	8,646	39.3	1,405	41.3	663	19.5	873	25.7	438	12.9
Willacy	11,046	18.6	713	34.7	759	36.9	442	21.5	131	6.4
Williamson	208,521	40.3	35,956	42.8	23,072	27.5	14,242	16.9	9,561	11.4
Wilson	24,894	43.9	2,989	27.3	2,702	24.7	3,456	31.6	1,726	15.8
Winkler	3,875	38.7	641	42.8	277	18.5	401	26.8	168	11.2
Wise	34,370	35.9	5,299	42.9	2,610	21.1	2,705	21.9	1,669	13.5
Wood	25,314	44.6	5,641	50.0	2,017	17.9	2,321	20.6	1,249	11.1
Yoakum	4,343	36.3	743	47.1	275	17.4	354	22.4	194	12.3
Young	11,483	41.3	2,393	50.4	851	17.9	958	20.2	521	11.0
Zapata	7,160	16.8	385	32.0	648	53.8	88	7.3	77	6.4
Zavala	7,967	22.1	322	18.3	1,078	61.4	232	13.2	110	6.3

Legislature Addresses Issues amid Political Discord

An insurgency against House Speaker Tom Craddick capped the final days of the 80th Legislature, producing political tensions for the 2008 elections and a battle over who would wield the gavel in the 2009 legislative session.

The 2007 session ended on an unusually discordant note, even though lawmakers had fewer thorny issues to deal with than usual and Republicans controlled both houses and the leadership.

Republicans occupied the positions of governor, speaker and lieutenant governor and a 20-11 majority in the Senate and 81-69 majority in the House.

The long-hovering school finance issue had finally been resolved, and the state was sitting on an historic $14 billion surplus. After Gov. Rick Perry pared down the Legislature's spending bill with his line-item veto, the budget for the 2008-2009 biennium was $151.9 billion, an increase of 11.8 percent over the previous two years.

The House began and ended with a speaker's fight. Craddick, the Midland Republican first elected in 2003 when Republicans captured a House majority, beat back a challenge at the session's opening to win his third term as speaker.

Although he promised to relax his tight grip, Craddick's detractors accused him of continued heavy-handed tactics and punishing Republicans who voted against the party leadership. Party conservatives labeled speaker opponents as RINOs – Republicans in Name Only – interested only in a power grab

In the session's final days, a bipartisan band again criticized Craddick's autocratic style and used parliamentary maneuvers to try to force a vote to remove him. Craddick declared that the presiding officer had "absolute authority" over any such motions. During several contentious days, the parliamentarian quit, members were restrained from storming the dais, and dozens of Democrats and Republicans staged a walkout hours before the session's end.

The House was able to complete most of its business, but several members declared as candidates to unseat Craddick as speaker in 2009. Democrats and Republi-

Rich Perry is sworn in as governor in the chamber of the House of Representatives Jan. 16. 2007. Erich Schlegel photo.

cans who defected from the speaker expected challenges in their party primaries in 2008, when House races were expected to divide candidates according to a pro- or anti-Craddick litmus test. The split in Republican ranks fostered hope among Democrats that they could regain a House majority in 2008.

Gov. Rick Perry also had a difficult session, after having been successful in finally fixing Texas' unconstitutional school funding system in a 2006 special session.

Perry persuaded John Sharp, a Democrat and former state comptroller, to chair the Texas Tax Reform Commission. It suggested overhauling the state's business taxes by closing franchise tax loopholes and creating a gross receipts tax on most businesses. The plan could produce new revenues that, with an increase in the state cigarette tax, would enable the state to reduce its reliance on property taxes for schools and allow property taxes to be cut by one-third. The Legislature approved the plan just before a Texas Supreme Court-imposed deadline of June 1, 2006, to fix school finance.

In the regular session, however, Perry saw much of his early agenda squashed. The Legislature overruled his attempt to mandate by executive order that teenage girls be vaccinated against the human papillomavirus vaccines. He also proposed, to deaf ears, that Texas sell its lottery to private interests.

Lawmakers responded to those Texans who opposed Perry's massive Trans-Texas Corridor toll road plan with a bill to restrict private toll road activity. Perry vetoed the bill, which resulted in a compromise that mandated a two-year moratorium on private toll contracts except for those already in the pipeline.

Taxpayers found that previously passed tax rate reductions meant little without property tax appraisal reform, but appraisal reform also sputtered, even after Perry appointed a task force to recommend changes

Lt. Gov. David Dewhurst also did not escape unscathed, getting into hot water when he tried to ram through the Senate a voter identification bill. Republicans wanted the bill to reduce the number of fraudulent voters, but Democrats said it would thwart legitimate voter participation. The issue failed. But Dewhurst was able to pass his pet bill, "Jessica's Law," to strengthen penalties on child molesters.

The 2007 Legislature did produce accomplishments, including more funds for cancer research, college financial aid, border security and disaster relief, and to help Texans purchase private and employer-sponsored health insurance. State park funding was boosted. And the first major water bill in more than a decade passed, addressing conservation and paving the way for the development of up to 19 reservoirs.

The Children's Health Insurance Program was expanded to reinstate many low-income youngsters who had been cut in a money-saving effort in 2003. Oversight of foster care was strengthened after reports of the beating deaths of three foster children, and the Texas Youth Commission that oversees juvenile lockups was overhauled after a sex abuse scandal. Lawmakers also created the largest high school athletes steroids testing program in the country.

A constitutional amendment requiring recorded votes was placed on the November 2007 ballot. The amendment, if passed, would require roll-call votes on final passage of new laws and the posting of votes in the House or Senate journals and on the Internet. For three sessions, *The Dallas Morning News*, other news organizations and good government groups had pressed for record votes.

Education issues took a back seat after several sessions dominated by school finance, but the much-maligned Texas Assessment of Knowledge and Skills (TAKS) test was replaced with end-of-course exams that would count for 15 percent of students' grades, beginning in the 2011-2012 school year.

Lawmakers, however, declined to change the college admission rule that guaranteed a spot in any public university to students who graduate in the top 10 percent of their school class, regardless of the rigors of the academic program. The rule, originally passed to guarantee diversity, drew protests from some parents and lawmakers who said it caused the state's flagship universities to lose talented students.

Among other unsuccessful legislation was a utility bill produced by growing unrest over high electric rates. Legislation failed that would have provided protections for low-income electricity customers and given regulators more tools to combat market abuses by power companies. — *Carolyn Barta.*

General Election, 2006

Below are the voting results for the general election held November 7, 2006, for all statewide races and for contested congressional, state senate, courts of appeals and state board of education races. These are official returns as canvassed by the State Canvassing Board. Abbreviations used are (Dem.) Democrat, (Rep.) Republican, (Lib.) Libertarian, (Ind.) Independent and (W-I) Write-in.

Governor

Rick Perry (Rep.)	1,716,792	39.02%
Chris Bell (Dem.)	1,310,337	29.78%
Carole Keeton Strayhorn (Ind.)	796,851	18.11%
Richard "Kinky" Friedman (Ind.)	547,674	12.44%
James Werner (Lib.)	26,749	0.60%
James "Patriot" Dillon (W-I)	713	0.01%
Total vote	4,399,116	

U.S. Senator

Kay Bailey Hutchison (Rep.)	2,661,789	61.69%
Barbara Ann Radnofsky (Dem.)	1,555,202	36.04%
Scott Lanier Jameson (Lib.)	97,672	2.26%
Total Vote	4,314,663	

Lieutenant Governor

David Dewhurst (Rep.)	2,513,530	58.19%
Maria Luisa Alvarado (Dem.)	1,617,490	37.44%
Judy Baker (Lib.)	188,206	4.35%
Total vote	4,319,226	

Attorney General

Greg Abbott (Rep.)	2,556,063	59.51%
David Van Os (Dem.)	1,599,069	37.23%
Jon Roland (Lib.)	139,668	3.25%
Total vote	4,294,800	

Comptroller of Public Accounts

Susan Combs (Rep.)	2,547,323	59.47%
Fred Head (Dem.)	1,585,362	37.01%
Mike Burris (Lib.)	150,565	3.51%
Total vote	4,283,250	

Commissioner of General Land Office

Jerry Patterson (Rep.)	2,317,554	55.13%
VaLinda Hathcox (Dem.)	1,721,964	40.96%
Michael A. French (Lib.)	164,098	3.90%
Total Vote	4,203,616	

Commissioner of Agriculture

Todd Staples (Rep.)	2,307,406	54.77%
Hank Gilbert (Dem.)	1,760,402	41.78%
Clay Woolam (Lib.)	144,989	3.44%
Total vote	4,212,797	

Railroad Commissioner

Elizabeth Ames Jones (Rep.)	2,269,743	54.03%

Dale Henry (Dem.)................................1,752,947 ...... 41.73%
Tabitha Serrano (Lib.).............................177,648 .... 4.22%
Total vote......................................4,200,338

U.S. HOUSE OF REPRESENTATIVES
(See map of new districts on p. 525. Those districts that are part of the special election due to redistricting are in italics below. In those districts, if a candidate did not get a majority of the vote, a runoff election was required.)

District 1
Louie Gohmert (Rep.)............................104,099 ...... 68.00%
Roger L. Owen (Dem.) ....46,303 ...... 30.24%
Donald Perkison (Lib.).............................2,668 .... 1.74%
Total Vote......................................153,070

District 2
Ted Poe (Rep.) ....90,490 ...... 65.63%
Gary E. Binderim (Dem) ....45,080 ...... 32.69%
Justo J. Perez (Lib.)..................................2,295 .... 1.66%
Total Vote......................................137,865

District 3
Sam Johnson (Rep.).................................88,690 ...... 62.51%
Dan Dodd (Dem.) ....49,529 ...... 34.90%
Christopher J. Claytor (Lib.).......................3,662 .... 2.58%
Total Vote......................................141,881

District 4
Ralph M. Hall (Rep.) ....106,495 ...... 64.43%
Glenn Melancon (Dem.) ....55,278 ...... 33.44%
Kurt G. Helm (Lib.)..................................3,496 ....2.11%
Total Vote......................................165,269

District 5
Jeb Hensarling (Rep.)..............................88,478 ...... 61.76%
Charlie Thompson (Dem.). ....50,983 ...... 35.58%
Mike Nelson (Lib.)....................................3,791 .... 2.64%
Total Vote 143,252

District 6
Joe L. Barton (Rep.) ....91,927 ...... 60.46%
David T. Harris (Dem.) ....56,369 ...... 37.07%
Carl Nulsen...3,740 .... 2.45%
Total Vote 152,036

District 7
John Culberson (Rep.) ....99,318 ...... 59.19%
Jim Henley (Dem.).................................64,514 ...... 38.45%
Drew Parks (Lib.).....................................3,953 .... 2.35%
Total Vote 167,785

District 8
Kevin Brady (Rep.) ....105,665 ...... 67.27%
James "Jim" Wright (Dem.)......................51,393 ...... 32.72%
Total Vote 157,058

District 10
Michael T. McCaul (Rep.) ....97,726 ...... 55.28%
Ted Ankrum (Dem.)................................71,415 ...... 40.40%
Michael Badnarik (Lib.)............................7,614 .... 4.30%
Total Vote 176,755

District 12
Kay Granger (Rep.) ....98,371 ...... 66.94%
John R. Morris (Dem.) ....45,676 ...... 31.08%
Gardner Osborne (Lib.) ....2,888 .... 1.96%
Total Vote 146,935

District 13
Mac Thornberry (Rep.) ....108,107 ...... 74.35%
Roger J. Waun (Dem.)............................33,460 ...... 23.01%
Jim Thompson (Lib.).................................3,829 .... 2.63%
Total Vote 145,396

District 14
Ron Paul (Rep.)......................................94,380 ...... 60.18%
Shane Sklar (Dem.)................................62,429 ...... 39.81%
Total Vote 156,809

District 15
Paul B. Haring (Rep.) ....16,601 ... 23.72%
Rubén Hinojosa (Dem.) ....43,236 ...... 61.77%
Eddie Zamora (Rep.) ....10,150 ...... 14.50%
Total Vote 69,987

District 16
Silvestre Reyes (Dem.)...........................61,116 ...... 78.66%
Gordon R. Strickland (Lib..).....................16,572 ...... 21.33%
Total Vote 77,688

District 17
Van Taylor (Rep.)....................................64,142 ...... 40.30%
Chet Edwards (Dem.)..............................92,478 ......58.11%
Guillermo Acosta (Lib.) ....2,504 ...... 1.57%
Total Vote 159,124

District 18
Ahmad R. Hassan (Rep.) ....16,448 ......19.11%
Sheila Jackson Lee (Dem.) ....65,936 ...... 76.62%
Patrick Warren (Lib.)..................................3,667 ...... 4.26%
Total Vote 86,051

District 19
Randy Neugebauer (Rep.) ....94,785 ...... 67.70%
Robert Ricketts (Dem.).............................41,676 ...... 29.76%
Fred C. Jones (Lib.)...................................3,349 .... 2.39%
Mike Sadler (W-I)...197 .... 0.14%
Total Vote 140,007

District 20
Charles A. Gonzalez (Dem.)...................68,348 ...... 87.35%
Michael Idrogo (Lib.)................................9,897 ...... 12.64%
Total Vote 78,245

District 21
Tommy Calvert (Ind.) ....5,280 ...... 2.59%
John Courage (Dem.)..............................49,957 ...... 24.51%
Gene Kelly (Dem.) ....18,355 .... 9.00%
James Lyle Peterson (Ind.).......................2,189 ...... 1.07%
Mark J. Rossano (Ind.) ....1,439 .... 0.70%
Lamar Smith (Rep.) ....122,486 ...... 60.10%
James Arthur Strohm (Lib.).......................4,076 .... 2.00%
Total Vote 203,782

District 22 *(unexpired term)*

(After Republican Tom DeLay resigned from Congress, the governor called a special election to coincide with the general election to fill the vacated seat until the new Congress convened in January 2007, when the winner of the general election took office.)

Shelley Sekula-Gibbs (Rep.) ....76,924 ...... 62.07%
Don Richardson (Rep.)............................7,405 .... 5.97%
M. Bob Smither (Lib.)..............................23,425 ...... 18.90%
Steve Stockman (Rep.) ....13,600 ...... 10.97%
Giannibecego Hoa Tran (Rep.)..................2,568 .... 2.07%
Total Vote 123,922

District 22
Nick Lampson (Dem.)..............................76,775 ...... 51.79%
Bob Smither (Lib.)....................................9,009 .... 6.07%
Joe Reasbeck (W-I)..89 .... 0.06%
Don Richardson (W-I)....................................428 .... 0.28%
Shelley Sekula-Gibbs (W-I) ....61,938 ...... 41.78%
Total Vote 148,239

District 23
August G. "Augie" Beltran (Dem.).............2,750 .... 2.22%
Rick Bolanos (Dem.).................................2,566 .... 2.07%
Henry Bonilla (Rep.) ....59,472 ...... 48.03%
Adrian DeLeon (Dem.).............................2,198 .... 1.77%
Lukin Gilliland (Dem.) ....13,728 ......11.08%
Ciro D. Rodriguez (Dem.) ....24,594 ...... 19.86%
Craig T. Stephens (Ind.) ....4,031 .... 3.25%
Albert Uresti (Dem.)................................14,460 ......11.68%
Total Vote 123,799

District 23 Runoff (Dec. 12)

Henry Bonilla (Rep.) ....*32,165* *45.68%*
Ciro D. Rodriguez (Dem.) ....*38,247* *54.32%*
   Total Vote *70,412*

District 24

Kenny E Marchant (Rep.) ....83,835 ...... 59.82%
Gary R. Page (Dem.).............................52,075 ...... 37.15%
Mark Frohman (Lib.) ....4,228 .... 3.01%
   Total Vote 140,138

District 25

Barbara Cunningham (Lib.) ....*6,942* *4.24%*
Lloyd Doggett (Dem.) ....*109,911* *67.25%*
Brian Parrett (Ind.) ....*3,596* *2.20%*
Grant Rostig (Rep.) ....*42,975* *26.29%*
   Total Vote *163,424*

District 26

Michael C. Burgess (Rep.) ....94,219 ...... 60.21%
Tim Barnwell (Dem.).............................58,271 ...... 37.23%
Rich Haas (Lib.).....................................3,993 ...... 2.55%
   Total Vote 156,483

District 27

Wm. "Willie" Vaden (Rep.) ....42,538 ...... 38.91%
Solomon P. Ortiz (Dem.)........................62,058 ...... 56.77%
Robert Powell (Lib.)................................4,718 ...... 4.31%
   Total Vote 109,314

District 28

Ron Avery (Con.) ....*9,383* *12.06%*
Henry Cuellar (Dem.)..............................*52,574* *67.61%*
Frank Enriquez (Dem.) ....*15,798* *20.31%*
   Total Vote *77,755*

District 29

Eric Story (Rep.) ....12,347 ...... 24.42%
Gene Green (Dem.).................................37,174 ...... 73.53%
Clifford Lee Messina (Lib.)........................1,029 ...... 2.03%
   Total Vote 50,550

District 30

Wilson Aurbach (Rep.)...........................17,850 ...... 17.59%
Eddie Bernice Johnson (Dem.)................81,348 ...... 80.18%
Ken Ashby (Lib.) ....2,250 ...... 2.21%
   Total Vote 101,448

District 31

John R. Carter (Rep.) ....90,869 ...... 58.48%
Mary Beth Harrell (Dem.).......................60,293 ...... 38.80%
Matt McAdoo (Lib.) ....4,221 ...... 2.71%
   Total Vote 155,383

District 32

Pete Sessions (Rep.)..............................71,461 ...... 56.42%
Will Pryor (Dem.) ....52,269 ...... 41.26%
John B. Hawley (Lib.) ....2,922 ...... 2.30%
   Total Vote 126,652

STATE COURTS

Chief Justice, Supreme Court

Wallace Jefferson (Rep.) ....2,575,696 ...... 76.13%
Tom Oxford (Lib.) ....799,373 ...... 23.62%
Charles E. Waterbury (W-I) ....8,045 .... 0.23%
   Total Vote 3,383,114

Justice, Supreme Court, Place 2

Don Willett (Rep.) ....2,135,612 ...... 51.04%
William E. "Bill" Moody (Dem.)...........1,877,909 ..... 44.88%
Wade Wilson (Lib.) ....169,918 .... 4.06%
   Total Vote 4,183,439

Justice, Supreme Court, Place 4

David M. Medina (Rep.)......................2,558,036 ...... 75.48%
Jerry Adkins (Lib.)...............................830,780 ...... 24.51%
   Total Vote 3,388,816

Justice, Supreme Court, Place 6

Nathan Hecht (Rep.)..........................2,560,036 ...... 75.93%
Todd Phillippi (Lib.) ....811,527 ...... 24.06%
   Total Vote 3,371,563

Justice, Supreme Court, Place 8

Phil Johnson (Rep.)...........................2,563,089 ...... 76.30%
Jay H. Cookingham (Lib.)....................795,718 ...... 23.69%
   Total Vote 3,358,807

Presiding Judge, Court of Criminal Appeals

Sharon Keller (Rep.) ....2,346,204 ...... 56.64%
J.R. Molina (Dem.)............................1,795,416 ...... 43.35%
   Total Vote 4,141,620

Judge, Court of Criminal Appeals, Place 7

Barbara Parker Hervey (Rep.)...........2,557,034 ...... 75.85%
Quanah Parker (Lib.) ....813,731 ...... 24.14%
   Total Vote 3,370,765

Judge, Court of Criminal Appeals, Place 8

Charles Holcomb (Rep.) ....2,548,406 ...... 76.02%
Dave Howard (Lib.).............................803,439 ...... 23.97%
   Total Vote 3,351,845

COURTS OF APPEALS

Justice, First District, Place 9

Elsa Alcala (Rep.) ....406,738 ...... 50.55%
Jim Sharp (Dem.) ....397,830 ...... 49.44%
   Total Vote 804,568

Justice, Third District, Place 2

Alan Waldrop (Rep.) ....248,966 ...... 51.30%
Jim Sybert Coronado (Dem.)................236,314 ...... 48.69%
   Total Vote 485,280

Justice, Third District, Place 3

Will Wilson (Rep.) ....241,811 ...... 49.52%
Diane Henson (Dem.)..........................246,411 ...... 50.47%
   Total Vote 488,222

Justice, Third District, Place 5

David Puryear (Rep.).............................256,044 ...... 52.26%
Mina A. Brees (Dem.) ....233,876 ...... 47.73%
   Total Vote 489,920

Justice, Third District, Place 6

Bob Pemberton (Rep.).........................250,567 ...... 51.24%
Bree Buchanan (Dem.).........................238,491 ...... 48.75%
   Total Vote 489,148

Justice, Fourth District, Place 3

Rebecca Simmons (Rep.) ....219,126 ...... 52.56%
Richard Garcia Jr. (Dem.) ....197,716 ...... 47.43%
   Total Vote 416,842

Justice, Fourth District, Place 4

Steve Hilbig (Rep.) ....215,264 ...... 50.99%
Dan Pozza (Dem.)................................206,857 ...... 49.00%
   Total Vote 422,121

Justice, Fourth District, Place 5

Karen Angelini (Rep.) ....229,229 ...... 54.62%
Lauro A. Bustamante (Dem.)................190,431 ...... 45.37%
   Total Vote 419,660

Justice, Fourth District, Place 7

Phylis Speedlin (Rep.)..........................218,787 ...... 52.53%
Eddie DeLaGarza (Dem.).......................197,646 ...... 47.46%
   Total Vote 416,433

Justice, Sixth District, Place 2

Bailey C. Moseley (Rep.).......................92,334 ...... 58.18%
Ben Franks (Dem.) ....66,351 ...... 41.81%
   Total Vote 158,685

Justice, Thirteenth District, Place 2

Rose Vela (Rep.) ....128,901 ...... 53.47%
Frederico "Fred" Hinojosa (Dem.)..........112,126 ...... 46.52%
   Total Vote 241,027

Justice, Fourteenth District, Place 6

Richard Edelman (Rep.) ....426,517 ...... 53.37%
Leora T. Kahn (Dem.) ....372,504 ...... 46.62%
   Total Vote 799,021

STATE BOARD OF EDUCATION
District 3

Tony Cunningham (Rep.)........................80,695 ...... 40.65%

Rick Agosto (Dem.)................................ 117,786 ...... 59.34%
  Total Vote 198,481

District 5
Ken Mercer (Rep.)................................234,807 ...... 71.10%
Bill Oliver (Lib.) ....95,406 ...... 28.89%
  Total Vote 330,213

District 9
Don McLeroy (Rep.) .... 192,218 ...... 59.58%
Maggie Charleton (Dem.) .... 130,375 ...... 40.41%
  Total Vote 322,593

District 10
Cynthia Dunbar (Rep.)........................221,808 ...... 70.30%
Martin Thomen (Lib.) ....93,679 ...... 29.69%
  Total Vote 315,487

District 12
Geraldine "Tincy" Miller (Rep.)...............186,295 ...... 77.84%
Matthew Havener (Lib.) ....53,013 ...... 22.15%
  Total Vote 239,308

District 15
Bob Craig (Rep.)................................202,999 ...... 83.81%
Brandon Stacker (Lib.)...........................39,191 ...... 16.18%
  Total Vote 242,190

STATE SENATE
District 1
Kevin Eltife (Rep.)................................ 109,450 ...... 83.13%
Jason Albers (Lib.) .... 22,211 ...... 16.86%
  Total Vote 131,661

District 2
Bob Deuell (Rep.) ....92,431 ...... 78.68%
Dennis Kaptain (Lib.).............................25,043 ...... 21.31%
  Total Vote 117,474

District 5
Steve Ogden (Rep.).............................105,979 ...... 61.48%
Stephen Wyman (Dem.) ....59,671 ...... 34.61%
Darrell R. Grear (Lib.) ....6,719 .... 3.89%
  Total Vote 172,369

District 7
Dan Patrick (Rep.) .... 118,067 ...... 69.18%
F. Michael Kubosh (Dem.) ....52,586 ...... 30.81%
  Total Vote 170,653

District 12
Jane Nelson (Rep.)............................... 109,513 ...... 63.98%
Dwight B. Fullingim (Dem.).....................55,380 ...... 32.35%
Morgan Ware (Lib.) ....6,273 .... 3.66%
  Total Vote 171,166

District 14
Kirk Watson (Dem.) .... 127,223 ...... 80.31%
Robert "Rock" Howard (Lib.)....................31,180 ...... 19.68%
  Total Vote 158,403

District 15
Angel DeLaRosa (Rep.) ....33,396 ...... 36.99%
John Whitmire (Dem.)..............................56,884 ...... 63.00%
  Total Vote 90,280

District 17
Kyle Janek (Rep.)...................................88,483 ...... 77.82%
Phil Kurtz (Lib.) ....25,212 ...... 22.17%
  Total Vote 113,695

District 18
Glenn Hegar (Rep.) .... 110,512 ...... 78.92%
Roy O. Wright II (Lib.).............................29,511 ...... 21.07%
  Total Vote 140,023

District 19 *(unexpired term)*

(After Democrat Frank Madla resigned, the governor called a special election to coincide with the general election to fill the vacated seat until the new Legislature convened in January 2007, when the winner of the general election took office.)

Dick Bowen (Rep.)................................38,070 ...... 40.02%
Carlos I. Uresti (Dem.)...........................57,045 ...... 59.97%
  Total Vote 95,115

District 19
Dick Bowen (Rep.)................................40,621 ...... 40.82%
Carlos I. Uresti (Dem.)............................58,876 ...... 59.17%
  Total Vote 99,497

District 22
Kip Averitt (Rep.) .... 112,765 ...... 80.60%
Phil Smart (Lib.).....................................27,141 ...... 19.39%
  Total Vote 139,906

District 25
Jeff Wentworth (Rep.)........................... 132,872 ...... 58.32%
Kathleen "Kathi" Thomas (Dem.).............84,816 ...... 37.22%
James R. "Bob" Thompson (Lib.) ....10,137 .... 4.44%
  Total Vote 227,825

District 29
Donald R. "Dee" Margo (Rep.) ....36,127 ...... 41.21%
Eliot Shapleigh (Dem.)............................51,531 ...... 58.78%
  Total Vote 87,658

Texas Primary Elections, 2006

Below are the official returns for the contested races only in the Republican and Democratic Party primaries held March 7, 2006. Included are statewide races and selected district races. The runoffs were held on April 12.

DEMOCRATIC PRIMARY

Governor
Chris Bell ....324,869 ...... 63.87%
Bob Gammage ....145,081 ...... 28.52%
Rashad Jafer ....38,652 ...... 7.59%
  Total vote..508,602

U.S. Senator
Darrel Reece Hunter................................93,609 ...... 18.69%
Gene Kelly ....191,400 ...... 38.21%
Barbara Ann Radnofsky........................215,776 ...... 43.08%
  Total Vote..500,785

Lieutenant Governor
Maria Luisa Alvarado ....207,835 ...... 41.51%
Adrian De Leon .... 112,011 ...... 22.37%
Benjamin Z. Grant ....180,769 ...... 36.10%
  Total vote..500,615

Commissioner of Agriculture
Hank Gilbert...323,517 ...... 71.14%
Koecadee Melton Jr..............................131,218 ...... 28.85%
  Total vote...454,735

U.S. HOUSE OF REPRESENTATIVES
District 1
Roger L. Owen ....10,121 ...... 53.34%
Duane Shaw..8,851 ...... 46.65%
  Total Vote...18,972

District 7
Jim Henley..3,950 ...... 67.49%
David Murff ....1,902 ...... 32.50%
  Total Vote...5,852

District 10
Ted Ankrum...3,703 ...... 36.73%
Paul Foreman ....3,610 ...... 35.81%
Pat Mynatt ....1,291 ...... 12.80%
Sid Smith ....1,475 ...... 14.63%

Total Vote..10,079

District 28
Henry Cuellar...24,256 ...... 53.09%
Victor Morales...2,943 ...... 6.44%
Ciro D. Rodriguez.................................18,484 ...... 40.46%
Total Vote..45,683

STATE SENATE
District 18
Bret Baldwin ....10,369 ...... 48.76%
Henry Boehm Jr......................................10,895 ...... 51.23%
Total Vote 21,264

District 19
Frank Madla...18,936 ...... 43.48%
Carlos I. Uresti...................................24,610 ...... 56.51%
Total Vote 43,546

Prop. 1 – Raising minimum wage
In Favor ....529,220 ...... 88.89%
Against...66,083 ....11.10%
Total Vote 595,303

Prop. 2 – Restoration of rights to trial by jury in civil cases
In Favor ....502,721 ...... 88.16%
Against...67,495 ....11.83%
Total Vote 570,216

COURTS OF APPEALS
Justice, Thirteenth District, Place 4
Esther Cortez......................................38,272 ...... 42.66%
Nelda Vidaurri Rodriguez ....51,431 ...... 57.33%
Total Vote 89,703

Justice, Thirteenth District, Place 5
Gina M. Benavides ....50,771 ...... 55.50%
Errlinda Castillo ....40,701 ...... 44.49%
Total Vote 91,472

DEMOCRATIC RUNOFF
U.S. Senator
Barbara Ann Radnofsky.......................124,663 ...... 60.15%
Gene Kelly ....82,589 ...... 39.84%
Total Vote 207,252

Lieutenant Governor
Maria Luisa Alvarado ....118,396 ...... 57.59%
Benjamin Z. Grant ....87,164 ...... 42.40%
Total Vote 205,560

U.S. House, District 10
Ted Ankrum...2,611 ...... 70.77%
Paul Foreman ....1,078 ...... 29.22%
Total Vote 3,689

REPUBLICAN PRIMARY
Governor
Rick Perry ....552,545 ... 84.23%
Star Locke ....23,030 .... 3.51%
Larry Kilgore ....50,119 .... 7.64%
Rhett R. Smith ....30,225 .... 4.60%
Total Vote 655,919

Lieutenant Governor
David Dewhurst ....492,052 ...... 78.25%
Tom Kelly ....136,707 ...... 21.74%
Total Vote 628,759

Railroad Commissioner
Elizabeth Ames Jones ....385,269 ...... 65.64%
Buck Werner..201,653 ...... 34.35%
Total Vote 586,922

Justice, Supreme Court, Place 2
Steve Smith ....274,302 ...... 49.45%
Don Willett ....280,356 ...... 50.54%
Total Vote 554,658

Presiding Judge, Court of Criminal Appeals
Sharon Keller.......................................294,862 ...... 52.80%
Tom Price...263,554 ...... 47.19%
Total Vote 558,416

Judge, Court of Criminal Appeals, Place 8
Robert W. Francis.................................128,078 ...... 24.29%
Charles Holcomb ....237,284 ...... 45.00%
Terry Keel ....161,913 ...... 30.70%
Total Vote 527,275

U.S. HOUSE OF REPRESENTATIVES
District 3
Sam Johnson..13,348 ...... 85.34%
Bob Johnson..2,292 ..... 14.65%
Total Vote 15,640

District 14
Ron Paul..24,086 ...... 77.64%
Cynthia Sinatra ....6,935 ...... 22.35%
Total Vote 31,021

District 15
Paul B. Haring ....5,552 ...... 70.90%
Eddie Zamora ....2,278 ...... 29.09%
Total Vote 7,830

District 17
Tucker Anderson ....14,712 ...... 45.97%
Van Taylor..17,291 ...... 54.02%
Total Vote 31,887

District 22
Tom DeLay ....20,563 ...... 61.99%
Tom Campbell.......................................9,941 ...... 29.97%
Mike Fjetland ....1,550 ...... 4.67%
Pat Baig ....1,115 ...... 3.36%
Total Vote 33,169

District 30
Wilson Aurbach.....................................1,614 ...... 44.51%
Amir Omar ....1,308 ...... 36.07%
Fred A. Wood.......................................704 ...... 19.41%
Total Vote 3,626

STATE SENATE
District 2
Dob Deuell...16,992 ...... 67.28%
Tim McCallum.......................................8,261 ...... 32.71%
Total Vote 25,253

District 3
Frank Denton..5,042 ...... 15.15%
Dave Kleimann ....6,721 ...... 18.05%
Robert Nichols ....20,190 ...... 54.22%
Bob Reeves ....4,678 ...... 12.56%
Total Vote 37,231

District 7
Dan Patrick ....28,870 ...... 68.81%
Mark Ellis ....2,548 ...... 6.07%
Peggy Hamric ....6,904 ...... 16.45%
Joe Nixon...3,630 .... 8.65%
Total Vote 41,952

District 18
Gary Gates ....12,985 ...... 35.53%
Glenn Hegar ....20,112 ...... 55.03%
David Stall ....3,449 .... 9.43%
Total Vote 36,546

District 19
Dick Bowen...3,513 ...... 51.32%
Darrel Brown...3,332 ...... 48.67%
Total Vote 6,845

Prop. 1 – Proposes requirement of photo ID to vote in any Texas election
In Favor ....592,862 ...... 87.66%
Against...83,403 ...... 12.33%
Total Vote...676,265

Prop. 2 – Prohibit takings of private property
In Favor ....635,075 ...... 94.08%
Against...................................39,931 .... 5.91%
Total Vote 675,006

Prop. 3 – Limit government spending increases with some exceptions
In Favor ....589,721 ...... 89.76%
Against...................................67,208 ...... 10.23%
Total Vote 656,929

Prop. 4 – Reduce property tax increase rate to 5% or less
In Favor ....614,026 ...... 91.90%
Against...................................54,109 .... 8.09%
Total Vote 668,135

COURTS OF APPEALS
Justice, Third District, Place 3
Bill Davidson................................15,143 ...... 24.37%
William Paul (Bill) Green.........................13,460 ...... 21.66%
Lee Parsley...................................12,610 ...... 20.29%
Will Wilson....................................20,906 ...... 33.65%
Total Vote 62,119

Justice, Fourth District, Place 4
Steve Hilbig ....28,663 ....66.11%
Grace Kunde ....14,693 ...... 33.88%
Total Vote 43,356

Justice, Sixth District, Place 2
M C Bruder...................................2,217 .... 8.30%
Andrew G. Khoury ....10,618 ...... 39.79%
Bailey C. Moseley..........................13,850 ...... 51.90%
Total Vote 26,685

Justice, Seventh District, Place 3
Pat Pirtle....................................27,821 ...... 55.58%

Walt Weaver ....22,232 ...... 44.41%
Total Vote 50,053

STATE BOARD OF EDUCATION
District 5
Mark Loewe................................7,613 ...... 15.23%
Ken Mercer...............................24,880 ...... 49.79%
Dan Montgomery ....17,471 ...... 34.96%
Total Vote 49,964

District 10
Tony Dale...................................18,114 ...... 35.72%
Cynthia Dunbar.............................32,589 ...... 64.27%
Total Vote 50,703

REPUBLICAN RUNOFF
U.S. House, District 30
Wilson Aurbach................................1,129 ...... 60.82%
Amir Omar ....727 ...... 39.17%
Total Vote 1,856

Judge, Court of Criminal Appeals, Place 8
Charles Holcomb ....89,395 ...... 53.64%
Terry Keel ....77,262 ...... 46.35%
Total Vote 166,657

Justice, Court of Appeals, Third District, Place 3
Will Wilson.....................................18,732 ...... 61.71%
Bill Davidson ....11,621 ...... 38.28%
Total Vote 30,353

State Board of Education, District 5
Ken Mercer ....12,359 ...... 61.38%
Dan Montgomery...............................7,776 ...... 38.61%
Total Vote 20,135

Political Party Organizations

DEMOCRATIC State Executive Committee
www.txdemocrats.org
Chair, Boyd Richie, Graham, 707 Rio Grande, Austin 78701; **Vice Chair**, Roy Laverne Brooks, Fort Worth; **Vice Chair for Finance**, Dennis Speight, Austin; **Secretary**, Ruby Jensen, Houston; **Treasurer**, Victor Garza, Edinburg; **Parliamentarians**, Ed Cogburn, Houston; Corinne Sabo, San Antonio; Gary Horton, Galveston; Sheryle Roppolo, Channelview; **Sergeant-at-Arms**, Bruce Elfant, Austin.

National Committee members: Alonzo Cantu, McAllen; Norma Fisher Flores, El Paso; Yvonne Davis, Dallas; Al Edwards, Houston; Jaime A. Gonzalez Jr., McAllen; David Holmes, Austin; Eddie Bernice Johnson, Dallas; Senfronia Thompson, Houston; Sue Lovell, Houston; Betty Richie, Graham; Bob Slagle, Sherman; C. Giovanni Garibay, Houston, Denise Johnson, Houston, Robert Martinez, North Richland Hills, and John Patrick, Friendswood.

District — Member and Hometown
1. Norma Narramore, Winfield; Johnny Weaver, Henderson.
2. Martha Williams, Terrell; Steve Tillery, Garland.
3. Kathleen Hawkins, Buna; Dennis Teal, Corrigan.
4. Sylvia McDuffie, Nederland; John Baker, Bridge City.
5. Kay Sweat, Lexington; Bill Holcomb, Crockett.
6. Rose A. Salas, Houston; Allan Jamail, Houston.
7. Joy Demark, Houston; Farrukh Shamsi, Houston.
8. Barbara Oldenburg, Plano; David Griggs, Addison.
9. Susan Culp, Grand Prairie; Marvin Sutton, Arlington.
10. Mary Edwards, Fort Worth; Marc House, Arlington.
11. Janet Mayeaux, Seabrook; Lloyd Criss, La Marque.
12. Danny Cooke, Fort Worth; Angela Wall, Watauga.
13. Jennifer Sanders, Houston; Rodney Griffin, Missouri City.
14. Fran Vincent, Austin; Rich Bailey, Austin.
15. Lenora Sorola-Pohlman, Houston; Ken Yarbrough, Houston.

16. Theresa Daniel, Dallas; Shannon Bailey, Dallas.
17. Ella Tyler, Houston; Arif Gafur, Houston.
18. Donald Bankston, Richmond; Vickie Vogel, La Grange.
19. Jo McCall, San Antonio; Bob Dean, Pecos.
20. Danny Noyola Jr., Corpus Christi; Rosalie Weisfeld, McAllen.
21. Tom Walker, Tilden; Linda Perez, Floresville.
22. JoAnn Jenkins, Ovilla; Danny Trull, Waxahachie.
23. Kenneth Molberg, Dallas; Natesha Wyrick-Cathey, Dallas.
24. Dian Ruud, Temple; Bill Perkison, Kerrville.
25. Zada True-Courage, San Antonio; Michael Wilson, Austin.
26. Madeleine Dewar, San Antonio; vacant.
27. Armando Martinez, Weslaco; Veronica De Lafuente, Harlingen.
28. J.B. Hall, San Angelo; Carolyn Salsberry, Amherst.
29. Yolanda Clay, El Paso; Michael Apodaca, El Paso.
30. Hal Ray Jr., Aledo; Victoria Winner, Celina.
31. Roberta Hicks, Amarillo; John James, Midland.

Senate Democratic Caucus: Leticia Van de Putte, San Antonio.

House Democratic Caucus: Roberto Alonzo, Dallas.

Texas Young Democrats: Shondra Wygal, Houston; Byron LaMasters, Dallas.

County Chairs Assn.: Philip Ruiz, Lockhart; Sharon Teal, Corrigan.

Texas Democratic Women: Gloria Caceres, Corpus Christi; Marcia Mainord, Greenville.

Asian American Democrats: AJ Durrani, Katy; Mini Timmaraju, Sugar Land.

Coalition of Black Democrats: Morris Overstreet, Prairie View; Beverly Hatcher, Beaumont.

Texas Environmental Democrats: Fidel Acevedo, Austin; Cecelia Crossley, Austin.

Non-Urban/Ag Caucus: Bill Brannon, Sulphur Springs; Susie Blackmon, Texarkana.

Tejano Democrats: Frank Ortega, Austin; Belinda Castro, Houston.

Stonewall Democrats: Lisa Thomas; Daniel Graney, San Antonio.

Statewide Organizations

Asian American Democrats.

Black Dems: blackdems.com

Coalition of Black Democrats: tcbd.org.

Mexican American Democrats.

Progressive Populist Caucus: www.texaspopulists.com

Stonewall Democrats: stonewalldemocratsofdallas.org/texas/.

Tejano Democrats.

Texas Environmental Democrats: texasenvironmentaldemocrats.org/index.html

Texas Democratic Veterans: texasdemocraticvets.org.

Texas Democratic Women: www.tdw.org.

Texas Young Democrats: www.texasyds.org.

REPUBLICAN State Executive Committee
www.texasgop.org

Chairman, Tina Benkiser, 900 Congress Ave. Ste. 300, Austin 78701; **Vice Chairman**, Robin Armstrong; **Secretary**, David Thackston; **Treasurer**, Wayne Tucker; **General Counsel**, Donna Davidson; **Associate General Counsel**, Dennis Donley; **Parliamentarian**, Butch Davis; **Finance Chairman**, Susan Howard-Chrane; **Sergeant-at-Arms**, John Larrison; **Chaplain**, Bob Long.

National Committee members: Bill Crocker, Austin; Denise McNamara, Dallas.

District — Member and Hometown

1. Dennis Boerner, Pittsburg; Ellen Guthrie, Tyler.
2. Cindy Burkett, Mesquite; John Cook, Terrell.
3. Dianne Caron; James Wiggins, Conroe.
4. Melina Fredricks, Conroe; Michael J. Truncale, Beaumont.
5. Bernice Lewis, College Station; Hal Talton, Round Rock.
6. Rex Teter, Pasadena; Linda Gonzales, Galena Park.
7. Valoree Swanson, Spring; Clint Moore, Spring.
8. Mandy Tschoepe, Plano; Neal J. Katz, Plano.
9. Timothy Hoy, Dallas; Jane Burch, Arlington.
10. James Borchert, Fort Worth; Leslie Recine, Arlington.
11. Kathy Haigler, Deer Park; Dennis Paul, Houston.
12. Tom Quinones, Haltom City; Mona Bailey, Roanoke.
13. Rex Lamb, Houston; Marcelyn Curry, Houston.
14. Brian Russell, Austin; Jan Galbraith, Austin.
15. Nelda Eppes, Houston; Josh Flynn, Houston.
16. Daniel Pickens, Garland; Chris B. Davis, Richardson.
17. Bruce Campbell, Houston; Terese Raia, Sugar Land.
18. Tim Von Dohlen, Goliad; Cress Ann Poston, Sugar Land.
19. Gayla Gabro Miller, Rio Frio; Darrel Brown.
20. Robert Jones, Corpus Christi; Sandra Cararas, McAllen.
21. John Larrison, La Vernia; Dawn Lothringer, Pleasanton.
22. Oneta Leutwyler, Woodway; Christopher DeCluitt, Waco.
23. John M. Fowler, Dallas; Marjorie Ford, DeSoto.
24. Rebecca Williamson, Hunt; Skipper Wallace, Lampasas.
25. Curt Nelson, San Antonio; Jan Koehne, Seguin.
26. Johnny E. Lovejoy II; Marian K. Stanko, San Antonio.
27. Humberto Zamora, Harlingen; Karen Ballard, Brownsville.
28. Jane Cansino, Lubbock; Russ Duerstine, San Angelo.
29. Cindy S. Facker, El Paso; David Thackston, El Paso.
30. Carolyn Nicholas, Wichita Falls; Clyde Siebman, Sherman.
31. Jason Moore; Benona Love, Amarillo.

Statewide Auxiliary Organizations

Texas Republican County Chairmen's Association: www.trcca.org.

Texas Federation of Republican Women: www.tfrw.org.

Republican National Hispanic Assembly of Texas.

Texas Federation of Pachyderm Clubs: www.pachyderms.org.

Texas Young Republican Federation: www.tyrf.org.

Texas Federation of Black Republicans: blackrepublicancounciloftexas.com/. ☆

Vote on Marriage Amendment

On November 8, 2005, an election was held on nine amendments to the Texas Constitution. The second proposed amendment drew the most voters. Proposition 2 stated: "The constitutional amendment providing that marriage in this state consists only of the union of one man and one woman and prohibiting this state or a political subdivision of this state from creating or recognizing any legal status identical or similar to marriage."

Below are the voting returns, by county, for Proposition 2 as canvassed by the State Canvassing Board. Travis County (Austin) was the only county where a majority voted against the amendment. The table shows the percentage of turnout of registered voters in each county, as well as the percentage for and against the ban. Some percentages may add up to more than 100.0 because of rounding off of the figures.

County	Turn-out	For	%	Against	%
TOTAL	18.0	1,723,782	76.3	536,913	23.7
Anderson	23.9	6,137	90.5	640	9.4
Andrews	21.9	1,617	92.0	140	8.0
Angelina	20.0	8,210	90.0	918	10.0
Aransas	17.9	2,117	76.0	668	24.0
Archer	26.0	1,522	91.9	134	8.1
Armstrong	33.0	462	93.1	34	6.9
Atascosa	12.5	2,565	84.7	463	15.3
Austin	22.9	3,401	88.0	462	12.0
Bailey	21.3	812	92.1	70	7.9
Bandera	22.4	2,485	81.3	573	18.7
Bastrop	22.6	5,974	71.1	2,432	28.9
Baylor	22.2	580	92.4	48	7.6
Bee	12.3	1,732	89.1	212	10.9
Bell	14.1	16,891	83.1	3,437	16.9
Bexar	16.7	100,308	69.2	44,578	30.8
Blanco	28.6	1,387	75.2	458	24.8

County	Turn-out	For	%	Against	%
Borden	39.5	162	90.5	17	9.5
Bosque	21.4	2,166	85.8	359	14.2
Bowie	17.0	8,651	91.5	800	8.5
Brazoria	21.4	27,582	82.7	5,789	17.3
Brazos	20.2	12,618	73.4	4,571	26.6
Brewster	20.2	774	64.4	427	35.6
Briscoe	39.9	471	93.8	31	6.2
Brooks	7.2	352	79.3	92	20.7
Brown	24.3	5,413	92.1	466	7.9
Burleson	19.1	1,815	87.9	249	12.1
Burnet	25.8	5,277	81.5	1,195	18.5
Caldwell	16.9	2,676	75.6	862	24.7
Calhoun	17.0	1,872	87.0	279	13.0
Callahan	21.5	1,782	92.8	138	7.2
Cameron	10.2	11,831	72.4	4,501	27.6
Camp	21.7	1,414	89.8	161	10.2
Carson	29.6	1,278	92.2	108	7.8

County	Turn-out	For	%	Against	%	County	Turn-out	For	%	Against	%
Cass	26.4	4,488	93.5	313	6.5	Guadalupe	19.0	9,844	80.7	2,358	19.3
Castro	22.6	938	91.2	91	8.8	Hale	18.9	3,568	92.3	299	7.7
Chambers	17.4	3,149	89.0	390	11.0	Hall	24.3	490	91.6	45	8.4
Cherokee	21.0	5,329	90.8	541	9.2	Hamilton	25.1	1,186	87.1	176	12.9
Childress	25.5	902	94.6	51	5.4	Hansford	29.7	904	95.1	47	4.9
Clay	27.7	1,942	91.6	177	8.4	Hardeman	20.3	545	90.7	56	9.3
Cochran	24.3	441	90.7	45	9.3	Hardin	16.6	5,121	93.7	342	6.3
Coke	22.3	506	91.0	50	9.0	Harris	17.5	236,071	72.5	89,652	27.5
Coleman	21.3	1,224	92.0	107	8.0	Harrison	17.7	6,717	91.0	662	9.0
Collin	16.6	44,765	74.5	15,359	25.5	Hartley	30.0	810	94.3	49	5.7
Collingsworth	26.0	563	93.5	39	6.5	Haskell	24.4	913	92.0	79	8.0
Colorado	19.9	2,302	88.9	287	11.1	Hays	20.3	9,253	58.1	6,665	41.9
Comal	20.5	10,826	81.1	2,515	18.9	Hemphill	28.6	593	91.7	54	8.3
Comanche	22.6	1,845	89.3	220	10.7	Henderson	21.7	9,310	87.8	1,293	12.2
Concho	21.6	367	90.6	38	9.4	Hidalgo	7.5	15,497	81.9	3,436	18.1
Cooke	26.6	5,632	89.8	640	10.2	Hill	20.4	3.911	88.2	523	11.8
Coryell	11.8	3,691	86.5	575	13.5	Hockley	21.2	2,663	91.9	235	8.1
Cottle	19.0	230	91.3	22	8.7	Hood	24.5	6,675	85.8	1,104	14.2
Crane	21.9	501	91.1	49	8.9	Hopkins	21.1	3,947	90.9	397	9.1
Crockett	16.1	392	87.9	54	12.1	Houston	19.8	2,717	91.3	258	8.7
Crosby	29.3	1,107	88.4	145	11.6	Howard	18.6	2,946	90.2	320	9.8
Culberson	8.9	132	82.0	29	18.0	Hudspeth	14.9	206	87.7	29	12.3
Dallam	20.3	615	94.3	37	5.7	Hunt	20.2	8,490	86.9	1,279	13.1
Dallas	18.8	144,559	66.5	72,973	33.5	Hutchinson	24.9	3,714	93.2	272	6.8
Dawson	19.1	1,482	91.7	135	8.3	Irion	25.9	272	84.7	49	15.3
Deaf Smith	18.6	1,664	93.2	121	6.8	Jack	24.1	1,075	91.2	104	8.8
Delta	24.9	766	90.5	80	9.5	Jackson	23.1	1,946	90.5	203	9.5
Denton	16.9	39,650	75.1	13,166	24.9	Jasper	19.1	3,690	93.5	258	6.5
DeWitt	21.6	2,281	88.8	288	11.2	Jeff Davis	22.8	294	75.8	94	24.2
Dickens	51.6	674	87.3	98	12.7	Jefferson	9.4	12,631	86.3	2,003	13.7
Dimmit	7.2	435	80.3	107	19.7	Jim Hogg	5.4	180	89.1	22	10.9
Donley	29.4	689	91.0	68	9.0	Jim Wells	7.3	1,677	88.7	214	11.3
Duval	11.2	833	77.8	238	22.2	Johnson	20.7	13,920	88.1	1,879	11.9
Eastland	25.2	2,386	92.3	199	7.7	Jones	20.9	1,927	90.6	201	9.4
Ector	17.7	10,465	88.3	1,382	11.7	Karnes	14.9	1,099	89.5	129	10.5
Edwards	22.4	299	89.3	36	10.7	Kaufman	16.5	7,535	88.9	939	11.1
Ellis	20.0	13,632	88.7	1,730	11.3	Kendall	23.9	4,044	81.4	923	18.6
El Paso	8.0	19,870	68.1	9,313	31.9	Kenedy	19.0	46	75.4	15	24.6
Erath	22.4	3,766	86.4	592	13.6	Kent	27.7	173	86.5	27	13.5
Falls	19.3	1,595	87.3	231	12.7	Kerr	24.0	6,518	84.4	1,205	15.6
Fannin	22.4	3,775	88.9	469	11.1	Kimble	25.7	668	91.5	62	8.5
Fayette	27.0	3,504	87.5	502	12.5	King	54.2	109	93.2	8	6.8
Fisher	26.0	659	88.8	83	11.2	Kinney	21.0	416	84.2	78	15.8
Floyd	27.1	1,134	95.4	55	4.6	Kleberg	9.3	1,364	80.6	329	19.4
Foard	19.2	154	81.9	34	18.1	Knox	24.2	563	92.1	48	7.9
Fort Bend	17.1	35,695	82.6	7,542	17.4	Lamar	23.0	6,134	91.7	554	8.3
Franklin	26.1	1,468	89.7	169	10.3	Lamb	28.3	2,360	89.4	279	10.6
Freestone	23.3	2,365	90.4	251	9.6	Lampasas	21.5	2,159	85.5	366	14.5
Frio	8.9	752	87.5	107	12.5	La Salle	8.5	303	82.6	64	17.4
Gaines	25.4	1,663	93.8	109	6.2	Lavaca	19.9	2,527	92.2	215	7.8
Galveston	13.6	18,331	74.6	6,241	25.4	Lee	25.4	2,001	87.6	284	12.4
Garza	23.6	646	94.9	35	5.1	Leon	23.0	2,318	90.9	233	9.1
Gillespie	30.9	4,132	82.9	852	17.1	Liberty	13.6	5,477	91.4	517	8.6
Glasscock	35.0	223	88.8	28	11.2	Limestone	18.8	2,294	88.1	311	11.9
Goliad	15.1	718	87.9	99	12.1	Lipscomb	33.5	602	94.1	38	5.9
Gonzales	16.5	1,703	87.2	249	12.8	Live Oak	15.6	1,033	91.5	96	8.5
Gray	30.8	4,099	91.5	379	8.5	Llano	33.5	3,722	82.2	806	17.8
Grayson	21.5	13,641	87.5	1,946	12.5	Loving	25.5	20	71.4	8	28.6
Gregg	20.0	13,213	89.9	1,480	10.1	Lubbock	20.1	25,594	82.6	5,380	17.4
Grimes	22.3	2,423	84.1	459	15.9	Lynn	19.7	758	93.3	54	6.7

County	Turn-out	For	%	Against	%	County	Turn-out	For	%	Against	%
Madison	21.1	1,314	91.9	116	8.1	San Patricio	8.8	3,525	84.9	628	15.1
Marion	15.7	1,046	85.9	171	14.1	San Saba	29.1	977	92.0	85	8.0
Martin	23.5	644	95.4	31	4.6	Schleicher	22.8	377	89.5	44	10.5
Mason	29.2	692	82.5	147	17.5	Scurry	19.6	1,955	92.5	159	7.5
Matagorda	21.8	3,957	87.5	566	12.5	Shackelford	21.9	506	92.8	39	7.2
Maverick	3.4	665	77.7	191	22.3	Shelby	21.9	2,942	92.8	229	7.2
McCulloch	22.3	1,088	90.4	115	9.6	Sherman	34.4	449	93.2	33	6.8
McLennan	17.9	18,819	80.9	4,445	19.1	Smith	21.6	22,357	89.7	2,559	10.3
McMullen	24.4	145	85.8	24	14.2	Somervell	23.6	1,158	88.6	149	11.4
Medina	14.7	3,121	87.3	453	12.7	Starr	3.0	665	81.0	156	19.0
Menard	17.7	266	82.9	55	17.1	Stephens	21.2	1,085	90.8	110	9.2
Midland	21.0	13,364	89.8	1,515	10.2	Sterling	24.4	193	91.9	17	8.1
Milam	23.7	2,767	82.0	606	18.0	Stonewall	30.8	340	92.9	26	7.1
Mills	27.0	805	91.3	77	8.7	Sutton	17.3	409	91.7	37	8.3
Mitchell	17.6	834	91.2	80	8.8	Swisher	23.6	991	91.8	89	8.2
Montague	22.8	2,655	90.6	274	9.4	Tarrant	19.0	128,456	76.8	38,831	23.2
Montgomery	17.1	31,600	86.4	4,956	13.6	Taylor	17.9	12,138	87.2	1,787	12.8
Moore	25.2	2,271	93.2	166	6.8	Terrell	22.8	145	84.3	27	15.7
Morris	22.1	1,755	91.1	172	8.9	Terry	20.0	1,381	92.2	117	7.8
Motley	38.1	327	94.5	19	5.5	Throckmorton	39.7	440	89.8	50	10.2
Nacogdoches	21.6	5,634	83.4	1,118	16.6	Titus	21.3	2,919	90.7	298	9.3
Navarro	21.5	5,276	89.7	604	10.3	Tom Green	21.9	11,418	82.6	2,400	17.4
Newton	18.0	1,552	93.5	108	6.5	Travis	25.2	54,246	40.1	81,170	59.9
Nolan	22.7	1,859	88.2	249	11.8	Trinity	17.0	1,673	89.5	197	10.5
Nueces	12.2	17,375	74.7	5,888	25.3	Tyler	18.7	2,332	92.8	181	7.2
Ochiltree	29.3	1,372	95.1	71	4.9	Upshur	23.9	5,194	91.6	477	8.4
Oldham	28.1	375	92.6	30	7.4	Upton	21.2	388	90.7	40	9.3
Orange	11.8	5,699	92.3	476	7.7	Uvalde	16.5	2,290	86.8	347	13.2
Palo Pinto	18.5	2,663	86.0	435	14.0	Val Verde	10.7	2,276	83.4	452	16.6
Panola	23.6	3,429	93.6	234	6.4	Van Zandt	24.9	7,189	91.6	663	8.4
Parker	21.0	11,905	87.7	1,669	12.3	Victoria	20.1	9,148	86.3	1,449	13.7
Parmer	24.5	1,141	95.1	59	4.9	Walker	21.4	5,012	83.4	998	16.6
Pecos	14.5	983	88.2	132	11.8	Waller	15.6	3,330	85.3	573	14.7
Polk	13.7	4,367	87.7	612	12.3	Ward	21.7	1,282	92.2	109	7.8
Potter	17.7	8,309	84.5	1,523	15.5	Washington	21.3	3,722	86.4	585	13.6
Presidio	5.3	195	67.2	95	32.8	Webb	6.3	4,619	75.9	1,463	24.1
Rains	24.4	1,421	91.0	141	9.0	Wharton	20.0	4,412	89.8	503	10.2
Randall	26.1	17,202	89.0	2,130	11.0	Wheeler	29.2	1,057	93.9	69	6.1
Reagan	21.1	353	89.1	43	10.9	Wichita	20.1	13,373	87.2	1,967	12.8
Real	30.2	637	86.5	99	13.5	Wilbarger	43.6	3,207	86.9	484	13.1
Red River	20.0	1,520	92.6	122	7.4	Willacy	7.4	671	82.7	140	17.3
Reeves	9.3	567	87.6	80	12.4	Williamson	24.6	33,677	69.9	14,508	30.1
Refugio	15.5	740	86.7	114	13.3	Wilson	16.0	3,275	87.3	478	12.7
Roberts	36.6	236	92.5	19	7.5	Winkler	23.3	805	90.3	86	9.7
Robertson	17.7	1,772	86.9	266	13.1	Wise	20.2	5,896	88.6	762	11.4
Rockwall	26.5	8,349	82.8	1,738	17.2	Wood	28.7	6,231	91.0	620	9.0
Runnels	21.4	1,319	89.9	148	10.1	Yoakum	22.9	919	93.4	65	6.6
Rusk	22.4	6,269	92.4	519	7.6	Young	32.5	3,228	89.3	387	10.7
Sabine	21.8	1,372	88.9	172	11.1	Zapata	7.9	444	82.2	96	17.7
San Augustine	15.1	897	87.3	130	12.7	Zavala	6.6	408	80.6	98	19.4
San Jacinto	19.0	2,624	89.3	316	10.7						

Government

The Texas Capitol in Austin. Harry Cabluck photo.

Historical Documents

Constitutional Amendments, 2005 & 2007

Chief Government Officials, 1691–2007

State Government

Local Government

Federal Government

Crime in Texas, 2006

Declaration of Independence of the Republic of Texas

The Declaration of Independence of the Republic of Texas was adopted in general convention at Washington-on-the-Brazos, March 2, 1836.

Richard Ellis, president of the convention, appointed a committee of five to write the declaration for submission to the convention. However, there is much evidence that George C. Childress, one of the members, wrote the document with little or no help from the other members. Childress is therefore generally accepted as the author.

The text of the declaration is followed by the names of the signers of the document. The names are presented here as the signers actually signed the document.

Our thanks to the staff of the Texas State Archives for furnishing a photocopy of the signatures.

UNANIMOUS

DECLARATION OF INDEPENDENCE,
BY THE

DELEGATES OF THE PEOPLE OF TEXAS,

IN GENERAL CONVENTION,

AT THE TOWN OF WASHINGTON,

ON THE SECOND DAY OF MARCH, 1836.

When a government has ceased to protect the lives, liberty and property of the people from whom its legitimate powers are derived, and for the advancement of whose happiness it was instituted; and so far from being a guarantee for the enjoyment of those inestimable and inalienable rights, becomes an instrument in the hands of evil rulers for their oppression; when the Federal Republican Constitution of their country, which they have sworn to support, no longer has a substantial existence, and the whole nature of their government has been forcibly changed without their consent, from a restricted federative republic, composed of sovereign states, to a consolidated central military despotism, in which every interest is disregarded but that of the army and the priesthood — both the eternal enemies of civil liberty, and the ever-ready minions of power, and the usual instruments of tyrants; When long after the spirit of the Constitution has departed, moderation is at length, so far lost, by those in power that even the semblance of freedom is removed, and the forms, themselves, of the constitution discontinued; and so far from their petitions and remonstrances being regarded, the agents who bear them are thrown into dungeons; and mercenary armies sent forth to force a new government upon them at the point of the bayonet. When in consequence of such acts of malfeasance and abdication, on the part of the government, anarchy prevails, and civil society is dissolved into its original elements: In such a crisis, the first law of nature, the right of self-preservation — the inherent and inalienable right of the people to appeal to first principles and take their political affairs into their own hands in extreme cases — enjoins it as a right towards themselves and a sacred obligation to their posterity, to abolish such government and create another in its stead, calculated to rescue them from impending dangers, and to secure their future welfare and happiness.

Nations, as well as individuals, are amenable for their acts to the public opinion of mankind. A statement of a part of our grievances is, therefore, submitted to an impartial world, in justification of the hazardous but unavoidable step now taken of severing our political connection with the Mexican people, and assuming an independent attitude among the nations of the earth.

The Mexican government, by its colonization laws, invited and induced the Anglo-American population of Texas to colonize its wilderness under the pledged faith of a written constitution, that they should continue to enjoy that constitutional liberty and republican government to which they had been habituated in the land of their birth, the United States of America. In this expectation they have been cruelly disappointed, inasmuch as the Mexican nation has acquiesced in the late changes made in the government by General Antonio Lopez de Santa Anna, who, having overturned the constitution of his country, now offers us the cruel alternative either to abandon our homes, acquired by so many privations, or submit to the most intolerable of all tyranny, the combined despotism of the sword and the priesthood.

It has sacrificed our welfare to the state of Coahuila, by which our interests have been continually depressed, through a jealous and partial course of legislation carried on at a far distant seat of government, by a hostile majority, in an unknown tongue; and this too, notwithstanding we have petitioned in the humblest terms, for the establishment of a separate state government, and have, in accordance with the provisions of the national constitution, presented the general Congress, a republican constitution which was without just cause contemptuously rejected.

It incarcerated in a dungeon, for a long time, one of our citizens, for no other cause but a zealous endeavor to procure the acceptance of our constitution and the establishment of a state government.

It has failed and refused to secure on a firm basis, the right of trial by jury; that palladium of civil liberty, and only safe guarantee for the life, liberty, and property of the citizen.

It has failed to establish any public system of education, although possessed of almost boundless resources (the public domain) and, although, it is an axiom, in political science, that unless a people are educated and enlightened it is idle to expect the continuance of civil liberty, or the capacity for self-government.

It has suffered the military commandants stationed among us to exercise arbitrary acts of oppression and tyranny; thus trampling upon the most sacred rights of the citizen and rendering the military superior to the civil power.

It has dissolved by force of arms, the state Congress of Coahuila and Texas, and obliged our representatives to fly for their lives from the seat of government; thus depriving us of the fundamental political right of representation.

It has demanded the surrender of a number of our citizens, and ordered military detachments to seize and carry them into the Interior for trial; in contempt of the civil authorities, and in defiance of the laws and constitution.

It has made piratical attacks upon our commerce; by commissioning foreign desperadoes, and authorizing them to seize our vessels, and convey the property of our citizens to far distant ports of confiscation.

It denies us the right of worshipping the Almighty according to the dictates of our own consciences, by the support of a national religion calculated to promote the temporal interests of its human functionaries rather than the glory of the true and living God.

It has demanded us to deliver up our arms; which are essential to our defense, the rightful property of freemen, and formidable only to tyrannical governments.

It has invaded our country, both by sea and by land, with intent to lay waste our territory and drive us from our homes; and has now a large mercenary army advancing to carry on against us a war of extermination.

It has, through its emissaries, incited the merciless savage, with the tomahawk and scalping knife, to massacre the inhabitants of our defenseless frontiers.

It hath been, during the whole time of our connection with it, the contemptible sport and victim of successive military revolutions and hath continually exhibited every characteristic of a weak, corrupt and tyrannical government.

These, and other grievances, were patiently borne by the people of Texas until they reached that point at which forbearance ceases to be a virtue. We then took up arms in defense of the national constitution. We appealed to our Mexican brethren for assistance. Our appeal has been made in vain. Though months have elapsed, no sympathetic response has yet been heard from the Interior. We are, therefore, forced to the melancholy conclusion that the Mexican people have acquiesced in the destruction of their liberty, and the substitution therefor of a military government — that they are unfit to be free and incapable of self-government.

The necessity of self-preservation, therefore, now decrees our eternal political separation.

We, therefore, the delegates, with plenary powers, of the people of Texas, in solemn convention assembled, appealing to a candid world for the necessities of our condition, do hereby resolve and DECLARE that our political connection with the Mexican nation has forever ended; and that the people of Texas do now constitute a FREE, SOVEREIGN and INDEPENDENT REPUBLIC, and are fully invested with all the rights and attributes which properly belong to the independent nations; and, conscious of the rectitude of our intentions, we fearlessly and confidently commit the issue to the decision of the Supreme Arbiter of the destinies of nations.

RICHARD ELLIS, president of the convention and Delegate from Red River.

Charles B Stewart

Tho⁵ Barnett
John S.D. Byrom

Fran^co Ruiz
J. Antonio Navarro
Jesse B. Badgett
Wm D. Lacey
William Menefee
Jn° Fisher
Mathew Caldwell
William Mottley
Lorenzo de Zavala
Stephen H. Everitt
Geo W Smyth

Elijah Stapp
Claiborne West

W^m B Scates
M.B. Menard

A.B. Hardin
J.W. Bunton
Tho⁵ J. Gasley
R. M. Coleman
Sterling C. Robertson
Benj Briggs Goodrich
G.W. Barnett
James G. Swisher
Jesse Grimes
S. Rhoads Fisher
John W. Moore
John W. Bower
Saml A Maverick from Bejar
Sam P. Carson
A. Briscoe
J.B. Woods
Jas Collinsworth
Edwin Waller
Asa Brigham
Geo. C. Childress
Bailey Hardeman
Rob. Potter
Thomas Jefferson Rusk
Chas. S. Taylor
John S. Roberts

Robert Hamilton
Collin McKinney
Albert H Latimer
James Power

Sam Houston
David Thomas

Edwd Conrad
Martin Parmer
Edwin O. LeGrand
Stephen W. Blount
Ja⁵ Gaines
Wm Clark, Jr
Sydney O. Penington
Wm Carrol Crawford
Jn° Turner

Test. H.S. Kimble, Secretary

Constitution of Texas

The complete official text of the Constitution of Texas, including the original document, which was adopted on Feb. 15, 1876, plus all amendments approved since that time, is available on the State of Texas Web page at this address: **http://tlo2.tlc.state.tx.us/txconst/toc.html.** An index at that site points you to the Article and Section of the Constitution that deals with a particular subject.

For election information, upcoming elections, amendment or other election votes and voter registration information, go to: **www.sos.state.tx.us/elections/index.shtml.**

According to the **Legislative Reference Library of Texas**: "The Texas Constitution is one of the longest in the nation and is still growing. As of 2005 (79th Legislature), the Texas Legislature has passed a total of 615 amendments. Of these, 439 have been adopted and 176 have been defeated by Texas voters. Thus, **the Texas Constitution has been amended 439 times since its adoption in 1876**."

Amendment of the Texas Constitution requires a two-thirds favorable vote by both the Texas House of Representatives and the Texas Senate, followed by a majority vote of approval by voters in a statewide election.

Prior to 1973, amendments to the constitution could not be submitted by a special session of the Legislature. But the constitution was amended in 1972 to allow submission of amendments if the special session was opened to the subject by the governor.

Constitutional amendments are not subject to a gubernatorial veto. Once submitted, voters have the final decision on whether to change the constitution as proposed.

The following table lists the total number of amendments submitted to voters by the Texas Legislature and shows the year in which the Legislature approved them for submission to voters; e.g., the 70th Legislature in 1987 approved 28 bills proposing amendments to be submitted to voters — 25 in 1987 and 3 in 1988.

Constitutional Amendments Submitted to Voters by the Texas Legislature

Year	No.	Year	No.	Year	No.
1879	1	1927	8	1973	9
1881	2	1929	7	1975	12
1883	5	1931	9	1977	15
1887	6	1933	12	1978	1
1889	2	1935	13	1979	12
1891	5	1937	7	1981	10
1893	2	1939	4	1982	3
1895	2	1941	5	1983	19
1897	5	1943	3	1985	17
1899	1	1945	8	1986	1
1901	1	1947	9	1987	28
1903	3	1949	10	1989	21
1905	3	1951	7	1990	1
1907	9	1953	11	1991	15
1909	4	1955	9	1993	18
1911	5	1957	12	1995	14
1913	7	1959	4	1997	15
1915	7	1961	14	1999	17
1917	3	1963	7	2001	20
1919	13	1965	27	2003	22
1921	5	1967	20	2005	9
1923	2	1969	16	2007	17
1925	4	1971	18		

For more information on bills and constitutional amendments, see the Legislative Reference Library of Texas Web site at: **www.lrl.state.tx.us/legis/lrlhome.cfm.**

Amendments, 2005

The following 9 amendments were submitted to the voters by the 79th Legislature in an election on **Nov. 8, 2005**:

HJR 6 — Providing that marriage in this state consists only of the union of one man and one woman and prohibiting this state or a political subdivision of this state from creating or recognizing any legal status identical or similar to marriage. **Passed:** 1,723,782 for; 536,913 against.

HJR 54 — Creating the Texas rail relocation and improvement fund and authorizing grants of money and issuance of obligations for financing the relocation, rehabilitation, and expansion of rail facilities. **Passed:** 1,112,718 for; 956,350 against.

HJR 79 — Authorizing the legislature to provide for a six-year term for a board member of a regional mobility authority. **Failed:** 913,358 for; 1,043,525 against.

HJR 80 — Clarifying that certain economic development programs do not constitute a debt. **Passed:** 1,025,173 for; 952,998 against.

HJR 87 — Including one additional public member and a constitutional county court judge in the membership of the State Commission on Judicial Conduct. **Passed:** 1,246,127 for; 744,585 against.

SJR 7 — Authorizing line-of-credit advances under a reverse mortgage. **Passed:** 1,201,740 for; 809,839 against.

SJR 17 — Authorizing the denial of bail to a criminal defendant who violates a condition of the defendant's release pending trial. **Passed:** 1,813,290 for; 322,168 against.

SJR 21 — Allowing the legislature to define rates of interest for commercial loans. **Failed:** 880,379 for; 1,147,628 against.

SJR 40 — Providing for the clearing of land titles by relinquishing and releasing and state claim to sovereign ownership or title to interest in certain lands in Upshur County and in Smith County. **Passed:** 1,153,241 for; 729,390 against.

Amendments, 2007

The following amendment was submitted to the voters by the 80th Legislature in an election on **May 12, 2007:**

SJR 13 — Authorizing the legislature to provide for a reduction of the limitation on the total amount of ad valorem taxes that may be imposed for public school purposes on the residence homesteads of the elderly or disabled to reflect any reduction in the rate of those taxes for the 2006 and 2007 tax years. **Passed:** 810,843 for; 113,734 against.

The following 16 amendments were submitted to the voters by the 80th Legislature in an election on **Nov. 6, 2007:**

HJR 6 — Authorizing the denial of bail to a person who violates certain court orders or conditions of release in a felony or family violence case.

HJR 19 — Requiring that a record vote be taken by a house of the legislature on final passage of any bill, other than certain local bills, of a resolution proposing or ratifying a constitutional amendment, or of any other nonceremonial resolution, and to provide for public access on the Internet to those record votes.

HJR 30 — Allowing governmental entities to sell property acquired through eminent domain back to the previous owners at the price the entities paid to acquire the property.

HJR 36 — Permitting a justice or judge who reaches the mandatory retirement age while in office to serve the remainder of the justice's or judge's current term.

HJR 40 — Authorizing the legislature to provide that the maximum appraised value of a residence homestead for ad valorem taxation is limited to the lesser of the most recent market value of the residence homestead as determined by the appraisal entity or 110 percent, or a greater percentage, of the appraised value of the residence homestead for the preceding tax year.

HJR 54 — Authorizing the legislature to exempt from ad valorem taxation one motor vehicle owned by an individual and used in the course of the owner's occupation or profession and also for personal activities of the owner.

HJR 69 — Abolishing the constitutional authority for the office of inspector of hides and animals.

HJR 72 — Clarifying certain provisions relating to the making of a home equity loan and use of home equity loan proceeds.

HJR 90 — Requiring the creation of the Cancer Prevention and Research Institute of Texas and authorizing the issuance of up to $3 billion in bonds payable from the general revenues of the state for research in Texas to find the causes of and cures for cancer.

HJR 103 — Providing for the continuation of the constitutional appropriation for facilities and other capital items at Angelo State University on a change in the governance of the university.

SJR 20 — Providing for the issuance of additional general obligation bonds by the Texas Water Development Board in an amount not to exceed $250 million to provide assistance to economically distressed areas.

SJR 29 — Authorizing the legislature to exempt all or part of the residence homesteads of certain totally disabled veterans from ad valorem taxation and authorizing a change in the manner of determining the amount of the existing exemption from ad valorem taxation to which a disabled veteran is entitled.

SJR 44 — Authorizing the legislature to permit the voters of a municipality having a population of less than 10,000 to authorize the governing body of the municipality to enter into an agreement with an owner of real property in or adjacent to an area in the municipality that has been approved for funding under certain programs administered by the Texas Department of Agriculture under which the parties agree that all ad valorem taxes imposed on the owner's property may not be increased for the first five tax years after the tax year in which the agreement is entered into.

SJR 57 — Providing for the issuance of $500 million in general obligation bonds to finance educational loans to students and authorizing bond enhancement agreements with respect to general obligation bonds issued for that purpose.

SJR 64 — Providing for the issuance of general obligation bonds by the Texas Transportation Commission in an amount not to exceed $5 billion to provide funding for highway improvement projects.

SJR 65 — Authorizing the issuance of up to $1 billion in bonds payable from the general revenues of the state for maintenance, improvement, repair, and construction projects and for the purchase of needed equipment. ☆

Joint Resolution for Annexing Texas to the United States

(For an overview of the subject, please see these discussions: The New Handbook of Texas, Texas State Historical Association, Austin, 1996; Vol. 1, pages 192–193. On the Web: **www.tsha.utexas.edu/handbook/online/articles/view/AA/mga2.html**. Also see the Texas State Library and Archives Web site: **www.tsl.state.tx.us/ref/abouttx/annexation/index.html**.)

Resolved

by the Senate and House of Representatives of the United States of America in Congress assembled, That Congress doth consent that the territory properly included within and rightfully belonging to the Republic of Texas, may be erected into a new State to be called the State of Texas, with a republican form of government adopted by the people of said Republic, by deputies in convention assembled, with the consent of the existing Government in order that the same may by admitted as one of the States of this Union.

2. And be it further resolved, That the foregoing consent of Congress is given upon the following conditions, to wit: First, said state to be formed, subject to the adjustment by this government of all questions of boundary that may arise with other government, --and the Constitution thereof, with the proper evidence of its adoption by the people of said Republic of Texas, shall be transmitted to the President of the United States, to be laid before Congress for its final action on, or before the first day of January, one thousand eight hundred and forty-six. Second, said state when admitted into the Union, after ceding to the United States all public edifices, fortifications, barracks, ports and harbors, navy and navy yards, docks, magazines and armaments, and all other means pertaining to the public defense, belonging to the said Republic of Texas, shall retain funds, debts, taxes and dues of every kind which may belong to, or be due and owing to the said Republic; and shall also retain all the vacant and unappropriated lands lying within its limits, to be applied to the payment of the debts and liabilities of said Republic of Texas, and the residue of said lands, after discharging said debts and liabilities, to be disposed of as said State may direct; but in no event are said debts and liabilities to become a charge upon the Government of the United States. Third — New States of convenient size not exceeding four in number, in addition to said State of Texas and having sufficient population, may, hereafter by the consent of said State, be formed out of the territory there-

of, which shall be entitled to admission under the provisions of the Federal Constitution; and such states as may be formed out of the territory lying south of thirty-six degrees thirty minutes north latitude, commonly known as the Missouri Compromise Line, shall be admitted into the Union, with or without slavery, as the people of each State, asking admission shall desire; and in such State or States as shall be formed out of said territory, north of said Missouri Compromise Line, slavery, or involuntary servitude (except for crime) shall be prohibited.

3. And be it further resolved, That if the President of the United States shall in his judgment and discretion deem it most advisable, instead of proceeding to submit the foregoing resolution of the Republic of Texas, as an overture on the part of the United States for admission, to negotiate with the Republic; then,

Be it resolved, That a State, to be formed out of the present Republic of Texas, with suitable extent and boundaries, and with two representatives in Congress, until the next appointment of representation, shall be admitted into the Union, by virtue of this act, on an equal footing with the existing States, as soon as the terms and conditions of such admission, and the cession of the remaining Texian territory to the United States shall be agreed upon by the governments of Texas and the United States: And that the sum of one hundred thousand dollars be, and the same is hereby, appropriated to defray the expenses of missions and negotiations, to agree upon the terms of said admission and cession, either by treaty to be submitted to the Senate, or by articles to be submitted to the two houses of Congress, as the President may direct.

Approved, March 1, 1845.

Source: Peters, Richard, ed., The Public Statutes at Large of the United States of America, v.5, pp. 797–798, Boston, Chas. C. Little and Jas. Brown, 1850.

Texas' Chief Governmental Officials

On this and following pages are lists of the principal administrative officials who have served the Republic and State of Texas with dates of their tenures of office. In a few instances there are disputes as to the exact dates of tenures. Dates listed here are those that appear the most authentic.

★ ★ ★ ★ ★ ★ ★

Governors and Presidents
*Spanish Royal Governors

Domingo Terán de los Rios	1691–1692
Gregorio de Salinas Varona	1692–1697
Francisco Cuerbo y Valdés	1698–1702
Mathías de Aguirre	1703–1705
Martín de Alarcón	1705–1708
Simón Padilla y Córdova	1708–1712
Pedro Fermin de Echevers y Subisa	1712–1714
Juan Valdéz	1714–1716
Martín de Alarcón	1716–1719
José de Azlor y Virto de Vera, Marqués de San Miguel de Aguayo	1719–1722
Fernando Pérez de Almazán	1722–1727
Melchor de Mediavilla y Azcona	1727–1731
Juan Antonio Bustillo y Ceballos	1731–1734
Manuel de Sandoval	1734–1736
Carlos Benites Franquis de Lugo	1736–1737
Joseph Fernández de Jáuregui y Urrutia	1737–1737
Prudencio de Orobio y Basterra	1737–1741
Tomás Felipe Winthuisen (or Winthuysen)	1741–1743
Justo Boneo y Morales	1743–1744
Francisco García Larios	1744–1748
Pedro del Barrio Junco y Espriella	1748–1750
Jacinto de Barrios y Jáuregui	1751–1759
Angel de Martos y Navarrete	1759–1767
Hugo Oconór	1767–1770
Juan María Vicencio, Barón de Ripperdá	1770–1778
Domingo Cabello y Robles	1778–1786
Rafael Martínez Pacheco	1787–1790
Manuel Muñoz	1790–1799
Juan Bautista de Elguezábal	1799–1805
Antonio Cordero y Bustamante	1805–1808
Manuel María de Salcedo	1808–1813
Juan Bautista de las Casas (revolutionary gov.)	1811–1811
Cristóbal Domínguez, Benito de Armiñan, Mariano Varela, Juan Ignacio Pérez, Manuel Pardo	1813–1817
Antonio María Martínez	1817–1821

*Some authorities would include Texas under adminis-trations of several earlier Spanish Governors. The late Dr. C.E. Castañeda, Latin-American librarian of The University of Texas and authority on the history of Texas and the Southwest, would include the following four: Francisco de Garay, 1523–26; Pánfilo de Narváez, 1526–28; Nuño de Guzmán, 1528–30; Hernando de Soto, 1538–43.

Governors Under Mexican Rule

The first two Governors under Mexican rule, Trespa-lacios and García, were of Texas only as Texas was then constituted. Beginning with Gonzáles, 1824, the Gover-nors were for the joint State of Coahuila y Texas.

José Felix Trespalacios	1822–1823
Luciano García	1823–1824
Rafael Gonzáles	1824–1826
Victor Blanco	1826–1827

José María Viesca	1827–1830
Ramón Eca y Músquiz	1830–1831
José María Letona	1831–1832
Ramón Eca y Músquiz	1832–1832
Juan Martín de Veramendi	1832–1833
Juan José de Vidáurri y Villasenor	1833–1834
Juan José Elguezábal	1834–1835
José María Cantú	1835–1835
Agustín M. Viesca	1835–1835
Marciel Borrego	1835–1835
Ramón Eca y Músquiz	1835–1835

Provisional Colonial Governor, Before Independence

Henry Smith (Impeached)	1835

James W. Robinson served as acting Governor just prior to March 2, 1836, after Smith was impeached.

Presidents of the Republic of Texas

David G. Burnet (provisional President)	Mar. 16, 1836–Oct. 22, 1836
Sam Houston	Oct. 22, 1836–Dec. 10, 1838
Mirabeau B. Lamar	Dec. 10, 1838–Dec. 13, 1841
Sam Houston	Dec. 13, 1841–Dec. 9, 1844
Anson Jones	Dec. 9, 1844–Feb. 19, 1846

Governors Since Annexation

J. Pinckney Henderson	Feb. 19, 1846–Dec. 21, 1847

(Albert C. Horton served as acting Governor while Henderson was away in the Mexican War.)

George T. Wood	Dec. 21, 1847–Dec. 21, 1849
Peter Hansbrough Bell	Dec. 21, 1849–Nov. 23, 1853
J. W. Henderson	Nov. 23, 1853–Dec. 21, 1853
Elisha M. Pease	Dec. 21, 1853–Dec. 21, 1857
Hardin R. Runnels	Dec. 21, 1857–Dec. 21, 1859
Sam Houston (resigned because of state's secession from the Union)	Dec. 21, 1859–Mar. 16, 1861
Edward Clark	Mar. 16, 1861–Nov. 7, 1861
Francis R. Lubbock (resigned to enter Confederate Army)	Nov. 7, 1861–Nov. 5, 1863
Pendleton Murrah (administration terminated by fall of Confederacy)	Nov. 5, 1863–June 17, 1865

Fletcher S. Stockdale (Lt. Gov. performed some duties of office on Murrah's departure, but is sometimes in-cluded in list of Governors. Hamilton's appointment was for immediate succession, as shown by the dates.)

Andrew J. Hamilton (Provisional, appointed by President Johnson)	June 17, 1865–Aug. 9, 1866
James W. Throckmorton	Aug. 9, 1866–Aug. 8, 1867
Elisha M. Pease (appointed July 30, 1867, under martial law)	Aug. 8, 1867–Sept. 30, 1869

Interregnum

Pease resigned and vacated office Sept. 30, 1869; no successor was named until Jan. 8, 1870. Some historians extend Pease's term until Jan. 8, 1870, but in reality Texas was without a head of its civil government from Sept. 30, 1869, until Jan. 8, 1870.

Edmund J. Davis (appointed provisional Governor after being elected)	Jan. 8, 1870–Jan. 15, 1874

Richard Coke (resigned to enter United States Senate) ....Jan. 15, 1874–Dec. 1, 1876
Richard B. Hubbard ....Dec. 1, 1876–Jan. 21, 1879
Oran M. Roberts .... Jan. 21, 1879–Jan. 16, 1883
John Ireland .... Jan. 16, 1883–Jan. 18, 1887
Lawrence Sullivan Ross ...... Jan. 18, 1887–Jan. 20, 1891
James Stephen Hogg .... Jan. 20, 1891–Jan. 15, 1895
Charles A. Culberson .... Jan. 15, 1895–Jan. 17, 1899
Joseph D. Sayers .... Jan. 17, 1899–Jan. 20, 1903
S. W. T. Lanham .... Jan. 20, 1903–Jan. 15, 1907
Thos. Mitchell Campbell ....Jan. 15, 1907–Jan. 17, 1911
Oscar Branch Colquitt ....Jan. 17, 1911–Jan. 19, 1915
James E. Ferguson (impeached) ....Jan. 19, 1915–Aug. 25, 1917
William Pettus Hobby ....Aug. 25, 1917–Jan. 18, 1921
Pat Morris Neff.................... Jan. 18, 1921–Jan. 20, 1925
Miriam A. Ferguson .... Jan. 20, 1925–Jan. 17, 1927
Dan Moody .... Jan. 17, 1927–Jan. 20, 1931
Ross S. Sterling.................. Jan. 20, 1931–Jan. 17, 1933
Miriam A. Ferguson .... Jan. 17, 1933–Jan. 15, 1935
James V. Allred................... Jan. 15, 1935–Jan. 17, 1939
W. Lee O'Daniel (*resigned to enter United States Senate*) ....Jan. 17, 1939–Aug. 4, 1941
Coke R. Stevenson...............Aug. 4, 1941–Jan. 21, 1947
Beauford H. Jester............... Jan. 21, 1947–July 11, 1949
Allan Shivers (*Lt. Governor succeeded on death of Governor Jester. Elected in 1950 and re-elected in 1952 and 1954*) .... July 11, 1949–Jan. 15, 1957
Price Daniel .... Jan. 15, 1957–Jan. 15, 1963
John Connally..................... Jan. 15, 1963–Jan. 21, 1969
Preston Smith .... Jan. 21, 1969–Jan. 16, 1973
*Dolph Briscoe.................... Jan. 16, 1973–Jan. 16, 1979
**William P. Clements .... Jan. 16, 1979–Jan. 18, 1983
Mark White .... Jan. 18, 1983–Jan. 20, 1987
**William P. Clements .... Jan. 20, 1987–Jan. 15, 1991
Ann W. Richards................. Jan. 15, 1991–Jan. 17, 1995
**George W. Bush ....Jan. 17, 1995–Dec. 21, 2000
**Rick Perry (*Lt. Governor succeeded on inauguration of Bush as U.S. President*) .....Dec. 21, 2000–present

*Effective in 1975, term of office was raised to 4 years, according to a constitutional amendment approved by Texas voters in 1972. See introduction to State Government chapter in this edition for other state officials whose terms were raised to four years.
**Republicans.

★ ★ ★ ★ ★ ★ ★

Vice Presidents and Lieutenant Governors

Vice Presidents of Republic
Date Elected
Lorenzo de Zavala (*provisional Vice President*)
Mirabeau B. Lamar..Sept. 5, 1836
David G. Burnet...Sept. 3, 1838
Edward Burleson ....Sept. 6, 1841
Kenneth L. Anderson....................................Sept. 2, 1844

Lieutenant Governors

Albert C. Horton...1846–1847
John A. Greer 1847–1851
J. W. Henderson...Aug. 4, 1851
D. C. Dickson 1853–1855
H. R. Runnels ....Aug. 6, 1855
F. R. Lubbock...Aug. 4, 1857
Edward Clark..Aug. 1, 1859
John M. Crockett...1861–1863
Fletcher S. Stockdale 1863–1866
George W. Jones..1866

(*Jones was removed by General Sheridan.*)
J. W. Flanagan..1869
(*Flanagan was appointed U.S. Senator and was never inaugurated as Lt. Gov.*)
R. B. Hubbard...1873–1876
J. D. Sayers...1878–1880
L. J. Storey 1880–1882
Marion Martin...1882–1884
Barnett Gibbs...1884–1886
T. B. Wheeler 1886–1890
George C. Pendleton......................................1890–1892
M. M. Crane........................ Jan. 17, 1893–Jan. 25, 1895
George T. Jester...1895–1898
J. N. Browning 1898–1902
George D. Neal...1902–1906
A. B. Davidson..1906–1912
Will H. Mayes...1912–1914
William Pettus Hobby 1914–1917
W. A. Johnson (*served Hobby's unexpired term and until*)..Jan. 1920)
Lynch Davidson 1920–1922
T. W. Davidson...1922–1924
Barry Miller 1924–1931
Edgar E. Witt 1931–1935
Walter Woodul 1935–1939
Coke R. Stevenson...1939–1941
John Lee Smith................................. 1943–Jan. 21, 1947
Allan Shivers........................Jan. 21, 1947–July 11, 1949

(*Shivers succeeded to the governorship on death of Governor Beauford H. Jester.*)

Ben Ramsey....................................1951–Sept. 18, 1961
(*Ben Ramsey resigned to become a member of the State Railroad Commission.*)

Preston Smith...1963–1969
Ben Barnes...1969–1973
William P. Hobby Jr...1973–1991
Robert D. Bullock...1991–1999
Rick Perry...1999–Dec. 21, 2000
*Bill Ratliff ....Dec. 28, 2000–Jan. 21, 2003
David Dewhurst .... Jan. 21, 2003–present

*Elected by Senate when Rick Perry succeeded to governorship on election of George W. Bush as U.S. President.

★ ★ ★ ★ ★ ★ ★

Secretaries of State

Republic of Texas

Raines Yearbook for Texas, 1901, gives the following record of Secretaries of State during the era of the Republic of Texas:

Under David G. Burnet — Samuel P. Carson, James Collingsworth and W. H. Jack.

Under Sam Houston (first term) — Stephen F. Austin, 1836. J. Pinckney Henderson and Dr. Robert A. Irion, 1837–38.

Under Mirabeau B. Lamar — Bernard Bee appointed Dec. 16, 1838; James Webb appointed Feb. 6, 1839; D. G. Burnet appointed Acting Secretary of State, May 31, 1839; N. Amory appointed Acting Secretary of State, July 23, 1839; D. G. Burnet appointed Acting Secretary of State, Aug. 5, 1839; Abner S. Lipscomb appointed Secretary of State, Jan. 31, 1840, and resigned Jan. 22, 1841; Joseph Waples appointed Acting Secretary of State, Jan. 23, 1841, and served until Feb. 8, 1841; James S. Mayfield appointed Feb. 8, 1841; Joseph Waples appointed April

30, 1841, and served until May 25, 1841; Samuel A. Roberts appointed May 25, 1841; reappointed Sept. 7, 1841.

Under Sam Houston (second term) — E. Lawrence Stickney, Acting Secretary of State until Anson Jones appointed Dec. 13, 1841. Jones served as Secretary of State throughout this term except during the summer and part of this term of 1842, when Joseph Waples filled the position as Acting Secretary of State.

Under Anson Jones — Ebenezer Allen served from Dec. 10, 1844, until Feb. 5, 1845, when Ashbel Smith became Secretary of State. Allen was again named Acting Secretary of State, March 31, 1845, and later named Secretary of State.

(In addition to the above, documents in theTexas State Archives indicate that Joseph C. Eldredge, Chief Clerk of the State Department during much of the Republic's existence, signed a number of documents in the absence of the office-holder in the capacity of "Acting Secretary of State.")

State Secretaries of State

Charles Mariner	Feb. 20, 1846–May 4, 1846
David G. Burnet	May 4, 1846–Jan. 1, 1848
Washington D. Miller	Jan. 1, 1848–Jan. 2, 1850
James Webb	Jan. 2, 1850–Nov. 14, 1851
Thomas H. Duval	Nov. 14, 1851–Dec. 22, 1853
Edward Clark	Dec. 22, 1853–Dec. 1857
T. S. Anderson	Dec. 1857–Dec. 27, 1859
E. W. Cave	Dec. 27, 1859–Mar. 16, 1861
Bird Holland	Mar. 16, 1861–Nov. 1861
Charles West	Nov. 1861–Sept. 1862
Robert J. Townes	Sept. 1862–May 2, 1865
Charles R. Pryor	May 2, 1865–Aug, 1865
James H. Bell	Aug. 1865–Aug. 1866
John A. Green	Aug. 1866–Aug. 1867
D. W. C. Phillips	Aug. 1867–Jan. 1870
J. P. Newcomb	Jan. 1, 1870–Jan. 17, 1874
George Clark	Jan. 17, 1874–Jan. 27, 1874
A. W. DeBerry	Jan. 27, 1874–Dec. 1, 1876
Isham G. Searcy	Dec. 1, 1876–Jan. 23, 1879
J. D. Templeton	Jan. 23, 1879–Jan. 22, 1881
T. H. Bowman	Jan. 22, 1881–Jan. 18, 1883
J. W. Baines	Jan. 18, 1883–Jan. 21, 1887
John M. Moore	Jan. ?1, 1887–Jan. 22, 1891
George W. Smith	Jan. 22, 1891–Jan. 17, 1895
Allison Mayfield	Jan. 17, 1895–Jan. 5, 1897
J. W. Madden	Jan. 5, 1897–Jan. 18, 1899
D. H. Hardy	Jan. 18, 1899–Jan. 19, 1901
John G. Tod	Jan. 19, 1901–Jan., 1903
J. R. Curl	Jan. 1903–April 1905
O. K. Shannon	April 1905–Jan. 1907
L. T. Dashiel	Jan. 1907–Feb. 1908
W. R. Davie	Feb. 1908–Jan. 1909
W. B. Townsend	Jan. 1909–Jan. 1911
C. C. McDonald	Jan. 1911–Dec. 1912
J. T. Bowman	Dec. 1912–Jan. 1913
John L. Wortham	Jan. 1913–June 1913
F. C. Weinert	June 1913–Nov. 1914
D. A. Gregg	Nov. 1914–Jan. 1915
John G. McKay	Jan. 1915–Dec. 1916
C. J. Bartlett	Dec. 1916–Nov. 1917
George F. Howard	Nov. 1917–Nov. 1920
C. D. Mims	Nov. 1920–Jan. 1921
S. L. Staples	Jan. 1921–Aug. 1924
J. D. Strickland	Sept. 1924–Jan. 1, 1925
Henry Hutchings	Jan. 1, 1925–Jan. 20, 1925
Mrs. Emma G. Meharg	Jan. 20, 1925–Jan. 1927
Mrs. Jane Y. McCallum	Jan. 1927–Jan. 1933
W. W. Heath	Jan. 1933–Jan. 1935
Gerald C. Mann	Jan. 1935–Aug. 31, 1935

R. B. Stanford	Aug. 31, 1935–Aug. 25, 1936
B. P. Matocha	Aug. 25, 1936–Jan. 18, 1937
Edward Clark	Jan. 18, 1937–Jan. 1939
Tom L. Beauchamp	Jan. 1939–Oct. 1939
M. O. Flowers	Oct. 26, 1939–Feb. 25, 1941
William J. Lawson	Feb. 25, 1941–Jan. 1943
Sidney Latham	Jan. 1943–Feb. 1945
Claude Isbell	Feb. 1945–Jan. 1947
Paul H. Brown	Jan. 1947–Jan. 19, 1949
Ben Ramsey	Jan. 19, 1949–Feb. 9, 1950
John Ben Shepperd	Feb. 9, 1950–April 30, 1952
Jack Ross	April 30, 1952–Jan. 9, 1953
Howard A. Carney	Jan. 9, 1953–Apr. 30, 1954
C. E. Fulgham	May 1, 1954–Feb. 15, 1955
Al Muldrow	Feb. 16, 1955–Nov. 1, 1955
Tom Reavley	Nov. 1, 1955–Jan. 16, 1957
Zollie Steakley	Jan. 16, 1957–Jan. 2, 1962
P. Frank Lake	Jan. 2, 1962–Jan. 15, 1963
Crawford C. Martin	Jan. 15, 1963–March 12, 1966
John L. Hill	March 12, 1966–Jan. 22, 1968
Roy Barrera	March 7, 1968–Jan. 23, 1969
Martin Dies Jr.	Jan. 23, 1969–Sept. 1, 1971
Robert D. (Bob) Bullock	Sept. 1, 1971–Jan. 2, 1973
V. Larry Teaver Jr.	Jan. 2, 1973–Jan. 19, 1973
Mark W. White Jr.	Jan. 19, 1973–Oct. 27,1977
Steven C. Oaks	Oct. 27, 1977–Jan. 16, 1979
George W. Strake Jr.	Jan. 16, 1979–Oct. 6, 1981
David A. Dean	Oct. 22, 1981–Jan. 18, 1983
John Fainter	Jan. 18, 1983–July 31, 1984
Myra A. McDaniel	Sept. 6, 1984–Jan. 26, 1987
Jack Rains	Jan. 26, 1987–June 15, 1989
George Bayoud Jr.	June 19, 1989–Jan. 15, 1991
John Hannah Jr.	Jan. 17, 1991–March 11, 1994
Ronald Kirk	April 4, 1994–Jan. 10, 1995
Antonio O. "Tony" Garza Jr.	Jan. 18, 1995–Dec. 2, 1997
Alberto R. Gonzales	Dec. 2, 1997–Jan. 10, 1999
Elton Bomer	Jan. 11, 1999–Dec. 31, 2000
Henry Cuellar	Jan. 2, 2001–Oct. 5, 2001
Gwyn Shea	Jan. 2, 2002–Aug. 4, 2003
Geoff Connor	Sept. 26, 2003–Jan. 1, 2005
J. Roger Williams	Jan. 1, 2005–July 1, 2007
Phil Wilson	July 1, 2007–present

★ ★ ★ ★ ★ ★ ★

Attorneys General
Of the Republic

David Thomas and Peter W. Grayson	Mar. 2–Oct. 22, 1836
J. Pinckney Henderson, Peter W. Grayson, John Birdsall, A. S. Thurston	1836–1838
J. C. Watrous	Dec. 1838–June 1, 1840
Joseph Webb and F. A. Morris	1840–1841
George W. Terrell, Ebenezer Allen	1841–1844
Ebenezer Allen	1844–1846

*Of the State

Volney E. Howard	Feb. 21, 1846–May 7, 1846
John W. Harris	May 7, 1846–Oct. 31, 1849
Henry P. Brewster	Oct. 31, 1849–Jan. 15, 1850
A. J. Hamilton	Jan. 15, 1850–Aug. 5, 1850
Ebenezer Allen	Aug. 5, 1850–Aug. 2, 1852
Thomas J. Jennings	Aug. 2, 1852–Aug. 4, 1856
James Willie	Aug. 4, 1856–Aug. 2, 1858
Malcolm D. Graham	Aug. 2, 1858–Aug. 6, 1860
George M. Flournoy	Aug. 6, 1860–Jan. 15, 1862
N. G. Shelley	Feb. 3, 1862–Aug. 1, 1864
B. E. Tarver	Aug. 1, 1864–Dec. 11, 1865
Wm. Alexander	Dec. 11, 1865–June 25, 1866
W. M. Walton	June 25, 1866–Aug. 27, 1867
Wm. Alexander	Aug. 27, 1867–Nov. 5, 1867

Ezekiel B. Turner .... Nov. 5, 1867–July 11, 1870
Wm. Alexander .... July 11, 1870–Jan. 27, 1874
George Clark .... Jan. 27, 1874–Apr. 25, 1876
H. H. Boone .... Apr. 25, 1876–Nov. 5, 1878
George McCormick................. Nov. 5, 1878–Nov. 2, 1880
J. H. McLeary .... Nov. 2, 1880–Nov. 7, 1882
John D. Templeton................... Nov. 7, 1882–Nov. 2, 1886
James S. Hogg .... Nov. 2, 1886–Nov. 4, 1890
C. A. Culberson .... Nov. 4, 1890–Nov. 6, 1894
M. M. Crane........................... Nov. 6, 1894–Nov. 8, 1898
Thomas S. Smith .... Nov. 8, 1898–Mar. 15,1901
C. K. Bell.......................... Mar. 20, 1901–Jan., 1904
R. V. Davidson........................... Jan. 1904–Dec. 31, 1909
Jewel P. Lightfoot................... Jan. 1, 1910–Aug. 31, 1912
James D. Walthall.................. Sept. 1, 1912–Jan. 1, 1913
B. F. Looney .... Jan. 1, 1913–Jan., 1919
C. M. Cureton .... Jan. 1919–Dec. 1921
W. A. Keeling .... Dec. 1921–Jan. 1925
Dan Moody .... Jan. 1925–Jan. 1927
Claude Pollard.............................. Jan. 1927–Sept. 1929
R. L. Bobbitt (Apptd.) .... Sept. 1929–Jan. 1931
James V. Allred............................. Jan. 1931–Jan. 1935
William McCraw .... Jan. 1935–Jan. 1939
Gerald C. Mann (resigned) .... Jan. 1939–Jan. 1944
Grover Sellers .... Jan. 1944–Jan. 1947
Price Daniel .... Jan. 1947–Jan. 1953
John Ben Shepperd................... Jan. 1953–Jan. 1, 1957
Will Wilson .... Jan. 1, 1957–Jan. 15, 1963
Waggoner Carr .... Jan. 15, 1963–Jan. 1, 1967
Crawford C. Martin .... Jan. 1, 1967–Dec. 29, 1972
John Hill................................. Jan. 1, 1973–Jan. 16, 1979
Mark White .... Jan. 16, 1979–Jan. 18, 1983
Jim Mattox .... Jan. 18, 1983–Jan. 15, 1991
Dan Morales .... Jan. 15, 1991–Jan. 13, 1999
John Cornyn .... Jan. 13, 1999–Dec. 2, 2002
Greg Abbott .... Dec. 2, 2002–present

*The first few Attorneys General held office by appointment of the Governor. The office was made elective in 1850 by constitutional amendment. Ebenezer Allen was the first elected Attorney General.

★ ★ ★ ★ ★ ★ ★

Treasurers
Of the Republic

Asa Brigham.. 1838–1840
James W. Simmons... 1840–1841
Asa Brigham.. 1841–1844
Moses Johnson 1844–1846

Of the State

James H. Raymond............. Feb. 24, 1846–Aug. 2, 1858
*C. H. Randolph.......................... Aug. 2, 1858–June 1865
*Samuel Harris .... Oct. 2, 1865–June 25, 1866
W. M. Royston .... June 25, 1866–Sept. 1, 1867
John Y. Allen .... Sept. 1, 1867–Jan. 1869
**George W. Honey .... Jan. 1869–Jan. 1874
**B. Graham (short term) .... beginning May 27, 1872
A. J. Dorn.. Jan. 1874–Jan. 1879
F. R. Lubbock.................................... Jan. 1879–Jan. 1891
W. B. Wortham .... Jan. 1891–Jan. 1899
John W. Robbins .... Jan. 1899–Jan. 1907
Sam Sparks...................................... Jan. 1907–Jan. 1912
J. M. Edwards................................... Jan. 1912–Jan. 1919
John W. Baker .... Jan. 1919–Jan. 1921
G. N. Holton.............................. July 1921–Nov. 21, 1921
C. V. Terrell .... Nov. 21, 1921–Aug. 15, 1924
S. L. Staples .... Aug. 16, 1924–Jan. 15, 1925
W. Gregory Hatcher.............. Jan. 16, 1925–Jan. 1, 1931
Charley Lockhart .... Jan. 1, 1931–Oct. 25, 1941

Jesse James...................... Oct. 25, 1941–Sept. 29, 1977
Warren G. Harding................... Oct. 7, 1977–Jan. 3, 1983
Ann Richards........................... Jan. 3, 1983–Jan. 2, 1991
Kay Bailey Hutchison................. Jan. 2, 1991–June 1993
†Martha Whitehead .... June 1993–Aug. 1996

*Randolph fled to Mexico upon collapse of Confederacy. No exact date is available for his departure from office or for Harris' succession to the post. It is believed Harris took office Oct. 2, 1865.

**Honey was removed from office for a short period in 1872 and B. Graham served in his place.

† The office of Treasurer was eliminated by Constitutional amendment in an election Nov. 7, 1995, effective the last day of August 1996.

★ ★ ★ ★ ★ ★ ★

Railroad Commission of Texas

(After the first three names in the following list, each commissioner's name is followed by a surname in parentheses. The name in parentheses is the name of the commissioner whom that commissioner succeeded.)

John H. Reagan................... June 10, 1891–Jan. 20, 1903
L. L. Foster .... June 10, 1891–April 30, 1895
W. P. McLean................... June 10, 1891–Nov. 20, 1894
L. J. Storey (McLean) .... Nov. 21, 1894–Mar. 28,1909
N. A. Stedman (Foster)............. May 1, 1895–Jan. 4, 1897
Allison Mayfield (Stedman)...... Jan. 5, 1897–Jan. 23, 1923
O. B. Colquitt (Reagan) ...... Jan. 21, 1903–Jan. 17, 1911
William D. Williams (Storey) ...April 28, 1909–Oct. 1, 1916
John L. Wortham (Colquitt)..... Jan. 21, 1911–Jan. 1, 1913
Earle B. Mayfield (Wortham) .Jan. 2, 1913–March 1, 1923
Charles Hurdleston (Williams) ....Oct. 10, 1916–Dec. 31,1918
Clarence Gilmore (Hurdleston). Jan. 1, 1919–Jan. 1, 1929
N. A. Nabors (A. Mayfield) ...March 1, 1923–Jan. 18, 1925
William Splawn (E. Mayfield) March 1, 1923–Aug. 1, 1924
C. V. Terrell (Splawn) .... Aug. 15, 1924–Jan. 1, 1939
Lon A. Smith (Nabors) ....Jan. 29, 1925–Jan. 1, 1941
Pat M. Neff (Gilmore)................. Jan. 1, 1929–Jan. 1, 1933
Ernest O. Thompson (Neff) ......Jan. 1, 1933–Jan. 8, 1965
G. A. (Jerry) Sadler (Terrell)......Jan. 1, 1939–Jan. 1, 1943
Olin Culberson (Smith) ....Jan. 1, 1941–June 22, 1961
Beauford Jester (Sadler) ....Jan. 1, 1943–Jan. 21, 1947
William J. Murray Jr. (Jester) Jan. 21, 1947–Apr. 10, 1963
Ben Ramsey (Culberson) ...Sept. 18, 1961–Dec. 31, 1976
Jim C. Langdon (Murray)..... May 28, 1963–Dec. 31, 1977
Byron Tunnell (Thompson) ..Jan. 11, 1965–Sept. 15, 1973
Mack Wallace (Tunnell) .....Sept. 18, 1973–Sept. 22, 1987
Jon Newton (Ramsey)..............Jan. 10, 1977–Jan. 4, 1979
John H. Poerner (Langdon)......Jan. 2, 1978–Jan. 1, 1981
James E. (Jim) Nugent (Newton) ....Jan. 4, 1979–Jan. 3,1995
Buddy Temple (Poerner)........Jan. 2, 1981–March 2, 1986
Clark Jobe (Temple) .... March 3, 1986–Jan. 5, 1987
John Sharp (Jobe .... Jan. 6, 1987–Jan. 2, 1991
Kent Hance (Wallace)........... Sept. 23, 1987–Jan. 2, 1991
*Robert Krueger (Hance).......... Jan. 3, 1991–Jan. 23, 1993
Lena Guerrero (Sharp) .... Jan. 23, 1991–Sept. 25, 1992
James Wallace (Guerrero)........ Oct. 2, 1992–Jan. 4, 1993
Barry Williamson (Wallace)....... Jan. 5, 1993–Jan. 4, 1999
Mary Scott Nabers (Krueger)... Feb. 9, 1993–Dec. 9, 1994
Carole K. Rylander (Nabers) . Dec. 10, 1994–Jan. 4, 1999
Charles Matthews (Nugent).... Jan. 3, 1995–Jan. 31, 2005
Michael L. Williams (Rylander) ....Jan. 4, 1999–present
Antonio Garza (Williamson)....Jan. 4, 1999–Nov. 18, 2002
Victor G. Carrillo (Garza) .... Feb. 19, 2003–present
Elizabeth A. Jones (Matthews) .... Feb. 2, 2005–present

* Robert Krueger resigned when Gov. Ann Richards appointed him interim U.S. Senator on the resignation of Sen.Lloyd Bentsen.

★ ★ ★ ★ ★ ★ ★

Comptroller of Public Accounts
Of the Republic

John H. Money ....Dec. 30, 1835–Jan. 17, 1836
H. C. Hudson ....Jan. 17, 1836–Oct. 22, 1836
E. M. Pease .... June 1837–Dec. 1837
F. R. Lubbock.................................. Dec. 1837–Jan. 1839
Jas. W. Simmons................ Jan. 15, 1839–Sept. 30, 1840
Jas. B. Shaw.......................Sept. 30, 1840–Dec. 24, 1841
F. R. Lubbock.......................... Dec. 24, 1841–Jan. 1, 1842
Jas. B. Shaw........................Jan. 1, 1842–Jan. 1, 1846

Of the State

Jas. B. Shaw........................ Feb. 24, 1846–Aug. 2, 1858
Clement R. Johns.................. Aug. 2, 1858–Aug. 1, 1864
Willis L. Robards...................Aug. 1, 1864–Oct. 12, 1865
Albert H. Latimer................. Oct. 12, 1865–Mar. 27, 1866
Robert H. Taylor.............. Mar. 27, 1866–June 25, 1866
Willis L. Robards.................June 25, 1866–Aug. 27, 1867
Morgan C. Hamilton...............Aug. 27, 1867–Jan. 8, 1870
A. Bledsoe .... Jan. 8, 1870–Jan. 20, 1874
Stephen H. Darden...............Jan. 20, 1974–Nov. 2, 1880
W. M. Brown ....Nov. 2, 1880–Jan. 16, 1883
W. J. Swain..........................Jan. 16, 1883–Jan. 18, 1887
John D. McCall .... Jan. 18, 1887–Jan. 15, 1895
R. W. Finley .... Jan. 15, 1895–Jan. 15, 1901
R. M. Love .... Jan. 15, 1901–Jan. 1903
J. W. Stephen ....Jan. 1903–Jan. 1911
W. P. Lane ....Jan. 1911–Jan. 1915
H. B. Terrell... Jan. 1915–Jan. 1920
M. L. Wiginton...................... Jan. 1920–Jan. 1921
Lon A. Smith .... Jan. 1921–Jan. 1925
S. H. Terrell.. Jan. 1925–Jan. 1931
Geo. H. Sheppard...................... Jan., 1931–Jan. 17, 1949
Robert S. Calvert........................ Jan. 17, 1949–Jan., 1975
Robert D. (Bob) Bullock.............. Jan. 1975–Jan. 3, 1991
John Sharp .... Jan. 3, 1991–Jan. 2, 1999
Carole Keeton Strayhorn .... Jan. 2, 1999–Jan. 1, 2007
Susan Combs................................. Jan. 1, 2007–present

★ ★ ★ ★ ★ ★ ★

U.S. Senators from Texas

U.S. Senators were selected by the legislatures of the states until the U.S. Constitution was amended in 1913 to require popular elections. In Texas, the first senator chosen by the voters in a general election was Charles A. Culberson in 1916. Because of political pressures, however, the rules of the Democratic Party of Texas were changed in 1904 to require that all candidates for office stand before voters in the primary. Consequently, Texas' senators faced voters in 1906, 1910 and 1912 before the U.S. Constitution was changed.

Following is the succession of Texas representatives in the United States Senate since the annexation of Texas to the Union in 1845:

Houston Succession

Sam Houston........................Feb. 21, 1846–Mar. 4, 1859
John Hemphill........................Mar. 4, 1859–July 11, 1861

Louis T. Wigfall and W. S. Oldham took their seats in the Confederate Senate, Nov. 16, 1861, and served until the Confederacy collapsed. After that event, the State Legislature on Aug. 21, 1866, elected David G. Burnet and Oran M. Roberts to the United States Senate, anticipating immediate readmission to the Union, but they were not allowed to take their seats.

†Morgan C. Hamilton.............Feb. 22, 1870–Mar. 3, 1877
Richard Coke..........................Mar. 4, 1877–Mar. 3, 1895
Horace Chilton.....................Mar. 3, 1895–Mar. 3, 1901
Joseph W. Bailey.....................Mar. 3, 1901–Jan. 8, 1913
Rienzi Melville Johnston..........Jan. 8, 1913–Feb. 3, 1913
‡Morris Sheppard (died)........ Feb. 13, 1913–Apr. 9, 1941
Andrew J. Houston ....June 2–26, 1941
W. Lee O'Daniel.....................Aug. 4, 1941–Jan. 3, 1949
Lyndon B. Johnson................ Jan. 3, 1949–Jan. 20, 1961
William A. Blakley .... Jan. 20, 1961–June 15, 1961
†John G. Tower .... June 15, 1961–Jan. 21, 1985
†Phil Gramm.........................Jan. 21, 1985–Dec. 2, 2002
†John Cornyn ....Dec. 2, 2002–present

Rusk Succession

Thomas J. Rusk (*died*) .... Feb 21, 1846–July 29, 1857
J. Pinckney Henderson (*died*) .Nov. 9, 1857–June 4, 1858
Matthias Ward (*appointed*
    interim)..........................Sept. 29, 1858–Dec. 5, 1859
Louis T. Wigfall .... Dec. 5, 1859–March 23, 1861

Succession was broken by the expulsion of Texas Senators following secession of Texas from Union. See note above under "Houston Succession" on Louis T. Wigfall, W. S. Oldham, Burnet and Roberts.

†James W. Flanagan............. Feb. 22, 1870–Mar. 3, 1875
Samuel B. Maxey ....Mar. 3, 1875–Mar. 3, 1887
John H. Reagan (*resigned*) ...Mar. 3, 1887–June 10, 1891
Horace Chilton (*filled vacancy on
    appointment*)...................Dec. 7, 1891–Mar. 30,1892
Roger Q. Mills......................Mar. 30, 1892–Mar. 3, 1899
‡Charles A. Culberson..............Mar. 3, 1899–Mar. 4, 1923
Earle B. Mayfield ....Mar. 4, 1923–Mar. 4, 1929
Tom Connally...........................Mar. 4, 1929–Jan. 3, 1953
Price Daniel ....Jan. 3, 1953–Jan. 15, 1957
William A. Blakley .... Jan. 15, 1957–Apr. 27, 1957
Ralph W. Yarborough .... Apr. 27, 1957–Jan. 12, 1971
§Lloyd Bentsen.....................Jan. 12, 1971–Jan. 20, 1993
Robert Krueger....................Jan. 20, 1993–June 14, 1993
†Kay Bailey Hutchison..................June 14, 1993–present

† Republicans
‡ First election to U.S. Senate held in 1916. Prior to that time, senators were appointed by the Legislature.
§ Resigned from Senate when appointed U.S. Secretary of Treasury by Pres. Bill Clinton.

★ ★ ★ ★ ★ ★ ★

Commissioners of the General Land Office
For the Republic

John P. Borden   Aug. 23, 1837–Dec. 12, 1840
H. W. Raglin   Dec. 12, 1840–Jan. 4, 1841
*Thomas William Ward Jan. 4, 1841–Mar. 20, 1848

For the State

George W. Smyth ....Mar. 20, 1848–Aug. 4, 1851
Stephen Crosby.......................Aug. 4, 1851–Mar. 1, 1858
Francis M. White....................Mar. 1, 1858–Mar. 1, 1862
Stephen Crosby.....................Mar. 1, 1862–Sept. 1, 1865
Francis M. White.................... Sept. 1, 1865–Aug. 7, 1866
Stephen Crosby.................... Aug. 7, 1866–Aug. 27, 1867
Joseph Spence..................Aug. 27, 1867–Jan. 19, 1870
Jacob Kuechler................... Jan. 19, 1870–Jan. 20, 1874
J. J. Groos .... Jan. 20, 1874–June 15, 1878
W. C. Walsh..........................July 30, 1878–Jan. 10, 1887
R. M. Hall............................. Jan. 10, 1887–Jan. 16, 1891
W. L. McGaughey............... Jan. 16, 1891–Jan. 26, 1895
A. J. Baker........................... Jan. 26, 1895–Jan. 16, 1899

George W. Finger	Jan. 16, 1899–May 4, 1899	
Charles Rogan	May 11, 1899–Jan. 10, 1903	
John J. Terrell	Jan. 10, 1903–Jan. 11, 1909	
J. T. Robison	Jan, 1909–Sept. 11, 1929	
J. H. Walker	Sept. 11, 1929–Jan., 1937	
William H. McDonald	Jan 1937–Jan. 1939	
Bascom Giles	Jan. 1939–Jan. 5, 1955	
J. Earl Rudder	Jan. 5, 1955–Feb. 1, 1958	
Bill Allcorn	Feb. 1, 1958–Jan. 1, 1961	
Jerry Sadler	Jan. 1, 1961–Jan. 1, 1971	
Bob Armstrong	Jan. 1, 1971–Jan. 1, 1983	
Garry Mauro	Jan. 1, 1983–Jan. 7, 1999	
David Dewhurst	Jan. 7, 1999–Jan. 3, 2003	
Jerry Patterson	Jan. 3, 2003–present	

Part of term after annexation.

★ ★ ★ ★ ★ ★ ★

Speaker of the Texas House

The Speaker of the Texas House of Representatives is the presiding officer of the lower chamber of the State Legislature. The official is elected at the beginning of each regular session by a vote of the members of the House.

Speaker, Residence	Year Elected	Legis- lature
William E. Crump, Bellville	1846	1st
William H. Bourland, Paris	1846	1st
James W. Henderson, Houston	1847	2nd
Charles G. Keenan, Huntsville	1849	3rd
David C. Dickson, Anderson	1851	4th
Hardin R. Runnels, Boston	1853	5th
Hamilton P. Bee, Laredo	1855	6th
William S. Taylor, Larissa	1857	7th
Matt F. Locke, Lafayette	1858	7th
Marion DeKalb Taylor, Jefferson	1859	8th
Constantine W. Buckley, Richmond	1861	9th
Nicholas H. Darnell, Dallas	1861	9th
Constantine W. Buckley, Richmond	1863	9th
Marion DeKalb Taylor, Jefferson	1863	10th
Nathaniel M. Burford, Dallas	1866	11th
Ira H. Evans, Corpus Christi	1870	12th
William H. Sinclair, Galveston	1871	12th
Marion DeKalb Taylor, Jefferson	1873	13th
Guy M. Bryan, Galveston	1874	14th
Thomas R. Bonner, Tyler	1876	15th
John H. Cochran, Dallas	1879	16th
George R. Reeves, Pottsboro	1881	17th
Charles R. Gibson, Waxahachie	1883	18th
Lafayette L. Foster, Groesbeck	1885	19th
George C. Pendleton, Belton	1887	20th
Frank P. Alexander, Greenville	1889	21st
Robert T. Milner, Henderson	1891	22nd
John H. Cochran, Dallas	1893	23rd
Thomas Slater Smith, Hillsboro	1895	24th
L. Travis Dashiell, Jewett	1897	25th
J. S. Sherrill, Greenville	1899	26th
Robert E. Prince, Corsicana	1901	27th
Pat M. Neff, Waco	1903	28th
Francis W. Seabury, Rio Grande City	1905	29th
Thomas B. Love, Lancaster	1907	30th
Austin M. Kennedy, Waco	1909	31st
John W. Marshall, Whitesboro	1909	31st
Sam Rayburn, Bonham	1911	32nd
Chester H. Terrell, San Antonio	1913	33rd
John W. Woods, Rotan	1915	34th
Franklin O. Fuller, Coldspring	1917	35th
R. Ewing Thomason, El Paso	1919	36th
Charles G. Thomas, Lewisville	1921	37th
Richard E. Seagler, Palestine	1923	38th
Lee Satterwhite, Amarillo	1925	39th

Robert L. Bobbitt, Laredo	1927	40th
W. S. Barron, Bryan	1929	41st
Fred H. Minor, Denton	1931	42nd
Coke R. Stevenson, Junction	1933	43rd
"	1935	44th
Robert W. Calvert, Hillsboro	1937	45th
R. Emmett Morse, Houston	1939	46th
Homer L. Leonard, McAllen	1941	47th
Price Daniel, Liberty	1943	48th
Claud H. Gilmer, Rocksprings	1945	49th
William O. Reed, Dallas	1947	50th
Durwood Manford, Smiley	1949	51st
Reuben Senterfitt, San Saba	1951	52nd
"	1953	53rd
Jim T. Lindsey, Texarkana	1955	54th
Waggoner Carr, Lubbock	1957	55th
"	1959	56th
James A. Turman, Gober	1961	57th
Byron M. Tunnell, Tyler	1963	58th
Ben Barnes, DeLeon	1965	59th
"	1967	60th
Gus F. Mutscher, Brenham	1969	61st
"	1971	62nd
Rayford Price, Palestine	1972	62nd
Price Daniel Jr., Liberty	1973	63rd
Bill Clayton, Springlake	1975	64th
"	1977	65th
"	1979	66th
"	1981	67th
Gibson D. Lewis, Fort Worth	1983	68th
"	1985	69th
"	1987	70th
"	1989	71st
"	1991	72nd
James M. (Pete) Laney, Hale Center	1993	73rd
"	1995	74th
"	1997	75th
"	1999	76th
"	2001	77th
Tom Craddick	2003	78th
"	2005	79th
"	2007	80th

★ ★ ★ ★ ★ ★ ★

Chief Justice of the Supreme Court
Republic of Texas

James Collinsworth	Dec. 16, 1836–July 23, 1838
John Birdsall	Nov. 19–Dec. 12, 1838
Thomas J. Rusk	Dec. 12, 1838–Dec. 5, 1840
John Hemphill	Dec. 5, 1840–Dec. 29, 1845

Under the Constitutions of 1845 and 1861

John Hemphill	Mar. 2, 1846–Oct. 10, 1858
Royall T. Wheeler	Oct. 11, 1858–April 1864
Oran M. Roberts	Nov. 1, 1864–June 30, 1866

Under the Constitution of 1866
(Presidential Reconstruction)

*George F. Moore	Aug. 16, 1866–Sept. 10, 1867

Removed under Congressional Reconstruction by military authorities who appointed members of the next court.

Under the Constitution of 1866
(Congressional Reconstruction)

Amos Morrill	Sept. 10, 1867–July 5, 1870

Under the Constitution of 1869

Lemuel D. Evans .... July 5, 1870–Aug. 31, 1873
Wesley Ogden .... Aug. 31, 1873–Jan. 29, 1874
Oran M. Roberts .... Jan. 29, 1874–Apr. 18, 1876

Under the Constitution of 1876

Oran M. Roberts .... Apr. 18, 1876–Oct. 1, 1878
George F. Moore .... Nov. 5, 1878–Nov. 1, 1881
Robert S. Gould .... Nov. 1, 1881–Dec. 23, 1882
Asa H. Willie .... Dec. 23, 1882–Mar. 3, 1888
John W. Stayton .... Mar. 3, 1888–July 5, 1894
Reuben R. Gaines .... July 10, 1894–Jan. 5, 1911
Thomas J. Brown .... Jan. 7, 1911–May 26, 1915
Nelson Phillips .... June 1, 1915–Nov. 16, 1921
C. M. Cureton .... Dec. 2, 1921–Apr. 8, 1940
†Hortense Sparks Ward .... Jan. 8, 1925–May 23, 1925
W. F. Moore .... Apr. 17, 1940–Jan. 1, 1941
James P. Alexander .... Jan. 1, 1941–Jan. 1, 1948
J. E. Hickman .... Jan. 5, 1948–Jan. 3, 1961
Robert W. Calvert .... Jan. 3, 1961–Oct. 4, 1972
Joe R. Greenhill .... Oct. 4, 1972–Oct. 25, 1982
Jack Pope .... Nov. 29, 1982–Jan. 5, 1985
John L. Hill Jr. .... Jan. 5, 1985–Jan. 4, 1988
Thomas R. Phillips .... Jan. 4, 1988–Sept. 3 2004
Wallace B. Jefferson .... Sept. 14, 2004–present

†Mrs. Ward served as Chief Justice of a special Supreme Court to hear one case in 1925.

Presiding Judges, Court of Appeals (1876–1891) and Court of Criminal Appeals (1891–present)

Mat D. Ector .... May 6, 1876–Oct. 29, 1879
John P. White .... Nov. 9, 1879–Apr. 26, 1892
James M. Hurt .... May 4, 1892–Dec. 31, 1898
W. L. Davidson .... Jan. 2, 1899–June 27, 1913
A. C. Prendergast .... June 27, 1913–Dec. 31, 1916
W. L. Davidson .... Jan. 1, 1917–Jan. 25, 1921
Wright C. Morrow .... Feb. 8, 1921–Oct. 16, 1939
Frank Lee Hawkins .... Oct. 16, 1939–Jan. 2, 1951
Harry N. Graves .... Jan. 2, 1951–Dec. 31, 1954
W. A. Morrison .... Jan. 1, 1955–Jan. 2, 1961
Kenneth K. Woodley .... Jan. 3, 1961–Jan. 4, 1965
W. T. McDonald .... Jan. 4, 1965–June 25, 1966
W. A. Morrison .... June 25, 1966–Jan. 1, 1967
Kenneth K. Woodley .... Jan. 1, 1967–Jan. 1, 1971
John F. Onion Jr. .... Jan. 1, 1971–Jan. 1, 1989
Michael J. McCormick .... Jan. 1, 1989–Jan. 1, 2001
Sharon Keller .... Jan. 1, 2001–present

★ ★ ★ ★ ★ ★ ★

Administrators of Public Education
Superintendents of Public Instruction

Pryor Lea .... Nov. 10, 1866–Sept. 12, 1867
Edwin M. Wheelock .... Sept. 12, 1867–May 6, 1871
Jacob C. DeGress .... May 6, 1871–Jan. 20, 1874
O. H. Hollingsworth .... Jan. 20, 1874–May 6, 1884
B. M. Baker .... May 6, 1884–Jan. 18, 1887
O. H. Cooper .... Jan 18, 1887–Sept. 1, 1890
H. C. Pritchett .... Sept. 1, 1890–Sept. 15, 1891
J. M. Carlisle .... Sept. 15, 1891–Jan. 10, 1899
J. S. Kendall .... Jan. 10, 1899–July 2, 1901
Arthur Lefevre .... July 2, 1901–Jan. 12, 1905
R. B. Cousins .... Jan. 12, 1905–Jan. 1, 1910
F. M. Bralley .... Jan. 1, 1910–Sept. 1, 1913
W. F. Doughty .... Sept. 1, 1913–Jan. 1, 1919
Annie Webb Blanton .... Jan. 1, 1919–Jan. 16, 1923
S. M. N. Marrs .... Jan. 16, 1923–April 28, 1932
C. N. Shaver .... April 28, 1932–Oct. 1, 1932
L. W. Rogers .... Oct. 1, 1932–Jan. 16, 1933

L. A. Woods .... Jan. 16, 1933–*1951

State Commissioner of Education

J. W. Edgar .... May 31, 1951–June 30, 1974
Marlin L. Brockette .... July 1, 1974–Sept. 1, 1979
Alton O. Bowen .... Sept. 1, 1979–June 1, 1981
Raymon Bynum .... June 1, 1981–Oct. 31, 1984
W. N. Kirby .... April 13, 1985–July 1, 1991
Lionel R. Meno .... July 1, 1991–March 1, 1995
Michael A. Moses .... March 9, 1995–Aug. 18, 1999
Jim Nelson .... Aug. 18, 1999–March 25, 2002
Felipe Alanis .... March 25, 2002–July 31, 2003
Shirley J. Neeley .... Jan. 12, 2004–July 1, 2007
Robert Scott (acting) .... July 1, 2007–present

The office of State Superintendent of Public Instruction was abolished by the Gilmer-Aikin act of 1949 and the office of Commissioner of Education created, appointed by a new State Board of Education elected by the people.

First Ladies of Texas

Martha Evans Gindratt Wood 1847–49
†Bell Administration 1849–53
Lucadia Christiana Niles Pease . 1853-57; 1867–69
‡Runnels Administration 1857–59
Margaret Moffette Lea Houston 1859–61
Martha Evans Clark 1861
Adele Barron Lubbock 1861–1863
Susie Ellen Taylor Murrah 1863–1865
Mary Jane Bowen Hamilton 1865–1866
Annie Rattan Throckmorton 1866–1867
Ann Elizabeth Britton Davis 1870–1874
Mary Home Coke 1874–1876
Janie Roberts Hubbard 1876–1879
Frances Wickliff Edwards Roberts 1879–1883
Anne Maria Penn Ireland 1883–1887
Elizabeth Dorothy Tinsley Ross 1887–1891
Sarah Stinson Hogg 1891–1895
Sally Harrison Culberson 1895–1899
Orlene Walton Sayers 1899–1903
Sarah Beona Meng Lanham 1903–1907
Fannie Brunner Campbell 1907–1911
Alice Fuller Murrell Colquitt 1911–1915
§Miriam A. Wallace Ferguson 1915–1917
Willie Cooper Hobby 1917–1921
Myrtle Mainer Neff 1921–1925
Mildred Paxton Moody 1927–1931
Maud Gage Sterling 1931–1933
Jo Betsy Miller Allred 1935–1939
Merle Estella Butcher O'Daniel 1939–1941
**Fay Wright Stevenson 1941–1942
**Edith Will Scott Stevenson 1942–1946
Mabel Buchanan Jester 1946–1949
Marialice Shary Shivers 1949–1957
Jean Houston Baldwin Daniel 1957–1963
Idanell Brill Connally 1963–1969
Ima Mae Smith 1969–1973
Betty Jane Slaughter Briscoe 1973–1979
Rita Crocker Bass Clements 1979–1983
Linda Gale Thompson White 1983–1987
Rita Crocker Bass Clements 1987–1991
Laura Welch Bush 1995–2000
Anita Thigpen Perry 2000–present

†Gov. Peter Hansbrough Bell was not married while in office
‡Gov. Hardin R. Runnels never married.
***Mrs. Coke R. (Fay Wright) Stevenson, the governor's wife, died in the Governor's Mansion Jan. 3, 1942. His mother, Edith Stevenson, served as Mistress of the Mansion thereafter.* ☆

State Government

Texas state government is divided into executive, legislative and judicial branches under the Texas Constitution adopted in 1876. The chief executive is the Governor, whose term is for four years. Other elected state officials with executive responsibilities include the Lieutenant Governor, Attorney General, Comptroller of Public Accounts, Commissioner of the General Land Office and Commissioner of Agriculture. The terms of those officials are also four years. The Secretary of State is appointed by the Governor.

Except for making numerous appointments and calling special sessions of the Legislature, the Governor's powers are limited in comparison with those in most states.

Current state executives "not-to-exceed" salaries are for the 2006–2007 biennium (maximum possible salaries; actual salaries can be lower); salaries for the 2008–2009 biennium were not available from the State Auditor at press time.

Governor: Rick Perry
P.O. Box 12428, Austin 78711
512-463-2000; www.governor.state.tx.us
$115,345

Attorney General: Greg Abbott
P.O. Box 12548, Austin 78711-2548
512-463-2100; www.oag.state.tx.us
$125,000

Land Commissioner: Jerry Patterson
P.O. Box 12873, Austin 78711-2873
512-463-5001; www.glo.state.tx.us
$125,000

Lt. Governor: David Dewhurst
P.O. Box 12068, Austin 78711
512-463-0001; www.senate.state.tx.us
For salary, see note* below.

Comptroller of Public Accounts: Susan Combs
PO Box 13528, Austin 78774
512-463-4000; www.windows.state.tx.us
$125,000

Commissioner of Agriculture: Todd Staples
P.O. Box 12847, Austin 78711-2847
512-463-7476; www.agr.state.tx.us
$125,000

Secretary of State: Phil Wilson
P.O. Box 12887, Austin 78711
512-463-5770; www.sos.state.tx.us
$117,516

Salary of Lt. Gov. is same as a Senator when serving as Pres.of the Senate; same as Gov. when serving as Gov.

The Governor's **Citizens' Assistance Hotline (1-800-843-5789)** can be used to make comments and complaints, which are passed to government officials who may offer sources of help.

Texas Legislature

The Texas Legislature has **181 members: 31 in the Senate** and **150 in the House of Representatives**. Regular sessions convene on the second Tuesday of January in odd-numbered years, but the governor may call special sessions. Article III of the Texas Constitution deals with the legislative branch. On the Web: **www.capitol.state.tx.us**.

The following lists are of members of the **80th Legislature**, which convened for its Regular Session on Jan. 9, 2007, and adjourned on May 28, 2007. The **81st Legislature** is scheduled to convene on Jan. 13, 2009, and adjourn June 1, 2009.

State Senate

Thirty-one members of the State Senate are elected to four-year, overlapping terms. Salary: The salary of all members of the Legislature, both Senators and Representatives, is $7,200 per year and $124 per diem during legislative sessions; mileage allowance at same rate provided by law for state employees. The per diem payment applies during each regular and special session of the Legislature.

Senatorial Districts include one or more whole counties and some counties have more than one Senator.

The **address of Senators** is Texas Senate, P.O. Box 12068, Austin 78711-2068; phone 512-463-0001; Fax: 512-463-0001. On the Web: **www.senate.state.tx.us**.

President of the Senate: Lt. Gov. David Dewhurst; **President Pro Tempore:** Mario Gallegos Jr.; **Secretary of the Senate:** Patsy Spaw; **Sergeant-at-Arms:** Rick De-Leon.

Texas State Senators

District, Member, Party-Hometown, Occupation

1. Kevin P. Eltife, R-Tyler; businessman.
2. Bob Deuell, R-Greenville; family physician.
3. Robert Nichols, R-Jacksonville; engineer.
4. Tommy Williams, R-The Woodlands; businessman.
5. Steve Ogden, R-Bryan; oil and gas producer.
6. Mario Gallegos Jr., D-Houston; retired firefighter.
7. Dan Patrick, R-Houston; broadcasting.
8. Florence Shapiro, R-Plano; former small business owner.
9. Chris Harris, R-Arlington; attorney.
10. Kenneth (Kim) Brimer, R-Fort Worth; businessman.
11. Mike Jackson, R-La Porte; businessman.
12. Jane Nelson, R-Lewisville; businesswoman.

13. Rodney Ellis, D-Houston; businessman.
14. Kirk Watson, D-Austin; attorney.
15. John Whitmire, D-Houston; attorney (**Dean of the Senate**).
16. John J. Carona, R-Dallas; company president.
17. Kyle Janek, R-Houston; anesthesiologist.
18. Glenn Hegar, R-Katy; farmer.
19. Carlos I. Uresti, D-San Antonio; attorney.
20. Juan (Chuy) Hinojosa, D-Mission; attorney.
21. Judith Zaffirini, D-Laredo; communications specialist.
22. Kip Averitt, R-Waco; tax consultant.
23. Royce West, D-Dallas; attorney.
24. Troy Fraser, R-Horseshoe Bay; businessman.
25. Jeff Wentworth, R-San Antonio; attorney, Realtor.
26. Leticia Van de Putte, D-San Antonio; pharmacist.
27. Eddie Lucio Jr., D-Brownsville; advertising executive.
28. Robert Duncan, R-Lubbock; attorney.
29. Eliot Shapleigh, D-El Paso; attorney.
30. Craig Estes, R-Wichita Falls; businessman.
31. Kel Seliger, R-Amarillo; businessman.

House of Representatives

This is a list of the 150 members of the House of Representatives in the 80th Legislature. They were elected for two-year terms from the districts shown below. Representatives and senators receive the same salary (see State Senate). The **address of all Representatives** is House of Representatives, P.O. Box 2910, Austin, 78768-2910; phone: 512-463-3000; Fax: 512-463-5896. On the Web: **www.house.state.tx.us/**

Speaker: Tom Craddick (R-Midland). **Speaker Pro Tempore**, Sylvester Turner (D-Houston). **Chief Clerk**, Robert Haney. **Sergeant-at-Arms**, Rod Welsh.

Members of Texas House of Representatives
District, Member, Party-Hometown, Occupation

1. Stephen Frost, D-Atlanta, attorney.
2. Dan Flynn, R-Van; businessman, rancher.
3. Mark Homer, D-Paris; small business owner.
4. Betty Brown, R-Terrell; rancher.
5. Bryan Hughes, R-Mineola; attorney.
6. Leo Berman, R-Tyler; retired military officer.
7. Tommy Merritt, R-Longview; small business owner.
8. Byron C. Cook, R-Corsicana; businessman, rancher.
9. Wayne Christian, R-Center; investment sales.
10. Jim Pitts, R-Waxahachie; attorney.
11. Charles (Chuck) Hopson, D-Jacksonville; pharmacist.
12. Jim McReynolds, D-Lufkin; petroleum landman.
13. Lois W. Kolkhorst, R-Brenham; business owner, investor.
14. Fred H. Brown, R-College Station; insurance.
15. Rob Eissler, R-The Woodlands; executive recruiter.
16. Brandon Creighton, R-Conroe; attorney, real estate.
17. Robert "Robby" Cook, D-Eagle Lake; farmer.
18. John C. Otto, R-Dayton; CPA.
19. Mike Hamilton, R-Mauriceville; catering.
20. Dan Gattis, R-Georgetown; attorney, rancher.
21. Allan B. Ritter, D-Nederland; business owner.
22. Joe Deshotel, D-Beaumont; attorney, businessman.
23. Craig Eiland, D-Galveston; attorney.
24. Larry Taylor, R-Friendswood; insurance agent.
25. Dennis H. Bonnen, R-Angleton; banking.
26. Charlie Howard, R-Sugar Land; Realtor, investor.
27. Dora F. Olivo, D-Rosenberg; attorney.
28. John Zerwas, R-Richmond; physician.
29. Mike P. O'Day, R-Pearland; contractor.
30. Geanie W. Morrison, R-Victoria; state representative.
31. Ryan Guillen, D-Rio Grande City; rancher, businessman.
32. Juan M. Garcia III, D-Corpus Christi; attorney, naval aviator.
33. Solomon P. Ortiz Jr., D-Corpus Christi; businessman.
34. Abel Herrero, D-Robstown; attorney.
35. Yvonne Gonzalez Toureilles, D-Alice; attorney.
36. Ismael (Kino) Flores, D-Palmview; businessman.
37. Rene O. Oliveira, D-Brownsville; attorney.
38. Eddie Lucio III, D-Brownsville; attorney.
39. Armando Martinez, D-Weslaco; firefighter, paramedic.
40. Aaron Peña, D-Edinburg; attorney.
41. Veronica Gonzales, D-McAllen; attorney.
42. Richard Peña Raymond, D-Laredo; businessman.
43. Juan M. Escobar, D-Kingsville; law enforcement, retired.
44. Edmund Kuempel, R-Seguin; salesman.
45. Patrick M. Rose, D-Dripping Springs; attorney, Realtor.
46. Dawnna M. Dukes, D-Austin; business consultant.
47. Valinda Bolton, D-Austin; non-profit consultant.
48. Donna Howard, D-Austin; nursing, public health.
49. Elliott Naishtat, D-Austin; attorney.
50. Mark Strama, D-Austin; technology consultant.
51. Eddie Rodriguez, D-Austin; policy consultant.
52. Mike Krusee, R-Round Rock; consultant.
53. Harvey Hilderbran, R-Kerrville; businessman.
54. Jimmie Don Aycock, R-Killeen; veterinarian, rancher.
55. Dianne White Delisi, R-Temple; state representative.
56. Charles (Doc) Anderson, R-Waco; veterinarian.
57. Jim Dunnam, D-Waco; attorney.
58. Rob D. Orr, R-Burleson; real estate broker.
59. Sid Miller, R-Stephenville; rancher, nurseryman.
60. James L. Keffer, R-Eastland; president, iron company.
61. Phil S. King, R-Weatherford; attorney.
62. Larry Phillips, R-Sherman, attorney.
63. Tan Parker, R-Flower Mound; businessman.
64. Myra Crownover, R-Denton; ranching, businesswoman.
65. Burt R. Solomons, R-Carrollton; attorney.
66. Brian McCall, R-Plano; businessman.
67. Jerry Madden, R-Richardson; insurance agent.
68. Rick L. Hardcastle, R-Vernon; rancher.
69. David Farabee, D-Wichita Falls; insurance agent.
70. Ken Paxton, R-McKinney; attorney.
71. Susan King, R-Abilene; surgical nurse.
72. Drew Darby, R-San Angelo; attorney, business owner.
73. Nathan Macias, R-Bulverde; businessman.
74. Pete P. Gallego, D-Alpine; attorney.
75. Inocente (Chente) Quintanilla, D-Tornillo; retired assistant superintendent, educator.
76. Norma Chávez, D-El Paso; business manager.
77. Paul C. Moreno, D-El Paso; attorney (Senior House Member).
78. Pat Haggerty, R-El Paso; real estate broker.
79. Joseph Pickett, D-El Paso; state representative.
80. Tracy O. King, D-Batesville; hearing aid specialist.
81. G.E. "Buddy" West, R-Odessa; retired safety engineer.
82. Tom Craddick, R-Midland; investor, sales representative (Speaker of the House)
83. Delwin Jones, R-Lubbock; businessman.
84. Carl H. Isett, R-Lubbock; CPA.
85. Joe Heflin, D-Crosbyton; attorney.
86. John T. Smithee, R-Amarillo; attorney.
87. David A. Swinford, R-Dumas; businessman.
88. Warren D. Chisum, R-Pampa; oil and gas producer.
89. Jodie Laubenberg, R-Parker; state representative.
90. Lon Burnam, D-Fort Worth; Dallas Peace Center director.
91. Kelly Hancock, R-North Richland Hills; business owner.
92. Todd Smith, R-Euless; attorney.
93. Paula Pierson, D-Arlington; businesswoman.
94. Diane Patrick, R-Arlington; university professor.
95. Marc Veasey, D-Fort Worth; consultant.
96. William (Bill) Zedler, R-Arlington; retired.
97. Anna Mowery, R-Fort Worth; state representative.
98. Vicki Truitt, R-Keller; small business owner.
99. Charlie L. Geren, R-Fort Worth; restaurant owner, real estate broker, rancher.
100. Terri Hodge, D-Dallas; retired.
101. Thomas R. Latham, R-Sunnyvale; law enforcement.
102. Tony Goolsby, R-Dallas; insurance.
103. Rafael Anchía, D-Dallas; attorney.
104. Roberto R. Alonzo, D-Dallas; attorney.
105. Linda Harper-Brown, R-Irving; CEO.
106. Kirk T. England, R-Grand Prairie; insurance agent.
107. Allen Vaught, D-Dallas; attorney.
108. Dan Branch, R-Dallas; attorney.
109. Helen Giddings, D-Dallas; small business owner.
110. Barbara Mallory Caraway, D-Dallas; business owner.
111. Yvonne Davis, D-Dallas; small business owner.
112. Fred Hill, R-Richardson; businessman.
113. Joe Driver, R-Garland; insurance agent.
114. Will Hartnett, R-Dallas; probate attorney, businessman.
115. Jim L. Jackson, R-Carrollton; retired.
116. Trey Martinez Fischer, D-San Antonio; attorney.
117. David M. Leibowitz, D-San Antonio; attorney.
118. Joe Farias, D-San Antonio; retired.
119. Robert Puente, D-San Antonio; attorney.
120. Ruth Jones McClendon, D-San Antonio; business owner.
121. Joe Straus III, R-San Antonio; insurance, investments.
122. Frank J. Corte Jr., R-San Antonio; real estate, property management.
123. Michael Villarreal, D-San Antonio; small business owner, investment banker.
124. José Menendez, D-San Antonio; marketing executive.
125. Joaquin Castro, D-San Antonio; attorney.
126. Patricia F. Harless, R-Spring; automobile dealer.
127. Joe Crabb, R-Atascocita; minister, attorney, rancher.
128. Wayne Smith, R-Baytown; civil engineer.
129. John E. Davis, R-Houston; roofing contractor.
130. Corbin Van Arsdale, R-Tomball; attorney.
131. Alma A. Allen, D-Houston; educator.
132. William A. Callegari, R-Houston; professional engineer.
133. Jim Murphy, R-Houston; businessman.
134. Ellen R. Cohen, D-Houston; CEO.
135. Gary Elkins, R-Houston; businessman, consultant.
136. Beverly Woolley, R-Houston; small business owner.
137. Scott Hochberg, D-Houston; software consultant.
138. Dwayne Bohac, R-Houston; businessman.
139. Sylvester Turner, D-Houston; attorney.
140. Kevin Bailey, D-Houston; college instructor.
141. Senfronia Thompson, D-Houston; attorney.
142. Harold V. Dutton Jr., D-Houston; attorney.
143. Ana E. Harnandez, D-Pasadena; attorney.
144. Robert E. Talton, R-Pasadena; attorney.
145. Richard J. (Rick) Noriega, D-Houston; businessman.
146. Borris L. Miles, D-Houston; insurance agent.
147. Garnet Coleman, D-Houston; business consultant.
148. Jessica Farrar, D-Houston; architect.
149. Hubert Vo, D-Houston; Realtor.
150. Debbie Riddle, R-Tomball; horse breeder. ☆

Texas State Judiciary

The judiciary of the state consists of 9 members of the State Supreme Court; 9 members of the Court of Criminal Appeals; 80 of the Courts of Appeals; 437 of the State District Courts, including 12 Criminal District Courts; 494 County Court judges; 821 Justices of the Peace; and 1,407 Municipal Courts judges.

In addition to its system of formal courts, the State of Texas has established 17 **Alternative Dispute Resolution Centers**. The centers help ease the caseload of Texas courts by using mediation, arbitration, negotiation and moderated settlement conferences to handle disputes without resorting to more costly, time-consuming court actions.

Centers are located in Amarillo, Austin, Beaumont, Bryan, Conroe, Corpus Christi, Dallas, Denton, El Paso, Fort Worth, Houston, Kerrville, Lubbock, Paris, Richmond, San Antonio and Waco. For the fiscal year ending Aug. 31, 2005, the mediation sections of the centers had closed 18,292 cases and had 2,997 cases pending.

(The list of U.S. District Courts in Texas can be found in the Federal Government section, page 528.)

State Higher Courts

The state's higher courts are listed below and are current as of **July 2007**. Notations in parentheses indicate dates of expiration of terms of office. Judges of the Supreme Court, Court of Criminal Appeals and Courts of Appeals are elected to 6-year, overlapping terms. District Court judges are elected to 4-year terms.

The salaries for judges as of July 2007 were as follows: Chief Justice of the Supreme Court and the Presiding Judge of the Court of Criminal Appeals: each $152,500; Justices, $150,000; Chief Justices of the Courts of Appeals, $140,000; justices, $137,500 from the state. A supplemental amount may be paid by counties, not to exceed $15,000 per year, and total salary must be at least $1,000 less than that received by Supreme Court justices. District Court judges receive $137,500 from the state, plus supplemental pay from various subdivisions. Their total salary must be $1,000 less than that received by justices of the Court of Appeals in which the district court is located.

Below is given information on only the Supreme Court, Court of Criminal Appeals and Courts of Appeals. The information was furnished by each court as of July 2007. Elsewhere in this section can be found names of county court judges by counties, names of District Court judges by district number, and the district numbers of the District Court(s) in each county.

Supreme Court

Chief Justice, Wallace B. Jefferson (12-31-08). **Associate Justices**: Scott Brister (12-31-10); Paul W. Green (12-31-10); Nathan L. Hecht (12-31-12); Phil Johnson (12-31-08); David M. Medina (12-31-12); Harriet O'Neill (12-31-10); Dale Wainwright (12-31-08); and Don R. Willett (12-31-12). **Clerk of Court**, Blake A. Hawthorne. Location of court, Austin. Web: **www.supreme.courts.state.tx.us.**

Court of
Criminal Appeals

Presiding Judge, Sharon Keller (12-31-12). **Judges**: Cathy Cochran (12-31-08); Barbara P. Hervey (12-31-12); Charles R. Holcomb (12-31-12); Cheryl Johnson (12-31-10); Michael E. Keasler (12-31-10); Lawrence E. Meyers (12-31-12); Tom Price (12-31-08); Paul Womack (12-31-08). State Prosecuting Attorney, Matthew Paul. **Clerk of Court**, Louise Pearson. Location of court, Austin. Web: **www.cca.courts.state.tx.us.**

Courts of Appeals

These courts have jurisdiction within their respective supreme judicial districts. A constitutional amendment approved in 1978 raised the number of associate justices for Courts of Appeals where needed. Judges are elected from the district for 6-year terms. An amendment adopted in 1980 changed the name of the old Courts of Civil Appeals to the Courts of Appeals and changed the jurisdiction of the courts. Web: **www.courts.state.tx.us/courts/coa.asp.**

First District — Houston. Chief Justice, Sherry Radack (12-31-10). **Justices**: Elsa Alcala (12-31-12); Jane Bland (12-31-12); George C. Hanks Jr. (12-31-12); Laura Carter Higley (12-31-08); Terry Jennings (12-31-12); Evelyn Keyes (12-31-10); Sam Nuchia (12-31-08); and Tim G. Taft (12-31-12). **Clerk of Court**, M Karinne McCullough. Counties in the First District: Austin, Brazoria, Chambers, Colorado, Fort Bend, Galveston, Grimes, Harris, Waller, Washington.

Second District — Fort Worth: Chief Justice, John H. Cayce (12-31-12). **Justices**: Lee Ann Dauphinot (12-31-12); Anne L. Gardner (12-31-10); Dixon W. Holman (12-31-08); Terrie Livingston (12-31-08); Bob McCoy (12-31-12); and Sue Walker (12-31-12). **Clerk of Court**, Stephanie Robinson. Counties in Second District: Archer, Clay, Cooke, Denton, Hood, Jack, Montague, Parker, Tarrant, Wichita, Wise, Young.

Third District — Austin: Chief Justice, W. Kenneth Law (12-31-08). **Justices**: Diane Henson (12-31-12); Jan P. Patterson (12-31-10); Bob Pemberton (12-31-12); David Puryear (12-31-12); Alan Waldrop (12-31-12). **Clerk of Court**, Diane O'Neal. Counties in the Third District: Bastrop, Bell, Blanco, Burnet, Caldwell, Coke, Comal, Concho, Fayette, Hays, Irion, Lampasas, Lee, Llano, McCulloch, Milam, Mills, Runnels, San Saba, Schleicher, Sterling, Tom Green, Travis, Williamson.

Fourth District — San Antonio: Chief Justice, Alma L. Lopez (12-31-08). **Justices**: Karen Anne Angelini (12-31-12); Steve Hilbig (12-31-12); Sandee Bryan Marion (12-31-10); Rebecca Simmons (12-31-12); Phylis J. Speedlin (12-31-12); and Catherine M. Stone (12-31-12). **Clerk of Court**, Dan E. Crutchfield. Counties in the Fourth District: Atascosa, Bandera, Bexar, Brooks, Dimmit, Duval, Edwards, Frio, Gillespie, Guadalupe, Jim Hogg, Jim Wells, Karnes, Kendall, Kerr, Kimble, Kinney, La Salle, Mason, Maverick, McMullen, Medina, Menard, Real, Starr, Sutton, Uvalde, Val Verde, Webb, Wilson, Zapata, Zavala.

Fifth District — Dallas: Chief Justice, Linda Thomas (12-31-12). **Justices**: David L. Bridges (12-31-08); Kerry P. FitzGerald, (12-31-12); Molly Meredith Francis (12-31-12); Douglas S. Lang (11-4-12); Elizabeth Lang-Miers (12-31-12); Amos L. Mazzant (12-31-12); Joseph B. Morris (12-31-12); Jim A. Moseley (12-31-12); Michael J. O'Neill (12-31-10); Martin E. Richter (12-31-12); Mark Whittington (12-31-08); Carolyn I. Wright (12-31-10). **Clerk of Court**, Lisa Matz. Counties in the Fifth District: Collin, Dallas, Grayson, Hunt, Kaufman, Rockwall.

Sixth District — Texarkana: Chief Justice, Josh R. Morris III (12-31-10). **Justices**: Jack Carter (12-31-08) and Bailey C. Moseley (12-31-12). **Clerk of Court**, Debbie Autrey. Counties in the Sixth District: Bowie, Camp, Cass, Delta, Fannin, Franklin, Gregg, Harrison, Hopkins, Hunt, Lamar, Marion, Morris, Panola, Red River, Rusk, Titus, Upshur, Wood.

Seventh District — Amarillo: Chief Justice, Brian P. Quinn (12-31-08). **Justices**: James T. Campbell (12-31-10); Mackey Hancock (12-31-12); and Patrick A. Pirtle (12-31-12). **Clerk of Court**, Peggy Culp. Counties in the Seventh District: Armstrong, Bailey, Briscoe, Carson, Castro, Childress, Cochran, Collingsworth, Cottle, Crosby, Dallam, Deaf Smith, Dickens, Donley, Floyd, Foard, Garza, Gray, Hale, Hall, Hansford, Hardeman, Hartley, Hemphill, Hockley, Hutchinson, Kent, King, Lamb, Lipscomb, Lubbock, Lynn, Moore, Motley, Ochiltree, Oldham, Parmer, Potter, Randall, Roberts, Sherman, Swisher, Terry, Wheeler, Wilbarger, Yoakum.

Eighth District — El Paso: Chief Justice, David Wellington Chew (12-31-08). **Justices**: Ann Crawford McClure (12-31-12); and Kenneth R. Carr (12-31-08). **Clerk of Court**, Denise Pacheco. Counties in the Eighth District: Andrews, Brewster, Crane, Crockett, Culberson, El Paso, Hudspeth, Jeff Davis, Loving, Pecos, Presidio, Reagan, Reeves, Terrell, Upton, Ward, Winkler.

Ninth District — Beaumont: Chief Justice, Steve McKeithen (12-31-08). **Justices**: David B. Gaultney (12-31-12); Henry Hollis Horton (12-31-12); and Charles Kreger (12-31-10). **Clerk of Court**, Carol Anne Flores. Counties in the Ninth District: Hardin, Jasper, Jefferson, Liberty, Montgomery, Newton, Orange, Polk, San Jacinto, Tyler.

Tenth District — Waco: Chief Justice, Thomas W. Gray (12-31-12). **Justices**: Felipe Reyna (12-31-10) and Bill Vance (12-31-08). **Clerk of Court**, Sharri Roessler. Counties in the Tenth District: Bosque, Brazos, Burleson, Coryell, Ellis, Falls, Freestone, Hamilton, Hill, Johnson, Leon, Limestone, Madison, McLennan, Navarro, Robertson, Somervell, Walker.

Eleventh District — Eastland: Chief Justice, Jim R. Wright (12-31-12). **Justices**: Terry McCall (12-31-10); and Rick Strange (12-31-08). **Clerk of Court**, Sherry Williamson. Counties in the Eleventh District: Baylor, Borden, Brown, Callahan, Coleman, Comanche, Dawson, Eastland, Ector, Erath, Fisher, Gaines, Glasscock, Haskell, Howard, Jones, Knox, Martin, Midland, Mitchell, Nolan, Palo Pinto, Scurry, Shackelford, Stephens, Stonewall, Taylor, Throckmorton.

Twelfth District—Tyler: Chief Justice, Jim Worthen (12-31-08). **Justices**: Sam Griffith (12-31-12) and Brian Hoyle (12-31-12). **Clerk of Court**, Cathy S. Lusk. Counties in the Twelfth District: Anderson, Angelina, Cherokee, Gregg, Henderson, Houston, Nacogdoches, Rains, Rusk, Sabine, San Augustine, Shelby, Smith, Trinity, Upshur, Van Zandt, Wood.

Thirteenth District—Corpus Christi: Chief Justice, Rogelio Valdez (12-31-12). **Justices**: Gina M. Benavides (12-31-12); Dori Contreras Garza (12-31-00); Nelda V. Rodriguez (12-31-12); Rose Vela (12-31-12) and Linda Reyna Yañez (12-31-10). **Clerk of court**, Cathy Wilborn. Counties in the Thirteenth District: Aransas, Bee, Calhoun, Cameron, DeWitt, Goliad, Gonzales, Hidalgo, Jackson, Kenedy, Kleberg, Lavaca, Live Oak, Matagorda, Nueces, Refugio, San Patricio, Victoria, Wharton, Willacy.

Fourteenth District—Houston†: Chief Justice, Adele Hedges (12-31-08). **Justices**: John S. Anderson (12-31-12); Richard H. Edelman (12-31-12); Wanda McKee Fowler (12-31-12); Kem Thompson Frost (12-31-08); Eva M. Guzman (12-31-10); J. Harvey Hudson (12-31-12); Charles W. Seymore (12-31-12); and Leslie Brock Yates (12-31-10). **Clerk of Court**, Ed Wells. Counties in the Fourteenth District: Austin, Brazoria, Chambers, Colorado, Fort Bend, Galveston, Grimes, Harris, Waller, Washington.

*The location of the First Court of Appeals was changed from Galveston to Houston by the 55th Legislature, with the provision that all cases originated in Galveston County be tried in that city and with the further provision that any case may, at the discretion of the court, be tried in either city.

†Because of the heavy workload of the Houston area Court of Appeals, the 60th Legislature, in 1967, provided for the establishment of a Fourteenth Appeals Court at Houston.

Administrative Judicial Districts of Texas

There are nine administrative judicial districts in the state for administrative purposes. An active or retired district judge or an active or retired appellate judge with judicial experience in a district court serves as the Presiding Judge upon appointment by the Governor. They receive extra compensation of $5,000 paid by counties in the respective administrative districts.

The Presiding Judge convenes an annual conference of the judges in the administrative district to consult on the state of business in the courts. This conference is empowered to adopt rules for the administration of cases in the district. The Presiding Judge may assign active or retired district judges residing within the administrative district to any of the district courts within the administrative district. The Presiding Judge of one administrative district may request the Presiding Judge of another administrative district to assign a judge from that district to sit in a district court located in the administrative district of the Presiding Judge making the request.

The Chief Justice of the Supreme Court of Texas convenes an annual conference of the nine Presiding Judges to determine the need for assignment of judges and to promote the uniform administration of the assignment of judges. The Chief Justice is empowered to assign judges of one administrative district for service in another whenever such assignments are necessary for the prompt and efficient administration of justice.

First District — John David Ovard, Dallas: Anderson, Bowie, Camp, Cass, Cherokee, Collin, Dallas, Delta, Ellis, Fannin, Franklin, Grayson, Gregg, Harrison, Henderson, Hopkins, Houston, Hunt, Kaufman, Lamar, Marion, Morris, Nacogdoches, Panola, Rains, Red River, Rockwall, Rusk, Shelby, Smith, Titus, Upshur, Van Zandt and Wood.

Second District — Olen Underwood, Conroe: Angelina, Bastrop, Brazoria, Brazos, Burleson, Chambers, Fort Bend, Freestone, Galveston, Grimes, Hardin, Harris, Jasper, Jefferson, Lee, Leon, Liberty, Limestone, Madison, Matagorda, Montgomery, Newton, Orange, Polk, Robertson, Sabine, San Augustine, San Jacinto, Trinity, Tyler, Walker, Waller, Washington and Wharton.

Third District — B.B. Schraub, Seguin: Austin, Bell, Blanco, Bosque, Burnet, Caldwell, Colorado, Comal, Comanche, Coryell, Falls, Fayette, Gonzales, Guadalupe, Hamilton, Hays, Hill, Johnson, Lampasas, Lavaca, Llano, McLennan, Mason, Milam, Navarro, San Saba, Travis and Williamson.

Fourth District — David Peeples, San Antonio: Aransas, Atascosa, Bee, Bexar, Calhoun, DeWitt, Dimmit, Frio, Goliad, Jackson, Karnes, LaSalle, Live Oak, Maverick, McMullen, Refugio, San Patricio, Victoria, Webb, Wilson, Zapata and Zavala.

Fifth District — J. Manuel Banales, Brownsville: Brooks, Cameron, Duval, Hidalgo, Jim Hogg, Jim Wells, Kenedy, Kleberg, Nueces, Starr and Willacy.

Sixth District — Stephen B. Ables, Kerrville: Bandera, Brewster, Crockett, Culberson, Edwards, El Paso, Gillespie, Hudspeth, Jeff Davis, Kendall, Kerr, Kimble, Kinney, Mason, Medina, Pecos, Presidio, Reagan, Real, Sutton, Terrell, Upton, Uvalde and Val Verde.

Seventh District — Dean Rucker, Midland: Andrews, Borden, Brown, Callahan, Coke, Coleman, Concho, Crane, Dawson, Ector, Fisher, Gaines, Garza, Glasscock, Haskell, Howard, Irion, Jones, Kent, Lynn, Martin, McCulloch, Menard, Midland, Mills, Mitchell, Nolan, Reeves, Runnels, Schleicher, Scurry, Shackelford, Sterling, Stonewall, Taylor, Throckmorton, Tom Green, Ward and Winkler.

Eighth District — Roger Jeffrey "Jeff" Walker, Fort Worth: Archer, Clay, Cooke, Denton, Eastland, Erath, Hood, Jack, Johnson, Montague, Palo Pinto, Parker, Somervell, Stephens, Tarrant, Wichita, Wise and Young.

Ninth District — Kelly G. Moore, Brownfield: Armstrong, Bailey, Baylor, Briscoe, Carson, Castro, Childress, Cochran, Collingsworth, Cottle, Crosby, Dallam, Deaf Smith, Dickens, Donley, Floyd, Foard, Gray, Hale, Hall, Hansford, Hardeman, Hartley, Hemphill, Hockley, Hutchinson, King, Knox, Lamb, Lipscomb, Lubbock, Moore, Motley, Ochiltree, Oldham, Parmer, Potter, Randall, Roberts, Sherman, Swisher, Terry, Wheeler, Wilbarger and Yoakum. ☆

Texas Courts by County

Below are listed the state district court or courts, court of appeals district, administrative judicial district and U.S. judicial district for each county in Texas as of July 2007. For the names of the district court judges, see table by district number on pages 479–480. For the names of other judges in the Texas court system, see listing on pages 475–480.

County	State Dist. Court(s)	Ct. of App'ls Dist.	Adm. Jud. Dist.	U.S. Jud. Dist.
Anderson	3, 87, 349, 369	12	1	E-Tyler
Andrews	109	8	7	W-Midland
Angelina	159, 217	9	2	E-Lufkin
Aransas	36, 156, 343	13	4	S-C.Christi
Archer	97	2	8	N-W. Falls
Armstrong	47	7	9	N-Amarilllo
Atascosa	81, 218	4	4	W-San Ant.
Austin	155	1, 14	3	S-Houston
Bailey	287	7	9	N-Lubbock
Bandera	216	4	6	W-San Ant.
Bastrop	21, 335	3	2	W-Austin
Baylor	50	11	9	N-W. Falls
Bee	36, 156, 343	13	4	S-C.Christi
Bell	27, 146, 169, 264	3	3	W-Waco
Bexar	37, 45, 57, 73, 131, 144, 150, 166, 175, 186, 187, 224, 225, 226, 227, 285, 288, 289, 290, 379, 386, 399, 407,408	4	4	W-San Ant.
Blanco	33	3	3	W-Austin
Borden	132	11	7	N-Lubbock
Bosque	220	10	3	W-Waco
Bowie	5, 102, 202	6	1	E-Texark.
Brazoria	23, 149, 239, 300	1, 14	2	S-Galves.
Brazos	85, 272, 361	1, 10, 14	2	S-Houston
Brewster	394	8	6	W-Pecos
Briscoe	110	7	9	N-Amarilllo
Brooks	79	4	5	S-C.Christi
Brown	35	11	7	N-S. Ang.
Burleson	21, 335	1, 14	2	W-Austin
Burnet	33	3	3	W-Austin
Caldwell	22, 207, 274	3	3	W-Austin
Calhoun	24, 135, 267	13	4	S-Victoria
Callahan	42	11	7	N-Abilene
Cameron	103, 107, 138, 197, 357, 404	13	5	S-Brownsville
Camp	76, 276	6	1	E-Marshall
Carson	100	7	9	N-Amarilllo
Cass	5	6	1	E-Marshall
Castro	64, 242	7	9	N-Amarilllo
Chambers	253, 344	1, 14	2	S-Galves.
Cherokee	2, 369	12	1	E-Tyler
Childress	100	7	9	N-Amarilllo
Clay	97	2	8	N-W. Falls
Cochran	286	7	9	N-Lubbock
Coke	51	3	7	N-S. Ang.
Coleman	42	11	7	N-S. Ang.
Collin	199, 219, 296, 366, 380, 401	5	1	E-Sherman
Collingsworth	100	7	9	N-Amarilllo
Colorado	25, 2nd 25	1, 14	3	S-Houston
Comal	22, 207, 274	3	3	W-San Ant.
Comanche	220	11	3	N-Ft. Worth
Concho	119	3	7	N-S. Ang.
Cooke	235	2	8	E-Sherman
Coryell	52	10	3	W-Waco
Cottle	50	7	9	N-W. Falls
Crane	109	8	7	W-Midland
Crockett	112	8	6	N-S. Ang.
Crosby	72	7	9	N-Lubbock
Culberson	205, 394	8	6	W-Pecos
Dallam	69	7	9	N-Amarilllo
Dallas	14, 44, 68, 95, 101, 116, 134, 160, 162, 191, 192, 193, 194,195, 203, 204, 254, 255, 256, 265, 282, 283, 291, 292, 298, 301, 302, 303, 304, 305, 330, 363, Cr.1, Cr2, Cr.3, Cr.4, Cr.5	5	1	N-Dallas

County	State Dist. Court(s)	Ct. of App'ls Dist.	Adm. Jud. Dist.	U.S. Jud. Dist.
Dawson	106	11	7	N-Lubbock
Deaf Smith	222	7	9	N-Amarillo
Delta	8, 62	6	1	E-Paris
Denton	16, 158, 211, 362, 367, 393	2	8	E-Sherman
DeWitt	24, 135, 267	13	4	S-Victoria
Dickens	110	7	9	N-Lubbock
Dimmit	293, 365	4	4	W-San Ant.
Donley	100	7	9	N-Amarilllo
Duval	229	4	5	S-C.Christi
Eastland	91	11	8	N-Abilene
Ector	70, 161, 244, 358	8	7	W-Midland
Edwards	63	4	6	W-Del Rio
Ellis	40, 378	10	1	N-Dallas
El Paso	34, 41, 65, 120, 168, 171, 205, 210, 243, 327, 346, 383, 384, 388, 409	8	6	W-El Paso
Erath	266	11	8	N-Ft. Worth
Falls	82	10	3	W-Waco
Fannin	6, 336	6	1	E-Paris
Fayette	155	3	3	S-Houston
Fisher	32	11	7	N-Abilene
Floyd	110	7	9	N-Lubbock
Foard	46	7	9	N-W. Falls
Fort Bend	240, 268, 328, 387, 400	1, 14	2	S-Houston
Franklin	8, 62	6	1	E-Texark.
Freestone	77, 87	10	2	W-Waco
Frio	81, 218	4	4	W-San Ant.
Gaines	106	8	7	N-Lubbock
Galveston	10, 56, 122, 212, 306, 405	1, 14	2	S-Galves.
Garza	106	7	7	N-Lubbock
Gillespie	216	4	6	W-Austin
Glasscock	118	8	7	N-S. Ang.
Goliad	24, 135, 267	13	4	S-Victoria
Gonzales	25, 2nd 25	13	3	W-San Ant.
Gray	31, 223	7	9	N-Amarilllo
Grayson	15, 59, 336	5	1	E-Sherman
Gregg	124, 188, 307	6, 12	1	E-Tyler
Grimes	12, 278	1, 14	2	S-Houston
Guadalupe	25, 2nd 25, 274	4	3	W-San Ant.
Hale	64, 242	7	9	N-Lubbock
Hall	100	7	9	N-Amarilllo
Hamilton	220	10	3	W-Waco
Hansford	84	7	9	N-Amarilllo
Hardeman	46	7	9	N-W. Falls
Hardin	88, 356	9	2	E-B'mont.
Harris	11, 55, 61, 80, 113, 125, 127, 129, 133, 151, 152, 157, 164, 165, 174, 176, 177, 178, 179, 180, 182, 183, 184, 185, 189, 190, 208, 209, 215, 228, 230, 232, 234, 245, 246, 247, 248, 257, 262, 263, 269, 270, 280, 281, 295, 308, 309, 310, 311, 312, 313, 314, 315, 333, 334, 337, 338, 339, 351	1, 14	2	S-Houston
Harrison	71	6	1	E-Marshall
Hartley	69	7	9	N-Amarilllo
Haskell	39	11	7	N-Abilene
Hays	22, 207, 274	3	3	W-Austin
Hemphill	31	7	9	N-Amarilllo
Henderson	3, 173, 392	12	1	E-Tyler
Hidalgo	92, 93, 139, 206, 275, 332, 370, 389, 398	13	5	S-McAllen
Hill	66	10	3	W-Waco
Hockley	286	7	9	N-Lubbock

County	State Dist. Court(s)	Ct. of App'ls Dist.	Adm. Jud. Dist.	U.S. Jud. Dist.
Hood	355	2	8	N-Ft. Worth
Hopkins	8, 62	6, 12	1	E-Paris
Houston	3, 349	12	1	E-Lufkin
Howard	118	11	7	N-Abilene
Hudspeth	205, 394	8	6	W-Pecos
Hunt	196, 354	5, 6	1	N-Dallas
Hutchinson	84, 316	7	9	N-Amarilllo
Irion	51	3	7	N-S. Ang.
Jack	271	2	8	N-Ft. Worth
Jackson	24, 135, 267	13	4	S-Victoria
Jasper	1, 1A	9	2	E-B'mont.
Jeff Davis	394	8	6	W-Pecos
Jefferson	58, 60, 136, 172, 252, 279, 317, Cr.	9	2	E-B'mont.
Jim Hogg	229	4	5	S-Laredo
Jim Wells	79	4	5	S-C.Christi
Johnson	18, 249	10	3	N-Dallas
Jones	259	11	7	N-Abilene
Karnes	81, 218	4	4	W-San Ant.
Kaufman	86	5, 12	1	N-Dallas
Kendall	216	4	6	W-San Ant.
Kenedy	105	13	5	S-C.Christi
Kent	39	7	7	N-Lubbock
Kerr	198, 216	4	6	W-San Ant.
Kimble	198	4	6	W-Austin
King	50	7	9	N-W. Falls
Kinney	63	4	6	W-Del Rio
Kleberg	105	13	5	S-C.Christi
Knox	50	11	9	N-W. Falls
Lamar	6, 62	6	1	E-Paris
Lamb	154	7	9	N-Lubbock
Lampasas	27	3	3	W-Austin
La Salle	81, 218	4	4	S-Laredo
Lavaca	25, 2nd 25	13	3	S-Victoria
Lee	21, 335	3	2	W-Austin
Leon	12, 87, 278	10	2	W-Waco
Liberty	75, 253	9	2	E-B'mont.
Limestone	77, 87	10	2	W-Waco
Lipscomb	31	7	9	N-Amarilllo
Live Oak	36, 156, 343	13	4	S-C.Christi
Llano	33	3	3	W-Austin
Loving	143	8	7	W-Pecos
Lubbock	72, 99, 137, 140, 237, 364	7	9	N-Lubbock
Lynn	106	7	7	N-Lubbock
Madison	12, 278	10	2	S-Houston
Marion	115, 276	6	1	E-Marshall
Martin	118	8	7	W-Midland
Mason	198	4	6	W-Austin
Matagorda	23, 130	13	2	C-Galves.
Maverick	293, 365	4	4	W-Del Rio
McCulloch	198	3	7	W-Austin
McLennan	19, 54, 74, 170	10	3	W-Waco
McMullen	36, 156, 343	4	4	S-Laredo
Medina	38	4	6	W-San Ant.
Menard	198	4	7	N-S. Ang.
Midland	142, 238, 318, 385	8	7	W-Midland
Milam	20	3	3	W-Waco
Mills	35	3	7	N-S. Ang.
Mitchell	32	11	7	N-Abilene
Montague	97	2	8	N-W. Falls
Montgomery	9, 221, 284, 359, 410	9	2	S-Houston
Moore	69	7	9	N-Amarilllo
Morris	76, 276	6	1	E-Marshall
Motley	110	7	9	N-Lubbock
Nacogdoches	145	12	1	E-Lufkin
Navarro	13	10	3	N-Dallas
Newton	1, 1A	9	2	E-B'mont.
Nolan	32	11	7	N-Abilene
Nueces	28, 94, 105, 117, 148, 214, 319, 347	13	5	S-C.Christi
Ochiltree	84	7	9	N-Amarilllo
Oldham	222	7	9	N-Amarilllo
Orange	128, 163, 260	9	2	E-B'mont.
Palo Pinto	29	11	8	N-Ft. Worth
Panola	123	6, 12	1	E-Tyler
Parker	43	2	8	N-Ft. Worth
Parmer	287	7	9	N-Amarilllo
Pecos	83, 112	8	6	W-Pecos
Polk	258, 411	9	2	E-Lufkin
Potter	47, 108, 181, 251, 320	7	9	N-Amarilllo
Presidio	394	8	6	W-Pecos
Rains	8, 354	12	1	E-Tyler
Randall	47, 181, 251	7	9	N-Amarilllo
Reagan	83, 112	8	6	N-S. Ang.
Real	38	4	6	W-San Ant.
Red River	6, 102	6	1	E-Paris
Reeves	143	8	7	W-Pecos
Refugio	24, 135, 267	13	4	S-Victoria
Roberts	31	7	9	N-Amarilllo
Robertson	82	10	2	W-Waco
Rockwall	382	5	1	N-Dallas
Runnels	119	3	7	N-S. Ang.
Rusk	4	6, 12	1	E-Tyler
Sabine	1, 273	12	2	E-Lufkin
San Augustine	1, 273	12	2	E-Lufkin
San Jacinto	258, 411	9	2	S-Houston
San Patricio	36, 156, 343	13	4	S-C.Christi
San Saba	33	3	3	W-Austin
Schleicher	51	3	7	N-S. Ang.
Scurry	132	11	7	N-Lubbock
Shackelford	259	11	7	N-Abilene
Shelby	123, 273	12	1	E-Lufkin
Sherman	69	7	9	N-Amarilllo
Smith	7, 114, 241, 321	12	1	E-Tyler
Somervell	18, 249	10	3	W-Waco
Starr	229, 381	4	5	S-McAllen
Stephens	90	11	8	N-Abilene
Sterling	51	3	7	N-S. Ang.
Stonewall	39	11	7	N-Abilene
Sutton	112	4	6	N-S. Ang.
Swisher	64, 242	7	9	N-Amarilllo
Tarrant	17, 48, 67, 96, 141, 153, 213, 231, 233, 236, 297, 322, 323, 324, 325, 342, 348, 352, 360, 371, 372, 396, Cr.1, Cr.2, Cr.3, Cr.4	2	8	N-Ft. Worth
Taylor	42, 104, 326, 350	11	7	N-Abilene
Terrell	63, 83	8	6	W-Del Rio
Terry	121	7	9	N-Lubbock
Throckmorton	39	11	7	N-Abilene
Titus	76, 276	6	1	E-Texark.
Tom Green	51, 119, 340, 391	3	7	N-S. Ang.
Travis	53, 98, 126, 147, 167, 200, 201, 250, 261, 299, 331, 345, 353, 390, 403	3	3	W-Austin
Trinity	258, 411	1, 14	2	E-Lufkin
Tyler	1A, 88	9	2	E-Lufkin
Upshur	115	6, 12	1	E-Marshall
Upton	83, 112	8	6	W-Midland
Uvalde	38	4	6	W-Del Rio
Val Verde	63, 83	4	6	W-Del Rio
Van Zandt	294	5, 12	1	E-Tyler
Victoria	24, 135, 267, 377	13	4	S-Victoria
Walker	12, 278	1, 14	2	S-Houston
Waller	9, 155	1, 14	2	S-Houston
Ward	143	8	7	W-Pecos
Washington	21, 335	1, 14	2	W-Austin
Webb	49, 111, 341, 406	4	4	S-Laredo
Wharton	23, 329	13	2	S-Houston
Wheeler	31	7	9	N-Amarillo
Wichita	30, 78, 89	2	8	N-W. Falls
Wilbarger	46	7	9	N-W. Falls
Willacy	103, 107, 138, 197, 357	13	5	S-Brownsville
Williamson	26, 277, 368, 395	3	3	W-Austin
Wilson	81, 218	4	4	W-San Ant.
Winkler	109	8	7	W-Pecos
Wise	271	2	8	N-Ft. Worth
Wood	402	6, 12	1	E-Tyler
Yoakum	121	7	9	N-Lubbock
Young	90	7	8	N-W. Falls
Zapata	49	4	4	S-Laredo
Zavala	293, 365	4	4	W-Del Rio

District Judges in Texas

Below are the names of all district judges in Texas, as of July 2007, listed in district court order. To determine which judges have jurisdiction in specific counties, refer to the table on pages 477–478.

Source: Texas Judicial System Directory 2007, Office of Court Administration.

Court	Judge	Court	Judge	Court	Judge
1	Joe Bob Golden	68	Martin J. Hoffman	137	Cecil G. Puryear
1A	Jerome P. Owens	69	Ronald E. Enns	138	Arturo Cisneros Nelson
2	Dwight L. Phifer	70	W. Denn Whalen	139	Jose Roberto Flores
3	Mark A. Calhoon	71	Bonnie Leggat-Hagan	140	Jim Bob Darnell
4	J. Clay Gossett	72	Ruben Gonzales Reyes	141	Len Wade
5	Ralph K. Burgess	73	Andy Mireles	142	George David Gilles
6	Jim D. Lovett	74	Alan M. Mayfield	143	Bob Parks
7	Kerry L. Russell	75	C.T. Hight	144	Catherine Torres-Stahl
8	Robert E. Newsom	76	Jimmy L. White	145	Campbell Cox II
9	Frederick E. Edwards	77	Horace Dickson Black Jr.	146	Jack Richard Morris
10	David Edward Garner	78	Roy T. Sparkman	147	Wilford Flowers
11	Mark Davidson	79	Richard Clark Terrell	148	Marisela Saldana
12	William Lee McAdams	80	Lynn M. Bradshaw-Hull	149	Robert E. May
13	John Howard Jackson	81	Donna S. Rayes	150	Janet P. Littlejohn
14	Mary L. Murphy	82	Robert Miller Stem	151	Caroline E. Baker
15	Jim Patrick Fallon	83	Carl Pendergrass	152	Kenneth Price Wise
16	Carmen Rivera-Worley	84	William D. Smith	153	Kenneth Charles Curry
17	Fred Wallis Davis	85	J.D. Langley	154	Felix Klein Littlefield
18	John Edward Neill	86	Howard Tygrett	155	Dan Raymond Beck
19	Ralph T. Strother	87	Deborah Oakes Evans	156	Joel B. Johnson
20	Edward Pierre Magre	88	Earl B. Stover III	157	Randall W. Wilson
21	Terry Flenniken	89	Mark Thomas Price	158	Jake Collier
22	Charles R. Ramsay	90	Stephen O'Neal Crawford	159	Paul E. White
23	Ben Hardin	91	Steven R. Herod	160	Jim Jordan
24	Joseph Patrick Kelly	92	Ricardo Rodriguez Jr.	161	John W. Smith
25	Dwight E. Peschel	93	Rodolfo Delgado	162	Lorraine Raggio
25A	William C. Kirkendall	94	Bobby Galvan	163	Dennis Robert Powell
26	Billy Ray Stubblefield	95	Karen Johnson	164	Martha Hill Jamison
27	Joe Carroll	96	Jeff Walker	165	Elizabeth Ray
28	Nanette Hasette	97	Roger E. Towery	166	Martha B. Tanner
29	Jerry D. Ray	98	W. Jeanne Meurer	167	Mike F. Lynch
30	Robert P. Brotherton	99	William Charles Sowder	168	Guadalupe Rivera
31	Steven R. Emmert	100	David M. McCoy	169	Gordon G. Adams
32	Glen N. Harrison	101	Martin Lowy	170	Jim Meyer
33	Guilford L. Jones III	102	John F. Miller Jr.	171	Bonnie Rangel
34	William E. Moody	103	Janet L. Leal	172	Donald J. Floyd
35	William Stephen Ellis	104	Lee Hamilton	173	Willis Daniel Moore
36	Mike E. Welborn	105	J. Manuel Banales	174	George H. Godwin
37	David A. Berchelmann Jr.	106	Carter Tinsley Schildknecht	175	Mary D. Roman
38	Mickey Ray Pennington	107	Benjamin Euresti Jr.	176	James Brian Rains
39	Shane Hadaway	108	Abe Lopez	177	Devon Diane Anderson
40	Gene Knize	109	James L. Rex	178	vacant
41	Mary Anne Bramblett	110	William P. Smith	179	J. Michael Wilkinson
42	John Wilson Weeks	111	Raul Vasquez	180	Debbie Mantooth-Stricklin
43	Don M. Chrestman	112	Pedro Gomez Jr.	181	John Boyd Board
44	Carlos Cortez	113	Patricia Ann Hancock	182	Jeannie S. Barr
45	Barbara Hanson Nellermoe	114	Cynthia Stevens Kent	183	Angela Vanessa Velasquez
46	Dan Mike Bird	115	Lauren L. Parish	184	Jan Krocker
47	Hal Miner	116	Bruce Priddy	185	Susan Brown
48	David Lettimore Evans	117	Sandra L. Watts	186	Maria Teresa Herr
49	Jose A. Lopez	118	Robert H. Moore III	187	Raymond C. Angelini
50	William Hawkins Heatly	119	Garland Benton Woodward	188	David Scott Brabham
51	Barbara Lane Walther	120	Maria A. Salas-Mendoza	189	William Rambo Burke Jr.
52	Phillip H. Zeigler	121	Kelly Glen Moore	190	Jennifer Walker Elrod
53	Scott H. Jenkins	122	John A. Ellisor	191	Gena Slaughter
54	Matt E. Johnson	123	Guy William Griffin	192	Craig Smith
55	Jeffrey V. Brown	124	Alvin G. Khoury	193	Carl H. Ginsberg
56	Lonnie Cox	125	John A. Coselli	194	Ernest B. White
57	Joe Frazier Brown Jr.	126	Darlene Byrne	195	Fred Tinsley
58	Robert J. Wortham	127	Sharolyn P. Wood	196	Joe M. Leonard
59	Rayburn M. (Rim) Nall Jr.	128	Patrick A. Clark	197	Migdalia Lopez
60	James Gary Sanderson	129	S. Grant Dorfman	198	Emil Karl Prohl
61	John Donovan	130	Craig Estlinbaum	199	Robert T. Dry Jr.
62	Robert Scott McDowell	131	John D. Gabriel Jr.	200	Gisela D. Triana
63	Thomas Franklin Lee	132	Ernie B. Armstrong	201	Suzanne Covington
64	Robert W. Kinkaid Jr.	133	Lamar McCorkle	202	Leon F. Pesek Jr.
65	Alfredo Chavez	134	Anne Ashby	203	Lana Rolf McDaniel
66	F.B. (Bob) McGregor Jr.	135	Kemper Stephen Williams	204	Lena Levario
67	Donald J. Cosby	136	Milton Gunn Shuffield	205	Kathleen H. Olivares

Court	Judge
206	Rose Guerra Reyna
207	Jack Hollis Robison
208	Denise M. Collins
209	Michael Thomas McSpadden
210	Gonzalo Garcia
211	Lawrence Dee Shipman Jr.
212	Susan Eliabeth Criss
213	Robert Keith Gill
214	Jose Longoria
215	Levi James Benton
216	Stephen B. Ables
217	Barry Randolph Bryan
218	Stella H. Saxon
219	Curt B. Henderson
220	James Edward Morgan
221	Suzanne Stovall
222	Roland Saul
223	Leland W. Waters
224	Gloria Saldana
225	Peter Sakai
226	Sid L. Harle
227	Philip A. Kazen Jr.
228	Marc C. Carter
229	Alex W. Gabert
230	Belinda Joy HIll
231	Randy Catterton
232	Mary Lou Keel
233	William W. Harris
234	Mauricio (Reece) Rondon
235	Janelle M. Haverkamp
236	Thomas Wilson Lowe III
237	Sam Medina
238	John Gary Hyde
239	Patrick Edward Sebesta
240	Thomas R. Culver III
241	Jack M. Skeen Jr.
242	Edward L. Self
243	David C. Guaderrama
244	William Stacy Trotter
245	Annette Galik
246	Jim York
247	Bonnie Crane Hellums
248	Joan Campbell
249	Dennis Wayne Bridewell
250	John K. Dietz
251	Ana E. Estevez
252	Layne W. Walker
253	Chap B. Cain III
254	David Hanschen
255	Lori Chrisman Hockett
256	Davis Lopez
257	Judy Lynne Warne
258	Elizabeth E. Coker
259	Brooks H. Hagler
260	Buddie J. Hahn
261	Lora J. Livingston
262	Mike Anderson
263	Jim Wallace
264	Martha Jane Trudo
265	Mark C. Stoltz
266	Donald Richard Jones
267	Juergen (Skipper) Koetter
268	Brady Gifford Elliott
269	John T. Wooldridge
270	Brent G. Gamble
271	John H. Fostel
272	Richard Davis
273	Charles R. Mitchell
274	Gary L. Steel
275	Juan R. Partida
276	William R. Porter
277	Ken Anderson
278	Kenneth H. Keeling
279	Jeffrey Randall Shelton
280	Tony D. Lindsay
281	David Jorge Bernal
282	Andy Chatham

Court	Judge
283	Rick Magnis
284	Cara Cordell Wood
285	Michael Parker Peden
286	Harold Phelan
287	Gordon Houston Green
288	Lori D. Massey
289	Carmen Kelsey
290	Sharon Sands MacRae
291	Susan Lynn Hawk
292	Larry Mitchell
293	Cynthia L. Muniz
294	Teresa Drum
295	Tracy E. Christopher
296	John R. Roach Jr.
297	Leo Everett Young Jr.
298	Emily G. Tobolowsky
299	Charlie F. Baird
300	Kenneth Randall Hufstetler
301	Lynn Cherry
302	Tena T. Callahan
303	Dennise Garcia
304	William A. Mazur Jr.
305	Cheryl Lee Shannon
306	Janis L. Yarbrough
307	Robin D. Sage
308	Georgia Dempster
309	Frank Barlow Rynd
310	Lisa Millard
311	Doug Warne
312	James D. Squier
313	Patrick Scott Shelton
314	John F. Phillips
315	Michael H. Schneider Jr.
316	John W. La Grone
317	Larry Edward Thorne III
318	Dean Rucker
319	Thomas F. Greenwell
320	Don R. Emerson
321	Carole W. Clark
322	Nancy L. Berger
323	Jean Hudson Boyd
324	Jerome S. Hennigan
325	Judith G. Wells
326	Aleta Hacker
327	Linda Yee Chew
328	Ronald R. Pope
329	Daniel Richard Sklar
330	Marilea Whatley Lewis
331	Robert A. Perkins
332	Mario E. Ramirez Jr.
333	Joseph James Halbach Jr.
334	Sharon McCally
335	Reva Townslee Corbett
336	Laurine Jean Blake
337	Don R. Stricklin
338	Tommy Brock Thomas Jr.
339	Caprice Cosper
340	Jay Weatherby
341	Elma Salinas Ender
342	Bob McGrath
343	Janna K. Whatley
344	Carroll E. Wilborn Jr.
345	Stephen A. Yelenosky
346	Angie Juarez Barill
347	Nelva Gonzales-Ramos
348	Dana M. Womack
349	Pamela Fletcher
350	Thomas Wheeler
351	Mark Kent Ellis
352	Bonnie Sudderth
353	Margaret A. Cooper
354	Richard (Rick) Beacom
355	Ralph H. Walton Jr.
356	Britton Edward Plunk
357	Leonel Alejandro
358	Bill McCoy
359	Kathleen A. Hamilton

Court	Judge
360	Debra Lehrmann
361	Steve Lee Smith
362	R. Bruce McFarling
363	Tracy F. Holmes
364	Bradley S. Underwood
365	Amado Jose Abascal III
366	Gregory Brewer
367	E. Lee Gabriel
368	Alfred Burton (Burt) Carnes
369	Bascom W. Bentley III
370	Noe Gonzalez
371	Mollee Bennett Westfall
372	David Scott Wisch
377	Robert C. Cheshire
378	Roy A. Scoggins Jr.
379	Robert C. (Bert) Richardson
380	Charles F. Sandoval
381	Jose Luis Garza
382	Brett Hall
383	Mike Herrera
384	Patrick Michael Garcia
385	Robin Malone Darr
386	Laura Lee Parker
387	Robert J. Kern
388	Patricia A. Macias
389	Leticia Lopez
390	Julie Harris Kocurek
391	Thomas J. Gossett
392	Carter William Tarrance
393	Vicki B. Isaacks
394	Kenneth Daly DeHart
395	Michael P. Jergins
396	George W. Gallagher
398	Aida Salinas Flores
399	Juanita A. Vasquez-Gardner
400	Clifford James Vacek
401	Mark Joseph Rusch
402	George Timothy Boswell
403	Brenda P. Kennedy
404	Abel C. Limas
405	Wayne Mallia
406	Oscar (O.J.) Hale Jr.
407	Karen Pozza
408	Larry E. Noll
409	Sam Medrano
410	K. Michael Mayes
411	Robert Hill Trapp
413	William C. Bosworth Jr.
414	Vicki Lynn Menard
415	Graham Quisenberry
416	John Christopher Oldner
417	Cynthia McCrann Wheless
419	Orlinda L. Naranjo
420	Edwin Allen Klein
421	Todd A. Blomerth
422	B. Michael Chitty
424	Daniel H. Mills
425	Mark J. Silverston
426	Fancy H. Jezek
428	William R. Henry
430	Thomas Wingate
433	Dibrell Waldrip
434	James H. Shoemake

Criminal District Courts

Dallas 1	Robert D. Burns III
Dallas 2	Don Adams
Dallas 3	Robert Francis
Dallas 4	John Coleman Creuzot
Dallas 5	Carter Thompson
Dallas 6	Jeanine L. Howard
Dallas 7	Michael Reuss Snipes
Jefferson	John B. Stevens Jr.
Tarrant 1	Sharen Wilson
Tarrant 2	Wayne Francis Salvant
Tarrant 3	Elizabeth Berry
Tarrant 4	Michael R. Thomas

Texas State Agencies

On the following pages is information about several of the many state agencies in Texas. Information was supplied to the *Texas Almanac* by the agencies, their Web sites and from news reports. The Web address for more information about state agencies, boards and commissions is: www2.tsl.state.tx.us/trail/agencies.jsp.

Texas Commission on Environmental Quality

Source: Texas Commission on Environmental Quality; www.tceq.state.tx.us

The Texas Commission on Environmental Quality (TCEQ) is the state's leading environmental agency. Known as the Texas Natural Resource Conservation Commission until September 2002, this agency works to protect Texas' human and natural resources in a manner consistent with sustainable economic development. The goals are clean air, clean water and the safe management of waste, with an emphasis on pollution prevention.

The TCEQ has about 2,900 employees; of those, about 1,000 work in the 16 regional offices. The operating budget for the 2007 fiscal year was $480.7 million, of which 85 percent ($409.8 million) was generated by program fees. The remaining revenues came from federal funds ($45.7 million or 10 percent); state general revenue ($5 million or 1 percent); and other sources ($20.2 million or 4 percent).

One of the TCEQ's major functions is issuing permits and other authorizations for the control of air pollution, the safe operation of water and wastewater utilities, and the management of hazardous and non-hazardous waste. More than 8,000 environmental permit applications are received annually.

The agency promotes voluntary compliance with environmental laws through pollution prevention programs, regulatory workshops, and assistance to businesses and local governments. But when environmental laws are violated, the TCEQ has the authority to levy penaltiesCas much as $10,000 a day per violation for administrative cases and $25,000 a day per violation in civil judicial cases. In a typical year, the agency investigates more than 70,000 regulated entities for compliance with state and federal laws, and it responds to about 6,000 environmental complaints.

In 2006, the TCEQ issued 1,531 administrative orders, which yielded $9.9 million in fines and directed another $3.2 million to supplemental environmental projects benefitting some of the communities in which the environmental violations occurred.

Air Quality

Texas is home to some of the largest U.S. cities, and therefore faces air quality challenges that are among the most difficult in the country. The state has a fast-growing population and a large industrial base, especially along the Gulf Coast. The TCEQ has worked with the U.S.

Environmental Protection Agency and local municipalities to craft a state implementation plan to bring metropolitan areas into compliance with federal ozone standards. The leading areas of concern are Houston, Dallas-Fort Worth and Beaumont-Port Arthur. Several other metropolitan areas have entered into voluntary compacts to institute programs that reduce emissions.

At an industrial facility in Beaumont, a TCEQ employee conducts fence-line screening for volatile organic compounds. The infrared-gas imaging camera is a new tool being used in pollution detection. Photo courtesy of TCEQ.

Water Quality

Surface water bodies in Texas are routinely monitored to determine whether they support their designated uses. The TCEQ coordinates a comprehensive sampling program to collect water quality data. The agency also conducts special studies to determine sources of pollution and the appropriateness of water quality standards. The TCEQ also is responsible for most of the state and federal regulatory programs that protect groundwater, and for state and federal storm water permits. It is the primary Texas agency authorized to enforce the federal Safe Drinking Water Act, and administers the supervision program for the state's 6,660 public water systems.

Waste Management

Waste management projects at the TCEQ include Superfund projects, pesticide collections and waste tire recycling. In 2006, there were 103 sites in the state and federal Superfund programs. Another major clean-up program focuses on leaking petroleum storage tanks. From 1988 to 2006, more than 21,000 such sites were corrected, and work continues at another 3,400 sites. The TCEQ also issues permits for municipal landfill operations and monitors landfill capacity on a regional basis.

Pollution Prevention

The TCEQ offers services to anyone interested in environmental stewardship. Staff members host workshops on recycling and disposal opportunities, and on regulatory and pollution prevention topics. They also offer free on-site technical assistance for regulatory compliance. Contact the TCEQ at PO Box 13087, Austin TX 78711; phone: 512-239-1000; www.tceq.state.tx.us. ☆

Health and Human Services Commission

Source: Texas Health and Human Services Commission; www.hhs.state.tx.us

The Texas Health and Human Services Commission (HHSC) is the oversight agency for the state's health and human services system. HHSC also administers state and federal programs that provide financial, health and social services to Texans.

In 2003, the 78th Texas Legislature mandated an unprecedented transformation of the state's health and human services system to create an integrated, effective and accessible health and human services enterprise that protects public health and brings high-quality services and support to Texans in need. The transformation blends 12 agencies into five to create a system that is client-centered, efficient in its use of public resources and focused on results and accountability.

The Health and Human Services Commission coordinates administrative functions across the system, determines eligibility for its programs, and administers Medicaid, Children's Health Insurance Program, Temporary Assistance for Needy Families (TANF), food stamps, family violence and disaster assistance, refugee resettlement and special nutrition programs.

The HHSC executive commissioner is Albert Hawkins. The executive commissioner is appointed by the governor and confirmed by the Senate.

The state's health and human services agencies spend nearly $20 billion per year to administer more than 200 programs, employ approximately 46,000 state workers, and operate from more than 1,000 locations.

The new state system includes four new departments, which operate under the oversight of HHSC. The four new departments under HHSC are:

The Department of Family and Protective Services includes the programs previously administered by the Department of Protective and Regulatory Services. DFPS began services Feb. 1, 2004.

The Department of Assistive and Rehabilitative Services combines the programs of the Texas Rehabilitation Commission, Commission for the Blind, Commission for the Deaf and Hard of Hearing, and Interagency Council on Early Childhood Intervention. DARS began services March 1, 2004.

The Department of Aging and Disability Services consolidates mental retardation and state school programs of the Department of Mental Health and Mental Retardation, community care and nursing home services programs of the Department of Human Services, and aging services programs of the Texas Department of Aging. DADS began services Sept. 1, 2004.

The Department of State Health Services includes the programs provided by the Texas Department of Health, the Texas Commission on Alcohol and Drug Abuse and the Health Care Information Council, plus mental-health community services and state hospital programs operated by the Department of Mental Health and Mental Retardation. DSHS began services on Sept. 1, 2004.

Major HHSC Programs at a Glance

The state's Medicaid program provides healthcare coverage for one out of every three children in Texas, pays for half of all births and accounts for 27 percent of the state's total budget. In 2004, an average of 2.68 million Texans received healthcare coverage through Medicaid.

The Children's Health Insurance Program (CHIP) is designed for families who earn too much money to qualify for Medicaid health care, yet cannot afford private insurance.

The Temporary Assistance for Needy Families (TANF) program provides basic financial assistance for needy children and the parents or caretakers with whom they live. As a condition of eligibility, caretakers must sign and abide by a personal-responsibility agreement. Time limits for benefits have been set by both state and federal welfare-reform legislation.

A typical TANF family of three (caretaker and two children) can receive a maximum monthly grant of $213. In fiscal year 2004, a monthly average of 255,081 individuals received TANF benefits.

The Food Stamp program is a federally funded program that assists low-income families, the elderly and single adults to obtain a nutritionally adequate diet. Those eligible for food stamps include households receiving TANF or federal Supplemental Security Income benefits and non-public assistance households having incomes below 130 percent of the poverty level.

Food stamp and TANF benefits are delivered through the electronic benefit transfer (EBT) system, through which clients access benefits at about 12,000 retail locations statewide with the Lone Star debit card.

In 2004, the monthly average number of recipients (individuals) who received food stamps benefits was 2,266,240. The average monthly food stamp benefit per individual was $81 per month or $213 per household.

Other HHSC programs

The Family Violence program educates the public about domestic violence and offers emergency shelter and support services to victims and their children. The program is administered through contracts with family-violence service providers.

The Disaster Assistance program processes grant applications for victims of presidentially declared disasters, such as tornados, floods and hurricanes. Victims are eligible for assistance from this state-administered federal program if they do not have insurance and cannot qualify for low-interest loans from the Small Business Administration.

The federally funded Refugee Resettlement program provides cash, health care and social services to eligible refugees to help them become self-sufficient as soon as possible after arriving in the United States.

Eight Special Nutrition programs, completely funded by the U.S. Dept. of Agriculture, provide meals to eligible recipients, including elderly or functionally impaired adults and to children and low-income individuals and families.

Information about Medicaid, CHIP and other health and human services programs, including eligibility requirements and how to apply, can be found online at www.hhsc.state.tx.us, www.helpintexas.com or by calling 2-1-1, a toll-free local resource for information on health and human service programs. ☆

The General Land Office

Source: General Land Office of Texas. On the Web: www.glo.state.tx.us

History of the General Land Office

The Texas General Land Office (GLO) is one of the oldest governmental entities in the state, dating back to the Republic of Texas. The first General Land Office was established in 1836 in the Republic's constitution, and the first Texas Congress enacted the provision into law in 1837. The GLO was established to oversee distribution of public lands, register titles, issue patents on land and maintain records of land granted.

In the early years of statehood, beginning in 1845, Texas established the precedent of using its vast public domain for public benefit. The first use was to sell or trade land to eliminate the huge debt remaining from Texas' War for Independence and early years of the Republic.

Texas also gave away land to settlers as homesteads; to veterans as compensation for service; for internal improvements, including building railroads, shipbuilding and improving rivers for navigation; and to build the state Capitol.

The public domain was closed in 1898 when the Texas Supreme Court declared there was no more vacant and unappropriated land in Texas. In 1900, all remaining unappropriated land was set aside by the Texas Legislature to benefit public schools.

Today, 19.9 million acres of land and minerals, owned by the Permanent School Fund, the Permanent University Fund, various other state agencies or the Veterans Land Board, are managed by the General Land Office and the Commissioner of the Texas General Land Office. This includes over 4 million acres of submerged coastal lands, which consist of bays, inlets and the area from the Texas shoreline to the three-marine-league area (10.36 miles) in the Gulf of Mexico. It is estimated that more than 1 million acres make up the public domain of the state's riverbeds and another 1.7 million acres are excess lands belonging to the Permanent School Fund.

The Permanent University Fund holds title to 2.1 million fee acres, and other state agencies or special schools hold title to another 2.3 million acres. The Permanent School Fund owns mineral rights alone in almost 7.4 million acres covered under the Relinquishment Act, the Free Royalty Act and the various sales acts, and it has outright ownership to about 747,522 upland acres, mostly west of the Pecos River. The Veterans Land Board has liens on more than 557,511 acres of land in active veterans accounts.

Veterans Land Board Programs

Veterans Land Program

In 1946, the Texas Legislature created a bond program to aid veterans in purchasing land. Up to $1.5 billion in bonding authority has been authorized over the years in a series of constitutional amendments; as of May 2005, about $1.4 billion of the bonds had been sold to fund loans.

Veterans Housing Assistance Program

The 68th Legislature created the Veterans Housing Assistance Program, which also is funded through bond proceeds. Over the years, Texans have passed constitutional amendments authorizing the sale of up to $2.5 billion in bonds to finance this program. As of May 2005, about $2.2 billion in bonds have been sold to fund housing loans. Eligible veterans may borrow up to $240,000 toward purchasing a home.

Veterans Home Improvement Program

In 1986, the Veterans Land Board implemented the Veterans Home Improvement Program, which is funded through the Veterans Housing Assistance Program. It allows Texas veterans to borrow up to $25,000 to make substantial home repairs and improvements. Since the program's inception, more than 3,300 veterans have received home improvement loans worth more than $50 million.

Texas State Veterans Homes

In 1997, the 75th Legislature approved legislation authorizing the Veterans Land Board to construct and operate Texas State Veterans Homes under a cost-sharing program with the U.S. Department of Veterans Affairs (USDVA) and to issue revenue bonds to obtain the state's necessary share. The homes provide affordable, quality, long-term care for Texas' aging veteran population.

Texas State Veterans Cemeteries

The Veterans Land Board owns and operates several cemeteries under USDVA guidelines. The USDVA funds the design and construction of the cemeteries, but the land must be donated. For more information on any of these veterans programs, call 1-800-252-VETS (8387), or visit the Texas Veterans Land Board Web site at www.texasveterans.com.

Voices of Veterans Oral History Program

The Voices of Veterans oral history program seeks to record the stories of Texas veterans and archive the transcripts in the Office of Veterans Records for future researchers and historians. Voices of Veterans represents the first time a state agency has ventured into the field of veterans' oral histories. The program is open to any Texas veteran who has served in the Armed Forces, from World War I to the War on Terror.

Any veteran interested in including his or her story in the Voices of Veterans program should contact the Veterans Land Board at 1-800-252-VETS, or send an e-mail to vlbinfo@glo.state.tx.us. Oral history interviews can be conducted in person at the Veterans Land Board in Austin or by telephone from anywhere in Texas.

Energy Resources

The General Land Office helps fund public education in Texas by maximizing the natural resources from state lands, including oil and gas. Millions of acres of Permanent School Fund land are leased through the GLO to energy firms for oil and gas exploration and production. Royalties and other fees from this production are paid to the GLO, which dedicates the money to the PSF for use in schools around the state.

Coastal Stewardship

The General Land Office is the steward of the Texas Gulf Coast, serving as the premier state agency for protecting and renourishing the coast and fighting coastal erosion. In 1999, the legislature created the Coastal Erosion Planning and Response Act (CEPRA) and put the GLO in charge of facilitating restoration and preservation of eroding beaches, dunes, wetlands and other bay shorelines along the Texas coast. ☆

Distribution of the Public Lands of Texas	
Purpose	**Acres**
Settlers	68,027,108
Spain and Mexico	24,583,923
Spanish and Mexican Grants south of the Nueces River, recognized by Act of Feb. 10, 1852	3,741,241
Headrights	30,360,002
Republic colonies	4,494,806
Preemption land	4,847,136
Military	9,874,262
Bounty	5,354,250
Battle donations	1,162,240
Veterans donations	1,377,920
Confederate	1,979,852
Improvements	37,155,714
Road 27,716	
Navigation	4,261,760
Irrigation	584,000
Ships 17,000	
Manufacturing	111,360
Railroads	32,153,878
Education	52,329,168
University, public school and eleemosynary institutions	52,329,168
Total of distributed lands	**167,386,252**

Texas Historical Commission

The Texas Historical Commission protects and preserves the state's historic and prehistoric resources. The Texas State Legislature established the Texas State Historical Survey Committee in 1953 to identify important historic sites across the state.

The Texas Legislature changed the agency's name to the Texas Historical Commission in 1973 and increased its mission and its protective powers. Today the agency's concerns include archaeology, architecture, history, economic development, heritage tourism, public administration and urban planning.

Among its many tasks, the commission:

• Provides leadership, training and preservation planning through its Visionaries in Preservation Program for county historical commissions, heritage organizations and museums in Texas' 254 counties;

• Assists citizens in obtaining historical designations for buildings, cemeteries, sites and other properties important to the state's historic and prehistoric past;

• Works with communities to help protect Texas' diverse architectural heritage, including historic county courthouses and other public buildings;

• Administers the state's historical marker program. There are more than 11,000 historical markers across Texas;

• Assists Texas cities in the revitalization of their historic downtowns through the Texas Main Street Program;

• Promotes travel to historic and cultural sites though its award-winning Texas Heritage Trails Program;

• Works with property owners to save archaeological sites on private land;

• Ensures that archaeological sites are protected when land is developed for highways and other public projects.

Mailing address: PO Box 12276, Austin 78711-2276; phone: 512-463-6100; fax: 512-463-8222; www.thc.state.tx.us.

Railroad Commission of Texas

The Railroad Commission of Texas has primary regulatory jurisdiction over the oil and natural gas industry, pipeline transporters, the natural gas and hazardous liquid pipeline industry, natural gas utilities, the liquefied petroleum gas (LP-gas) industry, rail industry, and coal and uranium surface mining operations. It also promotes the use of LP-gas as an alternative fuel in Texas through research and education.

The commission exercises its statutory responsibilities under provisions of the Texas Constitution, the Texas Natural Resources Code, the Texas Water Code, the Texas Utilities Code, the Coal and Uranium Surface Mining and Reclamation Acts, the Pipeline Safety Acts, and the Railroad Safety Act.

The commission has regulatory and enforcement responsibilities under federal law, including the Federal Railroad Safety Act, the Local Rail Freight Assistance Act, the Surface Coal Mining Control and Reclamation Act, Safe Drinking Water Act, the Pipeline Safety Acts, the Resource Conservation Recovery Act, and the Clean Water Act.

The Railroad Commission was established by the Texas Legislature in 1891 and given jurisdiction over rates and operations of railroads, terminals, wharves and express companies. In 1917, the legislature declared pipelines to be common carriers and gave the commission regulatory authority over them. It was also given the responsibility to administer conservation laws relating to oil and natural gas production.

The Railroad Commission exists to protect the environment, public safety, and the rights of mineral interest owners; to prevent waste of natural resources, and to assure fair and equitable utility rates in those industries over which it has authority. Mailing address: PO Box 12967, Austin 78711-2967; phone: 512-463-7288; www.rrc.state.tx.us.

Texas Workforce Commission

The Texas Workforce Commission (TWC) is the state government agency charged with overseeing and providing workforce development services to employers and job seekers of Texas.

For employers, TWC offers recruiting, retention, training and retraining, outplacement services and information on labor law and labor market statistics.

For job seekers, TWC offers career development information, job search resources, training programs, and, as appropriate, unemployment benefits. While targeted populations receive intensive assistance to overcome barriers to employment, all Texans can benefit from the services offered by TWC and our network of workforce partners.

The Texas Workforce Commission is part of a local and state network dedicated to developing the workforce of Texas. The network is composed of the statewide efforts of the commission coupled with planning and service provision on a regional level by 28 local workforce boards. This network gives customers access to local workforce solutions and statewide services in a single location—Texas Workforce Centers.

Primary services of the Texas Workforce Commission and our network partners are funded by federal tax revenue and are generally free to all Texans. Mailing address: 101 E. 15th Street, Austin 78778; 512-463-2222; www.twc.state.tx.us.

Texas Youth Commission

The Texas Youth Commission operates correctional facilities and halfway houses to provide for the care, custody and rehabilitation of chronically delinquent or serious youth offenders. In 2007, however, widespread sexual and physical abuse was uncovered at many of the TYC facilities. After a number of supervisors were dismissed, the entire TYC board resigned on March 15, 2007, and their powers were transferred to Acting Executive Ed Owens. Owens was named conservator of the agency on June 8, 2007, and will serve until June 2009. He replaced Jay Kimbrough, who led a sweeping investigation that restored order to the agency after his appointment by Gov. Rick Perry early in 2007. The 80th Texas Legislature approved a bill that was signed June 8, 2007, by Gov. Perry to overhaul the troubled agency. The legislation:

• Authorizes the governor to appoint an executive commissioner once the agency is out of conservatorship, and to appoint an ombudsman;

• Establishes an advisory board to the commission consisting of 9 members, with the governor, lieutenant governor and speaker each appointing 3 members;

• Requires TYC to maintain a ratio of one correctional officer for every 12 youth;

• Controls size of future population by requiring misdemeanor offenders to be held in local county probation detention centers instead of TYC;

• Requires TYC to evaluate minimum lengths of stay unique to each offense and to discharge youths at age 19;

• Establishes inspector generals, who must be peace officers, to investigate allegations of criminal conduct in the agency and all contract facilities;

• Requires ombudsman and the TYC chief inspector general to submit reports on investigations to the executive commissioner, advisory board, governor, lieutenant governor, speaker, Texas Department of Criminal Justice Special Prosecution Unit, state auditor, and appropriate legislative committees with TYC oversight;

• Requires TYC to implement strict guidelines to separate and group committed youth by age; and

• Authorizes TDCJ Special Prosecution Unit to prosecute crimes that occur in the agency or contract facilities.

Mailing address: PO Box 4260, Austin 78765; phone: 512-424-6130; www.tyc.state.tx.us. ☆

Texas Department of Criminal Justice

On the Web: www.tdcj.state.tx.us

The Texas Board of Criminal Justice (TBCJ or Board) is comprised of nine non-salaried members appointed by the Governor for staggered six-year terms. Charged with governing the Texas Department of Criminal Justice (TDCJ), the Board develops and implements policies that guide agency operations. The TBCJ also serves as the Board of Trustees for the Windham School District. For a list of members, see the Boards and Commission list following this article. Christina Melton Crain was appointed Board Chairman in February 2003.

The Executive Director of the TDCJ, who is appointed by the Board, is responsible for the day-to-day administration and operation of the agency. Brad Livingston has served as the executive director of the TDCJ since November 2003. The TDCJ is comprised of the following divisions: Administrative Review and Risk Management, General Counsel, Community Justice Assistance, Correctional Institutions, Private Facility Contract Monitoring/Oversight, Parole, Rehabilitation and Reentry Programs, Health Services, Victim Services, Human Resources and the Texas Correctional Office on Offenders with Medical or Mental Impairments. The departments within the Business and Finance Division report directly to the Chief Financial Officer. Additionally, the Chief Financial Officer provides oversight for the Manufacturing and Logistics Division, the Information Technology Division and the Facilities Division.

The State Counsel for Offenders Division, Internal Audit Division, the Office of the Inspector General and the Windham School District report directly to the Board. Coordinating with the Executive Director and the Deputy Executive Director is the Correctional Managed Health Care Committee.

Among the Agency's divisions, the Correctional Institutions Division (CID), Community Justice Assistance Division (CJAD), Parole Division and the Private Facility Contract Monitoring/Oversight Division are most involved in the everyday confinement and supervision of convicted felons. Supervision of probationers is the responsibility of local community supervision and corrections departments.

The CID is responsible for the confinement of adult felony and state jail offenders who are sentenced to prison. Prison facilities house offenders convicted of first, second, or third degree felonies. The state jail felony classification, which was created in 1993, contains certain offenses that were previously considered non-violent third degree felonies or Class A misdemeanors. Punishment can be up to two years in a state jail facility and a fine not to exceed $10,000, with possible community supervision after release. As of June 30, 2007, there were 136,043 institutional offenders; 13,739 state jail offenders; and 3,178 substance abuse felony punishment offenders for a total of 151,960 offenders. As of June 20, 2007, 13,195 offenders were housed in privately operated facilities monitored by the CID. Effective June 15, 2007, the private operated facilities were separated from the CID to commence as its own division.

The Private Facility Contract Monitoring/Oversight was created in May 2007 from the contract oversight and monitoring functions currently in the CID, Parole Division and the Rehabilitation and Reentry Programs Division. The number of treatment beds and contract expansion beds approved by the 80th Texas Legislative Session significantly increased the scope and size of that function.

The Parole Division processes offenders for release on parole or mandatory supervision and oversees the supervision and rehabilitative services for reintegration into the community. As of June 30, 2007, more than 77,000 adult offenders were under parole or mandatory supervision.

The CJAD oversees the community supervision and corrections departments that work directly with probationers. As of June 30, 2007, over 433,000 felony, misdemeanor and pre-trial probationers were under community supervision.

The Rehabilitation & Reentry Programs Division has broad based responsibilities that encompass every division within the Agency to ensure programs and services are administered efficiently and with consistency. Emphasis is placed on the rehabilitation and re-entry of offenders into the community.

Victim Services coordinates a central mechanism for crime victims to participate in the criminal justice process within an environment of integrity, fairness, compassion and dignity.

The Windham School District and the Continuing Education Program provide educational programming and services to meet the needs of the eligible offender population in TDCJ.

Correctional Institutions Division

The town listed is the nearest one to the facility, although the unit may actually be in another county. For instance, the Middleton Transfer Unit is in Jones County, but the nearest city is Abilene, which is in Taylor County. Units marked with an asterisk (*) are oper-

---

Inmate Profile

Age/Sex/Ethnicity

92% are male	37.6% are black
Average age: 37	31.9% are white
	30.0% are Hispanic

Average Sentences & Length of Time Served
Prison: 21.4 years　　　　State jail: 1 year
Average part of sentence served:
Prison: 60.5%; State jail: 99.0%

Education

Average IQ: 90.7
About 44.9% lack a high school diploma or GED.
Average education achievement score: 7.99

---

ated by private companies.

Prisons

Allred, Iowa Park, Wichita Co.; **Beto**, Tennessee Colony, Anderson Co.; **Boyd**, Teague, Freestone Co.; *Bridgeport, Bridgeport, Wise Co.; **Briscoe**, Dilley, Frio Co.; **Byrd** (diagnostic intake), Huntsville, Walker Co.; **Central**, Sugar Land, Fort Bend Co.; **Clemens**, Brazoria, Brazoria Co.; **Clements**, Amarillo, Potter Co.; *Cleveland, Cleveland, Liberty Co.; **Coffield**, Tennessee Colony, Anderson Co.; **Connally**, Kenedy, Karnes Co.; **Dalhart**, Dalhart, Hartley Co.; **Daniel**, Snyder, Scurry Co.; **Darrington**, Rosharon, Brazoria Co.; *Diboll, Diboll, Angelina Co.; **Eastham**, Lovelady, Houston Co.; **Ellis**, Huntsville, Walker Co.; **Estelle**, Huntsville, Walker Co.; *Estes, Venus, Johnson Co.; **Ferguson**, Midway, Madison Co.; **Gatesville**, Gatesville, Coryell Co. (Women's Unit); **Goree**, Huntsville, Walker Co.; **Hamilton**, Bryan, Brazos Co.; **Hightower**, Dayton, Liberty Co.; **Hilltop**, Gatesville, Coryell Co.; **Hobby**, Marlin, Falls Co.; **Hodge**, Rusk, Cherokee Co.; **Hospital Galveston**, Galveston, Galveston Co.; **Hughes**, Gatesville, Coryell Co.; **Huntsville**, Huntsville, Walker Co.; **Jester III and IV**, Richmond, Fort Bend Co.; **Jordan**, Pampa, Gray Co.; **Kyle**, Kyle, Hays Co.; **LeBlanc**, Beaumont, Jefferson Co.; **Lewis**, Woodville, Tyler Co.; *Lockhart, Lockhart, Caldwell Co.; **Luther**, Navasota, Grimes Co.; **Lynaugh**, Fort Stockton, Pecos Co.; **McConnell**, Beeville, Bee Co.; **Michael**, Tennessee Colony, Anderson Co.; **Montford**, Lubbock, Lubbock Co.; *B. Moore, Overton, Rusk Co.; **Mountain View**, Gatesville, Coryell Co.; **Murray**, Gatesville, Coryell Co.; **Neal**, Amarillo, Potter Co.; **Pack**, Navasota, Grimes Co.; **Polunsky**, Livingston, Polk Co.; **Powledge**, Palestine, Anderson Co.; **Ramsey I and II**, Rosharon, Brazoria Co.; **Roach**, Childress, Childress Co.; **Robertson**, Abilene, Jones Co.; **Scott**, Angleton, Brazoria Co.; **Segovia**, Edinburg, Hidalgo Co; **Skyview**, at Rusk State Hospital, Cherokee Co.; **Smith**, Lamesa, Dawson Co.; **Stevenson**, Cuero, DeWitt Co.; **Stiles**, Beaumont, Jefferson Co.; **Telford**, New Boston, Bowie Co.; **C.T. Terrell**, Rosharon, Brazoria Co.; **Torres**, Hondo, Medina Co.; **Vance**, Richmond, Fort Bend Co.; **Wallace**, Colorado City, Mitchell Co.; **Wynne**, Huntsville, Walker Co.; **C. Young**, Dickinson, Galveston Co.

Transfer Units

Cotulla, Cotulla, LaSalle Co.; **Duncan**, Diboll, Angelina Co.; **Fort Stockton**, Fort Stockton, Pecos Co.; **Garza East & West**, Beeville, Bee Co.; **Goodman**, Jasper, Jasper Co.; **Gurney**, Tennessee Colony, Anderson Co.; **Holliday**, Huntsville, Walker Co.; **Middleton**, Abilene, Jones Co.; **C. Moore**, Bonham, Fannin Co.; **Rudd**, Brownfield, Terry Co.; **Tulia**, Tulia, Swisher Co.; **Ware**, Colorado City, Mitchell Co.

State Jails

*Bartlett, Williamson Co.; *Bradshaw, Henderson, Rusk Co.; **Cole**, Bonham, Fannin Co.; *Dawson, Dallas, Dallas Co.; **Dominguez**, San Antonio, Bexar Co.; **Formby**, Plainview, Hale Co.; **Gist**, Beaumont, Jefferson Co.; **Havins**, Brownwood, Brown Co.; **Henley**, Dayton, Liberty Co.; **Hutchins**, Dallas, Dallas Co.; **Kegans**, Houston, Harris Co.; *Lindsey, Jacksboro, Jack Co.; **Lopez**, Edinburg, Hidalgo Co.; **Lychner**, Humble, Harris Co.; **Ney**, Hondo, Medina Co.; **Plane**, Dayton, Liberty Co.; **Sanchez**, El Paso, El Paso Co.; **Travis** County, Austin, Travis Co.; **Wheeler**, Plainview, Hale Co.; *Williacy County, Raymondville, Williacy Co.; and **Woodman**, Gatesville, Coryell Co.

SAFP Facilities

Glossbrenner, San Diego, Duval Co.; **Halbert**, Burnet, Burnet Co.; **Jester I**, Richmond, Fort Bend Co.; **Johnston**, Winnsboro, Wood Co.; **Sayle**, Breckenridge, Stephens Co.;

Contract Leased Beds

Bowie County Jail, Texarkana; **Jefferson County Jail**, Beaumont; **Limestone County Jail**, Groesbeck; and **Newton County Jail**, Newton. ☆

Texas State Boards and Commissions

Following is a list of appointees to state boards and commissions, as well as names of other state officials, revised to **July 15, 2007**. Information includes, where available, (1) date of creation of agency; (2) whether the position is elective or appointive; (3) length of term; (4) compensation, if any); (5) number of members; (6) names of appointees, their hometowns and the dates of the terminations of their terms. In some instances the dates of expiration of terms have already passed; in such cases, no new appointment had been made by press time, and the official is continuing to fill the position until a successor can be named. Most positions marked "apptv." are appointed by the Governor. Where otherwise, appointing authority is given. Most advisory boards are not listed. Salaries for commissioners and administrators are those that were authorized by the appropriations bill passed by the 80th Legislature for the 2006–2007 biennium (2008–2009 salaries were not available from the State Auditor at press time). They are "not-to-exceed" salaries: maximum authorized salaries for the positions. Actual salaries may be less than those stated here.

Accountancy, Texas State Board of Public – (1945 with 2-yr. terms; reorganized 1959 as 9-member board with 6-yr. overlapping terms; number of members increased to 12 in 1979; increased to 15 in 1989); per diem and expenses: J. Coalter Baker, Austin (1/31/07); Marcela E. Donadio, Houston (1/31/07); David D. Duree, Odessa (1/31/09); Gregory Lee Bailes, Austin (1/31/11); John W. Dunbar, El Paso (1/31/11); James Calvin Flagg, College Station (1/31/09); Dorothy M. Fowler, Corpus Christi (1/31/11); Evelyn M. Martinez, San Antonio (1/31/07); Orville W. Mills Jr., Sugar Land (1/31/09); Paula Martina Mendoza, Houston (1/31/11); Joseph W. Richardson, Houston (1/31/09); James W. Pollard, Canadian (1/31/11); John W. Steinberg, Converse (1/31/07); Melanie G. Thompson, Seguin (1/31/07); John A. Walton, Dallas (1/31/09). Exec. Dir., William Treacy ($70,000), 333 Guadalupe, Suite 3-900, Austin 78701-3900; (512) 305-7800.

Acupuncture Examiners, Texas State Board of– (1993); apptv.; 6 yrs.; per diem; 9 members: Sheng Ting Chen, Austin (1/31/09); Chung-Hwei Chernly, Hurst (1/31/11); Donald R. Counts, Austin (1/31/09); Pedro (Pete) V. Garcia Jr., Lubbock (1/31/09); Raymond J. Graham, Dallas (1/31/11); Hoang Xiong Ho, San Antonio (1/31/07); Meng-Sheng Linda Lin, Richardson (1/31/07); Terry Glenn Rascoe, Temple (1/31/07). Exec. Dir. Donald W. Patrick, 333 Guadalupe, Suite 1, #610, Austin, TX 78768; (512) 305-7010.

Ad Valorem Tax Rate, Board to Calculate the – (1907); ex officio; term in other office; 3 members: Governor, State Comptroller of Public Accounts and State Treasurer.

Adjutant General's Dept. – (1836 by Republic of Texas; present office established 1905); apptv.: Maj. Gen. Charles Gary Rodriguez (2/1/07); Assistant for Air, Maj. Gen. Allen Dehnert (2/1/07); Assistant for Army, Brig. Gen. John T. Furlow; PO Box 5218, Camp Mabry, Austin 78763-5218.

Administrative Judicial Districts of Texas, Presiding Judges – (Apptv. by Governor); serve terms concurrent with term as District Judge, subject to reappointment if re-elected to bench. No additional compensation. For names of judges, see Administrative Judicial Districts in index.

Aging and Disability Services Board, Department of – (2004); apptv.; 6 yrs.; 9 members: Abigail Rios Barrera, San Antonio (2/1/09); Frances Ann (Fran) Brown, Lewisville (2/1/07); Sharon Swift Butterworth, El Paso, (2/1/11); John A. Cuellar, Dallas (2/1/11); Jean I. Freeman, Galveston (2/01/07); Nancy L. Lund, Texarkana (2/1/09); Thomas E. Oliver, Houston, (2/01/07); Teresa D. (Terry) Wilkinson, Midland (2/1/09); David E. Young, Dallas (2/1/07); John H. Winters Human Servc. Complex, 701 W. 51st St., P.O. Box 149030, Austin, TX 78714-9030; (512) 438-3011.

Alcohol and Drug Abuse, Texas Commission on – (1953 as Texas Commission on Alcoholism); abolished by HB 2292 and functions merged into Department of State Health Services in January 2004.

Alcoholic Beverage Commission, Texas – (1935 as Liquor Control Board; name changed 1970); apptv.; 6-yr; per diem and expenses; administrator apptd. by commission; 3 members: Jose Cuevas Jr., Midland (11/15/09); Gail Madden, Dallas (11/15/05); John T. Steen Jr., San Antonio (11/15/07). Admin., Alan Steen ($91,000), PO Box 13127, Austin 78711-3127; (512) 206-3333.

Angelina and Neches River Authority, Board of Directors – (1935 as Sabine-Neches Conservation Dist.; reorganized 1950 and name changed to Neches River Conservation Dist.; changed to present name in 1977); apptv.; expenses; 6-yr.; 9 members: Karen Elizabeth Barber, Jasper (9/5/09); Dominick B. (Nick) Bruno, Jacksonville (9/5/09); Al Chavira, Jacksonville (9/5/07); Kenneth R. Darden, Livingston (9/5/09); Joe M. Deason, Lufkin (9/5/07); Julie Dowell, Bullard, (9/5/05); Carl Ray Polk Jr., Lufkin (9/5/05); James E. Raney, Nacogdoches (9/5/05); George S. Vorpahl, Lufkin (9/5/07). Gen. Mgr., Kenneth Reneau, PO Box 387, Lufkin 75902-0387; (936) 632-7795.

Animal Health Commission, Texas – (1893 as Texas Livestock Sanitary Commission; name changed in 1959, membership increased to 9 in 1973; raised to 12 in 1983); apptv.; per diem and expenses; 6-yr.; 13 members: Rita Esther Baca, El Paso (9/6/09); Reta K. Dyess, Jacksonville (9/6/11); William F. Edmiston Jr., El-

dorado (9/6/07); Thomas George Kezar, Dripping Springs (9/6/11); Coleman Hudgins Locke, Wharton (9/6/09); Rogelio (Roy) Martinez, McAllen (9/6/07); Ernesto A. Morales, Devine (9/6/11); Charles E. Real, Marion (9/6/07); Ralph Simmons, Center (9/6/09); Richard Traylor, Carrizo Springs (9/6/03); Michael Louis Vickers, Falfurrias, (9/6/11); Jerry P. Windham, College Station (9/6/07); Jill Bryar Wood, Wimberley (9/6/07);. Exec. Dir., Bob R. Hillman, DVM ($87,500), PO Box 12966, Austin 78711-2966; (512) 719-0700.

Appraiser Licensing and Certification Board, Texas – (1991); 2-yr.; apptd.; per diem on duty; 9 members: Exec. Sec. of Veterans' Land Board (Paul E. Moore) and 8 apptees: Malcolm J. Deason Jr., Diboll (1/31/07); William A. Faulk Jr., Brownsville (1/31/07); Larry D. Kokel, Georgetown (1/31/07); James Boyd Ratliff, Garland (1/31/07); Clinton P. Sayers, Austin (1/31/06); Shirley Ward, Alpine (1/31/08); Dona S. Scurry, El Paso (1/31/06). Commissioner, Wayne Thorburn, PO Box 12188, Austin 78711-2188; (512) 465-3950.

Architectural Examiners, Texas Board of – (1937 as 3-member board; raised to 6 members in 1951 and to 9 in 1977); apptv.; 6-yr.; per diem and expenses; 9 members: Gordon E. Landreth, Corpus Christi (1/31/07); Rosemary A. Gammon, McKinney (1/31/11); Kyle Garner, Amarillo (1/31/09); Peter L. Pfeiffer, Austin (1/31/09); Alfred Vidaurri Jr., Arlington (1/31/09); James S. Walker II, Houston (1/31/11); Janet F. Parnell, Canadian (1/31/07); Diane Steinbrueck, Austin (1/31/07); Peggy Lewene (Lew) Vassberg, Harlingen (1/31/11). Exec. Dir., Cathy L. Hendricks, ($65,000), PO Box 12337, Austin 78711-2337; (512) 305-9000.

Arts, Texas Commission on the – (1965 as Texas Fine Arts Commission; name changed to Texas Commission on the Arts and Humanities and membership increased to 18 in 1971; name changed to present form in 1979); apptv.; 6-yr.; expenses; 17 members: W.C. (Abby) Abernathy Jr., Archer City (8/31/07); Nelson H. Balido, San Antonio (8/31/09); Patty A. Bryant, Amarillo (8/31/11); Dorothy E. Caram, Houston (8/31/09); William W. Collins Jr., Fort Worth (8/31/09); Alphonse A. Dotson, Voca (8/31/07); David C. Garza, Brownsville (8/31/11); Susan Howard-Chrane, Boerne (8/31/07); Victoria Hodge Lightman, Houston (8/31/07); Loren O. McKibbens, Harlingen (8/31/07); Cobie Russell, Abilene (8/31/09); Billye Proctor Shaw, Abilene (8/31/11); George R. Snead, El Paso (8/31/09); Polly Sowell, Austin (8/31/11); Mary H. Teeple, Spicewood (8/31/09); Norma J. Webb, Midland (8/31/11); Mildred Anne Witte, Tyler (8/31/07). Exec. Dir., Ricardo Hernandez ($70,000), PO Box 13406, Austin 78711-3406; (512) 463-5535.

Athletic Trainers, Advisory Board of – (1971 as Texas Board of Athletic Trainers; name changed and membership increased to 6 in 1975); expenses; 6-yr.; 5 members: Lawrence M. Sampleton Jr., Austin (1/31/09); David R. Schmidt, San Antonio (1/31/07); Natalie Steadman, Lubbock (1/31/03); Michael Alan Waters, Lufkin (1/31/07); David J. Weir, College Station (1/3109); c/o Texas Dept. of State Health Services, 1100 W. 49th, Austin 78756-3183.

Attorney, State Prosecuting – (1923) apptv. by Court of Criminal Appeals: Matthew Paul (12/31/08); ($101,700), PO Box 13046, Austin 78711-3046; (512) 463-1660.

Auditor, State – (1929); apptv. by Legislative Audit Committee, a joint Senate-House committee; 2-yr.: John Keel, PO Box 12067, Austin 78711-2067; (512) 936-9500.

Banking Commissioner, State – (1923); apptv. by State Finance Commission; 2-yr.: Randall S. James ($118,427), 2601 N. Lamar Blvd., Austin 78705-4294 (See also Finance Commission of Texas); (512) 475-1300.

Bar of Texas, State – (1939 as administrative arm of Supreme Court); 30 members elected by membership; 3-yr. terms; expenses paid from dues collected from membership. President, president-elect, vice president and immediate past president serve as ex officio members. Exec. Dir., John Edwards, PO Box 12487, Austin 78711; (512) 463-1463.

Barbering Advisory Board, State – (1929 as 3-member Texas Board of Barber Examiners; membership increased in 1975; named changed to current in 2005 and functions transferred to TX Dept. of Licensing and Regulation); apptv. by department commissioners; 6-yr.; 5 members: Ronald L. Brown, Dripping Springs; Dwayne

Childers Jr., Waco; Linda G. Connor, Austin; Joseph B. Grondin, Round Rock; Aldene (Dene) Hudson Jr., Arlington; c/o Texas Department of Licensing and Regulation, 920 Colorado, Austin, TX 78711-2157; 512-463-6599.

Blind and Severely Disabled Persons, Committee on Purchases of Products of – (See **Disabilities, Texas Council on Purchasing from People with**)

Blind, Commission for the – Now the Division for Blind Services within the Department of Assistive and Rehabilitative Services of the Health and Human Services Commission as of 3/1/04.

Blind and Visually Impaired, Governing Board of Texas School for the – (1979); apptv.; 6-yr.; expenses; 9 members: Jesus H. Bautista, El Paso (1/31/07); Gene Iran Brooks, Austin (1/31/09); Donna Florence Vaden Clopton, Weatherford (1/31/09); Otilio (Toby) Galindo, San Angelo (1/31/05); Deborah Louder, San Angelo (1/31/11); Frankie D. Swift, Nacogdoches (1/31/07); Mary Sue Welch, Dallas (1/31/05); Jamie Lou Wheeler, North Richland Hills (1/31/09). Superintendent, Dr. Philip H. Hatlen ($84,000), 1100 W. 45th St., Austin 78756-3494; (512) 454-8631.

Board of (Note: In most instances, state boards are alphabetized under key word, as **Accountancy, Texas State Board of Public**.)

Brazos River Authority, Board of Directors – (1929 as Brazos River Conservation and Reclamation Dist.; name changed to present form in 1953); apptv.; 6-yr; expenses; 21 members: Chair: Steve Peña (2/1/05); M.G. Christopher, Granbury (2/1/11); Steve Adams Jr., Granbury (2/1/11); Roberto Bailon, Belton (2/1/09); Suzanne Alderson Baker, Lubbock (2/1/07); Truman Otis Blum, Clifton (2/1/11); Ronald D. Butler II, Stephenville (2/1/07); Mark J. Carrabba, Bryan (2/1/09); Jacqueline Baly Chaumette, Sugar Land (2/1/09); Robert M. Christian, Jewett (2/1/11; Christopher D. DeCluitt, Waco (2/1/11); P.J. Ellison, Brenham (2/1/07); Rodolfo Garcia, Alvin (2/1/03); Wade Compton Gear, Mineral Wells (2/1/09); Fred Lee Hughes, Abilene (2/1/07); Carolyn H. Johnson, Freeport (2/1/11); Roberta Jean Killgore, Somerville (2/1/11); Jere Lawrence, Sweetwater (2/1/09); Martha Stovall Martin, Graford (2/1/07); Billy Wayne Moore, Granbury (2/1/09); John R. Skaggs, Plainview (2/1/07); Salvatore A. Zaccagnino, Caldwell (2/1/07). Gen. Mgr., Phillip J. Ford, P. O. Box 7555, Waco 76714-7555; (254) 761-3100.

Building and Procurement Commission, Texas – apptv.; 6-yr.; 7 members: Chair, Brenda Pejovich, Dallas (1/31/09); Stuart Coleman, Brownwood (1/31/07); James S. Duncan, Houston (1/31/09); Bob Jones, Houston (1/31/07); Victor E. Leal, Amarillo (1/31/09); Mary Ann Newman-Buckley, Houston (1/31/05); Betty Reinbeck, Sealy (1/31/11). Exec. Dir. Cindy Reed ($115,000) PO Box 13047, Austin 78711-3047; (512) 463-6363.

Canadian River Compact Commissioner – (1951); apptv.; salary and expenses; (function is to negotiate with other states respecting waters of the Canadian): Roger S. Cox ($10,767), Amarillo (12/31/03).

Canadian River Municipal Water Authority – 2-yr; 17 members: Glenn Bickel, Plainview (8/31/04); Jerry Carlson, Pampa (7/31/03); James O. Collins, Lubbock (7/31/03); Tom Edmonds, Borger (7/31/04); Larry Hagood, Tahoka (7/31/03); William Hallerberg, Amarillo (7/31/04); Benny Kirksey, Pampa (7/31/04); Pat McCutchin, Levelland (7/31/03); E.R. Moore, O'Donnell (7/31/03); Ray Renner, Lamesa (7/31/03); L.J. Richardson, Brownfield (7/31/03); Robert Rodgers, Lubbock (7/31/04); George Sell, Amarillo (7/31/03); Carl Shamburger, Levelland (7/31/04); Steve Tucker, Slaton (7/31/03); JoAnn Wasicek, Borger (7/31/03); Norman Wright, Plainview (7/31/03). PO Box 9, Sanford 79078-0009; (806) 865-3325.

Cancer Council, Texas – (1985); 6-yr.; expenses; 15 members: James D. Dannenbaum, Houston (2/1/06); Donald C. Spencer, Austin (2/1/06); Karen Heusinkveld, Arlington (2/1/08); F. Diane Barber, Richmond (2/1/06); Karen Bonner, Corpus Christi (2/1/10); Clare Buie Chaney, Dallas (2/1/08); Lloyd K. Croft, Boerne (2/1/08); Sylvia P. Fernandez, San Antonio (2/1/10); Carolyn D. Harvey, Tyler (2/1/06); Rubye H. Henderson, Plainview (2/1/08); Larry Herrera, Temple (2/1/06); Courtney Townsend Jr., Galveston (2/1/04); J. Taylor Wharton, Houston (2/1/10). Ex officio member, Debra C. Stabeno. Exec. Dir. Sandra Balderrama ($57,691) PO Box 12097, Austin 78711; 512-463-3190.

Central Colorado River Authority (See **Colorado River Authority, Central.**)

Chemist, Office of State – (1911); ex officio, indefinite term: State Chemist, Tim Herrman, P.O. Box 3160, College Station 77841-3160; 979-845-1121.

Childhood Intervention, Interagency Council on Early – Combined into Department of Assistive and Rehabilitative Services of the Health and Human Services Commission as of 3/1/04. Exec. Dir. Mary Beth O'Hanlon.

Chiropractic Examiners, Texas Board of – (1949); apptv.; 6-yr.; expenses; 9 members: Chair Sandra Lee Jensen, Farmers Branch (2/1/07); Robert L. Coburn, West Columbia (2/1/05); Mar-

cia Olivia Daughtrey, Tyler (2/1/09); Paul H. Dickerson, Houston (2/1/05); Narciso Escareño, Brownsville (2/1/07); Serge Francois, Dallas (2/1/05); Scott Edward Isdale, Killeen (2/1/09); Steve Minors, Austin (2/1/07); David Alan Sime, El Paso (2/1/09). Exec. Dir. Sandra D. Smith ($52,000), 333 Guadalupe, Ste. 3-825, Austin 78701; 512-305-6700.

Coastal Water Authority, Board of Directors – (1967 as Coastal Industrial Water Authority, Board of Directors of; name changed in 1985); 7 members — 4 apptd. by mayor of Houston with advice and consent of governing body of Houston; 3 apptd. by Gov.; per diem and expenses; 2-yr.; Gov's. apptees: Dionel E. Aviles (3/31/01); Rick Cloutier (4/1/02); Buster E. French (4/1/00); Darryl L. King (4/1/01); Kurt Metyko (3/31/01); Gary R. Nelson (4/1/01); Dorothy M. Washington (3/31/02). Exec. Dir. Ralph T. Rundle, 1200 Smith St., Ste. 2260, Houston 77002; 713-658-9020.

Colorado River Authority, Central, Board of Directors – (1935); apptv.; 6-yr.; per diem on duty; 9 members: Ann Miller Hargett, Coleman (2/1/01); Alice B. Hemphill, Coleman (2/1/05); John S. Hensley, Santa Anna (2/1/05); Jack B. Horne, Coleman (2/1/03); Nan Knox Markland, Burkett (2/1/01); Ronald W. Owens, Coleman (2/1/01); Ben J. Scott, Coleman (2/1/05); Barbara A. Simmons, Santa Anna (2/1/03). Operations Mgr., Lynn W. Cardinas, PO Box 964, Coleman 76834.

Colorado River Authority, Lower, Board of Directors – (1934 as 9-member board; membership increased in 1951 and 1975); apptv.; 6-yr.; per diem on duty; 15 members: Chair Ray A. Wilkerson, Travis Co. (2/1/07); Vice-Chair G. Hughes Abell, Travis Co. (2/1/07); Secretary, Connie Granberg, Blanco Co. (2/1/07); Kay Morgan Carlton, Fayette Co. (2/1/09); Ida A. Carter, Burnet Co. (2/1/11); Lucy Ortiz Cavazos, Kerr Co. (2/1/09); John C. Dickerson, III, Matagorda Co. (2/1/09); Walter E. Garrett, Wharton Co. (2/1/09); Robert K. Long, Sr., Bastrop Co. (2/1/07); John H. Matthews, Colorado Co. (2/1/05); Woodrow Francis McCasland, Llano Co. (2/1/11); Charles R. Moser, Washington Co. (2/1/07); Clayborne L. Nettleship, San Saba Co. (2/1/09); Linda Clapp Raun, Wharton Co. (2/1/11); B.R. (Skipper) Wallace, Williamson Co. (2/1/11). Gen. Man., Joseph J. Beal, P. O. Box 220, Austin 78767-0220; 512-473-3200.

Colorado River Authority, Upper, Board of Directors – (1935 as 9-member board; reorganized in 1965); apptv.; 6-yr.; per diem and expenses; indefinite number of members: Chair Fred R. Campbell, Paint Rock (2/1/03); Vice/Chair Jeffie Harmon Roberts, Robert Lee (2/1/05); Secretary, Dorris M. Sonnenberg, Bronte (2/1/01); Treasurer, Hyman Sauer, Eldorado (2/1/05); Board Members: Ray Alderman, Winters (2/1/01); Ralph E. Hoelscher, Miles (2/1/01); Hope Huffman, San Angelo (2/1/03). Ellen Groth, Admin. Asst., 12 Orient, San Angelo 76903; 325-655-0565.

Commissioner of (See keyword, as **Agriculture, Commissioner of**.)

Concho River Water and Soil Conservation Authority, Lower – (1939); 6-yr.; 9 members: Chair Benjamin Orland Sims, Paint Rock (2/1/1997); Joseph Beach, Millersview (2/1/1997); Leroy Beach, Millersview (2/1/1999); Howard Loveless, Eden (2/1/1999); Billy J. Mikeska, Eola (2/1/1999); Eugene R. Rodgers, Eden (2/1/1997); Edwin T. Tickle, Eden (2/1/01); Harvey P. Williams, Eola (2/1/01). Office Address: Rt. 1, PO Box 4, Paint Rock 76866; 325-732-4371.

Consumer Credit Commissioner – Leslie L. Pettijohn ($90,000), 2601 N. Lamar, Austin 78705-4207.

Cosmetology Commission, Texas – (1935 as 3-member State Board of Hairdressers and Cosmetologists; name changed and membership increased to 6 apptv. and one ex officio in 1971); apptv.; per diem and expenses; 6-yr.; apptv. members: Leif Christiansen, Spring (12/31/07); Heliana L. Kiessling, Friendswood (12/31/03); Philip Lapp, Weatherford (12/31/07); Helen Quiram, Waco (12/31/05); Lucinda Shearer (Cindy) Sandoval, Edinburg (12/31/07); Elida Zapata, Lubbock (12/31/05). Ex officio member, Esther Camacho, Texas Education Agency. Exec. Dir. Antoinette Humphrey ($46,338), PO Box 26700, Austin 78755-0700; 512-380-7600.

Counselors, Texas State Board of Examiners of Professional – (1981); apptv.; 6-yr.; expenses; 9 members: Chair Judith D. Powell, The Woodlands (2/1/05); Ana C. Bergh, Edinburg (2/1/05); Diane J. Boddy, Henrietta (2/1/090: James Castro, San Antonio (2/1/09); Glenda Corley, Pearland (2/1/05); Michelle A. Eggleston, Amarillo (2/1/07); Alma Gloria Leal, Rancho Viejo (2/1/09); J. Helen Perkins, DeSoto (2/1/07); Dan F. Wilkins, Center (2/1/07). Exec. Dir. Bobbe Alexander, 1100 W. 49th, Austin 78756-3183; 512-834-6658.

Court Reporters Certification Board – (1977 as 9-member Texas Reporters Committee; name changed to present form and membership increased to 12 in 1983); apptv. by State Supreme Court; 6-yr.; expenses: Chair Catharina Haynes, Dallas (12/31/06); Attorney members: Olan Boudreaux, San Antonio (12/31/08); Wendy Tolson Ross, San Antonio (12/31/07). Official reporters: Albert

Alvarez, Austin (12/31/05); Judy Miller, Fort Worth (12/31/06). Freelance reporter: Paula Richards, Kerrville (12/31/08); one vacancy. Firm representatives: Audree Crutcher, Lubbock (12/31/08); Kim Tindall, San Antonio (12/31/06); Lay members: Sara Dolph, Austin (12/31/05); Michelle Herrera, San Antonio (12/31/07); Ly T. Nguyen, Austin (12/31/08. Director Michele L. Henricks ($52,000), 205 W. 14th St., Ste. 101, Austin 78701; 512-463-1630.

Credit Union Commission – (1949 as 3-member Credit Union Advisory Commission; name changed and membership increased to 6 in 1969; increased to 9 in 1981); apptv.; 6-yr.; expenses; 9 members: Presiding Officer Gary L. Janacek, Temple (2/15/09); Garold R. Base, Plano (2/15/07); Rufino Carbajal Jr., El Paso (2/15/07); Barbara K. Sheffield, Houston (2/15/11); Public members: Floyde Burnside, San Antonio (2/15/05); Thomas Felton Butler, La Porte (2/15/07); Richard A. Glasco Jr. Georgetown (2/15/03); Mary Ann Grant, Houston (2/15/09); Henry E. (Pete) Snow, Texarkana (2/15/11). Commissioner Harold E. Feeney, 914 E. Anderson Ln., Austin 78752-1699; 512-837/9236.

Crime Stoppers Advisory Council – (1981); apptv.; 4-yr.; per diem and expenses; 5 members: Janice C. Gillen, Rosenberg (9/1/04); Juan F. Jorge, Tomball (9/1/04); Tina Alexander Sellers, Lufkin (9/1/04); Dorothy Spinks, Marble Falls (9/1/05); Brian Thomas, Amarillo (9/1/05).

Criminal Justice, Texas Board of – (1989: assumed duties of former Texas Board of Corrections and Adult Probation Commission; also oversees Board of Pardons and Paroles Division); apptd; 6-yr.; expenses; 9 members: Chair Christina Melton Crain, Dallas (2/1/07); Vice-Chair Don B. Jones, Midland (2/1/05); Secretary William H. (Hank) Moody, Kerrville (2/1/05); Adrian A. Arriaga, McAllen (2/1/07); Mary Bacon, Houston (2/1/05); Oliver J. Bell, Austin (2/1/09); Greg S. Coleman, Austin (2/1/09); Patricia A. Day, Dallas (2/1/03); Pierce Miller, San Angelo (2/1/07). Exec. Dir, Dept. of Criminal Justice: Brad Livingston ($150,000), PO Box 13084, Austin 78711. 512-475-3250.

Deaf, Governing Board of the Texas School for the – (1979); 6-yr.; expenses; 9 members: Charles Estes, Denton (1/31/09); Beatrice M. Burke, Big Spring (1/31/07); Nancy E. Munger, Kyle (1/31/95); Jean Andrews, Beaumont (1/31/05); Walter Camenisch, Austin (1/31/09); Nancy Carrizales, Katy (1/31/07); Kenneth D. Kesterson, Big Spring (1/31/07); Lesa Thomas, Corpus Christi (1/31/05). Superintendent, Claire Bugen ($84,000), 1102 South Congress, Austin 78704; 512-462-5353.

Deaf and Hard of Hearing, Texas Commission for the – Combined into Department of Assistive and Rehabilitative Services of the Health and Human Services Commission as of 3/1/04.

Dental Examiners, State Board of – (1919 as 6-member board; increased to 9 members in 1971; increased to 12 in 1981; increased to 15 in 1991; sunsetted in 1994; reconstituted with 18 members in 1995); appt.; 6-yr.; per diem while on duty; 18 members: Presiding Officer J. Kevin Irons, Austin (2/1/05); Tammy Lynne Allen, Fort Worth (2/1/07); Oscar X. Garcia, Brownsville (2/1/07); Amy Landess Juba, Amarillo (2/1/09); Martha Lynn Manley Malik, Victoria (2/1/05); Norman Lewis Mason, Austin (2/1/09); Gary W. McDonald, Kingwood (2/1/09); Helen Hayes McKibben, Lubbock (2/1/09); Marti L. Morgan, Fort Worth (2/1/05); Phyllis A. Stine, Midland (2/1/07); George Strunk, Longview (2/1/09); Paul E. Stubbs, Austin (2/1/05); Nathaniel Tippit, Houston (2/1/05); Juan D. Villarreal, Harlingen (2/1/07); Charles Field Wetherbee, Jourdanton (2/1/09). Exec. Dir. Bobby Schmidt ($63,000), 333 Guadalupe, Ste. 3-800, Austin 78701; 512-463-6400.

Depository Board, State – (Abolished May 1997).

Diabetes Council, Texas – (1983; with 5 ex officio and 6 public members serving 2-yr. terms; changed in 1987 to 3 ex officio and 8 public members; changed to present configuration in 1991; term length changed from 4 to 6 years eff. 1997); 6-yr.; 17 members — 5 ex officio; 11 apptv. public members as follows: Chair Lawrence B. Harkless, San Antonio (2/1/07); Public members: Randy Bryon Baker, Mesquite (2/1/09); Belinda Bazan/Lara, San Antonio (2/1/05); Gene Fulton Bell, Lubbock (2/1/03); Victor Hugo Gonzalez, McAllen (2/1/03); Judith L. Haley, Houston (2/1/05); Richard S. (Rick) Hayley, Corpus Christi (2/1/05); Lenore Frances Katz, Dallas (2/1/07); Margaret G. Pacillas, El Paso (2/1/07); Avery Rhodes, Diboll (2/1/09); Jeffrey A. Ross, Bellaire (2/1/07). Director Jan Marie Ozias; c/o Texas Dept. of Health, 1100 W. 49th, Austin 78756; 512-458-7490.

Dietitians, Texas State Board of Examiners of – (1983); apptv.; 6-yr.; per diem and expenses; 9 members: Lucinda Flores, Brownsville (9/1/03); Georgiana S. Gross, San Antonio (9/1/09); Janet S. Hall, Georgetown (9/1/07); Ralph McGahagin, Austin (9/1/05); Amy N. McLeod, Lufkin (9/1/07); Gene Wisakowsky, Dallas (9/1/05); Public members: Carol Davis, Dallas (9/1/05); Linda W. Dickerson, Angleton (9/1/09); Claudia L. Lisle, Austin (9/1/07). Texas Dept. of Health, 1100 W. 49th, Austin 78756; 512-834-6601.

Disabilities, Texas Council for Developmental – (1971); apptv.; 6-yr.; 29 members — 8 ex offico: Representatives from Dept. of

Mental Health and Mental Retardation, Rehabilitation Commission, Dept. of Health, Dept. of Human Services, Texas Dept. on Aging, Texas Education Agency, Texas Commission for the Blind, Texas Commission for the Deaf; 19 apptv. members: Chair Jan R. Newsom, Dallas (2/1/07); Vice/Chair Richard A. Tisch, Spring (2/1/09). Public members: Raul Acosta, Lubbock (2/1/05); Susan Berkley, Alvin (2/1/07); Kristine Bissmeyer, San Antonio (2/1/05); Melonie S. Caster, Bedford (2/1/09); Brenda K. Coleman/Beattie, Austin (2/1/07); Mary M. Durheim, McAllen (2/1/05); Marcia Dwyer, Plano (2/1/05); Cindy Johnston, Dallas (2/1/07); Diana Kern, Cedar Creek (2/1/09); Amy L. Baxter Ley, Euless (2/1/09); Vickie J. Mitchell, Montgomery (2/1/09); John C. Morris, Austin (2/1/07); Dana S. Perry, Brownwood (2/1/09); Ed Rankin, Dallas (2/1/07); Joe Rivas, Denton (2/1/05); Raul Treviño, Mission (2/1/09); Susan Vardell, Sherman (2/1/07). Exec. Dir. Roger A. Webb, 6201 E. Oltorf, Ste. 600, Austin 78741; 512-437-5432.

Disabilities, Governor's Committee on People with – (1991); 16 members: 4 ex officio: Chmn., TEC; Commissioner, Texas Rehabilitation Comm.; Dir., Texas Commission for the Blind; member, Texas Comm. for the Deaf; 12 members apptd. by governor; 2-year terms: Chair Thomas P. Justis, Granbury (2/1/05); Kara Wilson Anglin, Houston (2/2/05); Douglas F. Grady Jr., Fort Worth (2/1/04); Peter Grojean, San Antonio (2/1/04); Roland Guzman, San Antonio (2/1/05); Anthony G. Jones, Lubbock (2/1/01); Judy Rae Scott, Dallas (2/1/04); Brian D. Shannon, Lubbock (2/1/05); Nancy Shugart, Austin (2/1/04); Kathy S. Strong, Garrison (2/1/04); Shane Whitehurst, Austin (2/1/05); one vacancy. Exec. Dir. Pat Pound, 4900 N. Lamar, Austin 78751-2613; 512-463-5739.

Disabilities, Texas Office for Prevention of Developmental – (1991) 9 members apptd. by governor; 6-year terms: Chair Theresa Mulloy, Stephenville; Vice-Chair J.C. Montgomery Jr., Dallas; Rep. Dwayne Bohac, Houston; Robert L. Carr, Lubbock; Dale Coln, Dallas; Joan Roberts-Scott, Austin; Marian Sokol, San Antonio; Mary S. Tijerina, San Marcos; Rep. Vicki Truitt, Southlake. Exec. Dir. Carolyn Smith, P.O. Box 12668, Austin 78711-2668; 512-206-4544.

Disabilities, Texas Council on Purchasing from People with – (1979 as 10-member Committee on Purchases of Products and Services of Blind and Severely Disabled Persons; name changed and members reduced to 9 in 1995); apptd.; expenses; 6-yr.; 9 members: Chair Margaret (Meg) Pfluger, Lubbock (1/31/05); Board Members: Chuck Brewton, San Antonio (1/31/05); Byron E. Johnson, El Paso (1/31/07); Howard K. Karnes, Dallas (1/31/07); John Luna, Euless (1/31/09); Floyd Glen Self, Jr., Dripping Springs (1/31/09); Wanda White Stovall, Fort Worth (1/31/09); Cathy J. Williams, Austin (1/31/05). Exec. Dir. Kelvin Moore. P.O. Box 13047, Austin 78711/3047; 512-463-3244.

Education, Board of Control for Southern Regional – (1969); apptv.; 4-yr.; 5 members: Gov. ex officio, 4 apptd.: Rep. Dianne White Delisi, Temple (6/30/07); Rep. Kent Grusendorf, Arlington (6/30/08); Shirley J. Neeley, Ed.D. (6/30/06); Sen. Florence Shapiro, Plano (6/30/05); Ex Officio Member, Governor Rick Perry, Austin); President, Mark D. Musick, Southern Regional Education Board, 592 10th St. N.W., Atlanta, GA 30318-5790; 404)-75-9211.

Education, Commissioner of – (1866 as Superintendent of Public Instruction, 1040 changed to present name by Gilmer-Aiken Law); apptv. by State Board of Education; 4-yr.: Robert Scott (acting commissioner) ($164,748) (See also Education, State Board of).

Education, State Board of – (1866; re-created 1928 and re-formed by Gilmer-Aikin Act in 1949 to consist of 21 elective members from districts co-extensive with 21 congressional districts at that time; membership increased to 24 with congressional redistricting in 1971, effective 1973; membership increased to 27 with congressional redistricting in 1981, effective 1983; reorganized by special legislative session as 15-member apptv. board in 1984 to become elective board again in 1988; expenses; 4-yr.; 15 members: Chair Geraldine (Tincy) Miller, Dallas, District 12 (2/1/07); Lawrence Allen Jr., Houston, District 4 (1/1/07); Mary Helen Berlanga, Corpus Christi, District 2 (1/1/07); Joe J. Bernal, San Antonio, District 3 (1/1/07); David Bradley, Beaumont, District 7 (1/1/09); Barbara Cargill, The Woodlands, District 8 (1/1/09); Bob Craig, Lubbock, District 15 (1/1/07); Patricia (Pat) Hardy, Weatherford, District 11 (1/1/09); Mavis B. Knight, Dallas, District 13 (1/1/09); Terri Leo, Spring, District 6 (1/1/09); Gail Lowe, Lampasas, District 14 (1/1/09); Don McLeroy, Bryan, District 9 (1/1/07); Dan Montgomery, Fredericksburg, District 5 (1/1/07); Rene Nuñez, El Paso, District 1 (1/1/07); Cynthia Thornton, Round Top, District 10 (1/1/07) Executive Assistant, Reneé Jackson. Commissioner of Education, Robert Scott (acting) ($164,748), Texas Education Agency, 1701 N. Congress Ave., Austin 78701-1494.

Educator Certification, State Board for – (1995); apptv.; 6-yr.; expenses; 15 members; 3 non-voting: rep. of Comm. of Education; rep of Comm. of Higher Education; 1 dean of a college of education apptd. by Gov.; 14 voting members apptd. by Gov.: Chair Annette T. Griffin, Carrollton (2/1/05); Vice/Chair Cecilia P. Abbott,

Austin (2/1/07); Secretary, Bonny L. Cain, Ed.D., Pearland (2/1/09); Board Members: Glenda Barron, Austin, at will of Comm.); John James Beck, Jr., San Marcos (2/1/05); Patti Lynn Johnson, Canyon Lake (2/1/09); Adele Quintana, Dumas (2/1/07); Cynthia M. Saenz, Austin (2/1/09); Antonio Sanchez, Mission (2/1/05); Robert Scott, Austin, at will of Comm.); John C. Shirley, Dallas (2/1/09); Troy Simmons, Longview (2/1/07); James Windham, Houston (2/1/05); Judie Zinsser, Houston (2/1/07). Exec. Dir. Herman Smith, ($78,000),1701 N. Congress Ave., 5th Fl, Austin 78701/1494; 512-936-8400.

Edwards Aquifer Authority – (1993); elected from single-member districts; 4-yr.; expenses; 15 apptv. members: Chair Doug Miller, Comal County, (12/1/06); Vice-Chair Rafael Zendejas, Bexar Co., (12/1/06); Sec., Levi Jackson III, Bexar Co., (12/1/08); Treas., Hunter Schuehle, Medina Co., (12/1/08); Ken Barnes, Hays Co., (12/1/08); Bailey Barton, Hays Co., (12/1/06); Luana Buckner, Medina Co., (12/1/06); Ramon Chapa, Jr., Comal Co., (12/1/08); Mario H. Cruz, Uvalde Co., (12/1/08); Bruce Gilleland, Uvalde Co., (12/1/06); Rogelio Muñoz, Uvalde Co. (12/1/08); Carol Patterson, Bexar Co., (12/1/06); George Rice, Bexar Co., (12/1/08); Johnny A. Rodriguez, Bexar Co., (12/1/06); Appt. Dir. Clay Binford, (12/1/08); at large, Susan Hughes, Bexar Co., (12/1/08); Appt. Dir. Bob Keith, (12/1/08). Gen. Mgr. Robert J. Potts, ($165,000) 1615 N. St. Mary's St., San Antonio 78215-1415.

Egg Marketing Advisory Board – (Abolished May 1997).

Election Commission, State – (1973); 9 members, ex officio and apptv. as indicated: Chmn. of Democratic State Executive Committee; Chmn. of Republican State Executive Committee; Chief Justice of Supreme Court; Presiding Judge, Court of Criminal Appeals; 2 persons to be named, one a justice of the Court of Appeals apptd. by Chief Justice of Supreme Court, one a District Judge apptd. by presiding judge of Court of Criminal Appeals; 2 county chairmen, one each from Democratic and Republican parties, named by the parties; Secretary of State.

Emergency Communications, Commission on State – (1985 as 17-member Advisory Commission on State Emergency Communications; name changed and membership reduced to 12, 2000); expenses; 12 members: 3 ex offico: exec. directors of Dept. of Health, Public Utilities Comm. and General Services Admin.; 9 public members (6 yr.): 2 apptd. by Lt. Gov.; 2 apptd. by Speaker; 5 apptd. by Gov. Gov's apptees: Presiding Officer, Dorothy Morgan, Brenham (9/1/05); James Beauchamp, Midland (8/31/07); Don Comedy, Haskell (8/30/03); John L. deNoyelles, Tyler (9/1/03); Herberto Gutierrez, San Antonio (9/1/03); Glenn O. Lewis, Fort Worth (9/1/07); James L. O'Neal, Lancaster (9/1/05); Lyn Phillips, Bastrop (9/1/03); H. T. Wright, Lockhart (9/1/07). Exec. Dir., Paul Mallett ($75,000), 333 Guadalupe St., Ste. 2-212, Austin 78701; 512-305-6911.

Emergency Services Personnel Retirement Fund, Texas Statewide – (1977; formerly the Fire Fighters' Relief and Retirement Fund); apptv.; expenses; 6-yr.; 9 members: Chair Francisco R. Torres, Raymondville (9/1/05); Vice-Chair John J. Scopel, Rosenburg (9/1/05); Sec., Paul V. Loeffler, Alpine (9/1/07); Oscar Choate, Mineral Wells (9/1/07); Kyle A. Donaldson, Sonora (9/1/09); Graciela G. Flores, Corpus Christi (9/1/09); Rex W. Klesel, Alvin (9/1/09); Maxie L. Patterson, Houston (9/1/07); Robert Weiss, Brenham (9/1/05); Commissioner, Lisa Ivie Miller, PO Box 12577, Austin 78711.

Employment Commission, Texas – (See **Workforce Commission, Texas**)

Engineers, State Board of Registration for Professional – (1937 as 6-member board; membership increased to 9 in 1981); apptv.; per diem and expenses; 6-yr.; 9 members: Chair James R. Nichols, P.E., Fort Worth (9/26/09); Jose F. Cardenas, P.E., El Paso (9/26/09); C. Roland Haden, Ph.D., P.E., College Station (9/26/07); Govind Nadkarni, P.E., Corpus Christi (9/26/05); Gerry E. Pate, P.E., Houston (9/26/07); Robert M. Sweazy, Ph.D., P.E., Lubbock (9/26/05); Public Members: William Lawrence, Highland Village (9/26/07); Shannon K. McClendon, Dripping Springs (9/26/09); Vicki T. Ravenburg, C.P.A., San Antonio (9/26/05). Exec. Dir., Dale Beebe Farrow ($75,000), 1917 S. IH-35, Austin 78741.

Environmental Quality, Texas Commission on – (1913 as State Board of Water Engineers; name changed in 1962 to Texas Water Commission; reorganized and name again changed in 1965 to Water Rights Commission; reorganized and name changed back to Texas Water Commission in 1977 to perform judicial function for the Texas Dept. of Water Resources; name changed to Texas Natural Resource Conservation Commission in 1993; changed to present form Sept. 1, 2002); apptv.; 6-yr.; 3 members full-time at $107,500–$111,792: Kathleen Hartnett White, Valentine (8/31/07); R.B. (Ralph) Marquez, Texas City (8/31/05); Larry Ross Soward, Austin (8/31/09). Exec. Dir., Glenn Shankle ($132,000), PO Box 13087, Austin 78711.

Ethics Commission, Texas – (1991); apptd.; 4-yr.; 8 members: 2 apptd. by Speaker, 2 apptd. by Lt. Gov, 4 apptd. by Gov.: Chair Wales H. Madden III, Amarillo (11/19/05); Vice-Chair Francisco Her-

nandez Jr., Fort Worth (11/19/03); Raymond R. (Trip) Davenport III, Dallas (11/19/07); Scott W. Fisher, Bedford (11/19/05); Warren Tom Harrison, Austin (11/19/07); Cullen R. Looney, Edinburg (11/19/07); James David Montagne, Orange (11/19/07); Ralph Wayne, Austin (11/19/05). Exec. Dir., David Allen Reisman ($97,000), 201 E. 14th St., 10th Fl., Austin 78701.

Finance Commission of Texas – (1923 as Banking Commission; reorganized as Finance Commission in 1943 with 9 members; membership increased to 12 in 1983; changed back to 9 members in 1989); apptv.; 6-yr.; per diem and traveling expenses; 9 members: Chair Vernon Bryant, Jr., Aledo (2/1/06); Gary D. Akright, Dallas (2/1/08); Mike Bradford (2/1/06); Hector Delgado, Dallas (2/1/10); Kenneth H. Harris, Austin (2/1/08); Cindy F. Lyons, El Paso (2/1/10); Allan B. Polunsky, San Antonio (2/1/08); John Snider, Center (2/1/06); William James White, Georgetown (2/1/10). Banking Commissioner, Randall S. James , 2601 N. Lamar, Austin 78705, appointee of Finance Commission. (See also Banking Commissioner, State.)

Fire Fighters' Pension Commissioner – (1937); apptv.; 2-yr.: Lisa Ivie Miller, Austin (7/1/07) ($57,000), PO Box 12577, Austin 78711.

Fire Protection, Texas Commission on – (1991; formed by consolidation of Fire Dept. Emergency Board and Commission on Fire Protection Personnel Standards and Education); apptv.; 6-yrs.; expenses; 12 members: Presiding Officer, Kelley M. Stalder, Parker (2/1/03); Commissioners: David Abernathy, Pittsburg (2/1/07); Juan J. Adame, Corpus Christi (2/1/07); Pat Barrett, College Station (2/1/03); Marvin G. Dawson, Brownfield (2/1/07); Mike Jolly, Georgetown (2/1/05); Alonzo Lopez, Jr., Kingsville (2/1/05); Arthur Lee Pertile, III, Waco (2/1/07); Ricardo Saldaña, Mission (2/1/05); Peggy Trahan, South Padre Island (2/1/03); G. Kent Worley, Fort Worth (2/1/03); Carl Wren, Manchaca (2/1/05). Exec. Dir., Gary L. Warren Sr. ($78,000), PO Box 2286, Austin 78768.

Food and Fibers Commission, Texas – (1941 as Cotton Research Committee; name changed in 1971 to Natural Fibers and Food Protein Committee; changed to commission in 1975; changed to present name 1989); 4 members are presidents and chancellor of four major universities (Pres., Texas Woman's University, Denton; Pres., Texas Tech University, Lubbock; Chancellor, Texas A&M University System, College Station; Pres., University of Texas at Austin) serving indefinite terms; and one ex officio member who is director of administrative office in Dallas, apptd. to 2-year term: Exec. Dir., Robert V. Avant Jr., 17360 Coit Rd., Dallas 75252.

Funeral Service Commission, Texas – (1903 as State Board of Embalming; 1935 as State Board of Funeral Directors and Embalmers; 1953 as 6-member board; membership increased to 9 in 1979; name changed to present form in 1987; membership reduced to 6 in 1999); apptv.; per diem and expenses; 6-yr.; 6 members: Presiding Officer, Harry Whittington, Austin (2/1/07); Laurens B. Fish, III, Austin (2/1/09); Dorothy Grasty, Arlington (2/1/05); Martha Greenlaw, Houston (2/1/07); Janice B. Howard, Missouri City (2/1/07); Martha (Marty) Rhymes, White Oak (2/1/03); Jim Wright, Wheeler (2/1/05). Exec. Dir., O.C. "Chet" Robbins ($45,816), 510 S. Congress, Ste. 206, Austin 78704-1716.

General Services Commission – (1919 as Board of Control; name changed to State Purchasing and General Services Commission in 1979; changed to present form and increased to 6 commissioners in 1991); apptv.; 6-yr.; expenses; 6 members: Tomás Cárdenas Jr., El Paso (1/31/05); James A. Cox Jr., Austin (1/31/05); Gilbert A. Herrera, Houston (1/31/07); Barbara Rusling, Waco (1/31/03); Gene Shull, Tyler (1/31/03). Acting Exec. Dir., Ann Dillon ($115,000), PO Box 13047, Austin 78711-3047.

Geoscientists, Texas Board of Professional – (2001); apptv.; expenses; 6-yr.; 9 members (6 professional geoscientists, 3 public members): William K. Coleman, Cedar Hill (2/1/05); Kelly K. Doe, Friendswood (2/1/09); Shiela B. Hall, Lubbock (2/1/07); Murray H. Milford, Bryan (2/1/07); Edward G. Miller, San Antonio (2/1/05); Rene D. Pena, El Paso (2/1/09); Danny R. Perkins, Houston (2/1/07); Kimberly R. Phillips, Houston (2/1/05); Gordon D. Ware, Corpus Christi (2/1/09). Exec. Dir., Michael D. Hess P.O. Box 12157, Austin, TX 78711.

Guadalupe River Authority, Upper – (1939); apptv.; 6-yr.; 9 members: Chair Fred R. Campbell, Paint Rock (2/1/03); Vice/Chair Jeffie Harmon Roberts, Robert Lee (2/1/05); Secretary, Dorris M. Sonnenberg, Bronte (2/1/01); Treasurer, Hyman Sauer, Eldorado (2/1/05); Board Members: Ray Alderman, Winters (2/1/01); Ralph E. Hoelscher, Miles (2/1/01); Hope Huffman, San Angelo (2/1/03). Gen. Mgr., Ellen Groth, 125 Lehman Dr., Ste. 100, Kerrville 78028.

Guadalupe-Blanco River Authority – (1935); apptv.; per diem and expenses on duty; 6-yr.; 9 members: Kathleen A. Devine, New Braunfels (2/1/05); Jack R. Gary, San Marcos (2/1/07); Margaret M. Grier, Boerne (2/1/09); Myrna P. McLeroy, Gonzales (2/1/07); Frank J. Pagel, Tivoli (2/1/07); Frederick S. Schlather, Cibolo (2/1/03); John P. Schneider, Jr., Lockhart (2/1/05); Clifton L. Thomas, Jr., Victoria (2/1/09); Stephen F. Wilson, D.V.M., Port Lavaca (2/1/05). Gen. Mgr., William E. West, 933 E. Court St., Seguin 78155.

Gulf Coast Waste Disposal Authority – (1969); apptv.; 2-yr.; per diem and expenses on duty; 9 members: 3 apptv. by Gov., 3 by County Commissioners Courts of counties in district, 3 by Municipalities Waste Disposal Councils of counties in district. Zoe Milian Barinaga, Houston (8/31/03); Ron Crowder, LaMarque (8/31/05); Louis S. (Sam) Dell'Olio, Jr., Galveston (8/31/02); Franklin Jones, Houston (8/31/05); James A. Matthews, Jr., Texas City (8/31/05); Irvin Osborne/Lee, Houston (8/31/04); Mark Schultz, Anahuac (8/31/06); Shirley Seale, Anahuac (8/31/02); Rita Standridge, Beach City (8/31/06). Gen. Mgr., Charles Ganze, 910 Bay Area Blvd., Houston 77058.

Gulf States Marine Fisheries Commission – (1949); apptv.; 3-yr.; 3 members — 2 ex officio: exec. dir., Texas Parks & Wildlife Dept.; one member of House; one apptd. by Gov.: L. Don Perkins, Houston (3/17/02). Exec. Dir., Larry B. Simpson, PO Box 726, Ocean Springs, MS 30564.

Health, Commissioner of – (1879 as State Health Officer; 1955 changed to Commissioner of Health; 1975 changed to Director, Texas Department of Health Resources; 1977 changed to Commissioner, Texas Department of Health; apptv.; 2-yr.: Albert Hawkins ($155,000), 1100 W. 49th, Austin 78756.

Health Coordinating Council, Statewide Rural – (1997); 17 members (6 representatives of care providers; 12 apptd. by Gov.); 6 yr.; Chair Ben G. Raimer, Galveston (8/1/09); Board Members: Joan Wood Biggerstaff, Plano (8/1/05); James A. Endicott, Jr., Harker Heights (8/1/05); Karl Alonzo Floyd, Stafford (8/1/09); Janie Martinez Gonzalez, San Antonio (8/1/09); Elva C. LeBlanc, Galveston (8/1/07); Jimmie Lee Mason, Lubbock (8/1/07); Thalia H. Munoz, Rio Grande City (8/1/09); Richard Madsen Smith,Amarillo (8/1/07); Patricia L. Starck, Houston (8/1/07); Russell K. Tolman, Fort Worth (8/1/05); David A. Valdez, San Antonio (8/1/07);1100 West 49th St., Austin, TX 78756/3199; 512-458-7261.

Health and Human Services Council – (1991); 9 members apptd.; 4-yr.; Presiding Officer Jerry Kane, Corpus Christi (2/1/09); Kathleen O. Angel, Round Rock (2/1/05); Sharon J. Barnes, Freeport (2/1/09); Maryann Choi, Temple (2/1/05); Manson B. Johnson, Houston (2/1/09); Leon J. Leach, Houston (2/1/07); Ronald Luke, Austin (2/1/07); Gwyn Shea, Irving (2/1/09); Robert A. Valadez, San Antonio (2/1/05). Commissioner Albert Hawkins III ($189,000), (2/1/05). 4900 N. Lamar Blvd., Austin 78751.

Health Services, Texas Department of State – (1975); apptv.; 7 members, 4-yr.; Chair Rodolfo (Rudy) Arredondo, Lubbock (2/1/09); Beverly Barron, Odessa (2/1/07); Jaime A. Davidson, Dallas (2/1/05); Lewis E. Foxhall, Houston (2/1/09); Glenda R. Kane, Corpus Christi (2/1/09); Jeffrey A. Ross, Houston, (2/1/07); James G. (Jim) Springfield, Harlingen (2/1/05). Exec. Dir., Eduardo J. Sanchez, 1100 W. 49th, Austin 78756-3199.

Hearing Instruments, State Committee of Examiners in the Fitting and Dispensing of – (1969); apptv.; 6-yr.; expenses; 9 members: Gordon L. Bisel, Houston (12/31/05); Richard R. Davila II, Lubbock (12/31/09); Kenneth W. Earl, Orange (12/31/07); Ronald J. Cnsweiler, Dallas (10/01/07); Cara Ann Garza, Penitas (10/01/00); V. Rosemary Geraci, Lufkin (12/31/09); Jerome Kosoy, Houston (12/31/07); James McCrae, Fredericksburg (12/31/05); Audrey McDonald, Georgetown (12/31/05);. Exec. Dir., Pam K. Kaderka, 4800 N. Lamar, Ste. 150, Austin 78756.

Higher Education Coordinating Board, Texas – (1953 as temporary board; 1955 as permanent 15-member Texas Commission on Higher Education; increased to 18 members in 1965; name changed to present form in 1987); apptv.; 6-yr.; expenses; 18 members: Jerry Farrington, Dallas (8/31/07); Robert W. Shepard, Harlingen (8/31/09); Neal W. Adams, Bedford (8/31/07); Laurie Bricker, Houston (8/31/09); Ricardo G. Cigarroa, Laredo (8/31/05); Paul Foster, El Paso (8/31/09); Cathy Obriotti Green, San Antonio (8/31/05) Gerry Griffin, Hunt (8/31/05); Carey Hobbs, Waco (8/31/05); George Louis McWilliams, Texarkana (8/31/07); Nancy R. Neal, Lubbock (8/31/07); Lorraine Perryman, Odessa (8/31/07); Curtis E. Ransom, Dallas (8/31/07); A.W. (Whit) Riter III, Tyler (8/31/05); Terdema L. Ussery II, Dallas (8/31/050). Commissioner of Higher Education, Raymond A. Paredes, ($150,000) PO Box 12788, Austin 78711; 512-427-6101.

Higher Education Tuition Board, Prepaid – (1995); apptv.; expenses; 6-yr.; 2 members: State Comptroller, 2 apptd. by Lt. Gov., 2 apptd. by Gov. Gov's apptees: Michael D. Gollob, Tyler (2/1/03); Beth Miller Weakley, San Antonio (2/1/05).

Historical Commission, Texas – (1953); apptv.; expenses; 6-yr.; 17 members: Chair John L. Nau III, Houston (2/1/09); Board Members: Thomas E. Alexander, Fredericksburg (2/1/09); Jane C. Barnhill, Brenham (2/1/07); Bob Bowman, Lufkin (2/1/09); Earl P. Broussard, Austin (2/1/11); Diane D. Bumpas, Dallas (2/1/11); Shirley W. Caldwell, Albany (2/1/07); Donna Dean Carter, Austin (2/1/11); Lareatha H. Clay, Dallas (2/1/07); Frank W. Gorman,

Jr., El Paso (2/1/07); David A. Gravelle, Dallas (2/1/07); Albert F. (Boo) Hausser, San Antonio (2/1/09); Sara Armstrong (Sarita) Hixon, Houston (2/1/11); Eileen Johnson, Ph.D., Lubbock (2/1/03); Thomas R. Phillips, Houston (2/1/05); Marcus Warren Watson, Plano (2/1/11); Frank D. Yturria, Brownsville (2/1/07); Commissioner Emeritus, T. R. Fehrenbach, San Antonio). Exec. Dir., F. Lawerence Oaks ($85,000), PO Box 12276, Austin 78711; 512-463-6100.

Historical Records Advisory Board, Texas – (1976); apptv.; 3-yr.; 9 members: State Archivist, 6 apptd. by by director and librarian of Texas State Library and Archives Comm.; two members apptd. by Gov. Public members: Martha Doty Freeman, Austin (2/1/02); Richard L. Hooverson, Belton (2/1/06). State Historical Records Coordinator, Chris LaPlante, State Library, PO Box 12927, Austin 78711.

Housing and Community Affairs, Board of Texas Dept. of – (1979 as Texas Housing Agency; merged with Department of Community Affairs and name changed in 1991); apptv.; expenses; 6-yr.; 7 members: Chair Elizabeth M. Anderson, Dallas (1/31/07); Board Members: Shadrick Bogany, Missouri City (1/31/05); Kent C. Conine, Frisco (1/31/09); Vidal Gonzalez, Del Rio (1/31/05); Patrick R. Gordon, El Paso (1/31/09); Norberto Salinas, Mission (1/31/07. Exec. Dir. Edwina Carrington ($112,352), 507 Sabine, Austin 78701.

Housing Corp, Texas State Affordable – 6-yr.; 5 members: Jesse Coffey, Denton (2/1/09); Jo Van Hovel, Temple (2/1/07); Thomas A. Leeper, Huntsville (2/1/07); Charles G. Rencher, Sugar Land (2/1/09); Jerry Romero, El Paso (2/1/05);. Pres. David Long, P.O. Box 12637, Austin, TX 78711-2637; 512-477-3555.

Industrialized Building Code Council, Texas – Martin J. Garza, Seguin (2/01/04); David L Beicher, San Antonio (2/01/03); Joe D. Campos, Dallas (2/01/04); Mark G. Delaney, Tomball (2/01/03); Craig N. Farmer, Lubbock (2/01/04); Rudy V. Gomez, Brownsville (2/01/04); James A. Kingham, Nacogdoches (2/01/04); Michael G. Mount, Burleson (2/01/03); Gary L. Purser, Amarillo (2/01/03); Douglas O. Robinson, Fort Worth (2/01/03); Ravi Shah, Carrollton (2/01/03); Arthur N. Sosa, Corpus Christi (2/01/04). Exec. Dir. William H. Kuntz Jr. 512-463-3173.

Information Resources, Department of – (1981 as Automated Information and Telecommunications Council; name changed in 1990); 6-yr.; expenses; 3 members recommended by Speaker of House, 3 by Lt. Gov.; 3 by Gov.: 9 members: Chair William L. Transier, Houston (2/1/09); Lance K. Bruun, Corpus Christi (2/1/07); Larry Leibrock, Austin (2/1/07); M. Adam Mahmood, Ph.D., El Paso (2/1/07); Phillip (Keith) Morrow, Southlake (2/1/11); Cliff Mountain, Austin (2/1/09); Willliam Michael Wachel, Dallas (2/1/09); Ex Officio Members: Robert Bray (2/1/07); Brian Rawson (2/1/07); George Rios (2/1/07). Chief Technology Officer, Larry Olson ($120,000), PO Box 13564, Austin 78711.

Insurance, Commissioner of – Mike Geeslin ($163,800), PO Box 149104, Austin 78714.

Interstate Mining Compact Commission – Melvin Hodgkiss, Austin. Exec. Dir.: Gregory Conrad, 459B Carlisle Drv., Herndon, VA 22070.

Interstate Oil and Gas Compact Commission, Texas Rep. – (1935); ex officio or apptv., according to Gov's. choice; per diem and expenses. (Approximately 150 other appointees serve on various committees.) Official representatives for Texas: Victor Carrillo, Michael L. Williams, Barry A. Williamson. Exec. Dir., Christine Hansen, PO Box 53127, Oklahoma City, OK 73152.

Interstate Parole Compact Administrator – (1951); apptv.: Knox Fitzpatrick, Dallas.

Jail Standards, Texas Commission on – (1975); apptv.; 6-yr.; expenses; 9 members: Chair David Gutierrez, Lubbock (2/1/09); Board Members: Albert L. Black, Austin (1/31/11); Stanley D. (Stan) Egger, Abilene (1/31/11); Gonzalo Gallegos, San Antonio (1/31/09); Mark D. Gilliam, Rockport (2/1/09); William C. Morrow, Midland (1/31/07); Evelyn (Kelly) Moyer, Magnolia (1/31/07); Michael M. Seale, M.D., Houston (1/31/05); Charles J. Sebesta, Caldwell (1/31/07). Exec. Dir., Terry Julian ($61,000), PO Box 12985, Austin 78711.

Judicial Conduct, State Commission on – (1965 as 9-member Judicial Qualifications Commission; name changed in 1977 to present form and membership raised to (11); expenses; 6-yr.; 11 members: 5 apptd. by Supreme Court; 2 apptd. by State Bar; 4 apptd. by Gov. as follows: Chair James A. Hall, San Antonio, (11/19/05); Vice-Chair Monica A. Gonzalez, San Antonio, (11/19/03); Secretary, Rex G. Baker, III, Dripping Springs, (11/19/09); Board Members: R.C. Allen, III, Corpus Christi, (11/19/05); Faye Barksdale, Arlington, (11/19/07); Michael R. Fields, Houston, (11/19/09); Gilbert A. Herrera, Houston, (11/19/09); Ronald D. Krist, Houston, (11/19/07); Joseph B. Morris, Dallas, (11/19/07); Kathleen H. Olivares, El Paso, (11/19/05); William A. (Buck) Prewitt, III, Temple, (11/19/09). Exec. Dir., Seana Beckerman Willing ($100,000), PO Box 12265, Austin 78711.

Judicial Council, Texas – (1929 as Texas Civil Judicial Council; name changed in 1975); ex officio terms vary; apptv.; 6-yr. terms; expenses; 19 members, increased to 22 in 1997: 16 ex officio and 6 apptd. from general public. Public members: Jean Birmingham, Marshall (6/30/03); Lance Richard Byrd, Dallas (6/30/07); Joseph Alan Callier, Kingwood (6/30/03); Delia Martínez-Carian, San Antonio (6/30/07); José Luis López, Crystal City (6/30/05); Ann Manning, Lubbock (6/10/05). Exec. Dir., Jerry L. Benedict, PO Box 12066, Austin 78711.

Judicial Districts Board – (1985); 12 ex officio members (term in other office); one apptv. (4 yrs.); ex officio: Chief Justice of Texas Supreme Court; Presiding Judge, Court of Criminal Appeals; Presiding Judge of each of 9 Administrative Judicial Districts; press. of Texas Judicial Council; apptee: Joseph W. Wolfe, Sherman (12/12/02).

Judicial Districts of Texas, Admin., Presiding Judges of – (See Administrative Judicial Districts, Presiding Judges).

Juneteenth Cultural and Historical Emancipation Commission, Texas – (1997); expenses; 6 yr.; 11 members; 5 ex officio, nonvoting: 2 apptd. by Lt. Gov., 2 apptd. by Speaker of House, and exec. dir. of Texas Historical Comm.; 6 apptd by Gov.: Chair Rep. Al Edwards, Houston); Board Members: Byron E. Miller, San Antonio (2/1/09); Eddie Price Richardson, Lubbock (2/1/05); Stella Wilson Roland, Austin (2/1/05); Willard Stimpson, Dallas (2/1/07); Linda Tarr, Houston (2/1/07).

Juvenile Probation Commission, Texas – (1981); apptv.; 6-yr.; expenses; 9 members — 3 judges of District Courts and 6 private citizens: Chair Cheryl Lee Shannon, Cedar Hill (8/31/09); Vice-Chair Betsy Lake, Houston (8/31/05); Board Members: Jean H. Boyd (2/1/11); Bob Ed Culver, Jr., Canadian (8/31/09); Keith H. Kuttler, College Station (8/31/07); Lyle T. Larson, San Antonio (8/31/05); Roberto I. Lopez, Pasadena (8/31/09); Barbara J. Punch, Missouri City (8/31/07); Carlos Villa, El Paso (8/31/05). Exec. Dir., Vicki Spriggs ($90,000), PO Box 13547, Austin 78711.

Land Board, School – (1939); one ex officio (term in other office); 2 apptd. — one by Atty. Gen. and one by Gov. for 2-yr. term; per diem and expenses; ex officio member: Comm. of General Land Office; appt'd members: Todd F. Barth, Houston (8/29/05); David S. Herrmann, San Antonio (8/29/05).

Land Surveying, Texas Board of Professional – (1979); formed from consolidation of membership of Board of Examiners of Licensed Land Surveyors, est. 1977, and State Board of Registration for Public Surveyors, est. 1955); apptv.; 6-yr.; 10 members — Commissioner of General Land Office serving by statute; 3 members of general public, 2 licensed land surveyors, 4 registered public surveyors, as follows: Chair Douglas Turner, League City (1/31/05); Board Members: Steve Hofer, Midland (1/31/05); Daniel Martinez, Lubbock (1/31/05); Kelly Neumann, San Antonio (1/31/09); A. W. Osborn, Tyler (1/31/07); Stephen Titus (Ty) Runyan, Austin (1/31/09); David G. Smyth, Devine (1/31/07); William C. Wilson, Jr., San Angelo (1/31/05). Exec. Dir., Sandy Smith ($47,000), 7701 N. Lamar, Ste. 400, Austin 78752.

Lands, Board for Lease of University – (1929 as 3-member board; membership increased to 4 in 1985); ex officio; term in other office; 4 members: Commissioner of General Land Office, 2 members of Board of Regents of University of Texas, 1 member Board of Regents of Texas A&M University.

Lavaca-Navidad River Authority, Board of Directors – (1954 as 7-member Jackson County Flood Control District; reorganized as 9-member board in 1959; name changed to present form in 1969); apptv.; 6-yr.; per diem and expenses; 9 members: John Alcus Cotten, Jr., Ganado (5/1/09); Jackie Ann Fowler, Ganado (5/1/09); Sherry Kay Frels, Edna (5/1/07); Basilio R. Jimenez, Edna (5/1/07); Ronald Edwin Kubecka, Palacios (5/1/09); Mike Myers, Edna (5/1/05); John J. Shutt, Edna (5/1/07); Sharla Vee Strauss, La Ward (5/1/05); Willard E. Ulbricht, Edna (5/1/05). Gen. Mgr., Patrick Brzozowski ($110,000) PO Box 429, Edna 77957.

Law Enforcement Officer Standards & Education, Comm. on – (1965); expenses; 14 members; 5 ex officio: Atty. Gen., Directory of Public Safety, Commissioner of Education, Exec. Dir. of Governor's Office Criminal Justice Division, and Commissioner of Higher Education; 9 apptv. members: Presiding Officer, Daniel J. Smith, Belton (8/30/07); Board Members: Steven M. Byrd, Dallas (8/30/07); Romulo Chavez, Houston (8/30/09); Cathy Ellison, Austin (8/10/07); Charles R. Hall, Midland (8/30/05); William B. Jackson, Arlington (8/30/05); Betty Harper Murphy, Fredericksburg (8/10/09); Joe A. Stivers, Huntsville (8/30/07); Gary M. Swindle, Brownsboro (8/30/09). Exec. Dir., D.C. Jim Dozier ($76,000), 6330 E. Hwy. 290, Ste. 200, Austin 78723.

Law Examiners, Board of – Nine attorneys apptd. by Supreme Court biennially for 2-year terms expiring September 30 of odd-numbered years. Compensation set by Supreme Court not to exceed $20,000 per annum. Exec. Dir., Julia Vaughan, PO Box 13486, Austin 78711.

Law Library Board, State – (1971); ex officio; expenses; 3 members: Chief Justice State Supreme Court, Presiding Judge Court of Criminal Appeals and Atty. General. Dir., Kay Schlueter ($58,000), PO Box 12367, Austin 78711.

Legislative Budget Board – (1949); 10 members; 6 ex officio members: Lt. Gov.; Speaker of House; Chmn., Senate Finance Comm.; Chmn., Senate State Affairs Comm.; Chmn., House Appropriations Comm.; Chmn., House Ways and Means Comm.; plus 4 other members of Legislature. Director, John Keel, PO Box 12666, Austin 78711-2666.

Legislative Council, Texas – (1949); 17 ex officio members — 4 senators named by Lt. Gov.; 9 representatives named by Speaker; Chmn., House Administration Committee; Chmn., Senate Administration Committee; Lt. Gov.; and Speaker. Exec. Dir. Mark Brown, PO Box 12128, Austin 78711.

Legislative Redistricting Board – (1948); 5 ex officio members; term in other office: Lt. Gov., Speaker of House, Atty. Gen., Comptroller and Commissioner of General Land Office.

Librarian, State – (Originally est. in 1839; present office est. 1909); apptv., indefinite term: Robert S. Martin ($65,000), PO Box 12927, Austin 78711.

Library and Archives Commission, Texas State – (1909 as 5-member Library and State Historical Commission; number of members increased to 6 in 1953; name changed to present form in 1979); apptv.; per diem and expenses on duty; 6-yr.; 6 members: Presiding Officer, Sandra Pickett, Liberty (9/28/09); Board Members: Chris A. Brisack, Edinburg (9/28/05); Diana Rae Hester Cox, Canyon (9/28/07); Martha Doty Freeman, Austin (9/28/09); Cruz G. Hernandez, Burleson (9/28/09); Sandra Gunter Holland, Pleasanton (9/28/07); Elizabeth Sanders, Arlington (9/28/05). Dir. and Librarian Peggy D. Rudd ($85,000), PO Box 12927, Austin 78711.

Library, State Legislative Reference – (1909); indefinite term; Director: Dale W. Propp, Box 12488, Austin 78711.

Licensing and Regulation, Texas Department on – (1989); apptv.; 6-yr.; expenses; 6 members: Chair Leopoldo R. Vasquez, III, Houston (2/1/05); Board Members: Frank S. Denton, Conroe (2/1/09); Luann Roberts Morgan, Midland (2/1/09); Fred N. Moses, Plano (2/1/09); Gina Parker, Waco (2/1/07); Bill C. Pittman, Austin (2/1/07); Patricia Stout, San Antonio (2/1/05). Exec. Dir., William H. Kuntz Jr. ($76,000), PO Box 12157, Austin 78711.

Lottery Commission, Texas – (1993); 6-yrs.; apptv.; expenses; 3 members: C. Thomas Clowe Jr., Waco (2/1/05); James A. Cox Jr., Austin (2/1/09); Rolando Olvera, Jr., Dallas (2/1/07). Exec. Dir, (vacancy) ($110,000), PO Box 16630, Austin 78761-6630.

Lower Colorado River Authority – (See Colorado River Authority, Lower).

Lower Concho River Water and Soil Conservation Authority – (See Concho River Water and Soil Conservation, Lower).

Lower Neches Valley Authority – (See Neches Valley Authority, Lower).

Marriage & Family Therapists, Texas State Board of Examiners of – (1991); apptd.; 6 yrs.; per diem and transportation expenses; 9 members: Chair Waymon R. Hinson, Abilene (2/1/07); Joe Ann Clack, Missouri City (2/1/09); Sandra L. DeSobe, Houston (2/1/07); B. W. McClendon, Austin (2/1/07); Asa Wesley Sampson, Sr., Houston (2/1/11); Brenda VanAmburgh, Fort Worth (2/1/05); Jackie Weimer, Plano (2/1/05); Beverly Walker Womack, Jacksonville (2/1/09). Exec. Dir., Andrew T. Marks, Dept. of Health, 1100 W. 49th St., Austin 78756-3183.

Medical Examiners, Texas State Board of – (1907 as 12-member board, membership raised to 15 in 1981, raised to 18 in 1993); apptv.; 6-yr.; per diem on duty; 18 members: Chair Roberta Kalafut, Abilene (4/13/07); Lee S. Anderson, M.D., Fort Worth (4/13/09); Jose Manuel Benavides, San Antonio (4/14/05); Christine L. Canterbury, Corpus Christi (4/13/07); David Garza, Laredo (4/14/05); Amanullah Khan, M.D., Dallas (4/13/09); Thomas D. Kirksey, Austin (4/13/07); Keith E. Miller, Center (4/13/09); Elvira Pascua/Lim, Lubbock (4/13/07); John W. Pate, El Paso (4/13/07); Larry Price, Temple (4/13/09); Public Members: Patricia Blackwell, Midland (4/13/07); Melinda S. Fredricks, Conroe (1/13/09); Eddie J. Miles, Jr., San Antonio (4/13/07); Annette P. Raggette, Austin (4/13/09); Nancy M. Seliger, Amarillo (4/14/05); Paulette B. Southard, Alice (4/14/05); Timothy J. Turner, Houston (4/13/09). Exec. Dir., Donald Patrick ($85,000), PO Box 149134, Austin 78714-9134.

Medical Physicists, Texas Board of Licensure for Professional – (1991); apptv.; 6-yrs.; 9 members: Presiding Officer, Philip D. Bourland, Ph.D., Temple (2/1/05); Board Members: Shannon D. Cox, M.D., Austin (2/1/03); Walter Grant, Ph.D., Bellaire (2/1/09); Lamk M. Lamki, M.D., Houston (2/1/07); Adrian D. LeBlanc, Ph.D., Houston (2/1/07); Isabel C. Menendez, M.D., Corpus Christi (2/1/03); Rebecca C. Middleton, Ph.D., De Soto (2/1/05); Richard E. Wendt, III, Ph.D., Houston (2/1/07); Public Member, Kumar Krishen, Ph.D., Houston (2/1/05). Exec. Sec., Jeanette Hilsabeck.

Midwestern State University, Board of Regents – (1959); apptv.; 6-yr.; 9 members: Chair Mac Cannedy, Jr., Wichita Falls

(2/25/06); Secretary, John C. Bridgman, Wichita Falls (2/25/06); Board Members: Pamela Odom Gough, Graham (2/25/08); Stephen A. Gustafson, Wichita Falls (2/25/10); Patricia A. Haywood, Wichita Falls (6/09/08); Munir A. Lanani, Wichita Falls (2/25/10); Don Ross Malone, Vernon (2/25/08); David Stephens, Plano (2/25/06); Ben F. Wible, Sherman (2/25/10). Pres., Dr. Jesse W. Rogers, 3400 Taft, Wichita Falls 76308.

Military Facilities Commission, Texas – (1935 as 3-member National Guard Armory Board; reorganized as 6-member board in 1981; name changed 1997); 6-yr.; 6 members: Chair Sandra Paret, Dallas (4/30/06); Treasurer, Jorge Perez, McAllen (4/30/05); Public Members: Regino J. Gonzales, Galena Park (4/30/09); Delores Ann Harper, San Antonio (4/30/07); Larry W. Jackson, Temple (4/30/09); Chao/Chiung Lee, Houston (4/30/09); National Guard Member, Michael H. Taylor Major Gen., Lufkin (4/30/07). Exec. Dir. John A. Wells ($57,000), PO Box 5426, Austin 78763.

Municipal Retirement System (See Retirement System, Municipal, Board of Trustees).

National Guard Armory Board, Texas – (see Military Facilities Commission, Texas).

Natural Resource Conservation Commission, Texas (See Environmental Quality, Texas Commission on).

Neches River Municipal Water Authority, Upper – (Est. 1953 as 9-member board; membership changed to 3 in 1959); apptv.; 6-yr.; 3 members: Joe Crutcher, Palestine (2/1/07); Jesse D. Hickman, Palestine (2/1/09); Robert E. McKelvey, Palestine (2/1/05). Gen. Mgr., T.G. Mallory, PO Box 1965, Palestine 75802.

Neches Valley Authority, Lower – (1933); apptv.; per diem and expenses on duty; 6-yr.; 9 members: Lonnie Arrington, Beaumont (7/28/07); Brian Babin, Woodville (7/28/07); Bill Clark, Beaumont (7/28/09); Sue Cleveland, Lumberton (7/28/09); Jimmie Ruth Cooley, Woodville (7/28/09); Kathleen Thea Jackson, Beaumont (7/28/09); Steven M. McReynolds, Groves (7/28/07); Cheryl Olesen, Beaumont (7/28/05); Olan Webb, Silsbee (7/28/05). Gen. Mgr. Robert Stroder, PO Box 5117, Beaumont 77726-5117.

Nueces River Authority Board of Directors – (1953 as Nueces River Conservation and Reclamation District; name changed in 1971); apptv.; 6-yr.; per diem and expenses; 21 members: President, Patty Puig Mueller, Corpus Christi (2/1/07); Vice President, J. R. Schneider, Sr., George West (2/1/05); Secretary, Roxana P. Tom, Campbellton (2/1/05); Board Members: Steve G. Beever, Pearsall (2/1/05); W. Scott Bledsoe, III, Oakville (2/1/03); Joe M. Cantu, Pipe Creek (2/1/07); William I. Dillard, Uvalde (2/1/07); Robert M. Dullnig, San Antonio (2/1/07); Eddie L. Garcia, Corpus Christi (2/1/07); Ernest R. Garza, Robstown (2/1/05); John William Howell, Portland (2/1/03); Yale Leland Kerby, Uvalde (2/1/11); Lindsey Alfred Koenig, Orange Grove); Dan S. Leyendecker, Corpus Christi (2/1/07); August Linnartz, Jr., Carrizo Springs (2/1/03); James Richard Marmion, III, Carrizo Springs (2/1/11); Rolando B. Pablos, San Antonio (2/1/09); Betty Ann Peden, Hondo (2/1/09); Scott James Petty, Hondo (2/1/07); Thomas M. Reding, Jr., Portland (2/1/03); Fidel R. Rul, Jr., Alice (2/1/11). Exec. Dir., Con Mims, PO Box 349, Uvalde 78802-0349.

Nurse Examiners, State Board of – (1909 as 6-member board; reorganized and membership increased to 9 in 1981); apptv.; per diem and expenses; 6-yr.; 9 members: President, Linda Rounds, Galveston (1/31/11); Vice President, Phyllis Caves Rawley, El Paso (1/31/09); Joyce M. Adams, Houston (1/31/07); George Buchenau, Amarillo (1/31/09); Virginia Milam Campbell, Mesquite (1/31/07); Blanca Rosa (Rosie) Garcia, Corpus Christi (1/31/11); Richard Gibbs, Mesquite (1/31/07); Rachel Gomez., Harlingen (1/31/07); Brenda S. Jackson, San Antonio (1/31/09); Beverly Jean Nutall, Bryan (1/31/11); Public Members: Deborah Hughes Bell, Abilene (1/31/11); Anita Palmer, Olney (2/1/09); Frank Sandoval, Jr., San Antonio (1/31/07). Exec. Dir., Katherine A. Thomas ($62,000), 333 Guadalupe, Suite 3-460, Austin 78701.

Nursing Facility Administrators, Texas Board of – (Abolished effective Sept. 1997; responsibilities transferred to the Texas Department of Human Services.)

Occupational Therapy Examiners, Texas Board of – (1983 as 6-member board; increased to 9 in 1999); apptv.; 6-yr.; per diem and expenses; 9 members: Chair Jean Polichino, Houston (2/1/05); Board Members: Judith E. Brown, Edinburg (2/1/05); Grace L. Butler., Pearland (2/1/05); David G. Cabrales, Dallas (2/1/07); Michael Carreon, El Paso (2/1/09); Dely De Guia Cruz, Houston (2/1/09); Cecilia Fierro, OTR, El Paso (2/1/07); Joseph A. Messmer, Corpus Christi (2/1/07); Clarissa A. Meyers, OTR, McAllen (2/1/07). Exec. Dir., John Maline ($51,198), 333 Guadalupe St., Ste. 2-510, Austin 78701.

Optometry Board, Texas – (1921 as 6-member State Board of Examiners in Optometry; name changed to present form in 1981 and membership increased to 9); apptv.; per diem; 6-yr.; 9 members: Fred Farias, III, McAllen (1/31/07); D. Dixon Golden, Center (1/31/09); Sharon Johnson, Arlington (1/31/07); Mark A. Latta, Ama-

rillo (1/31/05); Randall N. Reichle, Houston (1/31/09); Public Members: Ann Appling Bradford, Midland (1/31/05); Judy M. Eidson, San Antonio (1/31/07); Elsa Silva, El Paso (1/31/09). Exec. Dir., Chris Kloeris ($60,000), 333 Guadalupe St., Ste. 2-420, Austin 78701.

Orthotics and Prosthetics, Texas Board of – (1998); apptv.; compensation and travel expenses; 6-yr.; 6 members: Scott B. Atha, Pflugerville (2/1/03); Erin Elizabeth Berling, Coppell (2/1/07); Wanda Furgason, Brownwood (2/1/05); Richard Michael Neider, Lubbock (2/1/07); Stanley E. Thomas, San Antonio (2/1/03); Lupe M. Young, San Antonio (2/1/05).

Pardons and Paroles, Texas Board of – (1893 as Board of Pardon Advisers; changed in 1936 to Board of Pardons and Paroles with 3 members; membership increased to 6 in 1983; made a division of the Texas Department of Criminal Justice in 1990); apptv.; 6-yr.; (chairman, $85,500; members, $83,200 each); 7 members: Chair Rissie Owens, Huntsville (2/1/09); Jose L. Aliseda, Jr., Beeville (2/1/09); Charles Franklin Aycock, Amarillo (2/1/11); Jackie DeNoyelles, Flint (2/1/09); Linda F. Garcia, Angleton (2/1/07); Juanita M. Gonzalez, Round rock (2/1/09); Elvis Hightower, Georgetown (2/1/07).209 W. 14th St., Ste. 500, Austin 78701.

Parks and Wildlife Commission, Texas – (1963 as 3-member board; membership increased to 6 in 1971; increased to 9 in 1983); apptv.; expenses; 6-yr.; 9 members: Chair Joseph B.C. Fitzsimons, San Antonio (2/1/07); J. Robert Brown, El Paso (2/1/09); T. Dan Friedkin, Houston (2/1/11); Al Henry, Houston (2/1/05); Ned S. Holmes, Houston (2/1/09); Peter M. Holt, San Antonio (2/1/11); Philip Montgomery, Dallas (2/1/07); John D. Parker, Lufkin (2/1/09); Donato D. Ramos, Laredo (2/1/07). Chairman-Emeritus, Lee Marshall Bass, Fort Worth. Exec. Dir., Robert L. Cook ($115,000), 4200 Smith School Rd., Austin 78744.

Pecos River Compact Commissioner – (1942); apptv.; 6-yr.; expenses: Julian W. Thrasher Jr., Monahans (1/23/05). ($32,247).

Pension Board – For old age, blind and dependent children's assistance, see Human Services, State Board of. For retirement pay to state and municipal employees and teachers, see proper category under Retirement.

Pension Review Board, State – (1979); apptv.; 6-yr.; 9 members — one senator apptd. by Lt. Gov., one representative apptd. by Speaker, 7 apptd. by Gov. as follows: Chair Frederick E. Rowe, Jr., Dallas (1/31/09); Vice/Chair Rafael A. Cantu, Mission (1/31/05); Board Members: Paul A. Braden, El Paso (1/31/05); Roy Valentine Casanova, Jr., San Antonio (1/31/07); Richard Earl McElreath, Amarillo (1/31/07); Norman W. Parrish, The Woodlands (1/31/07); Rep. Allan B. Ritter, Nederland (1/31/05); Shari O. Shivers, Austin (1/31/09); Sen. John Whitmire, Houston (1/31/09). Exec. Dir., Virginia Smith ($52,000), PO Box 13498, Austin 78711.

Perfusionists, Texas State Board of Examiners of – (Abolished effective Sept. 2005; responsibilities transferred to the Texas Department of Human Services.)

Pest Control Board, Texas Structural – (1971 as 7-member board, membership raised to 9 in 1979); apptv.; 6-yr.; expenses; 9 members — 3 ex officio: Commissioner of Agriculture; Commissioner of Health; and head of Entomology Dept., Texas A&M University; 6 apptv. members: Chair John Lee Morrison, San Antonio (2/1/07); Board Members: Charles Brown, Bryan (2/1/07); Tomas Cantu, McAllen (2/1/05); Madeline Gamble, Dallas (2/1/05); Brenda Hill, Nacogdoches (2/1/09); Richard M. Hogers, Euless (2/1/09) Exec. Dir., Dale R. Burnett, ($92,000), 1106 Clayton Ln., Ste. 100 LW, Austin 78723-1066.

Pharmacy, Texas State Board of – (1907 as 6-member board; membership increased to 9 in 1981); apptv.; 6-yr.; 9 members: Pres. Oren M. Peacock Jr., Sachse (8/31/05); Vice Pres. Woodrow M. Brimberry, Austin (8/31/07); Treas. Kim A. Caldwell, Plano (8/31/09); Roger W. Anderson, Dr., Houston (8/31/05); Juluette Bartlett-Pack Houston (8/31/07); Rosemary F. Combs, El Paso (8/31/05); Wilson Benjamin Fry, San Benito (8/31/09); Doyle Eugene High, Haskell (8/31/07); Marcelo Laijas, Jr., Floresville (8/31/09). Exec. Dir., Gay Dodson ($70,000), 333 Guadalupe St., Ste. 3-600, Austin 78701.

Physical Therapy and Occupational Therapy Examiners, Executive Council of – (1971); apptv.; 2-yr.; expenses; 5 members: Presiding Officer, L. Suzan Kedron-Lyn, Dallas (2/1/07); Board Members: David Cabrales, Dallas (2/1/05); Sylvia A. Davila, San Antonio (2/1/05); Clarissa A. Meyers, McAllen (2/1/05); Dora Ochoa-Rutledge, San Antonio (2/1/05). Exec. Dir. John Maline, 333 Guadalupe St., Ste. 2-510, Austin 78701.

Physical Therapy and Occupational Therapy Examiners, Texas State Board of – (1971); apptv.; 6-yr.; expenses; 9 members: Chair Sylvia Davila, P.T., San Antonio (1/31/05); Board Members: Karen Gordon, P.T., Port O'Connor (1/31/07); Michael Grady Hines, P.T., Tyler (1/31/05); Manoranjan Mahadeva, The Woodlands (1/31/09); Dora Ochoa-Rutledge, San Antonio (1/31/07); Melinda A. Rodriguez, P.T., San Antonio (1/31/09); George Scott, Lubbock (1/31/07); Joseph J. Spano, P.T., Wharton (1/31/09); Mary Thompson, P.T., Celina (1/31/07). Exec. Dir. John Maline ($51,198), 333

Guadalupe St., Ste. 2-510, Austin 78701.

Plumbing Examiners, State Board of – (1947 as 6-member board; membership increased to 9 in 1981); apptv.; expenses; 6-yr.; Presiding Officer, John Hatchel, Woodway (9/05/07); Board Members: Tammy Betancourt, Houston (9/05/09); Min Chu, P.E., Houston (9/05/05); Louis A. Cortes, New Braunfels (9/05/07); Robert Franklin Jalnos, San Antonio (9/05/09); Richard Allen Lord, Pasadena (9/05/09); Carol McLemore, La Marque (9/05/05); Robert A. (Al) Tarver, Kingsland (9/05/07); Michael Thamm, Cuero (9/05/05). Exec. Dir. Robert L. Maxwell ($62,000), 929 E. 41st, Austin 78751.

Podiatric Medical Examiners, State Board of – (1923 as 6-member State Board of Chiropody Examiners; name changed to State Board of Podiatry Examiners in 1967; made 9-member board in 1981; name changed to present form in 1997); apptv.; 6-yr.; expenses; 9 members: Richard C. Adam, San Antonio (7/10/09); Sandra E. Cuellar, Dallas (7/10/05); Bradford Glass, Midland (7/10/05); Paul Kinberg, Dallas (7/10/09); Donald M. Lynch, Troy (7/10/07); Bruce A. Scudday, El Paso (7/10/07); Public Members: Doris A. Couch, Burleson (7/10/05); Carol Lee Roberts/Baker, Houston (7/10/07); Matthew Washington, Missouri City (7/10/09). Exec. Dir. Jim Zukowski, ($52,000), 333 Guadalupe St., Ste. 2-320, Austin 78701.

Polygraph Examiners Board – (1965); apptv.; 6-yr.; 6 members: Elizabeth P. Bellegarde, El Paso (6/18/07); Edward L. Hendrickson, Katy (6/18/05); Priscilla Jane Kleinpeter, Amarillo (6/18/09); Lawrence D. Mann, Plano (6/18/09); Horacio Ortiz, Corpus Christi (6/18/07); Andy Sheppard, Rowlett (6/18/09); Hugh Douglas Sutton, Lubbock (6/18/05). Exec. Officer, Frank Di Tucci ($40,000), PO Box 4087, Austin 78773.

Preservation Board, State – (1983); 2-yr.; 7 members — 4 ex officio: Gov., Lt. Gov., Speaker and Architect of Capitol; 3 apptv.: one apptd. by Gov., one senator apptd. by Lt. Gov. and one representative apptd. by Speaker. Gov's. apptee: Jocelyn Levi Straus, San Antonio (2/05). Exec. Dir., Gaye Polan ($115,000), PO Box 13286, Austin 78711.

Prison Board, Texas – (See Criminal Justice, Texas Dept. of)

Prison Industry Oversight Authority, Private Sector – (1997); 6-yr.; expenses; 6 ex officio: Senate member, House member, Texas Youth Commission, Department of Criminal Justice, Texas Work Force Commission, employer liaison; 9 apptd. members: Presiding Officer, Kathy L. Flanagan, Houston (2/1/07); Board Members: Lillian Barajas, El Paso (2/1/09); Burnis Brazil, Missouri City (2/1/09); William B. Brod, Granbury (2/1/11); S. Roxanne Carter, Amarillo (2/1/09); Suzanne C. Hart, Ph.D., San Antonio (2/1/11); Brian L. Hatley, El Paso (2/1/07); Raymond G. Henderson, Buda); Jeffery R. LaBroski, Richmond (2/1/07).

Private Security Bureau, Texas – (1969 as Board of Private Investigators and Private Security Agencies; name and makeup of board changed, 1999 to Texas Commission on Private Security; name changed in 2003 by 78th Leg.); apptv.; expenses; 6-yr.; 10 members — 1 ex officio: Dir., Dept. of Public Safety; 7 apptd. members: Chair George B. Craig, Corpus Christi (1/31/05); Secretary, Michael H. Samulin, San Antonio (1/31/07); Board Members: Stella Caldera, Houston (1/31/11); John E. Chism, Irving (1/31/09); Howard H. Johnsen, Dallas (1/31/11); Linda J. Sadler, Lubbock (1/31/07); Harold G. Warren, Austin (1/31/09).

Produce Recovery Fund Board – (1977 as 3-member board; membership increased to 6 in 1981); apptv.; expenses; 6-yr.; 6 members — 2 each from commission merchants, general public and producer representatives. Ralph Diaz, Corpus Christi (1/31/05); Steven Dexter Jones, Lubbock (1/31/01); Ly H. Nguyen, Lake Jackson (1/31/03); Joyce Cook Obst, Alamo (1/31/03); Jay Pack, Dallas (1/31/05); Byron Edward White, Arlington (1/31/01). Admin., Margaret Alvarez, PO Box 12847, Austin 78711.

Psychologists, Texas Board of Examiners of – (1969 as 6-member board; membership increased to 9 in 1981); apptv.; 6-yr.; per diem and expenses; 9 members: Pauline Amos Clansy, Houston, (10/31/07); Gary R. Elkins, Temple, (10/31/09); Arthur E. Hernandez, San Antonio, (10/31/07); Ruben Rendon, Jr., Dallas, (10/31/05); Carl E. Settles, Killeen, (10/31/09); Stephanie Sokolosky, Wichita Falls (10/31/05); Public Members: Betty Lou (Penny) Angelo, Midland, (10/31/07); Catherine Bernell Estrada, Dallas, (10/31/09); Michael D. Nogueira, Fredericksburg, (10/31/05). Exec. Dir., Sherry L. Lee ($52,000), 333 Guadalupe St., Ste. 2-450, Austin 78701.

Public Finance Authority, Texas – (1984, assumed duties of Texas Building Authority); apptv.; per diem and expenses; 6-yr.; membership increased from 3 to 6 in 1991: Chair R. David Kelly, Dallas (2/1/07); J. Vaughn Brock, Austin (2/1/07); Mark A. Ellis, Houston (2/1/09); Linda McKenna, Harlingen (2/1/11); H.L. (Bert) Mijares, Jr., El Paso (2/1/09); Ruth Schiermeyer, Lubbock (2/1/07); Marcellus A. Taylor, Dallas (2/1/11). Exec. Dir., Kimberly

K. Edwards ($95,000), 300 W. 15th St., Ste. 411, Austin 78711.

Public Safety Commission – (1935); apptv.; expenses; 6-yr.; 3 members: James B. Francis Jr., Dallas (12/31/05); Robert B. Holt, Midland (12/31/01); M. Colleen McHugh, Corpus Christi (12/31/03). Dir. of Texas Dept. of Public Safety, Col. Thomas A. Davis ($102,000), PO Box 4087, Austin 78773-0001.

Public Utility Commission – (1975); apptv.; 6-yr., 3 members at $105,000-$107,500: Chair Paul Hudson, Austin (9/1/09); Commissioners: Julie Caruthers Parsley, Austin (9/1/05); Barry Thomas Smitherman, Houston (9/1/07). Exec. Dir., W. Lane Lanford ($92,000), PO Box 13326, Austin 78711-3326.

Racing Commission, Texas – (1986); 6-yr.; per diem and expenses; 8 members — 2 ex officio: Chmn. of Public Safety Commission and Comptroller; 6 apptv.: Chair R. Dyke Rogers, Dalhart (2/1/05); Vice-Chair Michael G. Rutherford, Houston (2/1/07); Board Members: Jesse R. Adams, Helotes (2/1/09); Treva Boyd, Christoval (2/1/05); Gerald Ken Carter, Caldwell (2/1/09); Comer J. Cottrell, Plano (2/1/07); Charles L. Sowell, Houston (2/1/09); Louis E. Sturns, Arlington (2/1/07). Exec. Sec., Paula C. Flowerday ($77,760), PO Box 12080, Austin 78711.

Railroad Commission of Texas – (1891); elective; 6-yr.; 3 members, $92,217 each: Victor Carrillo (12/31/10); Michael L. Williams (12/31/08); Elizabeth Ames Jones (1/1/06). Dir., Ronald Kitchens ($106,381), PO Box 12967, Austin 78711.

Real Estate Commission, Texas – (1949 as 6-member board; membership increased to 9 in 1979); apptv.; per diem and expenses; 6-yr.; 9 members: Chair John Walton, Lubbock (1/31/07); Board Members: James N. Austin, Jr., Fort Worth (1/31/05); Mary Frances Burleson, Aubrey (1/31/09); Louise E. Hull, Victoria (1/31/07); Lawrence D. Jokl, Brownsville (1/31/05); Elizabeth Leal, El Paso (1/31/09); Public Members: Ramon Cantu, Houston (1/31/05); William H. Flores, Sugar Land (1/31/09); Paul H. Jordan, Georgetown (1/31/07). Admin., Wayne Thorburn ($70,000), PO Box 12188, Austin 78711.

Real Estate Research Center – (1971); apptv.; 6-yr.; 10 members — one ex officio: representative of Texas Real Estate Commission; 9 apptv. members: Joseph A. Adame, Corpus Christi (1/31/03); David E. Dalzell, Abilene (1/31/07); Tom H. Gann, Lufkin (1/31/07); Celia Goode/Haddock, College Station (1/31/05); Joe Bob McCartt, Amarillo (1/31/05); Catherine Miller, Fort Worth (1/31/03); Nick Nicholas, Dallas (1/31/05); Jerry L. Schaffner, Dallas (1/31/03); Douglas A. Schwartz, El Paso (1/31/07). Dir., R. Malcolm Richards, Texas A&M, College Station 77843-2115.

Red River Authority, Board of Directors – (1959); apptv.; 6-yr.; per diem and expenses; 9 members: George W. Arrington, Canadian (8/11/01); Nathan J. (Jim) Bell, IV, Paris (8/11/05); Lisa C. Brent, Amarillo (8/11/05); William K. Daniel, Wichita Falls (8/11/03); Carol C. Gunn, Ph.D., Wichita Falls (8/11/03); Janie Matteson, DeKalb (8/11/05); Patricia C. Peale, Lake Kiowa (8/11/01); Cliff A. Skiles, Jr., D.V.M., Hereford (8/11/03); W. F. Smith, Jr., Quanah (8/11/01). Gen. Mgr., Curtis W. Campbell, 900 8th St., Ste. 520, Wichita Falls 76301-6894.

Red River Compact Commissioner – (1949); apptv.; 4-yr.; (Function of commissioner is to negotiate with other states respecting waters of the Red.): William A. Abney ($24,225), El Paso (2/1/05).

Redistricting Board, Legislative – (See Legislative Redistricting Board).

Rehabilitation Commission, Texas – Combined into Department of Assistive and Rehabilitative Services of the Health and Human Services Commission as of 3/1/04..

Residential Construction Commission, Texas – apptv.; 6-yr.; expenses; 9 members: Chair Patrick Cordero, Midland (2/1/09); Vice/Chair Art Cuevas, Lubbock (2/1/11); Commissioners: Lewis Brown, Spring (2/1/11); Kenneth L. Davis, Weatherford (2/1/09); J. Paulo Flores, Dallas (2/1/11); John R. Krugh, Houston (2/1/09); Glenda C. Mariott, College Station (2/1/07); Scott M. Porter, Kerrville (2/1/07); Mickey R. Redwine, Ben Wheeler (2/1/07). Exec. Dir., Stephen D. Thomas, PO Box 13144, Austin 78711-3144.

Retirement System, Municipal, Board of Trustees – (1947); apptv.; 6-yr.; expenses; 6 members: Connie J. Green, Killeen (2/1/05); Patricia Hernandez, Plainview (2/1/05); Carolyn M. Linér, San Marcos (2/1/07); Rick Menchaca, Midland (2/1/07); H. Frank Simpson, Missouri City (2/1/09); Kathryn M. Usrey, Carrollton (2/1/09). Exec. Dir., Gary W. Anderson, PO Box 149153, Austin 78714-9153.

Retirement System of Texas, Employees – (1949); apptv.; 6-yr.; 6 members — one apptd. by Gov., one by Chief Justice of State Supreme Court and one by Speaker; 3 are employee members of the system serving 6-yr. overlapping terms: Chair Owen Whitworth, Austin (8/31/05); Vice-Chair Carolyn Lewis Gallagher, Austin (8/31/06); Appt'd Mem. Bill Ceverha, Dallas (8/31/08); Elected Members: Don Green, Austin (8/31/07); Yolanda Griego,

El Paso (8/31/09); Appointed Member, Milton Hixson, Austin (8/31/04); . Exec. Dir., Ann S. Fuelberg ($175,000), PO Box 13207, Austin 78711-3207; 512-867-7711.

Retirement System, Texas County and District – (1967); apptv.; 6-yr.; 9 members: Chair Robert Eckels, Houston (12/31/07); Vice-Chai Amador E. Reyna, Kountze (12/31/05); Jerry Bigham, Canyo (12/31/09); Martha Gustavsen, Conroe (12/31/05); Daniel R. Haggerty, El Paso (12/31/09); Jan Kennady, New Braunfels (12/31/09); Mitchell E. Liles, Garland (12/31/05); Bridget McDowell, Baird (12/31/07); Robert C. Willis, Livingston (12/31/09). Dir. Gene Glass, PO Box 2034, Austin 78768-2034; 512-328-8889.

Rio Grande Compact Commissioner of Texas – (1929); apptv.; 6-yr.: Joe G. Hanson, El Paso (6/9/07). Box 1917, El Paso 79950-1917 ($41,195).

Risk Management, State Office of – apptv.; 2-yr.; 5 members: Chair Martha Rider, Rosenberg (2/1/07); Vice/Chair Ronald D. Beals, M.D., Tyler (2/1/07); Board Members: Ernest C. Garcia, Austin (2/1/09); Kenneth N. Mitchell, El Paso (2/1/09); Ronald James Walenta, Dallas (2/1/11).

Rural Community Affairs, Office of – apptv.; 6-yr.; 9 members: Chair William M. Jeter, III, Bryan (2/1/07); Board Members: David Alders, Nacogdoches (2/1/09); Nicki Harle, Baird (2/1/07); Carol Harrell, Jefferson (2/1/07); Wallace Klussmann, Fredericksburg (2/1/07); Jim Roberts, Lubbock (2/1/05); Lydia Rangel Saenz, Carrizo Springs (2/1/09); Patrick Wallace, Athens (2/1/05); Michael Waters, Abilene (2/1/11). Exec. Dir. Charles S. (Charlie) Stone.

Rural Community Health System of Texas – (1975); apptv.; 7 members, 4-yr.; Chair Rodolfo (Rudy) Arredondo, Lubbock (2/1/09); Beverly Barron, Odessa (2/1/07); Jaime A. Davidson, Dallas (2/1/05); Lewis E. Foxhall, Houston (2/1/09); Glenda R. Kane, Corpus Christi (2/1/09); Jeffrey A. Ross, Houston, (2/1/07); James G. (Jim) Springfield, Harlingen (2/1/05). Exec. Dir., Eduardo J. Sanchez, 1100 W. 49th, Austin 78756-3199.

Sabine River Authority, Board of Directors – (1949); apptv.; per diem and expenses; 6-yr.; 9 members: Claudia J. Abney, Marshall (7/06/05); Don O. Covington, Orange (7/06/05); Sammy D. Dance, Center (7/06/07); Calvin E. Ebner, Deweyville (7/06/05); J. D. Jacobs, Jr., Rockwall (7/06/07); Richard A. Linkenauger, Greenville (7/06/09); Connie Wade, Longview (7/06/09); Constance Moore Ware, Marshall (7/06/09); Clarence Earl Williams, Orange (7/06/07). Gen. Mgr., Jerry Clark, PO Box 579, Orange 77630.

Sabine River Compact Commission – (1953); apptv.; 6-yr.; $8,487 each; 5 members — one member and chmn. apptd. by President of United States without a vote; 2 from Texas and 2 from Louisiana. Texas members: Frank Edward Parker, Center (7/12/01); Gary E. Gagnon, Orange (7/12/07). Box 579, Orange 77630.

San Antonio River Authority – apptv., 6 yr., 12 members: Chair H. B. (Trip) Ruckman, III, Karnes Co. (1/31/09); Vice-Chair Louis E. Rowe, Bexar Co. (1/31/09); Sec. JC Turner, Wilson Co. (1/31/09); Treas., Adair Ramsey Sutherland, Goliad Co. (1/31/07); Terry E. Baiamonte, Goliad Co. (1/31/09); Sara (Sally) Buchanan, Bexar Co. (1/31/05); James (lim) Johnson, Bexar Co. (1/31/07); Alois (Al) Kollodziej, Jr., Wilson Co. (1/31/07); Gaylon J. Oehlke, Karnes Co. (1/31/05); Roberto G. Rodriguez, Bexar Co. (1/31/07); Nancy Steves, Bexar Co. (1/31/05); Thomas G. Weaver, Bexar Co. (1/31/09). Gen. Mgr., Gregory E. Rothe, PO Box 839980, San Antonio 78283-9980.

San Jacinto River Authority, Board of Directors – (1937); apptv.; expenses while on duty; 6-yr.; 6 members: Linda Koenig, Houston, 10/16/05); R. Gary Montgomery, P.E., The Woodlands, 10/16/07); Mary L. Rummell, Spring, 10/16/09); John H. Stibbs, The Woodlands, 10/16/09); Lloyd B. Tisdale, Conroe, 10/16/07); Joseph V. Turner, Conroe, 10/16/05). Gen. Mgr., James R. Adams, PO Box 329, Conroe 77305.

Savings and Loan Commissioner – Apptv. by State Finance Commission: Danny Payne ($92,676), PO Box 1089, Austin 78767.

School Land Board – (See Land Board, School).

Securities Board, State – (Est. 1957, the outgrowth of several amendments to the Texas Securities Act, originally passed 1913); act is administered by the Securities Commissioner, who is appointed by the board members; expenses; 6-yr.; 3 members: Chair Jack D. Ladd, Midland (1//07); Kenneth W. Anderson, Jr., Dallas (1//05); Beth Ann Blackwood, Dallas (1//07); Bryan K. Brown, Pearland (1//11); William R. Smith, Campbell (1//07). Securities Commissioner, Denise Voigt Crawford ($90,000), PO Box 13167, Austin 78711-3167.

Sex Offender Treatment, Council on – (1997); apptv.; 6-yr.; expenses; 6 members: Chair Walter J. Meyer, III, M.D., RSOTP, Galveston (2/1/07); Board Members: Liles Arnold, L.P.C., RSOTP, Plano (2/1/09); Monica Hernandez, Harlingen (2/1/11); Dr. Glen Allen Kercher, Huntsville (2/1/09); Patricia Rae Lykos (2/1/07); Maria

Molett, MA, LPC, RSOTP, Garland (2/1/09); Aaron Paul Pierce, Rockdale (2/1/11). Exec. Dir., Allison Taylor, PO Box 12546, Austin 78711.

Social Worker Examiners, Texas State Board of – (1993); apptd.; 6-yr.; per diem and travel expenses; 9 members: Chair Jeannie McGuire, LBSW, College Station (2/1/07); Board Members: Tim M. Brown, LMSW, Bryan (2/1/09); Julia Dunaway, LCSW, Fort Worth (2/1/07); J. Steven Roberts, LCSW, San Marcos (2/1/05); Jamie B. Ward, LBSW, Boerne (2/1/05); Carrie Yeats, LMSW, Lubbock (2/1/09); Public Members: Holly L. Anawaty, Houston (2/1/07); Lt. Willie McGee, Plainview (2/1/05); Matt Shaheen, Plano (2/1/09). Exec. Dir. Andrew T. Marks.

Soil and Water Conservation Board, Texas State – (1939); elected by members of individual districts; 2 yrs.; 5 members: Guillermo (Memo) Benavides, Laredo (5/06/05); W. T. Crumley, Stephenville (5/06/05); Larry Jacobs, Montgomery (2/1/06); Jerry Nichols, Nacogdoches (5/07/06); Aubrey Russell, Panhandle (5/06/05); Reed Stewart, Sterling City (5/1/06); Joe L. Ward, Telephone (2/1/07). Exec. Dir., Rex Isom ($65,000), PO Box 658, Temple 76503.

Speech-Language Pathology and Audiology, State Board of Examiners for – (1983); apptv.; 6-yr.; per diem and expenses; 9 members: Presiding Officer, Cheryl Lynn Sancibrian, Lubbock (8/31/05); Board Members: Rosario R. Brusniak, Plano (8/31/07); Bertha Moore Campbell, Houston (8/31/05); Deborah L. Carlson, Galveston (8/31/05); Matthew H. Lyon, El Paso (8/31/07); Kerry Ormson, Amarillo (8/31/09); Public Members: Richard J. Caldwell, Houston (8/31/09); Crystal Dawn Perkins, DeSoto (8/31/05); Minnette Son, M.D., San Antonio (8/31/07). Exec. Secy., Sharon Williams, 1100 W. 49th, Austin 78756-3183.

Stephen F. Austin State University, Board of Regents – (1969); apptv.; expenses; 6-yr.; 9 members: Margarita de la Garza/Grahm, M.D., Tyler (1/31/07); Valerie E. Ertz, Dallas (1/31/09); Joe Max Green, Nacogdoches (1/31/09); Kenneth James, Kingwood (1/31/07); Gary Lopez, Dallas (1/31/05); Paul Gifford Pond, Port Neches (1/31/09); Raymond Lyn Stevens, Beaumont (1/31/05); Mike Wilhite, Henderson (1/31/05); Fredrick A. Wulf, Center (1/31/07). Pres. Tito Guerrero III, PO Box 6078, SFA Sta., Nacogdoches 75962.

Sunset Advisory Commission – (1977); 12 members: 5 members of House of Representatives, 5 members of Senate, one public member apptd. by Speaker, one public member apptd. by Lt. Gov.; 4-yr.; expenses. Public members: John Shields, San Antonio (9/1/05); Howard Wolf, Austin (9/1/05). Dir., Joey Longley, PO Box 13066, Austin 78711.

Tax Board, State – (1905); ex officio; term in other office; no compensation; 3 members: Comptroller, Secretary of State and State Treasurer.

Tax Professional Examiners, Board of – (1977 as Board of Tax Assessor Examiners; name changed to present form 1983); apptv.; expenses; 6-yr.; 5 members: Chair Deborah M. Hunt, Austin (3/1/05); Board Members: Michael Amezquita, Harlingen (3/1/05); James E. Childers, Canyon Lake (3/1/07); Linda Hatchel, Woodway (3/1/09); Dorye Kristeen Roe, Robert Lee (3/1/07). Exec. Dir., David E. Montoya ($52,000), 333 Guadalupe, Ste. 2-520 Austin 78701-3942.

Teacher Retirement System – (1937 as 6-member board; membership increased to 9 in 1973); expenses; 6-yr.; 9 members — 2 apptd. by State Board of Education, 3 apptd. by Gov. and 4 TRS members apptd. by Gov. after being nominated by popular ballot of members of the retirement system: Presiding Officer, Jarvis V. Hollingsworth, Missouri City (8/31/07); Board Members: Mary Alice Baker, Ph.D., Beaumont (8/31/05); Terence S. Ellis, New Ulm (8/31/05); James W. Fonteno, Jr., Houston (8/31/07); John Graham, Jr., Fredericksburg (8/31/09); Mark Henry, Ed.D., Galena Park (8/31/09); Greg Poole, Ed.D., Conroe (8/31/07); Dory A. Wiley, Dallas (8/31/09); Linus D. Wright, Dallas (8/31/05). Exec. Dir., Ronnie Jung, 1000 Red River, Austin 78701.

Texas A&M University System Board of Regents – (1875); apptv.; 6-yr.; expenses; 9 members: Phillip David Adams, Bryan, (2/1/07); Lupe Fraga, Houston (2/1/11); Wendy Lee Gramm, Helotes (2/1/07); Bill Jones, Austin (2/1/09); Lester Lowry Mays, San Antonio (2/1/07); Erle Allen Nye, Dallas (2/1/09); Gene Stallings, Powderly (2/1/11); Ida Clement Steen, San Antonio (2/1/11); John David White, Houston (2/1/09). Chancellor, Mike McKinney, PO Box C-1, College Station 77844-9021.

Texas Southern University, Board of Regents – (1947); expenses; 6-yr.; 9 members: J. Paul Johnson, Fresno (2/1/07); Regina Giovannini, Houston (2/1/05); Secretary, David Diaz, Corpus Christi (2/1/05); Board Members: Robert E. Childress, Ph.D., Richmond (2/1/09); Earnest Gibson, III, Houston (2/1/05); Belinda M. Griffin, Plano (2/1/09); Harry E. Johnson, Sr., Missouri City (2/1/09); Gerald E. Wilson, Katy (2/1/07); Second Vice/Chair George M. Williams, Houston (2/1/07). Pres., Dr. Priscilla Slade. Exec. Dir. for Board Relations, Karen A. Griffin 3100 Cleburne, Houston 77004.

Texas State Technical College, Board of Regents – (1960 as Board of the Texas State Technical Institute; changed to present name, 1991); apptv.; expenses; 6-yr.; 9 members: Chair C. Connie de la Garza, Harlingen (8/31/07); Vice/Chair Don Elliott, Wharton (8/31/05); Board Members: Nora Castañeda, Harlingen (8/31/09); James Virgil Martin, Sweetwater (8/31/09); Mike Northcutt, Longview (8/31/07); Jerilyn K. Pfeifer, Abilene (8/31/07); Terry W. Preuninger, Royse City (8/31/05); Linda Routh, Corpus Christi (8/31/05); Barbara N. Rusling, China Springs (8/31/09). Chancellor, Dr. Bill Segura, TSTC System, 3801 Campus Dr., Waco 76705; 254-867-4890.

Texas State University System, Board of Regents – (1911 as Board of Regents of State Teachers Colleges; name changed in 1965 to Board of Regents of State Senior Colleges; changed to present form in 1975); apptv.; per diem and expenses; 6-yr.; 9 members: Chair Alan W. Dreeben, San Antonio (2/1/07); Vice/Chair Kent M. Adams, Beaumont (2/1/07); Board Members: Dora G. Alcalá, Del Rio (2/1/09); Patricia D. Dennis, San Antonio (2/1/05); John E. Dudley, Comanche (2/1/09); Dionicio (Don) Flores, El Paso (2/1/05); Bernie C. Francis, Carrollton (2/1/09); James A. Hayley, Texas City (2/1/05); Pollyanna A. Stephens, San Angelo (2/1/07). Chancellor, Dr. Charles R. Matthews, Thomas J. Rusk Bldg., 200 E. 10th Street, Suite 600, Austin, TX 78701; 512-463-1808.

Texas Tech University, Board of Regents – (1923); apptv.; expenses; 6-yr.; 9 members: Larry Keith Anders, Dallas (1/31/11); C. Robert Black, Horseshoe Bay (1/31/07); F. Scott Dueser, Abilene (1/31/09); L. Frederick Francis, El Paso (1/31/07); Mark Griffin, Lubbock (1/31/11); J. Frank Miller, III, Dallas (1/31/09); Daniel T. (Dan) Serna, Arlington (1/31/11); Windy M. Sitton, Lubbock (1/31/09); Bob L. Stafford, M.D., Amarillo (1/31/07). Chancellor, Dr. David R. Smith, P.O. Box 42011, Lubbock 79409.

Texas Woman's University Board of Regents – (1901); apptv.; expenses; 6-yr.; 9 members: Therese B. Bevers M.D., Houston (2/1/07); Harry L. Crumpacker II, Plano (2/1/09); Virginia Chandler Dykes, Dallas (2/1/11); William H. Fleming, III, M.D., Houston (2/1/09); Kenneth L. Ingram, Denton (2/1/07); Tegwin Ann Pulley, Dallas (2/1/09); Lou Halsell Rodenberger, Baird (2/1/11); Sharon Venable, Dallas (2/1/11); Annie F. Williams, Dallas (2/1/07). Chancellor and Pres., Dr. Ann Stuart, PO Box 23925, TWU Sta., Denton 76204-1925.

Transportation Commission, Texas – (1917 as State Highway Commission; merged with Mass Transportation Commission and name changed to State Board of Highways and Public Transportation in 1975; merged with Texas Dept. of Aviation and Texas Motor Vehicle Commission and name changed to present form in 1991); apptv.; 6-yr.; ($15,914); 5 members: Hope Andrade, San Antonio (2/1/07); Ted Houghton, El Paso (2/1/09); John W. Johnson, Houston (2/1/05); Robert Lee Nichols, Jacksonville (2/1/09); Ric Williamson, Weatherford (2/1/07). Exec. Dir., Charles Heald ($155,000), 125 E. 11th St., Austin 78701.

Trinity River Authority, Board of Directors – (1955); apptv.; per diem and expenses; 6-yr.; 24 directors — 3 from Tarrant County, 4 from Dallas County, 2 from area-at-large and one each from 15 other districts: Chair Edd Hargett, Crockett (3/15/03); President, John W. Jenkins, Hankamer (3/15/03); Vice President, Hector Escamilla, Jr., Carrollton (3/15/03); Board Members: Russell B. Arnold, Trinity (3/15/05); Connie H. Arnold, Liberty (3/15/07); Harold L. Barnard, Waxahachie (3/15/05); Leslie C. Browne, Arlington (3/15/03); Karl R. Butler, Dallas (3/15/05); Patricia T. Clapp, Dallas (3/15/07); Michael Cronin, Terrell (3/15/05); Steve Cronin, Shepherd (3/15/05); Vincent Cruz, Jr., Fort Worth (3/15/05); Benny L. Fogleman, Livingston (3/15/03); Sylvia P. Greene, Arlington (3/15/03); Jerry F. House, Sr., D.Min., Leona (3/15/05); Katrina M. Keyes, Dallas (3/15/09); Nancy E. Lavinski, Palestine (3/15/07); Andrew Martinez, Huntsville (3/15/07); Lynn Hardy Neely, Madisonville (3/15/05); Nancy A. Perryman, Athens (3/15/07); AnaLaura Saucedo, Dallas (3/15/07); Louis E. Sturns, Fort Worth (3/15/07); Linda D. Timmerman Ed.D., Streetman (3/15/07); Kim C. Wyatt, Corsicana (3/15/09). Gen. Mgr., Danny F. Vance, PO Box 60, Arlington 76004-0060.

Tuition Board, Prepaid Higher Education – (1996); 6-yr.; 7 members: Comptroller; 4 apptd. by Lt. Gov.; 2 apptd. by Gov.

Uniform State Laws, Commission on – (1941 as 5-member Commissioners to the National Conference on Uniform State Laws; name changed to present form, membership increased to 6 and term of office raised to 6 years in 1977; membership raised to 9 in 2001); apptv.; 6-yr.; 9 members: Levi J. Benton, Houston (9/30/10); Cullen M. Godfrey, Austin (9/30/10); Debra H. Lehrmann, Colleyville (9/30/10); Peter K. Munson, Pottsboro (9/30/08); Marilyn Phelan, Lubbock (9/30/06); Rodney Wayne Satterwhite, Midland (9/30/08); Karen R. Washington, Dallas (9/30/02); Hon. Earl L.

Yeakel, III, Austin (9/30/06); Life Member, Patrick Guillot, Dallas).

University of Houston, Board of Regents – (1963); apptv.; expenses; 6-yr.; 9 members: Chair Morgan Dunn O'Connor, Victoria (8/31/05); Vice/Chair Leroy L. Hermes, Houston (8/31/07); Secretary, Raul A. Gonzalez, Austin (8/31/07); Board Members: Morrie K. Abramson, Houston (8/31/05); Michael J. Cemo, Houston (8/31/07); Dennis D. Golden, Carthage (8/31/09); Lynden B. Rose, Houston (8/31/09); Thad (Bo) Smith, Sugar Land (8/31/05); Calvin W. Stephens, Dallas (8/31/09). Chancellor, Dr. Jay Gogue, 3100 Cullen Blvd., Suite 205, Houston 77204-6001; 713-743-3444.

University of North Texas Board of Regents – (1949); apptv.; 6-yr.; expenses; 9 members: Charles Beatty, Waxahachie (5/22/05); Marjorie B. Craft, DeSoto (5/22/07); Tom Lazo, Sr., Dallas (5/22/05); Robert A. Nickell, Irving (5/22/09); Burle Pettit, Lubbock (5/22/07); Bobby Ray, Plano (5/22/07); C. Dan Smith, Jr., Plano (5/22/05); Gayle W. Strange, Denton (5/22/09); Rice M. Tilley, Jr., Fort Worth (5/22/09). Chancellor, Dr. Norval F. Pohl, PO Box 311220, Denton 76203.

University of Texas System, Board of Regents – (1881); apptv.; expenses; 6-yr.; 9 members: Chair James R. Huffines, Austin (2/1/09); Vice/Chairs: Rita C. Clements, Dallas (2/1/07); Woody L. Hunt, El Paso (2/1/05); Cyndi Taylor Krier, San Antonio (2/1/07); Board Members: John W. Barnhill, Jr., Brenham (2/1/09); H. Scott Caven, Jr., Houston (2/1/09); Judith L. Craven, M.D., M.P.H., Houston (2/1/07); Robert A. Estrada, Fort Worth (2/1/05); Robert B. Rowling, Dallas (2/1/11); Chancellor, Mark G. Yudof, 201 West Seventh St., Ste. 820, Austin, TX 78701.

Veterans Commission, Texas – (1927 as Veterans State Service Office; reorganized as Veterans Affairs Commission in 1947 with 5 members; membership increased to 6 in 1981; name changed to present form in 1985); apptv.; 6-yr.; per diem while on duty and expenses; 6 members: ames R. Adams Ph.D., Dallas, 12/31/05); Leonardo Barraza, El Paso, 12/31/05); John A. Brieden, III, Brenham, 12/31/07); Hector Farias, Weslaco, 12/31/07); Karen Summerfield Rankin, BGen, USAF (Ret.), San Antonio, 12/31/09). Exec. Dir., James E. Nier ($74,000), PO Box 12277, Austin 78711; 512-463-6564.

Veterans Land Board – (Est. 1949 as 3-member ex officio board; reorganized 1956); 4-yr.; per diem and expenses; 3 members: one ex officio: Comm. of General Land Office; 2 apptd.: Cephus S. Rhodes, El Paso, 12/29/06); M.S. Ussery, Amarillo, 12/29/04). Exec. Sec., Paul E. Moore, P.O. Box 12873, Austin 78701.

Veterinary Medical Examiners, Texas State Board of – (1911; revised 1953; made 9-member board in 1981); apptv.; expenses on duty; 6-yr.; 9 members: Pres, Gary Brantley, Richardson (8/26/05); Vice Pres., Robert L. Lastovica, Fredericksburg (8/26/07); Secy., Gary Wayne Johnsen, El Paso (8/26/07); Bud E. Alldrege, Jr., Sweetwater (8/26/09); Patrick Michael Allen, Lubbock (8/26/07); Dee A. Pederson, Austin (8/26/05); Public Members: Mario A. Escobar, Crystal City (8/26/05); Paul Martinez, Sonora (8/26/09); Dawn Elise Reveley, Cedar Park (8/26/07). Exec. Dir., Ron Allen ($60,000), 333 Guadalupe St., Ste. 2-330, Austin 78701-3998.

Water Development Board, Texas – (1957; legislative function for the Texas Dept. of Water Resources, 1977); apptv.; per diem and expenses; 6-yr.; 6 members: Chair E. G. (Rod) Pittman, Lufkin, 12/31/07); Board Members: Dario Vidal Guerra, Jr., Edinburg, 12/31/07); James Edward Herring, Amarillo, 12/31/09); Jack Hunt, Houston, 12/31/09); Thomas Weir Labatt, III, San Antonio, 12/31/05); William W. Meadows, Fort Worth, 12/31/05). Exec. Admin., J. Kevin Ward ($108,000), PO Box 13231, Austin 78711.

Workers' Compensation Commission, Texas – (1991); 6-yr.; apptv; expenses; 6 members: Mike Hachtman, Chair Houston (2/1/05); William A. Ledbetter, Jr., North Richland Hills (2/1/05); Edward J. Sanchez, Houston (2/1/05); Carolyn J. Walls, San Antonio (2/1/05); Lonnie Watson, Cleburne (2/1/05); Eddie Wilkerson, La Porte (2/1/05). Exec. Dir., Robert L. Shipe ($112,000), 7551 Metro Center Drive, Suite 100, Austin 78744.

Workforce Commission, Texas – (1936 as Texas Employment Commission; name changed 1995); apptv.; $97,000-$99,500; 6-yr.; 3 members: Chair Diane Rath, San Antonio (2/1/07); Ronald G. Congleto, (2/1/11); Ron Lehman, Round Rock (2/1/03). Exec. Dir., Larry Temple ($125,000), 101 E. 15th St., Ste. 618, Austin 78778-0001.

Youth Commission, Texas – (1949 as 9-member board; reorganized 1957 and again in 1975); 6-yr.; per diem on duty; 6 apptv. members: All board members resigned on March 16, 2007, and their powers were transferred to Conservator Ed Owens and Acting Executive Director Dimitria D. Pope; PO Box 4260, Austin 78765; 512-424-6130. ☆

State Government Income and Expenditures

Taxes are the state government's primary source of income. On this and the following pages are summaries of state income and expenditures, percent change from previous year, tax collections, tax revenue by type of tax, a summary of the state budget for the 2008–2009 biennium, Texas Lottery income and expenditures and the amount of federal payments to state agencies.

State Revenues by Source and Expenditures by Function

Amounts (in Millions) and Percent Change from Previous Year

Revenues by Source	2006	%	2005	%	2004	%	2003	%	2002	%
Tax Collections	33,544	12.4	28,838	6.9	$27,913	6.8	$26,127	-0.6	$26,279	-3.5
Federal Income	24,726	8.4	22,809	4.0	21,938	4.6	20,976	15.4	18,171	13.4
Licenses, Fees, Permits, Fines, Penalties	5,999	-2.5	6,155	11.0	5,546	15.9	4,785	9.6	4,366	2.4
Interest & Other Investment Income	1,949	27.5	1,529	8.8	1,406	-10.7	1,575	-7.2	1,696	-17.6
Net Lottery Proceeds	1,585	0.0	1,584	-0.8	1,597	13.6	1,406	1.0	1,392	-0.1
Sales of Goods & Services	492	43.1	344	4.5	329	-5.1	347	-36.6	547	34.5
Settlements of Claims	545	-1.1	551	8.2	510	-8.0	554	9.9	504	28.6
Land Income	860	31.6	654	31.3	498	27.8	390	19.9	325	-23.2
Contributions to Employee Benefits	220	12.0	197	10.7	178	11.3	160	12.7	142	11.6
Other Revenues	2,496	16.4	2,145	-0.6	2,158	8.4	1,991	10.8	1,798	19.2
Total Net Revenues	**$72,420**	**10.0**	**$65,810**	**6.0**	**$62,073**	**6.5**	**$58,310**	**5.6**	**$55,221**	**2.6**
Expenditures by Function										
General Government – Total	$2,214	8.9	$2,215	8.6	$2,040	1.8	$2,004	7.4	$1,867	-7.3
Executive	2,094	9.7	1,908	8.5	1,759	3.0	1,709	7.8	1,585	-9.5
Legislative	116	-4.4	122	9.0	112	-7.5	121	6.8	113	3.8
Judicial	201	9.1	185	9.6	169	-3.6	175	4.2	168	10.1
Education	23,185	6.1	21,844	5.4	20,734	-0.5	20,834	2.8	20,260	0.8
Employee Benefits	2,709	-1.3	2,745	2.2	2,685	-14.7	3,150	31.9	2,389	19.4
Health and Human Services	25,458	4.7	24,308	5.8	22,966	0.4	22,880	13.7	20,123	11.7
Public Safety and Corrections	4,218	27.8	3,301	0.8	3,276	-3.4	3,391	1.8	3,332	5.4
Transportation	7,316	10.2	6,641	26.6	5,248	6.4	4,934	-1.9	5,030	11.2
Natural Resources/Recreational Services	1,634	-2.3	1,672	-12.7	1,915	38.1	1,387	29.3	1,073	-0.3
Regulatory Agencies	229	-16.1	273	-12.0	310	28.4	242	13.9	212	1.9
Lottery Winnings Paid*	476	6.1	448	-13.3	517	25.0	414	-2.1	423	15.4
Debt Service – Interest	785	25.6	625	8.7	576	-8.1	626	11.0	564	-11.5
Capital Outlay	410	-33.7	618	36.9	452	10.2	410	-11.6	464	-18.6
Total Net Expenditures	**$68,833**	**6.4**	**$64,693**	**6.5**	**$60,719**	**0.7**	**$60,270**	**8.1**	**$55,739**	**5.8**

Does not include payments made by retailers. All amounts rounded. Expenditures exclude trust funds. Fiscal years end August 31. Source: State of Texas 2006 Annual Cash Report, Vol. One, Summary of Financial Information for the year ended August 31, 2006, Comptroller of Public Accounts' Office.

State Tax Collections, 1992–2006

Fiscal Year‡	State Tax Collections	Resident Population*	Per Capita Tax Collections	Taxes as % of Personal Income
1992	$15,848,915,148	17,641,580	$ 898.38	4.8
1993	17,010,737,258	17,989,926	945.57	4.9
1994	18,105,950,592	18,340,852	987.19	4.9
1995	18,858,790,042	18,693,032	1,008.87	4.8
1996	19,762,504,350	18,966,000	1,042.00	4.7
1997	21,187,868,237	19,312,000	1,097.13	4.7
1998	22,634,019,740	20,104,000	1,126.00	4.4
1999	23,614,611,235	20,507,000	1,152.00	4.4
2000	25,283,768,842	20,904,000	1,210.00	4.4
2001	27,230,212,416	21,317,000	1,277.00	4.5
2002	26,279,146,493	21,673,000	1,213.00	4.2
2003	26,126,675,424	22,052,000	1,185.00	4.1
2004	27,913,001,645	22,427,000	1,245.00	4.1
2005	29,838,277,614	22,835,000	1,307.00	4.1
2006	33,544,497,547	23,444,000	1,431.00	4.3

‡ Fiscal years end August 31.
* Revised fiscal year estimates

Sources: Texas Comptroller of Public Accounts, Annual Financial Reports of various years. Population and personal income figures, 1992 to 2005: U.S. Dept. of Commerce (U.S. Census Bureau and Bureau of Economic Analysis), adjusted to Texas fiscal years by Comptroller of Public Accounts. Data for 2006 include partial estimates by the Texas Comptroller of Public Accounts.

Tax Revenues, 2005–2006

Below are listed the major taxes and the amounts each contributed to the state in fiscal years 2005 and 2006.

Type of Tax	FY 2006	FY 2005
Sales	$18,275,209,754	$16,312,811,054
Motor Veh. Sales/Rnt*	3,075,153,783	2,847,653,057
Motor Fuels	2,993,569,575	2,934,580,537
Franchise	2,605,447,409	2,170,081,376
Insurance Occupation	1,233,493,584	1,208,866,496
Natural Gas Production	2,339,147,491	1,657,086,299
Cigarette/Tobacco	545,904,191	599,368,199
Alcoholic Beverages	680,748,138	626,277,831
Oil Production	862,360,868	681,890,801
Inheritance	13,360,123	101,674,348
Utility	480,792,722	380,006,470
Hotel/Motel	308,018,897	262,092,112
Other Taxes**	131,291,012	55,889,034
Totals	**$33,544,497,547**	**$29,838,277,614**

*Includes tax on manufactured housing sales and taxes on interstate motor carriers.
Source: State of Texas 2006 Annual Cash Report, Vol. One, Summary of Financial Information for the year ended August 31, 2006, Texas Comptroller of Public Accounts.

State Government Budget Summary, 2008–2009 Biennium

Source: Legislative Budget Board

Article (Govt. Division)	2008-09 Budget (all funds) (in millions)
Art. I, General Government	$ 3,406.6
Art. II, Health and Human Services	51,660.3
Art. III, Education	59,804.1
Art. IV, The Judiciary	546.0
Art. V, Public Safety & Criminal Justice	9,148.0
Art. VI, Natural Resources	2,126.0
Art. VII, Business & Economic Dev.	20,066.9
Art. VIII, Regulatory	549.1
Art. IX, General Provisions	0.0
Art. X, The Legislature	325.5
Total	**$ 147,632.5**

The Legislative Budget Board's (LBB) recommended baseline appropriations for state government operations for the 2008–09 biennium total $147.6 billion from all fund sources. This amount excludes $14.2 billion in appropriations for property tax relief. The recommendations provide a $3 billion, or 2.1 percent, increase from the 2006–07 biennial level.

General Revenue Funds, including funds dedicated within the General Revenue Fund, total $75.8 billion for the 2008–09 biennium, an increase of $2.3 billion, or 3.1 percent, over the anticipated 2006–07 biennial spending level.

The LBB recommended appropriations for the 2008–09 biennium are within the Comptroller's 2008–09 Biennial Revenue Estimate. www.lbb.state.tx.us. ☆

Texas Lottery

Source: Texas Lottery Commission

The State Lottery Act was passed by the Texas Legislature in July 1991. Texas voters approved a constitutional amendment authorizing a state lottery in an election on Nov. 5, 1991, by a vote of 1,326,154 to 728,994. Sales since the first ticket was sold on May 29, 1992, through June 2007 total more than $46.7 billion. Through the same period, more than $26.8 billion was paid out in prizes.

The Texas Lottery®, the 3rd largest in North America, offers players a wide range of choices, including approximately 80 instant ticket scratch-off games as well as its on-line games.

Approximately 27 percent (as of the end of Fiscal Year 2006) of all Texas Lottery revenue is transferred to the Foundation School Fund, which supports public education in Texas. Prior to September 1997, revenues were deposited in the General Revenue Fund.

Texas Lottery transfers to the state from May 1992 to June 2007 total $14,868,503,027, with $9,498,776,159 going to the Foundation School Fund and $5,078,658,983 to the General Revenue Fund.

Who Plays the Texas Lottery

The executive director of the Texas Lottery Commission is required to conduct a biennial demographic survey of lottery players to determine the income, age, sex, race, education and frequency of participation of players. This information, gathered by the Survey Research Center at the University of North Texas in September 2006, follows. A total of 1,700 usable interviews were completed with Texans age 18 and older. Since the survey relied solely on interviews, all demographic information and participation rates were self-reported and not independently verified. The data presented to the commission was given a +2.4 percent margin of error at a confidence level of 95 percent for the sample.

The percentage of Texans who reported purchasing at least one Texas Lottery ticket in 12 months preceding the survey was 45.4 percent. Of those respondents who reported purchasing a ticket, 84.8 percent of those reported playing Lotto Texas®; 67.2 percent, "scratch off" or instant games; 53.3 percent, Mega Millions®; 33.3 percent, Cash Five®; 33.9 percent, Pick 3™ day draw; 21.2 percent, Pick 3 night draw; and 16.2 percent, Texas Two Step®.

Age: The 55 to 64 age group had the highest participation rate. Younger players (18 to 24) reported spending more than those in other age categories despite having the lowest rate of participation.

Educational Level: Participation rates in Texas Lottery games were generally consistent across groups defined by level of education. Respondents with some college education or less than

Texas Lottery Financial Data

Start-up to Dec. 31, 2006

Period	Sales (millions)	Value of Prizes Won (millions)	Retailer Comm-issions (millions)	Admin-istration (millions)	To State of Texas (millions)
Start-up–FY 1993	$2,448	$1,250	$122	$170	$907
FY 1994	2,760	1,529	138	167	869
FY 1995	3,037	1,689	152	188	927
FY 1996	3,432	1,951	172	217	1,158
FY 1997	3,745	2,152	187	236	1,189
FY 1998	3,090	1,648	155	198	1,157
FY 1999	2,572	1,329	129	169	969
FY 2000	2,657	1,509	133	172	918
FY 2001	2,825	1,643	141	173	865
FY 2002	2,966	1,715	148	167	957
FY 2003	3,131	1,845	157	158	955
FY 2004	3,488	2,069	174	181	1,044
FY 2005	3,662	2,228	183	183	1,010
FY 2006	3,775	2,311	189	128	1,036

All figures accrued.

a high school diploma were somewhat more likely to play than other groups. The educational category that reported spending the most on lottery products per month (those respondents with a high school diploma) averaged approximately $40 monthly.

Income Level: Participation in Texas Lottery games was fairly consistent across income categories, with respondents in the $20,000 to $29,999 and $75,000 to $100,000 annual income ranges slightly more likely to play than other groups.

Ethnic Background: Hispanic residents were more likely to participate in the Texas Lottery, and black lottery players spent more per month than members of other racial/ethnic groups.

Sex: There was no statistical difference in participation rates of men and women, but male respondents who did play reported spending more, averaging $35.00 per month. Female lottery players reported spending $22.50 on average. . ☆

Federal Revenue by State Agency

Source: Texas Comptroller of Public Accounts, Annual Cash Report for the Year Ended August 31, 2006, Vol. One.

State Agency	2006	2005	2004	2003
Texas Health and Human Services Commission	$12,776,549,811	$12,148,742,005	$10,721,782,083	$10,365,443,434
Texas Department of State Health Services	1,028,932,697	913,038,794	763,798,877	669,436,838
Texas Department of Public Safety	969,835,174	155,148,088	174,212,898	250,958,337
Texas Education Agency	4,247,418,741	3,834,814,130	3,453,080,099	2,981,494,206
Texas Department of Transportation	3,090,574,205	3,250,361,011	2,776,411,283	2,604,116,090
Texas Workforce Commission	939,632,616	876,996,803	885,226,177	894,194,005
Department of Family and Protective Services	342,709,315	330,138,905	280,033,177	282,413,338
Texas Rehabilitative Services	346,265,781	302,975,841	251,630,297	260,347,382
Texas Department of Housing and Community Affairs	158,572,570	151,228,941	124,820,089	116,476,756
All Other Agencies	825,963,031	863,651,493	1,609,001,691	1,587,325,697
Total All Agencies	**$24,726,453,940**	**$22,809,751,233**	**$21,937,677,532**	**$20,975,686,726**

Local Governments

Texas has **254 counties,** a number which has not changed since 1931 when Loving County was organized. Loving had a population of 60 according to the 2006 estimate by the State Data Center, compared with 164 in 1970 and a peak of 285 in 1940. It is the **least-populous county** in Texas. In contrast, Harris County has the **most residents** in Texas, with a 2006 population estimate of 3,886,207.

Counties range in area from Rockwall's 148.7 square miles to the 6,192.78 square miles in Brewster, which is equal to the combined area of the states of Connecticut and Rhode Island.

The Texas Constitution makes a county a legal subdivision of the state. Each county has a commissioners court. It consists of four commissioners, each elected from a commissioner's precinct, and a county judge elected from the entire county. In smaller counties, the county judge retains judicial responsibilities in probate and insanity cases. For names of county and district officials, see tables on pages 513–523.

There are **1208 incorporated municipalities** in Texas that range in size from 32 residents in Los Ybanez to Houston's 2,085,737, according to the State Data Center's 2006 estimate. More than 80 percent of the state's population lives in cities and towns meeting the U.S. Census Bureau definition of urban areas.

Texas had 327 incorporated towns with more than

Boy Scouts from troop 175 in Irving served as the color guard May 15, 2007, during the rededication of Old Red Courthouse and dedication of Old Red Museum of Dallas County History & Culture. The courthouse had undergone 5 years of restoration. Jim Mahoney photo.

5,000 population, according to State Data Center estimates. Under law, these cities may adopt their own charters (called home rule) by a majority vote. Cities of less than 5,000 may be chartered only under the general law. Some home-rule cities may show fewer than 5,000 residents because population has declined since adopting home-rule charters. Home-rule cities are marked in this list by a single-dagger symbol (†) before the name. ☆

Mayors and City Managers of Texas Cities

The list below was compiled from questionnaires sent out immediately after the municipal elections in May 2007. Included is the name of each city's mayor, as well as the name of the city manager, city administrator, city coordinator or other managing executive of munipalities having that form of government. If a town's mail goes to a post office in a different town, the mailing address is included.

An asterisk (*) before the city name indicates that the *Texas Almanac* received no response to the questionnaire and that the information on city officials is from the Texas State Directory 2007, 50th edition.

— A —

Abbott .... Harry G. Nors
*Abernathy .... .Q.C. "Hoppy" Toler
  City Mgr., Mike Cypert
†Abilene .... Norm Archibald
  City Mgr., Larry D. Gilley
*Ackerly .... Jimmie L. Schuelke
†Addison .... Joe Chow
  City Mgr., Ron Whitehead
*Adrian .... Finis Brown
*Agua Dulce .... Carl Vajdos
†Alamo .... Rudy Villarreal
  City Mgr., Luciano Ozuna Jr.
†Alamo Heights (6116 Broadway, San Antonio 78209) .... Louis Cooper
  City Admin., Rebecca Waldman
Alba .... Orvin Carroll
Albany .... Harold Cox
  City Mgr., Bobby R. Russell
*Aledo .... Kit Marshall
  City Admin., Mack Wofford
*†Alice .... Grace Saenz-Lopez.
  City Mgr., Pete Anaya
†Allen .... Stephen Terrell
  City Mgr., Peter H. Vargas
Alma (140 Alma Dr., Ennis 75119)
  .... Scot Shepherd
†Alpine .... Mickey Clouse
  City Mgr., Chuy Garcia
Alto .... Carey Palmer
  City Admin., Debra Dannelley
*Alton (Box 9004, Mission 78572)
  .... Salvador Vela

City Mgr., Hilario (Larry) Rincones
Alvarado .... Tom Durington
  City Mgr., Mary Daly
†Alvin .... Gary Appelt
  City Mgr., Paul Horn
Alvord .... Frank Knittel
  City Admin., Ricky Tow
†Amarillo .... Debra McCartt
  City Mgr., Alan Taylor
Ames .... John White
Amherst .... George Thompson
*Anahuac .... Guy Robert Jackson
  City Admin., Stephone Taylor
Anderson .... Gail M. Sowell
†Andrews .... Robert Zap
  City Mgr., Glen E. Hackler
*†Angleton .... J. Patrick Henry
  City Admin., Michael Stoldt
*Angus (6008 S. I-45 W, Corsicana 75110)
  .... Eben Dale Stover
*Anna .... Kenneth L. Pelham
  City Mgr., Lee Lawrence
Annetta (Box 1150, Aledo 76008)
  .... Olan Usher
*Annetta North (Box 262, Aledo 76008).....
  .... Kenneth Hall
Annetta South (Box 61, Aledo 76008) ....
  .... Gerhard Kleinschmidt
Annona .... George H. English
  City Mgr., Garry L. Watkins
†Anson .... Tom Isbell
  City Mgr., Dowell Matthews
Anthony .... Art Franco

Anton .... Greg Hodges
  City Mgr., Larry Conkin
*Appleby (RR 10, Box 5186, Nacogdoches 75961) .... Gerald Herbert Sr.
*Aquilla .... James Hamner Sr.
†Aransas Pass .... Tommy Knight
  City Mgr., Mike Sullinger
*Archer City .... Carl Harrelson
  City Mgr., Robin Ross
Arcola .... Tom O. Tuffly
Argyle .... Greg Landrum
  City Admin., Lyle Dresher
†Arlington .... Robert Cluck
  City Mgr., Jim Holgersson
Arp .... Vernon L. Bedair
*Asherton .... Gilberto Gonzalez Jr.
Aspermont .... John Dane Gholson
  City Admin., Roger Parker
*†Athens .... Randy Daniel
  City Mgr., Pam J. Burton
†Atlanta .... Keith Crow
  City Mgr., Michael Ahrens
*Aubrey .... Tim Leslie
*Aurora (Box 558, Rhome 76078)
  .... Barbara Brammer
  City Admin., Toni Kelly-Richardson
†Austin .... Will Wynn
  City Mgr., Toby Futrell
*†Austwell .... Thomas L. Bernal
*Avery .... Bill Trimm
Avinger .... Marvin E. Parvino
†Azle .... Russ Braudis
  City Mgr., Craig Lemin

City Admin., Paul Shelley
†**Cleburne**.............................Ted Reynolds
  City Mgr., Chester Nolen
*†**Cleveland** .... Clifton Wilridge
  City Mgr., Philip Cook
Clifton .... Raymond Zuehlke
  City Admin., Charles McLean
***Clint** ....Dale T. Reinhardt
†**Clute**......................................Calvin Shiflet
  City Mgr., (vacancy)
***Clyde** .... Steve Livingston
  City Admin., Tim Atkinson
Coahoma .... Bill Read
***Cockrell Hill** (4125 W. Clarendon Dr.,Dallas 75211) .... Luis D. Carrera
***Coffee City** (Box 716, Frankston 75763)
  .... Michael Warren
Coldspring.............................. Pat Eversole
†**Coleman** ....Nick Poldrack
  City Mgr., Larry Weise
*†**College Station** .... Ron Silvia
  City Mgr., Glenn Brown
*†**Colleyville** ....David Kelly
  City Mgr., Bill Lindley
***Collinsville** .... Brad Kerr
Colmesneil ....Don Baird
  City Mgr., Carrie Edwards
†**Colorado City** ....Jim Baum
  City Mgr., Paul Catoe
***Columbus**........................ Richard Heffley
  City Mgr., David Meisell
***Comanche**........................... Brent Hagood
***Combes** ....Silvestre (Silver) Garcia
  City Mgr., Lonnie Bearden
Combine (123 Davis Road, Seagoville 75159) ....Keith Taylor
*†**Commerce**...................... Sheryl Zelhart
  City Mgr., Bill Shipp
***Como** ....Roy Darby
*†**Conroe**........................... Tommy Metcalf
  City Admin., Jerry McGuire
†**Converse** .... Al Suarez
  City Mgr., Sam Hughes
†**Cool** (150 So. FM 113, Millsap 76066)
  ....Dorothy Hall
Coolidge .... Bobby Jacobs
Cooper ....Thomas Scotty Stegall
  City Admin., Margaret Eudy
†**Coppell** ....Doug Stover
  City Mgr., Jim Witt
†**Copperas Cove** ....Roger P. O'Dwyer
  City Mgr., Steven J. Alexander
Copper Canyon (400 Woodland Dr., Lewisville 75077) .... Sue Tejml
  Town Admin., Quentin Hix
†**Corinth** (2003 S. Corinth St., Denton 76210) .... Victor J. Burgess
  City Mgr., Clovia English
†**Corpus Christi**.....................Henry Garrett
  City Mgr., George K. Noe
Corral City (14007 Corral City Dr., Argyle 76226)..........................James E. Draper
***Corrigan** ....Grimes Fortune
  City Mgr., Mandy K. Risinger
†**Corsicana** ..............................C.L. Brown
  City Mgr., Connie Standridge
Cottonwood (Box 293, Scurry 75158)
  .... Doug Harris
Cottonwood Shores ....Sylvia H. Breem
***Cotulla** ....Abel B. Gonzalez
  City Admin., Rachael Hernandez
Cove (Box 2251, Mont Belvieu 77580)
  ....Lee Wiley
Covington...................... Tommy L. Elkins
Crandall ....Josef Baker
  City Mgr., Judy Bell
Crane ....Kelly S. Nichols
  City Admin., Dru Gravens
Cranfills Gap ....David D. Witte
Crawford ....David C. Posten
***Creedmoor** (12108 FM 1625, Austin 78747) ....Robert L. Wilhite
  City Admin. Richard L. Crandal Jr.
Cresson .... W.R. "Bob" Cornett

†**Crockett** ....Wayne Mask
  City Admin., Ronald M. Duncan
Crosbyton............................Joe Hargrove
  City Admin., Margot Hardin
Cross Plains .... Ray Purvis
  City Admin., Debbie Gosnell
***Cross Roads** (11700 Hwy 380 E, Aubrey 76227) ....Harv Kitchens
***Cross Timber** (Box 2042, Burleson 76097)
  .... Wava McCullough
***Crowell** ....Robert Kincaid
†**Crowley**................................Billy P. Davis
  City Mgr., Truitt Gilbreath
*†**Crystal City** ....Norma R. Hernandez
  City Mgr., Diana Palacios
†**Cuero** .............................W.L. "Buzz" Edge
  City Mgr., Corlis Riedesel
Cumby .... Travis Baxley
Cuney...................................Jessie Johnson
Cushing .... Don Bruce Richards
Cut and Shoot (Box 7364, Conroe 77306)
  ....Lang Thompson

— D —

†**Daingerfield**...............................Lou Irvin
  City Mgr., Marty Byers
Daisetta.....................Edward "Lynn" Wells
  City Mgr., Harold G. Biano, Jr.
*†**Dalhart**................................ Kevin Caddell
  City Mgr., Greg Duggan
†**Dallas** ....Tom Leppert
  City Mgr., Mary K. Suhm
Dalworthington Gardens (2600 Roosevelt Dr., Arlington 76016)............ Michel Tedder
  City Admin., Melinda Brittain
Danbury ....Fred Williamson
Darrouzett............................. Bill Johnson
***Dawson** ....Paula Sears
†**Dayton** ....Steve E. Stephens
  City Mgr., David Douglas
***Dayton Lakes** (Box 1476, Dayton 77535)
  ....(vacancy)
***Dean** (6913 State Hwy. 79N, Wichita Falls 76035) ....Steve L. Sicking
†**Decatur** ....Joe A. Lambert
  City Mgr., Brett Shannon
***De Cordova** (4612 Cimmaron Tr., Granbury 76049) ....Dick Pruitt
†**Deer Park**.........................Wayne Riddle
  City Mgr., Ronald V. Crabtree
De Kalb ....Paul G. Meadows
  City Admin., Abbi Baker
†**De Leon** ....Danny Owen
Dell City ....Pamela Dean
  City Admin., Juanita R. Collier
*†**Del Rio** ....Efrain Valdez
  City Mgr., Rafael Castillo
†**Denison** .... Robert Brady
  City Mgr., Larry Cruise
†**Denton** ....Perry R. McNeill
  City Mgr., George Campbell
†**Denver City**...........................David Bruton
  City Mgr., Stan David
***Deport**................................ Edna Gifford
†**DeSoto** ....Bobby G. Waddle
  City Mgr., James Baugh
***Detroit**.................................. Travis Bronner
Devers.................................Edna Johnson
***Devine** .... Steve A. Lopez
  City Admin., Dora V. Rodriguez
Diboll............................Kenneth Williams
  City Mgr., Kenneth Williams
***Dickens** ....Lena Penick
†**Dickinson** ....Julie Masters
  City Admin., Julie Johnson
***Dilley**..............................Russell J. Foster
  City Admin., Felix (Ram) Arambula
*†**Dimmitt**..........................Wayne Collins
  City Mgr., David Denman
DISH ....Calvin Tillman
Dodd City.............................Jackie Lackey
***Dodson**....................................(vacancy)

Domino ....Marvin Campbell
†**Donna** .... Ricardo Morales
  City Mgr., Patricia Rene "P.R." Avila
Dorchester.........................Alice F. Stewart
Double Oak ....Pamela A. King
***Douglassville** ....Douglass B. Heath
Dripping Springs ....Todd Purcell
  City Mgr., Michelle Fischer
***Driscoll**..................................... Ted Ozuna
  City Admin., Roy Gonzalez
Dublin ....James "Red" Seigars
  City Mgr., David Carrothers
†**Dumas**...................................Mike Milligan
  City Mgr., Vince DiPiazza
†**Duncanville** .... David L. Green
  City Mgr., Kent Cagle

— E —

***Eagle Lake** .... Mike Morales
  City Mgr., Ronald W. Holland
†**Eagle Pass**.........................Chad Forester
  City Mgr., Marga Lopez
Early.................................Robert Mangrum
  City Admin., Ken Thomas
Earth.....................................Brad Freeman
***East Bernard**.................... Buck Boettcher
*†**Eastland**..............................Mark Pipkin
  Int. City Mgr., Don T. Wilson
East Mountain (RR 1, Box 500, Gilmer 75644) .... Ronnie Hill
  City Mgr., Tammy Hazel
Easton.................Willis Charles Sammons
East Tawakoni (288 Briggs Blvd., Point 75472) ....Gary Vaughan
***Ector** .... Mary Dean Norris
***Edcouch** ....Ramiro Silva
  City Admin., Ernesto Ayala Jr.
Eden...........................Charlie Rodgers, Jr.
***Edgecliff Village** (1605 Edgecliff Rd., Edgecliff 76134)........................ Mary King
Edgewood .... Charles Prater
†**Edinburg**.....................Richard H. Garcia
  Interim City Admin., Juan Jose "J.J." Roderiguez
***Edmonson**................. Wendell Edmonson
†**Edna**.....................................Joe D. Hermes
  City Mgr., Ken Pryor
Edom (150 PR 8279, Ben Wheeler 75754)
  .... Barbara Crow
*†**El Campo**.................. Kenneth G. Martin
  City Mgr., John Steelman
El Cenizo ....Raul L. Reyes
***Eldorado**.............................John Nikolauk
***Electra**...............................Glen Branch
  City Admin., Steve Giesbrent
*†**Elgin** .... Gladys Markert
  City Mgr., Jim D. Dunaway
Elkhart ....Joe B. Burris
El Lago..Brad Emel
Elmendorf.................. Thomas Preston Hicks
†**El Paso**..............................John F. Cook, Jr.
  City Admin., Joyce A. Wilson
†**Elsa** ....Senovio Castillo
  City Mgr., Maria Hilda Ayala
Emhouse (3825 Joe Johnson Dr., Corsicana 75110)...................Johnny Pattison
  City Mgr., Linda Maggard
Emory .... Cay Frances B. House
  City Admin., Clyde Smith
Enchanted Oaks (Box 5019, Gun Barrel City 75147) ....Donald G. Warner III
***Encinal** ....Javier Mancha
  City Admin., Matt Peter Olivera
†**Ennis**.................................Russell Thomas
  City Mgr., Steve Howerton
***Estelline** .... Don James
†**Euless** ....Mary Lib Saleh
  City Mgr., Joe Hennig
Eureka (1305 FM 2859, Corsicana 75110)
  .... Barney Thomas
Eustace.............................. Laura R. Ward
***Evant** ....Alma (Fritz) Green
†**Everman** ....Jim Stephenson

City Mgr., Donna Anderson

— F —

Fairchilds (8713 Fairchilds Rd., Richmond 77469) ....Richard G. Vacek
*Fairfield .... Roy Hill
  City Admin., Mike Gokey
Fair Oaks Ranch ...................E.L. Gaubatz
†Fairview (500 S. Hwy 5, McKinney 75069)
  ....Sim Israeloff
  Town Mgr., John Godwin
*Falfurrias ....J. Wesley Jacobs
Falls City...................................Vi Malone
†Farmers Branch ....Bob Phelps
  City Mgr., Gary D. Greer
*Farmersville ....Robbin H. Lamkin
  City Mgr., Alan Hein
Farwell ....Jimmie Mace
Fate ....David Hill
Fayetteville ....Ronald Pflughaupt
  City Mgr., Billy J. Wasut
Ferris...........................Jim E. Parks, Jr.
  City Mgr., Gus H.Pappas
Flatonia.....................................Bob Bizzell
  City Mgr., John Irvin
Florence....................................Paul Ward
*Floresville ....Daniel M. Tejada
  City Mgr., Gary Pelech
†Flower Mound....................Jody A. Smith
  Town Mgr., Harlan Jefferson
*Floydada ....Bobby Gilliland
  City Mgr., Gary Brown
Follett ....Lynn Blau
  City Mgr., Robert Williamson
*†Forest Hill (6800 Forest Hill Dr., Fort Worth 76140)........................James Gosey
  City Mgr., David Miller
†Forney............................Darrell Grooms
  City Mgr., Ron Patterson
Forsan....................................Roger Hudgins
Fort Stockton ....Tony Villarreal
  City Mgr., Danny Valenzuela
†Fort Worth ....Mike Moncrief
  City Mgr., Charles Boswell
Franklin..............................Charles Ellison
Frankston ....James Gouger
†Fredericksburg ....Jeryl Hoover
  City Mgr., Gary Neffendorf
*†Freeport............. James W. (Jim) Phillips
  City Mgr., Ron P. Bottoms
*Freer ....Arnoldo Cantu
*†Friendswood.............David J.H. Smith
  City Mgr., Roger Roecker
*Friona ....John C. Taylor
  City Mgr., Terri J. Johnson
†Frisco...............................Mike Simpson
  City Mgr., George A. Purefoy
*Fritch ....Kevin R. Keener
  City Mgr., Dottie Williams
Frost..Ken Reed
*Fruitvale ....Carl Waddell
Fulshear..........James "Jamie" W. Roberts
Fulton......................................Russel Cole

— G —

†Gainesville............................ Glenn Loch
  City Mgr., Mike Land
†Galena Park..............R.P. "Bobby" Barrett
  City Admin., John L. Cooper
*Gallatin ....Juanita Cotton
†Galveston ....Lyda Ann Thomas
  City Mgr., Steve LeBlanc
Ganado ....Clinton W. Tegeler
Garden Ridge.....................Jay Feibelman
  City Admin., Nancy Cain
†Garland............................Ronald Jones
  City Mgr., William E. Dollar
Garrett (208 N. Ferris St., Ennis 75119)
  ....Flo Smith
  City Admin., Bill Turnage
Garrison...............................Patsy Nugent

Gary ....Jean L. Heaton
†Gatesville........................David K. Byrom
  City Mgr., Roger L. Mumby
†Georgetown........................ Gary Nelon
  City Mgr., Paul Brandenburg
*†George West .... August E. Caron, Jr.
  City Mgr., Benjamin Tanguma
*Gholson (1277 Wesley Chapel Rd., Waco 76705) .... Larry Binnion
*†Giddings............................James Arndt
  City Mgr., Hector Forestier
†Gilmer......................................R.D. Cross
  City Mgr., Jeff Ellington
†Gladewater .... John Paul Tallent
  City Mgr., Jay Stokes
*Glenn Heights ....Clark C. Hoate
  City Mgr., Joseph Portugah
Glen Rose..................................Pam Miller
*Godley...............................David Wallis
  City Admin., Stephanie Hodges
Goldsmith.......................Billy Whittemore
  City Mgr., Vickie Emfinger
*Goldthwaite...................... Mike McMahan
  City Mgr., Bobby Rountree
*Goliad ....William J. Schaefer
  City Admin., Kenneth R. Bays
Golinda (7021 Golinda Dr., Lorena 76685)
  .... Mary Evelyn Hupp
†Gonzales........................Bobby G. O'Neil
  City Mgr., Buddy Drake
*Goodlow (Box 248, Kerens 75144)
  .... Willie H.Washington
Goodrich...................................Nita Gokey
*Gordon ....Pat M. Sublett
*Goree...................................Ray Hudson
†Gorman...............................Robert Ervin
Graford ....Carl Walston
  City Mgr., Tisha Sanchez
†Graham .... Wayne Christian
  City Mgr., Larry Fields
†Granbury ....David Southern
  City Mgr., Harold Sandel
Grandfalls.................. Mandy Brandenburg
  City Admin., Karen Thomas
†Grand Prairie................Charles England
  City Mgr., Tom Hart
Grand Saline ....Terry Tolar
  City Admin., Stephen G. Ashley
Grandview...................................Jack Orr
*Granger ....Jerry Lalla
  City Admin., Kathleen Vrana
†Granite Shoals ....Frank M. Reilly
  Interim City Mgr., John Gayle
Granjeno (6603 S. FM 494, Mission 78572) ....Alberto Magallan
  City Admin., Roy Garcia
Grapeland..............................Dan Walling
†Grapevine....................William D. Tate
  City Mgr., Bruno Rumbelow
Grayburg (17572 Grayburg Rd, Sour Lake 77659) ................................J.W. Floyd
Gray's Prairie (Box 116, Scurry 75158)
  ....Don Murray
*Greenville...........Thomas B. (Tom) Oliver
  City Mgr., Karen Daly
*Gregory ....Fernando P. Gomez
Grey Forest (18502 Scenic Loop Rd., Helotes 78023) ....Donald D. Darst
Groesbeck.................Jackie Levingston
  City Admin., Martha Stanton
Groom...................................Joe L. Homer
†Groves ....Brad Bailey
  City Mgr., D.E. Sosa
Groveton................................Troy Jones
Gruver................................Mark K. Irwin
  City Mgr., Linda Weller
†Gun Barrel City ....Paul Eaton
  City Mgr., (vacancy)
Gunter................................Mark A. Millar
*Gustine....................................Adam Stark

— H —

Hackberry (119 Maxwell Rd., Ste. B-7,

Frisco 75034)...................Brenda Lewallen
*Hale Center .... Sheryl Lyn Canales
*Hallettsville .... Warren Grindeland
  City Admin., Tom Donnelly
Hallsburg (1115 Wilbanks Dr., Waco 76705) .... Mike Glockzin
*Hallsville........................ T. Bynum Hatley
†Haltom City...........................Bill Lanford
  City Mgr., Tom Muir
Hamilton ....Roy Rumsey
  City Admin., Bill Funderburk
Hamlin...........................Jack W. Shields
Happy.......................................Sara Tirey
Hardin ....Lee Miller
†Harker Heights......................Ed Mullen
  City Mgr., Steve Carpenter
†Harlingen ....Chris Boswell
  City Mgr., Craig Lonon
Hart.....................................Stanley Dyer
*Haskell ....Ken Lane
  City Admin., Brandon Anderson
Haslet...................................Gary Hulsey
  City Coord., Diane Rasor
Hawk Cove (Box 670, Quinlan 75474)
  .... Ava Havens
Hawkins ....Sam Bradley
*Hawley..........................Ronnie Woodard
Hays (Box 1285, Buda 78610)
  .... Joleen B. Brown
*†Hearne .... Ruben Gomez
  City Mgr., Wendell Hughey
*Heath ....John Ratcliffe
  City Mgr., Edward Thatcher
*Hebron (Box 118916, Carrollton 75010)
  .... Kelly Clem
Hedley......................................Janie Hill
Hedwig Village (955 Piney Point Rd., Houston 77024) ....Sue V. Speck
  City Admin., Beth Staton
Helotes...........................Tom Schoolcraft
  City Mgr., (vacancy)
Hemphill ....Robert Hamilton
  City Mgr., Donald P. Iles
*Hempstead....................Michael S. Wolfe
  City Admin. (vacancy)
†Henderson.....................John W. Fullen
  City Mgr., Randy Freeman
Henrietta ....James Stanford
  City Admin., Robert Patrick
*†Hereford ....Robert D. Josserand
  City Mgr., Rick L. Hanna
†Hewitt .... Charles D. Turner
  City Mgr., Dennis H. Woodard
Hickory Creek (Box 453, Lake Dallas 75065) ....Jeff Price
*Hico .... Lavern Tooley
  City Admin., Lambert Little
*Hidalgo ....John David Franz
  City Mgr., Joe Vera III
Hideaway ....Bill Kashouty
Higgins .... Gary Duncan
Highland Haven ....Peter E. Freehill
†Highland Park (4700 Drexel Dr., Dallas 75205) .... William D. White Jr.
  City Admin., L.A. (George) Patterson
†Highland Village................Dianne Costa
  City Mgr., Mike Leavitt
Hill Country Village (116 Aspen Ln., San Antonio 78232) .... Kirk W. Francis
*Hillcrest Village (Box 1172, Alvin 77512)
  .... Craig Gilbert
†Hillsboro.........................John P. Erwin Jr.
  Acting City Mgr., Betty Harrell
Hilshire Village (8301 West View, Houston 77055) ....Robin S. Border
†Hitchcock ....Lee A. Sander
*Holiday Lakes (RR 4, Box 747, Angleton 77515) ....Charles Rushing
*Holland ....Dora Mae Smith
Holliday.................................. Allen Moore
Hollywood Park........Richard W. McIlveen
†Hondo........................James W. Danner
  City Mgr., Robert T. Herrera
*Honey Grove...................Monte Ashcraft

Hooks..............................Michael W. Babb
*†Horizon City.............Raymond Morales
Horseshoe Bay...................Bob Lambert
*†Houston.....................................Bill White
Howardwick (HC 2 Box 2230, Clarendon 79226)......................................Marvin Elam
*Howe...............................Michael Jones
City Admin., Steven McKay
Hubbard..........................Terry F. Reddell
City Mgr., Al Saldana
Hudson (201 Mount Carmel Rd., Lufkin 75904)...Robert Smith
City Admin., James M. Freeman
Hudson Oaks (150 N. Oakridge Dr., Weatherford 76087)..............................Par Deen
Hughes Springs.................Reba Simpson
City Mgr., George Fite
*†Humble................Donald G. McMannes
City Mgr., Darrell Boeske
*Hunters Creek Village (1 Hunters Creek Pl., Houston 77024)........Stephen Reichek
*Huntington................Herman Woolbright
City Admin., Robert Walker
*†Huntsville.................................J. Turner
City Mgr., Kevin Evans
†Hurst...................................Richard Ward
City Mgr., Allan Weegar
Hutchins...............................Artis Johnson
Hutto.............................Kenneth L. Love
City Mgr., Edward Broussard
*Huxley (RR 1, Box 1410, Shelbyville 75973)................................. Larry Vaughn

— I —

Idalou.......................................Jack Bush
City Admin., Jeffrey Snyder
Impact (Box 3116, Abilene 79604)
....Jack Sharp
Indian Lake (62 S. Aztec Cove Dr., Los Fresnos 78566)..........Luis C. Martinez Sr.
Industry.............................Alan W. Kuehn
*†Ingleside........................... Elaine Kemp
City Mgr., Walter Hill
Ingleside on the Bay (Box B, Ingleside 78362)..........................Cynthia B. Foster
Ingram.............................Howard Jackson
*Iowa Colony (12003 Cty. Rd. 65, Rosharon 77583)...............................Robert Wall
*Iowa Park.........................Randy Catlin
City Admin., Michael C. Price
*Iraan.....................................June Heck
Iredell..............................Royce P. Heath
†Irving..............................Herbert Gears
City Mgr., Tommy Gonzalez
Italy...................................Frank Jackson
City Admin., Cynthia Olguin
*Itasca.....................................David Heald
City Mgr., Mark Gropp

— J —

†Jacinto City.......................Mike Jackson
City Mgr., Jack Maner
Jacksboro............................ Tom Sessions
City Mgr., Shawna Dowell
*†Jacksonville...............Robert N. Haberle
City Mgr., Mo Raissi
Jamaica Beach (Box 5264, Galveston 77554)..................................Victor Pierson
City Admin., John Brick
Jarrell............................Wayne E. Cavalier
*†Jasper...........................David G. Barber
City Mgr., Alan Grindstaff
Jayton....................................Albert Brown
*Jefferson........................Ned Fratangelo
City Admin., Corby D. Alexander
†Jersey Village.................Russell Hamley
City Mgr., Mike Castro
Jewett.............................Judi Kirkpatrick
Joaquin...............................Steve Hughes
Johnson City....................Kermit Roeder
City Admin., David Dockery
Jolly (194 Milton St., Wichita Falls 76301)

.....................................Mary Y. Taylor
Jones Creek (7207 Stephen F. Austin Rd., Freeport 77541)................ George Mitchell
*Jonestown.....................James M. Brown
City Admin., Johnny Sartain
Josephine.......................Cameron Brooks
†Joshua.................Merle M. Breitenstein
City Mgr., Paulette Hartman
Jourdanton................................Larry Pryor
City Mgr., Daniel G. Nick
Junction.............................James C. Murr
City Admin., Mike Evans
Justin...Ed Trietsch

— K —

Karnes City............................ Don Tymrak
City Admin., Larry Pippen
†Katy..Don Elder Jr.
City Admin., Johnny Nelson
†Kaufman......................... William Fortner
City Mgr., Curtis Snow
†Keene.............................Roy W. Robinson
City Admin., James Minor
†Keller....................................Pat McGrail
City Mgr., (vacancy)
Kemah.....................................Greg Collins
City Admin., R.W. "Bill" Kerber
Kemp.....................................Billy M. Teel
City Admin., James Stroman
Kempner...........................Gene Isenhour
Kendleton..........................Carolyn Jones
Kenedy............................. Randy Garza
City Mgr., Reggie H. Winters
*Kenefick (3564 FM 1008, Dayton 77535)
..................Steven Douglas Ames Jr.
Kennard.....................................Bill Thomas
City Admin., Glenn Westbrook
†Kennedale...................Bryan Lankhorst
City Mgr., Bob Hart
Kerens............................Joe B. Baxter
City Admin., Cindy Scott
*†Kermit.......................Ted Westmoreland
City Mgr., Sam Watson
†Kerrville.....................Eugene C. Smith
City Mgr., Paul A. Hofmann
*Kilgore.............................Joe T. Parker
City Mgr., Jeffrey Howell
†Killeen.....................Timothy L. Hancock
City Mgr., Connie J. Green
*†Kingsville...........................Sam Fugate
City Mgr., Carlos Yerena
*†Kirby.................................Ray Martin
City Mgr., Zina Tedford
Kirbyville............................Giles Hom, Jr.
City Admin., Paul Brister
*Kirvin......................................(vacancy)
Knollwood Village (100 Collins Dr., Sherman 75090)..........................Richard Roelke
Knox City...............................Jeff Stanfield
City Mgr., Barbara Rector
Kosse......................................Ben Daniell
Kountze.............................Fred E. Williams
City Admin., Roderick Hutto
*Kress.................................Esther Mount
*Krugerville.......................Robert Cleversy
Krum....................................Terry Wilson
*Kurten (1888 N. FM 2038, Bryan 77808)
....Bobby Kurten
†Kyle................................Miguel Gonzalez
City Mgr., Thomas L. Mattis

— L —

La Coste.......................Henry A. Seay Jr.
City Admin., (vacancy)
†Lacy-Lakeview (Box 154549, Waco 76715)...............................Calvin Hodde
City Mgr., Michael Nicoletti
†Ladonia..............................Leon Hurse
†La Feria..............Stephen Page Brewer
City Mgr., Sunny K. Philip
*Lago Vista...........................Dennis Jones
City Mgr., Bill Angelo

†La Grange.........................Janet Moerbe
City Mgr., Shawn Raborn
*La Grulla.....................Oscar V. Gonzalez
Laguna Vista (122 Fernandez St., Port Isabel 78578)................................Stan Hulse
City Admin., Iris Hill
La Joya.................... William R. "Billy" Leo
City Admin., Mike Alaniz
Lake Bridgeport (301 S. Main St., Bridgeport 76426)..........................Doug Dunlap
Lake City (Box 177, Mathis 78368)
....Harold McCown
†Lake Dallas...................Marjory Johnson
City Mgr., Earl Berner
†Lake Jackson.......................Bob Sippie
City Mgr., William P. Yenne
Lakeport...........................Ricky L. Shelton
Lakeside (Box 787, Mathis 78368)
....Ed Gentry, Jr.
*Lakeside.......................Raymond E. Beck
City Mgr., Donald W. Seely
Lakeside City (Box 4287, Wichita Falls 76308)............................Steve Halloway
City Mgr., Sam Bownds
Lake Tanglewood (RR 8, Box 35-15, Amarillo 79118).........................John Langford
Lakeview..............................Kelly Clark
†Lakeway............................. Steve Swan
City Mgr., Steve Jones
Lakewood Village..............Frank Jaromin
City Mgr., Angela Rangel
†Lake Worth.................... Walter Bowen
City Mgr., Joey Highfill
*†La Marque.....................Larry E. Crow
City Mgr., Robert Ewart
†Lamesa........................ Kelvin Barkowsky
City Mgr., Fred Vera
*†Lampasas.........................Jack Calvert
City Mgr., Michael Talbot
†Lancaster............................Joe Tillotson
City Mgr., Rickey Childers
†La Porte.......................... Alton E. Porter
Interim City Mgr., John Joerns
*†Laredo............................. Raul Salinas
City Mgr., Larry Dovalina
Latexo.............................Deborah Bruner
La Vernia.......................D. Bradford Beck
*La Villa..............................Rene Castillo
City Mgr., Jaime Gutierrez
Lavon.....................................Norma Martin
*La Ward............................. Hunter A. Karl
Lawn...............................Mitchell Connel
†League City.........................Jerry Shults
City Admin., Chris Reed
*Leakey..............................Jesse Pendley
*†Leander.....................John D. Cowman
City Mgr., Anthony Johnson
*Leary (RR 5, Box 435, Texarkana 75501)
.... James Palma Sr.
Ledbetter...................................(vacancy)
Lefors..............................Michael R. Young
*Leona..............................Travis J. Oden
Leonard............................Willaim J. Yoss
City Admin., George Henderson
Leon Valley...........................Chris Riley
City Mgr., Lanny S. Lambert
*Leroy.............................David Williams
†Levelland..........................Hugh Bradley
City Mgr., Richard A. Osburn
†Lewisville............................. Gene Carey
City Mgr., Claude King
Lexington........................Robert Willrich Sr.
†Liberty................................. Carl Pickett
Interim City Mgr., Michael Ramirez
*Liberty Hill.........................Connie Fuller
*Lincoln Park (110 Parker Pkwy., Aubrey 76227)...............................Loretta Ray
City Mgr., Nat Parker III
*Lindale...............................James Ballard
City Admin., Jim Cox
Linden................................Kenny Hamilton
Lindsay............................Steven K. Zwinggi
Lipan......................................Mike Stowe
†Little Elm.........................Frank Kastner

City Mgr., Ivan Langford
*†Littlefield ....Shirley Mann
City Mgr., Danny Davis
*Little River-Academy (Box 521, Little
River 76554) ....Ronnie W. White
†Live Oak................. Henry O. Edwards Jr.
City Mgr., Matt Smith
*Liverpool............................Michael Peters
Livingston ....Ben R. Ogletree Jr.
City Mgr., Marilyn Sutton
Llano.................................Roger Pinchney
City Mgr., John T. Montgomery
*†Lockhart ....James Bertram
City Mgr., Clovia English
Lockney ....Rodger Stapp
City Admin., Ron Hall
Log Cabin ....Gene Bearden
*Lometa ....Mike McGarry
*Lone Oak............................Harold Slemmons
*Lone Star............................Maggie Curtis
†Longview ....Jay Dean
City Mgr., David Willard
Loraine.............................Ina Vay McAdams
*Lorena ....Stacy Garvin
City Mgr., John Moran
*Lorenzo ....Lester C. Bownds
City Admin., Dorothy Bristow
†Los Fresnos .... David N. Winstead Sr.
City Admin., Mark W. Milum
Los Indios..................Diamantina Bennett
*Los Ybañez (1919 CR M, Box 52A, Lame-
sa 79331)..........................Mary A. Ybañez
*Lott ....Juanita Hogg
Lovelady ....Michael R. Broxson
*Lowry Crossing (1405 S. Bridgefarmer
Rd., McKinney 75069) .... Greg Piatt
†Lubbock.............................David A. Miller
City Mgr., Lee Ann Dumbauld
Lucas (151 Country Club Rd., Allen 75002)
....Bill Carmickle
City Admin., Charles Fenner
Lueders...............................Russell Mullins
†Lufkin............................... Jack Gorden
City Mgr., Paul Parker
†Luling...............................Mike Hendricks
City Mgr., Robert W. Berger
*Lumberton ....Don Surratt
City Mgr., Norman P. Reynolds
Lyford...............................Rodolfo Saldaña
Lytle ....Horace E. Fincher
City Admin., Josie Campa

— M —

Mabank ....Larry Teague
City Admin., Louann Confer
Madisonville .... Don Dean
City Mgr., Ruth Smith
*Magnolia............................Jimmy Thornton
City Mgr., Roger D. Carlisle
Malakoff........................Pat Isaacson
City Admin., Glen Herriage, Ann Baker
Malone ....David Wood
Manor.................................Joe Sanchez
City Mgr., Phil Tate
†Mansfield............................Barton Scott
City Mgr., Clayton W. Chandler
Manvel ....Delores M. Martin
*†Marble Falls ....Raymond Whitman
City Mgr., George W. Russell
Marfa................................Daniel P. Dunlap
Marietta............................ Susan Brigance
Marion................................Glenn A. Hild
*†Marlin .... Norman D. Erskine
City Mgr., Randall Holly
Marquez................................Stynette Clary
*†Marshall.............................. Ed Carlile
City Mgr., Frank Johnson
Marshall Creek (Box 1070, Roanoke
76262) ....James Stimpson
City Admin., Diana Underwood
*Mart.................................Richard Bryant
Martindale......................Patricia Peterson
Mason ....Brent Hinckley

City Admin., Brain Boudreaux
Matador..................................Pat Smith
†Mathis ....Mario Alonzo
City Admin., Manuel Lara
Maud ....Patric McCoy
City Mgr., Betty Hamilton
Maypearl .... Kelly Jacobson
†McAllen ....Richard Cortez
City Mgr., Mike R. Perez
McCamey ....Sherry Phillips
City Mgr., Lou Ann Watson
*†McGregor ....James S. Hering
City Mgr., Dennis McDuffie
†McKinney ....Bill Whitfield
City Mgr., Lawrence Robinson
*McLean ....Bobby Martin
McLendon-Chisholm (1248 S. St. Hwy.
205 Rockwall 75032)..Michael D. Donegan
City Admin., David Butler
Meadow ....Eloisa Cuellar
City Admin., Katherine Saulters
*Meadowlakes ....John Aaron
Meadows Place ....Mark McGrath
*Megargel ....Danny Fails
Melissa..........................David E. Dorman
City Admin., Jason Little
Melvin ....Billy Joe Ferris
City Admin., Mike Hagan
Memphis ....Joe D. Rollo
City Admin., Nelwyn Ward
Menard...........................Johnny L. Brown
City Admin., Sharon L. Key
†Mercedes ....Joel Quintanilla
City Mgr., Ricardo Garcia
Meridian.................................Jeffery Keese
City Mgr., Tanya Ramer
Merkel .... Rusty Watts
City Mgr., Donnie Edwards
*Mertens ....Linda Maples
Mertzon.................................Patsy Kahlig
City Admin., Linda C. Harris
†Mesquite ....Mike Anderson
City Mgr., Ted Barron
†Mexia ....Steve Brewer
City Mgr., Carolyn Martin
Miami .... Rusty Early
*†Midland..........................Michael J. Canon
City Mgr., Rick Menchaca
†Midlothian......................Boyce L. Whatley
City Mgr., Don Hastings
Midway......................Patrick H. Wakefield
Milano ....Billy Barnett
*Mildred (5417 FM 637, Corsicana 75110)
.... Robert D. (Duane) Carpenter
Miles....................................Juan Ornelas
Milford.................................Carrie Wallace
*Miller's Cove (RR 3, Box 491, Mt. Pleas-
ant 75455) ....Grady Hughes
Millsap ....Jamie French
Mineola .........................N.R. (Pete) Smith
City Admin., Dion O. Miller
†Mineral Wells
.... Clarence Holliman
City Mgr., Lance Howerton
*Mingus .... Milo Moffit
†Mission ....Norberto Salinas
City Mgr., Julio Cerda
†Missouri City .... Allen Owen
City Mgr., Frank Simpson
*Mobeetie........................Gordon Estes
Mobile City (824 Lilac, Rock-
wall 75087) .... Wanda Cooper
*†Monahans ....David B. Cutbirth
City Mgr., David Mills
Mont Belvieu .... Nick Dixon
City Admin., Bryan Easum
*Montgomery.........................Edith Moore
City Admin., Vicky Rudy
Moody ....Michael Alton
City Admin., Charleen Dowell
*Moore Station (4818 FM 314
S, LaRue 75770) ....Arthur T. Earl
†Moran ....Lisa Clopton-Taggart
Morgan.................................Teresa Stacy

*Morgan's Point (Box 839, La
Porte 77572) ....Peggy Arisco
City Admin., Lance Avant
Morgan's Point Resort ..Malvin D. Fischer
City Mgr., Stacy Wayne Hitchman
Morton ....Edward Akin
City Mgr., Brenda Shaw
Moulton.............................Cindy McIntosh
City Admin., Michael Arnold
Mountain City (Box 1494, Buda 78610)
.............................LaVerne McClendon
City Mgr., Charlie Koehn
Mount Calm ....Jimmy Tucker
City Mgr., Tricia Law
Mount Enterprise...............Harvey Graves
City Mgr., Rosena J. Becker-Ross
†Mount Pleasant ....Jerry Boatner
City Mgr., Courtney Sharp
*Mount Vernon .............J.D. Baumgardner
City Mgr., Jim Blanchard
Muenster..............................Johnny Pagel
City Mgr., Stan Endres
†Muleshoe ....Cliff Black
City Mgr., David Brunson
*Mullin ....Larry Reese
Munday ....Robert Bowen
City Admin., Dwayne Bearden
*Murchison ....Larry Everett
*Murphy ....Bret Baldwin
City Mgr., Craig Sherwood
*Mustang (Box 325, Corsicana 75151)
....Jackie Bounds
Mustang Ridge (12800 Hwy. 183 S., Buda
78610) ....Alfred Vallejo II

— N —

†Nacogdoches ....Roger Van Horn
City Mgr., James P. Jeffers
*Naples ....John R. Anthony
*Nash ....Henry Slaton
City Mgr., Elizabeth Lea
†Nassau Bay (1800 NASA Rd. 1, Houston
77058) ....Donald C. Matter
City Mgr., John D. Kennedy
Natalia ....Ruberta C. Vera
City Mgr., Beth Leonesio
Navarro (222 S. Harvard Ave., Corsicana
75110).................................Benny Horn
†Navasota.................................. Bert Miller
City Mgr., Brad Stafford
Nazareth ....Ralph Brockman
†Nederland ..................R.A. "Dick" Nugent
City Mgr., André Wimer
*Needville ....Delbert Wendt
Nevada.................................Christy Schell
Newark..Bill Malone
New Berlin (9180 FM 775, La Vernia
78121) ....Gilbert R. Merkle
New Boston.................Johnny L. Branson
*†New Braunfels ....Bruce Boyer
City Mgr., Michael Morrison
*Newcastle .... Darlton Dyer
*New Chapel Hill (14039 Cty. Rd. 220, Ty-
ler 75707) ....Robert Whitaker
*New Deal ....Christopher Bruce
New Fairview (Box 855, Rhome 76078)
....Joe Max Wilson
City Mgr., Monica Rodriguez
*New Home......................Steve Lisemby
*New Hope (Box 562, McKinney 75070)
......................................Johnny Hamm
*New London......................Mollie Ward
New Summerfield ....Dan L. Stallings
Newton................................Rachel Martin
City Admin., Donald H. Meek
New Waverly....................Dan Underwood
*Neylandville (2469 Cty. Rd. 4311, Green-
ville 75401) ....Kathy Wilson
Niederwald.....................Shirley Whisenant
City Admin., Angie Schulze
Nixon.................................Don Chessher
City Admin., Marilyn Byrd
Nocona .... Robert H. Fenoglio

City Mgr., Lynn Henley
Nolanville..........................Carolyn Sterling
*Nome ....David Studdert
Noonday (Box 6425, Tyler 75711)
....J. Mike Turman
Nordheim.......................Katherine Payne
*Normangee ....Tim Taylor
*North Cleveland (Box 1266, Cleveland 77327) ....Robert Bartlett
Northlake (Box 729, Justin 76247)
....Peter Dewing
†North Richland Hills .... Oscar Trevino
City Mgr., Larry J. Cunningham
*Novice ....Wanda Motley

— O —

Oak Grove (Box 309, Kaufman 75142)
....Jerry G. Holder
Oak Leaf .... Paul Klooster
Oak Point.............................Tom Kanuch
City Mgr., Richard Martin
*Oak Ridge (129 Oak Ridge Dr., Gainesville 76240) .... Tommy Shugart
*Oak Ridge (Box 539, Kaufman 75142)
....Roy W. Perkins
Oak Ridge North (27424 Robinson Rd., Conroe 77385)............... Fred R. O'Connor
City Admin., Paul Mendes
*Oak Valley (2211 Oak Valley, Corsicana 75110).. Bob O'Dell
*Oakwood .... Teresa Brewer
*O'Brien .... Charlene Brothers
*Odem......................Jessie Rodriguez Sr.
†Odessa......................Larry L. Melton
City Mgr., Richard Morton
O'Donnell......................James E. Williams
*Oglesby......................Kenneth Goodwin
*Old River-Winfree (Box 1169, Mont Belvieu 77580)...........................Joe Landry
Olmos Park (119 W. El Prado Dr., San Antonio 78212)......................Ronald Teftellir
City Mgr., Amy Buckert
†Olney .... Mary Schoonover
City Admin., Danny C. Parker
Olton .... Tom B. McGill
City Mgr., Marvin Tillman
Omaha ....Dwaine Higgins
Onalaska........................... Lew Vail
Opdyke West (Box 1179, Levelland 79336)
.... Wayne Riggins
*†Orange.............. William Brown Claybar
City Mgr., Shawn Oubre
*Orange Grove .... Seale Brand
City Admin., Perry R. Young
Orchard ....Rodney Pavlock
*Ore City ....Glenn Breazeale
*Overton ....Robert Young
*Ovilla .... Bill Turner
City Admin., John McDonald
*Oyster Creek.......... Richard D. Merriman

— P —

Paducah.............................Howard Smith
†Paint Rock.......................... John Hruska
†Palacios......................Joseph Morton
City Mgr., Charles R. Winfield
†Palestine..........................Carolyn Salter
City Mgr., R Dale Brown
Palisades (115 Brentwood Rd., Amarillo 79118)...Pat Knight
*Palmer..........................Don Huskins
Palmhurst .... Ramiro J. Rodriguez Sr.
City Mgr., Lori A. Lopez
Palm Valley (1313 Stuart Place Rd., Harlingen 78552).............................Joe Neely
*Palmview (RR 11, Box 1000, Edinburg 78539) ....Jorge G. García
City Mgr., John V. Alaniz
*†Pampa ....Lonny Robbins
City Mgr., John Horst
*Panhandle.............................Dan Looten
City Mgr., Loren Brand

Panorama Village (98 Hiwon Dr., Conroe 77304) ....Howard L. Kravetz
Pantego ....Dorothy Anderhult
City Mgr., Doug Davis
Paradise.................... Nathan C. Cleveland
*†Paris .... Richard Manning
City Mgr., Tony N. Williams .
Parker (5700 E. Parker Rd., Allen 75002)
....Jerry Tartaglino
City Admin., Dina Daniel
*†Pasadena ....John Manlove
Pattison .... Bill Matthews
Patton Village (16940 Main St., Splendora 77372) ....Cecil Ray White
Payne Springs (Box 2, Mabank 75147)
....Michael McDonald
*†Pearland .... Tom Reid
City Mgr., Bill Eisen
†Pearsall........................ George Cabasos
City Mgr., José G. Treviño
*Pecan Gap...................... Warner Cheney
Pecan Hill (Box 443, Red Oak 75154)
....Rick Blake
*†Pecos.......................Richard L. Alligood
City Mgr., Joseph Torres
Pelican Bay (1300 Pelican Cir., Azle 76020)......................Thomas A. Reed
*Penelope ....Inez Arriola
Peñitas........................Servando Ramírez
City Admin., Oscar Cuellar Jr.
*Pernitas Point (HC 1, Box 1440, Sandia 78383) .... Jerry W. Hedrick
Perryton .... David C. Hale
City Mgr., David Landis
Petersburg.........................Darin Greene
City Mgr., Marie Parr
*Petrolia ....Cindy Armour
*Petronila (RR 3, Box 42, Robstown 78380) ....William J. Ordner
*†Pflugerville.................Catherine Callen
City Mgr., David Buesing
†Pharr ....Leopoldo "Leo" Palacios
City Mgr., Fred Sandoval
Pilot Point ....Jerry W. Alford
City Admin., Vicky Varnau
*Pine Forest (Box 1004, Vidor 77670)........
....Bruce Childs
Pinehurst (3640 Mockingbird, Orange 77630) ....Jerry D. Hussey
City Admin., Dan Robertson
*Pine Island (RR 3, Box 70AF, Hempstead 77445) ....Debra Ferris
*Pineland ....John O. Booker Jr.
Piney Point Village (7721 San Felipe, #100 Houston 77063) ....Carol Fox
City Admin., Lorena Briel
Pittsburg .... Shawn Kennington
City Mgr., Jim Blanchard
Plains ....Pamela Redman
City Admin., Terry B. Howard
†Plainview ....John C. Anderson
City Mgr., Greg Ingham
†Plano..............................Pat Evans
City Mgr., Thomas Muehlenbeck
Pleak Village (6621 FM 2218 Rd., Richmond 77469) ....Margie Krenek
*†Pleasanton .... Bill Carroll
City Mgr., Kathy Coronado
Pleasant Valley (4006 Hwy 287 E, Iowa Park 76367) ....Raymond Haynes
City Mgr., Norm Hodges
*Plum Grove (Box 1358, Splendora 77372) .... T.W. Garrett
Point.........................James Phillip Kerr
Point Blank.........................Lillian Bratton
Point Comfort....................Pam Lambden
*Point Venture (549 Venture Blvd. S. Leander 78645) ....Kevin Sheffer
Ponder ....Jeff Vardell
†Port Aransas ....Claude Brown
City Mgr., Michael Kovacs
*†Port Arthur ....Oscar G. Ortiz
City Mgr., Steve Fitzgibbons
*†Port Isabel................Patrick H. Marchan

City Mgr., Robert H. García
†Portland ....David R. Krebs
City Mgr., Michael Tanner
†Port Lavaca ....Jack Whitlow
City Mgr., Gary Broz
†Port Neches...............R. Glenn Johnson
City Mgr., Randy Kimler
Post .................................W.G. Pool Jr.
City Mgr., Ric Walton
Post Oak Bend (Box 758, Kaufman 75142) ....Raymond Bedrick
*Poteet ....Lino Z. Donato
City Admin., Adolfo F. Rodriguez
Poth ....Chrystal Eckel
Pottsboro...............................Frank Budra
City Mgr., Kevin M. Farley
Powell ....Dennis Bancroft
Poynor ....Dannie Smith
Prairie View ....Frank D. Jackson
Premont ....Norma Tullos
*Presidio ....Alcee M. Tavarez
City Admin., Lorenzo Cabrerra
Primera ....John David Osbourne
City Admin., Javier Mendez
Princeton ....Steven Deffibaugh
City Admin., Lesia Thornhill
*Progreso ....Omar Vela
City Admin., Alfredo (Fred) Espinosa
*Progreso Lakes (Box 760, Progreso 78579) ........................O.D. (Butch) Emery
*Prosper......................Charles E. Niswanger
City Admin., Douglas Mousel
*Putnam ....Roy Petty
Pyote...................................Earl Stoker

— Q —

†Quanah ....Gary Newsom
City Admin., Danny Felty
*Queen City ....Harold Martin
Quinlan ....Sharon Royal
*Quintana ....James Nevil
Quitaque .... Clyde Dudley
City Mgr., Maria Cruz Merrell
Quitman ....Sammy D. Lang

— R —

*Ralls.................................Kelly Wing
City Admin., J. Rhett Parker
Rancho Viejo.......................Craig B. Flood
City Admin., Cheryl J. Kretz
*Ranger ....John Casey
*†Rangerville (31850 Rangerville Rd., San Benito 78586) ....Wayne I Talbert
*Rankin ....Cora Gaynelle McFadden
Ransom Canyon ....Robert G. Englund
City Admin., Melissa Verett
Ravenna ....Claude L. Lewis
*†Raymondville.................Orlando Correa
Red Lick (Box 870, Nash 75569)
....Sheila K. Kegley
*†Red Oak.................................Ron Bryce
City Mgr., Ken Pfeifer
Redwater ....Beverly Phares
*Refugio ....Ray Jaso
Reklaw .... Bill Traweek
Reno (Lamar Co.) ....Weldon M. Coston
City Admin., Shannon Barrentine
Reno (195 W. Reno Rd., Azle 76020)........
..................Granville (Randy) Martin III
*Retreat (125 Ingham Rd., Corsicana 75110)........................Janice Barfknecht
Rhome ....Mark Lorance
*Rice.................................Larry Bailey
†Richardson .... Steve Mitchell
City Mgr., Bill Keffler
*Richland ....Dolores Baldwin
†Richland Hills...................David L. Ragan
City Mgr., James W. Quin
Richland Springs ....Jerry M. Benton
*Richmond....................... Hilmar G. Moore
City Mgr., R. Glen Gilmore
Richwood ....Sandra Boykin

*Riesel............................David Guenat, Jr.
  City Admin., Bill McLelland
Rio Bravo (1402 Centeno Ln., Laredo 78046) ....Juan G. Gonzalez
*Rio Grande City ....Kevin D. Hiles
  City Admin., Juan F. Zuniga
Rio Hondo ....Santiago A. Saldana Jr.
  City Admin., Arturo F. Prida
Rio Vista ....William Keith Hutchinson
*Rising Star ....Earl B. Harris
*†River Oaks (4900 River Oaks Blvd, Fort Worth 76114) ....Herman D. Earwood
  City Admin., Linda A. Ryan
Riverside .... G. Frank Rich
  City Mgr., Joan Harvey
Roanoke ....Carl E. Gierisch Jr.
  City Mgr., Jimmy Stathatos
*Roaring Springs ....Corky Marshall
  City Mgr., Robert Osborn
*Robert Lee ....Joe V. White
*Robinson........................Bryan Ferguson
  City Mgr., R.C. Fletcher
†Robstown ....Rodrigo Ramon Jr.
Roby.....................................Eli Sepeda
  City Mgr., Claude A. Day
*Rochester........Marvin Stegemoeller
  City Mgr., Gregg Hearn
*†Rockdale ....John C. Shoemake
  City Mgr., T. Flemming
†Rockport......................Todd W. Pearson
  City Mgr., Thomas J. Blazek
*Rocksprings ....Rachel Gallegos
†Rockwall........................William R. Cecil
  City Mgr., Julie Couch
Rocky Mound (Box 795, Pittsburg 75686) ....Noble T. Smith
Rogers ....Billy Ray Crow
Rollingwood ....Hollis Jefferies
  City Mgr., Vicky Rudy
Roma ....Rogelio Ybarra
  City Mgr., Crisanto Salinas
Roman Forest ....Floyd O. Jackson Jr.
Ropesville........................Victor Marrett
Roscoe...............Frank S. (Pete) Porter
  City Admin., Jack Brown
*Rosebud...........................Kenny Hensel
  City Mgr., Megan Henderson
*Rose City (370 S. Rose City Dr., Vidor 77662) ....David E. Bush
Rose Hill Acres (Box 8285, Lumberton 77657) ....Nannette Knight
†Rosenberg....................Joe M. Gurecky
  City Mgr., Jack S. Hamlett
Ross ....James L. Jaska Sr.
*Rosser ....Albert L. Davis
*Rotan ....Jerry A. Marshall
  City Mgr., Harold Sanders
*Round Mountain...............Alvin Gutierrez
*†Round Rock ....Nyle Maxwell
  City Mgr., Jim Nuse
Round Top.........................Barnell Albers
*†Rowlett ....C. Shane Johnson
  City Mgr., Craig S. Owens
Roxton ....James (Jimmy) Cooper
Royse City ....Jim Mellody
  City Mgr., Karen Philippi
Rule ....James M. Marquis
*Runaway Bay..........................A.L. Jowitt
Runge ....Homer Lott Jr.
†Rusk................................Angela Raiborn
  City Mgr., Mike Murray

— S —

Sabinal..............................Henry Alvarado
†Sachse ....Mike J. Felix
  City Mgr., Allen Barnes
Sadler....................................Jaime Harris
†Saginaw ....Gary Brinkley
  City Mgr., Nan Stanford
St. Hedwig ....Mary Jo Dylla
*Saint Jo ....Tom Weger
St. Paul (2505 Butcher's Block, Wylie 75098) ....Opie Walter

Salado..Rick Ashe
*†San Angelo...................Joseph W. Lown
  City Mgr., Harold Dominguez
†San Antonio................. Phil Hardberger
  Int. City Mgr., Sheryl L. Sculley
San Augustine....................Leroy Hughes
  City Mgr., James Duke Lyons Jr.
*†San Benito....................Joe Hernandez
  City Mgr., Victor Trevino
Sanctuary (Box 125, Azle 76098)
  ....Cliff Scallan
San Diego ....Alonzo Lopez Jr.
  City Mgr., Ernest Sanchez Jr.
*Sandy Point .... Curt Mowery
*San Felipe ....Bobby Byars
Sanford ....Rodney Ormon
*Sanger.................................Joe Higgs
  City Mgr., Jack L. Smith
*†San Juan ...San Juanita "Janie" Sanchez
  City Mgr., Jorge A. Arcaute
San Leanna (Box 1107, Manchaca 78652)
  ....James E. Payne
  City Admin., Kathleen Lessing
†San Marcos ....Susan Naruaiz
  City Mgr., Dan O'Leary
*San Patricio (5617 Main, Mathis 78368)
  .... Lonnie Glasscock III
*San Perlita........................Oscar de Luna
San Saba ....David Parker
*Sansom Park (5500 Buchanan St., Fort Worth 76114) ....Robert Armstrong
*Santa Anna....................Russell Fisher
*Santa Clara (Box 429, Marion 78124)
  ....David D. Mueller
†Santa Fe............................Ralph Stenzel
  City Mgr., Joe Dickson
Santa Rosa..................Ruben Ochoa Jr.
  City Mgr., Jose L. Lopez
Savoy ....Clete Stogsdill
†Schertz.......................Harold D. Baldwin
  City Mgr., Don Taylor
Schulenburg............Roger Moellenberndt
  City Admin., Ronald Brossman
Scotland ....Robert J. Krahl
*Scottsville ....Walter Johnson
Scurry ....Robert Stewart
*†Seabrook............................Robin Riley
  City Mgr., Chuck Pinto
Seadrift .... Billy F. Ezell
  City Mgr., Paula Moncrief
†Seagoville...................Sydney Sexton Jr.
  City Mgr., Denny Wheat
*Seagraves ....Ovidio Martinez Jr.
†Sealy ....Russell L. Koym
  City Mgr., John Maresh
*†Seguin ....Betty Ann Matthies
  City Mgr., Douglas Faseler
Selma ....Jim Parma
  City Admin., Kenneth Roberts
†Seminole...............................Mike Carter
  City Admin., Tommy Phillips
Seven Oaks (Box 540, Leggett 77350)
  .... Anna Wallace
Seven Points ....Gerald E. Taylor
*Seymour .... Dan Craighead
  City Admin., Joe Shephard
Shady Shores (Box 362, Lake Dallas 75065) ....Olive Stephens
Shallowater .... Don Blevins
Shamrock ....Wendell Morgan
  City Mgr., Johnny W. Rhodes
*Shavano Park (99 Saddletree Rd., San Antonio 78231) ....David Marne
  City Mgr., Matt Smith
*Shenandoah (29811 I-45, Spring 77381)
  ....Becky Altemus
  City Admin., Chip VanSteenberg
*Shepherd...........................Obie Daniels
†Sherman...............................Bill Magers
  City Mgr., George Olson
Shiner ....Henry Kalich
*Shoreacres...................Jayo Washington
  City Admin., David K. Stall
*†Silsbee.................... Herbert Muckleroy

  City Mgr., Tommy Barosh
Silverton ....Lane B. Garvin
  City Admin., Jerry Patton
Simonton ....Louis J. Boudreaux
†Sinton ....Jessica Thomas Bates
  City Mgr., Jackie Knox Jr.
Skellytown ....John Chaney
†Slaton.....................Laura Lynn Wilson
  City Admin., Roger McKinney
*Smiley................................Donald Janicek
Smithville............................Mark A. Bunte
  City Mgr., Tex Middlebrook
Smyer.............................Mary Beth Sims
Snook.............................John W. See III
†Snyder ....Francene Allen-Noah
  City Mgr., Jared H. Miller
Socorro...................................Trini Lopez
  City Mgr., Carol Garcia
Somerset ....Fred Gonzales
  City Admin., Melissa Gonzales
*Somerville ....Tommy Thompson
  City Admin., Barbara J. Pederson
Sonora ....Gloria Lopez
  City Mgr. JIm Polonis
Sour Lake ....Bruce Robinson
  City Mgr., Larry Saurage
South Houston .... Joe Soto
†Southlake ....Andy Wambsganss
  City Mgr., Shana Yelverton
*Southmayd............ Diana Skinner Barker
*South Mountain (107 Barton Ln., Gatesville 76528) ....Billy Mayhew
*South Padre Island...........Bob Pinkerton
  City Mgr., Dewey P. Cashwell Jr.
Southside Place (6309 Edloe St., Houston 77005) ....Richard L. Rothfelder
  City Mgr., David N. Moss
Spearman.......................Brian Gillispie
  City Mgr., Edward Hansen
Splendora .... Carol W. Carley
*Spofford ..........................J.B. Herndon
*Springlake.........................Harlon Watson
Springtown.........................Doug Hughes
  City Admin., Randall Whiteman
Spring Valley (1025 Campbell Rd., Houston 77055) ....T. Michael Andrews
  City Admin., Richard Rockenbaugh
*Spur ....Kenneth Gilcrease
*Stafford ....Leonard Scarcella
Stagecoach ....William Berger
†Stamford ....Johnny Anders
  City Mgr., Roy Rice
Stanton .... Lester Baker
  City Admin., Danny Fryar
Star Harbor (Box 949, Malakoff 75148)
  ....Walter W. Bingham
*†Stephenville.......................Rusty Jergins
  City Admin., Mark A. Kaiser
*Sterling City ....Ray Sparks
Stinnett ....Billy Murphy
  Interim City Mgr., Mike Lamberson
Stockdale.............................Johnny Stahl
  City Mgr., Carl Lambeck
*Stratford ....David Brown
  City Admin., Sean Hardman
Strawn.................................David G. Day
Streetman.......................Judith E. Wardle
Sudan.........................Robert K. Sisson Jr.
†Sugar Land..................David G. Wallace
  City Mgr., Allen Bogard
*Sullivan City....................Gumaro Flores
  City Mgr., Rolando Gonzalez
*†Sulphur Springs ....Freddie Taylor
  City Mgr., Marc Maxwell
Sundown ....Jim Winn
  City Admin., Barry Stephens
*Sunnyvale ....Jim Phaup
  City Admin., Larry Graves
*Sunray ....Casey Stone
  City Mgr., Greg Smith
Sunrise Beach Village .... Patricia Frain
*Sunset ....Danny Russell
Sunset Valley ....Cat Quintanilla
*Sun Valley (RR 2, Box 800, Paris

75462) ....Maria Z. Wagnon
Surfside Beach (1304 Monument Dr., Freeport 77541)................James Bedward
†Sweeny ....Larry G. Piper
  City Mgr., H.T. (Tim) Moss
†Sweetwater..............Gregory L. Wortham
  City Mgr., Edward P. Brown

— T —
Taft ....Filberto Rivera
  City Mgr., Dolores R. Topper
*Tahoka.......................Michael R. Mensch
  City Admin., Jerry W. Webster
*Talco...........................K.M. (Mike) Sloan
Talty (Box 565, Forney 75126) Todd Hutton
  City Admin., Connie Goodwin
Tatum ....Phil Cory
†Taylor ....Bennabe Gonzales
  City Mgr., Frank L. Salvato
Taylor Lake Village .... Natalie S. O'Neill
Taylor Landing ....John Durkay
Teague.........................Jacqueline Utsey
  City Admin., Don Doering
Tehuacana ....Herman Douglas East Jr.
†Temple ....William A. Jones III
  City Mgr., David A. Blackburn
Tenaha ....George N. Bowers
*†Terrell ....Frances Anderson
  City Mgr., Gordon C. Pierce
†Terrell Hills ....J. Bradford Camp
  City Mgr., James Mark Browne
*†Texarkana......................James Bramlett
  City Mgr., George T. Shackelford
*†Texas City ....Matthew T. Doyle
Texhoma.......................................Mel Yates
Texline ....Brad Riley
  City Mgr., Stacey Martinez
†The Colony ....John Dillard
  City Mgr., Dale A. Cheatham
Thompsons ....Freddie Newsome Jr.
*Thorndale ....Billy Simank
  City Admin., Keith Kiesling
*Thornton ....James W. Jackson Jr.
  City Admin., Beth Nolan
*Thorntonville (Box 740, Monahans 79756) ....David Mitchell
Thrall..Troy Marx
Three Rivers...........................James Liska
  City Admin., Marion R. Forehand
*Throckmorton.........................Will Carroll
*Tiki Island, Village of ...Charles E. Everts
Timbercreek Canyon (101 S. Timbercreek Dr., Amarillo 79118) ....Terri Welch
Timpson......................Douglas McDonald
*Tioga ....Stanley Kemp
Tira (RR 7, Box 220, Sulphur Springs 75482) ....John Hadley
*Toco (2103 Chestnut Dr., Brookston 75421) ....John Jason Waller
Todd Mission (390 N. Millcreek Dr., Plantersville 77363) .... George Coulam
Tolar ....Terry R. Johnson
†Tomball ....Gretchen Fagan
  Interim City Mgr., Mary Coker
*Tom Bean ....Tom Wilthers
Tool ....R. Scott Confer
*Toyah................................Bart F. Sanchez
Trent..Rocky Brian
*Trenton ....David Hamrick
Trinidad......................................Chris Quinn
  City Admin., Terri R. Newhouse
Trinity..Lyle Stubbs
  City Mgr., Phil Patchett
†Trophy Club...................C. Nick Sanders
  City Mgr., Brandon Emmons
Troup..John Whitsell
  City Admin., Russ Obar
*Troy.......................................Sammy Warren
†Tulia...Pat George
  City Mgr., Rick D. Crownover
Turkey.......................................Pat Carson
  City Mgr., Jerry Landry
Tuscola ....Russell Bartlett
*Tye ....Butch Schuman

*†Tyler.................................Joey Seeber
  City Mgr., Robert (Bob) Turner

— U —
Uhland ....Daniel Heideman
  City Admin., Diana T. Woods
*Uncertain...............................Sam Canup
*Union Grove (RR 2, Box 196FF, Gladewater 75647) .... Randy Simcox
*†Universal City.............Joseph Medinger
  City Mgr., Ken Taylor
†University Park (3800 University Blvd., Dallas 75205) .... James H. Holmes III
  City Mgr., Bob Livingston
†Uvalde.............................Josue Garza Jr.
  City Mgr., John H. Harrell

— V —
*Valentine ....Jesús Calderon
*Valley Mills ....Bill Lancaster
*Valley View ....Carl Kemplin
*Van...Billy B. Smith
  City Admin., Gary McDaniel
Van Alstyne .... Mike Parker
  City Mgr., Bill Harrington
Van Horn............................Okey D. Lucas
  City Admin., Rebecca L. Brewster
*Vega............................Mark J. Groneman
Venus ....Carolyn Welcher
  City Admin., Jerry Reed
†Vernon ....Ed Garnett
  City Mgr., Jim Murray
*†Victoria .... Will Armstrong
  City Mgr., Denny Arnold
†Vidor..Joe Hopkins
  City Mgr., Ricky Jorgensen
Village of the Hills (102 Trophy Dr., Austin 78738)...........................Virginia W. Jones
  City Admin., Dan Roark
*Vinton ....Madeleine Praino
*Volente .... Jan Yenawine

— W —
†Waco ....Virginia DuPuy
  City Mgr., Larry D. Groth
*Waelder .... Roy Tovar
Wake Village..............Michael Huddleston
  City Admin., Bob Long
Waller.................................Dwayne Hajek
Wallis ....Tony I. Salazar Jr.
Walnut Springs ....Benny Damron
Warren City (3004 George Richey Rd., Gladewater 75647) .... Ricky J. Wallace
Waskom ....Jesse Moore
†Watauga ....Henry J. Jeffries
  City Mgr., Kerry Lacy
†Waxahachie ....Joe Jenkins
  City Mgr., Paul Stevens
*†Weatherford............................Joe Tison
  City Mgr., George Campbell
*Webberville ....Hector Gonzales
†Webster ....Donna Rogers
  City Mgr., Michael W. Jez
*Weimar ....Bennie Kosler
  City Mgr., Randal W. Jones
*Weinert ....Julian Estrada
Weir......................Charles Mervin Walker
*Wellington ....Gary Brewer
  City Mgr., Jon Sessions
Wellman...................................Kent Davis
Wells ....Jim Maddox
  City Mgr., Lynette Bailey
†Weslaco .... Hector (Buddy) De La Rosa
  City Mgr., Anthony Covacevich
West.......................................Jerrol Bolton
Westbrook ....Ramiro Fuentes
West Columbia.................David E. Foster
  City Mgr., Debbie Sutherland
Westlake .... Scott Bradley
  City Mgr., Trent Petty
West Lake Hills ....Mark Urdahl
  City Admin., Robert Wood
Weston...Ed Town
†West Orange .... Roy C. McDonald

Westover Hills (5824 Merrymount, Fort. Worth 76107).............Earle A. Shields Jr.
  City Admin., James Rutledge
West Tawakoni (1533 E. Hwy 276, Quinlan 75474)................................Bill Stausing
  City Admin., Cloy Richards
†West University Place ....Bob Kelly
  City Mgr., Michael Ross
Westworth Village (311 Burton Hill Rd., Fort Worth 76114)................Andy Fontenot
  City Admin., Gary Robinson
†Wharton.........................Bryce D. Kocian
  City Mgr., Andres Garza Jr.
*Wheeler .... Wanda Herd
*White Deer .... Dick Pierce
Whiteface.................Vernon Shellenberger
  City Mgr., Belinda Terrel
*†Whitehouse..........B.D. (Jake) Jacobson
  City Mgr., Ronny Fite
*White Oak.................................Tim Vaughn
  City Coor., Ralph J. Weaver
Whitesboro.................................W.D. Welch
  City Admin., Michael Marter
*†White Settlement.........James O. Ouzts
  City Mgr., Dena Daniel
Whitewright............................ Bill Goodson
*Whitney .... Gwen Evans
†Wichita Falls.........................Lanham Lyne
  City Mgr., Darron Leiker
Wickett.............................Harold Ferguson
Willis ....Leonard Reed
  City Admin., James A. McAlister
*Willow Park .... Brad Johnson
  City Admin., Claud Arnold
Wills Point ....Scott McGriff
  City Mgr., Fred H. Hays
*Wilmer......................................Don Hudson
  City Admin., Bobbie Jo Martinez
Wilson.......................... Victor Steinhauser
*Wimberley ....Tom Haley
Windcrest .... Jack H. Leonhardt
  City Admin., Ronnie Cain
Windom...............................B.J.Stallings
*Windthorst...............Sue C. Steinberger
  City Mgr., Donald Frerich
Winfield.....................................John Walton
Wink..............................Betty Lou Dodd
  City Mgr., Tonya Todd
*Winnsboro ....Carolyn S. Jones
  City Admin., Ronny Knight
Winona ....Rusty Smith
  City Admin., James Bixler
Winters ....Nelan Bahlman
  City Mgr. Aref Hassan
Wixon Valley (Box 105, Kurten 77862) ....Ruby Clara Andrews
*Wolfe City........................Bethel Henslee
*Wolfforth..................................L.C. Childers
  City Admin., Frankie Pittman
*Woodbranch Village (Box 804, New Caney 77357)......................Sharon Frey
Woodcreek ....Gloria Whitehead
  City Admin., Peg Wolfe
Woodloch (Box 1379, Conroe 77305) ....Diane L. Lincoln
Woodsboro............George Hernandez Sr.
Woodson ....Bobby Mathiews
Woodville ....Tony Castillo
  City Admin., George K. Jones
*†Woodway ....Donald (Don) J. Baker
  City Mgr., Yousry Zakhary
Wortham ....Judy Edwards
*†Wylie.................................John Mondy
  City Mgr., Mindy Manson

— Y —
Yantis................................Jerry E. Miller
†Yoakum..........Anita R. (Annie) Rodriguez
  City Mgr., Calvin Cook
Yorktown .... Rene Hernandez

— Z —
*Zavalla ....Hulon Miller ☆

Regional Councils of Government

Source: Texas Association of Regional Councils; www.txregionalcouncil.org/

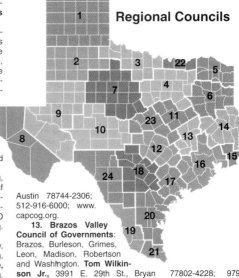

Regional Councils

The concept of regional planning and cooperation, fostered by enabling legislation in 1965, has spread across Texas since organization of the **North Central Texas Council of Governments** in 1966.

Regional councils are voluntary associations of local governments that deal with problems and planning needs that cross the boundaries of individual local governments or that require regional attention. These concerns may include criminal justice, emergency communications, job-training programs, solid-waste management, transportation needs, and water-quality management. The councils make recommendations to member governments and may assist in implementing the plans.

The **Texas Association of Regional Councils** is at 701 Brazos, Ste. 780, Austin 78701; 512-478-4715; fax: 512-478-9910. Financing is provided by the local governments, the state and the federal government. The map at right shows the locations of the **24 regional councils**, along with a list of the regional councils, the counties served and the executive director.

1. Panhandle Regional Planning Commission: Armstrong, Briscoe, Carson, Castro, Childress, Collingsworth, Dallam, Deaf Smith, Donley, Gray, Hall, Hansford, Hartley, Hemphill, Hutchinson, Lipscomb, Moore, Ochiltree, Oldham, Parmer, Potter, Randall, Roberts, Sherman, Swisher and Wheeler. **Gary Pitner**, PO Box 9257, Amarillo 79105-9257; 806-372-3381; www.prpc.cog. tx.us.

2. South Plains Association of Governments: Bailey, Cochran, Crosby, Dickens, Floyd, Garza, Hale, Hockley, King, Lamb, Lubbock, Lynn, Motley, Terry and Yoakum. **Tim Pierce**, PO Box 3730, Lubbock 79452-3730; 806-762-8721; www.spag. org.

3. Nortex Regional Planning Commission: Archer, Baylor, Clay, Cottle, Foard, Hardeman, Jack, Montague, Wichita, Wilbarger and Young. **Dennis Wilde**, PO Box 5144, Wichita Falls 76307-5144; 940-322-5281; www.nortexrpc.org.

4. North Central Texas Council of Governments: Collin, Dallas, Denton, Ellis, Erath, Hood, Hunt, Johnson, Kaufman, Navarro, Palo Pinto, Parker, Rockwall, Somervell, Tarrant and Wise. **R. Michael Eastland**, PO Box 5888, Arlington 76005-5888; 817-640-3300; www.nctcog.dst.tx.us.

5. Ark-Tex Council of Governments: Bowie, Cass, Delta, Franklin, Hopkins, Lamar, Morris, Red River, Titus and Miller County, Ark. **L.D. Williamson**, PO Box 5307, Texarkana 75505-5307; 903-832-8636; www.atcog.org.

6. East Texas Council of Governments: Anderson, Camp, Cherokee, Gregg, Harrison, Henderson, Marion, Panola, Rains, Rusk, Smith, Upshur, Van Zandt and Wood. **Glynn Knight**, 3800 Stone Rd., Kilgore 75662-6927; 903-984-8641; www.etcog.org.

7. West Central Texas Council of Governments: Brown, Callahan, Coleman, Comanche, Eastland, Fisher, Haskell, Jones, Kent, Knox, Mitchell, Nolan, Runnels, Scurry, Shackelford, Stephens, Stonewall, Taylor and Throckmorton. **Jim Compton**, PO Box 3195, Abilene 79601-3195; 325-672-8544; www.wctcog. org.

8. Rio Grande Council of Governments: Brewster, Culberson, El Paso, Hudspeth, Jeff Davis, Presidio and Doña Ana County, N.M. **Jake Brisbin Jr.**, 1100 N. Stanton, Ste. 610, El Paso 79902-4155; 915-533-0998; www.riocog.org.

9. Permian Basin Regional Planning Commission: Andrews, Borden, Crane, Dawson, Ector, Gaines, Glasscock, Howard, Loving, Martin, Midland, Pecos, Reeves, Terrell, Upton, Ward and Winkler. **Gary Gaston**, PO Box 60660, Midland 79711-0660; 432-563-1061.

10. Concho Valley Council of Governments: Coke, Concho, Crockett, Irion, Kimble, Mason, McCulloch, Menard, Reagan, Schleicher, Sterling, Sutton and Tom Green. **Jeffrey Sutton**, Box 60050, San Angelo 76906-0050; 325-944-9666; www.cvcog. org.

11. Heart of Texas Council of Governments: Bosque, Falls, Freestone, Hill, Limestone and McLennan. **Kenneth Simons**, PO Box 20847, Waco 76702-0847; 254-292-1800; www. hotcog.org.

12. Capital Area Council of Governments: Bastrop, Blanco, Burnet, Caldwell, Fayette, Hays, Lee, Llano, Travis and Williamson. **Betty Voights**, 6800 Burleson Rd., Bldg. 310, Ste. 165, Austin 78744-2306; 512-916-6000; www. capcog.org.

13. Brazos Valley Council of Governments: Brazos, Burleson, Grimes, Leon, Madison, Robertson and Washington. **Tom Wilkinson Jr.**, 3991 E. 29th St., Bryan 77802-4228; 979-595-2800; www.bvcog.org.

14. Deep East Texas Council of Governments: Angelina, Houston, Jasper, Nacogdoches, Newton, Polk, Sabine, San Augustine, San Jacinto, Shelby, Trinity and Tyler. **Walter G. Diggles**, 210 Premier Dr., Jasper 75951-7495; 409-384-5704; www.detcog.org.

15. South East Texas Regional Planning Commission: Hardin, Jefferson and Orange. **Chester R. Jourdan Jr.**, 2210 Eastex Fwy, Beaumont 77703; 409-899-8444; www.setrpc.org.

16. Houston-Galveston Area Council: Austin, Brazoria, Chambers, Colorado, Fort Bend, Galveston, Harris, Liberty, Matagorda, Montgomery, Walker, Waller and Wharton. **Jack Steele**, PO Box 22777, Houston 77227-2777; 713-627-3200; www.h-gac.com.

17. Golden Crescent Regional Planning Commission: Calhoun, DeWitt, Goliad, Gonzales, Jackson, Lavaca and Victoria. **Joe Brannan**, 568 Big Bend Dr., Victoria 77904-3623; 361-578-1587; www.gcrpc.org.

18. Alamo Area Council of Governments: Atascosa, Bandera, Bexar, Comal, Frio, Gillespie, Guadalupe, Karnes, Kendall, Kerr, Medina and Wilson. **Al J. Notzon III**, 8700 Tesoro Dr., Ste. 700, San Antonio 78217-6228 210-362-5200; www.aacog. com.

19. South Texas Development Council: Jim Hogg, Starr, Webb and Zapata. **Amanda Garza Jr.**, PO Box 2187, Laredo 78044-2187; 956-722-3995; www.stdc.cog.tx.us.

20. Coastal Bend Council of Governments: Aransas, Bee, Brooks, Duval, Jim Wells, Kenedy, Kleberg, Live Oak, McMullen, Nueces, Refugio and San Patricio. **John P. Buckner**, PO Box 9909, Corpus Christi 78469-9909; 361-883-5743; cb-cog98.org.

21. Lower Rio Grande Valley Development Council: Cameron, Hidalgo and Willacy. **Kenneth N. Jones Jr.**, 311 N. 15th, McAllen 78501-4705; 956-682-3481; www.lrgvdc.org.

22. Texoma Council of Governments: Cooke, Fannin and Grayson. **Frances Pelley**, 1117 Gallagher Dr., Ste. 100, Sherman 75090-3107; 903-893-2161; www.texoma.cog.tx.us.

23. Central Texas Council of Governments: Bell, Coryell, Hamilton, Lampasas, Milam, Mills and San Saba. **James Reed**, PO Box 729, Belton 76513-0729; 254-770-2200; www. ctcog.org.

24. Middle Rio Grande Development Council: Dimmit, Edwards, Kinney, La Salle, Maverick, Real, Uvalde, Val Verde and Zavala. **Leodoro Martinez Jr.**, PO Box 1199, Carrizo Springs 78834-1199; 830-876-3533; www.mrgdc.org. ☆

County Courts

Below are county courts, including county courts at law, probate courts, juvenile courts, domestic relations courts, criminal courts and criminal courts of appeals as reported by the county clerks as of July 2007. Other courts with jurisdiction in each county can be found in the list on pages 477–481. Other county and district officials can be found on pages 513–523.

Anderson — *Court at Law:* Jeff Doran. *Probate Courts:* No. 1, Linda Bostick Ray; No. 2, Jeff Doran. *Criminal Court at Law, Domestic Relations & Juvenile Courts:* Jeff Doran.

Andrews — *Probate Court, Criminal Court, Juvenile Court:* Richard Dolgener.

Aransas — *Court at Law:* William Adams.

Archer — Criminal and Domestic Relations Courts: Roger E. Towery; *Juvenile Court:* Gary W. Beesinger.

Armstrong — *All Courts:* Hugh Reed.

Austin — *Court at Law:* Daniel W. Leedy.

Bailey—Probate & Juvenile Courts: Sherri Harrison; *Domestic Relations Court:* Gordon Green.

Bandera —*Probate & Juvenile Courts:* Richard A. Evans.

Bastrop — *All courts:* Benton Eskew.

Baylor — *Probate Court:* Linda Rogers. *Juvenile Court:* William H. Heatly.

Bee — *Probate Court:* David Silva. *Juvenile Court:* Raul Casarez.

Bell — *Court at Law No. 1, Probate & Juvenile Courts:* Edward S. Johnson; *Courts at Law No. 2 & Criminal Court at Law,* John Mischtian.

Bexar — *Courts at Law: No. 1,* Al Alonso; *No. 2,* H. Paul Canales; *No. 3,* David J. Rodriguez; *No. 4,* Sarah E. Garrahan; *No. 5,* Timothy F. Johnson; *No. 6,* Ray Olivarri; *No. 7,* Monica E. Guerrero; *No. 8,* Karen Crouch; *No. 9,* Laura Salinas; *No. 10,* Irene Rios; *No. 11,* Jo Ann De Hoyos; *No. 12,* Michael Mery. *Probate Courts: No. 1,* Polly Jackson Spencer; *No. 2,* Tom Rickhoff.

Borden — *Probate Court:* Van L. York.

Bowie — *Court at Law:* Jeff Addison. *Probate Court:* James M. Carlow. Domestic Relations Court: Ralph Burgess. Juvenile: Court John F. Miller Jr. Criminal Court at Law: Leon Pesek Jr.

Brazoria — *Courts at Law & Probate Court: No. 1,* Jerri Lee Mills; *No. 2,* Marc W. Holder; *No. 3,* James A. Blackstock.

Brazos — *Courts at Law: No. 1,* Amanda Matzke; *No. 2,* Jim Locke.

Brooks — *Criminal Court at Law & Juvenile Court:* Joe B. Garcia.

Brown — *Court at Law:* Frank Griffin.

Burleson — Probate & Juvenile Courts: Mike Sutherland.

Burnet — *Court at Law:* W.R. Savage.

Caldwell — *Court at Law, Criminal Court at Law, Probate & Juvenile Courts:* Edward L. Jarrett.

Calhoun — All Courts: Alex R. Hernandez.

Cameron — *Court at Law: No. 1,* Arturo McDonald; *No. 2,* Laura Betancourt; No. 3, T. Daniel Robles.

Camp — *Probate Court:* Preston Combest. Domestic Relations & Juvenile Courts: William R. Porter and Jimmy White.

Carson — *Probate Court:* Lewis Powers.

Cass — *Court at Law:* Donald Dowd. Probate Court: Charles McMichael.

Castro — *Probate & Juvenile Courts:* William F. Sava.

Chambers — *Probate & Juvenile Courts:* Jimmy Sylvia; *Domestic Relations Court:* Carroll E. Wilborn Jr.

Cherokee — *Court at Law:* Daniel B. Childs.

Coke — *Probate Court:* Roy Blair. *Juvenile Court:* Barbara L. Walther.

Collin — *Courts at Law: No. 1,* Corinne Mason; *No. 2,* Jerry Lewis; *No. 3,* John Barry; *No. 4,* Raymond Wheless; *No. 5,* Gregory Brewer. *Probate Court:* Weldon Copeland. *Juvenile Court:* Cynthia Wheless.

Collingsworth — *Probate Court:* John A. James.

Colorado — *Probate & Juvenile Court:* Al Jamison.

Comal — *Court at Law:* Brenda Chapman.

Comanche — *Criminal Court at Law, Probate & Juvenile Court:* James R. Arthur.

Concho — Probate Court: Allen Amos. *Juvenile Court:* Ben Woodward.

Cooke — *Court at Law:* John H. Morris.

Coryell — *Court at Law:* Susan Stephens. *Probate Court:* John Hull.

Crocket — *Court at Law, Criminal Court at Law & Probate Court:* Fred Deaton.

Crosby — Probate & Juvenile Courts Davey Abell.

Culberson — *Court at Law, Probate & Juvenile:* John Conoly.

Dallam — *Probate & Juvenile Court:* David D. Field.

Dallas — *Courts at Law: No. 1,* DeMetria Benson *No. 2,* King Fifer;

No. 3, Sally Montgomery; *No. 4,* Ken Tapscott; *No. 5,* Mark Greenberg. *County Criminal Courts: No. 1,* Dan Patterson; *No. 2,* Lennox Bower; *No. 3,* Douglas Skemp; *No. 4,* Teresa Tolle; *No. 5,* Tom Fuller; *No. 6,* Angela King; *No. 7,* Elizabeth Crowder; *No. 8,* Jane Roden; *No. 9,* Peggy Hoffman; *No. 10,* Roberto Canas; *No. 11,* Elizabeth Frizell. *Probate Courts: No. 1,* Nikki DeShazo; *No. 2,* Robert E. Price; *No. 3,* Michael Miller. *County Criminal Courts of Appeals: No. 1,* Kristin Wade; *No. 2,* Jeff Rosenfield.

Dawson — *Probate & Juvenile Court:* Sam Saleh.

Deaf Smith — *Juvenile Court:* Tom Simons.

Delta — *Probate & Criminal Courts:* Ted Carrington. Domestic Relations Court: Scott McDowell. Juvenile Court: Robert. E. Newsom.

Denton — *Courts at Law: No. 1,* Darlene Whitten; *No. 2,* Margaret Barnes. *Probate Court:* Don Windle.

DeWitt — *All Courts:* Ben E. Prause.

Dimmit — All Courts: Francisco G. Ponce.

Donley — *Probate Court:* Jack Hall.

Eastland — *Probate Court:* Rex Fields. *Juvenile & Domestic Relations Courts:* Steven R. Herod.

Ector — *Courts at Law: No. 1,* J.A. "Jim" Bobo; *No. 2,* Mark Owens. *Juvenile Court:* J.A. "Jim" Bobo.

Edwards — *Probate & Juvenile Courts:* Nick Gallegos.

Ellis — *Court at Law: No. 1,* Bob Carroll; *No. 2,* A. Gene Calvert Jr. *Probate Court:* Bob Carroll. *Juvenile Court:* A. Gene Calvert Jr.

El Paso — *Courts at Law: No. 1,* Ricardo Herrera; *No. 2,* Julie Gonzalez; *No. 3,* Javier Alvarez; *No. 4,* Alejandro Gonzalez; *No. 5,* Carlos Villa; *No. 6,* M. Sue Kurita; *No. 7,* Jose Baca. *Probate Court:* Max D. Higgs. *Criminal Court at Law: No. 1,* Alma Trejo; *No. 2,* Robert Anchondo.

Erath — *Court at Law:* Bart McDougal. *Domestic Relations Court:* Don Jones.

Falls — *Probate Court:* Thomas B. Sehon.

Fayette — *Probate & Juvenile Courts:* Edward Janecka.

Fisher — *Probate & Juvenile Courts:* Marshall Bennett.

Fort Bend — *Courts at Law: No. 1,* Larry Wagenbach; *No. 2,* Walter McMeans; *No. 3,* Susan Lowery; *No. 4,* Sandy Bielstein.

Franklin — *Probate Court:* Gerald Hubbell.

Galveston — *Courts at Law:* No. 1, Mary Nell Crapitto; No. 2, C.G. Dibrell II. Probate: Gladys B. Burwell. *Domestic Relations Court:* Janis L. Yarbrough.

Garza — *All Courts:* Lee Norman.

Grayson — *Courts at Law: No. 1,* James C. Henderson; *No. 2,* Carol Siebman. *Probate Court:* Drue Bynum.

Gregg — *Court at Law No. 1, Criminal Court at Law, Probate & Juvenile:* Rebecca Simpson; *Court at Law No. 2, Probate & Criminal Court at Law:* Alfonso Charles. Domestic Relations: Robin Sage.

Guadalupe — *Court at Law No. 1:* Linda Z. Jones; *Court at Law No. 2 & Criminal Court at Law:* Frank Follis. *Probate & Juvenile Courts:* Linda Z. Jones and Mike Wiggins.

Hale — *Probate & Juvenile Courts:* Dwain Dodson.

Hamilton — *Probate & Juvenile Courts:* Randy Mills.

Hardin — *Probate Court:* Billy Caraway.

Harris — *Courts at Law: No. 1,* R. Jack Cagle; *No. 2,* Jacqueline Lucci Smith; *No. 3,* Linda Storey; *No. 4,* Roberta Lloyd. *County Criminal Courts at Law: No. 1,* Reagan C. Helms; *No. 2,* Bill Harmon; *No. 3,* Don Jackson; *No. 4,* James E. Anderson; *No. 5,* Margaret Stewart Harris; *No. 6,* Larry Standley; *No. 7,* Pam Derbyshire; *No. 8,* Jay Karahan; *No. 9,* Analia Wilkerson; *No. 10,* Sherman A. Ross; *No. 11,* Diane Bull; *No. 12,* Robin Brown; *No. 13,* Mark Atkinson; *No. 14,* Mike Fields; *No. 15,* Jean Spradling Hughes. *Probate Courts: No. 1,* Russell Austin; *No. 2,* Mike Wood; *No. 3,* Rory Robert Olsen; *No. 4,* William C. McCulloch.

Harrison — *Court at Law:* Jim Ammerman II.

Hays — *Court at Law No. 1, Criminal Court at Law, Probate & Juvenile Courts:* Howard S. Warner II. *Court at Law No. 2 & Criminal Court at Law,* Linda A. Rodriguez. *Domestic Relations Court:* Brenda Smith.

Henderson — *Court at Law: No. 1,* Matt Livingston; *No. 2,* Nancy Perryman. *Probate & Juvenile Courts:* David Holstein.

Hidalgo — *Courts at Law: No. 1,* Rodolfo Gonzalez; *No. 2,* Jaime Palacios; *No. 3 & Probate Court,* Homero Garza; *No. 4* Fred

Garza; No. 5 Arnoldo Cantu; No. 6, Albert Garcia. *Domestic Relations Court:* Homer Salinas and Fidencio Guerra. *Juvenile Court:* Maxine Longoria.

Hill — *Court at Law & Criminal Court at Law:* A. Lee Harris. *Probate Court:* Justin Lewis.

Hood — *Court at Law:* Vincent Messina.

Hopkins — *Court at Law:* Amy M. Smith.

Houston — *Court at Law & Juvenile:* Sarah Tunnell Clark.

Howard — *Probate & Juvenile Courts:* Mark J. Barr.

Hudspeth — *All Courts:* Becky Dean-Walker.

Hunt — *Court at Law:* J. Andrew Bench.

Hutchinson — *Probate Court:* Faye Blanks.

Jack — *Probate Court:* Mitchell G. Davenport.

Jackson — *Probate & Juvenile Courts:* Harrison Stafford II.

Jeff Davis — *All Courts:* George E. Grubb.

Jefferson — *Courts at Law: No. 1,* Alfred S. Gerson; *No. 2,* G.R. "Lupe" Flores; *No. 3,* John Paul Davis. *Domestic Relations Court:* Tom Mulvaney. *Juvenile Court:* Larry Thorne.

Johnson — *Courts at Law: No. 1,* Robert Mayfield; *No. 2,* Jerry Webber.

Jones — *Probate & Juvenile Courts:* Dale Spurgin.

Kaufman — *Court at Law No. 1 & Juvenile Court:* Erleigh Norville Wylie. *Court at Law No. 2:* David Lewis. *Probate Court:* Wayne Gent.

Karnes — *Probate & Juvenile Courts:* Alger H. Kendall Jr..

Kerr — *Court at Law & Criminal Court at Law:* Spencer W. Brown. *Probate & Juvenile Courts:* Pat Tinley.

Kimble — *Criminal Court & Probate:* Delbert R. Roberts.

Klegerg — *Court at Law:* Martin J. Chiuminatto Jr..

Lampasas — *Probate Court:* Wayne L. Boultinghouse. *Domestic Relations Court:* Joe Carroll & Charles Van Ordan. *Juvenile Court:* Joe Carroll.

La Salle — *Criminal Court at Law, probate & Juvenile Courts:* Joel Rodriguez Jr..

Lavaco — *Probate & Juvenile Courts:* Ronald L. Leck.

Lee — *Probate Court:* Evan Gonzales. *Juvenile Court:* Terry Flenniken.

Liberty — *Court at Law:* Don Taylor. *Probate & Juvenile Courts:* Phil Fitzgerald.

Limestone — *Court at Law & Probate:* Daniel Burkeen.

Lubbock — *Courts at Law: No. 1,* Larry B. (Rusty) Ladd; *No. 2,* Drue Farmer; *No. 3,* Paula Lanehart. *Probate:* Tome Head.

Lynn — *Probate & Juvenile Courts:* H.G. Franklin. *County Criminal Court at Law & Domestic Relations Court:* Carter Schildnecht.

Madison — *Probate & Juvenile Courts:* Arthur M. Henson.

Marion — *Probate Court:* Phil A. Parker.

Mason — *Probate Court:* Jerry M. Bearden.

Matagorda — *Probate:* Nate McDonald. *Domestic Relations:* Ben Hardin and Craig Estlinbaum. *Juvenile:* Craig Estlinbaum.

McCulloch — *Juvenile Court:* Karl Prohl.

McLennan — *Courts at Law & Criminals Courts at Law: No. 1,* Mike Freeman; *No. 2,* Michael B. Gassaway. *Probate Court:* Jim Lewis.

Medina — *Court at Law:* Vivian Torres.

Menard — *Probate Court:* Richard Cordes. *Domestic Relations & Juvenile Courts:* Emil Prohl.

Midland — *Courts at Law: No. 1,* Al Walvoord; *No. 2,* Marvin Moore. *Domestic Relations Court:* Dean Rucker.

Milam — *Probate Court:* Frank Summers. *Juvenile Court:* Ed P. Magre.

Montgomery — *Courts at Law: No. 1,* Dennis Watson; *No. 2,* Jerry Winfree; *No. 3,* Patrice McDonald; *No. 4,* Mary Ann Turner.

Moore — *Court at Law, Domestic Relations, Juvenile & Criminal Court at Law:* Delwin McGee. *Probate:* J.E. (Rowdy) Rhoades.

Morris — *Probate Court:* J.C. Jennings.

Motley — *All Courts:* Ed D. Smith.

Nacogdoches — *Court at Law & Criminal Court at Law:* John A. (Jack) Sinz.

Nolan — *Court at Law, Juvenile Court & Criminal Court at Law:* Gary D. Harger. *Probate Court:* Tim D. Fambrough.

Nueces — *Courts at Law: No. 1,* Robert J. Vargas; *No. 2,* Lisa Gonzales; *No. 3,* John Martinez; *No. 4,* James E. Klager; *No. 5:* Carl E. Lewis.

Orange — *Court at Law: No. 1,* Michael W. Shuff; *No 2,* Troy Johnson. *Probate:* Michael W. Shuff. *Juvenile & Criminal Court at Law:* Michael W. Shuff. and Troy Johnson.

Palo Pinto — *Probate & Juvenile Courts:* Mike A. Smiddy. *Domestic Relations Court:* Jerry Ray.

Panola — *Court at Law:* Terry D. Bailey.

Parker — *Court at Law: No. 1,* Deborah Dupont; *No. 2,* Ben Akers. *Probate:* Mark Riley. *Juvenile:* Mike Kidd. *Criminal Court at Law:* Don Crestman and Graham Quisenberry.

Parmer — *Juvenile Court:* Bonnie J. Heald.

Polk — *Court at Law:* Stephen Phillips.

Potter — *Courts at Law: No. 1:* W.F. (Corky) Roberts; *No. 2,* Pamela Cook Sirmon. *Probate Court:* Arthur Ware. *Juvenile Court:* W.F. (Corky) Roberts

Rains — *Probate Court:* Joe Ray Dougherty.

Randall — *Court at Law: No. 1,* James Anderson. *No. 2,* Ronnie Walker.

Reagan— *Probate & Juvenile Courts:* Morris Harville.

Red River— *Probate & Juvenile Courts:* Larry Isom.

Reeves — *All Courts:* Walter M. Holcombe.

Rockwall — *Court at Law:* David Rakow.

Rusk — *Court at Law, Domestic Relations & Juvenile:* Chad Dean. *Probate Court:* Sandra Hodges.

Sabine— *Probate Court:* Charles Watson. *Domestic Relations & Juvenile Courts:* Charles Watson and Joe Bob Golden.

San Augustine— *Probate Court:* Randy E. Williams.

San Jacinto— *Criminal Court at Law:* Fritz Faulkner.

San Patricio — *Court at Law:* Richard D. Hatch III.

Shackelford— *Probate & Juvenile Courts:* Ross Montgomery.

Smith — *Courts at Law: No. 1,* Thomas A. Dunn; *No. 2,* Randall L. Rogers. *Probate Court:* Joel Baker. *Juvenile:* Floyd Getz.

Somervell— *Probate & Juvenile Courts:* Walter Maynard.

Starr— *Court at Law, Criminal Court at Law & Juvenile Court:* Romero Molina. *Probate Court:* Eloy Vera and Romero Molina. *Domestic Relations Court:* Eloy Vera.

Stephens— *Probate Court:* Gary L. Fuller.

Sterling— *Probate Court:* Ralph Sides. *Juvenile Court:* Barbara Walther.

Stonewall— *Court at Law & Probate Court:* Bobby McGough. *Domestic Relations & Juvenile Courts:* Shane Hadaway.

Tarrant — *Courts at Law: No. 1,* R. Brent Keis; *No. 2,* Jennifer Rymell; *No. 3,* Vince Sprinkle. *County Criminal Courts at Law: No. 1,* Sherry Hill; *No. 2,* Mike Mitchell; *No. 3,* Billy D. Mills; *No. 4,* Deborah Nekhom Harris; *No. 5,* Jamie Cummings; *No. 6,* Molly Jones; *No. 7,* Cheril S. Hardy; *No. 8,* Daryl Coffee; *No. 9,* Brent A. Carr; *No. 10,* Phil Sorrels. *Probate Courts: No. 1,* Steve M. King; *No. 2,* Pat Ferchill.

Taylor — *Courts at Law and Criminal Courts at Law: No. 1,* Robert Harper; *No. 2,* Barbara B. Rollins. *Probate Court:* George A. Newman. *Domestic Relations:* Aleta Hacker. *Juvenile Court:* Robert Harper and Barbara B. Rollins.

Terrell— *Court at Law:* Leo Smith.

Titus— *Probate & Criminal Court at Law:* Sam W. Russell.

Tom Green — *Court at Law: No. 1,* Ben Nolan; *No. 2,* Penny Roberts.

Travis — *Courts at Law: No. 1,* J. David Phillips; *No. 2,* Eric Shepperd; *No. 3,* David Crain; *No. 4,* Mike Denton; *No. 5,* Nancy Hobengarten; *No. 6,* Jan Breland; *No. 7,* Elizabeth A. Earle. *Probate Court:* Guy Herman. *Juvenile Court:* Gardner Betts.

Trinity— *Probate & Criminal Court at Law:* Mark Evans.

Upshur— *Court at Law & Probate Court:* Dean Fowler. *Domestic Relations Court:* Lauren Parish. *Criminal Court at Law:* Dean Fowler and Lauren Parish.

Val Verde — *Court at Law:* Sergio J. Gonzalez.

Victoria — *Courts at Law: No. 1,* Laura A. Weiser; *No. 2,* Juan Velasquez III.

Walker — *Court at Law & Criminal Court at Law:* Barbara W. Hale. *Probate Court:* Barbara W. Hale and Danny Pierce.

Waller — *Court at Law:* June Jackson.

Washington — *Court at Law:* Matthew Reue.

Webb — *Courts at Law, Probate Court & Juvenile Court:* Alvino (Ben) Morales and Jesús (Chuy) Garza.

Wharton — *Court at Law, Probate & Criminal Court at Law:* John W. Murrile. *Domestic Relations & Juvenile:* Daniel Sklar.

Wichita — *Courts at Law: No. 1,* Jim Hogan; *No. 2,* Tom Bacus. *Probate, Domestic Relations & Juvenile:* Jim Hogan and Tom Bacus.

Willacy — *Court at Law, Probate & Criminal Court at Law:* Eliseo Barnhart.

Williamson — *Courts at Law: No. 1,* Suzanne Brooks; *No. 2,* Tim Wright; *No. 3,* Don Higginbotham; No. 4, John McMaster.

Wilson — *All Courts:* Marvin Quinney.

Winkler — *Criminal Court at Law, Probate & Juvenile Courts:* Bonnie Leck. *Domestic Relations Court:* James L. Rex.

Wise — *Court at Law & Criminal Court at Law:* Melton D. Cude.

Wood — *Probate Court:* Bryan Jeanes. *Juvenile Court:* G. Timothy Boswell.

Young — *Probate & Juvenile Courts:* Stanley H. Peavey III.

Zavala — *All Courts:* Joe Luna. ☆

County Tax Appraisers

The following list of Chief Appraisers for Texas counties was furnished by the State Property Tax Division of the State Comptroller's office. It includes the mailing address for each appraiser and is current to July 2006.

Anderson—Carson Wages, PO Box 279, Palestine 75802

Andrews—Ron Huckabay, 600 N. Main, Andrews 79714

Angelina—Keith Kraemer, PO Box 2357, Lufkin 75902

Aransas—Jad Smith, 601 S. Church, Rockport 78382

Archer—Kimbra York, PO Box 1141, Archer City 76351

Armstrong—Deborah J. Sherman, Drawer 835, Claude 79019

Atascosa—Edward A. Bridge, PO Box 139, Poteet 78065

Austin—Richard Moring, 906 E. Amelia St., Bellville 77418

Bailey—Kaye Elliott, 302 Main St., Muleshoe 79347

Bandera—Ed Barnes, PO Box 1119, Bandera 78003

Bastrop—Mark Boehnke, Drawer 578, Bastrop 78602

Baylor—Ronnie Hargrove, 211 N. Washington, Seymour 76380

Bee—Bruce Martin, PO Box 1262, Beeville 78104

Bell—Marvin Hahn, PO Box 390, Belton 76513

Bexar—Michael Amezquita, PO Box 830248, San Antonio 78283

Blanco—Hollis Boatright, PO Box 338, Johnson City 78636

Borden—Jill Freeman, PO Box 298, Gail 79738

Bosque—F. Janice Henry, PO Box 393, Meridian 76665

Bowie—Dolores Baird, PO Box 6527, Texarkana 75505

Brazoria—Cheryl Evans, 500 N. Chenango, Angleton 77515

Brazos—Gerald L. Winn, 1673 Briarcrest Dr., A-101, Bryan 77802

Brewster—Betty Jo Rooney, 107 W. Avenue E, #2, Alpine 79830

Briscoe—Pat McWaters, PO Box 728, Silverton 79257

Brooks—Marylou Cantu, Drawer A, Falfurrias 78355

Brown—Doran E. Lemke, 403 Fisk Ave., Brownwood 76801

Burleson—Curtis Doss, PO Box 1000, Caldwell 77836

Burnet—Stan Hemphill, PO Box 908, Burnet 78611

Caldwell—Matthew Allen, PO Box 900, Lockhart 78644

Calhoun—Andrew J. Hahn, PO Box 49, Port Lavaca 77979

Callahan—Bun Barry, 132 W. 4th St., Baird 79504

Cameron—Frutoso Gomez Jr., PO Box 1010, San Benito 78586

Camp—Geraldine Hull, 143 Quitman St., Pittsburg 75686

Carson—Donita Davis, PO Box 970, Panhandle 79068

Cass—Ann Lummus, 502 N. Main St., Linden 75563

Castro—Jerry Heller, 204 S.E. 3rd (Rear), Dimmitt 79027

Chambers—Michael Fregia, PO Box 1520, Anahuac 77514

Cherokee—Lee Flowers, PO Box 494, Rusk 75786

Childress—Anita Manley, 100 Ave. E NW, Childress 79201

Clay—A.G. Reis, PO Box 108, Henrietta 76365

Cochran—H. Loy Kern, 109 S.E. 1st, Morton 79346

Coke—Patsy N. Dunn, PO Box 2, Robert Lee 76945

Coleman—Bill W. Jones, PO Box 914, Coleman 76834

Collin—Jimmie Honea, 2404 Ave. K, Plano 75074

Collingsworth—Ann Wauer, 800 W. Ave., Wellington, Rm. 104 79095

Colorado—William T. Youens, PO Box 10, Columbus 78934

Comal—Lynn E. Rodgers, PO Box 311222, New Braunfels 78131

Comanche—Rhonda Woods, PO Box 6, Comanche 76442

Concho—Terry Farris, PO Box 68, Paint Rock 76866

Cooke—Doug Smithson, 201 N. Dixon St., Gainesville 76240

Coryell—Brett McKibben, 705 Main St., Gatesville 76528

Cottle—Rue Young, PO Box 459, Paducah 79248

Crane—Janet Wilson, 511 W. 8th, Crane 79731

Crockett—Rhonda Shaw, PO Drawer H, Ozona 76943

Crosby—Kathy Harris, PO Box 505, Crosbyton 79322

Culberson—Sally Carrasco, PO Box 550, Van Horn 79855

Dallam—Edward G. Carter, PO Box 579, Dalhart 79022

Dallas—Ken Nolan, 2949 N. Stemmons Fwy., Dallas 75247

Dawson—Tom Anderson, PO Box 797, Lamesa 79331

Deaf Smith—Danny Jones, PO Box 2298, Hereford 79045

Delta—Sarah Pruit, PO Box 47, Cooper 75432

Denton—Joe Rogers, PO Box 2816, Denton 76202

DeWitt—John Haliburton, PO Box 4, Cuero 77954

Dickens—Dexter Clay, PO Box 119, Dickens 79229

Dimmit—Elida Sanchez, 404 W. Peña St., Carrizo Springs 78834

Donley—Paula Lowrie, PO Box 1220, Clarendon 79226

Duval—Ernesto Molina, PO Box 809, San Diego 78384

Eastland—Steve Thomas, PO Box 914, Eastland 76448

Ector—Karen McCord, 1301 E. 8th St., Odessa 79761

Edwards—Jodie Greene, PO Box 858, Rocksprings 78880

Ellis—Kathy Rodrigue, PO Box 878, Waxahachie 75165

El Paso—Cora Viescas, 5801 Trowbridge, El Paso 79925

Erath—Jerry Lee, PO Box 94, Stephenville 76401

Falls—Sharon Scott, PO Box 430, Marlin 76661

Fannin—Mike Shannon, 831 W. State Hwy. 56, Bonham 75418

Fayette—Karen Schubert, PO Box 836, La Grange 78945

Fisher—Jacqueline Martin, PO Box 516, Roby 79543

Floyd—Shelia Faulkenberry, PO Box 249, Floydada 79235

Foard—Jo Ann Vecera, PO Box 419, Crowell 79227

Fort Bend—Glen Whitehead, 2801 B.F. Terry Blvd., Rosenberg 77471

Franklin—John Kirkland, PO Box 720, Mount Vernon 75457

Freestone—Bud Black, 218 N. Mount, Fairfield 75840

Frio—Irma Gonzalez, PO Box 1129, Pearsall 78061

Gaines—Betty Caudle, PO Box 490, Seminole 79360

Galveston—Ken Wright, 600 Gulf Fwy., Texas City 77591

Garza—Shirley A. Smith, PO Drawer F, Post 79356

Gillespie—David Oehler, 101 W. Main St., #11, Fredericksburg 78624

Glasscock—Royce Pruit, PO Box 89, Garden City 79739

Goliad—E.J. Bammert, PO Box 34, Goliad 77963

Gonzales—Glenda Strackbein, PO Box 867, Gonzales 78629

Gray—W. Pat Bagley, PO Box 430, Pampa 79066

Grayson—Larry Ward, 205 N. Travis, Sherman 75090

Gregg—Thomas Hays, 1333 E. Harrison Rd., Longview 75604

Grimes—Bill Sullivan, PO Box 489, Anderson 77830

Guadalupe—Chris Boenig, 3000 N. Austin, Seguin 78155

Hale—Nikki Branscum, PO Box 29, Plainview 79073

Hall—Marlin D. Felts, 512 W. Main St., Memphis 79245

Hamilton—Doyle Roberts, 119 E. Henry St., Hamilton 76531

Hansford—Alice Peddy, 709 W. 7th Ave., Spearman 79081

Hardeman—Twila Butler, PO Box 388, Quanah 79252

Hardin—Amador Reyna, PO Box 670, Kountze 77625

Harris—Jim Robinson, 10010 Northwest Fwy., Houston 77040

Harrison—David Whitmire, PO Box 818, Marshall 75671

Hartley—Mary M. Thompson, PO Box 405, Hartley 79044

Haskell—Kenny Watson, PO Box 467, Haskell 79521

Hays—David G. Valle (interim), 21001 N. IH-35, Kyle 78640

Hemphill—Duane Cox, PO Box 65, Canadian 79014

Henderson—Bill Jackson, PO Box 430, Athens 75751

Hidalgo—Alonzo Vega, PO Box 208, Edinburg 78540

Hill—Mike McKibben, PO Box 416, Hillsboro 76645

Hockley—Greg Kelley, PO Box 1090, Levelland 79336

Hood—Jeff Law, PO Box 819, Granbury 76048

Hopkins—William Sherman, PO Box 753, Sulphur Springs 75483

Houston—Kathryn Keith, PO Box 112, Crockett 75835

Howard—Keith Toomire, PO Box 1151, Big Spring 79721

Hudspeth—Zedoch L. Pridgeon, Box 429, Sierra Blanca 79851

Hunt—Mildred Compton, PO Box 1339, Greenville 75403

Hutchinson—Bill Swink, PO Box 5065, Borger 79008

Irion—Frances Grice, PO Box 980, Mertzon 76941

Jack—Kathy Conner, PO Box 958, Jacksboro 76458

Jackson—Damon D. Moore, 700 N. Wells, Ste. 204, Edna 77957

Jasper—David Luther, PO Box 1300, Jasper 75951

Jeff Davis—Zedoch L. Pridgeon, PO Box 373, Fort Davis 79734

Jefferson—Roland Bieber, PO Box 21337, Beaumont 77720

Jim Hogg—Arnoldo Gonzalez, PO Box 459, Hebbronville

78361
Jim Wells—Sidney Vela, PO Box 607, Alice 78333
Johnson—Jim Hudspeth, 109 N. Main, Cleburne 76033
Jones—Susan Holloway, PO Box 348, Anson 79501
Karnes—Oscar Caballero, 915 S. Panna Maria, Karnes City 78118
Kaufman—Richard L. Mohundro, PO Box 819, Kaufman 75142
Kendall—Leta Schlinke, PO Box 788, Boerne 78006
Kenedy—Bill Fuller, PO Box 701085, San Antonio 78270
Kent—Garth Gregory, PO Box 68, Jayton 79528
Kerr—P.H. "Fourth" Coates IV, PO Box 294387, Kerrville 78029
Kimble—John Dennis, PO Box 307, Junction 76849
King—Sandy Burkett, PO Box 117, Guthrie 79236
Kinney—William F. Haenn, PO Box 1377, Brackettville 78832
Kleberg—Tina Flores, PO Box 1027, Kingsville 78364
Knox—Kim McLemore, PO Box 47, Benjamin 79505
Lamar—Cathy Jackson, PO Box 400, Paris 75461
Lamb—Lesa Kloiber, PO Box 950, Littlefield 79339
Lampasas—Glenda January, Box 175, Lampasas 76550
La Salle—Joe R. Lozano, PO Box O, Cotulla 78014
Lavaca—Diane Munson, PO Box 386, Hallettsville 77964
Lee—Sheri Winn (interim), 218 E. Richmond, Giddings 78942
Leon—Jeff Beshears, PO Box 536, Centerville 75833
Liberty—Alan Conner, PO Box 10016, Liberty 77575
Limestone—Karen Wietzikoski, PO Drawer 831, Groesbeck 76642
Lipscomb—Jerry Reynolds, PO Box 128, Darrouzett 79024
Live Oak—Bob Johanson, PO Box 2370, George West 78022
Llano—Gary Eldridge, 103 E. Sandstone, Llano 78643
Loving—Sherlene Burrows, PO Box 352, Mentone 79754
Lubbock—Dave Kimbrough, PO Box 10542, Lubbock 79408
Lynn—Marquita Scott, PO Box 789, Tahoka 79373
Madison—Larry Krumnow, PO Box 1328, Madisonville 77864
Marion—David Sutton, PO Box 690, Jefferson 75657
Martin—Marsha Graves, PO Box 1349, Stanton 79782
Mason—Ted Smith, PO Box 1119, Mason 76856
Matagorda—Vince Maloney, 2225 Ave. G, Bay City 77414
Maverick—Victor Perry, 2243 Veterans Blvd., Eagle Pass 78852
McCulloch—Orlando Rubio, 306 W. Lockhart, Brady 76825
McLennan—Robert L. Waldrop, PO Box 2297, Waco 76703
McMullen—Jesse Bryan, PO Box 37, Tilden 78072
Medina—James Garcia, 1410 Ave. K, Hondo 78861
Menard—Dianna Miller, PO Box 1008, Menard 76859
Midland—Robert B. Kmiec, PO Box 908002, Midland 79708
Milam—Patricia Moraw, PO Box 769, Cameron 76520
Mills—Doug Stewart, PO Box 565, Goldthwaite 76844
Mitchell—Kaye Cornutt, 2112 Hickory St., Colorado City 79512
Montague—June Deaton, PO Box 121, Montague 76251
Montgomery—Mark Castleschouldt, PO Box 2233, Conroe 77305
Moore—Diane Ball, PO Box 717, Dumas 79029
Morris—Rhonda Hall, PO Box 563, Daingerfield 75638
Motley—Brenda Osborn, PO Box 779, Matador 79244
Nacogdoches—Gary Woods, 216 W. Hospital, Nacogdoches 75961
Navarro—Bill Worthen, PO Box 3118, Corsicana 75151
Newton—Margie Herrin, 109 Court St., Newton 75966
Nolan—Patricia Davis, PO Box 1256, Sweetwater 79556
Nueces—Ollie Grant, 201 N. Chaparral, Corpus Christi 78401
Ochiltree—Terry Symons, 825 S. Main, #100, Perryton 79070
Oldham—Jen Carter, PO Box 310, Vega 79092
Orange—Michael Cedars, PO Box 457, Orange 77631
Palo Pinto—Donna Rhodes, PO Box 250, Palo Pinto 76484
Panola—Loyd Adams, 2 Ball Park Rd., Carthage 75633
Parker—Larry Hammonds, 1108 Santa Fe Dr., Weatherford 76086
Parmer—Ron Procter, PO Box 56, Bovina 79009
Pecos—Sam Calderon Jr., PO Box 237, Fort Stockton 79735
Polk—Carolyn Allen, 114 W. Matthews, Livingston 77351
Potter—Jim Childers, PO Box 7190, Amarillo 79114
Presidio—Irma Salgado, PO Box 879, Marfa 79843
Rains—Carrol Houllis, PO Box 70, Emory 75440

Randall—Jim Childers, PO Box 7190, Amarillo 79114
Reagan—Byron Bitner, PO Box 8, Big Lake 76932
Real—LeAnn Rubio, PO Box 158, Leakey 78873
Red River—Jan Raulston, PO Box 461, Clarksville 75426
Reeves—Carol King-Markman, PO Box 1229, Pecos 79772
Refugio—Bettye Kret, PO Box 156, Refugio 78377
Roberts—DeAnn Williams, PO Box 458, Miami 79059
Robertson—Dan Brewer, PO Box 998, Franklin 77856
Rockwall—Ray Helm, 841 Justin Rd., Rockwall 75087
Runnels—Tylene Gamble, PO Box 524, Ballinger 76821
Rusk—Terry Decker, PO Box 7, Henderson 75653
Sabine—Jim Nethery, PO Box 137, Hemphill 75948
San Augustine—Jamie Doherty, 122 N. Harrison, San Augustine 75972
San Jacinto—Linda Lewis, PO Box 1170, Coldspring 77331
San Patricio—Rufino H. Lozano, PO Box 938, Sinton 78387
San Saba—Henry J. Warren, 423 E. Wallace, San Saba 76877
Schleicher—Scott Sutton, PO Box 936, Eldorado 76936
Scurry—Larry Crooks, 2612 College Ave., Snyder 79549
Shackelford—Teresa Peacock, PO Box 565, Albany 76430
Shelby—Robert Pigg, 724 Shelbyville St., Center 75935
Sherman—Teresa Edmond, PO Box 239, Stratford 79084
Smith—Michael Barnett, 245 South S.E. Loop 323, Tyler 75702
Somervell—Ronnie Babcock, 112 Allen Dr., Glen Rose 76043
Starr—Humberto Saenz Jr., PO Box 137, Rio Grande City 78582
Stephens—Troy Sloan, PO Box 351, Breckenridge 76424
Sterling—Linda Low, PO Box 28, Sterling City 76951
Stonewall—Ozella E. Warner, PO Box 308, Aspermont 79502
Sutton—Rex Ann Friess, 300 E. Oak St., Sonora 76950
Swisher—Cindy McDowell, PO Box 8, Tulia 79088
Tarrant—John Marshall, 2500 Handley-Ederville Rd., Fort Worth 76118
Taylor—Richard Petree, PO Box 1800, Abilene 79604
Terrell—Blain Chriesman, PO Box 747, Sanderson 79848
Terry—Ronny Burran, PO Box 426, Brownfield 79316
Throckmorton—Linda Carrington, Box 788, Throckmorton 76483
Titus—Katrina Perry, PO Box 528, Mount Pleasant 75456
Tom Green—Bill Benson, PO Box 3307, San Angelo 76902
Travis—Art Cory, PO Box 149012, Austin 78714
Trinity—Allen McKinley, PO Box 950, Groveton 75845
Tyler—Travis Chalmers, PO Drawer 9, Woodville 75979
Upshur—Louise Stracener (interim), 105 Diamond Loch, Gilmer 75644
Upton—Sheri Stephens, PO Box 1110, McCamey 79752
Uvalde—Alida Lopez (interim), 209 N. High, Uvalde 78801
Val Verde—Ricardo Martinez, PO Box 420487, Del Rio 78842
Van Zandt—Brenda Barnett, PO Box 926, Canton 75103
Victoria—Albert Molina (interim), 2805 N. Navarro, Ste. 300, Victoria 77901
Walker—Grover Cook, PO Box 1798, Huntsville 77342
Waller—David Piwonka, PO Box 159, Katy 77492
Ward—Arlice Wittie, PO Box 905, Monahans 79756
Washington—Willy Dilworth, PO Box 681, Brenham 77834
Webb—Sergio Delgado, 3302 Clark Blvd., Laredo 78043
Wharton—Larry Holub, 2407 1/2 N. Richmond Rd., Wharton 77488
Wheeler—Jeanine Hawkins, PO Box 1200, Wheeler 79096
Wichita—Eddie Trigg, PO Box 5172, Wichita Falls 76307
Wilbarger—Deborah Echols, PO Box 1519, Vernon 76385
Willacy—Augustin Colchado, Rt. 2, Box 256, Raymondville 78580
Williamson—Bill Carroll, 510 W. 9th St., Georgetown 78726
Wilson—Carlton R. Pape, Box 849, Floresville 78114
Winkler—Connie Carpenter, PO Box 1219, Kermit 79745
Wise—Mickey Hand, 400 E. Business 380, Decatur 76234
Wood—Tracy Nichols, PO Box 1706, Quitman 75783
Yoakum—Saundra Stephens, PO Box 748, Plains 79355
Young—Jerry Patton, PO Box 337, Graham 76450
Zapata—Amada Gonzalez, PO Box 2315, Zapata 78076
Zavala—Alberto Mireles, 323 W. Zavala, Crystal City 78839☆

Wet-Dry Counties

Source: Texas Alcoholic Beverage Commission; www.tabc.state.tx.us//

The list below shows the wet-or-dry status of counties in Texas as of August 31, 2007.

An **asterisk (*)** indicates counties in which the sale of mixed beverages (liquor by the drink) is legal in all or part of the county. In four counties marked with a **dagger (†)**, sale of mixed beverages in restaurants is permitted, but sale of distilled spirits for off-premise consumption is not permitted.

When approved in local-option elections in "wet" pre-

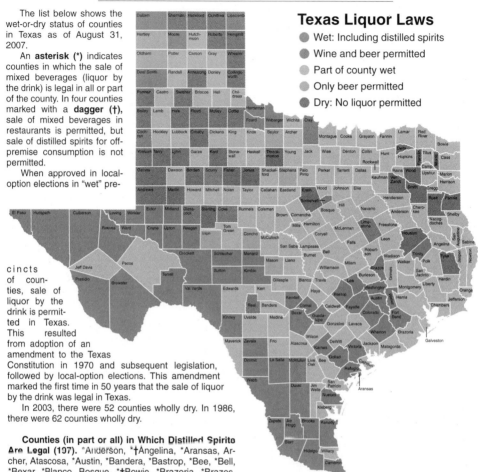

Texas Liquor Laws

- Wet: Including distilled spirits
- Wine and beer permitted
- Part of county wet
- Only beer permitted
- Dry: No liquor permitted

cincts of counties, sale of liquor by the drink is permitted in Texas. This resulted from adoption of an amendment to the Texas Constitution in 1970 and subsequent legislation, followed by local-option elections. This amendment marked the first time in 50 years that the sale of liquor by the drink was legal in Texas.

In 2003, there were 52 counties wholly dry. In 1986, there were 62 counties wholly dry.

Counties (in part or all) in Which Distilled Spirits Are Legal (197). *Anderson, *†Angelina, *Aransas, Archer, Atascosa, *Austin, *Bandera, *Bastrop, *Bee, *Bell, *Bexar, *Blanco, Bosque, *†Bowie, *Brazoria, *Brazos, *Brewster, Briscoe, *Brooks, *Brown, Burleson, *Burnet, *Caldwell, *Calhoun, Callahan, *Cameron, Camp, Carson, Cass, Castro, *Chambers, Cherokee, Childress, Coleman, *Collin, *Colorado, *Comal, Comanche, *Cooke, Coryell, Crane, Crockett, Culberson.

Also, Dallam, *Dallas, *Dawson, Deaf Smith, *Denton, *DeWitt, Dickens, *Dimmit, *Donley, *Duval, Eastland, *Ector, Edwards, *Ellis, *El Paso, Falls, Fannin, *Fayette, Foard, *Fort Bend, Freestone, *Frio, *Galveston, Garza, *Gillespie, *Goliad, Gonzales, Gray, *Grayson, *Gregg, *Grimes, *Guadalupe, Hall, Hamilton, *Hardeman, Hardin, *Harris, Harrison, Haskell, *Hays, *Henderson, *Hidalgo, *Hill, *Hockley, *Hood, Hopkins, *Howard, *Hudspeth, Hunt, Hutchinson, Jack, *Jackson, *Jasper, *Jeff Davis.

Also *Jefferson, *Jim Hogg, *Jim Wells, *†Johnson, *Karnes, *Kaufman, *Kendall, *Kenedy, *Kerr, *Kimble, King, *Kinney, *Kleberg, Knox, *Lamar, Lamb, *Lampasas, *La Salle, *Lavaca, *Lee, Leon, *Liberty, Live Oak, *Llano, *Lubbock, *†Madison, *Marion, *Matagorda, *Maverick, *McCulloch, *McLennan, *Medina, Menard, *Midland, Milam, Mills, Mitchell, Montague, *Montgomery, *Moore, Nacogdoches, *Navarro, Newton, Nolan, *Nueces.

Also, *Orange, Palo Pinto, *Parker, *Pecos, *Polk, *Potter, *Presidio, Rains, *Randall, Reagan, Red River, *Reeves, Refugio, Robertson, *Rockwall, Runnels, Sabine, San Augustine, San Jacinto, *San Patricio, San Saba, *Schleicher, Shackelford, Shelby, *Starr, Stonewall, *Sutton, *Tarrant, *Taylor, Terrell, Titus, *Tom Green, *Travis, Trinity, Upshur, Upton, Uvalde, *Val Verde, *Victoria, *Walker, Waller, Ward, *Washington, *Webb, *Wharton, *Wichita, *Wilbarger, *Willacy, *Williamson, *Wilson, Winkler, *Wise, Young, *Zapata, *Zavala.

Counties in Which Only Beer Is Legal (7): Baylor, Concho, Hartley, Irion, Mason, Oldham, Stephens.

Counties in Which Beer and Wine Are Legal (11): Clay, Cochran, Coke, Glasscock, Limestone, Lipscomb, Loving, McMullen, Real, Scurry, Somervell.

Counties Wholly Dry (39): Andrews, Armstrong, Bailey, Borden, Collingsworth, Cottle, Crosby, Delta, Erath, Fisher, Floyd, Franklin, Gaines, Hale, Hansford, Hemphill, Houston, Jones, Kent, Lynn, Martin, Morris, Motley, Ochiltree, Panola, Parmer, Roberts, Rusk, Sherman, Smith, Sterling, Swisher, Terry, Throckmorton, Tyler, Van Zandt, Wheeler, Wood, Yoakum. ☆

Texas County and District Officials — Table No. 1

County Seats, County Judges, County Clerks, County Attorneys, County Treasurers, Tax Assessors-Collectors and Sheriffs.

See Table No. 2 on pages following this table for District Clerks, District Attorneys and County Commissioners. Judges in county courts at law, as well as probate courts, juvenile/domestic relations courts, county criminal courts and county criminal courts of appeal, can be found beginning on page **508**. The officials listed here are elected by popular vote. An asterisk (*) before a county name marks a county whose county clerk failed to return our questionnaire; the names of officials for those counties are taken from most recent unofficial sources available to us.

County	County Seat	County Judge	County Clerk	County Attorney	County Treasurer	Assessor-Collector	Sheriff
Anderson	Palestine	Lnda Bostick Ray	Wanda Burke	NA	Sharon Peterson	Terri Garvey	Gregg Taylor
Andrews	Andrews	Richard H. Dolgener	F. Wm. Hoermann	John L. Pool	Office abolished 11-5-1985.	Robin Harper	Sam H. Jones
*Angelina	Lufkin	Joe Berry	Jo Ann Chastain	Ed Jones	Lois Warner	Bill Shanklin	Kent Henson
Aransas	Rockport	C.H. (Burt) Mills Jr.	Peggy L. Friebele	James L. Anderson Jr.	Marvine D. Wix	Jeri D. Cox	Mark Gilliam
Archer	Archer City	Gary W. Beesinger	Karren Winter	R.B. "Burk" Morris	Victoria Lear	Teresa K. Martin	Ed Daniels
Armstrong	Claude	Hugh Reed	Connie Spiller	Randy Sherrod	Sara Messer	Deborah Sherman	J.R. Walker
Atascosa	Jourdanton	Diana J. Bautista	Laquita Hayden	R. Thomas Franklin	Ray Samson	Barbara Schorsch	Tommy Williams
Austin	Bellville	Carolyn Cerny Bilski	Carrie Gregor		Cathleen V. Frank	Janice Kokemor	R. DeWayne Burger
Bailey	Muleshoe	Sherri Harrison	Paula Benton	Scott Say	Shonda Black	Berta Combs	Richard Willis
Bandera	Bandera	Richard A. Evans	Candy Wheeler	K.H. Schneider	Kay Welch	Mae Vion Meyer	Weldon B. Tucker
Bastrop	Bastrop	Ronnie McDonald	Rose Pietsch		Kathy Schroeder	Linda Harmon	Richard M. Hernandez
Baylor	Seymour	Linda Rogers	Clara "Carrie" Coker	Susan Elliott	Kevin Hostas	Jeanette Holub	Bob Elliott
Bee	Beeville	David Silva	Mirella Escamilla Davis	Michael J. Knight	Office abolished 11-2-1982.	Andrea W. Gibbud	Carlos Carrizales Jr.
Bell	Belton	Jon H. Burrows	Shelley Coston	Richard J. Miller	Charles Jones	Sharon Long	Dan Smith
Bexar	San Antonio	Nelson W. Wolff	Gerry Rickhoff	Position abolished	Office abolished 11-5-1985.	Sylvia S. Romo	Ralph Lopez
Blanco	Johnson City	Bill Guthrie	Karen Newman	Dean C. Myane	Camille Swift	Hollis Boatright	William R. "Bill" Elsbury
Borden	Gail	Van L. York	Joyce Herridge	Ben Smith	Kenneth P. Bennett	Billy J. Gannaway	Billy J. Gannaway
*Bosque	Meridian	Cole Word	Betty Outlaw	David Christian	Randy Pullin	Shana Wallace	Charles E. Jones
Bowie	Boston	James M. Carlow	Velma Moore	Carol Dalby	Donna Burns	Toni Barron	James Prince
Brazoria	Angleton	E.J. (Joe) King	Joyce Hudman	Jeri Yenne	Sharon Reynolds	Ro-Vin Garrett	Charles Wagner
Brazos	Bryan	Randy Sims	Karen McQueen	Jim Kuboviak	Kay Hamilton	Gerald L. "Buddy" Winn	Chris Kirk
Brewster	Alpine	Val Clark Beard	Berta Rios Martinez	Steve Houston	Carol Ofenstein	Betty Jo Rooney	Ronny Dodson
*Briscoe	Silverton	Wayne Nance	Bena Hester	Emily S. Roy	Mary Jo Brannon	Betty Ann Stephens	Jeff Fuston
Brooks	Falfurrias	Joe B. Garcia	Frutoso Garza Jr.	David T. Garcia	Gilberto Vela	Balde Lozano	Baldemar Lozano
Brown	Brownwood	E. Ray West III	Margaret Wood	Shane Britton	Ann Kroun	Cheryl Nelson	Bobby Grubbs
Burleson	Caldwell	Mike Sutherland	Anna L. Schielack	Joseph J. Skrivanek III	Beth Andrews Bills	Curtis Doss	A. Dale Stroud
*Burnet	Burnet	David Kithil	Janet Parker	Eddie Arredondo	Donna Klaeger	Sherri Frazier	Joe Pollock
Caldwell	Lockhart	H.T. Wright	Nina S. Sells	Trey Hicks	Lori Rangel-Pompa	Mary Vicky Gonzales	Daniel Law
Calhoun	Port Lavaca	Michael J. Pfeifer	Anita Fricke		Rhonda Sikes Kokena	Gloria A. Ochoa	Burnard B. Browning
Callahan	Baird	Roger Corn	Donna Bell	Joel Shane Deel	Dianne Alexander	Tammy T. Walker	Eddie Curtis
Cameron	Brownsville	Carlos H. Cascos	Joe G. Rivera	Richard O. Burts	David A. Betancourt	Antonio Yzaguirre Jr.	Omar Lucio
Camp	Pittsburg	Preston Combest	Elaine Young	James W. Wallace	Judy Croley	Gale Burns	Alan D. McCandless
Carson	Panhandle	Lewis Powers	Celeste Bichsel	Scott Sherwood	Denise Salzbrenner	Jackie Lewis	Tam Terry
Cass	Linden	Charles L. McMichael	Jannis Mitchell		Martha Fant Sheridan	Becky Watson	James Troup Estes
Castro	Dimmitt	William F. Sava	Joyce M. Thomas	James R. Horton	Janice Shelton	Billy Hackleman	Sal Rivera
Chambers	Anahuac	Jimmy Sylvia	Heather H. Hawthorne	Cheryl S. Lieck	Carren Sparks	Jerry Sparks	Joe LaRive
*Cherokee	Rusk	Chris Davis	Laverne Lusk	Craig D. Caldwell	Patsy Lassiter	Linda Beard	James E. Campbell
Childress	Childress	Jay Mayden	Zona Prince	Greg Buckley	Jeanie Thomas	Juanell Halford	Michael Pigg
Clay	Henrietta	Kenneth Liggett	Kay Hutchison	Eddy Atkins	Debra Alexander	Linda Sellers	Tim King
Cochran	Morton	James St. Clair	Rita Tyson	J.C. Adams Jr.	Doris Sealy	Linda Huckabee	R.Wallace Stalcup
Coke	Robert Lee	Roy Blair	Mary Grim	Nancy Arthur	Phelan Winkle	Josie Dean	Rick Styles
Coleman	Coleman	Jimmie D. Hobbs	JoAnn Hale	Heath A. Hemphill	Kay LeMay	Jamie Trammell	Robert Wade Turner
*Collin	McKinney	Ron Harris	Brenda Taylor		Brenda Taylor	Kenneth Maun	Terry Box
Collingsworth	Wellington	John A. James	Jackie Johnson	G. Keith Davis	Yvonne Brewer	Patsy Barnett	Joe D. Stewart
Colorado	Columbus	Al Jamison	Darlene Hayek	Ken Sparks	Diane Matus	Mary Jane Poenitzsch	R.H. "Curley" Wied
*Comal	New Braunfels	Danny Scheel	Joy Streater		Susan Patterson	Sherman Krause	Bob Holder
Comanche	Comanche	James R. Arthur	Ruby Lesley	Charles Williams	Billy Ruth Rust	Gay Horton Green	Jeff Lambert

County	County Seat	County Judge	County Clerk	County Attorney	County Treasurer	Assessor-Collector	Sheriff
Concho	Paint Rock	Allen Amos	Barbara K. Hoffman	Bill Campbell	Lisa J. Jost	Richard G. Doane	Richard G. Doane
Cooke	Gainesville	Bill Freeman	Rebecca Lawson	Tanya Davis	Judy Hunter	Billie Jean Knight	Mike Compton
Coryell	Gatesville	Riley Simpson	Barbara Simpson	Brandon Belt	Donna Meadford	Justin Carothers	Johnny Burks
*Cottle	Paducah	John D. Shavor	Beckey J. Tucker	John H. Richards	Kathy Biddy	Rue Young	Kenneth A. Burns
Crane	Crane	John Farmer	Judy Crawford	James McDonald	Cristy Tarin	Rebecca Gonzales	Robert DeLeon
Crockett	Ozona	Fred Deaton	Debbi Puckett	Jody Upham	Burl Myers	Rhonda Shaw	Shane Fenton
Crosby	Crosbyton	Davey Abell	Betty J. Pierce	C. Michael Ward	Debra Riley	Anna Rodriguez	Lavoice Udel (Red) Riley
Culberson	Van Horn	Manuel Molinar	Linda McDonald	Stephen L. Mitchell	Susana R. Hinojos	Amalia Y. Hernandez	Oscar E. Carrillo
Dallam	Dalhart	David D. Field	Terri Banks	Jon King	Wes Ritchey	Kay Howell	Bruce Scott
Dallas	Dallas	Jim Foster	John Warren		Joe Wells	David Childs	Lupe Valdez
Dawson	Lamesa	Sam Saleh	Gloria Vera	Steven B. Payson	Julie Frizel	Diane Hogg	Johnny Garcia
Deaf Smith	Hereford	Tom Simons	David Ruland	Jim English	Paula B. Price	Teresa Garth	Brent Harrison
Delta	Cooper	Ted Carrington	Jane Jones	H. Michael Bartley	Phyllis London	Brenda (Dawn) Curtis	Gaylon R. Wood
Denton	Denton	Mary Horn	Cynthia Mitchell		Cindy Yeatts Brown	Steve Mossman	Benny Parkey
DeWitt	Cuero	Ben E. Prause	Elva Petersen	Raymond H. Reese	Peggy Ledbetter	Susie Dreyer	Joe C. "Jode" Zavesky
Dickens	Dickens	Lesa Arnold	Winona Humphreys	vacant	Sandy Vickrey	Sherry Hill	Ken Brendle
Dimmit	Carrizo Springs	Francisco G. Ponce	Mario R. Garcia	Daniel M. Gonzalez	Estanislado Z. Martinez	Melinda Vega Campos	Douglas Sample
*Donley	Clarendon	Jack Hall	Fay Vargas	Kaye Messer (pro tem)	Rebecca Jackson	Wilma Lindley	Charles "Butch" Blackburn
Duval	San Diego	Abel Aragon	Oscar Garcia Jr.	Ricardo O. (Rocky) Carrillo	Lydia P. Molina	Carlos J. Montemayor Jr.	Santiago Barrera Jr.
Eastland	Eastland	Rex Fields	Cathy Jentho		Marti Baker	Sandra Cagle	Wayne Bradford
*Ector	Odessa	Jerry D. Caddel	Linda Haney	Cathy Linch	Carolyn Bowen	Barbara Horn	Mark Donaldson
Edwards	Rocksprings	Nick Gallegos	Joanna Baker	Allen Ray Moody	Lupe Sifuentes-Enriquez	Lonna Fry	Don G. Letsinger
*Ellis	Waxahachie	Chad Adams	Cindy Polley	Joe F. Grubbs	Ron Langenheder	John Bridges	Ray Stewart
El Paso	El Paso	Dolores Briones	Waldo Alarcon	José R. Rodriguez		Victor A. Flores	Leo Samaniego
*Erath	Stephenville	Tab Thompson	Gwinda Jones	Carey S. Fraser	Donna Kelly	Jennifer Carey	Tommy Bryant
Falls	Marlin	Thomas B. Sehon	Frances Breswell	Kathryn J. Gilliam	Sue Ryan	Bryant Hinson	Ben Kirk
Fannin	Bonham	Derrell Hall	Tammy Rich	Richard Glaser	Mike Towery	Pamela Sweet Richardson	Kenneth Moore
Fayette	La Grange	Edward F. Janecka	Carolyn Kutos Roberts	Peggy Supak	Office abolished 11-3-87.	Carol Johnson	Keith Korenek
Fisher	Roby	Marshal Bennett	Pat Thomson	Rudy V. Hamric	Marty Williamson	Jonnye Lu Brown	Mickey A. Counts
Floyd	Floydada	William D. Hardin	Marilyn Holcomb	Lex S. Herrington	Elva Martinez	Penny Golightly	Billy R. Gilmore
*Foard	Crowell	Charlie Bell	Sherry Weatherred	Daryl Halencak	Esther Kajs	Bobby Bond	Bobby Bond
*Fort Bend	Richmond	Robert E. Hebert	Dianne Wilson	Ben W. "Bud" Childers	Clifton Terrell	Patsy Schultz	Milton Wright
Franklin	Mount Vernon	Gerald Hubbell	Betty Crane	Cecil Solomon	Marla Carrell	Marjorie Jaggers	Charles J. (Chuck) White
Freestone	Fairfield	Linda K. Grant	Mary Lynn White	Jack Keith Meredith	Debra Kay Barger	Carolyn J. Varley	Ralph Billings
Frio	Pearsall	Carlos A. Garcia	Angie Tullis	Hector M. Lozano	Anna L. Hernández	Anna Alaniz	Lionel G. Treviño
Gaines	Seminole	Tom N. Keyes	Vicki Phillips	Sterling Harmon	Vicenta Munguia	Susan Shaw	Jon Key
Galveston	Galveston	James D. Yarbrough	Mary Ann Daigle	Harvey Bazaman	Kevin C. Walsh	Cheryl E. Johnson	Gean Leonard
Garza	Post	Lee Norman	Jim Plummer	Leslie C. Acker	Ruth Ann Young	Judy M. Bush	Cliff Laws
Gillespie	Fredericksburg	Mark Stroeher	Mary Lynn Rusche	Tamara Y.S. Keener	Laura Lundquist	Leola Brodbeck	Milton E. Jung
Glasscock	Garden City	Wilburn Bednar	Rebecca Betta	Hardy Wilkerson	Alan Dierschke	Royce Pruit	Royce Pruit
Goliad	Goliad	Harold F. Gleinser	Gail M. Turlay	Rob Baiamonte	June Bethke	Anna Breen	Robert de la Garza
Gonzales	Gonzales	David Bird	Lee Riedel	Robert B. Scheske	Sheryl Barborak	Norma Jean DuBose	Glen A. Sachtleben
Gray	Pampa	Richard Peet	Susan Wintorne	Joshua Seabourn	Scott Hahn	Gaye Whitehead	Don Copeland
Grayson	Sherman	Drue Bynum	Wilma Blackshear Bush	David Van Brunt Price	Virginia Hughes	John Ramsey	Keith Gary
Gregg	Longview	Bill Stout	Connie Wade	Janie Johnson	Office abolished 1-1-88.	William Kirk Shields	Maxey Cerliano
Grimes	Anderson	Betty Shiflett	David Paskat	Jon C. Fultz	Phillis Allen	Connie Perry	Donald Sowell
Guadalupe	Seguin	Mike Wiggins	Teresa Kiel	Elizabeth Murray-Kolb	Linda Douglass	Tavie Murphy	Arnold Zwicke
Hale	Plainview	Dwain Dodson	Latrice Kemp	James (Jim) Tirey	Ida A. Tyler	Kemp Hinch	David B. Mull
*Hall	Memphis	Jack Martin	Raye Bailey	John M. Deaver II	Janet Bridges	Pat Floyd	Earnest Neel
Hamilton	Hamilton	Randy Mills	Debbie Rudolph	Andy J. McMullen	Debbie Eoff	Terry Short	W.R. (Randy) Murphree
*Hansford	Spearman	Benny Wilson	Kim Vera	John L. Hutchison	Wanda Wagner	Linda Cummings	Gary Evans
Hardeman	Quanah	Ronald Ingram	Linda Walker	Stanley R. Watson	Mary Ann Naylor	Darlene Gamble	Randy L. Akers
Hardin	Kountze	Billy Caraway	Glenda Alston	David Sheffield	Sharon Overstreet	Shirley Stephens	Ed Jay Cain
Harris	Houston	Robert A. Eckels	Beverly B. Kaufman	Michael Stafford	Orlando Sanchez	Paul Bettencourt	Tommy Thomas
Harrison	Marshall	Richard M. Anderson	Patsy Cox		Jamie Noland Smith	Betty Wright	Tom McCool
*Hartley	Channing	Ronnie Gordon	Diane Thompson	M. Shane Turner	Dinkie Parman	Frank Scott	Franky Scott
Haskell	Haskell	David C. Davis	Rhonda Moeller	Kris Fouts	Janis McDaniel	Bobbye Collins	David Halliburton

County	County Seat	County Judge	County Clerk	County Attorney	County Treasurer	Assessor-Collector	Sheriff
Hays	San Marcos	Elizabeth (Liz) Sumter	Linda C. Fritsche	Sherri Tibbe	Michele Tuttle	Luanne Caraway	Allen Bridges
*Hemphill	Canadian	Steve Vandiver	Brenda Perrin	Ty M. Sparks	Cindy N. Bowen	Debra L. Ford	Gary S. Henderson
*Henderson	Athens	David Holstein	Gwen Moffeit	James Owen	Karin Smith	Milburn Chaney	J.R. "Ronny" Brownlow
Hidalgo	Edinburg	J.D. Salinas III	Arturo Guajardo Jr.	Steven Crain	Norma Garcia	Armando Barrera Jr.	Guadalupe Trevino
Hill	Hillsboro	Justin Lewis	Nicole Tanner	Mark Pratt	Becky Wilkins	Marchel Eubank	Brent Button
Hockley	Levelland	Larry D. Sprowls	Irene Gonzalez	Jay Michael (Pat) Phelan	Denise Bohannon	Christy Clevenger	David Kinney
*Hood	Granbury	Andy Rash	Sally Oubre	Kelton Conner	Kathy Davis	Sandy Tidwell	Gene Mayo
*Hopkins	Sulphur Springs	Cletis Millsap	Debbie Shirley	Dusty Hyde Rabe	Betty Bassham	Debbie Pogue Jenkins	Butch Adams
Houston	Crockett	Lonnie Hunt	Bridget Lamb	Donna Kaspar	Dina Herrera	Danette Millican	Darrell E. Bobbitt
Howard	Big Spring	Mark J. Barr	Donna Wright	C.E. (Mike) Thomas III	Teresa Thomas	Kathy A. Sayles	Dale Walker
Hudspeth	Sierra Blanca	Becky Dean-Walker	Paula L. Hoover	C.R. (Kit) Bramblett	Jennifer Canaba	L. Kay Scarbrough	Arvin West
Hunt	Greenville	John L. Horn	Linda Brooks	Joel Littlefield	Delores Shelton	Barbara Wiggins	Don Anderson
Hutchinson	Stinnett	Faye Blanks	Beverly Turner	Michael D. Milner	Kathy Sargent	Mary Lou Henderson	Guy D. Rowh
Irion	Mertzon	Leon Standard	Reba Criner	Kenneth Greer Jr.	Linda Pierce	Joyce Gray	Jimmy Martin
Jack	Jacksboro	Mitchell G. Davenport	Shelly Clayton	Michael G. Mask	Roger Sharp	Sharon Robinson	Danny R. Nash
Jackson	Edna	Harrison Stafford II	Kenneth W. McElveen		Mary Horton	Donna Atzenhoffer	Andy Louderback
Jasper	Jasper	Mark Allen	Debbie Newman		Rene Kelley	Bobby Biscamp	Ronnie McBride
Jeff Davis	Fort Davis	George E. Grubb	Sue Blackley	Bart Medley	Geen Parrott	Thomas Roberts	Thomas Roberts
*Jefferson	Beaumont	Carl R. Griffith Jr.	Carolyn L. Guidry	Tom Rugg	Linda Robinson	Miriam K. Johnson	Mitch Woods
Jim Hogg	Hebbronville	Guadalupe S. Canales	Noemi G. Salinas	Enrique A. Garza	Linda Jo G. Soliz	Norma Liza S. Hinojosa	Erasmo Alarcon Jr.
Jim Wells	Alice	L. Arnoldo Saenz	Ruben Sandoval	Jesusa Sanchez-Vera	Becky Dominguez	Lucila Reynolds	Oscar López
Johnson	Cleburne	Roger Harmon	Curtis H. Douglas	Bill Moore	Barbara Robinson	Scott Porter	Bob Alford
Jones	Anson	Dale Spurgin	Julia McCray	Dennis Brown	Tish McIntire	Mary Ann Lovelady	Larry Moore
Karnes	Karnes City	Alger H. Kendall Jr.	Alva Jonas	Rober L. Busselman	Nancy Duckett	Anne Franke	David A. Jalufka
Kaufman	Kaufman	Wayne Gent	Laura Hughes		Johnny Countryman	Richard Murphy	David Byrnes
*Kendall	Boerne	Eddie John Vogt	Darlene Herrin	Don Allee	Medana Crow	James A. Hudson Jr.	Roger Duncan
Kenedy	Sarita	J.A. Garcia Jr.	Veronica Vela	Jaime E. Tijerina	Cynthia M. Salinas	Eleuteria S. Gonzalez	Ramiro Medellin Jr.
Kent	Jayton	Jim White	Richard Craig Harrison	Howard Freemyer	Linda McCurry	Brenda Long	William Delmer Scogin
Kerr	Kerrville	Pat Tinley	Jannett Pieper	Melvin Rex Emerson	Mindy Williams	Diane Bolin	W.R. (Rusty) Hierholzer
Kimble	Junction	Delbert R. Roberts	Haydee Torres	Lawrence F. Harrison	Sheila D'Spain	Mike Chapman	Mike Chapman
King	Guthrie	Duane Daniel	Jammye D. Timmons	Marshall Capps	Traci Butler	Sadie Mote	Raymond C. Daniel Jr.
*Kinney	Brackettville	Herb Senne	Dora Elia Sandoval	Tully Shahan	Janis Floyd	Martha Pena Padron	Leland Burgess
Kleberg	Kingsville	Pete de la Garza	Leo Alarcon	Alfred Isassi	Priscilla Alaniz Cantu	Melissa T. de la Garza	Ed Mata
*Knox	Benjamin	Travis Floyd	Ronnie Verhalen	Bobby D. Burnett	Irma Bell	Linda Parker	Dean Homstad
*Lamar	Paris	Maurice Superville	Kathy Marlowe	Gary Young	Shirley Fults	Peggy Noble	B.J. McCoy
*Lamb	Littlefield	William A. Thompson Jr.	Bill Johnson	Mark Yarbrough	Janice B. Wells	Linda Charlton	Gary Maddox
Lampasas	Lampasas	Wayne L. Boultinghouse	Connie Hartmann	Larry W. Allison	Nelda DeRiso	Linda Crawford	Gordon Morris
La Salle	Cotulla	Joel Rodriguez Jr.	Margarita A. Esqueda	Elizabeth Martinez	Thelma R. Trevino	Elida A. Linares	Victor S. Villarreal
Lavaca	Hallettsville	Ronald L. Leck	Elizabeth A. Kouba	V'Anne Bostick Huser	Lois Henry	Margaret Kallus	Micah C. Harmon
Lee	Giddings	Evan Gonzales	Sharon Blasig	Ted Weems	Lyndy Krause	Virginia Jackson	Joe Goodson
Leon	Centerville	Byron Ryder	Carla Neyland McEachern	Jim Witt	Phil Skelton	Louise Wilson	Mike Pierce
Liberty	Liberty	Phil Fitzgerald	Delia Sellers	A.J. (Jack) Hartel	Kim Harris	Mark McClelland	Greg Arthur
Limestone	Groesbeck	Daniel Burkeen	Peggy Beck	Roy DeFriend	Carol Bostain	Charlene Black	Dennis D. Wilson
Lipscomb	Lipscomb	Willis V. Smith	Kim Blau	Matthew D. Bartosiewicz	Diana Schoenhals	Kathy Fry	James Robertson
Live Oak	George West	Jim Huff	Karen Irving	Gene Chapline	Peggy Benham	Virginia Horton	Larry R. Busby
Llano	Llano	Wayne Brascom	Bette Sue Hoy	Cheryl Mabray	Sandra Overstreet	Dexter Sagebiel	Nathan Garrett
Loving	Mentone	Skeet Jones	Beverly Hanson		Nicole Clark	Billy Burt Hopper	Billy Burt Hopper
Lubbock	Lubbock	Thomas V. Head	Kelly J. Pinion	Matt Powell	Sharon Gossett	Barbara Brooks	David Gutierrez
Lynn	Tahoka	H.G. Franklin	Susan Tipton	Donna Scott	Pam Miller	Sherry Pearce	Jerry D. Franklin
Madison	Madisonville	Arthur M. Henson	Charlotte Barrett	William C. (Bill) Bennett	Judy Weathers	Beverly Plumlee	Dan Douget
Marion	Jefferson	Phil A. Parker	Betty Smith	William Gleason	Terrie Neuville	Mary Alice Moseley Biggs	Bill McCoy
Martin	Stanton	Charles T. (Corky) Blocker	Susie Hull	James L. McGilvray	H.D. Howard	Kathy Hull	Randy Cozart
Mason	Mason	Jerry M. Bearden	Pam Beam	Shain V.H. Chapman	Polly McMillan	H. Clint Low	H. Clint Low
Matagorda	Bay City	Nate McDonald	Gail Denn	Jill Cornelius	Amy Perez	Cristyn Hallmark	James Mitchell
*Maverick	Eagle Pass	Jose Aranda	Sara Montemayor	Ricardo Ramos	Manuel Reyes Jr.	Esteban A. Luna	Tomas S. Herrera
McCulloch	Brady	Randy Young	Tina A. Smith	Mark Marshall	Donna Robinett	Treva A. Colen	Earl Howell
McLennan	Waco	Jim Lewis	J.A. (Andy) Harwell	John Segrest	Bill Helton	A.F. (Buddy) Skeen	Larry Lynch

County	County Seat	County Judge	County Clerk	County Attorney	County Treasurer	Assessor-Collector	Sheriff
McMullen	Tilden	Linda Lee Henry	Dorairene Garza	Roberto Varga	Donald Haynes Jr.	Angel Bostwick	Bruce Thomas
Medina	Hondo	James E. Barden	Lisa J. Barden	Ralph Bernsen	Cinthia Alles Ivy	Loraine Neuman	vacant
Menard	Menard	Richard Cordes	Polly Reeves	Ben Neel	Robert Bean	Angela McCain	Buck Miller
*Midland	Midland	William C. Morrow	Shauna Brown	Russell Malm	Mitzi Wohleking	Kathy Reeves	Gary Painter
Milam	Cameron	Frank Summers	Barbara Vansa	Kerry Spears	Danica Lara	Doug Bryan	Charles West
Mills	Goldthwaite	Robert E. Lindsey III	Beulah L. "Patty" Roberts	Ken Reynolds Roberts	Patsy E. Miller	Douglas Storey	Douglas Storey
Mitchell	Colorado City	Ray Mayo	Debby Carlock	Tom L. Rees Sr.	Ann Hallmark	Faye Lee	Patrick Toombs
Montague	Montague	Ted Winn	Glenda Henson	Jeb McNew	Linda McGaughey	Sydney Nowell	W.E. Keating
Montgomery	Conroe	Alan B. Sadler	Mark Turnbul	David Walker	Martha Gustavsen	J.R. Moore	Tommy Gage
Moore	Dumas	J.E. (Rowdy) Rhoades	Brenda McKanna	Scott Higginbotham	Pam Cox	Nikki McDonald	J.E. (Bo) Dearmond
Morris	Daingerfield	J.C. Jennings	Vicki Camp	J. Stephen Cowan	Nita Beth Traylor	Thelma L. Awtry	Jack. D. Martin
Motley	Matador	Ed. D. Smith	Kate Hurt	Tom Edwards	Eva Barkley	Elaine Hart	Jim Meador
Nacogdoches	Nacogdoches	Joe English	Carol Wilson	Jefferson Davis	Denise Baublet	Janie Weatherly	Thomas Kerss
*Navarro	Corsicana	Alan Bristol	Sherry Dowd		Joe Graves	Peggy Blackwell Moore	Leslie Cotten
Newton	Newton	Truman Dougharty	Mary Cobb		Karen Fuller Pousson	Melissa Burks	Joe A. Walker
Nolan	Sweetwater	Tim D. Fambrough	Patricia McGowan	Lisa Peterson	Gayle Biggerstaff	Fonda Holman	Donnie Rannefeld
Nueces	Corpus Christi	Samuel L. Neal	Diana T. Barrera	Laura Garza Jimenez	Office abolished 11-3-87.	Ramiro (Ronnie) Canales	Larry Olivarez Sr.
Ochiltree	Perryton	Earl McKinley	Jane Hammerbeck	Bruce Roberson	Ginger Hays	Helen Bates	Joe Hataway
Oldham	Vega	Don R. Allred	Becky Groneman	Kent Birdsong	Charlotte Cook	Cynthia Artho	David T. Medlin
Orange	Orange	Carol Thibodeaux	Karen Jo Vance	John Kimbrough	Vergie Moreland	Lynda Gunstream	Mike White
Palo Pinto	Palo Pinto	Mike A. Smiddy	Bobbie Smith	Phil Garrett	Mary M. Motley	Sandra R. Long	Ira Mercer
Panola	Carthage	David L. Anderson	Mickey Dorman		Gloria Portman	Jean Whiteside	Jack Ellett
Parker	Weatherford	Mark Riley	Jeane Brunson	John Forrest	Jim Thorp	Larry Lippincott	Larry Fowler
Parmer	Farwell	Bonnie J. Heald	Colleen Stover	Kathryn H. Gurley	Altha Herington	Bobbie Pierson	Randy Geries
Pecos	Fort Stockton	Joe Shuster	Judy Deerfield	Jesse Gonzáles Jr.	Barry McCallister	Santa Acosta	Cliff Harris
*Polk	Livingston	John P. Thompson	Barbara Middleton		Nola Reneau	Marion A. "Bid" Smith	Kenneth Hammack
Potter	Amarillo	Arthur Ware	Julie Smith	Scott Brumley	Leann Jennings	Robert Miller	Mike Shumate
*Presidio	Marfa	Jerry C. Agan	Brenda M. Silva		Mario S. Rivera	Norma Arroyo	Danny C. Dominguez
Rains	Emory	Joe Ray Dougherty	Linda Wallace	Robert F. Vititow	Teresa Northcutt	David Traylor	David Traylor
Randall	Canyon	Ernie Houdashell	Sue Wicker Bartolino		Glenna Canada	Carol Autry	Joel Richardson
Reagan	Big Lake	Larry Isom	Terri Pullig	J. Russell Ash	Nancy Ratliff	Cynthia Aguilar	Jeff Garner
Real	Leakey	W.B. Sansom Jr.	Bella A. Rubio	Garry A. Merritt	Kathy Brooks	Donna Brice	James Brice
Red River	Clarksville	Morris Harville	Lorie Moose	Val Varley	Glenda Garrison	Leslie Nix	Terry Reed
Reeves	Pecos	Sam Contreras	Dianne O. Florez	Alva E. Alvarez	Linda Clark	Elfida Zuniga	Arnulfo (Andy) Gomez
Refugio	Refugio	Roger Fagan	Ruby Garcia	Robert P. McGuill	Louise Null Aduddell	Veronica Rocha	Earl Petropoulos
Roberts	Miami	Vernon H. Cook	Donna L. Goodman	Leslie Breeding	Billie Lunsford	DeAnn Williams	Dana Miller
Robertson	Franklin	Jan Roe	Kathryn N. Brimhall	John C. Paschall	Mindy Turner	Carol Bielamowicz	Gerald Yezak
Rockwall	Rockwall	Chris Florance	Lisa Constant		Bill Sinclair	Kathryn Feldpausch	Harold Eavenson
Runnels	Ballinger	Marilyn Egan	Elesa Ocker	Stuart Holden	Margarette Smith	Robin Burgess	William Baird
Rusk	Henderson	Sandra Hodges	Joyce Lewis	Micheal E. Jimerson	Karen Vaughn	Matt B. Johnson	Glen Deason
Sabine	Hemphill	Charles Watson	Janice McDanial	Robert G. Neal Jr.	Tricia Jacks	Martha Stone	Thomas Maddox
San Augustine	San Augustine	Randy E. Williams	Diana Kovar	Heather Land Watts	Pamela Smith	Regina A. Barthol	Don Michael
San Jacinto	Coldspring	Fritz Faulkner	Angelia Steele		Charlene Everitt	Barbara Shelly	Lacy Rogers
San Patricio	Sinton	Terry Simpson	Gracie Alaniz-Gonzales	David Aken	Courtenay Dugat	Dalia Sanchez	Leroy Moody
San Saba	San Saba	Byron Theodosis	Kim Wells	David M. Williams	Gayla Hawkins	John L. Wells	John L. Wells
Schleicher	Eldorado	Johnny F. Griffin	Peggy Williams	Raymond C. Loomis Jr.	Karen Henderson	Jeanne Snelson	David R. Doran
Scurry	Snyder	Rod Waller	Joan Bunch	Michael Hartman	Nelda Colvin	Jana Young	Darrin Jackson
Shackelford	Albany	Ross Montgomery	Cathey Lee	Colton P. Johnson	Sherry Enloe	Richard Wagman	Richard Wagman
Shelby	Center	John Tomlin	Allison Harbison	Gary W. Rholes	Carolyn Golden	Janie Graves	Newton Johnson Jr.
*Sherman	Stratford	Kim Crippen	Mary Lou Albert	Kimberly Allen	Doris Parson	Valerie McAlister	Jack Haile
Smith	Tyler	Joe Baker	Judy Carnes	Michael Gary	Kelli White	Gary Barber	J.B. Smith
Somervell	Glen Rose	Walter Maynard	Candace Garret	Ronald Hankins	Barbara Hudson	Darlene Chambers	Greg Doyle
Starr	Rio Grande City	Eloy Vera	Dennis D. Gonzalez	Victor Canales	Jaime U. Maldonado	Carmen A. Peña	Reymundo Guerra
Stephens	Breckenridge	Gary L. Fuller	Helen Haddock	Gary Trammel	Sharon Trigg	Terry S. Sullivan	James D. (Jim) Reeves
Sterling	Sterling City	Ralph Sides	Susan Wyatt	Bill Stroman	Wanda Foster	Joy Manning	Don Howard
Stonewall	Aspermont	Bobby McGough	Belinda Page	vacant	Linda Messick	Jim Ward	Bill Mullen
Sutton	Sonora	Carla Garner	Veronica E. Hernandez	David W. Wallace	Joyce H. Chalk	Deedie McIntire	Joe Fincher

County	County Seat	County Judge	County Clerk	County Attorney	County Treasurer	Assessor-Collector	Sheriff
*Swisher	Tulia	Harold Keeter	Brenda Hudson	J. Michael Criswell	Tricia Speed	Brenda Gunnels	Larry P. Stewart
Tarrant	Fort Worth	R. Glen Whitley	Suzanne Henderson		Office abolished 4-2-83.	Betsy Price	Dee Anderson
Taylor	Abilene	George A. Newman	Laarry G. Bevill		Lesa Crosswhite	Lavena Cheek	Jack Dieken
Terrell	Sanderson	Leo Smith	Martha Allen	Marsha Monroe	Lynda Helmers	Clint McDonald	Clint McDonald
Terry	Brownfield	Douglas Ryburn	Ann Willis	Ramon Gallegos	Bobbye Jo Floyd	Rexann Turrentine	Jerry L. Johnson
Throckmorton	Throckmorton	Trey Carrington	Mary Walraven	Kristin L. Fouts	Brenda Rankin	John Riley	John Riley
Titus	Mt. Pleasant	Sam W. Russell	Teresa Price	Tim R. Taylor	Debbie Rhea	Judy Cook	Arvel Shepard
*Tom Green	San Angelo	Michael D. Brown	Elizabeth McGill	Chris Taylor	Dianna Spieker	Cindy Jetton	Joe Hunt
*Travis	Austin	Samuel T. Biscoe	Dana DeBeauvoir	David Escamilla	Dolores Ortega-Carter	Nelda Wells Spears	Greg Hamilton
Trinity	Groveton	Mark Evans	Diane McCrory	Joe Warner Bell	Jo Bitner-Bartee	Kathy McCarty	Jimmy Smith
Tyler	Woodville	Jacque Blanchette	Donece Gregory		Sharon Fuller	Lynette Cruse	Jessie Wolf
Upshur	Gilmer	Dean Fowler	Peggy LaGrone		Myra Harris	Michael L. Smith	Anthony Betterton
Upton	Rankin	Vikki Bradley	Phyllis Stephens	Melanie Spratt-Anderson	Nancy P. Poage	Dan W. Brown	Dan W. Brown
Uvalde	Uvalde	William R. Mitchell	Lucille C. Hutcherson	John P. Dodson	Joni Deorsam	Margarita (Maggie) Del Toro	Terry L. Crawford
*Val Verde	Del Rio	Manuel "Mike" L. Fernandez	Maria Elena Cardenas	Ana Markowski Smith	Morris Taylor	Beatriz I. "Bea" Munoz	A. D'Wayne Jernigan
Van Zandt	Canton	Rhita Koches	Charlotte Bledsoe		Terry Shepard	Vicki Looney	R.P. (Pat) Burnett Jr.
Victoria	Victoria	Donald R. Pozzi	Val D. Huvar		Sean Kennedy	Rena Scherer	T. Michael O'Connor
Walker	Huntsville	R.D. (Danny) Pierce	James D. Patton		Sharon Duke	Tom Cauthen	Clint McRae
Waller	Hempstead	Owen Ralston	Cheryl Peters	Kevin D. Acker	Susan Winfree	Ellen C. Shelburne	Randy Smith
Ward	Monahans	Greg M. Holly	Natrell Cain	Julie Renken	Teresa Perry Stoner	Dolores Fine	Mikel Strickland
Washington	Brenham	Dorothy Morgan	Beth A. Rothermel	J. Homero Ramirez	Norman Draehn	Candy Arth	J.W. Jankowski
Webb	Laredo	Danny Valdez	Margie Ramirez Ibarra		Delia Perales	Patricia Barrera	Rick Flores
Wharton	Wharton	John W. Murrie	Sandra K. Sanders	G.W. (Trey) Maffett	Donna Kocourek	Patrick L. Kubala	Jess Howell
Wheeler	Wheeler	Jerry Dan Hefley	Margaret Dorman	Misty L. Walker	Jauna Benefield	Lewis Scott Porter	Joel Finsterwald
Wichita	Wichita Falls	Woodrow (Woody) Gossom	Lori Bohannon		R.J. (Bob) Hampton	Lou Murdock	Thomas J. Callahan
Wilbarger	Vernon	Greg Tyra	Bettie Thompson	Michael Baskerville	Joann Carter	Chris Quisenberry	Larry Lee
Willacy	Raymondville	Eliseo Barnhart	Terry Flores	Juan Angel Guerra	Ruben Cavazos	LaQuita Garza	Larry G. Spence
Williamson	Georgetown	Dan A. Gattis	Nancy E. Rister	Jana Duty	Vivian Wood	Deborah Hunt	James R. Wilson
Wilson	Floresville	Marvin Quinney	Eva S. Martinez	Russell H. Wilson	Jan Hartl	Anna D. Gonzales	Joe D. Tackitt Jr.
Winkler	Kermit	Bonnie Leck	Shethelia Reed	Thomas Cameron	Eulonda Everest	Patti Franks	Robert L. Roberts Jr.
Wise	Decatur	Bill McElhaney	Sherry Parker-Lemon	Greg G. Lowery	Katherine Canova	Monte Shaw	David Walker
Wood	Quitman	Bryan Jeanes	Brenda Taylor		Beckie Cannon	Tommie Bradshaw	Dwaine Daugherty
*Yoakum	Plains	Dallas Brewer	Deborah L. Rushing	Richard Clark	Barbara Wright	Jan Parrish	Don Corzine
Young	Graham	Stanley H. Peavy III	Shirley Choate	Boyd L. Richie	Charlotte Farmer	Nanacy Thomas	Bryan Walls
*Zapata	Zapata	David Morales	Consuelo R. Villarreal	José Antonio López	Romeo Salinas	Rosalva D. Guerra	Sigifredo Gonzalez Jr.
Zavala	Crystal City	Joe Luna	Oralia G. Treviño	Eduardo Serna	Susie Perez	Florinda Perez	Eusevio Salinas

Texas County and District Officials — Table No. 2

District Clerks, District Attorneys and County Commissioners

See Table No. 1 on preceding pages for County Seats, County Judges, County Clerks, County Attorneys, County Treasurers, Tax Assessors-Collectors and Sheriffs. Judges in county courts at law, as well as probate courts, juvenile/domestic relations courts, county criminal courts and county criminal courts of appeal, can be found on page 508. An asterisk (*) before a county name marks a county whose county clerk failed to return our questionnaire; the names of officials for those counties are taken from the most recent unofficial sources available to us. If more than one district attorney is listed for a county, the district court number is noted in parentheses after each attorney's name. If no district attorney is listed, the county attorney, whose name is listed in Table No. 1, assumes the duties of that office.

County	District Clerk	District Attorney	Comm. Precinct 1	Comm. Precinct 2	Comm. Precinct 3	Comm. Precinct 4
Anderson	Janice Staples	Douglas E. Lowe	Joe W. Chaffin	Rashad Mims I	Ronny Smith	Randy Watkins
Andrews	Cynthia Jones	John L. Pool	Barney Fowler	Brad Young	Hiram Hubert	Jim Waldrop
*Angelina	Reba Squyres	Clyde Herrington	Rick Harrison	Kenneth Timmons	Robert Louis Loggins	Lynn George
Aransas	Pam Heard	Patrick Flanigan	Oscar Piña	Leslie (Bubba) Casterline	Charles Smith	Howard Murph
Archer	Jane Ham	Jack McGaughey	Richard Shelley	Darin Wolf	Pat Martin III	Darryl Lightfoot
Armstrong	Connie Spiller	Randall Sims	John Britten	Mike Baker	C.M. Bryant	Tom Ferris
Atascosa	Jerome T. Brite	Rene Pena	David Caballero	William (Bill) Torans	Freddie Ogden	Weldon P. Cude
Austin	Sue Murphy	Travis J. Koehn	David Ottmer	Robert Wayne Rinn	Randy Reichardt	David Hubenak
Bailey	Elaine Parker	Johnny Actkinson	Floyd J. "Butch" Vandiver	C. E. Grant Jr.	Joey Kindle	Juan Chavez
Bandera	Tammy Kneuper	E. Bruce Curry	H. Bruce Eliker	Robert A. Harris	Richard Keese	Doug King
Bastrop	Cathy Smith	Bryan Goertz	David Goertz	Clara Beckett	John Klaus	Lee Dildy
Baylor	Clara "Carrie" Coker	William H. Heatly	Travis Clark	John E. Nelson	Charles R. Morris	Charlie Piatt
Bee	Anna Marie Silvas	Martha Warren	Carlos Salazar Jr.	Susan C. Stasny	Eloy Rodriguez	Ronnie Olivares
Bell	Sheila Norman	Henry L. Garza	Richard Cortese	Tim Brown	Eddy Lange	John Fisher
Bexar	Margaret G. Montemayor	Susan D. Reed	Sergio "Chico" Rodriguez	Paul Elizondo	Lyle T. Larson	Tommy Adkisson
Blanco	Debby Elsbury	Sam Oatman	vacant	James Sultemeier	Robert A. "Bob" Mauck	Paul Granberg
Borden	Joyce Herridge	Dana W. Cooley	Monte Smith	Randy L. Adcock	Ernest Reyes	Joe T. Belew
*Bosque	Sandra L. Woosley	B.J. Shepherd	Kent Harbison	Durwood Koonsman	Jerry Smith	Jimmy Schmidt
Bowie	Billie Fox	Bobby Lockhart	Jack Stone	John Addington	Kelly Blackburn	Carl Teel
Brazoria	Jerry Deere	Jeri Yenne	Donald "Dude" Payne	Matt Sebesta	Jack Harris	Mary Ruth Rhodenbaugh
Brazos	Marc Hamlin	Bill Turner	Lloyd Wassermann	E. Duane Peters	Kenny Mallard Jr.	Carey Cauley Jr.
Brewster	Jo Ann Salgado	Frank Brown	Asa Stone	Kathy Killingsworth	Ruben Ortega	Matilde Pallanez
Briscoe	Bena Hester	Becky McPherson	Terry Grimland	Dale Smith	Larry Comer	John Burson
*Brooks	Noe Guerra	Joe Frank Garza	Gloria Garza	Ramon Navarro Jr.	Jose Garcia	Mae Saenz
Brown	Jan Brown	Michael Brandon Murra/	Steve Adams	Joel Kelton	Richard Gist	Larry Traweek
Burleson	Joy Brymer	Renee Mueller	Frank L. Kristof	Vincent Svec Jr.	David Hildebrand	John B. Landolt Jr.
*Burnet	Dana DeBerry	Sam Oatman	Bille Neve	Russell Graeter	Ronny Hibler	James Oakley
Caldwell	Tina Morgan	Trey Hicks	Tom D. Bonn	Charles Bullock	Neto Madrigal	Joe Ivan Roland
Calhoun	Pamela Martin-Hartgrove	Dan W. Heard	Roger C. Galvan	Vernon Lyssy	Neil E. Fritsch	Kenneth W. Finster
Callahan	Sharon Owens		Harold Hicks	Bryan Farmer	Tommy Holland	Cliff Kirkham
Cameron	Aurora de la Garza	Armando Villalobos	Sofia C. Benavidez	John Wood	David A. Garza	Edna Tamayo
Camp	Mignon Cook	Charles Bailey	Bart Townsend	Larry Shelton	Norman Townsend	Vernon Griffin
Carson	Celeste Bichsel	Stuart Messer	Mike Britten	Kenneth Ware	Jerry Strawn	Kevin Howell
Cass	Becky Wilbanks	Clint Allen	Kenneth L. Pate	Danny Joe Shaddix	Paul Cothren	Max Bain
Castro	Joyce M. Thomas	James R. Horton	Tom McLain	Larry Gonzales	W.A. Baldridge	Dan Schmucker
Chambers	Robert (Bobby) Scherer	Michael R. Little	Mark Huddleston	Judy Edmonds	Gary R. Nelson	W.O. (Bill) Wallace
*Cherokee	Marlys Mason	Elmer C. Beckworth Jr.	Mary Gregg	Kevin Pierce	Moody Glass Jr.	Billy McCutcheon

County	District Clerk	District Attorney	Comm. Precinct 1	Comm. Precinct 2	Comm. Precinct 3	Comm. Precinct 4
Childress	Zona Prince	Stuart Messer	Denzil Ray	Mark Ross	Lyall Foster	Don Ray Crook
Clay	Dan Slagle	Jack McGaughey	Lindy Choate	Johnny Gee	Wilson Scaling	Brice Jackson
Cochran	Rita Tyson	Gary Goff	Gerald Ramsey	Margaret Allen	Stacey Dunn	Jimmy Mullinax
Coke	Mary Grim	Stephen Lupton	Troy Montgomery	Robert Feil	Gaylon Pitcock	Bobby Blaylock
Coleman	JoDean Chapman	Joe Lee Rose	Jimmie R. Porter	Billy Don McCrary	Michael L. Barker	Alan Davis
*Collin	Hannah Kunkle	John R. Roach	Phyllis Cole	Jerry Hoagland	Joe Jaynes	Jack Hatchell
Collingsworth	Jackie Johnson	Stuart Messer	Dan Langford	Mike Hughs	Eddie Orr	Kirby Campbell
Colorado	Harvey Vornsand		Doug Wessels	Herbert Helmcamp	Tommy Hahn	Darrell Gertson
*Comal	Katherine "Kathy" Faulkner	Dib Waldrip	Jack Dawson	Jay Millikin	Gregory Parker	Jan Kennady
Comanche	Brenda Dickey	B.J. Shepard	Garry Steele	Kenneth Feist	Bobby Schuman	Jimmy D. Johnson
Concho	Barbara K. Hoffman	George E. McCrea	R.M. "Hoss" Kingston	Ralph Willberg	Ernest R. Gomez	Aaron B. Browning Jr.
Cooke	Patricia Payne	Cindy Stormer	Gary Hollowell	Steve Key	Al Smith	Virgil Hess
Coryell	Jaice Gray	David Castillo	Jack Wall	Darren Moore	Don Jones	Elizabeth Taylor
*Cottle	Beckey J. Tucker	David W. Hajek	Jim Sweeney	Hazel Biddy	Manuel Cruz Jr.	Gus Timmons
Crane	Judy Crawford	Mike Fostel	Jack Damron	Dennis Young	Domingo Escobedo	Roy Hodges
Crockett	Debbi Puckett	Laurie K. English	Frank Tambuga	Pleas Childress	Randy Branch	Alfredo Tobar
Crosby	Karla Isbell	C. Michael Ward	Gary Jordan	Frank Mullins	Larry Wampler	Billy Bob Wright
Culberson	Linda McDonald	Jaime Esparza	Cornelio Garibay	Duane Corrales	John Jones	Adrian Norman
Dallam	Terri Banks	David Green	Glenn Reagan	Oscar Przilas	Don Bowers	Carl French
Dallas	Gary Fitzsimmons	Craig Watkins	Maureen Dickey	Mike Cantrell	John Wiley Price	Kenneth Mayfield
Dawson	Carolyn Turner	Ricky Smith	Jerry Beaty	Gilbert Tejeda	Troy Howard	Foy O'Brien
Deaf Smith	Jean Schumacher Coody	Jim English	Pat Smith	Jerry Roberts	Troy Don Moore	Jerry O'Connor
Delta	Jane Jones	Martin Braddy	B.V. (Rip) Templeton	David Max Moody	Wayne Poole	Mark Brantley
Denton	Sherri Adelstein	Paul Johnson	Cynthia White	Ron Marchant	Bobbie J. Mitchell	Andy Eads
DeWitt	Tabeth Gardner	Michael Sheppard	Curtis G. Afflerbach	Joe L. Machalec	Gilbert Pargmann	Alfred Rangnow
Dickens	Winona Humphreys	Becky McPherson	Don Condron	Ricky West	Doc Edwards	Sheldon Parsons
Dimmit	Maricela G. Gonzalez	Roberto Serna	Larry Speer	Johnny Gloria	Jose P. Martinez	Rodrigo Jaime
*Donley	Fay Vargas	Stuart Messer	Ernest Johnston	Don Hall	Andy Wheatly	Bob Trout
Duval	Richard M. Barton	Heriberto Silva	Alejo C. Garcia	Rene M. Perez	Nestor Garza Jr.	Gilberto Uribe Jr.
Eastland	Karen Moore	Russ Thomason	Wayne Nance	Norman Christian	Bill Underwood	Reggie Pittman
*Ector	Janis Morgan	John W. Smith	Freddie Gardner	Greg Simmons	Barbara Graff	Bob Bryant
Edwards	Joanna Baker	Fred Hernandez	Robert Pena	Steve Nance	James E. Epperson Jr.	Mike Grooms
*Ellis	Billie Ann Fuller	Joe F. Grubbs	Dennis Robinson	Larry Jones	Heath Sims	Ron Brown
*El Paso	Gilbert Sanchez	Jaime E. Esparza	Barbara Perez	Betti Flores	Miguel A. Teran	Daniel R. Haggerty
*Erath	Wanda Pringle	John Terrill	Jerry Martin	Lynn Tidwell	Doug Eberhart	Randy Lowe
Falls	Larry Hoelscher	Kathryn J. Gilliam	Tom Zander	Robert Paul Sr.	Nelson Coker	Wendell Harris
Fannin	Nancy Young		Ronnie Rhudy	Stan Barker	Dewayne Strickland	Pat Hilliard
Fayette	Virginia Wied	Peggy Supak	Johns Saunders	Gary Weishuhn	James Kubecka	Tom Muras
Fisher	Tammy Haley	Mark Edwards	Gordon Pippin	Rodney Tankersley	Earnest Ragan	Gene Terry
*Floyd	Barbara Edwards	Becky McPherson	Ray Nell Bearden	Lennie Gilroy	Craig Gilly	Jon Jones
*Foard	Sherry Weatherred	Dan Mike Bird	Rick Hammonds	Rockne Wisdom	Larry Wright	Edward Crosby
*Fort Bend	Glory Hopkins	John Healey	Tom Stavinoha	Grady Prestage	Andy Meyers	James Patterson
Franklin	Ellen Jaggers	Martin Braddy	Danny Chitsey	Bobby Elbert	Deryl Carr	Sam Young
Freestone	Janet Chappell		Luke Ward Sr.	Craig Oakes	Stanley Gregory	Clyde E. Ridge Jr.
Frio	Ramona Rodriguez	Rene M. Peña	Jesus G. Salinas	Robert Cannizales	Arnulfo Luna	Jose Flores
Gaines	Virginia Stewart	Ricky Smith	Danny Yocom	Craig Belt	Blair Tharp	Charlie Lopez

County	District Clerk	District Attorney	Comm. Precinct 1	Comm. Precinct 2	Comm. Precinct 3	Comm. Precinct 4
Galveston	Latonia Wilson	Kurt Sistrunk	Patrick F. Doyle	Bryan Lamb	Stephen D. Holmes	Kenneth Clark
Garza	Jim Plummer	Ricky B. Smith	Gary McDaniel	Charles Morris	John Valdez	Mike Sanchez
Gillespie	Barbara Meyer	E. Bruce Curry	Curtis Cameron	William A. Roeder	Calvin Ransleben	Donnie Schuch
Glasscock	Rebecca Batla	Hardy Wilkerson	Jimmy Strube	Mark Halfmann	Marck Schafer	Michael Hoch
*Goliad	Gail M. Turley	Michael Sheppard	Arturo Rojas	Jerry Rodriguez	Jim Kreneck	Ted Long
Gonzales	Sandra Baker	Vicki Pattillo	Kenneth O. (Dell) Whiddon	Donnie R. Brzozowski	Kevin T. LaFleur	Otis S. (Bud) Wuest
Gray	Gaye Honderich	Lynn Switzer	Joe Wheeley	Gary Willoughby	Gerald Wright	James Hefley
Grayson	Tracy Brown	Joe Brown	Johnny Waldrip	David Whitlock	Jackie Crisp	Gene Short
Gregg	Barbara Duncan	William M. Jennings	Charles Davis	Darryl Primo	Bob Barbee	John Mathis
Grimes	Gay Wells	Tuck Moody McLain	John Bertling	Bill Pendley	Julian Melchor Jr.	Pam Finke
Guadalupe	Debi Crow	Vicki Pattillo	Roger Baenziger	Cesareo Guadarrama	Jim O. Wolverton	Judy Cope
Hale	Carla Cannon	Wally Hatch	Neal Burnett	Mario Martinez	Gary Koelder	Benny Cantwell
*Hall	Raye Bailey	Stuart Messer	Milton Beasley	Terry Lindsey	Buddy Logsdon	James Fuston
Hamilton	Leoma Larance	B.J. Shepherd	Jim Boatwright	Mike Lewis	Jon Bonner	Dickie Clary
*Hansford	Kim Vera	Clay Ballman	Ira G. "Butch" Reed	Joe T. Venneman	Tim Stedje	Danny Henson
Hardeman	Linda Walker	Stanley Heatley	Johnny Akers	Rodger Tabor	Barry Haynes	Rodney Foster
Hardin	Vicki Johnson	Henry A. Coe III	Bob Burgess	Patricia McGallion	Ken Pelt	Bobby Franklin
Harris	Charles Bacarrise	Chuck Rosenthal	El Franco Lee	Sylvia R. Garcia	Steve Radack	Jerry Eversole
Harrison	Sherry Griffis	Joe Black	Jerry Lomax	Emma Bennett	James Greer	Galen McBride
*Hartley	Diane Thompson	David Green	David Vincent	Andy Michael	John Newsom	Butch Owens
Haskell	Penny Anderson	Mike Fouts	Johnny Scoggins	Tiffen Mayfield	Kenny Thompson	Bobby Smith
Hays	Cecelia Adair	Sherri Tibbe	Debbie Gonzales Ingalsbe	Jeff Barton	Will Conley	Karen Ford
Hemphill	Brenda Perrin	Lynn Switzer	Joe Schaef	Ed Culver	John Ramp	Lynard G. Schafer
*Henderson	Becky Hanks	Donna Bennett	Joe D. Hall	Wade McKinney	Ronny Lawrence	Jerry West
Hidalgo	Laura Hinojosa	Rene A. Guerra	Sylvia Handy	Hector (Tito) Palacios	Joe M. Flores	Oscar L. Garza Jr.
Hill	Charlotte Barr	Dan V. Dent	Bob Atwell	Steven Sulak	Sam McClendon	Lee Harkins
Hockley	Dennis Price	Gary Goff	Marvin (Smitty) Smith	Larry Carter	J.L. (Whitey) Barnett	Thomas R. Clevenger
*Hood	Tonna Hitt	Rob Christian	Mike Sumpson	Charles Baskett	Leonard Heathington	Larry Shafer
*Hopkins	Patricia Dorner	Martin Braddy	Beth B. Wisenbaker	Burke Bullock	Don Patterson	Danny Evans
Houston	Carolyn Rains	David Cervantes	Jerry McLeod	Willie Kitchen	Pat Perry	Kennon Kellum
Howard	Colleen Barton	Hardy Wilkerson	Emma (Puga) Brown	Jerry Kilgore	W.B. (Bill) Crooker	Gary Simer
Hudspeth	Paula L. Hoover	Jaime Esparza	Wayne West	Curtis Carr	Jim Ed Miller	James Kiehne
Hunt	Stacey Landrum	F. Duncan Thomas	Kenneth Thornton	Ralph Green	Phillip Martin	Jim Latham
Hutchinson	Joan Carder	Clay L. Ballman	R.D. Cornelison	Jerry D. Hefner	S.T. (Red) Isbell Jr.	Eddie Whittington
Irion	Reba Criner	Stephen Lupton	Michael Dolan	Jeff Davidson	John Nanny	Barbara Searcy
Jack	Tracie Pippin	Jana Jones	Joe Paul Nichols	Bryson Sewell	James L. Cozart	Milton R. (Sonny) Pruitt
Jackson	Sharon Mathis	Bobby Bell	Wayne Hunt	Wayne Bubela	Johnny E. Belicek	Larry Deyton
Jasper	Linda Ryall	Steve Hollis	Charles Shofner Jr.	Roy Parker	Willie Stark	Vance Moss
Jeff Davis	Sue Blackley	Frank Brown	Larry Francell	Diane Lacy	Curtis Evans	Albert Miller
Jefferson	Lolita Ramos	Tom Maness	Eddie Arnold	Mark L. Domingue	Waymon D. Hallmark	Everette "Bo" Alfred
Jim Hogg	Noemi G. Salinas	Heriberto Silva	Antonio Flores	Abelardo Alaniz	Sandalio Ruiz	Ruben Rodriguez
Jim Wells	R. David Guerrero	Joe Frank Garza	Zenaida Sanchez	Ventura Garcia Jr.	Oswald Alanis	Javier N. Garcia
Johnson	David Lloyd	Dale Hanna	R.C. McFall	John Matthews	Mark Carpenter	Don Beeson
Jones	Lacey Hansen	Billy John Edwards	James Clawson	Mike Polk	Jimmy (Buz) Wylie	Steve Lollar
Karnes	Robbie Shortner	Rene Pena	Darrel Blaschke	Jeffrey Wiatrek	James Rosales	Isidro D. Rossett Jr.
Kaufman	Sandra Featherston	Rick Harrison	Jerry Rowden	Ray Clark	Kenneth Schoen	Jim Deller

County	District Clerk	District Attorney	Comm. Precinct 1	Comm. Precinct 2	Comm. Precinct 3	Comm. Precinct 4
*Kerdall	Shirley R. Stehling	E. Bruce Curry	Anne Reissig	Gene Mietschin	Darrel L. Lux	Russell C. Busby
Kenedy	Veronica Vela	Carlos Valdez	Leonard May	Roberto Salazar Jr.	Anne Armstrong	Gumecinda Gonzales
Kent	Richard Craig Harrison	Mike Fouts	Roy W. Chisum	Don Long	Tommy Stanaland	Robert Graham
Ker	Linda Uecker	E. Bruce Curry	H.A. (Buster) Baldwin	William Williams	Jonatha A. Letz	Bruce Oehler
Kimble	Haydee Torres	Ronald L. Sutton	Vicente Menchaca	Charles McGuire	Jim Watson	Tooter Schulze
King	Jammye D. Timmons	David Hajek	Stephen Brady	Larry Hajek	Bob Tidmore	Donna Marshall
*Kinney	Dora Elia Sandoval	Fred Hernandez	Marvin Davis	Joe Montalvo	Nat Terrazas	Pat Melancon
Kleberg	Martha L. Soliz	Carlos Valdez	David Rosse	Norma Nelda Alvarez	Roy Cantu	Romeo L. Lomas
*Knox	Ronnie Verhalen	David Hajek	Weldon Skiles	Jerry Parker	Jimmy Urbanczyk	Johnny Birkenfeld
*Lamar	Marvin Ann Patterson	Gary Young	Mike Blackburn	Carl Steffey	Rodney Pollard	Jackie Wheeler
*Lamb	Celia A. Kuykendall	Mark Yarbrough	Rodney Smith	Thurman Lewis	Emil Macha	Jimmy Young
Lampasas	Terri Cox	Larry W. Allison	Robert L. Vincent Jr.	Alex Wittenburg	Lowell B. Ivey	Jack B. Cox
La Salle	Margarita A. Esqueda	René M. Peña	Chris Hinojosa III	Maria Teresa Adams	Jose Jimenez	Raul Ayala
Lavaca	Calvin J. Albrecht	Vicki Pattillo	Charles A. Netardus	Mark H. Zimmerman	David Wagner	Dennis W. Kocian
Lee	Lisa Teinert	Ted Weems	Maurice Pits Jr.	Douglas Hartfield	O.B. (Butch) Johnson	Thomas Kovar
Leon	Diane Oden Davis	Whitney Smith	Joey Sullivan	David Ferguson	Ray Gaskin	Dean Player
Liberty	Melody Gilmore	Mike Little	Todd Fontenot	Lee Groce	Melvin Hunt	Norman Brown
Limestone	Carol Sue Jenkins	Roy DeFriend	John McCarver	William (Pete) Kirven	Morris Beaver	Milton Carroll
Lipscomb	Kim Blau	Lynn Switzer	Juan Cantu	Stanley Born	Scotty Schilling	John Fritzlen
Live Oak	Lois Shannon	Martha Warner	Richard Lee	Donna Mills	Jim Bassett	Emilio Garza
Llano	Joyce Gillow	Sam Oatman	Johnnie B. Heck	Henry Parker	Duane Stueven	Jerry Don Moss
Loving	Beverly Hanson	Michael Fostel	Harlan Hopper	Royce Creager	Zane Kiehne	Joe Renteria
Lubbock	Barbara Sucsy	Matt Powell	Bill McCoy	Mark Heinrich	Ysidro Gutierrez	Patti Jones
Lynn	Sandra Laws	Rickey Smith	Don Morton	Mike Braddock	Don Blair	Brad Hammonds
Madison	Joyce Batson	William C. (Bill) Bennett	Roland Standley	Phillip Grisham	Tommy Cornelius	Mary Andrus
Marion	Janie McCay	William Gleason	Bob Higgins	T. W. (Sam) Smith	C.E. (Cecil) Bourne	Charles Treadwell
Martin	Susie Hull	Hardy L. Wilkerson	Jesus Garza	Valentino Sotelo	Bobby Kelly	Bryan Cox
Mason	Pam Beam	Ronald L. Sutton	Wayne Hofmann	John Dalton Fleming	Stanley Toeppich	Eldon Kothmann
Matagorda	Becky Denn	Steven E. Reis	Daniel Pustka	George Deshotels	James Gibson	David Woodson
*Maverick	Irene Rodriguez	Roberto Serna	Eliaz Maldonado	Rudy Heredia	David Saucedo	Cesar Flores
McCulloch	Mackye Johnson	Ron Sutton	Joe Johnson	Jerry Bratton	Nelson Solsbery	Brent C. Deeds
McLennan	Karen Matkin	John Segrest	Wendall Crunk	Lester Gibson	Joe A. Mashek	Ray Meadows
McMullen	Dorairene Garza	Martha Warner	Tim Teal	Murray Swaim	Paul Koonce	Maximo G. Quintanilla Jr.
Medina	M. Eva Soto	Anton E. Hackebeil	Ronald	Beverly Keller	Arturo Barrientes	Kelly Carroll
Menard	Polly Reeves	Ronald Sutton	Boyd Murchison	James Taylor	Pete Crothers	Larry Burch
*Midland	Vivian Wood	Al Schorre	Jimmy Smith	Mike Bradford	Juluis Brooks	Randy Prude
Milam	Cindy Fechner	Kerry Spears	Clifford Whiteley	Kenneth Hollas	C. Dale Jaecks	Burke Bauerschlag
Mills	Beulah L. "Patty" Roberts	Michael Murray	John Mann	Carroll Bunting	Billy L. Hobbs	Farrel Thorne
Mitchell	Sharon Hammond	Glen Harrison	Jimmy Rees	Carl Guelker	Larry Johnson	Billy H. Preston
Montague	Lesia Darden	Jack McGaughey	Dickey J. Cox	Jerry Clement	Glenn Seay	Tommie Sappington
Montgomery	Barbara Gladden Adamick	Michael A. McDougal	Mike Meador	Craig Doyal	Ed Chance	Ed Rinehart
Moore	Diane Hoefling	David Green	A. Gordon Clark	Bobby Barker	Milton Pax	Lynn Cartrite
Morris	Gwen Oney	J. Stephen Cowan	Hubert L. Mitchell Jr.	Dearl Quarles	J.P. Cobb	Gary Camp
Motley	Kate Hurt	Becky McPherson	Ronnie Davis	Donnie Turner	Franklin Jameson	Russell Alexander
Nacogdoches	Donna Phillips	Stephanie Stephens	Tom Bush	Reggie Cotton	Charles Simmons	Tom Strickland
*Navarro	Marilyn Greer	Steve Keathley	Kit Herrington	Olin Nickelberry	William Baldwin	John Paul Ross

County	District Clerk	District Attorney	Comm. Precinct 1	Comm. Precinct 2	Comm. Precinct 3	Comm. Precinct 4
Newton	Bree Allen	Misti Spacek	William (Bill) Filler	Thomas Gill	Prentiss Hopson	Charles Brinson
Nolan	Patti Neill	Mark Edwards	Randall Smith	Terry Locklar	Tommy White	Tony Lara
Nueces	Patsy Perez	Carlos Valdez	Peggy Banales	Betty Jean Longoria	Oscar O. Ortiz	H.C. (Chuck) Cazalas
Ochiltree	Shawn Bogard		Duane Pshigoda	Doug Barnes	James W. Clark	Larry Hardy
Oldham	Becky Groneman	Kent Birdsong	Quincy Taylor	Donnie Knox	Roger Morris	Billy Don Brown
Orange	Vickie Edgerly	John Kimbrough	James Stringer	Owen Burton	John DuBose	Beamon Minton
Palo Pinto	Janie Glover	vacant	Ted Ray	Ed Laney	George Nowak	Jeff Fryer
Panola	Debra Johnson	Danny Buck Davidsen	Ronnie LaGrone	Douglas M. Cotton	Hermon E. Reed Jr.	Dale LaGrone
Parker	Elvera Johnson	Don Schnebly	Danny Choate	Joe Brinkley	John Roth	Jim Webster
Parmer	Sandra Warren	Johnny Actkinson	Kirk Frye	James Clayton	Michael Haseloff	Elvis Powell
Pecos	Gayle Henderson	Frank Brown (83rd) Laurie English (112th)	George Riggs	Juan Rodriguez	J.H. (Jay) Kent	Paul Valenzuela
*Polk	Kathy E. Clifton	John S. Holleman	Robert C. "Bob" Willis	Bobby Smith	James J. "Buddy" Purvis	Tommy Overstreet
Potter	Caroline Woodburn	Randall Sims	Lacy Borger	Manuel Perez Villasenor	Joe Kirkwood	Alphonso S. Vaughn
Presidio	Brenda M. Silva	Frank Brown	Felipe Cordero	Eloy Aranda	Carlos Armendariz	Danny Watts
Rains	Deborah Traylor		Herschel Bullard	Robert M. Sisk	Gary Mike Bishop	Jimmie Painter
Randall	Jo Carter	James Farren	Robert (Bob) Karrh	Gene Parker	George E. (Skip) Huskey	Buddy DeFord
Reagan	Terri Pullig	Laurie English	Jessie Barrera	Ron Galloway	Mikel Jones	Thomas Strube
Real	Bella A. Rubio	Anton (Tony) Hackebeil	Manuel Rubio	Wade Reagor	Castulo San Miguel	Joe W. Connell Sr.
Red River	Janice Gentry		Rufus Ward Jr.	David Barnett	Elmer Caton	Josef Hausler
Reeves	Patricia Tarin	Randall (Randy) Reynods	Rojelio (Roy) Alvarado	Gabriel Martinez	Saul Herrera	Ramiro (Ram)Guerra
Refugio	Ruby Garcia	Michael A. Sheppard	Rindle Wilson	Janis Gillespie	Gary Bourland	John Reyna
Roberts	Donna L. Goodman	Lynn Switzer	William H. Clark	Ken R. Gill	Kelly V. Flowers	James F. Duvall Jr.
Robertson	Barbara Axtell	John C. Paschall	John Anderson	Donald Threadgill	Keith Nickelson	Robert Bielamowicz
Rockwall	Kay McDaniel	Galen Ray Sumrow	Jerry Wimpee	Lorie Grinnan	Bruce Beaty	David Magness
Runnels	Tammy Burleson	George McCrea	Robert Moore	Ronald Presley	James Thurman Self	Richard W. Strube
Rusk	Jean Hodges	Michael E. Jimerson	W.D. (Bill) Hale	Michael Pepper	Freddy Swann	Harold Howell
Sabine	Tanya Walker	John Fisher	Keith C. Clark	Jimmy McDaniel	Doyle Dickerson	Fayne Warner
San Augustine	Jean Steptoe	John Fisher	Thomas Stracener	Edward Wilson	Dale Mixon	Rodney Ainsworth
San Jacinto	Rebecca Capers	Bill Burnett	Michael Griffith	Royce Wells	David Brandon Sr.	Mark Nettuno
San Patricio	Laura Miller	Patrick L. Flanigan	Nina G. Trevino	Fred P. Nardini	Alma V. Moreno	Jim Price Jr.
San Saba	Kim Wells	Sam Oatman	Otis Juckins	Rickey Lusty	Wayland Perry	Roger McGehee
Schleicher	Peggy Williams	Stephen Lupton	Johnny F. Mayo Jr.	Lynn Meador	Kirk Griffin	Matthews Brown
*Scurry	Trina Rodgers	Dana Cooley	Terry Williams	Jerry House	Howard Limmer	Chloanne Lindsey
Shackelford	Cathey Lee	Billy John Edwards	Danny Peacock	Larry Cauble	Jimmy T. Brooks	Stan West
Shelby	Lori Oliver	Lynda K. Russell	Donnie Borders	Jimmy Lout	Travis Rodgers	Bradley Asher
*Sherman	Mary Lou Albert	David Green	Steve Pemberton	Randy Williams	David Hass	Tommy Asher
Smith	Lois Rogers	Matt Bingham	JoAnn Fleming	Bill McGinnis	Bobby Van Ness	JoAnn Hampton
Somervell	Candace Garrett	Dale Hanna	Zach Cummings	Mike Ford	Lloyd Wirt	James Barnard
Starr	Eloy R. Garcia	Heriberto Silva	Jaime Alvarez	Raul Pena Jr.	Eloy Garza	Abel N. Gonzalez Jr.
Stephens	Christie Copeland	Steven Bristow	Jerry Toland	D.C. (Button) Sikes	Joe F. High	Rickie Ray Carr
Sterling	Susan Wyatt	Stephen Lupton	Billy Joe Blair	Russell Noletubby	Deborah H. Horwood	Reed Stewart
Stonewall	Belinda Page	Michael Fouts	W.D. Ellison	Kenny Spitzer	Billy Kirk Meador	Gary Myers
Sutton	Veronica E. Hernandez	Laurie English	Miguel (Mike) Villanueva	John Wade	Milton Cavaness	Fred Perez
Swisher	Brenda Hudson	Wally Hatch	Loyd Rahlfs	Joe Bob Thompson	Harvey N. Foster	Tim Reed
Tarrant	Tom Wilder	Tim Curry	Roy Brooks	Marti VanRavenswaay	Gary Fickes	J.D. Johnson
Taylor	Patricia Henderson	James Eidson	Jack Turner	Dwayne Tucker	Stan Egger	Charles (Chuck) Statler

County	District Clerk	District Attorney	Comm. Precinct 1	Comm. Precinct 2	Comm. Precinct 3	Comm. Precinct 4
Terrell	Martha Allen	Fred Hernandez	Yolanda G. Lopez	Delia Fuentes	Charles Stegall	Kenn Norris
Terry	Paige Lindsey	Ramon Gallegos	Eddie Ryburn	Dale Andrews	Don Robertson	Jessie Hartman
Throckmorton	Mary Walraven	Michael Fouts	Casey Wells	Johnny Jones	Carlton Sullivan	Wilton Cantrell
Titus	Debra Abston	Charles Bailey	Bob Fitch	Mike Fields	Phillip Hinton	Thomas Hockaday
*Tom Green	Sheri Woodfin	Stephen R. Lupton (51st) George McCrea (119th)	Ralph Hoelscher	Karl Booker	Steve Floyd	Richard S. Easingwood Jr.
*Travis	Amalia Rodriguez-Mendoza	Ronnie Earle	Ron Davis	Sarah Eckhardt	Gerald Daugherty	Margaret Gómez
Trinity	Cheryl Cartwright	Joe Ned Dean	Grover Worsham	Jannette Hortman	Cecil Webb	Travis Forrest
Tyler	Melissie Evans	Joe R. Smith	Martin Nash	James (Rusty) Hughes	Joe Marshall	Jack Walston
Upshur	Carolyn Bullock	William (Billy) Byrd	James Critteden	Joe (Buddy) Ferguson	Lloyd Crabtree	Glenn Campbell
Upton	Phyllis Stephens	Laurie English	Brent Wrinkle	Tommy Owens	W.M. (Willie) Martinez	Leon Patrick
Uvalde	Lydia Steele	Anton (Tony) Hackabeil	Randy Scheide	Mariano Pargas Jr.	Jerry W. Bates	Jesse R. Moreno
*Val Verde	Martha Mitchell	Fred Hernandez	Ramiro V. Ramon	Rogelio "Roy" H. Musquiz	Robert Beau Nettleton	Jesus E. "Cheo" Ortiz
Van Zandt	Karen Wilson	Leslie Poynter Dixon	Ricky LaPrade	Virgil Melton	Kelles Miller	Ron Carroll
Victoria	Cathy Stuart	Stephen B. Tyler	Chris F. Rivera	Kevin Janak	Gary E. Burns	Wayne Dierlam
Walker	Robyn Flowers	David P. Weeks	B.J. Gaines	Robert E. Autery	James (Buddy) Reynolds	Tim Paulsel
Waller	Patricia Spadachene	Elton Mathis	W.M. (Bill) Eplen	Terry Harrison	Milton Whiting	Glenn Beckendorff
Ward	Patricia Oyerbides	Randy Reynolds	Julian Florez	Larry Hanna	Dexter Nichols	Eddie Nelms
Washington	Vicki Lehmann	Renee Ann Mueller	Zeb Hackmann	Donald Ahrens	Kirk Hanath	Joy Fuchs
Webb	Manuel Gutierrez	Jose Rubio	Frank Sciaraffa	Rosaura (Wawi) Tijerina	Gerardo (Jerry) Garza	Sergio (Keko) Martinez
Wharton	Denice K. Malota	Josh McCown	Mickey Reynolds	D.C. (Chris) King	Philip Miller	James (Jimmy) Kainer
Wheeler	Sherri Jones	Lynn Switzer	Daryl Snelgrooes	Tom Puryear	Hubert Moore	John Walker
Wichita	Dorsey Trapp	Barry Macha	Joe Miller	Pat Norris	Gordon Griffith	William (Bill) Presson
Wilbarger	Brenda Peterson	Staley Heatly	Richard Jacobs	Phillip Graf	Rodney Johnston	Lenville Morris
Willacy	Gilbert Lozano	Juan Angel Guerra	Abiel Cantu	Erasmo Chapa	Emilio Vera	Aurelio Guerra
Williamson	Lisa David	John Bradley	Lisa Birkman	Cynthia Long	Valerie Covey	Ron Morrison
Wilson	Deborah Bryan	René M. Peña	Albert Gamez Jr.	Leonard Rotter Jr.	Robert (Bobby) H. Lynn	Larry A. Wiley
Winkler	Sherry Terry	Michael L. Fostel	Tommy R. Smith	James R. (Robbie) Wolf	Randy Neal	Billy Ray Thompson
Wise	Christi Fuqua	Jana Jones	Robert Rankin	Kevin Burns	Mikel Richardson	Terry Ross
Wood	Jenica Turner	Jim Wheeler	Roy Don Shipp	Jerry Gaskill	Roger Pace	Jerry Galloway
*Yoakum	Vicki Blundell	Richard Clark	Woody Lindsey	Ben Coston	Ty Earl Powell	Jack Cobb
Young	Carolyn Collins	Stephen Bristow	John C. Bullock	John L. Hawkins	R.L. Spivey	Jimmy R. Wiley
*Zapata	Consuelo R. Villarreal	Joe M. Rubio	Jose Emilio Vela	Angel Garza	Joseph Rathmell	Norberto Garza
Zavala	Rachel Ramirez	Roberto Serna	Alfredo Sanchez	Raul G. Gomez	David A. López	Matthew McHazlett

Texans in Congress

Besides the two members of the U.S. Senate allocated to each state, Texas is allocated 32 members in the U.S. House of Representatives. The term of office for members of the House is two years; the terms of all members will expire on Jan. 1, 2009. Senators serve six-year terms. Sen. John Cornyn's term will end in 2009. Sen. Kay Bailey Hutchison's term will end in 2013.

Addresses and phone numbers of the lawmakers' Washington and district offices are below, as well as the committees on which they serve. Washington **zip codes** are **20515** for members of the House and **20510** for senators. The telephone area code for Washington is **202**. On the Internet, House members can be reached through **www.house.gov/writerep**. In 2007, members of Congress received a salary of $162,100. Members in leadership positions received $180,100.

U.S. Senate

CORNYN, John. Republican (Home: Austin); Washington Office: 517 HSOB, Washington, D.C. 20510; (202) 224-2934, Fax 228-2856. Web site, cornyn.senate.gov.

John Cornyn.

Texas Offices: 221 W. 6th Ste. 1530, **Austin** 78701, (512) 469-6034; 5005 LBJ Ste. 1150, **Dallas** 75244, (972) 239-1310; 222 E. Van Buren Ste. 404, **Harlingen** 78550, (956) 423-0162; 5300 Memorial Dr. Ste. 980, **Houston** 77007, (713) 572-3337; 3405 22nd Ste. 203, **Lubbock** 79410, (806) 472-7533; 600 Navarro Ste. 210, **San Antonio** 78205, (210) 224-7485; 100 E. Ferguson Ste. 1004, **Tyler** 75702, (903) 593-0905.

Committees: Armed Services, Budget, Judiciary, Select Committee on Ethics (vice chairman).

Kay Bailey Hutchison.

HUTCHISON, Kay Bailey. Republican (Home: Dallas); Washington Office: 284 RSOB, Washington, D.C. 20510; (202) 224-5922, Fax 224-0776. Web site, hutchison.senate.gov.

Texas Offices: 961 Federal Bldg., 300 E. 8th St., **Austin** 78701, (512) 916-5834; 500 Chestnut Ste. 1570, **Abilene** 79602, (325) 676-2839; 10440 N. Central Expy. Ste. 1160, **Dallas** 75231, (214) 361-3500; 222 E. Van Buren Ste. 404, **Harlingen** 78550, (956) 425-2253; 1919 Smith Ste. 800, **Houston** 77002, (713) 653-3456; 145 Duncan Dr. Ste. 120, **San Antonio** 78226, (210) 340-2885.

Committees: Appropriations; Commerce, Science and Transportation; Rules and Administration; Veterans Affairs.

U.S. House of Representatives

BARTON, Joe, R-Ennis, District 6; Washington Office: 2109 RHOB; (202) 225-2002; **District Offices**: 6001 West I-20 Ste. 200, Arlington 76017, (817) 543-1000. **Committee**: Energy and Commerce.

BRADY, Kevin, R-The Woodlands, District 8; Washington Office: 301 CHOB; (202) 225-4901, Fax 225-5524. **District Offices**: 200 River Pointe Ste. 304, Conroe 77304, (936) 441-5700; 1202 Sam Houston Ave. Ste. 8, Huntsville 77340, (936) 439-9542; 420 Green Ave., Orange 77630, (409) 883-4197. **Committee**: Ways and Means.

BURGESS, Michael, R-Flower Mound, District 26; Washington Office: 1224 LHOB; (202) 225-7772. **District Offices**: 1660 S. Stemmons Fwy. Ste. 230, Lewisville 75067, (972) 434-9700; 1100 Circle Dr. Ste. 200, Fort Worth 76119, (817) 531-8454. **Committee**: Energy and Commerce.

CARTER, John R. R-Round Rock, District 31; Washington Office: 408 CHOB; (202) 225-3864. District Offices: 1717 N. I-35 Ste. 303, Round Rock 78664, (512) 246-1600; 6544B S. General Bruce Dr., Temple 76502, (254) 933-1392. **Committee**: Appropriations.

CONAWAY, K. Michael, R-Midland, District 11; Washington Office: 511 CHOB; (202) 225-3605. **District Offices**: 6 Desta Dr. Ste. 2000, Midland 79705, (432) 687-2390; 501 Center Ave. Brownwood 76801, (325) 646-1950; 104 W. Sandstone, Llano 78643, (325) 247-2826; 411 W. 8th, Odessa 79761, (866) 882-3811; 33 Twohig Ste. 307, San Angelo 76903, (325) 659-4010. **Committees**: Agriculture, Armed Services, Budget.

CUELLAR, Henry, D-Laredo, District 28; Washington Office: 336 CHOB; (202) 225-1640, Fax 225-1641. **District Offices**: 602 E. Carlton Rd., Laredo 78041, (956) 725-0639; 615 E. Houston Ste. 451, San Antonio 78205, (210) 271-2851; 320 N. Main Ste. 221, McAllen 78501, (956) 631-4826; 100 S. Austin, Seguin 78155, (830) 401-0457. **Committees**: Agriculture, Homeland Security, Small Business.

CULBERSON, John Abney, R-Houston, District 7; Washington Office: 428 CHOB; (202) 225-2571; Fax 225-4381; District Office: 10000 Memorial Dr. Ste. 620, Houston 77024, (713) 682-8828. **Committee**: Appropriations.

DOGGETT, Lloyd, D-Austin, District 25; Washington Office: 201 CHOB; (202) 225-4865; **District Office**: 300 E. 8th Ste. 763, Austin 78701, (512) 916-

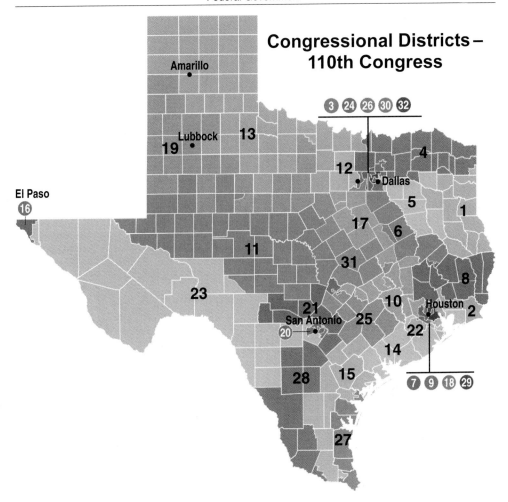

Congressional Districts – 110th Congress

Amarillo

Lubbock 13
19

El Paso
16

③ ㉔ ㉖ ㉚ ㉜

12
Dallas

4

5

1

17
6

11

31

8

23

21
San Antonio 25
20

10
Houston 2

22

14

28
15

⑦ ⑨ ⑱ ㉙

27

5921. **Committees**: Budget, Ways and Means.

EDWARDS, Chet, D-Waco, District 17; Washington Office: 2369 RHOB; (202) 225-6105, Fax 225-0350; **District Offices**: 600 Austin Ave. Ste. 29, Waco 76701, (254) 752-9600; 115 S. Main Ste. 202, Cleburne 76033, (817) 645-4743; 111 University Dr. Ste. 216, College Station 77840, (979) 691-8787; 115 S. Main Ste. 202, Cleburne 76033, (817) 645-4796. **Committees**: Appropriations, Budget.

GOHMERT, Louie, R-Tyler, District 1; Washington Office: 510 CHOB; (202) 225-3035, Fax 226-1230; **District Offices**: 1121 ESE Loop 323 Ste. 206, Tyler 75701, (903) 561-6349; 101 E. Methvin Ste. 302, Longview 75601, (903) 236-8597; 300 E. Shepherd, Lufkin 75901, (866) 535-6302; 102 W. Houston, Marshall 75670, (866) 535-6302; 202 E. Pilar Ste. 304, Nacogdoches 75961, (866) 535-6302. **Committees**: Judiciary, Natural Resources, Small Business.

GONZALEZ, Charlie A., D-San Antonio, District 20; Washington Office: 303 CHOB; (202) 225-3236, Fax 225-1915; **District Office**: 124-B Federal Building, 727 East Durango, Federal Building, San Antonio

78206, (210) 472-6195. **Committees**: Energy and Commerce, House Administration, Small Business.

GRANGER, Kay, R-Fort Worth, District 12; Washington Office: 440 CHOB; (202) 225-5071, Fax 225-5683; **District Office**: 1701 River Run Rd. Ste. 407, Fort Worth 76107, (817) 338-0909. **Committee**: Appropriations.

GREEN, Al, D-Houston, District 9; Washington Office: 425 CHOB; (202) 225-7508; **District Office**: 3003 South Loop West Ste. 460, Houston 77054, (713) 383-9234. **Committees**: Financial Services, Homeland Security.

GREEN, Gene, D-Houston, District 29; Washington Office: 2335 RHOB; (202) 225-1688, Fax 225-9903; **District Offices**: 256 N. Sam Houston Pkwy. E. Ste. 29, Houston 77060, (281) 999-5879; 11811 I-10 East Ste. 430, Houston 77029, (713) 330-0761; 10 North Gaillard, Baytown 77520, (281) 420-0502. **Committees**: Energy and Commerce, Standards of Official Conduct.

HALL, Ralph M., R-Rockwall, District 4; Washington Office: 2405 RHOB; (202) 225-6673, Fax 225-

3332; **District Offices**: 104 N. San Jacinto, Rockwall 75087, (972) 771-9118; 101 E. Pecan, Sherman 75090, (903) 892-1112; 710 James Bowie Dr., New Boston 75570, (903) 628-8309; 1800 N. Graves Ste. 101, McKinney 75069, (214) 726-9949; 320 Church Ste. 132, Sulphur Springs 75482, (903) 885-8138; 4303 Texas Blvd. Ste. 2, Texarkana 75503, (903) 794-4445. **Committees**: Energy and Commerce, Science and Technology.

HENSARLING, Jeb, R-Dallas, District 5; Washington Office: 132 CHOB; (202) 225-3484, Fax 226-4888. **District Offices:** 6510 Abrams Rd. Ste. 243, Dallas 75231, (214) 349-9996; 100 E. Corsicana Ste. 205, Athens 77571, (903) 675-8288. **Committees**: Budget, Financial Services.

HINOJOSA, Rubén, D-Mercedes, District 15; Washington Office: 2463 RHOB; (202) 225-2531, Fax 225-5688; **District Offices**: 2864 W. Trenton Rd., Edinburg 78539, (956) 682-5545; 107 S. St. Mary's St., Beeville 78102, (361) 358-8400. **Committees**: Education and Labor, Financial Services, Foreign Affairs.

JACKSON LEE, Sheila, D-Houston, District 18; Washington Office: 2435 RHOB; (202) 225-3816, Fax 225-3317; **District Offices**: 1919 Smith Ste. 1180, Houston 77002, (713) 655-0050; 420 W. 19th St., Houston 77008, (713) 861-4070; 6719 W. Montgomery Ste. 204, Houston 77091. **Committees**: Foreign Affairs, Homeland Security, Judiciary.

JOHNSON, Eddie Bernice, D-Dallas, District 30; Washington Office: 1511 LHOB; (202) 225-8885, Fax 225-1477; **District Office**: 3102 Maple Ave. Ste. 600, Dallas 75201, (214) 922-8885. **Committees**: Science and Technology, Transportation and Infrastructure.

JOHNSON, Sam, R-Plano, District 3; Washington Office: 1211 LHOB; (202) 225-4201, Fax 225-1485; **District Office**: 2929 N. Central Expressway, Ste. 240, Richardson 75080, (972) 470-0892. **Committee**: Ways and Means.

LAMPSON, Nick, D-Stafford, District 22; Washington Office: 436 CHOB; (202) 225-5951, Fax 225-5241. **Disrict Office**: 10701 Corporate Dr. Ste. 118, Stafford 77477, (281) 240-3700; 1020 Bay Area Blvd, Ste. 224, Houston 77058, (281) 461-6300. **Committees**: Agriculture, Education and Labor, Science and Technology, Transportation and Infrastructure.

MARCHANT, Kenny, R-Coppell, District 24; Washington Office: 1037 LHOB; (202) 225-6605, Fax 225-0074. **District Office**: 9901 E. Valley Ranch Parkway Ste. 3035, Irving 75063, (972) 556-0162. **Committees**: Education and Labor, Oversight and Government Reform, Transportation and Infrastructure.

McCAUL, Michael, R-Austin, District 10; Washington Office: 131 CHOB; (202) 225-2401, Fax 225-5955. **District Offices**: 903 San Jacinto Ste. 320, Austin 78701, (512) 473-2357; 2000 S. Market Ste. 303, Brenham 77833, (979) 830-8497; [Katy] 1550 Foxlake Ste. 120, Houston 77084, (281) 398-1247; 990 Village Sq. Ste. B, Tomball 77375. **Committees**: Homeland Security, Foreign Affairs, Science and Technology, Standards of Official Conduct.

NEUGEBAUER, Randy, R-Lubbock, District 19; Washington Office: 429 CHOB; (202) 225-4005, Fax 225-9615. **District Offices**: 500 Chestnut Rm. 819, Abilene 79602, (325) 675-9779; 1510 Scurry Ste. B, Big Spring 79720, (432) 264-7592; 611 University Ave. Ste. 220, Lubbock 79401, (806) 763-1611. **Committees**: Agriculture, Financial Services, Science and Technology.

ORTIZ, Solomon P., D-Corpus Christi, District 27; Washington Office: 2110 RHOB; (202) 225-7742, Fax 226-1134; **District Offices**: 3649 Leopard Ste. 510, Corpus Christi 78408, (361) 883-5868; 1805 Ruben Torres B-27, Brownsville 78526, (956) 541-1242. **Committees**: Armed Services, Natural Resources.

PAUL, Ron, R-Lake Jackson, District 14; Washington Office: 203 CHOB; (202) 225-2831. **District Offices**: 122 West Way Ste. 301, Lake Jackson 77566, (979) 285-0231; 601 25th Ste. 216, Galveston 77550, (409) 766-7013; 1501 Mockingbird Lane Ste. 229, Victoria 77904, (361) 576-1231. **Committees**: Financial Services, Foreign Affairs.

POE, Ted, R-Humble, District 2; Washington Office: 1605 LHOB; (202) 225-6565, Fax 225-5547. **District Offices**: 505 Orleans Ste. 100, Beaumont 77701, (409) 212-1997; 20202 U.S. Hwy 59 N. Ste. 105, Humble 77338, (281) 446-0242. **Committees**: Foreign Affairs, Transportation and Infrastructure.

REYES, Silvestre, D-El Paso, District 16; Washington Office: 2433 RHOB; (202) 225-4831, Fax 225-2016; **District Office**: 310 N. Mesa Ste. 400, El Paso 79901, (915) 534-4400. **Committees**: Armed Services, Intelligence (chairman).

RODRIGUEZ, Ciro, D-San Antonio, District 23; Washington Office: 2458 RHOB; (202) 225-4511. **District Offices**: 1950 SW Military Dr., San Antonio 78221, (210) 992-1874; Pecos County Courthouse, 103 W. Callaghan, Fort Stockton 79735; 1995 Williams Ste. B, Eagle Pass 78852. **Committees**: Appropriations, Veterans Affairs.

SESSIONS, Pete, R-Dallas, District 32; Washington Office: 1514 LHOB; (202) 225-2231, Fax 225-5878; **District Office**: 12750 Merit Dr. Ste. 1434, Dallas 75251, (972) 392-0505. **Committee**: Rules.

SMITH, Lamar S., R-San Antonio, District 21; Washington Office: 2409 RHOB; (202) 225-4236, Fax 225-8628; **District Offices**: 1100 NE Loop 410 Ste. 640, San Antonio 78209, (210) 821-5024; 3536 Bee Cave Rd. Ste. 212, Austin 78746, (512) 306-0439; 301 Junction Hwy. Ste. 346C, Kerrville 78028, (830) 896-0154. **Committees**: Homeland Security, Judiciary, Science.

THORNBERRY, William M. (Mac), R-Clarendon, District 13; Washington Office: 2457 RHOB; (202) 225-3706, Fax 225-3486; **District Offices**: 905 S. Fillmore Ste. 520, Amarillo 79101, (806) 371-8844; 4245 Kemp Ste. 506, Wichita Falls 76308, (940) 692-1700. **Committees**: Armed Services, Intelligence. ☆

Presidential Medal Honors Burnett, Robinson

The nation's highest civil honor from the president was awarded to San Antonio native Carol Burnett and baseball great Frank Robinson in 2005.

Burnett and Robinson received the Presidential Medal of Freedom from President George W. Bush at the White House in November 2005.

Frank Robinson.

Born Aug. 31, 1935, in Beaumont, Frank Robinson moved with his family to California when he was four and grew up in Oakland. As a member of the Cincinnati Reds, he was the Most Valuable Player of the National League. And, later, as a Baltimore Oriole, he was the Most Valuable Player of the American League.

He was the first African-American manager in Major League Baseball and was named manager of the year in both leagues.

Carol Burnett was born April 26, 1933. She left San Antonio when she was seven years old with her grandmother for California.

In her professional career, her television variety show ran for 11 years and received 25 Emmys.

President Bush said at the award ceremony, "It is far more than her talent that has endeared Carol Burnett

Carol Burnett.

to the American people. It is her goodness of heart, her sincerity, and the wonderful spirit that comes through."

The other eleven receipts of the 2005 Medals of Freedom included Muhammad Ali, Jack Nicklaus and Alan Greenspan.

President Harry Truman established the Medal of Freedom in 1945 to recognize civilians who had contributed to the efforts in World War II.

In 1963, President John F. Kennedy reintroduced the medal as an honor for distinguished civilian service in peacetime.

Other Texans who received the honor in the past include Barbara Jordan, Lloyd Bentsen, Lady Bird Johnson, J. Frank Dobie, James Farmer, Dr. Michael DeBakey, Van Cliburn, Gen. Tommy Franks and Willie Velásquez.

Also, several astronauts serving in Houston have been honored, as well as national figures who spent part of their lives in Texas, including author James Michener and artist Georgia O'Keeffe. ☆

Congressional Medal Honors Nelson, Borlaug

Two Texans were voted the highest civilian honor awarded by Congress in late 2006, the Congressional Gold Medal of Honor.

Nobel laureate Norman Borlaug, international agriculture professor at Texas A&M University, and the late golfer Byron Nelson of Fort Worth were honored with the medal, which dates back to 1776 when the Continental Congress awarded the first medal to Gen. George Washington.

Byron Nelson, born Feb. 4, 1912, in Waxahachie, played professionally from 1935 to 1946. In 1945, he won 11 consecutive tournaments and 18 total tournaments.

The congressional act awarding the medal pointed out that the "EDS Byron Nelson Championship is the only PGA tour event named in honor of a professional golfer." The medal, it said, was "in recognition of his significant contributions to the game of golf as a player, a teacher, and a commentator." The medal was presented posthumously to his widow Peggy Nelson at the nation's Capitol in June 2007.

Norman Borlaug received the Nobel Peace Prize in 1970 for his agricultural techniques that expanded

Byron Nelson in 1945. AP file photo.

crop production. The congressional act that awarded him a Gold Medal says, "Dr. Borlaug's 'green revolution' uplifted hundreds of thousands of the rural poor in Mexico and saved hundreds of millions from famine and outright starvation in India and Pakistan."

He was born March 25, 1914, in Iowa, and, although he travels a great deal each year, he has maintained a residence in Texas for the last 20 years.

In addition to all of the other honors that Dr. Borlaug has received, he was presented with the National Medal of Science at the White House in February 2006. (See photo on page 572.)

Legislation to award a Congressional Gold Medal of Honor must be co-sponsored by two-thirds of the House and at least 67 senators must also cosponsor the proposal in that chamber.

The medal was originally a military honor until the Medal of Honor (commonly called the Congressional Medal of Honor) was instituted during the Civil War for military valor.

Texans previously receiving the Congressional Gold Medal have been Lady Bird Johnson in 1984, Sam Rayburn in 1962, and Howard Hughes, who was raised in Houston, in 1939. ☆

Federal Courts in Texas

Source: The following list of U.S. appeals and district court judges and officials was compiled from court web sites.

Texas is divided into four federal judicial districts, each of which is comprised of several divisions. Appeal from all Texas federal courts is to the **U.S. Fifth Circuit Court of Appeals** in New Orleans.

U.S. COURT OF APPEALS, FIFTH CIRCUIT

The Fifth Circuit is composed of Louisiana, Mississippi and Texas. Sessions are held in each of the states at least once a year and may be scheduled at any location having adequate facilities. U.S. circuit judges are appointed for life and received a salary of $175,100 in 2006.

Circuit Judges — Chief Judge, Edith H. Jones, Houston. **Judges**: Fortunato P. Benavides and Priscilla R. Owen, Austin; Carolyn Dineen King, Jerry E. Smith and Harold R. DeMoss Jr., Houston; Rhesa H. Barksdale and E. Grady Jolly, Jackson, Miss.; W. Eugene Davis, Lafayette, La.; Jacques L. Wiener Jr., James L. Dennis and Edith Brown Clement, New Orleans; Emilio M. Garza and Edward C. Prado, San Antonio; Carl E. Stewart, Shreveport, La. **Senior Judges**: Thomas M. Reavley, Houston; Will Garwood and Patrick E. Higginbotham, Austin. **Clerk of Court**: Charles R. Fulbruge III, New Orleans.

U.S. DISTRICT COURTS

U.S. district judges are appointed for life and received a salary in 2006 of $165,200.

Northern Texas District
www.txnd.uscourts.gov

District Judges — Chief Judge, A. Joe Fish, Dallas. **Judges**: Mary Lou Robinson, Amarillo; Sidney A. Fitzwater, Jorge A. Solis, Sam A. Lindsay, Barbara M.G. Lynn, David C. Godbey, Ed Kinkeade, Jane Boyle, Dallas; John H. McBryde, Terry R. Means, Fort Worth; Sam R. Cummings, Lubbock. **Senior Judges**: Barefoot Sanders, Dallas; Robert B. Maloney, Dallas; Jerry Buchmeyer, Dallas. **Clerk of District Court**: Karen Mitchell, Dallas. **U.S. Attorney**: Richard Roper, Dallas. **Federal Public Defender**: (acting) G. Pat Black. **U.S. Marshal**: Randy Ely, Dallas. **Bankruptcy Judges**: Harlan D. Hale, Barbara J. Houser and Stacey G.C. Jernigan, Dallas; D. Michael Lynn and Russell F. Nelms, Fort Worth; Robert Jones, Lubbock. Court is in continuous session in each division of the Northern Texas District.

Following are the different divisions of the Northern District and the counties in each division:

Abilene Division
Callahan, Eastland, Fisher, Haskell, Howard, Jones, Mitchell, Nolan, Shackelford, Stephens, Stonewall, Taylor and Throckmorton. **Magistrate**: Phillip R. Lane, Abilene. **Deputy-in-charge**: Marsha Elliott.

Amarillo Division
Armstrong, Briscoe, Carson, Castro, Childress, Collingsworth, Dallam, Deaf Smith, Donley, Gray, Hall, Hansford, Hartley, Hemphill, Hutchinson, Lipscomb, Moore, Ochiltree, Oldham, Parmer, Potter, Randall, Roberts, Sherman, Swisher and Wheeler. **Magistrate**: Clinton E. Averitte, Amarillo. **Deputy-in-charge**: Lynn Sherman.

Dallas Division
Dallas, Ellis, Hunt, Johnson, Kaufman, Navarro and Rockwall. **Magistrates**: William F. Sanderson Jr., Jeff Kaplan, Paul Stickney and Irma C. Ramirez, Dallas.

Fort Worth Division
Comanche, Erath, Hood, Jack, Palo Pinto, Parker, Tarrant and Wise. **Magistrate**: Charles Bleil, Fort Worth. **Manager**: Pam Murphy.

Lubbock Division
Bailey, Borden, Cochran, Crosby, Dawson, Dickens, Floyd, Gaines, Garza, Hale, Hockley, Kent, Lamb, Lubbock, Lynn, Motley, Scurry, Terry and Yoakum. **U.S. District Judge**: Sam R. Cummings, Lubbock. **Magistrate**: Nancy M. Koenig, Lubbock. **Deputy-in-charge**: Kristy Weinheimer.

San Angelo Division
Brown, Coke, Coleman, Concho, Crockett, Glasscock, Irion, Menard, Mills, Reagan, Runnels, Schleicher, Sterling, Sutton and Tom Green. **Deputy-in-charge**: Beverly Roper.

Wichita Falls Division
Archer, Baylor, Clay, Cottle, Foard, Hardeman, King, Knox, Montague, Wichita, Wilbarger and Young. **Magistrate**: R. Kerry Roach, Wichita Falls. **Deputy-in-Charge**: Teena McNeely.

Western Texas District
www.txwd.uscourts.gov

District Judges — Chief Judge, Walter S. Smith Jr., Waco. **Judges**: Xavier Rodriguez, Orlando Garcia, Fred Biery and W. Royal Furgeson, San Antonio; Kathleen Cardone, Frank J. Montalvo, Philip R. Martinez and David Briones, El Paso; Sam Sparks and Lee Yeakel, Austin; Alia M. Ludlum, Del Rio; Robert A. Junell, Midland-Odessa. **Senior Judges**: Harry Lee Hudspeth, William Wayne Justice and James R. Nowlin, Austin. **Clerk of District Court**: William G. Putnicki, San Antonio. **U.S. Attorney**: Johnny Sutton, San Antonio. **Federal Public Defender**: Lucien B. Campbell. **U.S. Marshal**: Lafayette Collins, San Antonio. **Bankruptcy Judges**: Robert C. McGuire and Frank P. Monroe, Austin; Lief M. Clark and Ronald B. King, San Antonio.

Following are the different divisions of the Western District, and the counties in each division.

Austin Division
Bastrop, Blanco, Burleson, Burnet, Caldwell, Gillespie, Hays, Kimble, Lampasas, Lee, Llano, Mason, McCulloch, San Saba, Travis, Washington and Williamson. **Magistrates**: Andrew W. Austin and Robert Pitman, Austin. **Divisional Office Manager**: David O'Toole. **Bankruptcy Court Deputy-in-charge**: Maria Dozauer.

Del Rio Division
Edwards, Kinney, Maverick, Terrell, Uvalde, Val Verde and Zavala. **Magistrate**: Dennis Green and Vic-

tor R. Garcia, Del Rio. **Divisional Office Manager**: Rebecca Moore.

El Paso Division

El Paso County only. **Magistrates**: Norbert J. Garney, Michael S. McDonald and Richard P. Mesa, El Paso. **Divisional Office Manager**: Richard Delgado. **Bankruptcy Court Deputy-in-charge**: Julie Herrera.

Midland-Odessa Division

Andrews, Crane, Ector, Martin, Midland and Upton. Court for the Midland-Odessa Division is held at Midland, but may, at the discretion of the court, be held in Odessa. **Magistrate**: L. Stuart Platt, Midland. **District Court Divisional Office Manager**: Laura Gonzales, Midland. **Bankruptcy Court Deputy-in-charge**: Christy L. Carouth.

Pecos Division

Brewster, Culberson, Hudspeth, Jeff Davis, Loving, Pecos, Presidio, Reeves, Ward and Winkler. **Magistrate**: Durwood Edwards, Alpine. **Divisional Office Manager**: Karen J. White.

San Antonio Division

Atascosa, Bandera, Bexar, Comal, Dimmit, Frio, Gonzales, Guadalupe, Karnes, Kendall, Kerr, Medina, Real and Wilson. **Magistrates**: Pamela A. Mathy, John W. Primomo and Nancy Stein Nowak, San Antonio. **Bankruptcy Court Deputy-in-Charge**: Mary Croy, San Antonio. **Divisional Office Manager**: Michael F. Oakes.

Waco Division

Bell, Bosque, Coryell, Falls, Freestone, Hamilton, Hill, Leon, Limestone, McLennan, Milam, Robertson and Somervell. **Magistrate**: Jeffrey C. Manske, Waco. **Divisional Office Manager**: Mark G. Borchardt. **Bankruptcy Court Deputy-in-charge**: Bridget Hardage.

Eastern Texas District
www.txed.uscourts.gov

District Judges — Chief Judge, Thad Heartfield, Beaumont. **Judges**: Ron Clark and Marcia A. Crone, Beaumont; Michael H. Schneider and Leonard Davis, Tyler; T. John Ward, Marshall; Richard A. Schell, Sherman; David J. Folsom, Texarkana. **Clerk of District Court**: David J. Maland, Tyler. **U.S. Attorney**: John L. Ratcliff, Beaumont. **Federal Public Defender**: Pat Black. **U.S. Marshal**: John Moore, Tyler. **Bankruptcy Judges**: William Parker, Tyler, and Brenda T. Roades, Plano.

Following are the divisions of the Eastern District and the counties in each division:

Beaumont Division

Hardin, Jasper, Jefferson, Liberty, Newton, Orange. **Magistrates**: Earl Hines.

Lufkin Division

Angelina, Houston, Nacogdoches, Polk, Sabine, San Augustine, Shelby, Trinity, Tyler.

Marshall Division

Camp, Cass, Harrison, Marion, Morris, Upshur. **Magistrate**: Charles Everingham IV.

Paris Division

Delta, Fannin, Hopkins, Lamar and Red River.

Sherman Division

Collin, Cooke, Denton and Grayson. **Magistrate**: Don Bush.

Texarkana Division

Bowie, Franklin and Titus. **Magistrate**: Caroline M. Craven.

Tyler Division

Anderson, Cherokee, Gregg, Henderson, Panola, Rains, Rusk, Smith, Van Zandt and Wood. **Magistrates**: Judith Guthrie and John Love, Tyler.

Southern Texas District
www.txs.uscourts.gov

District Judges — Chief Judge, Hayden W. Head Jr., Corpus Christi. **Judges**: Nancy F. Atlas, Keith Ellison, Vanessa Gilmore, Melinda Harmon, Kenneth M. Hoyt, Lynn N. Hughes, Sim Lake, Gray H. Miller, John D. Rainey, Lee H. Rosenthal, Houston; Janis Graham Jack, Corpus Christi; Samuel B. Kent, Galveston; Hilda G. Tagle and Andrew S. Hanen, Brownsville; Ricardo H. Hinojosa and Randy Crane, McAllen; George P. Kazen and Micaela Alvarez, Laredo; John D. Rainey, Victoria. **Senior Judges**: David Hittner and Ewing Werlein Jr., Houston. **Clerk of Court**: Michael N. Milby, Houston. **U. S. Attorney**: Donald J. DeGabrielle Jr, Houston. **Federal Public Defender**: Alejandro G. Labanzat. **U.S. Marshal**: Ruben Montzon, Houston. **Bankruptcy Judges**: Chief, Karen K. Brown, Houston; Jeff Bohm, Marvin Isgur, and Wesley W. Steen, Houston; Richard S. Schmidt, Corpus Christi, and Letitia Z. Clark, Galveston.

Following are the different divisions of the Southern District and the counties in each division:

Brownsville Division

Cameron and Willacy. **Magistrates**: John Wm. Black, Felix Recio. **Deputy-in-charge**: Juan Barbosa.

Corpus Christi Division

Aransas, Bee, Brooks, Duval, Jim Wells, Kenedy, Kleberg, Live Oak, Nueces and San Patricio. **Magistrates**: B. Janice Ellington and Brian L. Owsley.

Galveston Division

Brazoria, Chambers, Galveston and Matagorda. **Magistrate**: John R. Froeschner.

Houston Division

Austin, Brazos, Colorado, Fayette, Fort Bend, Grimes, Harris, Madison, Montgomery, San Jacinto, Walker, Waller and Wharton. **Magistrates**: Calvin Botley, Frances H. Stacy, Nancy Johnson, Mary Milloy and Stephen W. Smith. **Deputy-in-charge**: Robbie Westmoreland.

Laredo Division

Jim Hogg, La Salle, McMullen, Webb and Zapata. **Magistrates**: Adriana Arce-Flores and Diana Saldaña.

McAllen Division

Hidalgo and Starr. **Magistrates**: Dorina Ramos and Peter Ormsby. **Deputy-in-charge**: Ed Leandro.

Victoria Division

Calhoun, DeWitt, Goliad, Jackson, Lavaca, Refugio and Victoria. **Magistrate**: Nancy K. Johnson. **Deputy-in-charge**: Joyce Richards. ☆

Federal Funds to Texas by County, 2004

Texas received **$141,858,480,000** in 2004 from the federal government. Below, the distribution of funds is shown by county. The first figure after the county name represents **total direct** expenditures to the county for fiscal year 2004. The second and third figures are that part of the total that went directly for **individuals**, either in **retirement** payments, such as Social Security, or **other** direct payments, principally Medicare. In the last column are direct payments other than to individuals, principally **agricultural** programs such as crop insurance. *For a more complete explanation, see end of chart. Source: Consolidated Federal Funds Report 2004, U.S. Department of Commerce.*

COUNTY	TOTAL	For INDIVIDUALS		other direct (ag., etc.)	COUNTY	TOTAL	For INDIVIDUALS		other direct (ag., etc.)
		retirement	other				retirement	other	
	(Thousands of dollars, 000)					(Thousands of dollars, 000)			
Anderson	$ 280,345	$ 128,900	$ 74,049	$ 162	Coryell	$ 286,802	$ 186,724	$ 37,079	$ 1,275
Andrews	58,387	26,842	15,625	4,524	Cottle	21,320	5,529	4,265	4,464
Angelina	434,925	198,548	117,985	913	Crane	14,954	7,195	5,786	28
Aransas	124,957	75,805	28,774	759	Crockett	24,412	7,503	3,590	744
Archer	61,341	30,630	7,779	2,437	Crosby	69,536	14,853	17,640	21,879
Armstrong	15,611	5,408	2,877	4,610	Culberson	15,234	4,384	4,106	870
Atascosa	182,403	84,774	38,392	3,376	Dallam	62,462	18,120	10,190	20,897
Austin	503,700	61,025	32,787	2,174	Dallas	12,174,161	3,476,275	2,035,616	24,127
Bailey	54,051	13,333	10,570	18,330	Dawson	129,243	28,121	32,759	36,604
Bandera	94,748	65,330	13,815	230	Deaf Smith	118,279	31,302	22,211	28,929
Bastrop	266,224	135,299	46,429	616	Delta	40,444	15,235	10,164	1,469
Baylor	36,869	14,485	9,675	4,007	Denton	1,057,753	497,996	195,832	5,984
Bee	162,367	59,101	45,910	5,462	DeWitt	116,815	44,493	33,159	990
Bell	3,735,942	733,937	189,270	5,092	Dickens	26,373	6,964	9,362	4,259
Bexar	12,574,848	4,137,656	1,664,551	19,450	Dimmit	87,569	17,175	16,104	946
Blanco	68,242	42,426	18,206	124	Donley	28,490	11,524	7,969	3,878
Borden	4,496	569	687	2,096	Duval	115,382	28,177	29,241	2,340
Bosque	104,271	57,177	25,785	676	Eastland	135,784	59,093	42,265	2,540
Bowie	811,899	285,566	134,384	3,990	Ector	508,244	239,062	156,354	284
Brazoria	820,038	441,458	194,404	15,188	Edwards	18,608	5,904	8,160	921
Brazos	927,938	214,314	101,578	6,499	Ellis	468,376	223,411	107,400	6,191
Brewster	62,885	22,364	13,482	336	El Paso	4,446,264	1,391,475	736,732	14,375
Briscoe	26,348	4,936	4,341	10,567	Erath	157,994	76,514	46,844	2,367
Brooks	73,980	16,600	14,609	934	Falls	128,234	44,515	27,764	5,164
Brown	237,512	106,410	67,574	1,645	Fannin	474,737	90,509	45,628	5,400
Burleson	99,322	44,450	21,189	2,466	Fayette	147,716	68,566	37,780	1,083
Burnet	187,680	121,103	33,956	307	Fisher	39,572	11,907	8,716	10,134
Caldwell	158,653	70,512	37,966	1,716	Floyd	78,650	15,917	18,078	31,088
Calhoun	111,533	46,127	21,366	6,626	Foard	18,845	5,272	3,442	4,787
Callahan	73,755	38,901	16,520	1,229	Fort Bend	882,588	411,698	123,478	39,032
Cameron	1,793,263	523,640	387,345	24,049	Franklin	53,727	24,480	12,932	297
Camp	84,013	36,943	20,994	577	Freestone	91,688	44,699	20,231	263
Carson	42,552	15,167	8,881	8,598	Frio	86,876	26,310	17,891	8,854
Cass	215,397	102,413	51,842	438	Gaines	124,148	21,839	17,514	59,681
Castro	64,410	13,075	9,857	29,238	Galveston	1,471,481	558,529	314,676	6,193
Chambers	154,061	37,737	26,277	10,569	Garza	38,305	10,007	9,795	4,338
Cherokee	241,687	100,309	69,974	345	Gillespie	130,498	84,894	30,249	940
Childress	44,944	16,335	10,343	7,057	Glasscock	18,704	1,881	1,066	9,640
Clay	48,575	24,692	12,210	2,108	Goliad	39,761	17,067	10,190	940
Cochran	42,669	7,741	5,643	21,464	Gonzales	145,275	50,753	27,072	1,009
Coke	20,124	10,329	5,458	868	Gray	132,597	60,031	46,931	4,332
Coleman	80,439	30,427	25,265	2,106	Grayson	583,347	299,068	154,126	3,670
Collin	1,674,560	645,060	176,313	3,648	Gregg	603,439	318,925	166,356	256
Collingsworth	41,220	8,527	6,937	13,057	Grimes	117,053	50,061	26,640	169
Colorado	137,944	52,220	30,967	15,467	Guadalupe	472,048	307,368	70,411	3,519
Comal	432,938	264,732	72,303	377	Hale	228,573	70,110	56,466	46,107
Comanche	94,577	38,199	28,081	3,138	Hall	41,578	10,621	8,413	10,958
Concho	27,556	7,249	5,730	4,527	Hamilton	52,155	22,688	18,001	624
Cooke	169,156	86,095	48,423	1,186	Hansford	39,587	11,018	6,013	16,343

COUNTY	TOTAL	For INDIVIDUALS		other direct (ag., etc.)
		retirement	other	
		(Thousands of dollars, 000)		
Hardeman	$ 41,731	$ 13,784	$ 9,288	$ 4,862
Hardin	228,015	119,442	65,046	413
Harris	15,798,626	4,921,784	3,132,368	27,068
Harrison	331,144	132,218	75,953	210
Hartley	22,839	2,545	1,340	16,622
Haskell	60,704	18,397	13,186	14,244
Hays	435,282	188,403	75,433	979
Hemphill	13,574	6,423	4,534	985
Henderson	339,081	163,593	90,993	484
Hidalgo	2,683,789	754,463	632,531	46,803
Hill	211,079	100,789	51,242	7,057
Hockley	153,007	43,589	40,909	30,719
Hood	230,024	159,425	45,851	385
Hopkins	168,121	77,479	44,172	1,919
Houston	171,225	66,316	39,637	1,582
Howard	301,078	86,570	59,621	12,547
Hudspeth	35,959	5,792	3,287	5,257
Hunt	884,554	186,917	104,687	2,332
Hutchinson	114,411	58,386	32,235	4,316
Irion	7,909	3,950	2,090	494
Jack	40,328	17,837	11,225	166
Jackson	97,035	30,642	23,173	22,632
Jasper	217,068	91,791	60,943	1,016
Jeff Davis	17,119	6,206	2,190	170
Jefferson	2,429,523	594,174	457,437	15,869
Jim Hogg	45,063	10,280	10,719	253
Jim Wells	253,746	84,110	67,589	5,032
Johnson	503,443	292,332	121,745	1,343
Jones	117,158	45,453	27,917	13,616
Karnes	101,711	32,786	23,519	1,901
Kaufman	410,005	217,020	109,128	778
Kendall	167,521	109,919	23,245	180
Kenedy	1,531	526	385	8
Kent	8,596	2,845	1,568	2,141
Kerr	343,932	200,269	68,612	123
Kimble	24,327	12,693	6,451	244
King	2,972	289	615	1,101
Kinney	30,204	12,987	5,370	709
Kleberg	286,147	64,642	47,635	7,055
Knox	42,489	11,200	9,598	7,553
Lamar	313,133	131,042	71,829	4,390
Lamb	121,169	32,488	26,898	38,090
Lampasas	121,428	78,680	25,952	154
La Salle	60,559	11,482	8,614	1,437
Lavaca	147,191	64,568	38,804	1,992
Lee	67,128	31,994	14,738	520
Leon	127,815	57,976	27,905	159
Liberty	356,767	157,443	108,550	11,644
Limestone	137,791	59,451	32,030	1,545
Lipscomb	17,283	6,932	4,064	3,178
Live Oak	74,394	20,761	13,965	2,209
Llano	115,678	75,049	28,231	167
Loving	595	280	52	86
Lubbock	1,268,803	493,826	351,192	30,055
Lynn	62,054	13,843	11,376	23,412
Madison	54,362	25,790	12,912	104
Marion	79,093	31,194	14,476	139
Martin	46,314	8,551	6,360	16,131

COUNTY	TOTAL	For INDIVIDUALS		other direct (ag., etc.)
		retirement	other	
		(Thousands of dollars, 000)		
Mason	$ 24,861	$ 11,969	$ 6,317	$ 783
Matagorda	216,919	82,584	43,121	22,956
Maverick	258,598	68,980	60,154	897
McCulloch	60,750	24,610	16,656	1,986
McLennan	1,367,054	550,539	264,270	6,626
McMullen	3,586	1,797	667	123
Medina	179,279	95,938	37,617	4,015
Menard	18,177	6,929	5,094	569
Midland	459,269	223,734	119,729	3,997
Milam	148,803	66,464	29,291	6,622
Mills	33,955	15,211	10,014	407
Mitchell	53,407	19,453	13,935	6,682
Montague	122,575	65,860	32,818	878
Montgomery	1,033,698	586,340	246,604	1,869
Moore	74,022	31,592	14,418	12,783
Morris	92,370	45,430	24,030	397
Motley	14,799	4,322	3,225	3,668
Nacgdoches	330,144	126,855	86,323	9,343
Navarro	269,804	115,593	66,172	3,936
Newton	59,474	33,485	19,978	116
Nolan	99,754	42,135	29,661	5,745
Nueces	2,407,886	728,999	403,893	26,308
Ochiltree	39,345	14,932	7,691	11,413
Oldham	13,993	5,409	2,556	3,207
Orange	462,919	218,298	134,577	1,772
Palo Pinto	155,619	71,108	39,468	337
Panola	125,892	56,870	34,445	79
Parker	357,667	209,564	70,540	563
Parmer	77,049	17,258	9,974	37,348
Pecos	59,231	23,962	13,895	2,534
Polk	372,097	235,701	78,907	2,515
Potter	2,081,657	399,294	168,394	1,244
Presidio	55,808	15,602	8,010	403
Rains	46,946	27,800	9,854	165
Randall	204,785	67,801	86,026	7,728
Reagan	17,344	5,159	3,203	4,384
Real	24,908	12,304	4,992	87
Red River	123,722	41,137	28,009	3,269
Reeves	85,637	22,948	16,818	3,523
Refugio	55,694	21,064	13,848	6,358
Roberts	4,664	1,644	1,131	996
Robertson	117,534	41,337	23,398	5,429
Rockwall	206,676	87,193	25,048	786
Runnels	79,964	31,257	18,939	8,110
Rusk	220,805	99,384	58,491	405
Sabine	98,578	50,279	26,068	193
S. Augustine	69,478	28,012	17,053	122
San Jacinto	105,960	49,348	26,923	35
San Patricio	481,697	153,222	84,959	16,927
San Saba	51,149	14,360	11,656	583
Schleicher	15,467	6,102	4,230	1,554
Scurry	90,692	35,886	24,849	7,309
Shackelford	20,538	10,241	4,850	946
Shelby	181,715	67,040	43,957	217
Sherman	27,751	5,385	3,387	16,005
Smith	972,825	461,180	231,715	363
Somervell	28,216	15,041	7,361	41
Starr	260,368	63,363	58,271	8,015

COUNTY	TOTAL	For INDIVIDUALS		other direct (ag., etc.)	COUNTY	TOTAL	For INDIVIDUALS		other direct (ag., etc.)
		retirement	other				retirement	other	
	(Thousands of dollars, 000)					(Thousands of dollars, 000)			
Stephens	$ 52,269	$ 23,965	$ 16,660	$ 501	Victoria	$ 399,973	$ 183,270	$ 101,756	$ 8,636
Sterling	6,151	2,027	1,545	456	Walker	229,224	100,254	57,850	374
Stonewall	14,055	4,840	3,244	3,302	Waller	148,608	49,973	42,451	4,463
Sutton	15,011	6,897	3,967	795	Ward	60,696	25,403	14,515	405
Swisher	71,732	18,848	12,350	27,502	Washington	176,664	76,463	42,004	630
Tarrant	15,410,163	2,632,629	1,209,192	20,942	Webb	961,064	244,125	188,278	1,995
Taylor	984,414	341,474	148,157	5,028	Wharton	272,006	92,085	61,633	43,531
Terrell	12,776	3,186	1,651	230	Wheeler	38,946	14,921	13,557	3,442
Terry	109,467	27,450	23,031	36,714	Wichita	1,210,379	394,270	155,190	4,968
Throckmrton	14,531	5,381	3,456	2,644	Wilbarger	94,463	35,427	28,653	9,651
Titus	137,243	56,598	40,843	210	Willacy	126,331	32,603	27,212	14,440
Tom Green	721,612	274,862	115,248	10,594	Williamson	1,405,961	451,380	10,5081	10,010
Travis	7,849,727	1,514,632	548,935	26,462	Wilson	139,267	80,445	25,063	2,412
Trinity	105,686	51,217	29,579	71	Winkler	34,726	15,361	12,630	102
Tyler	119,421	59,441	34,855	181	Wise	176,576	96,967	35,904	504
Upshur	194,828	105,150	48,929	426	Wood	239,345	133,912	59,947	587
Upton	18,242	7,410	5,337	1,788	Yoakum	48,257	13,948	8,411	19,836
Uvalde	154,065	52,005	38,457	6,096	Young	108,847	51,803	31,146	2,627
Val Verde	412,318	95,819	37,615	1,757	Zapata	61,552	18,190	19,304	322
Van Zandt	241,212	128,317	71,416	1,106	Zavala	75,522	18,458	17,129	3,984

*Total federal government expenditures include: grants, salaries and wages (Postal Service, Dept. of Defense, etc.), procurement contract awards, direct payments for individuals, and other direct payments other than for individuals, such as some agriculture programs.

Retirement and disability programs include federal employee retirement and disability benefits, Social Security payments of all types, and veterans benefit payments.

Other direct payments for individuals include Medicare, excess earned income tax credits, food stamps, unemployment compensation benefit payments and lower income housing assistance, but not salaries and wages.

Other direct payments other than for individuals include crop insurance, wool and mohair loss assistance program, conservation reserve program, production flexibility payments for contract commodities and postal service funds other than salaries and procurements.

Source: Consolidated Federal Funds Report, Fiscal Year 2004, U.S. Department of Commerce, Bureau of the Census.

U.S. Tax Collections in Texas

*Fiscal Year	Individual Income and Employment Taxes	Corporation Income Taxes	Estate Taxes	Gift Taxes	Excise Taxes	TOTAL U.S. Taxes Collected in Texas
	(Thousands of dollars, 000)	Information for fiscal years, furnished by the Internal Revenue Service.				
2005	$ 125,816,805	$ 29,186,478	$ 1,196,362	$ 118,231	$ 13,074,838	$ 169,392,715
2004	118,410,514	17,127,574	1,109,558	104,214	15,939,329	152,691,189
2003	116,353,959	11,487,059	958,791	147,351	12,987,394	141,934,554
2002	117,685,965	13,702,495	1,287,937	109,064	13,654,721	146,440,182
2001	127,738,858	17,598,181	1,242,130	248,892	14,350,268	161,178,329
2000	116,094,820	20,310,672	1,176,278	269,109	14,732,513	152,583,349
1999	104,408,504	13,098,033	968,736	446,168	16,729,589	135,651,029
1998	94,404,751	14,526,238	1,300,104	247,989	11,877,230	122,356,312
1997	90,222,786	13,875,653	933,616	159,111	12,185,271	117,376,440
1996	76,863,689	12,393,992	733,282	158,237	10,418,847	101,079,028
1995	69,706,333	10,677,881	869,528	152,683	11,135,857	92,342,282
1990	52,795,489	6,983,762	521,811	196,003	5,694,006	66,191,071
1985	41,497,114	5,637,148	528,106	41,560	6,058,110	53,762,038
1980	25,707,514	7,232,486	453,830	23,722	4,122,538	37,540,089
1970	6,096,961	1,184,342	135,694	20,667	843,724	8,281,389
1960	2,059,075	622,822	70,578	10,583	209,653	2,972,712

*Beginning in 1976, the fiscal year ending date was changed to Sept. 30, from June 30.

Navy mine warfare ships dock at Naval Station Ingleside. Paul Iverson photo.

Major Military Installations

Below are listed the major military installations in Texas in 2007. Data are taken from the U.S. Department of Defense *Base Structure Report 2006* and other sources. "Civilian" refers to Department of Defense personnel, and "other" refers to employees such as contractor personnel.

U.S. NAVY

Naval Air Station Corpus Christi
Location: Corpus Christi, in the Flour Bluff area (est. 1941).
Address: NAS Corpus Christi, 11001 D St., Corpus Christi 78419
Main phone number: (361) 961-2811
Personnel: 5,577 active-duty; 887 civilians.
Major units: Naval Air Training Command Headquarters; Training Air Wing Four; Commander of Mine Warfare Command; Coast Guard Air Group; Corpus Christi Army Depot (est. 1961).

Naval Air Station-Joint Reserve Base Fort Worth
Location: westside Fort Worth (est. 1994) [Carswell, est. 1942 as Fort Worth Army Air Field, closed 1993].
Address: NAS-JRB, 1215 Depot Ave., Fort Worth 76127
Main phone number: (817) 782-5000
Personnel: 4,064 active-duty; 6 civilians.
Major units: Fighter Attack Squadron 201, Navy Reserve; Marine Air Group 41; 14th Marine Regiment; Fleet Logistics Support Squadron 59; 136th Airlift Wing, Texas Air National Guard; 301st Fighter Wing, Air Force Reserve; 10th Air Force.

Naval Station Ingleside
(the station is scheduled to close in September 2010.)
Location: Ingleside (est. 1990).
Address: 1455 Ticonderoga Rd., #W123, Ingleside 78362
Main phone number: (361) 776-4200
Personnel: 2,620 active-duty; 113 civilians.

Major units: Mine Warfare Force; 3 Mine Countermeasures Squadrons with 15mine warfare ships.

Naval Air Station Kingsville
Location: Kingsville (est. 1942).
Address: NAS Kingsville, Texas 78363
Main phone number: (361) 516-6136
Personnel: 321 active-duty; 136 civilians.
Major units: Training Air Wing Two; Naval Auxiliary Landing Field Orange Grove; McMullen Target Range, Escondido Ranch.

U.S. ARMY

Fort Bliss
Location: El Paso (est. 1849).
Address: Fort Bliss, Texas 79916
Main phone number: (915) 568-2121
Personnel: 11,930 active-duty plus trainees; 2,276 civilians; 3,138 other.
Major units: 32nd Air and Missile Defense Command; 6th, 11th, 31st, and 108th Air Defense Artillery Brigades; 204th Military Intelligence Battalion; 76th Military Police Battalion; Biggs Army Airfield (est. 1916, originally called Bliss Field).

Fort Hood
Location: Killeen (est. 1942).
Address: Fort Hood, Texas 76544
Main phone number: (254) 287-2131
Personnel: 45,192 active-duty; 3,559 civilians; 5,380 other.
Major units: III Corps, Headquarters Command; 1st Cavalry Division; 4th Infantry Division; 13th Sustainment Command; 89th Military Police Brigade; 504th Military Intelligence Brigade; 3rd

Signal Brigade; 4th Battalion, 5th Air Defense Artillery; 21st Cavalry Brigade (Air Combat); 1st Infantry Division (Mechanized); Army Operational Test Command; Darnell Army Medical Center.

Fort Sam Houston
Location: San Antonio (est. 1878).
Address: Fort Sam Houston, Texas 78234
Main phone number: (210) 221-1211
Personnel: 13,648 active-duty; 4,328 civilians; 2,515 other.
Major units: Fifth U.S. Army; U.S. Army South; Brooke Army Medical Center; Institute of Surgical Research; Army Medical Command; Army Medical Dept. Center and School; 5th Recruiting Brigade; 12th Brigade, Western Region (ROTC); Camp Bullis (est. 1917), training area.

Red River Army Depot
Location: 18 miles west of Texarkana (est. 1941).
Address: Red River Army Depot, Texarkana 75507
Main phone number: (903) 334-2141
Personnel: 144 active-duty; 1,894 civilians; 1,838 other.
Major unit: Defense Distribution Center; U.S. Army Tank-Automotive and Armaments Command.

U.S. AIR FORCE

Brooks City-Base
Location: San Antonio (est. 1917, in 2002 the property was conveyed to the Brooks Development Authority for commercial use, but retains military missions.).
Address: Brooks City-Base, San Antonio 78235
Main phone number: (210) 536-1110
Personnel: 1,050 active-duty; 1,142 civilians.
Major units: 311th Human Systems Wing; 311th Mission Support Group; School of Aerospace Medicine; Air Force Institute for Occupational Health; 59th Medical Squadron; 68th Information Operations Squadron; 710th Intelligence Flight.

Dyess Air Force Base
Location: Abilene (est. 1942 as Tye Army Airfield, closed at end of World War II, re-established in 1956).
Address: Dyess Air Force Base, Texas 79607
Main phone number: (915) 696-0212
Personnel: 5,022 active-duty; 357 civilians.
Major units: 7th Bomb Wing (Air Combat Command); 317th Airlift Group.

Goodfellow Air Force Base
Location: San Angelo (est. 1940).
Address: Goodfellow AFB, San Angelo 76908
Main phone number: (915) 654-3231
Personnel: 1,512 active-duty, approximately 1,200 trainees; 531 civilians.
Major units: 17th Training Wing; 344th Military Intelligence Battalion; NCO Academy.

Lackland Air Force Base
Location: San Antonio (est. 1942 when separated from Kelly Field).

Address: Lackland Air Force Base, Texas 78236
Main phone number: (210) 671-1110
Personnel: 12,040 active-duty; 4,193 civilians.
Major units: 37th Training Wing; Defense Language Institute; Inter-American Air Force Academy; Kelly Field Annex (was Kelly Air Force Base, est. 1916, closed as base 2001).

Laughlin Air Force Base
Location: Del Rio (est. 1942).
Address: Laughlin Air Force Base, Texas 78843
Main phone number: (830) 298-3511
Personnel: 1,000 active-duty; 890 civilians.
Major units: 47th Flying Training Wing.

Randolph Air Force Base
Location: San Antonio (est. 1930).
Address: Randolph Air Force Base, Texas 78150
Main phone number: (210) 652-1110
Personnel: 3,201 active-duty; 5,355 civilians.
Major units: 12th Flying Training Wing; Air Education and Training Command; Air Force Personnel Center; Air Force Recruiting Service; Air Force Manpower Agency.

Sheppard Air Force Base
Location: Four miles north of Wichita Falls (est. 1941).
Address: Sheppard Air Force Base, Texas 76311
Main phone number: (940) 676-2511
Personnel: 3,173 active-duty; 1,304 civilians.
Major units: 82nd Training Wing; 80th Flying Training Wing.

TEXAS MILITARY FORCES

Camp Mabry
Location: 2210 W. 35th St. in Austin. Just west of MoPac Blvd.
Address: Box 5218, Austin, Texas 78763
Main phone number: (512) 465-5101
Web site: www.agd.state.tx.us
Personnel: 1,949 guard, 445 civilians, 238 other.
Adjutant General of Texas:
Lt. General Charles G. Rodriguez.
Major units:
36th Infantry Division, Headquarters;
Texas Air National Guard;
Texas National Guard Academy;
U.S. Property and Fiscal Office;
Texas National Guard Armory Board.

Texas Military Forces Museum,
open Wednesday–Sunday, 10 a.m. - 4 p.m.

Tracing their history to early frontier days, the Texas Military Forces are organized into the Army and Air National Guard, the Texas State Guard and the Adjutant General's Department.

When not in active federal service, Camp Mabry, in northwest Austin, is the main storage maintenance and administrative headquarters.

Camp Mabry was established in the early 1890s as a summer encampment of the Texas Volunteer Guard, a forerunner of the Texas National Guard. The name, Camp Mabry, honors Woodford Haywood Mabry, adjutant general of Texas from 1891-98.

The Texas State Guard, an all-volunteer backup force, was originally created by the Texas Legislature in 1941. It became an active element of the state military forces in 1965 with a mission of reinforcing the National Guard in state emergencies, and of replacing National Guard units called into federal service. The Texas State Guard has a membership of approximately 1,100 personnel.

When the forces were reorganized following World War II, the Texas Air National Guard was added. Texas Air National Guard units serve as augmentation units to major Air Force commands, including the Air Defense Command, the tactical Air Command and the Strategic Air Command. Approximately 3,500 men and women made up the Air Guard in 2007.

The Army National Guard is available for either national or state emergencies and has been used exten-

sively during hurricanes, tornadoes and floods. There are more than 180 units throughout Texas, with many recently serving in Afghanistan, Iraq, Kosovo, Bosnia and the Sinai.

The governor of Texas is commander-in-chief of the Texas National and State Guards. This command function is exercised through the adjutant general appointed by the governor and approved by both federal and state legislative authority.

The adjutant general is the active administrative head of the Texas Military Forces. In 2007, Adjutant General Rodriguez was responsible for commanding a total of 21,000 soldiers, airmen and civilians in the Texas Army and Air National Guard, the State Guard and the Adjutant General's Department.

When called into active federal service, National Guard units come within the chain of command of the Army and Air Force units. ☆

The Dallas-Fort Worth National Cemetery in southwest Dallas County. Robert Plocheck photo.

National Cemeteries in Texas

The United States Department of Veterans Affairs administers six cemeteries in Texas. The first cemetery was started in San Antonio in 1867, and the latest and largest of the cemeteries, Dallas-Fort Worth, was established in 2000. Veterans and their spouses are eligible for burial in the national cemeteries.

Cemetery year established	Interments (as of 2005)	Burial space	Acreage	Location / phone	Visitation hours
Dallas-Fort Worth 2000	13,166	Yes: Casket and Cremated	638.4	2000 Mountain Creek Parkway (214) 467-3374	dawn to dusk
Houston 1965	59,688	Yes: Casket and Cremated	419.2	10410 Veterans Memorial Drive (281) 447-8686	8 a.m. to sunset
San Antonio 1867	3,163	Cremated only	3.7	517 Paso Hondo Street (210) 820-3891	sunrise to sunset
Fort Sam Houston 1926	110,123	Yes: Casket and Cremated	154.7	1520 Wurzbach Road (210) 820-3891	7 to 7 weekdays 7 to 5 weekends
Kerrville 1923	463	No: Closed	1.7	3600 Memorial Blvd.	sunrise to sunset
Fort Bliss 1883	42,141	Yes: Casket and Cremated	82.1	5200 Fred Wilson Blvd. (915) 564-0201	sunrise to sunset

Source: U.S. Department of Veterans Affairs, 2007.

Crime in Texas — 2006

Source: Texas Department of Public Safety, Austin.

The **total number of major crimes** committed in Texas in 2006 decreased by 2.6 percent compared to 2005. In addition, the **2006 major crime rate** — the number of crimes per 100,000 population — decreased 5.3 percent from 2005. In 2006, there were 4,599.6 crimes per 100,000 people, compared with 4857.1 in 2005.

The **violent crime rate** decreased 2.3 percent from 2005 to 2006. The number of murders in 2006 was down 1.4 percent from 2005, and the number of rapes decreased by 1.2 percent over 2005.

The **nonviolent, or property, crime rate** decreased 5.7 percent from 2005 to 2006. The value of property stolen during the commission of index crimes in 2006 was more than $2 billion. The **value of stolen property recovered** by Texas law-enforcement agencies in 2006 was more than $697 million.

The total number of arrests in Texas increased 2.9 percent in 2006 over 2005. The number of juvenile arrests decreased 0.7 percent, while adult arrests increased 3.5 percent. There were 1.13 million arrests in 2006 compared with 1.10 million arrests in 2005.

The crime rate is tabulated on seven major offenses designated Index Crimes by the Federal Bureau of Investigation's **Uniform Crime Reporting program**. These seven categories include four violent offenses (murder, rape, robbery and aggravated assault) and three nonviolent crimes (burglary, larceny-theft and motor-vehicle theft). In Texas, these figures are collected by the Texas Department of Public Safety for the national UCR program. In 2006, 1,020 Texas law enforcement agencies (99.9 percent) participated in the Texas UCR program. Data are estimated for non-reporting agencies.

Arson

In 2006, reported arson offenses decreased 3.7 percent from 2005. Property damage from arson was reported at more than $93 million in 2006. There were 6,549 arsons in 2006, a drop from 6,800 arsons in 2005.

Family Violence in Texas in 2006

Family violence decreased by about 0.5 percent in 2006 from 2005. In 2006, there were 186,686 reported incidents of family violence committed against 200,803 victims by 197,037 offenders. In 2005, there were 187,811 incidents of family violence committed against 199,574 victims by 195,174 offenders. In 47.6 percent of the 2006 incidents, the relationship of victim to offender was marital. Of these victims, 20.1 percent were wives and 15.7 percent were common-law wives.

Of the remaining offenses, 15.5 percent involved parents against children or children against parents; and 36.9 involved other family/household relationships, such as grandparents, grandchildren, siblings, step-siblings, roommates or in-laws. The 77th Legislature amended the Texas Family Code to include violence in a "dating relationship."

There are six general categories of family violence: assault, homicide, kidnapping, robbery, forcible sex offenses and nonforcible sex offenses. Assaults (including aggravated, simple and intimidation) accounted for 96.7 percent of all family violence in 2006.

Investigation of reports of domestic violence can be hazardous to police officers. During 2006, 474 Texas law officers were assaulted while investigating such reports.

Hate Crimes in Texas in 2006

There were 247 reported incidents of hate crime in Texas in 2006. This is a decrease of 6.4 percent from the 264 incidents in 2005. These crimes involved 222 victims, 291 offenders, resulting in a total of 300 offenses.

These crimes were motivated by race (50.9%), ethnicity/national origin (19.1%), sexual orientation (18.7%), religion (10.5%) and disability (0.8%).

Hate crimes, as defined by the Texas Hate Crimes Act, are crimes motivated by prejudice and hatred. The Texas Hate Crimes Act directs all law enforcement agencies in Texas to report bias offenses to the DPS.

Law Enforcement Deaths, Injuries

In 2006, two Texas law enforcement officers were killed in the line of duty because of criminal activity, and five officers were killed in duty-related accidents.

There were 4,634 officers assaulted during 2006 compared to 4,619 in 2005. This represents a increase of 0.3 percent. ☆

Texas Crime History 1986–2006

Year	Murder	Rape	Robbery	Aggravated Assault	Burglary	Larceny-Theft	Motor Vehicle Theft	Rate per 100,000 Population
1986	2,255	8,605	40,018	59,002	341,560	664,832	119,095	7,408.2
1987	1,960	8,068	38,049	57,903	355,732	711,739	123,378	7,724.3
1988	2,021	8,122	39,307	60,084	362,099	739,784	134,271	8,019.6
1989	2,029	7,953	37,910	63,978	342,360	741,642	150,974	7,926.8
1990	2,388	8,746	44,316	73,860	314,346	730,926	154,387	7,823.7
1991	2,651	9,265	49,698	84,104	312,719	734,177	163,837	7,818.6
1992	2,240	9,368	44,582	86,067	268,864	689,515	145,039	7,055.1
1993	2,149	9,923	40,464	84,892	233,944	664,738	124,822	6,438.5
1994	2,023	9,101	37,639	81,079	214,698	624,048	110,772	5,873.1
1995	1,694	8,526	33,666	80,377	202,637	632,523	104,939	5,684.5
1996	1,476	8,374	32,796	80,572	204,335	659,397	104,928	5,708.3
1997	1,328	8,007	30,513	77,239	200,966	645,174	101,687	5,478.2
1998	1,343	7,914	28,672	73,648	194,872	606,805	96,614	5,110.7
1999	1,218	7,629	29,424	74,165	190,347	614,478	91,992	5,035.2
2000	1,236	7,821	30,186	73,987	188,205	634,575	92,878	4,952.4
2001	1,331	8,191	35,330	77,221	204,240	669,587	102,838	5,152.3
2002	1,305	8,541	37,599	78,713	212,702	690,028	102,943	5,196.7
2003	1,417	7,986	37,000	75,706	219,733	697,790	98,174	5,144.1
2004	1,360	8,401	35,811	75,983	220,079	696,220	93,844	5,032.0
2005	1,405	8,505	35,781	75,409	219,733	676,022	93,471	4,857.1
2006	1,385	8,407	37,271	74,624	215,754	648,083	95,750	4,599.6

Source: Texas Department of Public Safety, Austin, and the Federal Bureau of Investigation, Washington. Population figures used to determine crime rate per 100,000 population based on U.S. Bureau of Census. The population figure used in determining the crime rate for 2006 in Texas was 23,507,783.

Kristina Montet, left, president of Metroplex C.O.P.S. (Concerns of Police Survivors) discusses the program for the 2007 Peace Officers Candlelight Vigil and Memorial Services held May 6–7 in Austin. The Texas Peace Officers Memorial is on the grounds of the Capitol Complex and honors Texas law enforcement and corrections officers who were killed in the line of duty. The memorial was dedicated in 1999. Maria Alvarado photo.

Crime Profile of Texas Counties for 2006

County	Agencies	Commissioned Personnel †	Murder	Rape	Robbery	Assault	Burglary	Larceny-Theft	Auto Theft	Total Index Crimes (see page 532 for definition)	Crime Rate per 100,000
Anderson	3	68	2	21	14	159	359	710	76	1,341	2,311.8
Andrews	2	27	0	8	3	21	83	233	14	362	2,761.5
Angelina	5	148	2	50	50	363	654	1,350	156	2,625	3,129.9
Aransas	2	42	1	30	3	25	350	911	46	1,366	5,634.6
Archer	2	10	0	1	0	5	31	49	11	97	1,037.1
Armstrong	1	3	0	0	0	3	3	9	1	16	715.9
Atascosa	5	60	1	14	8	79	199	511	45	857	1,911.5
Austin	4	53	0	5	6	32	130	432	33	638	2,375.0
Bailey	2	12	1	3	0	15	59	107	7	192	2,775.8
Bandera	1	27	1	1	1	21	87	130	14	255	1,240.6
Bastrop	4	89	2	17	19	120	583	1,197	106	2,044	2,834.6
Baylor	2	10	0	1	1	29	18	62	5	116	2,935.2
Bee	2	38	1	5	2	55	206	381	21	671	1,984.9
Bell	12	553	10	153	335	629	3,546	6,902	538	12,113	4,584.0
Bexar	28	2,944	130	591	2,480	5,557	17,347	65,753	7,295	99,153	6,352.7
Blanco	3	17	0	1	0	5	60	51	4	121	1,291.6
Borden	1	2	0	0	0	1	1	3	0	5	750.8
Bosque ‡	4	20	0	3	4	21	61	130	15	234	1,260.2
Bowie	7	162	10	44	84	474	743	2,421	217	3,993	4,283.8
Brazoria	20	455	3	76	111	429	1,766	4,376	455	7,216	2,490.4
Brazos	4	325	7	84	137	635	1,763	5,590	359	8,575	5,334.9
Brewster	3	27	0	1	0	20	70	85	9	185	1,981.6
Briscoe	1	2	0	0	0	1	5	1	0	7	414.0
Brooks	2	20	0	2	3	23	78	142	5	253	3,200.5
Brown	4	67	0	20	15	124	376	1,010	60	1,605	4,036.7
Burleson	3	27	0	4	5	31	72	108	15	235	1,325.7
Burnet	7	93	0	13	3	60	208	556	60	900	1,963.4
Caldwell	4	71	0	16	25	124	249	646	48	1,108	3,035.5
Calhoun	4	46	0	13	2	46	125	336	35	557	2,628.6
Callahan	3	14	0	4	0	19	40	84	13	160	1,151.2
Cameron	16	628	12	125	277	1,264	3,882	13,316	1,094	19,970	5,133.3
Camp	2	18	1	2	7	33	113	162	14	332	2,638.1
Carson	2	9	0	0	0	5	6	8	0	19	280.5
Cass	5	36	1	14	14	48	195	368	56	696	2,244.4
Castro	3	17	0	2	1	12	76	130	6	227	2,889.1
Chambers	2	47	1	3	8	86	242	378	42	760	2,921.7
Cherokee ‡	6	70	1	28	20	155	457	717	101	1479	2,975.7
Childress	2	14	0	0	1	24	42	87	13	167	2,115.5
Clay	1	10	0	3	2	11	56	106	16	194	1,671.4
Cochran	1	7	0	0	1	2	32	34	2	71	2,099.3
Coke	1	5	0	0	0	0	5	4	0	9	242.3
Coleman	3	17	0	1	1	4	104	129	16	255	2,861.6
Collin	15	762	8	135	234	963	3,475	13,455	969	19,239	3,128.1
Collingsworth	1	5	0	0	0	0	0	0	0	0	0
Colorado	4	42	1	6	6	45	116	276	24	474	2,222.8
Comal	3	189	1	32	37	225	712	2305	119	3,431	3,417.4
Comanche	3	20	2	4	0	13	76	162	11	268	1,901.1
Concho	2	8	0	0	1	1	16	17	0	35	911.2

County	Agencies	Commissioned Personnel †	Murder	Rape	Robbery	Assault	Burglary	Larceny-Theft	Auto Theft	Total Index Crimes (see page 532 for definition)	Crime Rate per 100,000
Cooke ‡	4	61	3	10	23	153	325	747	88	1,349	3,376.9
Coryell	3	75	1	18	27	98	364	1,039	46	1,593	2,035.4
Cottle	2	3	0	0	0	2	7	2	0	11	612.8
Crane	2	13	0	0	0	5	16	44	5	70	1,773.9
Crockett	1	12	0	4	0	16	12	24	2	58	1,433.9
Crosby	2	8	0	0	0	6	4	4	0	14	203.6
Culberson	1	8	0	0	0	0	1	3	0	4	148.1
Dallam	2	18	0	3	5	32	65	158	9	272	3,032.7
Dallas	36	5,531	228	953	8,229	9,640	32,722	86,215	20,025	158,012	6,100.5
Dawson	2	22	0	2	6	48	90	144	16	306	2,103.1
Deaf Smith	2	32	0	1	5	60	123	476	42	707	3,708.8
Delta	1	9	0	0	2	2	52	53	2	111	1,969.8
Denton ‡	21	679	5	134	174	502	2,039	7,372	792	11,018	2,389.0
DeWitt	3	26	0	13	4	44	77	182	9	329	1,743
Dickens	2	4	2	0	0	1	9	0	0	12	441.0
Dimmit	1	12	1	2	1	41	136	147	32	360	3,367.6
Donley	1	5	0	0	1	4	16	12	2	35	875.2
Duval	3	29	0	3	0	45	135	181	14	378	2,733.4
Eastland	6	31	0	1	2	15	134	277	27	456	2,410.9
Ector	4	279	3	14	97	567	1,014	3,439	315	5,449	4,188.0
Edwards	1	4	0	0	1	2	8	19	2	32	1,566.3
Ellis	9	204	6	28	49	308	943	2,364	268	3,966	3,054.4
El Paso	10	1,503	22	335	546	1,914	2,771	17,059	3,822	26,469	3,567.0
Erath	4	75	0	12	3	52	181	684	51	983	2,805.2
Falls	3	31	1	6	6	34	74	135	17	273	1,504.6
Fannin	2	37	0	7	3	63	255	404	26	758	2,224.1
Fayette	3	28	1	2	2	5	96	139	6	251	1,083.0
Fisher	1	5	0	4	0	4	27	31	2	68	1,617.1
Floyd	3	13	0	1	2	11	31	39	4	88	1,192.9
Foard	2	4	0	1	0	2	2	1	0	6	384.4
Fort Bend ‡	11	676	18	85	288	837	2132	5,980	677	10,017	2,276.5
Franklin	1	8	1	1	0	2	42	77	11	134	1,378.5
Freestone	4	33	0	2	7	40	50	116	23	238	1,231.1
Frio	3	27	2	0	2	45	146	228	15	438	2,599.3
Gaines	3	24	1	3	3	10	45	124	6	192	1,269.1
Galveston	15	719	11	217	355	691	2,799	7,213	829	12,115	4,109.9
Garza	1	7	0	1	0	2	31	57	6	97	1,885.7
Gillespie	2	45	0	0	0	12	39	267	4	322	1,356.2
Glasscock	1	3	0	0	0	0	0	0	0	0	0
Goliad	1	11	0	0	0	1	14	18	1	34	465.6
Gonzales	3	39	0	12	11	116	231	345	7	722	3,584.5
Gray	2	38	0	31	10	135	270	642	63	1,151	5,211.0
Grayson	11	195	1	26	53	221	1,007	2,725	222	4,255	3,541.6
Gregg	5	269	12	91	141	616	1,556	4,893	680	7,989	6,340.7
Grimes	2	42	0	10	10	47	228	441	46	782	3,018.6
Guadalupe	5	162	1	37	22	190	612	2,080	135	3,077	2,908.1
Hale	4	66	0	20	13	88	332	1,099	54	1,606	4,232.1
Hall	2	8	0	1	0	6	36	34	9	86	2,260.2
Hamilton ‡	2	12	0	0	1	9	43	74	10	137	1,643.7
Hansford	3	8	0	3	0	11	9	33	1	57	1,059.9
Hardeman	2	8	0	4	3	3	62	74	8	154	3,489.7
Hardin	5	77	1	14	10	64	265	676	103	1,133	2,161.3
Harris ‡	39	9,130	461	1,380	14,177	17,749	41,838	112,658	28,584	216,847	5,667.2
Harrison	4	97	6	20	20	238	647	1,307	119	2,357	3,709.4
Hartley	1	4	0	0	0	0	7	8	3	18	603.2
Haskell	2	6	0	0	0	13	29	54	5	101	1,785.4
Hays	4	228	1	32	35	177	543	1,665	150	2,603	2,024.9
Hemphill	1	8	0	1	1	13	11	29	4	59	1,676.6
Henderson ‡	9	129	3	34	29	323	776	1,302	123	2,590	3,147.6
Hidalgo ‡	21	1,052	32	179	544	1,881	5,922	22,895	2,605	34,058	4,882.9
Hill	5	59	2	11	14	26	202	473	51	779	2,138.5
Hockley	5	40	0	18	5	57	162	343	25	610	2,603.2
Hood	3	56	1	0	12	50	213	850	70	1,196	2,426.6
Hopkins	2	55	0	14	2	48	185	363	34	646	1,881.9
Houston	3	35	0	5	6	61	157	341	27	597	2,500.4
Howard	2	56	1	19	16	114	378	778	64	1,370	4,096.4
Hudspeth	1	16	0	0	0	9	16	15	1	41	1,210.2
Hunt	8	125	5	18	67	236	850	1,877	240	3,293	3,879.5
Hutchinson ‡	3	34	0	14	9	68	205	682	64	1,042	4,506.7
Irion	1	4	0	0	0	0	15	14	1	30	1,661.1
Jack	2	21	0	4	0	5	21	34	5	69	740.3

County	Agencies	Commissioned Personnel †	Murder	Rape	Robbery	Assault	Burglary	Larceny-Theft	Auto Theft	Total Index Crimes (see page 532 for definition)	Crime Rate per 100,000
Jackson	3	22	0	5	0	23	60	168	6	262	1,776.9
Jasper	3	38	2	9	17	134	221	569	48	1,000	2,732.6
Jeff Davis	1	2	0	0	1	6	7	5	0	19	801.3
Jefferson	7	554	17	105	537	1,059	3,319	7,043	966	13,046	5,124.4
Jim Hogg	1	20	0	0	0	10	25	43	3	81	1,566.1
Jim Wells	4	78	2	20	9	335	506	1,531	91	2,494	6,051.0
Johnson	7	209	4	51	48	280	916	3,030	317	4,646	3,034.4
Jones	5	25	0	2	1	28	66	71	18	186	1,284.4
Karnes	3	19	0	3	1	23	65	122	2	216	1,368.3
Kaufman	6	128	4	35	56	337	998	1,915	337	3,682	4,019.9
Kendall	2	54	2	10	2	36	77	315	18	460	1,615.1
Kenedy	1	11	0	0	0	2	3	2	0	7	1,631.7
Kent	1	2	1	0	0	2	9	13	0	25	3,109.5
Kerr	3	102	2	19	13	39	268	828	48	1,217	2,545.3
Kimble	2	16	0	1	0	24	16	60	2	103	2,181.7
King	1	2	0	0	0	0	2	0	0	2	632.9
Kinney	1	7	0	0	0	0	1	1	3	5	146.2
Kleberg	3	84	0	7	21	249	434	1,807	50	2,568	8,119.1
Knox	3	7	0	0	0	14	21	39	3	77	1,980.5
Lamar	4	91	2	16	29	215	557	1,556	51	2,426	4,752.1
Lamb ‡	4	34	0	8	4	20	108	194	22	356	2,393.0
Lampasas ‡	3	37	0	18	0	15	51	194	15	293	1,471.6
La Salle	1	12	0	0	0	6	27	56	0	89	1,438.7
Lavaca	3	27	4	6	0	20	60	181	14	285	1,315.0
Lee	3	26	1	6	0	42	113	255	12	429	2,524.4
Leon	1	21	1	4	1	34	83	84	15	222	1,320.9
Liberty	4	88	6	28	24	155	473	1,075	224	1,985	2,568.9
Limestone	4	46	0	6	13	42	185	577	31	854	3,648.3
Lipscomb	1	5	0	0	0	3	5	6	0	14	439.0
Live Oak	2	17	1	0	0	3	41	65	8	118	979.3
Llano ‡	3	31	0	4	0	11	78	190	10	293	1,858.0
Loving	1	2	0	0	0	0	1	1	1	3	4,687.5
Lubbock	9	511	16	115	377	1,795	3,414	9,465	824	16,006	6,186.0
Lynn	3	11	0	1	1	3	30	52	5	92	1,410.2
Madison	2	16	1	0	9	28	74	172	26	310	2,289.5
Marion	2	19	0	8	9	41	109	135	25	327	2,903.6
Martin	2	8	0	1	1	1	8	24	2	37	850.0
Mason	1	6	0	1	1	7	16	43	1	69	1,729.3
Matagorda	4	92	3	5	62	173	361	957	54	1,615	4,149.3
Maverick	2	102	2	7	15	166	304	1,346	86	1,926	3,659.4
McCulloch	2	14	0	2	0	25	88	60	2	177	2,163.5
McLennan	17	506	10	122	292	859	2,960	7,219	640	12,102	5,238.2
McMullen	1	2	0	0	0	1	2	10	0	13	1,431.7
Medina	4	47	1	22	8	84	244	595	26	980	2,233.4
Menard	1	5	0	0	0	2	2	8	1	13	574.5
Midland	3	251	5	68	80	282	997	2,968	251	4,651	3,758.3
Milam	4	35	0	9	9	37	168	329	26	578	2,216.9
Mills	1	5	0	0	0	2	15	8	1	26	482.8
Mitchell	2	12	0	3	1	28	41	129	7	209	2,159.1
Montague ‡	4	27	1	13	2	24	93	399	33	565	2,792.2
Montgomery	9	476	15	73	187	810	2,435	6,650	873	11,043	2,846.3
Moore	3	38	0	2	10	58	87	334	18	509	2,432.5
Morris	4	23	0	0	1	34	77	129	14	255	1,916.9
Motley	1	3	0	0	0	0	2	1	0	3	224.6
Nacogdoches	3	138	4	30	30	118	380	1,054	88	1,704	2,740.3
Navarro	3	104	3	21	19	63	538	1,239	118	2,001	3,996.6
Newton	1	9	0	3	0	19	62	147	6	237	1,610.7
Nolan	3	34	1	3	13	24	159	257	14	471	3,078.4
Nueces	8	585	21	202	481	1,539	3,505	16,704	942	23,394	7,118.9
Ochiltree	2	17	0	0	1	11	26	114	7	159	1,647.5
Oldham	1	5	0	1	0	5	3	9	1	19	872.4
Orange	7	151	0	43	71	307	947	2,028	326	3,722	4,259.0
Palo Pinto	2	46	2	10	9	44	255	720	49	1,089	3,569.0
Panola	2	41	2	2	5	100	121	318	69	617	2,633.9
Parker	5	133	1	31	13	122	503	1425	144	2,239	2,219.2
Parmer	4	14	0	0	3	10	49	59	6	127	1,266.2
Pecos	2	31	0	3	1	19	101	180	12	316	1,937.7
Polk	4	74	2	40	16	67	390	620	86	1,221	2,545.8
Potter	4	408	7	98	404	1,145	2,466	7,786	1,099	13,005	6,391.4
Presidio	3	15	0	2	0	7	15	54	8	86	1,083.0
Rains	1	9	0	1	0	17	67	94	20	199	1,711.8

County	Agencies	Commissioned Personnel †	Murder	Rape	Robbery	Assault	Burglary	Larceny-Theft	Auto Theft	Total Index Crimes (see page 532 for definition)	Crime Rate per 100,000
Randall	3	97	0	5	4	54	120	367	31	581	1,763.6
Reagan	1	10	0	0	0	1	7	22	5	35	1,136.4
Real	1	3	0	0	0	0	8	5	0	13	417.1
Red River	3	21	1	1	2	23	91	112	9	239	1,712.0
Reeves	2	35	0	0	3	37	42	163	11	256	2,139.0
Refugio	2	19	0	0	0	24	31	64	5	124	1,578.6
Roberts	1	4	0	0	0	2	8	22	3	35	4,151.8
Robertson	4	32	1	2	2	42	109	243	25	424	2,546.4
Rockwall	4	101	0	14	12	110	280	878	78	1,372	2,443.8
Runnels	3	17	0	0	2	11	42	97	8	160	1,417.8
Rusk	4	82	4	15	19	169	396	1,012	138	1,753	3,728.7
Sabine	3	13	1	0	1	31	57	90	6	186	1,736.5
San Augustine	2	11	2	1	0	24	58	68	5	158	1,725.1
San Jacinto	1	14	0	0	4	56	218	255	67	600	2,352.6
San Patricio	9	127	3	23	24	105	497	1,893	84	2,629	3,630.6
San Saba	2	8	0	3	0	4	29	26	7	69	1,104.4
Schleicher	1	4	0	0	0	3	3	9	2	17	602.8
Scurry	3	25	2	12	1	83	101	159	15	373	2,236.6
Shackelford	1	4	0	2	0	5	4	11	3	25	767.6
Shelby	2	26	4	5	6	41	136	324	45	561	2,070.6
Sherman	2	7	0	2	0	2	6	29	3	42	1,360.5
Smith ‡	11	365	6	75	136	683	1,621	4,718	394	7,633	3,894.7
Somervell	1	19	2	0	0	8	30	81	3	124	1,591.2
Starr	3	77	5	6	16	66	325	511	179	1,108	1,768.0
Stephens	2	17	1	2	1	5	42	88	6	145	1,474.8
Sterling	1	3	0	0	0	0	4	4	0	8	597.0
Stonewall	1	2	0	0	0	2	0	5	0	7	496.1
Sutton	2	9	1	0	1	12	12	47	3	76	1,754.8
Swisher	2	14	0	0	2	40	49	137	8	236	2,931.7
Tarrant	38	3,685	75	618	2,735	5,327	17,436	54,235	6,968	87,394	5,344.1
Taylor	6	257	6	69	108	400	1,423	3,697	327	6030	4,485.4
Terrell	1	5	0	0	0	3	7	4	0	14	1,367.2
Terry	2	25	0	2	0	17	44	103	18	184	1,440.8
Throckmorton	1	2	0	0	0	1	1	4	0	6	360.6
Titus	2	51	2	18	12	78	221	503	63	897	2,962.4
Tom Green	3	218	2	56	62	303	1,060	3,577	232	5,292	4,966.8
Travis	14	2,277	24	373	1,420	2,248	8,919	35,944	2,810	51,738	5,592.4
Trinity	2	17	2	7	7	55	65	117	20	273	1,848.3
Tyler	2	27	1	6	3	46	126	80	8	270	1,273.5
Upshur ‡	5	56	0	4	11	96	296	639	83	1,129	3,111.5
Upton	1	9	2	2	0	2	4	13	0	23	731.8
Uvalde	3	45	1	8	13	98	337	998	30	1,485	5,357.3
Val Verde	2	105	0	0	11	29	249	810	117	1,216	2,484.4
Van Zandt	6	65	0	1	13	88	403	714	113	1,332	2,467.6
Victoria	3	193	7	45	90	250	819	2,443	223	3,877	4,401.9
Walker	2	75	3	23	45	144	328	1,014	92	1,040	2,556.1
Waller	6	79	4	15	21	65	357	544	100	1,106	3,144.9
Ward	2	26	2	0	1	17	53	109	4	186	1,766.9
Washington	2	55	1	16	15	72	193	318	52	667	2,057.8
Webb	6	604	24	96	271	872	1,780	9,966	1,247	14,256	6,169.8
Wharton	3	86	3	8	23	126	353	809	63	1,385	3,241.1
Wheeler	2	7	1	1	2	3	12	31	2	52	1,053.7
Wichita	6	252	9	36	170	296	1,496	4,907	448	7,362	5,686.6
Wilbarger	2	29	0	5	11	61	101	509	20	707	4,947.5
Willacy	3	31	0	13	7	175	263	690	24	1,172	5,591.6
Williamson	11	459	2	85	66	368	1,128	4610	259	6,518	1,972.4
Wilson	3	50	0	7	1	37	88	349	17	499	1,293.0
Winkler	3	21	0	1	0	12	29	76	4	122	1,773.3
Wise	4	81	1	12	5	161	292	820	35	1,326	2,274.3
Wood ‡	5	56	2	3	1	157	287	340	25	815	1,905.1
Yoakum	2	17	0	0	0	4	9	59	3	75	984.5
Young	3	37	0	5	2	25	98	336	21	487	2,631.0
Zapata	1	37	0	1	5	28	84	105	25	248	1,803.4
Zavala	2	21	0	0	3	18	72	171	5	269	2,217.6
STATE TOTAL			1,385	8,407	37,271	74,624	215,754	648,083	95,750	1,081,274	4,599.6

* County population figures used for calculation of crime rate are the U.S. Census Bureau revised figures for 2006.
† The commissioned officers listed here are those employed by sheriffs' offices and police departments of municipalities; universities, colleges and public-school districts; transit systems; park departments; and medical facilities. The Texas Department of Public Safety also has 3,407 commissioned personnel stationed statewide.
‡ County in which one or more law-enforcement agencies did not report data for 2006 to the DPS. The number of commissioned officers listed for this county does not include those employed by nonreporting agencies. The numbers of index crimes for the county includes estimates for nonreporting agencies to enable the DPS to provide comparable data for 2006.

Culture & the Arts

Dallas area gospel choirs perform with the Dallas Symphony Orchestra. Ricky Moon photo.

Cajuns in Texas

Performing Arts Organizations

Museums

Film and Television

Honored Artists

Religion

Cajuns of Texas: Let the Good Times Roll

By Robert Plocheck

Gumbo and crawfish boils, boudin sausage and steaming pots of étouffée, the rhythmic blend of fiddle and accordion of Cajun music: all these have become part of Texas cuisine and culture through the influence of Cajuns who came to the state from Louisiana.

So many of the Cajuns have settled in the southeastern corner of Texas known as the "Golden Triangle" of Beaumont, Port Arthur and Orange that the area has been referred to as the "Lapland", where Cajun culture overlaps into Texas. The whole state, however, has experienced the influence of this French-based culture. There are annual crawfish or "mudbug" festivals as far west as Odessa and Fredericksburg, which is mostly noted for its German background. Also in the Hill Country, there is an annual Cajun Festival and Gumbo Cookoff on Medina Lake.

Crawfish shells line a table top as couples dance to the music at the annual Cajun Fest in Grand Prairie. Brad Loper photo.

Cajuns are descendants of French colonists of the Maritime Provinces of Canada — Nova Scotia, New Brunswick and Prince Edward Island. In the 1600s and 1700s the area was called Acadia and its people were known in French as Acadien or Acadians. Most of these colonists had emigrated from west-central France beginning in large numbers in 1632.

Dr. Carl A. Brasseaux of the Center for Acadian Studies at the University of Louisiana–Lafayette says, "At least 55 percent — and possibly 70 percent — of Acadia's seventeenth-century immigrants were natives of the Centre-Quest provinces of Poitou, Aunis, Angoumois, and Saintonge, or the province of Anjou, in an adjacent geographical region." Many had close family ties including their extended families, a condition that has been reinforced by the history of persecution and wanderings that the Cajuns have endured.

While several generations lived in eastern Canada there was some intermarriage with the indigenous people, the Mikmaq, so that, like many people in the United States and Mexico, these North Americans acquired some Indian blood, as well.

Explusion

When the British gained final control of this part of Canada in 1713, the Acadian French Catholics tried to remain neutral in conflicts between Britain and France, agreeing to a "conditional" oath of allegiance to Britain that stipulated they not be required to take up arms against France. This attempt did not survive the various changes of British administrations, whose regimes varied from relaxed to strict.

Finally, after the Catholic Acadians refused to take an "unconditional" oath of loyalty to the British Protestant king, a policy of expulsion — a kind of ethnic cleansing — was implemented. It did not help, either, that when British forces took the French Canadian Fort Beausejour, they also captured some 300 Acadian conscripts who had been fighting by the side of the French soldiers.

This evidence of a lack of neutrality was the final straw. The Acadian settlers were forced off their lands by the British governors of Canada beginning in 1755, and were scattered around the world in what is called *Le Grand Derangement*. Some went to the American colonies, some fled to Quebec, and many returned to their ancestral homeland, living in the various port cities of northwestern France. Eventually, many would find their way to south Louisiana, another isolated island of French culture in North America. As American expansion evolved, the Acadian's new English-speaking neighbors' casual pronunciation of "Acadian" was corrupted to "Cadian" and then into "Cajun."

The first Cajuns in Texas arrived by mistake in the spring of 1770. The group of 30 refugees, who were trying to get to Louisiana from Maryland, was on the schooner Britain, which was blown off course, missing the Mississippi River and ending up at Matagorda Bay. Imprisoned by the Spanish authorities as suspected smugglers, they had to do hard labor at Goliad but were released in October and made a trek across East Texas to Natchitoches, La., and then down to Opelousas.

Spain, which had been given authority over Louisiana in 1763 in the Treaty of Paris, provided ships in 1785 to carry some 1,600 Acadians who had taken refuge in Europe to Louisiana, partly to be a buffer of Catholic subjects against Anglo-American expansion. In 1800, there were 3,000 to 4,000 Acadians or Cajuns in south Louisiana.

They did not stay long in the port of New Orleans

but moved to the remote prairies and bayous west of the city, into what would become the 22 civil parishes that now make up Acadiana, a designation proscribed by the Louisiana legislature in 1971, recognizing the uniqueness of the area as home to Cajun culture.

Across the Sabine

By the 1840s the first Cajuns began moving across the Sabine River into Texas, an emigration — always westward — that would ebb and flow into the 20th century. Among these first Cajun settlers was the Hébert family, who began farming along Taylor Bayou in Jefferson County in 1842. Around 1850 the Chaisson family followed.

The first U.S. census in Texas in 1850 found 600 "Franco-Louisianans" between Orange and Houston. Not all these Franco-Louisianans were Cajun, it should be pointed out, and here we encounter the sometimes confusing term "Creole" in Lousiana history (*See accompanying article, Creole and Cajun.*) In fact, probably most of these early Louisianan immigrants were French Creoles.

In the late 19th century, two factors brought an increased movement of Cajuns into Texas. One was the need for workers to cultivate rice in Southeast Texas. Another was the labor force needed on the Southern Pacific Railroad line that ran from the Sabine River to Houston. Many of these Cajun railroad workers settled in Houston where Southern Pacific had its district headquarters.

By the time these immigrations into Texas began, the Cajuns had blended through intermarriage with their German, Spanish, and Anglo neighbors in Louisiana. So, some Cajun families had names such as Martinez, Schexnaider and McGee.

Another impetus for this emigration was the poor economy in Louisiana. As Dr. Brasseaux writes about the Cajun migration in *The French in Texas*, "Because of the extensive devastation wrought by the Union invasions of south-central Louisiana during the Civil War, the region's economy virtually collapsed in the early postbellum period, and perhaps half the area's freeholders were reduced to tenantry."

As more and more Cajuns began living in Jefferson, Orange and neighboring counties of Texas, a Cajun middle class began to emerge. In 1892, Joseph Broussard established the Beaumont Rice Mills, and later, in 1898, he helped to found the Beaumont Irrigation Co.

Twentieth Century

Then there was Spindletop in 1901. The discovery of the massive oilfield in Southeast Texas forever changed the ethnic makeup of the area as Louisiana Cajuns streamed into Texas to work in the burgeoning oil industry. And, this oil industry would be a solid link between Louisiana and Texas: the primary catalyst in bringing the culture of Cajun Louisiana into the homes and offices of Texans, and Texans into Cajun Louisiana as the petroleum industry expanded there.

Into the 1910s, the Cajun presence increased in Southeast Texas, especially in 1915, when a severe hurricane hit the upper Texas coastal area. The destruction in Texas provided immediate work for rebuilding the infrastructure and thus, more Cajuns came to Texas for those jobs. This influx of Cajuns was sustained for another five years as the United States entry into World War I spurred growth in the oil refineries and shipyards in the Golden Triangle.

In the 1920s, a shift by Japanese rice growers in southeast Texas to truck farming provided a need for more Cajun labor, but the next sizeable influx was to come in the 1940s when a larger labor force was required for the industrial expansion during the World War II.

In the postwar period, another industry in which Cajuns had been important – shrimping – brought many to the better fishing grounds off the Texas Gulf Coast.

By the latter part of the 20th century, Cajun professionals and engineers in telecommunications, petroleum and construction began a different kind of migration. For the first time, it was white-collar experts and not laborers who were leaving Louisiana. In fact, during the 1990s, Louisiana had a net loss of population.

Today, there are probably at least 375,000 Cajuns who call Texas home. (*See census data on next page.*)

Language

Cajun French is a mix of Acadian French, standard 19th-century French, Creole and English. It also borrowed words from Spanish, African languages and American Indian languages ("bayou" from Choctaw, for example).

It is a dialect that is fading away, even in Louisi-

Continued on page 545.

Creole and Cajun

Creole is a confusing term, although, in Texas, it has come to refer to "Creoles of Color," those of mixed Afro-Carribbean and French ancestry. The Spanish, who ruled Louisiana from 1763–1801, used the term "*criollo*" for the first generation of colonists to be born in America, and the term evolved over time, in Louisiana, to include both the European or African descendants. So, Creole was used by both mixed-race and white non-Cajuns, especially in New Orleans, and has come to define the city's cuisine and culture.

Over the last two centuries, European French Creoles have intermarried with Cajuns, so that, says *The Encyclopedia of Cajun Culture,* "Many names of French Creole origin, like Soileau, Fontenot and François, are now widely considered Cajun." Thus, the distinction between Louisianans of French descent has became somewhat less so today.

The encyclopedia says that "today Creole is most often used in Acadiana [southwestern Louisiana] to refer to persons of full or mixed African heritage."

(Yet, in New Orleans, many of European French heritage still refer to themselves, their culture and their cuisine as French Creole.)

While the Cajun culture and the culture of the Creoles of color are distinct, each has had a profound impact on the other.

Some food historians insist that red beans and rice, along with any stews with tomatoes, are Creole; dirty rice and étouffée are Cajun. Both groups have their gumbo and jambalaya. But today there has been such a fusion of Creole/Cajun/Louisiana cooking you are likely to find dishes served as part of the other cuisine. – RP

Texas county	1990 census			2000 census	
	French Canadian* (including Cajun)	French (all, including French Canadian/Cajun)	% of total pop.	Acadian/Cajun	French (all, including French Canadian/ Cajun)
Jefferson	39,263	66,446	27.8	2,203	25,830
Orange	15,783	26,483	32.9	1,598	12,202
Liberty	3,488	7,769	14.7	128	3,453
Hardin	3,402	7,685	18.6	346	4,197
Chambers	3,233	5,349	26.6	174	2,160
Jasper	1,949	4,059	13.1	276	1,826
Tyler	771	2,329	14.0	53	1,178
Newton	1,009	1,817	13.4	108	921
Sabine	481	1,162	12.1	18	569
Harris (Houston)	59,345	192,019	6.8	2,619	97,433
Dallas	17,001	88,216	4.8	483	45,323
Tarrant (Ft. Worth)	13,690	67,991	5.8	578	39,539
Bexar (San Antonio)	12,780	51,735	4.4	415	32,142
Travis (Austin)	8,096	34,155	5.9	706	26,794
TEXAS total	**264,986**	**965,448**	**5.7**	**15,276**	**552,959**
Louisiana parish	**1990**			**2000**	
Orleans	13,818	66,927	13.4	826	30,514
Lafayette	99,107	138,041	83.8	5,145	53,689

*In 1990 totals, the bureau included Cajuns with French-Canadians.   Source: adapted from the U.S. Census 2000 and 1990.

French/Cajun Ancestry as Percent of Total Population

The U.S. census bureau does not provide a list on its long form in which respondents check off a selection such as "Cajun."

Instead, the form merely asks, "What is the person's ancestry or ethnic origin?" In 1990 and 2000, a few examples were provided (including French-Canadian on both).

The result of this procedure was that in 2000 in Lafayette Parish in Louisiana, which is called the Capital of Cajun Country, the census estimate was only 5,145 persons of Cajun origin in a civil parish of more than 190,000 people.

More likely, most of the respondents — 53,689 persons — replied "French," (see chart above for 2000) a figure down from 138,041 in 1990.

In fact, throughout the nation in 2000, census respondents were significantly less likely to put an ancestral origin, and the number who simply replied "American" increased by 62 percent from 1990.

Thus, the figures that more closely reflect the ethnic origins are probably the 1990 census estimates, which would be, for Lafayette, 83.8 percent of the population with some French background, many being Cajun.

Applied to Texas counties, this means Orange County has about a third of its population of some French origin, either single origin, primary or secondary. (Each census repondent may enter as many as two ethnic origins.)

Jefferson County (Beaumont-Port Arthur) and Chambers County (Anahuac-Winnie) have over one-quarter of their populations of French origin. That compares to a Texas statewide average of 5.7 percent with some French origin.

Of course, not all with French ancestry are Cajun. But, if even half are, that figure would be nearer a 1980 estimate by Canadian ethnographers of 375,000 Texas Cajuns.

That is far from the mere 15,276 Texas Cajuns estimated in the 2000 census.

The map at left shows the counties, all in the southeastern corner of the state, that according to the 1990 census, have more than 10 percent of their populations of French ancestry, probably the majority of whom are Cajun or Creole.

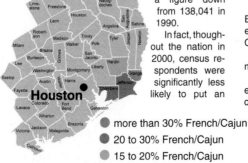

- more than 30% French/Cajun
- 20 to 30% French/Cajun
- 15 to 20% French/Cajun
- more than 10% French/Cajun

Note in the chart that Houston has more Cajuns than New Orleans, which, although it has many French Creoles, is not a Cajun city. – RP

ana where the state legislature banned all French from schools in the 1920s in an attempt to enforce assimilation and the use of English. That policy was abandoned in the 1970s when there was a reversal in sentiment to retain local cultures.

Probably for Texas Cajuns, the exposure to the world outside their communities — in the oilfield, the shipyards and especially service in World War II — had much more to do with diminishing the use of Cajun French.

Even in the Cajun homeland today, few of the recent generations know their ancestral language.

As Shane K. Bernard puts it in *The Cajuns: Americanization of a People,* "Among Cajuns born between 1966 and 1970, for example, only about 12 percent grew up speaking French as their primary language; for those born between 1971 and 1975, the figure dropped to about 8 percent."

According to recent U.S. census data, only about 0.3 Texans speak French of any dialect at home. (See accompanying chart, page 549.)

Music

Music has been an important part of the Cajun culture since their time in Acadia, but it developed into a different style in the Gulf Coast as it blended with the music and instruments of their neighbors.

Although the tragic history of the Cajuns might indicate mournful ballads, instead the melodies are festive, cheerful and upbeat, often played and sung loudly to be heard over a crowded dance floor.

The fiddle was important to the music from the beginning, and later the accordion was picked up from their German neighbors in south Louisiana.

In the 1930s, the strings came to the fore again, as Cajun bands were influenced by the Western swing style so popular in Texas at the time, and which relied heavily on strings. The accordion reemerged as an important part of Cajun music in the 1960s as younger people began to return to the roots of the music.

Ponty Bone and the Squeezetones perform at the Fredericksburg Crawfish Festival. The musician at left plays a frottoir. Debbie Farquhar photo.

There has always been a rapport between Cajun and Texas music.

In a cemetery in Port Arthur, written on a tombstone in French and English is, *"Parrain De La Musique Cajun* — The Godfather of Cajun Music." It is the grave of Harry Choates, who in his lifetime was called "the fiddle king of Cajun swing."

Choates died in an Austin jail in 1951, after being arrested for failure to pay child support. Born in Louisiana in 1922, Choates had come to Port Arthur with his mother in the 1930s and began to play in the dancehalls and taverns of southeast Texas. In 1946, he had a big regional hit with "Jole Blon", a song first recorded by the Breaux family in Louisiana in 1928.

Choates' rewritten version of the song was an even bigger hit in 1947 for Moon (Aubrey Wilson) Mullican, another Texan from southeast Texas.

Mullican, who was called "the king of hillbilly piano players," was born in Polk County but had performed on both sides of the Sabine, including leading the band that backed up Gov. Jimmie Davis in his successful bid for the Louisiana governorship in 1944.

"Jole Blon" was later a national hit for the Grand Ole Opry's Roy Acuff, and has become a mainstay in the repertoire of many a Texas singer from Waylon Jennings to Kenny Rogers, and later for Townes Van Zandt and Jimmy Dale Gilmore. It is almost always sung in Cajun French.

The real breakthrough for Cajun music into popular and country music came not from a Cajun but from an Alabama singer: Hank Williams Sr..

His 1952 hit, "Jambalaya", was based on the melody of a 1946 Cajun hit, "Grand Texas" by Chuck Guillory. Guillory's lyric, *"tu m'as quitté pour t'en aller au Grand Texas,"* is about a departure from Louisiana for "Big Texas." Hank Williams' lyrics were about "me cher amio" Yvonne. Some music historians say Moon Mullican, who was on the Grand Ole Opry at the same time as Hank Williams, co-wrote the lyrics.

When singer Jo Stafford covered "Jambalaya" in 1952, Cajun music was introduced to popular American culture.

As Cajun music evolved throughout the 20th century, drums, electric bass and electric guitars have been included and the triangle, long used to keep tempo, has sometimes been replaced with the *frottoir* or rub-board.

The frottoir, which is hung around the neck, is more closely identified with Zydeco music, the folk music of the Creoles of south Louisiana that has a fast-tempo with a syncopated back beat.

But, Cajun and Zydeco have influenced each other, so that some bands now blend the styles and instruments.

In fact, the frottoir used today was made by a Cajun welder, based on a design of a Creole musician when they both worked at a Port Arthur oil refinery in 1946.

Refinery worker Clifton Chenier, a legend today in Zydeco music, wanted to replace the washboard in his band with a sheet of ribbed metal that did not have the wooden frame along the outside. From his drawing, fellow worker, Willie Landry, a Cajun and fellow

A.J. Judice Jr., front, enjoys a ride with his son, Al III through a bayou near Port Arthur. Richard Michael Pruitt photo.

Louisiana native, made the first frottoir used solely as a musical instrument.

Besides traditional Cajun folk music, another influence on Texas dance halls and songwriters came from a special fusion called "swamp pop", which reached its peak of popularity in the late 1950s and early 1960s.

This blend of Cajun, Creole, rockabilly, rhythm & blues and rock 'n' roll resulted in such hits as "Sea of Love", the 1958 hit by Phil Phillips, a Creole artist from Lake Charles (his real name was John Phillip Baptiste). The songs were noted for their highly emotional lyrics.

Another swamp pop song, "I'm Leaving It Up to You," was a hit for Dale and Grace (Grace Broussard of Ascension Parish).

Their record producer was Huey P. Meaux, whose family, like many Cajuns, had moved across the Sabine River. When he was 12, they settled in Winnie, where he later barbered before getting into the music business in the mid-1950s.

As the Beatles craze shook up the American music scene in 1964, Meaux began producing and promoting San Antonio's Doug Sahm. Meaux told Sahm to grow his hair long, and he renamed Sahm's band the Sir Douglas Quintet to capitalize on the British invasion.

Meaux, writes Joseph Levy on his Vinyl Tourist website, analyzed the Beatle sound and decided their "beat was on the beat, just like the Cajun two-step." Meaux then told Sahm to write a song with such a beat. In 1965, the Sir Douglas Quintet's mix of Cajun, rock 'n' roll and conjunto, "She's About a Mover," became an international hit.

In 1975, San Benito's own Tex-Mex rocker Freddy Fender sought out Meaux, who convinced Fender to record "Before the Next Teardrop Falls." They followed

that hit with a remake of "Wasted Days and Wasted Nights," which, although first recorded in 1959 in the Rio Grande Valley, is still included in swamp pop collections today.

(*The Huey Meaux Papers, 1940-1994*, are now housed in The Center for American History at the University of Texas. Huey Meaux was released from a Texas prison in 2002, where he had been serving a sentence as a convicted sex offender.)

Food

Cajuns live to eat, it is said, and it is their cuisine that has had a profound impact on Texas. Long before the Cajun food craze of the 1980s, when chef Paul Prudhomme turned on the whole country to blackened redfish and other delicacies, Cajuns were introducing Texans to their pots of spicy dishes.

Many of those dishes begin with the "trinity" of aromatics for Cajun cooking, onion, celery and bell pepper. And, there is the ubiquitous roux, a blend of oil or fat and flour, darkened in a pot to shades ranging from blonde to very brown.

Although historically based on provincial French cooking, Cajun cooking — often done by the menfolk — adapted to available ingredients and incorporated various styles from their neighbors, the Germans, Spanish, American Indians and Afro-Carribbeans.

In fact, the word gumbo, comes from *guingombo*, an African word for okra. And, the filé used to season and thicken gumbo was borrowed from the Choctaw Indians who ground the sassafras leaves for their dishes. From the Afro-Carribbeans they adopted the hot peppers, cayenne and sauce piquantes.

The preeminent Cajun ingredient is the crawfish, so much a part of the cuisine it has become the icon of Cajun culture. These "crawdads" or "mudbugs" are a small relative of the lobster and are an example of how the Cajuns adopted the resources they found in southern Louisiana to create hearty, simple dishes, such as gumbo, étouffée (just about anything smothered), and jambalaya (based on the Spanish paella, some say).

And whether incorporated in the dish or as a side, there is almost always rice, which the Cajuns found to grow so easily in the damp climate of the Gulf Coast.

The sausages include *andouille*, made with pork and garlic and smoked, often over pecan wood and sugar cane, and boudin, pork and rice stuffed into a casing; this is *boudin blanc*. *Boudin rouge* is a blood sausage.

There are many other dishes that today are a fusion of the distinctly Cajun with other influences such as Creole cooking and New Orleans specialties.

That process of fusion has continued in Texas, so that among the many Cajun/Creole/Louisiana restaurants in the state, menus include crawfish tamales and crawfish étouffée enchiladas.

Festivals

Bon Ton Roulet, is French for, "Good Times Roll" (as in "Let the good times roll.."), and they do, all over the state of Texas, to Cajun or Cajun-related themes. Some of those include:

Alvin — Crawfest & Shrimp Boil in April.
Austin — Louisiana Swamp Romp and Crawfish Festival in April.
Clear Lake area — Crawfish Festival in April.
Columbus — Rajun Cajun Fest in May.
Comal County, Anhalt Hall — Gumbo Cookoff and Cajun Dance in May (sponsored by San Antonio's De Fa Tras chapter of the Cajun French Music Association).
Conroe — Cajun Catfish Festival in October.
Fredericksburg — Crawfish Festival in May.
Grand Prairie — Cajun Fest in May.
Houston — Bayou City Cajun Fest in April.
Lakehills — Medina Lake Cajun Festival and Great Gumbo Cookoff in September.

Longview — Harvest Festival Crawfish Boil in April.
Odessa — Mudbug Hurricane Party in June.
Orange — Texas Cajun Heritage Festival in May.
Spring — Texas Crawfish & Music Festival in April.
Wimberley — Cypress Creek Crawfish Boil in April.
Winnie — Texas Rice Festival in October.
Various Catholic parishes, in East Texas especially, have seasonal Cajun crawfish boils and festivals.

In addition, a French Louisiana tradition that transcends the Cajun culture, the Mardi Gras, has taken root in Texas.

Galveston stages its version on the Strand in the period preceding Lent. The 10-day celebration of dances, parties and parades has grown to draw an estimated 500,000 revelers.

Port Arthur also has the Mardi Gras of Southeast Texas, a four-day event with floats, street entertainment and food. ☆

Sources

"Acadian to Cajun: History of a Society Built on the Extended Family," Carl A. Brasseaux, Center for Acadian Studies, University of Louisiana–Lafayette, 1999.

The Cajuns: Americanization of a People, by Shane K. Bernard, University Press of Mississippi, Jackson, 2003.

The French in Texas: History, Migration, Culture, François Lagrande, editor, University of Texas Press, Austin, 2003.

Texas Zydeco, by Roger Wood, University of Texas Press, Austin, 2003.

The New Handbook of Texas, various, Texas State Historical Association, 1996.

"The Cajuns: Still Loving Life," by Griffin Smith Jr., *National Geographic*, October 1990.

Encyclopedia of Cajun Culture, online.

"Huey P. Meaux: The Crazy Cajun," by Joe Nick Patoski, *Texas Monthly*, May 1996.

A seafood and sausage gumbo.

Irwin Thompson photo.

TIMELINE — Acadians/Cajuns

1604   First settlers arrive in Acadia, Canada, from west central France.

1621   Scottish settlement in same region, called Nova Scotia.

1631   Treaty of Suza gives area to France and the following year, 1632, first large group of French settlers arrive.

1671   Census counts 340 people in Acadia.

[1699   French begin settlement of Louisiana.]

1704   Another census counts 1,450 in Acadia.

1713   In Treaty of Utrecht, after the (European) War of Spanish Succession, France cedes Acadia to the British.

1713-44 Population of Acadia grows rapidly.

1730   Acadians take an oath of allegiance to the king of England with the condition that they did not have to take up arms against France. British call them "French Neutrals."

[1731   Louisiana population estimated at 8,000.]

1749   British began moving English-speaking settlers to Nova Scotia. Edward Cornwallis (uncle of Charles Cornwallis, who surrendered to George Washington at Yorktown) led founding of Halifax, and, as governor of Nova Scotia, demanded Acadians take an unrestricted oath of allegiance that obliged them to bear arms for the British crown.
Acadians insist on keeping conditional oath. Cornwallis' superiors delay any punitive action against Acadians.

1754   French and Indian War begins (global conflict among colonial powers [France-Britain-Spain], which was called the Seven Years' War in rest of the world.

1755   Deportation, *Le Grand Dérangement*, begins after acting governor Charles Lawrence seeks to force French-speaking population to take the unconditional oath of allegiance to the British king. 6,000 Acadians are exiled in first year to England and British colonies, including Maryland, New York.

1758   Acadians who had fled to Ile St. Jean (Prince Edward Island) and Ile Royale (Cape Breton Island) are rounded up. More than 3,000 sent to France. Two ships sink and hundreds die. Many survivors stay in northwestern France, near St. Malo and Morlaix.

1763   Treaty of Paris settles French and Indian War. French Canada (Quebec) ceded to Britain, but there are treaty guarantees that protect French-speakers from same fate as Acadians. Spain receives Louisiana from France.

1764   First Acadians (20) arrive in Louisiana from New York.

1769   Census counts 14,000 people in Louisiana, the majority slaves.

1770   At Matagorda Bay, a group of Acadian exiles from Maryland, blown off course from mouth of Mississippi, arrive and are imprisoned at Goliad, eventually make their way to Natchitoches, La., then Opelousas.

1785   Spain provides ships to carry 1,600 Acadians from France to Louisiana. Spanish policy sought to provide a buffer zone between British colonies in North America and colonial Mexcio (and Texas).

1800   2,500 to 4,000 Acadians/Cajuns in Louisiana.

1842   Cajuns in Jefferson County on Taylor Bayou. (Hébert family.)

1850   Census indicates a number of arrivals in Orange and Jefferson County from Louisiana. (Chiasson family to Jefferson County). Report says 600 "Franco-Louisianans" between Houston and Orange.

1885   Influx of immigrants from Louisiana into rice-growing areas.

Late 19th Railroad (the Southern Pacific Line) in Southeast Texas employed many Cajuns, and many families of workers settle in Houston.

1892   Joseph Broussard establishes Beaumont Rice Mills.

1898   Broussard cofounds Beaumont Irrigation Co.

1901   Spindletop oil influx brings many Cajun workers.

1910   More significant immigration of Cajun French into Jefferson County.

1915   Hurricane in Southeast Texas brings workers for rebuilding efforts.

1942   War workers take jobs in refineries and shipyards in Texas.

1945   Louisiana shrimpers, looking for better fishing grounds, move to Texas coastal communities.

1990s   Educated workers attracted to telecommunications industry in Texas cities.

Language Spoken in Texas Homes

The following data from the 2000 U.S. census refer to language currently used by respondents at home, either "English only" or a non-English language which is used in addition to English or in place of English. Most respondents who reported speaking a language other than English at home also speak English. Persons who knew languages other than English but did not use them at home, or who only used them elsewhere, were excluded.

Language spoken	Number	Percent
Total Texas population 5 years or older	19,241,518	100.0
Speak only English	13,230,765	68.8
Speak a language other than English	6,010 753	31.2
Spanish	5,195,182	27.0
French (including Cajun, Patois, Creole)	65,778	0.3
Italian	11,158	0.1
Portuguese	9,716	0.1
German	82,117	0.4
Yiddish	905	0.0
Other West Germanic languages	7,288	0.0
Scandinavian languages	6,583	0.0
Russian	11,574	0.1
Serbo-Croatian	6,731	0.0
Polish	9,652	0.1
Other Slavic languages	15,448	0.1
Greek	6,571	0.0
Armenian	1,172	0.0
Persian	17,558	0.1
Gujarati	19,140	0.1
Hindi	20,919	0.1
Urdu	32,978	0.2
Other Indic languages	24,454	0.1
Other Indo-European languages	8,277	0.0
Chinese	91,500	0.5
Japanese	14,701	0.1
Korean	38,451	0.2
Mon-Khmer, Cambodian	7,870	0.0
Miao, Hmong	180	0.0
Thai	7,282	0.0
Laotian	10,378	0.1
Vietnamese	122,517	0.6
Other Asian languages	32,780	0.2
Tagalog [of Philippines]	39,988	0.2
Other Pacific Island languages	8,683	0.0
Arabic	32,909	0.2
Hebrew	4,622	0.0
African languages	36,087	0.2
Hungarian	2,140	0.0
Navajo	595	0.0
Other Native American languages	3,603	0.0
Other and unspecified languages	3,266	0.0

Source: U.S. Census 2000.

State Cultural Agencies Assist the Arts

Source: Principally, the Texas Commission on the Arts, along with other state cultural agencies.

Culture in Texas, as in any market, is a mixture of activity generated by both the commercial and the nonprofit sectors.

The commercial sector encompasses Texas-based profit-making businesses including commercial recording artists, nightclubs, record companies, private galleries, assorted boutiques that carry fine art collectibles and private dance and music halls.

Texas also has extensive cultural resources offered by nonprofit organizations that are engaged in charitable, educational and/or humanitarian activities.

The Texas Legislature has authorized five state agencies to administer cultural services and funds for the public good. The agencies are:

Texas Commission on the Arts, Box 13406, Austin (78711); Texas Film Commission, Box 13246, Austin (78711); Texas Historical Commission, Box 12276, Austin (78711); Texas State Library and Archives Commission, Box 12927, Austin (78711); and the State Preservation Board, Box 13286, Austin (78711).

Although not a state agency, another organization that provides cultural services to the citizens of Texas is Humanities Texas, 1410 Rio Grande, Austin 78701.

The Texas Commission on the Arts was established in 1965 to develop a receptive climate for the arts through the conservation and advancement of Texas' rich and diverse arts and cultural industries.

The Texas Commission on the Arts' primary goals are:
• provide grants for the arts and cultural industries in Texas.
• provide the financial, human, and technical resources necessary to ensure viable arts and cultural communities
• promote widespread attendance at arts and cultural performances and exhibitions in Texas.
• ensure access to arts in Texas through marketing, fund raising, and cultural tourism

The arts commission is responsible for several initiatives including:
• Arts Education – programs that serve the curricular and training needs of the state's school districts, private schools, and home schools.
• Technology – a full service network providing a one-stop location for the arts and cultural industry of Texas.
• Marketing and Public Relations – marketing and fund raising expertise to generate funds for agency operations and increase visibility of the arts in Texas.
• Cultural Tourism – programs that develop and promote tourism destinations featuring the arts.

Additional information on programs and services is available on the Texas Commission on the Arts' Web site at www.arts.state.tx.us or by calling (800) 252-9415 or (512) 463-5535. ☆

First grader Phil Jacunski plays with a violin at an 'instrument petting zoo' preview for the Plano Symphony Orchestra. Matt Nager photo.

Texas Performing Arts Organizations

Below are Internet links, listed by city, to Web sites of Texas performing arts organizations — theatre, dance and music. The information is from the Texas Commission on the Arts.

Abilene
Abilene Philharmonic
www.abilenephilharmonic.org/
Classical Chorus of Abilene
www.classicalchorus.org/
Paramount Theatre
www.paramount-abilene.org/
Addison
Water Tower Theatre
www.watertowertheatre.org/
Allen
Allen Philharmonic Symphony
www.allenphilharmonic.com/

Amarillo
Amarillo Boy Choir
www.boychoirs.org/amarillo/
Amarillo Little Theatre
www.amarillolittletheatre.org/
Amarillo Opera
www.amarilloopera.org/
Amarillo Symphony
www.amarillosymphony.org/
Chamber Music Amarillo
www.chambermusicamarillo.org/
Lone Star Ballet
www.lonestarballet.org/

Arlington
Creative Arts Theatre/School
www.creativearts.org/
Theatre Arlington
www.theatrearlington.org/

Athens
Henderson County Performing Arts Center
www.hcpac.org/index_files/Page772.html
Austin
A. Mozart Fest
www.amozartfest.org
Austin Chamber Music Center
www.austinchambermusic.org/
Austin Circle of Theaters
www.acotonline.org/Pages/Home.html
Austin Civic Orchestra
www.austincivicorchestra.org/
Austin Classical Guitar Society
www.austinclassicalguitar.org
Austin Lyric Opera
www.austinlyricopera.org

Austin Symphonic Band
www.asband.org/
Austin Symphony Orchestra
www.austinsymphony.org/
Aztlan Dance Company
www.aztlandance.com/
Ballet Austin
www.balletaustin.org/
Ballet East Dance Theatre
www.balleteast.org/
Blue Lapis Light
www.bluelapislight.org/
Capital City Men's Chorus
www.io.com/~ccmcaus/
Chorus Austin
www.chorusaustin.org/
Conspirare Choir
www.conspirare.org/
Creative Opportunity Orchestra
www.creop.org/
Forklift Danceworks
www.forkliftdanceworks.org/
Gilbert and Sullivan Society
www.gilbertsullivan.org/
Hyde Park Theatre
hydeparktheatre.org/
Johnson/Long Dance Company
www.jldc.org/index.htm
Kathy Dunn Hamrick Dance Company
www.kdhdance.com/
One World Theatre
www.oneworldtheatre.org/
Paramount Theater/State Theater
www.austintheatre.org/
Puerto Rican Folkloric Dance
www.prfdance.org/
Roy Lozano Ballet Folklorico of Texas
www.rlbft.org/
Rude Mechanicals Theatre Collective
www.rudemechs.com/
Salvage Vanguard Theater
www.salvagevanguard.org/
Second Youth Family Theatre
www.secondyouth.com/
Sharir+Bustamante Danceworks
www.sbdanceworks.org/
Tapestry Dance Company
www.tapestry.org/
Teatro Humanidad
www.teatrohumanidad.com/
University of Texas Performing Arts
Center
www.utpac.org/
Vortex Theatre
www.vortexrep.org/
Zachary Scott Theatre Center
www.zachscott.com/

Beaumont
Symphony of Southeast Texas
www.sost.org/

Big Spring
Big Spring Symphony
www.bigspringsymphony.com/

Boerne
Boerne Community Theatre
www.boernetheatre.org/

Bonham
Red River Theatre Company
www.redrivertheatre.com/

Brenham
Unity Theatre Company
www.unitybrenham.org/

Bryan-College Station
Brazos Valley Chorale
www.bvchorale.org/
Brazos Valley Symphony Orchestra
www.bvso.org/
Brazos Valley Troupe
www.bvtroupe.com/
The Theatre Company
www.thetheatrecompany.com/

Carrollton
Texas Chamber Orchestra
wwoww.com/csm/

Claude
Armstrong County Theater
www.searchtexas.com/gem-theatre/

Conroe
Crighton Players
www.crightonplayers.org/

Coppell
Coppell Community Theatre
www.theatrecoppell.com/

Corpus Christi
Corpus Christi Ballet
www.corpuschristiballet.com/
Corpus Christi Symphony Orchestra
www.ccsymphony.org/
Fryderyk Chopin Society of Texas
www.fryderykchopinsocietyoftexas.
org/
Harbor Playhouse
www.harborplayhouse.com/

Corsicana
Palace Theater
www.corsicanapalace.com/

Dalhart
La Rita Performing Arts Theatre
www.larita.org/
Anita Martinez Ballet Folklorico
www.anmbf.org/

Dallas
Beckles Dancing Company
www.becklesdancingcompany.org/
Cara Mia Theatre
www.caramiatheatre.net/
Dallas Bach Society
www.dallasbach.org/
Dallas Black Dance Theatre
www.dbdt.com/
Dallas Chamber Music Society
dallaschambermusic.org/
Dallas Chamber Orchestra
www.dallaschamberorchestra.org/
Dallas Children's Theater
www.dct.org/
Dallas Hub Theater
www.dallashubtheater.org/
Dallas Opera
www.dallasopera.org/
Dallas Theater Center
www.dallastheatercenter.org/
Dallas Wind Symphony
www.dws.org/
Fine Arts Chamber Players
www.fineartschamberplayers.org/
Greater Dallas Youth Orchestra
www.gdyo.org/
Kitchen Dog Theater
www.kitchendogtheater.org/

Maharlika Dancers
www.geocities.com/maharlika_
dancers/
Metropolitan Winds
www.metropolitanwinds.org/
Orchestra of New Spain
www.orchestraofnewspain.org/
Pocket Sandwich Theatre
www.dallas.net/~pst/
Teatro Dallas
www.teatrodallas.com/
Teco Theatrical Productions
www.tecotheater.org/
Texas Ballet Theatre
www.texasballettheater.org/
Theatre Three
www.theatre3dallas.com/
Turtle Creek Chorale
www.turtlecreek.org/
Undermain Theatre
www.undermain.com/
Women's Chorus of Dallas
www.twcd.org/

Del Rio
The Upstagers
upstagers.org/

Denton
Campus Theatre
www.campustheatre.com/

El Paso
Aardvark Theatre
www.goaardvark.com/
El Paso Opera
www.epopera.org/
El Paso Performing Arts Center
www.elpasocvb.com/cpac_index.
sstg
El Paso Playhouse
www.elpasoplayhouse.org/
El Paso Pro-Musica
www.eppm.org/
El Paso Symphony Orchestra
www.epso.org/

Flower Mound
Expressions Repertory Theatre
www.fmpat.org/

Fort Worth
Ballet Concerto
balletconcerto.com/
Bass Performance Hall
www.basshall.com/indexa.html
Bruce Wood Dance Company
www.brucedance.org/
Casa Mañana
www.casamanana.org/
Circle Theatre
www.circletheatre.com/
Contemporary Dance/Fort Worth
www.cdfw.org/
Fort Worth Opera
www.fwopera.org/
Fort Worth Symphony
www.fwsymphony.org/
Hip Pocket Theatre
www.hippocket.org/
Jubilee Theatre
www.jubileetheatre.org/
Schola Cantorum
www.scholacantorum-tx.com
Texas Ballet Theatre
www.texasballettheater.org/

Concert fans fill Bass Hall in Fort Worth. Ricky Moon photo.

Texas Boys Choir
www.texasboyschoir.org/
Texas Camerata
www.musichost.com/txcam/
Van Cliburn Foundation
www.cliburn.org/

Fredericksburg
Fredericksburg Theater Company
www.fredericksburgtheater.org/

Frisco
Frisco Community Theatre
www.friscocommunitytheatre.com/

Gainesville
Butterfield Stage Players Theatre
www.butterfieldstage.org/

Galveston
Galveston Symphony Orchestra
www.galvestonsymphony.org/
The Grand 1984 Opera House
www.thegrand.com/

Garland
Garland Civic Theatre
www.garlandcivictheatre.org/
Garland Symphony Orchestra
www.garlandsymphony.org/

Granbury
Granbury Opera House
www.granburyoperahouse.org/

Grand Prairie
Grand Prairie Arts Council
www.artsgp.com/

Harlingen
Fryderyk Chopin Society of Texas
www.fryderykchopinsocietyoftexas.
org/

Houston
Alley Theatre
www.alleytheatre.org/alley/Default_
EN.asp
Applause Theatre Company
www.applausetheatre.com/
Bayou City Performing Arts
www.gmch.org/
Bere'sheet Ballet

www.beresheetballet.com/
Bobbindoctrin Puppet Theatre
www.bobbindoctrin.org/
City Dance Company
www.houstoncitydance.com/
De Camera
dacamera.com/
Dominic Walsh Dance Theater
www.dwdt.org/
Express Children's Theatre
www.expresstheatre.com/
Fly Dance Company
www.flydance.com/
Gilbert and Sullivan Society
www.gilbertandsullivan.net/
Houston Ballet
www.houstonballet.org/
Houston Chamber Choir
www.houstonchamberchoir.org/
Houston Children's Chorus
www.houstonchildren.org/
Houston Civic Symphony
www.civicsymphony.org/
Houston Early Music
www.houstonearlymusic.org/
Houston Grand Opera
www.houstongrandopera.com/
Houston Metropolitan Dance
Company
www.houstonmetdance.com/
Houston Repertoire Ballet
www.hrbdance.org/
Houston Symphony
www.houstonsymphony.org/
Illuminations Theatre with the Deaf
www.illuminationstheatre.org/
Infernal Bridegroom Productions
www.infernalbridegroom.com/
Kuumba House
www.kuumbahouse.org/
Main Street Theater
www.mainstreettheater.com/
Mercury Baroque Ensemble
www.mercurybaroque.org/
Opera in the Heights
www.operaintheheights.org/
Samskriti Indian Performing Arts
www.samskritihouston.org/

Sandra Organ Dance Company
www.organdance.org/
Several Dancers Core
www.severaldancerscore.org/
Stages Repertory Theatre
www.stagestheatre.com/
Suchu Dance
www.suchudance.org/
The Houston Sinfonietta
www.houstonsinfonietta.org/
Theatre Under the Stars
www.tuts.org/

Ingram
Hill Country Arts Foundation
www.hcaf.com/

Irving
Irving Community Theater
www.irvingtheatre.org/
Las Colinas Symphony
Orchestra
www.lascolinassymphony.org/
New Philharmonic Orchestra
of Irving
home.earthlink.net/~youngj1/npoi.
htm

Kilgore
Texas Shakespeare Festival
www.texaasshakespeare.com

Killeen
Vive Les Arts
www.vlatheatre.com/

Lockhart
Baker Theater
www.bakertheater.org/
Gaslight Theater
www.gaslighttheater.com/

Longview
Longview Symphony
www.longviewsymphony.org/

Lubbock
Ballet Lubbock
www.balletlubbock.org/
Lubbock Symphony Orchestra
www.lubbocksymphony.org/

Marble Falls
Hill Country Community Theatre
www.hcct.org/

Marfa
Marfa Theatre
www.themarfatheatre.org/

Marshall
Marshall Symphony
www.marshall-chamber.com/pages/
symphony.php

McAllen
South Texas Symphony
www.valleyorchestra.org/

Mesquite
Mesquite Symphony Orchestra
www.mesquitesymphony.org

Midland
Midland Community Threatre
www.mctmidland.org/
Midland-Odessa Symphony & Chorale
www.mosc.org/

Mount Pleasant
Whatley Center for Performing Arts
www.ntcc.edu/Whatley/index.htm

Nassau Bay
Clear Lake Symphony Orchestra
nassaubay.com/clsymphony.htm

New Braunfels
Mid-Texas Symphony
www.mtsymphony.org/

Odessa
Globe of the Great Southwest
www.globesw.org/
Midland-Odessa Symphony & Chorale
www.mosc.org/

Orange
Lutcher Theater
www.lutcher.org/

Pasadena
Pasadena Little Theatre
web.wt.net/~plth/

Pampa
Community Center for the Arts
createabeat.org/

Plano
Chamberlain Ballet Company
www.chamberlainperformingarts.
com/
Plano Civic Chorus
www.planocivicchorus.org/
Plano Symphony Orchestra
www.planosymphony.org/
Classics Theatre and Art for Children
www.classicsplano.org/
The Living Opera
www.thelivingopera.org/
Younger Generation Chorus
www.youngergeneration.org/

Richardson
Chamber Music International
www.chambermusicinternational.
org/
Richardson Symphony
www.richardsonsymphony.org/
Richardson Theatre Centre
www.richardsontheatrecentre.com/
Tuzer Ballet

www.tuzerballet.com/

Rockwall
Rockwall Community Playhouse
www.rockwallcommunityplayhouse.
org/

Round Rock
Sam Bass Community Theatre
www.sambasstheatre.org/

Round Top
James Dick Foundation
www.festivalhill.org/

San Angelo
Angelo Civic Theatre
www.angelocivictheatre.com/
San Angelo Symphony
www.sanangelosymphony.org/

San Antonio
Alamo City Men's Chorale
www.imagen-design.com/acmc/
default.asp
Ballet San Antonio
www.balletsanantonio.org/
Josephine Theatrical Company
www.josephinetheatre.org/
Magik Children's Theatre
www.magiktheatre.org/
San Antonio Symphony
www.sasymphony.org/
San Antonio Theater Coalition
www.satheatre.com/
San Pedro Playhouse
www.sanpedroplayhouse.com/
Texas Bach Choir
www.texasbachchoir.org/
Texas Photographic Society
www.texasphoto.org/
Youth Orchestras of San Antonio
www.yosa.org/

Seguin
Mid-Texas Symphony
www.mtsymphony.org/

Southlake
Southlake Community Band
www.southlakeband.com/

Stephenville
Cross Timbers Fine Arts Council
crosstimbersarts.org/

Sugar Land
Fort Bend Symphony Orchestra
www.fbso.org/
Fort Bend Theater
www.fortbendtheatre.com/

Temple
Temple Symphony Orchestra
www.templesymphony.org/

Terrell
Kaufman County Civic Theatre
www.kcct.org/

Texarkana
Perot Theatre
www.trahc.org/perot.htm

The Woodlands
Woodlands Center for the
Performing Arts
www.woodlandscenter.org/

Tyler
Ballet Tyler
www.ballettyler.org/
East Texas Symphony Orchestra
www.etso.org/
Tyler Civic Theatre Center
www.tylercivictheatre.com/

Victoria
Victoria Ballet Theatre
www.victoriaballettheatre.com/
Victoria Symphony
www.victoriasymphony.com/

Waco
Waco Hippodrome
www.wacohippodrome.org/
Waco Symphony Orchestra
www.wacosymphony.com/

Webster
Bay Area Houston Ballet & Theatre
www.bahbt.org/

Wichita Falls
Backdoor Theatre
www.backdoortheatre.org/

Wimberley
EmilyAnn Theatre
www.emilyann.org/

Texas
Texas Living History Association
www.texanalivinghistory.org/ ☆

Public Libraries in Texas

The following information was furnished by the Library Development Division of the Texas State Library, Austin.

Texas public libraries continue to strive to meet the education and information needs of Texans by providing library services of high quality with oftentimes-limited resources.

Each year, services provided by public libraries to the citizens of Texas increase, with more visits to public libraries and higher attendance in library programs.

The challenges facing the public libraries in Texas are many and varied. The costs for providing electronic and on-line sources, in addition to traditional library services, are growing faster than library budgets.

Urban libraries are trying to serve growing populations, while libraries in rural areas are trying to serve remote populations and provide distance learning where possible.

National rankings of public libraries are published by the National Center for Education Statistics. These rankings may be found at:

http://nces.ed.gov/globallocator.

When comparing Texas statistics to those nationally, Texas continues to rank below most of the other states in most categories, with the exception of Reference Transactions and Public Use Internet Terminals.

Complete statistical information on public libraries is available on the Texas State Library's Web page at:

www.tsl.state.tx.us.

Many Texas public libraries have established pages on the Internet. You can find a list of Web addresses at:

www.tsl.state.tx.us/texshare/pl/texlibs.html. ☆

Texas Museums of Art, Science, History

Listed below are links to the Web pages of Texas museums. Where required some have indication of the area of emphasis of the exhibits.

Abilene
Frontier Texas! (History)
www.frontiertexas.com
Grace Museum (Art, History)
www.thegracemuseum.org
National Center for Children's Illustrated Literature
www.nccil.org

Addison
Cavanaugh Flight Museum
www.cavanaughflightmuseum.com/

Albany
Old Jail Art Center
www.theoldjailartcenter.org/

Alpine
Museum of the Big Bend (History)
www.sulross.edu/~museum/

Amarillo
Amarillo Museum of Art
www.amarilloart.org/
American Quarter Horse Heritage Center & Museum
www.aqha.com/foundation/museum/
Don Harrington Discovery Center (Science, Children's)
www.dhdc.org/
Texas Pharmacy Museum
www.ttuhsc.edu/sop/prospective/visitors/museum.aspx

Angleton
Brazoria County Historical Museum
www.bchm.org/

Arlington
Legends of the Game Baseball Museum
www.rangers.mlb.com/NASApp/mlb/tex/ballpark/tex_ballpark_museum.jsp

Austin
Austin Children's Museum
www.austinkids.org/
Austin Museum of Art
www.amoa.org/
Bob Bullock Texas State History Museum
www.thestoryoftexas.com/
Capitol Visitors Center (Historical)
www.tspb.state.tx.us/CVC/home/home.html
Elisabet Ney Museum (Art)
www.ci.austin.tx.us/elisabetney/html/main.html
French Legation Museum (History)
www.frenchlegationmuseum.org/
Harry Ransom Humanities Research Center (History, Literature)
www.hrc.utexas.edu/
Jack S. Blanton Museum of Art
www.blantonmuseum.org/

Jacob Fontaine Religious Museum
www.rootsweb.com/~txjfrm/
Jourdan-Bachman Pioneer Farms
www.heritagesocietyaustin.org/pioneerfarm.html
Lady Bird Johnson Wildflower Center
www.wildflower.org/
Lyndon B. Johnson Library
www.lbjlib.utexas.edu/
Mexic-Arte Museum (Art)
www.mexic-artemuseum.org/
O. Henry Museum (History)
www.ci.austin.tx.us/parks/ohenry.htm
Texas Memorial Museum (History, Natural History)
www.tmm.utexas.edu/
Texas Military Forces Museum
www.texasmilitaryforcesmuseum.org/
Texas Music Museum
www.texasmusicmuseum.org
Umlauf Sculpture Garden & Museum
www.umlaufsculpture.org
Wild Basin Wilderness Preserve
www.wildbasin.org/

Bay City
Matagorda County Museum
www.matagordacountymuseum.org/

Beaumont
Art Museum of Southeast Texas
www.amset.org/
Edison Museum (Science)
www.edisonmuseum.org/
Fire Museum of Texas
www.firemuseumoftexas.org/
McFaddin-Ward House (History)
www.mcfaddin-ward.org/
Spindletop/Gladys City Boomtown Museum (History)
www.spindletop.org/
Texas Energy Museum (History)
www.texasenergymuseum.org

Big Spring
Heritage of Big Spring
www.bigspringmuseum.com/

Bonham
Sam Rayburn Library/Museum
www.cah.utexas.edu/museums/rayburn.php

The Texas State Aquarium in Corpus Christi. Robert Plocheck photo.

Brownsville
Brownsville Museum of Fine Art
www.brownsvillemfa.org
Historic Brownsville Museum
www.brownsvillemuseum.org

Brownwood
Brown County Museum of History
www.browncountyhistory.org/
bcmoh.html

Bryan
Brazos Valley Museum of Natural
History
bvmuseum.myriad.net/

Buffalo Gap
Buffalo Gap Historic Village
www.mcwhiney.org/buffgap/
bghome.html

Burton
Burton Cotton Gin and Museum
(Historical)
www.cottonginmuseum.org/

Canadian
River Valley Pioneer Museum
www.rivervalleymuseum.org/

Canyon
Panhandle-Plains Historical Museum
www.panhandleplains.org

Carthage
Texas Country Music Hall of Fame
& Tex Ritter Museum
www.carthagetexas.com/tcmhof/
index.htm

Clarendon
Saints' Roost Museum (Historical)
www.saintsroost.org

Clifton
Bosque Museum (History)
www.bosquemuseum.org/

College Station
George Bush Presidential Library
bushlibrary.tamu.edu/
J. Wayne Stark University Center
Galleries
stark.tamu.edu/
Virtual Museum of Nautical
Archaeology
ina.tamu.edu/vm.htm

Conroe
Heritage Museum of Montgomery
County
www.heritagemuseum.us/

Corpus Christi
Art Museum of South Texas
www.stia.org/
Corpus Christi Museum of Science
and History
www.ccmuseum.com/museum/
index.cfm
Texas State Aquarium
www.texasstateaquarium.org/
Texas State Museum of Asian
Cultures
www.asianculturesmuseum.org/
USS Lexington Museum
www.usslexington.com/

Corsicana
Pearce Western Art/Civil War Museum
www.pearcecollections.us/

Cotulla
Brush Country Historical Museum

historicdistrict.com/museum/

Dalhart
XIT Museum (Historical)
www.xitmuseum.com/

Dallas
African American Museum
www.aamdallas.org/
Age of Steam Railroad Museum
www.dallasrailwaymuseum.com
Dallas Historical Society (Fair Park)
www.dallashistory.org/
Dallas Museum of Art
www.dm-art.org/
Dallas Museum of Natural History
www.natureandscience.org
Frontiers of Flight Museum
flightmuseum.com/
International Museum of Cultures
www.internationalmuseum
ofcultures.org/
Meadows Museum (Art)
www.meadowsmuseumdallas.
org/index_main.htm
Old City Park/Dallas Heritage Village
www.oldcitypark.org/
The Sixth Floor Museum (History)
www.jfk.org/

Del Rio
Whitehead Memorial Museum
whitehead-museum.com

Denison
Red River Railroad Museum
www.redriverrailmuseum.org

Denton
Courthouse-on-the-Square Museum
(Historical)
dentoncounty.com/dept/main.
asp?Dept=72
University of North Texas Art Galleries
Gallery.unt.edu/
Denton County Historical Museum
www.dentoncountyhistorical
museum.com

Dublin
Dr Pepper Bottling Company Museum
www.dublindrpepper.com/

Edgewood
Edgewood Heritage Park and
Historical Village
www.vzinet.com/heritage/

Edinburg
Museum of South Texas History
www.mosthistory.org/

El Campo
El Campo Museum of Natural History
www.elcampomuseum.com/

El Paso
Centennial Museum/Chihuahuan
Desert Gardens
www.museum.utep.edu/
El Paso Museum of Art
www.elpasoartmuseum.org/

Fort Davis
Chihuahuan Desert Research
Institute and Visitor Center
www.cdri.org/

Fort Stockton
Annie Riggs Museum (Historical)
www.tourtexas.com/fortstockton/ft
stockriggs.html

Fort Worth
Amon Carter Museum (Art)
www.cartermuseum.org/
Cattle Raisers Museum
www.cattleraisersmuseum.org/
Fort Worth Museum of Science
and History
www.fwmuseum.org/
Kimbell Art Museum
www.kimbellart.org/
Log Cabin Village (Historical)
www.logcabinvillage.org
Modern Art Museum of Fort Worth
www.mamfw.org/
National Cowgirl Museum
and Hall of Fame
www.cowgirl.net/
Sid Richardson Collection
of Western Art
www.sidrmuseum.org/
Texas Civil War Museum
www.texascivilwarmuseum.com/

Fredericksburg
Gillespie County Historical Society
www.pioneermuseum.com/
National Museum of the Pacific War
www.nimitz-museum.org/

Galveston
Lone Star Flight Museum
www.lsfm.org
Offshore Energy Center/Ocean Star
(Science, Industry)
www.oceanstaroec.com/
Texas Seaport Museum and Tallship
"Elissa"
www.tsm-elissa.org/

Gilmer
Flight of the Phoenix Aviation
Museum
www.flightofthephoenix.org/

Greenville
Audie Murphy/American Cotton
Museum
www.cottonmuseum.com/

Henderson
The Depot Museum (Historical)
www.depotmuseum.com/

Houston
Blaffer Gallery, University of Houston
www.hfac.uh.edu/blaffer/
Children's Museum of Houston
www.cmhouston.org/
Contemporary Arts Museum
www.camh.org/
Houston Center for Comtemporary
Craft
www.crafthouston.org/default.
asp?ID=1
Houston Center for Photography
www.hcponline.org/
Houston Fire Museum (History)
www.houstonfiremuseum.org/
Houston Museum of Natural Science
www.hmns.org/
Lawndale Art Center
www.lawndaleartcenter.org/
The Menil Collection (Art)
www.menil.org/
Museum of Fine Arts
mfah.org/
Museum of Health and

Medical Science
www.mhms.org/
Museum of Printing History
www.printingmuseum.org/
Rice University Art Gallery
www.ricegallery.org/
San Jacinto Museum of History
www.sanjacinto-museum.org/
Sarah Campbell Blaffer (Art)
www.rice.edu/projects/Blaffer/
Space Center Houston
www.spacecenter.org/

Huntsville
Sam Houston Memorial Museum
www.shsu.edu/~smm_www/
Texas Prison Museum
www.txprisonmuseum.org/

Kerrville
Museum of Western Art
www.museumofwesternart.org/

Kilgore
East Texas Oil Museum
www.easttexasoilmuseum.com/

Lake Jackson
Lake Jackson Historical Museum
www.lakejacksonmuseum.org/

La Porte
San Jacinto Monument and Museum
www.sanjacinto-museum.org/

Laredo
Republic of the Rio Grande Museum
www.webbheritage.org/riogrande
history.htm
Texas A&M International University
Planetarium
www.tamiu.edu/coas/planetarium/

League City
West Bay Common School
Children's Museum (Historical)
www.oneroomschoolhouse.org/

Longview
Longview Museum of Fine Arts
www.lmfa.org/

Lubbock
American Museum of Agriculture
www.agriculturehistory.org/
Buddy Holly Center (Historical)
www.buddyhollycenter.org/
Museum of Texas Tech University
(Art, Humanities, Science)
www.depts.ttu.edu/museumttu/
National Ranching Heritage Center
www.depts.ttu.edu/ranchhc/home.
htm
Science Spectrum
www.sciencespectrum.com/

Lufkin
Texas Forestry Museum
www.treetexas.com/

Marfa
The Chinati Foundation (Art)
www.chinati.org/

Marshall
Harrison County Historical Museum
txgenes.com/TXHarrison/
NewHome.htm
Michelson Museum of Art
www.michelsonmuseum.org/

McAllen
International Museum of Art & Science
www.imasonline.org/

McKinney
Heard Natural Science Museum
www.heardmuseum.org/

Midland
American Airpower Heritage
Museum/Commerative Air Force
www.airpowermuseum.org/
Museum of the Southwest
(Art, Science, Children's)
www.museumsw.org/
Petroleum Museum
www.petroleummuseum.org/

Mobeetie
Old Mobeetie Texas Association
www.mobeetie.com/

New Braunfels
New Braunfels Sophienburg
Museum (History)
www.sophienburg.org/

Odessa
Ellen Noel Art Museum
www.noelartmuseum.org/

Orange
Stark Museum of Art
www.starkmuseum.org/

Panhandle
Carson County Square House
Museum
www.squarehousemuseum.org/

Plano
Heritage Farmstead Museum
www.heritagefarmstead.org/

Port Arthur
Museum of the Gulf Coast
(Historical)
museum.lamarpa.edu/

Port Lavaca
Calhoun County Museum (Historical)
www.calhouncountymuseum.org/

Richmond
George Ranch Historical Park
www.georgeranch.org/

Rockport
Texas Maritime Museum
www.texasmaritimemuseum.org/

Round Top
Henkel Square (History)
www.texaspioneerarts.org/
henkel_square.html
Winedale Historical Center
www.cah.utexas.edu/museums/
winedale.php

San Angelo
San Angelo Museum of Fine Arts
and Children's Art Museum
www.samfa.org/

San Antonio
The Alamo
www.thealamo.org/
Hertzberg Circus Collection/Museum
www.sat.lib.tx.us/Hertzberg/hzmain.
html
Institute of Texan Cultures
www.texancultures.utsa.edu/public/
index.html
Magic Lantern Castle Museum
www.magiclanterns.org/
Museo Alameda
www.thealameda.org
The McNay Art Museum
www.mcnayart.org/

San Antonio Art League Museum
www.saalm.org/
San Antonio Museum of Art
www.samuseum.org/main/
Witte Museum (Science, Historical)
www.wittemuseum.org/

San Marcos
Southwestern Writers Collection and
Wittliff Gallery of Southwestern
& Mexican Photography
www.library.txstate.edu/swwc/

Sarita
Kenedy Ranch Museum of
South Texas
www.kenedymuseum.org/

Serbin
Texas Wendish Heritage Museum
www.wendish.concordia.edu

Sherman
Red River Historical Museum
hosting.texoma.net/rrhms/

Sulphur Springs
Southwest Dairy Center/Museum
www.southwestdairyfarmers.com/

Teague
The B-RI Railroad Museum
www.therailroadmuseum.com/

Temple
Railroad and Heritage Museum
www.rrhm.org/

Texarkana
Museum of Regional History
www.texarkanamuseums.org/
texarkana_historical_museum.htm

Thurber
W.K. Gordon Center for Industrial
History of Texas
www.tarleton.edu%7Egordoncenter/

Tyler
Discovery Science Place
www.discoveryscienceplace.com/
Smith County Historical Museum
www.smithcountyhistory.org/
Museum.htm
Tyler Museum of Art
www.tylermuseum.org/

Victoria
Museum of the Coastal Bend
(Historical)
www.museumofthecoastalbend.org/

Waco
Dr Pepper Museum (History)
www.drpeppermuseum.com/
Mayborn Museum Complex
(History, Science)
www.baylor.edu/mayborn/
Texas Ranger Hall of Fame/ Museum
www.texasranger.org/
Texas Sports Hall of Fame
www.tshof.org/

Washington
Star of the Republic Museum
(Historical)
www.starmuseum.org/

White Settlement
White Settlement Historical Museum
www.wsmuseum.com/

Wichita Falls
Kell House Museum (History)
www.wichitaheritage.org/
kellhouse.html ☆

Film and Television Work in Texas

Source: Texas Film Commission

For almost a century, Texas has been one of the nation's top film-making states, after California and New York.

More than 1,300 projects have been made in Texas since 1910, including **Wings**, the first film to win an Academy Award for Best Picture, which was made in San Antonio in 1927.

Texas' attractions to filmmakers are its diverse locations, abundant sunshine and moderate winter weather, and a variety of support services.

The economic benefits of hosting on-location filming over the past decade are estimated at more than $2.79 billion.

Besides salaries paid to locally hired technicians and actors, as well as fees paid to location owners, the production companies do business with hotels, car rental agencies, lumberyards, restaurants, grocery stores, utilities, office furniture suppliers, gas stations, security services, florists and more.

All types of projects come to Texas besides feature films, including television specials, commercials, corporate films and game videos. Many projects made in Texas originate in California studios, but Texas is also the home of many independent filmmakers who make films outside the studio system.

Some films and television shows made in Texas have become icons.

Giant, John Wayne's **The Alamo**, and the long-running TV series **Dallas** all made their mark on the world's perception of Texas and continue to draw tourists to their film locations.

The Texas Film Commission, a division of the Office of the Governor, markets to Hollywood Texas' locations, support services and workforce. The commission's free services include location research, employment referrals, red-tape-cutting, and information on laws, weather, travel and other topics affecting filmmakers.

The on-line Texas Production Manual includes more than 1,200 individuals and businesses serving every facet of the film industry. ☆

The set used in John Wayne's The Alamo *near Brackettville. Robert Plocheck photo*

Regional Commissions

Amarillo Film Office
  1000 S. Polk, Amarillo 79101
  (806) 374-1497
  amarillofilm.org
Austin Film Office
  301 Congress Ave. Ste. 200
  Austin 78701, (800) 926-2282
  austintexas.org
Brownsville Border Film Comm.
  P.O. Box 911, City Hall
  Brownsville 78520, (956) 548-6176
  filmbrownsville.com
Dallas Film Commission
  325 N. St. Paul Ste. 700
  Dallas 75201, (214) 571-1050
  filmdfw.com
El Paso Film Commission

One Civic Center Plaza
El Paso 79901, (800) 351-6024
elpasocvb.com
Houston Film Commission
  901 Bagby Ste. 100
  Houston 77002, (800) 365-7575
  filmhouston.texaswebhost.com
San Antonio Film Commission
  203 S. St. Mary's, 2nd Floor
  San Antonio 78205, (800) 447-3372
  filmsanantonio.com
South Padre Island Film Comm.
  7355 Padre Blvd
  South Padre Island 78597
  (800) 657-2373, sopadre.com
Texas Panhandle Film Commission
  P.O. Box 3293, Amarillo 79116
  (806) 679-1116
  txpanhandlefilm.com

Film/TV Projects in Texas

Year	All projects	Feature films	Budgets (in millions)
2005	45	26	$141.1
2004	55	25	214.8
2003	46	19	230.2
2002	59	23	84.8
2001	55	34	203.8
2000	51	35	231.6
1999	33	22	143.7
1998	49	39	206.6
1997	56	24	172.8
1996	58	35	245.7

Source: Texas Film Commission.

Movie Productions Made in Texas 1927–2005

Following is a partial list of major productions filmed in Texas, in descending order by date. The date is for the year of release of the film, while actual location shots occurred often a year or two earlier.

Location information is from the Texas Film Commission and other sources.

When only a small portion of the movie is known to have been filmed in Texas, "(part)" is listed next to the movie title.

Some of the major artists who worked on the project are listed in the far right column.

Sources: Texas Film Commission, and online.

YEAR	MOVIE	LOCATIONS	ARTISTS
2005	The Three Burials of Melquiades Estrada	Van Horn, Monahans, Santa Elena Canyon, Lajitas, Shafter, Midland/Odessa	Tommy Lee Jones
2004	The Alamo	Dripping Springs, Wimberley, Pedernales Falls State Park, Bastrop, Austin	Dennis Quaid, Jason Patric
2004	Friday Night Lights	Odessa, Notrees, Austin, Houston	Billy Bob Thornton
2003	Texas Chainsaw Massacre	Martindale, Taylor, Austin	
2002	25th Hour (part)	Granger, Hutto, Elgin, Austin, Salt Flats	Spike Lee (director), Edward Norton
2002	The Rookie	Thorndale, Taylor, Arlington, Big Lake	Dennis Quaid
2001	Pearl Harbor (part)	Battleship Texas, Houston, and USS Lexington, Corpus Christi	Ben Affleck, Cuba Gooding Jr.
2000	All the Pretty Horses	Boerne, Helotes, Pipe Creek, Big Bend	Matt Damon, Sam Shepard
2000	Miss Congeniality	Austin, San Antonio	Sandra Bullock, Michael Caine
1999	Boys Don't Cry	Greenville, Dallas area	Hilary Swank
1999	Office Space	Austin, Dallas	Jennifer Aniston, Ron Livingston
1999	Varsity Blues	Elgin, Coupland, Taylor, Georgetown	John Van Der Beek, Jon Voight
1998	Dancer, Texas Pop. 81	Fort Davis, Alpine	
1998	Home Fries	Coupland, Taylor, Bastrop, Austin, El Paso	Drew Barrymore, Luke Wilson
1998	Hope Floats	Smithville, Austin	Sandra Bullock, Harry Connick Jr.
1998	The Newton Boys	Bertram, Martindale, Bartlett, Lockhart, Austin, San Antonio	Matthew McConaughey, Ethan Hawke
1996	Bottle Rocket	Hillsboro, Grand Prairie, Dallas	Luke and Owen Wilson, James Caan
1996	Courage Under Fire	Bertram, Bastrop, San Marcos, Austin, El Paso	Denzel Washington, Meg Ryan
1996	Lone Star	Eagle Pass, Del Rio, Laredo	Matthew McConaughey, Kris Kristofferson
1996	Michael	Gruene, Muldoon, Granger, New Corn Hill, Gonzales, La Grange, Georgetown	John Travolta, William Hurt
1995	Ace Ventura: When Nature Calls (part)	Hondo, Hunt, San Antonio	Jim Carrey
1995	Apollo 13	Houston area	Tom Hanks, Kevin Bacon
1995	Powder	Texas City, Wharton, Richmond, Sugar Land	Mary Steenburgen, Jeff Goldblum
1995	Streets of Laredo (TV movie)	Lajitas, Terlingua, Alpine, Big Bend Ranch State Natural Area, Del Rio, Brackettville, Texas State Railroad (Rusk/Palestine)	James Garner, Sissy Spacek, Randy Quaid
1994	Jason's Lyric	Pearland, Houston	Allen Payne, Forest Whitaker
1993	Dazed and Confused	Austin, Georgetown, Seguin	Richard Linklater (director), Matthew McConaughey
1993	What's Eating Gilbert Grape	Manor, Lockhart, Austin	Johnny Depp, Leonardo DiCaprio
1992	Leap of Faith	Groom, Happy, Tulia, Plainview, Amarillo, Irving	Steve Martin, Debra Winger
1991	JFK	Dallas, Irving, Arlington, Fort Worth	Oliver Stone (director), Kevin Costner
1991	Rush	Richmond, Highlands, Houston	Jason Patric, Sam Elliott
1991	Slacker	Austin	Richard Linklater (director)
1990	Robocop 2 (part)	Houston	
1990	Texasville	Archer City, Wichita Falls	Peter Bogdanovich (director)
1989	Lonesome Dove	Del Rio, Brackettville, Bastrop State Park, Austin	Robert Duvall, Tommy Lee Jones
1989	Scary Movie	Driftwood	
1988	D.O.A.	San Marcos, Austin	Dennis Quaid, Meg Ryan
1988	Heartbreak Hotel	Austin	David Keith, Tuesday Weld
1988	Talk Radio	Dallas	Oliver Stone (director)
1987	Robocop (part)	Dallas area	
1985	Alamo Bay	Corpus Christi area	Ed Harris
1985	Blood Simple	Round Rock, Hutto, Austin, Houston	Joel and Ethan Coen (writers)
1985	Fandango	San Elizario, Lajitas, Pecos, Monahans Sand Dunes State Park, Austin	Kevin Costner, Judd Nelson

YEAR	MOVIE	LOCATIONS	ARTISTS
1985	The Trip to Bountiful	Venus, Five Points, Waxahachie, Dallas	Horton Foote (writer), Geraldine Page
1985	The Legend of Billie Jean	Corpus Christi area	Matthew Robbins (director), Christian Slater
1984	Paris, Texas	Marathon, Fort Stockton, El Paso, Nordheim, Galveston, Port Arthur, Houston	Harry Dean Stanton. Dean Stockwell
1984	Places in the Heart	Waxahachie area	Sally Field, Danny Glover
1983	Tender Mercies	Palmer, Waxahachie area	Robert Duvall, Tess Harper
1983	Terms of Endearment	Houston, Texas City	Shirley MacLaine, Jack Nicholson
1982	The Ballad of Gregorio Cortez (part)	Gonzales	Edward James Olmos, Barry Corbin
1982	Barbarosa	Lajitas, Brackettville, Fredericksburg	Willie Nelson
1982	The Best Little Whore-house in Texas	Hallettsville, Austin	Burt Reynolds, Dolly Parton
1981	Southern Comfort	Caddo Lake State Park	Keith Carradine, Powers Boothe
1980	The Long Riders (part)	Texas State Railroad (Rusk/Palestine)	Dennis and Randy Quaid
1980	Middle Age Crazy	Houston, Dallas	Ann-Margret, Bruce Dern
1980	Urban Cowboy	Pasadena, Houston, Wallis, Huntsville	John Travolta, Debra Winger
1979	Resurrection	Shiner, Goliad, El Paso	Ellen Burstyn, Sam Shepard
1977	Bad News Bears in Break-ing Training	Houston, El Paso	William Devane
1977	For the Love of Benji	Houston	
1977	Outlaw Blues	Huntsville, Austin	Peter Fonda, Susan Saint James
1977	Semi-Tough (part)	Dallas	Burt Reynolds, Kris Kristofferson
1976	Drive-In	Terrell	Rodney Amateau (director)
1976	Futureworld	Houston (NASA)	Peter Fonda, Blythe Danner
1976	Logan's Run	Dallas, Fort Worth, Houston	Michael York, Farrah Fawcett
1975	The Great Waldo Pepper	Elgin, Lockhart, Floresville, Seguin, Kerrville	Robert Redford
1975	Mackintosh and T.J.	Dickens, Guthrie	Roy Rogers
1974	Benji	McKinney	
1974	The Sugarland Express	Sugar Land, Clodine, Richmond, Seguin, Boerne, Pleasanton, Floresville, Del Rio, San Antonio	Steven Spielberg (director), Goldie Hawn
1974	Texas Chainsaw Massacre	Round Rock	Tobe Hooper (director)
1972	The Getaway	San Marcos, New Braunfels, Huntsville, San Antonio, El Paso, Fabens	Sam Peckinpah (director), Steve McQueen
1971	The Andromeda Strain (part)	Shafter	Robert Wise (director)
1971	The Last Picture Show	Archer City	Peter Bogdanovich (director), Larry McMurtry (writer)
1970	Brewster McCloud	Houston, Astrodome	Robert Altman (director)
1970	My Sweet Charlie (TV movie)	Port Bolivar, Galveston	Patty Duke
1969	Midnight Cowboy (part)	Big Spring, Sweetwater	Jon Voight
1969	Viva Max!	San Antonio	Peter Ustinov, Jonathan Winters
1968	Bandalero!	Brackettville, Del Rio, Turkey Mountain	James Stewart, Raquel Welch
1968	Hellfighters	Baytown, Houston	John Wayne
1967	Bonnie and Clyde	Pilot Point, Ponder, Red Oak, Waxahachie, Denton	Warren Beatty, Faye Dunaway
1965	Baby, the Rain Must Fall	Wharton, Columbus, Bay City	Horton Foote (writer), Steve McQueen, Lee Remick
1963	Hud	Claude, Goodnight	Paul Newman, Patricia Neal
1962	State Fair	Dallas (Fair Park)	Pat Boone, Ann-Margret
1961	Two Rode Together	Brackettville, Del Rio	John Ford (director), James Stewart, Richard Widmark
1960	The Alamo	Brackettville	John Wayne
1960	Home from the Hill	Paris area	Robert Mitchum
1956	Giant	Marfa, Valentine	Elizabeth Taylor, Rock Hudson, James Dean
1953	Arrowhead	Brackettville	Charlton Heston, Jack Palance
1952	Viva Zapata	San Ygnacio, Roma, Dolores	Marlon Brando, Anthony Quinn
1950	High Lonesome	Marfa	Alan LeMay (director), John Drew Barrymore, Chill Wills
1949	Bad Boy	Copperas Cove	Audie Murphy, Jane Wyatt
1938	The Texans	Cotulla, Port Lavaca, Laredo	Randolph Scott, Joan Bennett
1927	Wings (won Best Picture at first Academy Awards)	San Antonio	Clara Bow, Gary Cooper

Texas Medal of the Arts Awards

Source: Texas Commission on the Arts

The Texas Medals of the Arts were presented to artists and arts patrons with Texas ties in April 2007.

The awards are administered by the Texas Cultural Trust Council. The council was established to raise money and awareness for the Texas Cultural Trust Fund, which was created by the Legislature in 1993 to support cultural arts in Texas (www.txculturaltrust.org).

The medals, awarded every two years, were first presented in 2001. A concurrent proclamation by the state Senate and House of Representatives honors the recipients, and the governor presents the awards in Austin.

2007

A **Lifetime Achievement Award** was presented to broadcast newsman Walter Cronkite of Houston. He was inducted into the national Academy of Television Arts and Sciences Hall of Fame in 1985.

Music: Ornette Coleman of Fort Worth, jazz saxophonist.

Dance: Alvin Ailey American Dance Theater. The late Alvin Ailey, born in Rogers, was a creator of African American dance works.

Literary: Sandra Brown of Waco. Ms. Brown, raised in Fort Worth, is the author of more than 50 New York Times best-sellers.

Visual arts: Jesús Moroles of Corpus Christi/Rockport, internationally known sculptor.

Walter Cronkite, raised in Houston. Karen Stallwood photo.

Theater arts: Judith Ivey of El Paso. Tony Award winner, also in TV series *Designing Women*.

Multimedia: Bill Wittliff of Taft and Austin, publisher, writer, photographer, director, producer.

Arts education: Paul Baker of Hereford/Waelder. Headed drama departments at Baylor and Trinity universities.

Individual arts patron: Diana and Bill Hobby of Houston.

Corporate arts patron: Neiman Marcus, Dallas.

Foundation arts patron: Sid W. Richardson Foundation of Fort Worth.

2005

Lifetime Achievement Award: singer Vikki Carr of El Paso.

Television/theater: actress Phylicia Rashad of Houston.

Music: singer/songwriter Lyle Lovett of Klein.

Dance: Ben Stevenson of Houston and Fort Worth.

Literary arts: Naomi Shihab Nye of San Antonio.

Visual arts: Jose Cisneros of El Paso.

Theater: Robert Wilson of Waco.

Arts education: Ginger Head-Gearheart of Fort Worth, advocate of arts education in public schools.

Individual arts patron: Joe R. and Teresa Lozano Long of Austin, philanthropists.

Foundation arts patron: Nasher Foundation of Dallas.

2003

Lifetime Achievement: writer John Graves of Glen Rose, author of *Goodbye to A River*.

Media-film/television acting: Fess Parker of Fort Worth.

Music: country singer Charley Pride of Dallas.

Dance: choreographer, singer, director, dancer Tommy Tune of Wichita Falls and Houston.

Theater: Enid Holm of Odessa, actress and former executive director of Texas Nonprofit Theatres.

Literary arts: novelist Sandra Cisneros of San Antonio.

Visual arts: sculptor Glenna Goodacre of Dallas.

Folk arts: Tejano singer Lydia Mendoza of San Antonio.

Architecture: State Capitol Preservation Project of Austin, headed by Dealey Herndon.

Arts education: theater teacher Marca Lee Bircher of Dallas.

Individual arts patron: philanthropist Nancy B. Hamon of Dallas.

Corporate arts patron: Exxon/Mobil based in Irving.

   Foundation arts patron: Houston Endowment Inc.

2001

Lifetime Achievement: Van Cliburn of Fort Worth, cited as "acclaimed concert pianist and mentor."

Film: actor Tommy Lee Jones of San Saba.

Music: singer-songwriter Willie Nelson of Austin.

Dance: Debbie Allen of Houston, choreographer, director, actress and composer.

Theater: *Texas* musical-drama producer Neil Hess of Amarillo.

Literary arts: playwright Horton Foote of Wharton.

Visual arts: muralist John Biggers of Houston.

Folk arts: musician brothers Santiago Jimenez Jr. and Flaco Jimenez of San Antonio.

Architecture: restoration architect Wayne Bell of Austin.

Arts education: theater arts director Gilberto Zepeda Jr. of Pharr.

Individual arts patron: philanthropist Jack Blanton of Houston.

Corporate arts patron: SBC Communications Inc. of San Antonio.

Foundation arts patron: Meadows Foundation of Dallas. ☆

Texas Institute of Letters Awards

Each year since 1939, the **Texas Institute of Letters** (www.wtamu.edu/til/) has honored outstanding literature and journalism that is either by Texans or about Texas subjects. Awards have been made for fiction, nonfiction, Southwest history, general information, magazine and newspaper journalism, children's books, translation, poetry and book design. The awards of recent years are listed below:

Writer/Designer: Title

2006

Lawrence Wright: *The Looming Tower: Al-Qaeda and the Road to 9/11*
Cormac McCarthy: *The Road*
Dominic Smith: *The Mercury Visions of Louis Daguerre*
Marian Schwartz: translator of *White on Black* by Ruben Gallego
Tony Freemantle: "The Gulf Coast Revisited" in the Houston Chronicle
Mary Ann Jacob: *Timeless Texas*
John Sprong: "The Good Book and the Bad Book" in *Texas Monthly*
Mark Wisniewski: "Prisoners of War"
Tim Tingle: *Crossing Bok Chitto: A Choctaw Tale of Friendship and Freedom*
Heather Hepler: *Scrambled Eggs at Midnight*
Jerry Thompson: *Civil War to the Bloody End: The Life and Times of Major Samuel P. Heintzelman*
Christopher Bakken: *Goat Funeral*
Lon Tinkle Award (for career): William D. Wittliff

2005

Stephen Graham Jones: *Bleed Into Me: A Bood of Stories*
Karen Olsson: *Waterloo*
Nate Blakeslee: *Tulia*
Thad Sitton and James H. Conrad: *Freedom Colonies: Independent Black Texans in the Time of Jim Crow*
John Bricuth: *As Long As It's Big*
D.J. Stout and Julie Savasky: *Conjunto*
Edward Hegstrom, Tony Freemantle and Elena Vega: "One Nation: Two Worlds" in the *Houston Chronicle*
Kelly Bennett: *Not Norman: A Goldfish Story*
Pamela Porter: *The Crazy Man*
Rick Bass: "The Lives of Rocks"
Pamela Colloff: "Unholy Act" in *Texas Monthly*
Harvey Yunis: translator *Demosthenes: Speeches 18 and 19*
Lon Tinkle Award (for career): James Hoggard

2004

Steven Mintz: *Huck's Raft*
Laurie Lynn Drummond: *Anything You Say Can and Will Be Held Against You*
Bret Anthony Johnston: *Corpus Christi*
William Wenthe: *Not Till We Are Lost*
Andres Resendez: *Changing National Identities at the Frontier: Texas and New Mexico, 1800–1850*
Philip Boehm: translator of *Death in Danzig* by Stefan Chwin
Mike Nichols: *Balaam Gimble's Gumption*
Ben Fountain: "Bouki and the Cocaine"

Zanto Peabody: "The Search for Eddie Peabody" in the *Houston Chronicle*
DJ Stout and Julie Savasky: *Maps of the Imagination*
Lawrence Wright: "The Kingdom of Silence" in the *New Yorker*
Diane Stanley: *Jack and the Beanstalk*
Susan Abraham and Denise Gonzales: *Cecilia's Year*
Lon Tinkle Award (for career): T.R. Fehrenbach

2003

Betty Lou Phillips: *Emily Goes Wild*
Brian Yansky: *My Road Trip to the Pretty Girl Capital of the Word*
D.J. Stout and Julie Savasky: *The Texas Cowboy Kitchen*
Steve Barthelme: "Claire"
Dick J. Reavis: articles on homelessness in the *San Antonio Express-News*
Jan Reid: "End of the River" in *Texas Monthly*
John Blair: *The Green Girls*
Jennifer Grotz: *Cusp*
Lynn Hoggard: translator of *Nelida* by Marie D'Agoult
B.H. Fairchild: *Early Occult Memory Systems of the Lower Midwest*
Jack Jackson: *Almonte's Texas*, translated by John Wheat
Don Graham: *Kings of Texas*
Robert Ford: *The Student Conductor*
Joseph Skibell: *The English Disease*
Lon Tinkle Award (for career): Bud Shrake

2002

Kathi Appelt: *Where, Where Is Swamp Bear?*
Carolee Dean: *Comfort*
Juan Rulfo: *Pedro Paramo*
Ben Fountain III: "Near-Extinct Birds of the Central Cordillera"
Mark Lisheron and Bill Bishop: "Cities of Ideas" in the *Austin American-Statesman*
Lawrence Wright: "The Man Behind Bin Laden" in the *New Yorker*
Dan Rifenburgh: *Advent*
Reginald Gibbons: *It's Time*
Kinky Friedman: *Meanwhile Back at the Ranch*
Michael Gagarin: *Antiphon the Athenian: Oratory, Law, and Justice in the Age of the Sophists*
Ray Gonzalez: *The Underground Heart: A Return to a Hidden Landscape*
Lisa Schamess: *Borrowed Light*
Rick Bass: *Hermit's Story*
Lon Tinkle Award: Shelby Hearon

2001

Carmen Bredeson: *Animals that Migrate*
Lori Aurelia Williams: *When Kambia Elaine Flew from Neptune*
Vicki Trego Hill: *Folktales of the Zapatista Revolution*
Tom McNeely: "Tickle Torture"
Mike Tolson, James Kimberly, Steve Brewer, Allan Turner: "A Deadly Distinction" in the *Houston Chronicle*
Larry L. King: "The Book on Willie Morris" in *Texas Monthly*
Ted Genoways: *Bullroarer*
Susan Wood: *Asunder*
Wendy Barker and Saranindranath Tagore: *Final Poems* by Rabindranath Tagore

*William D. Wittliff, publisher, producer, director and screenwriter (*Raggedy Man *and* Lonesome Dove *[teleplay], among others), was honored for career excellence at the 2006 awards presentations. Harry Cabluck photo.*

Marco Perela: *Adventures of a No Name Actor*
Betje Klier: *Pavie in the Borderlands*
Larry McMurtry: *Sacagawea's Nickname: Essays on the American West*
Katherine Tannery: *Carousel of Progress*
Sarah Bird: *The Yokota Officers Club*
Lon Tinkle Award: William H. Goetzmann

2000

Rosa Shand: *The Gravity of Sunlight*
Laura Wilson: *Hutterites of Montana*
Richard V. Francaviglia: *The Cast Iron Forest*
Corey Marks: *Renunciation*
Edward Snow: *The Duino Elegies* by Rainer Maria Rilke
Glen Pourciau: "Deep Wilderness"
Pamela Colloff: "Sins of the Father"
Joe Holley: "The Hill Country: Loving It to Death"
Anne Coyle: *Crookwood*
Molly Ivins and Lou DuBose: *Shrub*
Bradley Hutchinson: *Willard Clark: Printer and Printmaker*
D.J. Stout and Julie Savasky: *John Graves and the Making of Goodbye to a River*
Lon Tinkle Award: Leon Hale

1999

Rick DeMarinis: *New and Selected Stories*
Robert Draper: *Hadrian's Walls*
Ann Rowe Seaman: *Swaggart: The Unauthorized Biography of an American Evangelist*
J.Gilberto Quezada: *Border Boss: Manuel B. Bravo and Zapata County*
Walt McDonald: "Whatever the Wind Delivers"
Jenny Lind Porter: *Verses on Death by Helinand of Froidmont*
Tracy Daugherty: *Comfort Me With Apples*
Steven and Rick Barthelme: "Good Losers"
James Hoggard: "Greetings from Cuba"
Benjamin Alire Saenz: *Grandma Fina and Her Wonderful Umbrellas/La Abuelita Fina y Sus Sombrillas Maravillosas*
Neil Barrett Jr.: *Interstate Dreams*
Margerie Adkins West: *Angels on High: Marton Varo's Limestone Angels on Bass Performance Hall*

Peter Brown: *On the Plains*
Lon Tinkle Award: Walt McDonald

1998

C.W. Smith: *Understanding Women*
Susan Choi: *The Foreign Student*
William C. Davis: *Three Roads to the Alamo: The Lives and Fortunes of David Crockett, James Bowie, and William Barret Travis*
Don Carleton: *A Breed So Rare: The Life of J.R. Parten, Liberal Texas Oil Man, 1896-1992*
B.H. Fairchild: "The Art of the Lathe"
Marian Schwartz: *The Ladies from St. Petersburg: Three Novellas*
James Hoggard: *Poems from Cuba: Alone Against the Sea*
Jane Roberts Wood: "My Mother Had a Maid"
Rick Bass: "Into the Fire"
Patrick Beach: "The Struggle for the Soul of Kreuz Market"
Bryan Woolley: "A Legend Runs Through It"
Pat Mora: *The Big Sky*
Lon Tinkle Award: Robert Flynn

1997

Lisa Sandlin: *A Message to the Nurse of Dreams*
Joseph Skibell: *A Blessing on the Moon*
Tara Holley with Joe Holley: *My Mother's Keeper: A Daughter's Memoir of Growing up in the Shadow of Schizophrenia*
John Miller Morris: *El Llano Estacado*
Bruce Bond: "Radiography"
Debbie Nathan and Willavaldo Delgadillo: *The Moon Will Forever Be a Distant Love*
Clifford Hudder: "Misplacement"
Skip Hollandsworth: "The Curse of Romeo and Juliet"
Michael Leahy: "Oswald: A Brother's Burden"
Jerry Herring: *Charles Schorre*
David Timmons: *The Wild and Vivid Land*
Naomi Shihab Nye: *Habibi*
Lon Tinkle Award: Rolando Hinojosa-Smith

In 1983, a Special Citation honored: *The Texas Almanac*. ☆

National Arts Medal Honors Amarillo native Cyd Charisse

The 2006 National Medal of Arts honored Amarillo native Cyd Charisse, actress and dancer, among ten recipients.

In the award presentation, Ms. Charisse was cited for being "one of Hollywood's greatest dancers best known for two acclaimed dance sequences, the 'Broadway Melody Ballet' from the movie *Singin' in the Rain* with Gene Kelly and the 'Girl Hunt Ballet' from *The Band Wagon*."

The dancer was born Tula Finklea in 1921 in Amarillo where she took ballet lessons. At age 13, she joined the Ballet Russe, touring in the United States and Europe.

Four years later, she appeared in her first film *Something to Shout*.

Besides Hollywood musicals and 14 theater productions, she appeared on television and performed in a nightclub revue with her husband, singer Tony Martin.

The Medal of Arts was established by Congress in 1984 to honor those who make outstanding contributions to the arts.

Each year, the National Endowment for the Arts seeks nominations from across the country. The president selects the recipients.

Previous Texas recipients include Lydia Mendoza, Tejano recording star since the 1920s; country singer George Strait, dancer Tommy Tune, as well as the *Austin City Limits* concert TV series. ☆

Cyd Charisse dances with Fred Astaire in the 1953 MGM musical The Band Wagon. *Loew's Inc. photo.*

Poets Laureate of Texas

Since 2001, a committee of seven members appointed by the governor, lt. governor, and speaker of the House selects the poet laureate, state artists and state musician based on recommendations from the Texas Commission on the Arts. Earlier, the Legislature made the nominations.

Sources: Texas State Library and Archives; Texas Commission on the Arts; Dallas Morning News.

1932-34	Judd Mortimer Lewis, Houston
1934-36	Aline T. Michaelis, Austin
1936-39	Grace Noll Crowell, Dallas
1939-41	Lexie Dean Robertson, Rising Star
1941-43	Nancy Richey Ranson, Dallas
1943-45	Dollilee Davis Smith, Cleburne
1945-47	DavidRiley Russell, Dallas
1947-49	Aline B. Carter, San Antonio
1949-51	Carlos Ashley, Llano
1951-53	Arthur M. Sampley, Denton
1953-55	Mildred Lindsey Raiborn, San Angelo Dee Walker, Texas City, alternate
1955-57	Pierre Bernard Hill, Hunt
1957-59	Margaret Royalty Edwards, Waco
1959-61	J.V. Chandler, Kingsville Edna Coe Majors, Colorado City, alternate
1961	Lorena Simon, Port Arthur
1962	Marvin Davis Winsett, Dallas
1963	Gwendolyn Bennett Pappas, Houston Vassar Miller, Houston, alternate
1964-65	Jenny Lind Porter, Austin Edith Rayzor Canant, Texas City, alternate
1966	Bessie Maas Rowe, Port Arthur Grace Marie Scott, Abilene, alternate
1967	William E. Bard, Dallas Bessie Maas Rowe, Port Arthur, alternate
1968	Kathryn Henry Harris, Waco Sybil Leonard Armes, El Paso, alternate
1969-70	Anne B. Marely, Austin Rose Davidson Speer, Brady, alternate
1970-71	Mrs. Robby K. Mitchell, McKinney Faye Carr Adams, Dallas, alternate
1971-72	Terry Fontenot, Port Arthur Faye Carr Adams, Dallas, alternate
1972-73	Mrs. Clark Gresham, Burkburnett Marion McDaniel, Sidney, alternate
1973-74	Violette Newton, Beaumont Stella Woodall, San Antonio, alternate
1974-75	Lila Todd O'Neil, Port Arthur C.W. Miller, San Antonio, alternate
1975-76	Ethel Osborn Hill, Port Arthur Gene Shuford, Denton, alternate
1976-77	Florice Stripling Jeffers, Burkburnett Vera L. Eckert, San Angelo, alternate
1977-78	Ruth Carruth, Vernon Joy Gresham Hagstrom, Burkburnett, alternate

Steven Fromholz, poet laueate for 2007, wrote such songs as "Texas Trilogy" and "I'd Have to Be Crazy." Kim Ritzenthaler photo.

1978-79	Patsy Stodghill, Dallas Dorothy B. Elfstroman, Galveston, alternate
1979-80	Dorothy B. Elfstroman, Galveston Ruth Carruth, Vernon, alternate
1980-81	Weems S. Dykes, McCamey Mildred Crabree Speer, Amarillo, alternate
1981-82	*none designated*
1982-83	William D. Barney, Fort Worth Vassar Miller, Houston, alternate
1983-87	*none designated*
1987-88	Ruth E. Reuther, Wichita Falls
1988-89	Vassar Miller, Houston
1989-93	*none designated*
1993-94	Mildred Baass, Victoria
1994-99	*none designated*
2000	James Hoggard, Wichita Falls
2001	Walter McDonald, Lubbock
2002	*none designated*
2003	Jack Myers, Mesquite
2004	Cleatus Rattan, Cisco
2005	Alan Brikelbach, Plano
2006	Red Steagall, Fort Worth
2007	Steven Fromholz, Kopperl, Sugar Land
2008	Larry Thomas, Houston

State Musicians of Texas

2003	James Dick, Round Top
2004	Ray Benson, Austin
2005	Johnny Gimble, Tyler
2006	Billy Joe Shaver, Waco
2007	Dale Watson, Pasadena, Austin
2008	Shelley King, Austin

State Artists of Texas

1971-72	Joe Ruiz Grandee, Arlington
1972-73	Melvin C. Warren, Clifton
1973-74	Ronald Thomason, Weatherford A.C. Gentry Jr., Tyler, alternate
1974-75	Joe Rader Roberts, Dripping Springs Bette Lou Voorhis, Austin, alternate
1975-76	Jack White, New Braunfels
July 4, 1975 -July 4, 1976	Robert Summers, Glen Rose Bicentennial Artist
1976-77	James Boren, Clifton Kenneth Wyatt, Lubbock, alternate
1977-78	Edward "Buck" Schiwetz, DeWitt County Renne Hughes, Tarrant County, alternate
1978-79	Jack Cowan, Rockport Gary Henry, Palo Pinto County, alternate Joyce Tally, Caldwell County, alternate
1979-80	Dalhart Windberg, Travis County Grant Lathe, Canyon Lake, alternate
1980-81	Harry Ahysen, Huntsville Jim Reno, Simonton, alternate
1981-82	Jerry Newman, Beaumont Raul Guiterrez, San Antonio, alternate
1982-83	Dr. James H. Johnson, Bryan Armando Hinojosa, Laredo, alternate
1983-84	Raul Gutierrez, San Antonio James Eddleman, Lubbock, alternate
1984-85	Covelle Jones, Lubbock Ragan Gennusa, Austin, alternate
1986-87	Chuck DeHaan, Graford

1987-88	Neil Caldwell, Angleton Rey Gaytan, Austin, alternate	
1988-89	George Hallmark, Walnut Springs Tony Eubanks, Grapevine, alternate	
	Two-dimensional	**Three-dimensional**
1990-91	Mondel Rogers, Sweetwater	Ron Wells, Cleveland
1991-92	Woodrow Foster, Center	Kent Ullberg, Corpus Christi
	Harold Phenix, Houston, alternate	Mark Clapham, Conroe, alternate
1993-94	Roy Lee Ward	James Eddleman, Lubbock
1994-95	Frederick Carter, El Paso	Garland A. Weeks, Wichita Falls
1998-99	Carl Rice Embrey, San Antonio	Edd Hayes, Humble
2000-02	*none designated*	
2003	Ralph White, Austin	Dixie Friend Gay, Houston
2004	Sam Caldwell, Houston	David Hickman, Dallas
2005	Kathy Vargas, San Antonio	Sharon Kopriva, Houston
2006	George Boutwell, Bosque	James Surls, Athens
2007	Lee Herring, Rockwall	David Keens, Arlington
2008	Janet Eager Krueger, Encinal	Damian Priour, Austin

2007 state artist David Keens, above, established and now heads the Glass Program at the University of Texas at Arlington. Randy Eli Grothe photo.

Holidays, Anniversaries and Festivals, 2008 and 2009

Below are listed the principal federal and state government holidays; Christian, Jewish and Islamic holidays and festivals; and special recognition days for 2008 and 2009. Technically, the United States does not observe national holidays. Each state has jurisdiction over its holidays, which are usually designated by its legislature. This list was compiled partially from *Astronomical Phenomena 2008* and *Astronomical Phenomena 2009,* published by the U.S. Naval Observatory, and from the Texas Government Code. See the footnotes for explanations of the symbols.

2008

†§New Year's Day .... Tues., Jan. 1
Epiphany ....Sun., Jan. 6
‡Sam Rayburn Day ....Sun., Jan. 6
§§Islamic New Year ....Thurs., Jan. 10
†*Confederate Heroes Day ....Sat., Jan. 19
†§Martin Luther King, Jr., Day .... Mon., Jan. 21
Ash Wednesday .... Wed., Feb. 6
Valentine's Day ....Thurs., Feb. 14
†§**Presidents' Day ....Mon., Feb. 18
†Texas Independence Day ....Sun., March 2
‡Sam Houston Day ....Sun., March 2
‡Texas Flag Day ....Sun., March 2
Primary Election Day ....Tues., March 4
Palm Sunday ....Sun., March 16
†§Good Friday ....Fri., March 21
Easter Day ....Sun., March 23
†César Chávez Day ....Mon., March 31
‡Former Prisoners of War
   Recognition Day ....Wed., April 9
¶Passover (Pesach), first day of ....Sun., April 20
†San Jacinto Day .... Mon., April 21
Ascension Day .... Thurs., May 1
Whit Sunday — Pentecost .... Sun., May 11
Mother's Day .... Sun., May 11
Armed Forces Day ....Sat., May 17
Trinity Sunday ....Sun., May 18
†§Memorial Day .... Mon., May 26
¶Shavuot (Feast of Weeks) .... Mon., June 9
Flag Day (U.S.) ....Sat., June 14
Father's Day ....Sun., June 15
†Emancipation Day in Texas
   (Juneteenth) .... Thurs., June 19
†§Independence Day .... Fri., July 4
†Lyndon Baines Johnson Day .... Wed., Aug. 27
†§Labor Day ....Mon., Sept. 1
§§Ramadan, first day of ....Tues., Sept. 2
Grandparents Day .... Sun., Sept. 7
¶Rosh Hashanah (Jewish New Year) ....Tues., Sept. 30
¶Yom Kippur (Day of Atonement) .... Thurs., Oct. 9
§‡Columbus Day .... Mon., Oct. 13
¶Sukkot (Tabernacles), first day of ....Tues., Oct. 14
Halloween .... Fri., Oct. 31
‡Father of Texas (Stephen F. Austin) Day .....Mon., Nov. 3
†General Election Day ....Tues., Nov. 4
†§Veterans Day ....Tues., Nov. 11
†§††Thanksgiving Day ....Thurs., Nov. 27
First Sunday in Advent .... Sun., Nov. 30
¶Hanukkah, first day of ....Mon., Dec. 22
†§Christmas Day .... Thurs., Dec. 25
§§Islamic New Year ....Tues., Dec. 30

2009

†§New Year's Day ....Thurs., Jan. 1
Epiphany ....Tues., Jan. 6
‡Sam Rayburn Day ....Tues., Jan. 6
†§Martin Luther King, Jr., Day .... Mon., Jan. 19
†*Confederate Heroes Day .... Mon., Jan. 19
Inauguration Day ....Tues., Jan. 20
Valentine's Day .... Sat., Feb. 14
†§**Presidents' Day ....Mon., Feb. 16
Ash Wednesday .... Wed., Feb. 25
†Texas Independence Day ....Mon., March 2
‡Sam Houston Day ....Mon., March 2
‡Texas Flag Day ....Mon., March 2
†César Chávez Day .... Tues., March 31
Palm Sunday ....Sun., April 5
¶Passover (Pesach), first day of ....Thurs., April 9
‡Former Prisoners of War
   Recognition Day ....Thurs., April 9
†§Good Friday .... Fri., April 10
Easter Day ....Sun., April 12
†San Jacinto Day .... Tues., April 21
Mother's Day .... Sun., May 10
Armed Forces Day ....Sat., May 16
Ascension Day .... Thurs., May 21
†§Memorial Day .... Mon., May 25
¶Shavuot (Feast of Weeks) .... Fri., May 29
Whit Sunday — Pentecost .... Sun., May 31
Trinity Sunday ....Sun., June 7
Flag Day (U.S.) ....Sun., June 14
†Emancipation Day in Texas
   (Juneteenth) .... Fri., June 19
Father's Day ....Sun., June 21
†§Independence Day .... Sat., July 4
§§Ramadan, first day of .... Sat., Aug. 22
†Lyndon Baines Johnson Day ....Thurs., Aug. 27
†§Labor Day ....Mon., Sept. 7
Grandparents Day .... Sun., Sept. 13
¶Rosh Hashanah (Jewish New Year) .... Sat., Sept. 19
¶Yom Kippur (Day of Atonement) ....Mon., Sept. 28
¶Sukkot (Tabernacles), first day of .... Sat., Oct. 3
§‡Columbus Day .... Mon., Oct. 12
Halloween ....Sat., Oct. 31
‡Father of Texas (Stephen F. Austin) Day .... Tues., Nov. 3
†§Veterans Day ....Wed., Nov. 11
†§††Thanksgiving Day ....Thurs., Nov. 26
First Sunday in Advent .... Sun., Nov. 29
¶Hanukkah, first day of .... Sat., Dec. 12
§§Islamic New Year .... Fri., Dec. 18
†§Christmas Day .... Fri., Dec. 25

¶ §§ In these tables, the Jewish (¶) and Islamic (§§) holidays are tabular, which means they begin at sunset on the previous evening.

  † State holiday in Texas. For state employees, the Friday after Thanksgiving Day, Dec. 24 and Dec. 26 are also holidays. Optional holidays are César Chávez Day, Good Friday, Rosh Hashanah and Yom Kippur. Partial-staffing holidays are Confederate Heroes Day, Texas Independence Day, San Jacinto Day, Emancipation Day in Texas and Lyndon Baines Johnson Day. State offices will be open on optional holidays and partial-staffing holidays.

  ‡ State Recognition Days, designated by the Texas Legislature. In addition, the legislature has designated the week of May 22–26 as International Trade Awareness Week.

  § Federal legal public holiday.

  * Confederate Heroes Day combines the birthdays of Robert E. Lee (Jan. 19) and Jefferson Davis (June 3).

  ** Presidents' Day combines the birthdays of George Washington (Feb. 22) and Abraham Lincoln (Feb. 12).

  †† Between 1939 and 1957, Texas observed Thanksgiving Day on the last Thursday in November. As a result, in all Novembers having five Thursdays, Texas celebrated national Thanksgiving on the fourth Thursday and Texas Thanksgiving on the fifth Thursday. In 1957, Texas changed the state observance to coincide in all years with the national holiday. ☆

Church Affiliation Change: 1990 to 2000

Texas remains one of the nation's more "churched" states, even though a smaller portion of Texans is affiliated with a church than ten years ago.

Texas ranks 18th among the states in percentage of the population belonging to a denomination. According to *Churches and Church Membership in the United States 2000*, at least 55.5 percent of Texans are adherents to a religion.

The survey, from the Glenmary Research Center in Nashville, is the only U.S. survey to report church membership at the state and county level. It relies on reports from the different denominations for membership numbers.

But in 2000, the African-American churches did not participate in the study. This probably leaves out more than one million church-going Texans.

In 1990, when the survey was done, it was estimated that there were 815,000 black Baptists in Texas. A conservative estimate of the membership in black Pentecostal churches in 2000 would be about 300,000. And, an estimate for black Methodists in Texas would be approximately 200,000.

Adjusting for those additions, then the percentage of Texans that are members of a religion would be closer to 61.7 percent. Although that is higher than the 55.5 percent figure compiled from the reporting churches, still, it would be down from 67.1 percent ten years ago, indicating a move away from church membership.

This decrease occurred while many indicators have been showing that Americans are more interested in their spiritual lives than at any time in recent decades. Churches reported an increase of 1.5 million members while the total population of Texas increased by 4 million from 1990 to 2000. During the same period, the number of Texans not attached to a religion rose by 2.5 million.

Thus, according to the Texas Almanac analysis from a variety of sources, there are 7.9 million persons in the state who are not claimed by a church and about 13 million who are church members. (The U.S. census counted 20,851,820 persons in Texas in 2000.)

From the 2000 church survey, diversity among religious believers can be seen in the congregations of Muslims, Hindus, Buddhists and other non-Christian faiths. In 1990, these groups were not surveyed, so increases cannot be determined.

The estimate of Jewish Texans, 128,000, is from the congregations in the state. The number increased by 20,000 from 1990.

During the decade, the number of Catholics increased by almost 800,000, the greatest numerical gain among the churches. However, the percentage of Texans who are Catholic remained at 21 percent.

The largest faith group, the Baptists, increased by 314,761 members, a rate less than the statewide population increase. Thus in 2000, Baptists made up 21.8 percent of the population, down from 24.9 percent in 1990.

The trend in the state's two largest denominations, Roman Catholic and Southern Baptist, which together

St. Louis Church in Castroville was been in use since 1870. Robert Plocheck photo.

According to *Churches And Church Membership in the United States 2000*, **Texas ranks**:

— **First** in number of Evangelical Protestants, with 5,083,087. California, which ranks second, has less than half as many, with 2,432,285.

— **Second**, behind Pennsylvania, in number of Mainline Protestants at 1,705,394.

— **Third** in number of Catholics, behind California and New York.

— **Third** in number of Buddhist congregations.

— **Fifth** in number of Muslims.

— **Fifth** in number of Hindu congregations.

— **Sixth** in number of Mormons.

— **Tenth** in number of Jews.

make up over 40 percent of the population, was especially noticeable in the four largest metropolitan areas. More than half of all Texans live in these areas.

In the eight-county Houston metro area, the percentage of Catholics rose from 17.3 percent to 18.2 percent, while the percentage of Southern Baptists went down slightly from 14.9 percent to 14.8.

In the five-county Austin metro area, the percentage of Catholics increased from 13.6 percent to 18.4 percent. The percentage of Southern Baptists decreased from 13.5 percent to 10.2 percent.

In the four-county San Antonio metro area, the percentage of Catholics increased from 36.0 to 38.8, while the percentage of Southern Baptists decreased from 10.4 to 8.8.

The 12-county Dallas-Forth Worth metro area is the only one of the four where the number of Southern Baptists, 855,680, is higher than Catholics, 808,167. But, here also, the percentage of Southern Baptists declined from 19.0 to 16.4, while the percentage of Catholics rose from 9.0 in 1990 to 15.5 in 2000.

As noted, while these shifts in religious make-up were occurring, the number of persons not affiliated with a religious group was increasing.

In Houston in 1990, the percentage of the population not counted as church members was 43.1. In 2000, that had risen to 50.1 percent.

In Austin, the figure increased from 52.4 percent to 55.3 percent.

In San Antonio, the percentage of non-adherents to a religion was 36.2 in 1990. In 2000, it had risen slightly to 37.0 percent.

In the Dallas-Fort Worth area, it increased from 43.6 percent in 1990, to 47.7 percent in 2000.

These trends reflect what was happening in the nation at large, where the percentage of the population not affiliated with a church rose from 44.9 to 55.1.

The Southern Baptists and Catholics also were the largest religious groups in the nation. And the percentage of Catholics remained about the same, 21.5 in 1990 and 22.0 in 2000, while the percentage of the total population that was Southern Baptist declined from 13.8 to 7.1.

The Glenmary study is a combined effort of the Catholic research center and the Church of the Nazarene, a Protestant denomination with headquarters in Kansas City, Mo..

The study distinguishes between members, which it defines as adult members only, and adherents, which includes adults and children. **All figures for members used by the Texas Almanac refer to children and adults.**

Sources

Churches and Church Membership in the United States 2000, Glenmary Research Center, Nashville, Tenn., 2002.

National Council of Churches of Christ in the USA, New York, *Yearbook of American and Canadian Churches*, annual.

New Handbook of Texas, 1996, various: "Christian Methodist Episcopal Church," by Charles E. Tatum; "African-American Churches," "African Methodist Episcopal Church," and "African Methodist Episcopal Zion Church," by William E. Montgomery; "Religion," by John W. Storey. — *Robert Plocheck*

Numbers of Members by Denomination

Religious Groups in Texas	1990	Change	2000
Baha'i			**10,777**
Baptist	**4,223,157**	**+ 314,761**	**4,537,918**
American Baptist Association			61,272
American Baptist Churches in the USA	12,905	- 5,848	7,057
Baptist General Conference	278	+ 62	340
Baptist Missionary Association of America	125,323	- 2,125	123,198
Conservative Baptist Association of America (1 congregation)			
Free Will Baptist, National Association of, Inc.	4,936	- 2,114	2,822
Interstate & Foreign Landmark Missionary Baptists Association	76	+ 17	93
Landmark Baptist, Indep. Assns. & Unaffil. Churches			964
National Primitive Baptist Convention, USA			4,463
North American Baptist Conference	1,634	- 65	1,569
Primitive Baptists Associations	2,544		
Primitive Baptist Church — Old Line (118 congregations)			NR
Progressive Primitive Baptists			197
Reformed Baptist Churches (10 congregations)			
Regular Baptist Churches, General Association of			684
Seventh Day Baptist General Conference	242		
Southern Baptist Convention	3,259,395	+ 260,064	3,519,459
Southwide Baptist Fellowship (13 congregations)			
Two-Seed-in-the-Spirit Predestinarian Baptists	53	- 24	29
(Black Baptists Estimate)*	(815,771)*	—	(815,771)*
Buddhism (88 congregations)			**NR**
Catholic Church	**3,574,728**	**+ 794,241**	**4,368,969**
(Independent) Christian Churches & Churches of Christ	**33,766**	**+ 9,836**	**43,602**
Churches of Christ	**380,948**	**- 3,684**	**377,264**
(Disciples of Christ) Christian Church	**105,495**	**+ 5,793**	**111,288**
Episcopal	**169,227**	**+ 8,683**	**177,910**
Episcopal Church, The	169,112	+ 8,798	177,910
Reformed Episcopal Church	115		
Hindu (34 congregations)			**NR**
Holiness	**61,487**	**+ 25,052**	**86,539**
Christian & Missionary Alliance, The	3,082	+ 776	3,858

Religious Groups in Texas	1990	Change	2000
Church of God (Anderson, Ind.)	5,854	- 1,185	4,669
Free Methodist Church of North America	886	- 12	874
Nazarene, Church of the	45,097	+ 5,431	50,528
Salvation Army	5,676	+ 19,394	25,070
Wesleyan Church, The	892	+648	1,540
Independent Non-Charismatic Churches	**132,292**	**+ 12,957**	**145,249**
Jain (6 congregations)			**NR**
Jewish, estimate	**107,980**	**+ 20,020**	**128,000**
Lutheran	**294,524**	**+ 6,994**	**301,518**
Church of the Lutheran Brethren of America	71		
Church of the Lutheran Confession	144		
Evangelical Lutheran Church in America	155,276	- 257	155,019
Evangelical Lutheran Synod	146		
Free Lutheran Congregations, The Association of	144	+ 224	368
Lutheran Church—Missouri Synod, The	134,280	+ 5,826	140,106
Wisconsin Evangelical Lutheran Synod	4,463	+ 1,562	6,025
Mennonite/Amish	**2,608**	**+ 2,011**	**4,619**
Amish, Old Order	400	- 376	24
Amish, other			68
Beachy Amish Mennonite Churches	70	+ 57	127
Church of God in Christ (Mennonite)	522	+ 327	849
Conservative Mennonite Conference			191
Evangelical Bible Churches, Fellowship of (was Ev. Menn. Bre.)	20		
Eastern Pennsylvania Mennonite Church	39	+ 26	65
Mennonite Brethren Churches, U.S. Conference of	329	+ 96	425
Mennonite, other			1,655
Mennonite Church USA	1,228	- 13	1,215
Methodist	**1,202,991**	**+ 16,542**	**1,219,533**
African Methodist Episcopal Zion	2,191	—	(2,191)*
(African Methodist Episcopal estimate)*(300 congregations)	(150,000)*	—	(150,000)*
(Christian Methodist Episcopal estimate)*	(45,000)*	—	(45,000)*
Evangelical Methodist Church	1,482		
United Methodist Church, The	1,004,318	+ 18,024	1,022,342
(Mormons) Church of Jesus Christ of Latter-day Saints	**111,276**	**+ 44,175**	**155,451**
Muslim, estimate			**114,999**
Orthodox	**2,082**	**+ 20,673**	**22,755**
Antiochian Orthodox of North America			4,642
Armenian Apostolic Church/Cilicia			80
Armenian Apostolic Church/Etchmiadzin			1,275
Assyrian Apostolic Church	282		
Coptic Orthodox Church (8 congregations)			NR
Greek Orthodox Archdiocese of America			9,444
Greek Orthodox Archdiocese of Vasiloupulis			135
Malankara Archdiocese/Syrian Orthodox Church in North Amer.			825
Malankara Orthodox Syrian Church, American Diocese of the			2,675
Orthodox Church in America (Romanian Diocese)			413
Orthodox Church in America (Territorial Dioceses)			2,096
Russian Orthodox Church Outside of Russia (4 congregations)			NR
Serbian Orthodox Church in the USA			1,110
Serbian Orthodox Ch./New Gracanica Metropolitanate (1 cong)			NR
Syrian Orthodox Church of Antioch	1,800	- 1,740	60
Pentecostal/Charismatic	**682,769**	**+ 80,301**	**763,070**
Assemblies of God	202,082	+ 26,016	228,098
Pentecostal Church of God	12,296	- 704	11,592
Pentecostal Holiness Church, International	5,517	+ 4,748	10,265
Church of God (Cleveland, Tenn.)	27,828	+ 10,431	38,259
Church of God of Prophecy	2,918	- 12	2,906
(Church of God in Christ estimate)*(268 congregations)	(300,000)*	—	(300,000)*
International Church of the Foursquare Gospel	4,278	+ 8,223	12,501
Independent Charismatic Churches	127,850	+ 31,599	159,449

Religious Groups in Texas	1990	Change	2000
Presbyterian	**217,277**	**- 12,473**	**204,804**
Associate Reformed Presbyterian Church			28
Cumberland Presbyterian Church	10,373	- 1,951	8,422
Evangelical Presbyterian Church	490	+ 959	1,449
Orthodox Presbyterian Church, The			644
Presbyterian Church (USA)	200,969	- 20,654	180,315
Presbyterian Church in America	5,445	+ 8,501	13,946
(Quakers) Friends	**2,548**	**- 1,474**	**1,074**
Seventh-day Adventists	**41,470**	**+ 4,798**	**46,268**
Sikh (13 congregations)			**NR**
Tao (1 congregation)			**NR**
United Church of Christ	**20,950**	**- 4,363**	**16,587**
Zoroastrian (3 congregations)			**NR**
OTHERS (less than 12,000 reported)			
Advent Christian Church	221		
Apostolic Christian Churches of America	13	+ 14	27
Brethren In Christ Church	73		
Calvary Chapel Fellowship Church (19 congregations)			NR
Christ Catholic Church	3		
Christian (Plymouth) Brethren	6,766		
Christian Reformed Church	866	+ 1,070	1,936
Church of Christ, Scientist (93 congregations)			NR
Church of God General Conference, Abrahamic Faith	93	- 38	55
Church of God (Seventh Day) Denver, Col., The	1,743		
Church of the Brethren	302	- 18	284
Community of Christ			2,817
Congregational Christian Churches, National Association of	721		
Congregational Christian Churches (Not part of CCC body)	23		
Conservative Congregational Christian Conference	104	- 79	25
Evangelical Covenant Church, The			1,022
Evangelical Free Church of America, The	5,463	+ 4,257	9,720
Independent Fundamental Churches of America (4 cong.)			NR
International Churches of Christ			4,041
International Council of Community Churches			1,152
Metropolitan Community Churches, Universal Fellowship of			5,570
Missionary Church USA			403
Open Bible Standard Churches, Inc. (2 congregations)			NR
Reformed Church in America	1,592	+ 448	2,040
Unitarian Universalist Association	5,843	+ 1,029	6,872
Vineyard USA			11,637
Statewide Totals	**11,391,401**	**+ 1,483,617**	**12,875,018**
Unclaimed (not counted as adherent to religion)	5,460,358	+ 2,516,444	7,976,802

*Compiled principally from Glenmary Research Center, also other sources. NR, not reported. *Almanac estimates.*

Christ Church in Matagorda traces its history to 1838, making it the oldest Episcopal parish in Texas. Parts of the church building date to 1856.

Robert Plocheck photo.

Health & Science

East Texas Medical Center in Tyler. Robert Plocheck photo.

Honored Scientists

Research Funding in Texas

Deaths and Health Care

Hospitals

Drug Treatment

Mental Care

Texans in the National Academy of the Sciences

Source: National Academy of Sciences

The National Academy of Sciences is a private organization of scientists and engineers dedicated to the furtherance of science and its use for the general welfare. A total of 73 scientists affiliated with Texas institutions have been named members or associates.

Established by congressional acts of incorporation, which were signed by Abraham Lincoln in 1863, the academy acts as official adviser to the federal government in matters of science or technology.

Selected to the academy in 2007 were: **Mary K. Estes**, professor of molecular virology and microbiology at Baylor College of Medicine in Houston, and **Helen H. Hobb**s, director of the Eugene McDermott Center for Human Growth and Development at the University of Texas Southwestern Medical Center in Dallas. Selected to the academy in 2006 were: **Paul F. Bar-**

bara, professor of chemistry at the University of Texas at Austin. Also, **Melanie H. Cobb**, professor of pharmacology and dean of the graduate school at the UT Southwestern Medical Center at Dallas. Also, **David W. Russell**, professor of molecular genetics at the UT Southwestern Medical Center, Dallas.

Election to the academy is one of the highest honors that can be accorded a U.S. scientist.

As of May 3, 2007, the number of active members was 2,025. In addition, 387 scientists with citizenship outside the United States are nonvoting foreign associates. In 1970, D.H.R. Barton from Texas A&M University, and, in 1997, Johann Deisenhofer of the University of Texas Southwestern Medical Center, Dallas, were elected as foreign associates.

In 1948, Karl Folkers of the University of Texas at Austin became the first Texan elected to the science academy. ☆

Academy Member	Affiliation*	Year Elected
Perry L. Adkisson	A&M	1979
Abram Amsel	UT-Austin	1992
Neal R. Amundson	U of H	1992
Charles J. Arntzen	A&M	1983
David H. Auston	Rice	1991
Paul F. Barbara	UT-Austin	2006
Allen J. Bard	UT-Austin	1982
Brian J.L. Berry	UT-Dallas	1975
Lewis R. Binford	SMU	2001
Norman E. Borlaug	A&M	1968
Michael S. Brown	UTSWMC	1980
Karl W. Butzer	UT-Austin	1996
Luis A. Caffarelli	UT-Austin	1991
C. Thomas Caskey	Baylor Medical	1993
Joseph W. Chamberlain†	Rice	1965
C.W. Chu	U of H	1989
Melanie H. Cobb	UTSWMC	2006
F. Albert Cotton†	A&M	1967
Robert F. Curl	Rice	1997
Gerard H. de Vaucouleurs†	UT-Austin	1986
Bryce DeWitt†	UT-Austin	1990
Stephen J. Elledge	Baylor Medical	2003
Ronald W. Estabrook	UTSWMC	1979
Mary K. Estes	Baylor Medical	2007
Karl Folkers†	UT-Austin	1948
Marye Anne Fox	UT-Austin	1994
David L. Garbers	UTSWMC	1993
Quentin H. Gibson	Rice	1982
Alfred G. Gilman	UTSWMC	1985
Joseph L. Goldstein	UTSWMC	1980
William E. Gordon	Rice	1968
Verne E. Grant	UT-Austin	1968
Norman Hackerman†	Welch	1971
Dudley Herschbach	A&M	1967
Helen H. Hobbs	UTSWMC	2007
A. James Hudspeth	UTSWMC	1991
James L. Kinsey	Rice	1991
Ernst Knobil†	UTHSC-Houston	1986
Jay K. Kochi	U of H	1982
Alan M. Lambowitz	UT-Austin	2004
Alan G. MacDiarmid†	UT-Dallas	2002
John L. Margrave†	Rice	1974
S.M. McCann	UTSWMC	1983

Academy Member	Affiliation*	Year Elected
Steven L. McKnight	UTSWMC	1992
Ferid Murad	UTHSC-Houston	1997
Jack Myers	UT-Austin	1975
Eric N. Olson	UTSWMC	2000
Bert W. O'Malley	Baylor Medical	1992
Kenneth L. Pike†	SIL	1985
Lester J. Reed	UT-Austin	1973
David W. Russell	UTSWMC	2006
Marlan O. Scully	A&M	2001
Richard E. Smalley†	Rice	1990
Esmond E. Snell†	UT-Austin	1955
Richard C. Starr†	UT-Austin	1976
Thomas Südhof	UTSWMC	2002
Max D. Summers	A&M	1989
Harry L. Swinney	UT-Austin	1992
John T. Tate	UT-Austin	1969
Karen K. Uhlenbeck	UT-Austin	1986
Jonathan W. Uhr	UTSWMC	1984
Roger H. Unger	UTSWMC	1986
Ellen S. Vitetta	UTSWMC	1994
Salih J. Wakil	Baylor Medical	1990
Xiaodong Wang	UTSWMC	2004
Steven Weinberg	UT-Austin	1972
D. Fred Wendorf	SMU	1987
Jean D. Wilson	UTSWMC	1983
James E. Womack	A&M	1999
Masahi Yanagisawa	UTSWMC	2003
Huda Y. Zoghbi	Baylor Medical	2004

†Deceased
Source: National Academy of Sciences

* A&M - Texas A&M University
UT-Austin - The University of Texas at Austin
U of H - University of Houston
UT-Dallas - The University of Texas at Dallas
UTSWMC - The University of Texas Southwestern Medical Center at Dallas
Baylor Medical - Baylor College of Medicine, Houston
Rice - Rice University
Welch - Robert A. Welch Foundation
UTHSC - Houston - The University of Texas Health Science Center at Houston
SIL - Summer Institute of Linguistics
SMU - Southern Methodist University

Science Funding at Universities

The following chart shows the funding for research and development by source at universities and colleges in Texas, in order of total R&D funding. The figures are from the National Science Foundation and are for fiscal year 2004.

(in thousands, 000)	All R&D expenditures	Federal government	State and local government	Industry	Institutional funds	All other sources
United States	$ 42,945,081	$ 27,379,233	$ 2,846,722	$ 2,107,322	$ 7,771,253	$ 2,840,551
Texas (statewide)	2,880,784	1,647,212	355,426	162,157	410,789	305,200
Baylor College of Medicine	476,075	312,669	3,140	18,642	52,100	89,524
Texas A&M University	456,809	173,705	118,622	32,094	121,998	10,390
U. Texas M.D. Anderson	353,034	150,529	89,902	22,338	51,215	39,050
University of Texas Austin	343,886	235,281	21,009	27,176	37,877	22,543
U. Texas Southwestern Med.	314,403	200,888	23,298	12,493	7,100	70,624
U. Texas Medical Branch	166,798	102,491	16,183	5,842	29,920	12,362
U.Texas Health Sci. Houston	147,328	106,737	5,752	7,373	12,239	15,227
U.TX Health Sci. SanAntonio	137,039	89,662	4,924	6,268	25,274	10,911
Texas A&M Health Sci. Ctr.	64,170	30,283	1,057	2,876	20,083	9,871
University of Houston	60,962	34,468	10,192	5,297	6,119	4,886
Rice University	60,872	51,157	1,909	2,265	0	5,541
Texas Tech University	57,592	23,181	14,291	6,224	11,430	2,466
University of Texas Dallas	31,274	15,733	9,113	1,016	1,368	4,044
University of Texas El Paso	25,440	16,900	6,008	1,792	740	0
Texas Tech Health Sci. Ctr.	19,827	7,604	4,831	950	6,442	0
University of Texas Arlington	19,003	10,498	2,517	1,984	4,004	0
U. North Texas Health Sci.	18,520	13,259	608	1,954	1,697	1,002
U. Texas San Antonio	15,738	11,644	3,211	116	767	0
Texas A&M Corpus Christi	12,266	5,685	3,061	34	2,700	786
University of North Texas	11,958	5,499	1,505	618	3,255	1,081
Texas A&M Kingsville	11,102	3,832	1,089	271	5,173	737
Prairie View A&M University	10,989	7,965	2,285	72	579	88
Southern Methodist U.	10,432	6,752	462	367	2,147	704
Texas State U. San Marcos	9,130	3,536	2,744	59	1,709	1,082
Tarleton State University	7,194	5,208	905	211	870	0
Baylor University	5,242	1,372	706	1,033	1,567	564
Texas Southern University	4,088	3,749	67	272	0	0

Colleges and universities not listed received less. Source: National Science Foundation, 2007.

Dr. Norman Borlaug, with President Bush, shows an Aggie gig'em sign at the White House ceremony Feb.13, 2006, where he was presented with the National Medal of Science. Congress also honored the Texas A&M University professor with a Gold Medal of Honor in 2006. See story, page 527. Reuters/Jim Young photo.

Science Research Funding by State

The following chart shows expenditures for scientific research by state, in order by the total for fiscal year 2004.

State	2004	2002	2000
	(in thousands of dollars, 000)		
United States	$42,945,081	$36,367,358	$30,068,664
California	5,714,383	4,888,197	4,065,130
New York	3,365,658	2,763,416	2,291,749
Texas	2,880,784	2,535,237	2,037,681
Maryland	2,269,201	1,886,027	1,507,549
Pennsylvania	2,206,023	1,912,760	1,552,417
Massachusetts	2,000,120	1,697,102	1,486,174
Illinois	1,707,597	1,440,716	1,170,743
North Carolina	1,442,854	1,276,823	1,039,812
Michigan	1,397,011	1,233,511	1,007,582
Ohio	1,318,420	1,115,710	918,241
Florida	1,306,810	1,085,764	851,932
Georgia	1,221,251	1,076,424	926,749
Wisconsin	955,802	805,813	661,470

Source: National Science Foundation, 2007.

Death, Birth Rates Continue Trends in Texas Vital Statistics

Source: Texas Department of State Health Services.

Heart disease and cancer remained the major causes of death in 2004, the latest year for which statistics were available from the Bureau of Vital Statistics, Texas Department of State Health Services.

Heart disease accounted for 26.3 percent of the 152,374 deaths. Cancer accounted for 22.2 percent of the deaths during the year. These two diseases have been the leading causes of death in Texas and the nation since 1950.

Cerebrovascular diseases (strokes), accidents and chronic lower respiratory diseases ranked third, fourth and fifth, respectively. Together, these five leading causes of death represented 60.4 percent of all deaths.

While the number of babies born to Texas mothers continued to increase in 2004 (381,441), the state's birth rate was at an all-time low of 17.0 per 1,000 population. In 1960, that figure was 25.7. (See chart comparing other state and world birth rates, page 576.)

Although there has been a general decrease since 1990 in the number of abortions, there was an increase in 2005 to 74,399 from 72,441 in 2004.

Health Care and Deaths in Texas Counties

County	Patient Care 2006		Total Deaths 2004	Misc., 2005		County	Patient Care 2006		Total Deaths 2004	Misc., 2005	
	Physicians	Hospital Beds		Pregnancy rate*	Abortions		Physicians	Hospital Beds		Pregnancy rate*	Abortions
Statewide Total	**42,584**	**72,416**	**152,374**	**92.9**	**74,399***	Coleman	4	25	136	81.0	4
Anderson	81	249	597	84.0	66	Collin	1,170	1,072	2,239	84.1	1,787
Andrews	15	85	110	79.8	22	Collingswrth	2	16	51	59.5	1
Angelina	144	406	773	82.6	146	Colorado	31	103	245	70.4	37
Aransas	14	0	300	80.7	34	Comal	135	132	766	75.1	186
Archer	1	0	66	70.7	15	Comanche	16	50	159	75.1	13
Armstrong	0	0	31	62.3	0	Concho	2	16	29	71.1	0
Atascosa	36	67	300	86.9	89	Cooke	28	99	382	78.4	52
Austin	8	32	310	75.7	56	Coryell	22	55	358	55.9	108
Bailey	4	31	68	108.7	7	Cottle	0	0	10	91.8	12
Bandera	7	0	141	60.5	31	Crane	2	25	43	81.3	8
Bastrop	33	36	486	76.2	115	Crockett	1	0	36	83.9	9
Baylor	4	49	66	92.2	6	Crosby	2	25	86	108.2	18
Bee	24	69	222	79.3	44	Culberson	0	25	27	70.2	1
Bell	775	961	1,653	116.1	891	Dallam	7	0	48	85.7	9
Bexar	4,008	5,738	10,426	96.9	6,727	Dallas	6,252	7,812	13,741	102.0	11,128
Blanco	5	0	93	64.7	15	Dawson	3	44	151	86.8	18
Borden	0	0	1	38.8	3	Deaf Smith	8	40	156	99.1	23
Bosque	11	40	247	72.3	29	Delta	1	0	55	78.1	6
Bowie	240	914	962	65.9	37	Denton	617	565	1,967	74.5	1,553
Brazoria	202	249	1,680	86.8	547	DeWitt	10	60	228	77.5	27
Brazos	360	423	743	60.8	514	Dickens	1	0	30	67.0	8
Brewster	8	40	81	79.5	19	Dimmit	8	48	70	96.2	10
Briscoe	0	0	14	85.3	17	Donley	1	0	55	72.9	5
Brooks	2	0	47	99.3	16	Duval	2	0	110	84.4	35
Brown	63	216	472	69.7	39	Eastland	11	83	319	78.9	19
Burleson	5	25	150	83.7	27	Ector	207	602	1,112	95.4	242
Burnet	70	42	397	81.0	45	Edwards	1	0	17	52.2	3
Caldwell	14	64	276	80.2	54	Ellis	94	114	963	81.9	210
Calhoun	18	49	173	82.8	22	El Paso	1,002	2,186	4,143	102.1	2,018
Callahan	2	0	150	64.4	15	Erath	43	98	349	70.0	68
Cameron	519	1,271	1,930	116.1	873	Falls	4	44	225	58.1	40
Camp	13	44	134	92.2	13	Fannin	27	75	413	71.7	50
Carson	0	0	54	70.5	5	Fayette	25	50	338	67.9	24
Cass	13	90	378	64.4	7	Fisher	4	14	65	49.4	3
Castro	3	23	59	92.0	3	Floyd	7	25	77	80.0	5
Chambers	7	39	198	57.4	58	Foard	0	0	9	73.4	3
Cherokee	69	104	548	87.8	54	Fort Bend	452	516	1,672	74.6	1,225
Childress	9	49	60	71.7	6	Franklin	8	49	92	78.1	13
Clay	3	32	100	48.5	7	Freestone	11	48	227	83.3	40
Cochran	0	18	39	73.0	0	Frio	8	40	119	95.4	42
Coke	2	0	54	49.3	12	Gaines	6	49	104	91.0	11
						Galveston	727	1,027	2,261	83.6	741

County	Patient Care 2006		Total Deaths 2004	Misc., 2005	
	Physicians	Hospital Beds		Pregnancy rate*	Abortions
Garza	1	0	46	84.8	5
Gillespie	74	77	279	80.4	24
Glasscock	0	0	5	59.3	2
Goliad	2	0	76	66.9	9
Gonzales	15	35	197	106.0	36
Gray	22	115	270	73.3	12
Grayson	221	664	1,223	77.6	180
Gregg	298	659	1,184	83.7	110
Grimes	13	25	229	81.2	48
Guadalupe	66	117	665	66.3	186
Hale	32	100	305	98.7	46
Hall	1	0	53	86.6	3
Hamilton	8	49	143	79.8	15
Hansford	2	25	61	107.6	1
Hardeman	6	45	43	75.4	12
Hardin	14	0	501	71.7	95
Harris	9,409	14,834	20,195	100.4	18,973
Harrison	45	149	585	65.8	17
Hartley	0	21	54	149.3	3
Haskell	2	30	103	70.1	5
Hays	143	113	563	65.7	355
Hemphill	3	26	39	86.8	6
Henderson	59	117	889	80.0	98
Hidalgo	761	1,505	3,050	122.1	1,629
Hill	24	141	401	84.9	55
Hockley	15	48	221	86.0	43
Hood	53	56	528	70.5	44
Hopkins	32	100	361	76.4	39
Houston	14	80	302	81.0	16
Howard	44	150	378	82.5	47
Hudspeth	0	0	18	71.1	2
Hunt	73	172	734	76.3	138
Hutchinson	19	99	251	76.8	20
Irion	1	0	14	49.4	1
Jack	4	41	81	75.5	6
Jackson	5	35	147	84.7	28
Jasper	35	86	421	85.3	54
Jeff Davis	1	0	23	87.2	3
Jefferson	560	1,946	2,518	80.2	592
Jim Hogg	2	0	46	84.2	15
Jim Wells	38	211	305	83.7	101
Johnson	108	137	1,043	74.7	244
Jones	6	95	184	62.3	25
Karnes	3	43	147	82.3	26
Kaufman	83	221	716	82.8	175
Kendall	39	0	238	76.2	43
Kenedy	0	0	2	118.4	1
Kent	0	0	20	68.7	0
Kerr	147	155	653	83.0	92
Kimble	4	15	61	83.0	4
King	0	0	3	72.5	2
Kinney	1	0	34	74.8	1
Kleberg	19	100	249	81.8	98
Knox	2	28	58	75.8	1
Lamar	106	389	584	70.4	52
Lamb	4	75	142	87.8	16
Lampasas	12	25	189	62.1	23
La Salle	1	0	44	99.0	15
Lavaca	19	68	268	77.4	22
Lee	5	0	130	72.2	37
Leon	3	0	206	76.0	15
Liberty	62	142	671	68.3	104
Limestone	22	79	290	89.5	38
Lipscomb	0	0	39	80.9	2
Live Oak	3	0	78	58.9	17
Llano	17	30	273	70.8	21
Loving	0	0	0	–	0
Lubbock	785	1,933	1,898	79.0	697
Lynn	3	24	51	85.3	6
Madison	8	25	142	89.0	9
Marion	3	0	127	57.9	5
Martin	2	25	57	70.6	6
Mason	0	0	53	66.9	1
Matagorda	36	117	316	75.3	61
Maverick	29	77	241	98.6	35
McCulloch	7	49	118	81.0	13
McLennan	428	566	1,956	79.7	610
McMullen	0	0	6	29.9	1
Medina	20	25	341	78.3	66
Menard	1	0	31	48.6	3
Midland	186	491	905	82.5	269
Milam	12	69	283	89.0	37
Mills	3	0	57	57.3	1
Mitchell	3	25	107	89.0	10
Montague	13	87	270	78.6	26
Montgomery	509	892	2,170	78.5	643
Moore	18	60	122	111.5	16
Morris	3	0	160	70.1	8
Motley	1	0	18	95.5	1
Nacgdoches	122	346	574	69.7	111
Navarro	48	162	500	82.3	73
Newton	5	0	155	53.0	8
Nolan	16	85	209	80.5	23
Nueces	781	1,583	2,407	89.2	1,115
Ochiltree	6	49	54	95.4	16
Oldham	0	0	19	61.9	0
Orange	44	239	870	73.5	136
Palo Pinto	28	99	331	74.1	36
Panola	19	49	278	72.0	3
Parker	63	99	754	69.3	167
Parmer	3	25	73	82.0	11
Pecos	9	40	120	77.5	10
Polk	34	35	592	73.1	47
Potter	468	941	1,164	94.7	225
Presidio	1	0	37	94.5	4
Rains	2	0	119	59.5	7
Randall	79	4	736	65.7	162
Reagan	1	14	20	97.0	5
Real	0	0	52	71.9	2
Red River	6	49	216	64.4	13
Reeves	10	49	108	91.5	16
Refugio	3	20	93	67.6	24
Roberts	0	0	10	13.2	0
Robertson	4	0	192	77.0	26
Rockwall	57	97	357	83.2	115
Runnels	5	50	139	78.7	16
Rusk	27	96	503	71.4	34
Sabine	3	36	156	60.8	2
S. Augustine	4	25	140	62.0	5
San Jacinto	4	0	225	65.1	26

County	Patient Care 2006		Total Deaths 2004	Misc., 2005		County	Patient Care 2006		Total Deaths 2004	Misc., 2005	
	Physicians	Hospital Beds		Pregnancy rate*	Abortions		Physicians	Hospital Beds		Pregnancy rate*	Abortions
San Patricio	23	75	519	87.6	167	Victoria	207	741	692	81.2	149
San Saba	2	0	72	92.2	1	Walker	71	127	433	60.5	152
Schleicher	1	14	36	66.9	3	Waller	4	0	246	67.7	102
Scurry	13	99	166	97.5	18	Ward	5	49	109	67.6	9
Shackelford	1	0	48	50.9	2	Washington	36	60	344	75.9	54
Shelby	13	54	310	82.2	3	Webb	205	623	946	129.6	425
Sherman	1	0	28	107.7	17	Wharton	57	210	451	84.7	72
Smith	676	1,108	1,575	84.2	356	Wheeler	7	41	71	74.1	6
Somervell	8	16	61	69.3	9	Wichita	284	745	1,286	77.9	243
Starr	24	49	283	120.7	65	Wilbarger	17	47	182	87.2	24
Stephens	9	40	122	82.4	16	Willacy	8	0	117	106.3	39
Sterling	0	0	14	56.5	1	Williamson	339	307	1,410	87.2	714
Stonewall	1	20	16	82.7	1	Wilson	15	44	301	72.0	64
Sutton	2	12	35	103.0	4	Winkler	2	25	85	103.1	7
Swisher	4	20	72	99.5	11	Wise	44	85	431	64.5	50
Tarrant	2,980	4,521	9,670	94.8	5,771	Wood	28	80	495	77.4	42
Taylor	281	710	1,203	79.2	177	Yoakum	5	24	50	91.8	7
Terrell	0	0	13	222.9	16	Young	21	86	255	80.4	24
Terry	7	45	122	97.6	11	Zapata	6	0	66	109.9	19
Throckmortn	1	14	25	22.1	2	Zavala	4	0	76	92.2	19
Titus	47	165	248	96.5	49						
Tom Green	225	608	1,000	79.8	184						
Travis	2,349	2,197	3,297	87.1	3,907						
Trinity	4	30	228	72.5	13						
Tyler	9	49	279	100.1	55						
Upshur	13	37	386	68.3	28						
Upton	2	29	18	68.3	9						
Uvalde	26	66	228	96.8	56						
Val Verde	38	93	281	103.5	67						
Van Zandt	13	52	567	73.6	68						

Sources: Texas Department of Health: Vital Statistics, 2004-2005(by county of residence) and **Center for Health Statistics**, January 2007. **Texas Medical Board**, January 2007.
Physicians - All practicing licensed M.D.s and D.O.s.
Hospital Beds - Licensed Acute Care Beds (2004), not including U.S. military and veteran's hospitals.
*Pregnancy Rate figured per 1,000 women age 15-44.
*Abortion total statewide includes abortions performed in Texas but county of residence unknown, plus abortions obtained outside the state by Texas residents.

Marriage and Divorce in Texas and the United States

These charts are for certain years, including 1946 when there was a significant increase in marriages after World War II, as well as a significant increase in divorces. Also included are the years 1979-81 when the marriage and divorce rates reached another peak. *Source:* Statistical Abstracts of the United States, *various, U.S. Census.*

Texas	Total marriages	Marriage rate*	Total divorces	Divorce rate*	U.S.	Total marriages	Marriage rate*	Total divorces	Divorce rate*
1940	86,500	13.5	27,500	4.3	1940	1,595,879	12.1	264,000	2.0
1946	**143,092**	**20.5**	**57,112**	**8.4**	**1946**	**2,291,045**	**16.4**	**610,000**	**4.3**
1950	89,155	11.6	37,400	4.9	1950	1,667,231	11.1	385,144	2.6
1955	91,210	10.4	34,921	4.0	1955	1,531,000	9.3	377,000	2.3
1960	91,700	9.6	34,732	3.6	1960	1,523,381	8.5	393,000	2.2
1965	111,500	10.5	41,300	3.9	1965	1,800,200	9.3	479,000	2.5
1970	139,500	12.5	51,500	4.6	1970	2,159,000	10.6	708,000	3.5
1975	153,200	12.5	76,700	6.3	1975	2,152,700	10.1	1,036,000	4.9
1979	**172,800**	**12.9**	**92,400**	**6.9**	**1979**	**2,331,300**	**10.6**	**1,181,000**	**5.4**
1980	**181,800**	**12.8**	**96,800**	**6.8**	**1980**	**2,390,300**	**10.6**	**1,189,000**	**5.2**
1981	**194,800**	**13.2**	**101,900**	**6.9**	**1981**	**2,422,100**	**10.6**	**1,213,000**	**5.3**
1985	213,800	13.1	101,200	6.2	1985	2,425,000	10.2	1,187,000	5.0
1990	182,800	10.5	94,000	5.5	1990	2,443,000	9.8	1,182,000	4.7
1995	188,500	10.1	98,400	5.3	1995	2,336,000	8.9	1,169,000	4.4
2000	196,400	9.6	85,200	4.2	2000	2,329,000	8.2	**NA	4.1
2004	176,300	7.8	81,900	3.6	2004	2,178,400	7.4	NA	3.7

*Rate per 1,000 population.

**Not Available. Since 1995, the federal government no longer publishes information on the total number of divorces.

Comparison of Vital Statistics

The most current data available, with selected states; those bordering Texas and other large states. **Lowest and highest with number in bold.**

State/ Country	BIRTH rate*	DEATH rate*	LIFE expectancy
Texas	17.0	6.8	77.4
Alaska	15.8	**4.9**	-
Arkansas	14.0	10.2	-
California	15.2	6.8	-
Florida	12.5	9.9	-
Georgia	15.7	7.7	-
Illinois	14.2	8.3	-
Louisiana	14.5	9.5	-
Massachusetts	12.2	8.8	-
Michigan	12.8	7.4	-
New Mexico	14.9	7.9	-
New York	13.0	8.1	-
Ohio	13.0	9.5	-
Oklahoma	14.6	10.2	-
Utah	**21.2**	5.7	-
Vermont	**10.6**	8.3	-
West Virginia	11.5	**11.8**	-
United States	14.0	8.4	77.9
Afghanistan	46.6	20.3	43.3
Brazil	16.6	6.2	72.0
Canada	10.8	7.8	80.2
China	13.3	7.0	72.6
Congo	42.6	12.9	52.8
Egypt	22.9	5.2	71.3
France	12.0	9.1	79.7
Germany	**8.6**	10.6	78.8
India	22.0	8.2	64.7
Iraq	32.0	5.4	69.0
Italy	8.7	10.4	79.8
Japan	9.4	9.2	**81.2**
Kuwait	21.9	**2.4**	77.2
Mexico	20.7	4.7	75.4
Niger	**50.7**	20.9	43.8
Pakistan	29.7	8.2	63.4
Philippines	24.9	5.4	70.2
Poland	9.9	9.9	75.0
Russia	10.0	14.7	67.1
South Africa	18.2	22.0	42.7
Spain	10.1	9.7	79.7
Swaziland	27.4	**29.7**	**32.6**
Ukraine	8.8	14.4	70.0
United Kingdom	10.7	10.1	78.5
World	20.1	8.7	64.8

*Rates are number during 1 year per 1,000 persons.

Sources: Statistical Abstract of the United States, 2007; CIA World Factbook, 2006; Texas Vital Statistics Annual Report 2004. Statistics are from 2004-2006.

Life Expectancy for Texans by Group

	All	Whites	Blacks	Hispanics
Total population	77.4	77.7	72.6	78.7
Males	74.8	75.2	69.5	76.1
Females	80.0	80.2	75.5	81.2

Source: Texas Department of State Health Services, 2004.

Texas Births by Race/Ethnicity and Sex

	2004	2000	1990	1980
All Races	381,441	363,325	316,257	273,433
All Male	195,024	185,591	161,522	139,999
All Female	186,417	177,734	154,735	133,434
White Total	136,659	142,553	150,461	151,725
White Male	70,203	72,972	77,134	78,086
White Female	66,456	69,581	73,327	73,639
Black Total	42,117	41,180	43,342	38,544
Black Male	21,300	21,128	21,951	19,501
Black Female	20,817	20,052	21,391	19,043
Hispanic Total	187,784	166,440	115,576	79,324
Hispanic Male	95,845	84,750	58,846	40,475
Hispanic Female	91,939	81,690	56,730	38,849
Other* Total	14,881	13,152	6,687	3,840
Other Male	7,676	6,741	3,591	1,937
Other Female	7,205	6,411	3,287	1,903

*Other includes births of unknown race/ethnicity.
Source: Texas Department of State Health Services, 2005.

Persons Without Health Insurance by State, 2004

Comparison with states bordering Texas, other large states, highest and lowest percentage of coverage (in bold).

State	Total covered (1,000)	Total not covered — Number (1,000)	Total not covered — Percent	Children not covered — Number (1,000)	Children not covered — Percent
Texas	16,741	5,583	**25.0**	1,353	**21.4**
Arkansas	2,282	448	16.4	47	6.8
California	29,140	6,710	18.7	1,194	12.4
Florida	13,987	3,479	19.9	611	15.1
Georgia	7,193	1,513	17.1	273	11.7
Illinois	10,832	1,764	14.0	368	11.4
Louisiana	3,661	761	17.2	92	8.0
Mass.	5,625	748	11.7	97	6.5
Michigan	8,816	1,156	11.6	174	6.8
Minnesota	4,667	458	**8.9**	85	6.8
New Mexico	1,504	399	21.0	76	15.3
New York	16,345	2,705	14.2	396	8.6
Ohio	9,987	1,282	11.4	212	7.5
Oklahoma	2,760	685	19.9	144	16.9
Wisconsin	4,898	566	10.4	67	**5.1**
U.S. total	245,335	45,820	15.7	8,269	11.2

Source: U.S. Census Bureau.

The Laredo Medical Center. Robert Plocheck photo.

Community Hospitals in Texas

Source: The Texas Hospital Association

– Of the 525 reporting hospitals in Texas in 2005, 415 were considered community hospitals.

(A community hospital is defined as either a non-federal, short-term general hospital or a special hospital whose facilities and services are available to the public. A hospital may include a nursing home-type unit and still be classified as short-term, provided that the majority of its patients are admitted to units where the average length-of-stay is less than 30 days.)

– These 415 hospitals employed 288,000 full-time equivalent people (FTEs) with a payroll, including benefits, of more than $16.5 billion.

– These hospitals contained some 58,000 beds.

– The average length-of-stay was 5.2 days in 2005, compared to 6.8 days in 1975. This was less than the U.S. average of 5.6 days.

– The average cost per adjusted admission in Texas was $8,300 or $1,636 per day. This was 2.5 percent less than the U.S. average of $8,500.

– There were 2,509,000 admissions in Texas, which accounted for 13,102,000 inpatient days.

– There were 32,829,000 outpatient visits in 2005, of which 8,206,000 were emergency room visits.

– Of the FTEs working in community hospitals within in Texas, there were 75,400 registered nurses and 13,100 licensed vocational nurses. ☆

U.S. Hospitals: By the Numbers

ITEM	1980	1990	1995	2000	2004
Hospitals	6,965	6,649	6,291	5,810	5,759
Beds (000)	1,365	1,213	1,081	984	956
Daily census of patients (000)	1,060	844	710	650	658
Personnel (000)	3,492	4,063	4,273	4,554	4,695
Outpatient visits (millions)	263.0	368.2	483.2	592.7	662.1
Emergency (millions)	82.0	92.8	99.9	106.9	116.9

Source: Statistical Abstract of the United States 2007, from Hospital Statistics.

U.S. Hospital Care: Source of Payments

Source of payment	1990	1995	2000	2004
Hospital care, total ($ billions)	$ 251.6	$ 340.7	$ 417.0	$ 570.8
Out-of-pocket payments	11.3	10.4	13.6	18.6
Third-party payments	240.2	330.3	403.5	552.2
Private health insurance	97.8	110.6	143.6	203.4
Federal Government	101.7	166.0	192.9	258.7
State/Local Government	30.3	39.2	45.2	62.4
Physician and clinical services, total ($ billions)	157.5	220.5	288.6	399.9
Out-of-pocket payments	30.2	26.0	32.2	40.0
Third-party payments	127.3	194.5	256.4	359.9
Private health insurance	67.3	106.1	136.8	194.0
Federal Government	38.0	56.2	79.0	113.8
State/Local Government	10.7	14.7	18.4	24.4

Source: Statistical Abstract of the United States 2007, from U.S. Centers for Medicare and Medicaid Services.

Drug Treatment in State-Funded Programs: 2004

Primary Drug	Percent White	Percent Black	Percent Hispanic	Percent Employed over last 12 months	Average education (years)	Percent homeless
All Drugs	48.9	19.4	29.7	48.5	11.3	11.1
Opiates	51.6	8.6	38.2	30.1	11.6	9.5
Alcohol	57.9	13.8	26.1	45.8	11.9	12.7
Depressants	76.2	5.4	17.0	44.2	11.5	6.4
Amphet/Methamph	88.9	0.9	8.2	51.6	11.6	8.4
Cocaine	36.0	11.2	50.8	50.7	11.2	7.0
Marijuana	32.5	21.9	43.1	75.7	10.0	7.4
Hallucinogens	19.4	70.0	10.6	58.9	11.0	9.4
Other Drugs	35.8	15.4	43.5	62.8	10.3	7.7
Crack Cocaine	33.3	49.0	16.3	36.4	11.7	17.8

Source: Texas Department of State Health Services, 2006.

Characteristics of Youth Clients in State-Funded Drug Programs

Primary Drug	Total Admissions		Average Age		Percent Male		Percent Involved w/Criminal Justice	
	2004	2000	2004	2000	2004	2000	2004	2000
Total	6,484	4,339	16	16	77	80	58	66
Alcohol	521	380	16	16	69	70	51	59
Amphet/Methamph	201	53	16	16	56	53	53	57
Cocaine	346	216	16	16	60	67	50	55
Crack	96	83	16	16	50	75	55	55
Downers	101	17	16	15	56	76	49	47
Hallucinogens	15	48	16	15	80	73	33	69
Heroin	63	132	16	16	57	83	59	36
Inhalants	65	90	15	15	66	68	54	49
Marijuana/Hash	4,938	3,181	15	15	82	83	69	70
Other Drugs	82	122	16	16	72	69	61	59
Other, Synthetic Opiates	36	17	16	16	81	94	64	82

Source: Texas Department of State Health Services, 2006.

Characteristics of Adult Clients in State-Funded Drug Programs

Primary Drug	Total Admissions		Average Age		Percent Male		Percent Involved w/Criminal Justice	
	2004	2000	2004	2000	2004	2000	2004	2000
Total	46,742	31,352	35	34	61	63	22	22
Alcohol	13,890	11,001	38	37	68	72	24	26
Amphet/Methamph	5,061	1,753	30	31	46	46	21	16
Cocaine	3,994	2,692	32	31	56	61	28	22
Crack	9,431	7,157	37	35	54	54	14	13
Downers	575	358	32	36	33	07	10	8
Hallucinogens	37	53	29	27	65	57	27	25
Heroin	5,356	4,005	36	37	65	69	11	11
Inhalants	52	63	30	29	52	70	27	29
Marijuana/Hash	5,313	3,207	27	27	63	65	50	47
Other Drugs	251	206	28	28	48	54	33	19
Other, Synthetic Opiates	2,782	857	35	37	41	39	7	8

Source: Texas Department of State Health Services, 2006.

Estimated Use of Drugs in Texas and bordering states: 2002-2003

State	Any illicit drug	Marijuana	Other than marijuana[1]	Cigarettes	Binge alcohol[2]
Current users[3] as percent of population. Selected states.					
U.S. total	8.2	6.2	3.7	25.7	22.7
Texas	**7.0**	**4.8**	**3.9**	**25.6**	**23.9**
Arkansas	7.8	5.6	3.9	32.8	21.8
Louisana	8.1	5.8	4.2	28.3	23.8
Oklahoma	8.6	5.6	4.4	30.3	19.0
New Mexico	10.0	7.4	4.6	24.0	24.0

[1]Marijuana users who have also used another drug are included. [2]Binge use is defined as drinking five or more drinks on the same occasion on a least one day in the past 30 days. [3]Used drugs at least once within month. *Source: U.S. Substance Abuse and Mental Health Services Administration*, National Household Survey on Drug Use and Health, 2003.

State Institutions for Mental Health Services

Source: Texas Department of State Health Services.

Mental health services are provided to some 100,000 Texans each year in various institutions with staffs totalling 11,500 people. In 2006, the Texas Department of State Health Services (TDSHS) budget included $324.4 million for mental hospitals and $632.7 million for community mental health centers and substance-abuse treatment.

On Sept. 1, 2004, the TDSHS was created, bringing together:

— the Texas Department of Health,
— the Texas Department of Mental Health and Mental Retardation,
— the Commission on Alcohol and Drug Abuse,
— the Texas Health Care Information Council.

With the consolidation of the four agencies, TDSHS now includes treatment and prevention for mental illness and substance abuse in its public health framework. The Web address is: www.dshs.state.tx.us

Following is a list of state hospitals, the year each was founded and numbers of admissions/discharges of patients in fiscal year 2005.

Hospitals for Persons with Mental Illness

Austin State Hospital — Austin; 1857; 4,280 patients.
Big Spring State Hospital — Big Spring; 1937; 1,129 patients.
El Paso Psychiatric Center — El Paso; 1974; 974 patients.
Kerrville State Hospital — Kerrville; 1950; 488 patients.
North Texas State Hospital — Wichita Falls (1922) and Vernon (1969); 2,647 patients.
Rio Grande State Center — Harlingen; 1962; 1,217 patients.
Rusk State Hospital — Rusk; 1919; 1,902 patients.
San Antonio State Hospital — San Antonio; 1892; 3,121 patients.
Terrell State Hospital — Terrell; 1885; 2,419 patients.
Waco Center for Youth — Waco; 1979; 151 patients.

Following is a list of community mental health centers, the year each was founded, and the counties each serves.

Community Mental Health Centers

Abilene — Betty Hardwick Center; 1971; Callahan, Jones, Shackleford, Stephens and Taylor.
Amarillo — Texas Panhandle MHMR; 1968; Armstrong, Carson, Collingsworth, Dallam, Deaf Smith, Donley, Gray, Hall, Hansford, Hartley, Hemphill, Hutchinson, Lipscomb, Moore, Ochiltree, Oldham, Potter, Randall, Roberts, Sherman and Wheeler.
Austin — Austin-Travis County Center; 1967; Travis.
Beaumont — Spindletop MHMR Services; 1967; Chambers, Hardin, Jefferson and Orange.
Big Spring — West Texas Centers; 1997; Andrews, Borden, Crane, Dawson, Fisher, Gaines, Garza, Glasscock, Howard, Kent, Loving, Martin, Mitchell, Nolan, Reeves, Runnels, Scurry, Terrell, Terry, Upton, Ward, Winkler and Yoakum.
Brownwood — Center for Life Resources; 1969; Brown, Coleman, Comanche, Eastland, McCulloch, Mills and San Saba.
Bryan-College Station — MHMR Authority of Brazos Valley; 1972; Brazos, Burleson, Grimes, Leon, Madison, Robertson and Washington.
Cleburne — Johnson-Ellis-Navarro County Center; 1985; Ellis, Johnson, Navarro.
Conroe — Tri-County Services; 1983; Liberty, Montgomery and Walker.
Corpus Christi — Nueces County Community Center; 1970; Nueces.
Dallas — Dallas MetroCare; 1967; Dallas.
Denton — Denton County Center; 1987; Denton.
Edinburg — Tropical Texas Center; 1967; Cameron, Hidalgo and Willacy.
El Paso — Community Center; 1968; El Paso.
Fort Worth — MHMR of Tarrant County; 1969; Tarrant.
Galveston — Gulf Coast Center; 1969; Brazoria and Galveston.
Houston — MHMR Authority of Harris County; 1965; Harris.
Jacksonville — Anderson-Cherokee Community Enrichment Services; 1995; Anderson, Cherokee.
Kerrville — Hill Country Community Center; 1997; Bandera, Blanco, Comal, Edwards, Gillespie, Hays, Kendall, Kerr, Kimble, Kinney, Llano, Mason, Medina, Menard, Real, Schleicher, Sutton, Uvalde and Val Verde.
Laredo — Border Region Community Center; 1969; Jim Hogg, Starr, Webb and Zapata.
Longview — Sabine Valley Center; 1970; Gregg, Harrison, Marion, Panola, Rusk and Upshur.
Lubbock — Lubbock Regional Center; 1969; Cochran, Crosby, Hockley, Lubbock and Lynn.
Lufkin — Burke Center; 1975; Angelina, Houston, Jasper, Nacogdoches, Newton, Polk, Sabine, San Augustine, San Jacinto, Shelby, Trinity and Tyler.
Lytle — Camino Real Community Center; 1996; Atascosa, Dimmit, Frio, La Salle, Karnes, Maverick, McMullen, Wilson and Zavala.
McKinney — LifePath Systems; 1986; Collin.
Midland — Permian Basin Community Centers; 1969; Brewster, Culberson, Ector, Hudspeth, Jeff Davis, Midland, Pecos and Presidio.
Plainview — Central Plains Center; 1969; Bailey, Briscoe, Castro, Floyd, Hale, Lamb, Motley, Parmer and Swisher.
Portland — Coastal Plains Community; 1996; Aransas, Bee, Brooks, Duval, Jim Wells, Kenedy, Kleberg, Live Oak and San Patricio.
Rosenberg — Texana Center; 1996; Austin, Colorado, Fort Bend, Matagorda, Waller and Wharton.
Round Rock — Bluebonnet Trails Community Center; 1997; Bastroop, Burnet, Caldwell, Fayette, Gonzales, Guadalupe, Lee and Williamson.
San Angelo — MHMR Services for the Concho Valley; 1969; Coke, Concho, Crockett, Irion, Reagan, Sterling and Tom Green.
San Antonio — The Center for Health Care Services; 1966; Bexar.
Sherman — MHMR Services of Texoma; 1974; Cooke, Fannin and Grayson.
Stephenville — Pecan Valley Region; 1977; Erath, Hood, palo Pinto, Parker and Somervell.
Temple — Central Counties Center; 1967; Bell, Coryell, Hamilton, Lampasas and Milam.
Terrell — Lakes Regional Center; 1996; Camp, Delta, Franklin, Hopkins, Hunt, Kaufman, Lamar, Morris, Rockwall and Titus.
Texarkana — Northeast Texas Center; 1974; Bowie, Cass and Red River.
Tyler — Andrews Center; 1970; Henderson, Rains, Smith, Van Zandt and Wood.
Victoria — Gulf Bend Center; 1970; Calhoun, DeWitt, Jackson, Lavaca, Refugio and Victoria.
Waco — Heart of Texas Region Center; 1969; Bosque, Falls, Freestone, Hill, Limestone and McLennan.
Wichita Falls — Helen Farabee Regional Centers; 1969; Archer, Bayor, Childress, Clay, Cottle, Dickens, Foard, Hardeman, Haskell, Jack, King, Knox, Montague, Stonewall, Throckmorton, Wichita, Wilbarger and Young. ☆

Education

St. Louis Hall at St. Mary's University in San Antonio. Photo courtesy of St. Mary's.

Texas Public Schools

UIL Winning Schools for 2005–2006 & 2006–2007

Higher Education in Texas

Universities and Colleges

Texas Public Schools

Source: Texas Education Agency; www.tea.state.tx.us

Enrollment in the Texas public schools **reached a peak of 4,594,942 in 2006–2007**, according to the Texas Education Agency. That is an increase of almost 600,000 students over the last six years; enrollment was 4,059,619 in 2000–2001.

The **seven largest districts** (listed in descending order by average daily attendance) are: Houston, Dallas, Cypress-Fairbanks (Harris Co.), Northside (Bexar County), Austin, Fort Worth, and Fort Bend (Fort Bend Co.)

In Texas, there are **1,033 independent and common school districts** and **190 charter districts**. Independent school districts are administered by an elected board of trustees and deal directly with the Texas Education Agency. Common districts are supervised by

Members of the 2007 Newman High School graduating class take part in the school's 29th commencement on May 27 in the University of North Texas Coliseum in Denton. The school is part of the Carrollton-Farmers Branch Independent School District. File photo.

elected county school superintendents and county trustees. Charter schools are discussed later in this article.

Brief History
of Public Education

Public education was one of the primary goals of the early settlers of Texas, who listed the failure to provide education as one of their grievances in the Texas Declaration of Independence from Mexico.

As early as 1838, President Mirabeau B. Lamar's message to the Republic of Texas Congress advocated setting aside public domain for public schools. His interest caused him to be called the "Father of Education in Texas." In 1839 Congress designated three leagues of land to support public schools for each Texas county and 50 leagues for a state university. In 1840 each county was allocated one more league of land.

The Republic, however, did not establish a public school system or a university. After being admitted into the Union, the 1845 Texas State Constitution advocated public education, instructing the Legislature to designate at least 10 percent of the tax revenue for schools. Further delay occurred until Gov. Elisha M. Pease, on Jan. 31, 1854, signed the bill setting up the Texas public school system.

The public school system was made possible by setting aside $2 million out of $10 million Texas received for relinquishing its claim to land north and west of its present boundaries in the Compromise of 1850 (see map on page 62).

During 1854, legislation provided for state apportionment of funds based upon an annual census. Also, railroads receiving grants were required to survey alternate sections to be set aside for public-school financing. The first school census that year showed 65,463 students; state fund apportionment was 62 cents per student.

When adopted in 1876, the present Texas Constitution provided: "All funds, lands and other property heretofore set apart and appropriated for the support of public schools; all the alternate sections of land reserved by the

Enrollment and Expenditures per Student

School Year	Enrollment	Spending per student
2005–2006	4,505,572	$9,269
2004–2005	4,383,871	8,916
2003–2004	4,311,502	7,708
2002–2003	4,239,911	7,088
2001–2002	4,146,653	6,913
2000–2001	4,059,619	6,638
1999–2000	3,991,783	6,354
1998–1999	3,945,367	5,853
1997–1998	3,900,488	5,597
1996–1997	3,628,975	5,282
1995–1996	3,740,260	5,358

Graduates and Dropouts

School Year	Graduates	*Dropouts
2004–2005	239,716	8,876
2003–2004	244,165	7,180
2002–2003	238,109	15,117
2001–2002	225,167	16,622
2000–2001	215,316	17,563
1999–2000	212,925	23,457
1998–1999	203,393	27,592
1997–1998	197,186	27,550
1996–1997	181,794	26,901
1995–1996	171,844	29,207
1994–1995	169,085	29,518

*Grades 7–12.

Texas School Personnel & Salaries

Year/ Personnel Type	Personnel (Full-Time Equivalent)*	Average Total Salaries†
2005–2006 Personnel	**596,298**	**$35,677**
Teachers	302,149	43,105
Campus Administrators	16,744	63,255
Central Administrators	5,910	78,477
Support Staff*	47,869	51,077
Total Professionals	***372,671***	***45,595***
Educational Aides	60,944	16,547
Auxiliary Staff	162,682	20,123
2004–2005 Personnel	**583,760**	**$34,898**
Teachers	294,258	42,345
Campus Administrators	16,219	62,114
Central Administrators	5,704	77,111
Support Staff*	46,785	49,747
Total Professionals	***362,967***	***44,729***
Educational Aides	59,540	16,158
Auxiliary Staff	161,253	19,690

*Support staff includes supervisors, counselors, educational diagnosticians, librarians, nurses/physicians, therapists and psychologists.
†Supplements for non-teaching duties and career-ladder supplements are not included in this figure.

Permanent School Fund

The Texas public school system was established and the permanent fund set up by the Fifth Legislature, Jan. 31, 1854.

Year	Total Investment Fund*	Total Income Earned by P.S.F.
1854	$ 2,000,000.00	...
1880	3,542,126.00	...
1900	9,102,872.75	$ 783,142.08
1910	16,752,406.93	1,970,526.52
1920	25,698,281.74	2,888,555.44
1930	38,718,106.35	2,769,547.05
1940	68,299,081.91	3,331,874.12
1950	161,179,979.24	3,985,973.60
1960	425,821,600.53	12,594,000.28
1970	842,217,721.05	34,762,955.32
1980	2,464,579,397.00	163000,000.00
1985	5,095,802,979.00	417,080,383.00
1988	6,493,070,622.00	572,665,253.00
1989	6,873,610,771.00	614,786,823.00
1990	7,328,172,096.00	674,634,994.00
1991	10,227,777,535.00	661,744,804.00
1992	10,944,944,872.00	704,993,826.00
1993	11,822,465,497.00	714,021,754.00
1994	11,330,590,652.00	716,972,115.00
1995	12,273,168,900.00	737,008,244.00
1996	12,995,820,070.00	739,996,574.00
1997	15,496,646,496.00	692,678,412.00
1998	16,296,199,389.00	690,802,024.00
1999	19,615,730,341.00	661,892,466.00
2000	22,275,586,452.00	698,487,305.00
2001	19,021,750,040.00	794,284,231.00
2002	17,047,245,212.00	764,554,567.00
2003	18,037,320,374.00	896,810,915.00
2004	19,261,799,285.00	54,922,310.00
2005	21,354,333,727.00	NA
2006	22,802,708,177.00	NA

*For years before 1991, includes cash, bonds at par and stocks at book value. For years beginning with 1991, includes cash, bonds and stocks at fair value.

PSF Apportionment, 1854–2006

The first apportionment by Texas to public schools was for school year 1854–1855

Years	Amount of P.S.F. Distributed to Schools
1854–55	$ 40,587
1880–81	679,317
1900–01	3,002,820
1910–11	5,931,287
1920–21	18,431,716
1930–31	27,342,473
1940–41	34,580,475
1950–51	93,996,600
1960–61	164,188,461
1970–71	287,159,758
1980–81	3,042,476
1985–86	807,680,617
1988–89	882,999,623
1989–90	917,608,395
1990–91	700,276,846
1991–92	739,200,044
1992–93	739,494,967
1993–94	737,677,545
1994–95	737,008,244
1995–96	739,996,574
1996–97	692,678,412
1997–98	690,802,024
1998–99	661,892,466
1999–00	698,487,305
2000–01	794,284,231
2001–02	764,554,567
2002–03	896,810,915
2003–04	825,059,655
2004–05	879,981,965
2005–06	841,878,709

Source: Texas Education Agency.

state of grants heretofore made or that may hereafter be made to railroads, or other corporations, of any nature whatsoever; one half of the public domain of the state, and all sums of money that may come to the state from the sale of any portion of the same shall constitute a perpetual public school fund."

More than 52 million acres of the Texas public domain were allotted for school purposes. (See table, Distribution of the Public Lands of Texas on page 483.)

The Constitution also provided for one-fourth of occupation taxes and a poll tax of one dollar for school support and made provisions for local taxation.

No provision was made for direct ad valorem taxation for maintenance of an available school fund, but a maximum 20-cent state ad valorem school tax was adopted in 1883 and raised to 35 cents in connection with provision of free textbooks in the amendment of 1918.

In 1949, the Gilmer-Aikin Laws reorganized the state system of public schools by making sweeping changes in administration and financing. The Texas Education Agency, headed by the governor-appointed Commissioner of Education, administers the public-school system.

The policy-making body for public education is the 15-member State Board of Education, which is elected from separate districts for overlapping four-year terms. Current membership of the board may be found in the State Government section of this Almanac.

Recent Changes in Public Education

Members of the 68th Legislature passed a historic education-reform bill in the summer of 1984. House Bill 72 came in response to growing concern over deteriorating literacy among Texas' schoolchildren over two decades, reflected in students' scores on standardized tests.

Provisions of HB 72 raised teachers' salaries, but tied those raises to teacher performance. It also introduced more stringent teacher certification and initiated competency testing for teachers.

Academic achievement was set as a priority in public education with stricter attendance rules; adoption of a no-pass, no-play rule prohibiting students who were failing courses from participating in sports and other extracurricular activities for a six-week period; and national norm-referenced testing throughout all grades to assure parents of individual schools' performance through a common frame of reference.

No-pass, no-play now requires only a three-week suspension for a failing course grade, during which time the student can continue to practice, but not participate in competition.

The 74th Legislature passed the Public Schools Reform Act of 1995, which increased local control of public schools by limiting the Texas Education Agency to recommending and reporting on educational goals; overseeing charter schools; managing the permanent, foundation and available school funds; administering an accountability system; creating and implementing the student testing program; recommending educator appraisal and counselor evaluation instruments; and developing plans for special, bilingual, compensatory, gifted and talented, vocational and technology education.

Texas students, beginning with the Class of 1987, have been required to pass an exit-level exam, along with their courses, in order to receive a diploma from a Texas public high school. Beginning with the Class of 2005, Texas students must pass the exit-level Texas Assessment of Knowledge and Skills (TAKS) to meet this graduation requirement. TAKS, which is the most rigorous graduation test ever given to Texas students, covers English language arts, mathematics, science and social studies.

To give Texas residents a sense of how schools are performing, the state has issued ratings for its public school districts and campuses since 1993. The new system is based on state test scores and high school completion rates.

A teacher also may remove a disruptive student from class and, subject to review by a campus committee, veto the student's return to class. The district must provide alternative education for students removed from class. A student must be placed in alternative education for assault, selling drugs or alcohol, substance abuse or public lewdness. A student must be expelled and referred to the appropriate court for serious offenses, such as murder or aggravated assault.

Actions of the 79th & 80th Texas Legislatures Affecting Public Schools

During the 79th Legislative session, lawmakers again wrestled with the issue of providing equitable and adequate funding for the public schools after a state district declared the existing school finance system, in place since 1993, unconstitutional. Efforts to pass a finance bill failed during the regular session. Gov. Rick Perry then vetoed all funding for the public schools and ordered lawmakers back to Austin. The Legislature was meeting in special session at press time.

Lawmakers during the regular session agreed to move the duties of the State Board of Educator Certification, which certifies Texas teachers, into the Texas Education Agency, essentially eliminating the 10-year-old SBEC.

Responding to concerns about the health of the state's children, they passed legislation requiring school districts to develop a treatment and management plan for each student with diabetes.

They also required the state to add personal financial literacy education to one or more courses required for high school graduation.

In reaction to revelations that some student athletes were using performance-enhancing drugs, lawmakers passed a bill that requires the University Interscholastic League to adopt rules related to steroid use and/or abuse. The UIL is to develop an educational program on the topic aimed at student athletes.

Education issues took a back seat in the 80th Legislature after several sessions dominated by school finance, but the much-maligned Texas Assessment of Knowledge and Skills (TAKS) test was replaced with end-of-course exams that would count for 15 percent of students' grades, beginning in the 2011-2012 school year.

Charter Schools

Charter-school legislation in Texas provides for three types of charter schools: the home-rule school district charter, the campus or campus-program charter and the open-enrollment charter.

As of April 2007, no district has expressed official interest in home-rule charter status, because of its complex developmental procedures. Houston, Dallas, Nacogdoches, San Antonio, Clear Creek, Colorado, Corpus Christi and Spring Branch school districts have created campus charter schools, which are overseen by each school district's board of trustees.

Open-enrollment charter schools are public schools released from some Texas education laws and regulations. These schools are granted by the State Board of Education (SBOE). This charter contract is typically granted for 5 years and can be revoked if the school violates its charter.

As of April 2007, a total of 260 open-enrollment charter schools have been chartered. As of the spring of 2007, 203 charters are open and educating more than 70,000 students. Many charter schools have focused their efforts on educating young people who are at risk of dropping out of school or who have dropped out and then returned to school. ☆

Students from Pleasant Run Elementary School take a horse and carriage ride during a field trip to the historic Strain Farmstead in Lancaster. Pleasant Run is in the Lancaster Independent School District. Ron Baselice photo.

University Interscholastic League Winning Schools for the School Years 2005–2006 to 2006–2007

Winners in the academic, music and the arts categories are listed first, then winners in sports categories. Winners in earlier years can be found in the Texas Almanac 2000—2001 and the Texas Almanac 2006–2007. If there is a dash (—) in the box, there was no competition in that conference in that category for that year. Source: University Interscholastic League.

Academics

Year	Conference A	Conference AA	Conference AAA	Conference AAAA	Conference AAAAA
Overall State Meet Academic Champions					
2005–06	Garden City	Argyle	Lindale	Friendswood	College Station A&M
2006–07	Lindsay	Salado	Longview Spring Hill	Friendswood	Katy Taylor
Accounting					
2005–06	Loop	Rosebud-Lott	Dalhart	Brownwood	Keller
2006–07	Sudan	Tuscola Jim Ned	Giddings	Mesquite Poteet	Keller
Accounting Team Event					
2005–06	Trenton	Rosebud-Lott	Dalhart	Brownwood	Keller
2006–07	Trenton	Tuscola Jim Ned	Hamshire-Fannett	Brownwood	Keller
Calculator Applications					
2005–06	Garden City	Argyle	Bridge City	El Paso	La Joya
2006–07	Garden City	Ballinger	Longview Spring Hill	Mount Pleasant	Lubbock
Calculator Applications Team Event					
2005–06	Garden City	Argyle	Bridge City	Longview Pine Tree	San Juan PSJA
2006–07	Garden City	Salado	Bridge City	Mission Veterans Mem.	Lubbock
Computer Applications					
2005–06	Wellington	Centerville	Hamshire-Fannett	Brownwood	Abilene Cooper
2006–07	Springlake Earth	Crawford	Princeton	Friendswood	College Station A&M
Computer Science					
2005–06	Savoy	Refugio	Center	Friendswood	Round Rock Westwood
2006–07	Garden City	Ozona	Gonzales	Midlothian	Katy Taylor
Computer Science Team					
2005–06	Savoy	Ozona	Center	Friendswood	Houston Cypress Falls
2006–07	Garden City	Ozona	Gonzales	Midlothian	Katy Taylor
Number Sense					
2005–06	Utopia	Argyle	Longview Spring Hill	Nacogdoches	Pearland
2006–07	Plains	Wichita Falls City View	Longview Spring Hill	Port Lavaca Calhoun	Sugar Land Clements
Number Sense Team Event					
2005–06	Garden City	Argyle	Bridgeport	Castroville Medina Val.	Klein
2006–07	Lindsay	Wichita Falls City View	Longview Spring Hill	Cor. Christi Flour Bluff	Helotes O'Connor
Mathematics					
2005–06	Silverton	Argyle	Bridgeport	Klein Oak	College Station A&M
2006–07	Lindsay	Wichita Falls City View	Bridgeport	Port Lavaca Calhoun	College Station A&M
Mathematics Team Event					
2005–06	Garden City	Argyle	Bridgeport	Klein Oak	College Station A&M
2006–07	Garden City	McGregor	Argyle	Port Lavaca Calhoun	Sugar Land Clements
Science					
2005–06	Garden City	Argyle	Cuero	Friendswood	Katy Taylor
2006–07	Garden City	Floydada	Cuero	Dallas Highland Park	San Antonio MacArthur
Science Team Event					
2005–06	Garden City	Argyle	Cuero	Dallas Highland Park	Sugar Land Clements
2006–07	Garden City	Floydada	Cuero	Dallas Highland Park	Sugar Land Clements
Social Studies					
2005–06	Gail Borden	Idalou	Zapata	Aledo	Katy Cinco Ranch
2006–07	Normangee	Idalou	Zapata	Katy Seven Lakes	Victoria Memorial
Social Studies Team Event					
2005–06	Comstock	Sadler S&S	Abilene Wylie	Aledo	College Station A&M
2006–07	Sabine Pass	Colorado City	Wimberley	Katy Seven Lakes	Katy Taylor
Current Issues & Events					
2005–06	Hedley	Sadler S&S	Mont Belvieu Barbers Hill	El Paso	College Station A&M
2006–07	Martin's Mill	Tuscola Jim Ned	Wimberley	Stephenville	Round Rock
Current Issues & Events Team					
2005–06	Apple Springs	Sadler S&S	Abilene Wylie	Stephenville	Round Rock
2006–07	Martin's Mill	Sadler S&S	Abilene Wylie	Mont Belvieu Barber's Hill	Round Rock
Literary Criticism					
2005–06	Quanah	Salado	Kemp	Dayton	Austin Westlake
2006–07	Martin's Mill	Weimar	Atlanta	Stephenville	Flower Mound

Richardson High School's Scott Howell, center, cross examines a witness as Courtney Mitchell, left, and Jessica Wilkin listen during a preparation for UIL competition in cross examination team debate.

John David Emmett photo.

Year	Conference A	Conference AA	Conference AAA	Conference AAAA	Conference AAAAA
Literary Criticism Team Event					
2005–06	Quanah	Sadler S&S	Mont Belvieu Barbers Hill	Aledo	Austin Westlake
2006–07	Martin's Mill	Sadler S&S	Liberty	Friendswood	Keller
Poetry Interpretation					
2005–06	Cherokee	Holliday	Canton	Houston Scarborough	Grand Prairie
2006–07	Lindsay	Hico	Athens	Ennis	Amarillo Tascosa
Prose Interpretation					
2005–06	Tolar	Grandview	Seminole	Bay City	Colleyville Heritage
2006–07	Lindsay	Boling	Athens	Red Oak	Colleyville Heritage
Ready Writing					
2005–06	Gail Borden	Hico	Bellville	New Braunfels Canyon	Harlingen
2006–07	Gail Borden	Panhandle	Decatur	Austin Crockett	Georgetown
Informative Speaking					
2005–06	Lindsay	Holliday	Monahans	Bay City	Humble Kingwood
2006–07	Lindsay	Aubrey	Athens	Bay City	San Angelo Central
Persuasive Speaking					
2005–06	Gail Borden	Salado	Royse City	Gregory-Portland	Plano West
2006–07	Gail Borden	Aubrey	Royse City	Mercedes	San Antonio Jay
Speech					
2005–06	Gail Borden	Holliday	Lindale	Bay City	Helotes O'Connor
2006–07	Lindsay	Aubrey	Athens	Bay City	Round Rock Westwood
Lincoln-Douglas Debate					
2005–06	Gail Borden	Paris Chisum	Brady	Montgomery	Katy Cinco Ranch
2006–07	Lindsay	Salado	Canyon	Lindale	Katy Cinco Ranch
Cross Examination Team Debate					
2005–06	Thorndale	Holliday	Wimberly	Bay City	Fort Bend Hightower
2006–07	Gail Borden	Blanco	Sealy	Crosby	Round Rock Westwood
Spelling & Vocabulary					
2005–06	Yantis	Hamilton	Borger	El Paso	Arlington Lamar
2006–07	Albany	Salado	Canton	El Paso	Arlington Lamar
Spelling & Vocabulary Team Event					
2005–06	Lindsay	Salado	Gonzales	Friendswood	Klein
2006–07	Lindsay	Salado	Canton	Friendswood	Arlington Lamar
Journalism Team					
2005–06	Tolar	Panhandle	Palestine Westwood	Texarkana Texas	San Antonio Clark
2006–07	Lindsay	Lockney	Llano	Pflugerville Connally	Alvin
Editorial Writing					
2005–06	Flatonia	Panhandle	Groesbeck	Jacksonville	Coppell
2006–07	Lindsay	Mason	Borger	Whitehouse	Garland North
Feature Writing					
2005–06	Harleton	Ballinger	Bandera	McKinney North	Sachse
2006–07	Archer City	Mildred	Emory Rains	Texarkana Texas	Alvin
Headline Writing					
2005–06	Muenster	Godley	Mineola	Texarkana Texas	Edinburg
2006–07	Yantis	Krum	Llano	Lindale	Mansfield
News Writing					
2005–06	Nazareth	Idalou	Texarkana Liberty-Eylau	Pflugerville Connally	Flower Mound Marcus
2006–07	Nazareth	Lockney	Canyon	Hallsville	McAllen

Publications

Year	Yearbooks	Newspapers
2005–06	Bellaire, Burges, Duncanville, Pleasant Grove, St. Mark's School of Texas.	Burges, Connally, Duncanville, Fulmore, Highland Park, LBJ Austin, Marcus, St. Mark's School of Texas, Westlake.
2006–07	Burges, Duncanville, McKinney, Pleasant Grove, Texarkana Texas, Westlake.	Burges, Connally, Fulmore, LBJ Austin, Marcus, St. Mark's School of Texas, Texarkana Texas.

Note: Before the 1991–92 school year, the UIL named only one top yearbook and one top newspaper each year. Beginning with the 1991-92 school year, awards were presented to all yearbooks and newspapers judged to be worthy of the honors, which were divided into gold, silver and bronze categories. Only the gold-award winners are listed here.

Year	Conference A	Conference AA	Conference AAA	Conference AAAA	Conference AAAAA

Music and Theatre

One-Act Play					
2005–06	Channing	Sonora	Decatur	Montgomery	Plano East
2006–07	Lindsay	Mount Pleasant Chapel Hill	Van	Friendswood	Temple
State Marching Band Contest					
2005–06	Sundown	Argyle	—	Poteet	—
2006–07	—	—	Canton	—	Flower Mound Marcus

Flower Mound Marcus High School band members warm-up prior to their turn to compete in the UIL marching band competition.

Pichi Chuang photo.

Athletics

Year	Conference A	Conference AA	Conference AAA	Conference AAAA	Conference AAAAA
Baseball					
2005–06	Anderson-Shiro	Brock	Texarkana Liberty-Eylau	New Braunfels	Conroe The Woodlands
2006–07	Archer City	Rogers	Jasper	Corpus Christi Moody	Houston Cypress Fairbanks
Basketball, Boys					
2005–06	I: Bogata Rivercrest II: Nazareth	Arp	Dallas Roosevelt	Dallas South Oak Cliff	Plano
2006–07	I: Thorndale II: Nazareth	Kountze	Sour Lake Hardin-Jefferson	Dallas South Oak Cliff	Duncanville
Basketball, Girls					
2005–06	I: Martin's Mill II: Kennard	Argyle	China Spring	Waxahachie	Plano West
2006–07	I: Lindsay II: Nazareth	Poth	Canyon	Fort Worth Dunbar	Rockwall
Cross Country, Boys					
2005–06	Sundown	Boys Ranch	Decatur	Fort Worth North Side	Corpus Christi King
2006–07	Hart	Wall	Decatur	Big Spring	Conroe The Woodlands
Cross Country, Girls					
2005–06	Sundown	Holliday	Decatur	Hereford	Southlake Carroll
2006–07	Sundown	Shallowater	Canyon	Hereford	Southlake Carroll
Golf, Boys					
2005–06	Throckmorton	Edgewood	Palestine	Dallas Highland Park	Fort Worth Pascal
2006–07	La Rue La Poynor	Edgewood	Castroville Medina Valley	Aledo	Conroe The Woodlands

Year	Conference A	Conference AA	Conference AAA	Conference AAAA	Conference AAAAA
Golf, Girls					
2005–06	Shamrock	Salado	Snyder	Montgomery	Allen
2006–07	Memphis	Wall	Andrews	Montgomery	Houston Clear Lake
Softball					
2005–06	Clyde Eula	Weimar	West Columbia Columbia	Orange Little Cypress-Mauriceville	Garland
2006–07	Bosqueville	Troy	Medina Valley	Boerne	Garland
Team Tennis					
2005–06	—	—	—	Dallas Highland Park	Plano West
2006–07	—	—	—	Dallas Highland Park	Plano West
Tennis, Boys Singles					
2005–06	Nazareth	Franklin	Clyde	Dallas Highland Park	Amarillo Tascosa
2006–07	Bronte	Franklin	Levelland	Austin Lake Travis	Victoria Memorial
Tennis, Boys Doubles					
2005–06	Garden City	Mason	Levelland	Dallas Highland Park	Richardson Pearce
2006–07	Garden City	Comfort	Canyon	Richardson Pearce	Austin Westlake
Tennis, Girls Singles					
2005–06	Gruver	Winona	Abilene Wylie	New Braunfels	Flower Mound Marcus
2006–07	Lenorah Grady	Winona	Abilene Wylie	New Braunfels	Westwood
Tennis, Girls Doubles					
2005–06	Nazareth	Mason	Abilene Wylie	Dallas Highland Park	Lubbock Coronado
2006–07	Nazareth	Mason	Longview Sping Hill	Dallas Highland Park	Lubbock Coronado
Tennis, Mixed Doubles					
2005–06	Nazareth	Mason	Vernon	Dallas Highland Park	Arlington Bowie
2006–07	Shiner	Franklin	Abilene Wylie	New Braunfels	Klein
Track & Field, Boys					
2005–06	Rotan	Crane	Cuero	Texas City	Houston Eisenhower
2006–07	Rule	Tatum	Dallas Madison	Copperas Cove	Fort Bend Hightower
Track & Field, Girls					
2005–06	Hubbard	Universal City Randolph	Dallas Madison	Lancaster	Alief Taylor
2006–07	Lindsay	Universal City Randolph	Dallas Madison	Lancaster	Fort Bend Hightower
Volleyball					
2005–06	Windthorst	Poth	Bellville	New Braunfels	Arlington Martin
2006–07	Collinsville	Poth	Wimberley	Dumas	Amarillo

Year	6-man	A	AA	AAA	AAAA	AAAAA
Football						
2005–06	Throckmorton	Stratford	I: Newton II: Celina	I: Wimberly II: Tatum	I: Dallas Highland Park II: Lewisville Hebron	I: Euless Trinity II: Southlake Carroll
2006–07	I: Richland Springs II: Vernon Northside	I: Alto II: Chilton	I: Tatum II: Mart	I: Texarkana Liberty-Eylau II: Liberty Hill	I: San Antonio Alamo Heights II: La Marque	I: Southlake Carroll II: Cedar Hill

	Girls		Boys	
Soccer				
Year	AAAA	AAAAA	AAAA	AAAAA
2005–06	McKinney North	Katy Taylor	Boerne	Brownsville Porter
2006–07	Lewisville The Colony	Plano West	Wichita Falls Rider	Flower Mound Marcus

	Girls		Boys	
Swimming & Diving				
Year	AAAA	AAAAA	AAAA	AAAAA
2005–06	Dallas Highland Park	Conroe The Woodlands	Frisco	Austin Westlake
2006–07	Dallas Highland Park	Austin Westlake	Richardson Pearce	Humble Kingwood

	Wrestling, Boys
2005–06	**Team**: Dallas Highland Park; **Weight Class 103**: Austin Bowie; **112**: Colleyville Heritage; **119**: Klein Oak; **125**: El Paso Americas; **130**: Arlington Martin; **135**: San Antonio Madison; **140**: El Paso Hanks; **145**: Arlington Bowie; **152**: Dumas; **160**: Katy Cinco Ranch; **171**: Coppell; **180**: Dallas Highland Park; **189**: Coppell; **215**: Klein Collins; **275**: Keller
2006–07	**Team**: ; **Weight Class 103**: Allen; **112**: Arlington; **119**: Conroe The Woodlands; **125**: Houston Cypress Fairbanks; **130**: Colleyville Heritage; **135**: San Antonio Madison; **140**: Richardson Lake Highland; **145**: Katy Cinco Ranch; **152**: Arlington Bowie; **160**: Katy Cinco Ranch; **171**: Dallas Highland Park; **180**: Dallas Jesuit; **189**: Coppell; **215**: Houston Strake Jesuit; **275**: Keller
	Wrestling, Girls
2005–06	**Team**: Amarillo Caprock; **Weight Class 95**: Frisco Centennial; **102**: El Paso Hanks; **110**: Amarillo Tascosa; **119**: Katy Taylor; **128**: El Paso Socorro; **138**: Frisco; **148**: Klein; **165**: Coppell; **185**: Cedar Park Vista Ridge; **215**: Katy
2006–07	**Team**: ; **Weight Class 95**: Frisco Centennial; **102**: Amarillo Caprock; **110**: Frisco Centennial; **119**: Houston Cypress Fairbanks; **128**: Coppell; **138**: Frisco; **148**: Klein; **165**: Katy Taylor; **185**: Cedar Park Vista Ridge; **215**: Arlington

Brief History of Higher Education in Texas

While there were earlier efforts toward higher education, the first permanent institutions established were church-supported schools:

• **Rutersville University,** established in 1840 by Methodist minister Martin Ruter in Fayette County, predecessor of Southwestern University, Georgetown, established in 1843;

• **Baylor University,** now at Waco, but established in 1845 at Independence, Washington County, by the Texas Union Baptist Association; and

• **Austin College,** now at Sherman, but founded in 1849 at Huntsville by the Brazos Presbytery of the Old School Presbyterian Church.

Other historic Texas schools of collegiate rank included: **Larissa College,** 1848, at Larissa, Cherokee County; **McKenzie College,** 1841, Clarksville; **Chappell Hill Male and Female Institute,** 1850, Chappell Hill; **Soule University,** 1855, Chappell Hill; **Johnson Institute,** 1852, Driftwood, Hays County; **Nacogdoches University,** 1845, Nacogdoches; **Salado College,** 1859, Salado, Bell County. **Add-Ran College,** established at Thorp Spring, Hood County, in 1873, was the predecessor of present *Texas Christian University,* Fort Worth.

Texas A&M and University of Texas

The **Agricultural and Mechanical College of Texas** (now **Texas A&M University),** authorized by the Legislature in 1871, opened its doors in 1876 to become the first publicly supported institution of higher education. In 1881, Texans established the University of Texas in Austin, with a medical branch in Galveston. The Austin institution opened Sept. 15, 1883, the Galveston school in 1891.

First College for Women

In 1901, the 27th Legislature established the Girls Industrial College, which began classes at its campus in Denton in 1903. A campaign to establish a state industrial college for women was led by the State Grange and Patrons of Husbandry.

A bill was signed into law on April 6, 1901, creating the college. It was charged with a dual mission, which continues to guide the university today, to provide a liberal education and to prepare young women with a specialized education "for the practical industries of the age."

In 1905 the name of the college was changed to the **College of Industrial Arts;** in 1934, it was changed to **Texas State College for Women.** Since 1957 the institution, which is now the largest university principally for women in the United States, has been the **Texas Woman's University.**

Historic, Primarily Black Colleges

A number of Texas schools were established primarily for blacks, although collegiate racial integration is now complete in the state. The black-oriented institutions include state-supported **Prairie View A&M University** (originally established as **Alta Vista Agricultural College** in 1876), Prairie View; **Texas Southern University,** Houston; and privately supported **Huston-Tillotson College,** Austin; **Jarvis Christian College,** Hawkins; **Wiley College,** Marshall; **Paul Quinn College,** originally located in Waco, now in Dallas; and **Texas College,** Tyler.

Predominantly black colleges that are important in the history of higher education in Texas, but which have ceased operations, include **Bishop College,** established in Marshall in 1881, then moved to Dallas; **Mary Allen College,** established in Crockett in 1886; and **Butler College,** originally named the **Texas Baptist Academy,** in 1905 in Tyler. ☆

Recent Developments in Texas Higher Education

Source: Texas Higher Education Coordinating Board; **www.thecb.state.tx.us/**

State Appropriations

For the 2008–2009 biennium, beginning Sept. 1, 2007, and ending Aug. 31, 2009, general revenue appropriations to higher education were $16,362,900,000, which represented a 12.2 percent ($1,773,600,000) increase from the $14,589,300,000 appropriated for the previous biennium (Sept. 1, 2005, through Aug. 31, 2007).

Enrollment

Enrollment in Texas public and independent, or private, colleges and universities in fall 2006 totaled 1,211,582 students, an increase of 27,209 from fall 2005.

Enrollment in the 35 public universities increased by 5,743 students to 490,742 students. Twenty-six universities reported enrollment increases, while 9 reported decreases.

The state's public community college districts and Lamar State Colleges, which offer two-year degree programs, reported fall 2006 enrollments totaling 574,775 students, an increase of 19,714 over fall 2005.

The public Texas State Technical College System, which also offers two-year degree programs, reported fall 2006 enrollments totaling 11,081 students, an increase of 71 students over fall 2005.

Enrollments for fall 2006 at the state's 37 independent senior colleges and universities increased to 115,281 students, up 995 students from fall 2005.

The state's two independent junior colleges reported 706 students in fall 2006, an increase of 8 students from the previous fall.

Public medical, dental, nursing, and allied health institutions of higher education reported enrollments totaling 16,228 students in fall 2006, up 692 from fall 2005.

Enrollment at independent health-related institutions totaled 2,769 students, down 14 students from the previous fall.

Closing the Gaps plan

Closing the Gaps by 2015, the state's higher education plan, was adopted in 2000. It establishes goals to "close the gaps"—both within Texas and in comparison with other states—in student participation, student success, educational excellence and research by 2015.

The plan's first goal calls for enrolling by 2015 an additional 300,000 academically prepared students in Texas higher education; this is above the 200,000 students already expected, based on past trends.

The second goal calls for the state to increase by 50 percent the number of degrees and other higher education academic credentials awarded by 2015.

The third goal challenges the state to substantially increase the number of nationally recognized programs and services at colleges and universities in our state.

The fourth goal aims at increasing federal science and research funding to Texas higher education institutions by 50 percent.

To support the plan, the Legislature in recent years has increased funding for financial aid programs to help students pay college costs, strengthened the curriculum for public school students, and established a statewide higher education awareness and motivational campaign (see College for Texans campaign web site: http://www.collegefortexans.com/. ☆

Universities and Colleges

Source: Texas Higher Education Coordinating Board and institutions. In some cases, dates of establishment differ from those given in the preceding discussion because schools use the date when authorization was given, rather than actual date of first classwork. For explanation of type of institution and other symbols, see notes at end of table. **www.thecb.state.tx.us**

Name of Institution; Location; (Type* - Ownership, if private sectarian institution); Date of Founding; President (unless otherwise noted)	Number of Faculty†	Enrollment		
		Fall Term 2006	Summer Session 2006	Extension or Continuing Ed.
Abilene Christian University—Abilene; (3 - Church of Christ); 1906 (as Childers Classical Institute; became **Abilene Christian College** by 1914; became university in 1976); Dr. Royce Money	347	4,786	1,042	
ALAMO COMMUNITY COLLEGE DISTRICT (9) — Dr. Bruce H. Leslie chancellor				
‡ Northwest Vista College — San Antonio; (7); 1995; Dr. Jacqueline Claunch	298	8,703	2,817	285
‡ Palo Alto College—San Antonio; (7); 1985; Dr. Ana M. "Cha" Guzmán	433	7,988	4,157	597
‡ St. Philip's College—San Antonio; (7); 1898; Dr. Patricia Candia	200	10,422	3,758	8,323
San Antonio College—San Antonio; (7); 1925; Dr. Robert E. Zeigler	1,028	21,639	10,528	13,817
Northeast Lakeview College—Live Oak; (7); 2007; Dr. Eric Reno	NA	NA	NA	NA
Alvin Community College—Alvin; (7); 1949; Dr. A. Rodney Allbright	92	4,079	4,043	2,387
Amarillo College—Amarillo; (7); 1929; Dr. Steven W. Jones	384	10,150	3,393	25,000
Amberton University—Garland; (3); 1971 (as **Amber University**; name changed in spring 2001); Dr. Melinda Reagan	45	1,582	1,339	NA
Angelina College—Lufkin; (7); 1968; Dr. Larry Phillips	110	4,940	2,613	2,574
Angelo State University—San Angelo (See **Texas State University System**)				
‡Arlington Baptist College—Arlington; (3 - Baptist); 1939 (as **Bible Baptist Seminary**; changed to present name in 1965); Dr. David Bryant	20	175	80	75
Austin College—Sherman; (3 - Presbyterian USA); 1849; Dr. Oscar C. Page	106	1,354	**	**
Austin Community College—Austin; (7); 1972; Dr. Robert Aguero	1,290	30,955	21,883	NA
Austin Presbyterian Theological Seminary—Austin; Presbyterian; 3-yr; 1902 (successor **Austin School of Theology**, est. 1884); Theodore J. Wardlaw	27	273	273	45
Baptist Missionary Association Theological Seminary—Jacksonville; Baptist Missionary, 3-yr.; 1955; Dr. Charley Holmes	8	168	140	175
‡ Baylor College of Medicine—Houston; (5 - Baptist until 1969); 1903 (Dallas; moved to Houston, 1943); Peter Traber, M.D.	**	1,287	**	**
‡ Baylor University—Waco; (3 - So. Baptist); 1845 (at Independence; merged with Waco University in 1887 and moved to Waco); Bill Underwood (interim)	777	13,799	5,851	**
Bee County College—Beeville (see **Coastal Bend College**)				
Blinn College—Brenham; (7); 1883 (as academy; jr. college, 1927); Dr. Donald E. Voelter	575	14,046	10,783	900
Brazosport College—Lake Jackson; (7); 1967; Dr. Millicent M. Valek	169	3,858	2,792	7,729
Brookhaven College—Farmers Branch (See **Dallas County Community College District**)				
Cedar Valley College—Lancaster (See **Dallas County Community College District**)				
Central Texas College District—Killeen; (7); 1965; Dr. James R. Anderson, chancellor	234	60,605	32,364	695
Cisco Junior College—Cisco; (7); 1909 (as private institution; became state school in 1939); Dr. Colleen Smith	150	3,600	1,500	200
Clarendon College—Clarendon; (7); 1898 (as church school; became state school in 1927); Dr. W. Myles Shelton	69	1,013	452	6
‡ Coastal Bend College—Beeville; (7); (1966 as **Bee Co. College**, name changed in 1999); Dr. John Brockman	99	3,821	2,266	588
‡ College of the Mainland—Texas City; (7); 1967; Dr. Homer M. Hayes	89	3,961	2,949	**
‡ College of St. Thomas More—Fort Worth; (3-Roman Catholic); 1981 (as St. Thomas More Inst.; became college 1989; accredited as 2-year college 1994); Dr. Dean M. Cassella, Provost	14	76	4	NA
‡ Collin County Community College—McKinney; (7); 1985; Dr. Cary A. Israel	904	19.332	12,701	4,982
Concordia University—Austin; (3 - Mo. Lutheran); 1926 (as **Concordia Lutheran College**; name changed in 1995); Dr. Tom Cedel	172	1,266	**	NA
Cooke County College—Gainesville (See **North Central Texas College**)				
Corpus Christi State University—(See **Texas A&M University–Corpus Christi** listing under **Texas A&M University System**)				
‡ Dallas Baptist University—Dallas; (3 - Southern Baptist).; 1891 (as **Northwest Texas Bible College**; name changed to Decatur Baptist College in 1897; moved to Dallas, name changed to Dallas Baptist College in 1965; became university in 1985); Dr. Gary Cook	488	5,153	2.432	NA
Dallas Christian College—Dallas; (3 - Christian); 1950; Dr. Dustin D. Rubeck	75	366	71	NA
DALLAS COUNTY COMMUNITY COLLEGE DISTRICT (9) — Dr. Wright Lassiter, chancellor				
Brookhaven College—Farmers Branch; (7); 1978; Dr. Alice W. Villadsen	533	10,123	6,813	4,366
Cedar Valley College—Lancaster; (7); 1977; Dr. Jennifer Wimbish	182	4,345	2,652	1,858
Eastfield College—Mesquite; (7); 1970; Dr. Rodger Pool	509	11,705	9.081	2,895
El Centro College—Dallas; (7); 1966; Dr. Wright Lassiter	372	6,015	1,937	5,127
Mountain View College—Dallas; (7); 1970; Dr. Monique Amerman	382	6,598	3,786	2,631
North Lake College—Irving; (7); 1977; Dr. Herlina M. Glassock	550	8,382	3,844	4,148
Richland College—Dallas; (7); 1972; Dr. Stephen K. Mittelstet	903	14,128	16,946§	8,200

Name of Institution; Location; (Type* - Ownership, if private sectarian institution); Date of Founding; President (unless otherwise noted)	Number of Faculty†	Enrollment		
		Fall Term 2006	Summer Session 2006	Extension or Continuing Ed.
Dallas Theological Seminary—Dallas; private, graduate; 1924 (as **Evangelical Theological College**; name changed in 1936); Dr. Mark L. Bailey	119	2,036	1,144	493
Del Mar College—Corpus Christi; (7); 1935; Dr. Carlos A. Garcia	739	11,345	7,388	10,111
Eastfield College—Mesquite (See **Dallas County Community College District**)				
East Texas Baptist University—Marshall; (3 - Baptist); 1913 (as **College of Marshall**; became **East Texas Baptist Coll.**, 1944; became university in 1984); Dr. Bob E. Riley	112	1,412	NA	NA
East Texas State University (see **Texas A&M University-Commerce** in **Texas A&M System** listing)				
East Texas State University at Texarkana (see **Texas A&M University-Texarkana** in **Texas A&M System** listing)				
El Centro College—Dallas (See **Dallas County Community College District**)				
# El Paso Community College District—El Paso; (7); 1969; three campuses: **Rio Grande, TransMountain** and **Valle Verde**; Dr. Richard Rhodes	1,200	26,435	**	**
Episcopal Theological Seminary of the Southwest—Austin; Episcopal; Graduate-level; 1952; Very Rev. Dr. Doug Travis	38	109	55	NA
‡ Frank Phillips College—Borger; (7); 1948; Dr. Herbert J. Swender	111	1,398	563§	NA
Galveston College—Galveston; (7); 1967; Dr. William R. Auvenshine	160	2,119	700	1,500
Grayson County College—Denison; (7); 1963; Dr. Alan Scheibmeir	175	4,000	1,560	3,000††
Hardin-Simmons University—Abilene; (3 - So. Baptist); 1891 (as **Simmons College**; became **Simmons University**, 1925; present name since, 1934); Dr. W. Craig Turner	198	2,372	1,572	0
‡ Hill College—Hillsboro; (7); 1923 (as **Hillsboro Junior College**; name changed, 1962); Dr. William R. Auvenshine	66	3,173	724	404
Houston Baptist University—Houston; (3 - Baptist); 1960; Dr. Robert B. Sloan Jr.	1,200	2,200	900	0
HOUSTON COMMUNITY COLLEGE SYSTEM—Houston; (9); 1971 Dr. Mary S. Spangler, chancellor. System consists of following colleges (president):	3,323	57,364	39,230	7.761
Central College — (Dr. Patricia Williamson)				
Northeast College — (Dr. Margaret Forde)				
Northwest College— (Dr. Zachary Hodges)				
Southeast College — (Dr. Diane Castillo)				
Southwest College— (Dr. Sue Cox)				
# Howard College—Big Spring; (7); 1945; (includes **SouthWest Collegiate Institute for the Deaf**, Ron Brasel, Provost); Dr. Cheryl T. Sparks	16	114	NA	NA
Howard Payne University—Brownwood; (3 - Baptist); 1889; Dr. Lanny Hall	146	1,328	248	303
Huston-Tillotson College—Austin; (3 - Methodist/Church of Christ); 1875 (**Tillotson College**, 1875, **Samuel Huston College**, 1876; merged 1952); Dr. Larry L. Earvin	37	685	133	0
International Bible College—San Antonio; (3); 1944; Rev. David W. Cook	15	75	NA	NA
Jacksonville College—Jacksonville; (8 - Missionary Baptist); 1899; Dr. Edwin Crank	20	310	144	34
‡ Jarvis Christian College—Hawkins; (3); 1912; Dr. Sebetha Jenkins	**	538	**	**
Kilgore College—Kilgore; (7); 1935; Dr. William M. Holda	139	4,968		4,968
Kingwood College—Kingwood (See **North Harris Montgomery Community College Dist.**)				
Lamar University and all branches (see Texas State University System)				
‡ Laredo Community College—Laredo; (7); 1946; Dr. Ramon H. Dovalina	337	9,030	4,480	3,545
‡ Lee College—Baytown; (7); 1934; Dr. Martha Ellis	364	5,854	4,615	2,616
‡ LeTourneau University—Longview; (3); 1946 (as **LeTourneau Technical Institute**; became 4-yr. college in 1961); Dr. Dale A. Lunsford	352	3,983	916	108
‡ Lon Morris College—Jacksonville; (8 - Methodist); 1854 (as **Danville Academy**; changed in 1873 to Alexander Inst.; present name, 1923), Dr. Clifford M. Lee	**	437	NA	NA
Lubbock Christian University—Lubbock; (3 - Church of Christ); 1957; Dr. L. Ken Jones	155	1,974	1,032	NA
McLennan Community College—Waco; (7); 1965; Dr. Dennis Michaelis	389	7,794		1,067
‡ McMurry University—Abilene; (3 - Methodist); 1923; Dr. John H. Russell	104	1,386	612	NA
‡ Midland College—Midland; (7); 1972; Dr. David E. Daniel	**	5,535	**	**
Midwestern State University—Wichita Falls; (2); 1922; Dr. Jesse W. Rogers	418	6,042	4,510	1,298
Montgomery College—Conroe (See North Harris Montgomery Community College Dist.)				
Mountain View College—Dallas (See **Dallas County Community College District**)				
‡ Navarro College—Corsicana; (7); 1946; Dr. Richard M. Sanchez	460	7,500	2,549	833
‡ North Central Texas College—Gainesville; (7); 1924 (as **Gainesville Jr. College**; **Cooke County College**, 1960; present name, 1994); Dr. Ronnie Glasscock	256	6,458	2,609	1,316
Northeast Texas Community College—Mount Pleasant; (7); 1984; Dr. Charles B. Florio	135	2,474	1,678	2,533
NORTH HARRIS MONTGOMERY COMMUNITY COLLEGE DISTRICT (9)— Dr. Richard Carpenter, chancellor. Includes these colleges, location (president)	2,040	42,500	22,196	14,000
Cy-Fair College — (Dr. Diane Troyer)	444	8,727	4,420	2,178
Kingwood College — Kingwood (Dr. Linda Stegall)	365	18,251	6,488	2,493
Montgomery College — Conroe (Dr. Thomas Butler)	300	7,219	3,300	5,000
North Harris College — Houston (Dr. David Sam)	10,114			
Tomball College — Tomball (Dr. Raymond H. Hawkins)	**	7,406	4,637	**
North Lake College—Irving (See **Dallas County Community College District**)				
Northwest Vista College (see **Alamo Community College District**)				
Northwood University—Cedar Hill; private; 1966; Dr. Kevin Fegan		57	1,135	524

Name of Institution; Location; (Type* - Ownership, if private sectarian institution); Date of Founding; President (unless otherwise noted)	Number of Faculty†	Enrollment		
		Fall Term 2006	Summer Session 2006	Extension or Continuing Ed.
Oblate School of Theology—San Antonio; Rom. Catholic, 4-yr.; 1903 (formerly **Scholasti** cate); Rev. Warren Brown, O.M.I.	24	133	126	273
Odessa College—Odessa; (7); 1946; Dr. Gregory Williams	287	4,596	1,426§	1,693
Our Lady of the Lake University of San Antonio—San Antonio; (3 - Catholic); 1895 (as. for girls; sr. college, 1911; university, in 1975); Dr. Tessa Martinez Pollock	238	2,783	594	801
Palo Alto College—San Antonio (See **Alamo Community College District**)				
Panola College—Carthage; (7); 1947 (as **Panola Junior College**; name changed, 1988); Dr. Gregory S. Powell	63	1,871	1,784	262
Paris Junior College—Paris; (7); 1924; Dr. Pamela Anglin	338	4,300	1,800	1,200
Paul Quinn College—Dallas; (3-AME Church); 1872 (Waco; Dallas, 1990); Dr. Dwight Fen nell	146	954	170	472
Prairie View A&M University—Prairie View (See **Texas A&M University System**)				
Ranger College—Ranger; (7); 1926; Dr. Ken Tunstall	30	873	525	**
Rice University (William Marsh)—Houston; (3); chartered 1891, opened 1912 (as **Rice Institute**; name changed in 1960); Dr. David W. Leebron	976	5,008	445	58
Richland College—Dallas (See **Dallas County Community College District**)				
St. Edward's University—Austin; (3 - Roman Catholic); 1885; Dr. George E. Martin	410	4,651	**	282
St. Mary's University—San Antonio; (3 - Catholic); 1852; Dr. Charles L. Cotrell	325	3,904	1,650	133
St. Philip's College—San Antonio (See **Alamo Community College District**)				
Sam Houston State University—Huntsville (See **Texas State University System**)				
San Antonio College—San Antonio (See **Alamo Community College District**)				
SAN JACINTO COLLEGE DISTRICT (9) — Dr. Bill Lindemann Includes these campuses, location (president):	1,122	23,441	16,381	22,50
Central, Pasadena — (Dr. Monte Blue)	11,540	8,470	10,000	
North, Houston — (Dr. Charles Grant)	250	5,497	4,540	784
‡South, Houston — (Dr. Linda Watkins)				
Schreiner University—Kerrville; (3 - Presbyterian); 1923; Dr. Charles Timothy Summerlin	94	930	125	NA
Southern Methodist University—Dallas; (3 - Methodist); 1911; Dr. R. Gerald Turner	528	10,901	4,029	NA
South Plains College—Levelland; (7); 1957; Dr. Gary D. McDaniel	289	9,561	2,500	**
South Texas College of Law—Houston; private, 3-yr.; 1923; James J. Alfiui, Dean and Pres.	100	1,200	NA	NA
South Texas Community College—McAllen; (7); NA; Dr. Shirley A. Reed	296	17,132	5,479	1,000††
Southwest Collegiate Institute for the Deaf — Big Spring (See **Howard College**)				
‡ Southwest Texas Junior College—Uvalde; (7); 1946; Dr. Ismael Sosa	**	5,202	**	**
Southwest Texas State University—San Marcos (see **Texas State University–San Marcos** under **Texas State University System**)				
Southwestern Adventist University—Keene; (3 - Seventh-Day Adventist); 1893 (as Keene Industrial Acad.; named **Southwestern Jr. College** in 1916; changed to **Southwestern Union College** in 1963, then to **Southwestern Adventist College** in1980; became university in 1996); Dr. Don Sahly	75	894	260	289
Southwestern Assemblies of God University—Waxahachie; (3 - Assemblies of God); 1927 (in Enid, Okla., as **Southwestern Bible School**; moved to Fort Worth and merged with **South Central Bible Institute** in 1941; moved to Waxahachie as **Southwestern Bible Institute** in 1943; changed to **Southwestern Assemblies of God College**,1963; university since 1996); Dr. Kermit S. Bridges	96	1,702	**	NA
Southwestern Baptist Theological Seminary—Fort Worth; Southern Baptist, 4-yr.; 1908; Dr. Kenneth Hemphill	91	3,005	1,179	26
Southwestern Christian College—Terrell; (3 - Church of Christ); 1948 (as **Southern Bible Inst.** in Fort Worth; moved to Terrell, changed name to present, 1950); Dr. Jack Evans Sr.	18	241	NA	NA
Southwestern University—Georgetown; (3 - Methodist); 1840 (**Southwestern University** was a merger of Rutersville (1840), Wesleyan (1846) and McKenzie (1841) colleges and **Soule University** (1855). First named **Texas University**; chartered under present name in 1875); Dr. Jake B. Schrum	120	1,277	NA	NA
Stephen F. Austin State University—Nacogdoches; (2); 1921; Dr. Baker Pattillo	627	11,756	NA	NA
Sul Ross State University—Alpine (See **Texas State University System**)				
Sul Ross State University-Rio Grande College —Uvalde (See **Texas State University System**)				
Tarleton State University—Stephenville (See **Texas A&M University System**)				
TARRANT COUNTY COLLEGE DISTRICT—Fort Worth; (7); 1965 (as **Tarrant County Junior College**; name changed 1999); Dr. Leonardo de la Garza, chancellor; four cam puses (location, campus president):	1,395	34,854	NA	14,019
Northeast (Hurst, Dr. Larry Darnel)	412	10,975	7,130	5,553
Northwest (Fort Worth, Dr. Michael Saenz)	261	5,259	2,987	8,597
‡South (Fort Worth, Dr. Ernest Thomas)				
‡Southeast (Arlington, Dr. Judith Carrier)				
Temple College—Temple; (7); 1926; Dr. Marc A. Nigliazzo	256	4,279	1,916	1,117
Texarkana College—Texarkana; (7); 1927; Dr. Frank Coleman	110	4,216	1,841	10,300
Texas A&I University—Kingsville (See **Texas A&M University-Kingsville** listing under **Texas A&M University System**)				

Name of Institution; Location; (Type* - Ownership, if private sectarian institution); Date of Founding; President (unless otherwise noted)	Number of Faculty†	Enrollment		
		Fall Term 2006	Summer Session 2006	Extension or Continuing Ed.
TEXAS A&M UNIVERSITY SYSTEM (1) —Dr. Michael D. McKinney, M.D., chancellor				
Prairie View A&M University—Prairie View; (2); 1876 (as **Alta Vista Agricultural College**; changed to **Prairie View State Normal Institute** in 1879; later **Prairie View Normal and Industrial College**; in 1947 changed to **Prairie View A&M College** as branch of **Texas A&M University System**; present name since 1973); Dr. George C. Wright	467	8,350	3,389	NA
‡ **Tarleton State University**—Stephenville; (2); 1899 (as John Tarleton College; taken over by state in 1917 as **John Tarleton Agricultural College**; changed 1949 to **Tarleton State College**; present name since 1973; includes campus in Killeen); Dr. Dennis McCabe	377	9,464	5,121	NA
Texas A&M International University—Laredo; (2); 1970 (as **Laredo State University**; name changed to present form 1993); Dr. Ray M Keck	266	4,272	3,755	NA
Texas A&M University—College Station; (2); 1876 (as **Agricultural and Mechanical of Texas**; present name since 1963; includes **College of Veterinary Medicine** and **College of Medicine** at College Station); Dr. Eddie J. Davis (interim pres.)	3,876	45,380	18,031	NA
Texas A&M University–Commerce; (2); 1889 (as **East Texas Normal College**; renamed **East Texas State Teachers College** in 1923; "Teachers" dropped, 1957; university status conferred and named changed to **East Texas State University**, 1965; transferred to Texas A&M system 1995; includes **ETSU Metroplex Commuter Facility**, Mesquite); Dr. Keith D. McFarland	330	8,566	4,834	152
‡ **Texas A&M University–Corpus Christi**–Corpus Christi; (2); 1973 (as upper-level Corpus Christi State Univ.; present name since 1993; 4-year in 1994); Dr. Flavius Killebrew	580	8,584	4,728	NA
‡ **Texas A&M University at Galveston**–Galveston; (2); 1962 (as **Texas Maritime Academy**; changed to **Moody College of Marine Sciences and Maritime Resources** and became 4-yr. college in 1971); Dr. R. Bowen Loftin (vice-pres. and C.E.O.)	83	1,553	673	0
Texas A&M University–Kingsville; (2); 1925 (as **South Texas Teachers College**; name changed to **Texas College of Arts and Industries** in 1929; to **Texas A&I University**, 1967; made part of **Univ. of South Texas System** in 1977; entered A&M system in 1993); Dr. Rumaldo Z. Juárez	470	6,689	5,596	243
Texas A&M University System Health Science Center—(Includes **Baylor College of Dentistry, College of Medicine, Graduate School of Biomedical Sciences, Institute of Biosciences and Technology, School of Rural Public Health**, and HSC Statellite locations)				
Texas A&M University–Texarkana; (2 - upper-level); 1971 (as **East Texas State University at Texarkana**, transferred to Texas A&M system and name changed,); Dr. Stephen R. Hensley	95	1,624	993	NA
West Texas A&M University—Canyon; (2); 1910 (as **West Texas State Normal College**; became **West Texas State Teachers College** in 1923; **West Texas State College**, 1949; changed to **West Texas State Univ.**, 1949; present name, 1993); Dr. J. Patrick O'Brien	237	7,412	4,651	21
Texas Baptist Institute-Seminary—Henderson; (3 - Calvary Baptist); 1948; Dr. Ray O. Brooks	15	35	NA	NA
Texas Christian University—Fort Worth; (3 - Disciples of Christ); 1873 (as **Add- Ran College at Thorp Spring**; name changed to **Add-Ran Christian Univ.** 1890; moved to Waco1895; present name, 1902; moved to Fort Worth 1910); Dr. Victor J. Boschini Jr.	478	8,865	2,711	2,278
Texas College—Tyler; (3 - C.M.E.); 1894; Dr. Billy C. Hawkins	42	757	109	0
Texas College of Osteopathic Medicine—Fort Worth (See University of North Texas Health Science Center at Fort Worth)				
‡ **Texas Lutheran University**—Seguin; (3 - Lutheran); 1891 (in Brenham as **Evangelical Lutheran College**; moved to Seguin, 1912 and renamed **Lutheran College of Seguin**; renamed **Texas Lutheran College**, 1932; changed to university, 1996); Rev. Ann Svennungsen	95	1,334		NA
‡ **Texas Southern University**—Houston; (2); 1926 (as **Houston Colored Junior Coll.**; upper level added, name changed to **Houston College for Negroes** in mid-1930s; became **Texas State University for Negroes**, 1947; present name, 1951); Dr. J. Timothy Boddie Jr. (inter. pres.)	578	11,224	2,818	50
Texas Southmost College—Brownsville (see **The University of Texas at Brownsville** under **University of Texas System** listing)				
‡ **TEXAS STATE TECHNICAL COLLEGE SYSTEM (6) — Dr. Willaim Segura, chancellor.** Includes extension centers in Abilene, Breckenridge and Brownwood, and the colleges listed below (location, president):	**	11,253	**	**
Texas State Technical College-Harlingen (Dr. J. Gilbert Leal)	**	4,350	**	**
Texas State Technical College-Marshall (Dr. J. Gary Hendricks)	46	687	393	246
Texas State Technical College- Waco (established as James Connally Technical Institute; name changed in 1969), (Dr. Elton E. Stuckly)	280	4,491	2,602	88
Texas State Technical College-West Texas—Sweetwater (Dr. Homer Taylor)	123	1,725	1,208	1,990
TEXAS STATE UNIVERSITY SYSTEM (1)—Dr. Charles R. Matthews, chancellor				
Angelo State University—San Angelo; (2); 1928; Dr. E. James Hindeman	347	6,265	3,644	1,102
Lamar University—Beaumont; (2); 1923 (as **South Park Junior Coll.**; name changed to **Lamar Coll.**, 1932; name changed to **Lamar State Coll. of Technology**, 1951; present name, 1971; transferred from Lamar Univ. System, 1995); Dr. James M. Simmons	559	9,906	4,845	
Lamar State College - Orange—Orange; (10); 1969 (transferred from **Lamar University System**, Sept. 1995; name changed to **State College**, 2000); Dr. J. Michael Shahan	97	2,011	694	97

Name of Institution; Location; (Type* - Ownership, if private sectarian institution); Date of Founding; President (unless otherwise noted)	Number of Faculty†	Fall Term 2006	Summer Session 2006	Extension or Continuing Ed.
Lamar State College - Port Arthur—Port Arthur; (10); 1909 (as **Port Arthur College**; became part of **Lamar Univ.** in 1975; part of **TSU system**, 1995; name changed to **State College**, 2000); Dr. W. Sam Monroe	130	2,916	2,268	225
Lamar Institute of Technology—Beaumont; (10); (part of TSU system, 1995); Dr. Robert D. Krienke	140	2,500	500	500
Sam Houston State University—Huntsville; (2); 1879; Dr. James F. Gaertner	926	15,935	10,146	292
Sul Ross State University—Alpine; (2); 1917 (as **Sul Ross State Normal Coll.**; changed to **Sul Ross State Teachers Coll.**, 1923; to **Sul Ross State Coll.**, 1949; present name since 1969) Dr. R. Vic Morgan	148	1,937	1,024	NA
Sul Ross State University-Rio Grande College—Uvalde, Eagle Pass and Del Rio (2 – up per level); 1973 (name changed from **Sul Ross State University**, Uvalde Center 1995) Dr. Joel Vela, vice president; Dr. Frank Abbott, dean.	50	948	701	795
Texas Chiropractic College—Pasadena (5) Richard G. Brassaro.	47	350	347	NA
Texas State University–San Marcos—San Marcos; (2); 1903 (as **Southwest Texas Normal School**; changed1918 to **Southwest Texas State Normal College**, in 1923 to **Southwest Texas State Teachers College**, in 1959 to **Southwest Texas State College**, in 1969 to **Southwest Texas State University**, and to present form in 2003);Dr. Denise M. Trauth	1,128	27,000	8,658	**
TEXAS TECH UNIVERSITY (1) —Kent Hance, chancellor				
Texas Tech University—Lubbock; (2); 1923 (as **Texas Technological College**; present name since 1969); Dr. Jon Whitmore	1,437	28,483	9,156	2,137
Texas Tech University Health Sciences Center—Lubbock; (4); 1972; Roy Wilson, M.D.	596	2,272	**	NA
Texas Wesleyan University—Fort Worth; (3 - United Methodist); 1891 (as college; present name since 1989); Dr. Harold G. Jeffcoat	254	2,774	953	0
Texas Woman's University—Denton; (2); 1901 (as **Coll. of Industrial Arts**; name changed to **Texas State Coll. for Women**, 1934; present name, 1957); Dr. Ann Stuart, Chancellor and President	428	11,831	8,215	500
Tomball College—Tomball (See North Harris Montgomery Community College Dist.)				
Trinity University—San Antonio; (3 - Presbyterian); 1869 (at Tehuacana; moved to Waxahachie, 1902; to San Antonio, 1942); Dr. John R. Brazil	240	2,693	433	NA
Trinity Valley Community College—Athens; also campus at Terrell; (7); 1946 (originally Henderson County Junior College); Dr. Ronald C. Baugh	124	6,456	2,500	1,400
Tyler Junior College—Tyler; (7); 1926; Dr. William R. Crowe	492	9,422	3,951	1,782
University of Central Texas—Killeen (see Texas A&M University System, Tarleton State University Systems Center/Central Texas)				
University of Dallas—Irving; (3 - Catholic); 1956; Dr. Francis M. Lazarus	234	2,941	1,641	183
UNIVERSITY OF HOUSTON SYSTEM (1) — Dr. John M. Rudley, chancellor				
‡ **University of Houston**—Houston; (2); 1927; Dr. Jay Gogue	3,036	35,100	NA	NA
University of Houston-Clear Lake—Houston; (2 - upper level and grad.); 1974; Dr. William A. Staples	602	7,706	4,218	NA
University of Houston-Downtown—Houston; (2); 1948 (as **North Texas College**; became part of **University of Houston** in 1974) ; Dr. Max Castillo	550	11,974	4,838	1,712
‡ **University of Houston-Victoria**—Victoria; (2 - upper-level); 1973; Tim Hudson	108	2,183	1,955	NA
University of the Incarnate Word—San Antonio; (3 - Catholic); 1881 (as **Incarnate Word College**; name changed 1996); Dr. Louis J. Agnese Jr.	147	4,800	**	NA
University of Mary Hardin-Baylor—Belton; (3 - So. Baptist); 1845; Dr. Jerry G. Bawcom	273	2,713	1,092	0
University of North Texas—Denton; (2); 1890 (as **North Texas Normal College**; name changed 1923 to **North Texas State Teachers Coll.**; in 1949 to **North Texas State Coll.**; university, 1961; present name since 1988); Dr. Gretchen M. Bataille	2,098	33,443	15,823	
University of North Texas Health Science Center at Fort Worth—Fort Worth; (4);1966 (as private college; came under direction of **North Texas State University** in 1975; present name since 1993); Dr. Ronald R. Blanck, D.O.		222	1,021	777
‡ **University of St. Thomas**—Houston; (3); 1947; Rev. J. Michael Miller, CSB	190	3,648	**	NA
UNIVERSITY OF TEXAS SYSTEM (1) — Mark G. Yudof, chancellor				
University of Texas at Arlington, The—Arlington; (2); 1895 (as **Arlington Coll.**; became state inst. in 1917 and renamed **Grubbs Vocational Coll.**; 1923 became **North Texas Agricultural and Mechanical Coll.**; became **Arlington State Coll.**, 1949; present name since 1967); Dr. James Spaniolo	1,081	25,297	12,310	3,374
University of Texas at Austin, The—Austin; (2); 1883; Dr. Larry R. Faulkner	2,137	50,403	**	**
University of Texas at Brownsville, The (2 - upper-level); 1973 (as branch of **Pan American Coll.**; changed to **Univ. of Texas-Pan American - Brownsville**; present name, 1991) and **Texas Southmost College** (7); 1926 (as **Brownsville Jr. Coll.**; name changed,1949) — Brownsville; Dr. Juliet V. Garcia	743	15,688	5,599	512
University of Texas at Dallas, The—Richardson; (2); 1961 (as **Graduate Research of the Southwest**; changed to **Southwest Center for Advanced Studies** in 1967; joined **U.T. System** and present name, 1969; full undergraduate program, 1975); David Daniel	855	14,523	6,825	NA
University of Texas at El Paso, The—El Paso; (2); 1913 (as **Texas Coll. of Mines and Metallurgy**; changed to **Texas Western Coll. of U.T.**, 1949; present name, 1967); Dr. Diana S. Natalicio	1,083	19,842	8,716	2,921

Name of Institution; Location; (Type* - Ownership, if private sectarian institution); Date of Founding; President (unless otherwise noted)	Number of Faculty†	Enrollment		
		Fall Term 2006	Summer Session 2006	Extension or Continuing Ed.
University of Texas-Pan American, The—Edinburg; (2); 1927 (as **Edinburg Junior Coll.**; changed to **Pan American College** and made 4-yr., 1952; became **Pan American Uni** in 1971; present name since 1991); Dr. Blandina Cardenas	842	17,337	10,487	NA
‡ **University of Texas of the Permian Basin, The**—Odessa; (2); 1969 (as 2-yr. upper- level institution; expanded to 4-yr., Sept. 1991); Dr. W. David Watts	158	3,347	1,185	NA
‡ **University of Texas at San Antonio**—San Antonio; (2); 1969; Dr. Ricardo Romo	**	26,175	10,530	512
University of Texas at Tyler—Tyler; (2 - upper-level); 1971 (as **Tyler State Coll.**; became **Texas Eastern University**, 1975; joined U.T. System, 1979); Dr. Rodney H. Mabry	378	5,926	2,219	NA
‡ **University of Texas Health Science Center at Tyler (4)** — Dr. Kirk A. Calhoun, M.D. Established 1949 as **East Texas Tuberculosis Sanatorium**; renamed **East Texas Chest Hospital**, 1971; joined UT system and gained present name in 1977). Primary emphasis is on pulmonary and heart disease	125	75	NA	NA
University of Texas Health Science Center at Houston (4) — Dr. James T. Willerson Established 1972; consists of following divisions (year of founding): **Dental Branch** (1905); **Graduate School of Biomedical Sciences** (1963); **Medical School** (1970); **School of Allied Health Sciences** (1973); **School of Nursing** (1972); **School of Public Health** (1967); **Division of Continuing Education** (1958).	1,224	3,399	1,961	25,559
‡ **University of Texas Health Science Center at San Antonio (4)** — Dr. Francisco G. Cigarroa, M.D. Established 1968; consists of following divisions (year of founding): Dental School (1970); Graduate School of Biomedical Sciences (1970); Health Science Center (1972); Medical School (1959 as South Texas Medical School of UT; present name, 1966); School of Allied Health Sciences (1976); School of Nursing (1969).	1,400	2,845	NA	NA
University of Texas M.D. Anderson Cancer Center — Dr. John Mendelsohn, M.D.	1,050	70	NA	2,252
‡ **University of Texas Medical Branch at Galveston (4)** — Dr. John D. Stobo Established 1891; consists of following divisions (year of founding): **Graduate School of Biomedical Sciences** (1952); **Medical School** (1891); **School of Allied Health Sciences** (1968); **School of Nursing** (1890).	1,984	2,149	1,481	NA
University of Texas Southwestern Medical Center at Dallas (4) — Dr. Kern Wildenthal, M.D. Established 1943 (as private institution; became **Southwestern Medical Coll. of UT** 1948; became **UT Southwestern Medical School at Dallas**, 1967; made part of **UT Health Science Center at Dallas**, 1972); consists of following divisions (year of founding): Graduate School of Biomedical Sciences (1947); **School of Allied Health Sciences** (1968); **Southwestern Medical School** (1943).	1,902	1,768	NA	NA
‡ **Vernon Regional Junior College**—Vernon; (7); 1970; Dr. Steve Thomas	132	2,793	1,057	1,291
Victoria College, The —Victoria; (7); 1925; Dr. Jimmy Goodson	110	4,036	2,046	924
Wayland Baptist University—Plainview; (3 -Southern Baptist); 1910; Dr. Wallace Davis Jr., Chancellor; Dr. Paul W. Ames, President	109	5,712	4,165	NA
Weatherford College—Weatherford; (7); 1869 (as branch of Southwestern Univ.; 1922, became denominational junior college; became muni. jr. college, 1949); Dr. Joe Birmingham.	252	4,512	4,889	NA
‡ **Western Texas College**—Snyder; (7); 1969; Dr. Gregory Williams	72	1,698	1,099	876
‡ **Wharton County Junior College**—Wharton; (7); 1946; Betty A. McCrohan	413	6,106	2,612	740
‡ **Wiley College**—Marshall; (3 - Methodist); 1873; Dr. Haywood L. Strickland	75	843	NA	67

Key to Table Symbols

Type:
(1) Public University System
(2) Public University
(3) Independent Senior College or University
(4) Public Medical School or Health Science Center
(5) Independent Medical or Dental School
(6) Public Technical College System
(7) Public Community College
(8) Independent Junior College
(9) Public Community College System
(10) Public Lower-Level Institution

NA - Not applicable

† Unless otherwise noted, faculty count includes professors, associate professors, adjunct professors, instructors and tutors, both full and part-time, but does not include voluntary instructors.

‡ No reply received to questionnaire. Name of president and number of students enrolled in fall 2004 was obtained from the institutions Web site or the Texas Higher Education Coordinating Board Web site: www.thecb.state.tx.us/DataAndStatistics/institutions.htm.

Includes faculty and enrollment at all branches or divisions.

§ Includes all students in two summer sessions.

¶ Full-time faculty only.

** Information not supplied by institution.

†† Approximate count.

§§ Latest figures available from institution's Web page were for 2002–2003 school year.

§§§ Enrollment in online courses only.

¶¶ Number of students in extension courses or continuing education for all of fiscal year 2002.

Business

Oil refineries and petrochemical plants along the Houston Ship Channel. Robert Plocheck photo.

Economy & Employment

Banking & Insurance

Oil & Gas

Minerals

Media

Construction

Utilities

Texas Economy Continues Upward Trend

Source: State of Texas Annual Cash Report 2006, Comptroller of Public Accounts.

The Texas economy grew briskly in 2006, as reflected in numerous statistics and illustrated by rising state tax collection. Nonfarm employment, adding jobs every month, was up 235,000 or 2.4 percent during the year.

At the end of fiscal 2006, Texas' unemployment rate was 5.1 percent, above its low of 3.8 in December 2000, but substantially lower than the 6.8 percent rate in mid-2003. Fiscal 2006 continued the upward trend in employment and was the third consecutive year of nonfarm job gains, following declines in fiscal 2002 and 2003. During the fiscal year, Texas outpaced national job growth rates in seven of the 12 months.

The Texas Index of Leading Economic Indicators improved on a year-to-year basis for 39 straight months, and at the end of fiscal 2006 the index was 2.9 percent above its level one year earlier.

In fiscal 2006, job creation remained, as always, a key driver for forecasting future state economic growth, but rising oil prices, up 23.9 percent, helped grow the leading indicators index even with negative effects higher energy prices have had on Texas consumers.

The oil price indicator has been a positive for the overall economy because Texas is a net energy exporter at current energy prices and the oil and natural gas industry provides Texas with a large number of relatively high-paying jobs. Rounding out the double-digit gainers in the latest indicators index, total retail sales growth climbed 13.9 percent, followed by initial claims for unemployment compensation which dropped by 13.5 percent.

Construction was the fastest growing major industry in Texas in 2006. File photo.

Of Texas' 11 major non-farm industries, as defined by the North American Industrial Classification System (NAICS), all but two (information and "other" services) added employment during fiscal 2006. The fastest growing major industry, with 7.1 percent employment growth and an increase of 40,300 jobs over the year, was construction. The sector that lost the most jobs was information, with a 1.0 percent decline during the year.

I. PRODUCTS

Manufacturing

Texas manufacturers are producing more with fewer workers, fueled by steady advances in information processing and technology. During 2006, the real (inflation adjusted) gross state product in Texas manufacturing rose 4.2 percent, but industry employment also grew for the second straight year, following four years of losses.

The durable goods sectors of manufacturing accounted for most of the growth in the industry in fiscal 2006. Two sectors with differing fortunes stood out over the past year. Fabricated metals and machinery benefited from supplying materials for renewed oil and gas exploration and a strong construction market. The sector added 3,500 jobs, a 3.0 percent increase.

High technology manufacturing, however, was still depressed as both prices and demand for computers and new technology slumped. Computer and electronic product manufacturing suffered a loss of 6.2 percent of its workforce, dropping 7,100 jobs, while electric equipment and appliances lost 300 jobs (1.7 percent).

In total, manufacturing's durable goods sectors gained 4,100 jobs (0.7 percent), with other sizable increases in transportation equipment (3,600 jobs or 4.1 percent) and furniture manufacturing (700 jobs, up 2.2 percent).

The nondurable goods sectors of manufacturing lost 1,900 jobs (0.6 percent) in fiscal 2006, with only food and beverage and pharmaceutical manufacturing adding jobs. Pharmaceuticals had the strongest increase, 5.4 percent, although this translated into only 500 jobs. Food manufacturing advanced by 900 jobs, a 1.0 percent increase, while beverages employment grew by 500, a 4.6 percent increase.

Petroleum refining had a flat year, neither losing nor gaining net employment, but all other sectors of nondurable manufacturing lost jobs. The largest declines were in printing (1,500 jobs or 4.1 percent) and plastics (1,000 jobs or 2.2 percent). There was also a net loss of 200 jobs in chemicals, with losses in the rest of nondurable goods more than counterbalancing the gain in pharmaceuticals.

Total manufacturing employment in Texas increased by 3,200 jobs, or 0.4 percent, in fiscal 2006, a smaller gain than a year earlier, but an improvement over the declines of the four preceding years. Texas' manufacturing industry fared better than the nation's, which saw jobs grow by only 0.1 percent.

Oil and Gas

The segments of Texas' oil and gas industry that have benefited the most from higher oil and gas prices are exploration and development.

Employment in the oil and gas extraction sector grew by 3,000 or 4.5 percent in fiscal 2006, spurred by the dramatic taxable price increases for crude oil (30 percent) and natural gas (29 percent).

For the fourth year, the support activities for the mining sector added jobs, with an additional 9,100 or 10.1 percent in fiscal 2006.

Worldwide demand for oil is increasing and quickly diminishing the buffer of excess capacity, particularly due to sizeable demand increases from China, the world's second largest consumer of oil.

Increased demand, plus concerns of supply disruptions, kept energy prices high during most of the fiscal year.

What happens on the energy front is of great concern because Texas is the national — and arguably the world — headquarters of the oil and gas industry, and it's no surprise that the natural resources and mining industry's share of Texas' total nonfarm earnings is over five times the national share.

In fiscal 2006, Texas added 10,200 jobs (up 6.1 percent) in natural resources and mining.

Construction

The Texas construction continued to rebound in fiscal 2006, after employment declines in fiscal 2002 through 2004, attributable in large part to new building construction. This, combined with expanding specialty trade construction, led to a net gain of 40,300 jobs (up 7.1 percent) for the industry.

The building construction sector (residential and non-residential combined) added 12,700 jobs, or 9.4 percent, with heavy and civil engineering construction growing at a slower pace (3,400 jobs or 3.2 percent).

In fiscal 2006, existing Texas home sales had another up year, by 5.1 percent, and the average price for a new or existing house reached a new high, suggesting the housing market is still growing. Single family housing starts in 2006 increased at the fastest rate since 1998.

II. SERVICES

Typically, Texas' service-providing sectors, which comprise more than 83 percent of the state's nonfarm employment, added jobs at a faster pace that the goods-producing sectors, although fiscal 2006 saw a reversal of this pattern for the first time in eight years. While service-providing industries added 77 percent of the state's

job increase, growing at 2.2 percent, the goods industries grew at 3.3 percent, due largely to strong construction and oil and gas hiring.

Professional and Business Services

The fastest-growing Texas service industry during fiscal 2006 was the professional and business services industry. Growing at 5.1 percent, the industry added 58,800 jobs, nearly one-third of the growth in all service-providing jobs and one-fourth of total nonfarm job growth.

Computer systems design services, which topped the list as the fastest growing sector of any industry in Texas by adding 9,900 jobs in fiscal 2006, recorded a 12.8 percent gain. Accounting, tax preparation, bookkeeping, and payroll services tacked on a 7.9 percent job growth, followed by the management of companies and enterprises, which grew by 6.4 percent and added 3,400 jobs, to reach 56,300 jobs.

Finance

The financial activities industry was the second fastest-growing service industry in Texas during fiscal 2006, adding 18,200 jobs (3.0 percent). All three major components (finance, insurance, and real estate) added jobs at a brisk pace. Securities and financial investments added 2,000 jobs (4.9 percent). The real estate market displayed continued strength in fiscal 2006 with the number of real estate jobs increasing by 1.9 percent. Insurance carriers boosted their employment by 3.0 percent. Banking and credit intermediation services grew by 7,100 jobs during the year (up 3.1 percent). No sector of financial activities lost net jobs during fiscal 2006.

Education and Health

While financial activities had its most active hiring year since 1999, the educational and health services industry experienced the opposite, with its slowest rate of hiring since 1999. Still, educational and health services added a substantial number of jobs, 26,700, and increased its overall employment by 2.2 percent in fiscal 2006. Nearly half of this employment growth was in the home health-care services segment. Home health care employment grew by 6.7 percent, with the addition of

Gross Domestic Product in Current Dollars

	Millions of $ dollars			Percent of U.S. total			GDP* 2005	
	2003	2004	2005	2003	2004	2005	China	8,859,000
United States	**10,896,356**	**11,655,355**	**12,402,967**	**100.0**	**100.0**	**100.0**	Japan	4,018,000
1. California	1,410,539	1,519,202	1,621,116	12.9	13.0	13.1	India	3,611,000
2. Texas	**828,456**	**903,208**	**989,443**	**7.6**	**7.7**	**8.0**	Germany	2,504,000
3. New York	847,123	906,783	957,873	7.8	7.8	7.7	United Kingdom	1,830,000
4. Florida	556,748	609,372	673,274	5.1	5.2	5.4	France	1,816,000
5. Illinois	509,161	533,735	560,032	4.7	4.6	4.5	Italy	1,698,000
6. Pennsylvania	439,241	463,752	489,025	4.0	4.0	3.9	Russia	1,589,000
7. Ohio	402,607	425,173	440,923	3.7	3.6	3.6	Brazil	1,556,000
8. New Jersey	388,645	410,306	431,079	3.6	3.5	3.5	Canada	1,114,000
9. Michigan	362,805	366,601	376,243	3.3	3.1	3.0	Mexico	1,067,000
10. Georgia	317,490	339,730	363,839	2.9	2.9	2.9	Spain	1,029,000

Source: Bureau of Economic Analysis, U.S. Department of Commerce.

*Estimated Gross Domestic Product in millions of U.S. dollars from the World Factbook of the CIA.

11,500 jobs. Employment in physicians' offices grew by 3.5 percent, while positions in Texas hospitals grew by a more modest 1.9 percent. The health care and social assistance sector alone now employs nearly 1.1 million Texans, with more people employed in this sector than in manufacturing.

The educational services component had an unusual year of very slow growth, rising by only 500 jobs or 0.4 percent. Private colleges, universities, and professional schools gave up 1,200 positions, or 2.3 percent.

Trade, Transportation, Utilities

The trade, transportation, and utilities industry is Texas' largest employer, accounting for more than one-fifth of all nonfarm jobs and providing wages for two million Texans. In fiscal 2006, the industry continued its upward trend and, unusually, more jobs were added in wholesale trade than in retail trade.

Retail trade grew by 15,100 jobs (1.4 percent), wholesale by 16,200 (3.4 percent), and transportation, warehousing, and utilities by a comparatively modest 2,300 jobs (0.6 percent).

There were large job increases in building materials and supplies (up 6.5 percent), while in-migration fueled job growth in grocery stores (5.0 percent), health and personal care retailers (5.8 percent), and clothing stores (3.6 percent).

Nonstore retailers, including Texas retailers selling from the Internet, saw job increases of 4.1 percent. On the other hand, department stores shrank their job count by 5.4 percent; gasoline stations lost 1.0 percent of their jobs.

Transportation and warehousing had comparatively slow job growth during fiscal 2006, partly due to continued losses in air transportation sector (down 3,000 jobs or 4.8 percent). Truck transportation added employment, with 3,100 more jobs (2.8 percent).

Because fuel price increases take a greater toll on trucks than railways, rail transportation had the fastest job growth of the transportation sectors, although its robust 5.2 percent job growth translated into only 900 jobs in this small sector. The greatest job growth was in warehousing and storage (port and harbor activities, freight packing, and household storage), which added 2,200 jobs or 5.7 percent.

Utilities, traditionally the most stable sector of this industry, continued its reputation by adding jobs at a moderate rate of 1.5 percent, an increase of 700 jobs.

Overall, trade, transportation, and utilities grew by 1.8 percent during fiscal 2006, adding 36,200 jobs and, based on job growth, landed in the middle of the pack for Texas industries.

Information Industry

The information industry has under performed in recent years, and it did again in fiscal 2006. No information industry sector added jobs in Texas in fiscal 2006. Information is a conglomerate of several industries, some old-economy (printing, publishing, data processing, television broadcasting, and wired telephone services) and some newer (cellular telephone providers, Internet providers, DSL, and software services). In fiscal 2006 the information industry lost 2,200 jobs, or 1.0 percent.

The Internet providers, web portals, and data processing sector led the industry in 2006, since it did not lose net jobs. However, the sector did not gain any jobs either, beginning and ending the year with 34,800 jobs.

The telecommunications sector had another year of losses, although the 400 job decline was only 0.4 percent of its total, so it appears to be stabilizing. About three-fourths of Texas telecommunications employment is in wired and cellular providers of telephone services, although there is also substantial employment in satellite and cable providers, paging services, and telecommunications reselling services.

The last few years have been difficult for publishers of newspapers, books, and magazines, both in Texas and nationwide. Challenged by electronic media, which can be updated immediately, publishers had another year of job losses, dropping 300 or 0.6 percent in fiscal 2006.

Restaurants and Hospitality

More than three-fourths of the jobs in Texas' leisure and hospitality industry are in restaurants and bars, and 84 percent of the jobs added in fiscal 2006 were in these food services and drinking establishments. Unlike professional and business services, this industry continued to grow through Texas' economic downturn in the early part of the decade.

The hotel sector tacked on 1,600 jobs during fiscal 2006, with employment near 100,000 and a growth rate of 1.6 percent. The sector decreasing the most during the year, losing 4,200 jobs or 5.1 percent, was amusement, gaming and recreation, a sector stressed by higher transportation costs, the closing of a major Houston amusement park, and increasing competition for recreational activities from across the state's borders.

This industry outperforms the overall economy during bad economic times, but it usually grows more slowly during economic booms. In fiscal 2006, the industry mostly matched the state's overall economic growth, adding 20,000 jobs or 2.2 percent.

Other Services

This industry group includes occupations such as automotive repair, automobile body shops, computer repair, beauty salons and hair stylists, laundry and dry cleaning, civic and social associations, religious organizations, professional organizations, and employment in private households.

Given that general statistics about such a broad range of sectors conceals the story in specific areas, this services group suffered a loss of 1,300 in fiscal 2006, a drop of 0.4 percent. Personal and laundry services gave up 2,200 jobs (2.5 percent) during the year. Associations and organizations were quite stable, but they still lost 100 jobs (down 0.1 percent).

Government

Government employment in Texas rose by 1.5 percent during fiscal 2006, adding 24,700 jobs. State government added just 400 jobs, a bit over 0.1 percent, while the civilian federal government component dropped by 600 jobs or 0.3 percent. U.S. Department of Defense staff increased by 900 jobs (1.9 percent). The real job growth in the Texas government sector, however, was at the local level, where 21,700 jobs were added in 2006, an increase of 2.0 percent. The great majority of local government job growth was for schools, with a small share (1,800) in local government.

Accounting for seasonal adjustments, of the jobs added to government in Texas in 2006, 93 percent were in local schools, continuing a long-term trend. ☆

Texas Gross Domestic Product, 1997–2006, By Industry (in millions)

Industry	1997	1998	1999	2000	2001	2002	2003	2004	2005	2006
Agriculture, Forestry, Fishing/Hunting	$6,691	$6,052	$6,752	$6,470	$6,394	$7,457	$8,394	$9,688	$10,587	$11,007
% change*	(5.0)	(9.6)	11.6	(4.2)	(1.2)	16.6	12.6	15.4	9.3	4.0
Natural Resources and Mining	34,047	23,237	27,652	45,182	44,072	39,219	57,422	67,832	82,505	94,066
% change	9.9	(31.8)	19.0	63.4	(2.5)	(11.0)	46.4	18.1	21.6	14.0
Construction	25,333	29,568	32,836	36,882	40,259	41,871	43,470	46,263	50,230	55,200
% change	8.0	16.7	11.1	12.3	9.2	4.0	3.8	6.4	8.6	9.9
Manufacturing	92,409	97,929	91,601	92,981	92,273	94,462	93,222	110,172	121,935	130,699
% change	7.6	6.0	(6.5)	1.5	(0.8)	2.4	(1.3)	18.2	10.7	7.2
Trade, Transportation, Utilities	126,618	135,536	146,595	155,785	160,789	164,723	171,109	183,414	196,895	213,934
% change	6.5	7.0	8.2	6.3	3.2	2.4	3.9	7.2	7.4	8.7
Information	27,370	30,603	33,295	35,865	36,992	36,531	35,414	38,293	41,544	44,948
% change	9.3	11.8	8.8	7.7	3.1	(1.2)	(3.10)	8.1	8.5	8.2
Financial Activities	92,684	99,250	107,929	117,200	125,928	128,219	134,745	141,345	150,602	162,804
% change	8.5	7.1	8.7	8.6	7.4	1.8	5.1	4.9	6.5	8.1
Professional and Business Services	56,380	62,928	69,387	73,208	82,195	83,937	87,194	97,296	106,849	118,784
% change	14.5	11.6	10.3	5.5	12.3	2.1	3.9	11.6	9.8	11.2
Educational and Health Services	35,507	37,182	39,357	42,359	46,797	51,380	54,608	58,572	62,459	67,344
% change	5.3	4.7	5.8	7.6	10.5	9.8	6.3	7.3	6.6	7.8
Leisure and Hospitality Services	18,642	19,960	21,764	23,106	23,993	25,492	26,387	27,976	29,783	32,041
% change	10.3	7.1	9.0	6.2	3.8	6.2	3.5	6.0	6.5	7.6
Other Private Services	14,674	15,922	16,576	17,603	18,106	18,679	19,522	20,451	21,530	22,971
% change	5.0	8.5	4.1	6.2	2.9	3.2	4.5	4.8	5.3	6.7
Government and Schools	69,136	71,044	75,249	80,590	84,448	91,512	96,969	101,906	107,484	114,417
% change	4.5	2.8	5.9	7.1	4.8	8.4	6.0	5.1	5.5	6.5
TOTAL	$599,491	$629,211	$668,993	$727,231	$762,246	$783,482	$828,456	$903,208	$982,403	$1,068,215
% change	7.7	5.0	6.3	8.7	4.8	2.8	5.7	9.0	8.8	8.7
TOTAL (in 2000 chained** dollars)	$627,501	$666,590	$699,101	$727,229	$745,325	$760,588	$771,082	$810,510	$845,459	$887,750
% change	9.1	6.2	4.9	4.0	2.5	2.0	1.4	5.1	4.3	5.0

*Percent change from the previous year. ** In 1996, the U.S. Department of Commerce introduced the chained-dollar measure. The new measure is based on the average weights of goods and services in successive pairs of years. It is "chained" because the second year in each pair, with its weights, becomes the first year of the next pair. *Source: U.S. Bureau of Economic Analysis.*

Per Capita Income by County, 2005

Below are listed data for 2005 for total personal income and per capita income by county. Total income is reported in millions of dollars. The middle column indicates the percent of change in total income from 2004 to 2005.

In the far right column is the county's rank in the state for per capita income. Loving County, a unique case — with a total population of only 60, leads in per capita income with $77,787. Sherman County, at the top of the Panhandle, is second with $47,084.

The lowest per capita income is in Starr County, along the Rio Grande, at $12,197.

Source: Bureau of Economic Analysis, U.S. Department of Commerce.

County	Total Income ($ mil)	% change 04/05	Per capita income	Rank
United States	$10,220,942	5.2	$ 34,471	—
Metropolitan	8,924,022	5.3	36,140	—
Nonmetro	1,296,920	4.6	26,161	—
Texas	$ 744,270	7.8	$ 32,460	—
Metropolitan	671,480	8.0	33,661	—
Nonmetro	72,791	6.2	24,425	—
Anderson	$ 1,142	4.1	$ 20,226	221
Andrews	354	11.3	27,727	77
Angelina	2,327	5.0	28,518	69
Aransas	679	7.3	27,504	81
Archer	274	4.4	29,838	50
Armstrong	62	1.6	28,612	68
Atascosa	936	6.8	21,631	207
Austin	787	7.0	30,259	45
Bailey	160	5.0	23,984	166
Bandera	559	6.0	27,935	73
Bastrop	1,656	5.9	23,725	173
Baylor	88	0.9	23,006	191
Bee	578	5.8	17,564	244
Bell	7,921	10.9	31,139	36
Bexar	46,777	6.6	30,843	38
Blanco	282	5.8	30,795	39
Borden	20	11.4	31,210	35
Bosque	441	5.5	24,529	155
Bowie	2,490	6.1	27,583	79
Brazoria	8,298	7.8	29,869	49
Brazos	3,915	7.7	24,994	136
Brewster	248	1.1	27,422	84
Briscoe	40	9.9	24,325	158
Brooks	143	6.2	18,591	233
Brown	920	6.8	23,780	171
Burleson	425	6.6	24,773	145
Burnet	1,214	8.5	29.262	60
Caldwell	804	6.6	21,992	205
Calhoun	505	5.9	24,561	154
Callahan	317	4.6	23,612	175
Cameron	6,597	6.0	17,410	246
Camp	347	2.6	28,350	71
Carson	177	5.4	26,841	96
Cass	746	4.1	24,894	140
Castro	297	-2.3	38,945	7
Chambers	947	9.7	33,249	20
Cherokee	1,200	5.2	24,879	142

County	Total Income ($ mil)	% change 04/05	Per capita income	Rank
Childress	$ 140	6.7	$ 18,248	237
Clay	306	6.1	27,328	87
Cochran	103	14.9	31,232	34
Coke	70	-2.7	19,198	229
Coleman	202	4.3	23,278	182
Collin	30,217	14.5	45,720	3
Collingsworth	94	8.1	31,650	31
Colorado	569	7.4	27,463	82
Comal	3,117	9.8	32,522	25
Comanche	349	3.9	25,377	129
Concho	70	5.1	18,644	232
Cooke	1,157	9.2	29,771	52
Coryell	1,908	11.1	25,278	132
Cottle	47	-8.3	27,565	80
Crane	90	10.4	23,447	179
Crockett	68	-3.0	17,318	247
Crosby	212	7.3	31,908	30
Culberson	46	3.8	17,727	241
Dallam	183	3.1	29,598	55
Dallas	93,073	5.4	40,317	6
Dawson	302	6.8	21,193	212
Deaf Smith	455	13.8	24,574	153
Delta	116	2.8	21,337	210
Denton	19,004	7.9	34,241	17
DeWitt	495	9.5	24,281	159
Dickens	49	3.9	18,493	234
Dimmit	185	5.5	17,837	239
Donley	100	0.2	26,656	121
Duval	263	6.6	20,925	215
Eastland	493	8.1	26,857	94
Ector	3,206	10.0	25,590	124
Edwards	39	-2.3	19,544	226
Ellis	3,687	5.6	27,613	78
El Paso	16,771	6.6	23,256	184
Erath	868	6.6	25,627	122
Falls	369	2.8	20,941	214
Fannin	753	6.0	22,755	193
Fayette	707	4.9	31,456	32
Fisher	107	9.9	26,459	106
Floyd	209	1.3	29,183	62
Foard	35	3.1	23,120	189
Fort Bend	16,918	10.7	36,286	13
Franklin	286	4.0	27,784	75
Freestone	416	5.9	22,285	201
Frio	294	6.6	17,997	238

County	Total Income ($ mil)	% change 04/05	Per capita income	Rank	County	Total Income ($ mil)	% change 04/05	Per capita income	Rank
Gaines	$ 373	10.8	$ 25,307	131	Knox	$ 93	2.4	$ 24,832	144
Galveston	9,192	6.8	33,146	21	Lamar	1,240	4.7	24,993	137
Garza	118	3.3	24,218	161	Lamb	349	8.7	24,058	164
Gillespie	756	5.5	32,852	24	Lampasas	599	14.0	30,234	46
Glasscock	38	9.3	29,404	57	La Salle	106	12.1	17,728	240
Goliad	166	5.2	23,353	180	Lavaca	539	7.1	28,507	70
Gonzales	519	6.3	26,586	103	Lee	427	8.4	25,873	118
Gray	651	8.0	30,261	44	Leon	415	3.9	25,461	128
Grayson	3,060	6.3	26,207	113	Liberty	1,981	7.2	26,332	108
Gregg	3,900	8.8	33,768	18	Limestone	532	4.7	23,531	177
Grimes	563	10.3	22,279	202	Lipscomb	84	1.1	27,394	86
Guadalupe	2,961	9.6	28,720	66	Live Oak	245	6.5	21,037	213
Hale	836	5.0	23,120	189	Llano	488	5.0	26,928	90
Hall	74	7.3	20,067	222	Loving	5	2.8	77,787	1
Hamilton	210	3.6	25,814	119	Lubbock	7,065	6.5	27,997	72
Hansford	189	10.7	36,283	14	Lynn	186	7.1	30,039	48
Hardeman	105	4.9	24,703	149	Madison	293	7.3	22,305	200
Hardin	1,416	9.4	27,778	76	Marion	229	5.8	20,871	216
Harris	156,921	9.4	41,703	4	Martin	113	5.9	25,719	120
Harrison	1,714	9.1	27,174	88	Mason	98	7.1	25,476	127
Hartley	153	-3.4	28,655	67	Matagorda	859	3.4	22,599	196
Haskell	147	3.3	26,519	105	Maverick	752	9.6	14,690	250
Hays	3,187	8.2	25,610	123	McCulloch	212	5.2	26,693	102
Hemphill	129	3.4	37,973	9	McLennan	6,026	6.2	26,860	93
Henderson	1,945	4.4	24,401	157	McMullen	24	-1.9	26,712	101
Hidalgo	11,102	8.5	16,359	248	Medina	997	6.1	23,224	186
Hill	823	5.2	23,309	181	Menard	44	1.6	20,013	224
Hockley	576	7.1	25,274	133	Midland	4,963	12.1	40,855	5
Hood	1,420	6.1	29,734	53	Milam	593	7.4	23,550	176
Hopkins	838	5.3	25,209	134	Mills	129	6.0	24,509	156
Houston	533	-2.8	23,121	188	Mitchell	165	4.6	17,519	245
Howard	776	4.6	23,858	168	Montague	527	9.1	26,847	95
Hudspeth	49	-7.1	14,804	249	Montgomery	13,258	10.1	34,978	15
Hunt	2,151	7.2	26,138	114	Moore	500	8.4	24,624	151
Hutchinson	560	7.6	24,969	138	Morris	348	8.3	26,879	92
Irion	46	4.2	26,392	107	Motley	31	7.2	24,255	160
Jack	206	9.9	22,668	195	Nacogdoches	1,384	5.5	22,844	192
Jackson	340	5.0	23,743	172	Navarro	1,127	5.5	23,136	187
Jasper	860	9.1	24,215	162	Newton	281	7.7	19,651	225
Jeff Davis	44	-2.6	19,499	227	Nolan	369	6.6	24,888	141
Jefferson	7,248	8.1	29,324	59	Nueces	9,428	6.7	29,541	56
Jim Hogg	118	1.4	23,480	178	Ochiltree	310	7.6	32,905	23
Jim Wells	992	8.3	24,184	163	Oldham	49	3.7	23,260	183
Johnson	3,813	5.9	26,024	117	Orange	2,275	9.4	26,763	98
Jones	400	5.9	20,239	220	Palo Pinto	703	6.9	25,543	125
Karnes	270	4.9	17,677	243	Panola	613	6.4	26,904	91
Kaufman	2,332	7.8	26,228	111	Parker	3,063	7.4	29,834	51
Kendall	1,058	9.1	36,868	11	Parmer	257	10.2	26,243	110
Kenedy	13	-2.1	33,108	22	Pecos	282	4.1	17,704	242
Kent	18	-9.4	23,825	169	Polk	1,274	7.0	27,432	83
Kerr	1,558	7.0	33,473	19	Potter	3,147	6.1	26,219	112
Kimble	95	4.4	20,746	219	Presidio	112	1.7	14,583	253
King	8	-3.4	25,367	130	Rains	240	7.3	21,334	211
Kinney	69	2.9	20,813	218	Randall	3,341	5.4	30,369	43
Kleberg	758	7.3	24,761	147	Reagan	80	18.8	26,725	99

County	Total Income ($ mil)	% change 04/05	Per capita income	Rank	County	Total Income ($ mil)	% change 04/05	Per capita income	Rank
Real	$ 65	4.7	$ 21,472	209	Throckmorton	$ 52	8.1	$ 31,960	28
Red River	293	5.1	21,595	208	Titus	732	2.9	24,756	148
Reeves	213	6.6	18,439	235	Tom Green	2,976	4.6	28,777	64
Refugio	223	4.9	29,195	61	Travis	33,777	7.0	37,972	10
Roberts	24	5.8	28,949	63	Trinity	316	3.3	22,076	204
Robertson	412	4.9	25,514	126	Tyler	462	8.3	22,422	198
Rockwall	2,286	9.8	36,373	12	Upshur	927	8.5	24,589	152
Runnels	240	0.3	21,853	206	Upton	83	9.2	26,935	89
Rusk	1,186	7.4	24,767	146	Uvalde	601	5.7	22,339	199
Sabine	260	7.1	24,938	139	Val Verde	1,055	6.1	22,133	203
San Augustine	199	4.6	22,533	197	Van Zandt	1,434	5.5	27,420	85
San Jacinto	592	7.9	23,898	167	Victoria	2,629	7.4	30,667	41
San Patricio	1,709	6.6	24,674	150	Walker	1,217	6.2	19,223	228
San Saba	137	2.8	22,676	194	Waller	924	6.6	26,543	104
Schleicher	58	4.5	20,854	217	Ward	244	8.5	23,802	170
Scurry	502	12.8	31,047	37	Washington	1,020	8.1	32,399	26
Shackelford	92	2.2	28,766	65	Webb	4,230	9.5	18,809	231
Shelby	624	4.7	23,722	174	Wharton	1,080	5.7	26,093	115
Sherman	139	-6.4	47,084	2	Wheeler	185	10.5	38,471	8
Smith	5,963	7.2	31,301	33	Wichita	3,852	4.8	30,639	42
Somervell	204	5.6	26,781	97	Wilbarger	371	8.6	26,316	109
Starr	738	9.7	12,197	254	Willacy	376	8.4	18,417	236
Stephens	228	8.6	23,989	165	Williamson	10,678	14.1	31,933	29
Sterling	24	-1.5	18,832	230	Wilson	980	8.9	26,039	116
Stonewall	44	4.1	32,354	27	Winkler	165	8.4	25,008	135
Sutton	117	12.7	27,832	74	Wise	1,411	8.1	24,872	143
Swisher	240	7.0	30,725	40	Wood	948	6.6	23,227	185
Tarrant	55,514	6.1	34,275	16	Yoakum	220	7.5	29,718	54
Taylor	3,673	5.5	29,395	58	Young	536	10.8	30,222	47
Terrell	20	-4.4	20,039	223	Zapata	196	8.8	14,592	252
Terry	331	5.7	26,723	100	Zavala	173	7.0	14,644	251

Average Work Hours and Earnings

The following table shows the **average weekly earnings**, **hours worked per week** and **average hourly wage** in Texas for selected industries in January 2007. Figures are provided by the Texas Workforce Commission.

Industry	Earnings	Hours	Wage
NATURAL RESOURCES	**$ 657.58**	**42.7**	**$ 15.40**
Oil/Gas Extraction	676.05	34.3	19.71
Support Activities	742.77	47.1	15.77
MANUFACTURING	**580.92**	**41.2**	**14.10**
Durable Goods	**576.45**	**42.2**	**13.66**
Lumber/Wood Products	403.35	39.7	10.16
Primary Metal	623.66	43.1	14.47
Fabricated Metal	607.01	44.6	13.61
Structural Metal	496.22	43.3	11.46
Machinery	579.03	43.7	13.25
Agriculture/Mining	605.19	42.8	14.14
Electronic	614.17	38.1	16.12
Transportation Equipment	723.48	43.4	16.67
Furniture	393.78	40.1	9.82
Non-Durable Goods	**589.25**	**39.6**	**14.88**
Food Manufacturing	522.86	42.2	12.39
Printing	496.43	36.8	13.49
Chemicals	824.59	41.9	19.68
Plastics/Rubber	533.48	39.4	13.54

Industry	Earnings	Hours	Wage
TRADE/TRANSPORT/UTIL	**101.04**	**34.9**	**14.07**
Wholesale Trade	**635.20**	**40.0**	**15.88**
Electronic/Electric Goods	549.36	42.0	13.08
Motor Vehicle/Parts	607.93	35.1	17.32
Machinery/Supplies	558.80	40.0	13.97
Grocery	531.07	38.4	13.83
Chemical Products	632.42	39.8	15.89
Retail Trade	**360.68**	**31.5**	**11.45**
Auto Dealers	609.38	32.5	18.75
Building/Garden Supply	363.10	32.8	11.07
Clothing Stores	222.75	22.5	9.90
Food/Beverage	300.82	31.9	9.43
Grocery Stores	300.81	31.4	9.58
Furniture	421.52	32.6	12.93
Electronics/Appliances	561.63	34.1	16.47
Gasoline Stations	328.05	39.1	8.39
Sporting Goods/Music	204.82	26.6	7.70
Office Supplies	290.18	29.4	9.87
Newspapers/Periodicals	414.20	30.3	13.67
Telecommunications	571.55	35.5	16.10
Internet Service	647.24	44.0	14.71
Finance, Depository Insts.	**474.40**	**40.0**	**11.86**

Employment in Texas by Industry

Employment in Texas increased to 10,061,100 in January 2007, up from 9,806,600 in January 2006. The following table shows Texas Workforce Commission estimates of the nonagricultural labor force by industry for January 2006 and 2007. The column at the extreme right shows the percent change during the year in the number employed. *Source: Texas Workforce Commission. Additional information available at the website www.twc.state.ts.us.*

Industry	2007	2006	Chng.
	(in thousands, 000)		
GOODS PRODUCING	1,720.0	1,655.1	3.9
Mining	195.4	173.3	12.8
Oil & Gas Extraction	72.2	67.9	6.3
Support Activities	108.6	94.0	15.5
Construction	602.2	576.1	4.5
Manufacturing	922.4	905.7	1.8
Durable Goods	598.7	581.4	3.0
Wood Products	26.9	28.0	-3.9
Furniture/Fixtures	32.6	31.9	2.2
Primary Metals	25.6	25.0	2.4
Fabricated Metal Industries	127.4	119.0	7.1
Machinery	88.1	83.0	6.1
Computers/Electronics	109.5	108.2	1.2
Electric/Appliances	19.1	18.4	3.8
Transportation Equipment	93.2	91.8	1.5
Misc. Manufacturing	32.3	32.6	-0.9
Non-Durable Goods	323.7	324.3	-0.2
Food	92.2	91.3	1.0
Beverage/Tobacco	11.5	10.6	8.5
Paper	20.3	21.0	-3.3
Printing	34.5	34.9	-1.1
Petroleum/Coal Products	23.9	23.1	3.5
Chemicals	72.6	73.0	-0.5
Rubber/Plastics	46.8	46.2	1.3
SERVICE PROVIDING	8,341.1	8,151.5	2.3
Trade/Transport/Utilities	2,037.8	2,015.1	1.1
Wholesale Trade	493.8	485.7	1.7
Merchants/Durable Goods	290.6	279.0	4.2
Merchants/Non-Durable	156.1	155.3	0.5
Retail Trade	1,123.4	1,119.4	0.4
Building/Garden Supplies	91.0	86.1	5.7
General Merchandise	244.4	254.3	-3.9
Food/Beverage Stores	195.2	190.5	2.5
Motor Vehicle/Parts	152.6	149.7	1.9
Clothing/Accessories	111.7	107.1	4.3
Furniture	43.7	43.9	-0.5
Electronics/Appliances	46.4	46.1	0.7
Gasoline Stations	64.9	66.3	-2.1
Sporting/Books/Music	36.7	39.1	-6.1
Misc. Store Retailers	60.5	60.2	0.5
Nonstore Retailers	18.3	19.5	-6.2

Industry	2007	2006	Chng.
Transportation/Utilities	420.6	410.0	2.6
Utilities	45.0	44.7	0.7
Transportation	375.6	365.3	2.8
Air	63.7	62.0	2.7
Trucking	114.3	109.8	4.1
Pipeline	13.4	12.2	9.8
Support Activities	67.9	66.4	2.3
Couriers/Messengers	36.0	37.2	-3.2
Warehousing/Storage	41.1	39.9	3.0
Information	221.2	221.4	-0.1
Publishing	50.1	49.9	0.4
Telecommunications	88.6	89.4	-0.9
Internet/Data Search	35.7	35.8	-0.3
Financial Activities	628.3	614.6	2.2
Finance/Insurance	452.6	442.6	2.3
Credit Intermediation	243.8	234.9	3.8
Securities/Investments	43.6	40.9	6.6
Insurance Carriers	155.3	156.2	-0.6
Real Estate/Rental	175.7	172.0	2.2
Real Estate	114.2	111.7	2.2
Rental/Leasing	60.3	58.1	3.8
Professional Services	1,231.2	1,180.9	4.3
Scientific/Tech	524.1	511.8	2.4
Management/Enterprises	60.7	54.7	11.0
Administration/Support	621.8	590.3	5.3
Education/Health	1,222.6	1,193.3	2.5
Educational Services	142.4	142.1	0.2
Health Care	1,080.2	1,051.2	2.8
Ambulatory	480.1	466.6	2.9
Hospitals	267.4	260.0	2.8
Residential Care	156.0	148.3	5.2
Social Assistance	176.7	176.3	0.2
Leisure/Hospitality	931.3	888.7	4.8
Accommodations	94.8	92.4	2.6
Food/Drinking Places	742.7	706.2	5.2
Amusements/Recreation	68.9	65.1	5.8
Other Services	344.1	341.1	0.9
Repair/Maintenance	103.8	102.2	1.6
Personal/Laundry	91.8	88.2	4.1
Religious/Civic	148.5	150.7	-1.5
Total Government	1,724.6	1,696.4	1.7
Federal	182.6	183.4	-0.4
State	353.7	348.9	1.4
Local	1,188.3	1,164.1	2.1

Cost of Living Index for Metro Areas

The comparison standard of all values is for the **United States set at 100**. Data are for the fourth quarter of 2005. The overall composite is excluding taxes. The column at the far right refers to miscellaneous goods and services.

Metro area	Overall	Groceries	Housing	Utilities	Transport	Health	Goods/ Services
Austin	96.1	91.9	84.0	91.8	99.1	101.9	107.4
Brownsville	86.3	81.0	71.2	103.3	103.7	90.4	90.9
Corpus Christi	88.3	79.3	78.1	93.6	98.4	90.7	95.6
Dallas	94.6	99.2	76.7	117.7	108.0	105.1	96.3
El Paso	91.1	106.0	72.2	96.3	98.6	99.0	96.8
Fort Worth	88.6	91.7	77.5	93.7	102.7	93.8	91.1
Houston	88.9	84.7	72.9	103.3	103.8	98.5	94.8
Lubbock	84.8	86.2	72.3	75.4	89.6	98.3	94.6
San Antonio	91.6	82.9	84.5	84.2	89.1	100.8	102.3

Source: Statistical Abstract of the United States 2007.

Construction Industry: Comparison of Awards, 1945–2007

The chart below shows the total value of construction contract awards in Texas by year: *Source Texas Contractor, 2007.*

Year	Total Awards	Year	Total Awards	Year	Total Awards
2007	$ 25,785,189,283	1994	$ 4,396,199,988	1981	$ 3,700,112,809
2006	20,566,889,250	1993	5,394,342,718	1980	3,543,117,615
2005	18,923,051,000	1992	4,747,666,912	1979	3,353,243,234
2004	13,014,672,068	1991	3,926,799,801	1978	2,684,743,190
2003	12,897,933,353	1990	3,922,781,630	1977	2,270,788,842
2002	7,297,909,363	1989	4,176,355,929	1976	1,966,553,804
2001	6,067,377,351	1988	3,562,336,666	1975	1,737,036,682
2000	5,232,788,835	1987	4,607,051,270	1970	1,458,708,492
1999	4,941,352,362	1986	4,636,310,266	1965	1,254,638,051
1998	4,951,275,224	1985	4,806,998,065	1960	1,047,943,630
1997	5,088,017,435	1984	3,424,721,025	1955	949,213,349
1996	4,383,336,574	1983	4,074,910,947	1950	1,059,457,667
1995	4,771,332,413	1982	3,453,784,388	1945	245,438,277

Approved Texas Construction, 2007

Federal:

General Services Administration	$ 6,900,000
Federal Aviation Administration	97,750,000
NASA	5,000,000
Department of Defense	360,000,000
Department of Veterans Affairs	20,350,000
Rural Utilities Service	114,000,000
U.S. Department of Agriculture	120,000,000
Department of Energy	6,700,000
Natural Res. Conserv. Service	6,000,000
Department of Justice	1,500,000
Department of the Interior	1,300,000
Federal Highway Administration	2,575,000,000
Total Federal	$ 3,314,500,000

State:

Texas Dept. of Transportation	$ 3,755,000,000
State Agencies	355,500,000
State Colleges and Universities	1,065,000,000
Total State	$ 5,175,500,000

Water Projects:

Corps of Engineers	$ 85,000,000
Bureau of Reclamation	500,000
River Authorities	945,000,000
Clean Water StateRevolvingFund	465,000,000
Drinking WaterState Revolving Fund	270,000,000
Total Water Projects	$ 1,765,500,000

Buildings Total | $ 15,529,689,283

Grand Total | $ 25,785,189,283

Source: Texas Contractor, 2007.

Texas Single-Family Building Permits

Year	Number of Dwelling Units		Avg. Value per Unit ($)	
	Units	% change	Value	% change
1980	67,870	–	$ 51,900	–
1981	66,161	-3	55,700	7
1982	78,714	19	53,800	-3
1983	103,252	31	63,400	18
1984	84,565	-18	68,000	7
1985	67,964	-20	71,000	4
1986	59,143	-13	72,200	2
1987	43,975	-26	77,700	8
1988	35,908	-18	83,900	8
1989	36,658	2	90,400	8
1990	38,233	4	95,500	6
1991	46,209	21	92,800	-3
1992	59,543	29	95,400	3
1993	69,964	18	96,400	1
1994	70,452	1	99,500	3
1995	70,421	0	100,300	1
1996	83,132	18	102,100	2
1997	82,228	-1	108,900	7
1998	99,912	22	112,800	4
1999	101,928	2	118,800	5
2000	108,782	7	127,100	7
2001	111,915	3	124,700	-2
2002	122,913	10	126,400	1
2003	137,493	12	128,800	2
2004	151,384	10	137,600	7
2005	166,203	10	144,300	5
2006	163,032	-2	155,100	7

Source: U.S. Bureau of Census and Real Estate Center at Texas A&M University, 2007.

Federal Aid to States for Highway Trust Fund, 2004

The chart below shows dispersement of federal funds for highway construction and maintenance in **millions of dollars** in the middle column. The column at right shows dollars per capita based on estimated population. *Source: U.S. Bureau of Census.*

State	Highway Fund		State	Highway Fund		State	Highway Fund	
	Total	Per capita		Total	Per capita		Total	Per capita
U.S.	$288,813	$23	Pennsylvania	$1,224	$99	New Jersey	$752	$87
Texas	2,827	126	North Carolina	977	114	Missouri	723	126
California	2,365	66	Ohio	958	84	South Carolina	670	160
Florida	1,563	90	Michigan	799	79	Tennessee	622	105
New York	1,470	76	Georgia	788	89	Illinois	611	48

Tourism Impact Estimates by County, 2005

This analysis covers most travel in Texas including business, pleasure, shopping, to attend meetings and other destinations. Expenditures by **visitors** are for purchases including lodging taxes and other applicable local and state taxes. **Earnings** are wages and salaries of employees and income of proprietors of businesses that receive travel expenditures. Employment associated with these businesses are listed under **jobs**. Local **tax receipts** are from hotel taxes, local sales taxes, auto rental taxes, etc, as separate from state tax receipts. *Source: Office of the Governor, Economic Development and Tourism.*

County	Visitor Spending	Earnings	Jobs	Local tax receipts	County	Visitor Spending	Earnings	Jobs	Local tax receipts
	($000)	($000)		($000)		($000)	($000)		($000)
Anderson	$ 44,710	$ 10,640	700	$ 680	Cooke	$ 41,410	$ 9,520	490	$ 590
Andrews	6,230	1,480	110	60	Coryell	38,180	9,560	550	560
Angelina	106,860	23,130	1,470	1,390	Cottle	1,420	140	10	0
Aransas	74,920	20,930	1,130	1,350	Crane	1,340	270	20	20
Archer	1,720	300	20	20	Crockett	22,270	2,090	170	100
Armstrong	1,060	80	10	0	Crosby	1,480	370	30	10
Atascosa	22,990	5,780	310	270	Culberson	28,630	3,840	190	290
Austin	33,120	7,510	460	310	Dallam	11,570	3,840	200	240
Bailey	4,930	1,230	100	80	Dallas	6,243,510	2,206,230	64,360	162,820
Bandera	22,280	13,100	690	420	Dawson	11,600	1,870	150	100
Bastrop	51,070	14,570	650	660	Deaf Smith	12,270	2,510	180	170
Baylor	5,770	710	30	30	Delta	1,090	200	10	10
Bee	23,060	5,330	320	300	Denton	410,940	112,920	4,370	8,080
Bell	323,450	79,010	5,120	5,850	DeWitt	32,480	5,270	290	230
Bexar	4,609,090	1,344,970	52,580	104,140	Dickens	470	130	10	10
Blanco	8,960	2,210	150	140	Dimmit	11,700	1,500	100	100
Borden	100	10	0	0	Donley	5,310	1,450	110	100
Bosque	11,450	5,030	200	180	Duval	9,710	1,040	70	100
Bowie	144,830	22,820	1,540	1,670	Eastland	12,140	2,890	210	230
Brazoria	215,770	55,080	3,440	3,070	Ector	178,650	48,450	2,410	3,290
Brazos	291,070	65,670	4,070	4,770	Edwards	1,130	260	20	10
Brewster	44,260	20,750	1,360	900	Ellis	107,210	24,590	880	1,650
Briscoe	1,150	140	10	0	El Paso	1,075,130	274,050	11,770	17,250
Brooks	12,170	1,790	110	160	Erath	32,990	7,820	410	460
Brown	40,870	12,290	690	780	Falls	7,180	1,520	90	90
Burleson	10,780	2,630	150	110	Fannin	10,170	1,570	100	90
Burnet	50,670	16,600	790	1,050	Fayette	26,680	4,720	310	280
Caldwell	23,350	5,160	210	210	Fisher	900	150	10	10
Calhoun	26,410	7,780	400	480	Floyd	4,640	660	50	20
Callahan	3,390	850	60	40	Foard	340	80	10	0
Cameron	605,520	135,420	7,980	13,350	Fort Bend	293,630	80,250	3,370	5,450
Camp	12,780	1,080	70	40	Franklin	7,430	1,330	100	90
Carson	6,180	560	40	20	Freestone	38,940	4,400	370	340
Cass	18,030	4,640	230	220	Frio	11,780	2,550	170	180
Castro	2,710	510	30	20	Gaines	8,880	1,430	100	70
Chambers	23,050	4,530	210	540	Galveston	638,790	172,820	9,040	16,580
Cherokee	29,860	6,720	470	370	Garza	8,150	2,610	110	80
Childress	10,610	2,410	190	300	Gillespie	59,660	17,430	950	1,490
Clay	16,280	1,050	80	20	Glasscock	210	30	0	0
Cochran	860	190	20	10	Goliad	7,410	1,320	60	70
Coke	3,190	600	50	20	Gonzales	16,270	1,970	120	110
Coleman	6,150	1,170	80	90	Gray	28,690	7,220	480	400
Collin	738,960	238,010	8,730	15,370	Grayson	166,460	27,660	1,570	2,020
Collingsworth	1,910	310	20	10	Gregg	184,260	46,060	2,650	2,700
Colorado	43,790	8,830	520	440	Grimes	15,490	4,020	210	220
Comal	225,740	63,720	2,730	4,560	Guadalupe	76,000	25,140	1,020	1,180
Comanche	10,540	1,790	130	90	Hale	49,980	11,590	940	760
Concho	1,520	930	40	20					

County	Visitor Spending ($000)	Earnings ($000)	Jobs	Local tax receipts ($000)	County	Visitor Spending ($000)	Earnings ($000)	Jobs	Local tax receipts ($000)
Hall	$ 2,140	$ 300	20	$ 20	Llano	$ 79,290	$ 30,450	1,860	$ 1,680
Hamilton	4,430	940	50	60	Loving	30	10	0	0
Hansford	1,560	260	20	20	Lubbock	508,900	151,860	6,740	7,060
Hardeman	4,700	690	50	40	Lynn	1,010	220	20	10
Hardin	32,480	6,450	440	440	Madison	7,950	1,690	120	150
Harris	7,737,080	3,673,290	95,650	187,950	Marion	8,450	2,290	200	170
Harrison	76,100	12,130	720	510	Martin	11,840	560	40	10
Hartley	750	120	10	10	Mason	2,470	610	50	40
Haskell	3,790	760	60	60	Matagorda	37,590	12,040	800	810
Hays	159,980	41,260	1,830	2,520	Maverick	39,500	8,490	510	650
Hemphill	4,200	750	40	120	McCulloch	12,620	1,650	150	140
Henderson	92,500	15,310	500	670	McLennan	385,970	83,130	4,860	5,520
Hidalgo	914,390	230,800	13,400	16,040	McMullen	660	120	10	0
Hill	52,570	9,160	600	520	Medina	32,920	5,820	330	260
Hockley	14,410	3,100	220	110	Menard	2,470	300	20	20
Hood	45,240	10,830	460	710	Midland	224,970	48,280	2,760	2,570
Hopkins	51,310	8,850	540	420	Milam	23,400	5,200	290	260
Houston	29,320	5,510	300	200	Mills	2,770	510	30	40
Howard	64,280	9,100	590	630	Mitchell	6,600	1,250	60	60
Hudspeth	4,520	330	20	0	Montague	14,280	3,450	290	190
Hunt	82,980	18,470	670	910	Montgomery	328,580	132,440	4,430	7,190
Hutchinson	28,170	5,930	410	360	Moore	29,350	4,410	340	460
Irion	8,720	320	20	0	Morris	4,360	750	50	40
Jack	4,050	680	50	40	Motley	610	80	10	0
Jackson	8,750	1,660	110	110	Nacogdoches	63,480	16,440	1,160	1,280
Jasper	34,490	9,660	660	650	Navarro	33,260	7,740	470	480
Jeff Davis	6,360	2,560	100	0	Newton	4,670	720	40	40
Jefferson	394,680	80,700	4,900	6,200	Nolan	15,090	4,480	310	400
Jim Hogg	4,040	880	50	40	Nueces	747,990	202,650	10,860	18,280
Jim Wells	50,930	10,760	630	400	Ochiltree	12,740	1,880	130	180
Johnson	98,400	15,540	700	940	Oldham	7,780	810	70	50
Jones	7,820	2,370	150	100	Orange	87,600	17,230	1,020	940
Karnes	14,140	2,210	120	80	Palo Pinto	61,480	11,320	580	510
Kaufman	100,110	14,450	560	870	Panola	11,660	2,270	160	240
Kendall	62,830	16,580	960	1,010	Parker	91,500	17,860	790	1,040
Kenedy	830	270	20	0	Parmer	4,210	580	40	30
Kent	680	120	10	0	Pecos	33,420	4,450	380	600
Kerr	81,830	32,750	1,870	1,640	Polk	43,900	12,160	710	420
Kimble	13,560	1,990	170	180	Potter	546,800	113,220	6,920	10,520
King	40	10	0	0	Presidio	6,800	1,340	60	160
Kinney	4,840	1,450	100	50	Rains	6,160	1,750	80	60
Kleberg	42,820	10,420	540	560	Randall	85,910	14,970	1,040	850
Knox	2,930	460	30	30	Reagan	1,750	320	30	10
La Salle	5,690	1,090	70	60	Real	4,590	1,370	70	40
Lamar	50,640	13,200	700	670	Red River	4,280	1,110	50	40
Lamb	9,350	1,070	80	60	Reeves	28,490	3,350	260	330
Lampasas	11,800	2,200	170	180	Refugio	17,740	1,790	110	110
Lavaca	11,700	2,550	130	160	Roberts	860	30	0	0
Lee	17,730	3,780	190	130	Robertson	14,850	2,540	190	270
Leon	25,620	3,640	250	280	Rockwall	42,520	9,540	400	700
Liberty	41,810	13,580	490	570	Runnels	5,860	1,050	80	50
Limestone	13,350	1,790	120	160	Rusk	31,120	5,630	300	350
Lipscomb	1,930	150	10	0	Sabine	10,280	1,850	150	30
Live Oak	23,700	2,670	170	200	S.Augustine	7,360	1,830	100	70

County	Visitor Spending ($000)	Earnings ($000)	Jobs	Local tax receipts ($000)
San Jacinto	$ 10,080	$ 2,020	160	$ 50
San Patricio	86,070	18,180	990	1,510
San Saba	3,560	830	60	30
Schleicher	440	110	10	10
Scurry	22,100	6,180	420	280
Shackelford	1,920	1,300	90	30
Shelby	23,220	4,760	380	280
Sherman	4,480	380	30	10
Smith	258,110	58,050	3,100	3,750
Somervell	13,130	3,150	170	320
Starr	21,860	4,180	240	330
Stephens	5,830	1,390	110	90
Sterling	1,920	150	10	10
Stonewall	910	230	20	10
Sutton	9,280	2,480	220	260
Swisher	3,180	730	50	30
Tarrant	3,394,050	2,531,190	57,660	59,540
Taylor	311,270	60,010	3,510	5,260
Terrell	1,340	260	20	0
Terry	5,080	1,400	110	90
Throckmrton	2,950	170	10	0
Titus	42,280	7,880	480	550
Tom Green	148,200	41,390	2,710	1,820
Travis	2,804,040	836,130	34,270	68,570
Trinity	9,690	4,370	270	120
Tyler	8,910	1,900	150	90
Upshur	19,260	2,830	180	170
Upton	1,420	320	30	20
Uvalde	51,180	9,630	630	830
Val Verde	46,060	13,420	730	910
Van Zandt	39,840	7,230	450	390
Victoria	151,430	30,750	1,630	2,020

County	Visitor Spending ($000)	Earnings ($000)	Jobs	Local tax receipts ($000)
Walker	$ 77,670	$ 15,860	1,150	$ 870
Waller	30,940	3,800	150	240
Ward	7,230	1,520	110	110
Washington	72,310	11,440	660	690
Webb	410,380	99,600	5,290	6,180
Wharton	27,330	7,190	500	440
Wheeler	15,350	2,340	170	180
Wichita	171,390	38,750	2,920	3,130
Wilbarger	14,380	3,060	220	210
Willacy	19,380	2,880	150	140
Williamson	338,890	75,220	3,440	6,350
Wilson	19,770	3,900	220	140
Winkler	3,470	590	40	40
Wise	34,610	9,150	560	540
Wood	22,080	6,690	400	210
Yoakum	3,650	750	60	40
Young	19,480	5,460	330	250
Zapata	11,700	2,050	140	80
Zavala	6,040	670	40	40

Traveler's Top Attractions, 2005

Rank	Texans	Rank	Non Texans
1.	San Marcos Outlets	1.	Alamo
2.	River Walk	2.	River Walk
3.	Alamo	3.	Six Flags
4.	Sea World	4.	South Padre Island
5.	Padre Island NS	5.	Sea World
6.	State Capitol	6.	Moody Gardens
7.	Space Center	6.	State Capitol
8.	Six Flags	8.	Texas State Fair
8.	State Aquarium	9.	San Marcos Outlets
10.	South Padre Island	10.	Padre Island NS

Source: Office of Governor, Economic Development and Tourism.

Visitors at the Texas State Aquarium in Corpus Christi watch a presentation on dolphins. Robert Plocheck photo.

Largest Banks Operating in Texas by Asset Size

Source: Texas Department of Banking, Dec. 31, 2006

Abbreviations: NA, not available; N.A. National Association.

	Name	City	Class	Assets	Loans
				(in thousands, 000)	
1	JP Morgan Chase Bank	New York NY	National	$ 63,502,000	NA
2	Countrywide Bank	Alexandria VA	National	50,326,000	NA
3	Bank of America	Charlotte NC	National	43,377,000	NA
4	Wells Fargo Bank	San Francisco CA	National	27,244,000	NA
5	Frost National Bank	San Antonio	National	13,306,861	$ 7,341,673
6	Amergy Bank N.A.	Houston	National	10,359,193	6,289,643
7	Compass Bank	Birmingham AL	State	9,794,000	NA
8	International Bank of Commerce	Laredo	State	9,181,474	4,437,604
9	Texas State Bank	McAllen	State	8,548,312	4,216,833
10	Capital One	New Orleans LA	National	5,086,000	NA
11	Prosperity Bank	El Campo	State	4,586,491	2,176,507
12	Laredo National Bank	Laredo	National	4,467,870	2,215,959
13	Sterling Bank	Houston	State	4,114,661	3,077,845
14	Bank of Texas N.A.	Dallas	National	3,868,058	2,169,907
15	First National Bank	Edinburg	National	3,737,457	2,173,543
16	Texas Capital Bank N.A.	Dallas	National	3,671,043	2,722,097
17	Comerica Bank	Detroit MI	State	3,536,000	NA
18	Wachovia Bank	Charlotte NC	National	3,248,000	NA
19	Regions Bank	Birmingham AL	State	2,863,000	NA
20	PlainsCapital Bank	Lubbock	State	2,857,914	2,203,618
21	Woodforest National Bank	Houston	National	2,239,606	1,408,860
22	Amarillo National Bank	Amarillo	National	2,174,957	1,599,035
23	American State Bank	Lubbock	State	2,094,471	797,788
24	Southside Bank	Tyler	State	1,890,155	759,147
25	Broadway National Bank	San Antonio	National	1,754,602	752,863
26	State National Bank	Fort Worth	National	1,715,694	1,169,857
27	Lone Star National Bank	Pharr	National	1,715,467	942,283
28	TIB Independent BankersBank	Irving	State	1,603,688	679,106
29	American National Bank of Texas	Terrell	National	1,554,711	965,971
30	Inter National Bank	McAllen	National	1,474,184	787,589
31	City Bank	Lubbock	State	1,255,307	1,091,578
32	Inwood National Bank	Dallas	National	1,252,482	867,835
33	Legacy Texas Bank	Plano	State	1,210,822	819,874
34	Century Bank N.A.	New Boston	National	1,207,658	924,054
35	First Victoria National Bank	Victoria	National	1,176,458	844,315
36	State Bank	La Grange	State	1,112,358	758,719
37	Metrobank N.A.	Houston	National	1,011,445	702,525
38	Extraco Banks N.A.	Temple	National	994,528	611,739
39	American Bank of Texas	Sherman	State	974,238	675,050
40	Moody National Bank	Galveston	National	948,100	306,110
41	North Dallas Bank & Trust Co.	Dallas	State	936,255	354,091
42	First Financial Bank N.A.	Abilene	National	926,227	368,205
43	Town North Bank N.A.	Dallas	National	867,972	372,073
44	Texas Bank and Trust Co.	Longview	State	843,490	682,223
45	First State Bank Central Texas	Temple	State	828,266	515,923
46	International Bank of Commerce	Brownsville	State	824,536	299,217
47	Austin Bank Texas N.A.	Jacksonville	National	796,981	571,074
48	American Bank N.A.	Corpus Christi	National	786,051	532,024
49	Western National Bank	Odessa	National	744,463	427,392
50	Citizens National Bank	Henderson	National	703,172	336,186

Deposits/Assets of Commercial Banks by County

Source: Federal Reserve Bank of Dallas as of Dec. 31, 2006.
(thousands of dollars, 000)

COUNTY	Banks	Deposits	Assets	COUNTY	Banks	Deposits	Assets
Anderson	3	$ 254,596	$ 286,570	Dimmit	1	$ 29,525	$ 36,111
Andrews	2	303,588	331,038	Donley	1	29,754	36,573
Angelina	2	646,870	723,191	Duval	2	78,056	85,440
Armstrong	1	79,800	89,721	Eastland	1	117,332	136,681
Atascosa	3	192,151	224,739	Ector	4	1,175,765	1,335,142
Austin	4	619,708	716,913	Edwards	1	41,580	46,396
Bailey	2	139,038	157,999	Ellis	5	650,642	731,189
Bandera	1	33,157	37,267	El Paso	3	845,877	936,582
Bastrop	1	243,699	279,931	Erath	4	453,244	516,300
Baylor	2	92,255	104,653	Fannin	3	233,991	284,046
Bee	2	181,611	200,450	Fayette	6	1,207,630	1,557,816
Bell	6	2,414,596	2,920,471	Fisher	1	34,881	40,106
Bexar	8	13,307,454	16,459,375	Floyd	1	75,862	86,851
Blanco	3	249,956	277,739	Foard	1	20,010	22,992
Bosque	3	213,497	243,334	Fort Bend	1	36,733	43,259
Bowie	4	1,494,997	1,655,753	Franklin	1	94,175	120,951
Brazoria	7	624,727	731,633	Freestone	2	157,994	180,902
Brazos	3	528,745	612,212	Frio	2	206,284	414,821
Briscoe	1	34,273	40,437	Galveston	6	1,544,202	1,764,794
Brooks	3	105,463	120,323	Gillespie	1	462,310	558,860
Brown	2	326,675	372,946	Gonzales	2	236,008	260,179
Burleson	2	232,059	257,436	Gray	1	10,874	12,664
Burnett	3	673,974	792,292	Grayson	5	1,180,735	1,335,311
Caldwell	2	152,528	171,622	Gregg	7	1,323,569	1,494,523
Calhoun	1	151,637	173,137	Grimes	3	206,537	235,822
Callahan	2	212,285	234,108	Guadalupe	3	237,180	270,845
Cameron	4	684,563	1,047,536	Hale	2	262,986	303,814
Camp	1	188,789	211,867	Hall	2	76,019	89,814
Carson	1	30,428	33,136	Hamilton	1	27,616	30,344
Cass	4	204,193	236,229	Hansford	3	183,443	208,618
Castro	1	481,774	578,524	Hardeman	2	61,774	69,622
Chambers	3	157,690	185,301	Harris	32	17,136,706	23,415,713
Cherokee	2	776,451	891,396	Harrison	2	91,050	102,374
Childress	1	74,948	80,268	Haskell	1	53,764	60,231
Clay	1	75,815	85,158	Hemphill	2	175,170	194,486
Coke	2	52,019	60,923	Henderson	2	339,211	379,632
Coleman	3	121,484	146,195	Hidalgo	9	12,887,385	16,040,153
Collin	10	2,521,558	2,958,444	Hill	2	116,027	138,958
Collingsworth	2	176,975	196,168	Hockley	2	108,609	117,034
Colorado	4	284,902	340,807	Hood	3	633,741	713,441
Comal	1	180,360	204,679	Hopkins	2	632,243	788,352
Comanche	2	152,226	173,743	Houston	4	257,839	286,327
Concho	2	90,877	103,620	Howard	2	273,112	306,289
Cooke	3	538,694	640,194	Hunt	1	34,364	37,752
Coryell	3	427,731	467,609	Hutchinson	1	36,383	42,922
Cottle	1	45,450	51,103	Irion	1	140,729	156,266
Crockett	2	324,621	390,024	Jack	2	245,601	277,880
Crosby	2	140,805	159,142	Jackson	1	47,319	50,495
Dallam	1	43,380	47,413	Jasper	1	178,287	204,671
Dallas	33	11,787,089	16,621,102	Jeff Davis	1	50,726	55,493
Dawson	2	274,524	312,975	Jefferson	1	124,078	158,597
Deaf Smith	2	180,507	203,163	Jim Hogg	1	103,723	119,217
Delta	3	46,965	54,294	Jim Wells	1	195,247	257,674
Denton	7	1,106,775	1,261,714	Johnson	3	459,426	509,198
DeWitt	2	179,175	208,436	Jones	2	112,835	131,714
Dickens	1	27,345	30,276	Karnes	2	154,118	177,319

Total bank assets in Dallas County were $16.6 billion, down from $44.1 billion in 2000. In Bexar County (San Antonio), assets were $16.5 billion, down from $31 billion, and, in Harris County (Houston), assets were $23.4 billion, up from $13.6 billion.

Besides the major metropolitan areas, banks in two counties on the border had assets over $10 billion, Webb County (Laredo) and Hidalgo County (McAllen).

No independent banks were reported in 37 counties: Aransas, Archer, Borden, Brewster, Cochran, Crane, Culberson, Falls, Gaines, Garza, Glasscock, Goliad, Hardin, Hartley, Hays, Hudspeth, Kendall, Kenedy, King, Kinney, Lipscomb, Loving, Marion, Maverick, McMullen, Moore, Motley, Oldham, Randall, Reagan, Real, Robertson, San Augustine, Somervell, Upton, Willacy and Winkler.

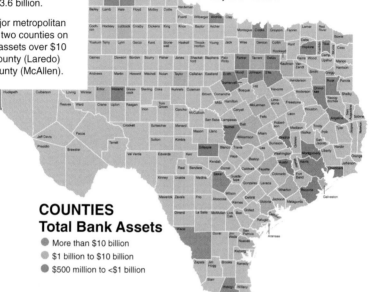

COUNTIES
Total Bank Assets

- ● More than $10 billion
- ◍ $1 billion to $10 billion
- ● $500 million to <$1 billion

COUNTY	Banks	Deposits	Assets
Kaufman	2	$ 1,383,636	$ 1,604,901
Kent	1	21,724	24,199
Kerr	1	22,742	24,563
Kimble	2	67,847	76,625
Kleberg	1	193,504	223,506
Knox	1	56,040	63,446
Lamar	4	373,061	436,668
Lamb	3	155,590	191,188
Lampasas	1	83,261	97,044
La Salle	1	34,084	38,145
Lavaca	2	217,915	257,570
Lee	1	78,211	104,602
Leon	4	269,380	303,157
Liberty	2	240,687	269,476
Limestone	3	200,534	221,703
Live Oak	2	199,031	222,893
Llano	2	171,854	193,455
Lubbock	10	6,518,406	8,042,234
Lynn	2	90,738	101,844
Madison	1	150,152	177,754
Martin	1	47,493	56,056
Mason	2	75,357	95,681
Matagorda	1	38,262	43,178
McCulloch	2	137,881	156,796
McLennan	11	1,831,926	2,073,897
Medina	7	402,753	454,121
Menard	2	54,245	60,243
Midland	3	857,226	974,818
Milam	3	399,319	449,478

COUNTY	Banks	Deposits	Assets
Mills	1	$ 142,400	$ 159,700
Mitchell	2	76,182	87,546
Montague	2	356,889	406,703
Montgomery	3	502,867	570,368
Morris	3	175,299	203,024
Nacogdoches	1	265,632	302,114
Navarro	5	253,253	298,746
Newton	1	115,764	134,417
Nolan	3	246,467	275,844
Nueces	5	1,211,133	1,337,918
Ochiltree	1	76,165	86,385
Orange	1	88,350	97,467
Palo Pinto	4	274,841	316,710
Panola	2	360,279	421,079
Parker	3	489,482	543,467
Parmer	2	147,947	183,622
Pecos	3	139,559	159,763
Polk	3	425,647	498,856
Potter	3	2,650,003	3,148,177
Presidio	2	54,815	63,918
Rains	1	72,904	83,671
Red River	1	15,134	17,504
Reeves	1	112,040	126,725
Refugio	2	77,855	90,051
Roberts	1	26,022	28,705
Rockwall	2	44,811	60,393
Runnels	4	186,358	205,140
Rusk	3	802,509	897,742
Sabine	1	45,094	51,986

COUNTY	Banks	Deposits	Assets	COUNTY	Banks	Deposits	Assets
San Jacinto	2	$ 99,247	$ 107,667	Tyler	1	$ 103,711	$ 119,430
San Patrico	2	109,775	122,283	Upshur	3	353,228	401,082
San Saba	1	42,173	49,192	Uvalde	2	420,614	470,008
Schleicher	1	40,343	46,226	Val Verde	1	10,548	13,442
Scurry	2	185,169	205,295	Van Zandt	5	254,157	288,020
Shackelford	1	233,675	262,509	Victoria	1	1,037,180	1,176,458
Shelby	3	295,848	333,035	Walker	2	329,390	367,614
Sherman	1	124,051	148,097	Waller	1	59,528	68,568
Smith	5	1,914,380	2,876,186	Ward	1	270,344	292,827
Starr	1	50,860	59,284	Washington	4	262,899	311,676
Stephens	1	75,351	84,798	Webb	4	10,231,420	14,812,700
Sterling	1	38,549	45,211	Wharton	4	4,270,251	5,168,611
Stonewall	1	23,848	34,338	Wheeler	1	46,418	49,518
Sutton	1	136,373	152,956	Wichita	5	854,904	975,656
Swisher	2	463,562	555,023	Wilbarger	2	188,640	238,228
Tarrant	24	3,905,683	4,637,267	Williamson	8	977,500	1,086,469
Taylor	3	854,830	1,028,617	Wilson	1	23,694	27,928
Terrell	1	22,613	37,110	Wise	2	149,467	165,827
Terry	1	107,494	127,090	Wood	4	295,272	371,024
Throckmorton	1	21,311	23,769	Yoakum	1	19,510	22,189
Titus	2	569,014	648,994	Young	5	379,100	434,036
Tom Green	2	388,566	474,029	Zapata	2	346,877	468,535
Travis	4	227,653	258,410	Zavala	1	48,276	56,522
Trinity	2	72,542	79,605				

Texas Total Bank Resources and Deposits: 1905–2006

On Dec. 31, 2006, Texas had a total of 608 national and state banks, the lowest number since before 1906 when there were 619. In 1986, the number of independent banks in the state peaked at 1,972. In 2006, the total assets were $181.8 billion. The peak for total assets was in 1997 with $235 billion. *Source: Federal Reserve Bank of Dallas*

Date	National Banks			State Banks			Combined Total		
	No. Banks	Assets (add 000)	Deposits (add 000)	No. Banks	Assets (add 000)	Deposits (add 000)	No. Banks	Assets (add 000)	Deposits (add 000)
Sept. 30, 1905	440	$ 189,484	$ 101,285	29	$ 4,341	$ 2,213	469	$ 193,825	$ 103,498
Nov. 10, 1910	516	293,245	145,249	621	88,103	59,766	1,137	381,348	205,015
Dec. 29, 1920	556	780,246	564,135	1,031	391,127	280,429	1,587	1,171,373	844,564
Dec. 31, 1930	560	1,028,420	826,723	655	299,012	231,909	1,215	1,327,432	1,058,632
Dec. 31, 1940	446	1,695,662	1,534,702	393	227,866	179,027	839	1,923,528	1,713,729
Dec. 31, 1950	442	6,467,275	6,076,006	449	1,427,680	1,338,540	891	7,894,955	7,414,546
Dec. 31, 1960	468	10,520,690	9,560,668	532	2,997,609	2,735,726	1,000	13,518,299	12,296,394
Dec. 31, 1970	530	22,087,890	18,384,922	653	8,907,039	7,958,133	1,183	30,994,929	26,343,055
Dec. 31, 1980	641	75,540,334	58,378,669	825	35,186,113	31,055,648	1,466	110,726,447	89,434,317
Dec. 31, 1985	1,058	144,674,908	111,903,178	878	64,349,869	56,392,634	1,936	209,024,777	168,295,812
Dec. 31, 1986	1,077	141,397,037	106,973,189	895	65,989,944	57,739,091	1,972	207,386,981	164,712,280
Dec. 31, 1987	953	135,690,678	103,930,262	812	54,361,514	47,283,855	1,765	190,052,192	151,214,117
Dec. 31, 1988	802	130,310,243	106,740,461	690	40,791,310	36,655,253	1,492	171,101,553	143,395,714
Dec. 31, 1989	687	133,163,016	104,091,836	626	40,893,848	36,652,675	1,313	174,056,864	140,744,511
Dec. 31, 1990	605	125,808,263	103,573,445	578	45,021,304	40,116,662	1,183	170,829,567	143,690,107
Dec. 31, 1991	579	123,022,314	106,153,441	546	46,279,752	41,315,420	1,125	169,302,066	147,468,861
Dec. 31, 1992	562	135,507,244	112,468,203	529	40,088,963	35,767,858	1,091	175,596,207	148,236,061
Dec. 31, 1993	502	139,409,250	111,993,205	510	44,566,815	39,190,373	1,012	183,976,065	151,183,578
Dec. 31, 1994	481	140,374,540	111,881,041	502	47,769,694	41,522,943	983	188,144,234	153,403,984
Dec. 31, 1995	456	152,750,093	112,557,468	479	49,967,946	42,728,454	935	202,718,039	155,285,922
Dec. 31, 1996	432	152,299,695	122,242,990	445	52,868,263	45,970,674	877	205,167,958	168,213,664
Dec. 31, 1997	417	180,252,942	145,588,677	421	54,845,186	46,202,808	838	235,098,128	191,791485
Dec. 31, 1998	402	128,609,813	106,704,893	395	50,966,996	42,277,367	797	179,576,809	148,982,260
Dec. 31, 1999	380	128,878,607	99,383,776	373	52,266,148	42,579,986	753	181,144,755	141,963,762
Dec. 31, 2000	358	112,793,856	88,591,657	351	53,561,550	43,835,525	709	166,355,406	132,427,182
Dec. 31, 2001	342	85,625,768	72,812,548	344	59,047,520	47,843,799	686	144,673,288	120,656,347
Dec. 31, 2002	332	95,308,420	79,183,418	337	62,093,220	49,715,186	669	157,401,640	128,898,604
Dec. 31, 2003	316	75,003,613	62,567,943	337	61,448,617	49,790,333	653	136,452,230	112,358,276
Dec. 31, 2004	311	82,333,800	67,977,669	328	69,127,411	54,950,601	639	151,461,211	122,928,270
Dec. 31, 2005	302	96,505,262	77,688,463	324	76,697,256	61,257,128	626	173,202,518	138,945,591
Dec. 31, 2006	286	$ 97,936,270	$ 79,389,737	322	$ 83,910,356	$ 66,132,394	608	$181,846,626	$145,522,131

Texas State Banks

Consolidated Statement, Foreign and Domestic
Offices, as of Dec. 31, 2006
Source: Federal Reserve Bank of Dallas

Number of Banks	322

(thousands of dollars, 000)

Assets

Cash and balances due from banks:
Non-interest-bearing balances
and currency and coin ....$ 2,729,124
Interest-bearing balances...829,616
Held-to-maturity securities....................................5,020,053
Available-for sale securities................................17,730,789
Federal funds sold in domestic offices 3,385,793
Securities purchases under agreements to resell 0
Loans and lease financing receivables:
Loans and leases held for sale 400,386
Loans and leases, net of unearned income 47,486,294
Less: allowance for loan and lease losses.............530,670
Loans and leases, net.......................................46,955,624
Trading Assets...897
Premises and fixed assets...................................1,808,549
Other real estate owned 89,240
Investments in unconsolidated subsidiaries
and associated companies..7,331
Intangible assets:
Goodwill 2,661,881
Other...261,265
Other assets 2,029,770

Total Assets ....$ 83,910,318

Liabilities

Deposits:
In domestic offices ....$ 66,132,394
Non-interest-bearing....................................14,989,516
Interest-bearing...51,142,878
In foreign offices, edge & agreement subsidiaries
and IBFs...216,678
Non-interest-bearing..0
Interest-bearing balances....................................216,678
Federal funds purchased and securities sold under
agreements to repurchase:
funds in domestic offices................................1,218,559
securities sold under agreement to repurchase ... 1,426,568
Trading liabilities..0
Other borrowed money (mortgages/leases)............4,474,184
Subordinated notes and debentures 46,745
Other liabilities... 613,629

Total Liabilities ....$ 74,128,757
Minority interest in consolidated subsidiaries 986

Equity Capital

Perpetual preferred stock ....$ 525
Common stock..532,969
Surplus (exclude surplus related to
preferred stock) 6,452,961
Retained earnings 2,931,503
Accumulated other comprehensive income...............-136,721
Other equity capital components.................................-662

Total Equity Capital ....$ 9,780,575

**Total liabilities, minority interest and
equity capital** ....$ 83,910,318

Texas National Banks

Consolidated Statement, Foreign and Domestic
Offices, as of Dec. 31, 2006
Source: Federal Reserve Bank of Dallas

Number of Banks	286

(thousands of dollars, 000)

Assets

Cash and balances due from banks:
Non-interest-bearing balances
and currency and coin ....$ 4,377,775
Interest-bearing balances......................................1,202,259
Held-to-maturity securities....................................2,156,396
Available-for sale securities................................20,031,453
Federal funds sold in domestic offices 5,292,438
Securities purchases under agreements to resell 115,405
Loans and lease financing receivables:
Loans and leases held for sale 622,368
Loans and leases, net of unearned income 56,917,584
Less: allowance for loan and lease losses.............669,663
Loans and leases, net.......................................56,247,921
Trading Assets...116,829
Premises and fixed assets...................................2,068,351
Other real estate owned 75,936
Investments in unconsolidated subsidiaries
and associated companies..5,962
Intangible assets:
Goodwill 2,945,993
Other...323,244
Other assets 2,536,464

Total Assets ....$ 97,936,494

Liabilities

Deposits:
In domestic offices ....$ 79,389,737
Non-interest-bearing....................................20,095,863
Interest-bearing...59,293,872
In foreign offices, edge & agreement subsidiaries
and IBFs..2,321,552
Non-interest-bearing..0
Interest-bearing balances.................................2,321,552
Federal funds purchased and securities sold under
agreements to repurchase:
funds in domestic offices...................................785,361
securities sold under agreement to repurchase ... 2,089,535
Trading liabilities..7,246
Other borrowed money (mortgages/leases)............1,123,502
Subordinated notes and debentures 376,000
Other liabilities... 746,599

Total Liabilities ....$ 86,839,525
Minority interest in consolidated subsidiaries 3,397

Equity Capital

Perpetual preferred stock ....$ 910
Common stock..488,330
Surplus (exclude surplus related to
preferred stock) 6,187,821
Retained earnings 4,630,254
Accumulated other comprehensive income...............-199,753
Other equity capital components.................................-13,990

Total Equity Capital ....$ 11,093,572

**Total liabilities, minority interest and
equity capital** ....$ 97,936,494

Credit Unions: Mid-Year 2006

	#Credit Unions	State Charter	Federal Charter	Members	Percent of Pop.*	Savings (000)	Loans (000)	Assets (000)
Texas	618	223	395	6,890,936	30.1	$41,048,060	$33,139,010	$48,723,469
U.S.	8,853	3,547	5,306	87,895,738	29.3	$613,297,338	$492,634,971	$719,231,364

In percent of population, each member counted once for every credit union they belong to. Source: Credit Union National Association.

	U.S. Credit Union History				Texas Credit Union History			
Year	# Credit Unions	Members	Savings ($ millions)	Loans ($ millions)	# Credit Unions	Members	Savings ($ millions)	Loans ($ millions)
2006	8,853	87,895,738	$ 613,297	$ 492,635	618	6,890,936	$ 41,048	$ 33,139
2005	9,198	86,987,764	591,388	449,891	625	6,832,172	40,273	32,745
2004	9,542	85,639,535	567,827	407,937	641	7,130,609	40,749	31,709
2003	9,875	84,240,057	538,033	367,065	667	7,000,010	39,148	29,199
2002	10,174	82,557,258	483,527	343,400	683	6,801,810	36,591	26,383
2001	10,514	80,937,530	427,411	318,027	695	6,626,098	32,838	24,128
2000	10,860	78,865,715	380,858	295,251	714	6,454,376	28,400	22,562
1995	12,230	69,305,876	278,813	198,337	819	5,360,020	20,306	14,701
1990	14,549	61,610,057	201,082	141,889	954	4,379,982	13,875	8,946
1980	21,465	43,930,569	61,724	48,703	1,379	3,202,066	4,818	3,691
1970	23,687	22,775,511	15,411	14,068	1,435	1,452,416	1,034	951
1960	20,094	12,025,393	4,976	4,376	1,159	688,517	282	265
1950	10,586	4,617,086	862	679	484	179,956	38	35

Source: Credit Union National Association.

Credit Unions in Texas

Source: Texas Credit Union Department, National Credit Union Administration and Credit Union National Association.

Credit unions are chartered at federal and state levels. The National Credit Union Administration (NCUA) is the regulatory agency for the federal-chartered credit unions in Texas.

The Texas Credit Union Department is the regulatory agency for the state-chartered credit unions. It was established in 1969 as a separate agency by the 61st Legislature. In 2006, besides the 223 active state-chartered credit unions, it also supervised the Texas branch offices of 23 out-of-state credit unions.

The state-chartered credit unions served 2.7 million Texans and had approximately $17.9 billion in assets in 2006. The department is supervised by the nine-member Texas Credit Union Commission, which is appointed by the governor to staggered terms of six years, with the terms of one-third of the members expiring Feb. 15 of each odd-numbered year.

The Texas Credit Union League has been the state association for federal and state chartered credit unions since October 1934.

The league's address is 4455 LBJ Freeway Ste. 909, Farmers Branch, 75244-5998.

The address for the Texas Credit Union Department is 914 East Anderson Lane, Austin, 78752-1699. Their Web site is www.tcud.state.tx.us. ☆

Distribution of Consumer Savings

$ billions. Mid-Year 2006

	Savings	Market share
Commercial banks	$ 3,916.9	60.1%
Money Market Mutual Funds	927.6	14.2%
Savings Institutions	849.8	13.0%
Credit Unions	**613.3**	**9.4%**
US Savings Securities	205.2	3.2%
Total	**$ 6,512.9**	

Credit Outstanding by Lenders

	Outstanding	Market share
Commercial banks	$ 694.8	29.9%
Pool of Securitized Assets	627.7	27.0%
Finance Companies	506.8	21.8%
Credit Unions	**230.2**	**9.9%**
Student Loans	102.6	4.4%
Savings Institutions	103.9	4.5%
Nonfinancial business	56.5	2.4%
Total	**$ 2,322.6**	

Source: Credit Union National Association.

Savings and Loan Associations in Texas

This table includes all thrifts that are not also classified as banks under federal law: that is, it includes federal savings and loan associations and federal savings banks. *Source: Texas Department of Savings and Mortgage Lending.*

Year ending	Number of Institutions	Total Assets	*Mortgage Loans	†Cash	†Investment Securities	Deposits	FHLB/ Borrowed Money	‡Net Worth
				in thousands of dollars (000)				
Dec. 31, 2006	20	$ 64,692,927	$ 22,908,898	$12,709,276	. . .	$ 39,661,286	$ 18,817,750	$ 4,993,335
Dec. 31, 2005	19	55,755,096	42,027,293	9,140,789	. . .	30,565,411	11,299,136	4,228,103
Dec. 31, 2004	20	51,000,806	40,740,030	6,648,858	. . .	26,526,138	12,786,086	3,647,046
Dec. 31, 2003	21	45,941,356	16,840,610	17,362,664	. . .	23,954,623	10,725,209	3,130,442
Dec. 31, 2002	24	43,940,058	31,604,285	4,900,880	. . .	23,264,510	11,662,118	3,189,629
Dec. 31, 2001	24	42,716,060	35,823,258	9,542,688	. . .	22,182,152	15,531,159	3,608,222
Dec. 31, 2000	25	55,709,391	43,515,610	1,512,444	. . .	28,914,234	17,093,369	4,449,097
Dec. 31, 1999	25	45,508,256	40,283,186	2,615,072	. . .	26,369,005	14,790,241	3,802,977
Dec. 31, 1998	30	40,021,239	35,419,110	5,236,596	. . .	21,693,469	15,224,654	3,101,795
Dec. 31, 1997	32	40,284,148	33,451,365	4,556,626	. . .	21,854,620	15,190,014	3,089,458
Dec. 31, 1996	37	54,427,896	27,514,639	5,112,995	. . .	28,053,292	20,210,616	4,345,257
Dec. 31, 1995	45	52,292,519	27,509,933	5,971,364	. . .	28,635,799	15,837,632	3,827,249
Dec. 31, 1994	50	50,014,102	24,148,760	6,790,416	. . .	29,394,433	15,973,056	3,447,110
Dec. 31, 1993	62	42,983,595	14,784,215	10,769,889	. . .	25,503,656	13,356,018	2,968,840
Dec. 31, 1992	64	47,565,516	14,137,191	14,527,573	. . .	33,299,278	10,490,144	2,917,881
Dec. 31, 1991	80	53,500,091	15,417,895	11,422,071	. . .	41,985,117	8,189,800	2,257,329
Dec. 31, 1990§	131	72,041,456	27,475,664	20,569,770	. . .	56,994,387	17,738,041	-4,566,656
Conservatorship	51	14,952,402	6,397,466	2,188,820	. . .	16,581,525	4,304,033	-6,637,882
Privately Owned	80	57,089,054	21,078,198	18,380,950	. . .	40,412,862	13,434,008	2,071,226
Dec. 31, 1989§	196	90,606,100	37,793,043	21,218,130	. . .	70,823,464	27,158,238	-9,356,209
Conservatorship	81	22,159,752	11,793,445	2,605,080	. . .	25,381,494	7,103,657	-10,866,213
Privately Owned	115	68,446,348	25,999,598	18,613,050	. . .	45,441,970	20,054,581	1,510,004
Dec. 31, 1988	204	110,499,276	50,920,006	26,181,917	. . .	83,950,314	28,381,573	-4,088,355
Dec. 31, 1987	279	99,613,666	56,884,564	12,559,154	. . .	85,324,796	19,235,506	-6,677,338
Dec. 31, 1986	281	96,919,775	61,489,463	9,989,918	. . .	80,429,758	14,528,311	109,807
Dec. 31, 1985	273	91,798,890	60,866,666	10,426,464	. . .	72,806,067	13,194,147	3,903,611
Dec. 31, 1980	318	34,954,129	27,717,383	3,066,791	. . .	28,439,210	3,187,638	1,711,201
Dec. 31, 1975	303	16,540,181	13,367,569	167,385	$ 1,000,095	13,876,780	919,404	914,502
Dec. 31, 1970	271	7,706,639	6,450,730	122,420	509,482	6,335,582	559,953	531,733
Dec. 31, 1965	267	5,351,064	4,534,073	228,994	230,628	4,631,999	286,497	333,948
Dec. 31, 1960	233	$ 2,508,872	$ 2,083,066	$ 110,028	$ 157,154	$ 2,238,080	$ 48,834	$ 166,927

Texas Savings Banks

The savings bank charter was approved by the Legislature in 1993 and the first savings bank was chartered in 1994. Savings banks operate similarly to savings and loans associations in that they are housing oriented lenders. Under federal law a savings bank is categorized as a commercial bank and not a thrift. Therefore savings-bank information is also reported with state and national bank information. *Source: Texas Department of Savings and Mortgage Lending.*

				in thousands of dollars (000)				
Dec. 31, 2006	22	$ 9,393,482	$ 6,444,178	$ 836,821	. . .	$ 5,721,314	$ 2,453,757	$1,138,780
Dec. 31, 2005	19	8,720,497	5,605,678	985,535	. . .	5,308,639	1,967,673	1,352,882
Dec. 31, 2004	22	12,981,650	6,035,081	1,654,978	. . .	8,377,409	3,000,318	1,482,078
Dec. 31, 2003	23	17,780,413	8,396,606	3,380,565	. . .	11,901,441	3,315,544	2,422,317
Dec. 31, 2002	24	15,445,211	7,028,139	3,147,381	. . .	10,009,861	3,422,600	1,910,660
Dec. 31, 2001	25	11,956,074	5,845,605	1,305,731	. . .	8,742,372	1,850,076	1,270,273
Dec. 31, 2000	25	11,315,961	9,613,164	514,818	. . .	8,644,826	1,455,497	1,059,638
Dec. 31, 1999	28	13,474,299	8,870,291	4,101,480	. . .	7,330,776	4,822,372	1,188,852
Dec. 31, 1998	23	12,843,828	7,806,738	193,992	. . .	7,299,636	4,477,546	1,067,977
Dec. 31, 1997	17	7,952,703	6,125,467	892,556	. . .	5,608,429	1,615,311	745,515
Dec. 31, 1996	15	7,872,238	6,227,811	856,970	. . .	5,329,919	1,930,378	611,941
Dec. 31, 1995	13	7,348,647	5,644,591	1,106,557	. . .	4,603,026	2,225,793	519,827
Dec. 31, 1994	8	$ 6,347,505	$ 2,825,012	$ 3,139,573	. . .	$ 3,227,886	$ 2,628,847	$ 352,363

* Beginning in 1982, net of loans in process.
† Beginning in 1979, cash and investment securities data combined.
‡ Net worth includes permanent stock and paid-in surplus general reserves, surplus and undivided profits.
§ In 1989 and 1990, the Office of Thrift Supervision, U.S. Department of the Treasury, separated data on savings and loans (thrifts) into two categories: those under the supervision of the Office of Thrift Supervision (Conservatorship Thrifts) and those still under private management (Privately Owned).

Insurance in Texas

Source: 2006 Annual Report, Texas Department of Insurance.

The Texas Department of Insurance reported that on Aug. 31, 2006, there were 2,732 firms licensed to handle insurance business in Texas and 273,502 insurance agents.

From 1957 to 1993, a three-member State Board of Insurance administered legislation relating to the insurance industry. This board, appointed by the governor, hired a commissioner of insurance. The establishment of this system followed discovery of irregularities in some firms. It succeeded two previous regulatory groups, established in 1913 and changed in 1927.

Under reforms in 1993-94, the board was replaced by the Texas Department of Insurance with a Commis-

sioner of Insurance appointed by the governor for a two-year term in each odd-numbered year and confirmed by the Texas Senate.

On Sept. 1, 2005, legislation passed by the 79th Legislature took effect, transferring functions of the Texas Workers' Compensation Commission to the Texas Department of Insurance and creating within it the Division of Worker's Compensation.

Also established was the office of Commissioner of Workers' Compensation, appointed by the governor, to enforce and implement the Texas Workers' Compensation Act. The division consists of five sections: dispute resolution, field services, legal and compliance, medical advisor, and workplace and medical services.

Companies in Texas

The following table shows the number and kinds of insurance companies licensed in Texas on Aug. 31, 2006.

Type of Insurance	Texas	Out-of-State	Total
Stock Life	119	483	602
Mutual Life	3	38	41
Stipulated Premium Life	34	0	34
Non-Profit Life	0	1	1
Stock Fire	2	4	6
Stock Fire & Casualty	104	665	769
Mutual Fire & Casualty	5	54	59
Stock Casualty	8	145	153
Mexican Casualty	0	11	11
Lloyds	61	0	61
Reciprocal Exchanges	10	15	25
Fraternal Benefit Societies	8	24	32
Title Insurance	5	29	34
Non-Profit Legal Services	3	0	3
Health Maintenance Organizations	49	3	52
Risk Retention Groups	2	0	2
Multiple Employer Welfare Arrang.	6	0	6
Joint Underwriting Associations	3	3	6
Third Party Administrators	269	478	747
Workers' Comp. Self Insurance	7	0	7
Continuing Care Retirement Communities	20	4	24
Total	**718**	**1,957**	**2,675**
Local Mutual Associations	3	0	3
Exempt Associations	9	0	9
Non-Profit Hospital Service	2	0	2
County Mutual Fire	24	0	24
Farm Mutual Fire	17	0	17
Total	**57**	**0**	**57**
Grand Total	**775**	**1,957**	**2,732**

Source: 2006 Annual Report, Texas Department of Insurance.

Premium Income and Losses Paid, 2005

(Texas business only)	Texas Companies	Out-of-State Companies
Legal Reserve Life Insurance Companies		
Life premiums	$ 694,771,220	$ 7,011,361,546
Claims & benefits paid	$ 4,010,026,902	$ 17,818,597,152
Accident & health premiums	$ 442,192,784	$ 10,275,346,650
Accident & health loss paid	$ 286,699,701	$ 7,227,744,034
Mutual Fire & Casualty Companies		
Premiums	$ 797,871,970	$ 3,400,995,089
Losses	$ 297,383,882	$ 2,006,058,374
Lloyds Insurance		
Premiums	$ 4,895,474,875	....
Losses	$ 2,270,739,405	....
Reciprocal Insurance Companies		
Premiums	$ 842,049,298	$ 709,372,059
Losses	$ 484,145,355	$ 346,940,828
Fraternal Benefit Societies		
Life Certificates Issued	8,658	17,192
Amount issued 2005	$ 164,142,583	$ 1,572,580,833
Considerations from members:		
Life	$ 75,934,281	$ 260,325,659
Accident & Health	0	$ 24,970,559
Benefits paid to members:		
Life	$ 54,787,049	$ 219,378,711
Accident & Health	0	$ 12,476,586
Insurance in force	$ 2,924,841,000	$273,114,547,000
Title Companies		
Premiums	$ 427,320,785	$ 1,060,147,440
Paid losses	$ 9,574,455	$ 27,221,939
Stock Fire, Stock Casualty, and Stock Fire & Casualty Companies		
Premiums	$ 1,674,758,413	$ 11,450,306,815
Losses	$ 897,571,473	$ 5,739,327,332

Texas Top 5 Auto Insurers

Company	% of market
1. State Farm Mutual	19.86
2. Progressive County Mutual	8.54
3. Mid-Century	6.34
4. Allstate County Mutual	6.17
5. Farmers Texas County Mutual	5.90

Texas Top 5 Homeowners Insurers

1. State Farm Lloyds	29.41
2. Allstate Texas Lloyds	16.53
3. Farmers Insurance Exchange	6.61
4. Travelers Lloyds of Texas	5.49
5. United Services	4.20

Texas Top 5 Accident/Health Insurers

1. Blue Cross/Blue Shield	22.29
2. United Healthcare	16.02
3. Humana	6.47
4. Aetna Life	5.00
5. Unicare	3.68

Texas Top 5 HMOs

1. Aetna Health	13.42
2. Pacificare of Texas	13.11
3. Amerigroup Texas	11.79
4. Blue Cross/Blue Shield	11.50
5. Humana	6.86

Texas Top 5 Life Insurers

1. Metropolitan Life	7.69
2. Northwestern Mutual Life	4.16
3. State Farm Life	3.01
4. Prudential	2.98
5. New York Life	2.81

Source: 2006 Annual Report, Texas Department of Insurance.

Homeowners Insurance: Average Premiums by State, 2003

The U.S. average is $668. Idaho has the least expensive at $433.

1. Texas	**$ 1,328**
2. Louisiana	975
3. Oklahoma	925
4. Florida	810
5. District of Columbia	806
6. Mississippi	793
7. Kansas	772
8. Colorado	762
9. California	753
10. Minnesota	733

In dollars. The Texas Insurance Commissioner promulgates residential policy forms which are similar but not identical to the standard national forms. Source: U.S. Statistical Abstract 2007.

Auto Insurance: Average for Coverage by State, 2003

The U.S. average is $821. North Dakota has the least expensive at $536.

1. New Jersey	$ 1,188
2. New York	1,161
3. District of Columbia	1,129
4. Massachusetts	1,052
5. Florida	1,015
6. Louisiana	1,014
7. Rhode Island	992
8. Connecticut	983
9. Delaware	973
10. Alaska	938
17. Texas	**837**

In dollars. The figures are actually reported as 'average expenditures', which equals total premiums divided by liability car-years. A car-year is equal to 365 days of insured coverage for a single vehicle. Source: U.S. Statistical Abstract 2007.

10-year history, number of insurance companies operating in Texas

	1997	1998	1999	2000	2001	2002	2003	2004	2005	2006
Life/Health										
In-State	263	248	233	220	216	213	206	196	190	186
Out-of-State	680	669	649	639	625	607	580	561	552	546
subtotal	943	917	882	859	841	820	786	757	742	732
Property/Casualty										
In-State	245	247	250	250	245	243	244	245	250	248
Out-of-State	854	861	877	888	910	913	916	915	917	926
subtotal	1,108	1,108	1,127	1,138	1,155	1,156	1,160	1,160	1,167	1,174
Other*										
In-State	308	333	359	367	373	368	362	348	352	341
Out-of-State	335	368	390	414	426	436	456	462	479	485
subtotal	643	701	749	481	799	804	818	810	831	826
Grand Total	**2,694**	**2,726**	**2,758**	**2,778**	**2,795**	**2,780**	**2,764**	**2,727**	**2,740**	**2,732****

*Other includes: Non-profit legal services corporations, third party administrators, continuing care retirement communities and health maintenance organizations.

**Does not include 270 premium finance companies and their 53 branch offices.

Source: 2006 Annual Report, Texas Department of Insurance.

Telecommunications in Transition to New Technology

The chart below shows the move to wireless and the decline in the number of telephone land lines to residences and business in Texas and nationwide, as well as the growth of high-speed Internet use in the state. (NA, for information not available). *Source: Trends in Telephone Service, Federal Communications Commission, February 2007.*

	2006	2005	2004	2003	2002	2001	2000
Mobile Wireless Telephone Subscribers							
Texas	16,902,077	14,402,814	12,091,134	10,776,234	9,650,715	8,294,338	6,705,423
U.S.	217,418,404	192,053,067	167,313,001	147,623,734	130,751,459	114,028,928	90,643,058
Local Telephone Lines							
Texas	NA	10,945,498	11,590,497	12,717,073	12,949,056	13,531,474	13,657,444
U.S.	NA	157,041,487	165,978,892	173,140,710	180,095,333	185,587,160	188,499,586
High-Speed Lines for Internet							
Texas	4,371,655	2,943,487	2,203,490	1,571,250	1,015,245	614,704	252,721
U.S.	64,614,270	42,436,904	31,950,574	22,995,444	15,787,647	9,241,996	4,106,918

Cell phones, even in Luckenbach. Robert Plocheck photo.

High-Speed Lines by Technology as of June 2006

Area	DSL	Cable Modem	Traditional Wireline	Fiber	Satellite	Fixed Wireless	Mobile Wireless	Power Line	Total
Texas	1,748,894	1,692,433	32,321	1,04,719	*	51,814	*	0	4,371,655
U.S.	22,9122,448	28,513,500	610,722	700,083	495,365	360,976	11,015,968	5,208	64,614,270

* Data withheld to maintain firm confidentiality.

Percent of U.S. Households with Internet Connections (as of October 2003)

	Rural	Urban	Total
Internet Service	54.1 %	54.8 %	54.6 %
Dial-Up	40.4 %	32.3 %	34.3 %
High-Speed	13.2 %	21.8 %	19.9 %
Cable Modem	7.7 %	12.4 %	11.2 %
DSL	5.0 %	9.4 %	8.3 %
Satellite/Fixed Wireless	0.6 %	0.3 %	0.4 %
Other	0.4 %	0.5 %	0.4 %

Top Telephone Carriers in U.S. as of December 2004

Company	Percent of total
Verizon	31.63
SBC	31.46
BellSouth	13.24
Qwest	8.93
Sprint	4.35
AllTel	1.68

Source: FCC 2007

The South Texas Nuclear Power Plant in Matagorda County. Robert Plocheck photo.

Nuclear Power Plants: 2004 *(788,528 represents 788,528,000,000 kilowatt-hours.)*

	Number of Units	Net Generation		Net Summer Capacity	
		Total mil. kWh	Percent of total	Total mil. kWh	Percent of total
Texas	4*	40,435	10.4	4.86	4.8
U.S.	104	788,528	19.9	99.63	10.3

*Texas has two nuclear plants; South Texas near Bay City and Comanche Peak near Glen Rose. Each has two units.

Electric Utilities: Capacity and Demand

Electric Power Generation and Summer Capacity: 2000 – 2005

	Net Generation (bil. kWh)						Net Summer Capacity (mil. kW)					
	2000	2001	2002	2003	2004	2005	2000	2001	2002	2003	2004	2005
Texas	377.7	372.6	385.6	379.2	390.3	396.7	81.7	88.0	94.5	99.6	101.1	101.0
U.S.	3,802.1	3,736.6	3,858.5	2,883.2	3,970.6	4,054.7	811.7	848.2	905.3	948.4	962.9	978.0
U.S. summer capacity margin *(amount of unused available capability at peak load as a percentage of capacity.)*							9.6	12.2	13.4	16.9	17.3	13.1

Source: Energy Information Administration, 2007.

Net Internal Demand, Capacity Margins for U.S. and Texas Grids

The Electric Reliability Council of Texas (**ERCOT**) operates the electric grid and manages the deregulated market for 75 percent of the state. The northern and western part of the Panhandle and a small corner of Northeast Texas is under the Southwest Power Pool (**SPP**). El Paso and the far western corner of the Trans Pecos is under the Western Electric Coordinating Council (**WECC**), and the southeast corner of Texas is under the **SERC** Reliability Corporation. The councils were first formed in 1968 to ensure adequate bulk power supply. *Source: Federal Energy Information Administration, 2005.*

	History *(in megawatts)*					Projections				
	2001	2002	2003	2004	2005	2006	2007	2008	2009	2010
U.S. demand	674,833	696,376	696,752	692,908	746,470	742,388	757,056	775,514	791,038	806,129
capacity	788,990	833,380	856,131	875,870	882,125	892,085	897,213	902,711	910,084	806,129
% margin	14.5	16.4	18.6	20.9	15.4	16.8	15.6	14.1	13.1	12.3
ERCOT demand	55,106	55,833	59,282	58,531	59,060	60,506	62,027	63,168	64,800	66,398
capacity	70,797	76,849	74,764	73,850	66,724	70,182	70,384	70,191	70,124	70,310
% margin	22.2	27.3	20.7	20.7	11.5	13.8	11.8	10.0	7.6	5.6
SPP demand	38,807	38,298	39,428	39,383	41,079	40,939	41,469	42,399	43,057	43,810
capacity	45,530	47,233	45,802	48,000	46,376	47,847	47,960	479,221	48,998	51,155
% margin	14.8	18.9	13.9	18.0	11.4	14.4	13.1	13.9	12.1	14.4
WECC demand	107,294	117,032	120,894	121,205	128,464	128,225	131,418	134,576	137,957	141,008
capacity	124,193	142,624	150,277	155,455	160,026	162,009	162,566	162,595	162,588	162,553
% margin	13.6	17.9	19.6	22,0	19.7	20.9	19.2	17.2	15.1	13.3
SERC demand	144,399	154,459	148,380	153,024	186,049	183,783	187,982	193,706	197,248	201,233
capacity	171,530	172,485	177,231	182,861	219,749	221,246	223,103	226,119	230,978	236,518
% margin	15.8	10.5	16.3	16.3	15.3	16.9	15.7	14.3	14.6	14.9

Wind Energy: A Small Part, But Growing

Source: State Energy Conservation Office, Austin, 2007.

Wind power is the fastest growing source of electricity generation in the world.

Wind energy installations in the United States now exceed 11,600 megawatts in generating capacity and produce enough daily electricity to power the equivalent of more than 2.9 million homes.

Texas accounted for nearly a third of the new wind power installed in 2006 and is now the largest wind energy producer in the nation with an installed wind generating capacity at 2,370 MW, which is enough power for over 600,000 average-sized homes a year.

One megawatt of wind power produces enough electricity to serve 250 to 300 homes on average each day.

In 2006, there were over 2,000 wind turbines in West Texas alone, and the numbers continue to increase. Additionally, Texas has the world's largest operating wind farm, the 735-MW Horse Hollow Wind Energy Center, located in Taylor and Nolan counties. Moreover, Texas has approved two offshore wind farms along the Gulf Coast — another national first.

Vast areas with high wind power potential exist in West Texas, the High Plains and along the Gulf Coast. The best locations, on top of mesas and along ridges, are being developed first.

Recent advances in wind energy technologies have lowered the cost of wind energy so dramatically that these immense turbines are becoming a familiar sight, silhouetted against Texas skies.

New wind farms consist of hundreds of skyscraper turbines, each a source of immense power, and each capable of generating electricity for entire communities.

Texas wind is also being harnessed on a smaller scale to provide on-site electricity and working power for ranches, homes and businesses at increasingly competitive costs. ☆

Wind turbines generating electricity on mesas near Iraan. Robert Plocheck photo.

Electric Cooperatives

Source: Texas Electric Cooperatives.

Electric cooperatives are non-profit, consumer-owned utilities providing electric service primarily in rural areas. Rates are regulated by the Public Utility Commission of Texas.

The nation's first electric cooperative was established in 1935 in Bartlett. Today Texas is home to 65 distribution co-ops and nine generation and transmission co-ops serving nearly 3 million member-customers. And, there are more than 286,000 miles of lines linking 232 of the 254 counties.

In 2007, there were 930 electric co-ops serving 34 million people throughout the nation. ☆

Average Retail Price for Electricity: 2005-06

The following table shows the price of power in the period from July 2005–June 2006 for major utilities with high dependence on natural gas generation.

Utility	State	Avg. price in cents per kWh	Gas share of generation
NSTAR	Massachusetts	19.38	45.0 %
Pacific Gas & Electric	California	14.30	47.6 %
Southern California Edison	California	14.80	47.6 %
San Diego Gas & Electric	Califormia	15.40	47.6 %
Gulf Power	Florida	13.57	38.1 %
Tampa Electric Company	Florida	14.55	38.1 %
Central Maine Power	Maine	15.03	48.3 %
Sierra Pacific	Nevada	13.04	46.4 %
TXU Price to Beat	Texas	15.00	48.6 %
Centerpoint Price to Beat	Texas	16.29	48.6 %
TXU Lowest Offer	Texas	13.48	48.6 %
Centerpoint Lowest Offer	Texas	14.23	48.6 %

Source: Public Utility Commission of Texas, 2007.

Summary Statistics for Natural Gas in Texas

	2001	2002	2003	2004	2005
Total Supply (MMcf, million cubic feet)	7,151,094	7,136,599	7,349,612	7,320,094	7,184,367
Consumption (million cubic feet) delivered to consumers					
Residential	208,449	209,951	206,694	191,507	184,895
Commercial	171,847	226,273	218,565	192,901	159,895
Industrial	2,029,809	1,978,184	186,138	1,814,173	1,466,824
Vehicle Fuel	1,715	1,811	2,2183	2,485	2,697
Electric Power	1,506,112	1,550,292	1,453,858	1,394,408	1,466,263
Number of Consumers					
Residential	3,738,260	3,809,370	3,859,647	3,939,101	2,978,755
Commercial	314,858	317,446	320,786	322,242	322,647
Industrial	10,047	9,143	9,015	9,359	9,141
Average Price for Natural Gas (dollars per thousand cubic feet)					
Residential	8.90	7.29	9.22	10.37	12.49
Commercial	6.48	5.49	7.59	8.36	10.48
Industrial	4.46	3.40	5.36	5.91	7.64
Vehicle Fuel	7.95	5.67	8.09	8.58	10.52
Electric Power	4.32	3.41	5.47	5.90	8.12

Source: Federal Energy Information Administration, Natural Gas Annual 2005.

Top Gas Distribution Utilities, 2004

Utility	Customers	Sales (MMcf)
Atmos Energy – Mid-Tex	1,509,661	130,573,860
CenterPoint Energy Entex	1,325,104	116,501,050
Texas Gas Service	555,287	35,866,577
San Antonio Public Service	309,293	53,520,673
Atmos Energy	285,796	27,906,849

These utilities represent 96% of all distribution in Texas.
Source: Gas Division, Texas Railroad Commission, 2007.

Texas Share of U.S. Total, 2005

Natural Gas	Percent of National Total
Dry Production	27.11
Residential Deliveries	3.85
Commercial Deliveries	5.16
Industrial Deliveries	21.74
Electric Power	24.98
Total Delivered	15.97

Source: Energy Information Administration, 2005.

Total Residential Gas Bill for 6,000 cubic feet in Selected Cities

City	Gas Co.	January 2005	June 2005	December 2005
Amarillo	Atmos	$ 52.89	$ 55.24	$ 72.00
Austin	Texas Gas Service	60.56	63.22	74.69
Beaumont	CenterPoint Entex	74.35	60.84	109.69
Corpus Christi	Municipal	63.55	73.93	80.08
Dallas	Atmos Mid-Tex	59.02	56.65	109.93
El Paso	Texas Gas Service	49.50	48.62	64.97
Fort Worth	Atmos Mid-Tex	67.93	56.65	109.93
Houston	CenterPoint Entex	71.51	78.13	87.23
Laredo	CenterPoint Entex	72.29	59.39	114.24
Lubbock	Atmos	53.53	54.19	83.35
McAllen	Texas Gas Service	53.02	55.52	64.23
Odessa	Atmos	51.48	52.86	67.86
San Angelo	Atmos Mid-Tex	67.93	56.65	109.93
San Antonio	Municipal	59.35	58.96	73.92
Texarkana	CenterPoint	79.06	80.57	88.49
Tyler	CenterPoint Entex	71.83	57.95	98.84
Waco	Atmos Mid-Tex	67.93	56.65	109.93
Wichita Falls	Atmos Mid-Tex	67.93	56.65	109.93
Average		**$ 63.39**	**$ 59.50**	**$ 91.68**

Source: Gas Division, Texas Railroad Commission, 2007.

Belo Covers the Nation

Belo Corp., a Dallas-based media company, has been a part of Texas history since the days of the Republic. The oldest continuously operating business in Texas, Belo had its origins in Galveston with the one-page *The Daily News*, which was first published in April 1842.

Today, Belo is one of the nation's largest media companies with a diversified group of market-leading broadcasting, publishing, cable and interactive media assets. A *Fortune* 1000 company with approximately 7,100 employees and $1.6 billion in annual revenues, Belo has news and information operations in some of the most desirable markets in Texas, the Northwest, the Southwest, the Mid-Atlantic and Rhode Island. Belo's media outlets reach more than 30 million viewers, readers and online users each week.

The company owns 20 television stations, six of which are in the 15 largest U.S. broadcast markets. The company also owns or operates six cable news channels and manages one television station through a local marketing agreement.

Belo's daily newspapers are *The Dallas Morning News* in Dallas, Texas, which publishes the *Texas Almanac; The Providence Journal* in Providence, R.I.; *The Press-Enterprise* in Riverside, Calif.; and the *Denton Record-Chronicle* in Denton, Texas. Belo operates more than 30 Web sites associated with its operating companies. The company also produces specialty publications targeting young adults and the fast-growing Hispanic market, including *Quick* and *Al Dia* in Dallas-Fort Worth, and *El D* and *La Prensa* in Riverside.

The Early Days

The Daily News in Galveston was established in 1842, three years before the Republic of Texas achieved statehood. The newspaper was printed on equipment owned by Massachusetts native Samuel Bangs, along with his brother-in-law and *The Daily News* publisher, George H. French. In June 1843, Bangs leased the printing equipment to Wilbur F. Cherry and Michael Cronican; Cherry soon acquired sole ownership of *The News*.

Another Massachusetts émigré, Willard Richardson, became editor of the paper in 1844 and its sole owner in 1845. He campaigned editorially for annexation, fiscal responsibility and railroads. In 1857, Richardson conceived and founded the *Texas Almanac*, which he hoped would help attract settlers to the new state. Eight years later, he hired Alfred Horatio Belo, a former Confederate colonel from North Carolina, as bookkeeper. Belo was made a full partner in the growing company after only three months. The company eventually was named for him.

In 1874, George Bannerman Dealey, a 15-year-old English emigrant, was hired as an office boy. Working tirelessly, he made his way from office boy to business manager and then to publisher of *The Dallas Morning News*. It was Dealey who chose the then-small settlement of Dallas as the site for a sister publication. Dealey and other members of the Galveston newspaper's staff relocated to Dallas to found the *Morning News* and the company prospered and grew.

Belo Was a Radio Broadcasting Pioneer

On June 26, 1922, Belo began operating a 50-watt radio station, WFAA-AM, which was the first network station in the state. The company sold this radio property in 1987.

The Newspaper Group

The Dallas Morning News began publication on Oct. 1, 1885, with a circulation of 5,000 subscribers. After being in operation only two months, *The Dallas Morning News* acquired its first competitor, the *Dallas Herald* (not to be confused with the *Dallas Times-Herald* that closed in December 1991). Rather than compete with each other for subscribers, the two newspapers combined, keeping the name *The Dallas Morning News*.

In 1906, on the 21st anniversary of *The Dallas Morning News*, Dealey gave a speech from which emerged the company's motto: "Build the news upon the rock of truth and righteousness. Conduct it always upon the lines of fairness and integrity. Acknowledge the right of the people to get from the newspaper both sides of every important question." Today these words are carved in a three-story-high space above the entrance to *The Dallas Morning News'* main office building. *The News* building, a long-standing dream of Dealey's, was completed in 1949, three years after his death.

While Belo has become one of the nation's largest, most diversified media companies, *The Dallas Morning News* remains the flagship newspaper of the company's publishing business.

In 1997, Belo purchased *The Press-Enterprise*, a daily newspaper serving Riverside County and the inland Southern California area. *The Press-Enterprise* also publishes *La Prensa,* the area's top-rated Spanish-language newspaper, and *The Business Press*. Also in 1997, through the acquisition of The Providence Journal Company, Belo acquired *The Providence Journal*, the leading newspaper in Rhode Island and southeastern Massachusetts, and Rhode Island Monthly Communications, Inc., the state's only full-service publisher of magazines and specialty publications. Founded in 1829, *The Providence Journal* is America's oldest major daily general circulation newspaper in continuous publication.

In 1999, Belo acquired the Denton Publishing Company, whose assets included the *Denton Record-Chronicle*, a daily newspaper serving Denton County and surrounding areas in North Texas.

In 2003, Belo expanded its portfolio of specialized publications to serve young adults, affluent populations and the fast-growing Hispanic market with the launch of *Quick* and *Al Dia* in Dallas-Fort Worth, and *El D* in Riverside.

The Television Group and Cable Operations

Belo entered the television broadcasting business in 1950 with the acquisition of its flagship station, ABC affiliate WFAA-TV in Dallas-Fort Worth. In 1983, in the nation's largest broadcast acquisition to date, Belo acquired KHOU-TV (CBS) in Houston; KXTV (ABC) in Sacramento/Stockton/Modesto, Calif.; WVEC-TV (ABC) in Hampton/Norfolk, Va.; and KOTV (CBS) in Tulsa, Okla. In June 1994, Belo acquired WWL-

TV (CBS) in New Orleans, La., and in Sept. 1994, the company acquired KIRO-TV in Seattle/Tacoma, Wash.

Belo's acquisition of The Providence Journal Company in 1997 is the largest transaction to date in the Company's history. The acquisition included five NBC affiliates (KING-TV in Seattle/Tacoma, Wash.; KGW-TV in Portland, Ore.; WCNC-TV in Charlotte, N.C.; KHNL-TV in Honolulu, Hawaii; and KTVB in Boise, Idaho); one ABC affiliate (WHAS-TV in Louisville, Ky.); one CBS affiliate (KREM-TV in Spokane, Wash.); two FOX affiliates (KASA-TV in Albuquerque/Santa Fe, N.M., and KMSB-TV in Tucson, Ariz.); and NorthWest Cable News (NWCN) in Seattle/Tacoma. Belo also assumed the management of four television stations through local marketing agreements and became the managing general partner of the Television Food Network, a cable channel in New York, N.Y.

In connection with the acquisition of The Providence Journal Company, Belo agreed to exchange KIRO-TV for a station in another market to comply with Federal Communications Commission regulations, which prohibited a company from owning multiple television stations in a single market. The agreement resulted in Belo's June 1997 acquisition of KMOV-TV (CBS) in St. Louis, Mo.

In early 1997, the company opened its Capital Bureau in Washington, D.C., which houses Washington-based journalists representing the company's 17 network-affiliated television stations as well as *The Dallas Morning News* and *The Providence Journal.*

In February 1997, Belo began operating Local News on Cable in Hampton/Norfolk, Va., through a partnership with Cox Communications and *The Virginian-Ledger,* which also leveraged WVEC-TV's local news programming and marketing strengths.

In December 1997, Belo exchanged its interest in the Television Food Network for KENS-TV (CBS) and KENS-AM in San Antonio.

Belo's WFAA-TV made television history in February 1998 by becoming the first VHF station in the country to transmit a digital signal on a permanent basis.

Belo expanded its cable operations in October 1998 with the addition of NewsWatch on Channel 15 through another partnership with Cox Communications, which extended the company's presence in New Orleans.

On Jan. 1, 1999, Belo launched Texas Cable News (TXCN), the first 24-hour regional cable news channel in Texas. On June 1, 1999, Belo exchanged KXTV (ABC) in Sacramento/Stockton/Modesto for KVUE-TV (ABC) in Austin. By the end of 1999, the combined reach of Belo's Texas television stations reached 67 percent of all television households in Texas.

In November 1999, Belo acquired KTVK (Ind.) in Phoenix, along with the rights to operate KASW-TV, the Phoenix WB affiliate; a 50-percent interest in the Arizona News Channel; and azfamily.com, Arizona's leading Web publishing and design services firm. Also in November 1999, Belo divested KHNL and KASA.

In March 2000, Belo acquired two television stations that it had previously operated under local marketing agreements, KONG-TV (Ind.) in Seattle/Tacoma and KASW-TV in Phoenix, creating the company's first two duopoly markets. Belo began operating KBEJ-TV (UPN) in San Antonio under a local marketing agree-

ment in August 2000.

Belo divested KOTV, its Tulsa station, in December 2000.

In October 2001, Belo acquired KSKN-TV, the WB/UPN affiliate in Spokane, Wash., which the company had operated under a local marketing agreement, creating the company's third duopoly market. In a similar move in March 2002, Belo acquired KTTU-TV, the UPN affiliate in Tucson, which also had been operated through a local marketing agreement, creating Belo's fourth duopoly market.

Between June 2002 and April 2003, Belo formed a joint venture with Time Warner that launched 24-hour cable news channels in Houston, San Antonio and Charlotte to augment its network-affiliated local television stations, KHOU-TV, KENS-TV and WCNC-TV. In October 2003, the company launched the 24/7 News Channel to complement its KTVB operation in Boise. In July 2004, as marketplace needs shifted, Belo discontinued its joint venture relationship with Time Warner in Houston, San Antonio and Charlotte. In November 2004, Belo identified new opportunities in Dallas-Fort Worth and formed a strategic alliance to provide sales, advertising, operations and programming support to KFWD-TV.

Belo sold its only remaining radio station, KENS-AM in San Antonio, in March 2003.

By January 2005, Belo's Television Group reached almost 14 percent of all U.S. television households.

In February 2006, Belo finalized the purchase of WUPL-TV, the UPN affiliate in New Orleans, creating the company's fifth duopoly market with WWL-TV.

Interactive Media

Belo Interactive Media is a corporate department within Belo, established in 1999, that focuses on interactive strategies that extend its core franchises to new media and audiences. Belo operates more than 30 Web sites, interactive alliances and partnerships, and a broad range of Internet-based products and services. By the first quarter 2007, Belo's network of news and information Web sites averaged more than 7 million unique visitors and more than 145 million page views each month.

Belo Corp. Officers

Officers of Belo Corp. are Robert W. Decherd, chairman of the board and chief executive officer; Dunia A. Shive, president and chief operating officer; James M. Moroney III, publisher and chief executive officer of *The Dallas Morning News*; Dennis A. Williamson, executive vice president and chief financial officer; Guy H. Kerr, senior vice president/Law and Government and secretary; and, Marian Spitzberg, senior vice president/ Human Resources.

Other officers include: Donald F. (Skip) Cass Jr., executive vice president; Peter L. Diaz, senior vice president; Richard J. Keilty, senior vice president; Daniel J. Blizzard, vice president/Operations; Russell F. Coleman, vice president/General Counsel and assistant secretary; David M. Duitch, vice president/Capital Bureau; Allison K. Engel, vice president/Corporate Controller; Carey P. Hendrickson, vice president/Human Resources; John P. Irvin, vice president/Facilities Planning; Brenda C. Maddox, vice president/Treasurer & Tax and assistant secretary; J. William Mosley, vice president/Financial Planning & Analysis; Anna R. Nicodemus, vice president/Internal Audit; David S. Starr, vice president/Deputy General Counsel; R. Paul Fry, vice president/Investor Relations and Corporate Communications; and, Steven J. McIntosh, vice president/BACS.

The Dallas Morning News

Officers of *The Dallas Morning News* are James M. Moroney III, publisher and chief executive officer; Robert W. Mong Jr., editor; Evelyn Miller, executive vice president; Gilbert H. Bailon, publisher and editor/ *Al Dia*; Laura Gordon, senior vice president/Marketing; John G. Walsh, senior vice president/Circulation; Alison L. Draper, publisher/*Quick;* and, Fran Wills, senior vice president/Interactive.

Other officers include: James T. Berry Jr., vice president/Financial Planning and Analysis; Cynthia S. Carr, vice president/Strategy; William H. May Jr., vice president/Production; R. Scott Messer, vice president/ Finance; George P. Rodrigue, vice president/managing editor; Darryl G. Thornton, vice president/Human Resources; Keven Ann Willey, vice president/Editorial Page editor; James R. Chandler, vice president/DFW Printing Co.; Bernard F. Heller, vice president/ Advertising; and Victor V. Savelli, vice president/ Interactive Sales.

The Denton Record-Chronicle

Officers of the *Denton Record-Chronicle* include F. William Patterson, publisher/chief executive officer; and Annette Fuller, managing editor.

The Providence Journal

Officers of *The Providence Journal* are Howard G. Sutton, chairman of the board, president /publisher and chief executive officer; Mark T. Ryan, executive vice president/general manager; John J. Palumbo, president/ publisher and general manager, *Rhode Island Monthly*; Sandra J. Radcliffe, senior vice president/Finance; Joel P. Rawson, senior vice president/executive editor; Michael J. Dooley, vice president/Circulation; Debra S. Hill, vice president/Publishing Technology; Wayne Pelland, vice president/Operations; and, Robert B. Whitcomb, vice president and Editorial Page editor.

The Press-Enterprise

Officers of *The Press-Enterprise* include Ronald Redfern, publisher and chief executive officer; Maria DeVarenne, vice president/News and editor; Edward B. Lasak, vice president/Finance and Publishing Operations; Karen Kokiko, vice president/Marketing and Public Affairs; Virginia Neal, vice president/Interactive; and, Kathy W. Weiermiller, vice president/Consumer Sales and Product Logistics.

The Television Group

Officers of Belo's television stations include: Katherine E. Clements, president and general manager, WFAA-TV; David F. Muscari, vice president/Product Development, WFAA-TV; Mike Devlin, vice president and station manager, WFAA-TV; and Angela E. Betasso, vice president/Sales.

Other officers of Belo television stations include: Peter L Diaz, president and general manager, KHOU-TV; Susan A. McEldoon, vice president and station manager, KHOU-TV; Ray B. Heacox, president and general manager, KING-TV, KONG-TV and North-West Cable News; Patrick J. Costello, vice president and executive news director, KING-TV; Mark A. Higgins, president and general manager, KTVK; Jamie T. Aitken, vice president and station manager, KTVK, and general manager, KASW-TV; Marie McGlynn-Peach, vice president/Sales and Marketing, KTVK; Allan R. Cohen, president and general manager, KMOV-TV; Stuart B. Powell, president and general manager, WCNC-TV; Robert G. McGann, president and general Manager, KENS-TV; Lawrence D. Nicholson, president and general Manager, WVEC-TV; Albert B. Brown Jr., president and general manager, WWL-TV; Patti C. Smith, president and general manager, KVUE-TV; Deborah J. Wilson, president and general manager, KREM-TV; Tod A. Smith, president and general manager, KMSB-TV; and Douglas L. Armstrong, president and general manager, KTVB.

Belo Corp. Directors

Robert W. Decherd

Robert W. Decherd has served as a director of Belo since March 1976. He has been Belo's chairman and chief executive officer since January 1987. Decherd served as president of Belo from January 1994 until February 2007 and previously served as president from January 1985 through December 1986. From January 1984 through December 1986, he served as chief operating officer. Decherd is a member of the board of directors, lead director, and chairman of the Executive Committee of Kimberly-Clark Corporation. He also serves on the Advisory Council for Harvard University's Center for Ethics and has been a member of the Graduate Council of *The Harvard Crimson* for more than three decades. He currently serves on the Board of Visitors of the Columbia Graduate School of Journalism.

Henry P. Becton Jr.

Henry P. Becton Jr. has served as a director of Belo since May 1997. He has been president of WGBH Educational Foundation, a public broadcasting organization, since 1984 and served as its general manager from 1978 until 1999. He is the lead director of Becton Dickinson and Company and is a trustee or director of 32 DWS Scudder Fund investment companies or trusts advised by Deutsche Bank. Becton served as a director of The Providence Journal Company from 1992 to 1997.

Becton is a trustee of the Boston Museum of Science and is a member of the boards of directors of the PBS Foundation, Public Radio International and America's Public Television Stations.

Louis E. Caldera

Louis E. Caldera has served as a director of Belo since July 2001. Caldera served as president of the University of New Mexico from August 2003 to February 2006 and is currently a tenured member of the University of New Mexico Law School faculty. He served as vice chancellor for university advancement at The California State University from June 2001 to June 2003. Caldera was Secretary of the Army in the Clinton Administration from July 1998 until January 2001. He previously served as managing director and chief operating officer for the Corporation for National and Community Service, a federal grant-making agency, from September 1997 to June 1998. Caldera also serves on the boards of directors of IndyMac Bancorp, Inc., and Southwest Airlines Co.

France A. Córdova, Ph.D.

France A. Córdova, Ph.D., has served as a director of Belo since May 2003. She has been chancellor of the University of California Riverside since July 2002. From August 1996 to July 2002, she was vice chancellor for research and professor of physics at University of California Santa Barbara. She served as chief scientist of the National Aeronautics and Space Administration (NASA) from 1993 to 1996. Córdova is a member of the board of directors of Edison International and its subsidiary, Southern California Edison, the American Council of Education, and the National Association of State Universities and Land Grant Colleges. She is vice chair of the board of the California Association for Research and Astronomy, and serves on the California Council of Science and Technology and on advisory committees for the National Academy of Sciences.

Judith L. Craven, M.D., M.P.H.

Judith L. Craven, M.D., M.P.H., has served as a director of Belo since December 1992. She is a member of the board of regents of The University of Texas System, a position she has held since March 2001, and serves on the boards of directors of SYSCO Corporation, Luby's, Inc., three Sun America Mutual Fund companies,

and two Variable Annuity Life Insurance Company of America mutual fund companies. From July 1992 until her retirement in October 1998, Craven served as president of the United Way of the Texas Gulf Coast. From 1983 to 1992, she was dean of the School of Allied Health Sciences of the University of Texas Health Science Center at Houston, and from 1987 to 1992 was vice president of multicultural affairs for the University of Texas Health Science Center.

Dealey D. Herndon

Dealey D. Herndon has served as a director of Belo since May 1986. She was president of Herndon, Stauch & Associates, a project and construction management firm, from September 1995 until the business was sold in April 2006. Herndon remains active in the new firm as executive project manager. From January 2001 to October 2001, she also served as director of appointments for Texas Gov. Rick Perry. From 1991 to September 1995, she was executive director of the State Preservation Board of the State of Texas and managed the Texas Capitol Restoration in that capacity. Herndon is trustee emeritus of the National Trust for Historic Preservation in Washington, D.C., and is a board member and past president of the Heritage Society of Austin.

Laurence E. Hirsch

Laurence E. Hirsch has served as a director of Belo since August 1999. He is the chairman of Eagle Materials, Inc., a construction products company, a position he has held since July 1999. He is also the chairman of Highlander Partners, L.P., a private equity firm. Hirsch is the former chairman and chief executive officer of Centex Corporation, one of the nation's largest homebuilders. He was chief executive officer of Centex from July 1988 through March 2004 and chairman of the board from July 1991 through March 2004. Hirsch serves as chairman of the Center for European Policy Analysis in Washington, D.C.

Wayne R. Sanders

Wayne R. Sanders has served as a director of Belo since May 2003. Sanders is the former chairman and chief executive officer of Kimberly-Clark Corporation. He served as president and chief executive officer of Kimberly-Clark from 1991 until September 2002 and as chairman of the board from 1992 until February 2003. Sanders joined Kimberly-Clark in 1975 and held other senior positions prior to 1991. He also serves on the board of directors of Texas Instruments Incorporated. Sanders is a member of the board of trustees of Marquette University and serves as national trustee and governor of the Boys and Girls Clubs of America.

William T. Solomon

William T. Solomon has served as a director of Belo since April 1983. He is chairman of the board of Austin Industries, Inc., a general construction company, a position he has held since 1987. Solomon was chairman and chief executive officer from 1987 to March 2001 and, prior to 1987, president and chief executive officer of Austin Industries. He also serves on the boards of the Hoblitzelle Foundation and the Southwestern Medical Foundation.

M. Anne Szostak

M. Anne Szostak has served as a director of Belo since October 2004. Since June 2004, she has been president and chief executive officer of Szostak Partners, a consulting firm that advises businesses on strategic and human resource issues. From February 1998 until her retirement in June 2004, Szostak served as executive vice president of FleetBoston Financial, a diversified financial services company. She also served as director of Human Resources and Diversity of Fleet from February 1998 until June 2004 and served as chairman and chief executive officer of Bank-Rhode Island from 2001 to 2003. During her 31-year career with Fleet, she held several executive positions. Szostak is a director of Choicepoint, Inc., Spherion Corporation and Tupperware Corporation. She chairs the board of Women & Infants Hospital in Providence and is governor emeritus of Boys and Girls Clubs of America. Szostak is a member of the boards of directors of The Rhode Island Foundation, Women & Infants Hospital Foundation, and Salve Regina University.

Lloyd D. Ward

Lloyd D. Ward has served as a director of Belo since July 2001. Ward has been chairman of BodyBlocks Nutrition Systems, Inc., a manufacturer of snack food and beverages, since April 2003. Since September 2006, he has also served as chief executive officer and general manager of Yuanzhen Org Dairy Co., Ltd., an Inner Mongolia Sino-American Joint Venture producing organic milk in China. Ward was chief executive officer and secretary general of the United States Olympic Committee from October 2001 until March 2003 and was chairman and chief executive officer of iMotors from January 2001 until May 2001. He was chairman and chief executive officer of Maytag Corporation from August 1999 to November 2000, president and chief operating officer from 1998 to August 1999, and executive vice president of Maytag from 1996 to 1998.

J. McDonald Williams

J. McDonald Williams has served as a director of Belo since April 1985. Williams is the former chief executive officer and chairman of Trammell Crow Company, a real estate services firm. He served as chief executive officer from 1977 through July 1994, as chairman of the board from August 1994 until May 2002, and as chairman emeritus from May 2002 until December 2006 when Trammell Crow Company merged with CB Richard Ellis. Williams serves on the boards of directors of Tenet Healthcare Corporation, Abilene Christian University, the Hoblitzelle Foundation, Southern Methodist University's Perkins School of Theology, and the Dallas Foundation for Community Empowerment. He also serves on the Dean's Council of Harvard University's John F. Kennedy School of Government. ☆

Texas Newspapers, Radio and Television Stations

In the list of print and broadcast media below, frequency of publication of subscription newspapers is indicated after the names by the following codes: (D), daily; (S), semiweekly; (TW), triweekly; (BW), biweekly; (SM), semimonthly; (M), monthly; all others are weeklies. "DT" following the call letters of a television station indicates digital transmission. The radio and TV stations are those with valid operating licenses as of April 2007. Not included are those with only construction permits or with applications pending. Sources: Newspapers: 2007 Texas Newspaper Directory, Texas Press Association, Austin; Broadcast Media: Federal Communications Commission Web site: http://svartifoss2.fcc.gov/prod/cdbs/pubacc/prod/cdbs_pa.htm.

Abernathy—Newspaper: Abernathy Weekly Review.

Abilene—Newspaper: Abilene Reporter-News (D). **Radio-AM:** KSLI, 1280 kHz; KWKC, 1340; KYYW, 1470; KZQQ, 1560. **Radio-FM:** KGNZ, 88.1 MHz; KACU, 89.7; KAGT, 90.5; KAQD, 91.3; KULL, 92.5; KFGL, 100.7; KEAN, 105.1; KKHR, 106.3; KEYJ, 107.9. **TV:** KRBC-Ch. 9; KXVA-Ch. 15; KTAB-Ch. 32.

Alamo—Radio-FM: KJAV, 104.9 MHz.

Alamo Heights—Radio-AM: KDRY, 1100 kHz.

Albany—Newspaper: Albany News.

Aledo—Newspaper: The Community News.

Alice—Newspaper: Alice Echo-News-Journal (D). **Radio-AM:** KOPY, 1070 kHz. **Radio-FM:** KOPY, 92.1 MHz; KNDA, 102.9.

Allen—Newspaper: The Allen American. **Radio-FM:** KESN, 103.3 MHz.

Alpine—Newspaper: Alpine Avalanche. **Radio-AM:** KVLF, 1240 kHz. **Radio-FM:** KALP, 92.7 MHz.

Alvarado—Newspapers: Alvarado Post; Alvarado Star.

Alvin—Newspaper: Alvin Sun. **Radio-AM:** KTEK, 1110 kHz. **Radio-FM:** KACC, 89.7 MHz. **TV:** KFTH-DT-Ch. 36; KFTH-Ch. 67.

Alvord—Newspaper: Alvord Gazette.

Amarillo—Newspaper: Amarillo Globe-News (D). **Radio-AM:** KGNC, 710 kHz; KIXZ, 940; KTNZ, 1010; KZIP, 1310; KDJW, 1360; KPUR, 1440. **Radio-FM:** KJRT, 88.3 MHz; KXLV, 89.1; KACV, 89.9; KAVW, 90.7; KXRI, 91.9; KQIZ, 93.1; KMXJ, 94.1; KMML, 96.9; KGNC, 97.9; KPRF, 98.7; KBZD, 99.7; KXGL, 100.9; KATP, 101.9; KRGN, 103.1; KJJP, 105.7. **TV:** KACV-Ch. 2; KAMR-Ch. 4; KVII-Ch. 7; KACV-DT-Ch. 8; KFDA-DT-Ch. 9; KFDA-Ch. 10; KCIT-Ch. 14.

Anahuac—Newspaper: The Progress.

Andrews—Newspaper: Andrews County News (S). **Radio-AM:** KACT, 1360 kHz. **Radio-FM:** KACT, 105.5 MHz.

Anna—Newspaper: The Anna/Melissa Tribune.

Anson—Newspaper: Western Observer. **Radio-FM:** KTLT, 98.1 MHz.

Aransas Pass—Newspapers: Aransas Pass Progress; The Coastal Bend Herald.

Archer City—Newspaper: Archer County News.

Arlington—Radio-FM: KLTY, 94.9 MHz. **TV:** KPXD-DT-Ch. 42; KPXD-Ch. 68.

Aspermont—Newspaper: Stonewall County Courier.

Athens—Newspaper: Athens Daily Review (D). **Radio-AM:** KLVQ, 1410 kHz. **Radio-FM:** KATG, 88.1 MHz.

Atlanta—Newspaper: Atlanta Citizens Journal (S). **Radio-AM:** KPYN, 900 kHz. **Radio-FM:** KNRB, 100.1 MHz.

Aubrey—Newspaper: The Town Charter.

Austin—Newspapers: Austin American-Statesman (D); Austin Business Journal; Austin Chronicle; Daily Texan (D); Texas Observer (BW); Texas Weekly; West Austin News; Westlake Picayune. **Radio-AM:** KLBJ, 590 kHz; KVET, 1300; KFON, 1490. **Radio-FM:** KAZI, 88.7 MHz; KMFA, 89.5; KUT, 90.5; KVRX, 91.7; KLBJ, 93.7; KKMJ, 95.5; KVET, 98.1; KASE, 100.7; KPEZ, 102.3. **TV:** KTBC-Ch. 7; KLRU-Ch. 18; KXAN-DT-CH. 21; KLRU-DT-Ch. 22; KVUE-Ch. 24; KVUE-DT-CH. 33; KXAN-Ch. 36; KEYE-Ch. 42; KEYE-DT-Ch. 43; KNVA-Ch. 54; KTBC-DT-Ch. 56.

Azle—Newspaper: Azle News. **Radio-FM:** KTCY,101.7 MHz.

Baird—Newspapers: Baird Banner; Callahan Co. Star. **Radio-FM:** KORQ, 95.1 MHz.

Balch Springs—Radio-AM: KSKY, 660 kHz.

Ballinger—Newspaper: Ballinger Ledger. **Radio-AM:** KRUN, 1400 kHz. **Radio-FM:** KKCN, 103.1 MHz.

Bandera—Newspapers: The Bandera Bulletin; Bandera County Courier. **Radio-FM:** KEEP, 103.1 MHz.

Bartlett —Newspaper: Tribune-Progress.

Bastrop—Newspaper: Bastrop Advertiser (S) **Radio-FM:** KHIB,

88.5 MHz; KGSR, 107.1.

Bay City—Newspaper: The Bay City Tribune (S). **Radio-FM:** KZBJ, 89.5 MHz; KXGJ, 101.7; KMKS, 102.5.

Baytown—Newspaper: Baytown Sun (D). **Radio-AM:** KWWJ, 1360 kHz. **TV:** KAZH-Ch. 57.

Beaumont—Newspaper: Beaumont Enterprise (D). **Radio-AM:** KLVI, 560 kHz; KZZB, 990; KRCM, 1380; KIKR, 1450. **Radio-FM:** KTXB, 89.7 MHz; KVLU, 91.3; KQXY, 94.1; KYKR, 95.1; KFNC, 97.5; KTCX, 102.5; KQQK, 107.9. **TV:** KFDM-Ch. 6; KBMT-Ch. 12; KFDM-DT-Ch. 21; KITU-DT-Ch. 33; KITU-Ch. 34.

Beeville—Newspaper: Beeville Bee-Picayune (S). **Radio-AM:** KIBL, 1490 kHz. **Radio-FM:** KVFM, 91.3 MHz; KTKO, 105.7; KRXB, 107.1.

Bellaire—Radio-AM: KILE, 1560 kHz.

Bells—Radio-FM: KMKT, 93.1 MHz.

Bellville—Newspaper: Bellville Times. **Radio-AM:** KNUZ, 1090 kHz.

Belton—Newspaper: The Belton Journal. **Radio-AM:** KTON, 940 kHz. **Radio-FM:** KOOC, 106.3 MHz. **TV:** KNCT-Ch. 46.

Benavides—Radio-FM: KXTM, 107.7 MHz.

Benbrook—Radio-AM: KDXX, 107.1 MHz.

Big Lake—Newspaper: Big Lake Wildcat. **Radio-FM:** KPDB, 98.3 MHz; KWTR, 104.1

Big Sandy—Newspaper: Big Sandy-Hawkins Journal. **Radio-FM:** KTAA, 90.7 MHz.

Big Spring—Newspaper: Big Spring Herald (D). **Radio-AM:** KBYG, 1400 kHz; KBST, 1490. **Radio-FM:** KPBD, 89.3 MHz; KBCX, 91.5; KBTS, 94.3; KBST, 95.7. **TV:** KWAB-Ch. 4.

Bishop—Newspaper: Kingsville Record and Bishop News. **Radio-FM:** KMZZ, 106.9 MHz.

Blanco—Newspaper: Blanco County News. **TV:** KNIC-Ch. 17.

Bloomington—Radio-FM: KHVT, 91.5 MHz; KLUB, 106.9.

Blossom—Newspaper: Blossom Times.

Boerne—Newspapers: Boerne Star & Recorder (S); Hill Country View. **Radio-AM:** KBRN, 1500 kHz.

Bogata—Newspaper: Bogata News.

Bonham—Newspaper: Bonham Journal. **Radio-AM:** KFYN, 1420 kHz.

Booker—Newspaper: Booker News.

Borger—Newspaper: Borger News-Herald (D). **Radio-AM:** KQTY, 1490 kHz. **Radio-FM:** KASV, 88.7 MHz; KQFX, 104.3; KQTY, 106.7. **TV:** KEYU-DT-Ch. 31.

Bowie—Newspaper: Bowie News (S). **Radio-AM:** KNTX, 1410 kHz.

Brackettville—Newspaper: The Brackett News.

Brady—Newspaper: Brady Standard-Herald (S). **Radio-AM:** KNEL, 1490 kHz. **Radio-FM:** KNEL, 95.3 MHz.

Breckenridge—Newspaper: Breckenridge American (S). **Radio-AM:** KROO, 1430 kHz. **Radio-FM:** KLXK, 93.5 MHz.

Bremond—Newspaper: Bremond Press.

Brenham—Newspaper: Brenham Banner-Press (D). **Radio-AM:** KWHI, 1280 kHz. **Radio-FM:** KULF, 94.1 MHz; KTTX, 106.1.

Bridgeport—Newspaper: Bridgeport Index. **Radio-FM:** KBOC, 98.3 MHz.

Brookshire—Newspaper: The Times Tribune. **Radio-AM:** KCHN, 1050 kHz.

Brownfield—Newspaper: Brownfield News (S). **Radio-AM:** KKUB, 1300 kHz. **Radio-FM:** KPBB, 88.5 MHz; KLZK, 104.3.

Brownsboro—Newspaper: Brownsboro and Chandler Statesman.

Brownsville—Newspaper: The Brownsville Herald (D). **Radio-AM:** KVNS, 1700 kHz. **Radio-FM:** KBNR, 88.3 MHz; KKPS, 99.5; KTEX, 100.3. **TV:** KVEO-Ch. 23; KVEO-DT-Ch. 24.

Brownwood—Newspaper: Brownwood Bulletin (D). **Radio-AM:** KXYL, 1240 kHz; KBWD, 1380. **Radio-FM:** KPBE, 89.3 MHz; KBUB, 90.3; KHPU, 91.7; KXYL, 96.9; KPSM, 99.3;

KOXE, 101.3.

Bryan—Newspaper: Bryan-College Station Eagle (D). **Radio-AM:** KTAM, 1240 kHz; KAGC, 1510. **Radio-FM:** KORA, 98.3 MHz; KNFX, 99.5; KKYS, 104.7. **TV:** KBTX-Ch. 3; KYLE-Ch. 28.

Buda—Newspaper: Free Press. **Radio-FM:** KROX, 101.5 MHz.

Buffalo—Newspapers: Buffalo Express; Buffalo Press.

Bullard—Newspaper: Bullard Banner News.

Buna—Newspaper: The Buna Beacon.

Burkburnett—Newspaper: Burkburnett Informer Star. **Radio-FM:** KYYI, 104.7 MHz.

Burleson—Newspaper: Burleson Star (S). **Radio-AM:** KHFX, 1460 kHz.

Burnet—Newspapers: Burnet Bulletin; Citizens Gazette. **Radio-AM:** KRHC, 1340 kHz. **Radio-FM:** KBEY, 92.5 MHz; KHLE, 106.9.

Bushland—Radio-FM: KTXP, 91.5 MHz.

Caldwell—Newspaper: Burleson County Tribune. **Radio-FM:** KLTR, 107.3 MHz.

Callisburg—Radio-FM: KPFC, 91.9 MHz.

Calvert—Newspaper: Calvert Tribune.

Cameron—Newspaper: The Cameron Herald. **Radio-AM:** KMIL, 1330 kHz. **Radio-FM:** KNVR, 94.3 MHz; KXCS, 103.9. **Campbell—Radio-FM:** KRVA, 107.1 MHz.

Camp Wood—Radio-FM: KAYG, 99.1 MHz.

Canadian—Newspaper: Canadian Record.

Canton—Newspapers: Canton Herald; Van Zandt News. **Radio-AM:** KRDH, 1510 kHz.

Canyon—Newspaper: The Canyon News (S). **Radio-AM:** KZRK, 1550 kHz. **Radio-FM:** KWTS, 91.1 MHz; KPUR, 107.1; KZRK, 107.9.

Canyon Lake—Newspaper: Times Guardian.

Carrizo Springs—Newspaper: Carrizo Springs Javelin. **Radio-AM:** KBEN, 1450 kHz. **Radio-FM:** KCZO, 92.1 MHz.

Carrollton—Radio-AM: KJON, 850 kHz.

Carthage—Newspaper: Panola Watchman (S). **Radio-AM:** KGAS, 1590 kHz. **Radio-FM:** KTUX, 98.9 MHz; KGAS, 104.3.

Castroville—Newspaper: Castroville News Bulletin.

Cedar Hill—Newspapers: Cedar Hill Today.

Cedar Park—Newspaper: Hill Country News Weekender. **Radio-FM:** KDHT, 93.3 MHz.

Celina—Newspaper: Celina Record.

Center—Newspaper: The Light & Champion (TW). **Radio-AM:** KDET, 930 kHz. **Radio-FM:** KQBB, 100.5 MHz.

Centerville—Newspaper: Centerville News. **Radio-FM:** KUZN, 105.9 MHz.

Chico—Newspaper: Chico Texan.

Childress—Newspaper: The Childress Index (TW). **Radio-AM:** KCTX, 1510 kHz. **Radio-FM:** KCTX, 96.1 MHz.

Cisco—Newspaper: Cisco Press (S).

Clarendon—Newspaper: Clarendon Enterprise. **Radio-FM:** KEFH, 99.3 MHz.

Clarksville—Newspaper: Clarksville Times. **Radio-AM:** KCAR, 1350 kHz. **Radio-FM:** KGAP, 98.5 MHz.

Claude—Newspaper: The Claude News. **Radio-FM:** KARX, 95.7 MHz.

Clear Lake—Newspaper: The Citizen.

Cleburne—Newspaper: Cleburne Times-Review (D). **Radio-AM:** KCLE, 1140 kHz.

Cleveland—Newspaper: Cleveland Advocate. **Radio-FM:** KTHT, 97.1 MHz.

Clifton—Newspaper: Clifton Record. **Radio-FM:** KWOW, 104.1 MHz.

Clute—Newspaper: The Facts (D).

Clyde—Newspaper: Clyde Journal.

Coahoma—Radio-FM: KWDC, 105.5 MHz.

Cockrell Hill—Radio-AM: KRVA, 1600 kHz.

Coleman—Newspaper: Chronicle & Democrat-Voice (S). **Radio-AM:** KSTA, 1000 kHz. **Radio-FM:** KQBZ, 102.3 MHz.

College Station—Newspaper: The Battalion (D). **Radio-AM:** KZNE, 1150 kHz, WTAW, 1620. **Radio-FM:** KEOS, 89.1 MHz; KLGS, 89.9; KAMU, 90.9; KNDE, 95.1. **TV:** KAMU-DT-Ch. 12; KAMU-Ch. 15.

Colorado City—Newspaper: Colorado City Record. **Radio-AM:** KVMC, 1320 kHz. **Radio-FM:** KAUM, 107.1 MHz.

Columbus—Newspapers: The Banner Press Newspaper; Colorado County Citizen. **Radio-FM:** KULM, 98.3 MHz.

Comanche—Newspaper: Comanche Chief. **Radio-AM:** KCOM, 1550 kHz. **Radio-FM:** KYOX, 94.3 MHz.

Comfort—Newspaper: The Comfort News. **Radio-FM:** KCOR, 95.1 MHz.

Commerce—Newspaper: Commerce Journal. **Radio-FM:** KETR, 88.9 MHz; KYJC, 91.3.

Conroe—Newspaper: The Courier (D). **Radio-AM:** KJOJ, 880 kHz; KYOK, 1140. **Radio-FM:** KAFR, 88.3 MHz; KHPT, 106.9. **TV:** KPXB-DT-Ch. 5; KTBU-DT-Ch. 42; KPXB-Ch. 49; KTBU-CH. 55.

Cooper—Newspaper: Cooper Review.

Coppell—Newspaper: Citizens' Advocate.

Copperas Cove—Newspaper: Copperas Cove Leader-Press (S). **Radio-FM:** KSSM, 103.1 MHz.

Corpus Christi—Newspapers: Corpus Christi Caller-Times (D); Coastal Bend Legal & Business News (D); South Texas Catholic (BW). **Radio-AM:** KCTA, 1030 kHz; KCCT, 1150; KSIX, 1230; KKTX, 1360; KUNO, 1400; KEYS, 1440. **Radio-FM:** KKLM, 88.7 MHz; KEDT, 90.3; KBNJ, 91.7; KMXR, 93.9; KBSO, 94.7; KZFM, 95.5; KLTG, 96.5; KRYS, 99.1.**TV:** KIII-Ch. 3; KRIS-Ch. 6; KZTV-Ch. 10; KEDT-Ch. 16; KORO-Ch. 28.

Corrigan—Newspaper: Corrigan Times.

Corsicana—Newspaper: Corsicana Daily Sun (D). **Radio-AM:** KAND, 1340 kHz.

Crane—Newspaper: Crane News. **Radio-AM:** KXOI, 810 kHz. **Radio-FM:** KMMZ, 101.3 MHz.

Crawford—Newspaper: Lone Star Iconoclast (M).

Creedmoor—Radio-AM: KZNX, 1530 kHz.

Crockett—Newspaper: Houston Co. Courier (S). **Radio-AM:** KIVY, 1290 kHz. **Radio-FM:** KCKT, 88.5 MHz; KIVY, 92.7; KBHT, 93.5.

Cross Plains—Newspaper: Cross Plains Review.

Crowell—Newspaper: Foard Co. News.

Crowley—Newspaper: Crowley Star.

Crystal Beach—Radio-FM: KSTB, 101.5 MHz; KPTI, 105.3.

Crystal City—Newspaper: Zavala County Sentinel. **Radio-FM:** KHER, 94.3 MHz.

Cuero—Newspaper: Cuero Record. **Radio-FM:** KTLZ, 89.9 MHz; KLTO, 97.7.

Cypress—Radio-AM: KYND, 1520 kHz.

Daingerfield—Newspaper: The Bee. **Radio-AM:** KNGR, 1560 kHz.

Dalhart—Newspaper: Dalhart Texan (TW). **Radio-AM:** KXIT, 1240 kHz. **Radio-FM:** KXIT, 96.3 MHz.

Dallas—Newspapers: The Dallas Morning News (D); Al Día; Dallas Business Journal; Daily Campus; Daily Commercial Record (D); Dallas Examiner; Oak Cliff Tribune; Park Cities News; Park Cities People; Texas Jewish Post; Texas Lawyer; The White Rocker. **Radio-AM:** KLIF, 570 kHz; KGGR, 1040; KRLD, 1080; KFXR, 1190; KTCK, 1310; KNIT, 1480. **Radio-FM:** KNON, 89.3 HMz; KERA, 90.1; KCBI, 90.9; KVTT, 91.7; KZPS, 92.5; KBFB, 97.9; KLUV, 98.7; KJKK, 100.3; WRR, 101.1; KDMX, 102.9; KKDA, 104.5; KLLI, 105.3. **TV:** KDFW-Ch. 4; WFAA-Ch. 8; WFAA-DT-Ch. 9; KERA-Ch. 13; KERA-DT-Ch. 14; KDFI-Ch. 27; KDAF-DT-Ch. 32; KDAF-Ch. 33; KDFW-DT-Ch. 35; KXTX-Ch. 39; KXTX-DT-Ch. 40; KDTX-Ch. 58.

Decatur—Newspaper: Wise County Messenger (S). **Radio-FM:** KDKR, 91.3 MHz; KRNB, 105.7. **TV:** KMPX-Ch. 29; KMPX-DT-Ch. 30.

Deer Park—Newspaper: Deer Park Progress.

De Kalb—Newspaper: De Kalb News (S).

De Leon—Newspapers: De Leon Free Press.

Dell City—Newspaper: Hudspeth County Herald.

Del Mar Hills—Radio-AM: KVOZ, 890 kHz.

Del Rio—Newspaper: Del Rio News-Herald (D). **Radio-AM:** KTJK, 1230 kHz; KWMC, 1490. **Radio-FM:** KDLK, 94.1 MHz; KTDR, 96.3. **TV:** KTRG-Ch. 10.

Del Valle—Radio-AM: KIXL, 970 kHz.

Denison—Newspapers: Herald Democrat (D); The Pottsboro/Denison Press. **Radio-AM:** KYNG, 950 kHz.

Denton—Newspaper: Denton Record-Chronicle (D). **Radio-FM:** KNTU, 88.1 MHz; KFZO, 99.1; KHKS, 106.1. **TV:** KDTN-Ch. 2; KDTN-DT-Ch. 43.

Denver City—Newspaper: Denver City Press.

Deport—Newspaper: Deport Times.

DeSoto—Newspapers: Focus Daily News (D); DeSoto Today.

Detroit—Newspaper: Detroit Weekly.

Devine—Newspaper: Devine News. **Radio-FM:** KRPT, 92.5 MHz.

Diboll—Newspaper: Diboll Free Press. **Radio-AM:** KSML, 1260 kHz. **Radio-FM:** KAFX, 95.5 MHz.

Dilley—Radio-FM: KVWG, 95.3 MHz; KLMO, 98.9.

Dimmitt—Newspaper: Castro County News. **Radio-AM:** 1470 kHz. **Radio-FM:** KNNK, 100.5 MHz.

Doss—Radio-FM: KGLF, 88.1 MHz.

Dripping Springs—Newspapers: Dripping Springs Century News; The News-Dispatch. **Radio-FM:** KXXS, 104.9 MHz.

Dublin—Newspaper: Dublin Citizen.

Dumas—Newspaper: Moore County News-Press (S). **Radio-AM:** KDDD, 800 kHz. **Radio-FM:** KDDD, 95.3 MHz.

Duncanville—Newspaper: Duncanville Today.

Eagle Lake—Newspaper: Eagle Lake Headlight.

Eagle Pass—Newspapers: The News Gram; Eagle Pass News-Guide. **Radio-AM:** KEPS, 1270 kHz. **Radio-FM:** KEPI, 88.7 MHz; KEPX, 89.5; KINL, 92.7. **TV:** KVAW-Ch. 16.

East Bernard—Newspaper: East Bernard Express.

Eastland—Newspaper: Eastland Telegram (S). **Radio-AM:** KEAS, 1590 kHz. **Radio-FM:** KATX, 97.7 MHz.

Eden—Newspaper: The Eden Echo.

Edgewood—Newspaper: Edgewood Enterprise.

Edinburg—Radio-AM: KURV, 710 kHz. **Radio-FM:** KOIR, 88.5 MHz; KBFM, 104.1; KVLY, 107.9.

Edna—Newspaper: Jackson Co. Herald-Tribune. **Radio-AM:** KTMR, 1130 kHz. **Radio-FM:** KEZB, 96.1 MHz.

El Campo—Newspaper: El Campo Leader-News (S). **Radio-AM:** KULP, 1390 kHz. **Radio-FM:** KIOX, 96.9 MHz.

Eldorado—Newspaper: Eldorado Success.

Electra—Newspaper: Electra Star-News. **Radio-FM:** KOLI, 94.9 MHz.

Elgin—Newspaper: Elgin Courier. **Radio-FM:** KKLB, 92.5 MHz.

El Paso—Newspaper: El Paso Times (D). **Radio-AM:** KROD, 600 kHz; KTSM, 690; KAMA, 750; KBNA, 920; KXPL, 1060; KSVE, 1150; KVIV, 1340; KHEY, 1380; KELP, 1590; KHRO, 1650. **Radio-FM:** KTEP, 88.5 MHz; KKLY; 89.5; KVER, 91.1; KOFX, 92.3; KSII, 93.1; KINT, 93.9; KYSE, 94.7; KLAQ, 95.5; KHEY, 96.3; KBNA, 97.5; KTSM, 99.9; KPRR, 102.1. **TV:** KDBC-Ch. 4; KVIA-Ch. 7; KTSM-Ch. 9; KCOS-Ch. 13; KFOX-Ch. 14; KFOX-DT-CH. 15; KTSM-DT-Ch. 16; KVIA-DT-Ch. 17; KDBC-DT-Ch. 18; KINT-Ch. 26; KCOS-DT-Ch. 30; KSCE-Ch. 38; KTFN-Ch. 65.

Emory—Newspaper: Rains Co. Leader.

Ennis—Newspaper: Ennis Daily News (D).

Everman—Newspaper: South Tarrant Star.

Fabens—Radio-FM: KPAS, 103.1 MHz.

Fairfield—Newspapers: Freestone County Times; The Fairfield Recorder. **Radio-FM:** KNES, 99.1 MHz.

Falfurrias—Newspaper: Falfurrias Facts. **Radio-AM:** KLDS, 1260 kHz. **Radio-FM:** KDFM, 103.3 MHz; KPSO, 106.3.

Fannett—Radio-FM: KZFT, 90.5 MHz.

Farmersville—Newspaper: Farmersville Times. **Radio-AM:** KFCD, 990 kHz. **Radio-FM:** KXEZ, 92.1 MHz.

Farwell—Newspaper: State Line Tribune. **Radio-AM:** 830 kHz; KIJN, 1060. **Radio-FM:** KIJN, 92.3 MHz; KICA, 98.3. **TV:** KPTF-Ch. 18.

Ferris—Newspaper: The Ellis County Press. **Radio-AM:** KDFT, 540 kHz.

Flatonia—Newspaper: The Flatonia Argus.

Floresville—Newspapers: Floresville Chronicle-Journal; Wilson County News. **Radio-FM:** KWCB, 89.7 MHz; KTFM, 94.1.

Flower Mound—Radio-FM: KTYS, 96.7 MHz.

Floydada—Newspaper: Floyd Co. Hesperian-Beacon. **Radio-AM:** KFLP, 900 kHz. **Radio-FM:** KFLP, 106.1 MHz.

Follett—Newspaper: The Golden Spread.

Forney—Newspaper: Forney Messenger.

Fort Davis—Newspaper: Jeff Davis Co. Mt. Dispatch.

Fort Stockton—Newspaper: Fort Stockton Pioneer. **Radio-AM:** KFST, 860 kHz. **Radio-FM:** KFST, 94.3 MHz.

Fort Worth—Newspapers: Fort Worth Business Press; Commercial Recorder (D); Fort Worth Star-Telegram (D); Fort Worth Weekly; NW Tarrant Co. Times-Record. **Radio-AM:** WBAP, 820 kHz; KFJZ, 870; KHVN, 970; KFLC, 1270; KKGM, 1630. **Radio-FM:** KTCU, 88.7 MHz; KLNO, 94.1; KSCS, 96.3; KEGL, 97.1; KPLX, 99.5; KDGE, 102.1; KMVK, 107.5. **TV:** KXAS-Ch. 5; KTVT-Ch. 11; KTXA-DT-Ch. 18;

KTVT-DT-Ch. 19; KTXA-Ch. 21; KXAS-DT-Ch. 41; KFWD-DT-Ch. 51; KFWD-Ch. 52.

Franklin—Newspapers: Franklin Advocate; Franklin News Weekly. **Radio-FM:** KZTR, 101.9 MHz.

Frankston—Newspaper: The Frankston Citizen. **Radio-AM:** KKBM, 890 kHz. **Radio-FM:** KOYE, 96.7 MHz.

Fredericksburg—Newspaper: Standard/Radio Post. **Radio-AM:** KNAF, 910 kHz. **Radio-FM:** KNAF, 105.7 MHz. **TV:** KCWX-Ch. 2.

Freeport—Radio-AM: KBRZ, 1460 kHz. **Radio-FM:** KJOJ, 103.3 MHz.

Freer—Newspaper: Freer Press. **Radio-FM:** KPBN, 90.7 MHz; KBRA, 95.9.

Friendswood—Newspapers: Friendswood Journal; Friendswood Reporter News.

Friona—Newspaper: Friona Star. **Radio-FM:** KGRW, 94.7 MHz.

Frisco—Newspaper: The Frisco Enterprise. **Radio-AM:** KATH, 910 kHz.

Fritch—Newspaper: The Eagle Press.

Gail—Newspaper: Borden Star.

Gainesville—Newspaper: Gainesville Daily Register (D). **Radio-AM:** KGAF, 1580 kHz. **Radio-FM:** KSOC, 94.5 MHz.

Galveston—Newspaper: Galveston Co. Daily News (D). **Radio-AM:** KHCB, 1400 kHz; KGBC, 1540. **Radio-FM:** KOVE, 106.5 MHz. **TV:** KLTJ-Ch. 22; KTMD-Ch. 47; KTMD-DT-Ch. 48.

Ganado—Radio-FM: KZAM, 104.7 MHz.

Gardendale—Radio-FM: KFZX, 102.1 MHz.

Garland—Radio-AM: KAAM, 770 kHz. **TV:** KUVN-Ch. 23; KUVN-DT-Ch. 24.

Garrison—Newspaper: Garrison In The News.

Gatesville—Newspaper: Gatesville Messenger and Star Forum (S). **Radio-FM:** KYAR, 98.3 MHz.

Georgetown—Newspapers: Sunday Sun; Williamson Co. Sun. **Radio-FM:** KHFI, 96.7 MHz; KINV, 107.7.

Giddings—Newspaper: Giddings Times & News. **Radio-FM:** KANJ, 91.1 MHz.

Gilmer—Newspaper: Gilmer Mirror (S). **Radio-FM:** KFRO, 95.3 MHz.

Gladewater—Newspaper: Gladewater Mirror. **Radio-AM:** KEES, 1430 kHz.

Glen Rose—Newspaper: Glen Rose Reporter. **Radio-FM:** KTFW, 92.1 MHz.

Goldthwaite—Newspaper: Goldthwaite Eagle.

Goliad—Newspaper: The Texan Express. **Radio-FM:** KHMC, 95.9 MHz.

Gonzales—Newspaper: Gonzales Inquirer (S). **Radio-AM:** KCTI, 1450 kHz. **Radio-FM:** KMLR, 106.3 MHz.

Gorman—Newspaper: Gorman Progress.

Graford—Newspaper: Lake Country Sun.

Graham—Newspaper: The Graham Leader (S). **Radio-AM:** KSWA, 1330 kHz. **Radio-FM:** KWKQ, 94.7 MHz.

Granbury—Newspaper: Hood Co. News (S). **Radio-AM:** KPIR, 1420 kHz.

Grand Prairie—Radio-AM: KKDA, 730 kHz.

Grand Saline—Newspaper: Grand Saline Sun.

Grandview—Newspaper: Grandview Tribune.

Grapeland—Newspaper: Grapeland Messenger.

Greenville—Newspaper: Herald-Banner (D). **Radio-AM:** KGVL, 1400 kHz. **Radio-FM:** KTXG, 90.5 MHz; KIKT, 93.5. **TV:** KTAQ-DT-Ch. 46; KTAQ-Ch. 47.

Gregory—Radio-FM: KPUS, 104.5 MHz.

Groesbeck—Newspaper: Groesbeck Journal.

Groom—Newspaper: Groom/McLean News.

Groves—Radio-FM: KCOL, 92.5 MHz.

Groveton—Newspaper: Groveton News.

Gun Barrel City—Newspaper: Cedar Creek Pilot.

Hale Center—Newspaper: Hale Center American.

Hallettsville—Newspaper: Hallettsville Tribune-Herald. **Radio-AM:** KHLT, 1520 kHz. **Radio-FM:** KTXM, 99.9 MHz.

Haltom City—Radio-FM: KDBN, 93.3 MHz.

Hamilton—Newspaper: Hamilton Herald-News. **Radio-AM:** KCLW, 900 kHz.

Hamlin—Newspaper: Hamlin Herald. **Radio-FM:** KCDD, 103.7 MHz.

Harker Heights—Radio-FM: KUSJ, 105.5 MHz.

Harlingen—Newspaper: Valley Morning Star (D). **Radio-AM:**

KGBT, 1530 kHz. **Radio-FM:** KMBH, 88.9 MHz; KFRQ, 94.5; KBTQ, 96.1. **TV:** KGBT-Ch. 4; KGBT-DT-Ch. 31; KMBH-DT-Ch. 38; KLUJ-Ch. 44; KMBH-Ch. 60.

Hart—Newspaper: Hart Beat.

Haskell—Newspaper: Haskell Free Press. **Radio-FM:** KVRP, 97.1 MHz.

Hawkins—Newspaper: Big Sandy-Hawkins Journal.

Hearne—Newspaper: Hearne Democrat. **Radio-FM:** KVJM, 103.1 MHz.

Hebbronville—Newspapers: Hebbronville View; Jim Hogg Co. Enterprise. **Radio-FM:** KAZF, 91.9 MHz; KEKO, 101.7.

Helotes—Radio-FM: KONO, 101.1 MHz.

Hemphill—Newspaper: The Sabine Co. Reporter. **Radio-AM:** KPBL, 1240 kHz. **Radio-FM:** KTHP, 103.9 Mhz.

Hempstead—Newspaper: Waller Co. News-Citizen. **Radio-FM:** KEZB, 105.3 MHz.

Henderson—Newspaper: Henderson Daily News (D). **Radio-AM:** KWRD, 1470 kHz.

Henrietta—Newspaper: Clay County Leader.

Hereford—Newspaper: Hereford Brand (D). **Radio-AM:** KPAN, 860 kHz. **Radio-FM:** KJNZ, 103.5 MHz; KPAN, 106.3.

Hewitt—Newspaper: Hometown News.

Hico—Newspaper: Hico News Review.

Highland Park—Radio-AM: KVCE, 1160 kHz. **Radio-FM:** KVIL, 103.7 MHz.

Highlands—Newspaper: Highlands Star/Crosby Courier.

Highland Village—Radio-FM: KWRD, 100.7 Mhz.

Hillsboro—Newspaper: Hillsboro Reporter (S). **Radio-AM:** KHBR, 1560 kHz. **Radio-FM:** KBRQ, 102.5 MHz.

Holliday—Newspaper: Archer County Advocate.

Hondo—Newspaper: Hondo Anvil Herald. **Radio-AM:** KCWM, 1460 kHz. **Radio-FM:** KMFR, 105.9 MHz.

Honey Grove—Newspaper: Weekly Gazette.

Hooks—Radio-FM: KPWW, 95.9 MHz.

Hornsby—Radio-FM: KOOP, 91.7 MHz.

Houston—Newspapers: Houston Business Journal; Houston Chronicle (D); Daily Court Review (D); Houston Forward Times; Houston Informer & Texas Freeman; Jewish Herald-Voice; Texas Catholic Herald (SM). **Radio-AM:** KILT, 610 kHz; KTRH, 740; KBME, 790; KEYH, 850; KPRC, 950; KLAT, 1010; KNTH, 1070; KQUE, 1230; KXYZ, 1320; KCOH, 1430; KMIC, 1590. **Radio-FM:** KUHF, 88.7 MHz; KPFT, 90.1; KTSU, 90.9; KTRU, 91.7; KKRW, 93.7; KTBZ, 94.5; KHJZ, 95.7; KHMX, 96.5; KBXX, 97.9; KODA, 99.1; KILT, 100.3; KLOL, 101.1; KMJQ, 102.1; KLTN, 102.9; KRBE, 104.1; KHCB, 105.7. **TV:** KPRC-Ch. 2; KUHT-Ch. 8; KUHT-DT-Ch. 9; KHOU-Ch. 11; KTRK-Ch. 13; KETH-Ch. 14; KTXH-DT-Ch. 19; KTXH-Ch. 20; KETH-DT-Ch. 24; KRIV-Ch. 26; KRIV-DT-Ch. 27; KHOU-DT-Ch. 31; KTRK-DT-Ch. 32; KPRC-DT-Ch. 35; KHCW-DT-Ch. 38; KHCW-Ch. 39; KZJL-Ch. 61.

Howe—Newspaper: Texoma Enterprise. **Radio-FM:** KHYI, 95.3 MHz.

Hubbard—Newspaper: Hubbard City News.

Hudson—Radio-FM: KLSN, 96.3 MHz.

Humble—Radio-AM: KGOL, 1180 kHz. **Radio-FM:** KSBJ, 89.3 MHz.

Huntington—Radio-FM: KSML, 101.9 MHz.

Huntsville—Newspaper: Huntsville Item (D). **Radio-AM:** KHCH, 1410 kHz; KHVL, 1490. **Radio-FM:** KSHU, 90.5 MHz; KSAM, 101.7.

Hurst—Radio-AM: KMNY, 1360 kHz.

Hutto—Radio-FM: KYLR, 92.1 MHz.

Idalou—Newspaper: Idalou Beacon. **Radio-FM:** KRBL, 105.7 MHz.

Ingleside—Newspaper: Ingleside Index. **Radio-FM:** KJKE, 107.3 MHz.

Ingram—Newspaper: West Kerr Current. **Radio-FM:** KTXI, 90.1 MHz.

Iowa Park—Newspaper: Iowa Park Leader.

Iraan—Newspaper: Iraan News.

Irving—TV: KSTR-DT-Ch. 48; KSTR-Ch. 49.

Jacksboro—Newspapers: Jacksboro Gazette-News; Jack County Herald. **Radio-FM:** KJKB, 95.5 MHz.

Jacksonville—Newspaper: Jacksonville Daily Progress (D). **Radio-AM:** KEBE, 1400 kHz. **Radio-FM:** KBJS, 90.3 MHz; KLJT, 102.3; KOOI, 106.5. **TV:** KETK-Ch. 56.

Jasper—Newspaper: The Jasper Newsboy. **Radio-AM:** KCOX, 1350 kHz. **Radio-FM:** KTXJ, 102.7 MHz; KJAS, 107.3.

Jefferson—Newspaper: Jefferson Jimplecute. **Radio-FM:** KHCJ, 91.9 MHz; KJTX, 104.5.

Jewett—Newspaper: Jewett Messenger.

Johnson City—Newspaper: Johnson City Record-Courier. **Radio-FM:** KFAN, 107.9 MHz.

Joshua—Newspaper: Joshua Star.

Jourdanton—Radio-FM: KLEY, 95.7 MHz.

Junction—Newspaper: Junction Eagle. **Radio-AM:** KMBL, 1450 kHz. **Radio-FM:** KOOK, 93.5 MHz.

Karnes City—Newspaper: The Countywide. **Radio-AM:** KAML, 990 kHz. **Radio-FM:** KTXX, 103.1 MHz.

Katy—Newspaper: Katy Times (S). **TV:** KNWS-Ch. 51.

Kaufman—Newspaper: Kaufman Herald.

Keene—Newspaper: Keene Star. **Radio-FM:** KJCR; 88.3 MHz.

Kenedy—Radio-AM: KAML, 990 kHz. **Radio-FM:** KTNR, 92.1 MHz.

Kerens—Newspaper: Kerens Tribune. **Radio-FM:** KRVF, 106.9 MHz.

Kermit—Newspaper: Winkler Co. News. **Radio-AM:** KERB, 600 kHz. **Radio-FM:** KERB, 106.3 MHz.

Kerrville—Newspapers: Kerrville Daily Times (D); Hill Country Community Journal. **Radio-AM:** KERV, 1230 kHz. **Radio-FM:** KKER, 88.7 MHz; KHKV, 91.1; KRNH, 92.3; KRVL, 94.3. **TV:** KMYS-Ch. 35.

Kilgore—Newspaper: Kilgore News Herald (D). **Radio-AM:** KBGE, 1240 kHz. **Radio-FM:** KTPB, 88.7 MHz; KKTX, 96.1.

Killeen—Newspaper: Killeen Daily Herald (D). **Radio-AM:** KRMY, 1050 kHz. **Radio-FM:** KNCT, 91.3 MHz; KIIZ, 92.3. **TV:** KAKW-DT-Ch. 13; KAKW-Ch. 62.

Kingsville—Newspaper: Kingsville Record & Bishop News (S). **Radio-AM:** KINE, 1330 kHz. **Radio-FM:** KTAI, 91.1 MHz; KKBA, 92.7; KFTX, 97.5.

Kirbyville—Newspaper: Kirbyville Banner.

Knox City—Newspaper: Knox Co. News.

Kress—Newspaper: Kress Chronicle.

Krum—Radio-FM: KNOR, 93.7 MHz.

La Feria—Newspaper: La Feria News.

La Grange—Newspaper: The Fayette County Record (S). **Radio-AM:** KVLG, 1570 kHz. **Radio-FM:** KBUK, 104.9 MHz.

Lake Dallas—Newspaper: The Lake Cities Sun. **TV:** KLDT-DT-Ch. 54.

Lake Jackson—Radio-FM: KYBJ, 91.1 MHz; KHTC, 107.5.

Lakeway—Newspaper: Lake Travis View.

Lamesa—Newspaper: Lamesa Press Reporter (S). **Radio-AM:** KPET, 690 kHz. **Radio-FM:** KBKN, 91.3 MHz; KTXC, 104.7.

Lampasas—Newspaper: Lampasas Dispatch Record (S). **Radio-AM:** KCYL, 1450 kHz.

Lancaster—Newspaper: Lancaster Today.

La Porte—Newspaper: Bayshore Sun (S). **Radio-FM:** KIOL, 103.7 MHz.

Laredo—Newspaper: Laredo Morning Times (D). **Radio-AM:** KLAR, 1300 kHz; KLNT, 1490. **Radio-FM:** KHOY, 88.1 MHz; KBNL, 89.9; KJBZ, 92.7; KQUR, 94.9; KRRG, 98.1; KNEX, 106.1. **TV:** KGNS-Ch. 8; KVTV-Ch. 13; KLDO-Ch. 27.

La Vernia—Newspaper: La Vernia News.

Leakey—Newspaper: The Leakey Star (BW). **Radio-FM:** KBLT, 104.3 MHz.

Leander—Radio-FM: KHHL, 98.9 MHz.

Leonard—Newspaper: Leonard Graphic.

Levelland—Newspaper: Levelland and Hockley Co. News-Press (S). **Radio-AM:** KLVT, 1230 kHz. **Radio-FM:** KLVT, 105.3 MHz.

Lewisville—Radio-FM: KESS, 107.9 MHz.

Lexington—Newspaper: Lexington Leader.

Liberty—Newspaper: Liberty Vindicator (S). **Radio-FM:** KSHN, 99.9 MHz.

Liberty Hill—Newspaper: The Liberty Hill Independent.

Lindale—Newspapers: Lindale News & Times.

Linden—Newspaper: Cass County Sun.

Little Elm—Newspaper: The Little Elm Journal.

Littlefield—Newspaper: Lamb Co. Leader-News (S). **Radio-AM:** KZZN, 1490 kHz.

Livingston—Newspaper: Polk Co. Enterprise (S). **Radio-AM:** KETX, 1440 kHz. **Radio-FM:** KETX, 92.3 MHz.

Llano—Newspaper: Llano News. **Radio-FM:** KAJZ, 96.3 MHz;

KITY, 102.9. **TV:** KXAM-Ch. 14.

Lockhart—Newspaper: Lockhart Post-Register; Lockhart Times-Sentinel. **Radio-AM:** KFIT, 1060 kHz.

Lometa—Radio-FM: KACQ, 101.9 MHz.

Longview—Newspaper: Longview News-Journal (D). **Radio-AM:** KFRO, 1370 kHz. **Radio-FM:** KYKX, 105.7 MHz. **TV:** KFXK-Ch. 51; KCEB-Ch. 54.

Lorenzo—Radio-FM: KKCL, 98.1 MHz.

Lubbock—Newspaper: Lubbock Avalanche-Journal (D). **Radio-AM:** KRFE, 580 kHz; KFYO, 790; KJTV, 950; KKAM, 1340; KJDL, 1420; KBZO, 1460; KDAV, 1590. **Radio-FM:** KTXT, 88.1 MHz; KOHM, 89.1; KAMY, 90.1; KKLU, 90.9; KXTQ, 93.7; KFMX, 94.5; KLLL, 96.3; KQBR, 99.5; KONE, 101.1; KZII, 102.5; KEJS, 106.5. **TV:** KTXT-Ch. 5; KCBD-DT-Ch. 9; KCBD-Ch. 11; KLBK-Ch. 13; KPTB-Ch. 16; KPTB-DT-Ch. 25; KAMC-Ch. 28; KJTV- Ch. 34; KTXT-DT-Ch. 39.

Lufkin—Newspaper: Lufkin Daily News (D). **Radio-AM:** KRBA, 1340 kHz. **Radio-FM:** KLDN, 88.9 MHz; KSWP, 90.9; KAVX, 91.9. KYBI, 100.1; KYKS, 105.1. **TV:** KTRE-Ch. 9; KTRE-DT-CH. 11.

Luling—Newspaper: Luling Newsboy and Signal. **Radio-FM:** KAMX, 94.7 MHz.

Lytle—Newspapers: Leader News; Medina Valley Times. **Radio-FM:** KZLV, 91.3 MHz.

Mabank—Newspaper: The Monitor (S).

Madisonville—Newspaper: Madisonville Meteor. **Radio-AM:** KMVL, 1220 kHz. **Radio-FM:** KHML, 91.5 MHz; KAGG, 96.1; KMVL, 100.5.

Malakoff—Newspaper: Malakoff News. **Radio-FM:** KCKL, 95.9 MHz.

Manor—Radio-AM: KELG, 1440 kHz.

Mansfield—Newspaper: Mansfield News-Mirror.

Marble Falls—Newspapers: The Highlander (S); The River Cities Daily Tribune (D). **Radio-FM:** KBMD, 88.5 MHz.

Marfa—Newspaper: The Big Bend Sentinel.

Marion—Radio-AM: KBIB, 1000 kHz.

Markham—Radio-FM: KZRC, 92.5 MHz.

Marlin—Newspaper: The Marlin Democrat. **Radio-FM:** KLRK, 92.9 MHz.

Marshall—Newspapers: Marshall News Messenger (D); Lone Star Eagle. **Radio-AM:** KCUL, 1410 kHz; KMHT, 1450. **Radio-FM:** KBWC, 91.1 MHz; KCUL, 92.3; KMHT, 103.9.

Mart—Newspaper: Mart Messenger. **Radio-FM:** KSUR, 88.9 MHz.

Mason—Newspaper: Mason County News. **Radio-FM:** KOTY, 95.7 MHz; KHLB, 102.5.

Matador—Newspaper: Motley County Tribune.

Mathis—Newspaper: Mathis News.

McAllen—Newspaper: The Monitor (D). **Radio-AM:** KRIO, 910 kHz. **Radio-FM:** KHID, 88.1 MHz; KVMV, 96.9; KGBT, 98.5. **TV:** KNVO-Ch. 48.

McCamey—Newspaper: McCamey News. **Radio-FM:** KPBM, 95.3 MHz.

McCook—Radio FM: KCAS, 91.5 MHz

McGregor—Newspaper: McGregor Mirror and Crawford Sun.

McKinney—Newspaper: McKinney Courier-Gazette (D); Collin County Commercial Record. **Radio-FM:** KNTU, 88.1 MHz.

Melissa—Newspaper: The Anna/Melissa Tribune.

Memphis—Newspaper: Hall County Herald. **Radio-FM:** KLSR, 105.3 MHz.

Menard—Newspaper: Menard News and Messenger.

Mercedes—Newspaper: Mercedes Enterprise. **Radio-FM:** KHKZ, 106.3 MHz.

Meridian—Newspaper: Bosque Co. News.

Merkel—Newspaper: Merkel Mail. **Radio-AM:** KMXO, 1500 kHz. **Radio-FM:** KHXS, 102.7 MHz.

Mertzon—Radio-FM: KMEO, 91.9 MHz.

Mesquite—Radio-FM: KEOM, 88.5 MHz.

Mexia—Newspaper: Mexia Daily News (D). **Radio-AM:** KRQX, 1590 kHz. **Radio-FM:** KWGW, 104.9 MHz.

Miami—Newspaper: Miami Chief.

Midland—Newspaper: Midland Reporter-Telegram (D). **Radio-AM:** KCRS, 550 kHz; KWEL, 1070; KJBC, 1150; KMND, 1510. **Radio-FM:** KPBJ, 90.1 MHz; KAQQ, 90.9; KNFM, 92.3; KZBT, 93.3; KQRX, 95.1; KCRS, 103.3; KCHX, 106.7. **TV:** KMID-Ch. 2; KUPB-Ch. 18.

Midlothian—Newspaper: Midlothian Mirror.

Miles—Newspaper: Miles Messenger.

Mineola—Newspaper: Mineola Monitor. **Radio-FM:** KMOO,

99.9 MHz.

Mineral Wells—Newspaper: Mineral Wells Index (D). **Radio-AM:** KJSA, 1120 kHz. **Radio-FM:** KFWR, 95.9 MHz.

Mirando City—Radio-FM: KBDR, 100.5 MHz.

Mission—Newspaper: Progress-Times. **Radio-AM:** KIRT, 1580 kHz. **Radio-FM:** KQXX, 105.5 MHz.

Missouri City—Radio-FM: KPTY, 104.9 MHz.

Monahans—Newspaper: The Monahans News (S). **Radio-AM:** KLBO, 1330 kHz. **Radio-FM:** KBAT, 99.9 MHz.

Moody—Newspaper: The Courier.

Morton—Newspaper: Morton Tribune.

Moulton—Newspaper: Moulton Eagle.

Mount Pleasant—Newspaper: Daily Tribune (D). **Radio-AM:** KIMP, 960 kHz.

Mount Vernon—Newspaper: Mount Vernon Optic-Herald.

Muenster—Newspaper: Muenster Enterprise. **Radio-FM:** KZZA, 106.7 MHz.

Muleshoe—Newspaper: Muleshoe Journal. **Radio-FM:** KMUL, 103.1 MHz.

Munday—Newspaper: The Munday Courier.

Murphy—Newspaper: Murphy Monitor.

Nacogdoches—Newspaper: Nacogdoches Daily Sentinel (D). **Radio-AM:** KSFA, 860 kHz. **Radio-FM:** KSAU, 90.1 MHz; KJCS, 103.3; KTBQ, 107.7. **TV:** KYTX-Ch. 19.

Naples—Newspaper: The Monitor.

Navasota—Newspaper: The Navasota Examiner. **Radio-AM:** KWBC, 1550 kHz. **Radio-FM:** KHTZ, 92.5 MHz.

Nederland—Radio-AM: KBED, 1510 kHz.

Needville—Newspaper: The Gulf Coast Tribune.

New Boston—Newspaper: Bowie County Citizen Tribune (S). **Radio-AM:** KNBO, 1530 kHz. **Radio-FM:** KEWL, 95.1 MHz; KZRB, 103.5.

New Braunfels—Newspaper: Herald-Zeitung (D). **Radio-AM:** KGNB, 1420 kHz. **Radio-FM:** KNBT, 92.1 MHz.

Newton—Newspaper: Newton Co. News.

New Ulm—Newspaper: New Ulm Enterprise. **Radio-FM:** KNRG, 92.3 MHz.

Nixon—Newspaper: Cow Country Courier.

Nocona—Newspaper: Nocona News.

Nolanville—Radio-FM: KLFX, 107.3 MHz.

Normangee—Newspaper: Normangee Star.

Odem—Newspaper: Odem-Edroy Times. **Radio-FM:** KLHB, 98.3 MHz.

Odessa—Newspaper: Odessa American (D). **Radio-AM:** KFLB, 920 kHz; KOZA, 1230; KRIL, 1410. **Radio-FM:** KBMM, 89.5 MHz; KFLB, 90.5 MHz; KOCV, 91.3; KMRK, 96.1; KMCM, 96.9; KODM, 97.9; KHKX, 99.1; KQLM, 107.9. **TV:** KOSA-Ch. 7; KWES-Ch. 9; KPEJ-Ch. 24; KWWT-Ch. 30; KPBT-Ch. 36; KMLM-Ch. 42.

O'Donnell—Newspaper: O'Donnell Index-Press.

Olney—Newspaper: The Olney Enterprise.

Olton—Newspaper: Olton Enterprise.

Orange—Newspaper: Orange Leader (D). **Radio-AM:** KOGT, 1600 kHz. **Radio-FM:** KKMY, 104.5 MHz; KIOC, 106.1.

Ore City—Radio-FM: KAZE, 106.9 MHz.

Overton—Newspaper: Overton Press. **Radio-FM:** KPXI, 100.7 MHz.

Ozona—Newspaper: Ozona Stockman. **Radio-FM:** KYXX, 94.3 MHz.

Paducah—Newspaper: Paducah Post.

Paint Rock—Newspaper: Concho Herald.

Palacios—Newspaper: Palacios Beacon. **Radio-FM:** KROY, 99.7 MHz.

Palestine—Newspaper: Palestine Herald Press (D). **Radio-AM:** KNET, 1450 kHz. **Radio-FM:** KYFP, 89.1 MHz; KYYK, 98.3.

Pampa—Newspaper: Pampa News (D). **Radio-AM:** KGRO, 1230 kHz. **Radio-FM:** KAVO, 90.9 MHz; KOMX, 100.3.

Panhandle—Newspaper: Panhandle Herald; White Deer News.

Paris—Newspaper: Paris News (D). **Radio-AM:** KZHN, 1250 kHz; KPLT, 1490. **Radio-FM:** KHCP, 89.3 MHz; KOYN, 93.9; KBUS, 101.9; KPLT, 107.7.

Pasadena—Newspaper: Pasadena Citizen (D). **Radio-AM:** KIKK, 650 kHz; KLVL, 1480. **Radio-FM:** KFTG, 88.1 MHz; KKBQ, 92.9.

Pearland—Newspapers: Pearland Journal; Pearland Reporter

News.

Pearsall—Newspaper: Frio-Nueces Current. **Radio-AM:** KVWG, 1280 kHz. **Radio-FM:** KRIO, 104.1 MHz.

Pecan Grove—Radio-AM: KREH, 900 kHz.

Pecos—Newspaper: Pecos Enterprise (S). **Radio-AM:** KIUN, 1400 kHz. **Radio-FM:** KGEE, 97.3 MHz; KPTX, 98.3.

Perryton—Newspaper: Perryton Herald (S). **Radio-AM:** KEYE, 1400 kHz. **Radio-FM:** KEYE, 96.1 MHz.

Petersburg—Newspaper: The Paper.

Pflugerville—Newspaper: Pflugerville Pflag. **Radio-AM:** KOKE, 1600 kHz.

Pharr—Newspaper: Advance News Journal. **Radio-AM:** KVJY, 840 kHz.

Pilot Point—Newspaper: Pilot Point Post-Signal. **Radio-FM:** KZMP, 104.9 MHz.

Pittsburg—Newspaper: Pittsburg Gazette. **Radio-FM:** KGWP, 91.1 MHz; KSCN, 96.9; KDVE, 103.1.

Plains—Newspaper: Cowboy Country News. **Radio-FM:** KPHS, 90.3 MHz.

Plainview—Newspaper: Plainview Daily Herald (D). **Radio-AM:** KVOP, 1090 kHz; KREW, 1400. **Radio-FM:** KPMB, 88.5 MHz; KBAH, 90.5; KWLD, 91.5; KSTQ, 97.3; KRIA, 103.9; KKYN, 106.9.

Plano—Newspaper: Plano Star Courier (D). **Radio-AM:** KMKI, 620 kHz.

Pleasanton—Newspaper: Pleasanton Express. **Radio-AM:** KFNI, 1380 kHz.

Point Comfort—Radio-FM: KJAZ, 94.1 MHz.

Port Aransas—Newspaper: Port Aransas South Jetty.

Port Arthur—Newspaper: Port Arthur News (D). **Radio-AM:** KDEI, 1250 kHz; KOLE, 1340. **Radio-FM:** KQBU, 93.3 MHz; KTJM, 98.5. **TV:** KBTV-Ch. 4.

Port Isabel—Newspaper: Port Isabel/South Padre Press (S). **Radio-FM:** KNVO, 101.1 MHz.

Portland—Newspaper: Portland News. **Radio-FM:** KSGR, 91.1 MHz; KMJR, 105.5.

Port Lavaca—Newspaper: Port Lavaca Wave (S). **Radio-FM:** KITE, 93.3 MHz.

Port Neches—Radio-AM: KUHD, 1150 kHz.

Post—Newspaper: Post Dispatch. **Radio-FM:** KPOS, 107.3 MHz.

Pottsboro—Newspaper: Pottsboro/Denison Press.

Prairie View—Radio-FM: KPVU, 91.3 MHz.

Premont—Radio-FM: KMFM, 100.7 MHz.

Presidio—Newspaper: The International Presidio Paper.

Princeton—Newspaper: Princeton Herald.

Quanah—Newspaper: Quanah Tribune-Chief (S). **Radio-AM:** KREL, 1150 kHz. **Radio-FM:** KWFB, 100.9 MHz.

Quinlan—Newspaper: The Quinlan-Tawakoni News.

Quitaque—Newspaper: Valley Tribune.

Quitman—Newspaper: Wood Co. Democrat.

Ralls—Newspaper: Crosby County News. **Radio-AM:** KCLR, 1530 kHz.

Ranger—Newspaper: Ranger Times. **Radio-FM:** KCUB, 98.5 MHz.

Rankin—Newspaper: Rankin News.

Raymondville—Newspaper: Chronicle/Willacy Co. News. **Radio-AM:** KSOX, 1240 kHz. **Radio-FM:** KBUC, 102.1 MHz; KBIC, 105.7.

Red Oak—Newspaper: Ellis Co. Chronicle.

Refugio—Newspaper: Refugio Co. Press. **Radio-FM:** KTKY, 106.1 MHz.

Richardson—Radio-AM: KKLF, 1700 kHz.

Richmond—Newspaper: Radio-AM. (see Rosenberg)

Riesel—Newspaper: Riesel Rustler.

Rio Grande City—Newspaper: Rio Grande Herald. **Radio-FM:** KQBO, 107.5 MHz. **TV:** KTLM-Ch. 40.

Rising Star—Newspaper: Rising Star.

Robert Lee—Newspaper: Observer/Enterprise.

Robinson—Radio-FM: KHCK, 107.9 MHz.

Robstown—Newspaper: Nueces Co. Record-Star. **Radio-AM:** KROB, 1510 kHz. **Radio-FM:** KLUX, 89.5 MHz; KSAB, 99.9; KMIQ, 104.9.

Rochester—Newspaper: Twin Cities News.

Rockdale—Newspaper: Rockdale Reporter. **Radio-FM:** KRXT, 98.5 MHz.

Rockport—Newspapers: Rockport Pilot (S); The Coastal Bend Herald. **Radio-FM:** KKPN, 102.3 MHz.

Rocksprings—Newspaper: Texas Mohair Weekly.

Rockwall—Newspaper: Rockwall County News.

Rollingwood—Radio-AM: KJCE, 1370 kHz.

Roma—Newspaper: South Texas Reporter. **Radio-FM:** KBMI, 97.7 MHz.

Rosebud—Newspaper: Rosebud News.

Rosenberg—Newspaper: Rosenberg Herald-Coaster (D). **Radio-AM:** KRTX, 980 kHz. **TV:** KXLN-Ch. 45; KXLN-DT-Ch. 46.

Rotan—Newspaper: Rotan Advance-Star-Record.

Round Rock—Newspaper: Round Rock Leader (TW). **Radio-FM:** KNLE, 88.1 MHz; KFMK, 105.9.

Rowena—Newspaper: Rowena Press.

Rowlett—Newspaper: The Rowlett Lakeshore Times.

Rudolph—Radio-FM: KTER, 90.7 MHz.

Rusk—Newspaper: Cherokeean Herald. **Radio-AM:** KTLU, 1580 kHz. **Radio-FM:** KWRW, 97.7 MHz.

Sachse—Newspaper: Sachse News.

Saint Jo—Newspaper: Saint Jo Tribune.

San Angelo—Newspaper: San Angelo Standard-Times (D). **Radio-AM:** KGKL, 960 kHz; KKSA, 1260; KCRN, 1340. **Radio-FM:** KLRW, 88.5 MHz; KNAR, 89.3; KUTX, 90.1; KDCD, 92.9; KCRN, 93.9; KIXY, 94.7; KGKL, 97.5; KELI, 98.7; KCLL, 100.1; KWFR, 101.9; KMDX, 106.1; KSJT, 107.5. **TV:** KSAN-Ch. 3; KIDY-Ch. 6; KLST-Ch. 8.

San Antonio—Newspapers: San Antonio Business Journal; Commercial Recorder (D); Express-News (D); North San Antonio Times; Today's Catholic. **Radio-AM:** KTSA, 550 kHz; KSLR, 630; KKYX, 680; KTKR, 760; KONO, 860; KRDY, 1160; WOAI, 1200; KZDC, 1250; KAHL, 1310; KCOR, 1350; KCHL, 1480; KEDA, 1540. **Radio-FM:** KPAC, 88.3 MHz; KSTX, 89.1; KSYM, 90.1; KYFS, 90.9; KRTU, 91.7; KROM, 92.9; KXXM, 96.1; KAJA, 97.3; KISS, 99.5; KCYY, 100.3; KQXT, 101.9; KJXK, 102.7; KZEP, 104.5; KXTN, 107.5. **TV:** WOAI-Ch. 4; KENS-Ch. 5; KLRN-DT-Ch. 8; KLRN-Ch. 9; KSAT-Ch. 12; KHCE-DT-Ch. 16; KHCE-Ch. 23; KABB-Ch. 29; KVDA-DT-Ch. 38; KWEX-DT-Ch. 39; KWEX-Ch. 41; KSAT-DT-Ch. 48; WOAI-DT-Ch. 58; KVDA-Ch. 60.

San Augustine—Newspaper: San Augustine Tribune. **Radio-FM:** KQSI, 92.5 MHz.

San Benito—Newspaper: San Benito News (S).

San Diego—Newspaper: Duval County Picture (S). **Radio-FM:** KUKA, 105.9 MHz.

Sanger—Newspaper: Sanger Courier. **Radio-FM:** KVRK, 89.7 MHz; KTDK, 104.1.

San Juan—Radio-AM: KUBR, 1210 kHz.

San Marcos—Newspaper: San Marcos Daily Record (D). **Radio-AM:** KUOL, 1470 kHz. **Radio-FM:** KTSW, 89.9 MHz; KBPA, 103.5.

San Saba—Newspaper: San Saba News & Star. **Radio-AM:** KBAL, 1410 kHz. **Radio-FM:** KBAL, 106.1 MHz.

Santa Fe—Radio-FM: KJIC, 90.5 MHz.

Schertz—Radio-FM: KBBT, 98.5 MHz.

Schulenburg—Newspaper: Schulenburg Sticker.

Seabrook—Radio-FM: KROI, 92.1 MHz.

Seadrift—Radio-FM: KMAT, 105.1 MHz.

Seagoville—Newspaper: Suburbia News.

Seagraves—Newspaper: Tri County Tribune.

Sealy—Newspaper: The Sealy News (S).

Seguin—Newspaper: Seguin Gazette-Enterprise (D). **Radio-AM:** KWED, 1580 kHz. **Radio-FM:** KSMG, 105.3 MHz.

Seminole—Newspaper: Seminole Sentinel (S). **Radio-AM:** KIKZ, 1250 kHz. **Radio-FM:** KSEM, 106.3 MHz.

Seymour—Newspaper: Baylor Co. Banner. **Radio-AM:** KSEY, 1230 kHz. **Radio-FM:** KSEY, 94.3 MHz.

Shamrock—Newspaper: County Star-News.

Shepherd—Newspaper: San Jacinto News-Times.

Sherman—Newspaper: Herald Democrat (D). **Radio-AM:** KJIM, 1500 kHz. **TV:** KXII-Ch. 12; KXII-DT-Ch. 20.

Shiner—Newspaper: The Shiner Gazette.

Silsbee—Newspaper: Silsbee Bee. **Radio-AM:** KSET, 1300 kHz. **Radio-FM:** KAYD, 101.7 MHz.

Silverton—Newspaper: Briscoe Co. News.

Sinton—Newspaper: San Patricio Co. News. **Radio-AM:** KDAE, 1590 kHz. **Radio-FM:** KNCN, 101.3 MHz; KOUL, 103.7.

Slaton—Newspaper: Slaton Slatonite. **Radio-FM:** KJAK, 92.7 MHz.

Smithville—Newspaper: Smithville Times.

Snyder—Newspaper: Snyder Daily News (D). **Radio-AM:**

KSNY, 1450 kHz. **Radio-FM:** KLYD, 98.9 MHz; KSNY, 101.5. **TV:** KPCB-DT-Ch. 10; KPCB-Ch. 17.

Somerset—Radio-AM: KYTY, 810 kHz.

Sonora—Newspaper: Devil's River News. **Radio-FM:** KHOS, 92.1 MHz.

South Padre Island—Radio-FM: KESO, 92.7 MHz; KZSP, 95.3.

Spearman—Newspaper: Hansford Co. Reporter-Statesman. **Radio-FM:** KTOT, 89.5 MHz; KXDJ, 98.3.

Springtown—Newspaper: Springtown Epigraph. **Radio-FM:** KSQX, 89.1 MHz.

Spur—Newspaper: Texas Spur.

Stamford—Newspaper: Stamford American. **Radio-AM:** KVRP, 1400 kHz. **Radio-FM:** KJTZ, 106.9 MHz.

Stanton—Newspaper: Martin Co. Messenger. **Radio-FM:** KFRI, 88.1 MHz.

Stephenville—Newspaper: Stephenville Empire-Tribune (D). **Radio-AM:** KSTV, 1510 kHz. **Radio-FM:** KQXS, 89.1 MHz; KEQX, 89.7.

Sterling City—Radio-FM: KNRX, 96.5 MHz.

Stratford—Newspaper: Stratford Star.

Sudan—Newspaper: Sudan Beacon-News.

Sugar Land—Newspaper: The Sugar Land Scoop.

Sulphur Springs—Newspaper: News-Telegram (D). **Radio-AM:** KSST, 1230 kHz. **Radio-FM:** KSCH, 95.9 MHz.

Sweetwater—Newspaper: Sweetwater Reporter (D). **Radio-AM:** KXOX, 1240 kHz. **TV:** KTXS-Ch. 12.

Taft—Newspaper: Taft Tribune.

Tahoka—Newspaper: Lynn Co. News. **Radio-FM:** KMMX, 100.3 MHz; KAMZ, 103.5.

Talco—Newspaper: Talco Times.

Tatum—Newspaper: Trammel Trace Tribune. **Radio-FM:** KXAL, 100.3 MHz.

Taylor—Newspaper: Taylor Daily Press (D). **Radio-AM:** KWNX, 1260 kHz. **Radio-FM:** KXBT, 104.3 MHz.

Teague—Newspaper: Teague Chronicle.

Temple—Newspaper: Temple Daily Telegram (D). **Radio-AM:** KTEM, 1400 kHz. **Radio-FM:** KVLT, 88.5 MHz; KBDE, 89.9; KLTD, 101.7. **TV:** KCEN-Ch. 6; KCEN-DT-Ch. 9.

Terrell—Newspaper: Terrell Tribune (D). **Radio-AM:** KPYK, 1570 kHz.

Terrell Hills—Radio-AM: KLUP, 930 kHz. **Radio-FM:** KPWT, 106.7 MHz.

Texarkana—Newspaper: Texarkana Gazette (D). **Radio-AM:** KCMC, 740 kHz; KTFS, 940; KKTK, 1400. **Radio-FM:** KTXK, 91.5 MHz; KTAL, 98.1; KKYR, 102.5. **TV:** KTAL-Ch. 6.

Texas City—Radio-AM: KYST, 920 kHz.

Thorndale—Newspaper: Thorndale Champion. **Radio-FM:** KLGO, 99.3 MHz.

Three Rivers—Newspaper: The Progress. **Radio-FM:** KEMA, 94.5 MHz.

Throckmorton—Newspaper: Throckmorton Tribune.

Timpson—Newspaper: Timpson & Tenaha News.

Tomball—Radio-AM: KSEV, 700 kHz.

Trenton—Newspaper: Trenton Tribune.

Trinity—Newspaper: Trinity Standard.

Tulia—Newspaper: Tulia Herald. **Radio-AM:** KTUE, 1260 kHz. **Radio-FM:** KBTE, 104.9 MHz.

Tuscola—Newspaper: Jim Ned Journal (BW).

Tye—Radio-FM: KBCY, 99.7 MHz.

Tyler—Newspapers: Tyler Morning Telegraph (D); Catholic East Texas (SM). **Radio-AM:** KTBB, 600 kHz; KZEY, 690; KGLD, 1330; KYZS, 1490. **Radio-FM:** KVNE, 89.5 MHz; KGLY, 91.3; KDOK, 92.1; KTYL, 93.1; KNUE, 101.5; KKUS, 104.1. **TV:** KLTV-Ch. 7; KLTV-DT-Ch. 10.

Universal City—Radio-AM: KSAH, 720 kHz.

University Park—Radio-AM: KTNO, 1440 kHz; KZMP, 1540.

Uvalde—Newspaper: Uvalde Leader-News (S). **Radio-AM:** KVOU, 1400 kHz. **Radio-FM:** KBNU, 93.9 MHz; KUVA, 102.3; KVOU, 104.9. **TV:** KPXL-Ch. 26.

Valley Mills—Newspaper: Valley Mills Progress.

Van—Newspaper: Van Banner.

Van Alstyne—Newspaper: Van Alstyne Leader.

Van Horn—Newspaper: Van Horn Advocate.

Vega—Newspaper: Vega Enterprise.

Vernon—Newspaper: Vernon Daily Record (D). **Radio-AM:**

KVWC, 1490 kHz. **Radio-FM:** KVWC, 103.1 MHz.

Victoria—Newspaper: Victoria Advocate (D). **Radio-AM:** KVNN, 1340 kHz; KNAL, 1410. **Radio-FM:** KAYK, 88.5 MHz; KXBJ, 89.3; KVRT, 90.7; KQVT, 92.3; KVIC, 95.1; KTXN, 98.7; KEPG, 100.9; KIXS, 107.9. **TV:** KVCT-Ch. 19; KAVU-Ch. 25.

Vidor—Newspaper: Vidor Vidorian.

Waco—Newspapers: The Waco Citizen; Waco Tribune-Herald (D). **Radio-AM:** KBBW, 1010 kHz; KWTX, 1230; KRZI, 1660. **Radio-FM:** KVLW, 88.1 MHz; KBCT, 94.5; KBGO, 95.7; KWTX, 97.5; WACO, 99.9; KWBU, 103.3. **TV:** KWTX-Ch. 10; KWBU-DT-Ch 20; KXXV-Ch. 25; KXXV-DT-Ch. 26; KWBU-Ch. 34; KWKT-Ch. 44; KWTX-DT-Ch. 53.

Wake Village—Radio-FM: KHTA, 92.5 MHz.

Wallis—Newspaper: Wallis News-Review.

Waxahachie—Newspaper: Waxahachie Daily Light (D). **Radio-AM:** KBEC, 1390 kHz.

Weatherford—Newspaper: Weatherford Democrat (D). **Radio-AM:** KZEE, 1220 kHz. **Radio-FM:** KMQX, 88.5 MHz; KYQX, 89.5.

Weimar—Newspaper: Weimar Mercury.

Wells—Radio-FM: KVLL, 94.7 MHz.

Wellington—Newspaper: Wellington Leader.

Weslaco—Radio-AM: KRGE, 1290 kHz. **TV:** KRGV-Ch. 5; KRGV-DT-Ch. 13.

West—Newspaper: West News.

West Lake Hills—Radio-AM: KTXZ, 1560 kHz.

West Odessa—Radio-FM: KLVW, 88.7 MHz.

Wharton—Newspaper: Wharton Journal-Spectator (S). **Radio-AM:** KANI, 1500 kHz.

Wheeler—Newspaper: The Wheeler Times. **Radio-FM:** KPDR, 90.5 MHz.

Whitehouse—Newspaper: Tri County Leader. **Radio-FM:** KISX, 107.3 MHz.

White Oak—Newspaper: White Oak Independent. **Radio-FM:** KAJK, 99.3 MHz.

Whitesboro—Newspaper: Whitesboro News-Record. **Radio-FM:** KMAD, 102.5 MHz.

Whitewright—Newspaper: Whitewright Sun.

Whitney—Newspaper: Lake Whitney Views (M).

Wichita Falls—Newspaper: Times-Record-News (D). **Radio-AM:** KWFS, 1290. **Radio-FM:** KMCU, 88.7 MHz; KMOC, 89.5; KZKL, 90.5; KNIN, 92.9; KLUR, 99.9; KWFS, 102.3; KQXC, 103.9; KBZS, 106.3. **TV:** KFDX-Ch. 3; KAUZ-Ch. 6; KJTL-Ch. 18.

Willis—Radio-FM: KVST, 99.7 MHz.

Wills Point—Newspaper: Wills Point Chronicle.

Wimberley—Newspaper: Wimberley View (S).

Winfield—Radio-FM: KALK, 97.7 MHz.

Winnie—Newspaper: The Hometown Press. **Radio-FM:** KKHT, 100.7 MHz.

Winnsboro—Newspaper: Winnsboro News. **Radio-FM:** KWNS, 104.7 MHz.

Winona—Radio-FM: KBLZ, 102.7 MHz.

Winters—Newspaper: Winters Enterprise. **Radio-FM:** KNCE, 96.1 MHz.

Wolfe City—Newspaper: Wolfe City Mirror.

Wolfforth—Radio-FM: KAIQ, 95.5 MHz. **TV:** KLCW-Ch. 22.

Woodville—Newspaper: Tyler Co. Booster. **Radio-AM:** KWUD, 1490 kHz.

Wylie—Newspaper: The Wylie News. **Radio-AM:** KHSE, 700 kHz.

Yoakum—Newspaper: Yoakum Herald-Times. **Radio-FM:** KYKM, 92.5 MHz.

Yorktown—Newspaper: Yorktown News-View.

Zapata—Newspaper: Zapata Co. News. **Radio-FM:** KBAW, 93.5 MHz.. ☆

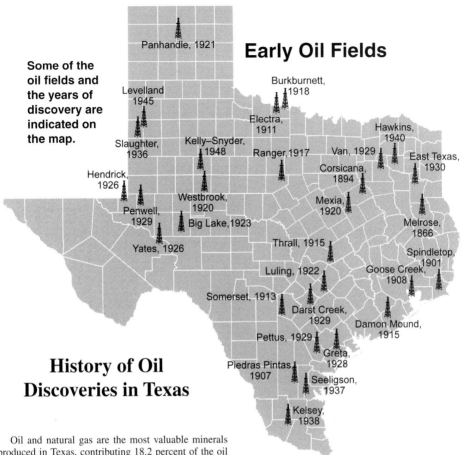

Early Oil Fields

Some of the oil fields and the years of discovery are indicated on the map.

Panhandle, 1921

Burkburnett, 1918

Levelland 1945

Electra, 1911

Hawkins, 1940

Slaughter, 1936

Kelly–Snyder, 1948

Ranger, 1917

Van, 1929

East Texas, 1930

Hendrick, 1926

Corsicana, 1894

Westbrook, 1920

Penwell, 1929

Big Lake, 1923

Mexia, 1920

Melrose, 1866

Yates, 1926

Thrall, 1915

Spindletop, 1901

Luling, 1922

Goose Creek, 1908

Somerset, 1913

Darst Creek, 1929

Damon Mound, 1915

Pettus, 1929

Greta, 1928

Piedras Pintas, 1907

Seeligson, 1937

Kelsey, 1938

History of Oil Discoveries in Texas

Oil and natural gas are the most valuable minerals produced in Texas, contributing 18.2 percent of the oil production in the United States in 2006, and nearly 30 percent of the gas production in the nation in 2005, the latest figures available.

Oil and gas have been produced from most areas of Texas and from rocks of all geologic eras except the Pre-cambrian. All of the major sedimentary basins of Texas have produced some oil or gas.

The Permian Basin of West Texas has yielded large quantities of oil since the Big Lake discovery in 1923, although there was a smaller discovery in the Westbrook field in Mitchell County three years earlier.

The 1923 discovery, Santa Rita No. 1 in Reagan County, was on University of Texas land, and it and Texas A&M University both have benefitted from the royalties.

Although large quantities of petroleum have been produced from rocks of Permian age, production in the area also occurs from older Paleozoic rocks. Pro-duction from rocks of Paleozoic age occurs primarily from North Central Texas westward to New Mexico and southwestward to the Rio Grande, but there is also sig-nificant Paleozoic production in North Texas.

Mesozoic rocks are the primary hydrocarbon reser-voirs of the East Texas Basin and the area south and east of the Balcones Fault Zone. Cenozoic sandstones are the main reservoirs along the Gulf Coast and offshore state waters.

Earliest Oil

Indians found oil seeping from the soils of Texas long before the first Europeans arrived. They told explorers that the fluid had medicinal values. The first record of Europeans using crude oil, however, was the caulking of boats in 1543 by survivors of the DeSoto expedition near Sabine Pass.

Melrose, in Nacogdoches County, was the site in 1866 of the first drilled well to produce oil in Texas. The driller was Lyne T. Barret.

Barret used an auger, fastened to a pipe and rotated by a cogwheel driven by a steam engine — a basic prin-ciple of rotary drilling that has been used since, although with much improvement.

In 1867 Amory (Emory) Starr and Peyton F. Edwards brought in a well at Oil Springs, in the same area.

Other wells followed and Nacogdoches County was the site of Texas' first commercial oil field, pipeline and effort to refine crude. Several thousand barrels of oil were produced there during these years.

First major refinery, 1899

Other oil was found in crudely dug wells in Bexar County in 1889 and in Hardin County in 1893. The three small wells in Hardin County led to the creation of two small refineries in 1896 and 1898.

Spindletop field in Jefferson County in 1902. Texas Energy Museum, Beamont, photo.

But it was not until June 9, 1894, that Texas had a major discovery. This occurred in the drilling of a water well for the city of Corsicana. Oil caused that well to be abandoned, but a company formed in 1895 drilled several producing oil wells.

The first well-equipped refinery in Texas was built there in 1898, and this plant, which shipped its first production in 1899, usually is called the state's first refinery, despite the earlier efforts. Discovery of the Powell Field, also near Corsicana, followed in 1900.

Spindletop, 1901

Jan. 10, 1901, is the most famous date in Texas petroleum history. This is the date that the great gusher erupted in the oil well being drilled at Spindletop, near Beaumont, by a mining engineer, Capt. A. F. Lucas.

Thousands of barrels of oil flowed before the well could be capped. This was the first salt dome oil discovery. Spindletop created a sensation throughout the world, and encouraged exploration and drilling in Texas that has continued since.

Texas oil production increased from 836,039 barrels in 1900 to 4,393,658 in 1901; and in 1902 Spindletop alone produced 17,421,000 barrels, or 94 percent of the state's production. Prices dropped to 3 cents a barrel, an all-time low.

Offshore, 1908

The first offshore drilling was in shallow northern Galveston Bay, where the Goose Creek Field was discovered in 1908. Several dry holes followed and the field was abandoned. But a gusher in 1916 created the real boom there. A water-well drilling outfit on the W. T. Waggoner Ranch in Wichita County hit oil, bringing in the Electra Field in 1911.

Salt dome oil fields followed at Damon Mound in 1915, Barbers Hill in 1916, and Blue Ridge in 1919.

In 1917 came the discovery of the Ranger Field in Eastland County. The Burkburnett Field in Wichita County was discovered in 1919.

About this time, oil discoveries brought a short era of swindling, with oil stock promotion and selling on a nationwide scale. It ended after a series of trials in federal courts.

The Mexia Field in Limestone County was discovered in 1920, and the second Powell Field in Navarro County in 1924.

Another great area really developed in 1921 in the Panhandle, a field with sensational oil and gas discoveries in Hutchinson and contiguous counties and the booming of Borger.

The Luling Field was opened in 1922, and 1925 saw the comeback of Spindletop with a production larger than that of the original field.

In 1925 Howard County was opened for production. Hendricks in Winkler County opened in 1926 and Raccoon Bend, Austin County, opened in 1927. Sugar Land was the most important Texas oil development in 1928.

The Darst Creek Field was opened in 1929. In the same year, new records of productive sand thickness were set for the industry at Van, Van Zandt County. Pettus was another contribution of 1929 in Bee County.

East Texas Field

The East Texas field, biggest of them all, was discovered near Turnertown and Joinerville, Rusk County, by veteran wildcatter C. M. (Dad) Joiner, in October 1930. The success of this well — drilled on land condemned many times by geologists of the major companies — was followed by the biggest leasing campaign in history.

The field soon was extended to Kilgore, Longview and northward. The East Texas field brought overproduction and a rapid sinking of the price. Private attempts were made to prorate production, but without much success.

On Aug. 17, 1931, Gov. Ross S. Sterling ordered the National Guard into the field, which he placed under martial law. This drastic action was taken after the Texas Railroad Commission had been enjoined from enforcing production restrictions. After the complete shutdown, the Texas Legislature enacted legal proration, the system of regulation still utilized.

West Texas

The most significant subsequent oil discoveries in Texas were those in West Texas. In 1936, oil was discovered west of Lubbock in the Duggan Field in Cochran County.

Originally it was thought to be one of two fields, it and the adjacent Slaughter Field, but in 1940 the Railroad Commission ruled that the two produced from one reservoir, called Slaughter. The prolific Levelland Field, in Cochran and Hockley counties, was discovered in 1945. A discovery well in Scurry County on Nov. 21, 1948, was the first of several major developments in that region. Many of the leading Texas counties in minerals value are in that section.

Austin Chalk

The Giddings Field on the Austin Chalk in Lee, Fayette and Burleson counties had significant drilling in the 1970s that continued into the 1980s. ☆

Chronological Listing of Major Oil Discoveries

The following list gives the name of the field, county and discovery date. Sources include Texas Mid-Continent Oil and Gas Association from records of the U.S. Bureau of Mines; the Oil and Gas Journal; previous Texas Almanacs, the New Handbook of Texas, and the Energy Information Administration of the U.S. Department of Energy.

FIELD	COUNTY	Year	FIELD	COUNTY	Year
Corsicana	Navarro	1894	Salt Flat	Caldwell	1928
Powell	Navarro	1900	Sugarland	Fort Bend	1928
Spindletop	Jefferson	1901	Darst Creek	Guadalupe	1929
Sour Lake	Hardin	1902	Penwell	Ector	1929
Batson-Old	Hardin	1903	Pettus	Bee	1929
Humble	Harris	1905	Van	Van Zandt	1929
Mission	Bexar	1907	Cowden North	Ector	1930
Piedras Pintas	Duval	1907	East Texas	Cherokee-Gregg-Rusk-Smith-Upshur	1930
Goose Creek	Harris	1908			
Panhandle Osborne	Wheeler	1910	Fuhrman-Mascho	Andrews	1930
Archer County	Archer	1911	Sand Hills	Crane	1930
Electra	Wichita	1911	Conroe	Montgomery	1931
Burk	Wichita	1912	Manvel	Brazoria	1931
Iowa Park	Wichita	1913	Tomball	Harris	1933
Orange	Orange	1913	Dickinson	Galveston	1934
Somerset	Bexar	1913	Hastings East	Brazoria	1934
Damon Mound	Brazoria	1915	Means	Andrews	1934
Thrall	Williamson	1915	Old Ocean	Brazoria	1934
Wilbarger County	Wilbarger	1915	Tom O'Connor	Refugio	1934
Barbers Hill	Chambers	1916	Anahuac	Chambers	1935
Stephens County Regular	Stephens	1916	Goldsmith	Ector	1935
			Keystone	Winkler	1935
Ranger	Eastland	1917	Plymouth	San Patricio	1935
Young County	Young	1917	Withers	Wharton	1936
Burkburnett Townsite	Wichita	1918	Pearsall	Frio	1936
Desdemona	Eastland	1918	Seminole	Gaines	1936
Hull	Liberty	1918	Slaughter	Cochran-Hockley	1936
West Columbia	Brazoria	1918	Talco	Titus-Franklin	1936
Blue Ridge	Fort Bend	1919	Wasson	Gaines	1936
KMA (Kemp-Munger-Allen)	Wichita	1919	Webster	Harris	1936
			Jordan	Crane-Ector	1937
Mexia	Limestone-Freestone	1920	Seeligson	Jim Wells-Kleberg	1937
Refugio	Refugio	1920	Dune	Crane	1938
Westbrook	Mitchell	1920	Kelsey	Brooks-Jim Hogg-Starr	1938
Panhandle	Carson-Collingsworth-Gray-Hutchinson-Moore-Potter-Wheeler	1921	Walnut Bend	Cooke	1938
			West Ranch	Jackson	1938
			Diamond M	Scurry	1940
Currie	Navarro	1921	Hawkins	Wood	1940
Mirando City	Webb	1921	Fullerton	Andrews	1941
Pierce Junction	Harris	1921	Oyster Bayou	Chambers	1941
Thompsons	Fort Bend	1921	Tijerina-Canales-Blucher	Jim Wells-Kleberg	1941
Aviators	Webb	1922			
High Island	Galveston-Chambers	1922	Quitman	Wood	1942
Luling-Branyon	Caldwell-Guadalupe	1923	Welch	Dawson	1942
Big Lake	Reagan	1923	Russell	Gaines	1943
Cooke County	Cooke	1924	Anton-Irish	Hale-Lamb-Lubbock	1944
Richland	Navarro	1924	Mabee	Andrews-Martin	1944
Wortham	Freestone	1924	Midland Farms	Andrews	1944
Boling	Wharton	1925	TXL Devonian	Ector	1944
Howard-Glasscock	Howard	1925	Block 31	Crane	1945
Lytton Springs	Caldwell	1925	Borregos	Kleberg	1945
McCamey	Upton	1925	Dollarhide	Andrews	1945
Hendrick	Winkler	1926	Levelland	Cochran-Hockley	1945
Iatan East	Howard	1926	Andector	Ector	1946
McElroy	Crane	1926	Kelly-Snyder	Scurry	1948
Yates	Pecos	1926	Cogdell Area	Scurry	1949
Raccoon Bend	Austin	1927	Pegasus	Upton-Midland	1949
Waddell	Crane	1927	Spraberry Trend	Glasscock-Midland	1949
Agua Dulce-Stratton	Nueces	1928	Prentice	Yoakum	1950
Greta	Refugio	1928	Salt Creek	Kent	1950
Kermit	Winkler	1928	Dora Roberts	Midland	1954

Top Oil Producing Counties since Discovery

There are 34 counties that have produced more than 500 million barrels of oil since discovery. The counties are ranked in the list below. The column at right lists the number of producing oil wells in the county in February 2007.

Rank	County	Barrels	Oil Wells	Rank	County	Barrels	Oil Wells
1.	Gregg	3,291,530,089	3,208	19.	Howard	823,562,727	3,358
2.	Ector	3,126,978,923	5,657	20.	Montgomery	776,896,233	122
3.	Andrews	2,832,121,927	6,824	21.	Ward	766,932,233	2,782
4.	Gaines	2,230,452,169	3,395	22.	Fort Bend	694,829,953	292
5.	Yoakum	2,113,888,412	3,469	23.	Jackson	683,336,072	238
6.	Scurry	2,064,917,257	2,580	24.	Gray	674,832,531	2,805
7.	Rusk	1,834,073,958	1,805	25.	Midland	639,609,940	4,584
8.	Pecos	1,777,116,324	2,962	26.	Duval	588,500,845	700
9.	Crane	1,762,302,749	3,877	27.	Kent	578,753,292	541
10.	Hockley	1,672,032,987	4,189	28.	Nueces	564,740,978	196
11.	Harris	1,378,238,534	338	29.	Van Zandt	552,443,544	571
12.	Refugio	1,328,724,031	786	30.	Jefferson	540,249,438	156
13.	Brazoria	1,275,748,641	332	31.	Liberty	537,275,225	603
14.	Wood	1,208,477,915	604	32.	Hutchinson	532,156,378	3,026
15.	Winkler	1,081,623,932	1,771	33.	Reagan	513,979,012	3,764
16.	Chambers	910,490,196	182	34.	Cochran	510,788,166	1,980
17.	Upton	850,669,179	2,314			Source: Texas Railroad Commission.	
18.	Wichita	881,879,598	5,612				

Oil Production since Discovery

- ● More than 1 billion barrels
- ● 500 million to 1 billion
- ● 250 million to 500 million

Texas Oil Production History

The table shows the year of oil or gas discovery in each county, oil production in 2005 and 2006 and total oil production from date of discovery to Jan. 1, 2007. The 17 counties omitted have not produced oil.

The table has been compiled by the Texas Almanac from information provided in past years by the Texas Mid-Continent Oil & Gas Assoc., which used data from the U.S. Bureau of Mines and the Texas state comptroller. Since 1970, production figures have been compiled from records of the Railroad Commission of Texas. The figures in the final column are cumulative of all previously published figures. The change in sources, due to different techniques, may create some discrepancies in year-to-year comparisons among counties.

| County | Year of Discovery | Production in Barrels* | | Total Production to Jan. 1, 2007 |
		2005	2006	
Anderson	1928	799,811	829,243	301,342,592
Andrews	1929	23,826,718	24,293,387	2,832,121,927
Angelina	1936	8,039	10,022	888,371
Aransas	1936	195,651	345,119	85,759,567
Archer	1911	1,056,221	1,087,335	496,223,936
Atascosa	1917	742,485	918,525	151,454,352
Austin	1915	403,670	329,416	115,522,750
Bandera	1995	1,524	2,056	25,411
Bastrop	1913	106,360	105,581	16,755,886
Baylor	1924	112,426	106,034	58,209,355
Bee	1929	530,251	539,429	108,951,799
Bell	1980	0	0	446
Bexar	1889	123,851	120,702	36,081,979
Borden	1949	4,395,833	3,846,412	413,848,223
Bosque	2006	0	35	35
Bowie	1944	105,035	81,786	6,592,242
Brazoria	1902	2,516,443	2,398,326	1,275,748,641
Brazos	1942	2,056,130	1,737,876	140,864,112
Brewster	1969	0	0	56
Briscoe	1982	0	0	3,554
Brooks	1935	1,424,624	1,971,615	172,509,066
Brown	1917	106,817	116,129	53,483,537
Burleson	1938	2,255,808	2,062,329	196,527,050
Caldwell	1922	926,344	942,555	283,236,333
Calhoun	1935	522,379	454,515	104,898,794
Callahan	1923	178,546	191,535	86,297,699
Cameron	1944	1,201	932	468,290
Camp	1940	230,684	261,637	29,460,771
Carson	1921	334,688	293,612	180,483,929
Cass	1936	327,717	318,325	114,776,911
Chambers	1916	1,306,079	1,287,701	910,490,196
Cherokee	1926	320,577	278,839	71,322,647
Childress	1961	32,684	29,588	1,643,761
Clay	1917	713,777	690,719	205,494,096
Cochran	1936	3,830,651	3,861,875	510,788,166
Coke	1942	469,506	471,700	224,172,647
Coleman	1902	281,568	278,885	95,252,001
Collin	1963	0	0	53,000
Collingsworth	1936	2,325	1,705	1,241,965
Colorado	1932	406,511	416,520	42,044,920
Comanche	1918	8,661	10,088	5,976,469
Concho	1940	440,271	427,518	26,814,568
Cooke	1924	1,614,642	1,548,034	391,781,750
Coryell	1964	0	0	1,100
Cottle	1955	108,018	111,615	4,764,150
Crane	1926	9,960,650	9,487,649	1,762,302,749
Crockett	1925	4,458,652	5,554,020	371,931,201

An oil well pump jack in Montague County.

| County | Year of Discovery | Production in Barrels* | | Total Production to Jan. 1, 2007 |
		2005	2006	
Crosby	1955	540,429	543,071	25,557,072
Culberson	1953	121,916	110,355	24,988,514
Dallas	1986	0	0	231
Dawson	1934	4,552,988	4,337,821	388,699,739
Delta	1984	0	0	65,089
Denton	1937	769,972	699,423	7,191,881
DeWitt	1930	767,593	828,058	68,064,393
Dickens	1953	1,538,123	1,373,018	20,078,759
Dimmit	1943	999,095	1,306,213	107,767,690
Donley	1967	0	261	261
Duval	1905	1,417,685	1,319,117	588,500,845
Eastland	1917	302,334	458,318	157,163,872
Ector	1926	19,130,720	18,037,005	3,126,978,923
Edwards	1946	3,592	3,296	534,514
Ellis	1953	17	121	840,024
Erath	1917	5,121	14,075	2,104,196
Falls	1937	1,894	2,494	852,294
Fannin	1980	0	0	13,281
Fayette	1943	1,745,359	1,586,687	154,367,925
Fisher	1928	570,071	585,003	249,523,760
Floyd	1952	1,628	1,720	158,961
Foard	1929	107,552	95,256	24,275,656
Fort Bend	1919	2,882,986	2,497,519	694,829,953
Franklin	1936	451,993	401,044	177,694,279

County	Year of Discovery	Production in Barrels* 2005	Production in Barrels* 2006	Total Production to Jan. 1, 2007
Freestone	1916	288,050	265,880	45,458,691
Frio	1934	542,949	570,277	146,946,999
Gaines	1935	28,976,415	27,731,472	2,230,452,169
Galveston	1922	1,386,028	1,387,866	455,729,871
Garza	1926	4,089,830	3,893,586	342,725,613
Glasscock	1925	3,681,498	3,635,291	273,270,196
Goliad	1930	956,270	873,979	84,437,586
Gonzales	1902	225,925	230,454	44,064,955
Gray	1925	1,290,577	1,215,956	674,832,531
Grayson	1930	1,480,378	1,364,171	258,286,703
Gregg	1931	2,954,383	2,924,531	3,291,530,089
Grimes	1952	178,312	146,806	18,545,016
Guadalupe	1922	1,489,774	1,416,339	206,503,541
Hale	1946	2,790,923	2,088,469	181,444,453
Hamilton	1938	1,990	918	153,454
Hansford	1937	167,347	158,733	39,373,359
Hardeman	1944	1,814,215	1,484,537	85,355,549
Hardin	1893	1,722,666	2,203,302	441,805,922
Harris	1905	2,046,159	1,929,783	1,378,238,534
Harrison	1928	1,022,379	1,153,353	91,190,047
Hartley	1937	212,668	174,568	7,736,383
Haskell	1929	351,898	328,402	117,256,511
Hays	1956	0	0	296
Hemphill	1955	1,229,404	1,279,536	39,633,275
Henderson	1934	619,635	484,150	178,368,464
Hidalgo	1934	2,841,130	2,635,373	115,634,304
Hill	1929	2	0	75,395
Hockley	1937	20,206,316	19,482,031	1,672,032,987
Hood	1958	31,065	123,739	268,057
Hopkins	1936	364,463	292,614	90,115,089
Houston	1934	773,179	738,684	58,041,914
Howard	1925	6,050,031	5,599,864	823,562,727
Hunt	1942	0	0	2,024,660
Hutchinson	1923	852,608	783,317	532,156,378
Irion	1928	1,461,363	1,589,241	103,830,702
Jack	1923	678,207	664,861	205,168,422
Jackson	1934	1,067,658	1,105,824	683,330,072
Jasper	1928	459,646	448,020	35,719,231
Jeff Davis	1980	0	0	20,866
Jefferson	1901	2,815,692	2,808,717	540,249,438
Jim Hogg	1921	309,301	377,880	112,831,527
Jim Wells	1931	202,088	169,803	462,949,296
Johnson	1962	16,296	13,593	230,491
Jones	1926	847,411	881,833	222,080,181
Karnes	1930	371,517	348,764	108,963,316
Kaufman	1948	55,585	68,091	24,722,437
Kenedy	1947	262,505	308,920	39,622,784
Kent	1946	4,940,084	4,538,137	578,753,292
Kerr	1982	1,039	0	78,946
Kimble	1939	489	460	98,399
King	1943	2,065,057	2,253,932	180,713,289
Kinney	1960	0	0	402
Kleberg	1919	445,092	417,436	337,219,641
Knox	1946	235,963	232,186	62,593,203
Lamb	1945	310,907	339,255	28,180,291
Lampasas	1985	859,130	673,707	39,100,217
La Salle	1940	0	0	111
Lavaca	1941	559,836	567,487	31,949,043
Lee	1939	1,687,746	1,449,948	137,001,625
Leon	1936	1,021,701	982,932	64,591,581
Liberty	1904	3,698,715	3,985,033	537,275,025
Limestone	1920	165,923	160,833	119,739,117
Lipscomb	1956	733,391	1,323,788	61,737,962
Live Oak	1930	635,826	717,815	85,177,603
Llano	1978	0	0	647
Loving	1921	1,049,958	1,170,972	112,558,607
Lubbock	1941	1,580,806	1,918,451	71,592,746
Lynn	1950	190,518	192,260	19,486,781
Madison	1946	533,767	546,797	34,068,318
Marion	1910	177,767	191,884	55,967,586
Martin	1945	5,156,549	5,464,301	319,183,815
Matagorda	1901	1,192,713	1,201,304	282,416,838
Maverick	1929	1,202,090	1,741,591	54,317,226
McCulloch	1938	91,626	75,194	1,980,048
McLennan	1902	1,787	1,379	339,203
McMullen	1922	1,268,055	1,333,841	106,377,556
Medina	1901	84,680	89,875	10,919,286
Menard	1946	123,331	111,799	7,544,150
Midland	1945	10,604,666	10,669,884	639,609,940
Milam	1921	512,616	426,808	21,611,325
Mills	1982	0	0	28,122
Mitchell	1920	3,157,272	3,158,955	230,834,310
Montague	1919	1,465,014	1,549,902	293,395,192
Montgomery	1931	898,729	873,636	776,896,233
Moore	1926	314,883	279,666	30,407,959
Morris	2004	2,218	2,012	6,384
Motley	1957	45,187	39,753	11,063,129
Nacogdoches	1866	292,495	369,353	4,491,739
Navarro	1894	275,361	330,200	218,966,135
Newton	1937	672,100	1,014,249	64,805,274
Nolan	1939	1,313,772	1,170,624	200,399,998
Nueces	1930	1,394,976	1,215,629	564,740,978
Ochiltree	1951	940,667	1,050,970	162,030,814
Oldham	1957	70,907	57,589	13,931,736
Orange	1913	965,945	792,025	159,419,473
Palo Pinto	1902	293,429	222,512	24,125,334
Panola	1917	2,215,682	2,414,646	96,912,971
Parker	1942	82,603	154,481	3,151,312
Parmer	1963	0	0	144,000
Pecos	1926	11,287,928	11,749,579	1,777,116,324
Polk	1930	1,072,146	1,303,966	126,715,936
Potter	1925	146,650	179,765	10,134,104
Presidio	1980	0	0	4,377
Rains	1955	0	1	148,897
Reagan	1923	5,175,105	5,486,375	513,797,012
Real	2003	4,152	2,756	23,256
Red River	1951	167,665	142,159	8,082,688
Reeves	1939	844,101	890,117	79,595,349
Refugio	1920	4,955,237	4,366,684	1,328,724,031
Roberts	1945	856,107	1,092,584	48,864,222
Robertson	1944	1,131,600	984,308	28,121,540

County	Year of Discovery	Production in Barrels*		Total Production to Jan. 1, 2007
		2005	2006	
Runnels	1927	469,239	676,614	148,233,217
Rusk	1930	2,723,979	2,792,601	1,834,073,958
Sabine	1981	5,246	9,271	4,916,348
SanAugustine	1947	5,760	6,574	2,482,303
San Jacinto	1940	228,714	222,041	26,403,260
San Patricio	1930	1,407,343	1,168,141	487,743,534
San Saba	1982	0	0	32,362
Schleicher	1934	439,215	450,991	88,695,173
Scurry	1923	16,297,363	15,775,548	2,064,917,257
Shackelford	1910	725,078	688,763	183,583,778
Shelby	1917	255,160	228,884	3,469,889
Sherman	1938	103,196	93,948	9,483,428
Smith	1931	1,629,634	1,641,300	267,734,489
Somervell	1978	0	31	172
Starr	1929	2,387,430	2,189,467	299,230,639
Stephens	1916	2,320,395	2,268,964	343,930,714
Sterling	1947	1,242,773	1,112,221	90,390,771
Stonewall	1938	1,034,319	990,995	264,294,833
Sutton	1948	82,349	90,746	7,929,228
Swisher	1981	0	0	6
Tarrant	1969	5,491	13,357	24,803
Taylor	1929	535,914	506,075	145,384,442
Terrell	1952	294,409	292,454	9,411,805
Terry	1940	4,162,641	4,084,317	446,550,512
Throckmorton	1925	851,628	795,342	222,512,565
Titus	1936	503,925	489,647	212,202,550
Tom Green	1940	490,520	569,610	93,238,161
Travis	1934	1,449	1,773	755,181
Trinity	1946	91,182	88,467	1,036,694

County	Year of Discovery	Production in Barrels*		Total Production to Jan. 1, 2007
		2005	2006	
Tyler	1937	2,490,876	3,303,698	48,237,381
Upshur	1931	670,287	663,271	288,612,959
Upton	1925	11,178,169	11,333,216	850,669,179
Uvalde	1950	0	0	1,814
Val Verde	1935	1,971	2,075	143,342
Van Zandt	1929	944,717	834,549	552,443,544
Victoria	1931	836,416	798,038	254,590,543
Walker	1934	5,983	6,921	533,899
Waller	1934	1,199,285	1,039,669	30,001,648
Ward	1928	4,769,458	5,262,961	766,932,233
Washington	1915	637,483	549,487	32,350,971
Webb	1921	1,471,955	1,297,706	163,226,266
Wharton	1925	2,017,041	1,792,955	346,633,340
Wheeler	1910	1,431,486	1,765,159	104,006,466
Wichita	1910	2,141,119	2,122,483	831,879,598
Wilbarger	1915	743,685	802,008	264,976,675
Willacy	1936	1,185,554	827,381	115,601,751
Williamson	1915	8,966	8,415	9,560,793
Wilson	1941	283,900	292,004	49,406,474
Winkler	1926	3,657,133	4,135,126	1,081,623,932
Wise	1942	1,040,890	1,078,689	102,726,890
Wood	1940	4,377,131	4,295,168	1,208,477,915
Yoakum	1936	25,493,596	25,005,127	2,113,888,412
Young	1917	1,269,048	1,284,824	312,023,067
Zapata	1919	347,681	346,358	48,169,513
Zavala	1937	867,681	784,142	47,953,549

*Total includes condensate production.

Source: Railroad Commission, 2005-06 production reports.

The oil fields in the Pecos Valley west of Iraan. Robert Plocheck photo.

Oil and Gas Production by County, 2006

In 2006 in Texas, the total natural gas production from gas wells was 5,518,954,895 thousand cubic feet (MCF) and total crude oil production was 344,394,906 barrels (BBL). Total condensate was 43,574,159 barrels. Total casinghead production was 682,443,776 MCF. Counties not listed in the chart below had no production in 2006. *Source: Texas Railroad Commission.*

County	Oil (BBL)	Casing-head (MCF)	Gas Well Gas (MCF)	Conden-sate (BBL)	County	Oil (BBL)	Casing-head (MCF)	Gas Well Gas (MCF)	Conden-sate (BBL)
Anderson	740,842	5,564,137	7,268,501	88,401	Ector	18,032,156	25,636,427	12,355,416	4,849
Andrews	24,284,167	32,039,291	1,682,495	9,220	Edwards	2,433	0	18,646,485	863
Angelina	4,423	0	3,455,185	5,599	Ellis	119	0	120,333	2
Aransas	72,857	457,851	8,322,728	272,262	Erath	3,409	35,859	3,558,589	10,666
Archer	1,087,256	596,302	14,834	79	Falls	2,494	0	0	0
Atascosa	903,301	273,605	6,322,163	15,224	Fayette	1,335,559	9,972,514	11,911,171	251,128
Austin	220,909	36,893	10,859,938	108,507	Fisher	583,972	763,851	78,760	1,031
Bandera	2,056	0	0	0	Floyd	1,720	0	0	0
Bastrop	89,879	159,032	176,612	15,702	Foard	95,256	23	740,516	0
Baylor	106,034	23	0	0	Fort Bend	1,828,618	1,467,099	33,097,114	668,901
Bee	315,083	468,460	34,417,017	224,346	Franklin	338,127	251,657	3,325,887	62,917
Bexar	120,702	73	0	0	Freestone	62,581	110,702	269,073,646	203,299
Borden	3,846,412	2,385,119	0	0	Frio	569,203	342,412	729,703	1,074
Bosque	0	0	30,806	35	Gaines	27,725,390	21,004,228	15,825,416	6,082
Bowie	77,242	46,992	216,378	4,544	Galveston	673,201	1,119,930	11,049,879	714,665
Brazoria	1,841,630	1,659,942	30,498,732	556,696	Garza	3,893,586	908,652	0	0
Brazos	1,664,182	4,987,480	6,051,851	73,694	Glasscock	3,592,442	11,408,019	1,709,172	42,849
Brooks	364,168	1,254,544	66,228,523	1,067,447	Goliad	342,817	739,584	78,473,739	531,162
Brown	114,730	410,662	1,087,478	1,399	Gonzales	219,186	90,592	1,093,384	11,268
Burleson	2,003,088	10,365,687	3,264,105	59,241	Gray	1,211,336	3,334,447	10,755,994	4,620
Caldwell	942,405	464,122	9,739	150	Grayson	1,352,078	4,594,153	1,750,033	12,093
Calhoun	296,687	1,189,627	9,735,489	157,828	Gregg	2,707,315	2,692,006	58,719,629	217,216
Callahan	186,487	327,798	635,002	5,048	Grimes	88,893	428,534	19,081,764	57,913
Cameron	661	428	167,117	271	Guadalupe	1,416,101	97,968	10,593	238
Camp	261,605	12	1,031,781	32	Hale	2,088,469	924,238	0	0
Carson	293,274	2,111,228	16,357,691	338	Hamilton	651	0	158,252	267
Cass	288,230	547,962	2,240,486	30,095	Hansford	134,153	603,509	25,167,005	24,580
Chambers	864,587	1,166,002	16,174,288	423,114	Hardeman	1,483,019	449,622	24,153	1,518
Cherokee	180,597	224,840	15,439,253	98,242	Hardin	1,263,613	1,674,731	11,343,501	939,689
Childress	29,588	180	0	0	Harris	1,603,720	1,270,994	23,369,897	326,063
Clay	679,577	435,214	283,441	11,142	Harrison	451,773	3,798,294	95,738,278	701,580
Cochran	3,859,673	2,162,023	230,499	2,202	Hartley	174,568	0	2,541,530	0
Coke	468,898	2,809,152	778,941	2,002	Haskell	328,402	57,388	0	0
Coleman	270,853	625,028	1,226,325	8,032	Hemphill	154,364	2,147,670	113,042,747	1,125,172
Collingswth	1,705	33,619	1,281,584	0	Henderson	441,155	13,423,524	22,997,844	42,995
Colorado	184,359	479,111	29,731,615	232,161	Hidalgo	55,992	192,830	209,222,545	2,579,381
Comanche	8,373	74,080	622,373	1,715	Hill	0	0	3,050,947	0
Concho	423,657	719,554	818,973	3,861	Hockley	19,480,060	10,036,021	108,139	1,971
Cooke	1,501,596	658,162	762,068	46,438	Hood	953	47,106	15,139,840	122,786
Cottle	47,754	52,653	5,564,308	63,861	Hopkins	290,267	160,707	845,908	2,347
Crane	9,403,654	43,188,563	12,074,563	83,995	Houston	713,966	272,403	9,732,320	24,718
Crockett	5,274,427	6,713,306	109,440,551	279,593	Howard	5,589,893	5,169,643	805,747	9,971
Crosby	543,071	66,350	0	0	Hutchinson	773,599	5,180,960	10,766,006	9,718
Culberson	107,244	150,995	1,042,476	3,111	Irion	1,526,680	6,545,436	5,579,371	62,561
Dawson	4,337,821	2,456,806	0	0	Jack	555,550	2,794,678	13,525,000	109,311
Denton	21,584	293,561	157,169,310	677,839	Jackson	688,444	1,496,721	27,048,006	417,380
DeWitt	62,464	9,007	34,866,559	765,594	Jasper	243,310	721,308	6,003,177	204,710
Dickens	1,373,018	98,947	0	0	Jefferson	834,643	1,315,755	41,926,538	1,974,074
Dimmit	1,278,444	2,281,631	2,508,807	27,769	Jim Hogg	56,489	98,180	29,776,749	321,391
Donley	0	0	16,868	261	Jim Wells	131,327	452,099	7,351,212	38,476
Duval	1,028,665	410,585	57,740,843	290,452	Johnson	0	0	151,726,864	13,593
Eastland	295,480	879,642	3,828,371	162,838	Jones	880,706	454,197	24,175	1,127

County	Oil (BBL)	Casing-head (MCF)	Gas Well Gas (MCF)	Condensate (BBL)
Karnes	272,195	516,271	6,142,078	76,569
Kaufman	68,091	7,336	0	0
Kenedy	97,699	170,279	44,930,466	211,221
Kent	4,538,137	8,099,594	0	0
Kimble	455	0	163,521	5
King	2,234,845	108,348	1,340,227	19,087
Kleberg	37,485	150,846	30,358,191	379,951
Knox	232,186	128	0	0
La Salle	157,495	338,900	14,887,092	181,760
Lamb	673,707	154,088	0	0
Lampasas	0	0	580	0
Lavaca	146,039	412,346	63,875,793	421,448
Lee	1,374,088	12,028,877	3,120,447	75,860
Leon	871,863	1,887,140	53,197,814	111,069
Liberty	1,921,498	2,729,485	64,017,403	2,063,535
Limestone	90,399	23,142	78,537,377	70,434
Lipscomb	856,247	5,204,589	49,854,950	467,541
Live Oak	491,953	579,701	22,746,546	225,862
Loving	1,040,457	2,932,441	87,484,968	130,515
Lubbock	1,918,451	302,769	0	0
Lynn	192,260	44,287	0	0
Madison	515,274	535,894	7,696,766	31,523
Marion	129,324	384,428	4,460,111	62,560
Martin	5,461,330	11,511,100	25,060	2,971
Matagorda	448,246	779,686	39,101,080	753,058
Maverick	1,715,450	176,709	3,165,194	26,141
McCulloch	75,194	2,354	18,337	0
McLennan	1,379	0	0	0
McMullen	1,142,708	3,118,849	38,274,835	191,133
Medina	89,875	650	90,444	0
Menard	111,799	17,585	56,511	0
Midland	10,310,318	37,260,559	15,309,780	359,566
Milam	426,570	395,714	24,047	238
Mills	0	0	8,710	0
Mitchell	3,158,955	451,037	0	0
Montague	1,544,238	2,691,950	300,888	5,664
Montgomery	737,415	759,592	10,004,941	136,221
Moore	279,147	2,473,797	39,673,062	519
Morris	2,012	0	0	0
Motley	39,753	0	0	0
Nacogdoches	3,765	56,903	82,147,258	365,588
Navarro	296,121	56,391	517,674	34,079
Newton	920,073	2,836,831	3,625,700	94,176
Nolan	1,168,948	1,411,721	482,408	1,676
Nueces	494,731	1,986,510	46,695,798	720,898
Ochiltree	935,980	4,088,076	23,189,183	114,999
Oldham	57,589	700	188,215	0
Orange	325,810	397,819	10,931,719	466,215
Palo Pinto	170,891	1,417,096	14,182,596	51,621
Panola	427,640	4,316,319	276,335,104	1,987,006
Parker	12,481	425,970	40,456,401	142,000
Pecos	11,623,531	62,939,568	131,109,818	126,048
Polk	531,467	302,818	25,619,120	772,499
Potter	179,505	370,691	17,844,478	260
Rains	0	0	5,067,169	1
Reagan	5,441,125	27,141,359	2,137,280	45,250
Real	2,756	50,024	133,599	0
Red River	142,159	3,110	0	0
Reeves	854,318	2,121,484	23,058,363	35,799

County	Oil (BBL)	Casing-head (MCF)	Gas Well Gas (MCF)	Condensate (BBL)
Refugio	4,287,480	23,626,485	24,407,044	79,204
Roberts	680,669	6,533,092	38,094,719	411,915
Robertson	951,909	634,081	132,274,565	32,399
Runnels	673,641	2,082,148	318,169	2,973
Rusk	2,192,044	1,641,163	113,873,360	600,557
Sabine	9,271	39,514	0	0
S.Augustine	6,467	4,890	47,260	107
San Jacinto	37,014	63,025	6,693,356	185,027
San Patricio	401,450	945,518	28,075,771	766,691
Schleicher	339,223	1,312,548	14,216,044	111,768
Scurry	15,775,548	27,032,673	0	0
Shackelford	671,233	924,249	2,460,984	17,530
Shelby	76,282	721,584	34,476,234	152,602
Sherman	89,902	176,766	22,037,520	4,046
Smith	1,236,257	1,976,596	56,368,437	405,043
Somervell	0	0	300,818	31
Starr	521,171	930,514	120,437,868	1,668,296
Stephens	2,235,795	3,196,462	10,166,432	33,169
Sterling	1,039,525	9,294,126	6,422,166	72,696
Stonewall	990,995	445,019	0	0
Sutton	14,285	23,663	81,944,498	76,461
Tarrant	0	0	168,248,127	13,357
Taylor	505,978	156,101	20,823	97
Terrell	21,457	643,578	78,064,455	270,997
Terry	4,084,317	1,015,629	27,723	0
Throckmorton	794,605	1,352,462	285,397	737
Titus	489,647	2,141	0	0
TomGreen	561,771	1,988,124	1,085,288	7,839
Travis	1,773	0	0	0
Trinity	86,952	128,814	81,907	1,515
Tyler	306,407	470,520	23,274,124	2,997,291
Upshur	152,493	93,067	52,201,197	510,778
Upton	10,169,987	30,476,006	42,986,224	1,163,229
Uvalde	0	0	2,991	0
Val Verde	1,852	5,612	15,388,067	223
Van Zandt	825,860	934,848	5,344,133	8,689
Victoria	664,302	804,930	15,628,939	133,736
Walker	3,082	55,361	1,360,906	3,839
Waller	976,070	470,206	6,296,770	63,599
Ward	5,162,991	15,265,886	32,429,807	99,970
Washington	418,768	2,615,297	19,543,514	130,719
Webb	147,350	297,152	234,879,917	1,150,356
Wharton	1,213,894	934,806	51,771,034	579,061
Wheeler	355,513	1,202,208	92,319,071	1,409,646
Wichita	2,122,483	265,976	0	0
Wilbarger	802,008	23,164	4,864	0
Willacy	425,736	761,920	23,008,514	401,645
Williamson	8,415	0	6,110	0
Wilson	291,911	35,912	10,304	93
Winkler	4,055,230	15,810,226	23,377,857	79,896
Wise	437,994	5,791,640	162,908,220	640,695
Wood	4,271,397	8,235,423	8,418,701	23,771
Yoakum	25,005,127	26,643,793	1,176,576	0
Young	1,273,496	1,782,611	1,520,393	11,328
Zapata	37,252	26,278	315,845,959	309,106
Zavala	783,973	439,053	871,904	169

Source: Texas Railroad Commission.

Top Gas Producing Counties, 1993–2007

In all, 36 counties have produced more than 500 billion cubic feet of natural gas since 1993. The counties are ranked in the list below. The column at the right lists the number of producing gas wells in the county in February 2007. (**MCF** is thousand cubic feet.) The map indicates areas of concentration of natural gas production in the state.

Rank	County	Gas (MCF)	Gas Wells	Rank	County	Gas (MCF)	Gas Wells
1.	Zapata	4,313,784,381	2,720	20.	Gregg	815,229,232	915
2.	Webb	4,179,422,024	4,331	21.	Moore	803,470,724	1,274
3.	Hidalgo	3,640,655,678	1,374	22.	Upshur	793,067,169	705
4.	Panola	3,570,820,895	4,540	23.	Harris	775,962,936	179
5.	Pecos	2,701,353,984	929	24.	Limestone	736,399,801	831
6.	Starr	2,070,633,096	1,103	25.	Washington	701,899,955	175
7.	Freestone	2,068,943,528	2,304	26.	Nueces	693,817,646	725
8.	Crockett	1,721,584,669	5,202	27.	Ward	680,341,849	285
9.	Wise	1,444,201,469	3,613	28.	Robertson	644,244,909	495
10.	Hemphill	1,231,494,753	1,946	29.	Wheeler	630,220,956	1,216
11.	Rusk	1,086,766,658	1,875	30.	Kenedy	607,116,497	179
12.	Lavaca	1,061,482,088	540	31.	Brazoria	594,465,880	176
13.	Sutton	978,113,544	5,225	32.	Grimes	583,359,559	191
14.	Terrell	935,030,749	586	33.	Lipscomb	557,938,983	1,164
15.	Duval	930,446,097	563	34.	Goliad	553,679,918	567
16.	Brooks	911,739,285	410	35.	Winkler	529,628,425	339
17.	Harrison	900,967,055	1,664	36.	Polk	505,499,180	139
18.	Wharton	838,377,175	519				
19.	Denton	835,521,952	2,052				

Source: Texas Railroad Commission.

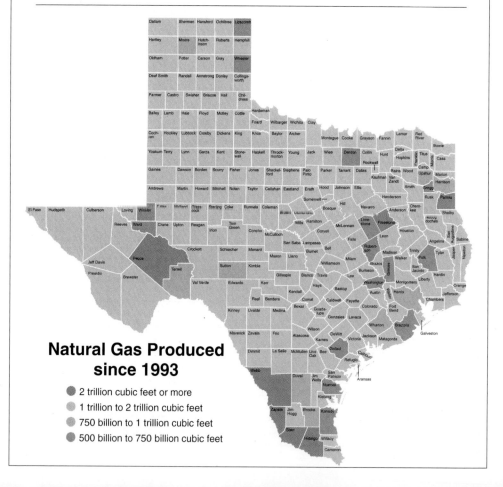

Natural Gas Produced since 1993

- 2 trillion cubic feet or more
- 1 trillion to 2 trillion cubic feet
- 750 billion to 1 trillion cubic feet
- 500 billion to 750 billion cubic feet

Petroleum Production and Income in Texas

Year	Crude Oil				Natural Gas		
	Production (thousand barrels)	Value (add 000)	Average Price per barrel (nominal)	*Average price per barrel (2000 dollars)	Production (million cubic feet)	Value (add 000)	Average Price (cents per MCF)
1915	24,943	$ 13,027	$ 0.52	–	13,324	$ 2,594	19.5
1925	144,648	262,270	1.81	–	134,872	7,040	5.2
1935	392,666	367,820	0.94	–	642,366	13,233	2.1
1945	754,710	914,410	1.21	–	1,711,401	44,839	2.6
1955	1,053,297	2,989,330	2.84	–	4,730,798	378,464	8.0
1965	1,000,749	2,962,119	2.96	–	6,636,555	858,396	12.9
1966	1,057,706	3,141,387	2.97	–	6,953,790	903,993	13.0
1967	1,119,962	3,375,565	3.01	–	7,188,900	948,935	13.2
1968	1,133,380	3,450,707	3.04	–	7,495,414	1,011,881	13.5
1969	1,151,775	3,696,328	3.21	–	7,853,199	1,075,888	13.7
1970	1,249,697	4,104,005	3.28	–	8,357,716	1,203,511	14.4
1971	1,222,926	4,261,775	3.48	–	8,550,705	1,376,664	16.1
1972	1,301,685	4,536,077	3.48	–	8,657,840	1,419,886	16.4
1973	1,294,671	5,157,623	3.98	–	8,513,850	1,735,221	20.4
1974	1,262,126	8,773,003	6.95	–	8,170,798	2,541,118	31.1
1975	1,221,929	9,336,570	7.64	–	7,485,764	3,885,112	51.9
1976	1,189,523	10,217,702	8.59	–	7,191,859	5,163,755	71.8
1977	1,137,880	9,986,002	8.78	$ 20.07	7,051,027	6,367,077	90.3
1978	1,074,050	9,980,333	9.29	20.30	6,548,184	6,515,443	99.5
1979	1,018,094	12,715,994	12.49	25.53	7,174,623	8,509,103	118.6
1980	977,436	21,259,233	21.75	40.41	7,115,889	10,673,834	150.0
1981	945,132	32,692,116	34.59	59.30	7,050,207	12,598,712	178.7
1982	923,868	29,074,126	31.47	50.65	6,497,678	13,567,151	208.8
1983	876,205	22,947,814	26.19	45.01	5,643,183	14,672,275	260.0
1984	874,079	25,138,520	28.76	42.67	5,864,224	13,487,715	230.0
1985	860,300	23,159,286	26.92	38.44	5,805,098	12,665,114	218.0
1986	813,620	11,976,488	14.72	20.67	5,663,491	8,778,410	155.0
1987	754,213	13,221,345	17.53	23.98	5,516,224	7,612,389	138.0
1988	727,928	10,729,660	14.74	19.43	5,702,643	7,983,700	140.0
1989	679,575	12,123,624	17.84	22.67	5,595,190	8,113,026	145.0
1990	672,081	15,047,902	22.39	27.42	5,520,915	8,281,372	150.0
1991	672,810	12,836,080	19.05	22.55	5,509,990	7,713,986	140.0
1992	642,059	11,820,306	18.41	21.21	5,436,408	8,643,888	159.0
1993	572,600	9,288,800	16.22	18.32	4,062,500	7,365,800	181.0
1994	533,900	7,977,500	14.94	16.60	3,842,500	6,220,300	162.0
1995	503,200	8,177,700	16.25	17.78	3,690,000	5,305,200	143.0
1996	478,100	9,560,800	20.00	21.64	3,458,100	6,945,000	200.0
1997	464,900	8,516,800	18.32	19.56	3,672,300	8,134,200	221.5
1998	440,600	5,472,400	12.42	12.73	3,557,900	6,362,900	178.8
1999	337,100	5,855,800	17.37	17.67	3,321,600	6,789,700	204.4
2000	348,900	10,037,300	28.60	28.60	3,552,000	12,837,600	361.4
2001	325,500	7,770,500	23.87	22.86	3,732,700	13,708,700	367.3
2002	335,600	8,150,400	24.29	22.81	3,476,800	9,840,800	283.0
2003	333,300	9,708,600	29.13	27.40	3,272,800	14,797,800	452.1
2004	327,910	12,762,650	38.92	35.55	3,336,200	17,077,700	511.9
2005	327,600	12,744,600	38.90	NA	3,206,600	16,399,400	511.4
2006	314,600	$ 19,353,500	$ 61.52	NA	4,029,300	$ 23,500,800	583.2

*In chained (2000) dollars, as calculated by the federal Energy Information Administration. (NA, not available.)
MCF (thousand cubic feet).
Sources: Previously from the Texas Railroad Commission, Texas Mid-Continent Oil & Gas Association and, beginning in 1979, data are from Department of Energy. Data since 1993 are from the state comptroller.
DOE figures do not include gas that is vented or flared or used for pressure maintenance and repressuring, but do include non-hydrocarbon gases.

A rig operating east of Palacios in Matagorda County. Robert Plocheck photo.

Rig Counts and Wells Drilled by Year

Year	Rotary rigs active*		Permits†	Texas wells completed		Wells drilled**
	Texas	U.S.	Texas	Oil	Gas	Texas
1982	994	3,117	41,224	16,296	6,273	27,648
1983	796	2,232	45,550	15,941	5,027	26,882
1984	850	2,428	37,507	18,716	5,489	30,898
1985	680	1,980	30,878	16,543	4,605	27,124
1986	313	964	15,894	10,373	3,304	18,707
1987	293	1,090	15,297	7,327	2,542	13,121
1988	280	936	13,493	6,441	2,665	12,261
1989	264	871	12,756	4,914	2,760	10,054
1990	348	1,009	14,030	5,593	2,894	11,231
1991	315	860	12,494	6,025	2,755	11,295
1992	251	721	12,089	5,031	2,537	9,498
1993	264	754	11,612	4,646	3,295	9,969
1994	274	775	11,030	3,962	3,553	9,299
1995	251	723	11,244	4,334	3,778	9,785
1996	283	779	12,669	4,061	4,060	9,747
1997	358	945	13,933	4,482	4,594	10,778
1998	303	827	9,385	4,509	4,907	11,057
1999	226	622	8,430	2,049	3,566	6,658
2000	343	918	12,021	3,111	4,580	8,854
2001	462	1,156	12,227	3,082	5,787	10,005
2002	338	830	9,716	3,268	5,474	9,877
2003	449	1,032	12,664	3,111	6,336	10,420
2004	506	1,192	14,700	3,446	7,118	11,587
2005	614	1,381	16,914	3,454	7,197	11,154
2006	746	1,648	18.952	4,761	8,412	12,764

Source for rig count: Baker Hughes Inc. This is an annual average from monthly reports.
†Totals shown for 1988 and after are number of drilling permits issued; data for previous years were total drilling applications received.
**Wells drilled are oil and gas well completions and dry holes drilled/plugged.*

Offshore Production History — Oil and Gas

The cumulative offshore natural gas production as of Jan. 1, 2007, was **3,949,523,724** thousand cubic feet (Mcf). The cumulative offshore oil production was **38,580,343** barrels.

Production in Recent Years

YEAR	Crude Oil BBL	Casing-head Mcf	Gas Well Gas Mcf	Conden-sate BBL
1993	1,685,177	1,370,634	86,264,924	275,945
1994	1,367,850	1,068,230	87,315,422	303,451
1995	1,108,868	807,468	64,295,758	223,103
1996	908,743	724,651	68,159,547	212,048
1997	765,283	698,488	76,974,574	328,025
1998	586,999	611,882	60,080,329	233,044
1999	433,958	382,566	48,816,099	132,827
2000	539,489	336,891	44,086,157	220,236
2001	516,677	370,317	53,535,529	475,389
2002	1,144,389	2,404,329	54,990,950	405,607
2003	760,824	1,370,696	52,662,329	409,416
2004	422,922	325,345	46,478,609	368,590
2005	449,888	396,269	36,699,164	392,647

Source: Texas Railroad Commission.

2006 Production by Area

Offshore Area	Crude Oil BBL	Casing-head Mcf	Gas Well Gas Mcf	Conden-sate BBL
Brazos-LB	0	0	2,411,603	3,800
Brazos-SB	0	0	821,704	297
Galveston-LB	0	0	3,744,372	96,780
Galveston-SB	0	0	0	0
High Island-LB	72,947	84,469	219,242	4,429
High Island-SB	72,373	28,181	56,735	0
Matagrda Island-LB	127,543	143,124	7,332,971	17,790
Matagrda Island-SB	0	0	2,825,012	46,610
Mustang Island-LB	39	0	3,078,251	18,040
Mustang Island-SB	39,168	58,329	3,439,443	35,843
N. Padre Island-LB	0	0	631,838	15,713
S. Padre Island-LB	0	0	0	0
Sabine Pass	0	0	0	0
Total	**312,070**	**314,103**	**24,561,171**	**239,302**

Offshore Areas

Based on a map of the Texas Railroad Commission.

Receipts by Texas from Tidelands

The Republic of Texas had proclaimed its Gulf boundaries as three marine leagues, recognized by international law as traditional national boundaries. These boundaries were never seriously questioned when Texas joined the Union in 1845. But, in 1930 a congressional resolution authorized the U.S. Attorney General to file suit to establish offshore lands as properties of the federal government. Congress returned the disputed lands to Texas in 1953, and the U.S. Supreme Court confirmed Texas' ownership in 1960. In 1978, the federal government also granted states a "fair and equitable" share of the revenues from offshore leases within three miles of the states' outermost boundary. The states did not receive any such revenue until April 1986.

The following table shows receipts from tidelands in the Gulf of Mexico by the Texas General Land Office to Aug. 31, 2005. It does not include revenue from bays and other submerged area owned by Texas. Source: General Land Office.

From	To	Total	Bonus	Rental	Royalty	Lease
6-09-1922	9-28-1945	$ 924,363.81	$ 814,055.70	$ 61,973.75	$ 48,334.36	...
9-29-1945	6-23-1947	296,400.30	272,700.00	7,680.00	16,020.30	...
6-24-1947	6-05-1950	7,695,552.22	7,231,755.48	377,355.00	86,441.74	...
6-06-1950	5-22-1953	55,095.04	—	9,176.00	45,919.04	...
5-23-1953	6-30-1958	54,264,553.11	49,788,639.03	3,852,726.98	623,187.10	...
7-01-1958	8-31-1959	771,064.75	—	143,857.00	627,207.75	...
9-01-1959	8-31-1960	983,335.32	257,900.00	98,226.00	627,209.32	...
9-01-1960	8-31-1961	3,890,800.15	3,228,639.51	68,578.00	593,582.64	...
9-01-1961	8-31-1962	1,121,925.09	297,129.88	127,105.00	697,690.21	...
9-01-1962	8-31-1963	3,575,888.64	2,617,057.14	177,174.91	781,656.59	...
9-01-1963	8-31-1964	3,656,236.75	2,435,244.36	525,315.00	695,677.39	...
9-01-1964	8-31-1965	54,654,576.96	53,114,943.63	755,050.12	784,583.21	...
9-01-1965	8-31-1966	22,148,825.44	18,223,357.84	3,163,475.00	761,992.60	...
9-01-1966	8-31-1967	8,469,680.86	3,641,414.96	3,711,092.65	1,117,173.25	...
9-01-1967	8-31-1968	6,305,851.00	1,251,852.50	2,683,732.50	2,370,266.00	...
9-01-1968	8-31-1969	6,372,268.28	1,838,118.33	1,491,592.50	3,042,557.45	...
9-01-1969	8-31-1970	10,311,030.48	5,994,666.32	618,362.50	3,698,001.66	...
9-01-1970	8-31-1971	9,969,629.17	4,326,120.11	726,294.15	4,917,214.91	...
9-01-1971	8-31-1972	7,558,327.21	1,360,212.64	963,367.60	5,234,746.97	...
9-01-1972	8-31-1973	9,267,975.68	3,701,737.30	920,121.60	4,646,116.78	...
9-01-1973	8-31-1974	41,717,670.04	32,981,619.28	1,065,516.60	7,670,534.16	...
9-01-1974	8-31-1975	27,321,536.62	5,319,762.85	2,935,295.60	19,066,478.17	...
9-01-1975	8-31-1976	38,747,074.09	6,197,853.00	3,222,535.84	29,326,685.25	...
9-01-1976	8-31-1977	84,196,228.27	41,343,114.81	2,404,988.80	40,448,124.66	...
9-01-1977	8-31-1978	118,266,812.05	49,807,750.45	4,775,509.92	63,683,551.68	...
9-01-1978	8-31-1979	100,410,268.68	34,578,340.94	7,318,748.40	58,513,179.34	...
9-01-1979	8-31-1980	200,263,803.03	34,733,270.02	10,293,153.80	155,237,379.21	...
9-01-1980	8-31-1981	219,126,876.54	37,467,196.97	13,100,484.25	168,559,195.32	...
9-01-1981	8-31-1982	250,824,581.69	27,529,516.33	14,214,478.97	209,080,586.39	...
9-01-1982	8-31-1983	165,197,734.83	10,180,696.40	12,007,476.70	143,009,561.73	...
9-01-1983	8-31-1984	152,755,934.29	32,864,122.19	8,573,996.87	111,317,815.23	...
9-01-1984	8-31-1985	140,568,090.79	32,650,127.75	6,837,603.70	101,073,959.34	...
9-01-1985	8-31-1986	516,503,771.05	6,365,426.23	4,241,892.75	78,289,592.27	$ 427,606,859.83
9-01-1986	8-31-1987	60,066,571.05	4,186,561.63	1,933,752.50	44,691,907.22	9,254,349.70
9-01-1987	8-31-1988	56,875,069.22	14,195,274.28	1,817,058.90	28,068,202.53	12,794,533.51
9-01-1988	8-31-1989	61,790,000.04	12,005,892.74	1,290,984.37	35,160,568.40	12,345,934.53
9-01-1989	8-31-1990	68,701,751.51	7,708,449.54	1,289,849.87	40,331,537.06	19,371,915.04
9-01-1990	8-31-1991	90,885,856.99	3,791,832.77	1,345,711.07	70,023,601.01	15,724,712.14
9-01-1991	8-31-1992	51,154,511.34	4,450,850.00	1,123,585.54	26,776,191.35	18,803,884.45
9-01-1992	8-31-1993	60,287,712.60	3,394,230.00	904,359.58	34,853,679.68	21,135,443.34
9-01-1993	8-31-1994	57,825,043.59	3,570,657.60	694,029.30	32,244,987.95	21,315,368.74
9-01-1994	8-31-1995	62,143,227.78	8,824,722.93	674,479.79	34,691,023.35	17,951,001.71
9-01-1995	8-31-1996	68,166,645.51	13,919,246.80	1,102,591.39	32,681,315.73	20,463,491.59
9-01-1996	8-31-1997	90,614,935.93	22,007,378.46	1,319,614.78	41,605,792.50	25,682,150.19
9-01-1997	8-31-1998	104,016,006.75	36,946,312.49	2,070,802.90	38,760,320.91	26,238,570.45
9-01-1998	8-31-1999	53,565,810.30	5,402,171.00	2,471,128.47	23,346,515.93	22,345,994.90
9-01-1999	8-31-2000	55,465,763.99	3,487,564.80	2,171,636.35	24,314,241.99	25,492,320.85
9-01-2000	8-31-2001	68,226,347.58	9,963,608.68	1,830,378.11	23,244,034.74	33,188,326.05
9-01-2001	8-31-2002	30,910,283.91	9,286,015.20	1,545,583.01	13,369,771.56	6,708,914.14
9-01-2002	8-31-2003	50,881,515.90	15,152,092.40	1,071,377.60	19,648,641.39	15,009,404.51
9-01-2003	8-31-2004	54,379,791.20	14,448,555.70	1,094,201.41	25,199,635.21	13,637,398.88
9-01-2004	8-31-2005	53,594,809.87	9,148,220.20	1,624,666.50	32,406,328.78	10,415,594.39
9-01-2005	8-31-2006	60,829,271.63	22,565,845.14	1,605,090.30	23,287,994.53	13,370,341.66
Total		$ 3,528,571,688.95	$ 737,859,824.31	$ 140,456,820.20	$1,861,,398,513.84	$ 788,856,510.60
Inside three-mile line		$ 501,517,079.99	$ 172,483,864.05	$ 37,353.744.33	$ 291,679,471.61	0
Between three-mile and three marine-league line		$ 2,235,372,712.78	$ 562,723,875.87	$ 102,929,794.68	$ 1,569,719,042.23	0
Outside three marine-league line		$ 791,681,876.18	$ 2,652,084.39	$ 173,281.19	0	$ 788,856,510.60

Nonfuel Mineral Production and Value, 2003, 2004 and 2005

Source: U.S. Geological Survey and the Texas Bureau of Economic Geology.
*(Production measured by mine shipments, sales or marketable production, including consumption by producers. Production and value data given in **thousand metric tons** and **thousand dollars**, unless otherwise specified.)*

MINERAL	2003		2004		2005*	
	Production	Value	Production	Value	Production	Value
Cement:						
Masonry................................	307	$ 36,100*	319	$ 38,000*	400	$ 48,500*
Portland................................	11,100	747,000*	11,200	800,000*	11,600	951,000*
Clays:						
Common...............................	2,110	8,890	2,160	8,890	2,300	8,700
Fuller's earth........................	27	2,400	W	W	W	W
Kaolin...................................	33	7,150	W	W	W	W
Gemstones................................	NA	201	NA	201	NA	200
Gypsum, crude	1,810	12,300	2,450	18,800	1,500	11,800
Lime	1,630	110,000	1,630	115,000	1,600	112,000
Salt...	9,640	116,000	9,870	118,000	9,600	117,700
Sand and gravel:						
Construction.........................	86,200	425,000	81,700	436,000	80,700	471,800
Industrial..............................	1,930	81,700	2,790	109,000	2,800	113,500
Stone:						
Crushed................................	126,000	595,000	122,000	582,000	133,800	823,400
Dimension............................	87	16,400	64	15,200	44	12,200
Talc, crude.................................	246	W	258	W	W	W
‡Combined value.....................	§	33,300	§	46,300	§	NA
††Total Texas Values...............	§	$2,080,000	§	$2,190,000	§	NA

** Estimated. † Preliminary. **NA:** not available. **W:** data withheld to avoid disclosing proprietary data; value included with "Combined value." § Not applicable. ‡ Includes value of brucite, clays (ball, bentonite), helium, zeolites (2004) and values indicated by symbol W. †† Data do not add to total shown because of independent rounding.*

Nonpetroleum Minerals

The nonpetroleum minerals that occur in Texas constitute a long list. Some are currently mined; some may have a potential for future development; some are minor occurrences only. Although overshadowed by the petroleum, natural gas and natural gas liquids that are produced in the state, many of the non-petroleum minerals are, nonetheless, important to the economy. In 2006, they were valued at an estimated $2.9 billion, representing a 17 percent increase from 2005 and ranking Texas fifth in overall U.S. production.

The **Bureau of Economic Geology**, which functions as the state geological survey of Texas, revised the following information about nonpetroleum minerals for this edition of the *Texas Almanac*. Publications of the Bureau, on file in many libraries, contain more detailed information. Among the items available is the Bureau map, "Mineral Resources of Texas," showing locations of resource access of many nonpetroleum minerals.

A catalog of Bureau publications is also available free on request from the Bureau Publications Sales, University Station, Box X, Austin, TX 78713-7508; 512-471-1534. On the Web: **www.beg.utexas.edu/**.

Texas' nonpetroleum minerals are as follows:

ALUMINUM — No aluminum ores are mined in Texas, but three Texas plants process aluminum materials in one or more ways. Plants in San Patricio and Calhoun counties produce **aluminum oxide (alumina)** from imported raw ore **(bauxite)**, and a plant in Milam County reduces the oxide to aluminum.

ASBESTOS — Small occurrences of amphibole-type asbestos have been found in the state. In West Texas, **richterite**, a white, long-fibered amphibole, is associated with some of the **talc deposits** northwest of **Allamoore** in Hudspeth County. Another type, **tremolite**, has been found in the **Llano Uplift** of Central Texas where it is associated with **serpen-**

tinite in eastern Gillespie and western Blanco County. No asbestos is mined in Texas.

ASPHALT (Native) — Asphalt-bearing Cretaceous limestones crop out in Burnet, Kinney, Pecos, Reeves, Uvalde and other counties. The most significant deposit is in southwestern Uvalde County where asphalt occurs naturally in the pore spaces of the Anacacho Limestone. The material is quarried and used extensively as **road-paving material**. Asphalt-bearing sandstones occur in Anderson, Angelina, Cooke, Jasper, Maverick, Montague, Nacogdoches, Uvalde, Zavala and other counties.

BARITE — Deposits of a heavy, nonmetallic mineral, barite (barium sulphate), have been found in many localities, including Baylor, Brown, Brewster, Culberson, Gillespie, Howard, Hudspeth, Jeff Davis, Kinney, Llano, Taylor, Val Verde and Webb counties. During the 1960s, there was small, intermittent production in the **Seven Heart Gap** area of the **Apache Mountains** in Culberson County, where barite was mined from open pits. Most of the deposits are known to be relatively small, but the Webb County deposit has not been evaluated. Grinding plants, which prepare barite mined outside of Texas for use chiefly as a **weighting agent** in well-drilling muds and as a **filler**, are located in Brownsville, Corpus Christi, El Paso, Galena Park, Galveston, and Houston.

BASALT (TRAP ROCK) — Masses of basalt — a hard, dark-colored, fine-grained igneous rock — crop out in Kinney, Travis, Uvalde and several other counties along the **Balcones Fault Zone**, and also in the Trans-Pecos area of West Texas. Basalt is quarried near Knippa in Uvalde County for use as **road-building material, railroad ballast and other aggregate**.

BENTONITE (see **CLAYS**).

BERYLLIUM — Occurrences of beryllium minerals at

several Trans-Pecos localities have been recognized for several years.

BRINE (see also **SALT, SODIUM SULPHATE**) — Many wells in Texas produce brine by solution mining of subsurface salt deposits, mostly in West Texas counties such as Andrews, Crane, Ector, Loving, Midland, Pecos, Reeves, Ward and others. These wells in the Permian Basin dissolve salt from the Salado Formation, an enormous salt deposit that extends in the subsurface from north of the Big Bend northward to Kansas, has an east-west width of 150 to 200 miles, and may have several hundred feet of net salt thickness. The majority of the brine is used in the petroleum industry, but it also is used in water softening, the chemical industry and other uses. Three Gulf Coast counties, Fort Bend, Duval and Jefferson, have brine stations that produce from salt domes.

Coal is loaded into a truck at the TXU's Big Brown mining site in 2006 near Fairfield in Freestone County. The mine provides coal for the neighboring TXU Corp.'s power plant. AP/David J. Phillip photo.

BUILDING STONE (DIMENSION STONE) — Granite and **limestone** currently are quarried for use as dimension stone. The granite quarries are located in Burnet, Gillespie, Llano and Mason counties; the limestone quarries are in Shackelford and Williamson counties. Past production of limestone for use as dimension stone has been reported in Burnet, Gillespie, Jones, Tarrant, Travis and several other counties. There has also been production of **sandstone** in various counties for use as dimension stone.

CEMENT MATERIALS — Cement is currently manufactured in Bexar, Comal, Dallas, Ector, Ellis, Hays, McLennan, Nolan and Potter counties. Many of these plants utilize Cretaceous limestones and shales or clays as raw materials for the cement. On the Texas High Plains, a cement plant near Amarillo uses impure **caliche** as the chief raw material. Iron oxide, also a constituent of cement, is available from the iron ore deposits of East Texas and from smelter slag. **Gypsum**, added to the cement as a retarder, is found chiefly in North Central Texas, Central Texas and the Trans-Pecos area.

CHROMIUM Chromite-bearing rock has been found in several small deposits around the margin of the Coal Creek **serpentinite** mass in northeastern Gillespie County and northwestern Blanco County. Exploration has not revealed significant deposits.

CLAYS — Texas has an abundance and variety of ceramic and non-ceramic clays and is one of the country's leading producers of clay products.

Almost any kind of clay, ranging from common clay used to make ordinary brick and tile to clays suitable for manufacture of specialty whitewares, can be used for ceramic purposes. **Fire clay** suitable for use as **refractories** occurs chiefly in East and North Central Texas; **ball clay**, a high-quality plastic ceramic clay, is found locally in East Texas.

Ceramic clay suitable for quality structural clay products such as **structural building brick, paving brick and drain tile** is especially abundant in East and North Central Texas. Common clay suitable for use in the manufacture of cement and ordinary brick is found in most counties of the state. Many of the Texas clays will expand or bloat upon rapid firing and are suitable for the manufacture of lightweight aggregate, which is used mainly in concrete blocks and highway surfacing.

Nonceramic clays are utilized without firing. They are used primarily as **bleaching and absorbent clays, fillers,** **coaters, additives, bonding clays, drilling muds, catalysts** and potentially as sources of alumina. Most of the nonceramic clays in Texas are **bentonites** and **fuller's earth**. These occur extensively in the Coastal Plain and locally in the High Plains and Big Bend areas. **Kaolin clays** in parts of East Texas are potential sources of such nonceramic products as **paper coaters and fillers, rubber fillers and drilling agents**. Relatively high in alumina, these clays also are a potential source of metallic aluminum.

COAL (see also LIGNITE) — **Bituminous coal**, which occurs in North Central, South and West Texas, was a significant energy source in Texas prior to the large-scale development of oil and gas. During the period from 1895 to 1943, Texas mines produced more than 25 million tons of coal. The mines were inactive for many years, but the renewed interest in coal as a major energy source prompted a revaluation of Texas' coal deposits. In the late 1970s, bituminous coal production resumed in the state on a limited scale when mines were opened in Coleman, Erath and Webb counties.

Much of the state's bituminous coal occurs in North Central Texas. Deposits are found there in Pennsylvanian rocks within a large area that includes Coleman, Eastland, Erath, Jack, McCulloch, Montague, Palo Pinto, Parker, Throckmorton, Wise, Young and other counties. Before the general availability of oil and gas, underground coal mines near **Thurber, Bridgeport, Newcastle, Strawn** and other points annually produced significant coal tonnages. Preliminary evaluations indicate substantial amounts of coal may remain in the North Central Texas area. The coal seams there are generally no more than 30 inches thick and are commonly covered by well-consolidated overburden. Ash and sulphur content are high. Beginning in 1979, two bituminous coal mine operations in North Central Texas — one in southern Coleman County and one in northwestern Erath County — produced coal to be used as fuel by the cement industry. Neither mine is currently operating.

In South Texas, bituminous coal occurs in the Eagle Pass district of Maverick County, and bituminous **cannel coal** is present in the **Santo Tomas district** of Webb County. The Eagle Pass area was a leading coal-producing district in Texas during the late 1800s and early 1900s. The bituminous coal in that area, which occurs in the Upper Cretaceous Olmos Formation, has a high ash content and a moderate moisture and sulfur content. According to reports, Maverick County coal beds range from four to seven feet thick.

The **cannel coals** of western Webb County occur near the Rio Grande in middle Eocene strata. They were mined for more than 50 years and used primarily as a boiler fuel. Mining ceased from 1939 until 1978, when a surface mine was opened 30 miles northwest of Laredo to produce cannel coal for use as fuel in the cement industry and for export. An additional mine has since been opened in that county. Tests show that the coals of the Webb County Santo Tomas district have a high hydrogen content and yield significant amounts of gas and oil when distilled. They also have a high sulfur content. A potential use might be as a source of various petrochemical products.

Coal deposits in the Trans-Pecos country of West Texas include those in the Cretaceous rocks of the Terlingua area of Brewster County, the Eagle Spring area of Hudspeth County and the **San Carlos** area of Presidio County. The coal deposits in these areas are believed to have relatively little potential for development as a fuel. They have been sold in the past as a soil amendment (see **LEONARDITE**).

COPPER — Copper minerals have been found in the **Trans-Pecos** area of West Texas, in the **Llano Uplift** area of Central Texas, and in redbed deposits of North Texas. No copper has been mined in Texas during recent years, and the total copper produced in the state has been relatively small. Past attempts to mine the North Texas and Llano Uplift copper deposits resulted in small shipments, but practically all the copper production in the state has been from the **Van Horn-Allamoore** district of Culberson and Hudspeth Counties in the Trans-Pecos area. Chief output was from the **Hazel copper-silver mine** of Culberson County that yielded over 1 million pounds of copper during 1891–1947. Copper ores and concentrates from outside of Texas are processed at **smelters** in El Paso and Amarillo.

CRUSHED STONE — Texas is among the leading states in the production of crushed stone. Most production consists of **limestone**; other kinds of crushed stone produced in the state include **basalt (trap rock), dolomite, granite, marble, rhyolite, sandstone and serpentinite**. Large tonnages of crushed stone are used as **aggregate** in concrete, as **road material** and in the manufacture of cement and lime. Some is used as **riprap, terrazzo, roofing chips, filter material, fillers** and for other purposes.

DIATOMITE (DIATOMACEOUS EARTH) — Diatomite is a very lightweight siliceous material consisting of the remains of microscopic aquatic plants (diatoms). It is used chiefly as a **filter and filler**; other uses are for **thermal insulation**, as an **abrasive**, as an **insecticide carrier** and as a **lightweight aggregate**, and for other purposes. The diatomite was deposited in shallow fresh-water lakes that were present in the High Plains during portions of the Pliocene and Pleistocene epochs. Deposits have been found in Armstrong, Crosby, Dickens, Ector, Hartley and Lamb counties. No diatomite is mined in Texas.

DOLOMITE ROCK — Dolomite rock, which consists largely of the mineral dolomite (calcium-magnesium carbonate), commonly is associated with limestone in Texas. Areas in which dolomite rock occurs include Central Texas, the Callahan Divide and parts of the Edwards Plateau, High Plains and West Texas. Some of the principal deposits of dolomite rock are found in Bell, Brown, Burnet, Comanche, Edwards, El Paso, Gillespie, Lampasas, Mills, Nolan, Taylor and Williamson counties. Dolomite rock can be used as crushed stone (although much of Texas dolomite is soft and not a good aggregate material), in the manufacture of lime and as a source of **magnesium**.

FELDSPAR — Large crystals and crystal fragments of feldspar minerals occur in the Precambrian pegmatite rocks that crop out in the **Llano Uplift** area of Central Texas — including Blanco, Burnet, Gillespie, Llano and Mason counties — and in the **Van Horn area** of Culberson and Hudspeth Counties in West Texas. Feldspar has been mined in Llano County for use as **roofing granules** and as a **ceramic material**. Feldspar is currently mined in Burnet County for use as an aggregate.

FLUORSPAR — The mineral fluorite (calcium fluoride), which is known commercially as fluorspar, occurs in both Central and West Texas. In Central Texas, the deposits that have been found in Burnet, Gillespie and Mason counties are not considered adequate to sustain mining operations. In West Texas, deposits have been found in Brewster, El Paso, Hudspeth, Jeff Davis and Presidio counties. Fluorspar has been mined in the **Christmas Mountains** of Brewster County and processed in Marathon. Former West Texas mining activity in the **Eagle Mountains** district of Hudspeth County resulted in the production of approximately 15,000 short tons of fluorspar during the peak years of 1942-1950. No production has been reported in Hudspeth County since that period. Imported fluorspar is processed in Brownsville, Eagle Pass, El Paso and Houston. Fluorspar is used in the **steel, chemical, aluminum, magnesium, ceramics and glass industries** and for various other purposes.

FULLER'S EARTH (see **CLAY**).

GOLD — No major deposits of gold are known in Texas. Small amounts have been found in the **Llano Uplift** region of Central Texas and in West Texas; minor occurrences have been reported on the **Edwards Plateau** and the **Gulf Coastal Plain** of Texas. Nearly all of the gold produced in the state came as a by-product of silver and lead mining at **Presidio mine**, near **Shafter**, in Presidio County. Additional small quantities were produced as a by-product of copper mining in Culberson County and from residual soils developed from gold-bearing quartz stringers in metamorphic rocks in Llano County. No gold mining has been reported in Texas since 1952. Total **gold production** in the state, 1889-1952, amounted to more than 8,419 troy ounces according to U.S. Bureau of Mines figures. Most of the production — at least 73 percent and probably more — came from the Presidio mine.

GRANITE — Granites in shades of red and gray and related intrusive igneous rocks occur in the **Llano Uplift** of Central Texas and in the **Trans-Pecos** country of West Texas. Deposits are found in Blanco, Brewster, Burnet, El Paso, Gillespie, Hudspeth, Llano, McCulloch, Mason, Presidio and other counties. Quarries in Burnet, Gillespie, Llano and Mason counties produce Precambrian granite for a variety of uses as **dimension stone and crushed stone**.

GRAPHITE — Graphite, a soft, dark-gray mineral, is a form of very high-grade carbon. It occurs in Precambrian schist rocks of the **Llano Uplift** of Central Texas, notably in Burnet and Llano counties. Crystalline-flake graphite ore formerly was mined from open pits in the **Clear Creek area** of western Burnet County and processed at a plant near the mine. The mill now occasionally grinds imported material. Uses of natural crystalline graphite are **refractories, steel production, pencil leads, lubricants, foundry facings and crucibles** and for other purposes.

GRINDING PEBBLES (ABRASIVE STONES) — Flint pebbles, suitable for use in **tube-mill grinding**, are found in the **Gulf Coastal Plain** where they occur in gravel deposits along rivers and in upland areas. Grinding pebbles are produced from **Frio River terrace** deposits near the McMullen-Live Oak county line, but the area is now part of the Choke Canyon Reservoir area.

GYPSUM — Gypsum is widely distributed in Texas. Chief deposits are bedded gypsum in the area east of the **High Plains**, in the **Trans-Pecos** country and in **Central Texas**. It also occurs in **salt-dome caprocks** of the Gulf Coast. The massive, granular variety known as rock gypsum is the kind most commonly used by industry. Other varieties include **alabaster, satin spar and selenite**.

Gypsum is one of the important industrial minerals in Texas. Bedded gypsum is produced from surface mines in Culberson, Fisher, Gillespie, Hardeman, Hudspeth, Kimble, Nolan and Stonewall counties. Gypsum was formerly mined at **Gyp Hill salt dome** in Brooks County and at **Hockley salt dome** in Harris County. Most of the gypsum is calcined and used in the manufacture of **gypsum wallboard, plaster, joint compounds** and other construction products. Crude gypsum is used chiefly as a **retarder in portland cement** and as a **soil conditioner**.

HELIUM — Helium is a very light, nonflammable, chemically inert gas. The **U.S. Interior Department has ended its helium operation** near Masterson in the Panhandle. The storage facility at **Cliffside gas field** near Amarillo and the 425-mile pipeline system will remain in operation until the government sells its remaining unrefined, crude helium. Helium is used in **cryogenics, welding, pressurizing and purging,**

leak detection, synthetic breathing mixtures and for other purposes.

IRON — Iron oxide (**limonite, goethite and hematite**) and **iron carbonate (siderite)** deposits occur widely in East Texas, notably in Cass, Cherokee, Marion and Morris counties, and also in Anderson, Camp, Harrison, Henderson, Nacogdoches, Smith, Upshur and other counties. **Magnetite (magnetic, black iron oxide)** occurs in Central Texas, including a deposit at **Iron Mountain** in Llano County. Hematite occurs in the **Trans-Pecos** area and in the **Llano Uplift** of Central Texas. The extensive deposits of **glauconite** (a complex silicate containing iron) that occur in East Texas and the hematitic and goethitic Cambrian sandstone that crops out in the northwestern Llano Uplift region are potential sources of low-grade iron ore.

Limonite and other East Texas iron ores are mined from open pits in Cherokee and Henderson counties for use in the preparation of **portland cement**, as a **weighting agent in well-drilling fluids**, as an **animal feed supplement** and for other purposes. East Texas iron ores also were mined in the past for use in the iron-steel industry.

KAOLIN (see **CLAY**).

LEAD AND ZINC — The lead mineral **galena (lead sulfide)** commonly is associated with zinc and silver. It formerly was produced as a by-product of West Texas silver mining, chiefly from the **Presidio mine at Shafter** in Presidio County, although lesser amounts were obtained at several other mines and prospects. Deposits of galena also are known to occur in Blanco, Brewster, Burnet, Gillespie and Hudspeth counties.

Zinc, primarily from the mineral **sphalerite (zinc sulphide)**, was produced chiefly from the **Bonanza** and **Alice Ray** mines in the **Quitman Mountains** of Hudspeth County. In addition, small production was reported from several other areas, including the **Chinati** and **Montezuma mines** of Presidio County and the **Buck Prospect** in the **Apache Mountains** of Culberson County. Zinc mineralization also occurs in association with the lead deposits in Cambrian rocks of Central Texas.

LEONARDITE — Deposits of weathered (oxidized) low-Btu value bituminous coals, generally referred to as "leonardite," occur in Brewster County. The name leonardite is used for a mixture of chemical compounds that is high in humic acids. In the past, material from these deposits was sold as **soil conditioner**. Other uses of leonardite include **modification of viscosity of drill fluids and as sorbants in water-treatment**.

LIGHTWEIGHT AGGREGATE (see CLAY, DIATOMITE, PERLITE, VERMICULITE).

LIGNITE — Almost all current coal production in Texas is located in the Tertiary-aged lignite belts that extend across the Texas Gulf Coastal Plain from the Rio Grande in South Texas to the Arkansas and Louisiana borders in East Texas. The Railroad Commission of Texas (RRC) reported that in 2005 Texas produced 47.2 million short tons of lignite in 13 mines. Cumulative production in 2005 was 1.33 billion short tons of lignite and coal. According to U.S. Energy Information Administration (EIA) 2005 preliminary numbers, Texas continued to rank as the fifth-largest coal-producing state.

The near-surface lignite resources, occurring at depths of less than 200 feet in seams of three feet or thicker, are estimated at 23 billion short tons. **Recoverable reserves of strippable lignite** — those that can be economically mined under current conditions of price and technology — are estimated by the EIA to be 722 million short tons.

Additional lignite resources of the Texas Gulf Coastal Plain occur as deep-basin deposits. Deep-basin resources, those that occur at depths of 200 to 2,000 feet in seams of five feet or thicker, are comparable in magnitude to near-surface resources. The deep-basin lignites are a potential energy resource that conceivably could be utilized by in situ (in place) recovery methods such as underground gasification.

As with bituminous coal, lignite production was significant prior to the general availability of oil and gas. Remnants of old underground mines are common throughout the area of lignite occurrence. Large reserves of strippable lignite have again attracted the attention of energy suppliers, and Texas is now the nation's **5th leading producer of coal**, 99 percent of it

lignite. Eleven large strip mines are now producing lignite that is burned for **mine-mouth electric-power generation**, and additional mines are planned. One of the currently operating mines is located in Bastrop, Milam and Lee counties, where part of the electric power is used for **alumina reduction**. Other mines are in Atascosa, Franklin, Freestone, Harrison, Hopkins, Leon, Limestone, McMullen, Panola, Robertson, Rusk and Titus counties. New permit applications have been submitted to the Railroad Commission of Texas for Freestone, Lee, Leon and Robertson counties.

LIME MATERIAL — **Limestones**, which are abundant in some areas of Texas, are heated to produce lime (calcium oxide) at a number of plants in the state. High-magnesium limestone and dolomite are used to prepare lime at a plant in Burnet County. Other lime plants are located in Bexar, Bosque, Comal, Hill, Johnson and Travis counties. Lime production captive to the kiln's operator occurs in several Texas counties. Lime is used in **soil stabilization, water purification, paper and pulp manufacture, metallurgy, sugar refining, agriculture, construction, removal of sulfur from stack gases** and for many other purposes.

LIMESTONE (see also **BUILDING STONE**) — Texas is one of the nation's leading producers of limestone, which is quarried in more than 60 counties. Limestone occurs in nearly all areas of the state with the exception of most of the Gulf Coastal Plain and High Plains. Although some of the limestone is quarried for use as **dimension stone**, most of the output is crushed for uses such as **bulk building materials (crushed stone, road base, concrete aggregate), chemical raw materials, fillers or extenders, lime and portland cement raw materials, agricultural limestone and removal of sulfur from stack gases**.

MAGNESITE — Small deposits of magnesite (natural magnesium carbonate) have been found in Precambrian rocks in Llano and Mason counties of Central Texas. At one time there was small-scale mining of magnesite in the area; some of the material was used as **agricultural stone** and as **terrazzo chips**. Magnesite also can be calcined to form magnesia, which is used in metallurgical furnace refractories and other products.

MAGNESIUM — On the Texas Gulf Coast in Brazoria County, magnesium chloride is **extracted from sea water** at a plant in Freeport and used to produce **magnesium compounds and magnesium metal**. During World War II, high-magnesium Ellenburger dolomite rock from Burnet County was used as magnesium ore at a plant near Austin.

MANGANESE — Deposits of manganese minerals, such as **braunite, hollandite and pyrolusite**, have been found in several areas, including Jeff Davis, Llano, Mason, Presidio and Val Verde counties. Known deposits are not large. Small shipments have been made from Jeff Davis, Mason and Val Verde counties, but no manganese mining has been reported in Texas since 1954.

MARBLE — Metamorphic and sedimentary marbles suitable for **monument and building stone** are found in the **Llano Uplift** and nearby areas of Central Texas and the **Trans-Pecos** area of West Texas. Gray, white, black, greenish black, light green, brown and cream-colored marbles occur in Central Texas in Burnet, Gillespie, Llano and Mason counties. West Texas metamorphic marbles include the bluish-white and the black marbles found southwest of Alpine in Brewster County and the white marble from **Marble Canyon** north of Van Horn in Culberson County. Marble can be used as **dimension stone, terrazzo and roofing aggregate** and for other purposes.

MERCURY (QUICKSILVER) — Mercury minerals, chiefly **cinnabar**, occur in the **Terlingua district** and nearby districts of southern Brewster and southeastern Presidio counties. Mining began there about 1894, and from 1905 to 1935, Texas was one of the nation's leading producers of quicksilver. Following World War II, a sharp drop in demand and price, along with depletion of developed ore reserves, caused abandonment of all the Texas mercury mines.

With a rise in the price, sporadic mining took place between 1951-1960. In 1965, when the price of mercury moved to a record high, renewed interest in the Texas mercury districts resulted in the reopening of several mines and the discovery of new ore reserves. By April 1972, however, the price had declined and the mines have reported no production since 1973.

MICA — Large crystals of flexible, transparent mica minerals in igneous pegmatite rocks and mica flakes in metamorphic schist rocks are found in the **Llano area** of Central Texas and the **Van Horn area** of West Texas. Most Central Texas deposits do not meet specifications for sheet mica, and although several attempts have been made to produce West Texas sheet mica in Culberson and Hudspeth counties, sustained production has not been achieved. A mica quarry operated for a short time in the early 1980s in the Van Horn Mountains of Culberson and Hudspeth counties to mine mica schist for use as an **additive in rotary drilling fluids**.

MOLYBDENUM — Small occurrences of molybdenite have been found in Burnet and Llano counties, and **wulfenite**, another molybdenum mineral, has been noted in rocks in the **Quitman Mountains** of Hudspeth County. Molybdenum minerals also occur at **Cave Peak** north of Van Horn in Culberson County, in the **Altuda Mountain area** of northwestern Brewster County and in association with uranium ores of the Gulf Coastal Plain.

PEAT — This spongy organic substance forms in bogs from plant remains. It has been found in the **Gulf Coastal Plain** in several localities including Gonzales, Guadalupe, Lee, Milam, Polk and San Jacinto counties. There has been intermittent, small-scale production of some of the peat for use as a **soil conditioner**.

PERLITE — Perlite, a glassy igneous rock, expands to a lightweight, porous mass when heated. It can be used as a **lightweight aggregate, filter aid, horticultural aggregate** and for other purposes. Perlite occurs in Presidio County, where it has been mined in the **Pinto Canyon area** north of the **Chinati Mountains**. No perlite is currently mined in Texas, but perlite mined outside of Texas is expanded at plants in Bexar, Dallas, El Paso, Guadalupe, Harris and Nolan counties.

PHOSPHATE — Rock phosphate is present in Paleozoic rocks in several areas of Brewster and Presidio counties in West Texas and in Central Texas, but the known deposits are not large. In Northeast Texas, sedimentary rock phosphate occurs in thin conglomeratic lenses in Upper Cretaceous and Tertiary rock units; possibly some of these low-grade phosphorites could be processed on a small scale for local use as a **fertilizer**. Imported phosphate rock is processed at a plant in Brownsville.

POTASH — The potassium mineral **polyhalite** is widely distributed in the subsurface Permian Basin of West Texas and has been found in many wells in that area. During 1927-1931, the federal government drilled a series of potash-test wells in Crane, Crockett, Ector, Glasscock, Loving, Reagan, Upton and Winkler counties. In addition to polyhalite, which was found in all of the counties, these wells revealed the presence of the potassium minerals **carnallite and sylvite** in Loving County and carnallite in Winkler County. The known Texas potash deposits are not as rich as those in the New Mexico portion of the Permian Basin and have not been developed.

PUMICITE (VOLCANIC ASH) — Deposits of volcanic ash occur in Brazos, Fayette, Gonzales, Karnes, Polk, Starr and other counties of the Texas Coastal Plain. Deposits also have been found in the Trans-Pecos area, High Plains and in several counties east of the High Plains. Volcanic ash is used to prepare **pozzolan cement, cleansing and scouring compounds and soaps and sweeping compounds**; as a **carrier for insecticides**, and for other purposes. It has been mined in Dickens, Lynn, Scurry, Starr and other counties.

QUICKSILVER (see **MERCURY**).

RARE-EARTH ELEMENTS AND METALS — The term, "rare-earth elements," is commonly applied to elements of the **lanthanide** group (atomic numbers 57 through 71) plus **yttrium**. Yttrium, atomic number 39 and not a member of the lanthanide group, is included as a rare-earth element because it has similar properties to members of that group and usually occurs in nature with them. The metals **thorium and scandium** are sometimes termed "rare metals" because their occurence is often associated with the rare-earth elements.

The majority of rare-earth elements are consumed as

catalysts in petroleum cracking and other chemical industries. Rare earths are widely used in the **glass industry for tableware, specialty glasses, optics and fiber optics**. Cerium oxide has growing use as a **polishing compound** for glass, gem stones, cathode-ray tube faceplates, and other polishing. Rare earths are alloyed with various metals to produce materials used in the **aeronautic, space and electronics** industries. Addition of rare-earth elements may improve resistance to metal fatigue at high temperatures, reduce potential for corrosion, and selectively increase conductivity and magnetism of the metal.

Various members of this group, including **thorium**, have anomalous concentrations in the **rhyolitic and related igneous rocks** of the **Quitman Mountains** and the **Sierra Blanca area** of Trans-Pecos.

SALT (SODIUM CHLORIDE) (see also **BRINES**) — Salt resources of Texas are virtually inexhaustible. Enormous deposits occur in the subsurface Permian Basin of West Texas and in the **salt domes of the Gulf Coastal Plain**. Salt also is found in the alkali **playa lakes** of the High Plains, the **alkali flats or salt lakes in the Salt Basin** of Culberson and Hudspeth counties and along some of the bays and lagoons of the South Texas **Gulf Coast**.

Texas is one of the leading salt-producing states. **Rock salt** is obtained from underground mines in **salt domes at Grand Saline** in Van Zandt County. Approximately one-third of the salt produced in the state is from rock salt; most of the salt is produced by solution mining as brines from wells drilled into the underground salt deposits.

SAND, INDUSTRIAL — Sands used for special purposes, due to **high silica content** or to unique physical properties, command higher prices than common sand. Industrial sands in Texas occur mainly in the **Central Gulf Coastal Plain** and in **North Central Texas**. They include **abrasive, blast, chemical, engine, filtration, foundry, glass, hydraulic-fracturing (propant), molding and pottery sands**. Recent production of industrial sands has been from Atascosa, Colorado, Hardin, Harris, Liberty, Limestone, McCulloch, Newton, Smith, Somervell and Upshur counties.

SAND AND GRAVEL (CONSTRUCTION) — Sand and gravel are among the most extensively utilized resources in Texas. Principal occurrence is along the major streams and in stream terraces. Sand and gravel are important **bulk construction materials, used as railroad ballast, base materials** and for other purposes.

SANDSTONE — Sandstones of a variety of colors and textures are widely distributed in a number of geologic formations in Texas. Some of the sandstones have been quarried for use as **dimension stone** in El Paso, Parker, Terrell, Ward and other counties. **Crushed sandstone** is produced in Freestone, Gaines, Jasper, McMullen, Motley and other counties for use as **road-building material, terrazzo stone and aggregate**.

SERPENTINITE — Several masses of serpentinite, which formed from the alteration of basic igneous rocks, are associated with other Precambrian metamorphic rocks of the **Llano Uplift**. The largest deposit is the **Coal Creek serpentinite mass** in northern Blanco and Gillespie counties from which **terrazzo chips** have been produced. Other deposits are present in Gillespie and Llano counties. (The features that are associated with surface and subsurface Cretaceous rocks in several counties in or near the **Balcones Fault Zone** and that are commonly known as "serpentine plugs" are not serpentine at all, but are altered igneous volcanic necks and pipes and mounds of altered volcanic ash — **palagonite** — that accumulated around the former **submarine volcanic pipes**.)

SHELL — Oyster shells and other shells in shallow coastal waters and in deposits along the **Texas Gulf Coast** have been produced in the past chiefly by dredging. They were used to a limited extent as raw material in the **manufacture of cement, as concrete aggregate and road base**, and for other purposes. No shell has been produced in Texas since 1981.

SILVER — During the period 1885-1952, the production of silver in Texas, as reported by the U.S. Bureau of Mines, totaled about **33 million troy ounces**. For about 70 years, silver was the most consistently produced metal in Texas, although always in moderate quantities. All of the production came from the **Trans-Pecos country** of West Texas, where the silver was mined in Brewster County (**Altuda Mountain**), Culberson and Hudspeth counties (**Van Horn Mountains and Van Horn-Allamoore district**), Hudspeth County (**Quitman Mountains and Eagle Mountains**) and Presidio County (**Chinati Mountains area, Loma Plata mine and Shafter district**).

Chief producer was the **Presidio mine in the Shafter district**, which began operations in the late 1800s, and, through September 1942, produced more than 30 million ounces of silver — more than 92 percent of Texas' total silver production. Water in the lower mine levels, lean ores and low price of silver resulted in the closing of the mine in 1942. Another important silver producer was the **Hazel copper-silver mine** in the **Van Horn-Allamoore district** in Culberson County, which accounted for more than 2 million ounces.

An increase in the price of silver in the late 1970s stimulated prospecting for new reserves, and exploration began near the old **Presidio mine**, near the old **Plata Verde mine** in the Van Horn Mountains district, at the Bonanza mine in the **Quitman Mountains** district and at the old **Hazel mine**. A decline in the price of silver in the early 1980s, however, resulted in reduction of exploration and mine development in the region. There is no current exploration in these areas.

SOAPSTONE (see **TALC AND SOAPSTONE**).

SODIUM SULFATE (SALT CAKE) — Sodium sulfate minerals occur in salt beds and brines of the alkali **playa lakes** of the High Plains in West Texas. In some lakes, the sodium sulfate minerals are present in deposits a few feet beneath the lakebeds. Sodium sulfate also is found in underground brines in the Permian Basin. Current production is from brines and dry salt beds at alkali lakes in Gaines and Terry counties. Past production was reported in Lynn and Ward counties. Sodium sulfate is used chiefly by the **detergent and paper and pulp industries**. Other uses are in the **preparation of glass and other products**.

STONE (see **BUILDING STONE** and **CRUSHED STONE**).

STRONTIUM — Deposits of the mineral **celestite (strontium sulfate)** have been found in a number of places, including localities in Brown, Coke, Comanche, Fisher, Lampasas, Mills, Nolan, Real, Taylor, Travis and Williamson counties. Most of the occurrences are very minor, and no strontium is currently produced in the state.

SULFUR — Texas is **one of the world's principal sulfur-producing areas**. The sulfur is mined from deposits of native sulfur, and it is extracted from sour (sulfur-bearing) natural gas and petroleum. **Recovered sulfur** is a growing industry and accounted for approximately 60 percent of all 1987 sulfur production in the United States, but only approximately 40 percent of Texas production. Native sulfur is found in large deposits in the caprock of some of the **salt domes** along the Texas Gulf Coast and in some of the surface and subsurface Permian strata of West Texas, notably in Culberson and Pecos counties.

Native sulfur obtained from the underground deposits is known as **Frasch sulfur**, so-called because of Herman Frasch, the chemist who devised the method of drilling wells into the deposits, melting the sulfur with superheated water and forcing the molten sulfur to the surface. Most of the production now goes to the users in molten form.

Frasch sulfur is produced from only one Gulf Coast salt dome in Wharton County and from West Texas underground Permian strata in Culberson County. Operations at several Gulf Coast domes have been closed in recent years. During the 1940s, acidic sulfur earth was produced in the **Rustler Springs district** in Culberson County for use as a **fertilizer and soil conditioner**. Sulfur is recovered from sour natural gas and petroleum at plants in numerous Texas counties.

Sulfur is used in the preparation of **fertilizers and organic and inorganic chemicals, in petroleum refining** and for many other purposes.

TALC AND SOAPSTONE — Deposits of talc are found in the Precambrian metamorphic rocks of the **Allamoore area** of eastern Hudspeth and western Culberson counties. Soapstone, containing talc, occurs in the Precambrian metamorphic rocks of the **Llano Uplift** area, notably in Blanco, Gillespie and Llano counties. Current production is from surface mines in the **Allamoore area**. Talc is used in **ceramic, roofing, paint, paper, plastic, synthetic rubber** and other products.

TIN — Tin minerals have been found in El Paso and Mason counties. Small quantities were produced during the early 1900s in the Franklin Mountains north of El Paso. **Cassiterite (tin dioxide)** occurrences in Mason County are believed to be very minor. The **only tin smelter in the United States**, built at **Texas City** by the federal government during World War II and later sold to a private company, processes tin concentrates from ores mined outside of Texas, tin residues and secondary tin-bearing materials.

TITANIUM — The titanium mineral **rutile** has been found in small amounts at the **Mueller prospect** in Jeff Davis County. Another titanium mineral, **ilmenite**, occurs in sandstones in Burleson, Fayette, Lee, Starr and several other counties. Deposits that would be considered commercial under present conditions have not been found.

TRAP ROCK (see **BASALT**).

TUNGSTEN — The tungsten mineral **scheelite** has been found in small deposits in Gillespie and Llano counties and in the **Quitman Mountains** in Hudspeth County. Small deposits of other tungsten minerals have been prospected in the **Cave Peak area** north of Van Horn in Culberson County.

URANIUM — Uranium deposits were discovered in the **Texas Coastal Plain** in 1954 when abnormal radioactivity was detected in the Karnes County area. A number of uranium deposits have since been discovered within a belt of strata extending more than 250 miles from the middle Coastal Plain southwestward to the Rio Grande.

Various uranium minerals also have been found in other areas of Texas, including the **Trans-Pecos**, the **Llano Uplift** and the **High Plains**. With the exception of small shipments from the High Plains during the 1950s, all the uranium production in Texas has been from the Coastal Plain. Uranium has been obtained from surface mines extending from northern Live Oak County, southeastern Atascosa County, across northern Karnes County and into southern Gonzales County. Uranium is produced by in-situ leaching, brought to the surface through wells, and stripped from the solution at recovery operations.

In 1999, uranium mining shut down because of decreased value and demand. Production resumed in Texas in late 2004, when inventories were depleted and market prices rose to economic levels that allowed resumption of production. A total of 1.325 million pounds of eU3O8 was produced in South Texas in 2006. Uranium Resources (URI) in Dallas reported a total of 259 thousand pounds of eU3O8 production. URI has operations at Kingsville Dome in Kleberg County and Vasquez Mine in Duval County. Mesteña Uranium LLC reported 1.066 million pounds of eU3O8 production from its Alta Mesa project in Brooks County. Cumulative production from 2004 through 2006 was 1.7 million pounds.

VERMICULITE — Vermiculite, a mica-like mineral that expands when heated, occurs in Burnet, Gillespie, Llano, Mason and other counties in the **Llano region**. It has been produced at a surface mine in Llano County. Vermiculite, mined outside of Texas, is exfoliated (expanded) at plants in Dallas, Houston and San Antonio. Exfoliated vermiculite is used for **lightweight concrete aggregate, horticulture, insulation** and other purposes.

VOLCANIC ASH (see **PUMICITE**).

ZEOLITES — The zeolite minerals **clinoptilolite** and **analcime** occur in Tertiary lavas and tuffs in Brewster, Jeff Davis and Presidio counties, in West Texas. Clinoptilolite also is found associated with Tertiary tuffs in the southern Texas Coastal Plain, including deposits in Karnes, McMullen and Webb counties, and currently is produced in McMullen County. Zeolites, sometimes called "**molecular sieves**," can be used in **ion-exchange processes to reduce pollution**, as a catalyst in **oil cracking**, in obtaining **high-purity oxygen and nitrogen** from air, in **water purification** and for many other purposes.

ZINC (see **LEAD AND ZINC**). ☆

Transportation

BNSF train in Chillicothe. Robert Plocheck photo.

Freight Gateways

Highways

Railroads

Aviation

Trucking

Ports

Foreign Trade Zones

Consulates

U.S. Freight Gateways, 2004

[In billions of dollars (125 represents $125,000,000,000)]. Top gateways ranked by value of shipments, with Texas gateways highlighted. *Source: U.S. Bureau of Transportation Statistics, National Transportation Statistics, annual.*

Rank	Port	Mode	Total trade	Exports	Imports	Exports as a percent of total
1	JFK International Airport, NY	Air	$ 125	$ 53	$ 73	42.0
2	Port of Los Angeles, CA	Water	121	16	105	13.5
3	Port of Long Beach, CA	Water	121	19	103	15.3
4	Port of Detroit, MI	Land	114	58	56	51.1
5	Port of New York and New Jersey	Water	114	23	90	20.4
6	Port of Laredo, TX	Land	90	38	51	42.9
7	Los Angeles International Airport, CA	Air	69	34	35	49.3
8	Port of Buffalo-Niagara Falls, NY	Land	68	32	37	46.4
9	Port of Houston, TX	Water	66	29	37	44.0
10	Port of Huron, MI	Land	66	24	42	35.8
11	Chicago, IL	Air	65	25	40	38.6
12	San Francisco International Airport, CA	Air	55	24	30	44.5
13	Port of Charleston, SC	Water	47	15	31	32.9
14	Port of El Paso, TX	Land	43	18	24	42.9
15	Port of Norfolk Harbor, VA	Water	33	12	21	35.8
16	Port of Baltimore, MD	Water	31	7	24	22.0
17	Dallas-Fort Worth, TX	Air	31	15	17	46.7
18	New Orleans, LA	Air	30	15	15	50.6
19	Port of Seattle, WA	Water	30	7	23	22.6
20	Port of Tacoma, WA	Water	29	5	24	18.3
21	Port of Oakland, CA	Water	27	8	19	31.1
22	Port of Savannah, GA	Water	26	10	17	36.9
23	Anchorage, AK	Air	26	6	21	21.8
24	Miami International Airport, FL	Air	25	16	9	64.0
25	Atlanta, GA	Air	25	10	15	41.6
26	Cleveland, OH	Air	23	13	10	55.6
27	Port of Otay Mesa Station, CA	Land	22	9	13	40.2
28	Port of New Orleans	Water	20	8	12	40.1
29	Port of Miami, FL	Water	18	8	11	41.5
30	Port of Beaumont, TX	Water	16	1	15	8.2
31	Port of Champlain-Rouses Pt., NY	Land	16	6	10	37.0
32	Port of Hidalgo, TX	Land	16	7	9	41.9
33	Newark, NJ	Air	15	3	12	22.3
34	Port of Blaine, WA	Land	14	6	8	44.3
35	Port of Morgan City, LA	Water	14	-	14	1.1
36	Port of Jacksonville, FL	Water	14	5	9	33.0
37	Boston Logan Airport, MA	Air	13	8	5	61.3
38	Port of Portland, OR	Water	12	3	9	24.7
39	Port of Nogales, AZ	Land	12	4	8	35.2
40	Port of Corpus Christi, TX	Water	12	2	10	16.6

Border Crossings at U.S. Ports of Entry, 2006

Below are listed 2006 statistics for selected states as to border traffic at official ports of entry into the United States. Data are from the U.S. Bureau of Transportation Statistics.

Entering at border crossing	Texas	California	Arizona	New Mexico	Michigan	U.S. total
Incoming vehicles	28,422,384	20,746,627	5,471,684	404,120	6,567,458	76,381,260
Privately-owned vehicles	26,472,790	20,011,499	5,223,191	379,581	4,967,782	69,428,390
Persons (total)	66,285,182	47,003,222	18,888,875	1,254,759	9,799,064	172,453,208
Persons on foot/bicycle	11,025,005	8,260,836	6,262,525	135,667	–	25,953,053
Loaded containers	1,419,956	401,202	206,827	18,164	1,637,949	6,288,786

Foreign Consulates in Texas

In the list below, these abbreviations appear after the name of the city: (CG) Consulate General; (C) Consulate; (VC) Vice Consulate. The letter "H" before the designation indicates honorary status. Compiled from "Foreign Consular Offices in the United States," U.S. Dept. of State, Fall/Winter 2006, and recent Internet sources.

Albania: Houston (HC); 10 Waterway Ct., Ste. 401, The Woodlands, 77380. (281) 548-4740.

Angola: Houston (CG); 3040 Post Oak Blvd., Ste. 780, 77056. (713) 212-3840.

Argentina: Houston (CG); 3050 Post Oak Blvd., Ste. 1625, 77056. (713) 871-8935.

Australia: Houston (HC); 4623 Feagan St., 77007. (713) 782-6009.

Austria: Houston (HCG); 1717 Bissonet St., Ste 306, 77005. (713) 526-0127.

Bangladesh: Houston (HCG); 35 N. Wynden Dr., 77056. (713) 621-8462.

Barbados: Houston (HC); 3027 Sleepy Hollow Dr., Sugar Land 77479. (832) 725-5566.

Belgium: Houston (HCG); 2009 Lubbock St., 77007. (713) 426-3933.
Fort Worth (HC); 6201 South Fwy., 76134. (817) 551-8389.
San Antonio (HC); 106 S. St. Mary's, Ste. 200, 78205. (210) 271-8820.

Belize: Houston (HCG); 7101 Breen, 77086. (713) 999-4484.
Dallas (HC); 1315 19th St., Ste. 2A, Plano, 75074. (972) 579-0070.

Bolivia: Houston (HCG); 800 Wilcrest, Ste. 100, 77042 (713) 977-2344.
Dallas (HC); 1881 Sylvan Ave., Ste. 110, 75208. (214) 571-6131.

Botswana: Houston (HC); 10000 Memorial Dr., Ste. 400, 77024. (713) 680-1155.

Brazil: Houston (CG); 1233 West Loop South, Ste. 1150, 77027. (713) 961-3063.

Cameroon: Houston (HC); 1319 Gamma, Crosby 77532. (713) 499-3502.

Canada: Dallas (CG); 750 N. Saint Paul, Ste. 1700, 75201. (214) 922-9806.
Houston (C); 5847 San Felipe St., Ste. 1700, 77057. (713) 821-1442.
San Antonio (HCG); 106 S. St. Mary's, Ste. 800, 78205. (210) 299-3525.

Chile: Houston (CG):1360 Post Oak Blvd., Ste. 1330, 77056; (713) 963-9066.
Dallas (HC); 3500 Oak Lawn, Apt. 200, 75219. (214) 528-2731.

China: Houston (CG); 3417 Montrose, Ste. 700, 77006. (713) 524-0780.

Colombia: Houston (CG); 5851 San Felipe, Ste. 300, 77057; (713) 527-8919.

Costa Rica: Houston (CG); 3000 Wilcrest, Ste. 112, 77042. (713) 266-0484.
Austin (C); 1730 E. Oltorf, 78741. (512) 445-0023.
Dallas (C); 7777 Forest Lane, Ste. B-445, 75230. (972) 566-7020.

Cyprus: Houston (HCG); 320 S. 66th St., 77011. (713) 928-2264.

Czech Republic: Houston (HC); 11748 Heritage Pkwy., West, 76691. (713) 629-6963.

Denmark: Dallas (HC); 2100 McKinney Ave., Ste. 700, 75201. (214) 661-8399.
Houston (HC); 4545 Post Oak Place, Ste. 347, 77027. (713) 622-9018.

Ecuador: Houston (CG); 4200 Westheimer, Ste. 218, 77027. (713) 622-1787.
Dallas (HC); 7510 Acorn Lane, Frisco, 75034. (972) 712-9107.

Egypt: Houston (CG); 1990 Post Oak Blvd., Ste. 2180, 77056. (713) 961-4915.

El Salvador: Dallas (CG); 1555 W. Mockingbird Lane, Ste. 216, 75235.
Houston (CG); 1702 Hillendahl Blvd. 77055. (713) 270-6239.

Ethiopia: Houston (HC); 9301 Southwest Freeway, Ste. 250, 77074. (713) 271-7567.

Finland: Dallas (HC); 1445 Ross Ave., Ste. 3200, 75202. (214) 855-4715.
Houston (HC); 14 Greenway Plaza, Ste. 22R, 77046. (713) 552-1722.

France: Houston (CG); 777 Post Oak Blvd. Ste. 600, 77056. (713) 572-2799.
Austin (HC); 515 Congress Ave, 78701. (512) 480-5605.
Dallas (HC); 12720 Hillcrest, Ste. 730, 75230. (972) 789-9305.
San Antonio (HC); X Route 1, 78109. 78209. (210) 659-3101.

Georgia: Houston (HC); 3040 Post Oak Blvd., Ste. 700, 77056. (281) 633-3500.

Germany: Houston (CG); 1330 Post Oak Blvd., Ste. 1850, 77056. (713) 627-7770.
Corpus Christi (HC); 615 N. Upper Broadway, Ste. 630,78477. (361) 884-7766.
Dallas (HC); 4265 Kellway, Addison, 75001. (972) 239-0788.
San Antonio (HC); 310 S. St. Mary's, 78205. (210) 226-1788.

Ghana: Houston (HC); 3434 Locke Lane, 77027. (713) 960-8806.

Greece: Houston (CG); 520 Post Oak Blvd., Ste. 450, 77027. (713) 840-7522.

Guatemala: Houston (CG); 3013 Fountain View, Ste 210, 77057. (713) 953-9531.
San Antonio (HC); 4840 Whirlwind, 78217.

Guyana: Houston (HC); 1810 Woodland Park Dr., 77077. (713) 497-4466.

Haiti: Houston (HC); 3535 Sage Rd., 77027.

Honduras: Houston (CG); 6700 West Loop South, Ste. 360, 77027. (713) 667-4693.

Hungary: Houston (HCG); 2221 Potomac B, 77057. (713) 977-8604.

Iceland: Dallas (HC); 17910 Windflower, Apt. 2201, 75252. (214) 540-9135.
Houston (HC); 2348 W. Settler's Way, The Woodlands, 77380. (713) 367-2777.

India: Houston (CG); 1990 Post Oak Blvd., Ste 600, 77056. (713) 626-2148.

Indonesia: Houston (CG); 10900 Richmond Ave., 77042.

Ireland: Houston (HC); 2630 Sutton Ct., 77027. (713) 961-5363.

Israel: Houston (CG); 24 Greenway Plz., Ste. 1500, 77046. (713) 627-3780.

Ivory Coast: Houston (HCG); 412 Hawthorne, 77006. (713) 529-4928.

Italy: Houston (CG); 1300 Post Oak Blvd., Ste. 660, 77056. (713) 850-7520.
Dallas (HC); 6255 W. Northwest Hwy., Apt. 304, 75225. (214) 368-4113.

Jamaica: Houston (HC); 7737 Southwest Fwy., Suite 580, 77074. (713) 541-3333.
Dallas (HC); 3068 Forest Lane, 75234. (972) 396-7969.

Japan: Houston (CG); 909 Fannin, Ste. 3000, 77010. (713) 652-2977.

Dallas (HCG); 5819 Edinburgh St., 75252. (972) 713-8683.

Jordan: Houston (HC); 723 Main St., Ste. 408, 77002. (713) 224-2911.

Korea: Houston (CG); 1990 Post Oak Blvd., Ste. 1250, 77056. (713) 961-0186.
Dallas (HC); 13111 N. Central Expy., 75243. (214) 454-1112.

Kyrgyzstan: Houston (HCG); 2302 Greens Ct., Richmond, 77469. (281) 920-1841.

Latvia: Houston (HC); 5847 San Felipe, Ste. 3400, 77057. (713) 785-0807.

Lebanon: Houston (HC); 1701 Hermann Dr., Ste. 1305, (713) 526-1141.

Lesotho: Austin (HC); 7400 Valburn Dr., 78731.

Lithuania: Houston (HC); 4030 Case, 77005 (713) 665-4218.

Luxembourg: Fort Worth (HC); 48 Valley Ridge Rd., 76107. (817) 738-8600.

Malaysia: Houston (HC); 700 Louisiana, Floor 46, 77002. (713) 222-1470.

Malta: Houston (HCG); 1221 Lamar, Ste. 1313, 77010. (713) 654-7900.
Dallas (HC); PO Box 830688, SM-24, Richardson, 75083. (972) 883-4785.
Austin (HC); 3925 W. Braker Lane, Ste. 300, 78759. (512) 305-0612.

Mexico: Austin (CG); 800 Brazos, Ste. 330, 78701. (512) 478,2803.
Brownsville (C); 301 Mexico Blvd., Ste. F3, 78520. (956) 542-4431.
Corpus Christi (C); 800 N. Shoreline, Ste. 410, 78401.
Dallas (CG); 8855 N. Stemmons Fwy, 75247. (214) 522-9740.
Del Rio (C); 2398 Spur 239, 78840. (830) 774-5031.
Eagle Pass (C); 140 Adams St., 78852. (830) 773-9255.
El Paso (CG); 910 E. San Antonio, 79901. (915) 533-3644.
Fort Worth (CG Dallas); 1801 Harrington Ave., 76106.
Houston (CG); 4507 San Jacinto St., 77004. (713) 271-6800. Tourism Office: 2707 North Loop, Ste. 450, 77008.
Laredo (CG); 1612 Farragut St., 78040. (956) 723-6369.
McAllen (C); 600 S. Broadway, 78501, (956) 686-0243.
Midland (C); 511 W. Ohio St., Ste. 121, 79701.
Presidio (C); 6717 Kelley Addition 1 Hwy, 79845. (915) 229-2788.
San Antonio (CG); 127 Navarro St., 78205. (210) 227-9145. Commercial Affairs Office: 203 S. Saint Mary's St., Ste. 450, 78213.
San Antonio (Office of Mexican Attorney General); 613 NW Loop 410 Ste. 610, 78216. (210) 344-1131.

Monaco: Dallas (HC); 8350 N. Central Expressway, Ste. 1900, 75206. (214) 234-4124.

Mongolia: Houston (HCAgent); 1221 Lamar, Ste. 1201, 77010. (713) 759-1922.

Netherlands: Houston (CG); 2200 Post Oak Blvd., Ste. 610, 77056. (713) 622-8000.

New Zealand: Houston (HC); 246 Warrenton Dr., 77024. (713) 973-8680.

Nicaragua: Houston (CG); 8989 Westheimer, Ste. 103, 77063. (713) 789-2762.

Norway: Houston (CG); 2777 Allen Parkway, Ste. 1185, 77019. (713) 521-2900.
Dallas (HC); 5500 Caruth Haven Lane, 75225. (214) 750-4222.

Pakistan: Houston (C); 11850 Jones Rd. 77070. (2810 890-8525.

Panama: Houston (CG); 24 Greenway Plaza, Ste. 1307, 77046. (713) 622-4451.

Papua New Guinea: Houston (HCG); 4900 Woodway Dr. Ste. 1200, 77056. (713) 966-2500.

Peru: Houston (CG); 5177 Richmond Ave., Ste. 695, 77056. (713) 355-9571.

Poland: Houston (HC); 35 Harbor View, Sugar Land, 77479. (281) 565-1507.

Portugal: Houston (HC); 4544 Post Oak Place, Ste. 350, 77027. (713) 759-1188.

Qatar: Houston (CG); 1990 Post Oak Blvd, Ste. 810, 77056. (713) 355-8221.

Romania: Dallas (HC); 220 Ross Ave., Ste. 2200, 75201. (214) 740-8608.
Houston (HC); 4265 San Felipe, Ste. 220, 77027. (713) 629-1551.

Russia: Houston (CG); 1333 West Loop South, Ste. 1300, 77027. (713) 337-3300.

Saint Kitts/Nevis: Dallas (HC); 6336 Greenville Ave., 75206.

Saudi Arabia: Houston (CG); 5718 Westheimer, Ste. 1500, 77057. (713) 785-5577.

Senegal: Houston (CG); 9701 Richmond, Ste. 212, 77042.

Slovenia: Houston (HC); 2925 Briarpark, Floor 7, 77042. (713) 430-7350.

Spain: Houston (CG); 1800 Bering Dr., Ste. 660, 77057. (713) 783-6200.
Corpus Christi (HC); 7517 Yorkshire Blvd., 78413 (361) 994-7517.
Dallas (HC); 5499 Glen Lakes Dr., Ste. 209, 75231. (214) 373-1200.
El Paso (HC); 420 Golden Springs Dr., 79912. (915) 534-0677.
San Antonio (HC); 8350 Delphian, 78148.

Sweden: Houston (HC); 2909 Hillcroft, Ste. 515, 77057. (713) 953-1417.
Dallas: (HC); 100 Cresent Ct., Ste. 880, 75201, (214) 220-9910.

Switzerland: Houston (CG); 1200 Smith St., Ste. 1040, 77002. (713) 650-0000.
Dallas (HC); 2651 N. Harwood, Ste. 455, 75201. (214) 965-1025.

Syria: Houston (HCG); 5433 Westheimer Rd., Ste. 1020, 77056. (713) 622-8860.

Thailand: Houston (HCG); 600 Travis St., Ste. 2800, 77002. (713) 229-8733.
Dallas (HCG); 1717 Main St., Ste. 4100, 75201.
El Paso (HCG); 4401 N. Mesa, Ste. 204, 79902. (915) 533-5757.

Trinidad/Tobago: Houston (HC); 2400 Augusta, Ste. 250, 77057. (713) 840-1100.

Tunisia: Dallas (HC); 4227 N. Capistrano Dr., 75287. (972) 267-4191.
Houston (HC); 12527 Mossycup, 77024. (713) 935-9427.

Turkey: Houston (CG); 1990 Post Oak Blvd., Ste.1300, 77056. (713) 622-5849.

Ukraine: Houston (HC); 2934 Fairway Dr., Sugar Land, 77478. (281) 242-2842.

United Kingdom: Houston (CG); 1000 Louisiana St., Ste. 1900, 77002. (713) 659-6270.
Dallas (C); 2911 Turtle Creek, Ste. 940, 75219. (214) 637-3600.
San Antonio (HC); 254 Spencer Lane, 78201. (210) 735-9393.

Venezuela : Houston (CG); 2925 Briarpark Dr., Ste. 900, 77027. (713) 961-5141. ☆

Foreign Trade Zones in Texas

Source: The International Trade Reporter, copyright 1979 by the Bureau of National Affairs, Inc., Washington, D.C.

Foreign-trade-zone status endows a domestic site with certain customs privileges, causing it to be considered outside customs territory and therefore available for activities that might otherwise be carried on overseas.

Operated as public utilities for qualified corporations, the zones are established under grants of authority from the Foreign-Trade Zones board, which is chaired by the

U.S. Secretary of Commerce. Zone facilities are available for operations involving storage, repacking, inspection, exhibition, assembly, manufacturing and other processing.

A foreign-trade zone is especially suitable for export processing or manufacturing operations when foreign components or materials with a high U.S. duty are needed to make the end product competitive in markets abroad.

Source: U.S. Department of Commerce

There were 33 Foreign-Trade Zones in Texas as of May 2007.

Amarillo, FTZ 252
City of Amarillo
600 S. Tyler Ste. 1503, Amarillo 79101

Athens, FTZ 269
Athens Economic Development Corp.
100 W. Tyler St., Athens 75751

Austin, FTZ 183
FTZ of Central Texas Inc.
301 W. Bagdad Ave., Round Rock 78664

Beaumont, FTZ 115
Port Arthur, FTZ 116
Orange, FTZ 117
FTZ of Southeast Texas Inc.
P.O. Drawer 2297, Beaumont 77704

Bowie County, FTZ 258
Red River Redevelopment Authority
107 Chapel Lane, New Boston 75570

Brownsville, FTZ 62
Brownsville Navigation District
1000 Foust Road, Brownsville 78521

Calhoun/Victoria Counties FTZ 155
Calhoun-Victoria FTZ Inc.
P.O. Drawer 397, Point Comfort 77978

Conroe, FTZ 265
City of Conroe
PO Box 3066, Conroe 77305

Corpus Christi, FTZ 122
Port of Corpus Christi Authority
P.O. Box 1541, Corpus Christi 78403

Dallas/Ft.Worth, FTZ 39
D/FW International Airport Board

P.O. Drawer 619428, D/FW Airport 75261

Dallas/Fort Worth, FTZ 168
FTZ Operating Company of Texas
P.O. Box 742916, Dallas 75374

Eagle Pass, FTZ 96
Maverick County Development Corp.
P.O. Box 3693, Eagle Pass 78853

Edinburg, FTZ 251
City of Edinburg
602 W. University Dr., Ste. B
Edinburg 78539

Ellis County, FTZ 113
Midlothian Trade Zone Corp.
1500 N. Service Road, Hwy. 67
Midlothian 76065

El Paso, FTZ 68
City of El Paso
501 George Perry, Ste. I,
El Paso 79906

El Paso, FTZ 150
Westport Economic Dev. Corp.
1865 Northwestern Dr.. El Paso 79912

Fort Worth, FTZ 196
Alliance Corridor Inc.
13600 Heritage Pkwy., Ste. 200
Fort Worth 76177

Freeport, FTZ 149
Brazos River Harbor Navigation Dist.
Box 615, Freeport 77542

Galveston, FTZ 36
Port of Galveston
P.O. Box 328, Galveston 77553

Gregg County, FTZ 234
Gregg County
269 Terminal Circle, Longview 75603

Harris County, FTZ 84
Port of Houston Authority
111 East Loop North, Houston 77029

Laredo, FTZ 94
Laredo International Airport
5210 Bob Bullock Loop, Laredo 78041

Liberty County, FTZ 171
Liberty Co. Economic Dev. Corp.
P.O. Box 857, Liberty 77575

Lubbock, FTZ 260
City of Lubbock
5401 N. Martin Luther King Blvd.
Lubbock 79403

McAllen, FTZ 12
McAllen Economic Development Corp.
6401 South 33rd St., McAllen 78501

Midland, FTZ 165
City of Midland
P.O. Box 60305, Midland 79711

San Antonio, FTZ 80
City of San Antonio
P.O. Box 839966, San Antonio 78283

Starr County, FTZ 95
Starr County Industrial Foundation
P.O. Box 502, Rio Grande City 78582

Texas City, FTZ 199
Texas City Harbor FTZ Corp.
P.O. Box 2608, Texas City 77592

Waco, FTZ 246
City of Waco
900 Washington Ave., Ste. 501
Waco 76701

Weslaco, FTZ 156
City of Weslaco
500 S. Kansas Ave., Weslaco 78596

Ships pass into Galveston Bay from the Gulf of Mexico. Robert Plocheck photo.

Tonnage Handled by Texas Ports, 1995–2005

Table below gives consolidated tonnage (x1,000) handled by Texas ports. All figures are in short tons (2,000 lbs.). Note that " - " indicates no commerce was reported, "0" means tonnage reported was less than 500 tons. *Source: Corps of Engineers, U.S. Army.*

Port	2005	2004	2003	2002	2001	2000	1999	1998	1997	1996	1995
Beaumont	78,887	91,698	87,541	85,911	79,131	76,894	69,406	60,052	48,665	35,705	20,937
Brownsville	5,105	4,171	3,731	4,739	4,100	3,268	2,487	2,799	2,284	2,401	2,656
Corpus Christi	77,637	78,921	77,216	71,939	77,576	81,164	78,003	86,140	86,806	80,436	70,218
Freeport	33,602	33,908	30,537	27,164	30,143	28,966	28,076	29,014	26,281	24,571	19,662
Galveston	8,008	8,113	7,545	9,136	9,038	10,402	10,336	11,049	10,126	11,641	10,465
Houston	211,666	202,047	190,923	177,561	185,050	186,567	158,828	169,070	165,456	148,183	135,231
Matagorda Chl. (Port Lavaca)	11,607	12,524	11,673	9,590	9,086	10,552	9,078	8,040	9,429	9,151	9,237
Port Arthur	26,385	27,570	27,170	22,676	22,802	20,524	18,308	29,557	37,318	37,158	49,800
Sabine Pass	641	929	894	1,214	1,203	910	949	1,200	725	135	231
Texas City	57,839	68,283	61,338	55,233	62,270	58,109	49,503	49,477	56,646	56,394	50,403
Victoria Chl.	3,224	3,712	4,750	4,734	4,733	5,104	5,522	5,298	5,000	4,351	4,624
Anahuac	-	-	-	-	-	-	-	-	-	0	-
Aransas Pass	128	142	127	207	15	6	169	48	91	39	181
Arroyo Colorado	791	779	964	898	1,132	837	940	992	928	964	994
Port Isabel	-	2	1			5	7	30	88	114	130
Cedar Bayou	1,172	1,151	972	965	871	1,002	955	666	435	404	473
Chocolate Byu.	3,537	3,534	3,338	2,932	3,411	3,488	3,329	4,048	3,983	3,845	3,480
Clear Creek	-	-	-	-	-	-	11	-	-	0	-
Colorado River	501	503	435	361	390	445	388	503	570	622	576
Dickinson	688	773	994	813	929	904	954	1,073	669	625	657
Double Bayou	257	-	0	-	-	0	-	0	0	0	-
Greens Bayou	3,768	1,138	1,017	0	0	0	0	0	0	0	0
Harbor Island (Port Aransas)	10	4	9	62	105	151	143	40	38	44	209
Liberty Chl.	-	92	18	9	-	-	-	18	-	39	-
Orange	627	609	825	764	798	681	873	756	691	616	693
Palacios	-	-	-	0	0	-	0	-	-	0	-
Port Mansfield	-	-	-	-	-	-	1	3	8	8	20
Rockport	-	-	-	1	-	-	2	-	-	1	-
San Bernard Rr.	773	910	878	662	613	633	666	565	578	565	653
Other Ports	0	0	0	0	0	0	0	0	0	0	0
TOTAL*	487,100	502,038	473,941	442,251	454,765	452,991	406,166	427,296	422,592	385,585	371,021

Totals exclude duplication.

Foreign/Domestic Commerce: Breakdown for 2005

Data below represent inbound and outbound tonnage for major ports. Note that "-" means no tonnage was reported. *Does not include Canadian. Source: U.S. Army Corps of Engineers*

(All figures in short tons x1000)

Port	Foreign		Domestic				Local
			Coastwise		Internal		
	Imports	Exports	Receipts	Shipments	Receipts	Shipments	
Beaumont	54,925	4,429	727	2,240	5,777	8,622	1,417
Brownsville	2,897	420	15	9	1,042	682	-
Corpus Christi	45,310	7,514	1,783	6,212	3,932	9,714	2,189
Freeport	25,388	2,680	1	484	2,483	2,187	-
Galveston	825	2,655	147	1,730	1,508	964	179
Houston	102,129	41,070	3,045	6,789	25,514	17,114	14,153
Matagorda Chl. (Port Lavaca)	7,358	1,778	-	194	348	1,835	-
Port Arthur	12,889	4,796	350	1,453	2,984	3,504	41
Sabine Pass	-	-	7	9	37	588	-
Texas City	37,690	5,333	306	3,154	4,827	5,577	508
Victoria	-	-	-	-	861	2,363	-

Gulf Intracoastal Waterway by Commodity (Texas portion)

(All figures in short tons x1000) *Source: U.S. Army Corps of Engineers*

Commodity	2005	2003	2001	1999	1997
Coal	335	168	105	136	126
Petroleum products	39,538	36,057	36,393	30,886	33,816
Chemicals	20,668	22,024	20,002	20,540	21,958
Raw materials	4,898	6,208	4,780	5,535	4,860
Manufactured goods	2,449	2,208	1,969	1,872	2,171
Food, farm products	473	643	900	789	759
Total	**69,517**	**68,517**	**65,097**	**61,563**	**65,112**

U.S. ports ranked by tonnage, 2005
(x1,000)

1. S. Louisiana 212,245
2. **Houston** 211,666
3. New York 152,132
4. Huntington, WV 83,889
5. Long Beach 79,858
6. **Beaumont** 78,887
7. **Corpus Christi** 77,647*
8. New Orleans 65,876
9. Baton Rouge 59,294
10. **Texas City** 57,839

includes Harbor Island

States ranked by tonnage, 2005
(x1,000)

1. **Texas** 487,100
2. Louisiana 456,713
3. California 216,042
4. Florida 133,281
5. New Jersey 127,375
6. Ohio 124,427
7. Washington 121,841
8. Illinois 117,132
9. Kentucky 111,846
10. Pennsylvania 107,728

Trucks and Trucking in Texas, 2002

This information shows the kind of products carried on Texas highways as reported in the *2002 Economic Census, Vehicle Inventory and Use Survey*. It also shows the kind of trucks driven, trip distances and kind of operator. (**Motor carrier** is a truck operated by a company and hired to carry other people's goods. **Owner operator** is a truck operated by an independent trucker hired to carry other people's goods. **Private** is a truck carrying goods owned by the company.). The U.S. Bureau of the Census conducts this survey every five years. This survey was published in December 2004. The total truck miles for the United States was 145.2 billion, with Texas making up 10.2 billion of that figure.

*[**Millions of miles**. Because of rounding, estimates may not be additive. Detail lines may not add to total because multiple products/hazardous materials may be carried at the same time.]*

Operational Characteristics	Truck miles distribution excluding pickups, minivans and SUVs
Total	10,189.9
TRAILER CONFIGURATION	
No trailer	3,700.1
Single trailer	6,308.7
Double trailers	174.8
RANGE OF OPERATION	
Off-road	254.4
50 miles or less	2,681.2
51-100 miles	1,707.3
101-200 miles	943.8
201-500 miles	1,105.4
501 or more	1,561.9
PRIMARY JURISDICTION	
Within Texas	6,938.9
Outside Texas	1,522.4
OPERATOR CLASSIFICATION	
Private	4,516.0
Motor carrier	3,380.7
Owner operator	1,099.4
Rental	1,164.4
For-hire characteristics	
Type of carrier:	
Contract	2,375.7
Common	1,593.2
Not reported	529.1
Not applicable (private)	5,691.9
Type of service:	
Truckload	1,101.6
Less-than truckload	2,859.9
Not reported	536.4
Not applicable (private)	5,691.9
PRODUCTS CARRIED	
Animal and fish, live	32.2
Animal feed/products of animal origin	100.1
Grains, cereal	49.2
All other agricultural products	206.2
Basic chemicals	109.1
Fertilizers/fertilizer materials	17.8
All other chemical products	68.5
Alcoholic beverages	56.6
Tobacco products	28.5
Bakery/milled grain products	185.7
Meat, seafood and preparations	227.9
All other prepared footstuffs	562.4
Logs	62.2
Paper/paperboard	131.8
Printed products	22.1

Operational Characteristics	Truck miles distribution excluding pickups, minivans and SUVs
Pulp, newsprint	17.9
Wood products	166.7
Articles of base metal	207.8
Base metal in semifinished form	102.8
Nonmetallic mineral products	265.0
Tools, nonpowered	406.6
Tools, powered	350.6
Electronic/electrical equipment	76.7
Furniture	52.7
Machinery	215.4
Precision instruments	38.8
Textile/leather	102.9
Vehichles/parts	328.2
Miscellaneous manufactured	178.9
Crude petroleum	62.3
Gravel or stone	292.1
Building stone	21.3
Natural sands	143.1
All other nonmetallic minerals	26.9
Fuel oils	99.8
Gasoline/aviation fuel	101.1
Plastics/rubber	68.6
All other refined petroleum products	95.8
Hazardous waste	6.4
All other waste/scrap	140.5
Recyclable products	55.0
Empty shipping containers	46.6
Mixed freight	364.2
Products not elsewhere classified	44.6
Products not specified	244.6
HAZARDOUS MATERIALS	
Explosives	1.0
Flammable gas	58.5
Nonflammable gas	35.8
Flammable	224.8
Combustible liquid	81.8
Oxygen	12.9
Flammable solid	6.2
Spontaneously combustible	1.9
Dangerous when wet	2.8
Oxidizer	18.6
Organic peroxide	7.3
Poison inhalation hazard	8.8
Poison	8.4
Corrosive	51.5
Hazardous material not specified	10.1

State Truck Registration Rankings: 2002 and 1997

State	2002 Trucks (000)	Rank	1997 Trucks (000)	Rank
United States	85,174.8		72,800.3	
California	**9,245.6**	**1**	**8,818.8**	**1**
*Light trucks	8,840.1			
*Med/Heavy	405.5			
Texas	**6,412.0**	**2**	**4,410.6**	**2**
Light trucks	6,015.7			
Med/Heavy	396.3			
Florida	**4,329.3**	**3**	**3,460.2**	**3**
Light trucks	4,147.2			
Med/Heavy	182.1			
Michigan	**3,581.3**	**4**	**2,734.5**	**6**
Light trucks	3,442.2			
Med/Heavy	139.1			
New York	**3,527.6**	**5**	**2,863.9**	**5**
Light trucks	3,346.7			
Med/Heavy	180.9			
Ohio	**3,499.3**	**6**	**2,985.1**	**4**
Light trucks	3,276.5			
Med/Heavy	222.8			
Illinois	**3,277.2**	**7**	**2,674.6**	**7**
Light trucks	2,991.2			
Med/Heavy	286.0			
Pennsylvania	**3,088.7**	**8**	**2,605.9**	**8**
Light trucks	2,931.2			
Med/Heavy	157.5			
Georgia	**2,733.2**	**9**	**2,258.4**	**9**
Light trucks	2,579.8			
Med/Heavy	153.4			
North Carolina	**2,528.3**	**10**	**1,996.1**	**10**
Light trucks	2,292.6			
Med/Heavy	235.7			

*Light trucks are 10,000 lbs. or less. Medium 10,001 to 19,500. Light-heavy 19,501 to 26,000. Heavy-heavy 26,001 or more.

Comparative Summary of Texas Trucks: 2002 and Earlier Years

*Estimates are shown as **percent** of total trucks.*

Characteristics	2002	1997	1992	1987
USE				
Agriculture, hunting	2.0	4.9	7.2	8.5
Mining	.2	.9	.8	.6
Construction	4.0	5.8	7.9	9.8
Manufacturing	1.0	1.0	2.5	1.5
Wholesale/retail trade	2.9	4.8	4.8	5.3
For-hire/warehousing	1.2	.9	1.1	1.6
Utilities	5.6	9.0	5.1	4.7
Personal transportation	80.1	71.4	69.4	67.9
Other	3.0	1.3	1.2	.3
BODY TYPE				
Pickup, minivan, SUV	95.2	94.1	94.0	91.8
Flatbed, stake, platform	1.2	2.0	1.9	2.9
Van	1.4	1.6	1.2	1.5
Service, utility	.2	.1	.3	.3
Van (step, walk-in)	.4	.3	.4	1.1
Dump	.4	.5	.5	.6
Tank for liquid, dry bulk	.4	.5	.4	.5
Other	.7	1.0	1.3	1.4
VEHICLE SIZE*				
Light	93.8	95.2	95.6	94.3
Medium	2.6	1.0	1.1	1.7
Light-heavy	1.0	.8	.7	.9
Heavy-heavy	2.6	2.9	2.5	3.1
TRUCK TYPE				
Single-unit trucks	95.3	97.0	96.5	96.5
2 axles	94.8	96.4	96.0	95.8
3 axles or more	.5	.6	.5	.7
Combinations	4.7	3.0	3.5	3.5
3 axles	.1	.7	.6	1.0
4 axles	3.2	.7	1.4	1.0
5 axles or more	1.2	1.7	1.5	1.5
FUEL TYPE				
Gasoline	88.9	91.3	92.2	94.3
All other fuels	9.2	8.7	7.5	5.7

Source: Vehicle Inventory and Use Survey, U.S. Census Bureau, 2002 Economic Census, Revised Dec. 1, 2004.

A truck stop along U.S. 287/82 at Jolly, east of Wichita Falls. Robert Plocheck photo.

Motor Vehicles Accidents, Losses

| Year | Number killed | † Number injured | Accidents by Kind | | | | ‡Vehicle Miles Traveled | | Economic loss (000,000) |
			Fatal	† Injury	† Non-injury	† Total	*Number (000,000)	Deaths per 100 mill miles	
1960	2,254	127,980	1,842	71,100	239,300	312,242	46,353	4.9	$ 350
1961	2,314	132,570	1,899	73,650	248,600	324,149	47,937	4.8	356
1962	2,421	144,943	2,002	80,524	277,680	360,206	49,883	4.9	388
1963	2,729	161,543	2,251	89,746	307,920	399,917	52,325	5.2	433
1964	3,006	182,081	2,486	101,156	351,120	454,762	55,677	5.4	487
1965	3,028	186,062	2,460	103,368	365,160	470,988	*52,163	5.8	498
1966	3,406	208,310	2,784	115,728	406,460	524,972	55,261	6.2	557
1967	3,367	205,308	2,778	114,060	768,430	885,268	58,124	5.8	793
1968	3,481	216,972	2,902	120,540	816,830	940,272	62,794	5.5	837
1969	3,551	223,000	2,913	124,000	850,000	976,913	67,742	5.2	955
1970	3,560	223,000	2,965	124,000	886,000	1,012,965	‡ 68,031	5.2	1,042
1971	3,594	224,000	2,993	124,000	890,000	1,016,993	70,709	5.1	1,045
1972	3,688	128,158	3,099	83,607	346,292	432,998	76,690	4.8	1,035
1973	3,692	132,635	3,074	87,631	373,521	464,226	80,615	4.6	1,035
1974	3,046	123,611	2,626	83,341	348,227	434,194	78,290	3.9	1,095
1975	3,429	138,962	2,945	92,510	373,141	468,596	84,575	4.1	1,440
1976	3,230	145,282	2,780	96,348	380,075	479,203	91,279	3.5	1,485
1977	3,698	161,635	3,230	106,923	393,848	504,001	96,998	3.8	1,960
1978	¶ 3,980	178,228	3,468	117,998	**304,830	**426,296	102,624	3.9	2,430
1979	4,229	184,550	3,685	122,793	322,336	448,814	101,909	4.1	2,580
1980	4,424	185,964	3,863	123,577	305,500	432,940	103,255	4.3	3,010
1981	4,701	206,196	4,137	136,396	317,484	458,017	111,036	4.2	3,430
1982	4,271	204,666	3,752	135,859	312,159	451,770	††124,910	3.4	3,375
1983	3,823	208,157	¶3,328	137,695	302,876	443,899	129,309	3.0	3,440
1984	3,913	220,720	3,466	145,543	293,285	442,294	137,280	2.9	§ 3,795
1985	3,682	231,009	3,270	151,657	300,531	452,188	143,500	2.6	3,755
1986	3,568	234,120	3,121	154,514	298,079	452,593	150,474	2.4	3,782
1987	3,261	226,895	2,881	146,913	246,175	395,969	151,221	2.2	3,913
1988	3,395	238,845	3,004	152,004	237,703	392,711	152,819	2.2	4,515
1989	3,361	243,030	2,926	153,356	233,967	390,249	159,679	2.1	4,873
1990	3,243	262,576	2,882	162,424	216,140	381,446	163,103	2.0	4,994
1991	3,079	263,430	2,690	161,470	207,288	371,448	162,780	1.9	5,604
1992	3,057	282,025	2,690	170,513	209,152	382,355	162,769	1.9	6,725
1993	3,037	298,891	2,690	178,194	209,533	390,417	167,988	1.8	§11,784
1994	3,142	326,837	2,710	192,014	219,890	414,614	172,976	1.8	12,505
1995	3,172	334,259	2,790	196,093	152,190	351,073	183,103	1.7	§13,005
1996	3,738	350,397	3,247	204,635	90,261	298,143	187,064	2.0	7,766
1997	3,508	347,881	3,079	205,595	97,315	305,989	194,665	1.8	7,662
1998	3,576	338,661	3,160	202,223	102,732	308,115	201,989	1.8	8,780
1999	3,519	339,448	3,106	203,220	105,375	311,701	213,847	1.6	8,729
2000	3,775	341,097	3,247	205,569	110,174	318,990	210,340	1.8	9,163
2001	3,739	340,554	3,319	207,043	113,596	323,958	216,276	1.7	$ 9,348

Last year statistics available.

*Vehicle miles traveled since 1964 were estimated on the basis of new data furnished by U.S. Bureau of Public Roads through National Safety Council.
† In August 1967, amended estimating formula received from National Safety Council. Starting 1972, actual reported injuries are listed rather than estimates.
‡ Vehicle miles traveled estimated by Texas Highway Department starting with 1970. Method of calculation varies from that used for prior years.
§ Economic loss formula changed. Last changed in July 1995, when only property damage accidents having at least one vehicle towed due to damages is tabulated.

¶ Change in counting fatalities. In 1978, counted when injury results in death within 90 days of accident. In 1983, counted when injury results in death within 30 days.
**Total accidents and non-injury accidents for 1978 and after cannot be compared with years prior to 1978 due to changes in reporting laws.
†† Method of calculating vehicle miles traveled revised 1982 by Texas Department of Transportation. The 1981 mileage adjusted for comparison purposes.

Source: Analysis Section, Accident Records Bureau of the Texas Department of Public Safety, Austin.

Accidents by Road Class

2001	Miles of road	Accidents
City/Town	78,671	124,884
Interstate	3,233	46,831
U.S./State	28,275	93,777
Farm-Market	40,991	34,974
County	142,357	21,431
Other*	7,624	2,061
Total	301,141	323,958

Toll roads, frontage roads and park roads.

Texas Dept. of Public Safety.

Driver Licenses

In 2006, the Texas Department of Public Safety issued 5,869,064 driver licenses and identification cards, including renewals.

The following list shows the number of licensed drivers by year for Texas and for all the states. Sources are the Texas Department of Public Safety and the Federal Highway Administration.

Year	Texas licensed drivers	Total U.S. licensed drivers
2006	16,096,985	NA
2005	15,831,852	200,548,972
2004	15,562,484	198,888,912
2003	15,091,776	196,165,666
2002	14,639,132	194,295,633
2001	14,303,799	191,275,719
2000	14,024,305	190,625,023
1999	13,718,319	187,170,420
1998	13,419,288	184,980,177
1997	12,833,603	182,709,204
1996	12,568,265	179,539,340
1995	12,369,243	176,628,482
1994	12,109,960	175,403,465
1993	11,876,268	173,149,313
1992	11,437,571	173,125,396
1991	11,293,184	168,995,076
1990	11,136,694	167,015,250
1989	11,103,511	165,555,295
1988	11,080,702	162,853,255
1987	11,153,472	161,818,461
1986	11,129,193	159,487,000
1985	10,809,078	156,868,277
1984	10,855,549	155,423,709
1983	11,406,433	154,389,178
1982	10,154,386	150,233,659
1981	9,673,885	147,075,169
1980	9,287,286	145,295,036
1975	7,509,497	129,790,666
1970	6,380,057	111,542,787
1965	5,413,887	98,502,152
1960	4,352,168	87,252,563
1955	3,874,834	74,685,949
1950	2,687,349	59,322,278

US 190 in Pecos County. Robert Plocheck photo.

Texas Highway Miles, Construction, Maintenance, Vehicles: 2006

Texans drove more than 20 million motor vehicles in 2006 over 300,000 miles of roadways, including city and county roads. That driving is calculated to have included more than 477.8 million miles driven daily on the 190,000 miles of state-maintained roads alone.

The Texas Department of Transportation is responsible for state highway construction and maintenance, motor vehicles titles and registration, commercial trucking, automobile dealer licensing and the state's official Texas Travel Information Centers.

The following mileage, maintenance and construction figures (listed by county) refer only to roads that are maintained by the state: Interstates, U.S. highways, state highways, farm-to-market roads and some loops around urban areas. Not included are city- or county-maintained streets and roads. A lane mile is one lane for one mile; i.e., one mile of four-lane highway equals four lane miles. Source: Texas Department of Transportation, 2007.

County	Vehicles Registered	Lane Miles of Highway	Vehicle Miles Driven Daily	State Construction Expenditures	State/ Contracted Maintenance Expenditures	State Net Receipts	County Net Receipts	Total Vehicle Registration Fees
Anderson	47,370	967	1,273,121	$ 6,982,886	$ 17,117,084	$ 1,842,629	$ 1,044,466	$ 2,887,095
Andrews	13,919	542	471,105	7	3,775,270	530,773	431,194	961,967
Angelina	80,142	926	2,158,448	37,634,298	6,626,746	3,634,805	1,695,133	5,329,938
Aransas	22,801	205	489,180	9,853,495	1,323,077	777,296	547,600	1,324,897
Archer	10,733	530	378,645	11,937,411	4,605,401	187,972	476,980	664,952
Armstrong	2,635	378	312,974	20,435,365	1,113,137	4,001	152,876	156,876
Atascosa	34,835	1,011	1,374,275	25,733,160	4,619,723	1,202,764	844,612	2,047,376
Austin	33,550	607	1,250,737	10,317,398	5,859,583	1,344,732	808,933	2,153,664
Bailey	6,708	490	226,893	4,049,880	1,994,486	65,814	391,161	456,974
Bandera	22,730	403	381,160	6,764,923	7,444,874	650,346	614,914	1,265,261
Bastrop	63,582	803	1,883,281	11,128,678	7,271,738	2,372,024	1,421,013	3,793,036
Baylor	4,289	437	181,728	3,240,644	11,684,044	18,204	240,211	258,415
Bee	20,696	643	697,615	20,107,813	2,945,415	607,669	630,213	1,237,881
Bell	238,169	1,495	6,375,254	57,252,418	14,267,043	9,771,510	5,377,366	15,148,877
Bexar	1,271,316	3,195	25,820,525	272,249,673	46,391,674	58,672,088	25,935,955	84,608,043
Blanco	12,548	462	570,773	317,201	2,752,442	367,185	419,047	786,232
Borden	963	344	58,274	2,220,360	1,087,813	1,075	39,170	40,245
Bosque	19,910	695	574,278	3,896,339	6,807,146	512,630	602,200	1,114,830
Bowie	90,295	1,201	2,918,274	13,168,011	8,401,015	3,595,881	1,865,075	5,460,956
Brazoria	259,146	1,255	4,578,947	47,397,544	7,430,155	11,571,663	4,698,180	16,269,843
Brazos	132,846	857	3,220,147	50,191,526	7,819,716	5,935,094	2,793,734	8,728,829
Brewster	8,920	591	246,485	2,386,119	4,349,200	191,158	353,668	544,826
Briscoe	2,153	326	58,433	2,439,528	857,845	3,579	131,435	135,014

County	Vehicles Registered	Lane Miles of Highway	Vehicle Miles Driven Daily	State Construction Expenditures	State/ Contracted Maintenance Expenditures	State Net Receipts	County Net Receipts	Total Vehicle Registration Fees
Brooks	6,044	317	623,243	211,250	2,614,462	97,811	259,986	357,798
Brown	40,640	755	786,754	10,381,504	5,122,842	1,428,504	995,298	2,423,803
Burleson	19,879	504	714,467	11,501,700	3,639,045	544,622	637,629	1,182,251
Burnet	46,926	804	1,270,175	10,082,402	4,511,649	1,725,175	1,122,734	2,847,909
Caldwell	30,790	606	914,198	10,595,305	4,589,180	1,108,693	762,523	1,871,215
Calhoun	22,365	384	467,344	13,546,687	3,376,734	630,698	676,914	1,307,612
Callahan	16,833	750	891,036	6,223,990	3,218,741	360,444	651,780	1,012,224
Cameron	238,765	1,644	5,597,186	116,282,492	11,669,316	11,012,576	4,337,630	15,350,206
Camp	13,515	265	306,090	3,845,547	3,661,664	857,622	607,328	1,464,950
Carson	6,835	776	817,864	3,467,737	5,173,561	61,451	337,302	398,753
Cass	32,386	985	1,059,381	19,329,976	7,850,385	1,048,585	814,950	1,863,535
Castro	7,688	534	285,056	5,691,872	2,433,407	132,004	452,034	584,037
Chambers	34,800	747	2,209,497	48,669,955	6,330,508	1,364,015	785,667	2,149,682
Cherokee	41,814	1,149	1,260,669	2,563,903	8,130,201	1,491,466	971,753	2,463,219
Childress	6,128	477	331,992	1,473,816	6,842,964	30,303	323,475	353,778
Clay	13,982	791	935,128	2,154,626	7,037,327	266,324	620,316	886,639
Cochran	3,070	468	100,172	1,817	1,883,786	5,569	193,585	199,154
Coke	4,348	356	184,804	232,463	1,407,990	10,946	225,988	236,934
Coleman	10,635	754	344,010	611,761	3,348,248	124,361	467,697	592,059
Collin	577,457	1,445	7,606,424	73,872,099	16,823,456	24,695,081	12,120,767	36,815,849
Collingsworth	3,238	446	99,636	3,234,383	1,681,216	5,604	192,077	197,682
Colorado	25,639	758	1,513,448	6,673,626	8,129,483	931,409	728,930	1,660,339
Comal	106,888	653	3,111,838	32,645,465	13,628,355	4,806,601	2,452,517	7,259,118
Comanche	15,933	737	466,029	6,643,269	3,549,109	367,925	612,767	980,692
Concho	3,302	453	263,226	2,421,657	2,307,610	4,837	164,671	169,507
Cooke	42,935	847	1,686,370	5,262,453	8,041,189	1,764,861	1,002,688	2,767,549
Coryell	47,681	684	1,087,043	16,463,688	4,110,964	1,653,591	1,081,823	2,735,414
Cottle	1,858	391	79,972	2,703,677	4,773,509	3,169	95,986	99,154
Crane	4,670	318	198,997	15,696	662,175	78,742	210,667	289,409
Crockett	4,567	789	512,045	7,412,357	3,124,875	25,057	252,897	277,954
Crosby	5,861	569	213,435	5,931,335	2,918,212	35,468	323,669	359,137
Culberson	1,996	748	608,981	8,186,270	6,027,374	3,603	125,135	128,738
Dallam	6,146	609	297,860	17,473,714	2,552,944	92,184	403,854	496,038
Dallas	1,940,677	3,305	39,290,145	335,757,635	57,138,259	93,515,669	37,365,559	130,881,229
Dawson	12,184	713	410,584	5,121,451	1,693,291	224,005	578,895	802,901
Deaf Smith	18,011	603	380,834	3,989,146	1,882,904	775,602	654,517	1,430,118
Delta	6,580	363	192,700	673,769	3,551,357	71,181	299,810	370,990
Denton	465,051	1,444	9,052,261	92,527,513	10,929,998	20,883,360	9,208,057	30,091,417
De Witt	20,354	656	511,203	3,816,773	10,719,140	541,318	629,205	1,170,523
Dickens	3,041	469	106,269	636,498	1,246,503	3,744	139,215	142,959
Dimmit	7,813	507	322,892	8,578,069	4,953,662	144,823	363,713	508,536
Donley	3,641	455	505,163	2,843,342	4,123,784	6,997	205,744	212,741
Duval	10,775	630	459,629	977,296	2,744,169	364,436	459,414	823,850
Eastland	21,873	1,023	1,058,343	10,005,343	7,057,045	802,140	709,045	1,511,185
Ector	127,381	951	1,804,144	18,509,661	6,389,362	6,293,302	2,934,734	9,228,037
Edwards	2,827	499	101,996	22,986	1,702,472	4,129	143,354	147,482
Ellis	137,367	1,507	4,521,862	75,079,485	13,867,116	6,620,596	2,281,351	8,901,947
El Paso	552,750	1,568	9,986,132	105,279,908	25,532,218	25,307,085	9,694,230	35,001,316
Erath	35,289	822	1,077,908	12,157,409	6,281,884	1,220,948	896,484	2,117,433
Falls	15,571	717	741,290	16,156,750	4,729,621	318,705	580,403	899,107
Fannin	37,022	963	813,347	1,700,572	5,066,251	1,191,046	983,354	2,174,400
Fayette	29,721	1,033	1,435,902	6,739,966	6,377,975	933,128	778,610	1,711,737
Fisher	4,456	555	154,775	1,321,395	2,694,974	7,131	226,766	233,897
Floyd	7,203	703	196,855	4,838,960	2,059,487	52,769	381,876	434,645
Foard	1,477	299	63,052	187,050	1,622,203	2,420	83,639	86,059
Fort Bend	361,048	1,143	5,808,989	164,540,598	9,817,173	17,210,735	6,273,345	23,484,079
Franklin	10,562	336	458,049	1,813,931	4,314,983	193,345	405,833	599,179
Freestone	22,392	810	1,728,702	6,303,757	8,509,865	592,008	728,214	1,320,221

County	Vehicles Registered	Lane Miles of Highway	Vehicle Miles Driven Daily	State Construction Expenditures	State/ Contracted Maintenance Expenditures	State Net Receipts	County Net Receipts	Total Vehicle Registration Fees
Frio	11,225	757	952,361	7,421,650	7,725,853	222,693	485,763	708,456
Gaines	14,952	668	511,081	177,944	2,989,952	486,834	421,459	908,293
Galveston	240,369	1,061	4,845,500	90,539,767	8,648,101	10,433,751	4,116,070	14,549,821
Garza	4,637	460	410,575	482,336	1,964,857	50,588	237,888	288,476
Gillespie	27,642	689	712,113	6,364,709	3,561,732	870,837	748,982	1,619,819
Glasscock	2,080	274	163,152	1,179,297	1,334,001	9,723	115,536	125,258
Goliad	7,434	503	400,594	15,845,958	4,790,200	66,516	314,278	380,793
Gonzales	20,491	878	1,073,273	13,781,417	4,945,493	652,830	662,445	1,315,274
Gray	24,411	773	696,619	5,798,832	3,235,307	807,033	765,767	1,572,800
Grayson	122,428	1,210	3,346,694	10,846,750	10,944,004	5,136,341	2,348,103	7,484,444
Gregg	125,254	786	2,731,184	9,775,017	5,926,152	5,960,436	2,836,313	8,796,748
Grimes	26,107	615	942,478	7,296,079	8,070,434	830,757	700,783	1,531,540
Guadalupe	101,989	904	2,716,624	34,043,685	16,015,347	4,439,124	1,903,830	6,342,954
Hale	29,239	1,057	868,538	412,120	5,871,324	1,074,430	786,544	1,860,974
Hall	3,338	460	226,301	3,780,621	2,635,893	5,133	196,352	201,485
Hamilton	10,219	580	359,026	382,388	3,136,519	134,474	477,153	611,627
Hansford	6,212	525	125,207	1,521,371	1,965,357	54,818	366,325	421,143
Hardeman	4,397	466	337,713	4,411,720	3,435,530	7,896	251,823	259,719
Hardin	56,051	573	1,420,335	12,358,042	6,970,214	2,108,382	1,296,362	3,404,744
Harris	3,040,626	4,748	58,362,938	913,311,762	74,789,184	146,538,647	63,250,202	209,788,848
Harrison	65,589	1,185	2,717,086	16,977,151	13,831,860	2,618,224	1,365,714	3,983,939
Hartley	5,360	540	300,480	2,110,094	3,546,129	112,666	334,339	447,006
Haskell	6,923	652	218,493	7,651,809	5,608,174	34,923	368,455	403,378
Hays	113,062	670	3,369,085	39,160,087	8,682,491	4,902,163	2,298,703	7,200,866
Hemphill	5,621	386	171,677	11,144,308	1,449,045	77,792	306,131	383,923
Henderson	81,624	992	1,824,391	17,117,426	6,799,817	3,365,683	1,450,957	4,816,640
Hidalgo	415,187	2,158	9,616,246	140,961,573	18,971,117	21,127,388	7,846,568	28,973,946
Hill	37,582	1,078	2,395,993	30,535,159	9,721,720	1,373,846	885,420	2,259,266
Hockley	21,343	752	624,443	4,085,608	4,056,537	809,502	669,382	1,478,884
Hood	57,028	389	988,368	2,259,966	2,487,697	2,109,863	1,299,062	3,408,925
Hopkins	36,489	953	1,535,197	17,044,951	6,332,800	1,516,104	906,242	2,422,347
Houston	22,257	844	588,966	8,030,330	5,312,780	647,205	649,557	1,296,763
Howard	26,859	856	929,640	6,844,825	4,232,808	914,873	778,520	1,693,393
Hudspeth	3,113	823	1,163,702	827,253	5,402,310	4,632	151,407	156,039
Hunt	87,091	1,285	2,618,698	11,633,184	15,215,196	3,321,233	1,761,614	5,082,847
Hutchinson	25,828	474	338,140	875,626	3,754,615	1,032,583	546,245	1,578,828
Irion	3,357	247	113,549	90,577	834,708	46,291	181,287	227,578
Jack	10,188	575	355,386	2,127,893	2,980,258	220,974	457,937	678,911
Jackson	15,051	636	917,447	3,926,619	5,116,450	340,146	556,155	896,301
Jasper	37,801	739	1,266,559	17,869,100	6,462,004	1,410,609	902,225	2,312,834
Jeff Davis	2,811	469	182,895	17,735,358	2,199,736	52,195	155,793	207,988
Jefferson	212,000	1,148	5,205,723	29,479,892	29,806,378	9,128,275	4,082,606	13,210,881
Jim Hogg	4,947	288	201,238	8,453	1,540,435	77,698	256,540	334,238
Jim Wells	35,984	715	1,406,235	4,037,420	5,672,494	1,614,957	989,625	2,604,582
Johnson	142,218	950	3,307,496	22,404,073	9,327,282	6,617,496	2,543,240	9,160,736
Jones	16,919	1,012	533,317	1,041,080	3,596,917	431,069	658,115	1,089,184
Karnes	11,712	696	413,663	459,340	4,928,651	153,229	508,173	661,402
Kaufman	91,536	1,203	3,909,816	15,610,237	8,822,198	3,568,643	1,964,525	5,533,168
Kendall	45,824	444	919,420	2,923,921	2,207,482	1,499,506	1,326,217	2,825,723
Kenedy	782	188	415,211	0	2,332,550	1,067	33,740	34,807
Kent	1,449	325	54,777	1,794,659	1,737,024	2,135	63,772	65,907
Kerr	52,417	707	1,146,139	17,617,415	4,147,197	1,951,423	1,142,454	3,093,877
Kimble	6,009	686	477,914	2,287,196	3,217,554	56,032	287,683	343,715
King	521	199	77,966	4,213,596	652,699	660	33,710	34,370
Kinney	3,106	407	197,391	1,791,652	1,004,656	36,309	147,930	184,238
Kleberg	27,308	369	916,496	2,780,811	1,575,973	869,679	808,727	1,678,406
Knox	4,291	439	132,435	13,625,648	3,489,549	23,109	267,599	290,708
Lamar	50,441	992	1,200,028	5,358,013	12,936,088	1,985,609	1,164,944	3,150,553

County	Vehicles Registered	Lane Miles of Highway	Vehicle Miles Driven Daily	State Construction Expenditures	State/ Contracted Maintenance Expenditures	State Net Receipts	County Net Receipts	Total Vehicle Registration Fees
Lamb	13,708	805	471,190	533,902	3,896,986	323,679	561,329	885,007
Lampasas	22,520	490	538,853	2,442,339	3,340,154	595,754	771,820	1,367,574
La Salle	5,060	649	657,941	6,693,684	4,961,215	234,485	358,156	592,641
Lavaca	23,647	640	565,522	7,483,536	5,173,123	760,543	664,663	1,425,206
Lee	19,862	529	677,696	4,397,760	3,185,114	669,094	615,869	1,284,963
Leon	19,322	834	1,421,056	7,063,475	9,959,894	644,843	574,313	1,219,157
Liberty	72,031	816	2,071,895	18,153,049	13,541,899	3,313,492	1,414,874	4,728,366
Limestone	23,302	769	731,069	8,671,314	4,340,608	671,684	693,431	1,365,114
Lipscomb	3,353	411	94,619	4,617,266	1,638,202	5,787	248,849	254,636
Live Oak	12,147	995	1,256,779	7,525,405	4,603,313	213,542	542,406	755,947
Llano	22,494	499	463,581	4,080,660	2,588,193	646,280	663,281	1,309,561
Loving	251	67	17,620	0	102,310	224	13,771	13,995
Lubbock	223,699	1,713	3,580,033	83,313,498	12,407,940	10,423,538	4,698,376	15,121,914
Lynn	5,928	710	354,609	7,988,342	2,564,653	25,375	325,541	350,916
Madison	14,262	572	890,213	210,783	5,282,416	234,809	574,360	809,169
Marion	11,217	323	345,395	4,460,341	2,714,752	162,312	486,194	648,506
Martin	5,648	574	376,488	1,763,425	3,611,277	8,246	316,235	324,481
Mason	5,116	423	166,477	275,784	2,565,469	32,962	247,144	280,106
Matagorda	34,889	679	811,358	11,082,910	6,600,166	1,277,022	846,081	2,123,103
Maverick	32,276	488	695,846	10,427,037	3,055,985	1,412,150	767,715	2,179,865
Mc Culloch	9,717	608	293,108	2,515,117	2,994,377	115,335	442,643	557,978
Mc Lennan	193,919	1,668	6,258,006	62,455,304	14,604,060	9,172,824	3,661,201	12,834,025
Mc Mullen	2,337	317	125,664	3,742,324	2,399,199	38,772	165,736	204,508
Medina	42,768	764	1,213,683	5,602,577	13,695,927	1,443,350	1,106,502	2,549,851
Menard	2,826	346	157,978	410,323	1,993,568	4,259	135,634	139,894
Midland	134,917	1,026	2,147,277	4,548,858	6,566,794	7,466,521	2,730,650	10,197,171
Milam	26,635	685	886,203	13,887,420	5,939,767	815,945	692,662	1,508,607
Mills	7,353	451	243,975	894,880	1,662,257	30,230	371,038	401,269
Mitchell	6,913	663	541,667	638,018	3,536,921	44,905	353,090	397,995
Montague	23,909	850	825,418	4,393,654	8,142,388	828,476	707,641	1,536,117
Montgomery	341,653	1,208	7,897,651	74,693,532	15,827,714	15,906,320	5,804,434	21,710,754
Moore	19,737	467	441,017	1,556,761	1,674,919	813,975	606,133	1,420,108
Morris	13,707	356	482,663	5,700,412	4,260,361	341,738	449,632	791,370
Motley	1,642	331	60,897	641,505	776,314	2,697	83,980	86,678

A visitor is assisted at the Texas Travel Information Center on Interstate 35 near Laredo. Robert Plocheck photo.

County	Vehicles Registered	Lane Miles of Highway	Vehicle Miles Driven Daily	State Construction Expenditures	State/ Contracted Maintenance Expenditures	State Net Receipts	County Net Receipts	Total Vehicle Registration Fees
Nacogdoches	54,660	952	1,731,759	9,436,378	11,923,585	1,956,921	1,232,489	3,189,411
Navarro	46,561	1,192	1,939,822	26,102,275	5,679,893	1,849,554	1,058,937	2,908,492
Newton	13,736	551	466,583	1,898,937	6,366,179	230,784	461,874	692,658
Nolan	14,329	695	870,128	3,533,729	3,669,331	335,249	587,550	922,799
Nueces	261,282	1,474	6,069,385	70,970,714	16,774,630	12,105,058	5,013,014	17,118,072
Ochiltree	12,035	430	238,925	2,915,951	1,056,862	292,094	557,808	849,901
Oldham	2,567	473	590,735	14,004,315	3,103,068	16,234	165,419	181,653
Orange	80,312	611	2,630,349	48,135,442	12,610,922	3,292,936	1,450,790	4,743,726
Palo Pinto	31,719	830	919,104	8,720,675	5,770,514	1,210,078	761,521	1,971,599
Panola	27,052	771	1,098,960	4,687,726	10,347,286	1,101,963	516,715	1,618,678
Parker	117,550	879	2,944,811	10,929,197	7,209,941	4,797,283	2,369,812	7,167,094
Parmer	9,777	614	411,777	11,002,627	3,076,575	180,474	486,251	666,726
Pecos	13,688	1,684	862,003	915,081	11,798,801	324,317	568,016	892,333
Polk	56,934	855	1,675,384	15,036,291	13,796,189	2,800,321	1,305,905	4,106,226
Potter	101,842	886	2,615,362	15,387,083	11,484,474	4,838,989	2,063,417	6,902,407
Presidio	7,076	545	190,740	44,122	3,771,438	123,441	315,794	439,235
Rains	13,890	268	325,163	5,438,048	1,356,328	288,410	443,541	731,951
Randall	116,793	901	1,296,178	5,883,771	4,109,281	4,840,031	2,581,251	7,421,283
Reagan	3,627	320	116,219	142,597	467,967	39,187	228,319	267,506
Real	3,743	296	110,555	3,588,831	1,182,375	34,619	188,662	223,281
Red River	14,131	748	436,522	8,822,013	3,867,880	236,548	527,301	763,850
Reeves	8,948	1,180	680,927	501,910	5,575,907	99,337	404,058	503,395
Refugio	7,351	465	862,011	3,746,004	3,567,496	113,558	331,808	445,366
Roberts	1,190	241	79,138	1,568,443	1,086,164	1,616	60,070	61,686
Robertson	17,006	627	850,869	13,696,518	6,051,002	346,549	624,523	971,072
Rockwall	61,610	339	1,628,583	6,052,950	4,311,923	2,813,712	1,162,585	3,976,296
Runnels	12,481	741	377,314	1,394,203	3,233,637	268,545	556,473	825,017
Rusk	49,177	1,172	1,404,492	5,729,589	7,527,551	1,936,056	1,077,564	3,013,619
Sabine	11,953	488	307,970	2,914,669	4,940,181	216,966	461,196	678,162
San Augustine	9,270	530	267,845	2,542,871	4,986,994	126,731	410,478	537,209
San Jacinto	22,904	510	720,403	11,375,204	7,392,984	819,270	647,153	1,466,424
San Patricio	60,223	945	2,235,261	28,203,405	7,667,320	2,513,373	1,281,031	3,794,404
San Saba	7,324	436	159,325	1,412,677	1,732,305	48,522	391,040	439,561
Schleicher	3,791	361	148,547	808,002	963,480	22,583	205,958	228,541
Scurry	19,502	680	572,982	3,666,704	2,957,001	841,152	680,051	1,521,204
Shackelford	4,055	353	159,521	330,267	1,605,292	36,548	224,731	261,279
Shelby	26,317	862	766,557	15,848,181	8,556,145	820,825	762,153	1,582,978
Sherman	2,708	429	207,090	840,959	2,159,391	4,574	172,000	177,400
Smith	199,709	1,587	5,212,275	50,429,647	19,111,146	8,401,593	3,971,831	12,373,424
Somervell	8,641	190	237,140	8,944,361	748,926	164,248	315,355	479,603
Starr	37,413	494	1,078,313	3,357,658	3,403,317	1,474,241	918,750	2,392,991
Stephens	10,809	560	224,769	221,685	2,846,748	212,057	456,350	668,406
Sterling	1,876	265	172,993	578,211	968,509	2,281	82,308	84,589
Stonewall	2,078	329	96,929	1,396,319	2,408,469	2,863	137,129	139,992
Sutton	6,412	592	531,709	1,539,216	1,964,692	181,114	317,379	498,493
Swisher	6,400	806	424,295	1,492,830	4,004,514	44,742	353,610	398,352
Tarrant	1,411,467	3,167	30,907,679	127,780,465	45,338,953	67,054,604	26,865,023	93,919,627
Taylor	122,916	1,203	2,158,219	13,296,248	17,334,113	5,530,724	2,607,817	8,138,541
Terrell	1,137	374	119,848	3,231,704	802,676	1,584	52,278	53,862
Terry	12,509	630	433,260	9,084,507	2,585,600	243,909	563,989	807,898
Throckmorton	2,040	341	73,742	3,382,135	1,713,333	2,783	103,307	106,090
Titus	32,691	541	1,085,666	7,576,691	3,353,489	1,077,533	859,202	1,936,735
Tom Green	102,706	975	1,555,836	12,639,778	10,233,098	4,309,667	2,296,177	6,605,843
Travis	757,153	1,774	16,011,971	717,688,987	24,249,875	34,099,837	15,323,614	49,423,451
Trinity	14,087	433	331,373	2,920,041	2,017,782	326,495	500,080	826,575
Tyler	19,361	521	616,320	5,986,650	4,443,928	518,411	588,644	1,107,055
Upshur	39,226	783	1,004,525	7,557,471	6,868,607	1,328,985	886,413	2,215,398
Upton	3,453	392	168,924	66	1,582,868	38,539	167,413	205,953

County	Vehicles Registered	Lane Miles of Highway	Vehicle Miles Driven Daily	State Construction Expenditures	State/ Contracted Maintenance Expenditures	State Net Receipts	County Net Receipts	Total Vehicle Registration Fees
Uvalde	23,754	729	727,197	11,162,988	6,482,029	977,109	649,681	1,626,790
Val Verde	40,137	713	499,653	5,693,647	5,461,225	1,526,235	983,119	2,509,353
Van Zandt	58,772	1,166	2,204,182	3,198,043	11,670,546	2,229,477	1,119,971	3,349,448
Victoria	86,712	854	2,019,613	12,720,340	8,272,183	3,780,796	1,885,775	5,666,571
Walker	44,644	791	2,232,683	22,329,560	5,304,088	1,611,297	1,079,664	2,690,961
Waller	43,501	584	1,763,853	16,246,168	5,841,578	1,363,898	1,319,894	2,683,792
Ward	10,757	667	492,819	683,756	12,326,231	350,004	321,832	671,835
Washington	37,755	659	1,299,554	2,187,842	7,283,556	1,552,969	941,916	2,494,885
Webb	144,165	1,110	2,704,467	83,058,854	5,233,055	8,046,040	2,996,532	11,042,572
Wharton	43,508	883	1,657,667	14,967,875	10,006,001	2,022,753	999,648	3,022,401
Wheeler	6,443	672	535,371	1,342,874	4,197,035	22,227	338,901	361,128
Wichita	115,218	1,122	2,279,582	33,741,986	11,167,182	4,854,366	2,343,237	7,197,603
Wilbarger	13,758	735	683,186	2,970,166	13,715,823	245,322	570,304	815,626
Willacy	13,601	479	440,721	1,546,517	4,031,597	290,710	573,653	864,362
Williamson	299,909	1,455	5,920,935	328,887,333	9,678,846	13,115,393	6,441,839	19,557,233
Wilson	37,501	746	811,785	2,018,546	9,104,166	1,273,888	849,091	2,122,979
Winkler	6,843	295	172,341	23,902	1,504,196	149,717	321,192	470,909
Wise	72,828	852	2,431,456	32,046,345	5,073,707	3,541,381	1,491,295	5,032,676
Wood	48,284	894	917,346	8,262,638	8,895,347	1,781,787	1,099,372	2,881,159
Yoakum	8,794	431	232,086	158,148	3,269,851	158,038	502,978	661,016
Young	22,324	707	376,993	4,292,197	4,588,315	780,910	674,848	1,455,759
Zapata	9,861	248	390,486	938,752	1,269,150	338,099	329,467	667,566
Zavala	7,259	543	313,890	323,136	6,585,580	141,972	338,674	480,646
Total:	20,084,036	190,764	477,769,968	5,888,173,040	1,672,560,096	$877,634,032	$436,539,893	$1,314,173,925
State collect.						63,552,941		63,552,941
Exempt reg.	420,829							
Special veh.	75,380							
Grand Total	20,580,245					$ 941,186,973	$436,539,893	$1,377,726,866

Drivers pass by bluebonnets and other wildflowers along Texas Business 35 in Rockport. Robert Plocheck photo.

A jet takes off from Dallas Love Field. Love and D/FW International Airport along with Houston's Hobby and Bush Intercontinental airports account for more than 80 percent of enplanements in Texas. Nathan Hunsinger photo.

Aviation: Passenger Service Returns to Pre-9/11 Levels

Source: Texas Transportation Institute.

Air transportation is a vital and vigorous part of the Texas economy, and Texans are major users of air transportation. The state's airport system ranks as one of the busiest and largest in the nation. The state's 47,196 active pilots represent 7.7 percent of the nation's pilots.

The economic impact of general aviation in Texas includes total employment of 61,943 jobs, a total payroll of $2,514,708,000, and total economic output of $8,738,586,000.

In 2005, Texas' commercial service airports with scheduled passenger service enplaned more than 65 million passengers; scheduled carriers served 27 Texas airports in 25 Texas cities; and more than 90 percent of the state's population lived within 50 miles of an airport with scheduled air passenger service.

Dallas/Fort Worth International, Dallas Love Field, Houston George Bush Intercontinental, and Houston's William P. Hobby together accounted for 81 percent of these enplanements.

The decline in air passenger activity in previous years is widely believed to be the result of a series of events. These include the prolonged recovery of the air transportation industry following the Sept. 11, 2001, terrorist attacks, the domestic economic downturn and its lingering recovery, volatile international conditions, and other specific factors related to the airline industry including over capacity, profitability, and sensitivity to oil prices.

These trends do indeed appear to be reversing as some of the uncertainty has stabilized and activity at many of the airports is reaching pre-9/11 levels.

Airport Changes

Commercial passenger service saw more changes than usual in Texas. Commercial service at Ellington Field ceased in 2005 but was initiated at Del Rio International Airport.

The City of Killeen and its surrounding market saw their commercial passenger service move from Killeen Municipal Airport to the new Killeen-Fort Hood Regional Airport/Robert Gray Army Airfield, which is now a joint-use facility.

Twenty-seven airports continue to provide commercial service to Texas communities including the Texarkana Regional Airport which is physically located in Arkansas.

Scheduled passenger traffic (air carrier and commuters) increased from 2003 to 2005 breaking a trend that bottomed in 2002. Scheduled passenger enplanements in Texas increased by more than 8 million or 14 percent over the two-year period.

Twenty-six airports saw their enplanements increase with only Longview's East Texas Regional Airport experiencing a decrease.

Twenty-one airports saw double-digit increases since 2003 with Abilene, Tyler, San Angelo, and Waco seeing their enplanements rise 63 percent, 52 percent, 49 percent, and 42 percent, respectively. (See chart, page 671.)

Air service continues to be a point of worry for some communities as the airlines have worked to remove excess capacity from the system and return to profitability. These communities have experienced a decrease in the number of flights and dropping passenger levels. This is the case for Texas' smaller communities particularly Victoria, Longview, Beaumont, College Station, and Wichita Falls.

Public Administration

The State of Texas has long been committed to providing air transportation to the public. In 1945, the Texas Aeronautics Commission (TAC) was created and directed by the legislature to encourage, foster, and assist in the development of aeronautics within the state, and to encourage the establishment of airports and air navigational facilities.

The commission's first annual report of Dec. 31, 1946, stated that Texas had 592 designated airports and 7,756 civilian aircraft.

In 1989, the TAC became the Texas Department of Aviation (TDA). And, on Sept. 1, 1991, when the Texas Department of Transportation (TxDOT) was created, the TDA became the Aviation Division within the department.

The primary responsibilities of the Aviation Division include providing engineering and technical services for planning, constructing, and maintaining aeronautical facilities in the state. It is also responsible for long-range aviation facility development planning (statewide system of airports), and applying for, receiving, and disbursing federal funds.

One of TxDOT's goals is to develop a statewide system of airports that will provide adequate air access to the population and economic centers of the state.

In the Texas Airport System Plan, TxDOT has identified 300 airports that are needed to meet the forecast aviation demand and to maximize access by aircraft to the state's population, business, and agricultural and mineral resource centers.

Of these 300 airports, 27 are commercial service airports, 23 are reliever airports, and 250 are general aviation airports.

Commercial service airports provide scheduled passenger service. The reliever airports provide alternative landing facilities in the metropolitan areas separate from the commercial service airports, and, together with the business service airports, provide access for business and executive turbine-powered aircraft.

The community service and basic service airports provide access for single- and multi-engine, piston-powered aircraft to smaller communities throughout the state.

Some community service airports are also capable of accommodating light jets.

TxDOT is charged by the legislature with planning, programming, and implementing improvement projects

Top U.S. Airports

Ranked by passengers arriving and departing, 2005

Rank	Airport	Passengers
1.	Atlanta	85,907,423
2.	Chicago (O'Hare)	76,510,003
3.	Los Angeles (LAX)	61,489,398
4.	**Dallas/Fort Worth (DFW)**	**59,176,265**
5.	Las Vegas	43,989,982
6.	Denver	43,387,513
7.	New York (JFK)	41,885,104
8.	Phoenix	41,213,754
9.	**Houston (IAH)**	**39,684,640**
10.	Minneapolis/St. Paul	37,604,373
11.	Detroit	36,389,294
12.	Orlando	34,128,048
13.	Newark	33,999,990
14.	San Francisco	32,802,363
15.	Philadelphia	31,495,385

Source: Airports Council International, March 2007.

at the general aviation airports. In carrying out these responsibilities, TxDOT channels the Airport Improvement Program (AIP) funds provided by the Federal Aviation Administration (FAA) for all general aviation airports in Texas.

Since 1993, TxDOT has participated in the FAA's state block grant demonstration program. Under this program, TxDOT assumes most of the FAA's responsibility for the administration of the AIP funds for general aviation airports.

The Aviation Facilities Development Program (AFDP) oversees planning and research, assists with engineering and technical services, and provides financial assistance through state grants and loans to public bodies operating airports for the purpose of establishing,

Passengers wait to go through security screening at D/FW airport. Mark M. Hancock photo.

Airport Rangers ride near a runway at George Bush Intercontinental Airport in Houston. The airport accepts equestrian volunteers, who undergo background checks before they are allowed to ride in the prairies and pine forests that surround the airport in far north Houston. The deputized security patrols, which include off-duty law enforcement officers, are part of a project begun in December 2003. AP photo.

constructing, reconstructing, enlarging, or repairing airports, airstrips, or navigational facilities.

The 79th Legislature appropriated funds to TxDOT who subsequently allocated a portion of those funds to the Aviation Division. TxDOT allocated approximately $15 million annually for the 2006-2007 biennium to the Aviation Division to help implement and administer the AFDP.

General Aviation

General aviation continues to be an important part of both the aviation industry and the national economy as the demand for and use of general aviation aircraft is closely related to economic growth.

According to industry data, the state of general aviation is strong. Aircraft shipments in all categories were up in 2006 and industry officials are confident about the future as well. The past two years have shown robust growth in all aspects of the general aviation aircraft market. Following some years of years of difficulty, the industry has rebounded.

Worldwide shipments and billings of general aviation aircraft have increased each year from 2004 through 2006. Piston-powered aircraft shipments have increased from 2,051 in 2004 to 2,465 in 2005 to 2,750 in 2007, representing a 34 percent increase. Over the same time period, turboprop aircraft shipments have increased from 321 to 365 to 407 for 2004, 2005, and 2006, respectively representing a 27 percent increase.

Business Jets

Most compelling was the increase in business jet shipments. Business jet shipments increased from 591 to 750 to 885 in 2004, 2005, and 2006, respectively, showing an impressive increase of nearly 50 percent over the time period.

Total shipments increased more than 36 percent from 2004 to 2006 with total billings increasing from $11.9 billion in 2004 to $18.79 billion in 2006.

Airplane shipments for those manufactured in the U.S. have been impressive as well. Total shipments for U.S. manufactured aircraft increased from 2,355 in 2004 to 3,146 in 2006, a 33 percent increase. Billings increased from $6.82 billion in 2004 to $10.36 billion in 2006, a 52 percent increase.

In both worldwide and U.S. manufacturing, business jets had the highest growth rates.

This is largely reflective of increased use of business jets. Two primary factors relating to this increase are the conveniences associated with post-9/11 travel and the capacity decreases among the commercial passenger carriers that left many cities with no or reduced air service.

This trend is expected to continue as technology advances and the advent of the very light jet makes this new form of personal travel accessible for corporations and the traveling public.

Sources: General Aviation Manufacturer's Association 2006 General Aviation Statistical Databook and Annual Industry Review and Market Outlook 2007; FAA Terminal Area Forecasts 2006; Texas Department of Transportation, Aviation Division; FAA Aerospace Forecasts 2006-2017; Wilbur Smith Associates, 2007.

Passenger Enplanement by Airport

Calendar year data. Source Texas Department of Transportation.

Airport	1995	1997	1999	2001	2003	Percent change*	2005
Abilene	69,555	52,864	48,624	57,645	46,166	63%	75,414
Amarillo	454,536	450,432	435,758	440,018	384,829	15%	442,327
Austin	2,658,039	2,948,701	3,235,560	3,595,173	3,157,961	14%	3,601,135
Beaumont	108,520	112,456	100,684	78,215	43,931	26%	55,484
Brownsville	—	81,439	71,530	74,411	60,087	22%	73,361
Brownwood**	2,015	—	1,475	2,232	2,008	-70%	603
College Station	85,331	93,331	92,691	85,875	67,459	24%	83,866
Corpus Christi	511,841	471,914	451,999	425,847	358,843	15%	413,364
D/FW International	27,013,761	28,152,220	28,077,898	26,929,286	24,601,481	14%	27,960,344
Dallas/Love	3,355,238	3,413,519	3,415,785	3,552,419	2,783,787	7%	2,976,972
Del Rio	—	—	889	0	0	N/A	7,638
El Paso	1,835,162	1,634,578	1,664,123	1,618,128	1,418,974	14%	1,617,793
Harlingen	489,082	461,619	465,516	461,067	392,733	9%	429,541
Houston/Bush Int'cont.	10,165,671	13,212,686	15,026,633	16,693,056	15,934,088	17%	18,636,208
Houston/ Hobby	4,111,175	3,949,236	4,222,144	4,265,890	3,691,967	7%	3,947,543
Houston/Ellington	NA	50,503	46,520	31,775	45,748	N/A	3,021
Killeen†	59,126	84,963	86,649	98,574	92,106	N/A	—
Fort Hood/Gray†	—	—	—	15,176	3,159	N/A	153,930
Laredo	59,948	67,664	88,969	82,215	73,210	28%	94,042
Longview	33,761	26,779	28,888	31,436	29,022	-20%	23,250
Lubbock	602,680	592,101	565,173	552,726	504,916	8%	545,340
McAllen	313,082	313,506	307,325	306,259	263,431	30%	341,824
Midland	566,904	527,760	486,709	452,889	399,334	10%	439,507
San Angelo	52,674	41,404	40,400	49,140	42,688	49%	63,785
San Antonio	3,058,274	3,343,818	3,384,107	3,434,894	3,121,545	13%	3,518,786
Texarkana	45,242	36,367	40,506	34,799	25,634	31%	33,573
Tyler	78,524	69,639	73,845	65,336	53,854	52%	81,723
Victoria	19,517	21,656	20,585	16,835	10,775	3%	11,115
Waco	55,824	58,742	61,668	62,228	49,915	42%	70,851
Wichita Falls	59,275	53,942	54,453	51,286	39,608	19%	47,126
Total	**57,751,285**	**60,329,687**	**62,597,136**	**63,564,830**	**57,699,259**	**14%**	**65,479,466**

*Percent change from 2003 to 2005. **Not a commercial airport. †Killeen-Fort Hood Regional/Robert Gray AAF replaced Killeen Municipal as the commercial service airport in the area. Commercial passenger service was recently initiated at Del Rio International Airport.

Texas Air History

Passengers enplaned in Texas by scheduled carriers.
Fiscal year data.

1950	1,169,051
1955	2,434,814
1960	3,113,582
1965	5,757,689
1970	10,256,691
1975	13,182,957
1980	26,280,646
1985	40,718,209
1990	49,317,029
1995	57,166,515
1996	58,180,769
1997	60,154,165
1998	61,712,342
1999	62,558,165
2000	65,090,784
2001	63,531,077
2002	57,638,423
2003	57,675,118
2004	62,835,571
2005	65,717,954

Source: Federal Aviation Administration.

Leading U.S. Routes, 2005

Rank	Route	Passengers
1.	New York to-from Fort Lauderdale	4.16 million
2.	New York to-from Orlando	3.59 million
3.	New York to-from Chicago	2.99 million
4.	New York to-from Los Angeles	2.74 million
5.	New York to-from Atlanta	2.62 million
15.	**Dallas/Fort Worth** to-from **Houston**	1.57 million
22.	New York to-from **Dallas/Fort Worth**	1.40 million

Source: Air Transport Association. Note: Includes all commercial airports in a metro area.

Leading U.S. Airlines, 2005

Rank	Airline	Passengers (000)	Planes
1.	**American**	98,037	699
2.	**Southwest**	88,379	445
3.	Delta	85,973	480
4.	United	66,717	458
5.	US Airways	63,981	374
6	Northwest	56,469	380
7.	**Continental**	42,776	356
8.	American Eagle	17,534	N/A
9.	Alaska	16,740	110
10.	AirTran	16,619	N/A

Source: Air Transport Association. Note: Texas-based airlines in bold type.

Freight Railroads in Texas

All data in these railroad charts are for the year 2005, except as noted. Included are reports for tons of freight transported by rail, the number of carloads moved within the state and comparison to the totals in the United States. A complete list of railroads operating in Texas is at the beginning of the Counties section on page 224.

Texas Freight Railroads	Miles Operated
Union Pacific Railroad Co.	6,377
BNSF Railway Co.	4,995
Kansas City Southern Railway Co.	893
Class I (total of three above)	12,265
Regional (1 - Texas Pacifico)	393
Local (19)	831
Switching & Terminal (21)	1,022
Total	14,511
TOTAL excluding trackage rights*	10,386

*Trackage rights — track provided by another railroad.
The numbers in parentheses represent the number
of railroads in each category.
Source: Association of American Railroads

Class I Railroads Nationwide 2005	
Number of railroads	7
Miles of road excluding trackage*	95,830
Locomotives in service	22,779
Freight cars in service	474,839
Carloads originated (millions)	31.14
Intermodal units (millions)	11.69
Tons originated (billions)	1.899
Operating Statistics	
Freight revenue per ton-mile	2.621 cents
Average tons per carload	61.0
Average tons per train	3,115
Average length of haul (miles)	893.2

Source: Association of American Railroads.

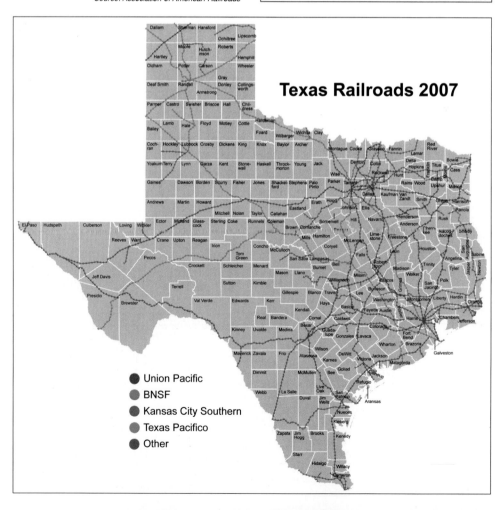

Texas Railroads 2007

- Union Pacific
- BNSF
- Kansas City Southern
- Texas Pacifico
- Other

A freight train moves along the Union Pacific line in northern Grayson County. Robert Plocheck photo.

Freight Traffic in Texas 2005 by Kind

Tons originated		Percent	Tons terminated		Percent
Chemicals	40,655,403	33%	Coal	59,486,670	27%
Nonmetallic Minerals	28,474,115	23%	Nonmetallic Minerals	41,506,896	19%
Petroleum Products	9,741,173	8%	Farm Products	26,861,959	12%
Mixed Freight	9,679,600	8%	Chemicals	22,081,168	10%
Stone/Glass Products	4,730,784	4%	Food Products	14,493,092	7%
All Other	29,619,601	24%	All Other	54,744,049	25%
Total	122,900,676		Total	219,173,834	

Source: Association of American Railroads.

Comparison of Texas Rail Traffic with Other States

State Rank	Miles of rail	State Rank	Carloads	State Rank	Freight tons carried
1. Texas	10,386	1. Illinois	11,780,610	1. Wyoming	518,899,126
2. Illinois	7,196	2. Texas	9,742,679	2. Illinois	513,722,448
3. California	5,791	3. Missouri	8,110,830	3. Nebraska	505,451,955
4. Ohio	5,354	4. California	7,124,010	4. Missouri	400,416,503
5. Pennsylvania	5,002	5. Ohio	6,809,864	5. Texas	384,437,616
6. Kansas	4,878	6. Indiana	6,751,549	6. Iowa	331,539,961
7. Georgia	4,738	7. New Mexico	6,451,038	7. Kansas	326,259,496
8. Minnesota	4,599	8. Iowa	6,372,589	8. Ohio	316,053,290
9. Indiana	4,165	9. Arizona	6,310,039	9. Indiana	297,850,892
10. Missouri	4,096	10. Kansas	6,222,800	10. Kentucky	288,266,528

Source: Association of American Railroads.

Freight Cars in Service in North America, Jan. 1, 2006

	Total all owners	Railroads		Car companies & shippers
		Class I	Other	
Canada	188,084	151,633	6,356	30,095
Mexico	34,388	22,348	5,870	6,170
United States	1,312,245	474,839	120,195	717,211
Total	1,534,717	648,820	132,421	753,476

Source: Association of American Railroads.

Agriculture

Donkeys graze on a small farm in Tarrant County. Elizabeth Alvarez photo.

Principal Crops

Vegetable Crops

Fruits & Nuts

Livestock and Their Products

Livestock Auctions 101

Agriculture in Texas

Information was provided by Texas Cooperative Extension specialists, Texas Agricultural Statistics Service, U.S. Department of Agriculture and U.S. Department of Commerce. Carl G. Anderson, professor and extension specialist–emeritus of Texas A&M University, coordinated the information. All references are to Texas unless otherwise specified.

Importance of Agriculture to the Texas Economy

Agribusiness, the combined phases of food and fiber production, processing, transporting and marketing, is a leading Texas industry. Most of this article is devoted to the phase of production on farms and ranches.

Agriculture is one of the most important industries in Texas. Many businesses, financial institutions and individuals are involved in providing supplies, credit and services to farmers and ranchers, and in processing and marketing agricultural commodities.

Including all its agribusiness phases, agriculture added about $33 billion to the economic activity of Texas in 2006. The estimated value of farm assets in Texas — the land, buildings, livestock, machinery, crops, inventory on farms, household goods and farm financial assets — totaled approximately $113 billion at the beginning of 2003.

Texas agriculture is a strong industry. Receipts from farm and ranch marketings in 2006 were estimated at $15.7 billion, compared with $16.4 billion in 2005. The decline in 2006 from the year before was due to a prolonged statewide drought.

The potential for further growth is favorable. With the increasing demand for food and fiber throughout the world, and because of the importance of agricultural exports to this nation's trade balance, agriculture in Texas is destined to play an even greater role in the future.

Major efforts of research and educational programs by the Texas A&M University System are directed toward developing the state's agricultural industry to its fullest potential. The goal is to capitalize on natural advantages that agriculture has in Texas because of the relatively warm climate, productive soils, and availability of excellent export and transportation facilities.

Texas Farms

The number and nature of farms have changed over time. The number of farms in Texas has decreased from 420,000 in 1940 to 230,000 in 2006, with an average size of 564 acres. Average value per farm of all farm assets, including land and buildings, has increased from $20,100 in 1950 to $705,000 in 2006. The number of small farms is increasing — but part-time farmers operate them.

Mechanization of farming continues as new and larger machines replace manpower. Although machinery price tags are high relative to times past, machines are technologically advanced and efficient. Tractors, mechanical harvesters and numerous cropping machines have virtually eliminated menial tasks that for many years were traditional to farming.

Revolutionary agricultural chemicals have appeared along with improved plants and animals, and methods of handling them. Many of the natural hazards of farming and ranching were reduced by better use of weather information, machinery and other improvements; but rising costs, labor availability and high-energy costs have added to concerns of farmers and ranchers. Changes in Texas agriculture in the last 50 years include:

1. More detailed record keeping that assists in management and marketing decisions.

2. More restrictions on choice or inputs/practices.

3. Precision agriculture will take on new dimensions through the use of satellites, computers and other high-tech tools to help producers manage inputs such as seed, fertilizers, pesticides and water.

Farms have become fewer, larger, specialized and much more expensive to own and operate, but far more productive. The number of small farms operated by part-time farmers is increasing. Land ownership is becoming more of a lifestyle used mostly for recreational purposes. Non-farm landowners are increasing.

Irrigation has become an important factor in crop production.

Crops and livestock have made major changes in production areas, as in the concentration of cotton on the High Plains and livestock increases in central and eastern Texas.

Pest and disease control methods have greatly improved. Herbicides are relied upon for weed control.

Ranchers and farmers are better educated and informed, and more science- and business-oriented. Today, agriculture operates in a global, high-tech, consumer-driven environment.

Feedlot finishing, commercial broiler production, artificial insemination, improved pastures and brush control, reduced feed requirements, and other changes have greatly increased livestock and poultry efficiency. Biotechnology and genetic engineering promise new breakthroughs in reaching even higher levels of productivity. Horticultural plant and nursery businesses have expanded. Improved wildlife management has increased deer, turkey and other wildlife populations. The use of land for recreation and ecotourism is growing.

Cooperation among farmers in marketing, promotion and other fields has increased.

Agricultural producers have become increasingly

Linda Slagle, owner of BuckBranch Farm and Equestrian Center in Wilmer, stands at the entrance of her 100-acre farm, which has been in her family since 1876. The Texas Department of Agriculture's Family Land Heritage Program recognized the farm in 2006 as being in continuous agricultural production for more than 100 years. The program has honored more than 4,000 Texas farms and ranches. Irwin Thompson photo.

dependent on off-the-farm services to supply production inputs such as feeds, chemicals, credit and other essentials.

Agribusiness

Texas farmers and ranchers have developed considerable dependence upon agribusiness. With many producers specializing in the production of certain crops and livestock, they look beyond the farm and ranch for supplies and services. On the input side, they rely on suppliers of production needs and services and, on the output side, they need assemblers, processors and distributors. The impact of production agriculture and related businesses on the Texas economy is about $33 billion annually.

Since 1940, the proportion of Texans whose livelihood is linked to agriculture has changed greatly. In 1940, about 23 percent were producers on farms and ranches, and about 17 percent were suppliers or were engaged in assembly, processing and distribution of agricultural products. The agribusiness alignment in 2004 was less than 2 percent on farms and ranches, with about 15 percent of the labor force providing production or marketing supplies and services, and retailing food and fiber products.

Cash Receipts

Farm and ranch cash receipts in 2005 totaled $16.355 billion. With estimates of $2.094 billion for government payments, $1.345 billion of non-cash income, and $1.620 billion of other farm-related income included, realized gross farm income totaled $21.414 billion. With farm production expenses of $15.118 billion, net farm income totaled $6.296 billion. The value of inventory adjustment was +$257.0 million.

Farm and Ranch Assets

Farm and ranch assets totaled $112.5 billion in 2003. This was up from the 2002 level of $107.5 billion. Value of real estate increased almost 5.3 percent to $90.9 billion in 2003. Liabilities totaled $13.3 billion, up slightly from $13.0 billion in 2002.

Percent of Income from Products

Livestock and livestock products accounted for 65.2 percent of the $16.355 billion cash receipts from farm marketings in 2005, with the remaining 34.8 percent from crops. Receipts from livestock have trended up largely because of increased feeding operations and reduced crop acreage associated with farm programs and low prices. However, these relationships change because of variations in commodity prices and volume of marketings.

Meat animals (cattle, hogs and sheep) accounted for 42 percent of total cash receipts received by Texas farmers and ranchers in 2005. Most of these receipts were from cattle and calf sales. Dairy products made up 5.3 percent of receipts; poultry and eggs, 9.4 percent; and miscellaneous livestock, 1.1 percent.

Cotton and cottonseed accounted for 10 percent of total receipts; feed crops, 5.3 percent; food grains, 2.1 percent; vegetables, 2.8 percent; greenhouse/nursery products, 8.1 percent; oil crops, 1.3 percent; fruits and nuts, 1.2 percent; and other crops, 0.2 percent.

Texas Rank Among States

Measured by cash receipts for farm and ranch marketings, Texas ranked second in 2005. California ranked first and Iowa third.

Texas normally leads all other states in numbers of farms and ranches and farm and ranch land, cattle slaughtered, cattle on feed, calf births, sheep and lambs, goats, cash receipts from livestock marketings, cattle and calves, beef cows, sheep and lambs, wool production, mohair production, and exports of fats, oils, and greases. The state also usually leads in production of cotton.

Texas Agricultural Exports

The value of Texas' share of agricultural exports in fiscal year 2005 was $3.526 billion. Cotton accounted for $1,337.4 million of the exports; feed grains and products, $251.9 million; wheat and products, $280.3 million; fats, oil and greases, $76.4 million; rice, $75.4 million; cottonseed and products, $34.1 million; hides and skins, $282.1 million; live animals and meat, excluding poultry, $281 million; fruits, $64.2 million; peanuts and products, $41 million; soybeans and products, $17.1 million; vegetables and products, $62.6 million; poultry and products, $160.3 million; dairy products, $63.6 million; and miscellaneous and other products, $475.4 million.

In 2004, Texas' exports of $3.74 billion of farm and ranch products compares with $3.407 billion in 2003 and $2.851 billion in 2002.

Hunting

The management of wildlife as an economic enterprise through leasing for hunting makes a significant contribution to the economy of many counties. Leasing the right of ingress on a farm or ranch for the purpose of hunting is the service marketed. After the leasing, the consumer — the hunter — goes onto the land to seek the harvest of the wildlife commodity. Hunting lease income to farmers and ranchers in 2006 was estimated at $588 million.

The demand for hunting opportunities is growing while the land capable of producing huntable wildlife is

Texas Crop Production
2006

Crop	Harvested Acres (000)	Yield Per Acre	Unit	Total Production (000)	Value (000)
Beans, dry edible	18.0	1,320	lb.	238	6,093
Corn, grain	1,450	121	bu.	175,450	561,440
Corn, silage	160	15.0	ton	2,400	—
Cotton, American-Pima	30.0	672	lb.	42.0	19,354
Cotton, upland	4,100	702	lb.	6,000	1,339,200
Cottonseed	—	—	ton	2,172	254,124
Grapefruit *	—	—	box	5,200	63,292
Hay, Alfalfa	150	4.5		675	107,325
Hay, Other	5,000	1.0		8,000	984,000
Hay, all	5,150	1.68	ton	8,675	1,091,325
Oats	100	37.0	bu.	3,700	8,510
Oranges†	—	—	box	1,600	10,598
Peaches	—	—	lb.	0.8	1,230
Peanuts	145	3,700	lb.	536,500	96,034
Pecans	—	—	lb.	36,000	61,390
Potatoes	19.9	358	cwt.	7,124	117,059
Rice	150	7,170	lb.	10,760	106,524
Sorghum, grain	1,300	2,688	lb.	34,944	174,720
Sorghum, silage	100	15.5	ton	1,550	—
Soybeans	155	24.0	bu.	3,720	20,088
Sugar cane	46.5	38.8	ton	1,804	—
Sunflowers	24	890	lb.	21,350	3,268
Sweet potatoes	2.1	100	cwt.	210	2,205
Vegetables, commercial:					
Fresh market ‡	64.7	—	cwt.	16,773	266,887
Processing §	20.4	—	cwt.	1,911	20,412
Wheat, winter	1,400	24.0	bu.	33,600	152,880
Total of Listed Crops	**19,585.6**	**—**	**—**	**—**	**5,467,958**

*Grapefruit, Texas 80-lb./box, reflects 2005–2006 crop year. †Oranges, Texas 85-lb./box, reflects 05/06 crop year. ‡Includes processing total for dual usage crops (asparagus, broccoli and cauliflower). Total Texas fresh market vegetables include: Bell peppers, cabbage, cantaloupes, carrots, cauliflower, celery, cucumbers, honeydew melons, onions, spinach, sweet corn, tomatoes and watermelons. §Total Texas processing vegetables include carrots, cucumbers, snap beans, spinach and tomatoes.
Source: "A Texas Ag Facts Annual Summary," TASS/USDA, 3/2/07.

decreasing. As a result, farmers and ranchers are placing more emphasis on wildlife management practices to help meet requests for hunting leases.

Irrigation

Agricultural irrigation in Texas peaked in 1974 at 8.6 million acres. Over the next 20 years, irrigation declined due to many factors including poor farm economics, falling water tables and conversion to more efficient technologies. In the 1990s, irrigation stabilized at 6.4 million acres. This puts Texas third in the nation, behind California and Nebraska in agricultural irrigation.

Although some irrigation is practiced in nearly every county in the state, about 50 percent of the total irrigated acreage is on the High Plains. Other concentrated areas of irrigation are the Gulf Coast rice-producing area, the Lower Rio Grande Valley, the Winter Garden area of South Texas, the Trans-Pecos area of West Texas, and the peanut producing area in North-Central Texas centered around Erath, Eastland and Comanche counties. The largest growth in irrigation is in the Coastal Bend area.

Sprinkler irrigation is used on about 65 percent of the total irrigated acreage, with surface irrigation methods, primarily furrow and surge methods, being used on the remaining irrigated area. Texas farmers lead the nation in

the adoption of efficient irrigation technologies, particularly LEPA (low energy precision application) and LESA (low elevation spray application) center pivot systems, both of which were developed by Texas A&M.

The use of drip irrigation is increasing, with current acreage estimated to be 450,000 acres. Drip irrigation is routinely used on vegetables and tree crops, such as citrus, pecans and peaches. Some drip irrigation of cotton and forages is being practiced in West Texas. Farmers continue to experiment with drip irrigation, but the high costs are limiting its widespread use.

Agricultural irrigation uses about 60 percent of all fresh water in the state, and landscape irrigation accounts for about 40 percent of total municipal water use. Texas is one of only a handful of states that require a state irrigator's license for the design and installation of landscape and residential irrigation systems. No license or certification, however, is required for agricultural irrigation systems.

To meet future water demand for our rapidly growing cities and industries, several regions of the state are looking at water transfers from agriculture. In recent years, major water transfer projects have been proposed, including transferring water from the Texas High Plains to the Metroplex and from the Colorado River to San Antonio. The potential economic, political and environmental benefits and consequences of such transfers are currently under investigation. Water utilities in San Antonio also have water transfer programs with irrigators in the Edwards Aquifer region. The effects of such transfers on farm and rural economies are uncertain.

In about 20 percent of the irrigated area, water is delivered to farms by irrigation and water districts through canals and pipelines. Many of these delivery networks are aging, in poor condition and have high seepage losses. In 2000, Congress passed Public Law 106-576 that, along with subsequent legislation, authorized federal cost-sharing for rehabilitation of districts along the Rio Grande in Texas. To date, Congress has appropriated about $10 million for such projects.

Approximately 80 percent of the state's irrigated acreage is supplied with water pumped from wells. Surface water sources supply the remaining area. Declining groundwater levels in several of the major aquifers is a serious problem for agriculture, particularly in the Ogallala Aquifer in the Texas High Plains and the southern portion of the Carizo-Wilcox formation. As the water level declines, well yields decrease and pumping costs increase.

Irrigation is an important factor in the productivity of Texas agriculture. The value of crop production from irrigated acreage is 50-60 percent of the total value of all crop production, although only about 30 percent of the state's total harvested cropland acreage is irrigated.

Principal Crops

In most recent years, the value of crop production in Texas is less than 40 percent of the total value of the state's agricultural output. Cash receipts from farm sales of crops are reduced somewhat because some grain and roughage is fed to livestock on farms where produced. Drought and low prices have reduced receipts in recent years.

Receipts from all Texas crops totaled $5.694 billion in 2005; $5.340 billion in 2004; and $5.036 billion in 2003.

Cotton, corn, grain sorghum and wheat account for a large part of the total crop receipts. In 2005, cotton contributed about 27.8 percent of the crop total; corn, 8.8 percent; grain sorghum, 4.2 percent; and wheat, 5.0 percent. Hay, cottonseed, vegetables, peanuts, rice and soybeans are other important cash crops.

Barley

Texas barley acreage and production falls far below that of wheat and oats. Barley is usually harvested from 10,000 of the 15,000 acres planted, with total production

*Realized Gross Income and Net Income from Farming, Texas, 1980–2005

Year	**Realized Gross Farm Income	Farm Production Expenses	Net Change In Farm Inventories	***Total Net Farm Income	***Total Net Income Per Farm
	— Millions of Dollars —				Dollars
1980	9,611.4	9,154.6	−542.5	456.8	2,330.6
1981	11,545.7	9,643.1	699.9	1,902.6	9,756.9
1982	11,404.5	10,016.2	−127.8	1,388.3	7,156.2
1983	11,318.1	9,796.5	−590.7	1,521.6	7,843.3
1984	11,692.6	10,285.7	186.1	1,406.9	7,252.1
1985	11,375.3	9,882.4	−9.0	1,492.9	7,775.5
1986	10,450.1	9,341.3	−349.0	1,108.8	5,835.8
1987	12,296.6	10,185.0	563.2	2,111.5	11,231.4
1988	12,842.8	10,816.8	−128.4	2,026.0	10,552.1
1989	12,843.1	10,703.7	−798.6	2,139.4	11,027.8
1990	14,463.2	11,412.4	343.9	3,050.8	15,565.3
1991	14,393.4	11,551.4	150.0	2,842.0	14,426.4
1992	14,392.5	10,994.9	464.1	3,397.6	17,159.6
1993	15,758.5	11,612.1	197.0	4,146.4	20,732.0
1994	15,450.5	11,593.4	107.7	3,857.1	17,532.0
1995	15,709.7	12,984.4	243.7	2,725.3	12,276.0
1996	15,076.8	12,552.9	−290.1	2,524.0	11,268.0
1997	16,515.8	13,240.5	709.2	3,275.3	14,557.0
1998	15,552.3	12,556.1	−817.1	2,996.2	13,258.0
1999	17,453.0	12,452.9	196.0	5,000.1	22,027.0
2000	16,106.1	12,180.4	−50.2	3,925.7	17,370.0
2001	17,574.8	12,576.4	113.4	4,998.4	22,019.0
2002	16,042.8	10,840.7	436.6	5,202.1	22,618.0
2003	19,418.7	13,214.2	−169.9	6,204.5	27,094.0
2004	21,003.4	13,975.3	473.3	7,028.1	30,690.0
2005	21,413.9	15,117.9	257.0	6,296.0	27,374.0

*Details for items may not add to totals because of rounding. Series revised, September 1981.
** Cash receipts from farm marketings, government payments, value of home consumption and gross rental value of farm dwellings.
*** Farm income of farm operators.
† A positive value of inventory change represents current-year production not sold by Dec. 31. A negative value is an offset to production from prior years included in current-year sales.
§ Starting in 1977, farms with production of $1,000 or more used to figure income.
Source: "Economic Indicators of the Farm Sector, State Financial Summary, 1985," 1987," 1989," 1993," USDA/ERS; "Farm Business Economics Report," August 1996, "Texas Agricultural Statistics Service, October 2006."

value of less than $500,000. Estimated production data was discontinued in 2000.

Corn

Interest in corn production throughout the state has increased since the 1970s as yields improved with new varieties. Once the principal grain crop, corn acreage declined as plantings of grain sorghum increased. Only 500,000 acres were harvested annually until the mid-1970s when development of new hybrids occurred.

Harvested acreage was 1.45 million in 2006; 1.85 million in 2005; and 1.68 million in 2004. Yields for the corresponding years were 121, 114 and 139 bushels per acre, respectively.

Most of the acreage and yield increase has occurred in Central and South Texas. In 2006, corn ranked fourth in value among the state's crops. It was valued at $561.44 million in 2006; $520.92 million in 2005; and $607.15 million in 2004. The grain is largely used for livestock feed, but other important uses are in food products.

The leading counties in production for 2005 were Dallam, Hartley, Castro, Sherman and Moore.

Cotton

Cotton has been a major crop in Texas for more than a century. Since 1880, Texas has led all states in cotton production in most years, and today the annual Texas cotton harvest amounts to approximately 25 percent of total production in the United States. The annual cotton crop has averaged 5.26 million bales since 1996.

Total value of Upland and Pima lint cotton produced in Texas in 2006 was $1.359 billion. Cottonseed value in 2004 was $254,124,000, making the total value of the Texas crop around $1.613 billion.

Upland cotton was harvested from 4.10 million acres in 2006, and American-Pima from 30,000 acres, for a total of 4.130 million acres. Yield for Upland cotton in 2006 was 702 pounds per harvested acre, with American-Pima yielding 672 pounds per acre. Cotton acreage harvested in 2005 totaled 5.624 million, with a yield of 723 pounds per acre for Upland cotton and 870 pounds per acre for American-Pima. Total cotton production amounted to 6.042 million bales in 2006 and 8.484 million in 2005. Counties

Export Shares of Commodities

Commodity*	2002	2003	2004	2005	2005 % of U.S. Total
	Millions of Dollars				
Rice	51.0	67.0	73.6	75.4	5.56
Cotton	425.6	841.5	1,486.2	1,337.4	34.54
Fats, oils & greases	68.4	85.5	89.5	76.4	16.01
Hides & skins	280.4	282.0	287.2	282.1	16.16
Meats other than poultry	700.8	748.5	333.7	281.0	5.71
Feed grains	261.1	313.9	307.8	251.9	3.63
Poultry products	121.6	109.3	140.1	160.3	5.32
Fruits	44.9	41.0	79.4	64.2	1.57
Vegetables	74.2	60.6	57.0	62.6	1.12
Wheat & flour	250.4	244.8	271.4	280.3	4.78
Soybeans & prod..	14.8	17.2	24.9	17.1	0.19
Cottonseed & prod.	22.6	30.8	36.7	34.1	35.10
Peanuts	67.5	36.7	39.9	41.0	18.87
Tree nuts	13.7	18.5	23.7	23.5	0.97
Dairy products	32.1	34.0	46.6	63.6	3.65
†All other	421.8	475.7	442.3	475.4	4.26
Total	**2,850.9**	**3,407.0**	**3,740.0**	**3,526.3**	**5.65**

Totals may not add due to rounding.
* Commodity and related preparations.
† Mainly, confectionary, nursery and greenhouse, essential oils, sunflower seed oil, beverages, and other miscellaneous animal and vegetable products.
Source: FATUS, Foreign Agricultural Trade of the United States, various issues, web site: www.ers.usda.gov for 2005 data. USDA/ERS.

leading in production of Upland cotton in 2005 included Hale, Lubbock, Gaines, Lynn, Terry and Dawson.

Cotton is the raw material for processing operations at gins, oil mills, compresses and a small number of textile mills in Texas. Less than 10 percent of the raw cotton produced is processed within the state.

Cotton in Texas is machine harvested. Field storage of harvested seed cotton is gaining in popularity as gins decline in number. Much of the Texas cotton crop is exported. China, Japan, South Korea and Mexico are major buyers. With the continuing development of fiber spinning technology and the improved quality of Texas cotton, more utilization of cotton by mills within the state may develop

Cotton bales are lined up on a farm in Medina County. The annual Texas cotton harvest amounts to about 25 percent of the total U.S. production. Robert Plocheck photo.

in the future. Spinning techniques can efficiently produce high-quality yarn from relatively strong, short or longer staple Upland cotton with fine mature fiber.

The first high-volume instrument cotton classing office in the nation was opened at Lamesa in 1980.

Flaxseed

Earliest flax planting was at Victoria in 1900. Since the first planting, Texas flax acreage has fluctuated depending on market, winterkill and drought. Flax acreage has dropped in recent years and estimates were discontinued in 1980.

Forest Products

For information on the Texas forest products, turn to the section titled "Texas Forest Resources," page 109.

Grain Sorghum

Grain sorghum in 2006 ranked sixth in dollar value. Much of the grain is exported, as well as being used in livestock and poultry feed throughout the state.

Total production of grain sorghum in 2006 was 34.94 million hundredweight (cwt), with a 2,688 pound per acre yield. With an average price of $5 per cwt., the total value reached $174.7 million. In 2005, 1.85 million acres of grain

sorghum were harvested, yielding an average of 3,360 pounds per acre for a total production of 62.16 million cwt. It was valued at $3.89 per cwt., for a total value of $241.8 million. In 2004, 2.05 million acres were harvested, with an average of 3,472 pounds per acre, or 71.17 million cwt. The season's price was $3.99 per cwt. for a total value of $283.99 million.

Although grown to some extent in all counties where crops are important, the largest concentrations are in the High Plains, Rolling Plains, Blackland Prairie, Coastal Bend and Lower Rio Grande Valley areas. Counties leading in production in 2005 were Nueces, Hidalgo, San Patricio, Cameron, Willacy and Floyd.

Research to develop high-yielding hybrids resistant to diseases and insect damage continues. A history of grain sorghum appeared in the 1972-1973 edition of the *Texas Almanac*.

Hay, Silage and Other Forage Crops

A large proportion of Texas' agricultural land is devoted to forage crop production. This acreage produces forage needs and provides essentially the total feed requirements for most of the state's large domestic livestock population, as well as game animals.

Approximately 83.4 million acres of pasture and rangeland, which are primarily in the western half of Texas, provide grazing for beef cattle, sheep, goats, horses and game animals. An additional 12.9 million acres are devoted to cropland used only for pasture or grazing. The average annual acreage of forage land used for hay, silage and other forms of machine-harvested forage is around 5 million acres.

Hay accounts for a large amount of this production, with some corn and sorghum silage being produced. The most important hay crops are annual and perennial grasses and alfalfa. Production in 2006 totaled 8.67 million tons of hay from 5.15 million harvested acres at a yield of 1.68 tons per acre. Value of hay was $1.09 million, or $130 per ton. In 2005, 9.14 million tons of hay was produced from 5.05 million harvested acres at a yield of 1.81 tons per acre. The value in 2005 was $769.27 million, or $92 per ton. In 2004, the production of hay was 12.29 million tons from 5.35 million harvested acres with a value of $832.72 million, or $77 per ton, at a yield of 2.30 tons per acre.

Alfalfa hay production in 2006 totaled 675,000 tons, with 150,000 acres harvested and a yield of 4.50 tons per acre. At a value of $159 per ton, total value was $107.32 million. In 2005, 810,000 tons of alfalfa hay was harvested from 150,000 acres at a yield of 5.40 tons per acre. Value was $102.87 million, or $127 per ton. Alfalfa hay was harvested from 150,000 acres in 2004, producing an average of 5.70 tons per acre for total production of 855,000 tons, valued at $112 million.

An additional sizable acreage of annual forage crops is grazed, as well as much of the small grain acreage. Alfalfa, sweet corn, vetch, arrowleaf clover, grasses and other forage plants also provide income as seed crops.

Nursery Crops

The trend to increase production of nursery crops continues to rise as transportation costs on long-distance hauling increases. This has resulted in a marked increase in the production of container-grown plants in Texas. This increase is noted especially in the production of bedding plants, foliage plants, sod and the woody landscape plants.

Plant rental services have become a multi-million dollar business. This relatively new service provides the plants and maintains them in office buildings, shopping malls, public buildings, and even in some homes for a fee. The response has been good as evidenced by the growth of companies providing these services.

The interest in plants for interior landscapes is confined

Value of Cotton and Cottonseed 1900–2006

Crop Year	Upland Cotton		Cottonseed	
	Production (Bales)	Value	Production (Tons)	Value
	(All Figures in Thousands)			
1900	3,438	$157,306	1,531	$20,898
1910	3,047	210,260	1,356	31,050
1920	4,345	376,080	1,934	41,350
1930	4,037	194,080	1,798	40,820
1940	3,234	162,140	1,318	31,852
1950	2,946	574,689	1,232	111,989
1960	4,346	612,224	1,821	75,207
1970	3,191	314,913	1,242	68,310
*1980	3,320	1,091,616	1,361	161,959
1981	5,645	1,259,964	2,438	207,230
1982	2,700	664,848	1,122	90,882
1983	2,380	677,443	1,002	162,324
1984	3,680	927,360	1,563	157,863
1985	3,910	968,429	1,634	102,156
1986	2,535	560,945	1,053	82,118
1987	4,635	1,325,981	1,915	157,971
1988	5,215	1,291,651	2,131	238,672
1989	2,870	812,784	1,189	141,491
1990	4,965	1,506,182	1,943	225,388
1991	4,710	1,211,789	1,903	134,162
1992	3,265	769,495	1,346	145,368
1993	5,095	1,308,396	2,147	255,493
1994	4,915	1,642,003	2,111	215,322
1995	4,460	1,597,037	1,828	201,080
1996	4,345	1,368,154	1,784	230,136
1997	5,140	1,482,787	1,983	226,062
1998	3,600	969,408	1,558	204,098
1999	5,050	993,840	1,987	160,947
2000	3,940	868,061	1,589	162,078
2001	4,260	580,723	1,724	159,470
2002	5,040	967,680	1,855	191,065
2003	4,330	1,199,237	1,616	202,000
2004	7,740	1,493,510	2,895	301,080
2005	8,440	1,879,757	2,869	289,739
2006	6,000	1,339,200	2,172	254,124

Beginning in 1971, basis for cotton prices was changed from 500 pound gross weight to 480 pound net weight bale; to compute comparable prices for previous years multiply price times 1.04167.
Source: "A Texas Agricultural Facts," Crop Value Annual Summary, February 2007 and "A Texas Ag Statistics," Texas Agricultural Statistics Service, Austin, Texas, annual summary. 2006 based on marketings and monthly prices received form August 1, 2006 – December 31, 2006.

The Triple-L Lavender farm in Kendall County is part of the boom in nursery crop production. Robert Plocheck photo.

to no specific age group as both retail nurseries and florist shops report that people of all ages are buying their plants — from the elderly in retirement homes to high school and college students in dormitory rooms and apartments.

Texas Cooperative Extension specialists estimated cash receipts from nursery crops in Texas to be around $1.7 billion in 2006. Ranking counties in specialty crops are Harris, Dallas, Montgomery, Bexar, Fort Bend and Cherokee. Texans are creating colorful and green surroundings by improving their landscape plantings.

Oats

Oats are grown extensively in Texas for winter pasture, hay, silage and greenchop feeding, and some acreage is harvested for grain.

Of the 760,000 acres planted to oats in 2000, 100,000 acres were harvested. The average yield was 37 bushels per acre. Production totaled 3.7 million bushels with a value of $8.51 million. In 2005, 690,000 acres were planted. From the plantings, 110,000 acres were harvested, with an average yield of 43 bushels per acre for a total production of 4.73 million bushels. Average price per bushel was $2.4 and total production value was $11.35 million.

Texas farmers planted 680,000 acres of oats in 2004. They harvested 160,000 acres that averaged 40 bushels per acre for a total production of 6.4 million bushels at an average price of $1.91 per bushel and an estimated value of $12.22 million. Most of the acreage was used for grazing.

Almost all oat grain produced in Texas is utilized as feed for livestock within the state. A small acreage is grown exclusively for planting seed. Leading oat grain-producing counties in 2005 were Hamilton, Falls, Medina, Coryell and Coleman.

Peanuts

Peanuts are grown on more than 250,000 acres in Texas. Well over three-fourths of the crop annually produced is on acreage that is irrigated. Texas ranked second nationally in production of peanuts in 2006. Among Texas crops, peanuts rank 10th in value.

Until 1973, essentially all of the Texas acreage was planted to the Spanish type, which was favored because of its earlier maturity and better drought tolerance than other types. The Spanish variety is also preferred for some uses due to its distinctive flavor. The Florunner variety, a runner market type, is now planted on a sizable proportion of the acreage where soil moisture is favorable. The variety matures later but produces better yields than Spanish varieties under good-growing conditions. Florunner peanuts have acceptable quality to compete with the Spanish variety in most products.

In 2006, peanut production totaled 536.5 million pounds from 145,000 harvested acres, yielding 3,700 pounds per acre. At 17.9 cents per pound, value of the crop was estimated at $96.03 million. In 2005, peanut production amounted to 975 million pounds from 265,000 acres planted and 260,000 harvested. Average yield of 3,750 pounds per acre and average price of 18.0 cents per pound combined for a 2005 value of $175.5 million. Production in 2004 amounted to 803.7 million pounds of peanuts from 240,000 acres planted and 235,000 acres harvested, or an average of 3,420 pounds per harvested acre valued at 19.2 cents per pound for a value of $154.31 million.

Leading counties in peanut production in 2005 included Gaines, Terry, Yoakum, Collingsworth, Cochran, Haskell and Dawson.

Rice

Rice, which is grown in about 20 counties on the Coast Prairie of Texas, ranked third in value among Texas crops for a number of years. However, in recent years, cotton, grain sorghum, wheat, corn, peanuts and hay have out-ranked rice.

Farms are highly mechanized, producing rice through irrigation and using airplanes for much of the planting, fertilizing, and application of insecticides and herbicides.

Texas farmers grow long- and medium-grain rice only. The Texas rice industry, which has grown from 110 acres in 1850 to a high of 642,000 acres in 1954, has been marked by significant yield increases and improved varieties. Record production was in 1981, with 27.23 million hundredweights harvested. Highest yield was 7,170 pounds per acre in 2006.

Several different types of rice milling procedures are in use today. The simplest and oldest method produces a product known as regular milled white rice, the most prevalent on the market today.

During this process, rice grains are subjected to additional cleaning to remove chaff, dust and foreign seed, and then husks are removed from the grains. This results in a product that is the whole unpolished grain of rice with only the outer hull and a small amount of bran removed. This product is called brown rice and is sometimes sold without further treatment other than grading. It has a delightful nutlike flavor and a slightly chewy texture.

When additional layers of the bran are removed, the rice becomes white in color and begins to appear as it is normally recognized at retail level. The removal of the bran layer from the grain is performed in a number of steps using two or three types of machines. After the bran is removed, the product is ready for classification as to size. Rice is more valuable if the grains are not broken. In many cases, additional vitamins are added to the grains to produce what is called "enriched rice."

Another process may be used in rice milling to produce a product called parboiled rice. In this process, the rice is subjected to a combination of steam and pressure prior to the time it is milled in the manner described above. This process gelatinizes the starch in the grain, the treatment aiding in the retention of much of the natural vitamin and mineral content. After cooking, parboiled rice tends to be fluffy, more separate and plump.

Still another type of rice is precooked rice, which is actually milled rice that, after milling, has been cooked. Then the moisture is removed through a dehydration process. Precooked rice requires a minimum of preparation time because it needs merely to have the moisture restored.

The United States produces only a small part of the world's total rice, but it is one of the leading exporters. American rice is popular abroad and is exported to more than 100 foreign countries.

Rice production in 2006 totaled 10.76 million cwt. from 150,000 harvested acres, with a yield of 7,170 pounds per acre. The crop value totaled $106.52 million. Rice production was 13.66 million cwt. in 2005 on 201,000 harvested acres, yielding 6,800 pounds per acre. Total value in 2005 was $106.2 million. Rice production was 14.69 million cwt. in 2004 on 218,000 harvested acres. Production in 2004 was valued at $118.65 million, with a yield of 6,840 pounds per acre. Counties leading in rice production in 2005 included Wharton, Colorado, Matagorda, Brazoria, Jefferson and Jackson.

Rye

Rye is grown mainly on the Northern and Southern High Plains, the Northern Low Plains, Cross Timbers, Blacklands and East Texas areas. Minor acreages are seeded in South-Central Texas, the Edwards Plateau and the Upper Coast. Rye is grown primarily as a cover crop and for grazing during the fall, winter and early spring. Estimated production data was discontinued in 1999.

Soybeans

Production is largely in the areas of the Upper Coast, irrigated High Plains, and Red River Valley of Northeast Texas. Soybeans are adapted to the same general soil climate conditions as corn, cotton or grain sorghum — provided moisture, disease and insects are not limiting factors. The major counties in soybean production in 2005 were Wharton, Victoria, Lamar, Ellis, Fannin, Ochiltree and Delta.

In low-rainfall areas, yields have been too low or inconsistent for profitable production under dryland conditions. Soybeans' need for moisture in late summer minimizes economic crop possibilities in the Blacklands and Rolling Plains. In the Blacklands, cotton root rot seriously hinders soybean production. Limited moisture at critical growth stages may occasionally prevent economical yields, even in high-rainfall areas of Northeast Texas and the Coastal Prairie.

Because of day length sensitivity, soybeans should be planted in Texas during the long days of May and June to obtain sufficient vegetative growth for optimum yields. Varieties planted during this period usually cease vegetative development and initiate reproductive processes during the hot, usually dry months of July and August. When moisture is insufficient during the blooming and fruiting period, yields are drastically reduced. In most areas of the state, July and August rainfall is insufficient to permit economical dryland production. The risk of dryland soybean production in the Coastal Prairie and Northeast Texas is considerably less when compared to other dryland areas because moisture is available more often during the critical fruiting period.

The 2006 soybean crop totaled 3.72 million bushels and was valued at $20.09 million, or $5.40 per bushel. Of the 225,000 acres planted, 155,000 were harvested with an average yield of 24.0 bushels per acre. In 2005, the Texas soybean crop averaged 26.0 bushels per acre from 230,000 acres harvested. Total production of 5.98 million bushels was valued at $32.59 million, or $5.45 per bushel. In 2004, the Texas soybean crop averaged 32 bushels per acre from 270,000 acres harvested. Total production of 8.64 million bushels was valued at $50.54 million, or $5.85 per bushel.

Sugarcane

Sugarcane is grown from seed cane planted in late summer or fall. It is harvested 12 months later and milled to produce raw sugar and molasses. Raw sugar requires additional refining before it is in final form and can be offered to consumers.

The sugarcane grinding mill operated at Santa Rosa, Cameron County, is considered one of the most modern mills in the United States. Texas sugarcane-producing counties are Hidalgo, Cameron and Willacy.

At a yield of 46.5 tons per acre, sugarcane production in 2006 totaled 1.8 million tons from 46,500 harvested acres. In 2005, 42,400 acres were harvested for total production of 1.62 million tons valued at $54.24 million, or $33.40 per ton. The yield was 38.3 tons per acre. In 2004, 44,000 acres were harvested, from which 1.63 million tons of sugarcane were milled. The yield averaged 37.3 tons per acre. The price averaged $27.70 per ton for a total value of $45.4 million.

Sunflowers

Sunflowers constitute one of the most important annual oilseed crops in the world. The cultivated types, which are thought to be descendants of the common wild sunflower native to Texas, have been successfully grown in several countries including Russia, Argentina, Romania, Bulgaria, Uruguay, Western Canada and portions of the northern United States. Extensive trial plantings conducted in the Cotton Belt states since 1968 showed sunflowers have considerable potential as an oilseed crop in much of this area, including Texas. This crop exhibits good cold and drought tolerance, is adapted to a wide range of soil and climate conditions, and tolerates higher levels of hail, wind and sand abrasion than other crops.

In 2006, sunflower production totaled 21.35 million pounds and was harvested from 24,000 acres at a yield of 890 pounds per acre. With an average price of $15.30 per cwt., the crop was valued at $3.26 million. In 2005, 140,000 of the 145,000 acres planted to sunflowers were harvested with an average yield of 1,403 pounds per acre. Total production of 196.4 million pounds was valued at $30.19 million, or $15.40 per cwt.

In 2004, of 41,000 acres planted to sunflowers, 38,000 acres were harvested, yielding 1,474 pounds per acre for a total yield of 56 million pounds, valued at $7.92 million, or $14.20 per cwt. The leading counties in production in 2005 were Moore, Sherman, Hidalgo, Dallam, Cameron and Hartley.

Reasons for growing sunflowers include the need for an additional cash crop with low water and plant nutrient requirements, the development of sunflower hybrids, and interest by food processors in Texas sunflower oil, which has high oleic acid content. Commercial users have found many advantages in this high oleic oil, including excellent cooking stability, particularly for use as a deep-frying medium for potato chips, corn chips and similar products.

Sunflower meal is a high-quality protein source free of nutritional toxins that can be included in rations for swine, poultry and ruminants. The hulls constitute a source of roughage, which can also be included in livestock rations.

Wheat

Wheat for grain is one of the state's most valuable cash crops. In 2006, wheat was exceeded in value by cotton, hay, corn, peanuts and sorghum. Wheat pastures also provide considerable winter forage for cattle that is reflected in value of livestock produced.

Texas wheat production totaled 33.6 million bushels in 2006 as yield averaged only 24.0 bushels per acre because of drought. Planted acreage totaled 5.55 million acres and 1.4 million acres were harvested. With an average price of $4.55 per bushel, the 2006 wheat value totaled $152.88 million. In 2005, Texas wheat growers planted 5.5 million acres and harvested 3 million acres. The yield was 32 bushels per acre for 2005, with total production of 96 million bushels at $3.44 per bushel valued at $330.24 million.

Texas wheat growers planted 6.3 million acres in 2004 and harvested grain from 3.5 million acres. The yield was 31.0 bushels per acre for a total production of 108.5 million bushels valued at $362.39 million.

Leading wheat-producing counties, based on production in 2005, were Ochiltree, Parmer, Hansford, Deaf Smith, Sherman and Dallam. The leading counties, based on acreage planted in 2005, were Hansford, Deaf Smith, Parmer, Ochiltree, Knox and Sherman.

Wheat was first grown

commercially in Texas near Sherman about 1833. The acreage expanded greatly in North-Central Texas after 1850 because of rapid settlement of the state and introduction of the well-adapted Mediterranean strain of wheat. A major family flour industry was developed in the area around Fort Worth, Dallas and Sherman between

Cash Receipts for Commodities, 2001–2005

Commodity *	2001	2002	2003	2004	2005	% of 2005
(All values in thousands of dollars)						
All Commodities:	13,508,535	12,567,541	15,349,424	16,545,022	16,355,268	100.00
Livestock & products	9,345,177	8,088,537	10,313,219	11,204,549	10,661,653	65.19
Crops, fruits & others	4,163,358	4,479,004	5,036,205	5,340,473	5,693,615	34.81
Livestock & Products						
Cattle & calves	6,812,228	5,862,734	7,872,092	8,092,721	7,580,168	46.35
Broilers	1,058,616	893,327	1,031,590	1,424,520	1,436,644	8.78
Milk	803,588	680,604	729,430	975,718	981,801	6.00
Eggs	267,077	273,312	310,007	306,322	236,843	1.45
Hogs	103,510	65,974	66,646	88,556	102,928	0.63
Sheep and lambs	40,175	44,766	50,428	57,893	60,133	0.37
Wool	3,122	4,046	5,040	5,712	5,328	0.03
Mohair	3,775	3,110	2,856	3,402	4,410	0.03
† Other livestock	253,086	260,664	245,130	249,705	253,398	1.55
Crops:						
Cotton lint	577,627	770,596	1,114,357	1,158,710	1,584,242	9.69
Corn	308,158	281,825	407,784	597,651	501,786	3.07
Wheat	270,756	225,665	246,390	329,907	283,880	1.74
Cottonseed	140,668	164,704	179,728	243,018	255,195	1.56
Sorghum grain	270,608	289,336	294,197	336,592	240,495	1.47
Hay	295,209	425,397	294,198	306,751	225,079	1.38
Peanuts	202,473	157,976	157,950	154,310	162,890	1.00
Onions	106,386	122,871	158,712	112,543	149,327	0.91
Rice	78,691	55,363	69,503	128,074	97,255	0.59
Potatoes	52,358	56,031	66,746	53,417	89,794	0.55
Watermelons	32,400	56,610	67,760	60,500	74,214	0.45
Soybeans	30,500	31,361	32,591	44,132	46,007	0.28
Sugarcane for sugar	56,702	52,480	51,381	45,400	45,400	0.28
Cabbage	66,011	39,917	53,869	60,208	41,499	0.25
Cantaloupes	69,720	80,798	63,444	26,760	34,206	0.21
Sunflowers	8,431	7,833	7,182	9,197	22,677	0.14
Carrots	26,934	12,305	14,295	19,119	20,865	0.13
Cucumbers	28,178	35,050	24,231	25,809	11,068	0.07
Peppers, chili	16,965	11,000	13,703	12,788	10,190	0.06
Tomatoes, fresh	6,480	7,680	7,605	7,540	8,625	0.05
Squash	9,259	5,530	10,317	7,080	5,320	0.03
Oats	2,725	7,990	5,255	4,850	4,437	0.03
Spinach	11,796	12,988	10,246	12,423	4,278	0.03
Dry Beans	5,274	6,315	8,510	6,447	3,931	0.02
Peppers, green fresh	11,083	7,520	5,670	3,984	3,539	0.02
Sweet potatoes	5,958	7,403	8,183	7,254	3,166	0.02
Corn, sweet	7,020	4,968	5,377	2,736	2,642	0.02
Honeydew melons	13,608	16,357	19,437	8,822	2,187	0.01
Barley	582	486	318	312	631	0.00
Other crops ‡	108,793	107,229	211,.139	212,716	217,683	1.33
Fruits & Nuts:						
Pecans	50,000	33,400	63,840	66,760	95,850	0.59
Grapefruit	21,258	20,567	17,396	34,755	83,403	0.51
Peaches	14,820	6,840	4,891	15,097	14,047	0.09
Oranges	7,867	6,525	5,224	7,227	8,065	0.05
Grapes	8,370	4,004	5,220	7,812	10,625	0.06
Other fruits and nuts	4,176	4,814	4,931	5,753	6,068	0.04
Other Farm Income:						
Greenhouse/nursery	1,235,512	1,341,270	1,324,625	1,204,019	1,323,040	8.09

* *Commodities are listed in order of importance for 2005 by crop items and by livestock items.*
† *For 2001–2005, includes milkfat, turkey eggs, equine, goats, goat milk, honey, catfish, and other poultry and livestock.*
‡ *For 2001, includes greens, okra, miscellaneous vegetables, field crops. For 2002–2005 includes miscellaneous vegetables and field crops. NA = Not Available; C = Confidential*
Source: 2005 Texas Agricultural Statistics, USDA/Texas Agricultural Statistics Service, October 2006; various issues of Texas Ag Statistics and Texas Agricultural Cash Receipts and Price Statistics, USDA/TASS.

1875 and 1900. Now, around half of the state's acreage is planted on the High Plains and about a third of this is irrigated. Most of the Texas wheat acreage is of the hard red winter class. Because of the development of varieties with improved disease resistance and the use of wheat for winter pasture, there has been a sizable expansion of acreage in Central and South Texas.

Most all wheat harvested for grain is used in some phase of the milling industry. The better-quality hard red winter wheat is used in the production of commercial bakery flour. Lower grades and varieties of soft red winter wheat are used in family flours. By-products of milled wheat are used for feed.

Vegetable Crops

Some market vegetables are produced in almost all Texas counties, but most of the commercial crop comes from about 200 counties. Hidalgo County is the leading Texas county in vegetable acres harvested, followed by Parmer and Uvalde counties. Other leading producing counties are: Hale, Frio, Yoakum, Zavala, Hudspeth and Gaines.

Texas is one of the five leading states in the production of fresh market vegetables. Nationally, in 2006, Texas ranked fifth in production, exceeded by California, Arizona, Florida and Georgia, and sixth in value of fresh-market vegetables. Texas had 3.6 percent of the production and 2.6 percent of the value of fresh-market vegetables produced. Onions were the top cash crop, with watermelons second. Other vegetables leading in value of production for 2006 were cabbage, cantaloupes, carrots, squash and tomatoes.

In 2006, total vegetable production of 18.68 million cwt. was valued at $287.29 million from 85,100 acres harvested. In 2005, Texas growers harvested total commercial vegetable crops valued at $371.27 million from 87,900 acres with a production of 18.41 million cwt. Texas growers harvested 20.21 million cwt. of commercial vegetable crops from 93,500 acres, valued at $366.25 million in 2004.

Bell Peppers

Bell pepper production in 2006 of 20,000 cwt. from 200 harvested acres was valued at $946,000, with a yield of 100 cwt. per acre. In 2005, bell peppers were harvested from 700 acres and valued at $3.54 million. At a yield of 150 cwt. per acre, 105,000 cwt. were produced. Bell peppers in 2004 were harvested from 500 acres and valued at $3.98 million. Production was 80,000 cwt. with a yield of 160 cwt. per acre.

Broccoli

Broccoli is primarily a South Texas crop. It is produced on 800 to 900 harvested acres. Estimated production data was discontinued in 2000.

Cabbage

In 2006, 7,600 acres were harvested and yielded total production of 2.89 million cwt. that was valued at $42.45 million. Yield was 380 cwt. per acre. In 2005, 8,700 acres of cabbage were harvested yielding total production of 2.61 million cwt., or 300 cwt. per acre, valued at $41.49 million. The 8,300 acres of cabbage harvested in Texas in 2004 brought a value of $60.21 million. At a yield of 390 cwt. per acre, total production was 3.24 million cwt.

Cantaloupe & Honeydew Melons

Cantaloupe production in 2006 totaled 559,000 cwt. from 4,300 harvested acres and was valued at $34.21 million at a yield of 130 cwt. per acre. In 2005, cantaloupes were harvested from 5,200 acres for total production of 1.14 million cwt., valued at $34.21 million, yielding 220 cwt. per acre. Of the 7,500 harvested acres in 2004, 1.2 million cwt. cantaloupes were produced at a yield of 160 cwt. per acre and were valued at $26.76 million.

Texas Vegetable Production 2006

Crop	Harvested Acres (000)	Yield Per Acre, Cwt.	Production (000) Cwt.	Value (000)
Bell Peppers	200	100	20	946
Cabbage	7,600	380	2,888	42,454
Cantaloupes	4,300	130	559	20,236
Carrots	2,000	310	620	12,338
Chile Peppers ‡	3,500	40	140	5,250
Cucumbers	1,300	110	143	3,375
Honeydew Melons	700	260	182	5,642
Onions, Spring	15,200	270	4,104	82,080
Onions, Summer	900	240	216	7,344
Spinach	2,200	80	176	4,682
Squash	1,300	220	286	12,269
Sweet Corn	1,800	54	97	2,367
Tomatoes	1,100	100	110	5,709
Watermelons	22,600	320	7,232	62,195
*Total Fresh Market**	*64,700*	—	*16,773*	*266,887*
Processed†	20,400	—	1,911	20,412
Total Vegetables	**85,100**	—	**18,684**	**287,299**

Numbers may not add due to rounding.
* Includes some quantities processed.
† Carrots, cucumbers, snap beans and spinach.
‡ Chile peppers are defined as all peppers, excluding bell peppers. Estimates include both fresh and dry product combined.
Source: "Texas Ag Facts", Texas Agricultural Statistics Service/ USDA. February 2007.

Honeydew production in 2006 totaled 182,000 cwt. and was valued at $5.64 million at a yield of 260 cwt. per acre in 2006. In 2005, 154,000 cwt. of honeydew melons were harvested from 700 acres for total value of $2.19 million, yielding 220 cwt. per acre. Honeydew melons valued at $8.82 million were harvested on 1,300 acres, producing a yield of 260 cwt. per acre and a total production of 338,000 cwt. in 2004.

Carrots

Carrot production in 2006 totaled 620,000 cwt. from 2,000 harvested acres at a yield of 310 cwt. per acre. Production was valued at $12.34 million. In 2005, carrots were harvested from 2,300 acres with a value of $20.01 million. At a yield of 300 cwt. per acre, 2005 production was 620,000 cwt. Carrot production was valued at $18.3 million in 2004 from 2,100 acres harvested. Production was 704,000 cwt. at a yield of 335 cwt. per acre.

The winter carrot production from South Texas accounts for about three-fourths of total production during the winter season.

Cucumbers

In 2006, 1,300 acres of cucumbers were harvested. Production totaled 143,000 cwt. and was valued at $3.37 million. The 2006 yield was 110 cwt. per acre. In 2005, 700 acres of cucumbers were harvested with a value of $2.64 million. Production was 98,000 cwt. with a yield of 140 cwt. per acre. At a yield of 350 cwt. per acre, the 525,000 cwt. cucumber crop in Texas during 2004 was harvested from 1,500 acres and valued at $11.02 million.

Onions

Onion production in 2006 totaled 4.32 million cwt. from 16,100 harvested acres and was valued at $89.42 million, at a yield of 268 cwt. per acre. In 2005, 4.98 million cwt. of onions were harvested from 16,400 acres and valued at $149.32 million, at a yield of 304 cwt. per acre. A total of 4.91 million cwt. of onions were produced from 15,300 harvested acres and valued at $112.54 million in 2004, yielding 321 cwt. per acre.

Potatoes

In 2006, all potatoes were harvested from 19,900 acres

with production of 7.12 million cwt. valued at $117.06 million and a yield of 358 cwt. per acre. All potatoes were harvested from 17,800 acres with production of 6.09 million cwt. valued at $73.38 million in 2005, yielding 342 cwt. per acre. This compares with 20,100 acres harvested and valued at $54.55 million in 2004, with production of 6.43 million cwt. and a yield of 320 cwt. per acre.

Spinach

Spinach production is primarily concentrated in the Winter Garden area of South Texas. The 2006 production value of spinach was estimated at $4.68 million. Production of 176,000 cwt. was harvested from 2,200 acres with a yield of 80 cwt. per acre. In 2005, 2,100 acres were harvested with a value of $3.23 million. At a yield of 100 cwt. per acre, production was 210,000 cwt. The 2,000 acres harvested in 2004 produced 250,000 cwt. at a yield of 125 cwt. per acre and valued at $9.62 million.

Lonnie Myers of Burleson, Mary Psencik of Kaufman and Sue Psencik of Fredericksburg enjoy homemade ice cream at Ham's Orchards Roadside Market on U.S. 80, east of Terrell in Kaufman County. Visitors can buy fresh-picked peaches grown at the orchard, along with other fruit. Kye R. Lee photo.

Sweet Corn

In 2006, 97,000 cwt. of sweet corn was harvested from 1,800 acres. Value of production was estimated at $2.37 million, with a yield of 54 cwt. per acre. In 2005, 119,000 cwt. of sweet corn was produced from 1,700 harvested acres at a yield of 70 cwt. per acre and valued at $2.64 million. Sweet corn was harvested in Texas from 1,900 acres and valued at $2.74 million in 2004. Production was 152,000 cwt. at a yield of 80 cwt. per acre.

Sweet Potatoes

In 2006, 210,000 cwt. of sweet potatoes were harvested from 2,100 acres for a value of $2.2 million at a yield of 100 cwt. per acre. Sweet potatoes in 2005 produced 169,000 cwt. from 2,600 harvested acres, with a value of $1.91 million. Yield was 65 cwt. per acre. This compared with 392,000 cwt. produced in 2004 at a yield of 140 cwt. from 2,800 harvested acres and valued at $0.59 million.

Tomatoes

Commercial tomatoes are marketed throughout the year from Texas partly as a result of recent increases in greenhouse production during the winter.

In 2006, 1,100 harvested acres of tomatoes at a yield of 100 cwt. per acre produced 110,000 cwt. of tomatoes with a value of $5.71 million. In 2005, 1,200 acres of tomatoes were harvested, producing 150,000 cwt. at a yield of 125 cwt. per acre for a value of $8.62 million. The tomato crop in 2004 was valued at $7.54 million from 1,100 harvested acres. Tomato production was 116,000 cwt. at a yield of 105 cwt. per acre.

Watermelons

Watermelon production in 2006 was 7.23 million cwt. from 22,600 acres, with a value of $62.19 million, yielding 320 cwt. per acre. In 2005, at a yield of 260 cwt. per acre, 5.8 million cwt. watermelons were harvested from 22,300 acres and valued at $74.21 million. Watermelon production was 6.05 million cwt. from 27,500 acres in 2004, with a value of $60.5 million, at a yield of 220 cwt. per acre.

Vegetables for Processing

In 2006, 1.91 million cwt. of cucumbers, carrots, snap beans and spinach for processing were harvested from 20,400 acres and valued at $20.41 million. In 2005, 21,300 acres were harvested and valued at $13.64 million, with a production of 1.98 million cwt. In 2004, 18,900 acres were harvested and valued at $24.34 million, producing 2.33 million cwt.

Fruits and Nuts

Texas is noted for producing a wide variety of fruits. The pecan is the only commercial nut crop in the state. The pecan is native to most of the state's river valleys and is the Texas state tree. Citrus is produced in the three southernmost counties in the Lower Rio Grande Valley. Some new orchards have been planted. Peaches represent the next most important Texas fruit crop, yet there is a considerable amount of interest in growing apples.

Apples

Small acreages of apples, usually marketed in the state, are grown in a number of counties. The leading counties in production are Montague and Gillespie. Other counties which have apples include: Callahan, Collingsworth, Clay, Cass, Donley, Eastland, Hudspeth, Jeff Davis, Lampasas, Parker, San Saba and Young. The crop is harvested and marketed from July to October.

A considerable number of apple trees have been planted in the Hill Country. Most of the trees are new varieties of Red and Golden Delicious types on semi-dwarfing rootstocks. Trees are established in high-density plantings of 100 to 200 trees per acre. Most of the apples are sold at roadside stands or go to nearby markets.

Apricots

Not a commercial crop, apricots are grown chiefly in Comanche, Denton, Wilbarger, Parker and Collingsworth counties. Others reporting apricots include: Martin, Clay, Young, Lampasas, Gillespie, Anderson, Erath, Wichita and Eastland counties.

Avocados

Avocados grow on a small acreage in the Lower Rio Grande Valley. Interest in this crop is increasing and production is expected to expand. Lulu is the principal variety.

Blackberries

Smith County is a blackberry center, with the Tyler-Lindale area having processed the crop since 1890. Other counties with blackberry acreage include Wood, Van Zandt and Henderson. The Brazos blackberry is grown as a local market or "pick-your-own" fruit in many sections of the state. New varieties of thornless vines have been developed. Dewberries grow wild in Central and East Texas and are gathered for home use and local sale in May and June.

Citrus

Texas ranks with Florida, California and Arizona as leading states in the production of citrus. Most of the Texas production is in Cameron, Hidalgo and Willacy counties of the Lower Rio Grande Valley. In 2005-2006, grapefruit production was estimated at 5.2 million boxes. At $12.17 per box, value of production was $63.29 million. Grapefruit production in 2004-2005, was 6.6 million boxes at $11.62 per box for a total value of $76.7 million. Production in 2003-2004 was 5.7 million boxes at $3.98 per box with a value of $22.71 million.

Production of oranges in 2005-2006 was 1.6 million boxes. At $6.62 per box, total value was $10.6 million. In 2004-2005, production was 1.77 million boxes at $6.77 per box for a total value of $11.98 million. Production was 1.65 million boxes in 2003-2004 at $4.29 per box for a value of $7.08 million.

Peaches

Primary production areas are East Texas, the Hill Country and the West Cross Timbers. Production varies substantially due to adverse weather conditions. Low-chilling varieties for early marketings are being grown in Atascosa, Frio, Webb, Karnes and Duval counties.

The Texas peach crop's utilized production totaled 750 tons in 2006 for a value of $1.23 million or $1,640 per ton. In 2005, utilized production was 8,350 tons. Value of production was $14.05 million or $1,680 per ton. In 2004, utilized production was 9,900 tons that was valued at $15.1 million or $1,520 per ton.

The demand for high-quality Texas peaches greatly exceeds the supply. Texas ranked 27th nationally in peach production in 2006. Leading Texas counties in production are Gillespie, Parker, Montague, Comanche, Limestone and Eastland.

Pears

Well adapted for home and small orchard production, the pear is not commercially significant in Texas. Comanche, Parker, Lampasas, Cooke, McCulloch and Eastland counties lead in trees. Usually the fruit goes for home consumption or to nearby markets.

Pecans

The pecan, the state tree, is one of the most widely distributed trees in Texas. It is native to over 150 counties and is grown commercially in some 30 additional counties. The pecan is also widely used as a dual-purpose yard tree. The commercial plantings of pecans have accelerated in Central and West Texas, with many of the new orchards being irrigated. Many new pecan plantings are being established under trickle-irrigation systems.

In 2006, utilized pecan production totaled 36 million pounds and was valued at $61.39 million, or $1.71 per pound. In 2005, 65 million pounds were produced. Total value was estimated at $95.85 million, and price averaged $1.47 per pound. The 2004 crop totaled 40 million pounds, valued at $66.76 million or $1.67 per pound.

Nationally, Texas ranked third behind New Mexico and Georgia in pecan production in 2006. Leading Texas counties in pecan production are Hood, El Paso, Pecos, San Saba, Mills, Comanche, Wharton and Gonzales.

Plums

Plum production is scattered over a wide area of the state with the heaviest production in East and Central Texas. The leading counties in production are Smith, Gillespie and Knox. Most of the production goes to nearby markets or to processors.

Strawberries

Atascosa County is the leading commercial area, although strawberries are grown for local markets in Wood, Van Zandt and Smith counties in East Texas. The most concentrated production occurs in the Poteet area south of San Antonio.

Livestock and Their Products

Livestock and their products accounted for about 65.2 percent of the agricultural cash receipts in Texas in 2005. The state ranks first nationally in all cattle, beef cattle, cattle on feed, sheep and lambs, wool, goats and mohair.

Meat animals normally account for around 72.7 percent of cash receipts from marketings of livestock and their products. Sales of livestock and products in 2005 totaled $7.74 billion, down from $8.24 billion in 2004.

Cattle and calves dominate livestock production in Texas, contributing more than 71 percent of cash receipts from livestock and products each year. On Jan. 1, 2007, inventory of all cattle and calves in Texas totaled 14 million head, valued at $11.06 billion, compared to 14.1 million as of Jan. 1, 2006, valued at $11.84 billion.

On Jan. 1, 2007, the sheep and lamb inventory stood at 1.07 million head, valued at $113.42 million, compared with 1.09 million head as of Jan. 1, 2006, valued at $124.26 million. Sheep and lambs numbered 3.21 million on Jan. 1, 1973, down from a high of 10.83 million in 1943. Sheep and lamb production fell from 148.29 million pounds in 1973 to 51.2 million pounds on Jan. 1, 2007. Wool production decreased from 26.35 million pounds valued at $23.19 million in 1973 to 4.9 million pounds valued at $4.46 million in 2006. Production was 5.55 million pounds in 2005, valued at $5.33 million. The price of wool per pound was 88 cents in 1973, 96 cents in 2005, and 91 cents in 2006.

Lamb prices averaged $92.40 per cwt. as of Jan. 1, 2007, $113 per cwt. in 2006, and $110 per cwt. in 2005. The average price of sheep was $37.10 per cwt. as of Jan. 1, 2007, $52.10 in 2006, and $43.40 in 2005.

Mohair production in Texas has dropped from a 1965 high of 31.58 million pounds to 1.1 million pounds in 2006. Production was valued at $4.4 million or $4 per pound. In 2005, production was 1.25 million pounds, valued at $3.75 million, or $3 per pound. Mohair production in 2004 was 1.62 million pounds, valued at $3.4 million, or $2.10 per pound.

Beef Cattle

Raising beef cattle is the most extensive agricultural operation in Texas. In 2005, 46.3 percent of total cash receipts from farm and ranch marketings — $7.59 million of $16.35 million —came from cattle and calves, compared with $8.09 million of $16.54 million in 2004 (48.9%), and $7.87 million of $15.35 million in 2003 (51.3%). The next leading commodity is cotton.

Nearly all of the 254 counties in Texas derive more revenue from cattle than from any other agricultural commodity, and those that don't usually rank cattle second in importance.

Within the boundaries of Texas are 14 percent of all the cattle in the U.S., as are 16 percent of the beef breeding cows, and 13 percent of the calf crop, as of the Jan. 1, 2007, inventory.

The number of all cattle in Texas on Jan. 1, 2007, totaled 14 million, compared with 14.1 million on Jan. 1, 2006; and 13.7 million in 2005.

Calves born on Texas farms and ranches by Jan. 1, 2007, totaled 5 million, compared with 5.13 million in 2006; and 5 million in 2005.

Sale of cattle and calves at approximately 154 livestock auctions inspected by the Texas Animal Health Commission totaled 5.22 million head in 2006; 4.89 million head in 2005; and 4.63 million in 2004. The number of cattle and calves shipped into Texas totaled 2.67 million head in 2006; 2.84 million head in 2005; and 3.26 million head in 2004.

Livestock Industries

A large portion of Texas livestock is sold through local auction markets. In 2005, the Texas Animal Health Commission reported 154 livestock auctions. In 2006, auctions sold 5.22 million head of cattle and calves; 42,000 hogs; and 1.37 million sheep and goats. This compared with 4.89 million cattle and calves; 45,000 hogs; and 1.19 million sheep and goats in 2005. Figures for 2004 were 4.64 million cattle and calves; 73,000 hogs; 1.13 million sheep and goats.

During 2006, the commission reported 1.06 million cattle and calves shipped from Texas to other states and 2.07 million shipped in; compared with 1.2 million shipped out and 2.22 million shipped in during 2005; and 1.26 million shipped out and 2.34 million shipped in during 2004. (Figures exclude cattle shipped direct to slaughter where no health certificates are required.)

During 2006, Texas shipped out 129,391 sheep and lambs and shipped in 28,252; compared with 91,105 shipped out and 42,707 shipped in during 2005; and 107,407 shipped out and 56,994 shipped in during 2004.

Feedlot Production

Feedlot production of livestock, mainly cattle, is a major industry in Texas. Annual fed cattle marketings totaled 5.77 million for feedlot capacity (head) of 1,000 and over in 2006. Texas lots marketed a total of 5.75 million head of grain-fed cattle in 2005, compared with 5.68 million in 2004 and 5.97 million in 2003. In recent years, more cattle have been fed in Texas than any other state in the United States.

During 2006, there were 130 feedlots in Texas with capacity of 1,000 animals or more. This compared with 130 in 2005, 131 in 2004, and 134 in 2003.

Federally inspected slaughter plants in Texas numbered 43 in 2006. This compared with 43 in 2005 and 41 in 2004. In 2006, the number of cattle slaughtered in Texas totaled 6.46 million cattle, 334,000 hogs, 41,300 sheep, and 8,300 calves. This compared with 6.22 million cattle, 339,800 hogs, 50,500 sheep, and 8,200 calves in 2005; and 6.15 million cattle, 319,200 hogs, 261,400 sheep, and 11,000 calves in 2004.

Feeding of cattle in commercial feedlots is a major economic development that has stimulated the establishment and expansion of beef slaughtering plants. Most of this development is in the Northern High Plains area of Northwest Texas. This area alone accounts for around 82 percent of the cattle fed in the state as of Jan. 1, 2007.

Total feedlot marketings represented about 24 percent of total U.S. fed cattle marketings in Jan. 1, 2007. Large amounts of capital are required for feedlot operations. This has forced many lots to become custom feeding facilities.

Feedlots are concentrated on the High Plains largely because of extensive supplies of corn, sorghum and other feed. Beef breeding herds have increased most in East Texas, where grazing is abundant.

Dairying

The state's dairy industry is spread out across the northern half of Texas, with the trend toward larger operations. As of Jan. 1, 2006, inventory, leading counties in milk production are Erath, Hopkins, Comanche, Lamb, Castro and Hale. Combined, these six counties produce 51.4 percent of the milk in Texas, with Erath producing 19 percent of the total.

All the milk sold by Texas dairy farmers is marketed under the terms of Federal Marketing Orders. Most Texas dairymen are members of one of four marketing

Texas Cattle Marketed by Size of Feedlots, 1965–2006

	Feedlot Capacity (head)						
Year	Under 1,000	1,000– 1,999	2000– 3,999	4,000– 7,999	8,000– 15,999	16,000 & Over	Total
	Cattle Marketed — 1,000 head —						
1965	104	108	205	324	107	246	1,094
1970	98	53	112	281	727	1,867	3,138
1975	50	22	51	134	485	2,325	3,067
1976	60	33	62	170	583	3,039	3,947
1977	146	22	38	206	604	3,211	4,277
1978	80	20	50	242	697	3,826	4,915
1979	54	19	46	227	556	3,543	4,445
1980	51	18	47	226	533	3,285	4,160
1981	50	20	50	220	510	3,110	3,960
1982	55	20	60	210	540	3,190	4,075
1983	100	20	80	130	490	3,580	4,400
1984	60	20	180	150	540	4,140	5,090
1985	70	10	20	170	620	4,140	5,030
1986	90	10	40	180	550	4,390	5,260
1987	90	20	35	170	625	4,375	5,255
1988	30	15	35	185	650	4,120	5,035
1989	40	15	40	165	675	3,810	4,745
1990	35	24	56	180	605	3,940	4,840
1991	35	25	45	225	500	4,250	5,080
1992	50	10	25	140	505	4,065	4,795
1993	30	20	70	160	640	4,370	5,290
1994	14	13	55	173	725	4,680	5,660
1995	12	24	43	166	630	4,665	5,540
1996	NA	17	43	180	460	4,800	5,500
1997	NA	17	48	250	485	5,000	5,800
1998	NA	10	20	140	420	5,470	6,060
1999	NA	10	20	140	385	5,510	6,065
2000	NA	8	17	125	470	5,570	6,190
2001	NA	8	22	90	450	5,460	6,030
2002	NA	10	15	85	390	5,480	5,980
2003	NA	10	15	75	420	5,450	5,970
2004	NA	20	20	485	485	5,180	5,685
2005	NA	20	20	475	475	5,260	5,755
2006	NA	25	25	470	470	5,280	5,755

Number of feedlots with 1,000 head or more capacity is number of lots operating any time during the year. Number under 1,000 head capacity and total number of all feedlots is number at end of year.
* Beginning in 2004 report, cattle marketed as 1,000–3,999 and 4,000–15,999 in feedlot capacity.
Source: "Texas Agricultural Facts, 1997," Texas Agricultural Statistics Service, September 1998. Numbers for 1986, '87, '88, '89, '90, '91, '92. 1993 Texas Livestock Statistics, Bulletin 252, August 1994; Cattle on Feed annual summary, USDA/ NASS, February 2007.

cooperatives. Associate Milk Producers, Inc., is the largest, representing the majority of the state's producers.

Texas dairy farmers received an average price for milk of $13.30 per hundred pounds in 2006, $15.30 in 2005, and $16.30 in 2004. A total of 7.124 billion pounds of milk was sold to plants and dealers in 2006, bringing in cash receipts from milk to dairy farmers of $947.49 million. This compared with 6.417 billion pounds sold in 2005 that brought in $981.8 million in cash receipts. In 2004, Texas dairymen sold 5.986 billion pounds of milk, which brought in cash receipts of $975.72 million.

The annual average number of milk cows in Texas was 347,000 head as of Jan. 1, 2007, inventory. This compared with 325,000 head as of Jan. 1, 2006, and 318,000 as of Jan. 1, 2005. Average milk production per cow in the state has increased steadily over the past several decades. The average milk production per cow was 21,328 pounds in 2006, 20,131 pounds in 2005, and 18,837 pounds in 2004. Total milk production in Texas was 7.145 billion pounds in 2006, 6.442 billion pounds in 2005, and 6.009 billion pounds in 2004.

There were 1,300 operations reporting milk cows in

Texas in 2006, 1,500 in 2005, and 1,700 in 2004.

Dairy Manufacturing

The major dairy products manufactured in Texas include condensed, evaporated and dry milk; creamery butter; and cheese. However, this data are not available because of the small number of manufacturing plants producing these products.

Frozen Desserts

Production of frozen desserts in Texas totaled 96.88 million gallons in 2006, 82.61 million gallons in 2005, and 80.49 million gallons in 2004. Production for regular ice cream in Texas in 2006 amounted to 64.58 million gallons, compared to 54.8 million gallons in 2005, and 44.18 million gallons in 2004. Regular ice cream mix produced in Texas in 2006 amounted to 35.27 million gallons; 30.86 million gallons in 2005; and 29.32 million gallons in 2004.

Sherbet mix in Texas totaled 709,000 gallons in 2006, 470,000 gallons in 2005, and 569,000 gallons in 2004. Sherbet production in 2006 totaled 939,000 gallons, compared with 719,000 gallons in 2005, and 906,000 gallons in 2004.

Goats and Mohair

Goats in Texas numbered 1.3 million on Jan. 1, 2007. This compares with 1.31 million on Jan. 1, 2006, and 1.27 million on Jan. 1, 2005. They had a value of $150.8 million or $116 per head in 2007; $140.17 million or $107 per head in 2006; and $138.43 million or $109 per head as of Jan. 1, 2005.

The goat herd consists of Angora goats for mohair production. Angora goats totaled 180,000 as of Jan. 1, 2007; 200,000 as of Jan. 1, 2006; and 210,000 as of Jan. 1, 2005. Spanish goats and others numbered 1.12 million as of Jan. 1, 2007; 1.11 million as of 2006; and 1.06 million as of Jan. 1, 2004. That is a sharp drop from 16.2 million pounds with a value of $42.6 million in 1987.

Mohair production during 2006 totaled 1.1 million pounds. This compares with 1.25 million in 2005, and 1.62 million pounds in 2004. Average price per pound in 2006 was $4 from 170,000 goats clipped for a total value of $4.4 million. In 2005, producers received $3 per pound from 200,000 goats clipped for a total value of $3.75 million. In 2004, producers received $2.10 per pound from 210,000 goats clipped for a total value of $3.4 million.

Nearly half of the world's mohair and 78 percent of the U.S. clip are produced in Texas. The leading Texas counties in Angora goats as of Jan. 1, 2006 are: Edwards, Sutton, Val Verde, Gillespie, Uvalde and Kinney.

Horses

Nationally, Texas ranks as one of the leading states in horse numbers and is the headquarters for many national horse organizations. The largest single-breed registry in America, the American Quarter Horse Association, has its headquarters in Amarillo.

The headquarters of the National Cutting Horse Association and the American Paint Horse Association are both located in Fort Worth. In addition to these national associations, Texas also has active state associations that include Palominos, Arabians, Thoroughbreds, Appaloosa and Ponies.

Horses are still used to support the state's giant beef cattle and sheep industries. However, the largest horse numbers within the state are near urban and suburban areas, where they are mostly used for recreational activities. State participation activities consist of horse shows, trail rides, play days, rodeos, polo and horse racing. Residential subdivisions have been developed within the state to provide facilities for urban and suburban horse owners.

Poultry and Eggs

Poultry and eggs contributed about 9.4 percent to the average yearly cash receipts of Texas farmers in 2005. In 2006, Texas ranked 6th among the states in broilers produced, 7th in eggs produced, and 7th in hens produced.

In 2005, cash receipts to Texas producers from the production of poultry and eggs totaled $1.729 billion. This compares with $1.799 billion in 2004 and $1.396 in 2003.

Value of production from eggs was $253.56 million in 2006; $238.8 million in 2005; and $306.32 million in 2004. Eggs produced in 2006 totaled 5.04 billion, compared with 4.76 billion in 2005 and 4.83 billion in 2004. The average price received per dozen in 2006 was 60.4 cents, compared with 60.2 cents in 2005, and 76.2 cents in 2004.

Broiler production in 2006 totaled 628.3 million birds, compared with 627.9 million in 2005, and 620.7 million in 2004. Value of production from broilers totaled $1.265 billion in 2006, $1.437 billion in 2005, and $1.425 billion in 2004. Price per pound averaged 38 cents in 2006, 44 cents in 2005, and 45 cents in 2004.

Sheep and Wool

Sheep and lambs in Texas numbered 1.07 million head on Jan. 1, 2007, compared to 1.09 million as of Jan. 1, 2006, and 1.07 million as of Jan. 1, 2005. All sheep were valued at $113.42 million or $106 per head on Jan. 1, 2007, compared with $124.26 million or $114 per head as of Jan. 1, 2006, and $112.35 million or $105 per head as of Jan. 1, 2005.

Breeding ewes one year old and over numbered 675,000 as of Jan. 1, 2007; 690,000 as of Jan. 1, 2006; and 650,000 as of Jan. 1, 2005. Replacement lambs less than one year old totaled 105,000 head as of Jan. 1, 2007; 135,000 as of Jan. 1, 2006; and 145,000 as of Jan. 1, 2005. Sheep operations in Texas were estimated to be 7,000 as of Jan. 1, 2007; 6,900 as of Jan. 1, 2006; and 7,200 as of Jan. 1, 2005.

Texas wool production in 2006 was 4.9 million pounds from 700,000 sheep. Value totaled $4.46 million or 91 cents per pound. This compared with 5.5 million pounds of wool from 800,000 sheep valued at $5.33 million or 96 cents per pound in 2005; and 5.6 million pounds from 810,000 sheep valued at $5.71 million or $1.02 per pound in 2004.

Most sheep and lambs in Texas are concentrated in the Edwards Plateau area of West-Central Texas and nearby counties. As of Jan. 1, 2006, the 10 leading counties are: Crockett, Val Verde, Pecos, Tom Green, Schleicher, Concho, Gillespie, Edwards, Castro and Sterling. Sheep production largely has a dual purpose, for both wool and lamb production.

San Angelo long has been the largest sheep and wool market in the United States and the center for wool and mohair warehouses, scouring plants and slaughterhouses.

Swine

Texas had 930,000 head of swine on hand, Dec. 1, 2006 — only 1.5 percent of the U.S. swine herd. Swine producers in the state produce about 1.45 million head marketed annually.

Although the number of farms producing hogs has steadily decreased over the years, the size of production units has increased substantially. There is favorable potential for increased production.

In 2006, 1.45 million head of hogs were marketed in Texas, producing 259.99 million pounds of pork valued at $40.80 per 100 pounds, or $106.24 million. In 2005, 1.4 million head of hogs were marketed, producing 223.37 million pounds of pork valued at $101.84 million, or $45.40 per 100 pounds.

Figures for 2004 were 1.43 million head marketed, and 202.2 million pounds of pork produced with a value of $90.81 million, or $44.90 per 100 pounds. ☆

Livestock Auctions 101
Action-Packed and Noisy, This Is How Animals Are Bought and Sold

By Mary G. Ramos

If you've traveled the highways of Texas, you've occasionally seen a big barn-like structure fronting the road with livestock pens out back. A sign identifies it as a "livestock auction," "commission company" or "livestock market." The sign may also say "Sale every Tuesday at 10" or "Auction every Thursday at 1 p.m." If you happen by on sale day, which might be any day of the week except Sunday, the parking area is swarming with pickup trucks and large cattle trailers. Most any other day of the week, it looks almost deserted.

Texas has 154 of these livestock auction houses spread across the state from Dalhart in the Panhandle down to Edinburg in the Lower Rio Grande Valley, and from El Paso at the western tip of the state to Texarkana in the extreme northeast.

A few Texas auctions sell only cattle, but most sell some combination of cattle, horses and mules, swine, sheep and goats. Other, more unusual animals are handled by some auctions: bison,

Texas has 154 livestock auctions spread across the state. In addition to cattle, most also sell goats, horses, sheep, mules, swine and even exotic animals. File photo.

emus, llamas and other "exotics." The exotics category includes any animal not native to the United States, including the emus and llamas, as well as the blackbuck or axis deer, which often end up as venison on upscale restaurant menus.

In 2006, Texas livestock auctions sold 5,217,156 cattle (including bison), 509,017 sheep, 861,913 goats, 41,625 swine, 64,463 horses and 28,418 exotics, according to the Texas Animal Health Commission.

How a Livestock Auction Works

This general description may vary in details from one auction to another. In many cases, though, the auction barn contains the company's offices, the auction ring, and, often, a café.

Although most sellers bring their animals the day of the sale, others bring them in a day or so before and unload them into pens. Sellers pay a "yardage charge," which can range from less than 50 cents up to $1 per head. The auction house also charges separately for any hay or feed required.

Sellers register with the auction's office the first time they sell there, and their information is kept on file.

Buyers may be other farmers or ranchers wanting to expand their herds or replace older animals that can no longer breed. Or, they may be buying agents for food processors; for example, buying hogs for a sausage-

making company or cows for a slaughterhouse. More common, are "order buyers" who are buying large numbers of calves to fill orders from feedlots or other ranches. Buyers pick up a "buyer's card" at the office -- a white card about 3 x 7 inches with spaces for the buyer to note number of animals bought, kind of animal, weight and price. They also may inspect the animals before the auction starts.

The center of the action is an indoor amphitheater, in which the auction ring, a semicircular pen, faces the sellers and buyers, who sit in a semicircle of steeply tiered rows of seats. The auction ring is surmounted by a booth occupied by the auctioneer, the ticket writer and the scale master.

The ticket writer prepares the official record of each sale, including the animal's auction-house tag number, a description of each animal and the amount of the winning bid. The scale master is in charge of the scales and of notifying the workers where to pen the animals as they leave the ring, since all of one buyer's animals are kept together.

A livestock auction is a noisy affair. There's a loud clang as each animal is let in to one side of the auction ring through a heavy, metal-bar gate. An auction staff member sets the starting bid, and the auctioneer starts his chant. The chant is a constant stream of short, rhythmic phrases, repeated so fast it sounds like a vocal machine gun. To someone whose ear is not attuned to it, the words are indecipherable.

The chant is made up of the amount of the current bid and the next-higher bid the auctioneer is looking for, intermixed with filler words. These filler words can be anything except numbers, but are often chosen to keep the numbers rolling, such as "Three dollar bid now. Who'll give me four? Three, now three, now three, will ya give me four?"

The blistering pace of the chant generates excitement, keeping the bidding pace fast and helping the auctioneer sell the most animals in the smallest amount of time.

As the auctioneer chants, he watches buyers for movements that signify bids -- a hardly noticeable twitch of a buyer's card, for example, or the movement of a finger. When the bidding is over, the auctioneer announces the name of the successful bidder, and the animal is herded out of the ring through the gate on the far side of the ring, with another loud clang, to be placed in its buyer's pen.

The commission paid by sellers to the auction house may be a charge per head or a percentage of the sale price. The Gonzales Livestock Market, for example,

An auctioneer watches for bidders at a livestock auction at the Gonzales Livestock Market. Mary G. Ramos photo.

charges a 3.5 percent commission on all cattle sales, with a minimum of $7.50 per head. The Mills County Commission Company in Goldthwaite charges $2.25 to $2.75 per head for sheep and goats, depending on the number of animals in the consignment.

How Auctions Are Regulated

As informal as they appear on the surface, the auction markets are subject to regulations from several government agencies:

1. The federal Grain Inspection, Packers and Stockyards Administration (GIPSA) oversees business aspects of the markets, including such details as bonding requirements, accurate weighing of all animals sold, and timely and accurate payments to sellers.

2. One of the Texas Animal Health Commission's more than 100 animal health inspectors is present at each auction house on sale days, checking for general soundness of the animals, and looking for disease-carrying ticks or signs of other diseases that would warrant a checkup by a veterinarian. Adult cattle are checked for brucellosis.

Sheep and goats must be identifiable in case scrapie, a brain-wasting disease, is found. Blood samples from swine sold for breeding are tested for brucellosis and a virus called pseudorabies. Inspectors check that each horse has a current blood test for an infectious disease commonly known as Coggins.

A state-federal laboratory headquartered in Austin, with satellite labs in Fort Worth, Lubbock and Palestine, runs some of the tests, including brucellosis, tick identification and TB tests. The Texas Veterinary Medical Diagnostic Laboratory of Texas A&M University, with locations in College Station and Amarillo, conducts tests that the TAHC does not perform.

3. Since concentrations of livestock in one location might lead to pollution, the Texas Commission on Environmental Quality administers the issuance of air and water permits for auction markets.

Consolidation has affected livestock auction markets as agriculture has changed through the years. But, the local auction barn remains the place where ranchers gather to buy and sell their livestock and exchange the news. They remain a vibrant part of Texas' ranching past and future.

Although outside the scope of this article, video and Web livestock auctions are becoming more popular among some ranchers. The electronic auctions sell large groups of animals in each lot, rather than the smaller numbers sold in local livestock auction markets. ☆

Mary G. Ramos is a Dallas free-lance writer and editor emerita of the Texas Almanac.

Sources & Acknowledgements:

The author wishes to thank Dr. David P. Anderson of Texas A&M University for his generous assistance with this article. Dr. Anderson is associate professor and Extension Economist, Livestock and Food Products Marketing. Any errors are, of course, the author's own.

The author also thanks Rita Scott of the Gainesville Livestock Market for cheerfully providing details about the workings of an auction house.

Grain Inspection, Packers and Stockyards Administration (www.gipsa.usda.gov)

Texas Department of Agriculture (www.tda.state.tx.us)

Texas Animal Health Commission (www.tahc.state.tx.us)

Appendix

The Shafter Cemetery in Presidio County. Robert Plocheck photo.

Pronunciation Guide

State Obituaries

Index of Entries

Texas Pronunciation Guide

Texas' rich cultural diversity is reflected nowhere better than in the names of places. Standard pronunciation is used in many cases, but purely colloquial pronunciation often is used, too.

In the late 1940s, George Mitchel Stokes, a graduate student at Baylor University, developed a list of pronunciations of 2,300 place names across the state.

Stokes earned his doctorate and eventually served as director of the speech division in the Communications Studies Department at Baylor University. He retired in 1983.

In the following list based on Stokes longer list, pronunciation is by respelling and diacritical marking. Respelling is employed as follows: "ah" as in the exclamation, ah, or the "o" in tot; "ee" as in meet; "oo" as in moot; "yoo" as in use; "ow" as in cow; "oi" as in oil; "uh" as in mud.

Note that ah, uh and the apostrophe(') are used for varying degrees of neutral vowel sounds, the apostrophe being used where the vowel is barely sounded. Diacritical markings are used as follows: bāle, băd, lĕt, rīse, rĭll, ōak, brōōd, fŏŏt.

The stressed syllable is capitalized. Secondary stress is indicated by an underline as in Atascosa— ăt uhs KŌ suh.

A
Abilene—ĂB uh leen
Acala—uh KĀ luh
Acuff—Ā kuhf
Addielou—ă dĭ LŌŌ
Agua Dulce—ah wuh DŌŌL sĭ
Agua Nueva—ah wuh nyŏŏ Ā vuh
Alamo—ĂL uh mō
Alba—ĂL buh
Aledo—uh LEE dō
Algoa—ăl GŌ uh
Alief—Ā leef
Alpine—ĂL pīn
Altair—awl TĂR
Alto—ĂL tō
Altoga—ăl TŌ guh
Alvarado—ăl vuh RĀ dō
Alvord—ĂL vord
Amarillo—ăm uh RĬL ŏl
Anahuac—ĂN uh wăk
Andice—ĂN dīs
Angelina—ăn juh LEE nuh
Annona—ă NŌ nuh
Antelope—ĂNT uh lōp
Anton—ĂNT n
Aquilla—uh KWĬL uh
Aransas—uh RĂN zuhs
Aransas Pass—uh răn zuhs PĂS
Arbala—ahr BĀ luh
Arcadia—ahr KĀ dĭ uh
Arcola—ahr KŌ luh
Argo—AHR gō
Argyle—ahr GĬL
Arlington—AHR lĭng t'n
Arneckeville—AHR nĭ kĭ vĭl
Artesia Wells—ahr tee zh' WĔLZ
Asherton—ĂSH er t'n
Aspermont—ĂS per mahnt
Atascosa—ăt uhs KŌ suh
Attoyac—AT uh yăk
Austin—AWS t'n
Austonio—aws TŌ nĭ ŏ
Austwell—AWS wĕl
Avalon—ĂV uhl n
Avinger—Ā vĭn jer
Avoca—uh VŌ kuh
Axtell—ĂKS t'l
Azle—Ā z'l

B
Baileyboro—BĀ lĭ ber ruh
Baird—bărd

Balch Springs— bawlch or bawlk SPRĬNGZ
Ballinger—BĂL ĭn jer
Balmorhea—băl muh RĀ
Bandera—băn DĔR uh
Banquete—băn KĔ tĭ
Bassett—BĀ sĭt
Bastrop—BĂS trahp
Batesville—BĀTS v'l
Batson—BĂT s'n
Beasley—BEEZ lĭ
Beaukiss—bō KĬS
Beaumont—BŌ mahnt
Bebe—bee bee
Becton—BĔK t'n
Bedias—BEE dīs
Belcherville—BĔL cher vĭl
Bellaire—bĕl ĂR
Bellevue—BĔL vyŏŏ
Bellmead—bĕl MEED
Belton—BĔL t'n
Benarnold—bĕn AHR n'ld
Benavides—bĕn uh VEE d's
Benchley—BĔNCH lĭ
Ben Hur—bĕn HER
Berclair—ber KLĂR

The Jackrabbit, Odessa. Gary Payne photo.

Bertram—BERT r'm
Bessmay—bĕs MĀ
Bettie—BĔT ĭ
Bexar—BA är or băr
Beyersville—BĪRZ vĭl
Biardstown—BĂRDZ t'n
Birome—bī RŌM
Bivins—BĬ vĭnz
Blanchard—BLĂN cherd
Blanco—BLĂNG kō
Boerne—BER nĭ
Bogata—buh GŌ duh
Boling—BŌL ĭng
Bolivar—BAH lĭ ver
Bomarton—BŌ mer t'n
Bonham—BAH n'm
Bonita—bō NEE tuh
Bon Wier—bahn WEER
Borger—BŎR ger
Bosque—BAHS kĭ
Bovina—bō VEE nuh
Bowie—BŌŌ Ĭ
Brachfield—BRĂCH feeld
Bracken—BRĂ kĭn
Brackettville—BRĂ kĭt vĭl
Brashear—bruh SHĬR
Brazoria—bruh ZŌ rĭ uh
Brazos—BRĂZ uhs
Breckenridge—BRĔK uhn rĭj
Bremond—bree MAHND
Brenham—BRĔ n'm
Britton—BRĬT n
Broaddus—BRAW d's
Bronte—brahnt
Brookshire—BRŎŌK sher
Browndel—brown DĔL
Brundage—BRUHN dĭj
Bruni—BRŌŌ nĭ
Bryarly—BRĪ er lĭ
Buchanan Dam—buhk hăn uhn DĂM
Buda—BYŌŌ duh
Buena Vista—bwă nuh VEES tuh
Bula—BYŌŌ luh
Bullard—BŎŌL erd
Bulverde—bŏŏl VER dĭ
Buna—BYŌŌ nuh
Burkburnett—berk ber NET
Burkett—BER kĭt
Burnet—BER nĕt
Burton—BERT n
Bushland—BŎŌSH l'nd

Bustamante—<u>buhs</u> tuh MAHN tǐ
Bynum—BǏ n'm

C

Cactus—KǍK t's
Caddo Mills—<u>kā</u> dō MǏLZ
Calallen—kǎl ǍL ǐn
Calaveras—kǎl uh VĚR's
Calhoun—kǎl HŌON
Calliham—KǍL uh hǎm
Callisburg—KǍ lǐs berg
Calvert—KǍL vert
Camilla—kuh MEEL yuh
Campbellton—KǍM uhl t'n
Canadian—<u>kuh</u> NǍ dǐ uhn
Candelaria—kǎn duh LĚ rǐ uh
Canton—KǍNT n
Canyon—KǍN y'n
Caplen—KǍP lǐn
Caradan—KǍR uh dǎn
Carlisle—KAHR lǐl
Carlsbad—KAHR uhlz bad
Carmine—kahr MEEN
Carmona—<u>kahr</u> MŌ nuh
Caro—KAH rō
Carrizo Springs—kuh <u>ree</u> zuh
    SPRǏNGZ
Carrollton—KǍR 'l t'n
Carthage—KAHR thǐj
Cason—KǍ s'n
Castell—kǎs TĚL
Castroville—KǍS tro vǐl
Catarina—kǎt uh REE nuh
Caviness—KǍ vǐ něs
Cayuga—kā YŌO guh
Cedar Bayou—<u>see</u> der BǏ ō
Cee Vee—<u>see</u> VEE
Celeste—suh LĚST
Celina—suh LǏ nuh
Centralia—sěn TRǍL yuh
Charco—CHAHR kō
Chatfield—CHǍT feeld
Cheapside—CHEEP sīd
Cherokee—CHĚR uh <u>kee</u>
Chico—CHEE kō
Chicota—chǐ KŌ tuh
Childress—CHǏL drěs
Chillicothe—<u>chǐl</u> ǐ KAH thǐ
Chireno—sh' REE nō
Chisholm—CHǏZ uhm
Chita—CHEE tuh
Chocolate Bayou—<u>chah</u> kuh lǐt BǏ ō
Chriesman—KRǏS m'n
Christine—krǐs TEEN
Christoval—krǐs TŌ v'l
Cibolo—SEE bō lō
Cisco—SǏS kō
Cistern—SǏS tern
Clairemont—KLǍR mahnt
Clairette—klǎr ǐ ĚT
Clarendon—KLǍR ǐn d'n
Cleburne—KLEE bern
Clemville—KLĚM vǐl
Clodine—klaw DEEN
Coahoma—kuh HŌ muh
Cockrell Hill—kahk ruhl HǏL
Colfax—KAHL fǎks
College Station—<u>kah</u> lǐj STǍ sh'n
Collingsworth—KAH lǐnz werth
Colmesneil—KŌL m's neel

*Popeye, Crystal City. Robert Plo-
check photo.*

Colorado—<u>kahl</u> uh RAH dō
Colorado City—kah luh <u>rā</u> duh SǏT ǐ
Columbus—kuh LUHM b's
Comal—KŌ mǎl
Comanche—kuh MǍN chǐ
Combes—kōmz
Comfort—KUHM fert
Como—KŌ mō
Concan—KAHN kǎn
Concepcion—kuhn sep sǐ ŌN
Concho—KAHN chō
Conlen—KAHN lǐn
Conroe—KAHN rō
Cooper—KŌO per
Copeville—KŌP v'l
Coppell—kuhp PĚL or kuh PĚL
Copperas Cove—kahp ruhs KŌV
Corbett—KAWR bǐt
Cordele—kawr DĚL
Corinth—KAH rǐnth
Corpus Christi—<u>kawr</u> p's KRǏS tǐ
Corrigan—KAWR uh g'n
Corsicana—<u>kawr</u> sǐ KǍN uh
Coryell—kō rǐ ĚL
Cottle—KAH t'l
Cotulla—kuh TŌO luh
Coupland—KŌP l'n
Crandall—KRǍN d'l
Cranfills Gap—krǎn f'lz GǍP
Creedmore—KREED mōr
Cresson—KRĚ s'n
Crockett—KRAH kǐt
Crowley—KROW li
Cuero—KWĚR o
Culberson—KUHL ber s'n
Cumby—KUHM bǐ
Cuney—KYŌO nǐ
Currie—KER rǐ
Cuthand—KUHT hǎnd
Cyclone—SǏ klōn
Cypress—SǏ prěs

D

Dabney—DǍB nǐ
Dacosta—duh KAHS tuh

Dacus—DǍ k's
Daingerfield—DǍN jer feeld
Daisetta—dä ZĚT uh
Dalby Springs—dǍl bǐ SPRǏNGZ
Dalhart—DǍL hahrt
Dallam—DǍL uhm
Dallas—DǍ luhs
Damon—DǍ m'n
Danbury—DǍN běrǐ
Danciger—DǍN sǐ ger
Danevang—DǍN uh vǎng
Darrouzett—dǎr uh ZĚT
Davilla—duh VǏL uh
De Berry—duh BĚ rǐ
Decatur—<u>dee</u> KǍT er
De Kalb—dǐ KǍB
De Leon—da lee AHN
Del Rio—děl REE o
Del Valle—děl VǍ lǐ
Delwin—DĚl wǐn
Denhawken—DǏN haw kǐn
Denison—DĚN uh s'n
Denton—DĚNT n
Deport—dǐ PŌRT
Desdemona—<u>děz</u> dǐ MŌ nuh
DeSoto—dǐ SŌ tuh
Detroit—dee TROIT
Devers—DĚ vers
Devine—duh VǏN
DeWitt—dǐ WǏT
D'Hanis—duh HǍ nǐs
Dialville—DǏ uhl vil
Diboll—DǏ bawl
Dilley—DǏL i
Dimmit—DǏM ǐt
Dinero—dǐ NĚ rō
Direct—duh RĚKT
Dobbin—DAH bǐn
Dobrowolski—<u>dah</u> bruh WAHL skǐ
Donie—DŌ nǐ
Doole—DOO lǐ
Dorchester—dawr CHĚS ter
Doucette—DŌO sět
Dougherty—DAHR tǐ
Dozier—DŌ zher
Dryden—DRǏD n
Duffau—DUHF ō
Dumas—DŌO m's
Dumont—DYŌO mahnt
Dundee—DUHN dǐ
Dunlay—DUHN lǐ
Durango—duh RǍNG go
Duval—DŌO vawl

E

East Bernard—<u>eest</u> ber NAHRD
Eastland—EEST l'nd
Ector—ĚK ter
Edcouch—ěd KOWCH
Edinburg—ĚD n <u>berg</u>
Edna—ED nuh
Edom—EE d'm
Edroy—ĚD roi
Egypt—EE juhpt
El Campo—ěl KǍM pō
Eldorado—<u>ěl</u> duh RǍ duh
Electra—ǐ LĚK truh
Elgin—ĚL gǐn
Eliasville—<u>ee</u> LǏ uhs vǐl
El Indio—ěl ǏN dǐ ō

Elkhart—ĔLK hahrt
Ellinger—ĔL ĭn jer
Elmendorf—ĔLM 'n dawrf
Elm Mott—ĕl MAHT
Eloise—ĔL o eez
El Paso—ĕl PĂS ō
Elysian Fields—uh lee zh'n FEELDZ
Emhouse—ĔM hows
Encinal—ĕn suh NAHL
Encino—ĕn SEE nō
Engle—ĔN g'l
Enloe—ĔN lō
Ennis—ĔN ĭs
Enochs—EE nuhks
Eola—ee Ō luh
Era—EE ruh
Erath—EE răth
Esperanza—ĕs per RĂN zuh
Estelline—ĔS tuh leen
Etoile—ĭ TOIL
Etter—ĔT er
Eula—YOŌ luh
Euless—YOŌ lis
Eureka—yōō REE kuh
Eustace—YOŌS t's
Evadale—EE vuh dāl
Evant—EE vănt
Everman—Ĕ ver m'n

F

Fabens—FĀ b'nz
Fairlie—FĀR lee
Falfurrias—făl FYOŌ rĭ uhs
Fannett—fă NĔT
Fannin—FĂN ĭn
Farrar—FĂR uh
Farrsville—FAHRZ vĭl
Farwell—FAHR w'l
Fashing—FĂ shĭng
Fayette—fă ĔT
Fayetteville—FĀ uht vĭl
Fentress—FĔN trĭs
Flatonia—flă TŌN yuh
Flomot—FLŌ maht
Floresville—FLŌRZ vil
Florey—FLŌ ri
Floydada—floi DĀ duh
Fluvanna—flōō VĂN uh
Fodice—FŌ dĭs
Follett—fah LĔT
Fordtran—fōrd TRĂN
Forney—FAWR nĭ
Forsan—FŌR săn
Fort Chadbourne—fŏrt CHĂD bern
Fort Worth—fŏrt WERTH
Fowlerton—FOW ler t'n
Francitas—frăn SEE t's
Fredericksburg—FRĔD er rĭks berg
Fredonia—free DŌN yuh
Freer—FREE er
Frelsburg—FRĔLZ berg
Frio—FREE ō
Friona—free O nuh
Frisco—FRĬS ko
Frydek—FRĬ dĕk
Fulshear—FUHL sher

G

Galena Park—guh lee nuh PAHRK
Gallatin—GĂL uh t'n

Galveston—GĂL vĕs t'n
Ganado—guh NĀ dō
Garceno—gahr SĀ nō
Garciasville—gahr SEE uhs vĭl
Garland—GAHR l'nd
Garza—GAHR zuh
Gause—gawz
Geneva—juh NEE vuh
Geronimo—juh RAH nĭ mō
Giddings—GĬD ĭngz
Gillespie—guh LĔS pĭ
Gillett—juh LĔT
Gilliland—GĬL ĭ l'nd
Gilmer—GĬL mer
Girard—juh RAHRD
Girvin—GER vĭn
Gladewater—GLĀD wah ter
Glasscock—GLĂS kahk
Glazier—GLĀ zher
Glidden—GLĬD n
Gober—GŌ ber
Godley—GAHD lĭ
Goldfinch—GŌLD fĭnch
Goldthwaite—GŌLTH wāt
Goliad—GŌ lĭ ăd
Golinda—gō LĬN duh
Gonzales—guhn ZAH l's
Goodland—GOŌD l'n
Goodlett—GOŌD lĕt
Goodrich—GOŌD rĭch
Goree—GŌ ree
Gouldbusk—GOŌLD buhsk
Granbury—GRĂN bĕ rĭ
Grand Saline—grăn suh LEEN
Granger—GRĂN jer
Grapeland—GRĀP l'nd
Greenville—GREEN v'l
Groesbeck—GRŌZ bĕk
Gruene—green
Grulla—GROŌL yuh
Gruver—GROŌ ver
Guadalupe—gwah duh LOŌ pĭ
Guerra—GWĔ ruh
Gunter—GUHN ter

Gustine—GUHS teen
Guthrie—GUHTH rĭ

H

Hagansport—HĀ gĭnz pōrt
Hallettsville—HĂL ĕts vĭl
Hamshire—HĂM sher
Handley—HĂND lĭ
Hankamer—HĂN kăm er
Hargill—HAHR gĭl
Harleton—HAHR uhl t'n
Harlingen—HAHR lĭn juhn
Haskell—HĂS k'l
Haslam—HĂZ l'm
Haslet—HĂS lĕt
Hasse—HĂ sĭ
Hatchell—HĂ ch'l
Hawley—HAW lĭ
Hearne—hern
Heath—heeth
Hebbronville—HĔB r'n vĭl
Hebron—HEE br'n
Hedley—HĔD lĭ
Heidenheimer—HĪD n hīmer
Helena—HĔL uh nuh
Helotes—hĕl Ō tĭs
Hemphill—HĔMP hĭl
Hermleigh—HER muh lee
Hewitt—HYOŌ ĭt
Hico—HĪ kō
Hidalgo—hĭ DĂL gō
Hillister—HĬL ĭs ter
Hiram—HĪ r'm
Hochheim—HŌ hĭm
Hondo—HAHN dō
Houston—HYOŌS t'n or YOŌS t'n
Huckabay—HUHK uh bĭ
Hudspeth—HUHD sp'th
Humble—UHM b'l
Hutto—HUH tō
Hye—hĭ
Hylton—HĬL t'n

I

Iago—ī Ā gō
Idalou—Ī duh lōō

Snoopy, Luling. Robert Plocheck photo.

Inadale—Ī nuh dāl
Industry—ĬN duhs trĭ
Inez—ī NĔZ
Ingram—ĬNG gr'm
Iola—ī Ō luh
Ira—Ī ruh
Iraan—ī ruh ĂN
Iredell—Ī ruh dĕl
Ireland—Ī rĭ l'nd
Irene—ī REEN
Irion—ĪR i uhn
Irving—ER vĭng
Italy—ĬT uh lĭ
Itasca—ī TĂS kuh
Ivan—Ī v'n
Ivanhoe—Ī v'n hō

J

Jardin—JAHRD n
Jarrell—JĂR uhl
Jeddo—JĔ dō
Jermyn—JER m'n
Jewett—JOŌ ĭt
Jiba—HEE buh
Joaquin—waw KEEN
Jonah—JŌ nuh
Joshua—JAH sh' wa
Jourdanton—JERD n t'n
Juliff—JOŌ lĭf
Juno—JOŌ nō

K

Kalgary—KĂL gĕ rĭ
Kamay—KĀ ĭm ā
Kanawha—KAHN uh wah
Karnack—KAHR năk
Karnes City—kahrnz SĬT ĭ
Katemcy—kuh TĔM sĭ
Kaufman—KAWF m'n
Keechi—KEE chĭ
Keene—keen
Kellerville—KĔL er vĭl
Kemah—KEE muh
Kempner—KĔMP ner
Kendalia—kĔn DĀL yuh
Kennard—kuh NAHRD
Kennedale—KĔN uh dāl
Kerens—KER 'nz
Kerrville—KER vĭl
Kilgore—KĬL gōr
Killeen—kuh LEEN
Kimble—KĬM b'l
Kinney—KĬN ĭ
Kirvin—KER vĭn
Kleberg—KLĀ berg
Knickerbocker—NĬK uh <u>bah</u> ker
Knippa—kuh NĬP uh
Kosciusko—kuh SHOŌS kō
Kosse—KAH sĭ
Kountze—koōntz
Kurten—KER t'n
Kyle—kīl

L

La Blanca—lah BLAHN kuh
La Coste—luh KAWST
Ladonia—luh DŌN yuh
LaFayette—lah fī ĔT
Laferia—luh FĔ rĭ uh
Lagarto—luh GAHR tō
La Gloria—lah GLŌ rĭ uh

The Peanut, Floresville. Robert Plocheck photo.

La Grange—luh GRĀNJ
Laguna—luh GOŌ nuh
La Joya—luh HŌ yuh
La Marque—luh MAHRK
Lamasco—luh MĂS kō
Lamesa—luh MEE suh
Lampasas—lăm PĂ s's
Lancaster—LĂNG k's ter
Langtry—LĂNG trĭ
Lanier—luh NĬR
La Paloma—<u>lah</u> puh LŌ muh
La Porte—luh PŌRT
La Pryor—luh PRĪ er
Laredo—luh RĀ dō
Lariat—LĂ ri uht
Larue—luh ROŌ
LaSalle—luh SĂL
Lasara—luh SĔ ruh
Lassater—LĂ sĭ ter
Latexo—luh TĔKS ō
Lavaca—luh VĂ kuh
La Vernia—luh VER nĭ uh
La Villa—<u>lah</u> VĬL uh
Lavon—luh VAHN
La Ward—luh WAWRD
Lazbuddie—LĂZ buh dĭ
Leakey—LĂ kĭ
Leander—lee ĂN der
Leary—LĬ er ĭ
Lefors—lĭ FŌRZ
Lela—LEE luh
Lelia Lake—<u>leel</u> yuh LĀK
Leon—lee AHN
Leona—<u>lee</u> Ō nuh
Leroy—LEE roi
Levita—luh VĬ tuh
Lindenau—lĭn duh NOW
Lipan—lĭ PĂN
Lissie—LĬ sĭ
Llano—LĂ nō
Lockney—LAHK nĭ
Lodi—LŌ dĭ
Lohn—lahn
Lolita—lō LEE tuh
Loma Alto—<u>lō</u> muh ĂL tō
Lometa—lō MEE tuh
Long Mott—lawng MAHT
Lopeno—lō PEE nō
Loraine—lō RĂN

Lorena—lō REE nuh
Los Angeles—laws AN juh l's
Los Ebanos—lōs ĔB uh nōs
Los Fresnos—lōs FRĔZ nōs
Los Indios—lōs ĬN dĭ ōs
Losoya—luh SAW yuh
Lott—laht
Louise—LOŌ eez
Lubbock—LUH buhk or LUH b'k
Lueders—LOŌ derz
Luella—loō ĔL uh
Lufkin—LUHF kĭn
Luling—LOŌ lĭng
Lund—luhnd
Lutie—LOŌ tĭ
Lyford—LĪ ferd
Lytton Springs—lĭt n SPRĬNGZ

M

Mabank—MĀ băngk
Macune—muh KOŌN
Malakoff—MĂL uh kawf
Manchaca—MĂN shäk
Manchester—MĂN chĕs ter
Manheim—MĂN hīm
Mankins—MĂN kĭnz
Manor—MĀ ner
Manvel—MĂN v'l
Marathon—MĂR uh th'n
Marfa—MAHR fuh
Markham—MAHR k'm
Marlin—MAHR lĭn
Marquez—mahr KĀ
Maryneal—mā rĭ NEEL
Mason—MĀ s'n
Matador—MĂT uh dōr
Matagorda—măt uh GAWR duh
Mathis—MĂ thĭs
Mauriceville—maw REES vĭl
Maverick—MĂV rĭk
Maxey—MĂKS ĭ
Maydell—MĀ dĕl
Maypearl—<u>mā</u> PERL
Maysfield—MĀZ feeld
McAdoo—MĂK uh doō
McAllen—măk ĂL ĭn
McCamey—muh KĀ mĭ
McCaulley—muh KAW lĭ
McCulloch—muh KUH luhk
McFaddin—măk FĂD n
McGregor—muh GRĔ ger
McKinney—muh KĬN ĭ
McLean—muh KLĂN
McLennan—muhk LĔN uhn
McLeod—măk LOWD
McMahan—măk MĂN
McMullen—măk MUHL ĭn
McNary—măk NĀ rĭ
McNeil—măk NEEL
McQueeney—muh KWEE nĭ
Medill—mĕ DĬL
Medina—muh DEE nuh
Megargel—muh GAHR g'l
Menard—muh NAHRD
Mendoza—mĕn DŌ zuh
Mentone—mĕn TON
Mercedes—<u>mer</u> SĀ deez
Mereta—muh RĔT uh
Meridian—muh RĬ dĭ uhn

Merkel—MER k'l
Mertens—<u>mer</u> TĔNZ
Mertzon—MERTS n
Mesquite—muhs KEET
Mexia—muh HĀ uh
Miami—mī ĂM uh or mī ĂM ĭ
Mico—MEE kō
Midland—MĬD l'nd
Midlothian—<u>mĭd</u> LŌ thĭ n
Milam—MĪ l'm
Milano—mĭ LĂ nō
Millett—MĬL ĭt
Millheim—MĬL hīm
Mineola—mĭn ĭ Ō luh
Minerva—mĭ NER vuh
Mingus—MĬNG guhs
Minter—MĬNT er
Mirando City—mĭ răn duh SĬT ĭ
Missouri City—muh zŏŏr uh SĬT ĭ
Mobeetie—mō BEE tĭ
Moline—mō LEEN
Monaville—MŌ nuh vĭl
Monkstown—MUHNGKS town
Monroe City—<u>mahn</u> rō SĬT ĭ
Montague—mahn TĀG
Montalba—mahnt ĂL buh
Mont Belvieu—mahnt BĔL vyōō
Montell—mahn TĔL
Montgomery—<u>mahnt</u> GUHM er ĭ
Monthalia—mahn THĀL yuh
Moore—mor
Morales—muh RAH lĕs
Moran—mō RĂN
Morgan Mill—<u>mawr</u> g'n MĬL
Morton—MAWRT n
Moscow—MAHS kow
Mosheim—MŌ shīm
Motley—MAHT lĭ
Moulton—MŌL t'n
Mount Selman—mownt SĔL m'n
Mount Sylvan—mownt SĬL v'n
Muenster—MYŌŌNS ter
Muldoon—muhl DŌŌN
Muleshoe—MYŌŌL shōō
Mullin—MUHL ĭn
Mumford—MUHM ferd
Munday—MUHN dī
Murchison—MER kuh s'n
Mykawa—mĭ KAH wuh
Myra—MĪ ruh

N

Nacogdoches—<u>năk</u> uh DŌ chĭs
Nada—NĀ duh
Naples—NĀ p'lz
Natalia—nuh TĀL yuh
Navarro—nuh VĂ rō
Navasota—năv uh SŌ tuh
Nazareth—NĂZ uh r'th
Neches—NĀ chĭs
Nederland—NEE der l'nd
Needville—NEED vĭl
Neuville—NYŌŌ v'l
Nevada—nuh VĀ duh
New Baden—nyōō BĀD n
New Boston—nyōō BAWS t'n
New Braunfels—nyōō BROWN fĕlz
New Caney—nyōō KĀ nĭ
Newcastle—NYŌŌ kăs uhl
Newlin—NYŌŌ lĭn

Paisano Pete in Fort Stockton. Robert Plocheck photo.

Newsome—NYŌŌ s'm
New Ulm—nyōō UHLM
New Waverly—nyōō WĀ ver lĭ
New Willard—nyōō WĬL erd
Nimrod—NĬM rahd
Nineveh—NĬN uh vuh
Nocona—nō KŌ nuh
Nopal—NŌ păl
Nordheim—NAWRD hīm
Normangee—NAWR m'n <u>jee</u>
Normanna—nawr MĂN uh
North Zulch—nawrth ZŌŌLCH
Nueces—nyōō Ā sĭs

O

Oakalla—ō KĂL uh
Ochiltree—AH k'l tree
Odell—Ō dĕl or ō DĔL
Odem—Ō d'm
Odessa—ō DĔS uh
Oenaville—ō EEN uh v'l
Oglesby—Ō g'lz bĭ
Oilton—OIL t'n
Oklaunion—<u>ōk</u> luh YŌŌN y'n
Olden—ŌL d'n
Oldham—ŌL d'm
Olivia—ō LĬV ĭ uh
Olmito—awl MEE tuh
Olmos Park—ahl m's PAHRK
Olney—AHL ni
Olton—ŌL t'n
Omaha—Ō muh haw
Omen—Ō mĭn
Onalaska—<u>uhn</u> uh LĂS kuh
Oplin—AHP lĭn
Osceola—ō sĭ Ō luh
Otey—Ō tĭ
Ottine—ah TEEN
Ovalo—ō VĂL uh
Ozona—ō ZŌ nuh

P

Paducah—puh DYŌŌ kuh
Palacios—puh LĂ sh's
Palestine—PAL uhs <u>teen</u>
Palito Blanco—p' <u>lee</u> to BLAHNG kō
Palo Pinto—<u>pă</u> lō PĬN tō

Paluxy—puh LUHK sĭ
Pampa—PĂM puh
Panna Maria—<u>păn</u> uh muh REE uh
Papalote—pah puh LŌ tĭ
Paris—PĂ rĭs
Parmer—PAH mer
Pasadena—<u>păs</u> uh DEE nuh
Patroon—puh TRŌŌN
Pattison—PĂT uh s'n
Pattonville—PĂT n vĭl
Pawnee—paw NEE
Pearland—PĂR lănd
Pearsall—PEER sawl
Peaster—PEES ter
Pecan Gap—pĭ kahn GAP
Pecos—PĀ k's
Penelope—puh NĔL uh pĭ
Penitas—puh NEE t's
Penwell—PĬN wĕl
Peoria—<u>pee</u> Ō rĭ uh
Percilla—per SĬL uh
Perrin—PĔR ĭn
Perryton—PĔ rĭ t'n
Petrolia—puh TRŌL yuh
Petteway—PĔT uh wā
Pettit—PĔT ĭt
Pettus—PĔT uhs
Pflugerville—FLŌŌ ger vĭl
Pharr—fahr
Phelps—fĕlps
Pidcoke—PĬD kōk
Piedmont—PEED mahnt
Pineland—PĬN land
Placedo—PLĂS ĭ dō
Placid—PLĂ sĭd
Plano—PLĀ nō
Plaska—PLĂS kuh
Plateau—plă TŌ
Pledger—PLĔ jer
Pointblank—pint BLĂNGK
Pollock—PAHL uhk
Ponta—pahn TĀ
Pontotoc—PAHNT uh tahk
Port Aransas—pōrt uh RĂN zuhs
Port Arthur—pōrt AHR ther
Port Bolivar—<u>pōrt</u> BAH lĭ ver

Port Isabel—pōrt ĬZ uh bĕl
Port Lavaca—pōrt luh VĂ kuh
Port Neches—pōrt NĂ chĬs
Posey—PŌ zĭ
Poteet—pō TEET
Poth—pŏth
Potosi—puh TŌ sĭ
Poynor—POI ner
Prairie Dell—prĕr ĭ DĔL
Prairie Lea—prĕr ĭ LEE
Premont—PREE mahnt
Presidio—pruh SĬ dĭ ō
Priddy—PRĬ dĭ
Primera—<u>pree</u> MĔ ruh
Pritchett—PRĬ chĭt
Progreso—prō GRĔ sō
Purdon—PERD n
Purley—PER lĭ
Purmela—per MEE luh
Pyote—PĪ ōt

Q

Quanah—KWAH nuh
Quemado—kuh MAH dō
Quihi—KWEE <u>hee</u>
Quintana—kwĭn TAH nuh
Quitaque—KĬT uh kwa
Quitman—KWĬT m'n

R

Ravenna—rĭ VĔN uh
Reagan—RĀ g'n
Real—REE awl
Realitos—<u>ree</u> uh LEE t's
Refugio—rĕ FYŌŌ rĭ ō
Reklaw—RĔK law
Reno—REE nō
Rhineland—RĪN l'nd
Rhome—rōm
Rhonesboro—RŌNZ buh ruh
Ricardo—rĭ KAHR dō
Richardson—RĬCH erd s'n
Riesel—REE s'l
Ringgold—RĬNG gōld
Rio Frio—<u>ree</u> ō FREE ō
Rio Grande City—ree ō grahn dĭ
    SĬT ĭ   or   ree ō grăn SĬT ĭ
Rio Hondo—<u>ree</u> ō HAHN dō
Riomedina—<u>ree</u> ō muh DEE nuh
Rios—REE ōs

Rio Vista—ree ō VĬS tuh
Riviera—ruh VĬR uh
Roane—rōn
Roanoke—RŌN ōk or RŌ uh <u>nōk</u>
Roans Prairie—rōnz PRĔR ĭ
Robstown—RAHBZ town
Roby—RŌ bĭ
Roma—RŌ muh
Romayor—rō MĀ er
Roosevelt—RŌŌ suh v'lt
Rosanky—rō ZĂNG kĭ
Rosenberg—RŌZ n berg
Rosenthal—RŌZ uhn thawl
Rosharon—rō SHĔ r'n
Rosita—rō SEE tuh
Rosser—RAW ser
Roswell—RAHZ w'l
Rotan—rō TĂN
Rowena—rō EE nuh
Rowlett—ROW lĭt
Royston—ROIS t'n
Ruidosa—<u>ree</u> uh DŌ suh
Runge—RUHNG ĭ

S

Sabinal—SĂB uh năl
Sabine—suh BEEN
Sabine Pass—suh <u>been</u> PĂS
Sabinetown—suh <u>been</u> TOWN
Sachse—SĂK sĭ
Sacul—SĂ k'l
Salado—suh LĀ dō
Salineno—suh LEEN yō
Salmon—SĂL m'n
Saltillo—săl TĬL ō
Samfordyce—săm FOR dis
Samnorwood—săm NAWR wŏŏd
San Angelo—<u>săn</u> ĂN juh lō
San Antonio—<u>săn</u> ăn TŌ nĭ ō
San Augustine—<u>săn</u> AW g's teen
San Benito—săn buh NEE tuh
Sandia—săn DEE uh
San Diego—<u>săn</u> dĭ Ā gō
San Felipe—<u>săn</u> fuh LEEP
San Gabriel—săn GĀ brĭ uhl
Sanger—SĂNG er
San Jacinto—<u>săn</u> juh SĬN tuh
San Juan—săn WAHN
San Marcos—<u>săn</u> MAHR k's
San Patricio—<u>săn</u> puh TRĬSH ĭ ō

San Perlita—<u>săn</u> per LEE tuh
San Saba—<u>săn</u> SĂ buh
Santa Anna—<u>săn</u> tuh ĂN uh
Santa Elena—săn tuh LEE nuh
Santa Maria—<u>săn</u> tuh muh REE uh
Santa Rosa—<u>săn</u> tuh RŌ suh
Santo—SĂN tō
San Ygnacio—<u>săn</u> ĭg NAH sĭ ō
Saragosa—<u>sĕ</u> ruh GŌ suh
Saratoga—<u>sĕ</u> ruh TŌ guh
Sargent—SAHR juhnt
Sarita—suh REE tuh
Saspamco—suh SPĂM kō
Savoy—suh VOI
Schattel—SHĂT uhl
Schertz—sherts
Schleicher—SHLĪ ker
Schroeder—SHRĀ der
Schulenburg—SHŌŌ lĭn berg
Schwertner—SWERT ner
Scurry—SKUH rĭ
Scyene—sĭ EEN
Sealy—SEE lĭ
Segno—SĔG nō
Segovia—<u>sĭ</u> GŌ vĭ uh
Seguin—sĭ GEEN
Seminole—SĔM uh nōl
Shafter—SHĂF ter
Shallowater—SHĂL uh wah ter
Shiner—SHĪ ner
Shiro—SHĪ rō
Shive—shĭv
Sierra Blanca—sĭer ruh BLĂNG kuh
Siloam—suh LŌM
Silsbee—SĬLZ bĭ
Sinton—SĬNT n
Sipe Springs—SEEP sprĭngz
Sisterdale—SĬS ter dāl
Sivells Bend—sĭ v'lz BĔND
Skellytown—SKĔ lĭ town
Skidmore—SKĬD mōr
Slaton—SLĂT n
Slayden—SLĀD n
Slidell—slī DĔL
Slocum—SLŌ k'm
Smiley—SMĪ lĭ
Smyer—SMĪ er
Snook—snŏŏk
Snyder—SNĪ der

Local – and alien – color in Marathon. Robert Plocheck photo.

Somerset—SUH mer sĕt
Somervell—SUH mer vĕl
Somerville—SUH mer vĭl
Sonora—suh NŌ ruh
South Bosque—sowth BAHS kĭ
South Houston—sowth HYŌŌS t'n
Southland—SOWTH l'nd
Southmayd—sowth MĀD
Sparenberg—SPĀR ĭn berg
Splendora—splĕn DŌ ruh
Spofford—SPAH ferd
Spurger—SPER ger
Sterley—STER lĭ
Stiles—stīlz
Stinnett—stĭ NĔT
Stoneham—STŌN uhm
Study Butte—styōō dĭ BYŌŌT
Sublime—s'b LĪM
Sudan—SŌŌ dăn
Sweeny—SWEE nĭ
Swisher—SWĬ sher
Sylvester— sil VES ter

T

Tahoka—tuh HŌ kuh
Talco—TĂL kō
Talpa—TĂL puh
Tankersley—TĂNG kers lĭ
Tarrant—TAR uhnt
Tarzan—TAHR z'n
Tascosa—tăs KŌ suh
Tatum—TĀ t'm
Tavener—TĂV uh ner
Tehuacana—tuh WAW kuh nuh
Telferner—TĔLF ner
Tenaha—TĔN uh haw
Terlingua—TER lĭng guh
Terrell—TĔR uhl
Texarkana—tĕks ahr KĂN uh
Texhoma—tĕks Ō muh
Texline—TĔKS lĭn
Texon—tĕks AHN
Thalia—THĀL yuh
Thrall—thrawl
Tioga—tī Ō guh
Tivoli—tī VŌ luh
Tokio—TŌ kĭ ō
Tolar—TŌ ler
Tolbert—TAHL bert
Tolosa—tuh LŌ suh
Tomball—TAHM bawl
Tornillo—tawr NEE yō
Tow—tow
Toyah—TOI yuh
Toyahvale—TOI yuh văl
Trawick—TRĀ wĭk
Trinidad—TRĬN uh dăd
Troup—trōōp
Truby—TRŌŌ bĭ
Trumbull—TRUHM b'l
Truscott—TRUHS k't
Tuleta—tōō LEE tuh
Tulia—TŌŌL yuh
Tulsita—tuhl SEE tuh
Tundra—TUHN druh
Tunis—TŌŌ nĭs
Tuscola—tuhs KŌ luh
Tuxedo—TUHKS ĭ dō
Twitty—TWĬ tĭ
Tye—tī

Tyler—TĪ ler
Tynan—TĪ nuhn

U

Uhland—YŌŌ l'nd
Umbarger—UHM bahr ger
Urbana—er BĀ nuh
Utley—YŌŌT lĭ
Utopia—yōō TŌ pĭ uh
Uvalde—yōō VĂL dĭ

V

Valdasta—văl DĂS tuh
Valera—vuh LĪ ruh
Van Alstyne—văn AWLZ teen
Van Vleck—văn VLĔK
Van Zandt—văn ZĂNT
Vashti—VĂSH tĭ
Vega—VĀ guh
Velasco—vuh LĂS kō
Vera—VĪ ruh
Veribest—VĔR ĭ bĕst
Vickery—VĬK er ĭ
Victoria—vĭk TŌ rĭ uh
Vidor—VĪ der
Vienna—vee ĔN uh
Vinegarone—vĭn er guh RŌN
Voca—VŌ kuh
Von Ormy—vahn AHR mĭ
Votaw—VŌ taw

W

Waco—WĀ kō
Waelder—WĔL der
Waka—WAH kuh
Walberg—WAWL berg
Waldeck—WAWL dĕk
Warda—WAWR duh
Waskom—WAHS k'm
Wastella—wahs TĔL uh
Watauga—wuh TAW guh
Waxahachie—wawks uh HĂ chĭ
Weches—WEE chĭz

Weesatche—WEE săch
Weimar—WĪ mer
Weinert—WĪ nert
Weir—weer
Weser—WEE zer
Weslaco—WĔS luh kō
Westhoff—WĔS tawf
Westminster— wĕst MĬN ster
Westphalia—wĕst FĀL yuh
Whitharral—HWĬT hăr uhl
Whitsett—HWĬT sĭt
Whitt—hwĭt
Whon—hwahn
Wichita Falls— wĭch ĭ taw FAWLZ
Wiergate—WEER găt
Wilbarger—WĬL bahr ger
Wildorado—wĭl duh RĀ dō
Willacy—WĬL uh sĭ
Wimberley—WĬM ber lĭ
Windom—WĬN d'm
Windthorst—WĬN thr'st
Wingate—WĬN găt
Winnie—WĬ nĭ
Winona—wĭ NŌ nuh
Woden—WŌD n
Wolfforth—WŌŌL forth
Wortham—WERTH uhm
Wylie—WĪ lĭ

Y

Yancey—YĂN sĭ
Yantis—YĂN tĭs
Yoakum—YŌ k'm
Ysleta—ĭs LĔT uh

Z

Zapata—zuh PAH tuh
Zavalla—zuh VĂL uh
Zephyr—ZĔF er
Zuehl—ZEE uhl

To the beach, Galveston. Elizabeth Alvarez photo.

Obituaries: July 2005-July 2007

Allen, J.B., 67; one of the West's best known cowboy poets who worked from his ranch in Whiteface, only starting to write poetry at age 50; in Lubbock, Dec. 13, 2005.

Armstrong, Tobin, 82; descendant of pioneer South Texas ranching family; director of the Texas and Southwestern Cattle Raising Association for 48 years; in Houston, Oct. 7, 2005.

Baker, O.T., 95; Center native who founded the Texas Folklife Festival in 1972 in San Antonio and served as director for its first five years; in Austin, Jan. 21, 2006.

Barr, Candy, 70; born Juanita Dale Slusher in Edna, she became famed stripper in Dallas in the 1950s, making headlines for her drug arrests; in Victoria, Dec. 30, 2005.

Barrow, Charles W., 84; Texas Supreme Court justice, chief judge of the U.S. 4th Court of Appeals and dean of the law school at Baylor University; in San Antonio, June 25, 2006.

Bass, Perry R., 91; prominent philanthropist and businessman whose family led the transformation of downtown Fort Worth; in Westover Hills, June 1, 2006.

Baugh, John F., 91; founder in 1946 of the nation's largest restaurant supplier, Sysco; gave $25 million to Baylor University in his hometown of Waco; founding trustee of Houston Baptist University; in San Antonio, March 5, 2007.

Bentsen, Lloyd M. Jr., 85; represented Texas in the U.S. Senate for 22 years; vice presidential candidate on the Democratic ticket in 1988; former secretary of Treasury; in Houston, May 23, 2006.

Bentsen.

Bond, Thomas Ross, 79; Dallas native played Butch the bully in the *Our Gang* and *Little Rascals* serials in the 1930s; in 1940s played Jimmy Olsen in two Superman movies; in Los Angeles, Sept. 24, 2005.

Bragg, George, 81; founder and director for 29 years of the Texas Boys Choir, which won numerous awards including two Grammys; in Fort Worth, May 31, 2007.

Brown, Clarence "Gatemouth," 81; singer and guitarist famous for juke-joint stomp numbers but who also performed jazz, country, blues, zydeco and Cajun; in Orange, where he grew up, Sept. 10, 2005.

Carothers, A J, 75; Houston native was screenwriter for *The Secret of My Success* and *The Happiest Millionaire*; associate producer of TV's *Playhouse 90* and *GE Theater*; in Los Angeles, April 9, 2007.

Carrol, Lou, 83; the "man down in Texas" (in Belton) who gave Richard Nixon the dog that led to the famous Checkers speech; in a Chicago suburb, April 3, 2006.

Chambers, James F. Jr., 93; former cop-beat reporter became president of the *Dallas Times Herald* in 1960 and publisher in 1967, retiring in 1980; in Dallas, Sept. 21, 2006.

Clayton, Billy, 78; Olney native was powerful speaker of the Texas House 1975-83; served on the board of the Texas A&M System; in Lubbock, Jan. 6, 2007.

Connally, Nellie, 87; former Texas first lady who was riding in John F. Kennedy's open car when he was shot along with her husband Gov. John Connally; in Austin, Sept. 1, 2006.

Corley, Pat, 76; Dallas native and a character actor for five decades; served advice along with drinks as the bartender on TV's *Murphy Brown*; in Los Angeles, Sept. 11, 2006.

Corley.

Cuellar, Claude "Poppy," 83; Dallas icon of Tex-Mex founded Tejano Restaurant in 1981 after working for El Chico chain; in Arlington, Oct. 16, 2005.

Cullum, Charles, 89; Dallas civic leader founded in 1948 with his brother the Tom Thumb food stores; served on Dallas city council; in Dallas, May 16, 2006.

Daniel, Bill, 90; member of prominent political family; former legislator appointed governor of Guam in 1961; in Liberty, June 20, 2006.

DeAnda, James, 81; Houston native was former federal judge who in 1954 helped successfully argue the pivotal case that made Hispanics a protected minority class; at his summer home in Michigan, Sept. 7, 2006.

Delaney, Joseph P., 70; bishop of the Catholic Diocese of Fort Worth for nearly 24 years; worked for inclusion of Hispanics, grappled with sexual abuse crisis; in Fort Worth, July 24, 2005.

Denney, Ruth, 92; noted drama educator and founding director in 1971 in Houston of one of the first public high schools devoted to the performing arts; in Austin, March 27, 2007.

Doss, Richard "Dick," 84; Harris County engineer who coordinated the construction of the Astrodome and was in charge of maintaining the finished structure; in Houston, March 16, 2007.

Dreibrodt, Irving Dingman, 86; founder in 1958 of the Southern Methodist University show band, dubbed "the Best Dressed Band in the Land;" in Dallas, Jan. 22, 2007.

Duckett, J. Fred, 74; public-address announcer for Texas Relays, Rice Owls and at the Astrodome where he started heralding "Jose Cruuuz"; in Houston, June 25, 2007.

East, Robert Claude, 87; great-grandson of Richard King and owner of San Antonio Viejo Ranch, one of the oldest ranching properties in South Texas; in Jim Hogg County, June 18, 2007.

Edwards, Doris, 96; widow of highway patrolman E.B. Wheeler, who was gunned down by Clyde Barrow's gang; later worked with Texas Rangers against illegal gambling; in Dallas, June 10, 2007.

Ellison, Ray Sr., 88; Greenville native was founder of San Antonio-based company than grew into one of the largest independent home builders in the nation; in San Antonio, Oct. 16, 2005.

Eure, Jim, 87; founder in 1969 of what would become Mr. Gatti's pizza chain, which grew to more than 200 stores; in Austin, Sept. 18, 2005.

Farb, Harold, 83; amassed a fortune beginning in the 1970s as "the king of the apartment business" in Houston with more than 30,000 units; in Houston, Oct. 10, 2006.

Fender, Freddy, 69; born Baldemar Huerta in San Benito, the Grammy-winning singer had hits with "Before the Last Teardrop Falls" and "Wasted Days and Wasted Nights"; in Corpus Christi, Oct. 14, 2006.

Fender.

Fitzpatrick, John J., 87; bishop of the Catholic Diocese of Brownsville 1971-91; noted for pastoral ministry to migrants and immigrants; in Brownsville, July 15, 2006.

Flanagan, Peggy, 85; one of the first women in Texas to be certified as an oil and gas landman in 1981; president of the American Business Women's Association 1964-65; in Houston, Jan. 11, 2007.

Friedman, Jeff, 62; the former "hippie mayor" of Austin in the 1970s, first serving at age 26 on the city council where he challenged the political establishment; June 7, 2007.

Fritsch, Toni, 60; popular Austrian-born kicker for the Luv Ya Blue-era Houston Oilers under coach Bum Phillips; earlier kicked for the Dallas Cowboys; in Vienna, Sept. 13, 2005.

Fürstenberg, Cecil Blaffer "Titi" von, 86; arts patron who was daughter of Humble Oil (ExxonMobil) founder Robert L. Blaffer and granddaughter of Texas Company (Texaco) founder William Thomas Campbell; married Prince Tassilo von Fürstenberg of Austria; in Houston, Nov. 17, 2006.

Gallego, Ernesto S. "Papo," 84; Air Force veteran born in Rowena who served as the first Hispanic mayor of Alpine and as a Brewster County commissioner; in Alpine, July 22, 2005.

Gonzalez Gonzalez, Pedro, 80; born in Aguilares as his show business parents were passing through; performed in San Antonio before breaking into movies, such as *Rio Bravo* and *The High and the Mighty*; in Culver City, Calif., Feb. 6, 2006.

Gonzalez Gonzalez.

Green, Howard L., 84; former Tarrant County judge and legislator; baseball enthusiast who helped bring Texas Rangers to Arlington; grandfather of actor Ethan Hawke; in Fort Worth, Oct. 13, 2005.

Hackerman, Norman, 95; former president of UT-Austin 1967–70 and Rice University 1970–85; respected chemist who worked on the Manhattan Project; member National Academy of the Sciences; in Temple, June 16, 2007.

Harrelson, Charles, 69; father of actor Woody Harrelson; convicted of the 1979 murder of San Antonio federal judge John Wood Jr.; in federal prison in Colorado, March 15, 2007.

Hearne, Grace Truman Dodson "Mimi," 102; daughter of a San Antonio attorney, she fished, was a talented markswoman, and played classical piano; ran her ranch near Blanco well into her 90s, where she died, July 22, 2005.

Hester, Darrell, 80; tough-minded jurist who presided over the trials that helped topple the dynasty of South Texas political boss George Parr; in Harlingen, Dec. 18, 2005.

Hildebrandt, Tim, 67; world-renowned illustrator and artist who, with his twin brother Greg, created posters for *Star Wars* and *The Lord of the Rings*; in San Antonio, June 11, 2006.

Hill, John L. Jr., 83; former Texas Supreme Court chief justice, secretary of state and attorney general; in 1978 became first Democrat in a century to lose the governor's race, falling to Republican Bill Clements; in Houston, July 9, 2007.

Hill, Margaret Hunt, 91; oldest child of oil tycoon H.L. Hunt; grew up in Tyler; active in resort development and her oil company, Hunt Petroleum, which gave $12 million to the Trinity River Corridor Project; in Dallas, June 14, 2007.

Hodgson, Jay, 78; known as Uncle Jay to baby boomers of Central Texas where he hosted an after-school children's show on Austin's KTBC for 25 years; May 27, 2007.

Howard, Merideth, 52; Corpus Christi native; oldest female soldier killed in action since military operations began in Iraq and Afghanistan; first female firefighter in Bryan; near Kabel, Sept. 8, 2006.

Hunt, Lamar, 74; as owner of the Dallas Texans was one of the founders of the AFL, instrumental in the merger of AFL and NFL; coined term "Super Bowl"; youngest son of legendary oilman H.L. Hunt; in Dallas, Dec. 13, 2006.

Ivins, Molly, 62; liberal newspaper columnist, commentator on Texas culture and politics, and former co-editor of the *Texas Observer*; in Austin, Jan. 31, 2007.

Ivins.

Jamail, Lee Hage, 76; prominent Houston philanthropist; former member of state college coordinating board, Houston Museum of Fine Arts, and other boards; wife of attorney Joseph D. Jamail; in Houston, Jan. 15. 2007.

Johnson, Jake, 75; colorful legislator

1960-73 known as a prankster; instrumental in creation of UT–San Antonio; in Austin, Sept. 9, 2006.

Johnson, Lady Bird, 94; born Claudia Taylor in Karnack, as first lady she championed wildflower conservation, and the policies of her husband President Lyndon Johnson, serving as his trusted adviser; in Austin, July 11, 2007.

Lady Bird Johnson.

Johnson, Richard J.V., 75; during four decades at the *Houston Chronicle* he served as publisher, president and chairman; in Houston, Jan. 14, 2006.

Jones, Garth, 88; longtime newsman for the Associated Press who covered nine governors and 19 regular sessions of the Legislature; in Austin, Jan. 18, 2006.

Jones, Wilford "Crazy Ray," 76; as a character at Dallas Cowboys games he became nationally recognizable and an unofficial mascot; in Dallas, March 17, 2007.

Ray Jones.

Jones, Woodrow Jr., 58; political science professor who became the first black dean at Texas A&M University in 1994 as head of the College of Liberal Arts; in College Station, Nov. 22, 2005, after a long battle with heart disease.

Keeter, Thomas Lee, 79; as head of horticulture services for the San Antonio parks department he devoted more than 30 years to beautifying the city, particularly the famed River Walk; in San Antonio, Jan. 1. 2007.

Kennedy, Ken, 61; Rice University scientist whose software design work paved the way for emergence of the commercial supercomputing industry of the 1980s; in Houston, Feb. 7, 2007.

Killingsworth, Jim, 83; basketball coach at Texas Christian University where his teams, known as "Killer's Frogs," won back-to-back championships in the Southwest Conference in 1986 and 1987; in Owasso, Okla., June 10, 2007.

Koy, Ernie Sr., 97; part of 1930-32 UT Longhorn football team with 22-7-1 record; played five years in major league baseball beginning with the Brooklyn Dodgers; in Bellville, Jan. 1, 2007.

Lancarte, David Allen, 53; co-owner of the landmark Fort Worth Tex-Mex restaurant Joe T. Garcia's, founded by his grandfather; in Plano, Aug. 12, 2005, of heart failure.

Lay, Kenneth, 64; founder of Houston's Enron Corporation who fell into disgrace amid national scandal and bankruptcy; in Aspen, Colo., July 5, 2006.

Lee, Gordon "Porky," 71; Fort Worth native was one of *The Little Rascals* in the 1930s, appearing in more than 40 *Our Gang* short films; later taught school in Post; in Minneapolis, Oct. 16, 2005.

Levitt, Zola, 67; national televangelist who emphasized his own Jewish roots and those of Christianity; in Dallas, April 19, 2006.

Levitt.

Long, Travis, 86; Bellville native and highway engineer for 37 years who oversaw the construction of Austin's main two expressways, I-35 and MoPac; Jan. 5, 2007.

Madla, Frank, 69; important political leader in San Antonio who represented Bexar County in the Legislature for 33 years, the last 13 in the state senate; in San Antonio, Nov. 24, 2006.

Magers, Judy; better known as the burro lady or *La Riena*, she wandered the Trans-Pecos for decades alone with her burro; in Sierra Blanca, Jan. 26, 2007.

Mahon, Eldon B., 87; Loraine native served as federal judge for 30 years; oversaw desegregation of Fort Worth schools and ruled that Dallas city council at-large districts diluted minority voting power; in Fort Worth, Dec. 3, 2005.

Marshall, E. Pierce, 67; son of oil tycoon J. Howard Marshall II who battled celebrity Anna Nicole Smith for his father's fortune; in Dallas area, June 20, 2006.

Maysel, Lou, 82; longtime sports editor and columnist for the *Austin American-Statesman*; Brenham native was also respected historian of UT Longhorn football; in Austin, Nov. 18, 2005.

McDermott, Robert F., 86; retired Air Force brigadier general was influential businessman and civic leader in San Antonio; former chairman of NBA Spurs; in San Antonio, Aug. 28, 2006.

McNutt, L.W. "Bill" Jr., 81; as president for 30 years built Collin Street Bakery into an international brand, mainly through direct-mail marketing; in Corsicana, Sept. 1, 2006.

Metcalf, Shelby, 76; in 27 seasons as basketball coach at Texas A&M, 1963-90, his teams won six Southwest Conference championships; in College Station, Feb. 8, 2007.

Moncure, Rhymes H. Jr., 61; first black man to lead the United Methodist Church as bishop in North Texas; in Dallas, Aug. 19, 2006.

Moroney, James M. Jr., 85; last surviving grandson of George Bannerman Dealey, founder of *The Dallas Morning News;* he served as publisher of *The News* 1980-85 and on the board of the parent company Belo for 48 years; in Dallas, Feb. 8, 2007.

Muse, M. Lamar, 86; airline executive raised in Palestine who helped launch Southwest Airlines in 1971; in 1981 he started Muse Air with his son; in Dallas, Feb. 5, 2007.

Nasher, Raymond D., 85; developer of Dallas' NorthPark shopping mall in the 1960s; philanthropist who donated sculpture collection and museum to the city; in Dallas, March 16, 2007.

Niekro, Joe, 61; knuckleball pitcher who came from obscurity to become the Houston Astros' all-time winner (1975–85); in Tampa, Fla., Oct. 27, 2006.

Nelson, Byron, 94; golf icon who dominated the game in the 1940s; went on to second career as TV commentator; at his Roanoke ranch, Sept. 26, 2006.

Nix, Emery, 86; nicknamed "Ice Water," he quarterbacked TCU in upsets over No. 1-ranked UT in 1941 and highly ranked UCLA in 1942; in Blanco, Dec. 6, 2005.

Norton, Jim, 68; one of the original AFL Houston Oilers and the franchise leader in pass interceptions; in Garland, June 12, 2007.

Olson, Lyndon L. Sr., 80; son of Swedish immigrants and Waco attorney who represented Midland in the 1968 U.S. Supreme Court case establishing proportional representation in local government districts; in Waco, Dec. 20, 2005.

Overton, Volma, 81; civil rights leader who in the 1960s led efforts through sit-ins and picket lines for public accommodations and in 1970 to desegregate Austin public schools; in Austin, Oct. 31, 2005.

Owens, Buck, 76; founder of the Bakersfield Sound, his country hits included "Act Naturally" and "Waitin' in Your Welfare Line"; co-host of TV's *Hee Haw;* was born on a farm outside Sherman; in Bakersfield,

Calif., March 25, 2006.

Pace, Linda, 62; heiress was patron of arts in San Antonio where she established an international artists residency program; her father created Pace Picante Sauce in 1947; in San Antonio, July 2, 2007.

Pappas, Pete H., 86; Dallas native was son of Greek immigrants who with his family built the chain of Pappas Restaurants; in Houston, Dec. 18, 2005.

Pass, Fred R., 87; Rogers native was a writer with *The Dallas Morning News* and served as editor of the *Texas Almanac* 1973-81; in Dallas, Aug. 6, 2006.

Peña, Albert A. Jr., 88; four-term Bexar County commissioner, municipal court judge and pioneering civil rights leader; in San Antonio, July 3, 2006.

Preston, Billy, 59; Houston native whose keyboards and vocals can be heard on songs of the Beatles and Rolling Stones; co-wrote Joe Cocker hit "You Are So Beautiful"; in Scottsdale, Ariz., June 6, 2006.

Preston.

Prince, William I. "Bill" Sr., 93; Buffalo Soldier in the 10th Cavalry, which he joined as a teenager in 1928, first serving at Fort Huachuca, Ariz.; worked to preserve history of this and other black units of U.S. Army; in Houston, June 1, 2007.

Quinn, J.M. "Mike" Jr., 76; newsman for *The Dallas Morning News* in Washington when Lyndon Johnson became president; went on to teach journalism at the University of Texas at Austin for 37 years; in Katy, Jan. 22, 2006.

Ragsdale, Charlotte, 57; longtime Dallas civil rights activist and local Democratic political figure; in Dallas, April 7, 2007, from cancer.

Rao, Raja, 97; award-winning author who wrote *Kanthapura* in 1938, considered the first major Indian novel written in English; in Austin, where he was UT emeritus professor of philosophy, July 8, 2006.

Rector, John A. Jr., 86; rose from advertising salesman to publisher 1985-86 of *The Dallas Morning News* in nearly 40 years of service; in Dallas, July 13, 2006.

Redman, Dewey, 75; jazz tenor saxophonist and bandleader born to schoolteachers in Fort Worth; attended Prairie View A&M; taught school in Bastrop; Sept. 2, 2006.

Reynolds, Herbert, 77; president of Baylor University 1981-95 where he led charter change to a governing board more independent of the Baptist General Convention of Texas; in Angel Fire, N.M., May 25, 2007.

Richards, Ann, 73; Waco area native was elected Democratic governor in 1990; known for her wit as well as her political savvy in the state and nationally; in Austin, Sept. 13, 2006.

Richards.

Ruiz, David, 63; convict whose 1972 lawsuit led to sweeping changes in the Texas prison system; in a prison hospital in Galveston, Nov. 15, 2005.

Rutherford, J.T. "Slick," 85; Democratic congressman 1954-62 from a district that spanned West Texas from Midland to El Paso; one of few from Texas to vote for the 1960 civil rights bill; in Arlington, Va., Nov. 6, 2006.

Schirra, Walter M. "Wally," 84; one of the original Mercury 7 astronauts working in Houston and the only one to fly in all three of NASA's manned spacecraft programs; in La Jolla, Calif., May 3, 2006.

Searcy, John Marvin, 90; raised in Fort Worth, started Interstate Battery in 1952, which grew to thousands of retail outlets nationwide; in Irving, June 2, 2007.

Shuford, Harry, 92; two-time All American and tri-captain of SMU's 1936 Rose Bowl team; president of Federal Reserve Bank of St. Louis and the Cotton Bowl Athletic Association; in Dallas, May 16, 2007.

Smalley, Richard E., 62; Nobel Prize winner and Rice University chemistry professor, championed nanotechnology to address energy needs; in Houston, Oct. 28, 2005.

Smith, Anna Nicole, 39; born Vicki Lynn Hogan in Houston; former *Playboy* centerfold and wife of elderly oil tycoon J. Howard Marshall II; in the Bahamas, Feb. 7, 2007, of a drug overdose; her 20-year-old son Daniel died the previous Sept. 10 of a drug overdose.

Spelling, Aaron, 83; noted Hollywood producer of *Dynasty, Love Boat,* and other TV hit shows; former SMU cheerleader grew up in South Dallas; in Los Angeles, June 23, 2006.

Sprague, Charles, 88; longtime head of the UT Southwestern Medical Center bringing it to international prominence; in Dallas, Sept. 17, 2005.

Steger, William M., 85; federal judge in East Texas for 35 years; in Tyler, June 4, 2006.

Stevenson, Edith W. "Scottie," 93; served as Texas' first lady for her father-in-law, Gov. Coke Stevenson, after his wife died; lived with her daughters in the Governor's Mansion while her husband served in WWII; in Austin, Dec. 24, 2006.

Stram, Hank, 82; Pro Football Hall-of-Famer, first coach of the AFL Dallas Texans in 1960-62, moving on to coach the Kansas City Chiefs to two Super Bowls; in Covington, La., July 4, 2005.

Strickland, Phil, 64; lobbied for Baptist Convention of Texas causes for 38 years in Austin, fighting gambling and advocating for children's care and for church-state separation; in Dallas, Feb. 11, 2006.

Temple, Arthur Jr., 86; businessman who turned his grandfather's sawmill firm into the Temple-Inland Inc. wood products empire; in Lufkin, April 12, 2006.

Templeton, Arleigh B., 90; headed three universities, Sam Houston State, UT–El Paso, and was first president of UT–San Antonio 1970-72; in San Antonio, Oct. 28, 2006.

Thomas, James B., 82; Galveston minister, city council member and NAACP president instrumental in bringing lawsuit to desegregate Galveston schools; March 16, 2007.

Thompson, Garfield, 89; black leader who organized his fellow maintenance workers at the Tarrant County Courthouse and later was elected to the Legislature 1984-94; in Fort Worth, Dec. 7, 2005.

Thornton, E.H. Jr., 95; legislator, chairman of the State Highway Commission, a director of the Texas Turnpike Authority and a member of the Texas Battleship Commission; in Houston, July 10, 2005.

Tweedy, Malcolm, 83; a catalyst beginning in the 1950s for creation of the Fort Davis National Historic Site; in Fort Davis, May 12, 2006.

Valenti, Jack, 85; Houston-born aide to President Lyndon Johnson who became president of the Motion Picture Association of America, where he instituted

Valenti.

the movie rating system; at his Washington, D.C., home, April 26, 2007.

Valentine, Foy, 82; Van Zandt County native was ethicist and civil rights advocate who headed the Southern Baptist Convention's public policy arm; in Dallas, Jan. 6, 2006.

Vowell, Jack, 79; El Paso Republican legislator 1980-94, named one of state's top lawmakers by *Texas Monthly*; championed education issues; in El Paso, Aug. 29, 2006.

Walker, Billy, 77; Ralls native and Grand Ole Opry star sang "Cross the Brazos at Waco" and "Charlie's Shoes"; in an accident on an Alabama interstate along with his wife and two band members, May 21, 2006.

Billy Walker.

Walker, Cindy, 87; Mexia resident wrote classic country songs, such as "You Don't Know Me," and "Bubbles in My Beer," and pop songs, including "Dream Baby" for Roy Orbison; in Waco, March 23, 2006.

Walser, Don, 72; country singer out of Brownfield and Lamesa whose yodel earned him the label "Pavarotti of the Plains"; in Austin, Sept. 20, 2006.

Westmoreland, Harry Lee Jr., 65; inventor of a portable drilling rig that could be carried in a pickup; founder of a charity to provide safe drinking water to Third World countries; in Sugar Land, Feb. 16, 2007.

Wilkin, Marijohn, 86; born Marijohn Melson in Kemp; was Nashville Hall of Fame songwriter, including "The Long Black Veil"; prominent Music Row publisher; Oct. 28, 2006.

Willis, Doyle Sr., 97; from 1947-97 served four separate stints as state representative and senator from Tarrant County and in between served on the Forth Worth city council; in Fort Worth, June 22, 2006.

Wilson, Will, 93; Dallas native was known as crime-busting Texas attorney general in the 1950s, taking on illegal gambling in Galveston; made unsuccessful runs for governor and senator in the 1960s; in Austin, Dec. 14, 2005.

Witts, David, 85; Dallas attorney who along with his friend Carroll Shelby started the famous Terlingua Chili Cook-off in 1967; chaired the Texas Aeronautics Commission; Oct. 25, 2006. ☆

General Index

For cities and towns not listed in the index, see lists of towns on pp. 414-442 and pp. 498-506. For full information about a county, also look under the cities and towns in the county.

For CITIES and TOWNS not listed in the index, see complete list on pages 414–442.

For CITIES and TOWNS not listed in the index, see complete list on pages 414–442.

For CITIES and TOWNS not listed in the index, see complete list on pages 414–442.

For CITIES and TOWNS not listed in the index, see complete list on pages 414–442.

For CITIES and TOWNS not listed in the index, see complete list on pages 414–442.

For CITIES and TOWNS not listed in the index, see complete list on pages 414–442.

For CITIES and TOWNS not listed in the index, see complete list on pages 414–442.

For CITIES and TOWNS not listed in the index, see complete list on pages 414–442.

For CITIES and TOWNS not listed in the index, see complete list on pages 414–442.

For CITIES and TOWNS not listed in the index, see complete list on pages 414–442.

For CITIES and TOWNS not listed in the index, see complete list on pages 414–442.

For CITIES and TOWNS not listed in the index, see complete list on pages 414–442.

For CITIES and TOWNS not listed in the index, see complete list on pages 414–442.

For CITIES and TOWNS not listed in the index, see complete list on pages 414–442.

For CITIES and TOWNS not listed in the index, see complete list on pages 414–442.

For CITIES and TOWNS not listed in the index, see complete list on pages 414–442.

For CITIES and TOWNS not listed in the index, see complete list on pages 414–442.

For CITIES and TOWNS not listed in the index, see complete list on pages 414–442.

For CITIES and TOWNS not listed in the index, see complete list on pages 414–442.

For CITIES and TOWNS not listed in the index, see complete list on pages 414–442.

For CITIES and TOWNS not listed in the index, see complete list on pages 414–442.

For CITIES and TOWNS not listed in the index, see complete list on pages 414–442.

For CITIES and TOWNS not listed in the index, see complete list on pages 414–442.

For CITIES and TOWNS not listed in the index, see complete list on pages 414–442.

For CITIES and TOWNS not listed in the index, see complete list on pages 414–442.

For CITIES and TOWNS not listed in the index, see complete list on pages 414–442.

For CITIES and TOWNS not listed in the index, see complete list on pages 414–442.

For CITIES and TOWNS not listed in the index, see complete list on pages 414–442.

For CITIES and TOWNS not listed in the index, see complete list on pages 414–442.

For CITIES and TOWNS not listed in the index, see complete list on pages 414–442.

For CITIES and TOWNS not listed in the index, see complete list on pages 414–442.

For CITIES and TOWNS not listed in the index, see complete list on pages 414–442.